Apostle Paul

Apostle Paul

His Life and Theology

Udo Schnelle

Translated by M. Eugene Boring

Baker Academic
Grand Rapids, Michigan

Originally published as *Paulus: Leben und Denken*
© 2003 by Walter de Gruyter GmbH & Co. KG, Berlin / New York. All rights reserved.

English translation ©2005 by Baker Publishing Group
Published by Baker Academic
a division of Baker Publishing Group
P.O. Box 6287, Grand Rapids, MI 49516-6287
www.bakeracademic.com

The publication of this work was supported by a grant from the Goethe-Institut.

Printed in the United States of America

Library of Congress Cataloging-in-Publication Data

Schnelle, Udo.
    [Paulus. English]
    Apostle Paul : his life and theology / Udo Schnelle ; translated by M. Eugene Boring.
       p.   cm.
    Includes bibliographical references and indexes.
    ISBN 0-8010-2796-9 (cloth)
       1. Paul, the Apostle, Saint. 2. Christian saints—Turkey—Tarsus—Biography.
    3. Bible. N.T. Epistles of Paul—Theology. I. Title
    BS2506.3.S3613 2005
    225.9′2—dc22   2005025534

Contents

Translator's Preface

In recent years Udo Schnelle has perhaps become best known for his works on the Gospel and Letters of John.[1] Udo Schnelle's doctoral dissertation, however, was a study of Paul's theology of baptism, *Gerechtigkeit und Christusgegenwart: Vorpaulinische und paulinische Tauftheologie* (Göttinger Theologische Arbeiten 24; Göttingen: Vandenhoeck & Ruprecht, 1983); and he has never ceased to be interested in the life, letters, and theology of Paul, as attested by his numerous articles listed in the bibliography of this book and by the extensive section on Paul in his introduction to the New Testament, *The History and Theology of the New Testament Writings* (trans. M. Eugene Boring; Minneapolis: Fortress, 1998). Now he has brought together his work on Paul in a comprehensive study that will take its place among the standard works in the field. In my judgment, it is the best single volume on Paul's life and work, providing to students and teachers at all levels a thorough survey of all major issues, integrating a careful and judicious engagement with the vast primary and secondary literature and his own balanced interpretation. I am thus very pleased to facilitate its use in the English-speaking world.

At the author's and the publisher's request, I have augmented the bibliography with English books and articles, mostly listing books and articles comparable to the ample German bibliography already present, for the benefit of students who do not read German. I have also complied with the author's and publisher's request that I occasionally provide translator's notes on the German text reflecting the European context with which the reader might not be familiar. In both cases, I have kept my own contributions to a minimum.

---

1. See especially his Habilitationsschrift, *Antidocetic Christology in the Gospel of John* (trans. Linda M. Maloney; Minneapolis: Fortress, 1992) and his valuable and readable commentary, *Das Evangelium nach Johannes* (Theologischer Handkommentar zum Neuen Testament 4; Leipzig: Evangelische Verlagsanstalt, 1998).

A valuable aspect of the volume is its extensive use of primary sources from the Hellenistic world. After the death of Georg Strecker, Schnelle assumed the editorship of the *Neuer Wettstein: Texte zum Neuen Testament aus Griechentum und Hellenismus* (Berlin: De Gruyter, 1996). His citation of such texts as are found there and insight into their relevance for New Testament interpretation greatly enrich this study of Paul. Except where otherwise indicated, translations of Aelius Aristides, Apostolic Fathers, Apuleius, Cicero, Dio Chrysostom, Diogenes Laertius, Epictetus, Euripedes, Eusebius, Homer, Iamblichus, Josephus, Lucian, Menander, Musonius Rufus, Ovid, Philostratus, Plato (Gorgias, Resp.), Plutarch, Quintilian, *Res gestae divi Augusti*, Seneca, Sophocles, Suetonius, Tacitus, and Xenophon are from the Loeb Classical Library editions listed in the bibliography.

This translation has been read by the author, Udo Schnelle, and by James Ernest, Joe Carey, and Paul Peterson for Baker Academic, all of whom have made helpful suggestions for which I hereby express my heartfelt thanks.

Preface to the German Edition

The goal of this book is to present a comprehensive introduction to the life and thought of the apostle Paul. It is intended as a textbook that takes a didactic perspective on the material as a whole and documents all important positions in Pauline research. At the same time, it is an independent contribution to the ongoing debate, outlining my own position on disputed points.

Since each section can be read as an independent unit, intended to be understandable on its own, some overlapping and repetition were unavoidable. I have attempted to reduce these to a minimum, although experience has taught that textbooks are usually not read straight through—and thus some repetition is in fact necessary and helpful.

I here express my gratitude to Dr. Michael Labahn and Dr. Manfred Lang, my coworkers at the University of Halle-Wittenberg, for their continuing expert advice as well as for their help in correcting the proofs. I am grateful to Dr. Claus-Jürgen Thornton not only for his customary good care regarding publication details but also for his discussions regarding the contents of this book.

Halle, November 2002
Udo Schnelle

Abbreviations

General Abbreviations

ca.	circa
ch(s).	chapter(s)
col(s).	column(s)
diss.	dissertation
ed(s).	editor(s), edited by
e.g.	*exempli gratia*, for example
enl.	enlarged
esp.	especially
ET	English translation
et al.	*et alii*, and others
exp.	expanded
f(f).	and the following one(s)
frg.	fragment
i.e.	*id est*, that is
ibid.	*ibidem*, in the same place
lit.	literally
LXX	Septuagint (the Greek Old Testament)
NF	*Neue Folge*, New Series
NIV	New International Version
NRSV	New Revised Standard Version
p(p).	page(s)
par.	parallel (to indicate textual parallels)
passim	here and there
pl.	plural
rev.	revised (by)
sc.	*scilicet*, namely
v(v).	verse(s)
viz.	*videlicet*, namely

Primary Sources

Old Testament Pseudepigrapha

As. Mos.	*Assumption of Moses*
2 Bar.	*2 Baruch (Syriac Apocalypse)*
1 En.	*1 Enoch (Ethiopic Apocalypse)*
2 En.	*2 Enoch (Slavonic Apocalypse)*
Jos. Asen.	*Joseph and Aseneth*
Jub.	*Jubilees*
L.A.B.	*Liber antiquitatum biblicarum (Pseudo-Philo)*
L.A.E.	*Life of Adam and Eve*
Let. Aris.	*Letter of Aristeas*
Pss. Sol.	*Psalms of Solomon*
Sib. Or.	*Sibylline Oracles*
T. Benj.	*Testament of Benjamin*
T. Dan	*Testament of Dan*
T. Iss.	*Testament of Issachar*
T. Jos.	*Testament of Joseph*
T. Levi	*Testament of Levi*
T. Naph.	*Testament of Naphtali*
T. Sim.	*Testament of Simeon*

Dead Sea Scrolls and Related Texts

CD	Cairo Genizah copy of the *Damascus Document*
1QH	*Hodayot* or *Thanksgiving Hymns*
1QM	*Milḥamah* or *War Scroll*
1QpHab	*Pesher Habakkuk*
1QS	*Serek Hayaḥad* or *Rule of the Community*
1QSa	*Rule of the Congregation* (Appendix a to 1QS)
1QSb	*Rule of the Congregation* (Appendix b to 1QS)
4QFlor (MidrEschat[a])	*Florilegium,* also *Midrash on Eschatology*[a]
4QMessAp	*Messianic Apocalypse*
4QMMT[a]	*Miqṣat Ma'aśê ha-Torah*[a]
11QMelch	*Melchizedek*
11QT[a]	*Temple Scroll*[a]

Philo

Abraham	*On the Life of Abraham*
Alleg. Interp. 1, 2, 3	*Allegorical Interpretation 1, 2, 3*
Confusion	*On the Confusion of Tongues*
Creation	*On the Creation of the World*
Decalogue	*On the Decalogue*
Dreams 1, 2	*On Dreams 1, 2*
Drunkenness	*On Drunkenness*
Embassy	*On the Embassy to Gaius*
Flaccus	*Against Flaccus*
Flight	*On Flight and Finding*
Giants	*On Giants*
Heir	*Who Is the Heir?*
Migration	*On the Migration of Abraham*
Moses 1, 2	*On the Life of Moses 1, 2*
Names	*On the Change of Names*
Planting	*On Planting*
Posterity	*On the Posterity of Cain*
Prelim. Studies	*On the Preliminary Studies*
QE 1, 2	*Questions and Answers on Exodus 1, 2*
Sobriety	*On Sobriety*
Spec. Laws 1, 2, 3, 4	*On the Special Laws*
Unchangeable	*That God Is Unchangeable*
Virtues	*On the Virtues*
Worse	*That the Worse Attacks the Better*

Josephus

Ag. Ap.	*Against Apion*
Ant.	*Jewish Antiquities*
J.W.	*Jewish War*
Life	*The Life*

Mishnah, Talmud, and Related Literature

t.	*Tosefta*
Šabb.	*Šabbat*

Apostolic Fathers

Barn.	*Barnabas*
1–2 Clem.	*1–2 Clement*
Did.	*Didache*
Ign. Magn.	Ignatius, *To the Magnesians*
Ign. Phil.	Ignatius, *To the Philadelphians*
Ign. Eph.	Ignatius, *To the Ephesians*
Ign. Rom.	Ignatius, *To the Romans*
Ign. Pol.	Ignatius, *To Polycarp*
Mart. Pol.	*Martyrdom of Polycarp*
Pol. Phil.	Polycarp, *To the Philippians*

New Testament Apocrypha and Pseudepigrapha

Ep. Paul Sen.	*Epistles of Paul and Seneca*

Other Early Christian Writers

Augustine
Civ.	*De civitate Dei*

Eusebius
Hist. eccl.	*Historia ecclesiastica*

Justin
Dial.	*Dialogus cum Tryphone*

Classical Authors

Apuleius
Metam.	*Metamorphoses*

Aristotle
Eth. nic.	*Nichomachean Ethics*
Pol.	*Politics*

Cicero
Amic.	*De amicitia*
Arch.	*Pro Archia*
Fin.	*De finibus*
Flac.	*Pro Flacco*
Leg.	*De legibus*
Nat. d.	*De natura deorum*
Off.	*De officiis*
Or.	*De oratore*
Parad.	*Paradoxa Stoicorum*
Rab. perd.	*Pro Rabirio perduellionis reo*
Resp.	*De re publica*
Tusc.	*Tusculanae disputationes*
Verr.	*In Verrem*

Demosthenes
Or.	*Orationes*

Dio Cassius

Dio Chrysostom
Alex.	*Ad Alexandrinos (Or. 32)*
Charid.	*Charidemus (Or. 30)*
Consuet.	*De consuetudine (Or. 76)*
De lege	*De lege (Or. 75)*
Lib.	*De libertate (Or. 80)*
1 Regn.	*De regno i (Or. 1)*
3 Regn.	*De regno iii 3 (Or. 3)*
Regn. tyr.	*De regno et tyrannide (Or. 62)*
1 Serv. lib.	*De servitute et libertate 1 (Or. 14)*
2 Serv. lib.	*De servitute et libertate 2 (Or. 15)*
1 Tars.	*Tarsica prior (Or. 33)*
2 Tars.	*Tarsica altera (Or. 34)*

Epictetus

Diatr.	Diatribae (Dissertationes) (Discourses)
Ench.	Enchiridion

Herodotus

Hist.	Historiae

Homer

Od.	Odyssea

Iamblichus

Prot.	Protrepticus
Vit. pyth.	De vita pythagorica

Livy

Urbe cond.	Ab urbe condita

Lucretius

Rer. nat.	De rerum natura

Menander

Sent.	Sententiae

Musonius Rufus

Diss.	Dissertationes

Philostratus

Vit. Apoll.	Vita Apollonii

Plato

Ep.	Epistulae
Gorg.	Gorgias
Leg.	Leges
[Min.]	Minos
Phaed.	Phaedo
Phaedr.	Phaedrus
Prot.	Protagoras
Resp.	Respublica

Pliny the Younger

Ep.	Epistulae

Plutarch

Alex.	Alexander
Alex. fort.	De Alexandri magni fortuna aut virtute
Is. Os.	De Iside et Osiride
Mor.	Moralia
Pel.	Pelopidas
Rom.	Romulus
Superst.	De superstitione

Quintilian

Inst.	Institutio oratoria

Seneca

Ben.	De beneficiis
Clem.	De clementia
Ep.	Epistulae morales
Ira	De ira
Marc.	Ad Marciam de consolatione
Tranq.	De tranquillitate animi

Sextus Empiricus

Math.	Adversus mathematicos

Strabo

Geogr.	Geographica

Suetonius

Tib.	Tiberius

Tacitus

Ann.	Annales
Hist.	Historiae

Xenophon

Anab.	Anabasis
Mem.	Memorabilia

Secondary Sources

AASFDHL	Annales Academiae scientiarum fennicae: Dissertationes humanarum litterarum
AAWGPH	Abhandlungen der Akademie der Wissenschaften in Göttingen: Philologisch-historische Klasse
AB	Anchor Bible
ABD	*The Anchor Bible Dictionary.* Edited by D. N. Freedman. 6 vols. New York: Doubleday, 1992
ABG	Arbeiten zur Bibel und ihrer Geschichte
ABRL	Anchor Bible Reference Library
AGJU	Arbeiten zur Geschichte des antiken Judentums und des Urchristentums
AKG	Antike Kultur und Geschichte
AMS	Asia Minor Studien
AnBib	Analecta biblica
ANRW	*Aufstieg und Niedergang der römischen Welt: Geschichte und Kultur Roms im Spiegel der neueren Forschung.* Edited by H. Temporini and W. Haase. Berlin: de Gruyter, 1972–
ANTC	Abingdon New Testament Commentaries
ARGU	Arbeiten zur Religion und Geschichte des Urchristentums
ATANT	Abhandlungen zur Theologie des Alten und Neuen Testaments
ATDan	Acta theologica danica
BA	*Biblical Archaeologist*
BBB	Bonner biblische Beiträge
BBET	Beiträge zur biblischen Exegese und Theologie
BDAG	Bauer, W., F. W. Danker, W. F. Arndt, and F. W. Gingrich. *Greek-English Lexicon of the New Testament and Other Early Christian Literature.* 3d ed. Chicago: University of Chicago Press, 1999
BETL	Bibliotheca ephemeridum theologicarum lovaniensium
BEvT	Beiträge zur evangelischen Theologie
BFCT	Beiträge zur Förderung christlicher Theologie
BGBE	Beiträge zur Geschichte der biblischen Exegese
BHT	Beiträge zur historischen Theologie
BKP	Beiträge zur klassischen Philologie
BN	*Biblische Notizen*
BNTC	Black's New Testament Commentaries
BTS	Biblisch-theologische Studien
BU	Biblische Untersuchungen
BWA(N)T	Beiträge zur Wissenschaft vom Alten (und Neuen) Testament
BWM	Bibelwissenschaftliche Monographien
BZ	*Biblische Zeitschrift*
BZNW	Beihefte zur Zeitschrift für die neutestamentliche Wissenschaft
Cath (M)	*Catholica* (Münster)
CBET	Contributions to Biblical Exegesis and Theology

CBQ	*Catholic Biblical Quarterly*
ConBNT	Coniectanea biblica: New Testament Series
CRINT	Compendia rerum iudaicarum ad Novum Testamentum
DDD	*Dictionary of Deities and Demons in the Bible.* Edited by K. van der Toorn, B. Becking, and P. W. van der Horst. 2nd ed. Leiden: Brill, 1999
DJD	Discoveries in the Judaean Desert
DPL	*Dictionary of Paul and His Letters.* Edited by Gerald F. Hawthorne and Ralph P. Martin. Downers Grove, IL: InterVarsity, 1993
EAW	Echoes of the Ancient World
EdF	Erträge der Forschung
EDNT	*Exegetical Dictionary of the New Testament.* Edited by H. Balz and G. Schneider. Translated by James W. Thompson and John W. Medendorp. 3 vols. Grand Rapids: Eerdmans, 1990–1993
EHS	Europäische Hochschulschriften
EKKNT	Evangelisch-katholischer Kommentar zum Neuen Testament
EKL	*Evangelisches Kirchenlexikon.* Edited by Erwin Fahlbusch et al. 5 vols. 3d ed. Göttingen: Vandenhoeck & Ruprecht, 1985–1997
EvT	*Evangelische Theologie*
FAT	Forschungen zum Alten Testament
FB	Forschung zur Bibel
FRLANT	Forschungen zur Religion und Literatur des Alten und Neuen Testaments
FSÖTh	Forschungen zur systematischen und ökumenischen Theologie
FWBKR	Frankfurter wissenschaftliche Beiträge: Kulturwissenschaftliche Reihe
GL	*Glaube und Lernen*
GNT	Grundrisse zum Neuen Testament
GTA	Göttinger theologischer Arbeiten
HAW	Handbuch der Altertumswissenschaft
HBS	Herders biblische Studien
HCS	Hellenistic Culture and Society
HE	Hermes: Einzelshriften
Hermeneia	Hermeneia: A Critical and Historical Commentary on the Bible
HEWS	Handbuch der europäischen Wirtschafts- und Sozialgeschichte
HNT	Handbuch zum Neuen Testament
HNTC	Harper's New Testament Commentaries
HRWG	*Handbuch Religionswissenschaftlicher Grundbegriffe.* Edited by Hubert Cancik, Burkhard Gladigow, and Matthias Laubscher. 5 vols. Stuttgart: Kohlhammer, 1988–2001
HTKNT	Herders theologischer Kommentar zum Neuen Testament
HTR	*Harvard Theological Review*
HUT	Hermeneutische Untersuchungen zur Theologie
ICC	International Critical Commentary
IdF	Impulse der Forschung
ILPPSM	International Library of Psychology, Philosophy, and Scientific Method

ILS	*Inscriptiones latinae selectae.* Edited by Herman Dessau. 3 vols. in 5. Berlin: Apud Weidmannos, 1892–1916.
JBL	*Journal of Biblical Literature*
JBTh	*Jahrbuch für biblische Theologie*
JJS	*Journal of Jewish Studies*
JRH	*Journal of Religious History*
JSHRZ	Jüdische Schriften aus hellenistisch-römischer Zeit
JSJ	*Journal for the Study of Judaism in the Persian, Hellenistic, and Roman Periods*
JSJSup	Supplements to the Journal for the Study of Judaism
JSNT	*Journal for the Study of the New Testament*
JSNTSup	Journal for the Study of the New Testament: Supplement Series
JSP	*Journal for the Study of the Pseudepigrapha*
JTC	*Journal for Theology and the Church*
JTS	*Journal of Theological Studies*
Jud	*Judaica*
KD	*Kerygma und Dogma*
KEK	Kritisch-exegetischer Kommentar über das Neue Testament (Meyer-Kommentar)
KuI	*Kirche und Israel*
LCL	Loeb Classical Library
LEC	Library of Early Christianity
LTK	*Lexicon für Theologie und Kirche*
MSÅAF	Meddelanden från Stiftelsens för Åbo akademi forskningsinstitut
MSSA	Moraltheologische Studien: Systematische Abteilung
MThSH	Münchener theologische Studien, 1: Historische Abteilung
MTS	Marburger theologische Studien
MTZ	*Münchener theologische Zeitschrift*
MySal	Mysterium salutis
NAWGPH	Nachrichten der Akademie der Wissenschaften in Göttingen 1: Philologisch-historische Klasse
NBL	*Neues Bibel-Lexikon.* Edited by Manfred Görg and Bernard Lang. Zurich: Benziger, 1988–
NEchtB	Neue Echter Bibel
NEchtBENT	Neue Echter Bibel: Ergänzungsband zum Neue Testament
Neot	*Neotestamentica*
NET	Neutestamentliche Entwürfe zur Theologie
NICNT	New International Commentary on the New Testament
NIGTC	New International Greek Testament Commentary
NovT	*Novum Testamentum*
NovTSup	Supplements to Novum Testamentum
NTAbh	Neutestamentliche Abhandlungen
NTD	Das Neue Testament Deutsch
NTL	New Testament Library
NTOA	Novum Testamentum et orbis antiquus

NTS	*New Testament Studies*
NUSPEP	Northwestern University Studies in Phenomenology and Existential Philosophy
NW	Johann Wettstein, *Neuer Wettstein: Texte zum Neuen Testament aus Griechentum und Hellenismus.* Edited by Georg Strecker et al. Berlin: de Gruyter, 1996–.
NZST	*Neue Zeitschrift für systematische Theologie*
OBO	Orbis biblicus et orientalis
OGG	Oldenbourg Grundriss der Geschichte
ÖTK	Ökumenischer Taschenbuch-Kommentar
OTL	Old Testament Library
OTP	*The Old Testament Pseudepigrapha.* 2 vols. Ed. James H. Charlesworth. Garden City, N.Y.: Doubleday, 1983.
OTS	Old Testament Studies
PhAnt	Philosophia antiqua
PTh	*Pastoraltheologie*
PW	Pauly, A. F. *Paulys Realencyclopädie der classischen Altertumswissenschaft.* Ed. G. Wissowa. 49 vols. in 58. New ed. Munich: Druckenmüller, 1894–1980
PWSup	Supplement to PW
PzB	*Protokolle zur Bibel*
QD	Quaestiones disputatae
RAC	*Reallexikon für Antike und Christentum: Sachwörterbuch zur Auseinandersetzung des Christentums mit der antiken Welt.* Edited by T. Klauser et al. Stuttgart: Hiersemann, 1950–
RGG	*Religion in Geschichte und Gegenwart Handwörterbuch für Theologie und Religionswissenschaft.* Edited by Hans Dieter Benz et al. 4th ed. Tübingen: Mohr, 1998–
RMP	*Rheinisches Museum für Philologie*
RNT	Regensburger Neues Testament
RTS	Rostocker theologische Studien
SANT	Studien zum Alten und Neuen Testaments
SBAB	Stuttgarter biblische Aufsatzbände
SBB	Stuttgarter biblische Beiträge
SBLDS	Society of Biblical Literature Dissertation Series
SBLSBS	Society of Biblical Literature Sources for Biblical Study
SBLSymS	Society of Biblical Literature Symposium Series
SBS	Stuttgarter Bibelstudien
SBT	Studies in Biblical Theology
SESJ	Suomen Eksegeettisen Seuran julkaisuja
SHAW	Sitzungen der heidelberger Akademie der Wissenschaften
SHR	Studies in the History of Religions (supplement to *Numen*)
SIJD	Schriften des Institutum judaicum delitzschianum
SJLA	Studies in Judaism in Late Antiquity
SJSHRZ	Studien zu den jüdischen Schriften aus hellenistisch-römischer Zeit

SLA	Studien der Luther-Akademie
SMBenSB	Serie monographica di Benedictina: Sezione biblico-ecumenica
SMBenSP	Série monographique de Benedictina: Section paulinienne
SNT	Studien zum Neuen Testament
SNTSMS	Society for New Testament Studies Monograph Series
SNTSU	Studien zum Neuen Testament und seiner Umwelt
SNTW	Studies of the New Testament and Its World
SPAWPH	Preussischen Akademie der Wissenschaften: Philosophisch-historische Klasse
SPhilo	*Studia philonica*
SR	*Studies in Religion*
ST	*Studia theologica*
STDJ	Studies on the Texts of the Desert of Judah
StPB	Studia post-biblica
SUNT	Studien zur Umwelt des Neuen Testaments
SVR	Studien zum Verstehen fremder Religionen
TA	Theologische Arbeiten
TANZ	Texte und Arbeiten zum neutestamentlichen Zeitalter
TB	Theologische Bücherei: Neudrucke und Berichte aus dem 20. Jahrhundert
TBei	*Theologische Beiträge*
TBLNT	*Theologisches Begriffslexikon zum Neuen Testament.* Edited by L. Coenen and K. Haacker. Rev. ed. Wuppertal: Brockhaus, 1997–.
TDNT	*Theological Dictionary of the New Testament.* Edited by G. Kittel and G. Friedrich. Translated by G. W. Bromiley. 10 vols. Grand Rapids: Eerdmans, 1964–1976
TDOT	*Theological Dictionary of the Old Testament.* Edited by G. J. Botterweck and H. Ringgren. Translated by J. T. Willis, G. W. Bromiley, and D. E. Green. Grand Rapids: Eerdmans, 1974–
TEH	Theologische Existenz heute
TGl	*Theologie und Glaube*
THKNT	Theologischer Handkommentar zum Neuen Testament
ThSt	Theologische Studiën
TLOT	*Theological Lexicon of the Old Testament.* Edited by E. Jenni, with assistance from C. Westermann. Translated by Mark E. Biddle. 3 vols. Peabody: Hendrickson, 1997
TQ	*Theologische Quartalschrift*
TRE	*Theologische Realenzyklopädie.* Edited by G. Krause and G. Müller. Berlin: de Gruyter, 1977–
TRu	*Theologische Rundschau*
TSAJ	Texte und Studien zum antiken Judentum
TSK	*Theologische Studien und Kritiken*
TTFL	Theological Translation Fund Library
TWNT	*Theologische Wörterbuch zum Neuen Testament.* Edited by G. Kittel and G. Friedrich. 10 vols. Stuttgart: Kohlhammer, 1932–1979
TZ	*Theologische Zeitschrift*

UNT	Untersuchungen zum Neuen Testament
VF	*Verkündigung und Forschung*
WBC	Word Biblical Commentary
WF	Wege der Forschung
WMANT	Wissenschaftliche Monographien zum Alten und Neuen Testament
WSt	*Wiener Studien*
WUNT	Wissenschaftliche Untersuchungen zum Neuen Testament
WZ(H)GS	*Wissenschaftliche Zeitschrift d. Martin-Luther-Universität Halle-Wittenberg*
ZAW	*Zeitschrift für die alttestamentliche Wissenschaft*
ZBKNT	Zürcher Bibelkommentare: NT
ZDPV	*Zeitschrift des deutschen Palästina-Vereins*
ZdZ	*Zeichen der Zeit*
ZNT	*Zeitschrift für Neues Testament*
ZNW	*Zeitschrift für die neutestamentliche Wissenschaft und die Kunde der älteren Kirche*
ZPE	*Zeitschrift für Papyrologie und Epigraphik*
ZTK	*Zeitschrift für Theologie und Kirche*
ZTKB	Zeitschrift für Theologie und Kirche: Beiheft
ZWT	*Zeitschrift für wissenschaftliche Theologie*

Part One

The Course of Paul's Life and the Development of His Thought

1

Prologue

Paul as Challenge and Provocation

1.1 Approaching Paul

Paul's life was the life of a traveler. Like no other before or after him, he bridged different continents, cultures, and religions and created a new continuing reality: Christianity as a world religion.[1] As the first Christian to really break through established boundaries, Paul set forth the meaning of the new being in Christ (ἐν Χριστῷ) and lived it out within the horizon of the Lord's parousia. This is the bond that unites him with Christians of every generation. Thus, to enter into his world of thought always means to trace out the contours of his faith. "What missionary is there, what preacher, what man entrusted with the cure of souls, who can be compared with him, whether in the greatness of the task he accomplished, or in the holy energy with which he carried it out?"[2]

Such a person could not remain uncontroversial. Even in New Testament times, his subtle thought processes already caused difficulties (cf. 2 Pet. 3:15–16). While in the course of church history Paul has served as the guar-

---

1. William Wrede, *Paul* (trans. Edward Lummis; Boston: American Unitarian Association, 1908), 179, calls Paul the "second founder of Christianity."

2. Adolf von Harnack, *What Is Christianity?* (trans. Thomas Bailey Saunders; New York: Harper & Row, 1900; repr., 1957), 188.

25

antor of the theology of some (Augustine, Martin Luther, Karl Barth) and a powerful source of theological renewal and church reform, others have seen in the apostle to the Gentiles only an inferior disciple who dissolved into theology Jesus' original teaching about God and thus falsified it. H. J. Schoeps finds it thought-provoking "that the Christian church has received a completely distorted view of the Jewish law at the hands of a diaspora Jew who had become alienated from the faith-ideas of his fathers."[3] Joseph Klausner states, "*First,* Paul, in spite of all his desire for authority and all the ridicule and hatred which he directed toward those who did not acknowledge his particular gospel or his authority as an apostle, did not have what may be called *genuine sovereignty.*"[4]

1.2 Reflections on Historiography

What is the best approach to this multifaceted personality? Is it at all possible to obtain an adequate grasp of the life and thought of Paul? How should a presentation of his life and thought be structured? Dealing with these issues requires hermeneutical and methodological reflections on two levels: (1) What epistemological theories are involved in the writing of history as such?[5] (2) What special problems arise in dealing with Paul?

How History Is Made and Written

At the center of recent discussion of historical theory stands the question of how historical reports and their incorporation into the thought world of the

---

3. Hans Joachim Schoeps, *Paul: The Theology of the Apostle in the Light of Jewish Religious History* (trans. Harold Knight; Philadelphia: Westminster, 1961), 261–62. On the Jewish interpretation, cf. Stefan Meissner, *Die Heimholung des Ketzers: Studien zur jüdischen Auseinandersetzung mit Paulus* (WUNT 2/87; Tübingen: Mohr Siebeck, 1996).

4. Joseph Klausner, *From Jesus to Paul* (trans. William F. Stinespring; New York: Macmillan, 1943), 582.

5. Regarding terminology, I use the German terms *Geschichte/geschichtlich* to refer to what happened, and *Historie/historisch* to indicate the ways in which historians attempt to reconstruct this. *Historik* refers to the philosophical theory of history. Cf. H.-W. Hedinger, "Historik," in *Historisches Wörterbuch der Philosophie* (ed. Karlfried Gründer et al.; Darmstadt: Wissenschaftliche Buchgesellschaft, 1974). *Geschichte* is never directly available except as *Historie,* but nonetheless the two concepts and terms must be distinguished because the questions posed from the point of view of philosophical theories of history are not simply identical with "what happened" as that was understood by people in the past. [Translator's note: The German language has two words for "history" whereas English has but one. Many German authors, including some quoted by Schnelle, use the two words interchangeably. The nuances distinguished by Schnelle are difficult to preserve in English. I have mostly rendered both words by "history," though sometimes using "event" for "Geschichte" to preserve the author's nuance].

historian/exegete relate to each other.[6] The classical ideal of historicism, namely, to present nothing more or less than "what actually happened,"[7] has proven to be an ideological postulate in several regards.[8] As the present passes into the past, it irrevocably loses its character as reality. For this reason alone it is not possible to recall the past without rupture into the present. The temporal interval signifies a fading away in every regard; it disallows historical knowledge in the sense of a comprehensive restoration of what once happened.[9] All one can do is declare in the present one's own interpretation of the past. The past is available to us exclusively in the mode of the present, again only in interpreted and selected form.[10] Only that is relevant from the past which is no longer merely past but influences world formation and world interpretation in the present.[11] The true temporal plane on which the historian/exegete lives is always the present,[12] within which he or she is inextricably intertwined, so that present understanding of past events is always decisively stamped by the historian's own cultural standards. The historian/exegete's social setting, its traditions, its political and religious values necessarily affect what he or she says in the present about the

6. Cf. Jörn Rüsen, *Historische Vernunft* (Grundzüge einer Historik 1; Göttingen: Vandenhoeck & Ruprecht, 1983); *Rekonstruktion der Vergangenheit: Die Prinzipien der historischen Forschung* (Grundzüge einer Historik 2; Göttingen: Vandenhoeck & Ruprecht, 1986); *Lebendige Geschichte: Formen und Funktionen des historischen Wissens* (Grundzüge einer Historik 3; Göttingen: Vandenhoeck & Ruprecht, 1989); Hans-Jürgen Goertz, *Umgang mit Geschichte: Eine Einführung in die Geschichtstheorie* (Reinbek: Rowohlt, 1995); Christoph Conrad and Martina Kessel, *Geschichte Schreiben in der Postmoderne: Beiträge zur aktuellen Diskussion* (Stuttgart: Reclam, 1994); V. Sellin, *Einführung in die Geschichtswissenschaften* (Göttingen: Vandenhoeck & Ruprecht, 1995). [Translator's note: Most of the works of Jörn Rüsen referred to here and in the following have not been translated, but his perspectives and major theses within the context of recent discussion are available in Jörn Rüsen, ed., *Western Historical Thinking: An Intercultural Debate* (New York: Berghahn Books, 2002); and Jörn Rüsen et al., eds., *Studies in Metahistory* (Pretoria: HSRC, 1993).]

7. Leopold von Ranke, "Geschichten der romanischen und germanischen Völker von 1494–1514," in *Sämmtliche Werke* (Leipzig: Duncker & Humblot, 1868–1890), vol. 33/34, p. VII: "People have conferred on history the responsibility of restoring the past to make it useful for the instruction of years to come. The present work does not accept such a high office: it only wants to set forth what actually happened." Cf. R. Vierhaus, "Rankes Begriff der historischen Objektivität," in *Objektivität und Parteilichkeit* (ed. W. J. Mommsen and J. Rüsen; Munich: Deutscher Taschenbuch-Verlag 1977), 63–76.

8. Goertz, *Umgang mit Geschichte*, 130–31.

9. Udo Schnelle, "Der historische Abstand und der Heilige Geist," in *Reformation und Neuzeit: 300 Jahre Theologie in Halle* (ed. Udo Schnelle; Berlin: de Gruyter, 1994), 87–103.

10. Hans-Jürgen Goertz, *Unsichere Geschichte: Zur Theorie historischer Referentialität* (Stuttgart: Reclam, 2001), 24.

11. Cf. Johann Gustav Droysen, *Outline of the Principles of History* (trans. E. Benjamin Andrews; New York: Fertig, 1893), 11: "The data for historical investigation are not past things, for these have disappeared, but things which are still present here and now, whether recollections of what was done, or remnants of things that have existed and of events that have occurred."

12. Paul Ricoeur, *Time and Narrative* (trans. Kathleen McLaughlin and David Pellauer; 3 vols.; Chicago: University of Chicago Press, 1984), 3:145: "The first way of thinking about the pastness of the past is to dull the sting of what is at issue, namely, temporal distance."

past.[13] Moreover, the very conditions of understanding, especially reason and the particular context, are subject to a process of continuing transformation, inasmuch as historical knowledge is determined by each period of intellectual history and its constantly changing goals and guidelines for obtaining knowledge.[14] Insight into the historicality of the knowing subject calls for reflection on his or her role in the act of understanding, for the knowing subject does not stand above history but is entirely involved in it. Therefore, if one wants to describe historical understanding, it is altogether inappropriate to contrast "objectivity" and "subjectivity."[15] The use of such terminology serves rather as a literary strategy of declaring one's own position as positive and neutral in order to discredit other interpretations as subjective and ideological.[16] The object known cannot be separated from the knowing subject, for the act of knowing also always effects a change in the object that is known. The awareness of reality attained in the act of knowing and the past reality itself are not related as original and copy.[17] One should thus speak not of the "objectivity" of historical arguments but of their plausibility and appropriateness to their subject matter.[18] After all, reports introduced into historical arguments as "facts" are as a rule themselves already interpretations of past events. The past event itself is not available to us but only the various understandings of the past event, mediated to us by various interpreters. History is not reconstructed but unavoidably and necessarily *constructed*. The common perception that things need only be "reported" or "re-constructed" suggests a knowledge of the original events that does not exist in the manner presupposed by this terminology. Nor is history simply identical with the past; rather, it always represents only a stance in the

13. J. Straub, "Über das Bilden von Vergangenheit," in *Geschichtsbewußtsein: Psychologische Grundlagen, Entwicklungskonzepte, empirische Befunde* (ed. Jörn Rüsen; Cologne: Böhlau, 2001), 45: "Representations of events and developments do not deliver mimetic models of events that once happened but perceptions of events bound to particular capacities of understanding and interpretation. Such interpretations are formed from the perspective of a particular present by particular persons and are thus directly dependent on the experiences, expectations, orientations, and interests of these persons."

14. Historical knowledge has available to it only what it supposes to be historical "truth," which means that "historical truth is constituted . . . in the process of a constant revision of the results of research in the academic discourse of scholars" (Friedrich Jaeger and Jörn Rüsen, *Geschichte des Historismus: Eine Einführung* [Munich: Beck, 1992], 70).

15. Goertz, *Umgang mit Geschichte*, 130–46.

16. A tendentious argument to this effect is found in Heikki Räisänen, *Neutestamentliche Theologie? Eine religionswissenschaftliche Alternative* (SBS 186; Stuttgart: Katholisches Bibelwerk, 2000); and (more moderately) in Gerd Theissen, *The Religion of the Earliest Churches: Creating a Symbolic World* (trans. John Bowden; Minneapolis: Fortress, 1999), 17–18, 306–7. They attempt to describe their history-of-religions approaches as "objective" and "value-neutral" although their theological perspectives fall at least implicitly under the verdict of ideology. For a delineation and critique of these proposals, cf. A. Lindemann, "Zur 'Religion' des Urchristentums," *TRu* 67 (2002): 238–61.

17. Cf. Goertz, *Unsichere Geschichte*, 55–56.

18. Cf. J. Kocka, "Angemessenheitskriterien historischer Argumente," in *Objektivität und Parteilichkeit* (ed. W. J. Mommsen and J. Rüsen; Munich: Deutscher Taschenbuch-Verlag, 1977), 469–75.

present from which one can view the past. Thus within the realm of historical constructions, there are no "facts" in the "objective" sense; interpretations are built on interpretations.[19] Hence the truth of the statement "Events are not [in themselves] history; they become history."[20]

In addition to these epistemological insights, we now come to reflections on the philosophy of language. History is always mediated to us in linguistic form; *history exists only to the extent that it is expressed in language.* Historical reports become history only through the semantically organized construction of the historian/exegete. In this process, language functions not only to describe the object of thought accepted as reality; language also determines and places its stamp on all perceptions that are organized as history.[21] For human beings, there is no path from language to an independent, extralinguistic reality, for reality is present to us only in and through language.[22] History is thus available only as memory—mediated and formed by language. And again, language itself is culturally conditioned and subject to constant social transformation,[23] so it is not surprising that historical events are construed and evaluated differently in situations shaped by different cultures and values. Language is much more than a mere reflection of reality, for it regulates and places its own stamp on

19. Classical examples are the differing pictures of Socrates in Xenophon and Plato and the contrasting portrayals of the Roman emperors in Tacitus and Suetonius.

20. Johann Gustav Droysen, *Historik: Rekonstruktion der ersten vollständigen Fassung der Vorlesungen* (Stuttgart–Bad Cannstatt: Frommann-Holzboog, 1857; repr., 1977), 69. On the same page Droysen judiciously comments regarding historical circumstances: "They are only historical because they are interpreted historically, not objective realities in and of themselves but in and through our observation and appropriation. We must, so to speak, transpose them into a different key." On the nature of historical knowledge as itself a construction, in addition to Droysen, cf. in the older literature esp. W. von Humboldt, "Ueber die Aufgabe des Geschichtsschreibers" (1822), in *Schriften zur Anthropologie und Geschichte* (vol. 1 of *Werke*; Darmstadt: Wissenschaftliche Buchgesellschaft, 1960), 585–606; J. Burckhardt, *Weltgeschichtliche Betrachtungen: Über geschichtliches Studium* (1870/1871; Munich: Deutscher Taschenbuch-Verlag, 1978); E. Troeltsch, "Was heißt 'Wesen des Christentums'?" in *Gesammelte Schriften* (4 vols.; 2nd ed.; Tübingen, 1922; repr., Aalen: Scientia, 1977), 2:386–451. The history and power of historicism's worldview is illustrated by Jörn Rüsen, *Konfigurationen des Historismus: Studien zur deutschen Wissenschaftskultur* (Frankfurt: Suhrkamp, 1993).

21. Cf. also R. Koselleck, *Vergangene Zukunft: Zur Semantik geschichtlicher Zeiten* (4th ed.; Frankfurt: Suhrkamp, 2000), who points out that the interpretation of sources and the formation of theories, as events that are mainly linguistically structured processes, always influence each other. In order to be able to write history/histories, one must have a theory of possible history/histories.

22. On the significance of these insights for exegesis, cf. Ulrich Luz, "Kann die Bibel heute noch Grundlage für die Kirche sein?" *NTS* 44 (1998) 317–39, who points out that the capacity of texts as the bearers of meaning is not denied by the claim that reality is linguistically constructed.

23. Cf. Günter Dux, "Wie der Sinn in die Welt kam und was aus ihm wurde," in *Historische Sinnbildung: Problemstellungen, Zeitkonzepte, Wahrnehmungshorizonte, Darstellungsstrategien* (ed. Klaus E. Müller and Jörn Rüsen; Reinbek bei Hamburg: Rowohlt, 1997), 203, who rightly objects to the mystification of language associated with the linguistic turn: "Pragmatism, which underlies the formative process of the mind, also underlies the formative process of language. The ability to act competently is inseparably bound to the way one constructs external reality. . . . Language has its genesis in the process of enculturation, just as does every other mental acquisition."

the appropriation of reality and thereby also on our pictures of what is real. At the same time, language is not *the* reality itself, for language too first comes into being in the course of human history and in the personal history of every human being within the framework of his or her biological and cultural development. In this process, language is decisively influenced by the varieties of human cultures and individual lives.[24] This constant process of change to which language is subject can only be explained in relation to the different social contexts by which it is conditioned;[25] that is, the connection between the signifier and the signified must be maintained if one does not want to surrender reality itself.

History as Meaning Formation

History is thus always a selective system by means of which the interpreter orders and interprets not merely the past but especially his or her own world. The linguistic construction of past events always therefore takes place as a *meaning-creating* process that confers meaning on both past and present; such constructions provide the sense-making capacity that facilitates the individual's orientation within the complex framework of life.[26] Historical interpretation means the creation of a coherent framework of meaning; facts only become what they are for us by the creation of such a historical narrative framework.[27] In this process historical reports must be made accessible to the present and expressed in language, so that in the presentation/narration of history, "facts" and "fiction"[28]—traditional data and the creative-

24. Günter Dux, *Historisch-genetische Theorie der Kultur: Instabile Welten: Zur prozessualen Logik im kulturellen Wandel* (Weilerswist: Velbrück Wissenschaft, 2000), 297: "The acquisition of language is the result of processing one's experiences. Language is not simply 'there,' prior to one's developing competence in dealing with the world, as a system already installed in the chromosomes. It is formed in the process of developing the capacity to interact with the external world and in the construction of this world."

25. Goertz, *Unsichere Geschichte*, 55–56.

26. On meaning formation as an aspect of historical theory, cf. Jörn Rüsen, "Historische Methode und religiöser Sinn—Vorüberlegungen zu einer Dialektik der Rationalisierung des historischen Denkens in der Moderne," in *Geschichtsdiskurs* (ed. Wolfgang Küttler et al.; 5 vols.; Frankfurt: Fischer, 1993–1999) 2:346. On the multilayered term "meaning formation," cf. E. List, "Sinn," in *Handbuch religionswissenschaftlicher Grundbegriffe* (ed. Günter Kehrer et al.; 5 vols.; Stuttgart: Kohlhammer, 1988), 5:62–71. [Translator's note: I have usually rendered *Sinnbildung* by "meaning formation," but note its relation to *Sinnwelt*, usually translated "universe of meaning" or "symbolic universe" (cf. n. 60 below)].

27. Cf. Chris Lorenz, *Konstruktion der Vergangenheit: Eine Einführung in die Geschichtstheorie* (trans. Annegret Böttner; Cologne: Böhlau, 1997), 17ff.

28. "Fiction" is not here used in the popular sense of "unreal" or "untrue" but is meant in the functional-communication sense and thus approaches the original meaning of *fictio*: "construction," "formation" [translator's note: cf. the use of "fabrication" in English]. Cf. Wolfgang Iser, *The Act of Reading: A Theory of Aesthetic Response* (Baltimore: Johns Hopkins University Press, 1978), 54: "If

fictive work of an author—necessarily combine.[29] As historical reports are combined, historical gaps must be filled in; reports from the past and their interpretation in the present flow together to produce something new.[30] Interpretation inserts the past event into a structure that it did not previously have.[31] There are only potential facts, for experience and interpretation are necessary to grasp the meaning potential of an event.[32] "Bare" facts must have a meaning attached to them, and the structure of this interpretation constitutes the understanding of facts.[33] It is the fictional element that first opens up access to the past, for it makes possible the unavoidable rewriting of the presupposed events. The figurative, symbolic level is indispensable for historical work, for it develops the prefigured plan of interpretation that shapes the present's appropriation and interpretation of the past. The fundamental principle is that history originates only after the event on which it is based has been discerned as relevant for the present, so that necessarily history cannot have the same claim to reality as the events themselves on which it is based.[34] This means that any outline of the history of the life and thought of Paul must always be only an approach to the past events themselves, an approach that must be aware of its theoretical presupposi-

---

it [fiction] is not reality, this is not because it lacks the attributes of reality, but because it tells us something about reality, and the conveyer cannot be identical to what is conveyed. Furthermore, once the time-honored convention has been replaced by the concept of communication, attention must be paid to the hitherto neglected recipient of the message. Now if the reader and the literary text are partners in a process of communication, and if what is communicated is to be of any value, our prime concern will no longer be the *meaning* of the text (the hobbyhorse ridden by the critics of yore) but its *effect*. Herein lies the function of literature, and herein lies the justification for approaching literature from a functionalist standpoint." Goertz, *Unsichere Geschichte*, 20: "The fictional element is not the free reign of poetic fantasy, which ignores, supplements, or trims the facts of the past to its own liking. It is, rather, the mediator, which first makes access to the past possible at all by facilitating its interpretation."

29. Cf. Goertz, *Umgang mit Geschichte*, 101–3.

30. See Luke 1:1–4; Plutarch, *Alex.* 1:1 (οὔτε γὰρ ἱστορίας γράφομεν ἀλλὰ βίους [for I am not writing history but portraying lives]). These two texts unmistakably illustrate that ancient authors, too, had a clear awareness of these connections.

31. Cf. the discussion in Goertz, *Unsichere Geschichte*, 16ff., oriented to how these issues have been dealt with in the history of scholarship.

32. This constructive aspect of the knowledge process also applies to the natural sciences. Constructiveness and contextuality determine the fabrication of knowledge; the natural sciences are always an interpreted reality that increasingly reflects the invisible currents of political and economic interests that involve us both individually and globally. Cf. K. Knorr-Cetina, *Die Fabrikation von Erkenntnis: Zur Anthropologie der Naturwissenschaft* (2nd ed.; Frankfurt: Suhrkamp, 1991). The criteria of rationality and objectivity brought to bear within the social debate mostly serve to conceal the process of domestication that the natural sciences have experienced worldwide.

33. Cf. Goertz, *Umgang mit Geschichte*, 87: "It is thus not pure facticity that constitutes a 'historical fact.' Rather, it is the significance of an event, which is only gradually perceived and adopted and which otherwise would have sunk unnoticed into the past, that confers this special quality upon it. Not in its own time but only after its time does a 'bare fact' become a historical fact."

34. Cf. Rüsen, *Historische Vernunft*, 58ff.

tions regarding the writing of history, its own constructive character, and the problems inherent in its task.

Paul as Maker of History and Meaning

What particular problems does Paul present to the writer of history? In the first place, one must reflect on the fact that Paul himself does all that has just been described: by narrating and interpreting the event of Jesus Christ in a particular way, *he himself writes history and constructs a new religious world.*[35] His interpretation allows a uniquely effective power to emerge, because its multifaceted nature allows it to proceed in several directions, uniting with other elements: the story of Jesus, Judaism, and Hellenism. This capacity for inclusion grew out of the apostle's own life journey, so that in Paul's case one must think of the relation of biography and theology in a particular way. In Paul, biography and theology congeal into a tensive unity, for "Paul is the only man of Primitive-Christian times whom we really know."[36] Of the ten New Testament documents whose authors are known, seven come from Paul. His letters from ca. 50–61 CE provide insight into his theological thought[37] but also illuminate his personal feelings. Extensive sections are charged with emotion and let Paul the human being come before our mind's eye with all his strengths and weaknesses. At the same time, the course of Paul's life prior to his emergence as a Pharisee zealous for the ancestral traditions lies more or less in the dark. The Christian socialization of the apostle, his activity

35. This insight is fundamental for the understanding of Paul here presented, for "what is decisive is not to get out of the circle but to come into it in the right way" (Martin Heidegger, *Being and Time* [trans. Joan Stambaugh; Albany: State University of New York Press, 1996; originally published in German, 1927;], 153).

36. Albert Schweitzer, *The Mysticism of Paul the Apostle* (trans. William Montgomery; London: A. & C. Black, 1931), 332.

37. A note on terminology: I use "thought" in a broad, general sense, on the level of forming, managing, and interpreting one's everyday life—the active use and intentional binding together of ideas and concepts. The issues are which concepts and ideas does Paul take up, by which rules does he relate them, to what sort of logic does he feel obligated, and what are the constructive elements in his worldview. As an active and formative event, theology is bound together with movements of thought whose rules are to be grasped. On the concept of "thinking/thought," cf. C. von Bormann et al., "Denken," in *Historisches Wörterbuch der Philosophie: Völlig neubearbeitete Auflage des "Wörterbuchs der Philosophischen Begriffe" von Rudolf Eisler* (ed. Karlfried Gründer et al.; Darmstadt: Wissenschaftliche Buchgesellschaft, 1971–), 2:60–102 (historical survey); H. Lenk, *Das Denken und sein Gehalt* (Munich: Oldenbourg, 2001) (philosophical explorations and definitions). Lenk sees the distinctive element in human thought (in contrast to animals) in its metalinguistic and metatheoretical capacities. He emphasizes the intentional and constructive character of thought—"Perception is a constructive process" (p. 368)—and points out the complexity of this achievement: "We are thus dealing with interpretative constructs that are cooperating cognitive or norming schemata. They are stabilized by both internal and external factors and by natural and social conditions and controls" (p. 369).

as a missionary for the Antioch church, and his independent mission prior to the composition of 1 Thessalonians can be glimpsed only as fragments. Nonetheless, this phase is of preeminent importance for understanding the apostle's personality, for his fundamental convictions were formed during this period. The different sources that provide the bases for constructing the individual phases of Paul's work and thought make it difficult to relate his biography and his theology to each other in a way that accounts for the data.

Furthermore, there are gaps in phases of Paul's life as documented by his letters. Since they were part of a comprehensive communications network between the apostle, his coworkers, and particular congregations, the letters were written not as world literature but to resolve urgent congregational problems. We do not know what Paul did and taught in the churches beyond what is contained in these letters. Within the framework of debates with congregations and opponents, as a rule we have only Paul's own position; divergent views are unknown or can only be surmised hypothetically. On the one hand, Paul's letters present us with an inexhaustible source of material for reflection on the apostle, reflection that has continued for almost two thousand years, with no end in sight; on the other hand, they are only historical and theological snapshots.

Finally, the Pauline letters present numerous questions regarding content:[38] What is their determinative theme? What are Paul's fundamental theological affirmations? What caused him to carry out a mission to almost the whole world (from the perspective of that time)? Was he aware that his work essentially called for the establishment of early Christianity[39] as an independent movement? Is it possible to locate the center of Paul's theological thinking, from which his thought may be grasped as a whole? Can pointed statements conditioned by particular situations be distinguished from, and meaningfully coordinated with, his fundamental theological principles? Does Paul's thought represent a comprehensive system free of contradictions? In tracing out the path of Paul's life and thought, is it better to grasp the material by a chronological or a thematic "handle"?

38. On the history of the research, cf. the recent studies of Hans Hübner, "Paulusforschung seit 1945," *ANRW* 25.4:2649–2840; and Otto Merk, "Paulus-Forschung 1936–1985," *TRu* 53 (1988): 1–81. For current work, see Christian Strecker, "Paul aus einer neuen 'Perspektiv,'" *KuI* 11 (1996): 3–18; Thomas Söding, "Rechtfertigung," *NBL* 3: 288–98; K.W. Niebuhr, "Die paulinische Rechtfertigungslehre in der gegenwärtigen exegetischen Diskussion," in *Worum geht es in der Rechtfertigungslehre? Das biblische Fundament der "Gemeinsamen Erklärung" von katholischer Kirche und Lutherischem Weltbund* (ed. Frank-Lothar Hossfeld and Thomas Söding; QD 180; Freiburg: Herder, 1999), 106–30.

39. Since there never existed a "primitive Christianity" [*Urchristentum*] in the sense of an epoch of uncorrupted beginnings, I use the term "early Christianity" [*frühes Christentum*]. Cf. Stefan Alkier, *Urchristentum: Zur Geschichte und Theologie einer exegetischen Disziplin* (BHT 83; Tübingen: Mohr Siebeck, 1993), 261–66.

1.3 Methodological "Handle": Meaning Formation in Continuity and Change

Human existence and action are characterized by their capacity for *meaning*.[40] No form of human life can be defined "without reference to meaning. It makes sense to understand meaning as the fundamental category of human existence."[41] The insights of cultural anthropology regarding the ability of human beings to transcend both themselves and the life world of their society and culture indicate this.[42] Moreover, human beings are always born into a world of meaning.[43] The drive to make sense of things is an unavoidable part of human life, for the human life world must be thought about, disclosed, and appropriated in some meaningful way—only thus are human life and action possible in this world.[44] As a form of meaning formation, every religion is such a process of disclosure and appropriation, including early Christianity and the theologies developed within it. Concretely, this process of disclosure and appropriation takes place as the formation of meaning, and Pauline theology is the result of a historical project of meaning formation in which Paul invested his whole life, a theology

40. The basic work is Alfred Schutz, *The Phenomenology of the Social World* (trans. George Walsh and Frederick Lehnert; London: Heinemann, 1972).

41. Dux, "Sinn in die Welt," 195.

42. Cf. Alfred Schutz and Thomas Luckmann, *The Structures of the Life-World* (trans. Richard M. Zaner, H. Tristram Engelhardt Jr., and David J. Parent; NUSPEP; Evanston, IL: Northwestern University Press, 1973, 1989), 2:99–157. Their point of departure is the undeniable experience of everyday life, experience that always necessarily transcends that of any individual, which means that existence is not livable without transcendence: we live in a world that was here before us and will be here after us. Reality almost always retreats from our efforts to grasp it, and the existence of other people, whose inner selves can never be truly known, provokes the question of our own selfhood. "By the fact that it constantly goes beyond itself in thematic field and horizon, every experience of every content whatsoever becomes, let us say, a 'co-experience' of transcendence. In the natural attitude this 'co-experience' is not itself taken into the group consciousness as theme; however, it forms the lowest stratum of the foundation on which knowledge of the 'transcendence' of the world rests" (p. 105). Schutz and Luckmann distinguish three forms of the experience of transcendence, which derive from the distinction between ego-referential and ego-surpassing experiences: (1) "Little" transcendent elements of everyday life (present experiences refer back to earlier experiences or nonexperiences); "medium" transcendent elements—other people (fellow human beings, contemporaries and generations); (3) "great" transcendent elements—other realities (sleep, dreams, ecstasies, crises, death).

43. Cf. Thomas Luckmann, "Religion–Gesellschaft–Transzendenz," in *Krise der Immanenz: Religion an den Grenzen der Moderne* (ed. Hans-Joachim Höhn and Karl Gabriel; Philosophie der Gegenwart; Frankfurt: Fischer, 1996), 114: "Meaning traditions transcend the mere natural state of the newborn." In the fundamental anthropological sense, this process can also be designated by the term "religion," which is to be distinguished from concrete historical manifestations of religions in the sense of confessional communities or denominations. Cf. p. 113: "I proceed from the fact that human life, in contrast to the life forms of other species, is characterized by a fundamental religious sense, namely, by the embedding of the individual in meaningful historical worlds."

44. Jörn Rüsen, "Was heißt: Sinn der Geschichte?" in *Historische Sinnbildung: Problemstellungen, Zeitkonzepte, Wahrnehmungshorizonte, Darstellungsstrategien* (ed. Klaus E. Müller and Jörn Rüsen; Reinbek bei Hamburg: Rowohlt, 1997), 17–47, here 38.

that already exercised its distinctive effect within the apostle's own lifetime. The "three components of experience, interpretation, and orientation" constitute historical meaning.[45] The meaningfulness of an event cannot be derived from its facticity alone; it still needs the experience of a particular person or persons before its meaning potential can be actualized.

Paul develops his experience of the resurrected Jesus Christ on the Damascus road into a new interpretation of God, world, and human existence, one that leads to a radically changed orientation to life.[46] The disclosure of God and the world that occurred in the light of the Damascus event generates an interpretation and an orientation within which the interpreted perceptions can be applied "to an intentional guide for action."[47] In order to come to terms with the world, the world must be interpreted. The fundamental constructive character of the historical formation of meaning is obvious in the case of Paul, for he confers new dimensions on the Christ event (the Jesus-Christ-history) (cf. 1 Cor. 11:23b–25; 15:3b–5), in that, as "minister of Jesus Christ to the Gentiles," he universalizes it and installs it into history through his successful mission. What is fundamental in the narration of any event[48] is also the case with Paul: he necessarily tells of the destiny of Jesus Christ in a selective manner and from a particular perspective; the beginning point and the course of the narration of the Jesus-Christ-history is qualified by its end point. Paul narrates not the story of Jesus but the event of Jesus Christ,[49] for throughout he presupposes the unity of the earthly Jesus and the crucified and risen one, which comprehends both the preexistence of Christ and his parousia.[50]

The quality of Pauline theology as meaning formation is seen in its *capacity for incorporation and combination.* "Historical meaning must fulfill the condition of the genetic capacity to incorporate and combine disparate elements in which subjective constructions proceed on the basis of given data in interpretive interaction with the human past and that develop in relation both to the given data and to the needs of the subjects determined by them."[51] Pauline theol-

---

45. Ibid., 36.

46. See below, chapter 4 ("The Call to Be Apostle to the Gentiles").

47. Rüsen, "Was heißt: Sinn der Geschichte?" 28.

48. Here a broader concept of narrative is presupposed that is not determined by specific literary genres. Proceeding from the fundamental insight that experience of time must be processed in the narrative mode, it is natural to interpret "narrative as a meaning- or sense-laden linguistic form, or one that creates sense or meaning. That is to say, the narrative form of human thematizing makes sense of, and confers meaning on, the happenings and actions—independently of the particular content of the narrative presentation" (Straub, "Bilden von Vergangenheit," 51f.). For a broad concept of narrative, cf. also Roland Barthes, *The Semiotic Challenge* (trans. Richard Howard; New York: Hill & Wang, 1988), 95–135.

49. See below, section 5.1 ("Rehearsal and Coaching: Paul and Early Christian Tradition").

50. Cf. Eckart Reinmuth, "Narratio und Argumentatio—zur Auslegung der Jesus-Christus-Geschichte im Ersten Korintherbrief," *ZTK* 92 (1995): 21.

51. Rüsen, "Was heißt: Sinn der Geschichte?" 38.

ogy manifests this inclusive capacity to incorporate and combine in regard to the Jesus-Christ-history and its first interpretations in early Christianity but also in regard to the Old Testament, to contemporary Judaism, and to Hellenism, the prevailing cultural power of the time. This capacity for inclusion grew out of Paul's background and the course of his life but also from the plausibility of his interpretation of the Jesus-Christ-history and his ability to create something new in response to historical challenges. Paul succeeded in translating his religious experiences into a multilayered system of thought and to differentiate it further in response to new historical challenges. The task of a presentation of Paul's life and thought must therefore be to interpret this process in its temporal and material dimensions. Meaning formation itself is always a historical process and only possible when there is a "relevance of the past-made-present for the problems of orienting oneself in the present."[52] Thus the task is to work out answers to the basic questions: *How did Pauline theology develop as an act of historical meaning formation? What gives this theology its persuasive power for a particular view of the world and for practical action within this world?*

Meaning Formation and the Formation of Identity

Meaning formation is always bound up with the projection of one's own sense of identity;[53] meaning formation functions successfully only when it projects a convincing sense of identity. Identity, in turn, develops as a constant interaction between the experience of differentiation and the positive determination of the self.[54] Identity can never be grasped as a static entity,[55] for it is part of an ongoing process of reformation, since, "as unity and selfhood of the subject," identity is "conceivable only as a synthesis of different, hetero-

---

52. Ibid., 35.

53. Cf. Thomas Luckmann, *Die unsichtbare Religion* (2nd ed.; Frankfurt: Suhrkamp, 1993), 93, who explains "worldview" as the matrix of meaning that forms the framework "within which human organisms formulate their identity and thereby transcend their biological nature."

54. On the concept of identity cf. B. Estel, "Identität," *HRWG* 3:193–210; for an introduction to the current ways of posing the issues in the widespread debate over "identity," cf. Jürgen Straub, *Erzählung, Identität, und historisches Bewußtsein: Die psychologische Konstruktion von Zeit und Geschichte* (2nd ed.; Frankfurt: Suhrkamp, 2000); Aleida Assmann and Heidrun Friese, eds., *Identities: Time, Difference, and Boundaries* (Making Sense of History 2; New York: Berghahn Books, 2001). The continuing complaint about the inflationary use of "identity" is, from one point of view, justified; on the other hand, one reason the complaint makes no progress is that there is no real alternative usage. A usable definition of "identity" is found in K. H. Hillmann, *Wörterbuch der Soziologie* (4th ed.; Stuttgart: A. Kröner, 1994), 350: "identity" is "the agreement of a person, social structure, or cultural objectification or a particular object of nature with what he, she, or it in fact is, thus with itself ('the self,' 'selfhood')."

55. Lorenz, *Konstruktion der Vergangenheit*, 407: "Persons and groups do not in fact find their identity in a prepackaged form in the given factual circumstances but form their identity in a reconstruction of the past within their view of the present and with a view to the future."

geneous elements that must be brought into relationship with each other."[56] The process of identity formation is determined by three equal factors: (1) the perceiving of one's difference from the surrounding world, (2) the encountering of boundaries set by one's inner self and by the world external to one's own experience, and (3) the positive perception of one's self. So also collective identities are formed by the processing of differentiating experiences and feelings of commonality.[57] Group identity is more than the sum of the identities of its members, for the new collective identity reacts with and affects the process of identity formation of the individual. At the same time, the interaction of the new group with its external world is of decisive significance, for identity is always an ascribed, imputed entity. The external perspective can evoke positive or negative reactions, which in turn have an effect on the internal perspective, that is, the self-perception of the group and its sense of self-worth. Moreover, collective identities are unstable compounds that always live from the continuing identification of the members with the new group.[58] *Symbols* play a decisive role in this process, for it is only with their help that collective identity can be created and maintained.[59] Universes of meaning must be able to articulate themselves in the world of secular reality and maintain their contents in a way that can be communicated. To a considerable degree this happens through symbols, which function in the life world as signs that open up new symbolic universes,[60] forming bridges of meaning "from one province of reality . . . into

56. J. Straub, "Temporale Orientierung und narrative Kompetenz," in *Geschichtsbewußtsein: Psychologische Grundlagen, Entwicklungskonzepte, empirische Befunde* (ed. Jörn Rüsen; Cologne: Böhlau, 2001), 15–44, here 39f.

57. Whether one can speak of collective identity formations at all is a disputed point; negative votes are cast by Peter L. Berger and Thomas Luckmann, *The Social Construction of Reality: A Treatise in the Sociology of Knowledge* (New York: Random House, 1966), 159; on the positive side is Jan Assmann, *Das kulturelle Gedächtnis: Schrift, Erinnerung, und politische Identität in frühen Hochkulturen* (Munich: Beck, 1992), 130ff. A balanced treatment is found in J. Straub, "Personal and Collective Identities," in *Identities: Time, Difference, and Boundaries* (ed. Aleida Assmann and Heidrun Friese; Making Sense of History 2; New York: Berghahn Books, 2001), 73–104. Straub rightly holds firm to the concept of collective identity, while at the same time tracing it back to individual identity: "According to the understanding here advocated, collective identities are constructs to be described as common elements (which can be specified in particular) in the practical relation to self and world as well as in the way individuals understand their relation to themselves and their world" (p. 103).

58. Cf. Straub, *Erzählung*, 102–3.

59. Cf. ibid., 97–98.

60. For comprehensive discussions of symbol, cf. G. Kurz, *Metapher, Allegorie, Symbol* (4th ed.; Göttingen: Vandenhoeck & Ruprecht, 1997); Michael Meyer-Blanck, *Vom Symbol zum Zeichen: Symboldidaktik und Semiotik* (2nd ed.; Rheinbach: CMZ, 2002); Loretta Dornisch, "Symbolic Systems and the Interpretation of Scripture: An Introduction to the Work of Paul Ricoeur," *Semeia* 4 (1975): 1–22, and the accompanying bibliographies, pp. 23–28 and *Semeia* 19 (1981) 23–32; Paul Tillich, "The Meaning and Justification of Religious Symbols," in *The Interpretation of Texts* (ed. David E. Klemm et al.; Hermeneutical Inquiry 1; Atlanta: Scholars Press, 1986), 165–71. [Translator's note: I have followed the convention of translating *Sinnwelt* (lit. "meaning-world") as "universe of meaning" or "symbolic universe" (cf. n. 26 above).]

another."[61] Particularly in the processing of the "large transcendent elements"[62] such as sickness, crises, and death, symbols play a fundamental role, for they belong to another level of reality and are themselves bearers of that reality and thus can establish communication with that realm. Symbols are a central category for the communication of religious meaning. Identity formation is thus always integrated into a complex process of interaction between the individual or collective subject, its experience of differentiation and boundaries, and its perception of self and nonself.

The respective determinations of identity are necessarily achieved through *universes of meaning* or *symbolic universes*, the interpretative models that as social constructions stand ready to facilitate the experience of reality in a meaningful way.[63] Symbolic universes are objectified as signs and symbols and thus represent reality in a communicable form. Among other things, symbolic universes legitimize social structures, institutions, and roles; that is, they explain and provide the basis for things as they are.[64] In addition, symbolic universes integrate these roles into a meaningful whole within which individual persons or groups can act. Just as human beings always unite different roles in themselves and belong to different groups, so they also always live in different symbolic universes at the same time. Family, race, education, friendships, school, education, work represent different levels of symbolic universes given by society; individual human beings locate themselves and live out their lives within these pre-given categories. For the most part, hierarchies are formed within this natural multiplicity of symbolic universes; the final hierarchical level must then serve as the overarching legitimation and integration of all the partial systems. This highest level can be called the "symbolic universe"[65] or the "worldview."[66] It confers a unifying meaningful sense on the individual meaning systems and, seen from the point of view of the sociology of knowledge, arises like all meaning systems in the process of social construction, objectification, and legitimization. Even these highest universes of meaning, the symbolic universes, can enter into competition with each other. For the most part, particular groups that bear and are borne by their respective symbolic universes will attempt to negate other symbolic universes by assimilating and integrating them into their own symbolic universe, by ignoring them, or by actively opposing them.

61. Schutz and Luckmann, *Structures*, 1:127.

62. Ibid., 99–134.

63. On the terms "universe of meaning" and "symbolic universe," cf. Berger and Luckmann, *Social Construction*, 73ff.

64. Ibid., 42–43, 48–50, 86.

65. Cf. ibid., 88: "Symbolic universes constitute the fourth level of legitimation. These are bodies of theoretical tradition that integrate different provinces of meaning and encompass the institutional order in a symbolic totality, using the term 'symbolic' in the way we have previously defined. To reiterate, symbolic processes are processes of signification that refer to realities other than those of everyday experience."

66. Cf. Luckmann, *Die unsichtbare Religion*, 114.

The Limits of Constructivism

The approach to these issues from the point of view of the sociology of knowledge proceeds from the presupposition that theological statements too are always interwoven into a social context that conditions both their origin and their later understanding. This does not mean, however, adopting the ideological presuppositions of radical constructivism now prevailing in various sociological and philosophical models.[67] In this view, reality as a whole, including religion, is exclusively a matter of human construction; we generate the world in which we live by living in it.[68] The theoreticians of constructivism must accept that their theories themselves are a construction. Epistemologically, the constructivists are obviously under the same suspicion that they themselves have postulated.[69] Everyday life, in particular, is only possible when one accepts it without question as a given reality. Reflection and construction are always secondary acts; the methods and results of interpretations of reality cannot claim to grasp reality as a whole, or even that they themselves are that reality. The absolutism of radical constructivism proposes an intellectual negation of the biological and

67. Peter L. Berger, *The Sacred Canopy: Elements of a Sociological Theory of Religion* (Garden City: Doubleday, 1967), 180, is aware of the limited range of issues with which sociology can deal: "Thus sociological theory must, by its own logic, view religion as a human projection, and by the same logic can have nothing to say about the possibility that this projection may refer to something other than the being of its projector. . . . Indeed, if a religious view of the world is posited, the anthropological ground of these projections may itself be the reflection of a reality that *includes* both world and man." On the methodological boundaries of issues posed from the point of view of constructivism and the sociology of knowledge, cf. also Peter Lampe, "Wissenssoziologische Annäherung an das Neue Testament," *NTS* 43 (1997): 354ff.; Regina Börschel, *Die Konstruktion einer christlichen Identität: Paulus und die Gemeinde von Thessalonich in ihrer hellenistisch-römischen Umwelt* (BBB 128; Berlin: Philo, 2001), 16–19.

68. Translator's note: The basic tenet of radical constructivism, a recent philosophical movement centered at the University of Vienna, is that any kind of knowledge is constructed rather than perceived through senses. Among its leading proponents are Heinz von Foerster and Humberto R. Maturana. Maturana, as the founder of the epistemological theory of autopoiesis, focuses on the central role of the observer in the production of knowledge. For an introduction to the topic, cf. Siegfried J. Schmidt, *Der Diskurs des radikalen Konstruktivismus* (8th ed.; Frankfurt: Suhrkamp, 2000); cf. further Paul Watzlawick, *The Invented Reality: How Do We Know What We Believe We Know? Contributions to Constructivism* (New York: Norton, 1984); Ernst von Glaserfeld, *Radikaler Konstruktivismus* (Frankfurt: Suhrkamp, 1997); and Lynn Segal, *The Dream of Reality: Heinz von Foerster's Constructivism* (2nd ed.; Berlin: Springer, 2001), who explicates the view that there is no objectivity at all, only our belief in it: we do not discover the world but invent it. On the comprehensive work of Humberto R. Maturana, cf., for an introduction and a critical evaluation from a theological point of view, Roija Friedrich Weidhas, *Konstruktion, Wirklichkeit, Schöpfung: Das Wirklichkeitsverständnis des christlichen Glaubens im Dialog mit dem Radikalen Konstruktivismus unter besonderer Berücksichtigung der Kognitionstheorie H. Maturanas* (Frankfurt: Lang, 1994).

69. Cf. Goertz, *Unsichere Geschichte*, 111; Dux, *Theorie der Kultur*, 160: "The blind spot in logical absolutism, as we have known it in the postmodern understanding of constructivism and the theoretical system associated with it, consists in the fact that constructivism does not understand itself to be subject to any systemic complex of conditions."

cultural presuppositions of every individual human life and disdains the world of human experience.[70] It is precisely on the sociological plane that experience in the human life world is to be taken seriously, experiences that point to a level of reality that is to be named "God." After all, every construction must be based on something previously given, so that the acceptance of transcendent elements is unavoidable. The methodological necessity of construction must therefore be affirmed and at the same time sharply distinguished and separated from the ontological implications of radical constructivism.

Religion simply constitutes *the* symbolic universe as such,[71] since, far more than law, philosophy, or political ideologies, it claims to represent reality as such, which transcends all other realities: God, or The Holy. As the all-encompassing reality within which every human life is lived, religion presents a symbolic universe that, especially by means of symbols, integrates both individuals and groups into the wholeness of the universe, interprets the phenomena of life, offers guidelines for how to live one's life, and ultimately opens up perspectives beyond death.[72]

The Pauline symbolic universe represents an independent model within the variety of symbolic universes already present not only in Judaism and the Roman Hellenistic world but also within early Christianity. The Pauline gospel to the Gentiles is the erection of a new symbolic universe offering a new identity not dependent on other such offers. Obviously, the possibility of a new identity set forth by Paul was very attractive to both Jews and Gentiles, as documented by its uniquely successful history. At the same time, conflicts were unavoidable, for the Pauline concept of identity was in competition with several others within early Christianity and its social context. Paul had to struggle especially with the particular concepts of identity present in Judaism and certain groups of Jewish Christians. Also, the classical identity concepts prevalent in the Greco-Roman world were not untouched by Paul's message.

Criteria for an Interpretation of Paul

The considerations discussed above lead to seven methodological requirements necessary for a valid interpretation of Pauline thought that does justice to its complexity:

(1) We must construct a delineation of Paul's life and thought *chronologically*, since his thought cannot be separated from his life. Because here origin,

---

70. Cf. Dux, *Theorie der Kultur*, 147: "Constructivistic absolutism always results in only one thing: world and worlds, reality and realities according to inconceivable models from the formative capacity of the mind, without regard to language, communication, society, history, etc."

71. Cf. Luckmann, *Die unsichtbare Religion*, 108.

72. Cf. Berger, *Sacred Canopy*, 32: "The tenuous realities of the social world are grounded [by religion] in the sacred *realissimum*, which by definition is beyond the contingencies of human meanings and human activity."

development, and theology all condition each other,[73] it is amiss to attempt to grasp Pauline theology only in terms of the history of ideas. In Paul's case, issues of origin and background already have theological status, and the course of his life and the development of his thought were stamped even more by historical events, some of which were uniquely his own; these events fundamentally affected his thoughts, feelings, and actions. Therefore the first order of business is to focus on Paul's intellectual and spiritual homeland and the path that led to his being called as an apostle of Jesus Christ. This, however, is only a first step in the direction of the Pauline thought represented in his letters. The "dark" years between Damascus (33 CE) and 1 Thessalonians (50 CE) must be illuminated. It was in this period that Paul made fundamental decisions. A chronological outline thus makes it necessary to determine the number and order of authentic Pauline letters. It makes a serious difference whether we read Colossians and 2 Thessalonians as authentic documents representing Paul's theology[74] or whether we adopt the consensus of scholarship, according to which only seven letters are considered to be authentically Pauline (1 Thessalonians, 1–2 Corinthians, Galatians, Romans, Philippians, Philemon).[75] The chronological location of Galatians plays a key role in the issue of the relative order of the letters.[76] For evaluating the place of the doctrine of justification in Paul's thought, it is of considerable significance whether one dates Galatians after 1 Thessalonians but before the Corinthians letters, or directly prior to Romans.

It is false to object against this approach that the whole presentation of Paul's theology is based on a chronology for the letters that in the final analysis is only hypothetical. There is no way to avoid positing some chronology, since Paul's letters were in fact written in some chronological order and thus were composed in different situations. Whoever abandons the attempt to base a chronology on the best available evidence will either tacitly presuppose some such chronology or else proceed as though all the letters were written at the same time from the same situation.

By respecting the letters as individual documents, a chronological approach—in contrast to a purely thematic outline—takes seriously the fact that each one was embedded in, and affected by, its own situation. We can understand neither the extant letters nor Pauline theology as a whole apart from their particular

73. Cf. W. Wiefel, "Paulus und das Judentum," *ZdZ* 40 (1986): 65–81.

74. Thus, somewhat tendentiously, Peter Stuhlmacher, *Biblische Theologie des Neuen Testaments* (2 vols.; Göttingen: Vandenhoeck & Ruprecht, 1992), 1:225; James D. G. Dunn, *The Theology of Paul the Apostle* (Grand Rapids: Eerdmans, 1998), 13 n. 39.

75. I consider Colossians and 2 Thessalonians to be deutero-Pauline. For arguments, cf. Udo Schnelle, *The History and Theology of the New Testament Writings* (trans. M. Eugene Boring; Minneapolis: Fortress, 1998), 281–98, 315–25.

76. Arguments for the order adopted in this book are found in sections 8.1, 9.1, 10.1, 11.1, 12.1, 13.2, 13.3.

historical setting. This applies to Romans also, which is embedded in a complex theological and political situation and is not simply *the* Pauline theology as such[77] but Pauline theology in the year 56 CE as set forth for the Roman church.[78] The apostle's theology cannot be delineated in the timeless form of a doctrinal system of central theological concepts; rather, we must give it its rightful place by carefully attending to its historical development and the basic theological affirmations that bore it along. We can understand Paul's theology in a nuanced way only when we see his ideas in the concrete context of each individual letter. Only in this way can we attend to both continuity and change as we trace the course of his thought.

(2) Only the *textual data of the individual letters* can decide whether and to what extent we should regard their theological views as constant basic principles or as contingent modifications conditioned by the situation. Among the constant basic principles are the ideas on the basis of which Paul structures his thought, ideas that are load pillars of his thought structure, ideas that determine it throughout. "Modifications" is a neutral term, referring to changes that we can document by comparing texts.[79] Rather than generalize here about how to interpret these changes, we will treat them in the exegesis of particular texts, whether as applications purely dependent on the situation; as the deepening,

77. For a fundamentally different approach, see, e.g., Dunn, *Theology of Paul*, 730, who in fact structures his whole presentation on the outline of Romans and emphasizes that he presents Pauline theology "at the time he wrote Romans, using Romans as a template."

78. See below, section 12.2 ("The Letter to the Romans as a Contextualized Document").

79. I am consciously avoiding the term "developments" [*Entwicklungen*] here because it has become baggage-laden in the discussion. [Translator's note: Schnelle prefers the term *Wandlungen* (changes, transformations). What he objects to is the concept of progress in the linear sense, evolutionary connotations of "development," or the idea that Paul's thought is the unfolding of a primal experience or concept. I have retained the English word "development" throughout, since it usually is without such connotations.]

Of course, where it can be documented in the texts that Paul has developed his thought further, I too will continue to speak of "developments." On this methodological approach, see the comprehensive treatment in Udo Schnelle, *Wandlungen im paulinischen Denken* (SBS 137; Stuttgart: Katholisches Bibelwerk, 1989); cf. further Hans Dieter Betz, "Paul," *ABD* 5:186–201; "Das Problem der Grundlagen der paulinischen Ethik," in *Paulinische Studien* (Tübingen: Mohr Siebeck, 1994), 184–205; Klaus Berger, *Theologiegeschichte des Urchristentums: Theologie des Neuen Testaments* (Tübingen: Francke, 1994), 440; Friedrich Wilhelm Horn, *Das Angeld des Geistes: Studien zur paulinischen Pneumatologie* (FRLANT 154; Göttingen: Vandenhoeck & Ruprecht, 1992), 118; Thomas Söding, *Das Liebesgebot bei Paulus: Die Mahnung zur Agape im Rahmen der paulinischen Ethik* (NTAbh 26; Münster: Aschendorff, 1995), 278–79; Joachim Gnilka, *Paulus von Tarsus, Apostel und Zeuge* (HTKNT 6; Freiburg: Herder, 1996), 15–16; Jürgen Roloff, *Einführung in das Neue Testament* (Stuttgart: Reclam, 1995), 98–100. The point of departure within the history of theology for this approach was provided by nineteenth-century liberal theology, in which various forms of developmental schemes were advocated. Cf., e.g., L. Usteri, *Entwickelung des paulinischen Lehrbegriffs mit Hinsicht auf die übrigen Schriften des Neuen Testaments: Ein exegetisch-dogmatischer Versuch* (2nd ed.; Zurich: Orell, Füssli, 1829); H. Luedemann, *Die Anthropologie des Apostels Paulus und ihre Stellung innerhalb seiner Heilslehre* (Kiel: Universitäts-Buchhandlung, 1872). The two most significant studies of Paul in the twentieth century, from William Wrede (1904) and Albert Schweitzer (first draft 1906; published 1930), still stand in this tradition of liberal theology.

clarification, variation, or logical development of previous statements; as the revision of prior standpoints; or as completely new ideas. These possibilities do not necessarily represent alternatives, since some statements are conditioned by their situation and the thinking through or revision of previous statements and the formation of completely new theologoumena are by no means mutually exclusive.[80] Not all of Paul's statements must be coherent in themselves; breaks and tensions within one's thought are indications of living convictions of faith and the active reception of tradition. Moreover, Paul continued to work on individual themes and attained new levels of intellectual penetration and presentation. And finally, the extant letters allow us to see clearly how complex and, to some extent, tension-filled the personality of the apostle is, from both personal and theological points of view.[81] At the same time we must remember that the letters by no means constitute a complete compendium of Pauline doctrine. Paul did not always have to say everything; for the most part, we do not know what he proclaimed and taught in his churches when present in person, whether in their founding period or during later visits. Thus we should only speak of modifications when substantial changes can be documented in the same theme in the course of several letters.

(3) The unique *historical and theological situation* of Paul must be perceived and evaluated in all its complexity and uniqueness. The apostle found himself in a unique situation of upheaval and deep-rooted change. He saw himself confronted with problems that at their core have not yet been resolved: How is God's first revelation to be related to the second? Why does the first covenant continue without qualification (cf. Rom. 9:4–5) when only the second covenant saves? What criteria must be fulfilled in order to belong to the elect people of God and at the same time maintain continuity with the people of God of the first covenant? What is the significance of the law/Torah for faith in Christ? In what relation do believers in Christ stand to empirical Israel? Must theological affirmations be changed because of the delay of the parousia? In view of these problems, instability and unresolved tensions in Pauline thought not only are to be expected but, in view of the subject matter, are absolutely unavoidable, for these are questions that in the final analysis only God can answer. Therefore tensions and contradictions in Pauline thought should not be denied on overriding theological or ideological grounds but accepted and interpreted. Paul does

---

80. Cf. also Werner Georg Kümmel, "Das Problem der Entwicklung in der Theologie des Paulus," *NTS* 18 (1971–1972): 457–58; Hans-Heinrich Schade, *Apokalyptische Christologie bei Paulus: Studien zum Zusammenhang von Christologie und Eschatologie in den Paulusbriefen* (GTA 18; Göttingen: Vandenhoeck & Ruprecht, 1981), 350–51.

81. The comment of J. Jervell is altogether appropriate: "There are obvious contradictions in Paul—theological and personal. He is the suffering, persecuted, and weak apostle and at the same time the charismatic full of divine power" (J. Jervell, "Der unbekannte Paulus," in *Die paulinische Literatur und Theologie = The Pauline Literature and Theology: Anlässlich der 50 jährigen Gründungs-Feier der Universität von Aarhus* [ed. Sigfred Pedersen; Århus: Aros, 1980], 34).

not comply with the wish for consistent unity and systemization,[82] for neither the ideal of Paul the thinker nor the thesis that Paul is a mere practitioner[83] deficient in theory corresponds to the historical truth. It is rather a matter of ascertaining the abiding deep insight, the determining structure, and the inner logic of Pauline thought and distinguishing them from his applications based on these guidelines but shaped by the actual situations.

(4) A plausible portrayal of Paul must be integrable into the *history of early Christianity* and able to explain the apostle's effects on both his opponents and his disciples. The success of the Pauline Gentile mission essentially determined the history of early Christianity and in turn evoked reactions that had no small influence on Paul's own thought. The constantly strained relations between Paul and early Christianity, the apostolic council, the incident in Antioch, and the demand of radical Jewish Christians that Gentile Christians be circumcised mark only four stations in a complex interaction between the successful new Paul and his supporters and/or opponents. Both Jews and Jewish Christians opposed Paul. Galatians shows how bitterly the disputes were carried on and how strongly they affected Paul's thinking. The opposing front became ever larger and stronger near the end of Paul's ministry, and this must have had a basis in the theological thinking of the apostle himself. Jews regarded him as an apostate, and radical Jewish Christians as a falsifier. That is, they perceived Pauline theology as hostile to Jewish or strict Jewish Christian self-understanding and not integrable into them. But Paul not only polarized; he also fascinated. Like no other theologian of early Christianity, he was able to gain coworkers, both men and women, in the service of his evangelistic mission. Not only that; he also triggered a literary tradition without parallel; not only the deutero-Paulines (Colossians, Ephesians, 2 Thessalonians, 1–2 Timothy, Titus) but also Acts must be read as attempts to extend Paul's writings and theology into changed times.[84] Along with all their contemporizing of Paul in their own independent manner, Paul's students not only adopted and developed secondary themes of the apostle's own thought; the way they appropriated Paul's thought also allows us to make inferences regarding Paul himself. What his students adopted and developed may well have been central and important for Paul himself.

(5) The inner logic of Pauline thought and its effects stand in a causal relationship with the *concept of identity* advocated by Paul. As the direct expression of his symbolic world, the Pauline construction of a Christian identity is a key

---

82. In this regard, Paul does not stand alone among the figures of antiquity. The extant works of Aristotle, for example, are also filled with tensions.

83. Cf. E. P. Sanders, *Paul* (Oxford: Oxford University Press, 1991), 128: "Paul was a theologian. . . . Paul was not systematic, however, since he did not reconcile his responses to these multifaceted problems with one another."

84. Cf. Jürgen Roloff, "Die Paulus-Darstellung des Lukas," in Jürgen Roloff, *Exegetische Verantwortung in der Kirche: Aufsätze* (ed. Martin Karrer; Göttingen: Vandenhoeck & Ruprecht, 1990), 255–78.

to the understanding of Pauline theology and the history of early Christianity. What interpretative model did Paul use on the Jesus-Christ-history in order to reveal its universal significance? Which symbols does he take up in order to facilitate the communication of the symbolic world? How did he succeed in implanting his symbolic universe in the meaning universes that already existed, in stabilizing threatened congregations, and in all the while advancing his evangelistic mission?

(6) If Pauline theology is understood as historical meaning formation, then it becomes clear, from insights derived from the related theory of history, that to pose such alternatives as external or internal perspective, theological or history-of-religions approach, confessional or nonconfessional is inappropriate.[85] These alternatives do not exist; what always does exist is the standpoint of the interpreter, which postulates them in order thereby to provide a foil for his or her own worldview. The past world emerges in the *act of interpretation*. All we can ever do is set forth our own present interpretation of the past, so that alternative category pairs such as subjective or objective lose their significance; all we have are arguments that may be deemed appropriate or inappropriate, adequate or inadequate. Given these presuppositions, no way of coming at the subject may be ruled out in advance; all realms of historical life are to be taken into account. All aspects of a cultural world must be inspected: psychological, sociological, linguistic, religious, theological. So also it is inappropriate to set up content and function as contrasting alternatives, for the functional description of a religion cannot be formulated apart from its contents and experience; contents, experiences, and functions constantly interact.[86]

(7) The previous discussion makes it clear that a historically and theologically appropriate interpretation of Paul must be multifactorial. Paul cannot be explained monocausally but must always be seen simultaneously as rooted in the Old Testament and ancient Judaism, anchored within the debates of Greco-

---

85. Räisänen, *Neutestamentliche Theologie?* 93, rejects theological interpretation of the New Testament writings with the claim that in this case the scholar identifies himself with the object of study and thus functions "as preacher, not as a scholar of religion." Theissen, *Religion of the Earliest Churches*, 17–18, justifies the adoption of general categories of the history of religion and the rejection of a theological interpretation with the claim that the latter approach would exclude many secularized contemporaries from access to the New Testament. Both authors deny that their standpoint itself has an ideological and confessional character, not seeing that there is no neutral no-man's-land where one can stand without taking a position and that the relation to a religion in one's own life history can never and must never be bracketed out.

86. Modern brain research has explicitly elaborated the view that a separation of our different knowledge worlds is a supplementary and secondary act. Cf. E. Pöppel, "Drei Welten des Wissens— Koordinaten einer Wissenswelt," in *Weltwissen—Wissenswelt: Das globale Netz von Text und Bild* (ed. Christa Maar et al.; Cologne: DuMont, 2000), 21–39, here 36: "A separation between reason and emotion can be made only retrospectively, when one reflects on what has been experienced and attempts to define and distinguish virtual realms of lived experience as independent entities."

Roman thinking, embedded within the conflicts of early Christian history, and as one whose creative power generated and shaped something new.

A consistent chronological and historical approach by no means excludes a *holistic interpretation* of Pauline thought but forms its presupposition. Among other things, Paul was a significant theological thinker; his work does have systematic quality. In order to present it in its continuity and change, the diachronic analyses must provide the basis for a comprehensive synchronic interpretation. Thus the fruits of the historical perspective can be brought into a comprehensive presentation of Paul's thought structured thematically. Social history and the history of ideas also interact with each other in the case of Paul, for his background and life struggles essentially determine his thought; at the same time it is true that precisely in the case of Paul, new knowledge changes the course of his life and thought. Accordingly, part 1 of this study begins with the pre-Christian Paul and his location in cultural history and then proceeds to examine the course of Paul's life and developing thought from Damascus to Rome in all its contexts.

On this foundation, part 2 presents a comprehensive, thematically structured interpretation of Pauline theology. It is intended to show how the Pauline meaning structure is constructed: How is Paul's talk of God structured? How are God and Jesus related to one another in Paul's thought? Which conceptual fields and symbols does Paul use in order to interpret the Jesus-Christ-history? How does he describe the believers' participation in salvation, and what determines their new life? How does he relate immanence and transcendence? What concepts of ethics and time does Paul set forth? What ideas give Paul's thought as a whole its characteristic stamp, and on what issues does he change his theological position? If meaning formation is always a constructed interpretation of the world in the present, then precisely in Paul is posed the issue of the model of the matrix used in this process. The conclusion consists of reflections on the capability of Pauline meaning formation in the present.

2

Sources and Chronology
for Paul's Life and Work

Definite and Hypothetical

Every event is bound to a particular place and time. The extant Pauline letters, however, name neither the place nor time of their composition.[1] Acts, it is true, gives extensive descriptions of Paul's missionary work, but here too we find no information on when and where Paul composed his letters. Luke does not place events important for early Christian history such as the apostolic council and the call of Paul in a chronological framework. Likewise we can only infer indirectly the year when the apostle to the Gentiles was born and the year he died. This is why it is so difficult to establish a chronology for Paul's life and work and why scholarly opinion on this issue is so divergent. Nonetheless, any presentation of the life and work of the apostle Paul, including any treatment that attempts to deal only with its content, will depend on some implicit or explicit chronology, and so we must begin by discussing this topic. As we develop this presentation, the goal is to establish a temporal framework within which we can integrate the central events of the *vita Pauli* and his letters.

---

1. One probable exception is 1 Cor. 16:8 (Ephesus).

47

In terms of method,[2] the historian's point of departure is the self-evident principle that primary sources always receive priority. We should thus always prefer the chronological data that one can glean from the undisputed Pauline letters when they are in tension or contradiction to other New Testament reports. We are not thereby disparaging the historical value of Acts, but when Acts and the undisputed Pauline letters contradict each other, we should follow the letters. On the other hand, when the information from Acts and Paul's letters can be combined, we obtain a solid basis for Pauline chronology. When Acts is the only source for events from the life of Paul, then one must probe the extent to which Luke transmits reliable older tradition or whether his presentation derives from his own redactional composition.

The obvious starting point for ascertaining an absolute chronology consists of the few places where the New Testament mentions events that make contact with the general data of world history documented by extracanonical sources or archaeological discoveries. This absolute chronology then provides the foundation on which we may construct the relative chronology of Paul's life and work.

2.1 Absolute Chronology

Two events enable us to reconstruct an absolute chronology of Paul's activity: the expulsion of Jews from Rome by Claudius (cf. Acts 18:2b) and the date when Gallio served as proconsul in Achaia.

The Edict of Claudius

Suetonius (*Divus Claudius* 25.4) reports that the emperor *Iudaeos impulsore Chresto assidue tumultuantis Roma expulit* (expelled the Jews from Rome because, instigated by Chrestus, they were constantly creating disturbances).[3] This event was dated by the later Christian historian Orosius (fifth century CE) to the ninth year of Claudius's reign (49 CE).[4] When Claudius died in October 54 CE, the edict was annulled.[5]

---

2. The methodological reflections of Niels Hyldahl, *Die paulinische Chronologie* (ATDan 19; Leiden: Brill, 1986), 1–17, deserve serious consideration.

3. For evidence that *impulsore Chresto* should not be taken as referring to some unknown Jewish agitator or messianic pretender with the common slave name Chrestus, cf. most recently Helga Botermann, *Das Judenedikt des Kaisers Claudius: Römischer Staat und Christiani im 1. Jahrhundert* (Hermes: Einzelschriften 71; Stuttgart: Steiner, 1996), 71.

4. Cf. Orosius, *Historia adversum paganos* 7.6.15. For an extensive supporting argument, cf. Rainer Riesner, *Paul's Early Period: Chronology, Mission Strategy, Theology* (trans. Douglas W. Stott; Grand Rapids: Eerdmans, 1998), 157–201.

5. Cf. Suetonius, *Nero* 33.1, who reports that Nero annulled decisions and decrees of Claudius; cf. further Rom. 16:3, where Prisca and Aquila have returned to Rome.

The Gallio Inscription

The time when Lucius Gallio, the brother of Seneca, was in office as the proconsul of Achaia may be determined with a fair degree of accuracy from an inscription documenting a letter from the emperor Claudius to the city of Delphi. The text correlates the date of its composition with the twenty-sixth acclamation of Claudius as emperor. Although the twenty-sixth acclamation itself cannot be exactly dated, data from other inscriptions document that the twenty-seventh acclamation had already taken place by August 1, 52 CE.[6] The letter is addressed to Gallio's successor (Gallio is mentioned in the text in the nominative case; cf. line 6 from the top, Γαλλίων)[7] and must therefore have been written in the summer of 52. Since proconsuls of senatorial provinces were usually in office one year, we may infer that Gallio was proconsul of Achaia from the early summer of 51 to the early summer of 52.[8] Since Prisca and Aquila were expelled from Rome and came to Corinth "not long" before Paul (Acts 18:2, προσφάτως), the apostle himself came to Corinth in the year 50. If one combines this with the information in Acts 18:11, Paul stayed one and a half years in Corinth. Assuming that the Jews would have brought complaints against Paul soon after the new proconsul entered office, we can date the Gallio scene of Acts 18:12–16 to the summer of 51.[9]

2.2 Relative Chronology

Paul's arrival in Corinth at the beginning of the year 50 provides a firm point from which the relative chronology of Paul's activity can be calculated both forwards and backwards. The goal is to establish a temporal frame-work within which the central events of the *vita Pauli* and his letters can be integrated.

6. Cf. Adolf Deissmann, *Paul: A Study in Social and Religious History* (trans. William E. Wilson; New York: Harper, 1957), 275; Karl Martin Fischer and Hans-Martin Schenke, *Einleitung in die Schriften des Neuen Testaments* (Gütersloh: Gütersloher Verlagshaus, 1978–), 1:52.

7. Fischer and Schenke, *Einleitung*, 1:50–51, provide the Greek text of the Gallio inscription, newly reconstructed and edited by A. Plassart and J. H. Oliver, with a German translation. For English translations of Claudius's decree and the Gallio inscription, see M. Eugene Boring et al., eds., *Hellenistic Commentary to the New Testament* (Nashville: Abingdon, 1995), §§ 521–22.

8. According to Seneca, *Ep.* 104.1, Gallio fell ill with a fever while in Achaia, and so it is possible that he did not serve out his full year in office.

9. This date is the only item in recent discussions of Pauline chronology on which there is general consensus. Cf. Alfred Suhl, *Paulus und seine Briefe: Ein Beitrag zur paulinische Chronologie* (SNT 11; Gütersloh: Gütersloher Verlagshaus, 1975), 325; Gerd Lüdemann, *Paul, Apostle to the Gentiles: Studies in Chronology* (trans. F. Stanley Jones; Philadelphia: Fortress, 1984), 164–65; Robert K. Jewett, *A Chronology of Paul's life* (Philadelphia: Fortress, 1979), 40; Hyldahl, *Chronologie*, 122; Riesner, *Paul's Early Period*, 202–8.

Events Prior to Corinth

We must begin with a reconstruction of the events prior to Paul's arrival in Corinth. In the Acts account Paul's stay in Corinth was part of the great Pauline mission in Asia Minor and Greece (the second missionary journey of Acts 15:36–18:22). We can reconstruct a list of individual missionary stations on the basis of the traditions reworked by Luke. Their journey first took Paul and Silas to the congregations that already exist in Syria and Cilicia (cf. Acts 15:40–41; also 15:23/Gal. 1:21). Then Paul came to Derbe and Lystra, where he converted Timothy (cf. 1 Cor. 4:17). Thereafter Paul and his coworkers proceeded through Phrygia and the Galatian country (Acts 16:6); from there they launched their mission in Europe. Philippi was the first station (Acts 16:11–12a; Phil. 4:15ff.); from there Paul proceeded to Thessalonica (Acts 17:1), then via Beroea to Athens (cf. Acts 17:10, 15). Early in the year 50 Paul journeyed from Athens to Corinth (cf. Acts 18:1). Paul's letters confirm the basic outline of these travels. Paul himself reports that he founded the congregation in Thessalonica after coming from Philippi (cf. 1 Thess. 2:2). His stay in Athens is also documented by 1 Thess. 3:1, so that both Acts and 1 Thessalonians confirm the following order of stations on Paul's journey: Philippi, Thessalonica, Athens, Corinth.[10] The missionary activity here portrayed occupied about a year and a half,[11] which brings one very near to the time of the incident in Antioch and the apostolic council, which preceded it. We can date these two events to the first half of 48 CE.[12]

According to Paul's account in Gal. 2:1–14, the Antioch incident occurred in direct proximity to the apostolic council. Granted, Paul does not explicitly place the two events in chronological order, but the sequencing of the text in Galatians and the Pauline line of argument suggest a strictly temporal succession of events. The Antioch incident thus falls in the summer of 48, after Paul and Barnabas had returned from Jerusalem and were staying in Antioch (cf. Acts 15:35).

In the portrayal of Paul's activities from his conversion to the apostolic council, there is considerable divergence between Acts and the undisputed Pauline letters. In Gal. 1:6–2:14 Paul gives a survey of his missionary work up to the apostolic council. In the first place, he emphasizes (Gal. 1:17) that after his conversion he did not go directly to Jerusalem but to Arabia and then

10. On the persistent differences between Acts and the letters, cf. Suhl, *Paulus und seine Briefe*, 96ff.; Lüdemann, *Chronology*, 13–14.

11. Jewett, *Chronology*, 57–62, points out that Paul's travels between the apostolic council and his arrival in Corinth could have lasted three or four years. He does consider it theoretically possible, however, for the trip described in Acts to have been made in eighteen months (p. 107). The chronology presupposed here reckons with a maximal travel time of two years.

12. For evidence, cf. most recently Riesner, *Paul's Early Period*, 319–21.

returned to Damascus.[13] The apostle wants this comment to underscore his independence from the original congregation in Jerusalem, and so the temporal connection in Gal. 1:18 (ἔπειτα μετὰ ἔτη τρία [three years later]) probably refers to his conversion. It was only after this relatively long period that Paul came to Jerusalem, where he stayed only fifteen days with Cephas and also saw James the Lord's brother. After this first Jerusalem visit Paul remained in Syria and Cilicia, far from Jerusalem, and only "afterwards, fourteen years later" (Gal. 2:1, ἔπειτα διὰ δεκατεσσάρων ἐτῶν), did he visit Jerusalem for the second time, with Barnabas and Titus on the occasion of the apostolic council. The reference to "fourteen years" in Gal. 2:1 probably refers to the first Jerusalem visit.[14] Paul confirms this himself by the comment that he "went up again" (πάλιν δὲ ἀνέβην) to Jerusalem. Since, in the ancient calculation of time, the year that had begun was counted as a full year, we may construct the following outline of Paul's activities from his conversion to the apostolic council. The apostolic council in the spring of 48 was preceded by missionary activity in Syria and Cilicia for about thirteen years, which had two phases: Paul probably remained for about six years in the area of Tarsus and Cilicia and then about 42 CE joined forces with the missionary program sponsored by the church in Antioch.[15] Paul's first visit to the church in Jerusalem falls in the year 35 CE. His visit to Arabia probably took place in 34, so that two years elapsed between his conversion in 33 and his first visit to Jerusalem. The year 33 as the date of Paul's call and commissioning near Damascus fits well with the presumed date of the death of Jesus, the 14th of Nisan (April 7) of 30 CE.[16] This date for Jesus' death is supported by two arguments: (1) both the calculations based on astronomy and the traditions about the date of Jesus' death support the hypothesis that in 30 CE the 14th of Nisan fell on a Friday; (2) according to Luke 3:1–2, John the Baptist made his public appearance in 27/28, and this was also the date of the beginning of Jesus' public ministry, which lasted two or three years. A period of about three years between Jesus' crucifixion and Paul's conversion corresponds to the missionary history of early Christianity, for Paul's actions as a persecutor presuppose a progressive expansion of the Christian movement.

The contradictions between the data in Gal. 1–2 and the testimony of Acts pose the central problem for a chronology of Paul's life and work: although Paul in Gal. 1:17 emphasizes that after his conversion he did not go directly to Jerusalem, according to Acts 9:26 he goes to Jerusalem immediately after his

13. This mission is reflected in the reference by 2 Cor. 11:32–33 to Paul's escape from the soldiers of the ethnarch of the Nabataean king Aretas IV (ca. 9 BCE–38/39 CE); on the problems, cf. Suhl, *Paulus und seine Briefe*, 314–15; Riesner, *Paul's Early Period*, 75–89.

14. Cf. Schnelle, *New Testament Writings*, 21.

15. For evidence and arguments for this chronology, see below, section 5.4 ("Paul as Missionary of the Antioch Church").

16. See the basic evidence presented by A. Strobel, "Der Termin des Todes Jesu," *ZNW* 51 (1960): 69–101.

flight from Damascus. The portrayal in Acts corresponds to Luke's ecclesiology, for the evangelist is interested in the unity of the developing church, which is here expressed in an exemplary fashion by Paul immediately establishing contact with the Jerusalem apostles.[17] Whereas in Gal. 1:18 Paul speaks of only one trip to Jerusalem prior to the apostolic council, in Acts he had already been in Jerusalem a second time before the council (11:27–30). Here, too, we should follow Paul's own testimony, especially since this second trip fits in with Luke's ecclesiology. In Acts 11:27–30 Luke is reworking individual elements of tradition in a way that emphasizes the continuity of salvation history and the unity of the church. Since in Acts 11:19–26 he has just reported on the founding of the congregation in Antioch, he now immediately adds in 11:27–30 that contacts were established between the new congregation in Antioch and the original church in Jerusalem.[18] For Luke, Paul's journeys to Jerusalem are a compositional strategy used to illustrate the spread of the gospel in the world. They stand in the service of his ecclesiology and provide the framework within which Luke reworked the extensive traditions available to him. The one great trip of Jesus to Jerusalem in the Gospel of Luke (cf. Luke 9:51–19:27), the five trips to Jerusalem by the missionary to the Gentiles (Acts 9:26; 11:27–30; 15:2, 4; 18:22; 21:15), and the journey of the martyr Paul to Rome form a unity for Luke. Historically, however, Paul's own testimony that as a Christian missionary he was in Jerusalem only three times is no doubt correct.

Whereas in Gal. 1:21 Paul speaks only of missionary activity prior to the apostolic council in the region of Syria and Cilicia, Acts 13–14 reports missionary work on Cyprus and in Pamphylia, Pisidia, and Lycaonia in Asia Minor. Is Acts' report of a first missionary journey thus only a "model mission"?[19] This is not a clear "yes or no" question. Although we must regard a missionary project on Cyprus as improbable[20] and we cannot easily harmonize the Pauline mission

17. Cf. Jürgen Roloff, *Die Apostelgeschichte* (17th ed.; NTD 5; Göttingen: Vandenhoeck & Ruprecht, 1981), 154.

18. Cf. the analysis of Georg Strecker, "Die sogenannte zweite Jerusalemreise des Paulus (Act. 11,27–30)," in *Eschaton und Historie: Aufsätze* (Göttingen: Vandenhoeck & Ruprecht, 1979), 132–41.

19. So Hans Conzelmann, *Acts of the Apostles: A Commentary on the Acts of the Apostles* (trans. James Limburg et al.; Hermeneia; Philadelphia: Fortress, 1987), xlii. The systematic periodizing of Paul's mission activity is doubtless the work of Luke: "Luke utilized the three missionary journeys of Paul as a means of structuring the narrative of Acts according to his own theological point of view: he legitimizes first the Gentile mission and then the independence of this mission from the synagogue, and finally the political relevance of this universalizing of Christianity becomes ever clearer" (C. Burfeind, "Paulus *muß* nach Rom," *NTS* 46 [2000]: 83). At the same time, the numerous traditions he has incorporated dealing with places, times, and people indicate that he has appropriately recounted and correctly characterized his formulation of the course of the Pauline mission.

20. According to Acts 11:19, Cyprus was evangelized by Hellenistic missionaries driven out of Jerusalem, so that Christians from Cyprus in turn were active in Antioch (cf. 11:20). Moreover, Barnabas and John Mark (cf. 13:5b) traveled back to Cyprus to do missionary work (cf. 15:39). Probably the Antiochene Cyprus traditions were connected with Barnabas (cf. 4:36–37); Luke took them up and related them secondarily to Paul in 13:1–3, 4–12 in order to bring together Barnabas, Paul, and John

in Pamphylia, Pisidia, and Lycaonia with Gal. 1:21.[21] Paul, on the other hand, is not intending in the Galatian passage to provide an extensive discussion of the individual stations of his mission but is only emphasizing his independence from Jerusalem. Moreover, the Lukan account in Acts 13–14 contains numerous traditions that speak for the historicity of the first missionary journey in the years 45–47.[22]

Events after Corinth

If the Gallio scene provides a point of departure for the absolute chronology and thus facilitates a relatively sure dating of the main stations of Paul's missionary work as far back as his conversion, on this basis we may now sort out the chronology of the Pauline mission in relation to Paul's stay in Corinth as pictured in Acts 18:1–17. The summarized travel report in Acts 18:18–23, however, already raises big problems. Paul at first remains some days in Corinth, then travels to Syria. He leaves the married couple Prisca and Aquila in Ephesus, has discussions with Jews in the synagogue, turns down their suggestion to remain in Ephesus for missionary work, and leaves Ephesus. Although Acts 18:18 names Syria as the actual destination of Paul's journey, in 18:22 he lands in Caesarea, "goes up" (ἀναβάς) to Jerusalem, and then proceeds from Jerusalem to Antioch.[23] Up to the point when Prisca and Aquila move from Corinth, these junctures in Paul's travels are undocumented in Paul's own letters. We also cannot find there a satisfactory explanation for the route and motivation for this trip. Why would Paul leave his successful mission work in Macedonia and Asia Minor in order to make a trip to Antioch? Nor is there an explanation for Paul's landing in Caesarea and visiting Jerusalem, when according to Acts 18:18 Syria is his destination and Acts 18:22 gives Antioch as his real goal. Explaining the landing in Caesarea as due to unfavorable winds[24] is hardly more than a makeshift solution. Moreover, the fourth Jerusalem visit

---

Mark. On the analysis of 13:4–12, cf. Gerd Lüdemann, *Early Christianity according to the Traditions in Acts: A Commentary* (trans. John Bowden; Minneapolis: Fortress, 1989), 148–51.

21. Cf. the evidence in Martin Hengel, "Die Ursprünge der christlichen Mission," *NTS* 18 (1971–1972): 15–38, at p. 18 n. 15, that Syria and Cilicia Pedias (with Tarsus) formed one Roman province in the time of Paul.

22. On the analysis and chronological arrangement of Acts 13:1–14:28, cf. Roloff, *Apostelgeschichte*, 194ff.; Riesner, *Paul's Early Period*, 264–79; Cilliers Breytenbach, *Paulus und Barnabas in der Provinz Galatien: Studien zu Apostelgeschichte 13f.; 16,6; 18,23 und den Adressaten des Galaterbriefes* (AGJU 38; Leiden: Brill, 1996), 276.

23. On the analysis of Acts 18:18–23, cf. esp. Alfons Weiser, *Die Apostelgeschichte* (2 vols.; ÖTK 5; Würzburg: Echter, 1981–1985), 2:496ff. A separation of tradition and redaction results in the following picture: 18:18:a–c, 19a, and 21b–23 could contain traditional elements, in contrast to 18:18d, 19b–21a, which correspond to the Lukan picture of Paul.

24. So, e.g., Ernst Haenchen, *The Acts of the Apostles: A Commentary* (Philadelphia: Westminster, 1971), 547; Roloff, *Apostelgeschichte*, 276.

in Luke's enumeration can hardly be historical,[25] for it is opposed to Paul's own statements in the letters. But what justification is there for striking Jerusalem from Acts 18:22 and still maintaining Caesarea and Antioch as original? On the other hand, the pre-Lukan tradition spoke of a trip by the apostle to Antioch, from where he visited the Galatian country and Phrygia en route to Ephesus. After all attempts to connect the traditions reworked in Acts 18:18–23 to a different Jerusalem trip have proven unsuccessful,[26] one must be satisfied with the insight that, according to the tradition available to Luke, Paul, in connection with his stay in Corinth, first returned to Antioch and from there made his way to Ephesus. Even if we should regard these particulars as historical, we cannot see this trip as including a visit to Jerusalem.

The reconstruction of Paul's mission in Ephesus is burdened with less uncertainty (Acts 19). The trips described in Acts 18:18–23 occupied the time from summer 51 to spring 52, after which Paul remained in Ephesus about two years and nine months (cf. Acts 19:8, 10; 20:31), from the summer of 52 until the spring of 55. Paul then left Ephesus in order to make the trip through Macedonia to Corinth, gathering the collection for the poor Christians in Jerusalem and Judea. According to Acts 19:21 and 1 Cor. 16:5, Paul intended to travel through Macedonia to Corinth. Acts 20:1–3 also gives Corinth as Paul's destination, where Paul arrived early in 56 and remained three months (cf. Acts 20:3). Originally Paul intended to travel by ship directly to Syria. Some Jews hindered this plan, and so he had to backtrack through Macedonia. This information in Acts 20:3 is in tension with Rom. 15:25, where Paul announces a trip back to Jerusalem in order to deliver the collection. Romans 15:25, however, does not speak of a trip directly from Corinth to Jerusalem, so that one need not understand the information in Acts as contradicting Paul's own testimony. According to Acts 20:6, Paul traveled from Corinth to Philippi, then to Troas, and from there via Assos to Miletus. He then continued his trip to Caesarea by ship in order to reach Jerusalem by Pentecost of 56 CE (cf. Acts 20:16).[27]

The date Festus succeeded Felix as procurator, as described in Acts 24:27, is decisive for establishing the later Pauline chronology. According to Acts 24:10, Felix had already been procurator for some years, and Paul had already spent two years in prison when Festus began his administration. Felix's time in office probably began in 52/53 (cf. Josephus, *J.W.* 2.247),[28] but the date of his

25. Cf. Weiser, *Apostelgeschichte*, 2:502; Roloff, *Apostelgeschichte*, 277.

26. Cf. Weiser, *Apostelgeschichte*, 2:495–502.

27. Acts 18:23–21:14 is traditionally described as the third missionary journey, which falls in the period 52–55/56 CE. Luke obviously intends such a periodization by having Paul return to Antioch in 18:22. At the same time, the problems mentioned regarding 18:18–23 show how difficult such a division of the material is. Whereas the first journey (13:1–14:28) and the beginning of the second journey (15:36) are clearly marked, the transition from the "second" to the "third" is vague.

28. Cf. Peter Schäfer, *The History of the Jews in Antiquity: The Jews of Palestine from Alexander the Great to the Arab Conquest* (trans. David Chowcat; Luxembourg: Harwood Academic Publishers, 1995), 115.

departure is disputed (either 55,[29] 58, or 59 CE[30]). Josephus (*J. W.* 2.250–270) dates the events associated with Felix to the reign of Nero. If Nero began to rule in October 54, it would have been necessary for all the events mentioned by Josephus to happen very quickly in order to have been complete by 55.[31] It is therefore better to assume that Festus's administration began in 58,[32] which also fits well with Acts 24:1, since the high priest Annas (Ananus) mentioned there was in office about 47–59.[33] Since Paul had appealed to Caesar during his trial before Festus (cf. Acts 25:11), it was probably still in 58 that he was sent to Rome on a prisoner transport led by a centurion (cf. Acts 27:1–28:16).[34] If the trip to Rome fell in the winter of 58–59, then Paul would have entered the capital of the empire in the spring of 59.[35] Acts 28:30 indicates that Paul as a prisoner was relatively free and that he preached in his residence for two years without hindrance. The year of Paul's death is unknown; one can only

29. Lüdemann, *Chronology*, 192–93 n. 4.

30. Among those who vote for 59 CE are Riesner, *Paul's Early Period*, 219–24; and A. Scriba, "Von Korinth nach Rom: Die Chronologie der letzten Jahre des Paulus," in *Das Ende des Paulus: Historische, theologische, und literaturgeschichtliche Aspekte* (ed. Friedrich Wilhelm Horn; BZNW 106; New York: de Gruyter, 2001), 163–64. Among other evidence, they appeal to Y. Meshorer, *Ancient Jewish Coinage* (2 vols.; Dix Hills, NY: Amphora Books, 1982), 183, who connects Festus's accession to office directly with a new minting of coins in Palestine in the fifth year of Nero's reign (58/59) and concludes, "Festus apparently assumed office in 59 C.E." It can happen that a new coinage is minted in the initial year of a procurator's office, but this need not necessarily be the case, especially since the end of the year 58 for the new minting is not to be excluded. Between 58 and 59, 58 has the advantage of allowing more room for the events that are to be placed in 58–59: the change of administration in the procurator's office, minting the new coins, and the change in the high priest's office (according to Josephus, *Ant.* 20.179, Agrippa II designated Ishmael high priest in 59).

31. Cf. the penetrating discussion of all the problems in Jewett, *Chronology*, 40–44.

32. Cf. Shemuel Safrai and M. Stern, eds., *The Jewish People in the First Century: Historical Geography, Political History, Social, Cultural and Religious Life and Institutions* (CRINT 1; Assen: Van Gorcum, 1974), 74–76. Felix entered the office in 52/53 CE, and since Albinos was already in the procurator's office by 62, there is a ten-year period for his and Festus's administrations (cf. Josephus, *J. W.* 6.301ff.). From the accounts in Josephus, *J. W.* 2.247–276, and Acts 24:10 we may infer that Felix's administration accounts for the greater part of this period.

33. Cf. Emil Schürer, *The History of the Jewish People in the Age of Jesus Christ (175 B.C.–A.D. 135)* (2nd ed.; 3 vols.; Edinburgh: T&T Clark, 1973), 2:231.

34. Heinz Warnecke, *Die tatsächliche Romfahrt des Apostels Paulus* (SBS 127; Stuttgart: Katholisches Bibelwerk, 1987), identifies the island mentioned in Acts 28:1 as Μελίτη (not Malta) but attempts to identify the place where Paul was stranded with the peninsula of the island of Kephallenia off the western coast of Greece. Alfred Suhl, "Gestrandet! Bemerkungen zum Streit über die Romfahrt des Paulus," *ZTK* 88 (1991): 1–28, votes for this theory; persuasive critiques of this view are presented by Jürgen Wehnert, "Gestrandet: Zu einer neuen These über den Schiffbruch des Apostels Paulus auf dem Wege nach Rom. (Apg 27–28)," *ZTK* 87 (1990): 67–99; M. Reiser, "Von Caesarea nach Malta: Literarischer Charakter und historische Glaubwürdigkeit von Acts 27," in *Das Ende des Paulus: Historische, theologische, und literaturgeschichtliche Aspekte* (ed. Friedrich Wilhelm Horn; BZNW 106; Berlin: de Gruyter, 2001), 49–74.

35. Riesner, *Paul's Early Period*, 201, and Scriba, "Von Korinth nach Rom," 171, place Paul's arrival in Rome in 60 CE.

suppose that during the persecution of Christians under Nero in the year 64, Paul died as a martyr in Rome (cf. *1 Clem.* 5.5–7).[36]

Chronology of Paul's Life and Work

Death of Jesus	30
Conversion of Paul	33
First visit to Jerusalem	35
Paul in Cilicia	ca. 36–42
Paul in Antioch	ca. 42
First missionary journey	ca. 45–47
Apostolic council	48 (spring)
Incident in Antioch	48 (summer)
Second missionary journey	48 (late summer)–51/52
Paul in Corinth	50/51
Gallio in Corinth	51/52
Trip to Antioch	51/52
Third missionary journey	52–55/56
Stay in Ephesus	52–54/55
Paul in Macedonia	55
Last stay in Corinth	56 (early in the year)
Arrival in Jerusalem	56 (early summer)
Imprisonment in Caesarea	56–58
Change of office, Felix/Festus	58
Arrival in Rome	59
Death of Paul	64

36. On the open questions regarding the end of Paul's life, see below, section 13.4 ("Paul the Martyr").

3

The Pre-Christian Paul

Open-Minded Religious Zealot

A first glance at the Pauline letters is already revealing: conviction, will, and energy shape the course of history. Paul has these at his disposal; even before his call to be apostle to the Gentiles, he was not a passive spectator but turned the wheel of history.

3.1 Background and Social Status

The exact year of Paul's birth is unknown; it was probably about the middle of the first decade CE. In Philem. 9 (written ca. 62 CE) he describes himself as πρεσβύτης (an old man), at which time he would have been about fifty-five years old.[1] Paul's family traced its descent from the tribe of Benjamin (cf. Rom. 11:1; Phil. 3:5), the tribe from which Israel's first king came (cf. 1 Sam. 9:1–2, 21; 10:20–21). This ancestry was important in the apostle's own

---

1. Cf. the listing of the stages of life in Philo, *Creation* 105 (*NW* 2/2:1064). According to Leonhard Schumacher, *Sklaverei in der Antike: Alltag und Schicksal der Unfreien* (Beck's archäologische Bibliothek; Munich: Beck, 2001), 42, the average life expectancy in the free population was about thirty years (the average reflects the high mortality rate among babies and children).

self-understanding, as indicated by 1 Cor. 15:8–9: just as Benjamin was the youngest son of Jacob, so Paul received his revelation from the Lord as the last and "least among the apostles."[2] Paul did not marry; he obviously lived alone out of conviction (cf. 1 Cor. 7:1, 8; 9:5). Like Epictetus,[3] he probably feared that a family would hinder the service to humanity to which he believed he was called. Paul was a city person; his urban socialization can be detected in his language and imagery (cf., e.g., 1 Cor. 3:12; 4:9; 9:24ff.; 14:8). The extant letters, like his missionary activity, reveal Paul as a dynamic, energy-filled personality who lived his life by fundamental convictions, one who pursued his goal with intense emotion. It is also true that Paul suffered from sickness for extended periods (2 Cor. 12:7, "Therefore, to keep me from being too elated, a thorn was given me in the flesh, a messenger of Satan to torment me"; Gal. 4:14, "though my condition put you to the test, you did not scorn or despise me, but welcomed me as an angel of God, as Christ Jesus"; 2 Cor. 10:10, "For they say, 'His letters are weighty and strong, but his bodily presence is weak, and his speech contemptible'").[4]

From Tarsus

Luke designates Paul's hometown as Tarsus (Ταρσός), the capital of Cilicia (cf. Acts 9:30; 11:25; 21:39; 22:3). The economic and political importance of Tarsus resulted from its favorable geographical location. The navigable lower course of the Cydnus river connected Tarsus to the open sea (cf. Acts 9:30), and an important commercial highway led from Antioch in Syria through the city to the Aegean coast of Asia Minor. Tarsus was also the first station on the business route that connected the Mediterranean with the Black Sea.[5] In 66

2. Cf. Klaus Haacker, "Zum Werdegang des Apostels Paulus," *ANRW* 26.2:824–26.

3. Cf. Epictetus, *Ench.* 15; *Diatr.* 3.22.67–82; 4.8.30–31. In principle, the Cynic should marry, but "in view of the how things are at the present, and the situation at the front, the Cynic must be unhindered from placing himself entirely in the service of God, must be able to travel freely among people without being hindered by bourgeois obligations, unbound by personal connections. If he contracted such obligations and violated them, he would no longer have the character of an honorable man; if he maintained them, it would destroy his mission as the messenger, scout, and herald of the gods" (*Diatr.* 3.22.69).

4. Cf. the famous characterization of the apostle's external appearance found in the *Acts of Paul and Thecla* near the end of the second century CE: "And he saw Paul coming, a man small of stature, with a bald head and crooked legs, in a good state of body, with eyebrows meeting and nose somewhat hooked, full of friendliness; for now he appeared like a man, and now he had the face of an angel" (cited from Edgar Hennecke and Wilhelm Schneemelcher, eds., *New Testament Apocrypha* [2 vols.; Philadelphia: Westminster, 1963–1964], 2:354).

5. On Tarsus, cf. esp. W. Ruge, "Tarsus," PW 4 A 2:2413–39; William M. Ramsay, *The Cities of St. Paul: Their Influence on His Life and Thought* (London: Hodder & Stoughton, 1907; repr. Grand Rapids: Baker, 1979), 85–224; H. Böhlig, *Die Geisteskultur von Tarsos im augusteischen Zeitalter mit Berücksichtigung der paulinischen Schriften* (FRLANT 19; Göttingen: Vandenhoeck & Ruprecht, 1913); Martin Hengel and Roland Deines, *The Pre-Christian Paul* (trans. John Bowden; Philadelphia: Trinity

BCE Tarsus became the capital of the new Roman province of Cilicia; Cicero was numbered among its governors (51/50 BCE). During the chaos of the civil war, in 47 CE Tarsus placed itself on the side of the emperor, which at first made great difficulties for the city but then earned it the favor and patronage of Antony and Augustus. In the first century CE, Tarsus was a city with a flourishing economic and cultural life. Xenophon praises Tarsus as a "large and happy" city;[6] numerous philosophers, rhetoricians, and poets thrived in the city.[7] Tarsus was considered a center of Stoic philosophy. About 140 BCE Antipatrus of Tarsus was the leading teacher in the Stoic school. According to Strabo, "the inhabitants [of Tarsus] exhibited such great zeal for philosophy and education in general that in this regard they surpassed even Athens, Alexandria and every other place."[8] Apollonius of Tyana studied rhetoric in Tarsus but then turned his back on the city because of its great wealth and the arrogance of its population.[9] Tarsus can thus in every respect be considered a metropolitan center of Hellenistic culture.

In Acts 21:39 Paul describes himself as "a Jew, from Tarsus in Cilicia, a citizen of an important city." He was probably from birth a member of the Jewish community, which in Tarsus as in other places was organized as its own ethnic group and had its own civil rights.[10] The Jews of Cilicia belonged to the Diaspora groups[11] that maintained their own synagogue in Jerusalem for pilgrims attending the festivals (cf. Acts 6:9). It is not clear whether Paul had full citizenship in the city of Tarsus,[12] since πολίτης (citizen, Acts 21:39) can refer to official citizenship or only to one's place of origin. In the imperial period, the rights of a citizen could be obtained in Tarsus for five hundred drachmas;[13]

Press International, 1991), 1–6; Martin Hengel and Anna Maria Schwemer, *Paul between Damascus and Antioch: The Unknown Years* (trans. John Bowden; Louisville: Westminster John Knox, 1997), 161–67. (Hengel polemically minimizes the Gentile influence on Paul.)

6. Xenophon, *Anab.* 1.2.23.

7. Cf. Dio Chrysostom, *Tarsica prior* and *Tarsica altera*. In *1 Tars.* 4 he says, "I have the impression that you have often heard of divine men who claim to know everything, and to give information about the essence and order on every subject: human beings, supernatural powers and gods, about the earth, sky, and sea, about sun, moon, and stars, about the whole universe, about growth and decay and innumerable other things" (*NW* 2/1:308–9).

8. Strabo, *Geogr.* 14.5.13.

9. Philostratus, *Vit. Apoll.* 1.7. Cf. further 6.34, which presupposes a Jewish community in Tarsus; cf. also Philo, *Embassy* 281.

10. Cf. Gerhard Delling, *Die Bewältigung der Diasporasituation durch das hellenistische Judentum* (Göttingen: Vandenhoeck & Ruprecht, 1987), 49–55.

11. On the Jews' assessment of their situation in the Diaspora, cf. W. C. van Unnik and Pieter Willem van Horst, *Das Selbstverständnis der jüdischen Diaspora in der hellenistisch-römischen Zeit* (AGJU 17; Leiden: Brill, 1993).

12. Heike Omerzu, *Der Prozess des Paulus: Eine exegetische und rechtshistorische Untersuchung der Apostelgeschichte* (BZNW 115; Berlin: de Gruyter, 2002), 34–36, casts a negative vote on this issue.

13. Cf. Dio Chrysostom, *2 Tars.* 21–23.

the apostle's ancestors[14] could have purchased it and Paul could have inherited it.[15] Being a citizen of Tarsus did not preclude also being a Roman citizen, for in Paul's time these were no longer strictly mutually exclusive.[16]

Paul as Roman Citizen

Regarding his legal status, Paul was a privileged Jew of the Diaspora; according to Acts 16:37–38; 22:35; 23:27, he possessed Roman citizenship, which could be obtained by birth, release or purchase from slavery, release from being a prisoner of war, discharge after long military service, adoption, or acceptance into a citizens' association (*adlectio*).[17] Doubt has been cast on the historicity of this Lukan tradition by the following arguments:[18] (1) The appeal to Roman citizenship in Acts 16:37–38 and 22:25ff. appears noticeably late in the narrative. *Counterargument*: This stylistic device derives from Lukan redaction, a way of enhancing the dramatic structure of the scene, and as such by no means speaks against Paul's having had Roman citizenship. (2) The appeal to Caesar (cf. Acts 25:9ff.; 26:31f.; 28:17ff.) and the transfer of Paul to Rome do not necessarily presuppose Roman citizenship, which Luke does not mention in this context.[19] *Counterargument*: Without the appeal to

---

14. On the tradition handed on by Jerome (*De viris illustribus* 5) that Paul's family and Paul himself came from Gischala in Galilee and moved to Tarsus, cf. Haacker, "Werdegang," *ANRW* 26.2:823–24, 828ff.

15. Cf. Hengel and Deines, *Pre-Christian Paul*, 6–14, 101–14.

16. A. N. Sherwin-White, *Roman Society and Roman Law in the New Testament* (Sarum Lectures, 1960–1961; Grand Rapids: Baker, 1978), 182; E. Kornemann, "Civitas," PWSup 1:310.

17. Cf. Omerzu, *Der Prozess des Paulus*, 28–39.

18. Cf. Wolfgang Stegemann, "War der Apostel Paulus ein römischer Bürger?" *ZNW* 78 (1987): 220–29; Klaus Wengst, *Pax romana: And the Peace of Jesus Christ* (Philadelphia: Fortress, 1987), 94–95; Ekkehard Stegemann and Wolfgang Stegemann, *The Jesus Movement: A Social History of Its First Century* (trans. O. C. Dean Jr.; Minneapolis: Fortress, 1999), 302, "The historical Paul was a citizen neither of Rome nor Tarsus"; David Alvarez Cineira, *Die Religionspolitik des Kaisers Claudius und die paulinische Mission* (HBS 19; Freiburg: Herder, 1999), 348–70. For critique, cf. Lüdemann, *Traditions in Acts*, 240–41; Gerd Lüdemann, *Paul, the Founder of Christianity* (Amherst, NY: Prometheus Books, 2002); Hengel and Deines, *Pre-Christian Paul*, 6–14, 100–111; Haacker, "Werdegang"; Riesner, *Paul's Early Period*, 147–56; Omerzu, *Der Prozess des Paulus*, 27–52. Noethlichs summarizes the matter with a note of skepticism: "A series of arguments that at first glance seem to speak against Paul's Roman citizenship have turned out to be ambivalent or not well founded. It does not necessarily follow, of course, that Paul was in fact a Roman citizen" (Karl-Leo Noethlichs, "Der Jude Paulus—ein Tarser und Römer?" in *Rom und das himmlische Jerusalem: Die frühen Christen zwischen Anpassung und Ablehnung* [ed. Raban von Haehling and Paul Mikat; Darmstadt: Wissenschaftliche Buchgesellschaft, 2000], 83).

19. Cf. Stegemann, "Römischer Bürger?" 213: "A plausible case can thus be made for the delivery of Paul to the imperial court without the presupposition of Roman citizenship. And one can at least pose the question whether Luke has not inferred Paul's Roman citizenship in the first place from the fact that Paul was sent to Rome for trial." Alvarez Cineira, *Claudius*, 364–70, after referring to the parallel in Josephus, *Life* 13–16, evaluates the transfer of Paul to the court in Rome as altogether a Lukan construction. In his view, Paul went to Rome as an ordinary traveler, and it was only there that

Caesar on the basis of Roman citizenship, it is difficult to explain the transfer of Paul's case to Rome.[20] (3) According to 2 Cor. 11:24–25, Paul five times suffered the synagogue penalty of being beaten with the lash (cf. also 2 Cor. 6:5; 1 Thess. 2:2). Had Paul been a Roman citizen, he would have needed only to say so in order to avoid this punishment.[21] *Counterargument:* Granted, it was forbidden to impose this punishment on citizens, but in practice this prohibition was not always observed.[22] (4) Paul's vocation does not point to a high social status, and so it is improbable that he either inherited Roman citizenship from his father or obtained it on his own. *Counterargument:* Paul's occupation is no sure indication of his social status and is related to his education as a Pharisee.[23] Like the Cynics,[24] Paul valued his work with his own hands as a craftsman, considering it a voluntary self-abnegation that assured his own independence (cf. 1 Thess. 2:9; 1 Cor. 4:12; 9:1–27; 2 Cor. 11:7). Moreover, in the early imperial period, citizenship was conferred not only on people from the upper class, as proven by the reference to "freedmen" (*libertini*) in Acts 6:9.[25] Finally, the apostle bears a Roman name, in which "Paul" (Παῦλος, *Paulus*) can be *cognomen* or *praenomen*.[26] It is hardly the case that the apostle himself devised and adopted the name Παῦλος in order to facilitate social contacts within the context of his missionary work (cf. Acts

---

he had "difficulties with the authorities, was arrested and executed" (p. 369). For a critique of this position, cf. Michael Labahn, "Paulus—ein homo honestus et iustus: Das lukanische Paulusportrait von Act 27–28 im Lichte ausgewählter antiker Parallelen," in *Das Ende des Paulus: Historische, theologische, und literaturgeschichtliche Aspekte* (ed. Friedrich Wilhelm Horn; BZNW 106; New York: de Gruyter, 2001), 98–99.

20. Since Paul was not a politically important or dangerous person, his appeal to Caesar can have been made only on the basis of his Roman citizenship; against Stegemann, "Römischer Bürger?" who puts forward the anti-Roman agitator Jonathan as a parallel (cf. Josephus, *J.W.* 7.449ff.). Cf. the issues of trial law esp. in Haacker, "Werdegang," 836ff.

21. Noethlichs, "Tarser und Römer," 70–74, argues that Roman citizens could be subject to punishment by the lash after a trial or within the legal framework of a magistrative *coercitio*. "No clear inferences for or against Paul's Roman citizenship can be drawn from the facts of Paul's having been bound, imprisoned, and subjected to corporal punishment" (p. 74).

22. Cf. Josephus, *J.W.* 2.308 (*NW* 1/2:798): Gessius Florus's scourging and crucifixion of Jerusalem Jews who had the same status as Roman knights. Suetonius, *Galba* 9: while governor of the province Hispania Tarraconensis, Galba had a Roman citizen crucified. Cicero, *Verr.* 2.5.161–167 (*NW* 1/2:800–801): Cicero reproaches Verres for having had Roman citizens whipped and crucified, Cf. further Livy, *Urbe cond.* 9.9.4–5 (*NW* 1/2:801–2), according to which the Porcian law "threatened severe punishments if a Roman citizen was scourged or executed."

23. Cf. Rudolf Meyer, "Das Arbeitsethos in Palästina zur Zeit der werdenden Kirche," in Rudolf Meyer, *Zur Geschichte und Theologie des Judentums in hellenistisch-römischer Zeit: Ausgewählte Abhandlungen* (ed. Waltraut Bernhardt; Neukirchen-Vluyn: Neukirchen, 1989), 17–18.

24. Cf. Martin Ebner, *Leidenslisten und Apostelbrief: Untersuchungen zu Form, Motivik, und Funktion der Peristasenkataloge bei Paulus* (FB 66; Würzburg: Echter, 1991), 69ff.

25. Cf. Hengel and Deines, *Pre-Christian Paul*, 56, 69, 136.

26. Cf. the documentation in Henry J. Cadbury, *The Book of Acts in History* (New York: Harper, 1955), 69–70. See also Hengel and Deines, *Pre-Christian Paul*, 6–14; and Omerzu, *Der Prozess des Paulus*, 39–42 (they suppose that Παῦλος was the apostle's *cognomen*).

13:7–12); rather, Παῦλος is the Roman name that Σαῦλος (Saul) bore from the very beginning (cf. Acts 7:58; 8:1, 3; 9:1, 8, 22, 24). In his missionary plans, Paul thinks in the geographical categories of the Roman Empire. He is oriented to the provincial capitals and constantly extends his missionary activity westward. Moreover, Rom. 13:1–7 reveals an apostle who thinks in Roman political categories (cf. also Phil. 3:20–21).[27] Paul probably had inherited Roman citizenship from a prior generation in his family who had received it as freed Jewish slaves (cf. Acts 22:28).[28] Philo reports Jews living in Rome, the majority of whom were freedmen and Roman citizens.[29] In addition, there were a considerable number of freed Jewish slaves who had returned to Judea and who had received Roman citizenship.

Vocation and Social Status

Paul's education and vocation essentially determined his social status. Although Paul himself only mentions that he worked day and night with his own hands, Acts 18:3 transmits the historically credible tradition that Paul and Aquila were tentmakers (σκηνοποιοί).[30] As independent craftsmen, Aquila and Paul would have made tents primarily for private customers[31] but possibly also for the military.[32] Cloth tents or tents with cloth roofs were widely used in the Mediterranean world and were constructed in various forms in order to reduce the heat from the sun.[33] The linen material for such tents was an important product in Tarsus (cf. Dio Chrysostom, 2 Tars. 21, 23), and so

27. Cf. Haacker, "Werdegang," 841. Romans 13:6–7 is to be noted in this connection, where Paul uses the second person plural; as a Roman citizen, he himself is not subject to tribute.

28. Omerzu, Der Prozess des Paulus, 39, supposes that Paul's family, "in the course of being released from slavery or from being prisoners of war, had been granted the status civitatis Romanae."

29. Cf. Philo, Embassy 155: "He [Augustus] was aware that the great section of Rome on the other side of the Tiber is occupied and inhabited by Jews, most of whom were Roman citizens who had been emancipated." Cf. also Embassy 157: "Yet nevertheless he neither ejected them from Rome nor deprived them of their Roman citizenship because they were careful to preserve their Jewish citizenship also." Josephus, Ant. 14.228, reports that in 49 BCE the consul Lucius Lentulus had excused from military service Jews in Ephesus who were Roman citizens (πολίτας Ῥωμαίων Ἰουδαίους). Many Jews possessed Roman citizenship: cf. M. Stern, "The Jewish Diaspora," in The Jewish People in the First Century: Historical Geography, Political History, Social, Cultural, and Religious Life and Institutions (ed. Shemuel Safrai and M. Stern; CRINT 1; Assen: Van Gorcum, 1974), 152; M. Smallwood, The Jews under Roman Rule from Pompey to Diocletian (SJLA 20; Leiden: Brill, 1981), 127–8.

30. On the historical reliability of this report, cf. Christoph Burchard, Der dreizehnte Zeuge: Traditions- und kompositionsgeschichtliche Untersuchungen zu Lukas' Darstellung der Frühzeit des Paulus (FRLANT 103; Göttingen: Vandenhoeck & Ruprecht, 1970), 39; Lüdemann, Traditions in Acts, 202.

31. So Peter Lampe, "Paulus-Zeltmacher," BZ 31 (1987): 256–61; Ronald F. Hock, The Social Context of Paul's Ministry: Tentmaking and Apostleship (Philadelphia: Fortress, 1980), 33–34, who, in contrast to Lampe, assumes that Aquila and Paul made leather tents.

32. Hengel and Deines, Pre-Christian Paul, 17.

33. Cf. Lampe, "Paulus-Zeltmacher," 258–59.

Paul could well have learned the handwork of such linen production in his hometown. But such tentmakers also usually worked with leather (cf. Epictetus, *Diatr.* 3.12.9). It is not possible to decide whether Paul's work included leather goods; in any case, the mobility of Paul's missionary work would have meant that he exercised his craft in a variety of ways. As a tentmaker, Paul would have belonged to the lower middle class.[34] But the social standing of the apostle was not determined by his vocational training alone. He worked as a missionary and founder of churches on the international level, composed lengthy letters with significant literary merit, knew how to utilize secretaries in his work (cf. Gal. 6:11; Rom. 16:22), coordinated and worked with numerous coworkers, and proved to be an outstanding theological thinker.[35] He had received both a Greek and a Jewish education,[36] and the linguistic and intellectual power[37] of his letters[38] (cf. 2 Cor. 10:10; 2 Pet. 3:15–16), alongside his Roman citizenship and his global activity, indicate that Paul belonged to the urban middle class.

34. Evaluations of the social status of Paul fall along a wide spectrum. Thus William M. Ramsay, *St. Paul, the Traveller and the Roman Citizen* (New York: G. P. Putnam, 1896; repr. Grand Rapids: Baker, 1962), 34, thinks Paul's family was very wealthy. For Eduard Meyer, *Die Apostelgeschichte und die Anfänge des Christentums* (Ursprung und Anfänge des Christentums 3; Stuttgart: Cotta, 1923), 308, Paul's father was the owner of a factory in Tarsus "in which cloth was processed from which tents were made." According to Hengel and Deines, *Pre-Christian Paul*, 17, and Hermann Lichtenberger, "Josephus und Paulus in Rom," in *Begegnungen zwischen Christentum und Judentum in Antike und Mittelalter: Festschrift für Heinz Schreckenberg* (ed. Dietrich-Alex Koch et al.; SIJD 1; Göttingen: Vandenhoeck & Ruprecht, 1993), 251, Paul came from at least the "petty bourgeoisie" middle class. Sanders, *Paul*, 10, argues for a "middle-class upbringing"; cf. also Anthony J. Saldarini, *Pharisees, Scribes, and Sadducees in Palestinian Society: A Sociological Approach* (Biblical Resource Series; Grand Rapids: Eerdmans, 2001), 140. On the basis of his occupation, Lampe locates Paul in the lower class ("Paulus-Zeltmacher," 259), as does Stegemann, "Römischer Bürger?" 227. Cf. Stegemann and Stegemann, *The Jesus Movement*, 302: "An investigation of Paul's self-testimonies, by contrast, strongly suggests that Paul belonged to the ancient lower stratum (above minimal existence, relatively poor) and also understood himself in that way." Justin J. Meggitt, *Paul, Poverty and Survival* (SNTW; Edinburgh: T&T Clark, 1998), 75–97, places Paul and his churches entirely within the lower class: "Paul and the Pauline churches shared in this general experience of deprivation and subsistence. Neither the apostle nor any members of the congregations he addresses in his epistles escaped from the harsh existence that typified life in the Roman Empire for the non-élite" (p. 75).

35. Cf. Betz, "Paul," 187.

36. Haacker, "Werdegang," rightly points out that Paul must have had at least an elementary ability in Latin, especially since in Rom. 13:1–7 and Phil. 3:20 he thinks in the categories of the Roman political system.

37. C. J. Classen, "Philologische Bemerkungen zur Sprache des Apostels Paulus," *WSt* 107–8 (1994–1995): 335, infers an educational level that corresponds to his use of the technical terminology of philosophy and rhetoric.

38. Cf. ibid.: "Paul was also familiar with a series of rhetorical technical terms. I dare not decide where and how he learned them, but his usage, together with his use of the technical terminology of philosophy, points to a level of education that in my opinion justifies the conclusion that he had acquired the rules and principles of rhetoric (and epistolography) from theoretical studies or from practice."

3.2 Paul: Pharisee in the Diaspora

In Phil. 3:5–6 Paul says regarding his Jewish past, "circumcised on the eighth day, a member of the people of Israel, of the tribe of Benjamin, a Hebrew born of Hebrews; as to the law, a Pharisee; as to zeal, a persecutor of the church; as to righteousness under the law, blameless." He thereby claims to belong to the elect covenant people of God. Like his family before him, he knows himself to be bound by the traditions of his Palestinian mother country although he lives in the Diaspora. Within the community of Pharisees, he lived according to the Torah, and it was his zeal for preserving the Torah that made him a persecutor of the Christian community. Paul also emphasizes his zeal for the traditions handed on by the fathers in Gal. 1:14. In Acts he appears as a Pharisee and "son of Pharisees" (Acts 23:6) who "belonged to the strictest sect of our religion and lived as a Pharisee." Paul thus joined the Pharisaic movement during his youth and distinguished himself by his strict adherence to the tradition of the fathers and his great zeal in the persecution of early Christian communities.

The Pharisaic Movement

The origins of the Pharisaic movement lie hidden in the darkness.[39] Most scholars have seen its beginning within the broader context of the Maccabean revolt[40] (cf. 1 Macc. 2:15–28), in the course of which the group of Hasidim first emerges: "Then there united with them a company of Hasideans, mighty warriors of Israel, all who offered themselves willingly for the law" (1 Macc.

---

39. On the Pharisees, cf. Schürer, *History of the Jewish People*, 2:381–403; Joachim Jeremias, *Jerusalem in the Time of Jesus: An Investigation into Economic and Social Conditions during the New Testament Period* (trans. F. H. Cave and C. H. Cave; Philadelphia: Fortress, 1975), 246–70; Rudolf Meyer and H. F. Weiss, "Φαρισαῖοι," *TDNT* 9:11–48; Rudolf Meyer, "Tradition und Neuschöpfung im antiken Judentum—dargestellt an der Geschichte des Pharisäismus," in Rudolf Meyer, *Zur Geschichte und Theologie des Judentums in hellenistisch-römischer Zeit: Ausgewählte Abhandlungen* (ed. Waltrauf Bernhardt; Neukirchen-Vluyn: Neukirchen, 1989), 130–87; G. Baumbach, *Jesus von Nazareth im Lichte der jüdischen Gruppenbildung* (Berlin: Evangelische Verlagsanstalt, 1971), 72–97; Jacob Neusner, *The Rabbinic Traditions about the Pharisees before 70* (3 vols.; Leiden: Brill, 1971); *From Politics to Piety: The Emergence of Pharisaic Judaism* (Englewood Cliffs, NJ: Prentice-Hall, 1973); Saldarini, *Pharisees, Scribes, and Sadducees*, 131–43 (esp. for Paul); Günter Stemberger, *Jewish Contemporaries of Jesus: Pharisees, Sadducees, Essenes* (trans. Allan W. Mahnke; Minneapolis: Fortress, 1995), passim; Peter Schäfer, "Der vorrabbinische Pharisäismus," in *Paulus und das antike Judentum: Tübingen-Durham-Symposium im Gedenken an den 50. Todestag Adolf Schlatters (19 Mai 1938)* (ed. Martin Hengel and Ulrich Heckel; WUNT 58; Tübingen: Mohr Siebeck, 1991), 125–72; H. F. Weiss, "Pharisäer," *TRE* 26:473–85; Roland Deines, *Die Pharisäer: Ihr Verständnis im Spiegel der christlichen und jüdischen Forschung seit Wellhausen und Graetz* (WUNT 101; Tübingen: Mohr Siebeck, 1997); "Pharisäer," *TBLNT* 2:1455–68; John P. Meier, *Companions and Competitors* (vol. 3 of *A Marginal Jew: Rethinking the Historical Jesus*; ABRL 3; New York: Doubleday, 2001), 189–388.

40. The revolt began ca. 167 BCE; for information, cf. Schäfer, *History of the Jews*, 44–64, 69–72.

2:42; cf. 7:13). Many scholars suppose that the common origin of Pharisees[41] and Essenes is found in this general setting, for the Hasidim were obviously characterized by a strict obedience to the law and a vigorous rejection of foreign elements within the Jewish faith.[42] Josephus appears to confirm this interpretation, since he mentions the existence of the three Jewish schools Pharisees, Sadducees, and Essenes in the context of his discussion of the time of the high priest Jonathan (161–142 BCE), who was a very controversial figure in the circles attempting to remain true to the law (cf. Josephus, *Ant.* 13.171–173).[43] The Pharisees attained recognizable contours by the time of John Hyrcanus (135/134–104 BCE), when they appear as a firmly established group in opposition to the policies of the king but greatly respected among the people (cf. Josephus, *Ant.* 13.288–292).[44] The Pharisees demanded that Hyrcanus give up the office of high priest, possibly because his mother had once been taken as a prisoner of war.[45] This seems to correspond to the original ideals of the Maccabean movement, which was interested above all in a legitimate temple cultus and the adherence to the Torah. There are also points of contact with the Essenes, for it was probably Jonathan's assumption of the high priesthood in 152 that caused the Teacher of Righteousness to lead his group to Qumran, establish the community there, and continue a vigorous polemic against the temple cult in Jerusalem (cf. CD 1:5–11).[46] The Pharisees became a dominant group in the time of Salome Alexandra (76–67 BCE); Josephus emphasizes their constantly increasing influence on the queen (cf. *J. W.* 1.110–112). Their influence seems to have declined in the reign of Herod the Great (40–4 BCE).[47] Josephus reports that they numbered six thousand at this time (*Ant.* 17.42),[48]

41. Deines, "Pharisäer," *TBLNT* 2:1456ff., presents an instructive outline of the history of the Pharisees and provides a good discussion of the origin of the term "Pharisees" as a designation for the group.

42. For a critical discussion of the problems, cf. Stemberger, *Pharisees, Sadducees, Essenes*, 91–98, who comes to this conclusion: "It is no more possible to reconstruct an exact prehistory of the three religious schools than it is to prove their direct origin from the Hasidic movement" (p. 98).

43. Stemberger, ibid., 91, considers the chronological location to be secondary.

44. Stemberger, ibid., 99–103, regards the account of the break between Hyrcanus and the Pharisees to be historically unreliable; so also Schäfer, "Der vorrabbinische Pharisäismus," 134–38, according to whom "Josephus in his *Antiquities* has retrojected the later political activities of the Pharisees into the time of Hyrcanus" (p. 138).

45. In Josephus, *Ant.* 13.372, this objection against Alexander Janneus recurs in the mouth of the people (instead of the Pharisees); on the analysis of the text, cf. Schäfer, "Der vorrabbinische Pharisäismus," 138f.

46. On this, cf. Hartmut Stegemann, *The Library of Qumran, on the Essenes, Qumran, John the Baptist, and Jesus* (Grand Rapids: Eerdmans, 1998) 147–48.

47. Cf. Stemberger, *Pharisees, Sadducees, Essenes*, 77–110.

48. On the statistics, cf. Berndt Schaller, "4000 Essener—6000 Pharisäer: Zum Hintergrund und Wert antiker Zahlenangaben," in *Antikes Judentum und frühes Christentum: Festschrift für Hartmut Stegemann zum 65. Geburtstag* (ed. Bernd Kollmann et al.; BZNW 97; Berlin: de Gruyter, 1999), 172–82 (round numbers as a widespread technique in historical fiction).

when they represented an influential minority within the Jewish population. About the end of the Herodian period, the Pharisees changed from a political group to a pietistic movement.[49] An important event occurred when a radical group within the Pharisees split off, calling themselves Zealots (οἱ ζηλωταί [the zealous ones, the enthusiasts]) in the line of Phinehas (Num. 25) and Elijah (1 Kings 19:9–10). This group was formed in 6 CE under the leadership of the Galilean Judas of Gamala and the Pharisee Zadduk (cf. Josephus, *Ant.* 18.3ff.).[50] The Zealots were characterized by their strict interpretation of the first commandment of the Decalogue, by rigid Sabbath practice, and by rigorous observance of the purity laws. They strove for a radical theocracy and thus rejected on religious grounds Roman rulership of the Jewish people. To a considerable extent, the criticism of the Pharisees in the Gospels reflects the debates between the Christian communities and Judaism after the destruction of the temple (70 CE). Nonetheless, the Gospels' numerous accounts of controversies between Jesus and the Pharisees reflect something authentically historical.[51] In the turmoil of the war against the Roman occupation forces (66–73/74 CE), the Pharisees lost influence to the radical groups (especially the Zealots),[52] but they must still be regarded as the strongest group in the first century in shaping the thought of Judaism.

Paul as Religious Zealot

As the distinguishing mark of his past life as a Pharisee, Paul names his zeal for the traditions of the fathers (Gal. 1:14, "I advanced in Judaism beyond many among my people of the same age, for I was far more zealous for the traditions of my ancestors"). Josephus also regards their understanding of tradition as the characteristic feature of the Pharisees[53] and that which distinguished them from the Sadducees:

> For the present I wish merely to explain that the Pharisees had passed on to the people certain regulations [νόμιμα] handed down by former generations [ἐκ πατέρων διαδοχῆς] and not recorded in the Laws of Moses, for which reason

49. Cf. Stemberger, *Pharisees, Sadducees, Essenes*, 110.

50. Cf. Martin Hengel, *Die Zeloten: Untersuchungen zur jüdischen Freiheitsbewegung in der Zeit von Herodes I. bis 70 nach Christus* (Leiden: Brill, 1961), 336ff.

51. As an introduction, see the sketch by Ulrich Luz, "Jesus und die Pharisäer," *Jud* 38 (1982): 111–24; cf. also Deines, "Pharisäer," *TBLNT* 2:1462–67. On the disputed issue of how much influence the Pharisees had before 70 CE and what form of continuity continued into the later rabbinic time, cf. D. Goodblatt, "The Place of the Pharisees in First Century Judaism: The State of the Debate," *JSJ* 20 (1989): 12–30.

52. On the details, cf. H. Schwier, *Tempel und Tempelzerstörung* (NTOA 11; Göttingen: Vandenhoeck & Ruprecht, 1989), 4–54.

53. On the basic theological views of the Pharisees, cf. Deines, "Pharisäer," *TBLNT* 2:1460–62.

they are rejected by the Sadducean group, who hold that only those regulations should be considered valid which were written down (in Scripture), and that those which had been handed down by former generations need not be observed. (*Ant.* 13.297)

Although John Hyrcanus set aside these regulations in his dispute with the Pharisees, according to Josephus, *Ant.* 13.408–409, Salome Alexandra reinstituted "whatever regulations [were] introduced by the Pharisees in accordance with the traditions of their fathers [κατὰ τὴν πατρῴαν παράδοσιν]." The agreements with Gal. 1:14 and the Synoptic tradition (cf. Mark 7:1–13) show that the παράδοσις (tradition) was the distinguishing mark of the Pharisees.[54] In New Testament times the content of the tradition was apparently composed of purity regulations (cf. Mark 7:1–8, 14–23; Rom. 14:14), rules concerning the tithe (cf. Matt. 23:23), and particular forms of vows (cf. Mark 7:9–13). According to Josephus (*Life* 191), the Pharisees distinguished themselves from others by "the reputation of being unrivalled experts with regard to the ancestral laws" (οἱ περὶ τὰ πάτρια νόμισμα δοκοῦσιν τῶν ἄλλων ἀκριβείᾳ διαφέρειν). They were more religious than others "and observed the law more conscientiously" (καὶ τοὺς ἀκριβέστερον ἀφηγεῖσθαι).[55] The term ἀκρίβεια (conscientious accuracy) is also found in Acts 22:3; 26:5 as a mark of Pharisaic education. Paul was "educated strictly according to our ancestral law" (πεπαιδευμένος κατὰ ἀκρίβειαν τοῦ πατρῴου νόμου) and had "belonged to the strictest sect of our religion and lived as a Pharisee" (κατὰ τὴν ἀκριβεστάτην αἵρεσιν τῆς ἡμετέρας θρησκείας ἔζησα Φαρισαῖος). Thus their exact knowledge and strict observance of the ancestral traditions, their piety and loyalty to the tradition were the distinctive marks of the Pharisees, who were "the most learned of the Jews and unrivalled interpreters of the ancestral laws [ἐξηγεταὶ τῶν πατρίων νόμων]" (*Ant.* 17.149; cf. further *J. W.* 2.162). They derived their specific traditions primarily from exposition of the Scripture, which did not particularly distinguish them from other Jewish groups.[56] The goal of the Pharisaic movement was the sanctification of everyday life by a comprehensive program of Torah observance in which the keeping of ritual purity laws had particular significance not only within the temple confines but in every realm of life.[57] Thus the Torah was extended in some cases in order to apply it to the multiplicity of everyday situations (cf., e.g., Aristobulus 139ff.; Josephus, *Ant.* 4.198; Mark 2:23–24; 7:4).

---

54. Cf. Stemberger, *Pharisees, Sadducees, Essenes,* 84ff.
55. Josephus, *J. W.* 1.110; cf. also 2.162; *Ant.* 17.41.
56. For Qumran, cf. CD 6:14ff.
57. Cf. Jacob Neusner and Hermann Lichtenberger, *Das pharisäische und talmudische Judentum: Neue Wege zu seinem Verständnis* (TSAJ 4; Tübingen: Mohr Siebeck, 1984), 24: "The Pharisees especially emphasize that eating must take place in a state of ritual purity, as though one were a priest in the temple, and that the greatest care must be exercised in tithing and obligatory gifts for the priesthood."

Alongside their particular understanding of Scripture and tradition, Josephus mentions that their view of fate and predestination characterized the Pharisees. They attributed much to the working of fate, but without negating human responsibility (cf. Josephus, *J. W.* 2.162; *Ant.* 13.72; 18.13; further *Avot* 3.5). In contrast to the Sadducees, the Pharisees advocated the doctrine of the resurrection of the dead as well as rewards and punishments after death (cf. Josephus, *J. W.* 2.163; *Pss. Sol.* 3:12; Mark 12:18–27; Acts 23:6–8). Messianic hopes were also apparently alive among the Pharisees, as indicated by *Pss. Sol.* 17–18. The *Psalms of Solomon*[58] also lets us see how Pharisaic circles thought of God's punishment of sinners and salvation of the righteous (cf. *Pss. Sol.* 14).

According to Acts 22:3, Paul received his pharisaic education[59] in Jerusalem: "I am a Jew, born in Tarsus in Cilicia, but brought up in this city at the feet of Gamaliel, educated strictly according to our ancestral law, being zealous for God, just as all of you are today." Gamaliel I was a highly respected teacher of the Torah in Jerusalem who, according to Acts 5:34–39, belonged to the Sanhedrin. That he belonged to the school of Hillel is not demonstrable.[60] Josephus (*Life* 191–192; *J. W.* 4.159) represents Simeon the son of Gamaliel as a leading member of the moderate wing of the Pharisaic group in Jerusalem, who opposed the goings-on of the Zealots during the tumultuous days during the siege of Jerusalem.

Where did Paul receive his education as a Pharisee? On the basis of Acts 22:3 and 26:4–5, W. C. van Unnik supposes that as a small child Paul moved with his parents from Tarsus to Jerusalem, that his mother tongue was Aramaic rather than Greek, and that he was reared and educated entirely in Jerusalem.[61] Paul's letters and his use of the Septuagint, however, point clearly to Greek as his native language, so that one must not postulate an early move of the apostle from Tarsus to Jerusalem.[62] Was Paul in Jerusalem at all before his call to be apostle to the Gentiles? In Gal. 1:22, while sharing his personal life story, the apostle states, "I was still unknown by sight to the churches of Judea that are in Christ." From this comment the inference is often drawn that Paul had never been in Jerusalem before his Damascus experience.[63] It is objected, however,

---

58. On the historical location and theological orientation of this document, see below, section 16.8.1 ("Cultural and Historical Milieu").

59. Haacker, "Werdegang," wants to understand Acts 22:3 generally in the sense of "education," not in the specific sense of "Torah study."

60. Cf. Neusner, *Pharisees before 70*, 1:341–76.

61. W. C. van Unnik, "Tarsus or Jerusalem: The City of Paul's Youth," in *Sparsa collecta* (3 vols.; NovTSup 29–31; Leiden: Brill, 1973–1983), 1:259–320.

62. Cf. Hengel and Deines, *Pre-Christian Paul*, 34.

63. Cf. Rudolf Bultmann, "Paul," in *Themes of Biblical Theology* (ed. Jaroslav Pelikan; Twentieth Century Theology in the Making 1; New York: Harper & Row, 1969), 169–214; Georg Strecker, "Der vorchristliche Paulus," in *Texts and Contexts: Biblical Texts in Their Textual and Situational Contexts: Essays in Honor of Lars Hartman* (ed. Tord Fornberg et al.; Boston: Scandinavian University Press, 1995), 713–41.

that one cannot base too much on this statement, since Paul could not have received a Pharisaic education outside Jerusalem, that convincing evidence of a Jewish educational program in the Diaspora is lacking, and that Jerusalem was the natural center for the education of Pharisees.[64] But we should not rate the silence of the sources on this point too highly.[65] In any case, it is remarkable that Paul himself never mentions Jerusalem when he speaks of his past life as a Pharisee. Moreover, in Paul's thought Jerusalem plays no significant role. The apostle is compelled to go twice to Jerusalem for particular occasions (the apostolic council, delivering the collection), and the first visit was demonstrably brief. It is also to be noted that Acts 5:34–39 presents Gamaliel as a tolerant scholar, and so Paul could not have learned his rigorous stance against those who believed differently from him.[66] The extant sources do not permit a clear decision on this issue. If Paul completed a program of Torah studies under Gamaliel, he probably came to Jerusalem at about the age of fifteen.[67]

At the time of Paul, the Pharisees were no longer a united movement, as is shown by the role of the Pharisee Zadduk in the founding of the Zealots and the disputes between the schools of Hillel and Shammai.[68] The noticeable emphasis on the theological category of "zeal"[69] in connection with the persecution of the first Christians (cf. Gal. 1:14; Phil. 3:6; Acts 22:3–4) could be an indication that Paul—unlike Josephus, for example[70]—inclined toward the radical wing of Pharisaism.[71] Whether this means that Paul belonged to the stricter school of Shammai[72] must remain an open question; what is clear is the zeal of Paul the Pharisee for the ancestral traditions.

64. Hengel and Deines, *Pre-Christian Paul*, 29–34, 38–39.

65. Cf. Stemberger, *Pharisees, Sadducees, Essenes*, 112: "We have no other evidence for Pharisees in the Diaspora, but we cannot draw any conclusion from this accidental silence of the sources, even though the observance of various religious laws, above all in the realm of purity, must have been very difficult in the Diaspora." Johann Maier, *Geschichte der jüdischen Religion: Von der Zeit Alexanders des Grossen bis zur Aufklärung mit einem Ausblick auf das 19./20. Jahrhundert* (Freiburg: Herder, 1992), 76–77, 81–82, reckons with the possibility of Diaspora Pharisees who were educated elsewhere than in Jerusalem. Jürgen Becker, *Paul: Apostle to the Gentiles* (trans. O. C. Dean; Louisville: Westminster John Knox, 1993), 39, does not exclude the possibility of a Jerusalem education for Paul but still comments, "Paul could also have easily received an education in the Pharisaic sense at any larger diaspora synagogue, even in Tarsus." Cf. further the reflections of Strecker, "Der vorchristliche Paulus," 732–37.

66. Cf. Sanders, *Paul*, 8.

67. Josephus (*Life* 10) began his study of the different Jewish school traditions (Pharisees, Sadducees, Essenes) when he was sixteen years old.

68. Cf. here Jacob Neusner, *Judaism in the Beginning of Christianity* (Philadelphia: Fortress, 1984), 63–89; R. Goldenberg, "Hillel/Hillelschule (Schammaj/Schammajschule)," *TRE* 15:326–30.

69. On the category "zeal" in ancient Judaism, cf. Hengel, *Zeloten*, 151ff.

70. Cf. Josephus, *Life* 10–12.

71. Cf. Klaus Haacker, "Die Berufung des Verfolgers und die Rechtfertigung des Gottlosen," *TBei* 6 (1975): 1–19.

72. So Hans Hübner, "Gal. 3,10 und die Herkunft des Paulus," *KD* 19 (1973): 215–31; Haacker, "Berufung des Verfolgers," 10; more hesitantly in Haacker, "Werdegang," 861–77.

3.3 The Religious and Cultural Background of Paul's Thought

The formation of one's identity always occurs under the influence of one or more cultural contexts. Thus such objectifiable factors as language, ancestry, religion, and their derivative traditions essentially determine one's awareness of ethnic identity. Such traditions are in turn the expression of cultural formation through texts, rites, and symbols.[73] Although identity formation as a rule occurs within such a pre-given framework, it always has a process character; it is fluid and involved in changing situations.[74] When one lives—as did Paul—in a situation of overlapping cultural realms, authentic personal identity develops only if it has the capacity to appropriate and integrate a variety of influences.

The Old Testament and Jewish Background

The theological thought of the apostle to the Gentiles is rooted in the fundamental convictions of the Hellenistic Judaism of his time. All Jewish theology, including that of the Jewish Christian Paul, proceeds from its basis in monotheism: the one true God, the father of Abraham, stands over against the Gentile gods as the true and living God. Paul takes up this creed of Hellenistic Judaism (cf., e.g., Aristobulus 124–169; *Jos. Asen.* 11:10–11; Philo, *Spec. Laws* 1.208; *Alleg. Interp.* 2.1–2; *Embassy* 115; Josephus, *Ant.* 8.91; 4.201; 5.112; 8.335, 337) and makes it the basis of his missionary preaching (cf. 1 Thess. 1:9–10). The Corinthian Christians may eat meat sacrificed to idols, for there is only one God, from whom all things come (cf. 1 Cor. 8:6; Rom. 11:36a). If the Galatians were to turn back to a religion of calendar observance, they would find themselves back in the time that has already become obsolete for them, the time in which they did not yet know God and served powers that in reality are not gods at all (cf. Gal. 4:8–9). As in ancient Judaism, Paul connects monotheism with faith in creation and election.[75] Only God calls the dead to life and nonbeing into being (compare Rom. 4:17 with *2 Bar.* 21.4; 48.8; *Jos. Asen.* 8.9). God, who sent forth light into darkness (cf. Gen. 1 in 2 Cor. 4:6), also shines into the hearts of believers (cf. 1QH 4:5, 27). God alone is the

73. Cf. Harald Welzer, "Das soziale Gedächtnis," in *Das soziale Gedächtnis: Geschichte, Erinnerung, Tradierung* (ed. Harald Welzer; Hamburg: Hamburger Edition, 2001), 9–21.

74. Assmann and Friese, eds., *Identities*, 269–87.

75. One need only note the first lines of the Eighteen Benedictions: "Blessed art thou, O Lord our God and God of our fathers, / God of Abraham, God of Isaac, and God of Jacob, / The great, the mighty, the revered God, the most high God, / Who bestowest lovingkindnesses, and possessest all things; / Who rememberest the pious deeds of the patriarchs; / And in love wilt bring a redeemer to their children's children." This translation is from *Authorized Daily Prayer Book of the United Hebrew Congregations of the British Empire* (trans. S. Singer; 9th American ed.; New York: Hebrew Publishing Co, 1932), 44. Cf. Hermann Strack and Paul Billerbeck, *Kommentar zum Neuen Testament aus Talmud und Midrasch* (6 vols. in 7; Munich: Beck, 1924), 4/1:208ff.

Creator, to whom the creature may offer no criticism (cf. Rom. 9:19ff.). In continuity with Jewish apocalyptic (cf. *Jub.* 1:29; 4:26; *1 En.* 72:1; *4 Ezra* 7:75; 1QS 4:25), Paul speaks of a καινὴ κτίσις (new creation)[76] that for Christians has already come into being through the gift of the Spirit in faith (2 Cor. 5:17). The concept of election, fundamental for Jewish faith (cf. *Jub.* 1:29; 2:20; *1 En.* 53:6; 56; 93; *2 Bar.* 48:20–24; *4 Ezra* 5:23–27; 6:54–56; *Avot* 1:7; 3:14), is adopted by Paul (cf. Rom. 3:1–2; 9:4; 11:2, 28–29) and reinterpreted within the Christian perspective. Christians now belong to the elect people of God (Rom. 8:33; cf. further 1 Thess. 1:4; Gal. 1:6; Rom. 1:6).

So also Paul's view of the judgment[77] is firmly rooted in the ideas of ancient Judaism. Thus a whole complex of ideas found in Paul's missionary proclamation was already present in the missionary preaching of Hellenistic Judaism, for example, the connections between the doctrine of the one true God, the failure of the Gentiles to acknowledge God and their turning to idolatry, the moral corruption of Gentiles resulting from their idolatry, the call to repentance, and the picturing of divine judgment to come (compare 1 Thess. 1:9–10; Rom. 1:18–32 with Wis. 13–15; Aristobulus 124–169; *T. Levi* 17; *T. Naph.* 3; 4; *T. Benj.* 9; 14; *1 En.* 91:7ff.; *Jos. Asen.* 11–13; *2 Bar.* 54:17–18).[78] The announcement of the wrath of God in the coming judgment applies to both Gentiles and Jews (cf. Rom. 2:1–3:20), for no one will escape condemnation by works of the law. Also for Paul, God judges every person by his or her works (compare 1 Cor. 3:14–15; 4:5; 2 Cor. 5:9–10; 9:6; 11:15; Gal. 6:7–8; Rom. 2:5–16 with *1 En.* 50:4; *2 Bar.* 85:12; Prov. 24:12; *Avot* 3:15; *Pss. Sol.* 2:16–18, 34; 9:5; *4 Ezra* 7:33–35).[79] Paul radicalizes the concept of judgment, since, for him, in the last judgment no person will be saved on the basis of works. There is no "treasury of good works" deposited with the Most High (cf. *Jub.* 30:17–23; *4 Ezra* 7:77; 8:33, 36; *2 Bar.* 14:12; 24:1; 52:7). Paul also speaks about a

---

76. For the background for Paul's use of καινὴ κτίσις in the history of religions, cf. Ulrich Mell, *Neue Schöpfung: Eine traditionsgeschichtliche und exegetische Studie zu einem soteriologischen Grundsatz paulinischer Theologie* (Berlin: de Gruyter, 1989), 47–257; Moyer V. Hubbard, *New Creation in Paul's Letters and Thought* (Cambridge: Cambridge University Press, 2002), 11–78.

77. Cf. K. Seybold, "Gericht," *TRE* 12:460–66; Gerbern S. Oegema, *Zwischen Hoffnung und Gericht: Untersuchungen zur Rezeption der Apokalyptik im frühen Christentum und Judentum* (WMANT 82; Neukirchen-Vluyn: Neukirchener Verlag, 1999); Ernst Synofzik, *Die Gerichts- und Vergeltungsaussagen bei Paulus: Eine traditionsgeschichtliche Untersuchung* (GTA 8; Göttingen: Vandenhoeck & Ruprecht, 1977), passim; Egon Brandenburger, "Gericht Gottes III," *TRE* 12:469–83.

78. Cf. here Claus Bussmann, *Themen der paulinischen Missionspredigt auf dem Hintergrund der spätjüdisch-hellenistischen Missionsliteratur* (EHS, Reihe 23, Theologie 3; Bern: Lang, 1971).

79. On the concept of judgment according to one's works in Greek thought, cf. Plato, *Phaed.* 113d: "And when the dead arrive at the place to which the genius of each severally guides them, first of all, they have sentence passed upon them, as they have lived well and piously or not. And those who appear to have lived neither well nor ill, go to the river Acheron, and embarking in any vessels which they may find, are carried in them to the lake, and there they dwell and are purified of their evil deeds, and having suffered the penalty of the wrongs which they have done to others, they are absolved, and receive the rewards of their good deeds, each of them according to his deserts."

person's being right before God and about right conduct that corresponds to God's will, but works of the law/Torah cannot effect salvation. Righteousness does not result from doing the commandments (as, e.g., in Deut. 6:25; Prov. 10:16a LXX; Aristobulus 168; *Pss. Sol.* 9:3; 14:2; *4 Ezra* 7:33ff.; 9:7–8; 13:23; *2 Bar.* 51:7; 67:6; 69:4; 85:2), and life does not come from fulfilling the law (cf., e.g., Neh. 9:29; Sir. 15:15–20; 17:11; *Pss. Sol.* 14:3; *4 Ezra* 7:21, 129). Paul thereby breaks the connection between keeping all the commandments of the Torah, received as the expression of God's unified saving will, and hearing the God's gracious word in the last judgment. This connection had been fundamental for his Jewish past (cf., e.g., Isa. 51:7a; Deut. 30:14ff.; Ps. 37:31; 40:9; Prov. 3:1–3; 7:1–3; Sir. 6:23–31; *Pss. Sol.* 2:36; *4 Ezra* 8:33; *2 Bar.* 46:3; *1 En.* 99; *Avot* 1:3, 17; 2:1).

In his concept of the resurrection, Paul recapitulates, with both continuity and discontinuity, an article of Pharisaic faith (cf., e.g., 1 Thess. 4:13–18; 1 Cor. 15:22–23; 2 Cor. 4:14ff.; Rom. 4:24; 8:11).[80] The resurrection of the righteous is understood as the reconstitution of individual bodily existence (cf., e.g., *1 En.* 91:10; 92:3; 100:5; *Pss. Sol.* 3:10–12; 13:11; 2 Macc. 7:11; 14:46; *2 Bar.* 30:1–5; 50; 51).[81] For Paul, the resurrection of Jesus from the dead validates the hope in the believers' resurrection, which is fulfilled as a new creation in which personal identity is preserved.

Paul's statements about the just God and human justification also show his rootedness in Jewish thought.[82] God is just and judges in righteousness (cf.

80. For the basis in Old Testament and early Jewish texts, cf., e.g., Isa. 26:19; Dan. 12:2–3; Ezek. 37:1–14; Ps. 73; 2 Macc. 7:14; *Pss. Sol.* 3:12. The resurrection hope is documented at Qumran by 4QMessAp 2:11–12: "And the LORD will accomplish glorious things . . . for he will heal the wounded, and revive the dead and bring good news to the poor" (Vermès, 245). Cf. Hermann Lichtenberger, "Auferstehung in den Qumrantexten," in *Auferstehung = Resurrection: The Fourth Durham-Tübingen Research Symposium: Resurrection, Transfiguration, and Exaltation in Old Testament, Ancient Judaism, and Early Christianity* (ed. Friedrich Avemarie and Hermann Lichtenberger; WUNT 135; Tübingen: Mohr Siebeck, 2001), 79–91. Lichtenberger judges the *Messianic Apocalypse* (4QMessAp) to be the only indisputable reference to the faith of the Qumran Essenes in the resurrection. The caution regarding this idea may be related to the influence of priestly-Sadducean circles at Qumran. Faith in the resurrection was not common property of ancient Judaism; the Sadducees rejected the idea (cf. Mark 12:18; Acts 4:2; 23:6–8; Josephus, *J.W.* 2.164–165; *Ant.* 18.16); on the concept of resurrection in early Judaism, cf. Günter Stemberger, *Der Leib der Auferstehung: Studien zur Anthropologie und Eschatologie des palästinischen Judentums im neutestamentlichen Zeitalter (ca. 170 v. C[h]r.–100 n. Chr.)* (AnBib 56; Rome: Biblical Institute Press, 1972).

81. Here after the resurrection all the righteous are transformed in glory while the godless suffer visible pain. The resurrection of both good and evil is also found in *1 En.* 22; *Sib. Or.* 3:178ff.; *4 Ezra* 7:29ff.; *L.A.E.* 51; *T. Benj.* 10:6ff.

82. A survey of the nuanced use of δικαιοσύνη (justice, righteousness, justification) in ancient Judaism is found in M. J. Fiedler, "Δικαιοσύνη in der diaspora-jüdischen und intertestamentarischen Literatur," *JSJ* 1 (1970): 120–43. The Old Testament data is documented in Klaus Koch, "צדק," *TLOT* 2:1046–62; B. Johnson, "צדק," *TDOT* 12:239–64; E. Otto, "Gerechtigkeit," *RGG* 3:702–4.

[Translator's note: In German as in Greek (but not in English), the same word is used for "justice" and "righteousness," and their adjectival and verbal cognates are from the same root. English

Pss. Sol. 2:15; 4:24; 8:24–26; 9:2, 4, 5; *Jub.* 5:16; *T. Levi* 3.2; *Sib. Or.* 3:704) according to one's works (Sir. 16:12; *4 Ezra* 8:33; *2 Bar.* 51:7). Therefore religious people know that their own righteousness can only come from God's righteousness (cf. *Pss. Sol.* 3:6; 5:17; *As. Mos.* 11:17; *4 Ezra* 8:32–33; 1QH 7:19–20; 13:17). The Psalms often celebrate how God helps his own people with God's own righteousness (cf. Ps. 22:32; 24:5; 31:2; 51:16; and passim). The Qumran texts often reflect on the connection between the righteousness of God and human righteousness.[83] Because human beings have no righteousness of their own (cf. 1QH 4:30; 9:14ff.), "My righteousness shall be by the righteousness of God" (1QS 11:12; cf. also 1QS 11:25; 1QM 4:6). The statements about justification present an instructive parallel to Paul, for here, on the basis of a deep awareness of human sin, there is reflection on the righteousness of God and how human beings can be righteous. At Qumran the righteousness of God means the merciful act of God for the sinner, for whom God is righteousness. On the basis of this divinely given righteousness, the fulfillment of the Torah first becomes possible. "As for me, if I stumble, the mercies of God shall be my eternal salvation. If I stagger because of the sin of the flesh, my justification shall be by the righteousness of God which endures forever" (1QS 11:12 [Vermès, 88]). Precisely because God is just and judges righteously and because human beings always fall short of the righteous demands of God, hope is finally based on God's mercy and compassion (cf. 1QH 1:31–32; 7:29–31; 9:34). The awareness of human nothingness before God and of dependence on the justifying act of God's grace alone did not, however, lead the Qumran believers to an *abrogatio legis* (abrogation of the law) but to an intensification of law observance. Precisely because justification comes from God, it is possible to call for a more rigorous observance of the commandments (cf. 1QS 1:8–9; 5:8–9; 8:1).

---

readers will note the connection between "justice" and "justification," but modern English has no verb for "make righteous." In his translation of Bultmann's *Theology of the New Testament,* Kendrick Grobel revived the Old English verb "rightwise" (i.e., "justify," "make right"). Cf. Grobel's explanatory footnote in Rudolf Bultmann, *Theology of the New Testament* (trans. Kendrick Grobel; 2 vols.; New York: Scribner, 1951), 1:253; and the adoption of this terminology by Schubert M. Ogden, ed., *Existence and Faith: Shorter Writings of Rudolf Bultmann* (New York: Meridian Books, 1960). Larry W. Hurtado, *Lord Jesus Christ: Devotion to Jesus in Earliest Christianity* (Grand Rapids: Eerdmans, 2003), 89, aptly comments, "It is clear that in Paul the Greek noun δικαιοσύνη and its verbal cognates (from δικαιόω) have to do with a positive relationship and standing with God. The English word 'righteousness' hardly communicates this effectively [nor does 'justice']. See the exhaustive study of the matter by Richard Kingsley Moore, 'Right with God: Paul and His English Translators' (Ph.D. diss., University of Queensland, 1978)."]

83. Cf. Siegfried Schulz, "Zur Rechtfertigung aus Gnaden in Qumran und bei Paulus," *ZTK* 56 (1959): 155–85; Jürgen Becker, *Das Heil Gottes: Heils- und Sündenbegriffe in den Qumrantexten und im Neuen Testament* (SUNT 3; Göttingen: Vandenhoeck & Ruprecht, 1964), 37ff.; Hermann Lichtenberger, *Studien zum Menschenbild in Texten der Qumrangemeinde* (SUNT 15; Göttingen: Vandenhoeck & Ruprecht, 1980), 87ff.

Paul's concept of sin also manifests clear parallels to that of the Judaism of his time.[84] The universally disastrous character of sin appears at the very beginning of the human race. From the time of Adam's sin, the nature of the world has been stamped by the inherent, all-determining connection between sin and death (compare Rom. 5:12 with *4 Ezra* 3:7, 21; 7:118; *2 Bar.* 23:4). As in Paul's writings (cf. Rom. 6:12ff.), Qumran's speak of "service to sin and deeds of deceit" (1QH 1:27; cf. 1QS 7:10; 1QM 13:5, "service to impurity").[85] Here, too, "flesh" is the realm of sin's dominion (cf. 1QS 4:20–21). Like Paul (cf. Rom. 3:20), *4 Ezra* advocates the view of universal human sinfulness (cf. 4:38; 7:68; 8:17, 35; 7:46, "who among the living is there that has not sinned, or who is there among mortals that has not transgressed your covenant?"). In contrast, extensive circles of Hellenistic Judaism regarded human beings as capable of living a righteous life by their own decision and the help of divine wisdom and thus of escaping the domination of sin and death (cf., e.g., Wis. 1:12–16; 2:23–3:3; 6:18–19; 9:10, 17–18). Insight into the fatal character of sin (cf. Rom. 5:12) leads Paul to the exact opposite of the view that human beings are able to proceed from their own situation to do what is good and right. Contrast *2 Bar.* 54:15 (cf. also *4 Ezra* 7:118–119):

> For, although Adam sinned first and has brought death upon all who were not in his own time, yet each of them who has been born from him has prepared for himself the coming torment. And further, each of them has chosen for himself the coming glory. . . . Adam is, therefore, not the cause, except only for himself, but each of us has become our own Adam.[86]

Ancient Judaism had also already intensively and with controversy discussed the question of human free will before Paul. Thus in Jesus ben Sira we find affirmations of freedom of the human will (cf. Sir. 15:11–15, 20) as well as statements that humans are not free to choose (cf. Sir. 33:11–15).[87] The *Psalms of Solomon*, from the Pharisaic tradition, gives further evidence that the issue of free will was a very disputed question in ancient Judaism.[88] On the one hand, we find statements that explicitly affirm human freedom of choice (cf. *Pss. Sol.*

---

84. Of course, Hellenistic philosophers were also aware of human guilt; cf. Seneca, *Ben.* 1.10.3 ("As for the rest, we always have to report the same: we are evil, we were evil, and—I am sorry to have to add—we will always be so"); cf. further *Ira* 1.14.3; 2.10.2; 2.28.1; 2.31.5; 3.25.2; 3.26.4; *Clem.* 1.6.3; *Ep.* 16.97.1.

85. On the understanding of sin in the Qumran texts, cf. Lichtenberger, *Studien zum Menschenbild*, 93ff.; and Seyoon Kim, "Heilsgegenwart bei Paulus: Eine religionsgeschichtlich-theologische Untersuchung zu Sündenvergebung und Geistgabe in den Qumrantexten sowie bei Johannes dem Täufer, Jesus, und Paulus" (diss., Georg August Universität, Göttingen, 1996), 35–40.

86. Trans. A. F. J. Klijn, *OTP* 1:640.

87. For an analysis of all important texts, cf. Gerhard Maier, *Mensch und freier Wille: Nach der jüdischen Religionsparteien zwischen Ben Sira und Paulus* (WUNT 12; Tübingen: Mohr Siebeck, 1971), 24–115.

88. Cf. ibid., 264–342.

9:4–7); on the other hand, *Pss. Sol.* 5:4 says, "For an individual and his fate are on the scales before you; he cannot add any increase contrary to your judgment, O God." Paul advocates a position very close to that of Sir. 33:11–15, which also has parallels in the Qumran literature (cf. 1QH 15:12–17; 1QS 3:13–4:26);[89] free will is exclusively a predicate of God, who in his freedom chooses and rejects and from whose decision there is no appeal (cf. Rom. 9:1–29).

Finally, Paul takes up the covenant concept central for ancient Judaism (cf., e.g., Sir. 24:23; 28:7; *Jub.* 1:17–18, 22–25; *Pss. Sol.* 9:10; 10:4; 17:15; *1 En.* 99:2 [Gr]; 1QS 1:16; 4:18–23; CD 15:5–11; Philo, *Dreams* 2.223–24, 237)[90] and uses it to describe the continuing covenant with Israel (Rom. 9:4; cf. also 1 Cor. 11:25; 2 Cor. 3:6, 14; Gal. 3:17; 4:24; Rom. 11:27). God's covenant with Israel remains firm.

The Greek and Hellenistic Background

Paul's native language was Greek, and he grew up in the Hellenistic metropolis Tarsus and carried out his missionary work primarily in Hellenistic Asia Minor or in Greece itself. Such a life history suggests an intensive influence of Greek-Hellenistic thought,[91] although this cannot always be demonstrated in detail. Whether and to what extent Paul knew the works of classic Greek literature and poetry and whether he attended the Greek theater must remain open questions. Only once (1 Cor. 15:33) does he specifically cite Greek literature, when he refers to a popular proverb of Euripides, found in Menander's comedy *Thais*: "Bad company ruins good morals."[92] The urban Hellenistic socialization of the apostle comes through in 1 Cor. 9:24–27, where, as a matter of course, he compares his life as an apostle to the competition in the arena of the Greek gymnasium.[93] He also compares himself to the Hellenistic image

89. These texts speak of God's having made humanity subject to the Spirit of Truth and the Spirit of Iniquity and of these two spirits completely determining human life: "The nature of the children of men is ruled by these [two spirits], and during their life all the hosts of men have a portion of their divisions and walk in [both] their ways. And the whole reward for their deeds shall be, for everlasting ages, according to whether each man's portion in their two divisions is great or small. For God has established the spirits in equal measure until the final age, and has set everlasting hatred between their divisions" (1QS 4:15–17 [Vermès, 74]). The Qumran texts, in massive form, assert that God predestined human beings either to salvation or damnation. The idea is interpreted positively in relation to the concept of election, which the Qumran community applied to itself; for analysis of the texts, cf. Maier, *Mensch und freier Wille*, 165–263.

90. For sorting out the data, cf. Manuel Vogel, *Das Heil des Bundes: Bundestheologie im Frühjudentum und im frühen Christentum* (TANZ 18; Tübingen: Francke, 1996), 225ff.

91. For an introduction to this topic, cf. Troels Engberg-Pedersen, ed., *Paul in His Hellenistic Context* (Minneapolis: Fortress, 1995).

92. Cf. *NW* 2/1:401.

93. Cf. O. Schwankl, "'Lauft so, daß ihr gewinnt': Zur Wettkampfmetaphorik in 1Kor 9," *BZ* 41 (1997): 174–91.

of the philosopher who exercises discipline every day in order to remain free and independent;[94] Paul likewise does his utmost for the proclamation of the gospel. What Seneca requires of philosophers also applies to Paul the teacher of ethics, namely, to make clear "what is right, what it means to have a sense of duty, what it means to be willing to suffer, to be brave, to have no fear of death, to know God, and the priceless value of a good conscience."[95]

Paul made his appearance in the Hellenistic cities as one preacher among a number of wandering philosophers, preachers, and miracle workers. It is thus not surprising to find some points of contact within the Pauline corpus with the traditions of these wandering philosophers. In 1 Thess. 2:1–12 Paul describes his interaction with the Thessalonians in the terminology and imagery that also belonged to the repertoire of the Cynic wandering philosophers.[96] Instruction on how to live one's life and cultivate one's mind, as well as modeling a way of life free from material needs and therefore oriented to freedom, was characteristic of both the apostle and the wandering philosophers. Epictetus says, "The true Cynic . . . must know that he has been sent by Zeus to men, partly as a messenger, in order to show them that in questions of good and evil they have gone astray, and are seeking the true nature of the good and the evil where it is not, but where it is they never think" (Epictetus, *Diatr.* 3.22.23). Like the Cynics, Paul practiced a radical lifestyle independent of family and economic obligations, understanding himself exclusively as a messenger of the gospel. In order to be a "scout" for the gods, the Cynic must be

> wholly devoted to the service of God, free to go about among men, not tied down by the private duties of men, nor involved in relationships which he cannot violate and still maintain his role as a good and excellent man, whereas, on the other hand, if he observes them, he will destroy the messenger, the scout, the herald [κῆρυξ] of the gods that he is. (Epictetus, *Diatr.* 3.22.69)[97]

94. Cf. Epictetus, *Diatr.* 4.1.112–114: "Look at everything carefully, and tear it from your hearts. Purify your judgments and examine yourself to see whether you are not dependent on something that does not belong to you, and whether you have not become attached to something that will only give you pain when it is taken away. And while you daily discipline yourself like an athlete on the playing field, do not say that you are philosophizing—a really highfalutin word—but that you are asserting your freedom. For that is true freedom. This is how Diogenes of Antisthenes became a free man, and thus established that he could no longer be enslaved by anyone" (*NW* 2/1:566–67).

95. Seneca, *Tranq.* 3.4.

96. Cf. Abraham J. Malherbe, *Paul and the Popular Philosophers* (Minneapolis: Fortress, 1989), 35–48; "Herakles," *RAC* 14:573: "Paul was familiar with Cynic traditions, including those about Hercules."

97. Cf. also Epictetus, *Diatr.* 4.8.30–31: "For such a person is a true Cynic, whom Zeus counts worthy of scepter and crown; such a one may say, 'In order that you may see, O people, that you must not seek happiness and peace of mind where it is, but where it is not, this is why I have been sent from God as a model [ἰδοὺ ἐγὼ ὑμῖν παράδειγμα ὑπὸ τοῦ θεοῦ ἀπέσταλμαι]. I have neither house nor property, neither wife nor children, no bed or coat, and just look at how healthy I am.'"

When Paul in 2 Cor. 11:16–12:10 slips into the role of a fool, in the view of his contemporaries he was presenting himself as a true philosopher.[98]

The Pauline style of argument, the diatribe (διατριβή), has a Hellenistic background.[99] The diatribe was a widespread technique of speaking and writing, characterized by dialogical elements and rhetorical questions, objections raised by the speakers or writers themselves, conversations with an imaginary partner whose objections are rejected, and the use of stock phrases. Among those who practiced the diatribe style were the Cynic Teles (third century BCE), the Stoic Musonius Rufus (ca. 30–100 CE), Epictetus (ca. 55–135 CE), and Seneca (ca. 4 BCE—65 CE).[100] Examples of Pauline texts strongly stamped by the diatribe are 1 Cor. 4:6–15; 9:1–18; 15:29–49; Rom. 1:18–2:11; 8:31–39; 11:1–24 (cf. also 1 Cor. 6:12–20; 12:12–13:13; 2 Cor. 11:16–33; Rom. 2:17–24; 7:7–15). The diatribe style prevails in Paul "wherever he cannot be sure of the positive acceptance of his theological arguments. When the Pauline corpus is considered as a whole, one thus notices that the letters are particularly characterized by 'diatribe style' that, on the one hand, have a strong theological argument and where, on the other hand, for whatever reason, communication has broken down."[101] This specific use of the diatribe by Paul explains its prevalence in Romans and 1 Corinthians. Paul's letters hardly belong to the elevated category of Greek literature; they do show, however, that Paul belongs to the class that used Greek fluently as its everyday language, at a level indicating the basics of a Hellenistic education.

The Pauline peristasis catalogues (recitals of personal hardships) are quite close to the Cynic-Stoic diatribes. They describe the life circumstances in which the philosopher or preacher finds himself and how he must endure as the representative of his teaching when it is put to the test.[102] The peristasis catalogues adopt the ideals of the time as their own themes: making do with what one has, the capacity to hold up under external stress, independence of either praise or blame, and the self-sufficiency of the sage. The Pauline peristasis catalogues

---

98. For analysis, cf. Hans Dieter Betz, *Der Apostel Paulus und die sokratische Tradition: Eine exegetische Untersuchung zu seiner Apologie 2 Korinther 10–13* (BHT 45; Tübingen: Mohr Siebeck, 1972), 43ff.

99. For a basic bibliography, see Rudolf Bultmann, *Der Stil der paulinischen Predigt und die kynisch-stoische Diatribe* (FRLANT 13; Göttingen: Vandenhoeck & Ruprecht, 1910); Stanley K. Stowers, *The Diatribe and Paul's Letter to the Romans* (SBLDS 57; Chico: Scholars Press, 1981); Thomas Schmeller, *Paulus und die "Diatribe": Eine vergleichende Stilinterpretation* (NTAbh NF 19; Münster: Aschendorff, 1987).

100. The diatribe style is also found in the preaching of the Hellenistic Jewish synagogues; cf. Folker Siegert, trans., *Drei hellenistisch-jüdische Predigten: Ps.-Philon, "Über Jona," "Über Simson," und "Über die Gottesbezeichnung 'wohltätig verzehrendes Feuer'"* (2 vols.; WUNT 20, 61; Tübingen: Mohr Siebeck, 1980–1992).

101. Schmeller, *Paulus und die "Diatribe,"* 423.

102. Cf. Epictetus, *Diatr.* 1.24.1: "Difficulties reveal who a person is" (αἱ περιστάσεις εἰσὶν τοὺς ἄνδρας δεικνύουσαι).

are very similar, in both form and content, to the catalogues of the Greek-Hellenistic world. First Corinthians 4:11–12 contains a peristasis catalogue that portrays the circumstances of the apostle's external life within which he carries out his preaching ministry.[103] The apostle's labors that are the content of the personal peristasis catalogue in 2 Cor. 11:23–29 manifest parallels to the labors of Hercules.[104] In 2 Cor. 12:10 Paul can evaluate the peristasis positively,[105] for endurance in difficult circumstances points to the power of Christ at work in the apostle (cf. Seneca, *Ep.* 41.4–5). In 2 Cor. 4:8–9 Paul orients himself to the model of the Stoic antitheses (cf. Epictetus, *Diatr.* 19.34); the peristases thus stand over against the attitudes that overcome them. Second Corinthians 6:4–10 contains a combination of peristasis catalogue and virtue catalogue.[106] In the adiaphora catalogue of Phil. 4:12 Paul emphasizes his self-sufficiency regarding external needs.[107] Like the philosophers, in the peristasis catalogues Paul represents himself as an example, in order to clarify for the churches the consequences and aspects of a life of discipleship to Jesus Christ. The peristasis lists preserve the faith in, and reveal the power of, the one who is crucified and risen.

Extensive sections of the Pauline letters have a rhetorical quality. For example, the overall structure of Galatians[108] and the subtle argument of Philemon[109] are formulated rhetorically. Numerous individual sections of Paul's letters (e.g., 2 Cor. 10–12; Rom. 9–11) are characterized by rhetorical elements, such as antitheses, questions, irony, comparisons, typologies, chains of inferences, aphorisms, examples, and complimentary addresses. If the goal of rhetoric is, as Quintilian says, "to speak to people in such a way that they do what the author wants,"[110] there is no doubt that Paul makes use of his rhetorical ability. Whether the rhetorical competence visible in his letters allows us to infer

103. Cf. Epictetus, *Diatr.* 3.22.45–48: "Yes, how can it be that one who has nothing, who is naked, without house and hearth, who struggles along pathetically, who has no slave, no homeland, still leads a happy life? Look, God has sent someone to you who shows you that it is in fact possible. Look at me—I have no house, no hometown, no property, no slave. I sleep on the ground, have no wife, child, or house, but only the earth beneath me and the sky above, and a single shabby cloak. But what else do I need?" (*NW* 1/1:169).

104. Ebner, *Leidenslisten und Apostelbrief*, 161–72; Markus Schiefer-Ferrari, *Die Sprache des Leids in den paulinischen Peristasenkatalogen* (SBB 23; Stuttgart: Katholisches Bibelwerk, 1991), 237–59. A classical example of self-presentation in antiquity is offered by Augustus, *Res gestae divi Augusti* (*Deeds of the Divine Augustus*).

105. For analysis, cf. Schiefer-Ferrari, *Peristasenkatalogen*, 260–70.

106. Cf. Ebner, *Leidenslisten und Apostelbrief*, 269ff., who points out the similarity to the descriptions of Hellenistic rulers.

107. Cf. Ebner's analysis, ibid., 331–64.

108. Cf. Hans Dieter Betz, *Galatians: A Commentary on Paul's Letter to the Churches in Galatia* (Hermeneia; Philadelphia: Fortress, 1979), 54–72.

109. Cf. Joachim Gnilka, *Der Philemonbrief* (HTKNT 10/4; Freiburg: Herder, 1982), 7–12.

110. Quintilian, *Inst.* 2.15.10.

that he had a standard education in such matters is a disputed point.[111] Two observations speak against this possibility: (1) Without any special instruction, Paul could have absorbed some rhetorical ability as one of the elements of his cultural environment. Then we would understand his rhetorical competence not as a part of his formal education but as a product of his general cultural formation. (2) The apostle's admission in 2 Cor. 11:6 that he was unskilled in speaking (ἰδιώτης τῷ λόγῳ) but not in knowledge relativizes the significance of the rhetorical elements in Paul's argumentation. Nevertheless, the potency of Paul's language points to a remarkably high level of Hellenistic culture.

The theme of conscience also reveals the apostle's rootedness in the prevailing culture of his time.[112] Paul develops his understanding of συνείδησις especially in the Corinthian correspondence: conscience is a court where one sits in judgment on oneself, where one's conduct is evaluated by given norms and concrete decisions are rendered (cf. 1 Cor. 10:25–29). Seneca can say about the conscience, "God is near to you, with you, in you. So I say, Lucilius: a holy spirit dwells in us, watching over our good and bad deeds. As we deal with it, so it deals with us."[113] As for Seneca, so also for Paul, conscience is active in all human beings (cf. Rom. 2:12–16), and thus Gentiles have an awareness of moral values just as do the Jews. The function of conscience is the same for all people, but the norms that provide its basis for judgment can be very different. For Seneca, the conscience functioning as internal judge is oriented to the universal laws of nature. In that it represents the ideal moral autonomy of the person, in the course of self-examination it can evaluate human conduct with either a "good or bad conscience" (cf. Seneca, *Ep.* 23.6–7; 24.12; 81.20; 97.15–16, 105.8, and often).

In Rom. 2:14–15 Paul takes up the Greco-Roman doctrine of the νόμος ἄγραφος (unwritten law).[114] The noble and free human being needs no externally imposed law; "he is a law unto himself."[115] There are numerous laws that function as valid in all cultures without being written down, and they therefore must have been given by God or the gods.[116]

---

111. Christopher Forbes, "Comparison, Self-Praise, and Irony: Paul's Boasting and the Conventions of Hellenistic Rhetoric," *NTS* 32 (1986): 23.

112. See below, section 19.5 ("Centers of the Human Self"); on the background of Paul's concept of conscience from the perspective of the history of religion, cf. Hans-Joachim Eckstein, *Der Begriff Syneidesis bei Paulus: Eine neutestamentlich-exegetische Untersuchung zum "Gewissensbegriff"* (WUNT 2/10; Tübingen: Mohr Siebeck, 1983), 35–104.

113. Seneca, *Ep.* 41.1–2 (*NW* 2/1:535). Granted, the word *conscientia* itself does not appear in this text, but there is no dispute among scholars that Seneca here attributes the function of conscience in us to the divine spirit; cf. Hans-Josef Klauck, "'Der Gott in dir' (Ep 41,1): Autonomie des Gewissens bei Seneca und Paulus," in *Alte Welt und neuer Glaube: Beiträge zur Religionsgeschichte, Forschungsgeschichte, und Theologie des Neuen Testaments* (NTOA 29; Göttingen: Vandenhoeck & Ruprecht, 1994).

114. See below, section 12.4 ("Knowledge of God among Jews and Gentiles").

115. Aristotle, *Eth. nic.* 4.1128a (*NW* 2/1:76).

116. Cf. Xenophon, *Mem.* 4.4.19–20 (*NW* 2/2:1574).

Clear lines of connection can be seen between the Pauline and the Stoic concept of freedom. Thus Seneca can specifically relate external slavery with internal freedom, and external freedom with real slavery (cf. Seneca, *Ep.* 47).[117] For Epictetus also, freedom is identical with inner independence, and they are slaves who allow themselves to be dominated by their own inclinations (cf. Epictetus, *Diatr.* 4.4.33). Just as no one can really give anything to the Stoic, neither can anything be taken away from him or her.[118] The Stoic concept of freedom is characterized by the idea of the agreement of one's own will with the will of God, which takes place in distinguishing oneself from the world, what is one's own from what is foreign. The freedom of the self means being integrated in the encompassing wholeness of the cosmos and at the same time distancing oneself from natural emotions. The ultimate ground of freedom is the person's relation to God: "No one has power over me. I have been freed by God, I have learned his commands, no one can make me a slave."[119] By understanding oneself as integrated into the divine order of the universe, where one is able to distinguish between self and world, the Stoic attains freedom, identity, and independence in harmony with the divine order of the cosmos. Thus freedom from the world is by no means identical with indifference to the world, but freedom and love belong together.[120]

Several aspects of this Stoic understanding of freedom are found in Paul. In 1 Cor. 7:20–22 the apostle advises slaves to remain in their social class and gives as his reason, "For whoever was called in the Lord as a slave is a freed person belonging to the Lord, just as whoever was free when called is a slave of Christ." Paul here defines freedom as inner freedom, a freedom made possible by Jesus Christ and having as its goal Jesus Christ alone. Social structures are irrelevant for this understanding of freedom, for they confer neither freedom nor slavery. The proximity to Stoic thinking is obvious. In 1 Cor. 9 Paul applies the freedom theme to financial independence and thus to freedom from human opinions.[121] Paul is here clearly dependent on Socratic tradition, for, like Socrates, he did not accept the pay that was really due him for his work and thus could deal with others in an independent manner.[122] So also the apostle's admonition in 1 Cor. 7:29–31, to make use of this world's goods as though one did not possess them, is closely related to the idea of freedom as inner independence. Though here framed within a context of apocalyptic thought, the concept of

---

117. Cf. also Seneca, *Ep.* 90.10: "A straw room protects free human beings, while slavery dwells in the midst of marble and gold."

118. Cf. Epictetus, *Diatr.* 4.1.112–113.

119. Epictetus, *Diatr.* 4.7.16, 17. Cf. also Epictetus, *Diatr.* 1.19.9; 4.1.131.

120. Cf. Samuel Vollenweider, *Freiheit als neue Schöpfung: Eine Untersuchung zur Eleutheria bei Paulus und in seiner Umwelt* (FRLANT 147; Göttingen: Vandenhoeck & Ruprecht, 1989), 56–57.

121. Cf. F. Stanley Jones, *"Freiheit" in den Briefen des Apostels Paulus: Eine historische, exegetische, und religionsgeschichtliche Studie* (GTA 34; Göttingen: Vandenhoeck & Ruprecht, 1987), 43–44.

122. Cf., e.g., Xenophon, *Apologia Socratis* 16, where Socrates asks, "What other human being is as free as I am, since I accept no money or payment from anyone?"

inner freedom vis-à-vis the things of this world is itself derived primarily from the Stoa (cf. Epictetus, *Ench.* 11, "Never say about anything, 'I have lost it,' but 'I have given it back.' Your child has died? It has been given back. Your wife has died? She has been given back. 'Somebody has stolen my property.' Well, that too has been given back.")[123] The renunciation of something and thus inner freedom from it is to be valued more highly than possessing it.[124]

Paul's Cultural Context

Paul was a citizen of the Roman Empire who had grown up in a significant cultural metropolis of the realm, had disciplined himself in an intensive Pharisaic education (possibly in Jerusalem), and had worked for about three decades in a province of the empire where Hellenistic culture prevailed. He was thus no wanderer between different cultural worlds; he united in himself—like Philo and Josephus—the cultures of Hellenistic Judaism and Greco-Roman Hellenism.[125] As a Jew of the Diaspora and an educated Pharisee, he lived in and from the Torah, the revealed saving will of the Creator of the whole world. At the same time, as a Greek-speaking citizen of Tarsus who also had Roman citizenship, he was not uninfluenced by his cultural formation and the spirit of his age.[126] Both his educational experience and his ability to enter into the intellectual horizon of his various audiences show the breadth of the apostle's formation. This ability gave Paul access to a broad spectrum of social groups and classes and predestined him to cross social and geographical boundaries in order to win people to the gospel.

We should therefore not describe the religious and educational background of Paul's thought monocausally or in terms of alternatives; he had been shaped by three great streams of tradition: the Old Testament, Hellenistic Judaism,

123. *NW* 2/1:297; cf. also Epictetus, *Diatr.* 3.24.

124. Cf. Epictetus, *Diatr.* 4.9.1–3.

125. [Translator's note: S. Ben-Chorim, *Paulus, der Völkerapostel in jüdischer Sicht* (Munich: P. List, 1970), describes the apostle as a wanderer and mediator between two worlds.] On the term "Hellenism," cf. Reinhold Bichler, *"Hellenismus": Geschichte und Problematik eines Epochenbegriffs* (IdF 41; Darmstadt: Wissenschaftliche Buchgesellschaft, 1983); Hans Dieter Betz, "Hellenismus," *TRE* 15:19–35; Hans-Joachim Gehrke, *Geschichte des Hellenismus* (2nd ed.; OGG 1A; Munich: Oldenbourg, 1995), 1–3, 129–31. In our context, "Hellenism" refers especially to the spread of the Greek language, architecture, art, literature, and philosophy in the Mediterranean world as a result of the conquests of Alexander the Great, and its meaning for cultural history. National cultures were partially transformed by it, and at the same time Greek and, later, Roman thought was opened up to oriental influences. On the political, economic, and social aspects of Hellenism not dealt with here, cf. Gehrke, *Geschichte*, 165ff. Cf. also Victor Tcherikover, *Hellenistic Civilization and the Jews* (Philadelphia: Jewish Publication Society of America, 1959; repr., Peabody, MA: Hendrickson, 1999), passim.

126. Contra M. Reiser, "Hat Paulus Heiden Bekehrt?" *BZ* 39 (1995): 77–83, who denies to Paul any close familiarity with the sophisticated Greek literature of his time. On Paul as missionary to Gentiles, cf. Thomas Söding, "Apostel der Heiden (Röm 11,13): Zur paulinischen Missionspraxis," in *Das Wort vom Kreuz: Studien zur paulinischen Theologie* (WUNT 93; Tübingen: Mohr Siebeck, 1997).

and the popular philosophical traditions of Greco-Roman Hellenism. All three realms are interwoven in multiple ways and together form the background and context of Paul's thought. Moreover, as a thinker who acts on his thought, Paul is always in the situation of leaving tradition behind and forming something new, and he is in part compelled to do so.

The old question of the influence of Hellenism on Judaism and subsequently on Christianity may not be reduced to the thesis that Hellenistic Judaism mediated everything Hellenistic in early Christianity.[127] It is rather the case—and it becomes clear precisely in the case of Paul—that early Christians participated in debates that were carried on both within Judaism and in the Greco-Roman realm. The success of the early Christian mission can be explained only by presupposing that early Christianity was quite capable of combining with elements of both traditional streams. The enculturation of the Pauline gospel is a necessary presupposition for the success of its mission. Paul moved within an encompassing cultural framework, took up impulses from different realms in varying intensity, and formed them into something new. Every language, on the basis of the cultural tradition that lies behind it, has available to it an encyclopedic competence[128] that can be activated by an author. This means that the Greek-speaking Diaspora Jew Paul must have had an extensive range of concepts and terminology at his disposal. Concepts, terminology, and their

127. Contra Martin Hengel, "Das früheste Christentum als eine jüdische messianische und universalistische Bewegung," *TBei* (1997): 198: "What in early Christianity is supposed to come from 'pagan influences' can consistently be traced back through Jewish mediation. Nowhere can a direct, lasting influence by pagan cults or non-Jewish thinking be demonstrated. Elements in the New Testament commonly called 'Hellenistic' derive, as a rule, from Jewish sources, which of course had no desire to separate themselves from the 'religious Koine' of the time, even if that had been possible." Reference to the extensive Hellenization of Jerusalem by no means suffices to explain the apostle's use in the metropolitan centers of Asia Minor and Greece of themes such as freedom, suffering, conscience, and financial and intellectual independence. Here one recognizes rather the writings of Cicero, Seneca, Epictetus and Dio Chrysostom. This is the thought world in and to which the Pauline letters speak. Cf., appropriately, Ebner, *Leidenslisten und Apostelbrief*, 105, according to whom Paul "was equipped with 'college-level' educational tools and knew how to use them." Two basic observations speak in favor of this assessment: the course of Paul's life, with its undeniable westward tendency, is a compelling argument for his knowledge of Greco-Roman culture; and in his correspondence with his churches in Asia Minor and Greece, Paul handles spheres of problems that originated in, and are peculiar to, the culture of the addressees.

128. Cf. Umberto Eco, *Lector in fabula: La cooperazione interpretativa nei testi narrativi* (Milan: Bompiani, 1979), 94–106; see also Stefan Alkier, *Wunder und Wirklichkeit in den Briefen des Apostels Paulus: Ein Beitrag zu einem Wunderverständnis jenseits von Entmythologisierung und Rehistorisierung* (WUNT 134; Tübingen: Mohr Siebeck, 2001), 72: "The alternative of reading Paul's letters as 'Jewish' or 'Hellenistic' is a very shaky approach when one takes into consideration that texts are indebted not only to the intertextual competence of their author and readers but to a general encyclopedic competence determined and conditioned by the culture. The composition of every text and the reading of every text must draw on an encyclopedia of knowledge that has been made conventional in that particular culture. Thus the cultural network of connections within which early Christian texts were written do not permit a dissection into 'Jewish' and 'Greek' elements." This is particularly true of the Pauline letters.

associated normativeness develop their force only within an already existing linguistic community that provides rules for their understanding, use, and evaluation—and is constantly reshaping them. This aspect of being bound to a tradition is only one element within a process of communication; at least as important is the way the culture has shaped the recipients, who have a lasting influence on the process of understanding. All the central concepts of Paul's thought have both a Jewish and a Greco-Roman history; these partly overlap, but we should consider them not only in combination but also each in its own right and with its own emphasis. "Context" refers not only to texts but also to the spiritual and intellectual realms in which perceptions and ideas originate and are advocated and variously modified. We can see the different contexts in which texts originate as forming a series of concentric circles, from the literary context to the dominant ideas within the culture as a whole. In accordance with this, we do not attain the goal of understanding an author and his or her texts until the whole circle of possible contexts has been examined.

3.4 The Persecutor of the Earliest Churches

The oldest traditions about Paul include reports on his persecution of Christians. Early in their history the churches in Judea received word from Christians elsewhere: "The one who formerly was persecuting us is now proclaiming the faith he once tried to destroy" (Gal. 1:23). In a similar stereotyped manner, the apostle himself reports in 1 Cor. 15:9, Gal. 1:13, and Phil. 3:6 that he persecuted the church(es) of God. It is clearly in the context of disputes about his apostleship that Paul refers back to his activity as a persecutor. In his debates with his opponents, the references to his activities as a persecutor are intended to affirm that only God could have effected the change from merciless persecutor of Christians to worldwide preacher of the gospel.[129] Whereas Paul gives no details about the place and manner of his acts of persecution, Acts provides a vivid account of the way Paul the Pharisee proceeded against the earliest church. Paul goes house to house in Jerusalem and has both men and women thrown into prison (Acts 8:3); he advocates the death penalty against Christians (cf. Acts 22:4; 26:10); and he forces them to recant their faith (cf. Acts 26:11). He has Christians whipped with the lash (Acts 22:19) and has himself deputized to persecute Christians as far away as Damascus (cf. Acts 9:2). The picture of Paul the merciless persecutor is doubtless to be attributed to Luke, as a dark foil that allows the great deeds of Paul, the apostle to the Gentiles, to shine all the brighter.[130]

---

129. Cf. Christian Dietzfelbinger, *Die Berufung des Paulus als Ursprung seiner Theologie* (WMANT 58; Neukirchen-Vluyn: Neukirchener Verlag, 1985), 6.

130. For analysis of the texts, cf. Karl Löning, *Die Saulustradition in der Apostelgeschichte* (NTAbh NF 9; Münster: Aschendorff, 1973), 12–25; 93–95; Burchard, *Der dreizehnte Zeuge*, 40–51 (cf. 50–51:

Location of the Persecution

Where did Paul persecute the first congregations of believers in Christ? Both Luke and his traditions presuppose Jerusalem as the place of persecution (cf. Acts 8:3; 9:1c, 2; 22:19). Paul himself, on the other hand, explicitly says, "I was still unknown by sight to the churches of Judea that are in Christ" (Gal. 1:22). It is only from other churches that the Christian believers in Judea hear that the one who was previously a persecutor now proclaims the faith himself (Gal. 1:23). Paul always includes Jerusalem when he speaks of Judea (cf. 2 Cor. 1:16; Rom. 15:31), and so we must eliminate Jerusalem from consideration as a location for Paul's persecuting activity.[131] Otherwise one would have to explain how it could be that the unrelenting persecutor of the first churches remained unknown to those he was persecuting. We cannot resolve this problem by supposing that Paul persecuted only the "Hellenists" in Jerusalem but not the earliest Aramaic-speaking church.[132] Granted, there was probably a relatively independent Christian congregation of Diaspora Jews in Jerusalem, whose leaders are mentioned in Acts 6:5 and who developed an independent mission after the death of Stephen (cf. Acts 8:4ff.; 11:19ff.). But if Paul's persecution had been a purely internal affair directed against the Greek-speaking synagogues in Jerusalem, it would still have to be explained why it was that the Aramaic-speaking Jewish Christians heard nothing about it. Against this possibility are the relatively small number of Christians who must have lived in Jerusalem at the time and the assumption that there must have been close contact between the two groups.[133] Moreover, the theological profiles of the two groups were probably not so different that a systematic persecution of one group would not have affected the other at all. Galatians 1:17 provides a pointer to the location of the persecution. Here the apostle mentions that after his conversion he did not go immediately to Jerusalem but went to Arabia and then returned to Damascus. It was thus before

---

"The persecution undertaken and carried out by Paul alone against all Christians in Jerusalem, a persecution that is supposed to have resulted in either denying the faith or execution, is essentially a purely Lukan construction").

131. Differently, e.g., Hengel and Schwemer, *Between Damascus and Antioch*, 35–38, who argue for Jerusalem as the place of persecution and see the persecuted "Hellenists" as the originators of the tradition in Gal. 1:23.

132. Contra Hengel and Deines, *Pre-Christian Paul*, 276–83; Karl-Wilhelm Niebuhr, *Heidenapostel aus Israel: Die jüdische Identität des Paulus nach ihrer Darstellung in seinen Briefen* (WUNT 62; Tübingen: Mohr Siebeck, 1992), 58–59; Wolfgang Kraus, *Zwischen Jerusalem und Antiochia: Die "Hellenisten," Paulus, und die Aufnahme der Heiden in das endzeitliche Gottesvolk* (SBS 179; Stuttgart: Katholisches Bibelwerk, 1999), 40.

133. Cf. Dietzfelbinger, *Berufung des Paulus*, 21–22. Among those who vote against a Pauline persecution in Jerusalem are Hans Conzelmann, *History of Primitive Christianity* (trans. John E. Steely; Nashville: Abingdon, 1973), 80; Wilhelm Schneemelcher, *Das Urchristentum* (Stuttgart: Kohlhammer, 1981), 107; Ludger Schenke, *Die Urgemeinde: Geschichtliche und theologische Entwicklung* (Stuttgart: Kohlhammer, 1990), 186; Becker, *Paul*, 66–69; Gerd Theissen, *The Gospels in Context: Social and Political History in the Synoptic Tradition* (trans. Linda M. Maloney; Minneapolis: Fortress, 1991), 156.

or at the time of his conversion in Damascus that he persecuted the Christian community there. At the very place where he was persecuting Christians, Paul became a disciple. "There, where he was attacking the message about Jesus, he was won over to it."[134]

In Gal. 1:13–14 and Phil. 3:5–6, Paul bases his actions as a persecutor on his previous life in Judaism and his zeal for the ancestral traditions.[135] Paul thus stands in the tradition of Jewish zeal for the Torah, which in imitation of Elijah (cf. 1 Kings 18:40; 19:10, 14) and Phinehas (cf. Num. 25:7–11) defended the Torah as the definitive norm of Jewish life (cf. Sir. 48:2; 1 Macc. 2:54, 58). Zeal for the Torah as the predominant mark of the Jewish way of life was not only characteristic of militant Zealots but also determinative for the Essenes (cf. 1QS 4:5–6, 17–18) and for radical Pharisees such as Paul. Paul characterizes the manner of his proceedings against the Christian believers with the strong verb πορθέω (destroy, Gal. 1:13, 23; Acts 9:21), which apparently refers to acts of violence (cf. Josephus, *J.W.* 4.405).[136]

Reasons for the Persecution

What impelled Paul to such a ruthless persecution? To the Pharisee zealous for the Torah, the Christian proclamation of a man who had been crucified as the promised Messiah of Israel must have appeared utterly scandalous.[137] The significance of the cross of Jesus Christ within Pauline theology (cf., e.g., 1 Cor. 1:17, 18, 23; 2:2, 8; Gal. 3:1; 5:11, 14; 6:14; Rom. 6:6; Phil. 2:8; 3:18) suggests that Paul had transformed what once was the great scandal into the center of his message. According to Deut. 21:23, "anyone hung on a tree is under God's curse." In 11QT^a 64:15–20, this curse also applies to those who were executed by crucifixion.[138] When Christian believers proclaimed Jesus of Nazareth, one

---

134. Dietzfelbinger, *Berufung des Paulus*, 22. Others who argue for Damascus as the place of persecution include Haenchen, *Acts*, 298; Suhl, *Paulus und seine Briefe*, 26–30; Schneemelcher, *Urchristentum*, 136; Strecker, "Der vorchristliche Paulus"; Becker, *Paul*, 66–69; Betz, "Paul," 187.

135. Cf. Bernd Schröder, *Die väterlichen Gesetze: Flavius Josephus als Vermittler von Halachah an Griechen und Römer* (TSAJ 53; Tübingen: Mohr Siebeck, 1996).

136. One can only make conjectures about the nature of violent compulsion; on synagogue punishments, cf. Strack and Billerbeck, *Kommentar*, 4/1:292ff.

137. It is doubtless the case that, from the Jewish perspective, not all victims of crucifixion were thought to have been cursed by God (so, rightly, Gerhard Friedrich, *Die Verkündigung des Todes Jesu im Neuen Testament* (BTS 6; Neukirchen-Vluyn: Neukirchener Verlag, 1982), 122–30), for among those crucified were Jewish martyrs (cf., e.g., Philo, *Flaccus* 72.83–85). Nonetheless, the idea of a crucified Messiah probably was beyond what was conceivable for most Jews, as still indicated in Justin, *Dial.* 90.1.

138. Cf. 11QT^a 64:19–20: "He who is hanged on the tree is accursed by God and men; you shall not pollute the ground which I give you to inherit" (Vermès, 179); for analysis, cf. H.-W. Kuhn, "Die Bedeutung der Qumrantexte für das Verständnis des Galaterbriefes," in *New Qumran Texts and Studies: Proceedings of the First Meeting of the International Organization for Qumran Studies, Paris, 1992* (ed. George J. Brooke and Florentino García Martínez; STDJ 15; Leiden: Brill, 1994), 231–38.

presumably crucified because of his blasphemy against God, as the Messiah of Israel, this was unbearable for Paul, a challenge to the very foundation of the faith to which he had devoted his life. Galatians 3:13 confirms this interpretation, for here the Christian Paul reworks Deut. 21:23 LXX and comes to the insight that Christ took the curse of the law/Torah on himself and thereby redeemed us from this curse. It was not that God had cursed Christ but that the innocent Christ took the curse of the law/Torah on himself in our behalf.[139] The idea of a crucified Messiah not only must have seemed absurd to Paul but also in his eyes represented a blasphemous challenge to the Jewish faith. He therefore denied the right of the followers of Jesus Christ to exist within the the synagogue assembly.[140]

139. Paul cites Deut. 21:23 LXX, with two weighty changes: he omits ὑπὸ Θεοῦ and changes the perfect passive participle into the passive adjective ἐπικατάρατος (cf. Deut. 27:26 LXX).

140. For a response to the thesis, now revived by Niebuhr, *Heidenapostel*, 62–65, and Hans Hübner, *Biblische Theologie des Neuen Testaments* (3 vols.; Göttingen: Vandenhoeck & Ruprecht, 1990), 2:32, that Paul persecuted segments of the Jerusalem Christian community because of their critical stance toward the law, see below, section 4.1 ("The Reports about the Damascus Event").

4

The Call to Be Apostle to the Gentiles

The New Horizon

Unanticipated events accelerate the course of history. What has gone before suddenly looses its attraction; something new begins to move people and comes on stage as a surprise.

4.1 The Reports about the Damascus Event

What happened to Paul in the year 33 CE in the neighborhood of Damascus?[1] Can it be shown from the apostle's own statements that his whole future theology was already contained in the Damascus experience, embryonically or even already clearly visible? Only the passages in which it is clear that Paul is referring back to the Damascus event can provide the textual basis: 1 Cor.

---

1. For the history of research, see most recently Larry W. Hurtado, "Convert, Apostate, or Apostle to the Nations," *SR* 22 (1993): 273–84; Christian Strecker, *Die liminale Theologie des Paulus: Zugänge zur paulinischen Theologie aus kulturanthropologischer Perspektive* (Göttingen: Vandenhoeck & Ruprecht, 1999), 81–96.

9:1; 15:8; 2 Cor. 4:6; Gal. 1:12–16; Phil. 3:4b–11.[2] What stands out about these texts is their almost stenographic brevity. Not only does Paul only rarely mention this event, which turned his whole life around;[3] he reduces its content to the language of visionary prophecy.[4]

Paul's Own Testimony to His Call

Paul speaks for the first time about his Damascus experience in 1 Cor. 9:1. He does not do this on his own initiative; it is clearly the Corinthian dispute about his apostleship that forces him to do so. In terms of text pragmatics, 1 Cor. 9:1ff.[5] and 15:1ff.[6] must be read as Paul's defense of his apostleship (cf. 1 Cor. 9:2a; 15:9–10); this is why they give information about the event on which his apostleship is based. In 1 Cor. 9:1 Paul defends his legitimation as an apostle above all by claiming that he had seen Ἰησοῦν τὸν κύριον (Am I not free? Am I not an apostle? Have I not seen Jesus our Lord?). In Corinth his apostleship was disputed because, among other reasons, he had never seen the Lord; it is no longer clear whether his opponents referred to the earthly or resurrected Jesus.[7] Paul connects his claim to have "seen" Jesus with the risen Lord, giving the content of the Damascus experience as Ἰησοῦν τὸν κύριον ἡμῶν ἑώρακα (I have seen Jesus our Lord). Paul provides no information about date and place; moreover, it remains unclear whether the apostle saw the Lord in heaven or on earth. In 1 Cor. 15:8 the apostle includes himself in the series of witnesses to the resurrection and derives his apostleship from an appearance of the Lord that was granted to him as it was to the others mentioned (Last of all, as to one untimely born, he appeared also to me). We see this in the parallel uses of ὁράω (see) in 15:5, 7, and 8 and in the way 15:8 is connected to the rest of the paragraph. The altered perspective and linguistic formulation in contrast to 1 Cor. 9:1 probably reflects 1 Cor. 15:3–5 and its background in the tradition.[8] It is to Paul as the least of all the apostles that Christ has appeared, which means that

---

2. For analysis of the texts, see esp. Bernhard Heininger, *Paulus als Visionär: Eine religionsgeschichtliche Studie* (Freiburg: Herder, 1996), 182–211.

3. Strictly speaking, only Galatians clearly refers to the Damascus event (cf. Gal. 1:17).

4. On models of communication between heaven and earth, cf. the analyses from the history-of-religions perspective in Heininger, *Paulus als Visionär*, 46–179ff.; on prophetic "seeing," cf. Amos 9:1; 3 Kings 22:19 LXX (1 Kings 22:19); Isa. 6:1.

5. Hans Conzelmann, *1 Corinthians: A Commentary on the First Epistle to the Corinthians* (trans. James W. Leitch; Hermeneia; Philadelphia: Fortress, 1975), 151ff.

6. Peter von der Osten-Sacken, "Die Apologie des paulinischen Apostolats in 1Kor 15,1–11," in *Evangelium und Tora: Aufsätze zu Paulus* (TB 77; Munich: Kaiser, 1987), 131–49.

7. Johannes Weiss, *Der erste Korintherbrief* (9th ed.; KEK; Göttingen: Vandenhoeck & Ruprecht, 1910), 232, supposes that Paul's opponents disputed his apostleship by arguing that he had never known the earthly Jesus.

8. Whereas Paul himself is the active subject in 1 Cor. 9:1 (ἑώρακα [I saw]), in 1 Cor. 15:8 he is the passive object (ὤφθη [appeared, was seen]).

here also, as in 1 Cor. 9:1, the ὁράω must have an exclusively christological-soteriological meaning. Both 1 Cor. 9:1 and 15:8 manifest a firm connection between vision/appearance and election to apostleship; that is, his call serves as Paul's proof of his (theological and financial) independence.[9]

Galatians 1:12–16 points in the same direction: In response to the attacks on his gospel and his apostleship, Paul objects in Gal. 1:12 that he did not receive his gospel from any human being ἀλλὰ δι᾽ ἀποκαλύψεως Ἰησοῦ Χριστοῦ (but through a revelation of Jesus Christ).[10] On the basis of 1:16a, "to reveal his Son to me," this "revelation of Jesus Christ" is to be construed as an objective genitive, that is, "a revelation about [not 'from'] Jesus Christ."[11] This revelation impelled Paul to break with his splendid past as a Jew and persecutor of the church of God. In 1:15–16 Paul describes his call, installation into office, and commissioning as a preacher of the gospel: "But when God, who had set me apart before I was born and called me through his grace, was pleased to reveal his Son to me, so that I might proclaim him among the Gentiles. . . ." Echoes of the call stories of Old Testament prophets are clearly recognizable (compare 1:15b with Jer. 1:5; Isa. 49:1, 5; Gal. 1:16b with Isa. 49:6);[12] it is even possible that Paul here takes up a stereotyped schema of prophetic calls based on the Old Testament.[13] Paul clearly understands his call, installation, and commissioning in analogy to the great prophets of the Old Testament, with a particularly close connection to Deutero-Isaiah (cf. Isa. 49:1–6).[14] Paul is now to fulfill the proclamation—announced in the Old Testament but not yet carried out—of the saving will of God that includes the Gentiles. As apostle of Jesus Christ and proclaimer of the gospel to the Gentiles, Paul understands himself to be a

---

9. One should strictly distinguish "call" from "conversion." Whereas, in calling, God alone is the acting subject and a human being is torn out of his or her previous (successful) life, the center of gravity in conversion lies on subjective considerations that (for the most part within the framework of a process) lead to a change of attitude. Cf. F. Wagner, "Bekehrung III," *TRE* 5:475: "Since conversion is not a once-for-all act but represents a lifelong process of realization, it cannot be fixed at a certain point in time." For discussion of the issue, cf. Haacker, "Werdegang," 896–98; Strecker, *Die liminale Theologie des Paulus*, 155–57.

10. Paul thereby primarily emphasizes the supernatural quality of his gospel, and only in a secondary sense might there also be a reference to a particular revelatory event; cf. Udo Borse, *Der Brief an die Galater* (Regensburg: Pustet, 1984), 55.

11. Cf. Georg Strecker, "Befreiung und Rechtfertigung: Zur Stellung der Rechtfertigungslehre in der Theologie des Paulus," in *Eschaton und Historie: Aufsätze* (Göttingen: Vandenhoeck & Ruprecht, 1979), 235; Franz Mussner, *Der Galaterbrief* (HTKNT 9; Freiburg: Herder, 1974), 68.

12. Dependence on the typical features of the prophetic call is also seen in comparing Gal. 1:16 and Rev. 1:1.

13. Cf. Werner Stenger, "Biographisches und Idealbiographisches in Gal. 1,11–2,14," in *Kontinuität und Einheit: Für Franz Mussner* (ed. Paul-Gerhard Müller and Werner Stenger; Freiburg: Herder, 1981), 123–40.

14. Cf. Florian Wilk, *Die Bedeutung des Jesajabuches für Paulus* (FRLANT 179; Göttingen: Vandenhoeck & Ruprecht, 1998), 48: "When all is said and done, the book of Isaiah makes it clear that, from an existential point of view, God chose Paul to be the mediator of salvation for the Gentiles included in the Christ event."

prophet called by God.[15] Like Amos and Jeremiah (cf. Amos 3:8; Jer. 20:9), his whole life stands under the compulsion to proclaim the message he has received from God (cf. 1 Cor. 9:16). As the Servant of the Lord in Deutero-Isaiah was separated from his mother's womb and dedicated to the task of bringing light to the Gentiles (cf. Isa. 49:1, 6), so Paul sees himself as called by God to be the apostle to the Gentiles (cf. Gal. 1:16; Rom. 1:1ff.). In Gal. 1:15a εὐδόκησεν (it pleased [God]) emphasizes the soteriological dimension of the event for the person of Paul, and God's separating him for the ministry of preaching the gospel among the Gentiles emphasizes the universal aspect of this event. Galatians 1:16a, where ἐν ἐμοί (in me) is to be translated as the simple dative, refers to the event of the call itself.[16] The content of the revelation granted to Paul is restricted to the reality of Jesus as the "Son of God,"[17] which suggests an exclusively christological-soteriological interpretation of the Damascus event.[18] Paul describes neither his call nor commissioning in the usual terminology of justification that he employs elsewhere in his polemical argumentation in Galatians, which one would expect if the origin of the Pauline critique of the Torah had already been present in his Damascus experience. According to the testimony of the Galatian letter, we should not interpret the Damascus event in the categories of law/Torah versus Christ; its scope is limited to the revelation of the identity of Christ as such, which forms the basis for Paul's call and commissioning.

Whether there is a reference to the Damascus event in 2 Cor. 4:6 is a disputed point: "For it is the God who said, 'Let light shine out of darkness,' who has shone in our hearts to give the light of the knowledge of the glory of God

---

15. Cf. also the echoes of Jer. 1:5 in Rom. 1:1, 5; for comprehensive evidence, cf. Karl Olav Sandnes, *Paul, One of the Prophets? A Contribution to the Apostle's Self-Understanding* (WUNT 2/43; Tübingen: Mohr Siebeck, 1991), 48–70. Cf. M. Eugene Boring, *Sayings of the Risen Jesus: Christian Prophecy in the Synoptic Tradition* (SNTSMS 46; Cambridge: Cambridge University Press, 1982), 30–36, and the literature there given; and David E. Aune, *Prophecy in Early Christianity and the Ancient Mediterranean World* (Grand Rapids: Eerdmans, 1983), 160, 202–3, 248–49, 344, 409, 422.

16. As parallel, cf. Rom. 1:19.

17. Cf. Antje Labahn and Michael Labahn, "Jesus als Sohn Gottes bei Paulus," in *Paulinische Christologie: Exegetische Beiträge: Hans Hübner zum 70. Geburtstag* (ed. Udo Schnelle et al.; Göttingen: Vandenhoeck & Ruprecht, 2000), 97–120.

18. Peter Stuhlmacher, *Das paulinische Evangelium* (FRLANT 95; Göttingen: Vandenhoeck & Ruprecht, 1968), 71; Seyoon Kim, *The Origin of Paul's Gospel* (Tübingen: Mohr Siebeck, 1981), 271; and Georg Luck, "Die Bekehrung des Paulus und das paulinische Evangelium," *ZNW* 76 (1985): 203ff., all appropriately interpret ἀποκάλυψις Ἰησοῦ Χριστοῦ in terms of the Pauline concept of the gospel. But when they presuppose an antinomian connotation for the term "gospel" itself, they introduce an element that is distinctly absent from Gal. 1:12ff. For a critique of this position, cf. also Heikki Räisänen, "Paul's Call Experience and His Later View of the Law," in *The Torah and Christ: Essays in German and English on the Problem of the Law in Early Christianity* (SESJ 45; Helsinki: Finnish Exegetical Society, 1986), 67, who rightly notes regarding Gal. 1:11ff., "If the possibility of hindsight is recognized, the lack of justification language appears even more striking"; cf. further Kraus, *Zwischen Jerusalem und Antiochia*, 89.

in the face of Jesus Christ." The plural formulation ἐν ταῖς καρδίαις ἡμῶν (in our hearts) could indicate that Paul is not referring to a particular event but to what is typical for the preacher of the gospel and all believers. The light that illuminates the believer comes from God, who has already revealed his light at creation.[19] To be sure, in 2 Corinthians Paul often uses the plural when speaking of himself (compare, e.g., 2:12 with 2:15; 3:1; 4:1 and passim). Moreover, 2 Cor. 7:3 shows clearly that the expression "in our hearts" can stand for Paul himself. The following observations speak in favor of a connection between 2 Cor. 4:6 and the Damascus experience:[20] (1) The aorist ἔλαμψεν refers to a particular event in the past. (2) The light metaphor appears in numerous Old Testament texts in the context of calling and commissioning (cf. esp. Isa. 42:6 LXX: "I, the Lord God, have called you . . . to be a light to the nations"; cf. also Isa. 42:16; 60:1–3). (3) As in Gal. 1:16, 2 Cor. 4:6 is concerned with an internal event, an inner "seeing." (4) The context of 2 Cor. 4:6 deals with the founding and essential nature of Paul's apostleship and his gospel. From the viewpoint of the history of traditions, the motif of the glory of the chosen one points to a throne room vision (cf. Ezek. 1:26, 28; *1 En.* 45:1–6; 49:1–4). At Damascus God revealed his glory in the face of Jesus Christ. Thus Paul attained the insight that Christ belongs to the realm of God's throne. The exalted one, as the εἰκὼν τοῦ θεοῦ (image/icon of God, 2 Cor. 4:4), is the continuing bearer of the divine δόξα (glory; cf. also 1 Cor. 2:8).

In Phil. 3:4b–11 Paul debates with Jewish Christian opponents, holding up to them, as the "gain" he once had, his own Jewish origin and his activity as a persecutor. All this has now for him become "loss" for the sake of Christ (3:7). The purely christological-soteriological dimension of the Damascus event becomes completely visible in 3:8, where Paul describes it as τῆς γνώσεως Χριστοῦ Ἰησοῦ τοῦ κυρίου μου (knowing Christ Jesus my Lord). This expression is found only here in Paul and has a very personal character.[21] The knowledge of Christ effects a radical new orientation through the power of the present Lord. In 3:8–10 the doctrine of justification and ontological teaching about redemption, juridical and participatory ways of thinking, cannot be separated from each other:[22] "I regard everything as loss because of the surpassing value of knowing Christ Jesus my Lord. For his sake I have suffered the loss of all things, and I

19. Hans Windisch, *Der zweite Korintherbrief* (9th ed.; Göttingen: Vandenhoeck & Ruprecht, 1924), 139.

20. Dietzfelbinger, *Berufung des Paulus*, 62ff.; Kim, *Origin*, 230–31; Hengel and Deines, *Pre-Christian Paul*, 79; Christian Wolff, *Der zweite Brief des Paulus an die Korinther* (THKNT 8; Berlin: Evangelische Verlagsanstalt, 1989), 8–9; Heininger, *Paulus als Visionär*, 201–9. Among those who vote against a reference to Damascus are Windisch, *Korintherbrief*, 140; and Victor Paul Furnish, *II Corinthians* (AB; Garden City, NY: Doubleday, 1984), 250–51.

21. Cf. Joachim Gnilka, *Der Philipperbrief* (3rd ed.; HTKNT 10/3; Freiburg: Herder, 1980), 192.

22. Cf. Strecker, "Befreiung und Rechtfertigung," 237; and Ulrich B. Müller, *Der Brief des Paulus an die Philipper* (THKNT 11/1; Leipzig: Evangelische Verlagsanstalt, 1993), 155.

regard them as rubbish, in order that I may gain Christ and be found in him, not having a righteousness of my own that comes from the law, but one that comes through faith in Christ, the righteousness from God based on faith. I want to know Christ and the power of his resurrection and the sharing of his sufferings by becoming like him." If, on the one hand, Paul speaks of being found ἐν αὐτῷ (in him), on the other hand, faith in Jesus Christ appears as the effective basis of his "own righteousness" (ἐμὴν δικαιοσύνην). Grammatically, 3:9 is to be understood as a parenthesis;[23] accordingly the passage in Philippians 3, from late in Paul's career, supports the interpretation "that Paul did not originally understand his call in the categories of the doctrine of justification but in a christological-ontological sense, as the beginning point of his knowledge of Jesus Christ the Lord."[24] Moreover, the abrupt antithesis ἐκ νόμου / ἐκ θεοῦ (from the law / from God) is obviously conditioned by the situation in Philippi and may not be simply projected back onto the Damascus event.[25]

Gerd Theissen interprets Rom. 7:7–23 and Phil. 3:4–6 from a psychological perspective, as Paul's working through his subconscious conflict with the law: "The thesis defended here . . . is that Phil. 3:4–6 reflects the consciousness of the pre-Christian Paul, while Romans 7 depicts a conflict that was unconscious at the time, one of which Paul became conscious only later."[26] Gerd Lüdemann argues similarly that Paul's subconscious "Christ complex" was "formally brought to the boil by the Christians whom he persecuted." "He wanted to find release by fighting an external enemy. That became his 'destiny.' And Saul became Paul."[27]

Doubtless a call also includes psychological dimensions,[28] but these can be understood as reactions to the prior act of God. When explanatory psycho-

---

23. Cf. Gnilka, *Philipperbrief*, 194.

24. Strecker, "Befreiung und Rechtfertigung," 237. Cf. Räisänen, "Paul's Call Experience," 72–73; Siegfried Schulz, *Neutestamentliche Ethik* (Zurich: Theologischer Verlag, 1987), 298.

25. Becker, *Paul*, 75: "Thus he reinterprets his experience, among other things, with means that were not at his command until later." Cf. further Eckhard Rau, "Der urchristliche Kurioskult und die Bekehrung des Paulus," in *Kulte, Kulturen, Gottesdienste—öffentliche Inszenierung des Lebens: Peter Cornehl zum 60. Geburtstag* (ed. Peter Stolt and Wolfgang Grünberg; Göttingen: Vandenhoeck & Ruprecht, 1996), 156–71 (p. 157: "The conversion of Paul originally had nothing directly to do with the issue of the validity of the law. Whenever these are related to each other, we have a retrospective insight that Paul had come to in his long missionary career, in which he had had to think through his painful experiences").

26. Gerd Theissen, *Psychological Aspects of Pauline Theology* (trans. John P. Galvin; Philadelphia: Fortress, 1987), 235.

27. Gerd Lüdemann, *The Resurrection of Jesus: History, Experience, Theology* (Minneapolis: Fortress, 1994), 83.

28. A survey of research on attempts to explain the Damascus experience in psychological terms is presented in Michael Reichardt, *Psychologische Erklärung der paulinischen Damaskusvision? Ein Beitrag zum interdisziplinären Gespräch zwischen Exegese und Psychologie seit dem 18. Jahrhundert* (Stuttgart: Katholisches Bibelwerk, 1999), 17–88. Two theories are of significance in the current discussion. One is the theory of cognitive dissonance, according to which Paul, who had previously persecuted the

logical models go beyond this and claim to be able to explain in this-worldly terms not only the repercussions but also the ultimate cause of the event, they confuse call with conversion, deny the possibility of God's acting in history, and make absolute claims. The subjective personal experience of the exegete is projected beneath the text and presented as "objective" knowledge. Moreover, the psychological theories used for such explanations have themselves recently been subjected to massive criticism within the field of psychology regarding both their presuppositions and their practical application (authoritarian self-preservation mechanisms), raising questions about their scientific validity.[29] The following holds true for Paul: (1) Before the Damascus event he was blameless with regard to the law; a (conscious or subconscious) conflict with the law cannot be inferred from the texts. (2) At Damascus something happened to him at God's initiative, he saw the one who had been crucified had been raised, and he acknowledged the crucified Jesus of Nazareth to be the Messiah. No interpretation can get behind this statement of recognition and faith; the experienced reality of God can neither be confirmed nor disproved by psychology or history. Paul understood the resurrection of Jesus obviously as an authentic event sui generis, not subject to historical demonstration as an event in space and time.

Paul never speaks voluntarily of the Damascus event; he always brings up the subject only when provoked by his opponents. All the texts show that Damascus is to be interpreted in christological-soteriological terms and is centered on the overwhelming revelation that Jesus Christ belongs to the realm of God and on the call of Paul to be an apostle.[30] From the Damascus event Paul derived his right to belong to the circle of the original Jerusalem disciples, a group firmly fixed in history and bound to a particular place, even though in fact he was a

---

church, was able to stabilize his own standpoint. Competing with this model from social psychology is the psychoanalytic model, according to which Paul's conduct was determined by his subconscious conflict with the law.

29. Cf. the fundamental critique of psychoanalysis by Manfred Pohlen and Margarethe Bautz-Holzherr, *Psychoanalyse: Das Ende einer Deutungsmacht* (Reinbek: Rowohlt, 1995), 12: "The psychoanalysis business has, in the course of a century, analyzed the psyche as far as it is possible to go. The explanatory work of psychoanalysis has penetrated into the farthest corner of the soul and brought it into public view, and has completely brought all the psychological dimensions of life within the grasp of its interpretative machinery. The soul no longer exists, for the inner life has been taken away from the subject and has become the total externalizing of the pathetic discourse of depth psychology. And psychoanalysis has itself come close to this cultural faith in a mysterious depth that alleges some hidden meaning to underlie everything we say or do, meanings that, with the help of psychoanalytic procedures, can be given a social and subjective explanation. At the end of this process, it is the psychoanalytical confessional, rather than the church's, where secret desires are revealed."

30. Cf. also Becker, *Paul*, 69–75, who rightly places the concept of apostleship at the center of the Damascus event; further Berger, *Theologiegeschichte*, 436–39; Haacker, "Werdegang," 909–16. Rau gives a different emphasis in Rau, "Bekehrung des Paulus," 159ff., seeing a close connection between the early Christian Kyrios cult and Paul's recognition of Jesus as Kyrios at Damascus.

wandering apostle.[31] The legitimacy of his apostleship was disputed throughout his life: he had not known the historical Jesus, he appealed to a prophetic revelation and call, he in fact operated as a missionary scribal teacher—"All in all, the exact opposite of what had previously been understood as an apostle."[32]

The Testimony of Acts

Three times Luke pictures the great turn in the life of Paul that transformed him from persecutor to preacher of the gospel (Acts 9:3–19a; 22:6–16; 26:12–18),[33] thereby signaling the epoch-making importance of this event. It is likely that behind Acts 9:3–19a there lies an earlier legend about Paul, current in the church of Damascus, which told how Paul, the persecutor of Christians, near Damascus had been brought to a new realization of the identity of Jesus Christ and how his traveling companions had brought him to Damascus (cf. Acts 9:11).[34] Nonetheless, serious tensions between the testimony of Acts and Paul's own statements cannot be overlooked: (1) According to 1 Cor. 9:1; 15:8, Paul himself understands the Damascus event as an Easter Christophany, of which there is nothing in Acts 9. For Luke, the period of Easter appearances obviously came to an end with Jesus' ascension, so that at Damascus Paul only saw a bright light and heard a voice[35] but saw no face and encountered no person. (2) The commission to preach, which was for Paul constitutive of the Damascus event (cf. Gal. 1:16b), is absent from Acts 9:3–19a and is only appended in a modified form in Acts 9:20. (3) The fundamental connection between the Damascus event and his apostleship, so important for Paul, does not appear in Acts 9.[36]

But had not Paul persecuted parts of the Christian community because of its critical stance toward the Torah? Did he not first become aware of the Christian message in the form purportedly advocated by the Stephen group, so that Paul's own later theology, with its critical stance toward the Torah, must go all the way back to Damascus? The answer to these questions can only come from Acts 6:8–15, which reports the appearance of Stephen on the scene.[37] According to

---

31. On wandering apostles, cf. Acts 14:4, 14; *Did.* 11:4; 1 Cor. 12:28; 2 Cor. 11:13; Rom. 16:7. We should distinguish these from the apostles sent out by particular congregations in 2 Cor. 8:23; Phil. 2:25; on the complex of issues regarding "apostles," cf. Jürgen Roloff, "Apostel I," *TRE* 3:430–45.

32. Paul Wernle, *Die Anfänge unserer Religion* (2nd ed.; Tübingen: Mohr Siebeck, 1904), 119.

33. For analysis of the texts, cf. Burchard, *Der dreizehnte Zeuge,* 51–36; Dietzfelbinger, *Berufung des Paulus,* 75–82; Heininger, *Paulus als Visionär,* 211–34; other accents are set by Haacker, "Werdegang," 900–909; Hengel and Schwemer, *Between Damascus and Antioch,* 38–47; 341–44.

34. For analysis, cf. Lüdemann, *Traditions in Acts,* 106–16; Heininger, *Paulus als Visionär,* 221–22 (a reconstruction of what is possibly the oldest tradition).

35. The outright contradiction between Acts 9:7 and 22:9 is to be noted.

36. Cf. Dietzfelbinger, *Berufung des Paulus,* 81–82.

37. A. Weiser, "Zur Gesetzes- und Tempelkritik der 'Hellenisten,'" in *Das Gesetz im Neuen Testament* (ed. Johannes Beutler and Karl Kertelge; QD 108; Freiburg: Herder, 1986), 146ff., presents a balanced presentation of the recent discussion about "Hellenists" and Stephen.

Acts 6:1–6[38] and the summarizing note in 6:7,[39] the charismatic leader Stephen emerges in 6:8 with hardly any transition. By placing him in this context, Luke seems to number Stephen among the "Hellenists," though he is never specifically identified as such.[40] Hellenistic Jews emerge as Stephen's opponents, but they are not able to withstand him, a fulfillment of the promise of Luke 21:15.[41] Then men are instigated to make libelous charges against Stephen. Here we should note two things: (1) It is not the disputants themselves who libel Stephen but men who have not even heard him. (2) Luke explicitly designates the charges as libel, showing he considers them to be untrue.[42] In 6:13–14 false witnesses appear again, in a passage that clearly represents Lukan redaction. They are the false witnesses whom Luke leaves unmentioned at the trial of Jesus (compare Mark 14:55–60 with Luke 22:66–67). Luke has also intentionally relocated the purported saying of Jesus about the destruction of the temple into this passage, since here—as the testimony of false witnesses, dissociated from Jesus—there is no longer any need to tone it down or get around it (cf. Mark 14:58; Matt. 26:61; John 2:19).[43] The charge of attacking Mosaic tradition goes back to texts such as Mark 2:23ff.; 7:14; 10:5–6. Proceeding from this basis in the tradition, Luke places the statement in Acts 6:13b, that Stephen had spoken against the temple and the law/Torah, and the summary of 6:14 in the mouth of the false witnesses (not Stephen's; cf. also Acts 7:48–50). He composes 6:15 in view of the following speech, also anticipating the vision report in 7:55–56, which manifests parallels to Luke's portrayal of Jesus' transfiguration (cf. Acts 6:15/Luke 9:29; Acts 7:55–56/Luke 9:32).

In summary, it may be said that in Acts 6:8–15 Luke intentionally reworks material from his tradition of the trial of Jesus in order to present the trial of the first martyr in this same light.[44] Here we also see an additional Lukan interest: "According to Luke, Stephen advocates the same basic position that will later be adopted by Paul (compare 6:13–14 and 7:48 with 21:21, 28; 7:58 with

---

38. For detailing the inconsistencies of this section, one need only consult Haenchen, *Acts*, 259–70.

39. To be noted is the very vague designation of this group as τίνες (some). Luke cannot describe them any more closely, since he knows nothing about them. Luke could have known the names of the synagogue members, just as the terms Ἑλληνισταί and Ἑβραῖοι (Hellenists, Hebrews) in Acts 6:1, μαθηταί (disciples, 6:1, 2, 7), and γογγυσμός (grumbling), παραθεωρέω (neglect), and καθημερινός (daily) in 6:1 could already have been present in Luke's tradition. All this, of course, is still no evidence for an "Antioch source" beginning in Acts 6.

40. Cf. Haenchen, *Acts*, 271.

41. Ibid.

42. Nothing supports the view of Martin Hengel, "Zwischen Jesus und Paulus: Die 'Hellenisten,' die 'Sieben,' und Stephanus," *ZTK* 72 (1975): 187, that Acts 6:11 derives from the source.

43. Cf. Haenchen, *Acts*, 274.

44. See the listing of parallels in Gerhard Schneider, *Die Apostelgeschichte* (HTKNT 5; Freiburg: Herder, 1980–), 1:433 n. 6.

9:29)."[45] Especially the redactional agreements between Acts 6:13 and 21:28[46] indicate that Acts 6:13 represents the Lukan view of the event, not an old, historically reliable tradition. It is obvious that by drawing parallels between Stephen and Paul, Luke wants to emphasize the salvation-historical continuity in early Christian theology and mission. The generally redactional character[47] of Acts 6:8–15 and the inconsistencies in its content mean we cannot consider it a reliable historical report of the theology of Stephen or the "Hellenists."

It is not demonstrable that the narrative of Stephen and the "Hellenists" represents a stance more critical of the Torah than what would have been possible in Judaism at the beginning of the Christian era, a position that would have justified persecution. Thus we must consider improbable the claim that they were driven out of Jerusalem because of this anti-Torah stance, and it is unlikely that Paul received his own Torah-critical attitude standpoint from them.[48] The better view is that what led to persecution of the new movement, including Paul's own activity as a persecutor, was the proclamation of the crucified Jesus of Nazareth as the Messiah of Israel, in connection with the movement's critical view of the temple[49] and the growing independence of its organizational structure and missionary practice.[50]

45. Weiser, *Apostelgeschichte*, 1:173; cf. also Karl Löning, "Der Stephanuskreis und seine Mission," in *Die Anfänge des Christentums: Alte Welt und neue Hoffnung* (ed. Jürgen Becker; Stuttgart: Kohlhammer, 1987), 86, who rightly comments on the paralleling of Stephen and Paul: "This Lukan conception of Paul serves to characterize Stephen indirectly by summarizing the 'charges' of the opponents in two points: critique of the temple and critique of the law. In this way the impression is created that the 'Hellenists' represented by Stephen constitute the bridge from the earliest Jerusalem church to Paul, which is a typical Lukanism." Also on target is E. Larsson, "Die Hellenisten und die Urgemeinde," *NTS* 33 (1987): 205–25, who emphasizes that we are not able to ascribe any particular theology to the Hellenists. The comments of Lüdemann, *Traditions in Acts*, 79–85, are somewhat out of focus, since he underestimates the redactional character of Acts 6:8–15 and does not attend to the Lukan paralleling of Stephen and Paul.

46. Cf. Heikki Räisänen, "The 'Hellenists'—a Bridge between Jesus and Paul?" in Heikki Räisänen, *The Torah and Christ: Essays in German and English on the Problem of the Law in Early Christianity* (ed. Anne-Marit Enroth; SESJ 45; Helsinki: Finnish Exegetical Society, 1986), 262, who also points out the parallels between Acts 6:13 and 21:28.

47. Weiser, *Apostelgeschichte*, 171; Löning, "Stephanuskreis," 86.

48. Dietzfelbinger bases his interpretation of the Damascus event as the origin of Paul's theology as a whole above all on Paul's activity as a persecutor, which in his view meant persecuting a community that, like Stephen, had adopted a critical stance to temple and law (cf. *Berufung des Paulus*, 16ff., 29). The apostle's own new attitude to the Torah, then, of course, is grounded in the Damascus event, both chronologically and in terms of its content. Dietzfelbinger's line of argument is especially subject to criticism for its uncritical acceptance of Luke's portrayal of Stephen, for he considers Acts 6:8–15 to be a historically reliable report (cf. p. 19); cf. further critique of Dietzfelbinger in Räisänen, "Paul's Call Experience," 87ff.

49. Emphasized by Eckhard Rau, *Von Jesus zu Paulus: Entwicklung und Rezeption der antiochenischen Theologie im Urchristentum* (Stuttgart: Kohlhammer, 1994), 15–77.

50. Cf. Strecker, "Befreiung und Rechtfertigung," 234. Contra Günter Klein, "Gesetz III," *TRE* 13:62, who fails to consider the redactional character of Acts 6:8–15 and claims that only the basic annulment of the authority of the law by the Hellenists can explain the events Luke recounts. In contrast is the more balanced view of Löning, "Stephanuskreis," 86–87, who considers neither the narrative of Acts 6:8–15 nor the following speech by Stephen to be critical of the law and supposes that "the pre-Lukan nucleus

4.2 Significance of the Damascus Event

Several interpreters have regarded Damascus as the origin of the whole of Paul's theology, especially of his doctrine of justification. They identify his new decision regarding Christ with a new decision regarding the Torah,[51] and Rom. 10:4 then describes the content of the Damascus event.[52] By attributing Pauline theology to the Damascus experience and seeing it as nothing else than the explication of this event, they can consider its unity a proven fact. They then see all changes as developments of this primal event or as applications of it, conditioned by particular situations. Paul's own statements, however, do not support the claim for such sweeping implications. Paul never mentions any biographical details of the event at Damascus; he stamps his presentation with standard expressions and refers strictly to his new knowledge of Jesus Christ and the founding of his apostleship. In Paul's own writings there are no terms or concepts for the interpretation of the Damascus event, and in no passage where he is developing his theology does he appeal to Damascus.

The New Knowledge

It is clear from the apostle's own statements that we must understand Damascus as a gracious act of God that granted Paul new knowledge on four fundamental points:[53]

---

of the charge against Stephen is the dispute concerning the temple as the place of God's presence and eschatological atonement" (p. 86). Similarly Kraus, *Zwischen Jerusalem und Antiochia*, 55: "Regarding the question of the persecution of the 'Hellenists' here dealt with, the most plausible hypothesis is that their criticism of the temple and its cult was the decisive reason they were driven out of Jerusalem."

51. Dietzfelbinger, *Berufung des Paulus*, 90–116; Klein, "Gesetz," 13:64–65; Luck, "Bekehrung des Paulus," 203ff.; Hübner, *Biblische Theologie*, 2:32: "Thus Damascus is the birthday of theological freedom from the law"; Stuhlmacher, *Biblische Theologie*, 1:234–52; Niebuhr, *Heidenapostel*, 179ff.; Martin Hengel, "Die Stellung des Paulus zum Gesetz in den unbekannten Jahren zwischen Damaskus und Antiochien," in *Paul and the Mosaic law* (ed. James D. G. Dunn; Grand Rapids: Eerdmans, 2001), 33: "For him, the encounter with the risen one at Damascus placed Paul before the question *law or Christ* in the form of a *soteriological* alternative."

52. Cf. in this sense, e.g., Peter Stuhlmacher, "Das Gesetz als Thema biblischer Theologie," in *Versöhnung, Gesetz, und Gerechtigkeit: Aufsätze zur biblischen Theologie* (Göttingen: Vandenhoeck & Ruprecht, 1981), 155: "Paul stands in the tradition of the Stephen group. He owes his dialectical theology of the law, however, directly to his call to be an apostle. In this call Christ appears to him as 'the end of the law' (Rom. 10:4)." For a critique of this position, cf. Klaus Haacker, "Der 'Antinomismus' des Paulus im Kontext antiker Gesetzestheorie," in *Geschichte–Tradition–Reflexion: Festschrift für Martin Hengel zum 70. Geburtstag* (ed. Hubert Cancik et al.; Tübingen: Mohr Siebeck, 1996), 394–95; Gerhard Dautzenberg, "Freiheit im hellenistischen Kontext," in *Der neue Mensch in Christus: Hellenistische Anthropologie und Ethik im Neuen Testament* (ed. Johannes Beutler; QD 190; Freiburg: Herder, 2001), 75; Ingo Broer, *Einleitung in das Neue Testament* (2 vols.; NEchtBENT 2/1; Würzburg: Echter, 1998), 2:242.

53. Theissen, *Religion of the Earliest Churches*, 219, underestimates the importance of Damascus when he states, "Paul's conversion and call is therefore the adoption of a completely new social position; he changes from being a persecutor of Christians to being a missionary of precisely this group."

(1) Theological knowledge: God again speaks and acts; at the end of the age God reveals his saving act in a new way. Through God's intervention, completely new perspectives are opened up in and for history.

(2) Christological knowledge: The crucified and risen Jesus of Nazareth now belongs forever at God's side; he is God's representative who takes his place in heaven as the "second power."[54] As "Lord" (1 Cor. 1:9, κύριος), "the Anointed One" (1 Cor. 15:3, Χριστός [Christ, Messiah]), "Son" (Gal. 1:16, υἱός) and "image of God" (2 Cor. 4:4, εἰκὼν τοῦ Θεοῦ), Jesus Christ is the permanent mediator of God's power and revelation. His exaltation and proximity to God reveal the honor of his unique office.

(3) Soteriological knowledge: In the present, the exalted Christ already grants believers participation in his reign. They are already incorporated within a process of universal transformation that began with Christ's resurrection, continues in the power of the Spirit, and will soon move to its climactic conclusion at the parousia and judgment.

(4) The biographical dimension: God has elected Paul and called him to announce this unheard-of good news to the nations. Paul himself thus becomes an integral element in God's plan of salvation, for he is the one through whom the gospel must be delivered to the world in order to save those who believe.

The texts have only a minimum to say about the way in which this new knowledge came to Paul. The Damascus experience no doubt had both external (cf. 1 Cor. 9:1; 15:8) and internal (Gal. 1:16; 2 Cor. 4:6) dimensions, possibly including an audition (cf. καλέω [call] in Gal. 1:15). But any additional interpretation of the content or of the psychology involved is lacking in Paul, so that we should draw no further conclusions beyond what these texts themselves say.[55]

The Consequences

If the contents of the Damascus event were Christophany and induction into office, apostolic call and commissioning,[56] so that from Paul's own point of view his recognition that Jesus Christ belongs to the category of deity and

---

54. For this concept, see Alan Segal, *Two Powers in Heaven: Early Rabbinic Reports about Christianity and Gnosticism* (Leiden: Brill, 1977).

55. Cf. Werner Georg Kümmel, *Römer 7 und das Bild des Menschen im Neuen Testament: Zwei Studien* (TB 53; Munich: C. Kaiser, 1974), 160, who warns against further-reaching interpretations of the Damascus event: "All psychological hypotheses and all claims that go beyond what can be extracted from the sources only pass by the facts and forget the appropriate respect for historical reality."

56. Strecker, *Die liminale Theologie des Paulus*, 155–57, would like to dispense with the terms "conversion" and "call" with reference to the Damascus event and speak instead of "initiation." He can appeal to the language and imagery of initiation (cf. 1 Cor. 15:8, the apostle as "abortion" or "stillborn"; 2 Cor. 4:6, new creation, light; Gal. 1:15–16, initiation into, and instruction in, a new vocation; Phil. 3, dying to a previous life and a completely new beginning). In my opinion, the initiation model is not an alternative to the call model but is complementary to it: Paul does obviously

his concept of apostleship give the key to understanding the Damascus event, then we cannot simply equate the significance of the Damascus event with the doctrine of justification found in the Galatian and Roman letters, written decades later, or with Pauline theology as a whole. There can be no dispute, however, that Damascus must have had an effect on the Pauline understanding of the law/Torah and justification and on Paul's thought as a whole. [57] But every reconstruction that goes beyond Paul's own statements is misguided, for such reconstructions represent a later stage of Pauline theology when Paul's whole line of argument had been conditioned by later situations, a theology that cannot simply be traced back point by point to the Damascus experience. [58] First Thessalonians and the Corinthian correspondence, in which νόμος (law) either is entirely absent or does not appear in the reflective sense found in the Galatian and Roman letters, confirm this understanding of the Damascus event. And the considerable tensions between the ways the law is understood even in Galatians and Romans[59] indicate that there can be no talk of a unified doctrine of the law already conveyed at Damascus.[60] Granted, the radical turn in the course of Paul's life at Damascus and the fundamentally new orientation could not, in the long run, remain without consequences for the former Pharisee Paul, but a point-for-point identification of Paul's new knowledge of Christ at Damascus with his critique of the law cannot be found in the Pauline texts.[61]

---

understand his Damascus call as an initiation that will be completed by participation in the resurrection body of Christ (Phil. 3:10–11).

57. This is worked out by Mark A. Seifrid, *Justification by Faith: The Origin and Development of a Central Pauline Theme* (NovTSup 68; Leiden: Brill, 1992), 136–80, without, however, simply equating the statements in Galatians, Romans, and Philippians with Damascus. "Nevertheless, a difference must be recognized between the shift in Paul's soteriology following his conversion, which can be described only in the most general language, and the arguments which he later enunciates in Galatians, Phil. 3 and Romans. The arguments regarding 'justification by faith apart from works of the Law' constitute a development in Paul's thought, which was precipitated by the struggle over the issue of Gentile circumcision and table-fellowship between Jewish and Gentile believers" (p. 180).

58. The 1908 statement of Wrede, *Paul*, 146, was already on target: "And so disappears every inducement to derive the doctrine of justification and the rejection of the works of the law directly from the conversion. To experience grace is not by any means the same thing as to set it up in contrst to human conduct. Belief in the death and resurrection of Christ is far from implying the necessity of doing away with circumcision and other rites, expecially as Christ, in Paul's belief, had himself kept the law" (Wrede refers to Gal. 4:4; Rom. 15:8).

59. See below, section 12.8 ("Sin, Law, and Freedom in the Spirit").

60. Cf. Heikki Räisänen, *Paul and the Law* (2nd ed.; WUNT 29; Tübingen: Mohr Siebeck, 1987), 256: "It is my contention that the theory of the theology of the law which was basically 'ready' with Paul's conversion cannot adequately explain the nature of the extant material."

61. Cf. Heikki Räisänen, "Paul's Conversion and the Development of His View of the Law," *NTS* 33 (1987): 416: "General considerations about the nature of Paul's theology of the Law and the historical context of mission suggest that theology was not complete with his conversion." Cf. also Berger, *Theologiegeschichte*, 436: "No connection is visible between Paul's conversion and the issue of the law"; Gnilka, *Apostel und Zeuge*, 45: "The crucified as one cursed by the law [not by God], Christ as the end of the law, salvation through the grace of Jesus Christ alone were insights that likely came to Paul

Paul certainly had already thought about the significance of the law/Torah for Gentile and Jewish Christians before his composition of the letters to the Galatians and Romans.[62] But whether he had always thought about this in the categories found in Galatians and Romans must remain an open question. The *subject matter* of justification and law had always been present with Paul since his conversion, but not the *doctrine* of justification and law as found in Galatians and Romans.

Damascus as Experience of Transcendence

When understood in this way, the significance of the Damascus event for Pauline theology is by no means belittled. On the contrary, the overwhelming experience of the risen Jesus Christ determined the life of the apostle from that point forward, without being reducible to statements of theological doctrine. At the beginning of every foundational religious experience stands the sense of being grasped, the experience of participation, but not systematic analysis. Damascus is an external experience of transcendence[63] that lays the foundations for a new identity. The concept of identity is particularly appropriate as a means of grasping the content of the Damascus experience and its consequences.[64] God acts to open new horizons for Paul: human judgment on the crucified Jesus was nullified; Jesus had not died on the cross as one under God's curse, but he belongs at God's side, he is God's representative, the bearer of God's glory who continues forever. Paul experiences Damascus as the intersection of two worlds—the Son of God appears to him in the world of space and time. Seeing the risen one leads Paul to surrender his former "I," a "divesting

---

later"; Kraus, *Zwischen Jerusalem und Antiochia*, 90: "Not being able to separate Paul's problem with the law entirely from the Damascus event thus still does not mean that the doctrine of justification or talk about the 'end of the law' can be moved back to that point"; Dautzenberg, "Freiheit im hellenistischen Kontext," 75: "I consider it very unlikely that at the beginning of Paul's Gentile mission, he disputed the claim of the Torah to universal validity."

62. Referring to Paul's Jewish past may well be reason enough to suppose that the Christian Paul, too, must have had an exceptional interest in questions dealing with the law and justification, but it still says nothing about the concrete form of his reflections; contra Ferdinand Hahn, "Gibt es eine Entwicklung in den Aussagen über die Rechtfertigung bei Paulus?" *EvT* 53 (1976): 346.

63. Schutz and Luckmann, *Structures*, 2:121–30, within their study oriented to experiences in the life world, by definition deal only with "internal" experiences of transcendence, within which they do, however, find a place to deal with death. "Knowledge that death is a final boundary is indubitable. But knowledge of what lies beyond is not indubitable. Since, in contrast with other transcendencies, this boundary is crossable in only one direction, what—if anything at all—could lie beyond it is certainly not immediately derivable from everyday experience. The other experiences of transcendence, however, offer some indications. Sleep has understandably time and time again been offered as a point of departure for the assumption that another reality awaits us beyond the boundary of death." (p. 127).

64. Cf. Straub, "Temporale Orientierung," 40: "The contingency of emerging events compels people to reconstruct their images of themselves and their world."

of self"[65] that is the negative presupposition for the new being in Christ. Paul is given the knowledge that with the resurrection of Jesus Christ from the dead, God has opened up the decisive epoch of salvation history, an epoch in which Paul himself is incorporated as preacher of this gospel.[66] Paul experienced Damascus as participation in the Christ event, which gave him a new identity and at the same time compelled him to restructure his picture of himself and the world. God granted him a new knowledge of the person of Jesus Christ and gave him a new assignment: to proclaim the gospel of Jesus Christ to the Gentiles.[67] Paul understood his apostolic office on the basis of this event. Paul did also take up elements from his former symbolic universe into his new identity, but in this process they were reevaluated within the new system of coordinates.[68] From the perspective of temporal theory, identity is necessarily a process of constant reformation;[69] from the viewpoint of identity theory, we must also regard it as improbable that at Damascus Paul already had at his disposal all the elements in his later symbolic universe as represented in Galatians and Romans.

Nonetheless, Damascus is undoubtedly the fundamental point of departure for Pauline meaning formation. Whereas he could formerly understand the proclamation of the crucified Messiah only as provocation, the Damascus experience led him to the insight that the cross was filled with the inherent potential for unexpected meaning. Paul now combines biographical thinking with universal perspectives, for he stands before the task of taking his experience and interpretation of a past event that happened to one individual and erecting a meaning structure that provides orientation in the present and hope for the future.[70] A mere historical fact such as the crucifixion is not in itself a bearer of

65. Rudolf Otto, "Mystische und gläubige Frömmigkeit," in *Sünde und Urschuld, und andere Aufsätze zur Theologie* (Munich: Beck, 1932), 144.

66. The primary marks of conversion given by Thomas Luckmann, "Kanon und Konversion," in *Kanon und Zensur* (ed. Aleida Assmann and Jan Assmann; Beiträge zur Archäologie der literarischen Kommunikation 2; Munich: Fink, 1987), 40, also apply to Paul: "biographical reconstruction, accepting one key to the nature of reality, bracketing analogical thinking and roles, 'totalizing,' that is, summing everything up under one heading."

67. Kraus, *Zwischen Jerusalem und Antiochia*, 105, rightly reemphasizes that this also includes the theme of the people of God. Still, it is a matter of a resulting phenomenon, not something at the center of the Damascus event itself.

68. Jörn Rüsen, "Krise, Trauma, Identität," in *Zerbrechende Zeit: Über den Sinn der Geschichte* (Cologne: Böhlau, 2001), 164: "In the procedures and practice of identity formation through historical consciousness, events play a decisive role. They are remembered and represented in such a way that their particular factuality (their character as a contingent event) stands for the particularity and uniqueness of the person or social self."

69. Cf. Straub, "Temporale Orientierung," 39, who argues that the "formation and maintenance of identity is only possible as a process of reformation that in principle cannot be definitively concluded."

70. Jörn Rüsen, "Historisches Erzählen," in *Zerbrechende Zeit: Über den Sinn der Geschichte* (Cologne: Böhlau, 2001), 54: "'Meaning' is an integration of perception, interpretation, orientation, and motivation in such wise that both one's relation to the world and one's relation to oneself can be intellectually mastered in its temporal structure and carried out in a practical and intentional way."

meaning; it requires an additional constructive procedure in order to "clothe facts with meaning and significance, to create from the chaos of meaningless factuality a cosmos of meaningful and significant history."[71] From the religious certainty of the Damascus event, Paul sets in motion a process of universalistic meaning formation that was to have unparalleled effects, making it possible for all people to understand their own existence within the whole scheme of things. He constructs and presents a network of meaning that relates one's individual existence to its social obligations, and binds together one's secure everyday world and crucial experiences with transcendent reality.

71. Rüsen, "Historische Methode," 353. Cf. also his comment in Jörn Rüsen, "Anmerkungen zum Thema Christologie und Narration," in *Gegenwart des Absoluten: Philosophisch-theologische Diskurse zur Christologie* (ed. Klaus-Michael Kodalle; Gütersloh: Gütersloher Verlagshaus, 1984), 91: "Strictly speaking, the writing of history is not primarily a matter of presenting the human past in its pure facticity but one of presenting the meaningful connections of human actions in their temporal dimension."

5

The Christian Paul

A Volcano Begins to Rumble

Paul does not make his entrance onto the stage of history as a solo performer; he is accompanied, instructed, and sent forth. By no means is Paul already a finished product; a difficult path still lay before him that would lead through numerous internal and external struggles. At the same time, it became clear early on that the apprentice would become a master, the follower would become the leader.

5.1 Rehearsal and Coaching: Paul and Early Christian Tradition

His activities as a persecutor would have made Paul familiar with the basic views of the Christian faith—then comes Damascus. In Gal. 1:11–12 Paul emphasizes that the gospel he preaches is not of a human sort, "for I did not receive it from a human source, nor was I taught it, but I received it through a revelation of Jesus Christ." The apostle accents this differently in 1 Cor. 15:1–3a,[1] where

---

1. The terminology of 1 Cor. 11:23a and 15:3a (παραλαμβάνω, παραδίδωμι) reflects the language used in Jewish tradition; cf. Conzelmann, *1 Corinthians,* 250.

he tells the community what he himself has received from others (cf. 1 Cor. 15:3b–5). In 1 Cor. 11:2 Paul praises the church "because you remember me in everything and maintain the traditions just as I handed them on to you." According to 1 Cor. 11:23a, Paul received the eucharistic tradition from the Lord and now hands it on to the church (1 Cor. 11:23b–26). In Paul's self-understanding, the gospel came to him both as a direct revelation of Christ and through human mediation. We can say nothing further about when and where Paul received instruction that gave him prior and special knowledge in the Christian faith. According to Acts 9:17–18, he received the Spirit and was baptized in Damascus; perhaps instruction in the Christian faith was included in this event.[2] In any case, Paul very early received such catechetical instruction, for soon after his apostolic call he begins his independent work as a missionary (cf. Gal. 1:17), but its extent, character, and results still lie shrouded in darkness. Paul's later letters do give some indications of the kind and extent of the ideas he had received.

Among the traditions transmitted by Paul were "sayings of the Lord."[3] He quotes them in 1 Thess. 4:15ff.; 1 Cor. 7:10–11; 9:14; 11:23ff. but does not always present them as sayings known to us from the Synoptic tradition of Jesus' sayings. The prohibition of divorce—without the parenthesis of 1 Cor. 7:11a—has a direct parallel in Mark 10:9–11,[4] and the Pauline eucharistic tradition repeats traditional material from the earliest time.[5] The "command of the Lord" in 1 Cor. 9:14 could refer to Luke 10:7/Matt. 10:10; there is no parallel to 1 Thess. 4:15ff. in the Gospel tradition. Paul does not distinguish between sayings of the earthly Jesus and those of the exalted Lord. Under the authority of the one Lord Jesus Christ, he can be thinking more of the earthly Jesus (1 Cor. 9:14),[6] or quoting a saying of the exalted Christ (2 Cor. 12:9),

2. The present order reflects Lukan redaction; cf. Weiser, *Apostelgeschichte*, 1:222.

3. A critical analysis of the history of research is given by Frans Neirynck, "Paul and the Sayings of Jesus," in Frans Neirynck, *Collected Essays, 1982–1991* (vol. 2 of *Evangelica: Gospel studies = Evangelica: Études d'évangile;* ed. Frans van Segbroeck; BETL 99; Leuven: Leuven University Press, 1991), 511–68. He rightly emphasizes that, strictly speaking, no letter of Paul cites a saying of Jesus. Similarly Nikolaus Walter, "Paulus und die urchristliche Jesustradition," *NTS* 31 (1985): 498–522. For the contrasting point of view, cf., e.g., Peter Stuhlmacher, "Jesustraditionen im Römerbrief?" *TBei* 14 (1983): 240–50; David Wenham, *Paul: Follower of Jesus or Founder of Christianity?* (Grand Rapids: Eerdmans, 1995), 373–407; Rainer Riesner, "Paulus und die Jesus-Überlieferung," in *Evangelium, Schriftauslegung, Kirche: Festschrift für Peter Stuhlmacher zum 65. Geburtstag* (ed. Otfried Hofius et al.; Göttingen: Vandenhoeck & Ruprecht, 1997), 347–65, who see a comprehensive continuity between Jesus and Paul.

4. For analysis, cf. Berndt Schaller, "Die Sprüche über Ehescheidung und Wiederheirat in der synoptischen Überlieferung," in *Der Ruf Jesu und die Antwort der Gemeinde* (ed. Eduard Lohse et al.; Göttingen: Vandenhoeck & Ruprecht, 1970), 226–46.

5. Cf. Joachim Jeremias, *The Eucharistic Words of Jesus* (trans. Norman Perrin; New York: Scribner, 1966), 138–201.

6. Cf. 1 Cor. 9:5.

or emphasizing both aspects equally (1 Cor. 11:23).[7] Paul seems quite close to the traditional Jesus sayings in Rom. 12:14–21 (cf. Luke 6:27–36) and Rom. 14:14 (cf. Mark 7:15).[8] Here Paul takes up (anonymous) Jesus tradition that has received a sapiential stamp—but without emphasizing its authority as words of Jesus. In Gal. 6:2 Paul has recourse to the "law of Christ" as an ethical norm, but the reference is probably to an ethical interpretation of Jesus' life as a whole rather that to a particular saying of Jesus.[9] It is altogether probable that Paul knew sayings of Jesus and that he was more aware of the historical Jesus than indicated in his extant letters.[10] Nonetheless, it is remarkable that the apostle makes only very limited use of this possible knowledge and does not integrate it into the line of argument followed in his letters.[11] There is no indication of Paul's having known the narrative Jesus tradition, nor does Paul cite sayings of Jesus when he is elaborating his own distinctive theology. For Paul, the significance of Jesus Christ is not revealed by the Synoptic tradition of Jesus' words and deeds; he concentrates on the saving significance of the death and resurrection of Jesus Christ as this had been delivered to him in the tradition. Pre-Pauline baptismal tradition is found in 1 Cor. 1:30; 6:11; 2 Cor. 1:21–22; Gal. 3:26–28; Rom. 3:25; 4:25; 6:3–4;[12] eucharistic traditions are found in 1 Cor. 11:23b–25 and 16:22. The apostle adopted early Christian creedal formulations in 1 Thess. 1:9–10; 1 Cor. 8:6; 15:3b–5; Rom. 1:3b–4a; 10:9; Phil. 2:6–11. Traditional paraenetic topoi lie behind 1 Cor. 5:10–11; 6:9–10; 2 Cor. 12:20–21; Gal. 5:19–23; Rom. 1:19–31; 13:13.[13]

These restrictive findings do not, however, justify the opinion that for Pauline theology the earthly Jesus was mostly irrelevant.[14] On the contrary, running

---

7. This is indicated by the introductory expression παρέλαβον ἀπὸ τοῦ κυρίου (I received [by tradition] from the [exalted] Lord) in 1 Cor. 11:23a.

8. Neirynck, "Paul and the Sayings of Jesus," 515ff., gives a detailed listing.

9. Walter, "Jesustradition," 508ff., rightly points out that Paul's references to the Jesus tradition are primarily paraenesis.

10. Dunn, *Theology of Paul*, 185–89, emphasizes this.

11. Thomas Schmeller, "Kollege Paulus: Die Jesusüberlieferung und das Selbstverständnis des Völkerapostels," *ZNW* 88 (1997): 260–83, attempts to explain this data by positing a complementary role for early Christian missionaries, so that Paul did not see the handing on of the Jesus tradition as the responsibility of his own group but of other missionaries.

12. For analysis, cf. Udo Schnelle, *Gerechtigkeit und Christusgegenwart: Vorpaulinische und paulinische Tauftheologie* (GTA 24; Göttingen: Vandenhoeck & Ruprecht, 1983), 33–88; 175–215.

13. On this, cf. Philipp Vielhauer, *Geschichte der urchristlichen Literatur: Einleitung in das Neue Testament, die Apokryphen, und die Apostolischen Väter* (Berlin: de Gruyter, 1975), 9–57; Georg Strecker, *History of New Testament Literature* (trans. Calvin Katter and Hans-Joachim Mollenhauer; Harrisburg, PA: Trinity Press International, 1997), 77–81; Wiard Popkes, *Paränese und Neues Testament* (SBS 168; Stuttgart: Katholisches Bibelwerk, 1995), who provides a good bibliography.

14. Rudolf Bultmann, "Die Bedeutung des geschichtlichen Jesus für die Theologie des Paulus," in *Glauben und Verstehen: Gesammelte Aufsätze* (4 vols.; Tübingen: Mohr Siebeck, 1933–), 1:188–213, can postulate a material continuity between Jesus and Paul but at the same time asserts that "Jesus Christ meets human beings no place else than in the kerygma, just as he met Paul, and forces them to a decision. . . . It is not the historical Jesus but the proclaimed Jesus Christ who is the Lord" (p. 228);

through Paul's letters, we find narrative elements and references that deal thematically with the story of the earthly Jesus and his resurrection and parousia
at one and the same time.[15] Thus the eucharistic tradition of 1 Cor. 11:23b–25
and the creedal tradition of 1 Cor. 15:3b–5 are narrative abbreviations[16] in styl-
ized language that contain the decisive basic data of the Jesus-Christ-history
and thus thematically present and reflect on the theological significance of
the proexistence (i.e., pre-Easter life) of the earthly Jesus.[17] These include his
intentional self-giving for his own on the night he was delivered over, his death,
his burial, his resurrection on the third day, and his appearances as the risen
one. The earthly Jesus does not fade from view in Paul's theology but is interpreted in the light of Easter. The cross, as the central narrative abbreviation, is
much more than an item determined by the kerygma; it always maintains its
reference to a particular historical place and the gruesome death that occurred
there, even in texts where Paul integrates it into mythological narratives (Phil.
2:6–11).[18] Wherever the cross appears in Paul's writings, it contains the whole
Jesus-Christ-history, which in 1 Cor. 1:18 he calls the "message about the
cross." The cross is at one and the same time a past event in history and the

---

cf. further Bultmann, *Theology of the New Testament*, 1:293: "Jesus' death-and-resurrection, then, is
for Paul the decisive thing about the person of Jesus and his life experience, indeed, in the last analysis
it is the sole thing of importance for him—implicitly included are the incarnation and the earthly life
of Jesus as bare facts. That is, Paul is interested only in the *fact* that Jesus became man and lived on
earth. *How* he was born or lived interests him only to the extent of knowing that Jesus was a definite,
concrete man, a Jew." Bultmann understands 2 Cor. 5:16 as evidence for his own view of the relation
between Jesus and Paul: "The Χριστὸς κατὰ σάρκα is Christ as he can be encountered in the world,
before his death and resurrection. He should no longer be viewed as such" (Rudolf Bultmann, *The
Second Letter to the Corinthians* [ed. Erich Dinkler; trans. Roy A. Harrisville; Minneapolis: Augsburg,
1985], 155).

    On the history of the Jesus/Paul question, cf. Werner Georg Kümmel, "Jesus und Paulus," in
Heilsgeschehen und Geschichte (ed. Erich Grässer et al.; MTS 3; Marburg: Elwert, 1965), 1:81–106; Josef
Blank, *Paulus und Jesus: Eine theologische Grundlegung* (SANT 18; Munich: Kösel, 1968), 61–132.

    15. Cf. Reinmuth, "Jesus-Christus-Geschichte," 21, according to whom Paul does not narrate an
abstract history of the historical Jesus but the Jesus-Christ-history, just as he "knows it and proclaims
it—thus the Jesus-Christ-history that includes the history of the earthly Jesus within the framework
of preexistence and parousia." Cf. further A. J. M. Wedderburn, "Paul and the Story of Jesus," in *Paul
and Jesus: Collected Essays* (JSNTSup 37; Sheffield: JSOT Press, 1989), 161–89.

    16. Cf. Jürgen Straub, "Geschichten erzählen, Geschichte bilden," in *Erzählung, Identität, und
historisches Bewußtsein: Die psychologische Konstruktion von Zeit und Geschichte* (2nd ed.; Frankfurt:
Suhrkamp, 2000), 123: "Narrative abbreviations contain histories or point to histories without themselves being histories. Narrative abbreviations may be expounded hermeneutically only in recourse to
histories, to which they refer or allude."

    17. Cf. Klaus Scholtissek, "'Geboren aus einer Frau, geboren unter das Gesetz' (Gal. 4,4): Die
christologisch-soteriologische Bedeutung des irdischen Jesus bei Paulus," in *Paulinische Christologie:
Exegetische Beiträge: Hans Hübner zum 70. Geburtstag* (ed. Udo Schnelle et al.; Göttingen: Vanden-
hoeck & Ruprecht, 2000), 211–12. H. Schürmann coined the term *Pro-Existenz*; cf., e.g., Heinz
Schürmann, *Gottes Reich—Jesu Geschick: Jesu ureigener Tod im Licht seiner Basileia-Verkündigung*
(Freiburg: Herder, 1983), 205ff.

    18. Ibid. 209–10.

enduring event of salvation, for its real significance can be grasped only as the act of God in Jesus Christ.[19]

The factual, material unity of the earthly Jesus and the risen Lord comes through wherever the historical dimensions of the life of Jesus come into view. These dimensions are theologically determined in every instance but at the same time point back to the indispensable historical event. In the fullness of time, Jesus of Nazareth was born of a woman and made subordinate to the law (Gal. 4:4). Paul binds together the facts of the natural birth of Jesus and his cultural incorporation within Judaism with the idea of fulfillment and the concept of the Son of God. God sent his Son in the "likeness of sinful flesh" (Rom. 8:3); the Messiah is Jesus the Jew (Rom. 9:5), who comes from Davidic ancestry (Rom. 1:3) and had at least two brothers (1 Cor. 9:5; Gal. 1:19). Jesus did not live for himself but took (loaded) on himself the insults of others (Rom. 15:3). He divested himself of his equality with God, assumed the form of a slave, became a human being, was obedient to the point of dying on the cross (Phil. 2:7–8; Gal. 3:1), and was buried (1 Cor. 15:4; Rom. 6:4). Although he was rich, for our sakes he became poor in order to make us rich (2 Cor. 8:9). He himself knew no sin but was made to be sin for our sakes so that in him we might become the righteousness of God (2 Cor. 5:21). He was crucified in weakness but now lives by the power of God (2 Cor. 13:4). Paul wants to preach nothing else but the crucified one (1 Cor. 2:2) who died for our sins (1 Cor. 15:3; Gal. 1:4) and has now been exalted by God (Phil. 2:9–11). The Pauline challenge to discipleship also points to the earthly Jesus[20] (cf. 1 Thess. 1:6; 2:14; 1 Cor. 4:6; 11:1; Phil. 2:5; 3:17), for the church should orient its own life to the meekness and gentleness of Christ (cf. 2 Cor. 10:1; Rom. 15:5; Phil. 1:8). Paul's letters presuppose a knowledge of the Jesus-Christ-history and continually refer to it.[21]

Paul avoids posing an alternative between a factual history of the earthly Jesus and an abstract kerygma Christology disconnected with this early life, which would have been inappropriate both historically and in terms of the realities themselves. On the contrary, for him the history of the earthly Jesus only comes in view from the perspective of the present reality of salvation created by the resurrected Christ (cf., e.g., Gal. 1:3–4, "the Lord Jesus Christ, who gave himself for our sins to set us free from the present evil age, according to the will of our God and Father").[22] Jesus' significance is not revealed

---

19. Cf. Reinmuth, "Jesus-Christus-Geschichte," 24–25.

20. Differently Otto Merk, "Nachahmung Christi," in *Neues Testament und Ethik: Für Rudolf Schnackenburg* (ed. Helmut Merklein and Rudolf Schnackenburg; Freiburg: Herder, 1989), 172–206.

21. Cf. Reinmuth, "Jesus-Christus-Geschichte," 22–23: "This Jesus-Christ-history is also to be presupposed as the content of Paul's oral preaching."

22. This is not contradicted by 2 Cor. 5:16, for κατὰ σάρκα (according to the flesh) modifies the verb, not Χριστόν (Christ). On the interpretation of 2 Cor. 5:16, see below, section 10.5 ("The Message of Reconciliation").

as the sum of his individual sayings and deeds but only through the history created by God's act in Jesus Christ, which validated him as the eschatological and definitive bringer of God's salvation. Within this Jesus-Christ-history, the earthly Jesus and risen Christ constitute a unity that cannot be dissolved in either direction. By narrating the act of God in Jesus Christ, Paul avoids the false alternative of "fact or interpretation" and thus preserves the wholeness of the Jesus-Christ-history.[23]

5.2 Paul's Bible

Paul's Bible was the Greek translation of the Old Testament, the Septuagint.[24] Not all Paul's quotations from Scripture, however, can be found in the Septuagint as it has been transmitted to us; especially in Job and Isaiah, one must postulate a recension of the Septuagint text that was closer to the Hebrew.[25] The undisputed Pauline letters contain eighty-nine citations from the Old Testament.[26] The majority of these quotations are from a limited selection of documents, with Isaiah, the Psalter, and the Pentateuch clearly the focus but Jeremiah, Ezekiel, and Daniel, for example, entirely passed over.[27] A further process of reduction and selection is seen in the concrete application of these

23. Blank, *Paulus und Jesus*, 183, is on target with his comment: "After all, it was not despite Easter that the early church continued to affirm Jesus' cross and his life history but precisely because of Easter and on the basis of Easter."

24. For an introduction, cf. Ernst Würthwein, *The Text of the Old Testament: An Introduction to the Biblia Hebraica* (trans. Erroll F. Rhodes; Grand Rapids: Eerdmans, 1979), 48–74. Cf. also Robert Hanhart, "Die Bedeutung der Septuaginta in neutestamentlicher Zeit," *ZTK* 81 (1984): 395–416; Martin Hengel, *The Septuagint as Christian Scripture: Its Prehistory and the Problem of Its Canon* (trans. Mark E. Biddle; OTS; Edinburgh: T&T Clark, 2002); and Karen H. Jobes and Moises Silva, *Invitation to the Septuagint* (Grand Rapids: Baker, 2000).

25. Dietrich-Alex Koch, *Die Schrift als Zeuge des Evangeliums: Untersuchungen zur Verwendung und zum Verständnis der Schrift bei Paulus* (BHT 69; Tübingen: Mohr Siebeck, 1986), 57–81.

On the Pauline reception of the Old Testament, see, in addition to the studies of D. A. Koch and H. Hübner, esp. Anthony Tyrrell Hanson, *Studies in Paul's Technique and Theology* (London: SPCK, 1974); *The New Testament Interpretation of Scripture* (London: SPCK, 1980); Richard B. Hays, *Echoes of Scripture in the Letters of Paul* (New Haven: Yale University Press, 1989); Christopher D. Stanley, *Paul and the Language of Scripture: Citation Technique in the Pauline Epistles and Contemporary Literature* (SNTSMS 69; Cambridge: Cambridge University Press, 1992); Craig A. Evans and James A. Sanders, eds., *Paul and the Scriptures of Israel* (JSNTSup 83; Sheffield: JSOT Press, 1993); Nikolaus Walter, "Alttestamentliche Bezüge in christologischen Ausführungen bei Paulus," in *Paulinische Christologie: Exegetische Beiträge: Hans Hübner zum 70. Geburtstag* (ed. Udo Schnelle et al.; Göttingen: Vandenhoeck & Ruprecht, 2000), 246–71.

26. Cf. Koch, *Schrift als Zeuge*, 21–23; for different counts, cf. Otto Michel, *Paulus und seine Bibel* (Gütersloh: C. Bertelsmann, 1929; repr., Darmstadt: Wissenschaftliche Buchgesellschaft, 1972), 12–13 (eighty-three citations); E. Earle Ellis, *Paul's Use of the Old Testament* (Edinburgh: Oliver & Boyd, 1957), 150–52 (eighty-eight citations).

27. Cf. the list in Koch, *Schrift als Zeuge*, 33.

citations. Within the Pentateuch Paul only rarely chooses texts from the legal tradition in the strict sense, mostly drawing on the narrative sections. Thus the only two citations from Leviticus (Lev. 18:5 in Rom. 10:5/Gal. 3:12, and Lev. 19:18 in Rom. 13:9/Gal. 5:14) are not at all typical of the legal sections of that book. Paul makes no use of Genesis 22 (the sacrifice of Isaac), which was constitutive for the picture of Abraham characteristic of ancient Judaism, although he does make extensive use of the Abraham tradition as such.[28] Of the eighty-nine quotations, sixty-six are provided with introductory formulae, mostly γέγραπται (it is written) or λέγει (it/he says). Paul edits several of the Old Testament texts in interpreting and applying them,[29] making use of a variety of techniques. He changes the word order and modifies the person, number, part of speech, tense, or mood, just as he shortens or expands the text by omissions and additions. Sometimes parts of the quotations are replaced by other formulations or exchanged with materials from other texts (mixed quotations), so that texts from several locations are cited together. Although this style of quotation is not peculiar to Paul,[30] biblical citations in ancient Judaism generally manifest less intentional alteration of the text than we find in Paul. For Paul, it is a matter of integrating the quotations into the new context, for the intertextual connections that are thereby generated accomplish two things: they place the Old Testament reference in a new horizon of meaning and at the same time legitimate the Pauline gospel. Paul in this way transcends the Hellenistic synagogue's horizon of understanding, for it is not the biblical text itself but God's act of eschatological salvation in Christ that forms the material center of his thought. From this point of departure, he thinks through the central contents of Jewish theology (Torah, election) in a new way and integrates Scripture texts into a productive intertextual process of interpretation. "The freedom in dealing with the wording of Scripture, which sets him at some distance from contemporary Jewish exegesis, is thus not to be separated from the content of his biblical interpretation and signals a fundamental change in his understanding of the nature of the Scripture."[31]

In his interpretation of Scripture, Paul makes use of contemporary exegetical methods. We thus find allegorical (cf. 1 Cor. 9:9; 10:4; Gal. 4:21–31) and typological interpretation (cf. 1 Thess. 1:7; Rom. 5:14; Phil. 3:17).[32] Romans 4

---

28. Cf. Dietrich-Alex Koch, "'. . . Bezeugt durch das Gesetz und die Propheten': Zur Funktion der Schrift bei Paulus," in *Sola scriptura: Das reformatorische Schriftprinzip in der säkularen Welt* (ed. Hans Heinrich Schmid and Joachim Mehlhausen; Gütersloh: Mohn, 1991), 169–79.

29. On the details, cf. Koch, *Schrift als Zeuge*, 186ff.

30. David Instone-Brewer, *Techniques and Assumptions in Jewish Exegesis before 70 CE* (TSAJ 30; Tübingen: Mohr Siebeck, 1992); Stanley, *Language of Scripture*, 267–360; Barbara Fuss, *"Dies ist die Zeit, von der geschrieben ist . . .": Die expliziten Zitate aus dem Buch Hosea in den Handschriften von Qumran und im Neuen Testament* (NTAbh NF 37; Münster: Aschendorff, 2000).

31. Koch, *Schrift als Zeuge*, 198.

32. Still valuable on this point is Leonhard Goppelt, *Typos: The Typological Interpretation of the Old Testament in the New* (trans. Donald H. Madvig; Grand Rapids: Eerdmans, 1982).

is composed somewhat in the style of a midrash, where Paul structures a whole block of material on the basis of one biblical text. The step-by-step commentary on a quotation (cf. Rom. 10:6–8) manifests a certain similarity to the pesher commentaries of Qumran. Paul has parallels to two of the seven middot (hermeneutical norms) of Hillel that rabbinic Judaism had taken over from Hellenistic rhetoric and made into hermeneutical principles: the application of the conclusion by analogy in 1 Cor. 9:9–10 and the inference from context in Rom. 4:10–11. Paul's manner of biblical interpretation is at home in contemporary Jewish exegesis and documents the apostle's background of Hellenistic Diaspora Judaism in the area of Asia Minor and Syria.[33]

The quotations are not distributed evenly among the letters but in a manner that calls for comment. Of the extant letters, Old Testament citations are entirely missing from the oldest (1 Thessalonians) and the two latest letters (Philippians, Philemon). Paul quotes the Old Testament twenty-eight times in 1 Corinthians, ten times in 2 Corinthians, ten times in Galatians, and sixty-five times in Romans.[34] This unequal distribution of citations led A. von Harnack to propose that it was the issues debated in the major letters that compelled Paul to make an intensive use of the Scriptures, that the apostle had not introduced Scripture into the newly founded churches on his own initiative, and that although Scripture continued to have great importance for him personally, it played only a subordinate role in his missionary work.[35] D.-A. Koch took up Harnack's thesis and developed it in a modified form. From the lack of quotations in 1 Thessalonians, Philippians, and Philemon, Koch infers that Paul did not always have at his disposal a firm collection of Scripture references upon which he could draw whenever he was composing a letter. It was only in composing particular letters that he sought out relevant texts and worked them into his composition. Koch understands Paul's engagement with the Scripture as a purely literary process. This meant that, as a rule, the apostle could only refer to particular quotations when he had sufficient time and could support his argument with written texts. This would explain the lack of quotations in Philippians and Philemon, both of which were written from prison. Against this hypothesis one could object that during his rather lenient incarceration in Rome, Paul would have had a copy of the Old Testament available and that as a trained Pharisee he probably had a considerable body of texts at his disposal.[36] Nonetheless, Koch's hypothesis is based on the correct observation

---

33. On the whole topic, cf. Koch, *Schrift als Zeuge*, 199–256.

34. Cf. ibid., 90. The higher total results from taking combinations and mixed quotations into consideration; cf. p. 33 n. 3.

35. Cf. Adolf von Harnack, *Das Alte Testament in den paulinischen Briefen und in den paulinischen Gemeinden* (SPAWPH 12; Berlin: Reimer, 1928), 124–41.

36. Cf. Hermann von Lips, "Paulus und die Tradition," *VF* 36 (1991): 35. Hengel and Deines, *Pre-Christian Paul*, 35, emphatically assert that "Paul's use of Scripture developed out of constant oral teaching."

that Paul did not work with a firm collection of texts already assembled at the very beginning of his missionary activity. Instead, for the most part he had to relate the statements of Scripture to his own theology when the necessity arose for introducing biblical citations for the clarification of controversial theological problems. The apostle could not simply join a project of Scripture interpretation that was already under way; rather, he worked references to Scripture into discussions of particular situations as they arose. This is confirmed by the Letter to the Romans, which deals with authentic Pauline themes (the righteousness of God, the right understanding of law/Torah, the place of Israel in God's plan) and where citations from Scripture are particularly frequent. In Rom. 3:21 the apostle himself points to this process when he claims the law and the prophets as support for his own critical view of the law. Especially Galatians and Romans show Paul reaching for his Bible to find texts that can serve to resolve the severe conflicts and arguments in which he is engaged.

Paul's use of Scripture thus confirms what we have found to be characteristic for Paul's theology as a whole: it was not simply "there," all at once, but grew and developed under the challenges of his missionary work.

5.3 First Steps as a Missionary

After his call Paul neither consulted with other people nor went to Jerusalem to those who were apostles before him, "but I went immediately into Arabia and later returned to Damascus" (Gal. 1:17b).[37] We have no information regarding Paul's stay in Arabia, but the designation probably refers to the rocky desert area southeast of Damascus, which formed the northern part of the Arab kingdom of Nabataea.[38] At that time the economic influence of Nabataea also embraced Damascus (2 Cor. 11:32),[39] where Paul returned and for the first time worked within an established Christian community. Damascus, a Hellenistic city that included a large Jewish population, had belonged to the Decapolis[40]

37. Why did Paul go to Arabia? A possible answer is given by Hengel, "Stellung des Paulus," 38: "In terms of genealogy and geography, the 'Arabs,' as descendants of Ishmael, were the closest relatives of Israel among the 'Gentiles,' for they too were descendants of Abraham."

38. Hengel, ibid., 37, defines "Arabia" as follows: "By 'Arabia,' the apostle probably refers to the Nabataean kingdom bordering Eretz Israel on the south and east, including a few cities of the Decapolis in Transjordan." Jerome Murphy-O'Connor, "Paul in Arabia," *CBQ* 55 (1993): 732–37, supposes Paul stayed in the area of Bosra.

39. It is not clear whether the Nabataeans controlled Damascus in the political-legal sense; somewhat skeptical are Riesner, *Paul's Early Period*, 75–89; and E. A. Knauf, "Die Arabienreise des Apostels Paulus," in *Paulus zwischen Damascus und Antiochien: Die unbekannten Jahre des Apostels* (ed. Martin Hengel and Anna Maria Schwemer; WUNT 108; Tübingen: Mohr Siebeck, 1998), 465–71 [translator's note: this appendix was not included in the English translation of Hengel and Schwemer].

40. H. Bietenhard, "Die Dekapolis von Pompejus bis Trajan," *ZDPV* 79 (1963): 24–58.

since 63 BCE.[41] Historians are still in the dark concerning the origins of the Christian community in Damascus.[42] The church there could have begun very early, since the city lay on a main commercial route, and was perhaps formed by refugees fleeing Jerusalem. According to Acts 22:12, Paul was introduced to the Damascus church by Ananias, who was regarded in the Jewish community as a respected, God-fearing man who was loyal to the Torah. This suggests that Christianity first began in Damascus within the Jewish community. "In Damascus the governor under King Aretas had the city of the Damascenes guarded in order to arrest me. But I was lowered in a basket from a window in the wall and slipped through his hands" (2 Cor. 11:32–33; cf. Acts 9:23–25). This ethnarch was probably the ruler of the Nabataean business colony in Damascus who represented the interests of the Nabataean kingdom there.[43] The intervention by the ethnarch was likely in response to Paul's missionary activity in Damascus, which caused disruption not only in the Jewish community but also among the Nabataeans. The relations between Nabataeans and Jews were severely strained at that time because of continuing border disputes and military confrontations; Rome's attempt to deal with these conflicts had only exacerbated the situation (cf. Josephus, *Ant.* 18.109ff.). Paul's description of his adventurous flight reflects the influence of Josh. 2:5—he escapes the efforts of the ethnarch's agents by concealing himself in one of the large baskets used for transporting food provisions.

Paul did not visit the original church in Jerusalem until the third year after his call to be an apostle (35 CE).[44] In Gal. 1:18–19 Paul gives a very terse description of both the intention and the duration of this first visit to Jerusalem. He stayed only fifteen days, in order to become acquainted with Cephas; of the other apostles, he saw only James the Lord's brother. We know nothing about the contents of the discussions between Peter and Paul.[45] The way in which he describes this visit reflects the self-understanding of the apostle to the Gentiles. Because he was called by the risen one himself, Paul needed no legitimization by the Jerusalem authorities. He seeks contact with Jerusalem but at the same time wants to avoid any appearance of dependence and subordination. He accords the revelation granted to him from the risen Christ the same objective quality as the appearances of the risen one to Peter and the other apostles, even

41. According to Josephus, *J. W.* 2.561; 7.368, ten thousand or eighteen thousand Jews were massacred in these conflicts.

42. On the city of Damascus and the history of the Christian community there, cf. Hengel and Schwemer, *Between Damascus and Antioch*, 50–90, 127–32.

43. E. A. Knauf, "Zum Ethnarchen des Aretas 2Kor 11,21," *ZNW* 74 (1983): 145–47.

44. According to Acts 9:26–30, directly after his flight from Damascus, Paul returned to Jerusalem and informed the apostles there; this cannot be harmonized with the apostle's own statements. Even Hengel and Schwemer acknowledge a contradiction here (*Between Damascus and Antioch*, 127–32).

45. Differently Hengel and Schwemer, ibid., 133–50.

though Paul himself is the least of all the apostles because he had previously been a persecutor (cf. 1 Cor. 15:3b–8).

Following his brief visit to Jerusalem, about 36/37 Paul went into the areas of Syria and Cilicia (Gal. 1:21). Syria most likely means the area around Antioch on the Orontes, and Cilicia the environs of Tarsus.[46] Paul probably worked at first in the area of Tarsus and Cilicia. We cannot determine the character of this mission either from Paul's own later letters or from Acts. Was Paul alone? How long did he stay in Cilicia before transferring his work to Antioch? Was his mission in Cilicia fruitful, or was it lack of success that caused him after a few years to continue his work in Antioch? No persuasive answers to these questions are available; one can only speculate. Tarsus was not only Paul's hometown; this major city of Cilicia also was home to a large Jewish community, and so it presented itself as a great missionary opportunity. The reference to Christian congregations in Cilicia in Acts 15:23, 41 could be a reflection of Paul's earlier mission in and around Tarsus. This missionary work of about six years[47] had probably not been overly successful, for about 42 CE Paul joined the Antioch mission as "junior partner" of Barnabas.

5.4 Paul as Missionary of the Antioch Church

Syrian Antioch on the Orontes was the third largest city of the Roman Empire,[48] at the end of the first century CE having a population of three hundred thousand to six hundred thousand.[49] Josephus presupposes that there was a very large Jewish community in Antioch that probably included about twenty

---

46. Compare Gal. 1:21 with Acts 9:29–30, according to which Paul was sent to Tarsus to protect him from the Jerusalem Jews. Moreover, Gal. 1:23 shows that Paul did not consider Judea a part of Syria and thus that he did not think of Syria in terms of the Roman province. Cf. Betz, *Galatians*, 157. On this phase of the Pauline mission, cf. also Riesner, *Paul's Early Period*, 264–72.

47. The length of this mission is difficult to calculate; as arguments for the duration mentioned above, we may mention the following: (1) With the expression "About that time" in Acts 12:1a, Luke makes a temporal connection between the beginning of the work of Barnabas and Paul in Antioch and the persecution in Jerusalem by Agrippa I (cf. Acts 12:1b-17). This persecution probably occurred in 42 CE (Cf. Riesner, *Paul's Early Period*, 117–23). (2) The famine mentioned in Acts 11:28 and the support given by the Antioch Christians to Jerusalem (Acts 11:29) fall in the period between 42 and 44 CE (cf. Riesner, ibid., 125–36). Somewhat different are Hengel and Schwemer, *Between Damascus and Antioch*, 171–78, who calculate Paul's stay in Cilicia as lasting three or four years (36/37–39/40 CE), during which time he had an independent and successful mission before joining the Antioch project, within which he worked nine or ten years (ca. 39/40–48/49).

48. Cf. Josephus, *J.W.* 3.29, where Antioch is described as "the capital of Syria, and a city which, for extent and opulence, unquestionably ranks third among the cities of the Roman world" [translator's note: after Rome and Alexandria]. On Antioch, cf. the recent study of F. Kolb, "Antiochia in der frühen Kaiserzeit," in *Geschichte–Tradition–Reflexion: Festschrift für Martin Hengel zum 70. Geburtstag* (ed. Hubert Cancik et al.; Tübingen: Mohr Siebeck, 1996), 97–118.

49. Cf. Fred W. Norris, "Antiochien I," *TRE* 3:99.

or thirty thousand persons (cf. *J. W.* 7.43–45). Antioch presented optimum conditions for the early Christian mission, for here numerous Greeks were already positively inclined toward the Jewish faith.[50] The proselyte Nicholas, a member of the group associated with Stephen, came from Antioch (Acts 6:5), and according to Acts 11:19, the church in Antioch was founded by Christians who had been forced to leave Jerusalem by persecution of this group. In Antioch, Hellenistic Jewish Christians from Cyprus and Cyrene made the transition to a successful preaching mission among the Greek population (Acts 11:20).[51] It was thus at Antioch that the decisive epoch of early Christianity began: the programmatic proclamation of the gospel to Gentiles as well as Jews. As the story is told in Acts, Barnabas and Paul did not themselves belong to the Antioch church from its beginnings but first began their work there after the Gentile mission had been launched (cf. Acts 11:22, 25). Clearly, Paul first came in contact with the Jerusalem Hellenists in Antioch.[52] The mission of the Antioch church among Jews and especially among Gentiles must have been successful, for, according to Acts 11:26, it was in Antioch that the term Χριστιανοί (Christians) was first applied to the followers of the new teaching, now predominantly Gentile. Ignatius confirms that this designation originated in Antioch, assuming without question that it is the normal term for followers of Christ.[53] Early in the 40s Christians were thus perceived for the first time to be a distinct group alongside Jews and Gentiles. From the Gentile perspective, they were a non-Jewish movement, and they must have attained a recognizable theological profile and their own organizational structure.[54] Formally, Χριστιανοί is a Latin term that has been given a Greek imprint,[55] which suggests that the Roman provincial administration already had an interest in the new movement.[56]

---

50. Cf. Josephus, *J. W.* 7.45: The Jews "were constantly attracting to their religious ceremonies multitudes of Greeks, and these they had in some measure incorporated with themselves." On Antioch, cf. also Hengel and Schwemer, *Between Damascus and Antioch*, 178–203.

51. The fact that this report does not correspond to Luke's own view speaks for its historicity; Luke understands Paul and Barnabas to have been the initiators of the Christian mission on Cyprus (cf. Acts 13:4; 15:39). It was not Peter (cf. 10:1–11:18) who instigated the decisive epoch in the history of early Christianity but those unknown Christian missionaries of 11:19–30. For analysis of this text, cf. Weiser, *Apostelgeschichte*, 1:273–80. This, of course, does not mean that before Antioch there had been no preaching to Greek-speaking non-Jews. The mission in Samaria, Damascus, Arabia, and Cilicia certainly included this group; cf. Hengel and Schwemer, *Between Damascus and Antioch*, 201.

52. Julius Wellhausen, *Kritische Analyse der Apostelgeschichte* (Berlin: Weidmann, 1914), 21.

53. Cf. Ign. *Eph.* 11.2; *Magn.* 4; *Rom.* 3.2; *Pol.* 7.3.

54. Adolf von Harnack, *The Mission and Expansion of Christianity in the First Three Centuries* (trans. James Moffatt; 2nd ed.; New York: Putnam, 1908), 411–12.

55. Friedrich Blass and A. Debrunner, *A Greek Grammar of the New Testament and Other Early Christian Literature* (trans. Robert W. Funk; Chicago: University of Chicago Press, 1961), 14, 23–24.

56. A. Mehl, "Sprachen im Kontakt, Sprachen im Wandel: Griechisch/Latein und antike Geschichte," in *Zur Evolution von Kommunikation und Sprache—Ausdruck, Mittelung, Darstellung* (ed. M. Liedtke; Graz: Austria Medien Service, 1998), 198, who sees an official action reflected in the creation of this term, "primarily for internal official use."

Moreover, the word formation indicates that, for outsiders in Antioch, the title Χριστός (Christ, anointed one) had already become a proper name.

Why did Christian preaching have such success in Antioch? For the first time the gospel was widely proclaimed in a major city where there were numerous sympathizers for the Jewish faith and where the connection with the synagogue was probably not so close as in Palestine. There occurred the formation of house churches in which the emphasis was on the new message, not on the old religion from which it derived. The previous religious, social, and national distinctions lost some of their importance, and a new spiritual community was formed that from the outside appeared to be an independent group and a new religion. Giving up ties with the synagogue enhanced the numbers and influence of Gentile Christians,[57] and so the later disputes about the function of the Torah for Gentile Christians were unavoidable consequences.

In Acts 13:1 Barnabas and Paul appear together in a list of names taken from the tradition of the Antioch church: "In the church at Antioch there were prophets and teachers: Barnabas, Simeon called Niger, Lucius of Cyrene, Manaen (who had been brought up with Herod the tetrarch), and Saul." The placing of Barnabas at the head of the list and Paul (Saul) at the end is probably Luke's editorial work, emphasizing in this way the two main actors in the following story.[58] The church at Antioch had obviously not yet developed fixed official roles for its leaders. Those who had previously been itinerant missionaries were now at work in this location, but they were prepared at any time to reactivate their itinerant mission activity (cf. Acts 13:2–3). The functions of prophets and teachers are not separated and are exercised by the same persons. Originally, in the power of the Spirit, the prophets had declared the will of the exalted Lord for the current situation whereas teachers were responsible for handing on and interpreting the tradition, but in practice these were not kept separate. Prophets and teachers were proclaimers of the word, givers of instruction, and leaders of the worship services. One must in fact include "apostles" (in the sense of "missionaries") in this group, for in Acts 14:4, 14 the same group is referred to as "apostles." Paul himself considered the term "apostle" very important (cf. 1 Cor. 9:1), and may have adopted this title for himself within the context of his work in Antioch.

Barnabas was one of the leading personalities in the history of the early Christian mission. The personal legend of Acts 4:36–37 and the list in Acts 13:1 indicate his special importance (also in relation to Paul); in Gal. 2:1, 9 he appears in the discussion at the apostolic council as a spokesperson with a status equal to Paul's. Paul fully acknowledged and accepted Barnabas (cf. 1 Cor. 9:6) but withstood him at the incident in Antioch. We can perceive Barnabas's

---

57. Cf. Hengel and Schwemer, *Between Damascus and Antioch*, 200–204.
58. Cf. Lüdemann, *Traditions in Acts*, 146.

theological views only indirectly, but alongside Paul he was certainly an open advocate of a Gentile mission overtly free from the law.[59]

The Significance of Antioch

The outstanding place held by Antioch in the history of early Christian theology has always been the occasion for inferring far-reaching historical and theological conclusions. For the history-of-religions school, Antioch not only provided the missing link between the earliest Jerusalem church and Paul but also was the birthplace of Christianity as a syncretistic religion. Here the radical development took place that was so important for the history of early Christianity, where, "out of the future Messiah Jesus, the present cult-hero as Kyrios of his community came into being."[60] On Hellenistic soil the church came in contact with the mystery cults and Gnosticism, movements that had a lasting affect on the young congregations.[61] Bultmann's interpretation of Paul represents the high point of this approach:

> The historical position of Paul may be stated as follows: Standing within the frame of Hellenistic Christianity he raised the theological motifs that were at work in the proclamation of the Hellenistic Church to the clarity of theological thinking; he called to attention the problems latent in the Hellenistic proclamation and brought them to a decision; and thus—so far as our sources permit an opinion on the matter—became the founder of Christian theology.[62]

As the connections of Pauline theology to Gnosticism and the mystery cults became less and less certain,[63] the flow of this imposing historical outline also became less and less distinct. There is no clear evidence that Paul's theology was related to the thought world of Gnosticism. Contacts between ideas from the mystery cults and Pauline theology are found only in Rom. 6:3–4, and there is no indication that these originated in Antioch.

J. Becker makes Antioch the native soil of Pauline theology in a different sense: Not only had Paul been taught here the fundamentals of Christian faith; all the important distinctive views of Pauline theology had already been

59. On Barnabas, cf. esp. Bernd Kollmann, *Joseph Barnabas: Leben und Wirkungsgeschichte* (SBS 175; Stuttgart: Katholisches Bibelwerk, 1998); Hengel and Schwemer, *Between Damascus and Antioch*, 211–20.

60. Wilhelm Bousset, *Kyrios Christos: A History of the Belief in Christ from the Beginnings of Christianity to Irenaeus* (trans. John E. Steely; Nashville: Abingdon, 1970), 136.

61. Johannes Weiss, *Earliest Christianity: A History of the Period A.D. 30–150* (trans. Frederick C. Grant; 2 vols.; New York: Harper, 1959), 1:171–77.

62. Bultmann, *Theology of the New Testament*, 1:187.

63. Martin Hengel, "Die Ursprünge der Gnosis und das Urchristentum," in *Evangelium, Schriftauslegung, Kirche: Festschrift für Peter Stuhlmacher zum 65. Geburtstag* (ed. Otfried Hofius et al.; Göttingen: Vandenhoeck & Ruprecht, 1997), 190–223.

developed in his Antioch period. "Thus on the whole we can say that what Paul used later from the old tradition essentially came from the knowledge of the Antiochene community."[64] According to Becker, the Pauline message of freedom, the new being in Christ, the foundational significance of baptism and Spirit, as well as the universal statements of Pauline Christology and soteriology go back to the Antiochene theology.

> There is, however, one viewpoint that can substantiate the Antiochene contribution to the development of Christology: it is the viewpoint of universalization, which is typical in general for Antiochene theology and doubtless also influenced Christology in various respects, namely, in regard to the eschatological salvific function of the Son, the universal lordship in missions, the mediation of all creational reality, and the comprehensive salvific death of Jesus.[65]

In this understanding, Pauline theology is nothing more or less than an explication of the kerygma of the Antioch church. According to Becker, all the fundamental insights of Pauline thought had already been shaped in Antioch before Paul and thus cannot be regarded as indications of distinctive elements of Paul's own theology.[66] Klaus Berger goes a step further; for him, Antioch is the decisive junction of all important streams in early Christian theology.[67] Here is where the "Antioch theologies" were developed, among which Berger would include the four Gospels, the Pauline corpus, and the Petrine and Johannine streams, including the Apocalypse. For Berger, Antioch was *the* early Christian metropolis, and it was within its vicinity and realm of influence that all the essential theological developments of early Christianity took place.

We cannot verify these far-ranging historical and theological conclusions by the texts.[68] (1) The conduct of Barnabas and other Jewish Christians at the Antioch incident (cf. Gal. 2:13) shows that a universalistic perspective by no

---

64. Becker, *Paul*, 104.

65. Ibid., 111.

66. Ibid., 102–12. A comparable argument is found, e.g., in Rau, *Von Jesus zu Paulus*, 114, who asks to what extent Paul "during his work in Antioch moved beyond the horizon of the theology prevalent there. In the present situation, I consider it a reasonable working hypothesis that this was possibly only minimally the case." Rau speaks of an "Antiochene substructure of Pauline thought" (ibid.). Here in fact Rau finds Pauline theology as a whole to be based on the intellectual achievements of the pre-Pauline churches. He thereby underestimates Paul's creativity and how necessary it was for him to give new answers to historical challenges. A comprehensive catalogue of the Pauline texts various scholars have attributed to Antioch can be found in Anton Dauer, *Paulus und die christliche Gemeinde im syrischen Antiochia: Kritische Bestandsaufnahme der modernen Forschung mit einigen weiterführenden Überlegungen* (Weinheim: Beltz Athenäum, 1996), 77–119.

67. Cf. Berger, *Theologiegeschichte*, 177ff.

68. For a critique of the widespread "pan-Antiochism" in scholarly literature, see also Hengel and Schwemer, *Between Damascus and Antioch*, 286–91.

means characterized in toto the Antioch church.[69] (2) According to Acts 11:26, Barnabas and Paul worked together only one year in Antioch itself,[70] and Luke portrays them as teachers of the Antioch church. Luke minimizes the direct residence of Paul in Antioch, which, in comparison with the residence of the apostle in Corinth (Acts 18:4, a year and a half) and Ephesus (Acts 19:10, over two years), must be regarded as entirely normal. Paul did return to Antioch at the conclusion of his first missionary tour (cf. Acts 14:28), but again, in comparison with the stations of his later missionary journeys, this is his normal procedure. (3) Paul mentions Antioch only in Gal. 2:11, in connection with the time between his first and second visits to Jerusalem, and so he is in fact entirely silent about the period of his initial work at Antioch.[71] (4) No passage in Paul's letters indicates where he received the traditions he adopted. Antioch is one possible source among several. Moreover, that the pre-Pauline traditions themselves reflect no particularly consistent background clearly speaks against their all being assigned almost exclusively to one location. (5) How can we distinguish the Antiochene theology from Paul's own thought when both must be constructed from Paul's own letters? The only specific item that can be attributed to the Antioch church is the transition to the Gentile mission. Acts does not discuss which theological views in particular were associated with this move. In no passage in his letters does Paul distinguish between generally accepted views that he could have received in Antioch and his own opinion.[72] (6) The interpretation of Pauline theology as the explication of the Antiochene kerygma represents a leveling-down of the independent theological thinking of the apostle himself.[73]

There can be no doubt about the special place of the Antioch church in the history of early Christian theology, just as its influence on Paul is unquestioned. Antioch was a significant station in the course of Paul's life. At the same time, we must guard against "allowing [Antioch] to become a 'holding tank' for our ignorance about early Christian connections."[74] Pauline theology does present itself as oriented to tradition, but it may never be reduced and simplified to the mere repetition of materials provided to Paul by others.

69. Thomas Söding, "Der Erste Thessalonicherbrief und die frühe paulinische Evangeliumsverkündigung: Zur Frage einer Entwicklung der paulinischen Theologie," *BZ* 35 (1991): 202–3.

70. Cf. Weiss, *Earliest Christianity*, 204; Lüdemann, *Traditions in Acts*, 136.

71. Dauer, *Paulus und die christliche Gemeinde*, 127, gives the Antioch incident as the reason, since Paul is supposed to have been traumatized by it and thus suppressed the memory of his time in Antioch.

72. Andreas Wechsler, *Geschichtsbild und Apostelstreit: Eine forschungsgeschichtliche und exegetische Studie über den antiochenischen Zwischenfall (Gal. 2, 11–14)* (BZNW 62; Berlin: de Gruyter, 1991), 306 n. 61.

73. Becker, *Paul*, 104, attempts to respond to this objection: "The Gentile-Christian thinking in Antioch is to a considerable extent determined by Paul himself. His leading role in the church is beyond question. In the end he is more consistently Gentile Christian than Antioch itself."

74. Wechsler, *Geschichtsbild und Apostelstreit*, 266.

The First Missionary Journey

At the center of the Antioch phase of Paul's work stands the first missionary journey (ca. 45–47 CE), the account of which in Acts 13:1–14:28 presents numerous problems.[75] Whereas in Gal. 1:21 Paul speaks of missionary activity in the regions of Syria and Cilicia before the apostolic council, Luke reports mission work on Cyprus and in the Asia Minor districts of Pamphylia, Pisidia, and Lycaonia. Luke portrays the mission on Cyprus in Acts 13:4–12 in a way that corresponds to his own interests.[76] Luke here reworks individual units of tradition into a dramatic event that climaxes with the conversion of the proconsul Sergius Paulus. After the conversion of the Roman military officer Cornelius in Acts 10, there follows the account of how even a Roman proconsul became a Christian. It is hardly an accident that Paul's first convert bears the same name by which he had become known in the story of the early Christian mission.[77] Luke here introduces the Roman name of the apostle because the apostle's Gentile mission has now begun. Cyprus was connected in the tradition with the name of Barnabas, who came from there (cf. Acts 4:36), and according to Acts 15:39, he and John Mark headed back to Cyprus after his separation from Paul. On this basis, Luke could have created the common mission of Barnabas, Paul, and John Mark on Cyprus.[78] In favor of this view are not only the Lukan interests that come to expression in the story but the factual difficulties in the present text.[79]

Paul's own letters do not directly confirm the trip of Barnabas and Paul to Perga, Antioch in Pisidia, and Iconium, but it is still likely that Barnabas and Paul worked in this area as missionaries commissioned by the Antioch church. Luke represents Paul here as an apostle of the Antioch church who is subordinated to Barnabas (cf. Acts 14:4, 12, 14). On the other hand, Paul's speech in Antioch of Pisidia is a product of Lukan redaction; within the structure of Luke's two-volume work, it corresponds to Jesus' inaugural sermon in Nazareth (Luke 4:16–30).[80] So also the portrayal of the missionary work of Barnabas and

75. Evidence for this chronology is that, in Luke's presentation, the death of Agrippa I in 44 CE (cf. Acts 12:18–23) and the apostolic council in the spring of 48 CE form the fixed points between which the first missionary journey took place.

76. For analysis, cf. Lüdemann, *Traditions in Acts*, 148–51.

77. Cf. the introduction of Peter's name in Luke 6:14; also to be noted is the parallel to the name change Bar-Jesus/Elymas (Acts 13:6, 8).

78. Riesner, *Paul's Early Period*, 272–73, considers Acts 13:4–12 historically reliable.

79. The essential points are found in Lüdemann, *Traditions in Acts*, 149: Instead of the expected clash between Paul and the magician Bar-Jesus, a new character is introduced with Sergius Paulus. In Acts 13:8 the magician is suddenly called Elymas, without specifically indicating that this is the same as Bar-Jesus. The punitive miracle results in the faith of the proconsul. As in Acts 8, Luke is concerned to point out the superiority of Christianity to competing religious groups.

80. Cf. Walter Radl, *Paulus und Jesus im Lukanischen Doppelwerk: Untersuchungen zu Parallelmotiven im Lukasevangelium und in der Apostelgeschichte* (EHS, Reihe 23, Theologie 49; Frankfurt: Lang, 1975), 82–100.

Paul in Iconium (Acts 14:1–7) and Lystra (Acts 14:8–20) essentially goes back to Luke in its present form, but also contains old tradition. Whereas previously the Christian message had been addressed to Jews and God-fearers (cf. Acts 13:43, 50; 14:1), now Barnabas and Paul turn for the first time to Gentiles (cf. Acts 13:11–13). Here the mission strategy of Paul and Barnabas is reflected, in which Jews and God-fearers were first evangelized but then Gentiles were very early included. In Acts 14:5 Luke reports the reaction to the apostles' preaching in summary form, as their abuse and stoning by both Jews and Gentiles. On the other hand, Acts 14:19–20a contains old tradition about Paul.[81] The verses can be abstracted from their context, and Paul himself refers to a stoning in 2 Cor. 11:25 (cf. also 2 Tim. 3:11). Probably Paul suffered this life-threatening punishment in Lystra. It is no longer clear whether Jews or Gentiles were responsible. It was probably the spontaneous act of a lynch mob, in which the victim was pelted with stones until he collapsed.

Is this account "history or story"? This often-posed alternative is not helpful for the narrative in Acts 13:1–14:28. In this section Luke is reworking numerous older traditions while at the same time narrating this journey of the apostle Paul within the framework of a theological concept.[82] He frames the report by the term ἔργον (work, assignment; Acts 13:2; 14:26), which signals the theological significance of the event: set apart by the Holy Spirit, Barnabas and Paul accomplish the work assigned to them by God and made possible by God's help, namely, to open the door of faith to the Gentiles. This gives the material grounds for resolving the problem of the Gentile mission that follows in Acts 15:1–35. Whereas the Gentile mission had been previously accepted with amazement (cf. Acts 10:1–11:18), there now follows in Luke's presentation an official agreement between the original Jerusalem church and Paul, so that from Acts 15:36 to the end of the book the reader's view rests only on the real hero of Acts: Paul.

81. For the evidence, cf. Lüdemann, *Traditions in Acts*, 163–64.
82. Burfeind, "Paulus *muß* nach Rom," 78.

6

The Apostolic Council
and the Incident at Antioch

The Problems Remain Unresolved

———————————

Some events promise clarification and resolution but in fact are only the occasion for new conflicts. Agreements can be understood differently by the parties involved; when viewed in a later perspective, many things do not look the same as they originally did.

6.1 The Apostolic Council

After completing their mission in Syria and parts of Asia Minor, Barnabas and Paul returned to Antioch.[1] Here "certain individuals" came down from Judea who "were teaching the brothers, 'Unless you are circumcised according to the custom of Moses, you cannot be saved'" (Acts 15:1). This resulted in a fierce debate between the strict Jewish Christians on the one side and Barnabas and Paul on the other. The Antioch congregation then decided to send

1. On the problems of Acts 14:20b–28, cf. Lüdemann, *Traditions in Acts*, 163.

Paul, Barnabas, and some other coworkers to Jerusalem to resolve the issue in discussion with the earliest church (cf. Acts 15:2; Gal. 2:1). Paul himself in Gal. 2:2a gives a somewhat different picture of the concrete occasion of the Jerusalem trip: "I went up in response to a revelation."[2] He thus no longer represents his presence at the apostolic council within the framework of the mission program of the Antioch church. One can suppose that it is the Lukan view of history that causes Luke to place the connection of Barnabas and Paul to the Antioch church in the foreground at the apostolic council. On the other hand, Paul himself also formulates his own portrayal tendentiously, for he wants to emphasize his independence from Jerusalem and the other churches. Furthermore, he discloses his own understanding of why he participated in the apostolic council: μή πως εἰς κενὸν τρέχω ἢ ἔδραμον (in order to make sure that I was not running, or had not run, in vain, Gal. 2:2). Torah-observant Jewish Christians had intervened in the congregations founded by the apostle, took note of their freedom (from the Torah), and come to the apostolic council to insist that Gentile Christians be circumcised (Gal. 2:4–5).[3] Paul had been conducting a mission to the Gentiles in which circumcision was not required to become Christians (which strict Jewish Christians then saw as in fact Torah-free).[4] Paul was obviously afraid that the agitation of these opponents would influence the Jerusalem leaders to reject his mission and thus cause it to be nullified. This would mean that his apostolic commission to found churches could not be carried out (cf. 1 Thess. 2:19; 1 Cor. 9:15–18:23; 2 Cor. 1:14). Even more drastic: the apostle saw that if he were to fail in the task to which he alone had been commissioned, his glory on the day of Christ, his eschatological salvation, was in danger (cf. Phil. 2:16).[5]

The apostolic council is also indirectly a result of significant changes in the history of the early Jerusalem church. In the circumstances related to Agrippa I's persecution in 42 CE, James the son of Zebedee was killed (Acts 12:2) and Peter gave up the leadership of the Jerusalem church and left the city (Acts 12:17). It

2. Paul here adopts an ancient mode of argument; cf. Xenophon, *Anab.* 3.1.5–7; Philo, *Moses* 1.268.

3. With Jürgen Wehnert, *Die Reinheit des "christlichen Gottesvolkes" aus Juden und Heiden: Studien zum historischen und theologischen Hintergrund des sogenannten Aposteldekrets* (FRLANT 173; Göttingen: Vandenhoeck & Ruprecht, 1997), 115–16, I refer Gal. 2:4–5 to the events in the Pauline/Antiochene churches and to the current situation as it is being discussed in Jerusalem.

4. Paul had never conducted a Gentile mission that was in principal "free from the law," for the central ethical contents of the Torah (e.g., the Decalogue) were, of course, also valid for Gentile Christians. Abandoning the requirement of circumcision for Gentile Christians while at the same time affirming that they belonged to the elect people of God turned out in practice to be something like a mission advocating "freedom from the law," for the contents of the Pauline ethic could be accepted and integrated into their own cultural background without difficulty, without any basis in the Old Testament–Jewish law.

5. Cf. Traugott Holtz, "Die Bedeutung des Apostelkonzils für Paulus," in *Geschichte und Theologie des Urchristentums: Gesammelte Aufsätze* (WUNT 57; Tübingen: Mohr Siebeck, 1991), 149–50.

is clear that James the Lord's brother (cf. Mark 6:3) took over Peter's position, as indicated by a comparison of Gal. 1:18–19 with Gal. 2:9 and 1 Cor. 15:5 with 1 Cor. 15:7 and by the last words of Peter in Acts 12:17b ("Tell this to James and to the [Jerusalem] believers") and the picture of the church in Acts 15:13; 21:18.[6] Although Peter himself probably had a liberal stance on the question of accepting uncircumcised Gentiles into the new movement (cf. Acts 10:34–48; Gal. 2:11–12) and was later a sympathetic participant in the Gentile mission (cf. 1 Cor. 1:12; 9:5), we must see James and his group as representatives of a strict Jewish Christianity (cf. Gal. 2:12a) that consciously understood itself as a part of Judaism and considered Torah observance a requirement for acceptance into the new movement.[7] James adopted this position not only as a political necessity but as a matter of conviction.[8] He rejected table fellowship between Jewish Christians and Gentile Christians (Gal. 2:12a) and was obviously highly respected by the Pharisees. Josephus reports that after the martyrdom of James in the year 62 CE, the Pharisees bitterly demanded the deposition of Ananus, the high priest who was responsible for James's death.[9] Very likely those who advocated the circumcision of Gentile Christians felt that their demand was strongly supported by the theological position of James.

The Issue

The issue at the apostolic council is clear: which criteria must be fulfilled in order to belong to the elect church of God and at the same time maintain continuity with the people of God of the first covenant?[10] Should circumcision, as the sign of God's covenant (cf. Gen. 17:11) and thus of membership in the elect people of God, also be a general requirement for Gentile Christians?[11] Must a Gentile who wants to become a Christian first become a Jew? Since,

---

6. Cf. Gerd Lüdemann, *Opposition to Paul in Jewish Christianity* (trans. M. Eugene Boring; Minneapolis: Fortress, 1989), 44–52.

7. Cf. also Kraus, *Zwischen Jerusalem und Antiochia*, 134–39.

8. In *Gospel of Thomas* 12 he appears as "James the Just [Righteous]" (cf. also Eusebius, *Hist. eccl.* 2.1.3 and passim; on the analysis of the James tradition, cf. Martin Hengel, "Jakobus, der Herrenbruder—der erste 'Papst'?" in *Paulus und Jakobus* (WUNT 141; Kleine Schriften 3; Tübingen: Mohr Siebeck, 2002), 549–82; and Wilhelm Pratscher, *Der Herrenbruder Jakobus und die Jakobustradition* (FRLANT 139; Göttingen: Vandenhoeck & Ruprecht, 1987).

9. Cf. Josephus, *Ant.* 20.199–203. On the analysis of the texts, cf. Lüdemann, *Opposition to Paul*, 62–63.

10. The Pauline terminology is noticeable, for the apostle himself speaks consistently of the ἐκκλησία (τοῦ) θεοῦ (church of God; cf., e.g., 1 Thess. 2:14; 1 Cor. 1:2; 10:32; 11:22; 15:9; 2 Cor. 1:1; Gal. 1:13), referring to the "people of God" (λαός, in a salvation-historical sense) only in Old Testament citations (cf. 1 Cor. 10:7; Rom. 9:25–26; 10:21; 11:1–2; 15:10) even though the relation of Christian believers to Israel is a central theme of his theology. On the issue as a whole, see below, section 21.1 ("Primary Vocabulary and Foundational Metaphors of Pauline Ecclesiology").

11. Cf. Otto Betz, "Beschneidung II," *TRE* 5:716–22.

from the Jewish perspective, a person became a proselyte and thus a member of the elect people of God only by circumcision and ritual immersion, it seemed clear from the strict Jewish Christian point of view that the new status among the redeemed people of God came only by baptism in the name of Jesus Christ and by circumcision.[12] The problem that occupied the apostolic council (and the conflict at Antioch) thus emerged in a time when the definition of what Christianity required on the ritual and social level had not been fully decided. Neither the Christian identity markers nor the lifestyle that this implied had yet been clarified. Could Gentile Christian churches be recognized as belonging to the same church as Jewish Christians, who for the most part still participated in the life of the synagogue? Previous Jewish self-understanding had considered it fundamental that one's national-cultural community and one's religious community were one and the same—must this now be given up? Does maintaining the codes of holiness and ritual purity matter? How do believers in Jesus come to participate in the people of God, and how do the promises of God's covenant with Israel come to apply to them? To what extent should the markers of Jewish identity such as circumcision, table fellowship only with one's own people, and Sabbath observance also apply to the emerging Gentile churches? Does the fundamental change of status that has already occurred when one professes Christian faith entail additional changes in one's status that must be worked out? Are baptism *and* circumcision obligatory initiation rites for all believers in Christ, or does baptism alone make possible full acceptance into the people of God? The successful mission work of the Antioch church generated these issues,[13] especially the mission of Barnabas and Paul among the Gentiles (cf. Gal. 2:2c). But the Gentile mission of the Antioch church was not the only one in early Christianity, as shown by the founding of the Roman church and the appearance of Apollos of Alexandria in Corinth (cf. 1 Cor. 3:4ff.; Acts 18:24–28).

The difficulty of finding a solution to this problem was intensified by the fact that the Torah contains no clear statements about Jews (or Jewish Christians) and Gentiles (or Gentile Christians) living together *outside the land of Israel.* The young churches composed of Jewish and Gentile Christians were an entity sui generis; the Torah had not foreseen such a situation and made no provisions for it.[14] As instruction for Israel, the Torah had no validity for

12. The possibility of becoming a full member of the Jewish community without circumcision probably never existed; cf. the analysis of the texts in Wolfgang Kraus, *Das Volk Gottes: Zur Grundlegung der Ekklesiologie bei Paulus* (WUNT 85; Tübingen: Mohr Siebeck, 1996), 96–107.

13. How long this missionary work had already been going on and why it did not result in conflicts before are questions that can no longer be answered. Holtz, "Apostelkonzils," 159ff., supposes that the practice of accepting Gentiles without circumcision became prevalent in Antioch only shortly before the apostolic council. Paul, too, made a radical turn on this issue. But this view cannot be confirmed by either Acts or Paul's letters.

14. In the Old Testament and ancient Jewish literature, one finds only the idea that the Gentiles, too, will glorify or worship Yahweh (cf. Isa. 19:16–25; Mal. 1:11; Zeph. 2:11; 3:9–10; *L.A.B.* 11.1–2; *Sib. Or.* 3.716–20; Tob. 14:6–7).

Gentiles (cf. Exod. 34:10–17; Lev. 20:2–7). No text in it calls for Gentiles to keep the command of circumcision or Sabbath, since it was acknowledged that Yahweh had assigned the gods of other peoples to them (cf. Deut. 4:19). The solution attempted by the apostolic decree regulated the relations between Jewish Christians and Gentile Christians in a manner analogous to those between Israel and foreigners *living in the land,* but this could not be a permanent solution. The commands regarding resident aliens (cf. Lev. 17–18, and esp. Exod. 12:43–49; 20:10; 23:12; Lev. 16:29; 20:2; 22:18–20; 24:10–22; Num. 9:14; 15:30; 19:1–11) do not facilitate their living together on an equal basis but throughout have an overtone of subordination.

What Happened at the Council?

We can reconstruct the basic outline of the course of events at the apostolic council from Acts 15:1–34 and Gal. 2:1–10,[15] even though the two reports have variations in details: (1) Paul and Barnabas came to Jerusalem as authorized delegates of the Antioch church (Acts 15:2, 4; Gal. 2:1, 9). (2) The agenda of the conference was the fundamental justification for the Gentile mission, and the practical procedures for carrying it out (Acts 15:12/Gal. 2:2, 9). (3) At the conference one group insisted on the circumcision of Gentile converts (Gal. 2:4–5, "false brethren"; Acts 15:5, Christian Pharisees). (4) The conference proceeded on two levels: a plenary meeting of the whole church (Acts 15:12/Gal. 2:2a) and discussions within a smaller circle (Acts 15:6, apostles and elders; Gal. 2:9, the "pillars"). Paul's account of the council reflects this division of responsibilities, for Gal. 2:3–5 reports the events of the plenary session and Gal. 2:6–10 refers to the agreement with the leadership of the Jerusalem church. (5) According to both reports, the council recognized the Gentile mission that did not require circumcision (Acts 15:10–12, 19/Gal. 2:9). The Lukan presentation does deviate sharply from Paul's own account. According to Luke, the Jerusalem church bound its basic approval of the Gentile mission to the condition that Gentiles observe a minimum of ritual prescriptions (Acts 15:19–21, 28–29; 21:25)—abstinence from idol worship, meat from animals that have been strangled, blood, and sexual immorality. These four abstinence prescriptions are oriented to the prescriptions for Jews and resident aliens in Lev. 17–18 and were understood as a model for how Jewish Christians and Gentile Christians could participate together in the same congregations.[16] Luke also

15. A list of the similarities and differences between Gal. 2:1–10 and Acts 15 is found in Mussner, *Galaterbrief,* 128–32, and in Lüdemann, *Traditions in Acts,* 171–72.

16. Cf. Lev. 17:10–14; 18:6–18, 26 for these minimal ritual requirements of the "Holiness Code" (Lev. 17–26) for "foreigners" living in the land. For the background of the apostolic decree in tradition history, cf. Wehnert, *Hintergrund des sogenannten Aposteldekrets,* 235: "The individual analyses have shown that the abstinence prescriptions of the apostolic decree can be derived from the terminology of the targums on Lev. 17–18, in particular from a tradition close to that of Pseudo-Jonathan."

fails to mention the dispute about the Gentile Christian Titus (Gal. 2:3) and postpones the agreement about the collection (Gal. 2:10; cf. Acts 11:27–30). Furthermore, in Luke's portrayal of the apostolic council, Paul plays only a minor role, for it is Peter (Acts 15:7–11) and James (Acts 15:13–21) who make the real decisions.

The matter is portrayed differently in Gal. 2:1–10, where the real decision takes place in the discussion between Paul on the one side and James, Peter, and John on the other. Whereas Acts 15:5ff. recounts a discursive explanation of the problem, Paul's own account contains no indication that the content of his gospel received by revelation was a matter for debate. He emphasizes, rather, that the Jerusalem authorities acknowledged his gospel qualitatively, in terms of a theology of revelation (καὶ γνόντες τὴν χάριν τὴν δοθεῖσάν μοι [recognizing the grace that had been given to me], Gal. 2:9),[17] so that the basis of the accord they sought was given in a revelation to Paul. According to Paul, this agreement included an ethnographic division of the world mission: "agreeing that we should go to the Gentiles and they to the circumcised" (Gal. 2:9c). But did this arrangement in fact result in the unity of the people of God?

The Gospel of Uncircumcision and the Gospel of Circumcision

Are the Pauline εὐαγγέλιον τῆς ἀκροβυστίας (gospel of uncircumcision) and the Petrine εὐαγγέλιον τῆς περιτομῆς (gospel of circumcision) actually congruent in terms of their content? On the basis of Gal. 2:8–9c (εἰς τὰ ἔθνη . . . εἰς τὴν περιτομήν [to the Gentiles . . . to the circumcised]), the genitive case of τῆς ἀκροβυστίας and τῆς περιτομῆς are to be understood as "the gospel for the uncircumcised . . . the gospel for the circumcised." At first the contents of these two formulations seem to manifest great agreement: both sides certainly understand the nucleus of the gospel as it is transmitted in, for example, 1 Cor. 15:3b–5: "that Christ died for our sins in accordance with the scriptures, and that he was buried, and that he was raised on the third day in accordance with the scriptures, and that he appeared to Cephas, then to the twelve." Furthermore, the typical marks of Jewish identity, such as monotheism and numerous ethical admonitions, were not disputed. After all, everyone concerned presupposed that salvation for those who believed in Jesus was attained only in continuity with Israel.

At the same time, the difference between these two formulae may not be passed over too lightly, for Paul usually speaks of the "gospel of Christ" (on εὐαγγέλιον τοῦ Χριστοῦ, cf. Gal. 1:7 and also 1:6, 11, 12) or the "gospel of

---

17. Burkhard Jürgens, *Zweierlei Anfang: Kommunikative Konstruktionen heidenchristlicher Identität in Gal 2 und Apg 15* (Berlin: Philo, 1999), 214–15.

God" (εὐαγγέλιον θεοῦ).[18] These two formulae probably reflect the wording to which those engaged in the apostolic council had agreed.[19] Distinctive details in language and content point to the traditional character of Gal. 2:7–8: (1) only here do we have "*Peter* and *Paul*" as a contrasting pair; in Gal. 2:9 Paul returns to his normal usage of the name Cephas; (2) the terms εὐαγγέλιον τῆς ἀκροβυστίας and εὐαγγέλιον τῆς περιτομῆς appear only in Gal. 2:7 in Paul, and they are not found elsewhere in the whole literature of antiquity; and (3) stylistically, Gal. 2:7–8 is a parenthesis (ὅτι πεπίστευμαι . . . εἰς τὰ ἔθνη [that I had been entrusted . . . to the Gentiles]). The decisive difference in their content certainly lay in the way circumcision was evaluated in terms of salvation history and the extent of Torah observance to be inferred from this. Circumcision was by no means to be considered an adiaphoron (matter of indifference), for it was the entrance gate to the whole law (cf. Philo, *Spec. Laws* 1.1ff.). It documents Israel's special status among the nations, was a guarantee of this identity (cf. *Jub.* 15:25–34),[20] and at the same time separated Israel from all other peoples (cf. Josephus, *Ant* 1.192; Tacitus, *Hist.* 5.5.2). For strict Jewish Christians, there was a natural connection between faith in the Messiah Jesus of Nazareth, circumcision as a mark of belonging to God's chosen people, and, of course, observance of the Torah. For them, baptism did not take the place of circumcision, and salvation did not occur as something that transcended the law. The incident at Antioch, the position of Pharisees who had come to faith in Christ (Acts 15:1, 5), and the demand made in Galatia

---

18. On εὐαγγέλιον τοῦ Χριστοῦ, cf. further 1 Thess. 3:2; 1 Cor. 4:15; 9:12; 2 Cor. 2:12; 4:4; 9:13; 10:14; Rom. 1:9; Phil. 1:27. On εὐαγγέλιον τοῦ θεοῦ, cf. 1 Thess. 2:2, 8, 9; 2 Cor. 11:7; Rom. 1:1; 15:16, 19.

19. E. Barnikol recognized the un-Pauline character of Gal. 2:7–8 and regarded it as a post-Pauline interpolation; see E. Barnikol, *Der nichtpaulinische Ursprung des Parallelismus der Apostel Petrus und Paulus (Galater 2,7–8)* (Forschungen zur Entstehen des Urchristentums des Neuen Testaments und der Kirche 5; Kiel: Mülau, 1931); ET "The Non-Pauline Origin of the Parallelism of the Apostles Peter and Paul: Galatians 2:7–8" (trans. Darrel J. Doughty with B. Keith Brewer), *Journal for Higher Criticism* 5 (1988): 285–300. Barnikol was followed by Fischer and Schenke, *Einleitung*, 79–80; and see now William O. Walker Jr., "Galatians 2:7b–8 as a Non-Pauline Interpolation," *CBQ* 65, (2003): 568–87. Many exegetes, however, rightly regard the core element of Gal. 2:7–8 as pre-Pauline tradition; cf., e.g., Erich Dinkler, "Der Brief an die Galater," in *Signum crucis: Aufsätze zum Neuen Testament und zur christlichen Archäologie* (Tübingen: Mohr Siebeck, 1967), 278–82; Günter Klein, "Galater 2,6–9 und die Geschichte der Jerusalemer Urgemeinde," in *Rekonstruktion und Interpretation: Gesammelte Aufsätze zum Neuen Testament* (BEvT 50; Munich: Kaiser, 1969), 99–128, here 110–11; Oskar Cullmann, "Πέτρος," *TDNT* 6:100; Betz, *Galatians*, 186; Lüdemann, *Chronology*, 64–68, who, however, refers Gal. 2:7–8 to Paul's first Jerusalem visit. The order in the Pauline text speaks clearly against this; Peter as the first witness represents the Jewish mission whereas Paul represents the Gentile mission. Galatians 2:7–8 is considered to be a Pauline formulation by, e.g., Mussner, *Galaterbrief*, 115–18, and Joachim Rohde, *Der Brief des Paulus an die Galater* (THKNT 9; Berlin: Evangelische Verlagsanstalt, 1989), 88–89.

20. *Jub.* 15:25–26: "This law is for all the eternal generations. . . . And anyone who is born and whose own flesh is not circumcised on the eighth day is not from the sons of the covenant which the Lord made for Abraham" (trans. O. Wintermute, *OTP* 2:87).

and Philippi that Gentile Christians be circumcised point in this direction.[21] In contrast, Paul can point to the obvious work among the Gentiles by God who shows no partiality (Gal. 2:6).[22] By baptism and reception of the Spirit, Gentile Christians are already full and equal members in the people of God (cf. Gal. 3:1–5, 26–28; Acts 10:44–48), and so any additional legitimizing signs would put in question God's previous saving acts among the Gentiles. Thus James, Cephas, and John acknowledge the grace conferred on Paul (Gal. 2:9a), and for his part, he accepts both the responsibility for the collection (Gal. 2:10) and the "gospel to the circumcision." We can no longer determine with certainty whether the singular formulation in Gal. 2:7 was coined at the apostolic council or whether it goes back to Paul himself. The decisive factor for interpretation, however, continues to be the realization that εὐαγγέλιον τῆς ἀκροβυστίας and εὐαγγέλιον τῆς περιτομῆς are *not* simply *identical*, that this singular contrast does not deal with the "one" Pauline gospel.[23] This is indicated in no small way by the expression φοβούμενος τοὺς ἐκ περιτομῆς (for fear of the circumcision faction) in Gal. 2:12. "Certain people from James" demand that the "gospel for the circumcision" be maintained, and charge Peter with violating its identity markers.

The Interpretations

At the apostolic council, both sides recognized that the one God calls people through the gospel in more than one way and that believers serve the will of

---

21. For the enduring presence of strict Jewish Christian positions in Asia Minor, cf. Ign. *Magn.* 8–11; *Phil.* 5–9.

22. Not to be overlooked is the vague formulation in Gal. 2:6 ("what they actually were makes no difference to me"); here Paul is keeping his distance from the Jerusalem "pillars"; cf. Jürgens, *Zweierlei Anfang*, 215–16.

23. Recent exegesis mostly underestimates the implications of Gal. 2:7. The problem either goes unmentioned (cf. Mussner, *Galaterbrief,* 115–17; Borse, *Galater,* 89; Betz, *Galatians,* 184–87) or is reduced to the level of different terminology without a material difference (cf. Heinrich Schlier, *Der Brief an die Galater* [10th ed.; Göttingen: Vandenhoeck & Ruprecht, 1949], 76; Stuhlmacher, *Das paulinische Evangelium,* 96 ["Although we are dealing with a Pauline formulation, it remains significant enough that Paul sees himself in the situation of subsuming his own message and that of Peter under one and the same term. For Paul there is only one gospel, the one revealed to him by God and that he is charged to proclaim"]; Jürgen Becker et al., *Die Briefe an die Galater, Epheser, Philipper, Kolosser, Thessalonicher, und Philemon* [14th ed.; NTD 8; Göttingen: Vandenhoeck & Ruprecht, 1976], 24; Dieter Lührmann, *Galatians* [trans. O. C. Dean; Minneapolis: Fortress, 1992], 39–40; Rohde, *Galater,* 87; Richard N. Longenecker, *Galatians* [WBC 41; Dallas: Word Books, 1990], 55). But cf. Gerd Theissen, "Judentum und Christentum bei Paulus," in *Paulus und das antike Judentum: Tübingen-Durham-Symposium im Gedenken an den 50. Todestag Adolf Schlatters (19 Mai 1938)* (ed. Martin Hengel and Ulrich Heckel; WUNT 58; Tübingen: Mohr Siebeck, 1991), 339 n. 17: "According to the agreement at the 'apostolic council' in the 40s, Paul was responsible [only] for the gospel to the Gentiles; but must not Paul himself have once shared the view that waiving many of the requirements of the law for entrance into the church applied only to Gentiles, not to Jews?

God in different ways.[24] Although differing concepts of mission were advocated at the apostolic council, the council did not unite these into a single view but acknowledged each as a legitimate expression of Christian faith. *It was the equal status, not the identity, of each version of the gospel that was confirmed at the apostolic council.*[25] For Paul, this was already clear, for he was the real innovator; before Paul and during the time of his mission with the Antioch church, the obvious marks of belonging to the people of God were circumcision, Torah observance, and faith in Jesus of Nazareth as the Messiah.

We should probably explain the differing evaluations of circumcision[26] at the apostolic council in terms of the differing backgrounds of the negotiating partners. Whereas in Palestinian Judaism a strict practice of circumcision prevailed,[27] in the Diaspora only a portion of those who were won over to

24. This was already clearly recognized by Ferdinand Christian Baur and Eduard Zeller, *Paul the Apostle of Jesus Christ: His Life and Works, His Epistles and Teachings: A Contribution to a Critical History of Primitive Christianity* (trans. Allan Menzies; 2nd ed.; TTFL; London: Williams and Norgate, 1873), 2:125: "The κοινωνία was a separation as well as an agreement; the agreement was simply that one party should go εἰς τὰ ἔθνη, the other εἰς τὴν περιτομήν, i.e., the Jewish apostles could really allege nothing against the principles on which Paul founded his evangelical labors, and were obliged so far to recognize them; but this recognition was a mere outward one; they left it to him to work further on these principles in the cause of the Gospel among the Gentiles; but they would have nothing to do with these principles themselves. The apostolic sphere of operation therefore became divided into two parts; there was a εὐαγγέλιον τῆς περιτομῆς and a εὐαγγέλιον τῆς ἀκροβυστίας, an ἀποστολὴ εἰς τὴν περιτομήν and an ἀποστολὴ εἰς τὴν ἀκροβυστίαν [gospel for the circumcision and gospel for the uncircumcised; apostolate for the circumcision and an apostolate for the uncircumcised]; in one the Mosaic law had force, in the other it had none, and these two systems simply co-existed without being in any way harmonized."

Albert Schweitzer noted regarding the problems in Paul's understanding of the law, "That believers from Judaism should continue to live according to the Law seems to him quite proper and in no way detrimental to their redemption. But if believers from among the Gentiles do the same thing, this is for him a denial of the Cross of Christ" (*Mysticism*, 187). The comment by Rudolf Meyer, "περιτέμνω," *TDNT* 6:83, is also on target: "Gal. 2:7 shows us, of course, that fundamentally freedom from Ἰουδαϊσμός was simply noted in Jerusalem; in fact, for all the mutual loyalty, the two fronts remained. Paul was now accepted as a preacher of the εὐαγγέλιον τῆς ἀκροβυστίας, and Peter as the preacher of the εὐαγγέλιον τῆς περιτομῆς, with no clarification of the theological antithesis. Neither then nor later was any compromise reached which would have finally united the two parties." W. Schneemelcher, *Das Urchristentum* (Stuttgart: Kohlhammer, 1981), 160: "The decision, however, stated: 'In the Gentile mission, you need not enforce the circumcision requirement, but we, the Jerusalem Jewish Christians, will continue to observe it.'"

25. Cf. Lothar Wehr, *Petrus und Paulus, Kontrahenten und Partner: Die beiden Apostel im Spiegel des Neuen Testaments, der apostolischen Väter, und früher Zeugnisse ihrer Verehrung* (NTAbh 30; Münster: Aschendorff, 1996), 53. He appropriately comments further: "On the contrary, the agreement included not only different territories for which each was responsible . . . but also a different content for the Christian message." Wehnert, *Hintergrund des sogenannten Aposteldekrets*, 120, even speaks of an "agreement to separate."

26. Cf. the thorough treatment of Andreas Blaschke, *Beschneidung: Zeugnisse der Bibel und verwandter Texte* (TANZ 28; Tübingen: Francke, 1998).

27. But cf. 1 Macc. 1:15, where it is said of the Hellenizing Jews in Jerusalem ca. 175 BCE that they "removed the marks of circumcision, and abandoned the holy covenant" (cf. also Josephus, *Ant.*

Judaism became members of the Jewish community in the fully legal sense, by circumcision and ritual immersion (along with sacrifice).[28] It even appears that there was a small stream within the Judaism of the Hellenistic Diaspora that did not regard circumcision as absolutely necessary. Philo reprimanded some allegorizers (*Migr.* 89–93)[29] who probably belonged to such a group, taking the law in a symbolic sense and neglecting its literal practice. In the context of his critique of this position, Philo mentions circumcision: "It is true that receiving circumcision does indeed portray the excision of pleasure and all passions, and the putting away of the impious conceit, under which the mind supposed that it was capable of begetting by its own power: but let us not on this account repeal the law laid down for circumcising" (*Migr.* 92). Although Philo does not share the position of the allegorists, the content of his own position is not so far removed:

> [Scripture] first makes it clearly apparent and demonstrable that in reality the sojourner is one who circumcises not his uncircumcision but his desires and sensual pleasures [ὅτι προσήλυτός ἐστιν οὐχ ὁ περιτμηθεὶς τὴν ἀκροβυστίαν ἀλλ᾽ ὁ τὰς ἡδονὰς καὶ τὰς ἐπιθυμίας καὶ τὰ ἄλλα πάθη τῆς ψυχῆς]. For in Egypt the Hebrew nation was not circumcised but being mistreated with all kinds of mistreatment by the inhabitants in their hatred of strangers, it lived with them in self-restraint and endurance [Ἐν Αἰγύπτῳ γὰρ τὸ Ἑβραῖον γένος οὐ περιτέτμητο, κακωθὲν δὲ πάσαις κακώσεσι τῆς παρὰ τῶν ἐγχωρίων περὶ τοὺς ξένους ὠμότητος, ἐγκρατείᾳ καὶ καρτερίᾳ συνεβίου]. (*QE* 2.2)

The vast majority of the Gentiles attracted to Judaism adopted its monotheism and basic ethical norms, attended worship at the synagogue, received instruction in the Torah, and observed the major aspects of the Sabbath commandment and the food laws but were not circumcised. As "God-fearers" (σεβόμενοι or οἱ φοβούμενοι τὸν θεόν), they became the first among the Gentiles to accept the Christian faith (cf. Acts 10:2; 13:16, 26; 16:14; 17:4, 17; 18:7, 13).[30] When Paul abandoned the requirement of circumcision for Gentile Christians, he who had previously been a Pharisee of the Diaspora was maintaining continuity with his background—and the same is true of his opponents.

From Paul's perspective, the apostolic council not only sanctioned the Gentile mission without reservations; Paul also understood it to have confirmed the special status of the apostle to the Gentiles as an equal partner with the Jerusa-

---

12.241). For the first half of the second century CE, *t. Šabb.* 15.9 reports, "In the days of Ben Koziba, many had themselves (re-)circumcised" (cited from Strack and Billerbeck, *Kommentar*, 4/1:34).

28. K. G. Kuhn and Hartmut Stegemann, "Proselyten," PWSup 9:1257ff.

29. For analysis, cf. David M. Hay, "Philo's References to Other Allegorists," *SPhilo* 6 (1979–1980): 41–75.

30. On this, cf. F. Siegert, "Gottesfürchtige und Sympathisanten," *JJS* 4 (1973): 109–64; and Bernd Wander, *Gottesfürchtige und Sympathisanten: Studien zum heidnischen Umfeld von Diasporasynagogen* (WUNT 104; Tübingen: Mohr Siebeck, 1998).

lem "pillars." This interpretation of the apostolic council, however, was by no means uncontested, as shown by the Antioch incident, the later agitation by Judaists in the Pauline churches, and especially by the Lukan tradition of the apostolic decree.[31] Whereas Paul's reading of the agreements at the apostolic council regarded them as binding obligations, these other streams within early Christianity saw them merely as a temporary concession for one particular situation or interpreted them in a completely different sense. The parallel co-existence of ultimately incompatible concepts of identity was only sanctioned, not overcome. And finally, we must remember that the apostolic council was in fact only a meeting involving the churches of Antioch and Jerusalem; to what extent other churches subscribed to the results of the council remains unclear. Thus after the apostolic council there were at least three different positions on the question of the validity of the Torah for Gentile Christians: (1) freedom from the requirement of circumcision, which in fact meant freedom from the Torah as such with the exception of its ethical core (Paul, parts of the Antioch church? Apollos?); (2) limited observance of the Torah but without the require-ment of circumcision (the apostolic decree); and (3) the comprehensive validity of the Torah, including circumcision, as binding also on Gentile Christians (the Jewish Christian missionaries in Galatia and Philippi who opposed Paul; parts of the Jerusalem church).

The Origin of the Different Reports

How did it come about that Paul and Luke produced different versions of the apostolic council? Students of early Christianity have always noticed the connection between the minimal ritual requirements of Acts 15:20, 29; 21:25 and the issues at stake in the Antioch incident: (1) Which rules must Gentile Christians observe in order to maintain the state of ritual purity required by God? The apostolic decree sees the solution of this problem to be the observance of a minimum of the purity laws. (2) In Acts 15:20 James first formulates the apostolic decree; then, according to Gal. 2:12, it is "certain people from James" who call for the separation of Jewish and Gentile Christians in Antioch. (3) The limited purview of the apostolic decree in Acts 15:23 (Antioch, Syria, and Cilicia) coincides with the Antiochene/Pauline mission territory (cf. Acts 13–14; Gal. 1:21); the decision at the apostolic council regarding the freedom of Gentile Christians from the requirement of circumcision was a matter of principle, without geographic restrictions. One could thus easily imagine that

31. The Pauline letters betray no knowledge of the apostolic decree; whether Paul was aware of it is a disputed point. Among those who argue against such knowledge are Roloff, *Apostelgeschichte*, 227; Schneider, *Apostelgeschichte*, 2:189 n. 3; Hans-Josef Klauck, *1. Korintherbrief* (3rd ed.; NEchtB 7; Würzburg: Echter, 1992), 75–76; on the other side are, e.g., Lüdemann, *Chronology*, 71–75; Rohde, *Galater*, 99–101.

Luke has intertwined two originally separate issues:[32] (1) the settlement agreed upon at the apostolic council, according to which Gentile Christians need not be circumcised, and (2) the apostolic decree formulated in the context of the Antioch incident, intended to regulate the common life of Jewish and Gentile Christians in the territory of the Antiochene/Pauline mission. We can still recognize traces of this fusion of the two traditions in Acts 15:1–29. It accords with Lukan redaction that the account, harking back to Acts 10:1–11:15, has Peter make the first speech and then has James present the solution to the problem, with Paul virtually silent.[33] Peter's speech once again provides the fundamental and unrestricted legitimization for the Gentile mission without the requirement of circumcision (cf. Acts 15:10). It climaxes in the declaration, with a Pauline tone, "we believe that we will be saved through the grace of the Lord Jesus, just as they [the Gentile Christians] will." The legitimization of the Pauline position is placed in the mouth of Peter, who affirms a mission in which Gentiles are accepted into the Christian community without the requirement of circumcision or any other stipulations of the law—a declaration that clearly stands in tension with the following apostolic decree. Also, the line of argument followed by James in Acts 15:19, 29 still shows traces of his original agreement made at the apostolic council, acknowledging a Gentile mission unconditionally free from the requirement of circumcision (15:19, "Therefore I have reached the decision that we should not trouble those Gentiles who are turning to God"; 15:28, "For it has seemed good to the Holy Spirit and to us to impose on you no further burden [except for . . .]"). Thus the restrictive combination with the conditions of the apostolic decree would stem from Lukan redaction. The content of the earlier tradition in the Lukan version thus confirms Paul's own account. The negotiating partners were Paul on the one side and James and Peter on the other. The agreed-upon settlement stated that it is not necessary for Gentile Christians to be circumcised in order to become full members of the people of God.

6.2 The Antioch Incident

The Antioch incident occurred in proximity to the apostolic council, both in chronological terms[34] and regarding the disputed issues. The apostolic council recognized both missionary models: the Jewish mission of the Jerusalem church

---

32. Cf. the exemplary argument in Weiser, *Apostelgeschichte*, 2:375–77.

33. It is mentioned only in Acts 15:12 that Barnabas and Paul (note the order) give a summary report of the success of their missionary work.

34. In Gal. 2:11 the grammatical signal ὅτε δέ indicates that Paul is presenting the events in chronological order; for the evidence, cf. Wechsler, *Geschichtsbild und Apostelstreit*, 297–305; Wehnert, *Hintergrund des sogenannten Aposteldekrets*, 120–23. There must have been some temporal gap, however, between the apostolic council and the Antioch conflict, since in Gal. 2:7–9 Peter still appears

and the Gentile mission not requiring circumcision. The contending parties there also worked out an agreement about the division of missionary territory, but the problems of *mixed* churches composed of both Jewish Christians and Gentile Christians were clearly not on the agenda. These problems emerged in Antioch, where the assumed practice of the church was obviously table fellowship between Jewish Christians and uncircumcised Gentile Christians who were considered ritually unclean in terms of Jewish law.

Different Concepts of Purity

According to Gal. 2:11, Peter participated in the integrated table fellowship in Antioch. He thereby documented that the Jewish food laws and prescriptions for ritual purity did not apply to Gentile Christians, that Jewish Christians could not simply place Gentile Christians in the same category as Gentiles per se. This liberal attitude suddenly changed with the arrival of τινες ἀπὸ Ἰακώβου (certain people from James).[35] Peter withdrew, and abandoned his previous practice of table fellowship with Gentile Christians. He separated himself, as recommended in *Jub.* 22:16: "And you also, my son Jacob, remember my words, and keep the commandments of Abraham your father. Separate yourself from the gentiles, and do not eat with them, and do not perform deeds like theirs. Because their deeds are defiled, and all their ways are contaminated, and despicable, and abominable."[36] The food laws (cf., e.g., Deut. 14:3–21) at this time were a central focus of Jewish (and thus also of Jewish Christian) understanding of the law,[37] so that the simple fact of their existence led the James people to reject the idea of eating together with Gentiles.[38] The application of the demand for ritual separation from the unclean to the relation between Gentile Christians and Jewish Christians would have effectively equated Gentile Christians with unbelieving Gentiles (heathen) and would have made eucharistic table fellowship between the two groups impossible. The motive Paul gives for Peter's momen-

---

as a representative of the Jerusalem preaching ministry among the Jews but in Antioch he has been practicing table fellowship with Gentile Christians.

35. The "false brothers" of Gal. 2:4 are not identical with the "certain people from James," for they accept the agreement at the apostolic council. Cf. Betz, *Galatians*, 203–4, who rightly sees James in the background.

36. Trans. O. Wintermute, *OTP* 2: 98; cf. also Dan. 1:8ff.; Tob. 1:10–12; *Jos. Asen.* 8; *Let. Aris.* 139–142, 182–183; 4 Macc. 1:33–35; Tacitus, *Hist.* 5.5; on the separating character of the Torah, cf. 2 Esd. 10). Cf. also Strack and Billerbeck, *Kommentar*, 4/1:374–8.

37. Cf. the extensive evidence in Christoph Heil, *Die Ablehnung der Speisegebote durch Paulus: Zur Frage nach der Stellung des Apostels zum Gesetz* (BBB 96; Weinheim: Beltz Athenäum, 1994), 23–123 (p. 299: "Paul's Jewish context regards the ritual food laws as representing the Torah as a whole").

38. For James D. G. Dunn, "The Incident at Antioch (Gal. 2.11–18)," *JSNT* 18 (1983): 15–16, from the point of view of the James people, the objectionable feature regarding the food was that it had not been tithed, and this is what precipitated their intervention, but this supposition has no adequate basis.

tous decision and resulting conduct is φοβούμενος τοὺς ἐκ περιτομῆς.[39] It was obviously the consistent Jewish Christian standpoint of the Jerusalem church as led by James that prompted Peter to change his conduct. For James and his followers, a Christian could remain within Judaism only by consistent observance of the Torah. Although Peter's previous practice in Antioch indicated he had already abandoned this standpoint (cf. also Acts 11:3), he now returned to it. This is why Paul charges him with being condemned by his own conduct (Gal. 2:11b). Peter's inconsistency now causes the other Jewish Christians, including even Barnabas, to assume this hypocritical stance and abandon their previous table fellowship with Gentile Christians (2:13). Paul evaluates this conduct as theological inconsistency because thereby the actual fellowship between Gentile and Jewish Christians is abolished. This is why Peter, Barnabas, and the other Jewish Christians were not living in accord with the truth of the gospel (2:14), just as had been done previously by the "false brothers" at the apostolic council who attempted to make circumcision compulsory for Gentile Christians (cf. 2:4–5). The verb ὀρθοποδέω (to walk on the right way/path/road) and the expression ἀλήθεια τοῦ εὐαγγελίου (the truth of the gospel) show very precisely that both for Paul and his opponents, practical and theological issues are always woven together. The truth of the gospel does not call for Gentiles to obey the ritual requirements of the Jewish law (cf. 2:5, 14). Thus Paul tells Peter to his face, "If you, though a Jew, live like a Gentile and not like a Jew, how can you compel the Gentiles to live like Jews?" Jews are not to be compelled to give up their own way of life, but at the same time, the Jewish way of life is not to be imposed on Gentiles (ἰουδαΐζειν). The context (2:12, συνήσθιεν [he used to eat with]) indicates that compelling Gentiles to live in the Jewish way refers primarily to the keeping of the Jewish food laws. The same subject matter as the apostolic decree is clearly in view. It is still debatable, however, whether the apostolic decree authorized by James was the trigger for the Antioch conflict[40] or its result.[41] On the other hand, it is clear that the Antioch conflict led Paul to separate from Barnabas and the Antioch mission (cf. Gal. 2:13/Acts 15:39) and the apostolic decree continued to be valid in the territory of this mission and its sphere of influence (Acts 15:23).

Paul and his opposing partners were not so different in the material content of their respective understandings of purity;[42] it was a matter of how each party

---

39. The expression οἱ ἐκ τῆς περιτομῆς does not describe a wider group but refers to "certain people from James." Peter's fear can be explained only by the arrival of influential authorities, namely, the representatives of James (cf. Günter Klein, "Die Verleugnung des Petrus," in *Rekonstruktion und Interpretation: Gesammelte Aufsätze zum Neuen Testament* (BEvT 50; Munich: Kaiser, 1969), 83 n. 205. The οἱ λοιποὶ Ἰουδαῖοι (the other Jews) in Gal. 2:13 are Jewish Christians from Antioch.

40. So, e.g., Wehnert, *Hintergrund des sogenannten Aposteldekrets*, 126ff.

41. So, e.g., Ferdinand Hahn, "Die Bedeutung des Apostelkonvents für die Einheit der Christenheit," in *Exegetische Beiträge zum ökumenischen Gespräch* (Göttingen: Vandenhoeck & Ruprecht, 1986), 107.

42. Cf. Wehnert, *Hintergrund des sogenannten Aposteldekrets*, 255–56.

understood its own foundational structure. Paul demands from his churches a sanctification of life, expressed especially by avoiding πορνεία ([sexual] immorality; cf. 1 Thess. 4:3–4, 7; 1 Cor. 1:30; 2 Cor. 12:21; Gal. 5:19; Rom. 1:24; 6:19, 22). In 1 Thess. 4:7 (For God did not call us to impurity but in holiness) and Rom. 6:19, ἁγιασμός (sanctification) appears as the counterpart to ἀκαθαρσία (impurity), so that for Paul sanctification includes the aspect of purity. The basis for this demand for purity is not the Torah but the separation from the power of sin accomplished in baptism (cf. 1 Cor. 6:11; 2 Cor. 1:21–22). In contrast, the understanding of purity presupposed in the apostolic decree is something in addition to baptism and thus reduces its exclusive importance.

The Perspective from Which the Account Is Presented

The rhetorical formation of Paul's account of the Antioch incident shows clearly that he is reporting the events in Antioch in the light of the Galatian crisis. In Gal. 2:14 Paul makes the transition into the actual context of the dispute with the Galatian church. The "James people" were insisting not on some sort of ἰουδαΐζειν (Judaizing) of Gentile Christians in the comprehensive sense[43] but merely that Peter and the other Jewish Christians maintain their separation from (ritually unclean) Gentile Christians. Paul's opponents in Galatia, however, advocated that the status of Gentile Christians be that of proselytes; they insisted on a compulsory Jewish way of life for Gentile Christians.[44] Galatians 2:15 also alludes to the current situation in Galatia.[45] Paul summarizes the main points of Jewish (and Jewish Christian) self-understanding on which both the separation in Antioch and the agitation in Galatia were based. Paul, like Peter and the other Jewish Christians, belonged from his birth to the elect people of God (Ἡμεῖς φύσει Ἰουδαῖοι); they belong to the righteous whereas Gentiles eo ipso are numbered among the sinners. This "natural" Jewish self-understanding is then transcended and relativized in that Paul adds adversatively,[46] "yet we know that a person is justified not by the works of the law but through faith in Jesus Christ. And we have come to believe in Christ Jesus, so that we might be justified by faith in Christ, and not by doing the works of the law, because no one will be justified by the works of the law" (Gal. 2:16). With the expression ἐξ ἔργων νόμου οὐ δικαιωθήσεται πᾶσα σάρξ (2:16d), Paul goes far beyond the agreement at the apostolic council and the disputed issue in the

43. The verb ἰουδαΐζω includes an obligation to keep the whole Torah, including the circumcision command; cf. Betz, *Galatians*, 211 n. 485. Thus the issue of ἰουδαΐζειν cannot be restricted to the apostolic decree but clearly has the Galatian conflict in mind.

44. Cf. Ulrich Wilckens, "Was heißt bei Paulus: 'Aus Werken des Gesetzes wird kein Mensch gerecht'?" in *Rechtfertigung als Freiheit: Paulusstudien* (Neukirchen-Vluyn: Neukirchener Verlag, 1974), 86–87.

45. Cf. Wechsler, *Geschichtsbild und Apostelstreit*, 376ff.

46. Cf. Wilckens, "Werken des Gesetzes," 88; Wechsler, *Geschichtsbild und Apostelstreit*, 378–79.

Antioch incident. The agreement in Gal. 2:9d (ἡμεῖς εἰς τὰ ἔθνη, αὐτοὶ δὲ εἰς τὴν περιτομήν [we to the Gentiles, they to the circumcised]) does contain for the Gentiles the affirmation of freedom from the law of circumcision, but at the same time Paul also accepts the basic obligation of Jewish Christians to observe the regulations of the Torah. He also took this position at the Antioch incident, for he does not criticize the "James people" but only the inconsistent conduct of Peter and those who followed his example.[47] At both the apostolic council and the Antioch incident, the only issue was whether the Torah was binding on non-Jews, and the consequences that follow from this decision.[48] The status of Jewish Christians remained unchanged; it is exclusively the ritual status of Gentile Christians that was at issue. The exclusive doctrine of justification found in the letters to the Galatians and to the Romans goes a decisive step further in that it also poses the issue of the jurisdiction of the Torah for *Jewish* Christians. There is no special status granted by circumcision; Jewish Christians and Gentile Christians stand before God in the same situation. Paul did not advocate the fundamental affirmation of Gal. 2:16d, that no one can be justified by works of the law/Torah, either at the apostolic council in Jerusalem or in Antioch, nor could he have done so at that time. The parties involved could hardly have reached an agreement if Paul had already at that time disputed the importance of the Torah for Jewish Christians, as he does in Gal. 3 or in the sharply formulated thesis statement of Rom. 3:21a: Νυνὶ δὲ χωρὶς νόμου δικαιοσύνη θεοῦ πεφανέρωται, "But now, apart from law, the righteousness of God has been disclosed." The gift of the Torah still established election and righteousness (Deut. 4:8, "And what other great nation has statutes and ordinances as just as this entire law that I am setting before you today?"). The commandments are still easy to fulfill, and Israel chooses the path of life when it places itself under the blessing of the Torah (Deut. 30:11–14, "Surely, this commandment that I am commanding you today is not too hard for you, nor is it too far away. It is not in heaven, that you should say, 'Who will go up to heaven for us, and get it for us so that we may hear it and observe it?' Neither is it beyond the sea, that you should say, 'Who will cross to the other side of the sea for us, and get it for us so that we may hear it and observe it?' No, the word is very near to you; it is in your mouth and in your heart for you to observe").

47. Differently, Räisänen, *Paul and the Law*, 256–63, who sees the Antioch incident as an intensification of a development toward restoration that had already begun at the apostolic council. He thinks "that the Antiochian episode reveals [to] us a great deal of how Paul's 'final' theology of the law took shape" (p. 259).

48. This is not noticed by Hübner, *Biblische Theologie*, 2:51, when he states that Paul had "already championed fundamental freedom from the law at the mission synod." Hübner must attribute to Paul a misinterpretation of the apostolic council (cf. pp. 31–32, 34), since he himself attributes the doctrine of justification found in Galatians to the apostle already at the time of the apostolic council.

The "pillars" could not have extended their hand to Paul if at the apostolic council he had already claimed that the Torah was secondary to the promise, both temporally and in its essential function (cf. Gal. 3:17, 19), that it was enslaving (cf. Gal. 3:23–24), that through the Torah comes (only) an awareness of sin (Rom. 3:20b), or that the Torah as the presupposition for sin had (merely) "come in between [in a temporary status]" (Rom. 5:20). The history of early Christian theology and missions also suggests such an interpretation. At the beginning, faith in Christ and observance of the Torah belonged in the same united category, and the new convert Paul never questioned this regarding Jewish Christians. He merely hesitated to make the Torah binding on Gentile Christians. Thus it is a mistake to connect the origin of the Pauline doctrine of justification in the exclusive sense with the apostolic council or the Antioch incident.[49] The foundational thesis of Gal. 2:16 does not accord with the outcome of the apostolic council, nor does it represent the issue that was debated at the Antioch incident. At that time Paul defended the view that his churches were clearly free from the requirement of circumcision (while observing the nucleus of the Torah's ethical requirements), but at the same time he acknowledged the obligation of the Jewish Christians to the Torah. In contrast, at the time Paul wrote Galatians, there was for him only one gospel, his gospel that was critical of the law/Torah, the gospel that was valid for Gentiles *and* Jews. In reaction to the challenge to his mission work, Paul expands his identity concept, for now the Torah has constitutive significance for neither Jew (Jewish Christians) nor Gentile (Gentile Christians).

49. Cf. below, section 11.5 ("Inclusive and Exclusive Doctrine of Justification in Paul").

7

Paul's Independent Mission

The Volcano Erupts

History is also made by human beings. While it is true enough that Paul is not the "second founder of Christianity," it is also true that without his accomplishment and ability a Jewish renewal movement would hardly have become, with breathtaking speed, a world religion with great drawing power.

7.1 Presuppositions of the Pauline Mission

The events relating to the apostolic council and the conflict at Antioch led to a parting of the ways between Paul and Barnabas and to a final separation of the apostle from the Antioch mission. We must consider the way this is presented in Acts as unhistorical on two points: (1) The conflict over John Mark, which obviously was a personal matter (cf. Acts 15:36–39), could hardly have been the real cause of the split between Paul and Barnabas. It is more likely that the Antioch incident was the occasion for the separation, for Paul and Barnabas obviously advocated differing understandings of purity. (2) In Acts 16:4 Paul appears as the leading protagonist in behalf of the apostolic decree, which from Luke's perspective has validity beyond the territory in which the Antioch mission was influential (Acts 15:23). We cannot be sure whether Paul actually knew the apostolic decree; his conduct during the Antioch conflict, however, speaks in favor of his having known it, for he strictly rejects its presupposed concept of purity. Paul, in contrast to Barnabas, did not accept the apostolic decree, which was regarded as authoritative in the territory of the Antioch mission, and this difference was probably the cause of their separation. The course of events drove Paul westward. Strengthened by the decisions of the apostolic council and now having lost his home within the area of his previous mission work when the churches in that area accepted the apostolic decree, at the end of the year 48 CE Paul began an independent mission.

Greek as a World Language

The external conditions for this mission work were very good,[1] for in the Roman Empire of the first century CE there existed a well-developed communications infrastructure, basically made possible by the linguistic situation. In the first place, inscriptions show that in Palestine of the first century CE two different linguae francae overlapped.[2] Alongside Aramaic, Koine Greek was widespread, and Greek was spoken in even the most uncultured social classes.[3] A comparable linguistic situation was found in Syria; here also both Aramaic and Greek were prevalent.[4] After the conquests of Alexander, Asia Minor lay under Greek influence, with the result that here also Greek was the dominant language in the first century.[5] Local dialects were preserved alongside Greek (cf., e.g., Acts 2:5–11; 14:11). Greek was, of course, the primary language in Greece and Macedonia, but the circumstances in Italy and Rome are difficult to

---

1. Cf. Harnack, *Mission and Expansion of Christianity*, 18–23. The cultural conditions within which the early Christian mission took place are sketched by W. Speyer, "Hellenistisch-römische Voraussetzungen der Verbreitung des Christentums," in *Der neue Mensch in Christus: Hellenistische Anthropologie und Ethik im Neuen Testament* (ed. Johannes Beutler; QD 190; Freiburg: Herder, 2001), 25–35: the decline of classical Greco-Roman culture, the development of monotheism, the concept of the divine origin of exceptional individuals, and the significance of ethics.

2. Cf. H. B. Rosén, "Die Sprachsituation im römischen Palästina," in *Die Sprachen im römischen Reich der Kaiserzeit* (ed. G. Neumann and J. Untermann; Cologne: Rheinland, 1980), 215–39; A. R. Millard, *Pergament und Papyrus, Tafeln und Ton: Lesen und Schreiben zur Zeit Jesu* (Giessen: Brunnen, 2000), 81–114; A. W. Argyle, "Greek among the Jews of Palestine in New Testament Times," *NTS* 20 (1973): 87–89; Stanley E. Porter, "Jesus and the Use of Greek in Galilee," in *Studying the Historical Jesus: Evaluations of the State of Current Research* (ed. Bruce Chilton and Craig A. Evans; Leiden: Brill, 1994), 123–54.

3. Cf. Rosén, "Sprachsituation," 236–37.

4. Cf. R. Schmitt, "Die Ostgrenze von Armenien über Mesopotamien, Syrien bis Arabien," in *Die Sprachen im römischen Reich der Kaiserzeit* (ed. G. Neumann and J. Untermann; Cologne: Rheinland, 1980), 198–205.

5. Cf. G. Neumann, "Kleinasien," in *Die Sprachen im römischen Reich* (ed. Neumann and Untermann), 167–85.

evaluate. Educated Romans knew Greek, just as did the large number of slaves who had been brought to Rome from the east. There is thus a limited sense in which Rome can also be considered bilingual.[6] Thus Paul could get along in "his" world with one language and communicate with all social classes. The language of Diaspora Judaism of the Mediterranean world likewise was Greek. Alongside Paul and other New Testament authors, one thinks here especially of Philo, who refers to Greek as "our language."[7]

Transportation

Paul's mission work was made easier by the excellent possibilities for travel available in the Roman Empire of the first century CE.[8] The network of roads comprised about 186,000 miles, of which 56,000 miles were improved highways.[9] The quality of this network of Roman roads is indicated by the fact that the system as a whole was still intact in the High Middle Ages and that some roads built by the Romans are still in use today. Paul and his coworkers traveled either on foot or by ship; there is no reference in the New Testament to Paul's traveling by wagon. An overland traveler could cover about nineteen miles a day through normal terrain.[10] When traveling by ship with a favorable wind, the average speed was about 4.5–6 knots, so that, for example, one could travel from Corinth to the Roman harbor Puteoli in four or five days. There were many travelers in the first century. These included merchants and peddlers as well as people traveling for educational value. Groups traveled from city to city, and Jews were not the only group for whom pilgrimages were a normal part of life.[11] And finally, the wandering Cynic philosophers[12] were an

6. I. Kajanto, "Minderheiten und ihre Sprachen in Rom," in *Die Sprachen im römischen Reich* (ed. Neumann and Untermann), 84ff. On the significance of Greek as the international language in the time of the Roman Empire, see ibid., 121–45; Gerard Mussies, "Greek as the Vehicle of Early Christianity," *NTS* 29 (1983): 356–69. An instructive example is offered by Josephus, who writes in Greek in order to include Romans in his readership (*J. W.* 1.3). Cf. also Cicero, *Arch.* 23: "Whoever thinks that Greek verses enhance one's reputation less than Latin greatly errs, since Greek books are read in almost every country while Latin is limited to its own linguistic area, which is quite small" (trans. M.E.B.).

7. Cf. Philo, *Prelim. Studies* 44.

8. A good survey with relevant bibliography is given by Riesner, *Paul's Early Period*, 307–17.

9. Reinhold Reck, *Kommunikation und Gemeindeaufbau: Eine Studie zu Entstehung, Leben, und Wachstum paulinischer Gemeinden in den Kommunikationsstrukturen der Antike* (SBS 22; Stuttgart: Katholisches Bibelwerk, 1991), 82.

10. Cf. ibid., 86; Riesner, *Paul's Early Period*, 311, estimates twenty to thirty kilometers (12.4–18.6 miles) per day.

11. Cf. Ludwig Friedlaender and Georg Wissowa, *Sittengeschichte Roms* (Vienna: Phaidon, 1934), 389–488; M. Giebel, *Reisen in der Antike* (Düsseldorf: Artemis & Winkler, 1999), 131–214.

12. On the Cynic movement and philosophy, cf. Donald Reynolds Dudley, *A History of Cynicism: From Diogenes to the 6th Century A.D.* (London: Methuen, 1937; repr., Hildesheim: G. Olms, 1967); an introduction is provided by Hans-Josef Klauck, *The Religious Context of Early Christianity:*

important factor in shaping the way Christian missionaries were perceived. They traveled throughout the Hellenistic-Roman world, bringing their message of moral renewal,[13] preaching especially on the streets and public squares, at the entrances of theaters and temples. As was the case for Paul, it was the cities that provided the real setting for the work of the Cynic preachers.[14] Their unconventional appearance (cloak, satchel, staff, long unkempt hair) and especially their addressing current themes and problems of everyday life gained them general respect but also often evoked opposition from the ruling class.[15] Many wandering philosophers had no permanent address; they traveled barefoot, begged for their food, and slept on the floors of public buildings. In the ancient world, Christian missionaries were not the only wandering preachers who proclaimed their message in public settings.

Religious Pluralism

The religious pluralism and tolerance of the Roman Empire in the first century CE was also propitious for the spread of Christianity. Greeks and Romans generally did not doubt that other gods besides their own existed; this perspective contributed to the coexistence and amalgamation of different religions.[16] Thus the Greek mystery cults (Eleusis, Dionysus, Attis) were open to the integration of Egyptian (Osiris, Isis, Sarapis) and oriental (Mithras) deities.[17] The classical Roman and Greek gods were in part identified with these

---

A Guide to Graeco-Roman Religions (trans. Brian McNeil; Minneapolis: Fortress, 2003), 377–85. The current state of research is documented in Robert Bracht Branham and Marie-Odile Goulet-Cazâe, eds., *The Cynics: The Cynic Movement in Antiquity and Its Legacy* (HCS 23; Berkeley: University of California Press, 1996).

13. E. Zeller rightly describes the Cynics as "voluntary moral preachers and soul doctors" (Eduard Zeller and Wilhelm Nestle, *Outlines of the History of Greek Philosophy* [trans. L. R. Palmer; 13th ed.; ILPPSM; New York: Humanities Press, 1931, repr., 1963], 111).

14. Cf. Dio Chrysostom, *Alex.* 9: "The city also has a fairly large number of so-called Cynics, and like the rest, these too are quite popular—a coarse bunch of bastards who know nothing and have nothing. On street corners, back streets, and at the temple gates they gather around themselves riffraff, sailors, and the like and put on a deceitful show—a burlesque actually—trot out one joke after another, and dish up familiar answers one can get anyplace at the market" (trans. M.E.B.). Cf. further Lucian, *Fugitivi* 16: "Every city is now full of such deceit, especially from those who have enlisted with Diogenes, Antisthenes, and Crates and who serve under the flag of the 'Dogs'" (trans. M.E.B.).

15. Cf. Walter L. Liefeld, *The Wandering Preacher as a Social Figure in the Roman Empire* (Ann Arbor, MI: University Microfilms, 1967).

16. For Greek religions, cf. Martin P. Nilsson, *A History of Greek Religion* (trans. F. J. Fielden; Westport, CT: Greenwood, 1980); for Roman religions, cf. Margaret Lyttelton and Werner Forman, *The Romans: Their Gods and Their Beliefs* (EAW; London: Orbis, 1984); Georg Wissowa, *Religion und Kultus der Römer* (2 ed.; HAW 4/5; Munich: Beck, 1971); Jörg Rüpke, *Die Religion der Römer: Eine Einführung* (Munich: Beck, 2001).

17. A masterful portrayal of this process can still be found in Franz Cumont, *The Oriental Religions in Roman Paganism* (Chicago: Open Court, 1911); in addition, cf. Reinhold Merkelbach, *Die Hirten des Dionysos: Die Dionysos-Mysterien der römischen Kaiserzeit und der bukolische Roman des Longus* (Stuttgart:

new gods, alongside whom some of the healing gods, such as Asclepius, attained great importance. Finally, within this syncretism the worship of stars and sun continued to play a considerable role, as did magic and superstition.[18] Oracle shrines were heavily visited,[19] and faith in such oracles was widespread. It was not merely a particular social class that tolerated and fostered this religious pluralism; merchants, soldiers, slaves, and travelers all propagated their deities and organized themselves into private cultic associations.

The pax romana

The Romans attempted to hold together, restrict, and channel the variety of religious and cultural streams within their empire through a common bond: the *pax romana* (Roman peace).[20] Since Augustus,[21] at the center of this image had stood the person of the emperor, who as *pontifex maximus* guaranteed the continued existence and cohesion of the Roman Empire as a sacral-legal reality; in this image the empire was held together by the emperor, who by astute politics provided peace and prosperity.[22] The political unity of the empire, its economic growth, and its legal stability were all gifts of the *pax romana*, which was based on Rome's military might. Peace in external affairs made possible an intact infrastructure and a thriving trade between the eastern and western parts of the empire, and these also enhanced the spread of the gospel by business

---

Teubner, 1988); *Mithras* (Königstein: Hain, 1984); *Isis Regina, Zeus Sarapis: Die griechisch-ägyptische Religion nach den Quellen dargestellt* (Stuttgart: Teubner, 1995); Walter Burkert, *Ancient Mystery Cults* (Cambridge: Harvard University Press, 1987); Eduard Zeller, "Mysterien/Mysterienreligionen," *TRE* 23:504–26; Luther H. Martin, *Hellenistic Religions: An Introduction* (New York: Oxford University Press, 1987); Klauck, *Religious Context*; Marvin W. Meyer, ed., *The Ancient Mysteries: A Sourcebook* (San Francisco: Harper, 1987).

18. Texts from the sphere of magic are presented in Georg Luck, ed., *Magie und andere Geheimlehren in der Antike: Mit 112 neu übersetzten und einzeln kommentierten Quellentexten* (Stuttgart: Kröner, 1990); Hans Dieter Betz, *The Greek Magical Papyri in Translation, Including the Demotic Spells* (Chicago: University of Chicago Press, 1986).

19. See M. Giebel, ed., *Das Orakel von Delphi: Geschichte und Texte* (Stuttgart: Reclam, 2001).

20. Wengst, *Pax romana*, 19–71.

21. As the prime example, cf. Augustus, *Res gestae divi Augusti*; on the religious development of Octavian/Augustus, cf. S. R. Price, *Rituals and Power: The Roman Imperial Cult in Asia Minor* (Cambridge: Cambridge University Press, 1984); Manfred Clauss, *Kaiser und Gott: Herrscherkult im römischen Reich* (Stuttgart: Teubner, 1999), 54–75; Karl Christ, *Geschichte der römischen Kaiserzeit: Von Augustus bis zu Konstantin* (Munich: Beck, 1988), 158–68; Adela Yarbro Collins, *Crisis and Catharsis: The Power of the Apocalypse* (Philadelphia: Westminster, 1984), 69–73; Leonard L. Thompson, *The Book of Revelation: Apocalypse and Empire* (Oxford: Oxford University Press, 1990), passim, esp. 191.

22. Cf., e.g., Seneca, *Clem.* 2.1.2, where he says of Nero, "That kindness of your heart will be recounted, will be diffused little by little throughout the whole body of your empire, and all things will be molded into your likeness. It is from the head that comes the health of the body; it is through it that all parts are lively and alert or languid and drooping according as the animating spirit has life or withers. There will be citizens, there will be allies worthy of this goodness, and uprightness will return to the whole world."

people, travelers, and slaves. The economic upturn also included social mobility; the boundaries between social classes became more relaxed, and the possibilities of upward mobility for the lower classes were improved.[23] Paul respected the *pax romana* (cf. Rom. 13:1–7), for it was an essential presupposition for the successful earlier mission: the boundaries of linguistic and cultural circles could be crossed without difficulty, and new views quickly found interested hearers. So long as the (for Christians) critical threshold of emperor worship was not crossed, the *pax romana* provided the framework for the success of the early Christian mission.

Diaspora Judaism

Within this complex historical and cultural setting, Judaism maintained its character as a national religion. It was precisely for this reason that as Christianity became a missionary religion, it found Judaism to be its first conversation partner. In the first century the Jewish Diaspora[24] comprised about five or six million people.[25] Outside Palestine more Jews lived in Egypt than in any other country; Philo gives the number of Egyptian Jews as approximately one million.[26] Other centers of Jewish population were Cyrene, Syria, and Phoenicia. Antioch and Damascus in particular were home to large Jewish communities. In Asia Minor hardly a city was found without a Jewish community. For example, Pergamon, Smyrna, Ephesus, and Tarsus were centers of Diaspora Judaism. Southern Italy and Rome also were home to important Jewish communities. In the first century CE, the center of Diaspora communities was the synagogue.[27] In the larger cities the synagogue was located within the Jewish residential section or at least on a Jewish street. As portrayed in Acts, upon his arrival in a new town, Paul always went first to the Jewish synagogue, where he recorded his first missionary successes (cf. Acts 9:20; 13:5, 14–43; 14:1–2; 17:1–3; 18:4; 19:8). This procedure was readily available, since as a Diaspora Jew Paul was familiar with the communication structures of the synagogue,

---

23. Cf. Henneke Gülzow, "Pontifikalreligion und Gesellschaft," in Henneke Gülzow, *Kirchengeschichte und Gegenwart: Studien, Aufsätze, Predigten, Meditationen* (ed. Bärbel Dauber; Hamburg: LIT, 1999), 13–14.

24. A survey is found in Johann Maier, *Zwischen den Testamenten: Geschichte und Religion in der Zeit des zweiten Tempels* (NEchtB: Ergängzungsband zum Alten Testament 3; Würzburg: Echter, 1990), 176–83; cf. also Tcherikover, *Hellenistic Civilization*, passim; Shaye J. D. Cohen, *From the Maccabees to the Mishnah* (Philadelphia: Westminster, 1987), 27–60.

25. On the statistics, cf. A. Kasher, "Diaspora I/2," *TRE* 8:711–12; Hans Conzelmann, *Gentiles, Jews, Christians: Polemics and Apologetics in the Greco-Roman Era* (trans. M. Eugene Boring; Minneapolis: Fortress, 1992), 24–44; Arye Ben-David, *Talmudische Ökonomie* (Hildesheim: Olms, 1974), 41–57; Günter Stemberger, "Juden," *RAC* 19:172–73.

26. Cf. Philo, *Flaccus* 43; on the spread of Judaism, cf. Stemberger, "Juden," *RAC* 19:162–65.

27. Cf. Stemberger, "Juden," *RAC* 19:169–70, 182–83, 194–95, 211–13.

and as Christianity developed, it began to separate from Judaism.[28] The synagogue was the center of all the activities of the Jewish community. Here people gathered for common worship,[29] with prayer, Scripture readings, sermons, lessons, and blessings, and for community meetings and other public events. The importance of the synagogue as a cultural and communication center was increased even more by libraries, schools, hostels, and homes for the aged. Pilgrimages from the Diaspora to Jerusalem not only fostered the connection with the temple and the holy city but thereby facilitated a lively exchange of reports and information between Palestine and the various centers of the Diaspora. Diaspora Jews also may have engaged in missionary work, as indicated by Matt. 23:15 and Horace, *Sermones* 1.4.142–143. However that may be, the existing communication system of the Jewish Diaspora communities presented Paul with the first opportunity to proclaim his new message. Those addressed by this message included, besides ethnic Jews and proselytes, especially the God-fearers. Paul probably received a significant response to his missionary preaching from within this segment, for—like Judaism—Christianity offered them a monotheistic faith and an appealing ethic but without denying them full membership in the community. Gentiles who had no previous contact with the synagogue constituted another central target group of the Pauline mission.[30] This is indicated by texts such as 1 Thess. 1:9–10; 2:16 (Paul speaks polemically against the Jews because they hinder him from preaching the gospel τοῖς ἔθνεσιν [to the Gentiles]); 1 Cor. 12:2; Gal. 2:3 (Τίτος ὁ σὺν ἐμοί, Ἕλλην ὤν [Titus, who was with me, . . . though he was a Greek]); 4:8–9; 5:2–3; 6:12; Rom. 1:13–15, 18ff.; 10:1–3; 11:13 (Ὑμῖν δὲ λέγω τοῖς ἔθνεσιν· ἐφ᾽ ὅσον μὲν οὖν εἰμι ἐγὼ ἐθνῶν ἀπόστολος [Now I am speaking to you Gentiles. Inasmuch then as I am an apostle to the Gentiles . . .]), 17–18, 24, 28, 30–31; 15:15–16, 18; Acts 28:28. We cannot understand the numerous conflicts in Corinth[31] and Rome (cf. Rom. 14:1–15, 13) unless those who had previously been Gentiles were involved in them. The abolition of the distinction between Jews and Gentiles (cf. 1 Cor. 12:13; Gal. 3:28, οὐκ ἔνι Ἰουδαῖος οὐδὲ Ἕλλην

28. E. P. Sanders challenges the Acts portrayal on the basis that the Israel problematic plays a minor role in Paul's letters (except for Rom. 9–11): "Had he spent the previous twenty years preaching in synagogues, the letters to his own churches would reflect the effort in some way or other. . . . It seems, then, that we must think of Paul as preaching directly to Gentiles" (*Paul*, 19).

29. Peter Schäfer, "Der synagogale Gottesdienst," in *Literatur und Religion des Frühjudentums: Eine Einführung* (ed. Johann Maier and Josef Schreiner; Würzburg: Echter, 1973), 391–413.

30. Contra Reiser, "Heiden Bekehrt?" 83–91, who claims Paul did not convert Gentiles in the classical sense but only God-fearers. In contrast, Wolfgang Reinbold, *Propaganda und Mission im ältesten Christentum: Eine Untersuchung zu den Modalitäten der Ausbreitung der frühen Kirche* (FRLANT 188; Göttingen: Vandenhoeck & Ruprecht, 2000), 164–82, argues for Gentiles as the target group of the Pauline mission. To be sure, Reinbold's argument is somewhat one-sided when he states, "To date there is no evidence that Paul had taken part in the mission to Jews during (or even before) his work as apostle to the Gentiles" (p. 174).

31. See below, section 9.1 ("Conflict in Corinth").

[There is no longer Jew or Greek]) makes sense only on the presupposition that the churches included both Gentile Christians and Jewish Christians. Finally, we can adequately explain neither the unique dynamic of the early Christian mission history nor the stormy debates that accompanied it, unless Paul had converted Gentiles in appreciable numbers. Among these Gentiles were both those who had previously been sympathizers with Judaism and those who had no previous relationship with Judaism.[32]

7.2 Beginnings of the Independent Mission

After the directions for the future had been set at the apostolic council and the debates in Antioch and the separation from Barnabas, Paul began his own full-scale independent missionary work. He crossed the boundaries established by the previous Antioch mission, which had been confined to the areas of Palestine, Syria, and southeast Asia Minor, and devoted himself to proclaiming the Christian message in western Asia Minor and Greece. He took the gospel to the cultural centers of the world of that time.

Luke traces the individual stations of this missionary expansion and thus generates the image of the tireless missionary. In company with Silas and Timothy, Paul's way leads from Syria through Cilicia and Phrygia to Galatia and from there to Troas, whence they set out for Macedonia and for the first time set foot on European soil. By portraying the arrival of the gospel in Europe as the result of direct revelation (Acts 16:9–10), Luke underscores the significance of Paul's decision for salvation history.

In Philippi Paul begins his mission work in the context of the synagogue and converts Lydia, a God-fearing businesswoman who dealt in purple goods.[33] The powerful appeal of the Jewish faith had produced a situation in which many people had abandoned worship of the pagan gods and, as worshipers of the one God, had accepted Jewish monotheism, though they were not formally converts to Judaism by circumcision. Particularly in Asia Minor, Paul could evidently win many converts to the new faith from within this group. It is also to be noted that the well-to-do Lydia decided to join the Christian community. The success of Paul's missionary work in Philippi had already resulted in the mistreatment of the apostle and his coworkers. Although the narrative in Acts 16:16–40 has legendary embellishments, its historical kernel is confirmed by 1 Thess. 2:2 (though we had already suffered and been shamefully mistreated at Philippi). From Philippi Paul proceeded westward along the Via Egnatia to Thessalonica. The account in Acts and the data in 1 Thessalonians agree on

32. Dieter Sänger, "Heiden–Juden–Christen," *ZNW* 89 (1998): 159–72, points to this group.
33. Peter Pilhofer, *Philippi* (2 vols.; WUNT 87, 119; Tübingen: Mohr Siebeck, 1995), 1:234–40.

two basic points: (1) Paul had great missionary success (cf. 1 Thess. 1:6–10; Acts 17:4), and (2) the Jews responded with persecutions, which in Acts 17:5ff. affect Paul, and in 1 Thess. 2:14–16 strike the church in Thessalonica. Acts 17:5ff. pictures Paul spending barely a month in Thessalonica. A different picture is given in Phil. 4:15–16, according to which the church in Philippi twice sent financial support to Paul while he was in Thessalonica. While there, Paul and his coworkers also supported themselves by their own work in order not to burden the church (1 Thess. 2:9). Each of these details speaks in favor of a somewhat longer stay of about three months.[34] After his departure, Paul attempted to visit the new church again but without success (cf. 1 Thess. 2:17–18). Paul also had a successful mission in Beroea, and later someone from this church accompanied him on the trip to Jerusalem to deliver the offering (Acts 20:4, Sopater [cf. Rom. 16:21]). From Beroea Paul and his coworkers went to Athens (cf. 1 Thess. 3:1–2). Paul spent a longer time there, and from Athens he sent Timothy to Thessalonica. Except for the fact that he was there, Paul gives no other information about his work in Athens. Paul himself does not mention Luke's accounts of his preaching to Jews and Gentiles in Athens, his encounters with Greek philosophers, and his impressions of the many idols and pagan altars in the city. Paul could hardly have given a speech such as the Areopagus address of Acts 17:22–31.[35] In particular, the idea of a relationship between God and human beings based on natural theology, as recounted in Acts 17:28–29, is inconceivable for Paul, since the point of departure for his own theology is the human alienation from God because of human sin. Presumably Paul's missionary work in Athens had only minimal success. Acts 17:32–34 confirms this assumption, for only Damaris and Dionysius the Areopagite are mentioned by name as having become Christians. Paul appears in Athens as one among many wandering preachers, and his preaching there seems to have had no lasting effect. The tradition says nothing about a church being established in Athens. Among the Pauline churches in Greece, and in the broader history of early Christianity, Athens plays no role, and it is only about 170 CE that we have reports of a Christian community there (Eusebius, *Hist. eccl.* 4.23.2–3).

7.3 The Pauline School and the Structure of Paul's Work with the Churches

To grasp the theological and historical complexity of Paul's life and thought, one must consider that his ministry was embedded in a complex of school traditions. Paul was certainly the outstanding theologian of his time, who developed a new theology that was to have powerful effects. At the same time,

34. Cf. Riesner, *Paul's Early Period*, 364.
35. For analysis, cf. Lüdemann, *Traditions in Acts*, 189–95.

he both came from a school tradition and founded a new school himself. Both the undisputed and the deutero-Pauline letters, in their different ways, show this to have been the case.[36]

As a Pharisee, Paul himself had developed his faith and theology within the tradition of a particular school,[37] and this influence continued throughout his life.[38] Moreover, his letters indicate that within his context of Diaspora Judaism he incorporated a large body of authentic Hellenistic material into his educational development and that he was familiar with the ancient philosophical schools. There are unmistakable similarities between these schools and the Pauline school:[39] a founder,[40] the discussion and interpretation of written documents, table fellowship, the ideal of friendship, the establishment of identity by marking itself off from the outside world, teaching activity in different locations, traveling in the company of disciples, and the founding of circles of sympathizers.[41] After all, Paul did not become a Christian simply as an individual but

36. To the best of my knowledge, the first to speak of a "Pauline school" was Heinrich Julius Holtzmann, *Die Pastoralbriefe* (Leipzig: Wilhelm Engelmann, 1880), 117.

37. Philo, *Spec. Laws* 2.61–62, connects the prohibition of work on the Sabbath with an exhortation to use this day for the study of philosophy: "So each seventh day in every city thousands of schools are open, in which good sense, temperance, courage, justice and other virtues are studied by scholars who sit quietly in order, with ears alert and with full attention." On the nature of contemporary Jewish instruction, cf. Shemuel Safrai, "Education and the Study of the Torah," in *The Jewish People in the First Century: Historical Geography, Political History, Social, Cultural, and Religious Life and Institutions* (ed. Shemuel Safrai and M. Stern; CRINT 1; Assen: Van Gorcum, 1974), 945–70.

38. See above, sections 3.1 ("Background and Social Status") and 3.2 ("Paul: Pharisee in the Diaspora").

39. Cf. the survey in Thomas Schmeller and Christian Cebulj, *Schulen im Neuen Testament? Zur Stellung des Urchristentums in der Bildungswelt seiner Zeit* (Freiburg: Herder, 2001), 46–92; and L. Alexander, "Paul and the Hellenistic Schools: The Evidence of Galen," in *Paul in His Hellenistic Context* (ed. Troels Engberg-Pedersen; Minneapolis: Fortress, 1995), 60–83.

40. Classically expressed in Diogenes Laertius 1.13–15, 18; 2.47, where Socrates is father of numerous philosophical schools. Epicurus says about the sage, "He will found a school, but not for instructing the masses; on request, he will also give public lectures. His doctrine will be firmly established [δογματιεῖν] and will teach with confidence" (Diogenes Laertius 10.121b).

41. On the definition of schools in antiquity, cf. Schmeller and Cebulj, *Schulen*, 91: "A philosophical school is an institutionalized association, between a teacher and several disciples from socially privileged circles, in which philosophical traditions that derive from a particular founder are taught and learned, at the same time being interpreted and ethically actualized." Schmeller infers with regard to Paul, "We can speak of a Pauline school during Paul's own lifetime only with great hesitation" (p. 182). Of course, the Pauline and deutero-Pauline letters do not deal with every characteristic of ancient schools with the same degree of specificity (cf. the listing of critical points, 179–82: there is a stronger consciousness of group identity among Christians, there is no possibility of being promoted to become a teacher of the same rank as Paul, teaching activities are not simply identical with school activities, and the teacher-disciples groups are not separated so sharply from the rest of the community). Six objections may be raised to Schmeller's views: (1) On the methodological plane, one must allow for the fact that new social movements are never merely copies of traditional forms. It always depends on how the traditional pattern is drawn and how closely the new element being compared must be subjected to this pattern. (2) The observed agreements already mentioned between Paul, his coworkers, and ancient philosophical schools are still evidence that they should be understood

after his conversion was introduced into the basics of the Christian faith by the group of coworkers in the Antioch mission, in which Paul himself worked for some time. In 1 Cor. 11:23a and 15:3a he emphasizes the importance of early Christian traditions for his own thought and documents his solidarity with earlier traditions by adopting eucharistic (cf. 1 Cor. 11:23b–25) and baptismal traditions (cf. 1 Cor. 1:30; 6:11; 12:13; 2 Cor. 1:21–22; Gal. 3:26–28; Rom. 3:25; 4:25; 6:3–4), by integrating christological traditions (cf. Rom. 1:3b-4a), and by taking up early Christian hymns (cf. Phil. 2:6–11).

Structures of the Pauline School

In varying degrees of intensity, school traditions had played a formative role in Paul's development prior to his own independent mission, and so it is not surprising that he founded a school himself. Several observations point to the existence of such a school:

(1) Paul makes his appearance on the stage of history as *one who receives revelations* (cf. 1 Cor. 9:1; 15:8; Gal. 1:1, 12, 15–16), as a *model example* for his followers (cf. 1 Thess. 1:6–7, 1 Cor. 4:16; 7:7–8, 11:1; 2 Cor. 4:2; 6:11–13; Gal. 4:12; Phil. 4:9), and as an inspired *teacher* (cf. 1 Cor. 2:12–16; 4:17; 7:40; 14:6, 19, 37–38; Gal. 1:8–9; Phil. 3:15).[42] The apostle is a prime example of one commissioned to mediate the gospel (1 Cor. 9:23); his ministry is part and parcel of God's own act of reconciliation (cf. 2 Cor. 5:19–20).[43]

(2) To a considerable extent, it is Paul's *coworkers* who carry on the work of the Pauline mission, who place their own stamp on it.[44] The undisputed Pauline

---

as comparable phenomena within cultural history. (3) Luke already represents the Christians as a school (cf. Acts 11:26; 26:28, Χριστιανοί [Christians]), and Paul as teacher and founder of a school (one need only note the "lecture hall of Tyrannus" in Acts 19:9 and the portrayal of Paul in Athens in Acts 17:16–34). (4) The high theological level of both the Pauline and (with some limitations) the deutero-Pauline letters indicates that there must have been institutionalized associations and patterns of behavior between Paul and his coworkers, even though these cannot be proven from case to case because of the nature and extent of our sources. (5) Pagan authors understood the Christians as having formed a new school (cf. Galen, *De pulsuum differentiis* 2.4; Lucian, *Alexander* 25.38; *De morte Peregrini* 11, 12, 13, 16). (6) Finally, one may ask about the heuristic value of accepting the school concept and terminology. Are terms such as "community," "mission," "association," "group," or "movement" *better* suited for grasping and understanding the phenomena?

42. Appropriately, Klaus Scholtissek, "Paulus als Lehrer," in *Christologie in der Paulus-Schule: Zur Rezeptionsgeschichte des paulinischen Evangeliums* (ed. Klaus Scholtissek; SBS 181; Stuttgart: Katholisches Bibelwerk, 2000), 34: "Paul worked de facto as a teacher, in the sense of the activity of the historical Paul himself (preaching the gospel, circle of coworkers, founding churches) and regarding its effect as perceived and received by his contemporaries (coworkers, members of the churches, non-Christians) and by later generations."

43. Cf. K. Backhaus, "Mitteilhaber des Evangeliums," in *Christologie in der Paulus-Schule* (ed. Scholtissek), 46–69.

44. Essential on this point is Wolf-Henning Ollrog, *Paulus und seine Mitarbeiter: Untersuchung zu Theorie und Praxis der paulinischen Mission* (WMANT 50; Neukirchen-Vluyn: Neukirchener Verlag,

letters mention about forty people as the apostle's coworkers. Barnabas was the first member of this inner circle, replaced by Silvanus and Timothy when the independent mission began, and later Titus. Silvanus (1 Thess. 1:1) and Timothy (1 Thess. 1:1, 1 Cor. 1:1; 2 Cor. 1:1; Phil. 1:1; Philem. 1:1) serve as co-senders of letters (cf. also Sosthenes in 1 Cor. 1:1), which documents their joint responsibility for the work of the different Pauline churches. In particular, Timothy and Titus emerge as independent missionaries, sent at Paul's behest to resolve problems in the mission churches (cf. 1 Cor. 4:17; 2 Cor. 8). There were also independent missionaries and teachers, both men and women, who worked alongside Paul and with whom the apostle worked from time to time. Apollos (cf. 1 Cor. 1–4; Acts 18:24) and the married couple Prisca and Aquila (cf. 1 Cor. 16:9; Rom. 16:3–4; Acts 18:2, 26) are particular examples of such teachers and mission workers. The majority of Paul's coworkers mentioned in the letters were envoys sent by various churches. They came out of churches founded by the apostle, and they participated in the Pauline mission as delegates of these churches (e.g., Erastus, Gaius, Aristarchus, Sosipater, Jason, Epaphras, and Epaphroditus). They maintained contact with their home churches, supported Paul in various ways, and carried on their independent mission work in the environs of the churches founded in the Pauline enterprise. As the mission continued to expand, Paul himself could maintain only occasional contact with the churches. His letters indicate how dissatisfied the churches were with what they perceived as minimal attention from Paul and how difficult it was for him to provide cogent arguments that would mollify their annoyance (cf. 1 Thess. 2:17–20; 1 Cor. 4:18).

(3) There is a causal connection between the large number of church envoys and Paul's new missionary method. He did not continue the previous practice of missionary journeys but developed an independent *mission center.* Whereas other missionaries or early Christian prophets wandered from place to place, Paul attempted to found a church, that is, one or more house churches, in each provincial capital. He remained in each location long enough for the church to develop its own leadership structure, and his own presence was no longer necessary.[45] Out of the Pauline mission center there grew independent congregations that in turn provided the basis for the broader Pauline mission and took responsibility for their own missionary work (cf. 1 Thess. 1:6–8).

(4) Within this large *circle of coworkers*, it is not likely that Paul's own work was limited to matters of organization. The συνεργοί (coworkers) were not commissioned by Paul but called into service by God (cf. 1 Cor. 3:9). Like Paul, they are committed to the same "work" of preaching the gospel among

---

1979). Cf. also Reck, *Kommunikation und Gemeindeaufbau*; Ulrich Heckel, "Paulus als 'Visitator' und die heutige Visitationspraxis," *KD* 41 (1995): 252–91.

45. On the leadership structures of the house churches, cf. Roger W. Gehring, *House Church and Mission: The Importance of Household Structures in Early Christianity* (Peabody, Mass.: Hendrickson, 2004), 196–225.

the Gentiles (cf. 1 Thess. 3:2; 1 Cor. 3:5–9; 16:10, 15–18; 2 Cor. 8:16–23; Phil. 2:22). We can presume that this work included intensive theological reflection, especially within the inner circle of coworkers.[46] Texts in the Pauline corpus that stand out from their context by their form, theology, and location confirm this supposition. Thus 1 Cor. 13 manifests only a loose connection with its context, and the transition from 1 Cor. 12:31 to 14:1 is seamless.[47] The content also manifests distinctive features, for the charismata of faith, hope, and love here stand above all other spiritual gifts. First Corinthians 13 had clearly been drafted before the composition of the letter itself; it points to the theological work of the Pauline school. Comparable texts are found in 1 Cor. 1:18ff.; 2:6ff.; 10:1ff.; 2 Cor. 3:7ff.; Rom. 1:18ff.; 7:7ff. All these texts are typified by their nonpolemic character, their thematic unity and compactness, and their rootedness in the tradition of Hellenistic Judaism. Their proximity to wisdom literature suggests that here too Paul picks up the thread of his pre-Christian period.[48]

(5) The *deutero-Paulines* (Colossians, Ephesians, 2 Thessalonians, the Pastorals)[49] explicitly confirm the existence of a Pauline school that continued after the death of the apostle. This legacy, found in the writings of four of Paul's disciples, makes clear how Pauline theology was further developed and applied in changed situations. In all the deutero-Paulines, Paul's emphasis on the doctrine of justification, as found in Galatians and Romans, remarkably subsides.[50] Apocalyptic motifs in Christology likewise decline in importance, and an emphasis on present eschatology prevails. The focus is on matters of church order and problems of ethics that have emerged because of the altered situation in the life of the church (the appearance of false teachers; coming to terms with the fading expectation of the parousia). In this situation Paul the sufferer (Colossians, Ephesians, and 2 Timothy present themselves as written from prison) becomes *the* authority of the foundational period. Paul's students appeal to their teacher and attempt to develop his theology within changed

---

46. Cf. Hans Conzelmann, "Paulus und die Weisheit," in *Theologie als Schriftauslegung: Aufsätze zum Neuen Testament* (BEvT 65; Munich: Kaiser, 1974), 177–90; H. Ludwig, "Der Verfasser des Kolosserbriefes: Ein Schüler des Paulus" (dissertation, Georg August Universität, 1974), 201–29; Hans Conzelmann, "Die Schule des Paulus," in *Theologia crucis, signum crucis: Festschrift für Erich Dinkler zum 70. Geburtstag* (ed. Carl Andresen and Günter Klein; Tübingen: Mohr Siebeck, 1979), 85–96; Angela Standhartinger, *Studien zur Entstehungsgeschichte und Intention des Kolosserbriefs* (NovTSup 94; Leiden: Brill, 1999), 1–10, 277–89.

47. Conzelmann, *1 Corinthians*, 217, 233.

48. Conzelmann, "Paulus und die Weisheit," 179; for critiques of Conzelmann's thesis, see Ollrog, *Mitarbeiter*, 115–18; Schmeller and Cebulj, *Schulen*, 102ff.

49. Peter Müller, *Anfänge der Paulusschule: Dargestellt am zweiten Thessalonicherbrief und am Kolosserbrief* (ATANT 74; Zurich: Theologischer Verlag, 1988), 270–320, limits the phenomenon of the Pauline school to the deutero-Paulines.

50. Cf. Ulrich Luz, "Rechtfertigung bei den Paulusschülern," in *Rechtfertigung: Festschrift für Ernst Käsemann zum 70. Geburtstag* (ed. Johannes Friedrich et al.; Göttingen: Vandenhoeck & Ruprecht, 1976), 365–83.

circumstances. Although the deutero-Paulines deviate from Paul's own theology in essential points, they still manifest familiarity with the apostle's thought. The Pauline school tradition, especially Romans, had a deep influence on the author of Colossians in particular. He probably acquired his knowledge of the basic themes of Pauline theology in the Pauline school and then developed them independently in accordance with the challenges of his own time. Acts, too, must be read as a document of the Pauline school tradition. Paul is the true hero of the story and repeatedly steps forth as the teacher who sets the agenda (cf. Acts 11:26; 13:12; 15:35; 17:19; 18:11; 20:20; 21:21, 28; 28:31).[51]

Ephesus is the most likely candidate for the location of the Pauline school.[52] This multicultural city (the Artemis temple, mystery religions, an important Jewish community, the emperor cult, Hellenistic philosophy) was the center of the early Christian mission.[53] Among those who worked here are Prisca and Aquila (cf. Acts 18:19–21; 1 Cor. 16:19), the Alexandrian Apollos (cf. Acts 18:24–28; 1 Cor. 16:12), and Paul himself from the summer of 52 until the spring of 55. In no other city did Paul spend as much time as in Ephesus, where he gathered a large staff and, according to Acts 19:9–10, preached for two years in the lecture hall of Tyrannus the rhetorician. Paul wrote 1 Corinthians in Ephesus, and it is likely that some of the deutero-Paulines were also written there (Colossians, Ephesians [?], the Pastorals).

Paul provided his coworkers and churches with solutions to disputed issues, with corrective theological reflections, and with ethical instructions, and at the same time his own thought was being strongly influenced by his coworkers and the changing situations in the churches. When all is said and done, the hypothesis of a Pauline school grants insight into the process of theological formation, as reflected in the Pauline letters by the interweaving of arguments conditioned by particular situations, general instruction, and foundational tradition.

Mission Strategies

Some passages in Paul's letters afford us a detailed view of how the mission was carried out.[54] Paul proclaimed the gospel not only in the local synagogues but also in private houses (cf. Acts 18:7–8; 20:7–11; 28:30–31; also Rom. 16:23),[55]

---

51. Cf. Bernhard Heininger, "Einmal Tarsus und zurück (Apg 9,30; 11,25–26): Paulus als Lehrer nach der Apostelgeschichte," *MTZ* 49 (1998): 125–43.

52. Cf. Conzelmann, "Paulus und die Weisheit," 179.

53. On Ephesus, cf. esp. Winfried Elliger, *Ephesos: Geschichte einer antiken Weltstadt* (Stuttgart: Kohlhammer, 1985).

54. On the modalities of the Pauline mission, see most recently Reinbold, *Propaganda und Mission*, 188–225. Reinbold places heavy emphasis on the function of Paul's personal contacts: "He makes contact with small groups and structures: incidental acquaintances, members of his own circles, families, colleagues, small interest groups and the like" (p. 195).

55. Cf. the extensive treatment by Gehring, *House Church and Mission*, 179–90.

in public places (cf. Acts 17:16–34),[56] and in prison (cf. Acts 28:30–31; Phil.
1:12ff.; Philemon). He rented halls open to the public (cf. Acts 19:9–10)[57]
and also made use of his craftsman's occupation as a context for his missionary
work (cf. 1 Thess. 2:9).[58] His own labor assured his financial independence
(cf. 1 Cor. 9:18) and freedom of thought, so that he was as independent as
the Cynic preachers.[59] Finally, his close contact with his coworkers served the
cause of the gospel, for Paul trained them to carry on their own missionary
work.[60] The initial preaching of the Christian message led to the founding of
new congregations.[61] According to Rom. 15:20, Paul saw his specific task to
be proclaiming "the good news, not where Christ has already been named, so
that I do not build on someone else's foundation."

The methods by which the gospel was communicated were appropriate to the
content of the gospel itself. Promotion of the gospel and zeal for the Christian
message (cf. 2 Cor. 11:2; Gal. 4:18) must correspond to the proclamation of
the crucified Christ (cf. 1 Cor. 1:17; 2 Cor. 13:4). The conduct of the apostle
has nothing to do with secrecy, cunning, or the profit motive (cf. 2 Cor. 4:1–2;
7:2; 11:7–11). On the contrary, he cares for his churches as a mother cares for
her children (cf. 1 Thess. 2:1–12; 1 Cor. 4:14–16; 2 Cor. 12:14; Gal. 4:9). The

---

56. Cf. Christoph vom Brocke, *Thessaloniki, Stadt des Kassander und Gemeinde des Paulus: Eine
frühe christliche Gemeinde in ihrer heidnischen Umwelt* (WUNT 2/125; Tübingen: Mohr Siebeck, 2001),
151 n. 37, who states regarding Thessalonica what is also likely true of other cities: "One can hardly
imagine that Paul did not make use of the great auditorium of the agora, with its many businesses and
pubic institutions, for his proclamation of the gospel. Along with the harbor, there was hardly any
other place in the city where public and business life pulsated more strongly than here."

57. Cf. Epictetus, *Diatr.* 3.23.30.

58. Cf. Hock, *Social Context*, 37–42. Less fruitful are the alternatives preferred by, e.g., Stanley K.
Stowers, "Social Status, Public Speaking, and Private Teaching: The Circumstances of Paul's Preaching
Activity," *NovT* 16 (1984): 59–82 (the private house as the central location of Paul's preaching); or
Reiser, "Heiden Bekehrt?" 91 ("Paul won Gentile converts in the synagogue, not in the marketplace").
David E. Aune, "Romans as a *logos protreptikos*," in *Paulus und das antike Judentum: Tübingen-Durham-
Symposium im Gedenken an den 50. Todestag Adolf Schlatters (19 Mai 1938)* (ed. Martin Hengel and
Ulrich Heckel; WUNT 58; Tübingen: Mohr Siebeck, 1991), 112–13, counts seven different settings
for Paul's work (synagogue, private homes, rented lecture halls, the Pauline school, workshops, public
places, prison) and then rightly states, "There is no reason, however, why any of these settings should
be considered inappropriate for Paul's teaching ministry" (p. 113).

59. Cf. the evidence in Ebner, *Leidenslisten und Apostelbrief*, 70–71. Musonius, *Diss.* 11: "Clearly
we should expect of a free man that he works for his own necessities rather than taking them from
others. After all, it is more honorable to need no one else to provide for one's needs than to be
dependent on others." Cynics counted manual labor as part of their comprehensive program of
contrast. Indeed, they considered it especially appropriate, alongside their teaching and preaching, to
demonstrate the agreement between their doctrine and their life and to preserve their independence
by doing occasional work. Cf. H. Schulz-Falkenthal, "Zum Arbeitsethos der Zyniker," *WZ(H)GS*
29 (1980): 91–101.

60. One need only note 1 Cor. 16:10, where Paul says of Timothy, "he is doing the work of the
Lord just as I am." The resolution of the conflict between Paul and the Corinthians was mainly the
work of Titus (cf. 2 Cor. 2:13; 7:6, 13–14; 8:6, 16, 23; 12:18).

61. Reck, *Kommunikation und Gemeindeaufbau*, 165ff.

restless life of the apostle is moved by anxious care "for all the churches" (2 Cor. 11:28). He deals with his churches and their individual members with pastoral care (cf. 1 Thess. 2:11); the apostle's words of encouragement and comfort, and his corresponding deeds, belong to the inner core of his missionary work from the very beginning. He responds to his congregations with candor and love and fights for them when they are in danger of being led away from the truth of the gospel (cf. 2 Cor. 11:4, 29; Gal. 3:1–5). Although Paul is driven by the fear that he may have worked in vain for his churches (cf. 1 Thess. 3:5; Gal. 2:2; 4:11; Phil. 2:16), his mission is not merely oriented toward "success." He does not depend on human approval; his sole obligation is to carry out his call as apostle to the Gentiles (cf. 1 Thess. 2:4, 6; 1 Cor. 9:16; Gal. 1:10). Paul has confidence in the truth's own power of persuasion, and this is exactly why he works tirelessly for the truth (1 Thess. 2:13). This dimension of depth gives stability to his restless life.

The lasting significance of the initial preaching of the Christian message is documented in 1 Thess. 1:6–10; 2:1; 4:2ff.; 1 Cor. 3:6, 10–11; 4:15; Gal. 4:13; 5:21; Phil. 1:5; 4:15. Paul reminds the churches of this founding event and derives his own authority from it. As ambassador of the gospel (cf. 2 Cor. 5:19–21; Rom. 10:14–17), he found access to people's hearts because it was the gospel of Jesus Christ that itself persuaded his hearers (cf. 1 Cor. 15:11). It is the Spirit that makes the apostle's preaching effective (cf. 1 Thess. 1:5; 1 Cor. 2:4–5; 4:19–20; Gal. 3:5). Proclamation of the word and the demonstration of power are clearly a single event (cf. 1 Thess. 1:5; 1 Cor. 2:4–5; 4:19–20; 2 Cor. 6:7; 12:12; Gal. 3:5; Rom. 15:18–19). The word δύναμις (power) appears in 2 Cor. 12:12 and Rom. 15:18–19 in connection with σημεῖα (signs) and τέρατα (miracles). Paul too works miracles in his churches, and they confirm his apostolic authority.

The new churches experienced the multidimensional event of the initial preaching as decisive for their future life. The communication of the gospel to them was an event with several layers of meaning, in which foundational faith experiences were combined with cognitive elements. The act of baptism, directly related to conferral of the Spirit, was an existential event. As a symbolic-ritual act, it mediated the new being founded in Jesus Christ and, as baptism in the name of the Lord Jesus, introduced believers into a new existence determined by the Spirit (cf. 2 Cor. 1:21–22; Gal. 3:26–28; Rom. 6:3–4). The induction of converts into the kind of conduct called for in the new Christian life (cf. Gal. 5:21) played a central role in founding a new church (cf. Gal. 5:21). On the positive side, the love command stood at the center; negatively, avoidance of immorality was primary.

House Churches

Since the household was the center of religious life within this general frame of reference, the house became the natural starting point for early Christian

communities, especially since they did not have public buildings available to
them. The house as the central location of religious life had a long tradition in
antiquity; private cultic associations, groups of initiates in the mystery cults, and
philosophical schools chose this location.[62] Furthermore, Jewish congregations
also sometimes met in house synagogues,[63] and the Christian mission began
in the synagogue context. It is thus not surprising that Paul's letters presuppose the existence of house churches (cf. the expression ἡ κατ' οἶκον ἐκκλησία
[the church that meets in their house] in 1 Cor. 16:19; Rom. 16:5; Philem. 2;
cf. also Rom. 16:14–15, 23; Acts 12:12; 18:7; Col. 4:15).[64] To outsiders, the
Christian congregations, like the Hellenistic Jewish synagogue congregations,
appeared to be clubs or associations.[65] Just as the social life of Hellenistic-Roman
antiquity was carried on in social clubs[66] and had its center and high point in

62. Cf. Hans-Josef Klauck, *Hausgemeinde und Hauskirche im frühen Christentum* (SBS 103; Stuttgart: Katholisches Bibelwerk, 1981), 83–97; David L. Balch and Carolyn Osiek, *Families in the New
Testament World: Households and House Churches* (Louisville: Westminster John Knox, 1997)

63. On this, see Carsten Claussen, *Versammlung, Gemeinde, Synagoge: Das hellenistisch-jüdische
Umfeld der frühchristlichen Gemeinden* (Göttingen: Vandenhoeck & Ruprecht, 2002), 160–64.

64. House churches clearly existed in Thessalonica, Philippi, Corinth, Cenchreae, Ephesus, and
Rome; for the post-Pauline time, we may mention Colossae and Laodicea. For analysis, cf. Gehring,
House Church and Mission, 130–55.

65. For the pioneering work on this subject, see G. Heinrici, "Die Christengemeinde Korinths
und die religiösen Genossenschaften der Griechen," *ZWT* 17 (1876): 465–26; then Klauck, *Religious
Context*, 42–54; Thomas Schmeller, *Hierarchie und Egalität: Eine sozialgeschichtliche Untersuchung
paulinischer Gemeinden und griechisch-römischer Vereine* (SBS 162; Stuttgart: Katholisches Bibelwerk,
1995); Stegemann and Stegemann, *The Jesus Movement*, 288–302; Richard S. Ascough, *What Are
They Saying about the Formation of Pauline Churches?* (New York: Paulist, 1998) (a comprehensive
history of research). Schmeller, *Hierarchie und Egalität*, 92ff., emphasizes that clubs, associations, and
congregations reflected the dual structure of a strongly hierarchical social environment: there was,
on the one hand, a more upper-class group of leaders "who, on the one hand, improved their status
within the group by material gifts and other acts in its behalf; on the other hand, there was a strong
emphasis on the unity and fundamental equality of all members, that is, an overcoming of social
barriers that could be expressed, for example, in the image ('fiction') of the Christian family" (p. 94).
In the Pauline churches, however, a higher degree of unity and equality of the membership prevailed
than in the clubs and associations.

66. The legal situation of clubs and associations is summarized by M. Öhler, "Römisches
Vereinsrecht und christliche Gemeinden," in *Zwischen den Reichen: Neues Testament und römische
Herrschaft: Vorträge auf der ersten Konferenz der European Association for Biblical Studies* (ed. Michael
Labahn and Jürgen Zangenberg; TANZ 36; Tübingen: Francke, 2002), 61, as follows: "At least
since the time of Augustus, the formation of clubs and associations had been carefully regulated.
A *collegium* could apply to the senate for permission, which was granted when a case could be
made that some public good would derive from it and no activities damaging to the state were
anticipated. Certain associations that had long existed, including Jewish synagogues, were always
licensed on the basis of their tradition. Alongside these there were innumerable unlicensed groups
that were tolerated as long as they did nothing illegal or offensive." At first, the early Christians
could claim to be a licensed *collegium* on the basis that they were a movement within Judaism;
this was hardly possible from the mid-50s on, as indicated by the persecution under Nero. They
could then continue as an unlicensed club or association like many pagan *collegia* so long as they
appeared politically harmless.

the fellowship of common meals,[67] so also the life of the Christian congregation was structured around the common meal. The establishment of a new group[68] could have taken place only within the framework of regular meetings and common meals in private homes.

We can only guess the size of these first congregations. From 1 Cor. 11:20 and 14:23 we may infer that the whole Corinthian church gathered in one place, that is, in a private house. The atrium of a residence could accommodate thirty to fifty people,[69] and these figures would also define the approximate size of a new congregation; where several house churches existed in larger cities, such as Rome, the total number of members of the church would be larger. The house church was an exceptional place within a somewhat hostile environment, a place where Christians could cultivate and practice their faith. Here they prayed (cf. Acts 12:12), preached the word (cf. Acts 16:32; 20:20), celebrated baptisms and the Eucharist, and provided for traveling missionaries (cf. Acts 16:15). First Corinthians 14:23 speaks of gatherings of the congregation in a house, and Pauline letters were read aloud to the congregation gathered in house churches (cf. 1 Thess. 5:27; Col. 4:16). The house church, as a center of early Christian mission, thus permitted a relative undisturbed practice of religious life and facilitated an efficient competition with synagogue congregations and cultic associations. Finally, the house church also offered a setting for breaking through the conventions of social structure and value systems and for living out the new identity in Christ (cf. Gal. 3:26–28). Within the Christian house churches, the differences between people lost their importance. God had torn all of them out of their old life and placed them in a new reality, which Paul describes as being in Christ.

67. On this, cf. Matthias Klinghardt, *Gemeinschaftsmahl und Mahlgemeinschaft: Soziologie und Liturgie frühchristlicher Mahlfeiern* (TANZ 13; Tübingen: Francke, 1996), 21–174, who elaborates the points of similarity between the table fellowship of the early Christians and the common meals of private groups and various clubs and associations. As in the clubs and other groups, so among the early Christians, table fellowship embodied the values of κοινωνία (fellowship), φιλία (friendship), and χάρις (benevolence); they were the setting of acts of social welfare by the wealthier members and forums for the discussion of basic religious, philosophical, and political issues. Cf. also Dennis Edwin Smith, *From Symposium to Eucharist: The Banquet in the Early Christian World* (Minneapolis: Fortress, 2003)

68. On the definition of a social group, cf. Bernhard Schäfers, "Entwicklung der Gruppensoziologie und Eigenständigkeit der Gruppe als Sozialgebilde," in *Einführung in die Gruppensoziologie: Geschichte, Theorien, Analysen* (ed. Bernhard Schäfers, 2nd ed.; Heidelberg: Quelle & Meyer, 1994), 21: (1) a limited number of members (a small group has a maximum of twenty-five persons); (2) a common goal for the group and "a motive for group and individual behavior"; (3) a "we-feeling" of belonging to the group; (4) a system of common norms and values; (5) "a mesh of interrelated social roles (role differential), oriented to the goal of the whole group, that, among other things, helps the group attain its goal and resolve internal conflicts."

69. Cf. Jerome Murphy-O'Connor, "The Corinth That Saint Paul Saw," *BA* 47 (1984): 147–59; Gehring, *House Church and Mission*, 140–41 (who thinks of a house church of forty to fifty persons).

Faith in Jesus Christ did not separate; it tore down the old walls and built no new ones. Believers really became one in Jesus Christ. The struggle between poor and rich, slave and free, male and female did not determine the reality of the early Christian house churches, but mutual participation in the unity of the one community established by Christ. In the house churches, the new identity was not merely announced or postulated; it was really lived. The attractiveness of the house churches within the Pauline mission was probably due to the fact that here believers no longer had to separate their Christian life and their social life but here could really live the new, liberating life of being in Christ. Small, manageable units with a high level of individual participation of the members on the social, emotional, and intellectual levels were sure to produce results. The young churches broke through the ancient norms by their orientation to the dawning new age, by their self-designation ἐκκλησία, by their lack of official structure, and by their inclusive spectrum of members (women, slaves).[70] The expression ἡ ἐκκλησία ὅλη (the whole church) in 1 Cor. 14:23 and Rom. 16:23 indicates that in larger places, such as Corinth or Rome, there was a "whole church" that included a number of house churches.[71]

For the most part, social stratification in the Pauline house churches reflected the society in which they were located.[72] None of the elite upper class (senators, governors, members of the emperor's family) belonged to the early churches, but their membership likely included some high-ranking local officials (cf. Erastus as "city treasurer" in Rom. 16:23;[73] members of the *familia Caesaris* ["Caesar's household"], Phil. 4:22). Members of upper-class families are greeted in Rom. 16:10–11. Among the wealthy class in their own cities are Gaius (1 Cor. 1:14; Rom. 16:23), Phoebe (Rom. 16:1–2), Stephanas (1 Cor. 1:16; 16:15, 17), and Philemon (Philem. 2). They owned houses, some of them owned slaves, and, most important, they provided financial support for the church as its patrons.[74] The collection for Jerusalem organized by Paul is inconceivable apart from the inclusion of patrons of the congregation. When

70. Cf. Stegemann and Stegemann, *The Jesus Movement*, 252–53.

71. Gehring, *House Church and Mission*, 155–59.

72. For the history of research, cf. Stegemann and Stegemann, *The Jesus Movement*, 288–89; Gehring, *House Church and Mission*, 165–71. Two directions are forming in current research: on the one side, some advocate the thesis of a structural congruence between the Pauline churches and society as a whole (cf. esp. Wayne A. Meeks, *The First Urban Christians: The Social World of the Apostle Paul* [New Haven: Yale University Press, 1983], 51–110); others see their members as belonging to the lower socioeconomic class, whether primarily (Stegemann and Stegemann, *The Jesus Movement*, 295–96) or exclusively (Meggitt, *Poverty*, 75ff.).

73. Cf. Gerd Theissen, "Social Stratification in the Corinthian Community," in *The Social Setting of Pauline Christianity* (trans. and ed. John H. Schütz; Philadelphia: Fortress, 1982), 69–119.

74. On the nature of patronage in Roman society, cf. P. Garnsey and R. Saller, "Patronal Power Relations," in *Paul and Empire: Religion and Power in Roman Imperial Society* (ed. Richard A. Horsley; Harrisburg, PA: Trinity Press International, 1997), 96–103.

Paul emphasizes in 1 Cor. 1:26 that the church did not have "many . . . wise by human standards, not many . . . powerful, not many . . . of noble birth," this presupposes that there were some who were wealthy and influential.[75] Like Paul himself, handworkers and merchants especially can be regarded as belonging to the middle class (cf. Prisca and Aquila, Rom. 16:3; Acts 18:2, 18, 26; cf. also the members mentioned in 1 Thess. 4:11–12).[76] Still, most of the membership of the early churches did belong to the lower socioeconomic class, including numerous slaves (cf. 1 Cor. 7:21–24; Gal. 3:28; Philemon; the slave names in Rom. 16:8–9, 22).[77]

Paul's church visitations and letters both were means of proclaiming the Christian message and for working out conflicts. He often laments the difference between being present with the congregations and being away from them,[78] for he longed to be with his churches in person.[79] Both care for his churches and anxiety about them[80] drove Paul to try to visit his congregations despite the difficulties of doing so. The goal of his visits was to encourage and comfort the churches, to support and admonish them;[81] Paul was concerned about not only their survival but their unity as the body of Christ. Paul also intervened in the spirited life of his congregations with the written word, to guide and lead them and win them over to his point of view. His letters were not only a substitute for his personal presence; the apostle also employed letters as a special means of preaching the gospel. On certain subjects, the letters were a better means of conflict resolution than face-to-face speech.[82]

75. Differently, Stegemann and Stegemann, *The Jesus Movement*, 294–95, who regard the formulation as rhetorical. But the way Paul develops his argument here speaks against this, namely, that God's paradoxical act in the crucifixion of Jesus is also reflected in the social structure of the church.

76. Whether there was any such thing in Roman society as a middle class in the modern sense is a disputed point. Among those who vote against it are Géza Alföldy, *Römische Sozialgeschichte* (Wiesbaden: Steiner, 1975), 94–132. K. Christ (among others) is critical of this division of all Roman society into only two strata (lower class and elite), finding the approach heuristically unfruitful and leveling out the complications of history. See Karl Christ, "Grundfragen der römischen Sozialstruktur," in *Römische Geschichte und Wissenschaftsgeschichte* (3 vols.; Darmstadt: Wissenschaftliche Buchgesellschaft, 1982), 3:152–76; and Friedrich Vittinghoff, "Gesellschaft," in *Europäische Wirtschafts- und Sozialgeschichte in der römischen Kaiserzeit* (ed. Friedrich Vittinghoff and John H. D'Arms; HEWS 1; Stuttgart: Klett-Cotta, 1990), 163–277.

77. According to Schumacher, *Sklaverei*, 42, around the beginning of the first century CE, slaves made up ca. 15–20 percent of the population of the Roman Empire, i.e., ca. ten million persons.

78. Cf. 1 Cor. 5:3; 16:27; 2 Cor. 10:1–2, 11; 13:2, 10; Gal. 4:18; Phil. 1:27; 2:12.

79. Cf. 1 Thess. 2:17; 3:10; Rom. 1:11; 15:23; Phil. 1:8; 4:1.

80. Cf. only 1 Thess. 2:17; 1 Cor. 12:25; 2 Cor. 7:7, 11; 9:2; 11:2; Gal. 2:10.

81. Cf. only παρακαλέω in 1 Thess. 2:12; 1 Cor. 1:10; 4:16; 2 Cor. 1:4–6; Rom. 12:1, 8; 15:31; Phil. 4:2; Philem. 9–10.

82. Cf. the extensive treatment by Bärbel Bosenius, *Die Abwesenheit des Apostels als theologisches Programm: Der zweite Korintherbrief als Beispiel für die Brieflichkeit der paulinischen Theologie* (TANZ 11; Tübingen: Francke, 1994).

7.4 The Self-Understanding of the Apostle to the Gentiles

We can only understand Paul's letters, his missionary work, and the conflicts involved in it when we recognize that the apostle's self-understanding was the driving force of his life. At least from the time when he began his independent Gentile mission, Paul's life was marked by a certain view of world history and his role in how it was unfolding, a view that we can see reflected in basic outline within his letters. Paul was convinced that there is only one God and that this God is carrying out a grand historical plan through Jesus Christ. God had chosen Paul as the apostle to the Gentiles to carry out this plan (cf. Gal. 1:16).

In view of the imminent judgment of God on all people, which would occur with the return of Christ (cf. 1 Thess. 1:9–10), Paul was obligated to fulfill the special task of proclaiming the gospel of Jesus Christ's cross and resurrection in order to save at least some (1 Cor. 9:16, "If I proclaim the gospel, this gives me no ground for boasting, for an obligation is laid on me, and woe to me if I do not proclaim the gospel!"; cf. also 1 Thess. 2:16; 1 Cor. 9:22). Paul considered himself to be especially qualified for this task. In 1 Cor. 15:9 he acknowledges that he is least of all the apostles because of his previous persecution of the church, but then continues: "But by the grace of God I am what I am, and his grace toward me has not been in vain. On the contrary, I worked harder than any of them—though it was not I, but the grace of God that is with me" (1 Cor. 15:10). Paul is doubtless correct when he counts himself among the best of the apostles (cf. also 2 Cor. 11:5, 21–23; Gal. 1:13–14; Phil. 3:4–6), and he successfully undertook the task of proclaiming the gospel to the ends of the world as then understood.

Paul repeatedly explains to his churches that they owe their existence to his bringing the gospel to them (cf. the begetting and birth metaphors in 1 Thess. 2:13; 1 Cor. 3:6–11; 9:1–2; 2 Cor. 2:14–3:3; 10:14–16; Rom. 15:18–21).[83] He especially values his coworkers, who work hard at the missionary task just as he himself does (cf. 1 Cor. 16:16; Rom. 16:6), and expects the Gentile converts to follow his lead without reservations in both their proclamation of the Christian message and in their ethical conduct. Thus not only can he appeal to the Corinthians, "be imitators of me!"[84] (1 Cor. 4:16; 11:1);[85] he can also in the realm of sex ethics express his wish "I wish that all were as I myself am"

---

83. Backhaus, "Mitteilhaber," 46ff.

84. Epictetus, *Diatr.* 8.31–32, has the true Cynic say, "'That you may see yourselves, O men, to be looking for happiness and serenity, not where it is, but where it is not, behold, God has sent me to you as an example; I have neither property, nor house, nor wife, nor children, no, not even so much as a bed, or a shirt, or a piece of furniture, and yet you see how healthy I am. Make trial of me, and if you see that I am free from turmoil, hear my remedies and the treatment which cured me.' For this, at length, is an attitude both humane and noble. But see whose work it is; the work of Zeus, or of him whom Zeus deems worthy of this service" (*NW* 1/2:39–40; Boring et al., eds., *Hellenistic Commentary*, § 455).

85. The philosophers likewise call their disciples to imitate them; cf. Xenophon, *Mem.* 1.6.3.

(1 Cor. 7:7). As founder of the churches and their example to be followed, Paul is the model of what it means to be a follower of Christ (cf., e.g., 1 Cor. 11:1–2; 2 Cor. 6:11–13; 7:2–4a; Gal. 4:12; Phil. 3:17). Paul is himself a participant in the gospel he proclaims (cf. 1 Cor. 9:23). Of course, it is not the life of the apostle in and of itself that is representative but only as derived from and within its relation to Christ (cf. 2 Cor. 12:9–10; Phil. 3:7–8). The metaphor of the Roman triumphal procession in 2 Cor. 2:14 expresses with great poignancy and power Paul's understanding of himself and the nature of reality (Thanks be to God, who in Christ always leads us in triumphal procession, and through us spreads in every place the fragrance that comes from knowing him):[86] Christ is the triumphant victor over the anti-God powers and now leads Paul through the world as a conquered prisoner so that he can announce the victory everywhere. Paul is thus not only one who bears the incense within the victory parade;[87] he understands that he himself is the incense emanating from the procession (2 Cor. 2:15, "For we are the aroma of Christ to God among those who are being saved and among those who are perishing"). The gospel he proclaims separates saved and lost.

In view of his unswerving commitment to the gospel, it is not surprising that for Paul the most alarming possibility was that he had worked in vain and that at the last judgment he could not point to any churches he had founded or at least influenced in the right direction (cf. 1 Thess. 2:19–20; 3:5; 1 Cor. 3:10–17; 2 Cor. 1:13–14; Gal. 4:11; Phil. 2:16). For him, the churches are "the seal of my apostleship" (1 Cor. 9:2). Paul drew from the Spirit the strength and endurance for his indefatigable missionary work. Like the prophets, he understood himself to be one grasped by the πνεῦμα,[88] one who possessed the Spirit and who lived and worked by its guidance (cf., e.g., 1 Cor. 1:10ff.; 14:1, 18, 37–38; Gal. 6:1; Phil. 3:15).

7.5 The Development of Early Christianity as an Independent Movement

In the first two decades of their existence, the successful mission of believers in Christ increasingly led to conflicts with the Jewish mother religion but also to disputes between Romans and Jews and between Romans and the new movement itself as it became increasingly more distinct from Judaism, devel-

---

86. Cf. Seneca, *Ben.* 2.11.1, *Ep.* 71.22. For analysis, cf. Cilliers Breytenbach, "Paul's Proclamation and God's 'Thriambos': Notes on 2 Corinthians 2:14–16b," *Neot* 24 (1990): 257–71; Jens Schröter, *Der versöhnte Versöhner: Paulus als unentbehrlicher Mittler im Heilsvorgang zwischen Gott und Gemeinde nach 2 Kor 2,14–7,4* (TANZ 10; Tübingen: Francke, 1993), 13–33.

87. Cf. Dionysius of Halicarnassus, *Antiquitates romanae* 7.72.13.

88. Cf. Isa. 42:1 LXX, ἔδωκα τὸ πνεῦμά μου ἐπ᾽ αὐτόν, κρίσιν τοῖς ἔθνεσιν ἐξοίσει, "I have put my Spirit upon him; he shall bring forth judgment to the Gentiles."

oping its own shape and self-definition. This development is only natural, for "intersubjective reconstructions of experiences of transcendence are potentially dangerous for the existing social order. 'Other' realities can disturb or even explode the assumed order of everyday life."[89] The successful mission of Jewish believers in Christ, and later of Gentile believers, was such a "reconstruction of experiences of the transcendent" and had important religious and political aftereffects.

The Parting of the Ways

The increasing period of conflict, leading toward separation, that began about 50 CE had multiple causes:[90]

(1) At a time when ancient Judaism was seeking to preserve its religious and ethnic identity, early Christianity, in the process of formation, was consciously and programmatically crossing ethnic, cultural, and religious boundaries.[91] It propagated a *universal plan of messianic redemption* that included people of all nations and cultures. The early Christian mission was not characterized by the demarcation of a particular group from others but by acculturation (cf. 1 Cor. 9:20–22) and enculturation as well as transethnic conceptions (cf. Gal. 3:26–28). The missionary message of early Christianity was consciously transnational and transcultural and transcended class distinctions. It has no analogy in antiquity regarding its magnitude, speed, and results.[92] Early Christianity created a new

89. Luckmann, "Religion–Gesellschaft–Transcendenz," 121.

90. Cf. also Ulrich Luz, "Das 'Auseinandergehen der Wege': Über die Trennung des Christentums vom Judentum," in *Antijudaismus—christliche Erblast* (ed. Walter Dietrich et al.; Stuttgart: Kohlhammer, 1999), 56–73. These events are described from the point of view of the classical historian in J. Molthagen, "Die ersten Konflikten der Christen in der griechische-römischen Welt," *Historia* 40 (1991): 42–76.

91. Differently, N. Elliott, "Paul and the Politics of Empire," in *Paul and Politics: Ekklesia, Israel, Imperium, Interpretation: Essays in Honor of Krister Stendahl* (ed. Richard A. Horsley; Harrisburg, PA: Trinity Press International, 2000),19ff., who challenges the contrast between a Christian universalism and a Jewish particularism with the argument that Paul's universalism is the legacy of his *Jewish* roots, that Paul's thought is not to be contrasted with Judaism but with the Roman Empire. In my opinion, this sets up false alternatives, for although it is true that Paul sometimes bases his support for a universal view of history on Old Testament traditions (esp. Deutero-Isaiah), he completely reinterprets these from the perspective of Christian faith. Paul abandons the particular marks of Jewish identity (election by belonging to a particular ethnic group, land, temple, and circumcision) and thus inevitably and logically comes into conflict with local Jewish authorities and strict Jewish Christian missionaries. At the same time, again inevitably and consistently with the logic of the situation, Paul's eschatology brings him into conflict with Roman authorities, for the claim made for the unique place of Jesus Christ could be understood as relativizing the claims of the emperor.

92. Cf. Martin Goodman, *Mission and Conversion: Proselytizing in the Religious History of the Roman Empire* (Oxford: Clarendon Press, 1994). Thomas Schmeller, "Neutestamentliches Gruppenethos," in *Der neue Mensch in Christus: Hellenistische Anthropologie und Ethik im Neuen Testament* (ed. Johannes Beutler; QD 190; Freiburg: Herder, 2001), 120–34, regards the membership recruitment carried on by philosophical schools as an analogy to the early Christian mission, but this does

cognitive identity that in part took up previous cultural identities and at the same time fundamentally reformed them.

(2) Early Christianity offered the same attractions as Judaism—a monotheistic message and a high ethical standard—but did so without Judaism's restrictions and hurdles. On the one hand, the *early Christian identity concept* integrated and transformed basic Jewish convictions even as, on the other hand, it separated them from the classic pillars of Judaism (election, Torah, temple, and land).

(3) The proclamation of the crucified and risen Messiah clearly had a deeply attractive power for *the God-fearers*. When they became Christians, the synagogue lost numbers of wealthy and politically influential people (cf. Acts 16:14–15; 17:4) and thus an important connection to pagan society. In many places this would disturb the delicate balance in Jewish-Gentile relations.

(4) The *edict of Claudius* had far-reaching effects on the relations between Christianity and Judaism and on the whole history of the early Christian mission. It prevented an early trip to Rome by Paul (cf. Rom. 1:13; 15:22) and changed the constituency of the Roman church. But above all, the success of the early Christian mission among Gentile sympathizers of the synagogue in Rome (and in other areas of the empire) led to a defensive reaction within Judaism. This became so fierce in Rome that it attracted the attention of the emperor, who intervened in order to prevent even greater disruptions. Although the edict of Claudius probably did not result in the expulsion of all Jews and Jewish Christians from Rome,[93] numerous leaders of both groups were forced to leave the world capital.[94] This produced a dangerous situation for Judaism. If at the heart of the Roman Empire Judaism was being looked upon as a notorious disruptive influence, it would be only a small step for the Romans to institute harsher measures against Jews—for example, to drive all Jews from Rome and to declare Judaism a *collegium illicitum*. Although Claudius had confirmed the special rights granted the Jews by Augustus,[95] further disturbances could lead

---

not take sufficient note of the differences, since such recruitment lacked the strategic dimensions of a mission such as Paul's.

93. The Jewish population of Rome is estimated at about forty thousand in the early imperial period; cf. Karl-Leo Noethlichs, *Das Judentum und der römische Staat: Minderheitenpolitik im antiken Rom* (Darmstadt: Wissenschaftliche Buchgesellschaft, 1996), 10. Rudolf Brändle and Ekkehard Stegemann, "Die Entstehung der ersten 'christichen Gemeinde' Roms im Kontext der jüdischen Gemeinden," *NTS* 42 (1996): 4, calculate that there were about twenty thousand Jews in Rome at the time of Nero.

94. Cf. Riesner, *Paul's Early Period*, 199–200.

95. Cf. Josephus, *Ant.* 14.259–260; 19.280–291, 299–311; 20.10–14. The Jews had special rights to assemble, to pay the temple tax, to have their own courts for internal affairs, to refrain from work on the Sabbath, and to keep their food laws and were not required to participate in the emperor cult or to offer sacrifice to foreign gods. On this, cf. Delling, *Diasporasituation*, 49–55; Günter Stemberger, "Die Juden im römischen Reich: Unterdrückung und Privilegien einer Minderheit," in *Christlicher Antijudaismus und jüdischer Antipaganismus: Ihre Motive und Hintergründe in den ersten drei*

to the loss of these privileges.[96] Moreover, the emperor's action would quickly become known in the provinces, so that it would no longer be only a matter of a local conflict. There were thus adequate grounds for the Jews to clarify their relationship to the new movement so as not to precipitate even more dangerous conflicts. From their perspective, Jews had to regard Christian beginnings as a destabilizing element: Christians obtained many of their members from people associated with the synagogue, and so long as the new group was considered a segment of Judaism, it endangered the sensitive relationship between Jews and the Roman government. In particular, the expulsions of Jews from Rome that are known to us always occurred in the context of missionary-syncretistic activities.[97] The expulsion of 139 BCE, mentioned by Valerius Maximus,[98] happened when some syncretistic Jews in Rome began propagating a cultic mixture of Judaism and religious ideas and practices from Asia Minor.[99] As a result of aggressive proselytizing propaganda,[100] in 19 CE Tiberius expelled the Jews from Rome as part of a general action against oriental cults.[101] From the Roman perspective, the edict of Claudius was in line with this previous action, and especially statements critical of Judaism in Cicero[102] and Seneca indicate that the ruling class in Rome was inclined to keep its distance from Judaism. Especially revealing are the statements of Seneca, a contemporary of Paul, handed on by Augustine

---

Jahrhunderten (ed. Herbert Frohnhofen; Hamburger theologische Studien 3; Hamburg: Steinmann & Steinmann, 1990), 6–22; Alvarez Cineira, *Claudius*, 165–70.

96. In the years 47–49 Claudius intensified his efforts to stimulate a revival of Roman religion; in 49 he extended the *pomerium*, i.e., the area in which only Roman gods could be worshiped; cf. Rainer Riesner, *Die Frühzeit des Apostels Paulus: Studien zur Chronologie, Missionsstrategie, und Theologie* (Tübingen: Mohr Siebeck, 1994), 105–7.

97. The 186 BCE court trial regarding the Bacchanalia, reported in Livy, *Urbe cond.* 39, shows clearly that the religious tolerance of the Romans ended at the point where they became nervous about the destabilizing of public order. On the relation of Roman religion to other religions, cf. Ursula Berner, "Religio und superstitio," in *Der Fremden wahrnehmen: Bausteine für eine Xenologie* (ed. Theo Sundermeier; SVR 5; Gütersloh: Gütersloher Verlagshaus, 1992), 45–64.

98. Valerius Maximus, *Facta et dicta memorabilia* 1.3.3; text and commentary in Menahem Stern, *Greek and Latin Authors on Jews and Judaism* (3 vols.; Jerusalem: Israel Academy of Sciences and Humanities, 1974), 1:357–60.

99. Cf. Martin Hengel, *Judaism and Hellenism: Studies in Their Encounter in Palestine during the Early Hellenistic Period* (trans. John Bowden; 2 vols.; London: SCM Press, 1974), 1:263–64.

100. Cf. Suetonius, *Tib.* 36: "He abolished foreign cults, especially the Egyptian and the Jewish rites, compelling all who were addicted to such superstitions to burn their religious vestments and all their paraphernalia. . . . The others of that same race or of similar beliefs he banished from the city, on pain of slavery for life if they did not obey." Cf. also Tacitus, *Ann.* 2.85; Josephus, *Ant.* 18.81–83, who reports that a teacher of the Jewish law in Rome could win prominent women over to Judaism, to which the emperor Tiberius responded by driving all the Jews from Rome.

101. Cf. Seneca, *Ep.* 108.22: "I grew up in the early years of the reign of the emperor Tiberius. Foreign cults were then removed, and refusal to eat the meat of certain animals was taken as evidence of superstition."

102. Cf. Cicero, *Flac.* 66, where he comments on the presence of a Jewish group at Flaccus's trial: "You know how influential they are, how they stick together, and the role they play at assemblies."

with the comment that already at that time the Christians were hated enemies of the Jews. Seneca says of the Jews, "The ways of this ignominious people have attained such influence that they have found their way into almost every country. The conquered have given laws to the conquerors."[103] The dangerous political and cultural constellation as a whole must have led the Jews to see that Christianity appeared to the Romans to be an aggressive missionary and syncretistic movement and that Jews needed to distance themselves from it.

Some passages in Paul's letters and Acts indicate, however, that even after the edict of Claudius the local Jewish communities took actions against the new Christian movement. Acts 17:1–9 gives an account of the Pauline mission in Thessalonica and the related conflicts. Paul was in Thessalonica around the turn of the year from 49 to 50 CE[104] and won over a considerable number of people who had been previously related to the synagogue (Acts 17:4). This resulted in tumults instigated by Jews, and Christians were dragged before the city authorities and charged with two political offenses: Christians had thrown the whole world into turmoil (Acts 17:6), and they violated the "decrees" (δόγματα) of the emperor. The plural δόγματα probably refers to the edict of Claudius,[105] which in this context also makes understandable the charge that Christians were upsetting the whole world. When the early Christians preached that, in view of the near parousia of Christ, *Roma aeterna* would also pass away, the Roman authorities were also concerned.[106] First Thessalonians 2:14–16 confirms the Acts reports of actions against Paul and his coworkers, in which Jews also were involved.[107] Only so can the sharp anti-Jewish polemic in 1 Thess. 2:15–16 be explained. It seems clear that Jews lodged charges against the apostle with the Roman authorities, charging him with disturbing the peace and violating the religious policy of Claudius.[108] The explosiveness of Paul's missionary success for the political stability of Judaism clarifies a narrative unit that Luke places immediately before Thessalonica. In Philippi Paul's preaching had led to economically motivated countermeasures from the Gentiles that climaxed in their charge of disturbing the peace: "These men are disturbing our city; they are Jews and are advocating customs that are not lawful for us as Romans to adopt or observe" (Acts 16:20b–21). For Jews, such charges were dangerous

---

103. Augustine, *Civ.* 7.11; cf. Seneca, *Ep.* 95.47; 108.22.

104. Cf. Riesner, *Paul's Early Period*, 364–65.

105. Cf. Alvarez Cineira, *Claudius*, 268.

106. Cf. Karl P. Donfried, "The Imperial Cults of Thessalonica and Political Conflict in 1 Thessalonians," in *Paul and Empire: Religion and Power in Roman Imperial Society* (ed. Richard A. Horsley; Harrisburg, PA: Trinity Press International, 1997), 215–23, who explicates the process of how the emperor attained divine status in Thessalonica and displaced even Zeus. Against this background, Paul's preaching could have seemed anti-empire to those responsible for law and order in Thessalonica.

107. Cf. Riesner, *Paul's Early Period*, 352–53; Alvarez Cineira, *Claudius*, 280–86; for interpretation of the texts, see below, section 8.2 ("The Theology of 1 Thessalonians").

108. E. Bammel, "Judenverfolgung und Naherwartung," *ZTK* 56 (1959): 294–315, had already made the connection between 1 Thess. 2:14–16 and the edict of Claudius.

in a double perspective: (1) Jews were identified with the new movement of believers in Christ and regarded as also responsible for the agitation they were causing, and (2) the message and practice of the new movement was classified as politically explosive and anti-Roman. On both counts the Jews must have had grounds for distancing themselves from the new agitators.

Galatians 6:12 also documents the conflict between the Pauline mission and the Jews. Regarding the motivation of his Jewish opponents, Paul says, "It is those who want to make a good showing in the flesh that try to compel you to be circumcised—only that they may not be persecuted for the cross of Christ." This verse contains two items of valuable historical information: (1) The real occasion for the arrival of Judaists in Galatia was the pressure of Judaism on Jewish Christians, especially in Jerusalem. The Judaists evidently were convinced that the problem could be avoided only by a full integration of the Gentile Christians into the broader framework of Judaism. (2) By using the word μόνον (only), Paul points to a decisive difference between himself and his Judaist opponents. They pervert the gospel only so that they will not be persecuted; that is, Paul too is persecuted by Jews, but without letting it cause him to betray the gospel. A reflection of these events is also found in Gal. 4:21–31, where Paul alludes to the current state of relations between Jews and Christians, especially in 4:29: "But just as at that time the child who was born according to the flesh persecuted the child who was born according to the Spirit, so it is now also." The expression οὕτως καὶ νῦν (so it is now also) alludes to the present persecutions of Jewish Christians by Jews. Galatians 5:11 must also be understood within this context: "my friends, why am I still being persecuted if I am still preaching circumcision? In that case the offense of the cross has been removed." Only the reality of persecution testifies to the truth of the Pauline message of the cross. In contrast to his opponents, Paul does not falsify the gospel under the pressure of persecution.

The Pauline Gentile mission, free from the requirement of circumcision and thereby in fact free from the Torah (except for its core of ethical requirements), was obviously attacked from two sides, which also opposed each other. The Jews put pressure not only on Paul but also on his Judaist opponents. Their goal was probably to prohibit the new movement from being regarded as a part of Judaism with its privileged status and to expose it as a *collegium illicitum*. The events related to the fire in Rome in 64 CE permit us to suppose that they were successful in achieving this goal. Christians were now seen as an independent movement that one could charge with responsibility for the trouble without reason and without opposition.

The Situation of the Earliest Jerusalem Church

This situation was especially dangerous for the original Jerusalem church. It had been subject to pressures from the Jewish side from the very beginning, and these increased after the persecutions associated with Stephen in the early 40s (Acts 8:1–3). Acts 12:1ff. reports the execution of James son of Zebedee and the imprisonment of Peter by Agrippa I, who from 41 to 43/44 CE ruled the whole realm that had once been subject to Herod the Great. He advocated a political program that was consciously religious and national in character[109] and persecuted segments of the early Jerusalem church. Apparently Agrippa I regarded the new movement as a destabilizing factor for Diaspora Judaism and also saw it making problems for Jewish relations with Rome.[110] He thus probably moved against the parts of the original church that had no objection to the acceptance of Gentiles into the new movement without requiring circumcision. In contrast, James the brother of Jesus was spared, since on this issue he adopted a negative or at least hands-off stance. The success of the Pauline mission, however, hampered the Jerusalem church's strategy for remaining within Judaism. Obviously the Jewish Christians in Jerusalem placed themselves under suspicion within the synagogue, for they maintained their contacts with an ever-growing number of "unclean" Gentile Christians. Two fundamental changes in contrast to the situation at the time of the apostolic council clarify this development: (1) As war with the Romans drew nearer and nearer, Jewish nationalism intensified under influence of the Zealot movement,[111] which meant increasing separation from Gentiles. (2) The rapidly growing number of Gentile Christians and their claim to be members of the elect people of God without meeting the requirement of circumcision must have been understood in the synagogue as provocation and threat. Thus, under the leadership of James the brother of Jesus, the Jerusalem church probably decided to shift its ground from the agreements made at the apostolic council or to activate a reservation it always had with regard to the Pauline position. So that Christians would continue to be regarded as a group within Judaism, a countermission to the Pauline mission was launched with the goal of compelling Gentile Christians to be circumcised and to adopt the Jewish festival calendar. Galatians, Romans, and Philippians must be read against this background. The Jerusalem church now categorized the Gentile mission's not requiring circumcision as theologically dangerous and politically illegitimate. The distant attitude of the Jerusalem Christians toward Paul is also seen in their refusal to accept the collection and their failure to give Paul any support during his final trials by the Romans.[112] Nonetheless, this pointed dissociation of itself from Paul was

---

109. Cf. Schürer, *History of the Jewish People*, 1:442–54.

110. Cf. Bernd Wander, *Trennungsprozesse zwischen frühem Christentum und Judentum im 1. Jahrhundert nach Christus: Datierbare Abfolgen zwischen der Hinrichtung Jesu und der Zerstörung des Jerusalemer Tempels* (TANZ 16; Tübingen: Francke, 1994), 212–30, who points to the Caligula crisis and the difficult situation of the Jews in Alexandria.

111. Cf. Martin Hengel, *The Zealots: Investigations into the Jewish Freedom Movement in the Period from Herod I until 70 A.D* (trans. David Smith; Edinburgh: T&T Clark, 1989), 313–58.

112. See below, section 13.1 ("Prehistory: Paul en Route to Rome").

unable to improve the relation of the Jerusalem church to Judaism, as shown
by the death of James and other members of the Jerusalem church in 62 CE
(cf. Josephus, *Ant.* 20.197–203).[113]

The Pauline Gentile mission was thus carried on within the framework of
extremely complex political and religious conditions and to no small degree
accelerated the separation of Christianity from Judaism. The success of the
Gentile mission with no requirement of circumcision considerably aggravated
the competitive situation that had actually been present from the very beginning. Judaism's defensive reaction then accelerated the new movement's process
of self-definition and thus also its separation from Judaism, for, as a rule, the
identity of a group as perceived from outside strengthens the internal process
of self-discovery. The persecutions show that also from within Judaism there
were those who perceived believers in Christ to be foreign and threatening,
which is to say that the separation was not a matter of fate but an unavoidable conclusion consciously drawn by each side. Not only did the Christianity
being formed separate from Judaism; Judaism separated itself from emerging
Christianity. Judaism was not interested in being brought into direct connection
with a movement that regarded as the Son of God one who had been executed
by the Romans as a rabble-rouser.[114]

An Independent Movement

The development of early Christianity as an independent movement and
the separation from Judaism this process entailed doubtless included recipro-
cal actions. For an extended period, various options had existed on each side,
but developments were simultaneously under way that irrevocably determined
the course of events. Especially the successful Gentile mission of the Antioch
church, followed by that of Paul and his school, which was followed in turn by
reactions from the Jewish side, influenced and accelerated both early Christian
identity formation and the separation of the Χριστιανοί from the Judaism
within which Christianity had originated.

At what point can we begin to speak of the Christians as an independent
and identifiable movement? When did Jewish and Gentile believers in Christ
become Jewish and Gentile Christians? It is difficult to pinpoint a precise date,
but lines of historical development can be identified:

(1) The persecution of Christians in Rome in 64 CE, in contrast to the edict
of Claudius (49 CE), presupposes a comprehensive *process of differentiation*
between Jews, on the one hand, and Jewish and Gentile Christians, on the
other. There were two aspects to this process: (a) As the proportion of Jewish

---

113. For interpretation, cf. Wander, *Trennungsprozesse*, 263–72.
114. On this point, cf. F. Vittinghoff, "'Christianus sum': Das 'Verbrechen' von Außenseitern der
römischen Gesellschaft," *Historia* 33 (1984): 336ff.

Christians within the Roman church declined, Gentile Christians became more influential, and this forced the separation of Jewish congregations from the church in Rome. (b) The dominance of Gentile Christians probably also led to a situation in which the Roman authorities began to identify Christians as an independent movement distinguishable from Judaism. Moreover, the "enormous mass" of Christians who were arrested during the Neronian persecution (Tacitus, *Ann.* 15.44.4) presupposes that the Roman church had grown very quickly. If Nero, without further argument and with the applause of the population, could charge the Christians with responsibility for the fire in Rome, then the new movement must have come to public attention some time before and was already popularly regarded as blameworthy.[115] A development (which Paul's letter to Rome attempted to guide) must already have been in its final stage at the end of the 50s: the separation of the predominantly Gentile congregations in Rome from the synagogue. Thus early Christianity in Rome and undoubtedly elsewhere was recognizable and known as an autonomous movement, and it was now headed for conflicts with the claims of the Roman state.

(2) When did this development begin, when did a messianic reform group within Judaism become *a recognizably independent movement?* Just as the year 64 CE marks the first decisive endpoint, the designation Χριστιανοί about 40 CE in Antioch marks the beginning point. The geographical separation from Jerusalem, Judea, and Galilee, partially corresponding to a difference in substance, made the formation of a new identity somewhat easier, and Jewish and Gentile believers in Christ became Jewish Christians and Gentile Christians. In the context of the progressive extension of the mission (e.g., to Rome and North Africa), individual groups of believers in Christ modulated into a movement with its own identity and a network with a variety of interconnections, both of which were indispensable presuppositions for its success. In Antioch about 40 CE all necessary conditions were fulfilled for speaking of an independent and identifiable movement:[116] believers in Christ appealed to their founder as

---

115. On the Neronian persecution, see below, section 13.4 ("Paul the Martyr").

116. Regarding terminology, in the academic study of religion and the social sciences in the German-speaking world, the prevalent term is "group"; cf. Günter Kehrer, "Religiöse Gruppenbildung," in *Religionswissenschaft: Eine Einführung* (ed. Hartmut Zinser; Berlin: Dietrich Reimer, 1988), 97–113. Cf. also Schäfers, "Entwicklung," 23, who, along with many others, differentiates between small groups (up to twenty-five persons), large groups (twenty-five to one thousand persons), and institutions. Regarding both language and content, the differentiation between "small groups" and "large groups" is problematic, since in everyday language "group" has come to mean mostly "small group." "The structure and size of the 'small group' is thus almost identical with that of the social group as such" (Schäfers, "Entwicklung," 23). It thus makes sense to me to restrict the term "group" to the "small group" and to replace the term "large group" with "movement." Thereby the dynamic character of larger social structures is emphasized, an aspect of great importance in early Christianity. Moreover, among scholars in the English-speaking world, the word "movement" for the formation of new religious structures has become common (cf., e.g., John A. Saliba, *Understanding New Religious Movements* [2nd ed.; Walnut Creek, CA: AltaMira, 2003]). Other sociological classifications of early Christians include *millenarian movement* (John G. Gager, *Kingdom and Community: The Social World of Early Christianity*

authority, had a name, emerged in public with a provocative and controversial doctrine, were well organized, had an international network, and carried on an organized campaign for members, that is, engaged in mission.

(3) It is no accident that the growth of Gentile Christianity in Syria, Asia Minor, Greece, and Rome greatly strengthened the *independence* of the new movement, for in Paul we already find a clearly recognizable consciousness of the theological and sociological independence of Christians: (a) Early Christians have formed their own concept of identity, targeted at overcoming the Greek and Jewish identity concepts (Gal. 3:26–28, "here there is neither Jew nor Greek"). (b) Paul and the early churches choose for their self-description not συναγωγή (synagogue) but the political term ἐκκλησία (church) (both mean literally "gathering," "assembly"). (c) According to 1 Thess. 2:14–16, God has condemned the Jews for hindering the efforts of Paul and his coworkers in proclaiming the saving message to the nations. (d) Paul protests that the concept and terminology of freedom belong exclusively to the new movement (cf. Gal. 4:31; 5:1). (e) The "new covenant" is not an improved version of the old one but a qualitatively new event characterized by the Spirit and unsurpassable glory (2 Cor. 3:6, 10). Only what was previously together can experience separation. But the Pauline churches in the urban centers of the Mediterranean world existed from the very beginning mainly outside the realm of the synagogue and also represented something new and independent over against the early Palestinian church. They assured their existence by insisting that newly converted members must be loyal exclusively to their new faith,[117] by a high religious and intellectual level,[118] by a social network, and by a new way of life within the churches that transcended previous social status, relating to each other as brothers and sisters of one family.

(4) New forms of meaning formation such as early Christianity can only originate if they have *the capacity to unite with existing historical realities.*[119] Pre-Pauline and Pauline Christianity manifested this unitive capacity, for it integrated ideas from traditional Palestinian Judaism, Hellenistic Judaism, and Greco-Roman religion and culture, simultaneously transforming them.

[Englewood Cliffs, NJ: Prentice-Hall, 1975], 20–65); *scholastic community* (E. A. Judge, "The Early Christians as a Scholastic Community," *JRH* 1 [1960]: 4–15, 125–37); *philosophical school/association* (Robert L. Wilken, "Collegia, Philosophical Schools, and Theology," in *The Catacombs and the Colosseum* [ed. Stephen Benko and John J. O'Rourke; Valley Forge, PA: Judson, 1971], 268–91); *cult movement* (Rodney Stark, *The Rise of Christianity: A Sociologist Reconsiders History* [Princeton: Princeton University Press, 1996], 44).

117. Stark, *The Rise of Christianity*, 203–8.

118. The evidence of Paul's letters and the Gospels shows that the early Christians *must have* worked at a high intellectual level; cf. François Vouga, "Die religiöse Attraktivität des frühen Christentums," *TGl* 88 (1998): 26–38. To this very day, the pagan propaganda of the second century has prevented people from seeing this.

119. Cf. Rüsen, "Was heißt: Sinn der Geschichte?" 38.

(5) Paul took materials and ideas that had already been developed and gave them a *systematic quality*: the schema of an event of universal judgment and salvation with no distinctions, into which those who believe and are baptized are incorporated.[120] With the resurrection of Jesus Christ from the dead, God inaugurated a process of universal transformation in which Christians already fully participate, a process God will soon bring to its consummation at the parousia.

(6) This theological concept of a universal plan of God cannot be combined with a theology oriented to particular Jewish identity based on election, Torah, temple, and land.[121] Instead, *faith in Jesus Christ as the only ground of salvation*, along with membership in the worshiping Christian community, shapes the awareness that, already in the present, believers participate in God's eschatological act of salvation.

(7) The lingering Jewish identity concepts partially adopted by some first-century Christian authors (e.g., Matthew, James) is *not* evidence against the thesis that Christianity became an independent movement rather early.[122] The *development took place in different ways and at different speeds* in different geographical areas and periods, but in the course of a painful process of separation, the Christianity that bore a Pauline stamp, and the Judaism that differentiated itself from such Christians, set the unavoidable directions for the future. Later authors partly repeated in their own ways what had essentially already been decided. This is a natural process, for identity formation always occurs with others in view; they are needed as a foil in order to articulate one's own sense of identity.[123]

(8) Paul is the decisive representative of the formation of early Christianity as an independent movement.[124] If, as in 1 Cor. 9:20–21, he can become a

120. On this, cf. David G. Horrell, "'No Longer Jew or Greek': Paul's Corporate Christology and the Construction of Christian Community," in *Christology, Controversy, and Community: New Testament Essays in Honour of David R. Catchpole* (ed. David G. Horrell and C. M. Tuckett; Leiden: Brill, 2000), 321–44.

121. From the point of view of the sociology of religions, early Christianity developed very quickly from a subcultural ethnic religion (as one direction within ancient Judaism) to a subcultural universal religion with the character of a religion of redemption and reconciliation; on the typology, cf. G. Mensching, *Soziologie der Religion* (2nd ed.; Bonn: Röhrscheid, 1968), 24ff.

122. For a completely different view, see ibid., 112–29; Mensching vehemently rejects the model of a "parting of the ways" and instead argues for understanding the relation of Jews and Christianity "as a single circulatory system, in which discursive elements could move from non-Christian Jews and back to them and could develop new aspects in the course of moving through the system" (p. 120). From this he concludes that still in the second century "the boundary between them became so blurred that no one could say exactly where the one ended and the other began" (121). This model simply ignores the historical facts presented above and is oriented to the boundless religious pluralism of the United States in the twenty-first century rather than to the intensive disputes and demarcations between Jews and Christians in the first and second centuries CE.

123. Rüsen, *Historische Vernunft*, 78.

124. But this is a long way from implying that Paul was the "real" founder of Christianity, as Lüdemann, *Founder*, 213–27, wants to suggest with his anti-Christian ideology. There is no "founder

Jew to Jews and a Gentile to Gentiles, then he is neither Jew nor Gentile in the full sense of either word but the representative of a new movement and religion. The awareness of early Christians that they were a "third race" of humanity alongside Jews and Greeks also comes to expression in 1 Cor. 1:22–23 and 10:32. In 1 Cor. 9:22–23 Paul designates the theology of the cross as the decisive difference between Christian faith and the symbolic universes of both Jews and Greeks. *The message of the cross is not compatible with these symbolic universes* and therefore must appear to the Jews as an offense and to the Greeks as foolishness. In 1 Cor. 10:32 Paul admonishes the Corinthian church not to cause any offense to the Jews, the Greeks, and the ἐκκλησία τοῦ θεοῦ (church of God). Paul positions the church as a whole[125] as an independent reality alongside Jews and Greeks and expresses this semantically through the neologism ἐκκλησία τοῦ θεοῦ.[126]

(9) Historical meaning formations are thus only successful if they are combined with *attractive identity concepts*. It is especially Paul who developed and practiced a new universal identity concept: "being in Christ," which transcends all traditional religious privileges. This transnational and transcultural concept, ritually transmitted (by baptism),[127] was not integrable into the Jewish and Greco-Roman identity structures and consequently led to the formation of early Christianity as an independent movement.

---

of Christianity"; rather, this new movement is based on the experiences and faith of a large number of (mostly) nameless men and women, some of whom had already been followers of Jesus of Nazareth and who, before and apart from Paul, had founded the churches of Damascus, Antioch, Alexandria, and Rome, and were still active in Paul's own time (one need think only of the congregations in Rome and of Apollos in Corinth). Within the tension-filled history of early Christianity, Paul gets the credit for presenting the landmark theological interpretation of the Christ event.

125. Cf. Jürgen Roloff, "ἐκκλησία," *EDNT* 1:411–12.

126. On ἐκκλησία τοῦ θεοῦ, see below, section 21.1 ("Primary Vocabulary and Foundational Metaphors of Pauline Ecclesiology").

127. Gerd Theissen, "Die urchristliche Taufe und die soziale Konstruktion des neuen Menschen," in *Transformations of the Inner Self in Ancient Religions* (ed. Gedaliahu A. G. Stroumsa and Jan Assmann; SHR 83; Leiden: Brill, 1999), 90ff., rightly emphasizes that the differentiation between early Christianity and Judaism entailed a new understanding of baptism that had been developed in the context of the Gentile mission and is found in its fully developed form in Paul. "The origin of baptism is closely related to the origin of a new subculture religion, independent of its origins and oriented to reconciliation, that brought together people from many national and ethnic backgrounds into small Christian communities. Relationship-through-rebirth took the place of relationship-through-birth. The construct of a ritually mediated new birth replaced physical birth. The social construction of the new person is thus not an incidental marginal phenomenon of this new religion but its constitutive presupposition" (pp. 93–94).

8

Paul and the Thessalonians

Consolation and Confidence

Paul and his churches—a continuing love story. The restless apostle had the capacity to be truly concerned with the problems of the young churches. He was able to offer consolation, encouragement, and confidence.

8.1 Prehistory and Initial Preaching

The city of Thessalonica was newly founded about 315 BCE. Its excellent location in the innermost cove of the Gulf of Thermai and on the Via Egnatia guaranteed its importance for all time as a port city and hub of transportation and commerce.[1] The city also possessed great drawing power as a cultural and religious center. Thus the intellectual life of the city was flavored by its many philosophers, rhetoricians, and poets;[2] excavations and literary evidence docu-

---

1. On the history of the city, see Winfried Elliger, *Paulus in Griechenland: Philippi, Thessaloniki, Athen, Korinth* (Stuttgart: Katholisches Bibelwerk, 1987), 78–116; Riesner, *Paul's Early Period*, 337–41; Vom Brocke, *Thessaloniki*, 12–101.

2. Cf. Vom Brocke, *Thessaloniki*, 143–51.

ment the worship of cult deities such as Serapis, Isis, Dionysus, or the pre-Greek deities known as the Cabiri.[3] The Roman emperor cult and its connection with the martial arts were also important.[4]

The Church

The successful mission that resulted in founding the church at Thessalonica had not occurred very long before the composition of 1 Thessalonians. After leaving the church, Paul had twice wanted to return, but "Satan blocked our way" (1 Thess. 2:17–20). Nonetheless, the apostle wanted to strengthen the church's faith by seeing the Thessalonian Christians face-to-face. Since Paul could not come to Thessalonica in person, his presence is represented by the letter. Neither the letter itself nor the account in Acts indicates Paul's location when he composed the letter. It is clear, however, that Timothy has returned from Thessalonica and that Paul now has Silvanus working with him (cf. 1 Thess. 1:1; 3:6; Acts 18:5). Since it was in Corinth that Paul met his coworkers who had returned from Macedonia, most interpreters assume that 1 Thessalonians was written there. The generally accepted date for its composition is 50/51 CE on the basis of combining the reference to the governor Gallio in Acts 18:12 and the note in Acts 18:2 about Claudius's expulsion of Jews from Rome, including Prisca and Aquila.[5] Paul's church-founding visit to Thessalonica would, then, fall in 49/50 CE.

The church in Thessalonica was composed primarily of Gentile Christians (cf. 1 Thess. 1:9; 2:14). Acts 17:1 documents the existence of a synagogue in the city, and so we must consider the likelihood of some Jewish Christians and Gentile sympathizers with Judaism belonging to the church as well (Acts 17:4).[6]

---

3. Cf. Karl P. Donfried, "Cults of Thessalonica and the Thessalonian Correspondence," *NTS* 31 (1985): 336–56; Robert K. Jewett, *The Thessalonian Correspondence: Pauline Rhetoric and Millenarian Piety* (Philadelphia: Fortress, 1986), 126ff.; Riesner, *Paul's Early Period*, 373–74; Vom Brocke, *Thessaloniki*, 115–38.

4. Cf. Vom Brocke, *Thessaloniki*, 138–41.

5. First Thessalonians is dated in 50/51 by, e.g., Martin Dibelius, *An die Thessalonicher I, II* (3rd ed.; Tübingen: Mohr Siebeck, 1937), 33; Werner Georg Kümmel and Paul Feine, *Introduction to the New Testament* (trans. Howard Clark Kee; 2nd ed.; NTL; London: SCM Press, 1975), 256–57; Vielhauer, *Geschichte der urchristlichen Literatur*, 88; Willi Marxsen, *Der erste Brief an die Thessalonicher* (Zurich: Theologischer Verlag, 1979), 14; cf. Willi Marxsen, *Introduction to the New Testament: An Approach to Its Problems* (trans. G. Buswell; Philadelphia: Fortress, 1968), 22; Helmut Koester, *History and Literature of Early Christianity* (vol. 2 of *Introduction to the New Testament*; 2nd ed.; New York: de Gruyter, 1995), 103; Jewett, *Thessalonian Correspondence*, 60; Riesner, *Paul's Early Period*, 364–66; Günter Haufe, *Der erste Brief des Paulus an die Thessalonicher* (THKNT 12/1; Leipzig: Evangelische Verlagsanstalt, 1999), 15; Abraham J. Malherbe, *The Letters to the Thessalonians: A New Translation with Introduction and Commentary* (AB 32B; New York: Doubleday, 2000), 73; opinions deviating from this consensus are reviewed by Traugott Holtz, *Der erste Brief an die Thessalonicher* (Neukirchen-Vluyn: Neukirchener Verlag, 1986), 20–23.

6. Cf. Riesner, *Paul's Early Period*, 344–48; and Vom Brocke, *Thessaloniki*, 207–33. A tomb inscription from the late third century CE documents the existence of a synagogue; cf. M. N. Pantelis,

We cannot say much about the social composition of the church; most members were probably merchants (cf. 1 Thess. 4:6), laborers, and handworkers at various crafts (cf. 1 Thess. 4:11) who belonged to the lower and middle classes. Acts 17:4 explicitly mentions some "leading women" of the city as members of the church, and Jason is portrayed as a wealthy homeowner who was able to go bail for the endangered missionaries (cf. Acts 17:5–9).[7] The house of Jason, who could also have been the leader of the house church, was probably the church's assembly room and a place where traveling missionaries could lodge. Moreover, we see from 1 Thess. 5:12–13 that there were other persons in the congregation with leadership abilities.[8] The church had existed only a short time before the letter's composition (cf. 2:17), but nevertheless news of the new church had already spread throughout Greece (cf. 1:7–8). Despite the positive report from Timothy (3:6), Paul still expresses concern about the state of the church.[9] The Christians in Thessalonica have had to endure a continuing experience of suffering that began when they first accepted the gospel (cf. 1:6) and obviously is still going on as Paul writes the letter. The members of the church in Thessalonica have been persecuted by people of their own country, just as the churches in Judea were persecuted by the Jews there (cf. 2:14–16). Residents of Thessalonica evidently perceived the formation of the new Christian community as a threat to the existing social and religious structures. The sharp polemic suggests that also in Thessalonica Paul regards Jews as the real instigators of the persecution.[10] Probably the successful enticing of people with a certain social status into the ranks of the new group evoked a continuing hostile reaction among both Gentiles and Jews. Alongside the disputes motivated by social and religious concerns among both Jews and Gentiles, the church was probably also burdened by everyday frictions with its environment (cf. 4:10b–12). The young church was likewise harassed by concrete theological questions (cf. 3:10). Thus the thrice repeated περί (now concerning) in 4:9, 13; 5:1 seems to take up specific questions the church in Thessalonica had posed to Paul. In particular, the fact that some members of the church had unexpectedly died before the Lord's return had created anxiety, to which Paul responds in 4:13–18; 5:1–11 with a discussion of the date and course of events when God brings the present age to a close at the parousia of Christ.

"Synagoge(n) und Gemeinde der Juden in Thessaloniki: Fragen aufgrund einer neuen jüdischen Grabinschrift der Kaiserzeit," *ZPE* 102 (1994): 297–306. Philo, *Embassy* 281, who reports on Jews in Macedonia, provides indirect evidence for the existence of a synagogue in Paul's time.

7. On Jason, cf. Vom Brocke, *Thessaloniki*, 249: "He is relatively wealthy, owns a house, and as a citizen is surely also entitled to local civil rights."

8. Cf. Gehring, *House Church and Mission*, 132–34, 197–201.

9. On the different hypotheses found in older research on "gnostic" or "enthusiastic" streams in Thessalonica, cf. Jewett, *Thessalonian Correspondence*, 135–57.

10. On the persecution of the church, see also Riesner, *Paul's Early Period*, 352–58; and Vom Brocke, *Thessaloniki*, 152–56.

The Initial Preaching

In a few passages, 1 Thessalonians lets us still see something of the content of Paul's original message during his initial church-founding visit to Thessalonica and how his preaching mediated the new symbolic universe generated by the gospel.[11] At the very beginning of the letter, Paul reminds the church of his initial message that called the church into being: "our message of the gospel came to you not in word only, but also in power and in the Holy Spirit and with full conviction" (1 Thess. 1:5).[12] This text already shows the determinative dimension of pneumatology, that the success of the gospel consisted not of human speaking but of the powerful work of the Spirit. The triad δύναμις, πνεῦμα ἅγιον, and πληροφορία (cf. 1 Cor. 2:4; 4:19–20, 2 Cor. 12:11–12; Rom. 15:18–19) designates the means by which the preaching of the gospel opens up its own way in the world. By accepting the gospel, the church validates its election (cf. 1 Thess. 1:4), which in turn reveals the love of God to the Thessalonians. The sole actor in election is God (cf. 2:12; 4:7; 5:9, 24), who at the end of time saves the believing community from the judgment that is already breaking in. The Thessalonians are addressed as the eschatological congregation; during his church-founding visit, Paul had proclaimed to them the sufferings of the last days that they must face (3:4). Nevertheless, the church received the apostle's preaching not as a mere human word but as God's word, which continued to work among them (cf. 2:13). The gospel had been preached among the Thessalonians with such enduring effects that people in Achaia are talking about what Paul taught them while he was there (1:6–9a). Paul recapitulates this message in 1:9b-10 with a *summarium* of the early Christian missionary message: "how you turned to God from idols, to serve a living and true God, and to wait for his Son from heaven, whom he raised from the dead—Jesus, who rescues us from the wrath that is coming."

The traditional character of 1 Thess. 1:9b–10 is made especially clear by analysis of its vocabulary:[13] hapax legomena in Paul's undisputed letters are ἀληθινός (real, true; cf. *Jos. Asen.* 11.10), ἀναμένω (await, expect; cf. Job 7:2; Jdt. 8:17), and ἐκ τῶν οὐρανῶν (from heaven; but cf. 2 Cor. 5:1; Phil. 3:20). Paul uses the verb ἐπιστρέφω (turn [toward]) elsewhere only in the sense of conversion (cf. 2 Cor. 3:16; Gal. 4:9); only here does ῥύομαι have a christological-apocalyptic sense (cf. 2 Cor. 1:10; Rom. 15:31; the quotation in Rom. 11:26). We should also note that only here does the article appear in the Pauline-sounding expression ἤγειρεν ἐκ τῶν νεκρῶν (he raised from *the* dead;

---

11. Cf. Raymond F. Collins, "Paul's Early Christology," in *Studies on the First Letter to the Thessalonians* (BETL 66; Leuven: Leuven University Press, 1984), 253–84; J. Plevnik, "Pauline Presuppositions," in *The Thessalonian Correspondence* (ed. Raymond F. Collins and Norbert Baumert; BETL 87; Leuven: Leuven University Press, 1990), 50–61; Börschel, *Konstruktion*, 91–137.

12. For analysis, cf. Horn, *Angeld des Geistes*, 120–23.

13. Cf. Bussmann, *Paulinischen Missionspredigt*, 38–56.

cf. Gal. 1:1; Rom. 4:24) and that ἐκ τῆς ὀργῆς τῆς ἐρχομένης (the wrath that is coming) is not a typical Pauline expression for the last judgment. In terms of content, the message is reminiscent of Jewish missionary preaching, with its monotheistic emphasis, rejection of idolatry, and expectation of coming judgment providing the background for its eschatological hope. Thus, in the Jewish conversion novel *Joseph and Aseneth,* the pagan Aseneth says before her great prayer of repentance, "But I have heard many saying that the God of the Hebrews is a true God, and a living God, and a merciful God, and compassionate and long-suffering and pitiful and gentle, and does not count the sin of a humble person. . . . Therefore I will take courage too and turn to him, and take refuge with him" (*Jos. Asen.* 11:10–11 [trans. C. Burchard, *OTP* 2:218]; cf. 54:5ff.). The central content of Paul's initial missionary preaching is the one true God, whose absoluteness and exclusivity mean that all other deities are idols. Paul constructs his symbolic universe around this center, relating to the fundamental hope for the parousia of the Son of God the Thessalonians' turn from idols to the true and living God. Because God raised up Jesus Christ from the dead, he will shortly appear and save believers from the coming judgment. God's saving act of election and Jesus' eschatological act of deliverance determine Paul's missionary message on which the church in Thessalonica was founded, and also shapes the line of thought in the letter. The Son will reappear as judge, and so the Thessalonians should live lives that correspond to their call (1 Thess. 2:11–12), "for God did not call us to impurity but in holiness" (4:7). Paul had previously assured the church that the Lord alone is the judge of all (4:6). Finally, as part of the apostle's missionary preaching, the church received its ethical instruction through the Lord himself (4:2). Paul stamped the essence of the Christian life on the community's consciousness under the three headings of "faith," "love," "hope" (1:3, 5:8). In the course of his early mission preaching, Paul had evidently adopted some ideas from Hellenistic Judaism and/or Jewish Christianity and crafted them into this brief and easily remembered formula, both theologically and rhetorically to the point.[14] This triad served the Thessalonians as the Christian response to God's eschatological act in Jesus Christ. God's present activity of election in the power of the Spirit, the coming saving act of the Son at the last judgment, and the life of holiness this requires thus form the central core of Paul's church-founding message in Thessalonica.

Paul's initial visit to Thessalonica concerned not only the message he proclaimed but the life and conduct of the apostle, which itself had a missionary dimension, qualifying Paul and his coworkers as mediators of a new symbolic universe. The acceptance of a symbolic universe is also bound to the person of those who mediate it; their appearance on the scene is itself a part of the

---

14. Evidence is given in Thomas Söding, *Die Trias Glaube, Hoffnung, Liebe bei Paulus: Eine exegetische Studie* (SBS 150; Stuttgart: Katholisches Bibelwerk, 1992), 38–64.

symbolic universe (cf. 1 Thess. 2:8). The authority of Paul does not rest on staking out arbitrary claims but is established by the one living God. Thus Paul can address the church with the words "You are witnesses, and God also, how pure, upright, and blameless our conduct was toward you believers" (2:10). The apostolic ministry that takes place in their midst is sincere and exemplary; the gospel is addressed to the Thessalonians in a pastoral, encouraging tone (2:3). Paul is concerned about every member of the church, just as a father cares for each of his children (2:11). Paul addresses them personally, attempting to help those who stand at the very beginning of their Christian journey to develop a path of life that corresponds to their call from God. In his initial, foundational instruction, Paul admonished, encouraged, and consoled the Thessalonians to live their lives now, in the present, in the light of the final saving event soon to come (2:12). One of the primary emphases of apostolic ministry during Paul's initial, founding visit was thus the pastoral care of the church and its individual members. The letter, then, functionally represents the presence of the apostle, who develops these basic concerns further. The letter evokes the memory of the founding visit and goes more deeply into the new converts' problems, such as their break with society, the fading of their first enthusiasm, and the emergence of new issues.[15]

8.2 The Theology of 1 Thessalonians

First Thessalonians contains an independent theological conception that we can determine with some precision, a conception which we should not smooth out with ideas from the later letters.

Election and Parousia as Theological Cornerstones

The foundation of the theology of 1 Thessalonians is the *concept of election*;[16] its temporal horizon is the expectation of the coming of κύριος Ἰησοῦς Χριστός (the Lord Jesus Christ) in the immediate future.[17] These two views are directly related, since election designates the present reality of salvation for the Thessalonians, and the parousia of Christ the basis of their hope. Paul proclaims the electing God, thereby reminding the church of the primary datum of its existence: "For we know, brothers and sisters beloved by God, that he has chosen you" (1 Thess. 1:4; cf. Rom. 9:11; 11:5, 7, 28). Just as ἐκλογή (election)

15. Cf. Riesner, *Paul's Early Period*, 371–84.
16. The significance of election has recently been elaborated in the work of Schade, *Apokalyptische Christologie*, 117ff. Cf., in addition, Becker, *Paul*, 130–40.
17. Cf. Marxsen, *Thessalonicher*, 21; Söding, "Der Erste Thessalonicherbrief," 187–88.

designates God's foundational act of election,[18] so καλέω (call) refers primarily to putting this act into effect. God has called the church to an upright life worthy of its call (1 Thess. 2:12), and election is concretely realized in being delivered from the general lostness and condemnation of humanity (cf. 4:7; 5:9). Thus the (in the Greek) participial expression "the one who calls you" (2:12; 5:24) becomes a designation for God. Paul assures the church, "The one who calls you is faithful, and he will do this" (5:24). The Thessalonians can thus understand their call as the gracious eschatological act of God's election; they are the church of God called together in the last days (1:1). God is therefore the origin and subject of the entire saving event, which underscores the primacy of *theo*logy (not Christology, pneumatology, eschatology, etc.) in the oldest extant Pauline letter.

Paul deliberately concludes every chapter of the letter with a forward look to the parousia (cf. 1:9–10; 2:19; 3:13; 4:13ff.; 5:23).[19] Both the compositional structure and the content make clear that the primary issue for both apostle and church is the eschatological event that is determinative for all humanity. Who will be saved when God's judgment breaks into history at the parousia? How can human beings escape the righteous judgment of God? What happens to those who die before the parousia? The pressure of these questions shapes the letter's train of thought; its strategy of communication is targeted on overcoming doubt and providing comfort and assurance on precisely these nagging issues.[20]

Discipleship as Imitation of Paul in Tribulation

The coordinate system of election/parousia also provides the framework for understanding the central theological conception of the first three chapters: the apocalyptic-eschatological idea of *imitation of the apostle* in the present es-

---

18. Within the context of the *pax romana*, Seneca, *Clem.* 1.2, presents a contrasting text when he portrays Nero as talking to himself: "Have I of all mortals found favor with Heaven and been chosen to serve on earth as vicar of the gods? I am the arbiter of life and death for the nations; it rests in my power what each man's lot and state shall be; by my lips Fortune proclaims what gift she would bestow on each human being; from my utterance peoples and cities gather reasons for rejoicing."

19. The word παρουσία was not a technical term of pre-Christian Jewish apocalyptic (cf. Walter Radl, "παρουσία," *EDNT* 3:43–44; Helmut Koester, "Imperial Ideology and Paul's Eschatology in 1 Thessalonians," in *Paul and Empire: Religion and Power in Roman Imperial Society* (ed. Richard A. Horsley; Harrisburg, PA: Trinity Press International, 1997), 158–66). In the Hellenistic world, the word designates, among other things, the visit of a ruler to a place where preparations must be made for his advent. Early Christians could well have adopted the term from this context: "Christ is anticipated as Savior and as Lord. Since, however, the Caesar could be received not just as a ruler but also as savior, official παρουσία terminology with its sacral elements probably stands closest to Christian usage" (Radl, "παρουσία," 3:44).

20. Jutta Bickmann, *Kommunikation gegen den Tod: Studien zur paulinischen Briefpragmatik am Beispiel des ersten Thessalonicherbriefes* (FB 86; Würzburg: Echter, 1998), 89ff.

chatological tribulations to which believers are subject (cf. 1:6; 2:2, 14, 17–18; 3:3–4).[21] Here Paul takes up a central idea of the Jewish apocalyptic and wisdom traditions: the suffering of the righteous in the last days.[22] By accepting the gospel in faith, love, and hope in this time of eschatological troubles (1:3), the Thessalonians manifest their election by God. Faith is not thereby defined in antithesis to "works" but as steadfastness and faithfulness in tribulation (1:6). Despite their sufferings, the Thessalonians accepted the message with joy and have become models for the churches in Macedonia and Achaia. Their life shaped by imitation of the apostle has missionary consequences, as the exemplary existence of the church includes the power of attracting others to the faith (cf. 1:7ff.). God's all-embracing act of salvation in raising up the Son confers a universal dimension on the act of preaching the gospel. Many Gentiles are following the Thessalonians by turning to the one true God and living in joyful expectation of the return of his Son. Especially 1 Thess. 1:9–10 recalls this reality to memory,[23] as it binds addressees and writer together: God's saving act in his Son qualifies the present as the time of eschatological salvation; church and apostle live their lives toward the day of the Son's return, in the assurance that they are called not to wrath but to salvation (1 Thess. 5:9).

In 1 Thess. 2:1–12 Paul applies the concept of imitation to the missionaries, who by their exemplary imitation of Christ gave the church no reason to doubt the credibility of their message.[24] In contrast to the numerous wandering preachers and philosophers, Paul did not weasel his way into the church's confidence with an insincere hidden agenda. He never attempted to win them over with flattering words, only then to take advantage of them. His primary concern was not his own reputation, but just as a mother cares for her children, so the apostle cares for the church. Paul contrasts his conduct with that of the wandering preachers and thus represents himself as a true philosopher, as described by Dio Chrysostom, *Alex.* 11–12: "But to find a man who in plain terms and without guile speaks his mind in frankness, and neither for the sake of reputation nor for gain makes false pretensions, but out of good will and concern for his fellow men stands ready, if need be, to submit to ridicule and to the disorder and the uproar of the mob—to find such a man as that is not easy, so great is the dearth of noble, independent souls and such the abundance of toadies, mountebanks, and sophists." The "gospel of God" (εὐαγγέλιον τοῦ θεοῦ, 1 Thess. 2:2, 8, 9) must not be obscured by the conduct of the preacher,

---

21. Schade, *Apokalyptische Christologie*, 117–34.
22. Cf. Ps. 33:20; 36:39; Dan. 12:1; Hab. 3:16; Zeph. 1:15; 1QM 1:11–12; 1QH 2:6–12; *4 Ezra* 7:89; *2 Bar.* 15:7–8; 48:50: "For surely, as you endured much labor in the short time in which you live in this passing world, so you will receive great light in that world which has no end" (trans. A. F. J. Klijn, *OTP* 1:637).
23. Cf. Alkier, *Wunder und Wirklichkeit*, 91–107.
24. For analysis of 1 Thess. 2:1–12, see Malherbe, *Thessalonians*, 133–63.

for his proclamation of salvation also includes the Gentiles. Agreement of teaching and life characterizes the true philosopher just as it does Paul the apostle.

Just as the missionaries' exemplary imitation of Christ gives no cause to doubt the credibility of their message, so in 1 Thess. 2:13 Paul again emphasizes the exemplary life of the church that accepted the word of Paul's preaching as the word of God. The message proclaimed expresses not merely the opinions of the individual preacher but God's saving act for the world. Paul understands his own actions to be an expression of God's own acceptance of them.

The Jews and the Wrath of God

In 1 Thess. 2:14–16 the apostle further develops the motif of the church in Thessalonica as an example to others. The work of God's word among them is seen in the fact that the Thessalonian Christians have become imitators of the churches in Judea, since the Thessalonians suffer from their compatriots the same as the Judean Christians did from the Jews there. The expression καὶ ὑμεῖς ὑπὸ τῶν ἰδίων συμφυλετῶν (and you . . . from your own compatriots) in 2:14 points, in the first place, to Gentile fellow citizens in Thessalonica as the source of the persecutions, for φυλή (race, tribe, class, nation, people) here indicates an organized group within the polis.[25] The polemic against those Jews hostile to the Christian faith in 2:15–16, however, presupposes that Paul sees Jews as also involved in the duress of the church in Thessalonica.[26] Partly by taking up traditional materials, in 2:15 he levels five accusations against them, each connected with the conjunction καί (and, also, even). The charge in 2:15a, that the Jews were guilty of the death of Jesus and the prophets, has parallels in Matt. 23:34–36/Luke 11:49–51; Mark 12:1–9; Acts 7:52 and repeats the substance of an old kerygmatic tradition that had connected the murder of the prophets with the death of Jesus.[27] By the addition of καὶ ἡμᾶς ἐκδιωξάντων (and drove us out), Paul places his own sufferings on the same level as the actions of the Jews against Jesus and the prophets. Whereas the reproach that the

---

25. Cf. Vom Brocke, *Thessaloniki*, 157–58: These organized groups (φυλαί) "facilitated political organization as well as classification of the population for various purposes. Each citizen belonged to a φυλή, usually as a matter of birth. New citizens were assigned to a particular φυλή. Freed slaves and their descendents, slaves or citizens of other towns, as well as foreigners usually did not belong to a φυλή, since they did not have citizenship in the city."

26. Differently, Vom Brocke, ibid., 162–65, who bases his view on the fact that Jews were not enrolled in the φυλαί of a polis. This observation, while presumably historically correct, does not exclude the possibility that Paul nonetheless regards the Jews as also responsible for the persecutions, since we can understand the polemic of 1 Thess. 2:15–16 only with this presupposition; cf. Dietrich-Alex Koch, "Die Christen als neue Randgruppe in Makedonien und Achaia im 1. Jahrhundert n. Chr.," in *Antike Randgesellschaften und Randgruppen im östlichen Mittelmeerraum: Ringvorlesung an der Westfälischen Wilhelms-Universität Münster* (ed. Hans-Peter Müller and F. Siegert; Münsteraner judaistische Studien 5; Münster: Universitätsverlag, 2000), 174 n. 28.

27. Cf. Holtz, *Thessalonicher*, 105–6.

Jews "displease God" is to be attributed to Paul,[28] with the words "and oppose everyone" the apostle takes up an often repeated slur of ancient anti-Jewish polemic that the Jews were "haters of humanity."[29] In 1 Thess. 2:16 we see what actually triggered Paul's attack: Jews hostile to the gospel were hindering the mission to the Gentiles that brings them salvation, so that their measure of sin is now full and the saying applies, ἔφθασεν δὲ ἐπ' αὐτοὺς ἡ ὀργὴ εἰς τέλος (God's wrath has overtaken them at last).[30] Hindering the Gentile mission has brought God's judgment on them; that is, God has withdrawn his election from them.

We cannot reconstruct a cohesive tradition in 2:15, for καὶ ἡμᾶς ἐκδιωξάντων (and drove us out), though expressed in vocabulary not elsewhere used by Paul, must be attributed to the apostle himself because of its content (ἡμᾶς [us]). Likewise καὶ θεῷ μὴ ἀρεσκόντων (they displease God) is a Pauline construction (cf. 1 Thess. 4:1; Rom. 8:8).[31] We do find unusual formulations in 1 Thess. 2:16 (ἀναπληρῶσαι αὐτῶν τὰς ἁμαρτίας [filling up the measure of their sins] is a singular expression for Paul [cf. L.A.B. 26:13; 36:1; 41:1]), and φθάνειν ἐπί τι[να] . . . εἰς τέλος (overtaken . . . at last) is not found elsewhere in Paul, but the verse is not to be regarded as un-Pauline. There are no indications of a post-Pauline origin for 1 Thess. 2:13–16.[32] The partially un-Pauline expressions derive from his adoption of traditional materials, and the tensions with Rom. 9–11 are not really an argument for interpolation hypotheses, for Paul could have changed his thinking on such matters.

Paul charges the Jews with doing what he himself had done as a Pharisee: putting obstacles in the way of the saving message of the gospel. At the time of the composition of 1 Thessalonians, the greatest threat to the expansion of the Christian mission was posed by agitations among the Jews and the adjustments within their ranks that were occurring as reactions to the success of Christian

28. Cf. ibid., 105.

29. Cf. especially Tacitus, *Hist.* 5.5.1: "Again, the Jews are extremely loyal toward one another, and always ready to show compassion, but toward every other people they feel only hate and enmity. They sit apart at meals, and they sleep apart, and although as a race, they are prone to lust, they abstain from intercourse with foreign women; yet among themselves nothing is unlawful. They adopted circumcision to distinguish themselves from other peoples by this difference. Those who are converted to their ways follow the same practice, and the earliest lesson they receive is to despise the gods, to disown their country, and to regard their parents, children, and brothers as of little account" (*NW* 2/1:777; Boring et al., eds., *Hellenistic Commentary,* § 815); on anti-Jewish polemic in antiquity, cf. Conzelmann, *Gentiles, Jews, Christians,* 45–133.

30. Both the parallels in Ezek. 13:13; 2 Chron. 12:12; *T. Levi* 6:11 and the aorist ἔφθασεν (it has come) suggest that εἰς τέλος (to the end, completely) is to be understood here in the sense of a complete destruction; cf. Schade, *Apokalyptische Christologie,* 127.

31. Contra Gerd Lüdemann, *Paulus und das Judentum* (TEH; Munich: Kaiser, 1983), 22.

32. For an extensive debate with interpolation hypotheses, cf. ibid., 25–27; J. Broer, "'Antisemitismus' und Judenpolemik im Neuen Testament: Ein Beitrag zum besseren Verständnis von 1. Thess. 2,14–16," in *Religion und Verantwortung als Elemente gesellschaftlicher Ordnung: Für Karl Klein zum 70. Geburtstage* (ed. Bodo B. Gemper; 2nd ed.; Siegen: Vorländer, 1983), 739–46.

missionaries operating in the context of the synagogue (cf. Acts 17:4ff.) and as the aftereffects of the edict of Claudius. The sharpness of Paul's polemic here is to be explained within this historical situation. For Paul, God had already pronounced his judgment on the Jews, and God's wrath had come upon them. Persecution can endanger the new symbolic universe that had just been communicated,[33] and so Paul not only gives the church theological interpretations of its experience of suffering but also stabilizes the church by expressing definitive pronouncements of judgment.

Paul continues his thoughts on the hindering of the Gentile mission in 1 Thess. 2:17ff., where now Satan himself appears as the one who places obstacles in its path. Satan had several times frustrated Paul's efforts to revisit his church, and so he is very concerned about the faith of the Thessalonians, who now must persevere in the eschatological θλίψις (tribulation, trouble) that is already beginning. After all, it is the Thessalonians who are his hope, joy, and crown when the Lord returns (2:19). They will be the visible demonstration that the Pauline missionary project was not in vain, even if the powers of darkness now threaten it. Both Paul (3:4) and the Thessalonians (3:3a, 5b) are presently in the grasp of the eschatological troubles, but their salvation manifests itself precisely in their imitation of him. Steadfastness in tribulations comes from faith in the present (3:11–13) and future saving act of God in the Lord Jesus (κύριος Ἰησοῦς). But also the Thessalonians' love, as reported by Timothy, comforts Paul and his coworkers in their distress (3:6ff.). The apostle is sure that God himself will overcome the adversary and strengthen Paul and the Thessalonians in their mutual love (3:11–13).

The Coming of the Lord

First Thessalonians as a whole is dominated by the *expectation that the Lord's parousia would occur in the immediate future*, and the two central eschatological passages must be understood in this comprehensive context (1 Thess. 4:13–18; 5:1–11). Occasioned by the unexpected death of some members of the church,[34] in 4:13–18 Paul first relates images of the parousia to the resurrection of Christians who have died.[35] Since actual deaths have called into question the new symbolic universe they accepted when they became Christians, dealing with this theme was absolutely necessary; Paul had to bridge the chasm that had

---

33. Cf. Börschel, *Konstruktion*, 214–24.

34. Differently, Andreas Lindemann, "Paulus und die korinthische Eschatologie," in *Paulus, Apostel und Lehrer der Kirche: Studien zu Paulus und zum frühen Paulusverständnis* (Tübingen: Mohr Siebeck, 1999), 68–69, who takes "those who have fallen asleep" to include both Christians and non-Christians; cf. the opposing view argued by Helmut Merklein, "Der Theologe als Prophet," in *Studien zu Jesus und Paulus* (2 vols.; WUNT 43, 105; Tübingen: Mohr Siebeck, 1987), 2:378–79.

35. Cf. Marxsen, *Thessalonicher*, 65.

opened up between his initial preaching in Thessalonica and the present reality of the church's experience.

Paul introduces the problem in 4:13, responding to the church's prevailing grief with a word of hope.[36] The kerygmatic formulation in 14a contains the apostle's initial answer. He presupposes that the faith confessed by the Thessalonian Christians includes the death and resurrection of Jesus, and on this basis affirms that God will not abandon those who have died. At the parousia Jesus will fill the role of eschatological mediator,[37] for διὰ τοῦ Ἰησοῦ (through Jesus)[38] God will bring "with him" (μετ᾽ αὐτοῦ) those who have fallen asleep. The Pauline argument continues in 4:15–17 without, however, explaining how this "bringing" (ἄγω) takes place. First Thessalonians 4:15 is a summary of the "word of the Lord" cited in 4:16–17, and thus an application of the following tradition to the situation in Thessalonica. The affirmations of 4:15 lie on the same temporal plane as 4:17, from which Paul evidently derived them (cf. οἱ ζῶντες οἱ περιλειπόμενοι [we who are alive, who are left]).[39] The traditional character of 4:16–17 is clear on both linguistic and thematic grounds.[40]

Hapax legomena for the New Testament are κέλευσμα (command) and περιλείπομαι (left). Hapax legomena for Paul are σάλπιγξ (trumpet; 1 Cor. 15:52 is dependent on 1 Thess. 4:16), ἀρχάγγελος (archangel; found elsewhere in the New Testament only in Jude 9), ἀπάντησις (meeting; elsewhere in the New Testament only in Matt. 25:6; Acts 28:15). Atypical Pauline word usage is represented by φωνή (voice; though cf. the nonapocalyptic use in 1 Cor. 14:7, 8, 10, 11; Gal. 4:20), καταβαίνω (descend; elsewhere only Rom. 10:7), ἀνίστημι for "rise" (elsewhere in Paul only in the immediate context, 1 Thess. 4:14), ἁρπάζω (caught up; cf. 2 Cor. 12:2, 4; only in 1 Thess. 4:17 in reference to the eschatological events), νεφέλη (cloud; elsewhere only in 1 Cor. 10:1, 2 in the midrash about Israel in the wilderness), and ἀήρ (air; in 1 Cor. 9:26; 14:9

---

36. On the special problems of 1 Thess. 4:13–18 not dealt with extensively here, in addition to the standard commentaries, cf. the foundational analyses of Ulrich Luz, *Das Geschichtsverständnis des Paulus* (BEvT: Theologische Abhandlungen 49; Munich: Kaiser, 1968), 318–31; Peter Siber, *Mit Christus Leben: Eine Studie zur paulinischen Auferstehungshoffnung* (Zurich: Theologischer Verlag, 1971), 13–59; W. Wiefel, "Die Hauptrichtung des Wandels im eschatologischen Denken des Paulus," *TZ* 30 (1974): 66–70; Lüdemann, *Chronology*, 205–38; Schade, *Apokalyptische Christologie*, 157–72; Walter Radl, *Ankunft des Herrn: Zur Bedeutung und Funktion der Parusieaussagen bei Paulus* (BBET 15; Frankfurt: Lang, 1981), 113–56; Jörg Baumgarten, *Paulus und die Apokalyptik: Die Auslegung apokalyptischer Überlieferungen in den echten Paulusbriefen* (WMANT 44; Neukirchen-Vluyn: Neukirchener Verlag, 1975), 91–98; Merklein, "Der Theologe als Prophet," 378ff.

37. Cf. Schade, *Apokalyptische Christologie*, 158.

38. Διά (through) is here to be understood causally, for Jesus' death and resurrection (1 Thess. 4:14a) is the salvific basis for the event of 4:14b.

39. Cf. Lüdemann, *Chronology*, 236.

40. Cf. esp. Siber, *Mit Christus Leben*, 35ff.; Lüdemann, *Chronology*, 221–38; differently, Merklein, "Der Theologe als Prophet," 410ff., who regards only 4:15b as the quotation.

in a figurative sense). Motifs parallel to the tradition here adopted by Paul are found in *4 Ezra* 13 and *2 Bar.* 29–30, 50–51.[41]

Paul took this early Christian "word of the Lord"[42] from the tradition and gave it a temporal structure (πρῶτον [first]; ἔπειτα [then]), combining past and present (ἅμα σὺν αὐτοῖς [together with them])[43] and actualizing it regarding the situation in Thessalonica (ἡμεῖς οἱ ζῶντες [we who are alive]), in order to show the soteriological goal of the whole event with the expression καὶ οὕτως πάντοτε σὺν κυρίῳ ἐσόμεθα (and so we will be with the Lord forever). The traditional word of the Lord begins the portrayal of the final events with the triumphal coming of the Lord from heaven, followed first by the resurrection of the νεκροὶ ἐν Χριστῷ (the dead in Christ), then by their being caught up together with those who are still alive to meet the Lord in the clouds in order to be and remain with him forever. In the course of these events, the resurrection of the dead members of the congregation plays only a subordinate role. The resurrection of the dead in Christ is only the prerequisite for the real eschatological act when all are caught up to meet the returning Lord, the condition for σὺν κυρίῳ ἐσόμεθα (we will be with the Lord).

Since, for the Thessalonians, the unexpected death of some members of the church before the parousia precipitated their question to Paul, we may assume that Paul did *not* speak of the resurrection of dead Christians as a part of his initial preaching that founded the church. The Thessalonians were obviously unacquainted with this idea,[44] though Paul himself, as a former Pharisee, was very likely familiar with it. We can explain these findings, which do seem strange at first, only by supposing that in his initial preaching in Thessalonica Paul made no reference to the resurrection of believers who had died, since he expected the parousia in the near future. The death of some believers before the parousia evoked the problem of the delay of the parousia and the relation of the Christian faith to history. It was this unanticipated situation that first compelled him to introduce the idea of a resurrection of believers who had died. In favor of this assumption is the observation that also in 4:13–18 the resurrection of dead Christians has only an auxiliary function and Paul still holds fast to his original conception of all believers being caught up to meet the returning Lord at the parousia. The soteriological goal of the whole event is expressed in the phrase καὶ οὕτως πάντοτε σὺν κυρίῳ ἐσόμεθα. The Lord's parousia provides the ultimate

---

41. Analysis of the texts is found in Lüdemann, *Chronology*, 225–37.

42. Reconstructions are attempted by Schade, *Apokalyptische Christologie*, 160; Heinrich Hoffmann, "Auferstehung I/3," *TRE* 4:453–54; Lüdemann, *Chronology*, 225; Gerhard Sellin, *Der Streit um die Auferstehung der Toten: Eine religionsgeschichtliche und exegetische Untersuchung von 1 Korinther 15* (FRLANT 138; Göttingen: Vandenhoeck & Ruprecht, 1986), 43.

43. Cf. Lüdemann, *Chronology*, 224.

44. Cf. Günther Bornkamm, *Paul* (trans. D. M. G. Stalker; New York: Harper & Row, 1971), 222; E. Brandenburger, *Auferstehung der Glaubenden*, 20; W. Marxsen, *Thessalonicher*, 65 and elsewhere; for a discussion of other possibilities, see Riesner, *Paul's Early Period*, 384–87.

horizon for this goal, which presupposes that all will be caught up together to meet him, and the resurrection of dead members of the church is what makes this possible—but these two latter events are only introduced as preliminaries to the ultimate goal. We can also understand the ἐν Χριστῷ (in Christ) statement in 4:16 against the background of the problem posed by the deaths in Thessalonica. By describing the deceased church members as νεκροὶ ἐν Χριστῷ, he emphasizes that the incorporation into Christ that began with their baptism does not end with their death. As in the pre-Pauline baptismal traditions in 1 Cor. 1:30; 6:11; Gal. 3:26–30; Rom. 3:25; 6:3–4, we should understand ἐν Χριστῷ here in both a soteriological and an ontological sense. It expresses the new existence that is constituted by baptism, being-in-the-realm-of-Christ and the personal communion with Christ, which even death cannot end.

In 1 Thessalonians, the death of Christians before the parousia is still the exception, and so 1 Thess. 4:13–17 is evidence of the unbroken acute expectation of the near parousia. Paul numbers himself and the church in Thessalonica among those who will still be alive at the parousia (ἡμεῖς οἱ ζῶντες, 4:15, 17), presumably still sure that it would occur in the immediate future. The following statements about God's bringing those who have died with Jesus (4:14b), the Pauline summary of the "word of the Lord" (4:15), and the word of the Lord itself and its concrete application by Paul cannot be derived directly from the kerygma of 4:14a but bear the marks of Christian prophecy.[45] The kerygma does not answer the question of the exact course of eschatological events and the place of those who have already died and those who will still be alive when they occur. "There is a gap in the argument, that needs to be filled out discursively."[46] This function is taken over by prophetic speech, which seeks to answer basic questions by a didactic expansion of the kerygma. For Paul, revelation about God's future acts has not ceased.

In 1 Thess. 5:1–11 Paul continues his discussion, begun in 4:13ff., about the "how" of the eschatological events by dealing with the question of "when?"[47] Making use of traditional motifs,[48] he first rejects speculation about the setting of dates (5:1–3), in the course of which he takes up a slogan of the *pax romana* (εἰρήνη καὶ ἀσφάλεια [peace and security]).[49] Over against the Roman ideology[50] of peace, security, and prosperity Paul places his view of the approaching

45. M. Eugene Boring, *The Continuing Voice of Jesus: Christian Prophecy and the Gospel Tradition* (Louisville: Westminster John Knox, 1991), 61–62; Merklein, "Der Theologe als Prophet," 394ff.

46. Merklein, "Der Theologe als Prophet," 395.

47. Börschel, *Konstruktion*, 151–56.

48. We also find Jewish apocalyptic rejecting speculation about the date of the end (*4 Ezra; 2 Baruch*); cf. Wolfgang Harnisch, *Eschatologische Existenz: Ein exegetischer Beitrag zum Sachanliegen von 1. Thessalonicher 4, 13–5, 11* (FRLANT 110; Göttingen: Vandenhoeck & Ruprecht, 1973), 60ff.

49. Cf. Wengst, *Pax romana*, 97–99; Vom Brocke, *Thessaloniki*, 139–40.

50. Cf. Seneca, *Clem.* 1.2, quoting Caesar: "All those many thousands of swords which my peace restrains will be drawn at my nod"; 1.5, "This pronouncement, Caesar, you may boldly make, that whatever has passed into your trust and guardianship is still kept safe."

end. History will attain its goal not as a this-worldly consummation achieved through the Roman Empire but by God's eschatological act that will bring ultimate justice to the world. This is why Paul exhorts individual believers to orient their lives toward the arrival of the day of the Lord, whose date cannot be calculated (5:4–8). The advent of the Lord who is still to come stamps the substance of the Christian life; it is precisely this that makes such a life eschatological existence. On the one hand, this existence is not at our disposal; on the other hand, by its orientation to the day of the Lord, it shows its assurance and manifests the reality and presence of God's future act in the here and now. In 5:9 the previous statements are grounded in God's election of the church not for wrath but for salvation. Again with the help of traditional imagery,[51] Paul emphasizes that the existence of believers—whether living or dead—has its goal in life with the Lord.[52] Thus not only in 4:13–17 but also here the apostle summarizes the hope and goal of Christian existence in being with Christ (4:17) or living with him (5:10). As in 4:18, he concludes the section by challenging the Thessalonians in 5:11 to comfort and build one another up with the answer they receive, as they are in fact doing.

Paul responds in 4:13–5:11 to questions about the fate of Christians who die before the Lord's parousia—questions raised by the unanticipated death of some Christians in Thessalonica—by a reminder of eschatological knowledge held in common.[53] The Son of the living God has been raised from the dead and will return from heaven in the near future to save the church from the eruption of eschatological wrath. All Christians accept this reality, and Paul derives from it his response to this particular problem. He postulates an equality of dead and living believers at the coming of the Lord. The soteriological goal of the eschatological events is to be with the Lord, which will be preceded and facilitated by the resurrection of dead Christians and their being caught up with all the rest to meet the Lord. Precisely because Paul expected the Lord to return in his own lifetime, he rejected speculation about particular dates and called the Thessalonians to live lives oriented to the near eschaton. They should encourage and admonish one another in the assurance that at the coming of the Lord they will be with him and live with him.

8.3 The Ethic of 1 Thessalonians

The expectation of the advent of the Lord Jesus Christ in the immediate future also shapes 1 Thessalonians statements about ethics. Paul vigorously challenges the Thessalonians to live "blamelessly" (ἄμεμπτοι, 3:13; 5:23) and

---

51. On the traditional elements in 5:9–10a, cf. Schade, *Apokalyptische Christologie*, 139–40.
52. The aorist subjunctive ζήσωμεν of 5:10 is to be understood in the future sense.
53. Cf. Alkier, *Wunder und Wirklichkeit*, 115–21.

in holiness (3:13; 4:3, 4, 7; 5:23), for the Lord is near. As Paul motivates his ethical challenge by pointing to the brief period remaining before the end, the parousia does not function to validate each individual ethical injunction but serves within the macrostructure of the letter as the basis for ethics as such.[54] Paul explicitly emphasizes this connection with the inferential particle λοιπὸν οὖν (therefore, it follows that . . .; NRSV, "finally," 4:1), which refers directly to 3:13.

The beginning point of the Christian life, from which all else proceeds, is God's call, which results in the believer's response to the proclaimed gospel in faith, love, and hope (1:4–5; 2:12; 4:7–8). In 2:12 Paul already points to the call's relevance for ethics, to the causal connection between God's call and a worthy life. *Love* (ἀγάπη) determines the content of the ethics of 1 Thessalonians (cf. 1:3; 5:8).[55] The exhortations to abound in love for one another (3:12a; 4:9) and for non-Christians (3:12b; 5:15) are self-evident themes of Pauline instruction (cf. 1:3; 5:8).[56] First Thessalonians 4:1–2 functions as the programmatic introduction to particular paraenetic instructions; Paul emphasizes that salvation necessarily includes a specific kind of life pleasing to God. After all, the ethical instruction the church receives in the apostle's missionary preaching comes from the Lord himself (4:2b). Thus the apostle confirms that the church is living a model ethical life (4:1, καθὼς καὶ περιπατεῖτε [as, in fact, you are doing]) and at the same time points out the goal of his instruction as ἵνα περισσεύητε μᾶλλον (that you do so more and more; cf. 3:10; 4:10). Paul develops the normative "how" that characterizes the Christian life in 4:3–8, in which "holiness," as the goal of what God wills, serves as a bracket in 4:3 and 4:7 for the catalogue of virtues and vices listed in 4:4–6. Here the content of Paul's exhortation to a moral and honorable life remains within the conventional ethical framework of Hellenistic Judaism.[57] During his initial preaching that founded the church, Paul had already taught that the parousia would involve a judgment according to one's works (4:6b; cf. 5:9). Apostle and church must appear together before God's throne (cf. 2:19; 3:13). Thus those who do not give heed to the apostle's instruction are rejecting God (4:8). The Thessalonians, as people who "have been taught by God" (θεοδίδακτοι; cf. John 6:45), are

---

54. Udo Schnelle, "Die Ethik des 1 Thessalonikerbriefes," in *The Thessalonian Correspondence* (ed. Raymond F. Collins and Norbert Baumert; BETL 87; Leuven: Leuven University Press, 1990), 295–305.

55. Cf. Söding, "Der Erste Thessalonicherbrief," 196–97.

56. Cf. the comprehensive treatment by Söding, *Liebesgebot*, 68–100.

57. Thorough analyses are found in Otto Merk, *Handeln aus Glauben: Die Motivierungen der paulinischen Ethik* (Marburg: Elwert, 1968), 46–51; Franz Laub, *Eschatologische Verkündigung und Lebensgestaltung nach Paulus: Eine Untersuchung zum Wirken des Apostels beim Aufbau der Gemeinde in Thessalonike* (BU 10; Regensburg: Pustet, 1973), 50ff., 179ff.; Helmut Umbach, *In Christus getauft, von der Sünde befreit: Die Gemeinde als sündenfreier Raum bei Paulus* (Göttingen: Vandenhoeck & Ruprecht, 1999), 67–81; Börschel, *Konstruktion*, 241–326.

not the objects of this warning,[58] for God himself instructs the community in the right way (1 Thess. 4:9). The exhortation in 4:11 to live a quiet, honorable, and industrious life (cf. 1 Cor. 10:32) is then, in 1 Thess. 4:12, based on projecting a favorable image toward outsiders (cf. 1 Cor. 5:12). Here Paul thus clearly proceeds on the basis of common ethical norms held by Christians and non-Christian Gentiles.[59] Gentiles are capable of evaluating the conduct of Christians on the basis of the general moral law. In 1 Thess. 4:11–12 Paul is evidently referring to particular wrongs that have occurred, for the reference to the ethical competence of the Gentiles presupposes events within the church that were generally known and that could be critically evaluated.[60]

In the concluding paraenesis of 1 Thess. 5:12–25 Paul exhorts the church to honor deserving coworkers (5:12–13a). The congregation as a whole is then admonished in a twofold way, as the apostle gives first a list of general moral instructions (5:13b–18) and then adds five directions centered around the phenomenon of prophecy in the church (5:19–22). In the first series, the exhortation to maintain peace in the congregation (5:13b; cf. 2 Cor. 3:11; Rom. 12:18), to renounce vengeance (5:15; cf. Rom. 12:17, 21), and to "rejoice always, pray without ceasing, give thanks in all circumstances" (5:16–18; cf. Rom. 12:12; Phil. 4:6), fall within the category of conventional paraenesis.[61] In contrast, the listing of "idlers," the "fainthearted," and the "weak" in 5:14 indicates that here the apostle has in mind particular groups within the church.[62] The instructions in 5:19–20 indicate the vigorous pneumatic and prophetic elements in the congregation's worship. The working of the Spirit should not be quenched, nor should the word of prophets be either disdained or uncritically accepted, but the congregation as a whole must test all such manifestations of the Spirit (5:21–22). That they have the criteria of "what is good" and "every form of evil" at their disposal indicates that the congregation is to evaluate the pneumatic phenomena in their midst by the standards of ethics generally prevailing in their situation.

We see the central importance of pneumatology for 1 Thessalonians from the way the gift of the Spirit is connected with their call to become Christians. The initial preaching that founded the church in Thessalonica came to them not only as a matter of words but ἐν δυνάμει καὶ ἐν πνεύματι ἁγίῳ (1:5, in power and in the Holy Spirit). Thus the Spirit of God manifests itself in the present as the power that makes the proclamation of the gospel real as the call of God and that gives the confidence that comes from faith in the midst of

---

58. Merk, *Handeln*, 51–52.

59. Schulz, *Neutestamentliche Ethik*, 303.

60. Riesner, *Paul's Early Period*, 375–78, supposes that the admonition to work with their own hands in 1 Thess. 4:11 was addressed to circles within the congregation who refused to work and expected charity from the wealthy members of the church.

61. Merk, *Handeln*, 57.

62. Holtz, *Thessalonicher*, 250–51.

the present persecutions (cf. 1:6). For Paul, the call of God and the gift of the Spirit are obviously not events that lie in the past but acts of God that determine present and future. God gives his Spirit in the present (note the present participle διδόντα in 4:8), and God still calls believers in the present (5:24 has the present participle καλῶν). God's saving act affects the whole person (cf. 5:23) and, by the gift of the Spirit, brings the church in Thessalonica into being and continues to preserve it. The church in the present is always endowed with the Spirit of God, which gives it the power to live in holiness, to hold fast to the gospel, and to proclaim it in the time between the members' call and the coming of the Lord. Their experiences of the presence of the Spirit confirm the believers' own self-understanding that they stand in a unique relation to God and that they live and act on the basis of this new relationship.

Paul understands the church to be a realm of salvation made possible by Christ and determined by the Spirit (cf. τοὺς ἔξω [those outside], 4:12), a realm in which baptized believers live in holiness in the brief period before the coming of the Lord. This conception is very important for the formation of a new Christian identity,[63] for the community defines itself over against the surrounding world in terms of its ethics. At the same time, however, it renounces exclusivism, for it also shares the general ethos and knows that the community is observed and evaluated by its neighbors according to these standards. By this dual strategy, Paul strengthens the ethical and social identity of the church, which at the same time remains a group open to all who will accept the gospel.

8.4 First Thessalonians as a Document of Early Pauline Theology

The particular theological profile of 1 Thessalonians is seen first of all in the absence of the anthropological terms σάρξ (flesh), ἁμαρτία (sin),[64] θάνατος (death), σῶμα (body), ἐλευθερία (freedom), and ζωή (life). The word groups deriving from δικ- (right-, just-) and σταυρ- (cross, crucify) are likewise missing from 1 Thessalonians. The Old Testament is not explicitly quoted, the polemic against the Jews in 1 Thess. 2:14–16 has no parallel elsewhere in the Pauline corpus, and the eschatological statements in 1 Thessalonians are considerably different from those in the later letters.

Negative Findings

At the time of the composition of 1 Thessalonians, the doctrine of justification by faith alone apart from works of the law, as found in different forms

---

63. Cf. Börschel, *Konstruktion*, 327–36.
64. The plural ἁμαρτίαι in 1 Thess. 2:16 has no particular anthropological significance.

on Galatians and Romans,[65] was not yet a constitutive element of Pauline theology. Otherwise one would expect to find at least hints of this central complex of ideas, so important for the soteriology and ethics of Galatians and Romans—but both the terminology (e.g., νόμος) and the subject matter are missing. This remarkable circumstance cannot be relativized by appealing to the apostolic council and the Antioch incident, for these prior events had only established that Gentile Christians need not be circumcised and that the "gospel for the circumcision" was the particular arrangement for Jewish Christians, which also is assumed by 1 Thessalonians.[66] One could object against this view of the development of early Christian theology that the "thing itself," or the "substance of the matter" of the later doctrine of justification as found in Galatians and Romans is also present in Paul's oldest extant letter.[67] Those who advocate this line of argument mostly point to the εὐαγγέλιον (gospel) terminology, which is taken to be an abbreviation for the Pauline doctrine of justification.[68] A Torah-critical understanding of the Pauline gospel derived from Rom. 1:16–17 is presented as evidence for this interpretation, but it is precisely this connotation of "gospel" that is *not* found in 1 Thessalonians. The content of the Pauline gospel as found in 1 Thessalonians can be precisely described: God's eschatological act of salvation in Jesus Christ, the risen one who will return in the near future to save believers from the divine wrath erupting as part of the final events (cf. 1 Thess. 1:10; 5:9). This gospel proclaimed to the Gentiles Paul describes as "our gospel" (1:5), as εὐαγγέλιον θεοῦ (gospel of God, 2:2, 4, 8, 9) and εὐαγγέλιον Χριστοῦ (gospel of Christ, 3:2). It forms the foundation and core of Pauline theology as a whole and in Galatians and Romans was extended in a direction critical of the law/Torah.

65. For evidence and argument, see below, section 11.3 ("The Doctrine of the Law and of Justification in Galatians"), 11.5 ("Inclusive and Exclusive Doctrine of Justification in Paul"), and 16.8 ("Jesus Christ as God's Righteousness/Justice"). Cf. further Schnelle, *Gerechtigkeit und Christusgegenwart*, 62ff., 89ff.

66. Contra Hübner, *Biblische Theologie*, 2:51, who believes that Gal. 2:15–16 relates "what Paul had polemically held up to Peter in Antioch. In view of these historical considerations, which rest on the chronological sequence of the events of Paul's life, it is extremely unlikely that the substance of his theology of justification, first found *expressis verbis* in Galatians, was not yet part of Paul's theology when he wrote 1 Thessalonians." Galatians 2:15–16 makes the significance of the Torah problematic for Gentile Christians *and* Jewish Christians, a topic that was debated neither at the apostolic council nor during the Antioch incident.

67. So again most recently Reinhard von Bendemann, "'Frühpaulinisch' und/oder 'spätpaulinisch'? Erwägungen zu der These einer Entwicklung der paulinischen Theologie am Beispiel des Gesetzesverständnisses," *EvT* 60 (2000): 225: "In terms of its subject matter, however, the language of holiness and sanctification characteristic of 1 Thessalonians is not far removed from the language of δικαιοσύνη ['justification'] and δικαιόω ['justify'] in the later Pauline letters."

68. Cf., e.g., Hahn, "Entwicklung," 344, "What the gospel is in regard to its content and effect is elaborated with the help of the justification thematic"; Riesner, *Paul's Early Period*, 400–401, wants to connect "our message of the gospel" in 1 Thess. 1:5 to "the particular understanding of the Pauline gospel culminating in justification without works."

The imagery of call and election, like the statements about the final judgment, in any case do not presuppose the doctrine of justification as found in Galatians and Romans, for these realms of traditional images reflect the status of human beings as acceptable to God, a constituent ingredient of the culture of the times[69] and an independent and pervasive theme of Pauline theology that can by no means simply be equated with a particular understanding of the law. The pre-Pauline missionary preaching of early Christianity had already connected the anticipated advent of Jesus with the traditional judgment theme (cf. 1:9–10). Likewise the repeated admonition to appear blameless before the Lord at his coming (2:19; 3:13) implies a judgment before the heavenly throne. Believers must stand before the judgment seat of Christ (2 Cor. 5:10), where the Lord will preside over the last judgment and will bring to light things now hidden (1 Cor. 4:4–5). The wrath of God that erupts as part of the eschatological events (cf. 1 Thess. 1:10; 5:19) raises the question of salvation and thus of how people can be acceptable before God. When disputes arise within the Christian community, believers should no longer seek justice in court, for in baptism Christians have been made just and they will themselves participate in the final judgment of the world, which will include even angels (1 Cor. 6:1–11). The "day of the Lord" (cf. 1 Thess. 5:1–10; 1 Cor. 1:7–8; 5:5; 2 Cor. 1:14) demands the holiness of the church, for the fiery judgment of that day will reveal the quality of human deeds (1 Cor. 3:12–15). The declarations about the last judgment in 1 Thessalonians and the two Corinthian letters thus point to the acceptance of human beings *coram Deo* (before God) as a pervasive theme of Pauline theology. It belongs to the *theme* of justification but by no means has a causal connection to the specific *doctrine* of justification as found in Galatians and Romans, nor is it an anticipation of this later doctrine. Rather, Paul was able to refer especially to the missionary preaching of Hellenistic Judaism or Jewish Christianity in order to express within various speaking and conceptual contexts the situation of human beings before God. Although it is true that in Galatians and Romans Paul relates his specific doctrine of justification to his statements about God's judgment (e.g., Gal. 1:8; 5:18–25; Rom. 1:17–3:20; 5:1, 8ff.), this does not allow us to infer that this connection was already present in the previous letters. And finally, the distinction between the constant "substance" and the contingent "form" of Paul's theology of justification ends up in leveling out the textual data of the letters instead of interpreting them in their actual complexity.[70]

---

69. On the ideas about the last judgment in ancient Judaism, cf. Marius Reiser, *Jesus and Judgment: The Eschatological Proclamation in Its Jewish Context* (trans. Linda M. Maloney; Minneapolis: Fortress, 1997), 19–144.

70. Marxsen, *Thessalonicher*, 74–77, emphasizes "that we have within the Pauline letters something like a development" (p. 74). On the other hand, he restricts this development exclusively to the "form" and thinks that the "substance" of Paul's theology always remained the same. Cf. here Johan

Early Pauline Theology

The particular features discussed appear to justify our regarding 1 Thessalonians as evidence of an early Pauline theology.[71] The theology of 1 Thessalonians can be designated early Pauline because it evidently provides the point of departure for Pauline theology both in a temporal sense and in terms of its subject matter and because it does not yet presuppose the central themes and conflicts that characterize the later letters. Reference to the specificity of each letter and the situation to which each letter was addressed is not adequate to explain the large number of distinctive features in 1 Thessalonians. We must finally conclude that the letter contains a coherent theological conception in and of itself, which does not need interpretative theological supplements from the later letters and which by no means can be considered deficient.[72] The point of departure for this theology is the conviction, common to Paul and the church, that the Jesus Christ whom God has raised from the dead will soon return to save the elect and holy community from the coming wrath. The world of 1 Thessalonians is determined by a concept of reality at the center of which stands God's saving act in Jesus Christ. As the living God, he can awaken the dead. This God is the one who graciously elects the church in Thessalonica and gives it the Spirit, so that God is the Father of all believers. The community derives its new identity from this event. In the present time it lives by faith, love, and hope; in the perfection of those who have been chosen for salvation, the Christians in Thessalonica live toward the saving advent of the Son. The fundamental story of the gospel is the resurrection of the Son from the dead, a reality in which the church itself participates. This means that 1 Thessalonians manifests a self-contained system of theological thought and its related identity concept: believers participate (σύν ["with"], 4:14, 17; 5:10) in the transformation of the Son (cf. 1:9–10; 4:14) and from it derive their own new self-understanding as those who are saved. This symbolic universe needs no supplementation from the statements about law and justification found in the later letters; on the contrary, it is itself the basis of all the Pauline letters.

Christiaan Beker, "Contingency and Coherence in Paul's Letters," in *Paul the Apostle: The Triumph of God in Life and Thought* (Philadelphia: Fortress, 1980), 23–36.

71. On the term "early Pauline theology," cf. Earl Richard, "Early Pauline Thought: An Analysis of 1 Thessalonians," in *Thessalonians, Philippians, Galatians, Philemon* (ed. Jouette M. Bassler; vol. 1 of *Pauline Theology*; Minneapolis: Fortress, 1991), 39–51; and Friedrich Wilhelm Horn, "Paulusforschung," in *Bilanz und Perspektiven gegenwärtiger Auslegung des Neuen Testaments: Symposion zum 65. Geburtstag von Georg Strecker* (ed. Friedrich Wilhelm Horn; BZNW 75; New York: de Gruyter, 1995), 51 n. 79. Horn rightly points out that this is above all a *theological* category. But a temporal element is also involved, for with the beginning of Paul's independent mission in connection with the apostolic council and near in time to the writing of 1 Thessalonians, no doubt something new was emerging.

72. Börschel, *Konstruktion*, 355.

9

First Corinthians

High and True Wisdom

Sometimes the course of events takes on a dynamic of its own. In Corinth, not only did the Pauline gospel fall on fertile soil in Corinth; the Corinthians took it into their own hands.

9.1 Conflict in Corinth

Like no other letters in the Pauline corpus, 1 Corinthians presents the reader with insight into the line of argument Paul follows when thinking through and applying his theology. The letter reveals a church existing within the conflicting force fields of its new faith and the omnipresent pagan religiosity, in a setting where the prevailing ethical norms and social conditions continue to have validity and must be taken into account. It is in this setting that we see it struggling to find its own identity.

192

Corinth: The City

In Paul's time Corinth had become, as the capital of the Roman province of Achaia, a very Roman city. The city had been destroyed in 146 BCE. Although the site continued to be populated, Caesar had refounded it in 44 CE as a Roman colony for military veterans.[1] In 27 BCE the city then became the capital of the senatorial province of Achaia. Alongside the influential Roman element, the proportion of Greeks and people from the eastern Mediterranean must have been large. Philo indicates there was a noteworthy Jewish colony in Corinth (Philo, *Embassy* 281), and Acts 18:4 reports the presence of a synagogue.[2] The unique location of the city with its two harbors, Cenchrea and Lechaeum, explains the importance of Corinth as a commercial center between Asia and Rome/Greece. It was considered a wealthy city that thrived on commerce, banking, and skilled trades,[3] a city in which numerous Hellenistic-oriental cults flourished. In the second century CE, Pausanias reports that Corinth had altars and shrines to Poseidon, Dionysus, Isis and Sarapis, and the Ephesian Artemis and a temple to Asclepius.[4] Apuleius portrays an initiation ceremony into the Isis cult as taking place in Corinth (*Metam.* 11.22.7ff.).[5] Corinth was certainly a hub of the Cynic movement, which experienced a revival in the first century CE. The city had been one of the favorite places of Diogenes (Dio Chrysostom, *De tyrannide* [*Or. 6*] 3), and the famous Cynic Demetrius[6] lived and taught there (cf. Lucian, *Bis accusatus* 19; Philostratus, *Vit. Apoll.* 4.25). Moreover, Corinth was the site of the Isthmian Games (cf. 1 Cor. 9:24–27), which were second only to the Olympic Games in all of antiquity. Finally, to the north of the city, an Asclepius temple has been excavated; its three banquet halls illustrate the problematic behind 1 Cor. 8–10.[7]

1. On Corinth, cf. esp. J. Wiseman, "Corinth and Rome, I: 228 B.C.–A.D. 267," *ANRW* 25.4:438–548; Elliger, *Paulus in Griechenland*, 200–51; Jerome Murphy-O'Connor, *St. Paul's Corinth: Texts and Archaeology* (Wilmington: Michael Glazier, 1983); W. J. Gill, "Corinth: A Roman Colony in Achaea," *BZ* 37 (1993): 259–64; Bruce W. Winter, *After Paul Left Corinth: The Influence of Secular Ethics and Social Change* (Grand Rapids: Eerdmans, 2001), 7–25.

2. Our inscriptional evidence for a synagogue in Corinth comes from the second to third centuries CE; cf. Hans-Josef Klauck, *Herrenmahl und hellenistischer Kult: Eine religionsgeschichtliche Untersuchung zum ersten Korintherbrief* (NTAbh NF 15; Münster: Aschendorff, 1982), 234 n. 3.

3. Cf. Strabo, *Geogr.* 7.6.20–21, 23: "Corinth was nicknamed 'the rich,' because it was situated as a commercial center on the isthmus, controlling two harbors, one in the direction of Italy, the other toward Asia. This made trade between these people so distant from each other much easier. . . . This is the reason the city and its population became so wealthy, for the sailors and sea captains immediately spent there the money they had earned" (*NW* 2/1:235).

4. Cf. Pausanias 2.1.7–2.5.5.

5. On the worship of Egyptian deities in Corinth, cf. Dennis E. Smith, "Egyptian Cults at Corinth," *HTR* 70 (1977): 201–31.

6. See Margarethe Billerbeck, *Der Kyniker Demetrius: Ein Beitrag zur Geschichte der frühkaiserzeitlichen Popularphilosophie* (PhAnt 36; Leiden: Brill, 1979).

7. Murphy-O'Connor, *St. Paul's Corinth*, 161–67.

The Church

Paul founded the church in the year 50 CE, after his work in Philippi, Thessalonica, Beroea, and Athens.[8] He came alone to Corinth (cf. Acts 18:5), followed soon by Silvanus and Timothy. Paul remained there about a year and a half (cf. Acts 18:11), and Corinth developed alongside Ephesus as a center of the Pauline mission. The Corinthian church reflected the cultural, religious, and social pluralism of the city. The majority of church members were Gentile converts from pagan religions (cf. 1 Cor. 12:2; 8:10; 10:27), as indicated by the deplorable state of affairs in the congregation (participation in cultic festival meals, going to court before pagan judges, prostitution). The account of the conversion of Crispus, an official in the synagogue, and the effect of this event (cf. Acts 18:8) as well as 1 Cor. 1:22–24; 7:18; 9:20; 10:32; Rom. 16:21 document the existence of a significant Jewish Christian element in the church. Proselytes and God-fearers had also joined the community (cf. Acts 18:7), which was composed primarily of the lower social classes (cf. 1 Cor. 1:26; 7:21; 11:22b). But there were also some rich Christians in Corinth, such as the synagogue official Crispus, already mentioned (cf. 1 Cor. 1:14), and Erastus, who occupied a high city office in Corinth (cf. Rom. 16:23). Corinthian Christians owned houses (cf. 1 Cor. 1:16; 11:22a; 16:15ff.; Rom. 16:23; Acts 18:2, 3, 8), and the church made a substantial contribution for the saints in Jerusalem (cf. 1 Cor. 16:1–4; 2 Cor. 8:7ff.; 9:1ff.; Rom. 15:31).[9] The Corinthian Christians were organized in several house churches (cf. 1 Cor. 14:23, plenary gatherings of the church; 1:16; 16:15, Stephanas; 16:19, Prisca and Aquila; Rom. 16:23, Gaius, Erastus; Acts 18:7–8, Titius Justus, Crispus).[10] We can only speculate about the size of the whole church; it may have consisted of about a hundred members.[11] The organizational structure of the church may also shed some light on the church's internal conflicts, for its division into several house churches could have contributed to the formation of separate groups.

Structure of the Letter

The complex situation within the church is reflected in the structure of 1 Corinthians and in its line of argument; in contrast to the other Pauline

8. Cf. Wolfgang Schrage, *Der erste Brief an die Korinther* (4 vols.; EKKNT 7; Zurich: Benziger, 1991), 1:34.

9. On the social structure of the Corinthian church, cf., most recently, Helmut Merklein, *Der erste Brief an die Korinther* (ÖTK 7; Gütersloh: Gütersloher Verlagshaus, 1992–), 1:31–42, with good bibliography. The judgment of Meeks, *First Urban Christians*, 73, is also on target: "A Pauline congregation generally reflected a fair cross-section of urban society."

10. See Gehring, *House Church and Mission*, 134–42.

11. Cf. Suhl, *Paulus und seine Briefe*, 115; Klauck, *1. Korintherbrief*; Gehring, *House Church and Mission*, 139.

letters, it cannot be divided into two major sections. The situation in Corinth and the preceding communication between apostle and church shape Paul's line of argument. In 5:9 Paul mentions a letter to the Corinthians that has not been preserved and to which the church had obviously responded. Their letter had contained a series of questions that the apostle takes up and answers one by one. This section of the letter begins at 7:1, with each item signaled by the phrase περὶ δέ (now concerning): 7:1 (marriage and celibacy), 7:25 (virgins), 8:1 (eating food sacrificed to idols), 12:1 (spiritual gifts), 16:1 (the collection for Jerusalem) and 16:12 (Apollos). In addition, Paul has oral information (cf. 1:11; 5:1; 11:18), which especially shapes his argument in 1 Cor. 1–4, 5, and 6, and 11:17–34. One of the peculiarities of 1 Corinthians is that it has no single connected line of thought. Instead, beginning with the παρακαλέω (I appeal to you) clause of 1:10, we already find the kind of paraenesis that characterizes the letter as a whole.[12]

In the first major section (1 Cor. 1–4), Paul relativizes the Corinthians' striving after wisdom, then goes into the questions of their letter and the current problems in the church (1 Cor. 5; 6:1–11, 12–24; 7; 8–10). First Corinthians 11 is closely related to 1 Cor. 12–14; on the compositional plane, 1:7–8 has prepared for the sequence charismatic gifts–eschatological expectation (1 Cor. 12–14 to 1 Cor. 5). There is a clear connection between the subject matter of 1 Cor. 12–14 and 1 Cor. 15, for the exaggerated pneumatic enthusiasm of the Corinthians (cf. 1 Cor. 15:46) triggers the discussion of the future resurrection.

The numerous partition hypotheses regarding 1 Corinthians raise a possibility at the most but in no case offer a compelling argument. Put positively, two considerations, in addition to arguments based on particular passages, support the literary integrity of 1 Corinthians: (1) The particular manner of argumentation represented by stringing together loosely connected sections corresponds to the particular communication situation between apostle and

---

12. On the possible rhetorical structure of 1 Cor. 1–4, 15, cf. M. Bünker, *Briefformular und rhetorische Disposition im 1. Korintherbrief* (GTA 28; Göttingen: Vandenhoeck & Ruprecht, 1984). A survey of recent studies of the literary-rhetorical structure of 1 Corinthians is found in Schrage, *Korinther,* 1:71–94; for Schrage, 1 Corinthians is primarily a "paraenetic-advisory" (from Aristotle's rhetorical category συμβουλευτικός, "advising," "deliberative") letter. Margaret Mary Mitchell, *Paul and the Rhetoric of Reconciliation: An Exegetical Investigation of the Language and Composition of 1 Corinthians* (HUT 28; Tübingen: Mohr Siebeck, 1991), 20–64, understands 1 Corinthians as a document of deliberative rhetoric. Against the background of the political rhetoric of the time, 1 Corinthians appears as a call to unity and concord. According to Richard A. Horsley, "Rhetoric and Empire—and 1 Corinthians," in *Paul and Politics: Ekklesia, Israel, Imperium, Interpretation: Essays in Honor of Krister Stendahl* (ed. Richard A. Horsley; Harrisburg, PA: Trinity Press International, 2000), 72–102, in 1 Corinthians Paul intentionally adopts the language of imperial rhetoric, turning it against the imperial ideology: "Paul is using the deliberative rhetoric of political unity and concord for the virtual opposite of its usual purpose" (p. 74).

church. (2) The sequence 1 Cor. 12–14 to 1 Cor. 15 (spiritual gifts–parousia) is already anticipated in the structure of 1:4–6 to 1:7–8.[13]

Tensions in the Church

The Corinthian church experienced numerous tensions because of theological, ethical, and social questions.[14] Thus in 1 Cor. 1–4 Paul grapples with the issue of belonging to theologically motivated groups, connected to particular understandings of baptism, that had led to divisions within the church. In 1 Cor. 5 the apostle deals with someone who had grossly violated the community's sexual standards, and 6:1–11 presupposes that Corinthian Christians were taking each other to court before pagan judges. The warning against widespread (cultic) prostitution (6:12–20) is followed in 1 Cor. 7 by recommendations on sexual asceticism and remaining in one's present status. Religious and social reasons have evoked the conflict between "strong" and "weak" (cf. esp. 8:1–13; 10:14–23). In contrast to the Cynic wandering preachers,[15] Paul accepted no pay for his missionary work among them; the Corinthians evidently considered this a violation of social norms and disparagement of their willingness to support him (cf. 1 Cor. 9; 2 Cor. 11:7–8).[16] In 1 Cor. 11:17–34 Paul criticizes abuses of the Lord's Supper; in Corinth the sacramental celebration was included in the context of an ordinary meal (cf. 11:23–25), reflecting the original practice, in which sharing the bread and the cup formed the framework for the meal (cf.

13. Christian Wolff, *Der erste Brief des Paulus an die Korinther* (THKNT 7; Leipzig: Evangelische Verlagsanstalt, 1996), 351.
On the unity of 1 Corinthians in the most recent exegesis, see esp. Helmut Merklein, "Die Einheitlichkeit des ersten Korintherbriefes," in *Studien zu Jesus und Paulus* (2 vols.; WUNT 43, 105; Tübingen: Mohr Siebeck, 1987), 1:345–75; Dieter Lührmann, "Freundschaftsbrief trotz Spannungen," in *Studien zum Text und zur Ethik des Neuen Testaments: Festschrift zum 80. Geburtstag von Heinrich Greeven* (ed. Wolfgang Schrage; BZNW 47; Berlin: de Gruyter, 1986), 298–314; Becker, *Paul*, 187–96; Schrage, *Korinther*, 1:63–71; Mitchell, *Rhetoric of Reconciliation*, 184ff.; Andreas Lindemann, *Der erste Korintherbrief* (HNT 9/1; Tübingen: Mohr Siebeck, 2000), 3–6.
14. The Corinthian church was embroiled in several conflicts springing from different causes and therefore must be understood methodologically on different planes (sociological, theological, cultural, and the history of religions); cf. William R. Baird, "'One against the Other': Intra-church Conflict in 1 Corinthians," in *The Conversation Continues: Studies in Paul and John* (ed. Robert T. Fortna and Beverly R. Gaventa; Nashville: Abingdon, 1990), 116–36; Richard A. Horsley, "1 Corinthians: A Case Study of Paul's Assembly as an Alternative Society," in *Paul and Empire: Religion and Power in Roman Imperial Society* (ed. Richard A. Horsley; Harrisburg, PA: Trinity Press International, 1997), 242–52.
15. Cf. Diogenes the Cynic, *Epistle 10*, to Metrocles: "Be bold, not only with regard to your dress, name, and way of life, Metrocles, but also in begging people for sustenance, for it is not at all disgraceful. To be sure, kings and lords ask for money, soldiers, ships, and food from their subjects. And those who are sick ask remedies of their doctor" (in Malherbe, *Cynic Epistles*, 103).
16. Horsley, "Case Study," 250, argues that "Paul's personal concern was surely to avoid becoming a 'house apostle' to some Corinthian patron." On the nature of patronage in Corinth, cf. J. K. Chow, "Patronage in Roman Corinth," in *Paul and Empire: Religion and Power in Roman Imperial Society* (ed. Richard A. Horsley; Harrisburg, PA: Trinity Press International, 1997), 104–25.

11:25, μετὰ τὸ δειπνῆσαι [after supper]). In Corinth this earlier practice had given way to having a festive meal prior to the sacramental observance itself. In this manner the difference between poor and rich members of the congregation became painfully evident, for some feasted and others went hungry (cf. 11:21–22, 33–34). As in the pagan cultic meals involving sacrificial meat, table fellowship groups were formed among the wealthy from which the poor were excluded. Disputes also existed in Corinth about the relative significance of the various spiritual gifts (cf. 1 Cor. 12–14). Obviously, segments of the church considered glossolalia very important, regarding ecstatic, unintelligible speech directed to God as the highest spiritual gift (cf. 1 Cor. 14); other spiritual gifts were devalued accordingly. Paul stands this scale on its head, placing prophecy above glossolalia, and love as the spiritual gift par excellence (1 Cor. 13). Finally, the future resurrection of the dead was a disputed issue among the Corinthian Christians. Some were teaching that "there is no resurrection of the dead" (ἀνάστασις νεκρῶν οὐκ ἔστιν, 15:12).

No other letter provides us such a window into the diversity within the Pauline churches as does 1 Corinthians, and shows how forcefully Paul's fundamental convictions and situationally conditioned arguments interact in his theology.[17]

9.2 The Wisdom of the World and the Foolishness of the Cross

Paul begins his communication with the Corinthians by acknowledging that the church is blessed with spiritual gifts (1 Cor. 1:4–9). This spiritual richness is God's gift and manifests itself in speech and knowledge; God's grace strengthens the church in its testimony to Christ.[18] Paul builds into the letter's opening words a line from which he will not deviate: the Corinthians are rich only by God's gracious act among them. God has come to the Corinthians in Jesus Christ, and so they are not lacking in any spiritual gift. But in Corinth numerous conflicts revolve around the χαρίσματα (spiritual gifts; more literally, gifts of grace), which evidently are based on a specific understanding of baptism and the presence of the Spirit. With rhetorical power, Paul places the κοινωνία (fellowship) of the Corinthians with Jesus Christ (1:9) over against the divisions that in reality characterize the life of the church. Paul thereby specifies the theme of the letter as a whole: the Corinthians' quarrels and divisions show that they are not living up to their claim that the Spirit is truly at work among them.

---

17. Gordon D. Fee, "Toward a Theology of 1 Corinthians," in *1 and 2 Corinthians* (ed. David M. Hay; vol. 2 of *Pauline Theology*; SBLSymS 2; Minneapolis: Fortress Press, 1991), 37–58, provides a survey of Paul's argument in 1 Corinthians; cf. also Victor Paul Furnish, "Theology in 1 Corinthians," in *1 and 2 Corinthians* (ed. Hay), 59–89.

18. Merklein, *Korinther*, 1:89.

Groups in Corinth

In 1 Cor. 1:10–17 Paul grapples with the problem of the formation of groups within the church; membership in such groups is related to baptism. There were four groups in Corinth, designated by the names of their postulated heads—Paul, Apollos, Cephas, and Christ.[19] In 1:12 ἐγὼ δὲ Χριστοῦ (I belong to Christ) is parallel to the preceding slogans. There is no particular accent within the list, and so we must reckon with a "Christ party" at Corinth.[20] Moreover, μεμέρισται ὁ Χριστός; (has Christ been divided?) in 1:13a presupposes the ἐγὼ δὲ Χριστοῦ of 1:12. After all, Paul himself would hardly have introduced the name of Christ into the list of slogans, for this would mean that he would be putting Christ in the same category as Peter, Apollos, and himself.[21] Evidently the particular relationship of individual church members to the one who baptized them had led to divisions within the body of Christ, into which they had all been incorporated.[22] Individual candidates for baptism probably understood the baptismal act as introducing them into a realm of spiritual wisdom essentially mediated by the one who baptized them.[23] The Corinthians thought it was important to be known by particular names, by which one's Christian identity was established; in contrast, Paul points only to the name of Christ. He subjects this religiously motivated salvation-individualism to a series of theological critiques based on the substance of the Christian faith itself. In the first place, he points out that he himself had baptized only a few members of the Corinthian church. Even if there were any value in the claim to have been baptized by Paul, only a very few could make that claim. He emphasizes that, after all, Christ had not sent him to baptize but to preach the gospel. This is no depreciation of baptism itself; Paul is only clarifying his personal commission as apostle and missionary in view of the current situation in Corinth.[24] With a sober evaluation of his own person and role, Paul opposes the obvious importance the Corinthians give to baptism and who performed

---

19. An instructive survey of research is given ibid., 115–19; and by Schrage, *Korinther*, 1:142–52.

20. Cf. Conzelmann, *1 Corinthians*, 33–35; Weiss, *Korintherbrief*; 15ff.; and Ulrich Wilckens, *Weisheit und Torheit: Eine exegetisch-religionsgeschichtliche Untersuchung zu 1. Kor. 1 und 2* (BHT 26; Tübingen: Mohr Siebeck, 1959), 17 n. 2, who are among those who regard the fourth slogan as a gloss. Merklein, *Korinther*, 1:146–47, speaks not of a "Christ party" but a "Christ slogan" that should be adopted by the other groups. Schrage, *Korinther*, 1:148, thinks in terms of a rhetorical exaggeration by Paul, "as a reduction ad absurdum of the forming of groups as such."

21. Cf. Lindemann, *Der erste Korintherbrief*, 39.

22. Cf. Horn, *Angeld des Geistes*, 162–63.

23. Winter, *After Paul Left Corinth*, 31–43, sees the cultural background of the Corinthian interest in forming parties to be the special relationship and obligation of students to their teacher, particularly as it was required and cultivated among the Sophists.

24. Contra Hans Lietzmann and Werner Georg Kümmel, *An die Korinther I, II* (5th ed.; HNT 9; Tübingen: Mohr Siebeck, 1969), 9; Gerhard Barth, *Die Taufe in frühchristlicher Zeit* (BTS 4; Neukirchen-Vluyn: Neukirchener Verlag, 1981), 103; Hans Weder, *Das Kreuz Jesu bei Paulus: Ein*

it. He too considers baptism very important, but without making it a means of cultivating one's own individualistic image. Paul then supplements this biographical argument with two theological viewpoints. In 1:13a he again takes up the idea of the church's unity, already introduced with πάντες (all) in 1:10. In the form of a rhetorical question, he points out that the Christian community may not be divided because Christ is not divided. Thus ὁ Χριστός (Christ), in connection with 12:22, makes clear that in this opening section Paul already has in mind the concept of the church as σῶμα Χριστοῦ (body of Christ).[25] Because baptism means incorporation into the unity of the church established by Christ, it cannot be the object of divisive individualistic pursuits but can only mean their defeat.

The Cross as Epistemological Criterion

Finally, Paul introduces the cross of Christ as the criterion for knowledge of God, the world, and oneself. The cross, of all things, cannot be the object of human self-assertion but rather is that which destroys every καύχησις (boasting, self-glorification, overevaluation of oneself), which Paul describes in 1:17 as σοφία λόγου (eloquent wisdom), alluding to the Corinthian's theology. The truth is, "For the message about the cross is foolishness to those who are perishing, but to us who are being saved it is the power of God" (1:18).[26] For Paul, the cross of Christ is the decisive theological criterion; he gives no argument for the cross but speaks from the cross as the axiomatic foundation of what he has to say. Even more, the cross of Christ is a present reality in the message of the cross (1:17–18). The Scripture has already testified that the content of God's wisdom can never be filled in from the wisdom of the world (1:19); both must be strictly distinguished from each other, for they are not derived from comparable sources of knowledge. It is not in the heights of human wisdom and knowledge but in the depths of suffering and death that the father of Jesus

---

Versuch, über den Geschichtsbezug des christlichen Glaubens nachzudenken (Göttingen: Vandenhoeck & Ruprecht, 1981), 126, who see a minimizing of the importance of baptism.

25. Gerhard Friedrich, "Christus: Einheit und Norm der Christen," in *Auf das Wort kommt es an: Gesammelte Aufsätze zum 70. Geburtstag* (ed. Johannes H. Friedrich; Göttingen: Vandenhoeck & Ruprecht, 1978), 153; Rolf Baumann, *Mitte und Norm des Christlichen: Eine Auslegung von 1 Korinther 1, 1–3, 4* (NTAbh NF 5; Münster: Aschendorff, 1968), 56.

26. On the exegesis of 1 Cor. 1:18–3:4, in addition to the commentaries, see Ulrich Wilckens, "Zu 1Kor 2,1–16," in *Theologia crucis, signum crucis: Festschrift für Erich Dinkler zum 70. Geburtstag* (ed. Carl Andresen and Günter Klein; Tübingen: Mohr Siebeck, 1979), 501–37; Weder, *Das Kreuz Jesu bei Paulus*, 137–73; Thomas Söding, "Das Geheimnis Gottes im Kreuz Jesu (1Kor)," *BZ* 38 (1994): 174–94; Horn, *Angeld des Geistes*, 262–81; Joachim Theis, *Paulus als Weisheitslehrer: Der Gekreuzigte und die Weisheit Gottes in 1 Kor 1–4* (BU 22; Regensburg: Pustet, 1991) (comprehensive history of research and thorough exegetical work); Florian Voss, *Das Wort vom Kreuz und die menschliche Vernunft: Eine Untersuchung zur Soteriologie des 1. Korintherbriefes* (FRLANT 199; Göttingen: Vandenhoeck & Ruprecht, 2002), 51–211.

Christ has shown himself to be the God hospitable to humanity. God's act in Jesus Christ is thus manifest as a paradoxical event that both anticipates and contradicts human doing and human wisdom.[27] This surprising and paradoxical act of God on the cross comes to expression in the election of the church, for God has not chosen many of the wise and mighty but what the world regards as foolishness. To shame the strong, God chose things that are nothing in order to reduce to nothing things that are (1:27–28). The existence of the church is itself already an application of the theology of the cross. This reality already excludes καύχησις: "Let the one who boasts, boast in the Lord" (1:31b). The Corinthians' striving after wisdom thus goes astray when it orients itself to the heights of what the world respects. God chose to locate his wisdom at the cross; here Jesus Christ becomes σοφία θεοῦ (the wisdom of God) for the church.

In 1:30 Paul utilizes traditional baptismal language as a means of interpreting the reality of the church in regard to the paradoxical revelation of God on the cross. This is indicated not only by the expression ὑμεῖς ἐστε ἐν Χριστῷ (you are in Christ; cf. Gal. 3:28b) and the context, which concerns their original call, but especially by the triadic formulation in 1:30c. All three terms have a soteriological function and portray the new situation of the church in light of the paradoxical revelation of God in Jesus Christ. Whereas in the exclusive doctrine of justification as found in Galatians and Romans the significance of δικαιοσύνη (righteousness) is determined by the connection to νόμος (law) and πίστις (faith), here it refers to the righteousness grounded in Jesus Christ and characteristic of the church. Sin, which had afflicted people before faith, had been removed in baptism, and they are really righteous.[28] Ἁγιασμός (sanctification) appears elsewhere in baptismal contexts, designating the holiness mediated by baptism (cf. 6:11; Rom. 6:19, 22). Again, we should think here of a real change, for it is not only one's status before God that is changed; the one who has been sanctified is now essentially separated from the world.[29] The term ἀπολύτρωσις (redemption) is firmly anchored in the tradition (cf. Rom. 3:24; Col. 1:14; Eph. 1:7; Heb. 9:15).[30] Paul uses this word only rarely, in places where he is making a particular emphasis (Rom. 3:24; 8:23); in 1 Cor. 1:30c it points to the redemption effected by the crucifixion of Jesus Christ and made real for the church in baptism.

27. How radically Paul's theology of the cross contradicts the contemporary Greek-Hellenistic picture of God is seen, e.g., in Diogenes Laertius 10.123, where Epicurus challenges his students to construct an appropriate idea of God: "First, think of God as an immortal and happy being, corresponding to the idea of God usually held, and do not impute anything to him that clashes with his immortality or his eternal bliss."

28. J. A. Ziesler, *The Meaning of Righteousness in Paul: A Linguistic and Theological Enquiry* (SNTSMS 20; Cambridge: Cambridge University Press, 1972), 158, is on target with his comment that for 1 Cor. 1:30 "a purely forensic meaning is impossible."

29. Cf. Weiss, *Korintherbrief*, 113.

30. Cf. Karl Kertelge, "ἀπολύτρωσις," *EDNT* 1:331–36.

True Wisdom

In the context of pneumatic enthusiasm, Paul consciously points to baptism as the locus of redemption and righteousness, which come from beyond ourselves. In baptism God constitutes the new reality of εἶναι ἐν Χριστῷ (being in Christ), something the Corinthians did not attain but which has been given to them. Righteousness and holiness are gifts of God, not attributes of intensified human self-realization. Paul's point of departure is the status of the Corinthians as persons who have been baptized and are therefore justified, sanctified, and redeemed. He then appeals to their experience in order to make clear that they must renounce boasting about themselves, which, after all, only leads to divisions within the church, and must now live out their new existence constituted in baptism. The "depths of God" (1 Cor. 2:10) cannot be fathomed by exaggerated ecstatic experiences. Whereas the Corinthians' "way of wisdom misunderstands the Spirit as the instrument of individualistic participation in salvation and as the guarantor of insight into hidden divine mysteries, Paul had preached, from his initial founding visit onwards, only Jesus Christ as the crucified one (cf. 2:2).[31] The apostle had intentionally made his appearance in Corinth "in weakness," and his message came to them "not with plausible words of wisdom, but with a demonstration of the Spirit and of power, so that your faith might rest not on human wisdom but on the power of God" (2:4b–5). Thus God himself is the ground, agent, and goal of a revelatory event in which the Spirit of God gives the human spirit insight into the saving plan of God in Jesus Christ (cf. 2:12). Paul knows that he himself and his preaching have been this foundational event and that in his letter to the Corinthians, as in his other teaching, he is interpreting spiritual things as himself a person endowed with the Spirit (πνευματικοῖς πνευματικὰ συγκρίνοντες of 2:13 is best translated "in that we interpret spiritual things by spiritual means"). Paul's preaching of the gospel is thus not merely a matter of words but a revelation of the Spirit and power of God. Pauline proclamation is not oriented to the superficial rules of rhetorically skilled communication; Paul ignored the effect of his external appearance[32] and renounced systems of thought that flattered the human intellect. His preaching was oriented exclusively to the subject matter: the cross.[33]

---

31. On the "way of wisdom," cf., e.g., Philo, *Unchangeable* 143: "This way, you must know, is wisdom. For wisdom is a straight high road, and it is when the mind's course is guided along that road that it reaches the goal which is the recognition and knowledge of God [τὸ δὲ τέρμα τῆς ὁδοῦ γνῶσίς ἐστι καὶ ἐπιστήμη θεοῦ]. Every comrade of the flesh hates and rejects this path and seeks to corrupt it. For there are no two things so utterly opposed as knowledge and the pleasure of the flesh."

32. Differently, e.g., Quintilian, *Inst.* 10.1.119, where the effect of the rhetorician Trachalus is described: "He had every possible external advantage—a lovely voice, unique in my experience, a delivery which would have graced the stage, and great personal beauty."

33. This also, of course, manifests some competence in rhetoric, for according to Cicero, *Or.* 1.31.138, rhetoric should serve not merely to talk people into doing something but actually to convince them with reasonable arguments.

Nevertheless, the apostle's preaching was not ineffective, for God himself was and is at work in it. That this work was not at Paul's own disposal is seen precisely in the paradoxical course of events through which it moves, for the word has its effect by the power of the Spirit despite the inadequacy of the methods used by the preacher. The Corinthians can recognize cause and effect here, namely, that they owe their faith not to human wisdom but to the power of God. Paul knows that his own life has always been enveloped and grasped by this power of God, and he by no means thinks lightly of the Spirit of God and the Spirit's gifts.

Thus he can say great things about the wisdom of God, the Spirit of God, and people who are filled by the Spirit (cf. 2:6–16).[34] God's wisdom is hidden from the world because world and divine wisdom are structured in opposition to each other: the wisdom of the world is based on what is visible and superficial, but the wisdom of God emerges from hiddenness and works in a manner hidden from human wisdom. In 2:6–16 Paul falls back on the motif of the preexistent, hidden wisdom sent by God (cf. Prov. 8:22–31; Sir. 1:4; 24:9; Job 28:12–14, 20–23; Wis. 9:13–18)[35] in order to emphasize the fundamental difference between God's acts and human criteria. Human wisdom is incapable of recognizing the wisdom of God because it can grasp the event of the cross only superficially, as foolishness (2:8). In contrast, God has revealed it to those who are spiritually mature (2:6) διὰ τοῦ πνεύματος (through the Spirit, 2:10). Paul counts himself among the spiritual, just as the Corinthians so regard themselves (πνευματικοί, 2:15–16). Both base their self-understanding on the gift of the Spirit that comes from God, which makes them fundamentally different from those who are only ψυχικοί (NRSV, "unspiritual"; NIV, "without the Spirit"; more literally, psychic, having only a human soul; cf. 2:14–15). Although Paul and the Corinthians have in common this fundamental concept of the Spirit, in each case it is bound up with a different anthropological conception. The Corinthians, too, attributed the noetic capacities of the spirit-endowed person to the Spirit of God (2:12b, "understand"; 2:13, "taught," "interpret"; 2:14–15, "discern"), but at the same time understood and employed them individualistically. Paul and the Corinthians proceeded on the basis of analogical knowledge, according to which the Spirit can only be recognized by those who have the Spirit, but they made different applications of this basic idea.[36] The Corinthians integrated the revealed divine wisdom into the creaturely abilities of human

34. He thereby makes use of a tripartite revelatory scheme: (1) that which was previously hidden (1 Cor 2:6–9) (2) has now been revealed to the person endowed with the Spirit (2:10–12), (3) so that it can now be proclaimed to other spiritual people (2:13–16). As parallel texts, cf. Col. 1:26–28; Eph. 3:5–8; 2 Tim. 1:9–11; Titus 1:2–3. A terse but extremely rich analysis is found in Conzelmann, *1 Corinthians*, 57–69 (Paul develops the schema in the internal discussions of the Pauline school).

35. Cf. Theissen, *Psychological Aspects*, 345–53, who appropriately designates 1 Cor. 2:6–16 a "wisdom speech"; cf. also Voss, *Das Wort vom Kreuz*, 102ff.

36. Cf. Merklein, *Korinther*, 1:219–20.

beings in order to make them more powerful. As they understood the matter, divine wisdom and knowledge worked as *movens* (mover, inciter, inspirer) of human intellectual power. Thereby the real basis of divine wisdom, the event of the cross, fell into the background while human intellectual powers stepped into the foreground. Paul and the Corinthians had differing understandings of the "mystery of God" (μυστήριον θεοῦ; cf. 2:1, 7; 4:1). As the "Lord of glory" (2:8, κύριος τῆς δόξης), Christ was evidently regarded by the Corinthians as the prototype of the "divine man," who by baptism had transformed the Spirit-endowed into the life of the transcendent world even while they still lived by faith in this present world. In contrast, Paul binds the "mystery of God" exclusively to the cross, for, in the form of the crucified one as the "Lord of glory," the "wisdom of God" (σοφία θεοῦ) prevails over the "wisdom of human beings" (σοφία ἀνθρώπων). The Corinthians do not eliminate the cross,[37] but they neutralize it in that they see the death of Jesus as the transitional passage-way to that true spiritual existence from which the preexistent one came. By this means they provide a rational basis for the unfathomable acts of God and make their own wisdom equal to that of God.

Paul demonstrates to the Corinthians their inadmissible paralleling of divine and human wisdom by pointing out to them the actual situation in their church. When jealousy and strife characterize the life of the church, the Corinthians still actually belong to the "fleshly" and "immature" (cf. 3:1–4). If the reality of their congregational life is dominated by slogans such as "I belong to Paul" or "I belong to Apollos" (3:4), then the Corinthians have not at all attained a true knowledge of God. The wisdom of God may not be confused with the wisdom of this world, since only the crucified Jesus Christ is the wisdom of God. Thus the wisdom of God cannot lead to the formation of such groups in the church, where individuals claim the deepest revelations for themselves. Paul, Apollos, and Peter are merely fellow laborers who belong to God, not architects in the construction of truth. The truth of the matter is that "no one can lay any foundation other than the one that has been laid; that foundation is Jesus Christ." If the Corinthians place their confidence in some other foundation, this will be revealed in the judgment. In this judgment by works (cf. 3:13–15), the quality of what everyone has done will be tested by fire.[38] The one who is tested can lose his or her work (and body) but will still share in the eschatological σωτηρία (salvation). Paul bases this on the reality that believers are the temple of God in whom God's Spirit dwells (3:16). The πνεῦμα (Pneuma, Spirit) given in baptism evidently confers an irrevocable quality that endures even through the judgment.

---

37. Cf. Söding, "Geheimnis Gottes," 178–79.
38. For analysis of the text, see Synofzik, *Vergeltungsaussagen*, 39–41.

Backgrounds: Cultural History

The Corinthian feeling of superiority and perfection (cf. 1 Cor. 4:8, "Already you have all you want! Already you have become rich! Quite apart from us you have become kings!";[39] cf. also 2:6; 4:10, 18, 20; 5:2; 6:12; 10:1ff., 23; 15:12) manifests a variety of partly overlapping religious, cultural, and social influences. Hellenistic Jewish wisdom thought is seen in the sophia theology of 2:6–16, the σάρξ/πνεῦμα (flesh/spirit) dualism, the high priority placed on knowledge (cf. 8:1–6; 13:2), the disdaining of the body (cf. 6:12–20), and the concept of the two archetypal human beings in 15:45.[40] Philo indicates that only the wise are the "free," "lords," (*Posterity* 138, ὁ σοφὸς μόνος ἐλεύθερος τε καὶ ἄρχων) and "kings" (*Dreams* 1.2, μόνος ὁ σοφὸς ἄρχων καὶ βασιλεύς; cf. *Names* 152; *Sobriety* 57; *Migration* 197). Only the wise receive the designation τέλεια (perfect, *Sobriety* 9); only they are "rich" and "mighty" (*Sobriety* 56).[41]

The influence of Hellenistic Jewish wisdom thought was strengthened by the great respect already accorded sages and wisdom in the Greco-Roman intellectual tradition. Cicero repeats a fundamental conviction of the ancient thought world: "Only the wise man is free, and every fool is a slave."[42] Epictetus can speak of the Cynic's kingdom (*Diatr.* 3.22.79, ἡ δὲ τοῦ Κυνικοῦ βασιλεία);[43] for him, the sage participates in Zeus's own rulership.[44] Seneca states, "Everything belongs to the wise."[45] Whereas an ordinary person on the way toward wisdom can be thrown back at any time, it can be said of the one who has perfected

---

39. For analysis of this passage, see Horn, *Angeld des Geistes*, 228–29.

40. Sellin, *Auferstehung*, 68, supposes that Apollos had introduced a wisdom theology from Alexandrian Judaism into Corinth that had become popular in the predominantly Gentile church in Corinth. Sellin can point to notable agreements between Philo and the Corinthian theology, but there are also objections to his proposal: (1) We do not in fact know anything about the theology of the Alexandrian Christian Apollos (cf. Acts 18:24), and so all such agreements are purely hypothetical. (2) If Apollos had been the cause of the conflict between Paul and the Corinthians, then it is difficult to explain why Paul has no criticism of him but rather accepts him as an independent missionary on a par with himself (cf. 1 Cor. 3:5, 8). (3) According to 1 Cor. 16:12, Paul encouraged Apollos several times to return to Corinth. This would mean that Paul had repeatedly asked him to leave Ephesus and return to the place where he was the source of the problems.

On Hellenistic Jewish wisdom thought, see, e.g., Egon Brandenburger, *Fleisch und Geist: Paulus und die dualistische Weisheit* (WMANT 29; Neukirchen-Vluyn: Neukirchener Verlag des Erziehungsvereins, 1968), passim; Karl-Gustav Sandelin, *Die Auseinandersetzung mit der Weisheit in 1. Korinther 15* (MSÅAF 12; Åbo, Finland: Åbo Akademi, 1976); Richard A. Horsley, "Wisdom of Word and Words of Wisdom in Corinth," *CBQ* 39 (1977): 224–39; Sellin, *Auferstehung*, passim; Theissen, *Psychological Aspects*, 358–67; Merklein, *Korinther*, 1:119–33; Voss, *Das Wort vom Kreuz*, 146–52.

41. Cf. also Philo, *Dreams* 2.230: "The Sage . . . is an intermediate being, superior to human beings but less than God."

42. Cicero, *Parad.* 33 (*NW* 1/2:438).

43. Cf. further Epictetus, *Diatr.* 3.22.49, 63.

44. Cf. Epictetus, *Diatr.* 3.22.95.

45. Cf. Seneca, *Ben.* 7.2.5; (3.2–3); and Zeno in Diogenes Laertius 7.125: τῶν σοφῶν δὲ πάντα εἶναι (Everything belongs to the wise).

wisdom, "The wise person cannot fall back, can never again get sick."[46] According to the *Cynic Epistles*, Diogenes taught "that everything belongs to God [πάντα τοῦ θεοῦ], and since friends share everything in common, everything belongs to the wise as well."[47] That which is due the ideal ruler is claimed by the Corinthians for themselves: everything is permitted.[48]

The Corinthians' beliefs also have some points of contact with the way salvation is understood in the mystery religions.[49] In both instances there is a deep interest in the possibilities and means of illuminating one's own nature, a concern for one's self that finds fulfillment in the realization of one's true self. In the face of blind, raging destiny and the inevitability of suffering and death, the initiates hope to participate in the dramatized destiny of a god who has experienced death as the passageway to new life. After fulfilling the rites of the cult, the initiate is "reborn" to a happy and successful new life that already begins in the present (cf. Apuleius, *Metam.* 11.16.2–4; 21.7).

Finally, we should not underestimate the influence of pagan ethics and the social conduct related to it.[50] In the ancient world, religious identity was always connected with social identity, that is, group identity (family, polis [city]), and so Paul expects the Corinthians not only to adopt a new faith but to change their whole pattern of life. Some members of the Corinthian church had not yet taken this step, still living within their usual ethical and social customs.[51] They were either unwilling to accept a complete break with their previous social relationships and/or believed that their new faith and the old pattern of life could be combined.

---

46. Seneca, *Ep.* 72.6 (*NW* 2/1:1436). Cf. also the concept of the purifying fire that frees the wise from all negative things: "Just so wisdom, like a purifying fire, releases the wise from all those things that other people regard as admirable and desirable, since they are not able to make discerning judgments" (Lucian, *Hermotimus [De sectis]* 7); cf. also Plutarch, *Mor.* 499c.

47. Cf. Crates, *Epistle 27* (in Malherbe, *Cynic Epistles*, 77).

48. Cf. Dio Chrysostom *3 Regn.* 10, concerning the ideal ruler: "For who needs more insight than the one who must give counsel about the most important issues? Who has a more refined sense of justice than the one who stands above the law? Who is more level-headed than the one to whom everything is permitted?" Cf. also Dio Chrysostom *Regn. tyr.* 2.

49. Cf. Söding, "Geheimnis Gottes," 181–82.

50. Cf. esp. Winter, *After Paul Left Corinth*, passim; see also Peter Marshall, *Enmity in Corinth: Social Conventions in Paul's Relations with the Corinthians* (WUNT 2/23; Tübingen: Mohr Siebeck, 1987), who argues that it was not theology but ethical and social issues that stand behind the conflict between Paul and the Corinthians.

51. How such ideas could have been regarded is seen in Philo, *Worse* 33, 34, who polemically reproduces the arguments of the Sophists: "Did nature create pleasures and enjoyments and the delights that meet us all the way through life, for the dead, or for those who have never come into existence, or for the living? And what is to induce us to forego the acquisitions of wealth and fame and honors and offices and everything else of that sort, things which secure for us a life not merely of safety but of happiness?" Whereas those who pursue virtue are disdained, "those, on the other hand, who take care of themselves are men of mark and wealth, holding leading positions, praised on all hands, recipients of honors, portly, healthy and robust, reveling in luxurious and riotous living, knowing nothing of labor, conversant with pleasures which carry the sweets of life to the all-welcoming soul by every channel of sense."

Differing Concepts of Identity

On the basis of the wisdom theology that had taken over their understanding of the Christian message, the Corinthians had evidently come to regard salvation as something "already" present in a comprehensive way, as indicated by the repeated ἤδη (already) of 1 Cor. 4:8. Paul and the church agree in thinking very highly of the Spirit and of baptism.[52] Both are convinced that in baptism believers fully participate in the death and resurrection of the deity, that here the door to new life is opened. In contrast to Paul, however, the Corinthians understand the gift of the Spirit primarily as the overcoming of the limitations of their previous creaturely being, as increasing their vital forces and life expectancy.[53] In the context of their present and individualistic beginnings in this new life, suffering is expected to fade away, and they have only a minimal understanding of the nature of sin. The central idea is the intensification of life's possibilities through a deity whose destiny has already overcome the limitations of death and who now guarantees the reality of the transcendent world in the present life. Thus the Corinthians can skip over the boundaries set by the Creator as no longer applying to them and degrade God to a means of religious fulfillment. They fail to recognize the basic maxim of Christian anthropology, "What do you have that you did not receive?" (4:7a). Their pursuits go beyond what is written, and people relate to each other in terms of inflated egos (4:6b).[54] The Corinthians want to evade their creaturely limitations, and not humility but exaltation and lordship appear to them as the appropriate expression of their redeemed state.

In contrast to this, the apostles are "fools for Christ's sake" (4:10). They provide a different model of the saved life in that, for the sake of the church, they conduct their ministry in weakness, danger, and poverty (cf. 4:11–13). They thus represent the category of the truly wise, who know themselves to be independent of all external evaluation, obligated only to their commission and their message. Thus Paul can call the Corinthians to be imitators of him:

52. It is hardly an accident that Paul repeatedly comes back to the subject of baptism throughout the letter (cf. 1 Cor. 1:30; 6:11; 10:1–4; 12:13; 15:29).

53. Cf. Horn, *Angeld des Geistes*, 248, who rightly advocates the view that the Corinthians' Spirit enthusiasm grew out of their baptismal theology; he gives two principal arguments: (1) "The early Christian interpretation of baptism as the place where the Spirit is conferred. The metaphoric that combined water and spirit was common in the ancient world, and gives us a glimpse of how the baptismal rite could be seen as the place where the πνεῦμα ['Spirit'] was transmitted as a substance and the one baptized became a πνευματικός [a 'spiritual,' 'Spirit-endowed' person] in a magical sense." (2) "The baptismal act is interpreted as a ritual reenactment of Christ's own fate, his death and resurrection. As one who has been baptized, the initiate now participates in the heavenly world."

54. The difficult expression τὸ μὴ ὑπὲρ ἃ γέγραπται (nothing beyond what is written) refers, in my opinion, to what was, in Paul's view, the Spirit-enthusiastic Scripture interpretation practiced by the Corinthians. On the numerous interpretations that have been given this phrase, cf. Christian Wolff, "'Nicht über das hinaus, was geschrieben ist,'" in *". . . Das tiefe Wort erneun": Festgabe für Jürgen Henkys zum 60. Geburtstag* (ed. Harald Schultze; Berlin: Wichern, 1989), 187–94.

μιμηταί μου γίνεσθε (be imitators of me, 4:16b). This is an appeal to their reason: they are not to imitate his person but appropriate for themselves the God-given new understanding of existence they see in Paul's life. In contradiction to human expectations, God chooses the weak and destroys the strong. The God who elects through the gospel has given his self-interpretation on the cross and crossed out human ideas and expectations.

The identity concepts held by Paul and the Corinthians are both based on the life-giving power of God, who raised Jesus Christ from the dead. At the same time, however, they differ on a central point: Paul understands the cross to be an identity marker that includes suffering and lowliness in one's relation to God and expects visible glory (only) at the parousia, which is to arrive in the near future.

9.3 The Power of the Spirit and the Purity of the Community

The Corinthians also grounded their consciousness of freedom in their understanding of Spirit enthusiasm. They evidently understood freedom as a matter of each individual's right as a Christian, which was maintained in continuity with their social identity outside the church. Thus they did not present their legal disputes before a forum within the church but before pagan courts (6:1–11).[55] Paul issues a fundamental challenge against this conduct: if the saints are going to judge the world and even the angels, then why are they looking to pagan courts for justice? The apostle suggests a different way of dealing with such problems: they should be resolved under the chairmanship of a σοφός (wise person, sage) within the church. In fact, this is not Paul's final word in regard to such problems in the future, for in 6:7 he questions whether there should be such legal disputes among Christians at all. Insisting on one's rights is the real mistake.[56] Christians must be ready to suffer injustice and to divest themselves of their rights. Renunciation of one's rights is the Christian's appropriate response in legal matters. The Corinthians must not attempt to establish their right before the courts, for it has already been granted them. To clarify this fundamental state of affairs, in 6:11b–c the apostle harks back to a

55. For comprehensive interpretations, cf. Erich Dinkler, "Zum Problem der Ethik bei Paulus," in *Signum crucis: Aufsätze zum Neuen Testament und zur christlichen Archäologie* (Tübingen: Mohr Siebeck, 1967), 204–40, and Winter, *After Paul Left Corinth*, 58–75 (74, "The Corinthians were simply acting as the élite had always done in Corinth when a conflict situation arose"). Horsley, "Rhetoric and Empire," 100, regards 1 Cor. 6:1–11 as evidence for his thesis that Paul understands the church as an "alternative society . . . independent of the larger society, having no dealings with institutions such as the civil courts."

56. Cf. Plato, *Gorg.* 509c: "Socrates: 'Seeing then that there are these two evils, the doing injustice and the suffering injustice—and we affirm that to do injustice is a greater, and to suffer injustice a lesser evil.'"

baptismal tradition[57] that defines the new being of Christians in contrast to their old existence (6:9–11a): "But you were washed, you were sanctified, you were justified in the name of the Lord Jesus Christ and in the Spirit of our God." The adverbial qualifiers refer to all three verbs and define the baptismal event more closely. The preposition ἐν (in, by) has here its instrumental function: the invocation of the name and the presence of the Spirit effect the washing, sanctification, and justification.[58] The invocation of the name corresponds to the assurance of the Lord's presence, made real in the conferral of the Spirit on the baptismal candidate. The Spirit is given in baptism, and the sacramental effect of baptism is effected by the Spirit.[59] The baptized person now is incorporated by baptism into the number of those who invoke the name of Christ and belong to the eschatological community of salvation (1:2). Because the Corinthians have not lived up to the status of holiness and righteousness conferred on them by baptism, Paul calls on them to live lives that correspond to their new being.

From Paul's point of view, the Corinthian motto πάντα μοι ἔξεστιν (All things are lawful for me, 1 Cor. 6:12; cf. 10:23) raises the question of the relation of freedom and responsibility. Responsibility is located concretely in bodily life and thus also in human sexuality. The freedom attained by wisdom and knowledge evidently allowed some members of the Corinthian church to treat the body as a matter of indifference. Thus the Corinthians tolerated a serious instance of incest among them, in which a member of the church was sexually involved with his stepmother (cf. 5:1–5).[60] Instead of excluding the offender, the church boasted of this demonstration of sexual libertinism.[61] Not

57. This is indicated both by the verbs ἀπελούσασθε (you were washed), ἡγιάσθητε (sanctified) and ἐδικαιώθητε (justified) and by the adverbial qualifiers ἐν τῷ ὀνόματι τοῦ κυρίου Ἰησοῦ Χριστοῦ καὶ ἐν τῷ πνεύματι τοῦ θεοῦ ἡμῶν (in the name of the Lord Jesus Christ and in the Spirit of our God). For extensive evidence, see Schnelle, *Gerechtigkeit und Christusgegenwart*, 39–42.

58. The verb δικαιωθῆναι (be made right/just) designates a onetime act in the past, with the passive voice emphasizing the gracious act of God. Here we should understand it in the sense of "being made right"; the effect of baptism is to actually make the one baptized righteous (cf. Strecker, "Befreiung und Rechtfertigung," 254). "The use of δικαιωθῆναι here should hardly cause us to think in terms of the precise sense of the word in the later letters to the Galatians and Romans. The specific doctrine of justification can hardly be dependent on baptism" (Wilhelm Heitmüller, *Taufe und Abendmahl bei Paulus: Darstellung und religionsgeschichtliche Beleuchtung* [Göttingen: Vandenhoeck & Ruprecht, 1903], 12). [Translator's note: Note that here and throughout the discussion, "right," "justice" and their variations are all forms of the same Greek word. This correspondence can be preserved in German but not in the English translation. See p. 72 n. 82 above.]

59. Cf. Conzelmann, *1 Corinthians*, 107 n. 46.

60. For analysis, see Ingrid Goldhahn-Müller, *Die Grenze der Gemeinde: Studien zum Problem der Zweiten Busse in Neuen Testament unter Berücksichtigung der Entwicklung im 2. Jh. bis Tertullian* (GTA 39; Göttingen: Vandenhoeck & Ruprecht, 1989), 121–35; Schrage, *Korinther*, 1:367–78; Umbach, *In Christus getauft*, 106–35. The relevant Old Testament prohibitions are conspicuously absent (cf. Lev. 18:8; 20:11; Deut. 23:1; 27:20).

61. Schrage, *Korinther*, 1:372, supposes that it was a "public, intentional, and, so to say, provocative-ideological act."

only was the social status of the church thereby set at risk;[62] the ritual purity of the church itself was at stake (cf. 5:6), for this case affected the holiness of the church at its very core. Paul sees himself compelled to take immediate action and makes a decision that opposes the tolerance (or indifference) of the church: they must immediately exclude the offender by assembling, with Paul also present in the Spirit,[63] and in the name of the Lord delivering the person to Satan (5:4–5).[64] The execution of the sentence clearly takes place by the power of the Spirit and with Paul's own participation, even though he is not present in person.[65] In this judgment "flesh" (σάρξ) and "spirit" (πνεῦμα) are distinguished, with the goal of saving the inner self of the offender, which had been renewed and embraced by the Holy Spirit given in baptism.[66] In 1 Corinthians, penalty is not a matter of vengeance but is for the salvation of both the offender and the church.

A comparable argument is found in 3:5, where Paul speaks of a judgment in which the Christian can in fact be punished for his or her works but nevertheless still shares in eschatological σωτηρία. Paul bases this on his view that the community of believers is the temple of God in which God's Spirit dwells (3:16), so that God's power can also be present in it to destroy: "If anyone destroys God's temple, God will destroy that person. For God's temple is holy, and you [pl.] are that temple" (3:17). Here, too, in Paul's view the Spirit conferred in baptism evidently has an irrevocable quality that endures even through the final judgment. An additional impressive example of the realism of Paul's sacramental understanding is found in 11:30: because the Lord's Supper was eaten in an unworthy manner, there are many who "are weak and ill, and some have died." Here Paul makes a direct connection between partaking of the sacrament and what happens to one physically. Doubtless in the background of this statement is the idea that when the Lord's Supper is eaten in an unworthy manner, the sacrament itself has deadly results.[67] As portrayed in 15:29, an inner power

---

62. Winter, *After Paul Left Corinth*, 55, emphasizes this aspect.

63. Cf. Wilhelm Bousset, "Der erste Brief an die Korinther," in *Die Schriften des Neuen Testaments neu übersetzt und für die Gegenwart erklärt* (ed. Otto Baumgarten et al., 4 vols.; 3rd ed.; Göttingen: Vandenhoeck & Ruprecht, 1917–1920), 2:94: "He [Paul] is really thinking of a spiritual effect by long distance."

64. On παραδοῦναι . . . τῷ Σατανᾷ, cf. Adolf Deissmann, *Light from the Ancient East: The New Testament Illustrated by Recently Discovered Texts of the Graeco-Roman World* (trans. Lionel R. M. Strachan; New York: Doran, 1927), 301–4.

65. Cf. Bousset, "Korinther," 94. It is presupposed that it is the present Lord himself who acts through the Spirit.

66. Ernst Käsemann, "Sentences of Holy Law in the New Testament," in *New Testament Questions of Today* (London: SCM Press, 1969), 72, rightly states that the baptismal event cannot be annulled.

67. Differently, Peter Lampe, "Das korinthische Herrenmahl im Schnittpunkt hellenistisch-römischer Mahlpraxis und paulinischer theologia crucis," *ZNW* 82 (1991): 211 n. 79: "[The phrase] ὑπὸ κυρίου excludes an automatic working of the elements, thought of in a magical sense: the elements do not function like a poison that causes illness when they are eaten in an unworthy manner. It is rather the Lord who causes the sickness." Of course, it is the Lord who punishes, but it is through

resides in the sacrament that operates independently of human acts, whether for good or for ill.

In yet another way, the Corinthians negate bodily existence as the place where life is lived in holiness and obedience to God. Even after becoming Christians, they continued their previous practice of visiting prostitutes (cf. 6:13b, 15b, 16, 18), since sexual activity did not involve the internal spiritual self but only the body (which belongs to a lower order of existence).[68] Paul, in contrast, uses σῶμα as a comprehensive term for the whole person. Precisely because human beings have bodies and *are* bodies, God's saving act in Christ includes and determines the concrete existence and history of the person as a whole.[69] The body is, then, essentially much more than eating and drinking (6:13a); it is not defined merely in terms of biological functions but itself belongs to the Lord (The body is meant not for fornication but for the Lord, and the Lord for the body, 6:13b). As the locus of sexuality (cf. 6:18; 7:4; Rom. 1:24), the body may not be defiled. Because the whole bodily existence of believers belongs to the Lord, they belong together as members of the body of Christ (1 Cor. 6:15). Therefore fornication belongs to a different category than other types of misconduct, for, since it involves the body, it involves the unity of believers with each other and with Christ (6:18) and endangers the purity of the church as the body of Christ.[70] Thus bodily existence appears as the locus where faith attains visible form. As the dwelling of the Holy Spirit, the body is no longer available for one's individual, independent desires (6:19).[71] The self-centered "I" no longer has charge of the body because God has claimed the body as the place where he is to be glorified: δοξάσατε δὴ τὸν θεὸν ἐν τῷ

the sacramental elements that this happens, as is made clear in the context by the direct connection between eating the elements and the judgment: "For all who eat and drink without discerning the body, eat and drink judgment against themselves" (1 Cor. 11:29).

68. On the cultural background, cf. Renate Kirchhoff, *Die Sünde gegen den eigenen Leib: Studien zu pornē und porneia in 1 Kor 6, 12–20 und dem sozio-kulturellen Kontext der paulinischen Adressaten* (SUNT 18; Göttingen: Vandenhoeck & Ruprecht, 1994); Winter, *After Paul Left Corinth*, 86–93. Contact with prostitutes was part of everyday life in Corinth and carried no social stigma.

69. Defiling one's own body through unbridled sexuality (homosexuality, illegitimate sexual relations with the free or slaves) is also a theme within Stoicism; cf. Musonius, *Diss.* 12: "I must emphatically point out that everyone who fails in this matter does wrong, even if it affects none of the people about him, yet immediately reveals himself as a worse and a less honorable person; for the wrong-doer by the very fact of doing wrong makes himself worse and less honorable"; cf. Gerhard Dautzenberg, "Φεύγετε τὴν πορνείαν," in *Neues Testament und Ethik: Für Rudolf Schnackenburg* (ed. Helmut Merklein; Freiburg: Herder, 1989), 271–98.

70. In 1 Cor. 6:18 Paul is obviously avoiding the noun ἁμαρτία for sin, describing wrong behavior with the related noun ἁμάρτημα and the verb ἁμαρτάνω; cf. Umbach, *In Christus getauft*, 106ff.

71. Cf. Epictetus, *Diatr.* 2.8.11–12: "But you are a being of primary importance; you are a fragment of God; you have within you a part of Him. Why, then, are you ignorant of your own kinship? Why do you not know the source from which you are sprung? Will you not bear in mind, whenever you eat, who you are that eat, and whom you are nourishing? Whenever you indulge in intercourse with women, who you are who do this?" (*NW* 2/1:253; Boring et al., eds., *Hellenistic Commentary*, § 631).

σώματι ὑμῶν (therefore glorify God in your body, 6:20; cf. also Phil. 1:20). Because the body is the intersection between the point where human beings interact with the world and the point where God deals with human beings, it is necessary to resist temptation and conduct one's life in holiness. The apostle wishes that all people would choose to abstain from sexual activity entirely, as he had done, but not all have this gift (χάρισμα, 1 Cor. 7:7). Whoever can live in celibacy should take advantage of this possibility; but those who cannot resist temptation should choose marriage as the natural setting for sexuality (cf. 7:8–9, 25–28). The massive degree to which the apostle thinks of holiness and spiritual things in tangibly realistic terms is indicated by 7:14: "For the unbelieving husband is made holy through his wife, and the unbelieving wife is made holy through her husband. Otherwise, your children would be unclean, but as it is, they are holy."[72] Paul obviously thinks of the communication of holiness in such wise that the unbelieving spouse and children of the Christian partner are included within the objective holiness of the believer and are thereby included within the realm where the Spirit is effective. They are thus snatched from the clutches of the other powers, but they do not yet share in eschatological σωτηρία (7:16).

Paul does not advocate the view of the church as a *corpus permixtum* (mixed body);[73] for him, the church is, rather, the realm of purity and holiness within which those who have been baptized live, separated from the power of sin. Thus, both for their own sake and for the sake of the church, evildoers must be excluded.

9.4 Freedom and Obligation in Christ

The understanding and use of Christian freedom also comes to expression in the conflict between the "strong" and the "weak" in Corinth (cf. 1 Cor. 8:1–13; 10:14–33). The issue was triggered by practical questions about life together in the Christian community, questions in which social, ethical, and theological aspects were interwoven: May Christians purchase meat from the public marketplace (10:25)? May Christians accept invitations to dinner parties given by their non-Christian friends and neighbors? Can belief in the new faith be combined with participation in banquets (8:10) or even cultic celebrations in pagan temples (10:14–22)?[74] Paul discusses the questions in a manner that allows the church to become aware of the basic conflict that lies behind them.

---

72. On the exegesis of this passage, see Horn, *Angeld des Geistes*, 298–99.

73. On the relation of Pauline and Matthean ecclesiology, cf. Umbach, *In Christus getauft*, 120–35.

74. On determining the historical situation here presupposed, cf. Dietrich-Alex Koch, "'Seid unanstößig für Juden und für Griechen und für die Gemeinde Gottes' (1Kor 10,32)," in *Paulus, Apostel Jesu Christi: Festschrift für Günter Klein zum 70. Geburtstag* (ed. Michael Trowitzsch; Tübingen:

The "Strong" and the "Weak"

The "strong" in Corinth doubtless belonged in part to the upper social class, who could sometimes be freed from traditional religious ideas by religious knowledge (cf. 1 Cor. 8:1, 4; 10:23).[75] We should not, however, simply identify these strong Christians with the upper class, for the knowledge that there is only one God and that gods and demons have no real existence is the expression of a monotheism that could be adopted by people of all social classes, Jews and Gentiles alike (cf. 1 Thess. 1:9–10). Cynic traditions could also have been important, since the Cynics, like elements of the Corinthian church, also made their monotheistic confession the basis of their freedom to ignore dietary taboos and eat anything.[76] Thus Gentile Christians as well as liberal Jewish Christians could be numbered within the group of the strong. Without giving it a thought, they ate meat that had been sacrificed to idols (1 Cor. 8:9; 10:25–30), continued to be invited to pagan banquets (10:27), and even participated in pagan cultic celebrations (14:20–21). Their social position alone was enough to make it impossible for them to completely avoid eating meat sacrificed to idols. The strong justified their practice by appealing to their "knowledge" (cf. γνῶσις, 8:1–2, 4). They evidently understood the gospel and its message of freedom primarily as individual independence, as emancipation from the conventions of religion and morality.[77]

The "weak" in the Corinthian church were clearly a minority composed mostly of Gentile Christians (cf. 8:7).[78] Some in this group probably abstained from eating any meat that had been sacrificed to idols, from fear of the gods that they considered to be real. Others struggled with the economic necessity of participating in public religious festivals and eating idol meat within such cultic settings, which gave them a bad conscience.[79] Still others were misled by the practice of the strong to eat idol meat despite the reservations of their own conscience, while the strong continued to participate in the cultic sacrificial

---

Mohr Siebeck, 1998), 38–40; see also Nikolaus Walter, "Christusglaube und heidnische Religiosität in paulinischen Gemeinden," in Nikolaus Walter, *Praeparatio evangelica: Studien zur Umwelt, Exegese, und Hermeneutik des Neuen Testaments* (ed. Wolfgang Kraus and Florian Wilk; WUNT 98; Tübingen: Mohr Siebeck, 1997), 99–103.

75. This aspect is emphasized by Gerd Theissen, "Die Starken und Schwachen in Korinth," in *Studien zur Soziologie des Urchristentums* (WUNT 19; Tübingen: Mohr Siebeck, 1992), 282–83. The article has been published in English as "The Strong and the Weak in Corinth: A Sociological Analysis of a Theoretical Quarrel," in *The Social Setting of Pauline Christianity* (ed. and trans. John H. Schütz; Philadelphia: Fortress, 1982), 121–43.

76. Thus Epictetus, *Diatr.* 3.22.50, can designate as one characteristic of the Cynics that "they will eat anything you give them." According to Diogenes Laertius 6.64, Diogenes had his breakfast in the shrine, his only complaint being that he was offered bread of poor quality; see additional text and interpretative notes in Jones, *"Freiheit,"* 59–61.

77. Cf. Thomas Söding, "Starke und Schwache," *ZNW* 85 (1994): 70–75.

78. Cf., e.g., ibid., 75–77.

79. Cf. Theissen, "Die Starken und die Schwachen," 276–79.

meals unproblematically for themselves but also without consideration of the others.

The Pauline Model

Paul discusses the disputed issues in their paradigmatic dimensions; it is not only a matter of particular practices but of understanding what the gospel requires on this issue. The contrast between γνῶσις (knowledge) and ἀγάπη (love) made in 1 Cor. 8:1 has already established the basic principle. Knowledge trusts in one's own strength, but love "builds up" because it takes into consideration the weakness of the other. Paul thereby pulls the rug out from under the motto of the strong, just as he relativizes it and makes it more precise in 10:23: "'All things are lawful,' but not all things are beneficial. 'All things are lawful,' but not all things build up." Christian freedom finds its authentic expression not in limitless self-affirmation and self-realization but rather is *essentially a relational concept*: it attains its real character only in relation to one's fellow Christians and the Christian community. Freedom can thus not be understood as an attribute of an autonomous subject but discovers its boundary in the conscience of the other: "But take care that this liberty of yours does not somehow become a stumbling block to the weak" (8:9). The freedom of the strong to eat idol meat without distress must not lead to a situation in which the weak thereby are no longer free. Unlimited freedom leads inevitably to loss of freedom because it does not observe the boundaries set for it by the neighbor. Above all, such a concept of freedom denies and disdains the death of Jesus Christ, who died for the weak brother and sister (8:11). Paul defines Jesus' existence-for-others as the embodiment of his love.[80] The salvation of the strong is not based on their knowledge but only on the cross and resurrection of Jesus Christ. Paul understands ἐλευθερία (freedom) in strictly christological terms: "But when you thus sin against members of your family, and wound their conscience when it is weak, you sin against Christ" (8:12). The Pauline concept of freedom becomes clear in this admonition to the strong. For Paul, Christian freedom is the freedom won for us by Jesus Christ, so that a misuse of this freedom is an offense not only against one's fellow Christians but against Christ. Paul thus issues the Corinthians a strong warning, reminding them of the fate of the wilderness generation (10:1–13).[81] As their Israelite ancestors fell in the wilderness, so the Corinthian Christians will also fall if they absolutize the sacraments and the gifts they confer. The salvation mediated by the sacraments does not happen apart from expression

---

80. Cf. Söding, "Starke und Schwache," 85ff.

81. For interpretation, cf., most recently, Horn, *Angeld des Geistes*, 167–71; Schrage, *Korinther*, 380–429.

in concrete ethical decisions; rather, "the sacramental good is rendered invalid by unethical conduct."[82]

By binding freedom to Christ and orienting it to the neighbor, Paul gains some maneuvering room as he attempts to resolve the complex problem posed by eating sacrificial meat. Although he himself basically inclines toward the position of the strong (cf. 8:4–6), Paul extends two guidelines: (1) for Christians, actual participation in pagan sacrificial and cultic meals is excluded (cf. 10:21), and (2) when, at a private dinner party, meat sacrificed to idols is explicitly designated as such, Christians should not eat it (cf. 10:26). Either case would be an offense against the honor of the one true God (cf. 10:31).[83] Within these clear limits, one need not inquire more closely; one can buy meat in the marketplace and accept invitations to private dinner parties (cf. 10:25, 27). The Corinthians are guided toward a kind of conscious, intentional action that must always decide from case to case, taking into consideration and balancing the current situation, the conscience of one's Christian brothers and sisters, and one's own knowledge. Paul formulates his agreement with the position of the strong without withdrawing his positive valuation of the weak, thus facilitating dialogue between the two groups as equals. Moreover, the Pauline model of resolving such issues secures the church its place between Jews and Greeks (cf. 10:32). With regard to the Jews, the offensive nature of participating in the pagan sacrificial cults is avoided; with regard to the Greeks, Christians are not excluded from being able to accept dinner invitations from their non-Christian friends.[84]

Freedom as Service

The service character of the Pauline concept of freedom is further developed in 1 Cor. 9.[85] Here Paul discusses the relation of freedom to personal rights, using himself as an example. As an apostle of Jesus Christ, he is free and has the right to be supported by the congregations he has founded (cf. 9:4–6, 12–18). He intentionally waives this right, however, in order not to place any obstacle in the way of the proclamation of the gospel (9:12, 15–16). Paul takes up standard themes of the Socratic tradition:[86] just as the true philosopher accepts no pay for

---

82. Schweitzer, *Mysticism*, 260.

83. Koch, "Seid unanstößig," 44–45, rightly emphasizes that for Paul the interpretation of each situation is the determining factor.

84. Cf. ibid., 49ff.

85. With what appears to be only a digression, Paul explains that he fulfills the Corinthians' demands with his own person; on the position of 1 Cor. 9 in the macrocontext, cf. Mitchell, *Rhetoric of Reconciliation*, 243–50; Schrage, *Korinther*, 2:213–15.

86. Cf. Xenophon, *Mem.* 1.2.5–7, where it is said of Socrates, "Nor, again, did he encourage love of money in his companions. For while he checked their other desires, he would not make money himself out of their desire for his companionship. He held that this self-denying ordinance ensured his liberty [τούτου δ' ἀπεχόμενος ἐνόμιζεν ἐλευθερίας ἐπιμελεῖσθαι]. Those who charged a fee for their society he denounced for selling themselves into bondage, since they were bound to converse with

his instruction and thus presents himself as truly independent and persuasive, so Paul foregoes the support he is due from the church in Corinth, in order to preach the gospel freely. The apostle even goes a step further—he uses his freedom to make himself a slave to others. In 9:20–22 Paul describes his freedom as proclaimer of the gospel paradoxically as the service of a slave, a service that comes to expression among the Jews as being under the Torah, "though I myself am not under the law" (9:20). In the same way, he can live as one without the Torah to those without the Torah, "though I am not free from God's law but am under Christ's law" (9:21). Paradoxically, freedom is the result of being bound by the "law" of Christ (cf. Gal. 6:2).[87] Here "law" cannot refer to the Torah, for in the previous statement it is the variable that may be observed or not.

Whereas in antiquity freedom and slavery were for the most part considered mutually exclusive alternatives, for Paul they condition each other: the apostle's freedom comes to expression precisely as bondage to the gospel (1 Cor. 9:19). Waiving his right to support by the church only serves the unhindered extension of the gospel; Paul can be a Jew to Jews and a Gentile to Gentiles in order to win them to the gospel. Here, too, freedom is a concept that has to do with relationships. It can express itself paradoxically as the service of a slave because its essence and content are determined by Christ, who himself assumed the form of a slave (Phil. 2:6). It is not that slavery as such can claim on its own to define itself as a kind of freedom, but the freedom manifest in Jesus Christ is fulfilled in the mode of slavery to the gospel. For Paul the missionary, this means, "I do it all for the sake of the gospel, so that I may share in its blessings" (1 Cor. 9:23).

The Question of Slavery

The issue of slavery brings up the social-ethical dimension of the Pauline concept of freedom. In 1 Cor. 7:21b, does Paul advise slaves to strive to obtain

---

all from whom they took the fee. He marveled that anyone should make money by the profession of virtue, and should not reflect that his highest reward would be the gain of a good friend; as though he who became a true gentleman could fail to feel deep gratitude for a benefit so great."
Cf. also Seneca, *Ep.* 108.36: "But no one treats humanity as a whole worse, in my opinion, than those who consider philosophy to be a means of making money, those who live differently than they prescribe for others."

87. Here, too, Paul approximates a philosophical understanding of freedom, for like Epictetus or Diogenes, the apostle feels himself bound only to God and God's law; cf. Epictetus, *Diatr.* 3.24.64; 4.1.89–90; 4.1.159: "Take Socrates and observe a man who had a wife and little children, but regarded them as not his own, who had a country, as far as it was his duty, and in the way in which it was his duty, and friends, and kinsmen, one and all subject to the law and to obedience to the law." Cf. further *Diatr.* 4.1.153–154, where it is said of Diogenes that he would have given away all he had if it were asked of him: "The same is true regarding his relatives, his friends, and his fatherland. He knew from where he had received them, from whom and under what conditions. His true ancestors, the gods [τοὺς θεούς] and his real fatherland, however, he would never have given up" (*NW* 2/1:566–67).

their freedom, or should they be content to remain in their status as slaves?[88] It is not clear grammatically whether the aorist verb χρῆσαι (make use of) refers to τῇ δουλείᾳ (service as a slave) or ἐλευθερίᾳ. The conjunction introducing 7:21b (ἀλλά [but, even]) can be understood as introducing a clause contrasting with the preceding, which would then be translated with "however" or "nevertheless" and would speak for "freedom" as the object of the verb.[89] On the other hand, ἀλλά can function to further strengthen the following clause, in the sense of "and not only but also" or "yes, even," which suggests that the meaning is that the slave should remain a slave.[90] The context, 7:17–24, speaks clearly in favor of the latter interpretation, where the emphasis of the paraenesis is on "remaining" in the status in which one was called (μένω ["remain"], 7:20, 24; also 7:8, 11, 40; cf. κλῆσις ["calling"], 7:20; καλέω (to call) in active forms, 7:15, 17; and in passive forms, 7:18 (bis), 20, 21, 22, 24). The explanatory 7:22 also points in this direction: "For whoever was called in the Lord as a slave is a freed person belonging to the Lord, just as whoever was free when called is a slave of Christ." Paul here defines freedom as an inner freedom made possible by Jesus Christ and having its only goal in him. Social structures are not very important for this concept of freedom because they can neither grant freedom nor remove slavery.

Here Paul clearly stands close to Stoic ideas.[91] Thus Seneca can say of the slave, "He is a slave—but perhaps free in his soul. He is a slave—will that hurt him? Show me someone who is not a slave: one is a slave to his sensuality, another to his greed, another to his ambition, all are slaves to hope, all to

---

88. Extensive exegetical studies are found in Vollenweider, *Freiheit als neue Schöpfung*, 233–46; Schrage, *Korinther*, 2:138–44.

89. Among those who argue for the freedom option are Vollenweider, *Freiheit als neue Schöpfung*, 234–35; Wolff, *Der erste Brief an die Korinther*, 150; Schrage, *Korinther*, 139–40; Merklein, *Korinther*, 2:133–34; James Albert Harrill, *The Manumission of Slaves in Early Christianity* (2nd ed.; HUT 32; Tübingen: Mohr Siebeck, 1998), 127 ("In 1 Cor. 7:21, the Apostle exhorts slaves who are offered manumission indeed to avail themselves of the opportunity and to use freedom"); Richard A. Horsley, *1 Corinthians* (ANTC; Nashville: Abingdon, 1998), 102–3. On the manumission of slaves (especially as the honoring of loyal service), cf. Schumacher, *Sklaverei*, 291–302.

90. Cf., in this sense, e.g., Weiss, *Korintherbrief*, 187–88; Lietzmann and Kümmel, *Korinther*, 152. Lindemann, *Der erste Korintherbrief*, 173, advocates a mediating position: "Paul instructs the Christian slaves not to be concerned about their manumission; but *if* they have the chance to go free, they should rather (μᾶλλον) take advantage of it.

91. Cf., e.g., Epictetus, *Diatr.* 1.9.24–25, where, with an appeal to Socrates, he calls upon people to remain at the post they have been assigned by God: "'You make yourselves laughable by thinking that, if one of our officers has appointed me to a certain post, it is my duty to remain there, and to resolve to die a thousand times rather than desert it; but if God has assigned us to any place and way of life, we are free to desert it.' Socrates speaks like a man who is really a kinsman of the gods." Antisthenes had already been credited with the saying "Whoever lives in fear of others is a slave without knowing it" (Stobaeus 3.8.14; cf. Georg Luck, ed., *Die Weisheit der Hunde: Texte der antiken Kyniker in deutscher Übersetzung mit Erläuterungen* [Stuttgart: Alfred Kröner, 1997], 47). An extensive presentation of the background of the saying in the history of religions and the history of law is found in Jones, *"Freiheit,"* 27–37.

fear. I will show you a man who was once a consul who is now the slave of an old woman; I will show you a rich man, who is enslaved to his young female slave; I will show you highly distinguished gentlemen who are slaves, and that of stage-actors. No slavery is more despicable than slavery to one's own will" (*Ep.* 47). For Epictetus, freedom is identical with inner independence: "You must let go of everything, body and property, your good reputation and your books, society, office, and your private life. For wherever your inclination attracts you, there you become a slave, there you are subjected, bound, compelled, in short: you are completely dependent on the other" (*Diatr.* 4.4.33; cf. *Ench.* 11). Just as no one can give anything to the Stoic, so no one can take anything away. The goal is to live in harmony with oneself and thereby to fit into the harmony of the cosmos.

In the cosmos that is passing away (cf. 1 Cor. 7:29–31), Paul counsels an internal freedom over against the things of this world[92] and advises people to remain in the state in which they were called. The distancing from the world bound up with the cross and resurrection of Jesus Christ demands neither conformity to the world nor flight from it. It maintains the believer's freedom over against the powers that want to enslave human beings to themselves. It is not an unchanging cosmic order given to the world by God that calls for such conduct but God's present and future saving act. Whereas the Corinthians' understanding of freedom focuses on the rights of the individual as a means of self-realization, Paul regards ἐλευθερία as a relational concept. It is not the potential of my own "I" but the needs of the "you" that shape Paul's understanding of freedom. Human beings are not freed from their permanent fixation on themselves and their sense of self-worth until they commit themselves to God as Lord and master. Only service to God places human life in the realm of freedom, where people find their true selves, where they discover other human beings as their fellow creatures, and where they learn to respect the creation itself as the gift of God.

9.5 The Power of the Spirit and Building Up the Church

For Paul as for the Corinthians, the reality of God in the world is the reality of the Spirit.[93] God is always the source of the πνεῦμα that manifests the life-giving

---

92. Cf. Epictetus, *Ench.* 11.

93. From the viewpoint of the history of religions, Paul's understanding of spirit is rooted in Hellenistic Judaism, especially close to that of Philo (cf. Brandenburger, *Fleisch und Geist*, 114ff.; Burton L. Mack, *Logos und Sophia: Untersuchungen zur Weisheitstheologie im hellenistischen Judentum* [SUNT 10; Göttingen: Vandenhoeck & Ruprecht, 1973], 176ff.): (1) Like Paul (e.g., Gal. 5:16–18; Rom. 8:4ff.), Philo also knows the antithesis σάρξ/πνεῦμα (*Heir* 55–56; *Giants* 19–20, 29; *Unchangeable* 140ff.). (2) The contrast of flesh and spirit corresponds in both Paul and Philo to contrasting groups of human beings (1 Cor. 3:1ff.; Gal. 6:1ff.; Philo, *Unchangeable* 144, 159–160; *Giants* 65–66) who

power of the Creator (cf. 1 Cor. 2:12–14). The normal location for the Spirit's work is the ἐκκλησία θεοῦ (church/congregation of God). The Corinthians had a deep and lasting experience of the manifold power of the Spirit, but at the same time their attempt at individualizing the Spirit and making it the instrument of their own agenda threatened to destroy the edification and unity of the church (12:25, "that there may be no dissension within the body, but the members may have the same care for one another"). Because of their special evaluation of themselves, the "Spirit-endowed" (πνευματικοί [spiritual], 12:1; cf. 2:13; 3:1; 14:37; Gal. 6:1)[94] were in danger of disdaining other members of the church as less important and separating themselves from the rest of the church as a special group. Thus Paul warns the Corinthians by referring to the fate of the wilderness generation (1 Cor. 10:1–13). As their Israelite ancestors fell in the wilderness, so the Corinthian Christians will also fall if they absolutize the sacraments and the gifts they confer, if they fail to recognize that the new being they have received is inseparably bound to new actions. Clearly the prevailing tendency in Corinth was to value only the extraordinary gifts of the Spirit and to regard the inconspicuous gifts as second-rate. Their worship services, filled with pneumatic phenomena, threatened to lose their real mission and function of communicating the gospel of Jesus Christ in a manner that could be understood (cf. 14:6, 26). As in 1 Cor. 8–10, so also in 1 Cor. 12–14, Paul faced the task of affirming the valid theological arguments of the "spiritual" without putting a damper on the work of the Spirit, but at the same time resisting the distortions of the Spirit's effects and developing his argument for his own view of the gospel.[95] The apostle is no opponent of spiritual gifts; ecstatic and

---

are dragged into the conflict of hostile powers that control them. (3) Both Paul and Philo presuppose that putting the flesh to death is the prerequisite for life in the Spirit (Gal. 5:24; Rom. 6:6; 8:13; Philo, *Drunkenness* 65–76) (4) Like Christ (1 Cor. 6:17; 15:45b; 2 Cor. 3:17), so also σοφία (wisdom) can be understood as Spirit (Wis. 1:6; 7:7, 22ff.; Philo, *Giants* 22–27). (5) Both Paul (1 Cor. 3:16; 6:19; 2 Cor. 6:16–17; Rom. 8:9, 11) and wisdom texts (Wis. 1:4; 7:28; 8:16–18; Philo, *Heir* 265; *Spec. Laws* 4.49) have the idea of the indwelling of the Spirit in human beings. (6) Also found in wisdom literature is the idea that the means of knowledge is identical with the content of knowledge, so that knowledge of God is possible only through the Spirit (1 Cor. 2:10ff.; 12:3; cf. Wis. 7:7; 9:17; Philo, *Alleg. Interp.* 1.38). Above all, Paul shares with Philo the idea that the Spirit is the ultimate, unsurpassable gift of God (1 Cor. 2:15), opposed to everything of an earthly, material, fleshly nature. It manifests the nearness and presence of God, has transformative power, and must be understood as the saving gift. Although the wisdom literature comes closest to providing the horizon of understanding for the Pauline pneumatology, there are still two significant differences: (1) For Paul, the πνεῦμα is *the* expression that communicates the presence and power of the divine whereas in Philo, e.g., πνεῦμα is used alongside σοφία, λόγος (word, reason), and νοῦς (mind, thought). (2) Paul binds his idea of the Spirit consistently to Christology and eschatology.

94. In Corinth one group evidently claimed this title exclusively for itself; cf. Horn, *Angeld des Geistes*, 180–88.

95. On the line of argument in 1 Cor. 12–14, cf. the extensive discussion in Ulrich Brockhaus, *Charisma und Amt: Die paulinische Charismenlehre auf dem Hintergrund der frühchristlichen Gemeindefunktionen* (Wuppertal: Brockhaus, 1972), 156–92; Oda Wischmeyer, *Der höchste Weg: Das 13. Kapitel des 1. Korintherbriefes* (SNT 13; Gütersloh: Gütersloher Verlagshaus, 1981), 27–38; Wolff, *Der erste*

miraculous phenomena are for him the obvious and expected manifestations of divine activity in and on the church.[96] We must not confuse this positive evaluation with an uncritical enthusiasm for spiritual phenomena as such, for Paul binds the spiritual gifts to norms and goals. For him, the primary mark of having received the gift of the Spirit is the confession Κύριος Ἰησοῦς (Jesus is Lord), and only those who join in this confession are inspired by the Spirit (12:3).[97] The charismata of "utterance of wisdom" (λόγος σοφίας), "utterance of knowledge" (λόγος γνώσεως), "healing" (χαρίσματα ἰαμάτων), "working of miracles" (ἐνεργήματα δυνάμεων), "prophecy" (προφητεία), "discernment of spirits" (διακρίσεις πνευμάτων), and "[speaking in] tongues" (γλῶσσα) are not instruments of individualistic self-realization but the expression of the church's diversity in unity given and maintained by the Spirit (12:8–11).[98]

The Church as Body

In 1 Cor. 12:12–31 Paul elaborates his view of the integration of charismatic gifts in the organism of the body of Christ. He takes up the imagery of the human organism that was widespread and popular in antiquity and applies it to the situation of the church in Corinth: as the body is one even though it has many members, so the church has many members but is still one body.[99] But not only does the church stand in some relation to the body of Christ; it is itself the body of Christ: Ὑμεῖς δέ ἐστε σῶμα Χριστοῦ (you are the body of

---

Brief an die Korinther, 282–348; Schrage, *Korinther*, 3:108ff.; Lindemann, *Der erste Korintherbrief*, 261–316.

96. Cf. Alkier, *Wunder und Wirklichkeit*, 191–205.

97. Here is a critical distinctive feature in contrast to pagan spiritual phenomena; cf. Eduard Schweizer, "πνεῦμα," *TDNT* 6:421.

98. On the term χάρισμα (charisma, spiritual gift), which is found only in Paul and in literature dependent on him, cf. Brockhaus, *Charisma und Amt*, 128–42; Horn, *Angeld des Geistes*, 282–83. For an interpretation of the lists of charismatic gifts in 1 Cor. 12:7–11, 28–30, see Heinrich Schürmann, "Die geistlichen Gnadengaben in den paulinischen Gemeinden," in *Das Kirchliche Amt im Neuen Testament* (ed. Karl Kertelge; WF 439; Darmstadt: Wissenschaftliche Buchgesellschaft, 1977), 362–412.

On the opposition of the Pauline doctrine of charismatic gifts to Spirit enthusiasm, cf. Horn, *Angeld des Geistes*, 281–91.

99. Eduard Schweizer and Friedrich Baumgärtel, "σῶμα," *TDNT* 7:1032–36, give numerous examples of body imagery in antiquity, especially handed on and further developed in Stoic circles; cf. also Matthias Walter, *Gemeinde als Leib Christi: Untersuchungen zum Corpus Paulinum und zu den "Apostolischen Vätern"* (NTOA 49; Göttingen: Vandenhoeck & Ruprecht, 2001); and *NW* 2/1:363–66. In the background of 1 Cor. 12:14–25 stands the fable of Menenius Agrippa (cf., e.g., Conzelmann, *1 Corinthians*, 211 n. 7). Epictetus, *Diatr.* 2.10.4, also uses this motif with an ethical implication. Those who examine themselves recognize their duty by virtue of their place in the universe: "What is not the duty of a citizen? He seeks no personal advantage and formulates no plans as though he were an isolated individual, but precisely as the hand or foot, if they could think and reflect on the natural organization of the body, would never move or extend themselves without taking the body as a whole into consideration."

Christ, 12:27). It is this identification that first permits the full application
of the organism imagery, for its ethical implications function only by equating the one body with Christ himself. It is not the case that the church must
form the body of Christ by its conduct; rather, the church's conduct must
conform to the reality of its being already in his body. The organism metaphor
provides an excellent image for the development of this metaphor, for with
its help both the church's relation to Christ and, based on this, the relation of
individual Christians to each other can be presented, the point of which is not
the similarity of members but that they are all of equal value.[100] All members
of the body are equally important and equally necessary; they are coordinated
with one another and depend on one another.

The church exists in and as the body of Christ because its individual members have been incorporated into his body by baptism (12:13).[101] The body
of Christ existed before its individual members; it is not brought into being
by human decisions and mergers but is a given reality existing before them
and providing their basis.[102] Baptism does not constitute the body of Christ,
but it is the historical locus for incorporation into this body and the concrete
expression of the church's unity, grounded in Christ. Those who are baptized
are incorporated into the body of Christ, whose reality and unity is established
by Christ; the believer is to live up to this reality. In Corinth, baptism and the
possession of the Spirit had triggered individualism, divisions, and seeking after
glory; Paul opposes to these centrifugal and destructive tendencies his concept
of the unity of the church maintained in Christ, appropriated in baptism, a
given unity that is to be preserved in the church's life.

In 12:13b–c Paul takes up traditional motifs (cf. Gal. 3:26–27) to interpret
the church's unity, given in baptism and made present in the Spirit, as the
abrogation of fundamental alternatives in the religious and social world. The
Jews have no advantage based on salvation history, the Greeks are not preferred
on ethnic-cultural grounds, and in the Christian community the distinctions
that have determined world history no longer exist—the distinctions between
servant and lord, slave and free, oppressed and oppressor. Rather, in baptism all
were given the one Spirit to drink,[103] the Spirit that makes the given unity of
the church a concrete reality in the present and whose visible expression is the

---

100. Cf. Conzelmann, *1 Corinthians*, 213–14.

101. For analysis, cf., most recently, Horn, *Angeld des Geistes*, 172–75.

102. Cf. Conzelmann, *1 Corinthians*, 212. Ferdinand Hahn, "Einheit der Kirche und Kirchen-
gemeinschaft in neutestamentlicher Sicht," in *Exegetische Beiträge zum ökumenischen Gespräch* (Göttingen:
Vandenhoeck & Ruprecht, 1986), 144, appropriately comments regarding σῶμα Χριστοῦ: "It is a
description of a given, comprehensive reality into which believers are incorporated as members."

103. Also 1 Cor. 12:13d refers to baptism (καὶ πάντες ἓν πνεῦμα ἐποτίσθημεν [we were all made
to drink of one Spirit]). The aorist form of the verb points to a single event of the past, analogous to the
ἐβαπτίσθημεν (we were baptized) in 12:13a. Differently, Ernst Käsemann, "The Pauline Doctrine of
the Lord's Supper," in *Essays on New Testament Themes* (SBT 41; London: SCM Press, 1964), 110–11,
who sees here a reference to the Eucharist.

abolition of those distinctions. The church, as body of Christ, lives from the closeness of God, which created its unity, in baptism and from the presence of Christ in the Spirit, which maintains this unity—and it documents this new reality also in its social form. It is only through a common life beneficial to all and serving the community of faith as a whole that the Corinthians live up to the new being established in baptism.

The Goal: Building Up the Church

The Spirit that proceeds from God and is effective in Christ is manifest in a variety of ways, but it is always "one and the same Spirit" (1 Cor. 12:4, τὸ δὲ αὐτὸ πνεῦμα). It leads into a wealth of diversity but not into the poverty of division. It belongs to its essence to establish unity, because it is itself ἕν πνεῦμα (one Spirit). The Spirit's unifying work is seen especially in the fact that it generates what benefits the church (12:7, τὸ συμφέρον [the common good]) and what serves its οἰκοδομή (edification, building up; cf. 1 Cor. 14). All charismatic gifts must be measured by this fundamental principle: πάντα πρὸς οἰκοδομὴν γινέσθω (Let all things be done for building up, 14:26). Those who speak in tongues[104] and have received the ability to praise God in the language of angels should pray that they can interpret such heavenly language to the church, for only this leads to building up the church (14:4, 5). Glossolalia, a charisma obviously highly valued in Corinth and limited to this church,[105] is not rejected by Paul but is bound by him to the critical goal of οἰκοδομή and thus can no longer be the means of individualistic showmanship. If glossolalia is translated, it has the same significance as prophecy: it strengthens the brothers and sisters in the faith (14:16–17), serving the church and the individual Christian.

Like the Corinthians, Paul treasures the gifts of the Spirit. At the same time, he emphasizes that the Spirit wants to work through the elements of order—of sober self-restraint and lining up with the interests of the church—and through consideration for others and mutual help. The gifts of the Spirit are, then, only present in the church if they can be shared. But Paul offers the Corinthians an even more excellent way: the way of love (ἀγάπη). It is no accident that 1 Cor. 13 stands between two chapters dealing with the misuse of charismatic gifts.[106] In 13:1–3 Paul makes clear that even the most extraordinary charismatic gifts are of no use if they are not pervaded by love. Their ephemeral character also relativizes the value of the gifts most treasured by the Corinthians, for they

---

104. On glossolalia, see Gerhard Dautzenberg, "Glossolalie," *RAC* 11:225–46; and Horn, *Angeld des Geistes*, 201–19, 291–97.

105. Cf. Horn, *Angeld des Geistes*, 204.

106. On the location of the chapter in its context and for an analysis, see Söding, *Liebesgebot*, 127–46; and Voss, *Das Wort vom Kreuz*, 239–71.

stand under the eschatological reservation (13:12). When the charismatic gifts have passed away and knowledge has ceased, love remains, which surpasses even faith and hope, because love is the most complete expression of God's essential being. Love is the very opposite of individualism and egoism; it does not seek its own good but reveals its nature precisely in bearing evil and doing the good. The ἀγάπη (love) of 1 Cor. 13 includes love for the neighbor and love for the enemy; it is not limited to ethics. Love is above all an eschatological power: the love of God that has appeared in Jesus Christ, which determines the whole life of the believer. Its field of operations is the church; Paul pulls the rug out from under the Corinthian consciousness of fulfillment, for apart from ἀγάπη there can be no real knowledge and no real fulfillment.

Paul structures his ecclesiology on a christological model: Jesus Christ exists in the church and as church, inasmuch as it is the community of those called and led by the Spirit, the realm in which the crucified and risen works historically and concretely. This does not mean that the ἐκκλησία is the *Christus prolongatus,* the prolongation of the Christ event, but the church is created and determined by this Christ. Christ is present there, and therefore it is σῶμα Χριστοῦ. Christ creates his church himself, and the church is only Christ's church so long as it is determined by the Spirit of Christ.[107]

9.6 The Resurrection of the Dead

First Corinthians 15 constitutes the high point of the letter as Paul, proceeding from the cross/resurrection creedal statement, elaborates on the final events at the Lord's parousia. The essential subject is the temporality of the world and human existence; Paul's struggle with this subject is tightly interwoven with Christology, anthropology, soteriology, and eschatology.[108]

The Foundational Story

Christianity's christological confession is the point of departure and basis for his reflections. Paul places the Corinthians under obligation to the reality of the gospel, the gospel that is accepted by all and that alone can save. It is the gospel that tells the Jesus-Christ-history, the gospel that has bound author and readers to each other since Paul's initial preaching in Corinth, which founded the church. The pre-Pauline tradition of 1 Cor. 15:3b–5 shows that five ele-

---

107. This priority of Christology to ecclesiology is especially emphasized by Ernst Käsemann, "The Theological Problem presented by the Motif of the Body of Christ," in *Perspectives on Paul* (Philadelphia: Fortress, 1971), 113–14, 116–17, 121.

108. On the history of research, cf., most recently, Oda Wischmeyer, "1. Korinther 15: Der Traktat des Paulus über die Auferstehung der Toten," in *Was ist ein Text?* (ed. Oda Wischmeyer and Eve-Marie Becker; NET 1; Tübingen: Francke, 2001), 172–78.

ments form the basic framework of the Easter event:[109] (1) a statement about Jesus' death (15:3, "Christ died for our sins in accordance with the scripture"); (2) a reference to the grave (15:4a, "he was buried"); (3) a statement about the resurrection (15:4b, "he was raised on the third day in accordance with the scriptures"); (4) a report of an appearance (15:5a, "he appeared to Cephas"); (5) a report of appearing to a group of disciples (15:5b, "then to the Twelve"). The basic structure of 15:3b–5 is clearly seen in the Greek text, which is character-ized by the naming of each event, followed by its interpretation:

ὅτι	Χριστὸς		
		ἀπέθανεν	
			ὑπὲρ τῶν ἁμαρτιῶν ἡμῶν
			κατὰ τὰς γραφὰς
καὶ ὅτι		ἐτάφη	
καὶ ὅτι		ἐγήγερται	
			τῇ ἡμέρᾳ τῇ τρίτῃ
			κατὰ τὰς γραφὰς
καὶ ὅτι		ὤφθη Κηφᾷ	εἶτα τοῖς δώδεκα.

that	Christ		
		died	
			for our sins
			in accordance with the scriptures,
and that		he was buried,	
and that		he was raised	
			on the third day
			in accordance with the scriptures,
and that		he appeared to Cephas,	then to the twelve.

The grammatical subject is Χριστός; the sentence concerns the destiny of the decisive figure of all humanity;[110] personal, individual history and universal history are united in one story. This is possible because God is to be thought of as the actual subject throughout, as indicated by the passive forms of the verbs θάπτω (bury) and ἐγείρω (raise) and the twofold interpretative κατὰ τὰς γραφάς (according to the scriptures). The series "dead–buried" and "raised–appeared" names the events in their chronological and objective order. The death of Christ is mentioned in general terms; there is no suggestion of an explicit theological interest in the tradition of the cross as the place and means of Jesus' death. That he was buried underscores the reality of Jesus' death and indicates some

109. On the interpretation of this text, cf. Hans Conzelmann, "On the Analysis of the Confes-sional Formula in 1 Corinthians 15:3–5," *Int* 20 (1966): 15–25; Wolff, *Der erste Brief an die Korinther*, 354–70; Schade, *Apokalyptische Christologie*, 191–202; Sellin, *Auferstehung*, 231–55; Schrage, *Korinther*, 4:31–53; Lindemann, *Der erste Korintherbrief*, 328–33. Cf. further in section 16.2.1 ("Jesus Christ as the Risen One").

110. Wolff, *Der erste Brief an die Korinther*, 361, points out that Χριστός is not to be taken here as a proper name but designates the salvific destiny of the Messiah.

knowledge of the events of the burial. The tenses of the verbs are significant, for the aorist forms of ἀποθνήσκω and θάπτω designate an event completed in the past whereas the perfect passive ἐγήγερται[111] stresses the continuing effect of the event.[112] Christ has been raised from the dead, and the resurrection means the continuing impact of Christ as the crucified one. The passive ὤφθη in 15:5, in connection with the Old Testament theophanies, emphasizes that the appearances of the risen one are according to God's will.[113] Within the line of argument in the thought world of 1 Corinthians, ὤφθη points to eyewitness testimony, which, combined with the other groups of eyewitnesses, characterizes the resurrection of Jesus Christ as a bodily event.[114] The fact that several independent witnesses are mentioned speaks against the supposition that we are dealing with a subjective vision in the modern sense.[115] That the first epiphany was to Cephas is firmly anchored in the tradition (cf. 1 Cor. 15:5; Luke 24:34), as are the appearances to the group of disciples (cf. Mark 16:7; Matt. 28:16–20; Luke 24:36–53; John 20:19–29). The interpretation is based on the testimony of Scripture; for the tradition, as for Paul, Christology is expressed in the language of Scripture.[116] The ὑπέρ-expression (for . . .) could be an allusion to Isa. 53:10–12; Ps. 56:14; 116:8, and the "third day" has several hermeneutical possibilities (historical memory; reference to Hos. 6:2; the significance of the third day in ancient cultures' views of death).[117] In any case, the essential content is a theological statement about God's saving act in the crucifixion of Jesus. God acts to deliver Jesus from the realm of death. Otherwise one must say, "if Christ has not been raised, then our proclamation has been in vain and your faith has been in vain" (1 Cor. 15:14). If the Corinthians accept the fact that God has raised Christ from the dead (15:12a, 15), then they cannot also say, "there is no resurrection of the dead" (15:12:b).

The line of argument of 15:3–10 as a whole is determined by a constantly increasing emphasis on the reality of the resurrection of Jesus Christ from the dead. At the beginning stands the witness of the tradition, then follows an extensive listing of eyewitnesses, in which the reference to more than five hundred brothers and sisters is especially significant: many of them are still alive and

---

111. On ἐγείρω, cf. 1 Thess. 1:10; 2 Cor. 4:14; Rom. 4:24b; 6:4; 7:4; 8:11b.

112. Cf. Blass and Debrunner, *Grammar*, § 342.

113. Cf. Wolff, *Der erste Brief an die Korinther*, 368.

114. Cf. ibid., 369; Alkier, *Wunder und Wirklichkeit*, 212, who appropriately comments, "But this is also not a countermove that establishes the reality of the resurrection in the positivistic sense of nineteenth-century historiography. After all, the context for the whole argumentation of 1 Corinthians is not the encyclopedic knowledge sought by modern historical positivism."

115. Already pointed out by Weiss, *Korintherbrief*, 349–50; cf. also Alkier, *Wunder und Wirklichkeit*, 212.

116. Cf. Martin Karrer, *Jesus Christus im Neuen Testament* (GNT 11; Göttingen: Vandenhoeck & Ruprecht, 1998), 335–37.

117. All possibilities are discussed by Wolff, *Der erste Brief an die Korinther*, 364–67, and Karrer, *Jesus Christus*, 42–43.

can be interrogated. And after all, it is the last witness to whom the risen one appeared who is at this very moment writing them a letter.

The Denial of the Resurrection

Some members of the Corinthian church denied a future resurrection because they had a different anthropology from Paul's.[118] They probably thought of the human person as a dichotomy, distinguishing between the self, as the invisible I-soul, and the visible body.[119] In contrast to later gnostic views, for the Corinthians, the body was not as such regarded negatively; rather, in their view, it was merely an earthly-temporary entity excluded from the eschatological redemption.[120] It is only the higher part of the person, the spiritual I-soul,[121] that has hope for a life beyond this one. Since the body is the earthly house for the soul, it has no bearing on the matter of salvation, and the Corinthians could regard it as irrelevant; this way of thinking could find expression both in unbridled sexual license and in sexual asceticism (cf. 1 Cor. 6:12–20; 1 Cor. 7). Because the body is transitory and doomed to die[122] but the soul was thought of as immortal, the Corinthians rejected the idea of an eschatological bodily resurrection. Evidently, for the Corinthians, life is not finally attained when death is overcome at the Lord's parousia but when the Spirit is conferred at baptism;[123] this is the place where the essential

118. For the reasons that exegetes have given for their denial of the resurrection, cf. the survey of research in Sellin, *Auferstehung*, 17–37.

119. Cf. ibid., 30: "The Corinthians denied the resurrection from the dead as such because they could not accept the ideas of bodily existence in eternal salvation that were bound up with it."

120. From the realm of popular piety, cf., e.g., Plutarch's account in *Is. Os.* 78: "This idea at the present time the priests intimate with great circumspection in acquitting themselves of this religious secret and in trying to conceal it: that this god Osiris is the ruler and king of the dead, nor is he any other than the god that among the Greeks is called Hades and Pluto. But since it is not understood in which manner this is true, it greatly disturbs the majority of people who suspect that the holy and sacred Osiris truly dwells in the earth and beneath the earth, where are hidden away the bodies of those that are believed to have reached their end. But he himself is far removed from the earth, uncontaminated and unpolluted and pure from all matter that is subject to destruction and death; but for the souls of men here, which are compassed about by bodies and emotions, there is no association with this god except in so far as they may attain to a dim vision of his presence by means of the apperception which philosophy affords. But when these souls are set free and migrate into the realm of the invisible and the unseen, the dispassionate and the pure, then this god becomes their leader and king, since it is on him that they are bound to be dependent in their insatiate contemplation and yearning for that beauty which is for men unutterable and indescribable."

121. Cf. Schade, *Apokalyptische Christologie*, 192–93.

122. For other texts from the history of religions, see below, section 22.2 ("The Course of the Final Events and Life after Death") and 22.4 ("Eschatology as Time Construal").

123. Traditions from Hellenistic Judaism illuminate this idea; cf. Wolff, *Der erste Brief an die Korinther*, 214. In Wis. 8:13 it can be said of the wisdom that is identical with spirit, "Because of her [wisdom] I shall have immortality, and leave an everlasting remembrance to those who come after me" (cf. Wis. 1:6; 7:7, 22; 8:17; 9:17). Wisdom enters into the soul of the pious (Wis. 10:16), which after death is in God's hand (Wis. 3:1).

transformation of the self occurs. For them, the irrevocable gift of the Spirit was already the absolute assurance of salvation because it not only granted entrance into the new being but was itself already the new being. For the Corinthians, the soul obviously already participated in immortality through the gift of the Spirit appropriated in baptism. The apostle shares this view of the objective reality of the Spirit expressed in such ideas (cf. 5:5; 3:15–16); in contrast to the Corinthian theology, however, Paul cannot think of the human self as a disembodied "I." Human existence is constituted in bodily terms; the body is not excluded from God's saving acts in the present and future. This was already true in God's saving act in Jesus of Nazareth, for not only did the crucified one have a body but the risen one has a body as well (cf. 10:16; 11:27; Phil. 3:21). Baptism grants incorporation into the whole destiny of Jesus, both with the bodily crucified one and with the bodily risen one. Thus Paul intentionally defers until 1 Cor. 15:29 the strange practice of vicarious baptism[124] because, against the intention of the Corinthians, it shows that a purely spiritual understanding of the resurrection does not square with the essence of baptism. In Corinth, Christians had themselves baptized on behalf of their relatives who had died without baptism, in the hope that they too would benefit from the power, operative in baptism, that overcomes death. Thus, in Paul's view, the Corinthians' own practice confirms that the Spirit must determine life after death. The salvific character of baptism consists in the overcoming of θάνατος, which begins with the conferral of the Spirit and is completed at the parousia of Christ. Baptism by no means protects one from natural death, but it bears within it the promise that at the eschaton the one who is baptized will be saved from death, God's eschatological opponent, the "last enemy" (15:26).

Existence and the Body

For Paul, there is no human existence apart from bodily existence, and so reflection on life after death must include the question of bodily life after death. For him, the question of the "how" of the resurrection can thus be only the question of what sort of body the resurrection body will be (cf. 1 Cor. 15:35b).[125] Paul opens this discussion in 1 Cor. 15:35ff.,[126] but the context is

---

124. For older interpretations, see Mathias Rissi, *Die Taufe für die Toten: Ein Beitrag zur paulinischen Tauflehre* (ATANT 42; Zurich: Zwingli, 1962). Selections from more recent literature can be found in Schnelle, *Gerechtigkeit und Christusgegenwart*, 150–52; Sellin, *Auferstehung*, 277–84; Wolff, *Der erste Brief an die Korinther*, 392–97; Horn, *Angeld des Geistes*, 165–67; Gordon D. Fee, *The First Epistle to the Corinthians* (NICNT; Grand Rapids: Eerdmans, 1987), 762–67; Joel R. White, "Baptized on account of the Dead," *JBL* 116 (1997): 487–99.

125. Lietzmann in Lietzmann and Kümmel, *Korinther*, 83, is on target with his comment that in 15:35 Paul responds "to the main objection of those who opposed the resurrection, that after death a *body* is inconceivable."

126. For interpretation, cf. Schade, *Apokalyptische Christologie*, 204ff.; Wolff, *Der erste Brief an die Korinther*, 402ff.; Lindemann, *Der erste Korintherbrief*, 354ff.; Schrage, *Korinther*, 4:266ff.; Jeffrey

important. In 15:12–19 the dominant theme was the correspondence between Christ and Christians, who are connected by an irreversible timeline, the beginning of which is constituted entirely by the resurrection of Jesus Christ. This was supplemented in 15:20 by the designation of Christ as the "first fruits of those who have died" (ἀπαρχὴ τῶν κεκοιμημένων) and the portrayal of the final events in 15:23–28.[127] In 15:36–38 Paul takes up the idea, widespread in antiquity, that death is the necessary condition of new life.[128] In 15:38 the apostle applies the factor of discontinuity, inherent in this view, to the free creative act of God, who gives to each its own σῶμα according to God's own will. God's ability to create earthly as well as heavenly bodies is for Paul a sign of God's creative power (15:39–41), which is the guarantee of the creation and receipt of an individual body of glory. In 15:42–44 Paul exploits hermeneutically what he has just said by interpreting the resurrection of what has been sown: just as the perishable is sown and the imperishable rises, so the σῶμα ψυχικόν (physical body) is sown and the σῶμα πνευματικόν (spiritual body) is raised. Paul answers the question of the "how" of the resurrection with this antithesis,[129] in that, on the one hand, bodily life is the basic presupposition of the resurrection and, on the other hand, the resurrection body is defined as a spiritual body and thus sharply distinguished from the present perishable world. In 15:45–49 Paul provides the basis for his thinking of the resurrection body as a σῶμα πνευματικόν. As a πνεῦμα ζῳοποιοῦν (life-giving spirit), Christ creates the spiritual resurrection body (15:45), and as the originator of the new being, he is at the same time its prime example and model. Just as the earthly state of the πρῶτος ἄνθρωπος (first human being), Adam, caused and determined the perishable nature of humans, so the heavenly state of the δεύτερος ἄνθρωπος (second human being) will cause and determine the future imperishable being. In 15:50a Paul summarizes the foregoing anthropological argument: σάρξ (flesh) and αἷμα (blood), the anthropological designation for the perishable nature of creaturely existence, cannot inherit the βασιλεία τοῦ θεοῦ (kingdom of God) because what is perishable cannot attain an imperishable nature.

With this antithesis of perishable and imperishable, in 15:50b Paul refers to the dominant (antithetical) line of argument since 15:35 and prepares his resolution of the problem. In 15:51 he presents an application of this solution

---

R. Asher, *Polarity and Change in 1 Corinthians 15: A Study of Metaphysics, Rhetoric, and Resurrection* (HUT 42; Tübingen: Mohr Siebeck, 2000), 91–145.

127. For exposition of this text, see below, section 22.2 ("The Course of the Final Events and Life after Death").

128. Cf. Herbert Braun, "Das 'Stirb und werde' in der Antike und im Neuen Testament," in *Gesammelte Studien zum Neuen Testament und seiner Umwelt* (3rd ed.; Tübingen: Mohr Siebeck, 1971), 136–58.

129. The antithesis πνευματικός/ψυχικός (spiritual/physical) is found for the first time in Paul; in terms of the history of religions, it probably derives from Jewish wisdom theology (cf. Philo, *Creation* 134–147; *Alleg. Interp.* 1.31–42, 88–95; 2.4–5); cf. Richard A. Horsley, "Pneumatikos vs. Psychikos," *HTR* 69 (1976): 269–88; Sellin, *Auferstehung*, 90–175; Horn, *Angeld des Geistes*, 194–98.

when he gives the church instruction, as a mystery disclosed by revelation, that not all will sleep but that all, living and dead, will be transformed.[130] First Corinthians 15:52 gives a more precise explanation of the relation of dead and living: the dead will be raised in an imperishable state, and "we" will be transformed. Since ἄφθαρτοι (imperishable) already describes the state of the future consummation (15:42, 50, 53–54), ἡμεῖς ἀλλαγησόμεθα (we will be changed) can only refer to those still living at the parousia, among whom Paul counts himself.[131] The explanation continues in 15:53ff., again framed antithetically, in which the metaphor of "putting on" imperishability or immortality clearly includes the element of identity between the old and the new being. Paul's argument takes account of the changed situation since writing 1 Thess. 4:13–18, for the death of Christians before the Lord's parousia is no longer the exception but the rule (cf. 1 Cor. 7:39; 11:30; 15:6, 18, 29, 51).[132] Paul deals with the problem constituted by thus temporal prolongation by introducing the motif of transformation,[133] which emphasizes equally both continuity and discontinuity between earthly life and life after death and affirms the parity of those who will have already died and those still alive at the parousia, while providing, in terms of his anthropological argument, the answer the Corinthians had called for regarding the "how" of the resurrection of Christians. In the course of this explanation, he is also affected by two central categories of Greek philosophy and cosmology: polarity and change.[134] The antitheses perishable/imperishable, earthly/heavenly are overcome through the work of the divine Spirit and transferred to the world of life after death by means of the concept of transformation.[135]

---

130. Cf. Lüdemann, *Chronology*, 1:242–42.

131. Cf. Henning Paulsen, "ἐνδύω," *EDNT* 1:451–52.

132. Cf. Lüdemann, *Chronology*, 1:240–41; Klauck, *1. Korintherbrief*, 123; differently, e.g., Lindemann, "Paulus und die korinthische Eschatologie," 79–80; Merklein, "Der Theologe als Prophet," 397.

133. Cf. Jürgen Becker, *Auferstehung der Toten im Urchristentum* (SBS 82; Stuttgart: KBW, 1976), 99.

134. Cf. Asher, *Polarity and Change*, 176–205. One example is that within Stoic thought, classifications in terms of polarities plays a significant role; cf. Diogenes Laertius 7.61: "Species is that which is comprehended under genus: thus man is included under animal. The highest or most universal genus is that which, being itself a genus, has no genus above: namely, reality or the real; and the lowest and most particular species is that which, being itself a species, has no species below itself, e.g., Socrates." Stoicism also understands as transformation the origination of what is qualitatively new; thus, e.g., Diogenes Laertius 7.142: "The world, they hold, comes into being when its substance has first been converted from fire through air into moisture and then the coarser part of the moisture has condensed as earth, while that whose particles are fine has been turned into air, and this process of rarefaction goes on increasing till it generates fire. . . . Chrysippus goes on to claim that the cosmos is a reasonable, body-like essence, with soul and spirit."

135. Cf. Asher, *Polarity and Change*, 206: "The thesis that has been argued in this investigation is that Paul attempts to persuade the Corinthians that there is a resurrection of the dead by showing them that the resurrection is compatible with the principle of cosmic polarity and that change is a solution to the problem of contrariety and the resurrection."

Their cultural background causes the Corinthians to exclude bodily existence from the realm of immortality and to regard the Spirit as the true realm of God's activity. In contrast, Paul adopts Greek models of argument to include the body within the realm of God's act and reverses the Corinthians order of things: "But it is not the spiritual that is first, but the physical, and then the spiritual" (1 Cor. 15:46). For him, the Jesus-Christ-history is in several aspects both the prototype and cause of the Corinthians' own history. The miraculous creative power of God raised Jesus from the dead, and it is God who will also act in the resurrection of the dead and the transformation of the Corinthians who are still alive at the parousia. As with Jesus Christ, so also with the Corinthians: God's creative power embraces the bodily existence of both.

9.7 The Cross, Justification, and the Law

We can give a relatively exact description of both the theological views prevailing in the Corinthian church and the ways in which Paul worked through the conflict. Paul takes up the basic concerns of the Corinthians in a positive manner, understanding, like them, the reality of the new being as the all-embracing, effective work of the Spirit.[136] At the same time, he points to decisive theological deficits: (1) Exclusive orientation to the pneumatic Christ as the "Lord of glory" neutralizes the death of Jesus Christ on the cross. (2) Their consciousness of being already in the fulfilled state of salvation relieves the Corinthians of their ethical responsibility and negates the greatest spiritual gift of all: love. (3) The saving, creative act of God also includes the body, and so the future existence of believers will always include bodily existence.

Justification and Law in 1 Corinthians

Within this line of argument, what significance does the thematic field "righteousness and law" have? The verb δικαιόω (justify, be/make righteous) is found in 1 Cor. 4:4; 6:11.[137] In 4:4 it means to be declared righteous before the court; in 6:11 δικαιωθῆναι describes an act in the past and is to be understood in the sense of "make righteous." This making righteous has an effective sense; those who are baptized are righteous through baptism, their sins are blotted out. Likewise δικαιοσύνη (righteousness) in the pre-Pauline baptismal tradi-

---

136. Cf. Hans von Soden, "Sakrament und Ethik bei Paulus: Zur Frage der literarischen und theologischen Einheitlichkeit von 1.Kor. 8–10," in *Das Paulusbild in der neueren deutschen Forschung* (ed. Karl Heinrich Rengstorf and Ulrich Luck; WF 24; Darmstadt: Wissenschaftliche Buchgesellschaft, 1964), 364: "For all the participants in the discussion thought in sacramental terms: the strong . . ; the weak . . . ; and also Paul himself."

137. The adverb δικαίως in 1 Cor. 15:34 should be translated as "rightly" in the moral sense. On the difficulty of consistently rendering this Greek word group in English, see p. 72 n. 82 above.

tion in 1:30 has no reference to the law; it means the righteousness attained in baptism that characterizes the church, grounded in Jesus Christ.

Νόμος occurs in 1 Corinthians eight times in four different passages.[138] In 9:9, in the context of the defense of his apostleship, Paul cites a law from Deut. 25:4 originally intended as protection for animals. With the formula "in the law it is written," in 1 Cor. 14:21 the apostle cites a text from Isa. 28:11–12 (and thus not a text from the law) that agrees with neither the Hebrew nor the Septuagint text.[139] In 1 Cor. 9:19–23 Paul portrays his life as a missionary with examples from the law/Torah (νόμος four times). He describes his freedom as a preacher of the gospel paradoxically as service as a slave because, for him, service is not a renunciation of freedom but its concrete expression.[140] He expresses this freedom when he is among Jews by being under the Torah, although Paul himself does not live under the Torah (9:20d). In the same way, the apostle conducts himself without the Torah in his dealings with Gentiles, although before God he lives "within the law of Christ" (ἔννομος Χριστοῦ, 9:21). Depending on the circumstances, Paul can sometimes bind himself to the Torah and at other times not do so. Such an accommodation does not apply, however, to the "law" of Christ, which is identical with the love command. Carrying out the commission to preach the gospel in obedience to Christ is the real driving power of Paul's ministry.[141] Because he feels himself to be wholly and exclusively bound to Christ, Paul can adjust to different situations without subjecting himself to a new norm. *The* norm of his freedom and identity is exclusively Christ. With this paradox Paul demonstrates his inner independence from human judgment, the judgment of those with whom he conducts his missionary labors. Like Diogenes, in every situation he knows himself to be bound to God alone.[142] It is not a matter of "freedom from the law"[143] but freedom ἐκ πάντων (9:19a, "from all"). The theologically reflective, conceptually accented, and essentially negative understanding of the law found in Galatians and Romans is not yet present in 1 Corinthians.

---

138. First Corinthians 14:34 is in fact a gloss; for evidence, see Jürgen Roloff, *Der erste Brief an Timotheus* (EKKNT 15; Neukirchen-Vluyn: Neukirchener Verlag, 1988), 128ff.

139. For the details, cf. Koch, *Schrift als Zeuge*, 63–66.

140. Cf. Merklein, *Korinther*, 2:228.

141. Cf. Lindemann, *Der erste Korintherbrief*, 212: "Paul thus speaks of the norm of obedience to Jesus Christ."

142. Cf. Epictetus, *Diatr.* 3.24.64–65: "Come, was there anybody that Diogenes did not love, a man who was so gentle and kind-hearted that he gladly took upon himself all those troubles and physical hardships for the sake of the common good? I would think he was a man who loved others. But what was the manner of his loving? As became a servant of Zeus, caring for human beings indeed, but at the same time subject [only] to God."

143. Differently, Vollenweider, *Freiheit als neue Schöpfung*, 213: "Eleutheria [freedom] is now treated thematically in its relation to nomos [law]." For a critique of this view, cf. Gerhard Dautzenberg, "Streit um Freiheit und Gesetz: Zu zwei neuen Arbeiten über die ELEUTHERIA in den Paulusbriefen," *JBTh* 5 (1990): 265–76, here 270.

To be sure, 1 Cor. 15:56 is already pointing in this direction. In a piece of eschatological instruction that concludes with a mixed quotation from Isa. 25:8 and Hos. 13:14,[144] 1 Cor. 15:56 is added to 15:51–55 as an exegetical explanation: "The sting of death is sin, and the power of sin is the law." The key words κέντρον (sting) and θάνατος are taken from 15:55, but surprisingly ἁμαρτία also appears, and then, with no preparation whatsoever, the word νόμος. Direct parallels are found in Rom. 6:16–17; 7:7ff. (esp. 7:25); these references, along with the feeling that the verse is out of place here, has repeatedly led interpreters to suppose that 1 Cor. 15:56 is a post-Pauline gloss.[145] Evidence for this assumption is not compelling, for one can make sense of 15:56 as a brief interjection in which the spotlight briefly flashes on a theme that will be explicitly treated in Romans: the relation between sin, law/Torah, and death. Nonetheless, there are two weighty differences between 15:56 and the doctrine of justification extensively elaborated in Galatians and Romans: (1) the constitutive antithesis between "faith" (πίστις) and "works of the law/Torah" (ἔργα νόμου) is missing in 1 Corinthians, and (2) the characteristic contrast νόμος/πνεῦμα, which permeates the deep structure of the doctrine of justification found in Galatians and Romans, goes unmentioned in 1 Corinthians—and this in a letter in which Paul uses the word πνεῦμα forty times. Moreover, it is not clear that the Corinthians could have known what Paul was talking about in this short, concentrated tangential comment. The complex discussions in Galatians and Romans indicate that this would have been very unlikely unless one wants to assume that Paul had already discussed these connections when he was in Corinth.[146] Thus 1 Cor. 15:56 cannot be considered an exposition of the doctrine of justification for Gentile Christians (in the sense of Galatians and Romans), for the essential ideas are missing (πίστις contra ἔργα νόμου; faith contra works of the law) and the thematic combination law/Torah–sin–death is dealt with in a form unique in 1 Corinthians.[147] Why the law/Torah plays an active role in the realm where sin rules cannot be found elsewhere in the letter. In sum, there emerges in 1 Cor 15:56 a partial aspect of the argumentation of

144. For details, see Koch, *Schrift als Zeuge*, 168–70.

145. Cf. the formidable evidence and argument presented by Friedrich Wilhelm Horn, "1Korinther 15,56—ein exegetischer Stachel," *ZNW* 82 (1991): 88–105. His three primary arguments: (1) the verse holds an isolated place in the context; (2) singularly for Paul, here an exegetical comment is inserted between a mixed Old Testament citation and a pronouncement of thanksgiving; (3) the presupposed relationship between law and sin is paralleled elsewhere only in Romans in the whole Pauline corpus.

146. So Andreas Lindemann, "Die biblischen Toragebote und die paulinische Ethik," in *Paulus, Apostel und Lehrer der Kirche: Studien zu Paulus und zum frühen Paulusverständnis* (Tübingen: Mohr Siebeck, 1999), 94.

147. Differently, F. Thielmann, "The Coherence of Paul's View of the Law: The Evidence of First Corinthians," *NTS* 38 (1992): 235–53, who regards 1 Cor. 15:56 as evidence that Paul did not advocate his doctrine of the law (as found in Galatians and Romans) only in polemical situations.

the Letter to the Romans (not Galatians);[148] this verse cannot be introduced as evidence that at the time of the composition of 1 Corinthians, Paul was already advocating the essentially different doctrine of justification found in the later letters to Galatia and Rome.[149]

Paul speaks thematically of "the commandments" in 7:19; he bases his instruction to married people and slaves, that they should remain in the status in which they were called, on the affirmation "Circumcision is nothing, and uncircumcision is nothing; but obeying the commandments of God is everything" (ἡ περιτομὴ οὐδέν ἐστιν καὶ ἡ ἀκροβυστία οὐδέν ἐστιν, ἀλλὰ τήρησις ἐντολῶν θεοῦ).[150] The word ἐντολαί (commandments) cannot here refer to the Torah, for circumcision belongs to its central commands.[151] Since Paul does not explain how this keeping of the commands is in fact carried out, it must refer to generally accepted ethical principles, that is, God's commands that are directly available to Christians. Comparable ideas are found in Epictetus, according to whom the true philosopher does not harken to human commandments but to God alone: "What instructions should I give you. Has not Zeus already given you commandments? Has he not already made available to you what really belongs to you as an inalienable possession, while that which does not belong to you places serious impediments upon you?" (*Diatr.* 1.25.3). As the philosopher has direct access to knowledge, so the Christian knows the will of God.[152] The variations in Gal. 5:6 and 6:15 (cf. also 1 Cor. 12:13; Gal. 3:28) indicate that Paul has the love command in mind as the fundamental orientation of the new existence. A comparison with the later statements in Galatians and Romans makes clear how distant 1 Cor. 7:19 is from the conceptually accented understanding of the law and from that type of "doctrine of justification."

Something similar is true with regard to the theme of freedom central to 1 Corinthians. Paul does not develop this theme as "freedom from the law/ Torah." Instead he falls back on ideas of freedom current in the Hellenistic world in order to define the true character of Christian freedom as being bound to

148. Galatians 3:21–22 is not a precise parallel to 1 Cor. 15:56.

149. As argued, e.g., by Klein, "Gesetz," 13:65. Thomas Söding, "'Die Kraft der Sünde ist das Gesetz' (1Kor 15,56): Anmerkungen zum Hintergrund und zur Pointe einer gesetzeskritischen Sentenz des Apostels Paulus," *ZNW* 83 (1992): 74–84, assumes a nuanced position; he clearly sees the special status of this verse.

150. Comparable expressions are found in Sir. 32:23 LXX: "Guard yourself in every act, for this is the keeping of the commandments" (ἐν παντὶ ἔργῳ πίστευε τῇ ψυχῇ σου καὶ γὰρ τοῦτό ἐστιν τήρησις ἐντολῶν); Wis. 6:18 says of wisdom, "and love of her is the keeping of her laws, and giving heed to her laws is assurance of immortality" (ἀγάπη δὲ τήρησις νόμων αὐτῆς προσοχὴ δὲ νόμων βεβαίωσις ἀφθαρσίας).

151. Cf. Lindemann, *Der erste Korintherbrief*, 171.

152. Will Deming, *Paul on Marriage and Celibacy: The Hellenistic Background of 1 Corinthians 7* (2nd ed.; Grand Rapids: Eerdmans, 2003), 170–73.

Christ and to demonstrate the believer's own independence from conventional human judgments.[153]

An Independent Conception

First Corinthians turns out to have an independent and coherent conception of righteousness/justification. Righteousness is understood as a new reality conferred through baptism; in the sacrament, under the invocation of the name of Christ, the effective making-righteous of the sinner takes place as the making-present of Christ's saving work through the salvific power of the Spirit. The Spirit thus appears as both the means of making-righteous and the determining power of the new being until the parousia of Christ. Believers and baptized are incorporated into the realm of the Kyrios, whereby they are snatched from the power of sin and are really righteous. Baptism thus appears simultaneously as the locus of liberation and the place where one is taken into service as an obedient slave to live according to God's will. This doctrine of righteousness, which has a causal connection with baptism, has no antinomian point; it had already been advocated in early Christianity prior to Paul and presents a coherent theological conception in and of itself. It can be designated an *inclusive* doctrine of righteousness/justification because it is not primarily oriented outwardly but inwardly, to the new being of the baptized.[154] This inclusive doctrine of justification needs no supplementation by the *exclusive* doctrine of justification found in Galatians and Romans, which has a primarily outward orientation, nor is it the case that it simply exhibits their basic ideas in a different form.[155] The understanding of the cross and the righteousness bound to it found in 1 Corinthians should be read in its own terms, without dragging in basic ideas derived elsewhere.[156] In this central issue, the perspective of the reader is decisive: If 1 Corinthians is read under the auspices of the later letters, then it is not difficult to point out anticipations and structural analogies to them. But if one reads within the limitations of the concrete historical location of the letter itself, one comes to a very different conclusion: the world

153. Appropriately, Jones, *"Freiheit,"* 69: "The references to freedom in 1 and 2 Corinthians guard themselves from being subordinated to the schema of 'freedom from law, from sin, and from death' that has become traditional among scholars.

154. Cf. Udo Schnelle, "Taufe II: Neues Testament," *TRE* 32:668–69.

155. Among those who understand the matter differently are Eduard Lohse, *Paulus: Eine Biographie* (Munich: Beck, 1996), 213–14; Stuhlmacher, "Gesetz als Thema," 156; Lindemann, "Toragebote," 94–95; Hübner, *Biblische Theologie,* 2:139ff., who argue that the Corinthian letters (primarily with their theology of the cross) presuppose the substance of the doctrine of justification found in Galatians and Romans. For a critique of the mixing of cross theology with a monodimensional understanding of the doctrine of justification, see also Berger, *Theologiegeschichte,* 482–83.

156. This methodological principle appears to be more and more accepted on the international scene; cf. Seifrid, *Justification by Faith,* 262–63; and the essays in David M. Hay, ed., *1 and 2 Corinthians* (vol. 2 of *Pauline Theology;* SBLSymS 2; Minneapolis: Fortress Press, 1991).

within which the argument of 1 Corinthians takes place is complete in itself. Over against the Corinthians' identity concept related to the potency of the Spirit, Paul sets a different, nuanced model, which develops the transformation of Jesus Christ and the baptized and Spirit-endowed believer's participation in this event in both its grandeur and its lowliness.

10

Second Corinthians

Peace and War

Second Corinthians begins a new chapter in the turbulent history of Paul with the Corinthian church: Paul attempts once again to refute personal charges against him, to explain the nature of his apostolic ministry, and to defeat his opponents.

10.1 The Events between 1 and 2 Corinthians

It is possible to understand this letter only if the events between the writing of 1 Corinthians and 2 Corinthians are taken into consideration. In 2 Cor. 12:14; 13:1, Paul announces a third visit to Corinth, and so he must have made a visit to Corinth between the writing of the two letters. In 2 Cor. 1:15–16 the apostle speaks of having planned to make a trip directly to Corinth, then to Macedonia, from Macedonia back to Corinth, and from there to Judea. Which trip is he talking about here? Information is provided in 2 Cor. 2:1, where Paul mentions that he does not want to make another painful visit to Corinth. Thus he had made a trip to Corinth after the initial founding visit, and during this second visit he had been insulted and in reaction had written the "tearful let-ter" (cf. 2 Cor. 2:4; 7:8, 12). This is the visit to which he refers in 2 Cor. 1:15, which had resulted from the change of the travel plans mentioned in 1 Cor. 16:5ff. Moreover, after the incident Paul did not carry through on the plans mentioned in 2 Cor. 1:16, but probably returned to Ephesus and wrote the "tearful letter" from there. Finally, during the painful visit, Paul had evidently promised to come to Corinth a third time (cf. 2 Cor. 1:23), but instead of mak-ing this visit, he had sent the "tearful letter" (cf. 2:3, 4), which was presumably brought to Corinth by Titus (cf. 7:5–9). It was especially these changes in his announced travel plans that occasioned the Corinthians' accusations that he had not been honest in his dealings with them (cf. 1:17).

From Ephesus the apostle then made a dangerous trip (cf. 1:8) via Troas (2:12) to Macedonia, where he met Titus (7:6–7). Titus brought him good news from Corinth, which set the stage for the third visit, announced in 12:14 and 13:1. The successful completion of the collection in Macedonia (cf. 8:1ff.; Rom. 15:26) was probably arranged by Timothy, who had made the trip to Macedonia by the land route and is the co-sender of 2 Corinthians (cf. 1 Cor. 4:17; 16:10; 2 Cor. 1:1).

The events of the time between the composition of 1 and 2 Corinthians may thus be reconstructed as follows:

(1) Paul travels from Ephesus to Corinth, the apostle's second visit to the church (cf. 2 Cor. 12:14; 13:1).
(2) He hastily returns to Ephesus because he was mistreated by a member of the church (cf. 2:3–11; 7:8, 12).
(3) He writes the "tearful letter," brought to Corinth by Titus (cf. 7:5–9).
(4) His life is endangered in Asia (1:8).
(5) He travels from Troas to Macedonia (cf. 2:12–13).
(6) In Macedonia he meets Titus returning from Corinth (7:5ff.).

These events would require more than six months, and so 2 Corinthians was probably written in the late autumn (cf. 8:10) of the year 55 CE in Macedonia (cf. 7:5; 8:1–5; 9:3–4).[1]

We learn from 8:10 that a new year had begun in the interval between the writing of 1 and 2 Corinthians. If Paul is following the Macedonian calendar familiar to him, this new year would have begun in the fall.[2] On the other hand, if one reckons with a year and a half between the two Corinthian let-

---

1. Cf. Lietzmann and Kümmel, *Korinther*, 135; Friedrich Lang, *Die Briefe an die Korinther* (17th ed.; NTD 7; Göttingen: Vandenhoeck & Ruprecht, 1994), 320 (2 Cor. 1–9); Furnish, *II Corinthians*, 55 (2 Cor. 1–9); Wolff, *Der zweite Brief an die Korinther*, 10.

2. Jack Finegan, *Handbook of Biblical Chronology: Principles of Time Reckoning in the Ancient World and Problems of Chronology in the Bible* (rev. ed.; Peabody, MA: Hendrickson, 1998), 51ff.

ters,[3] there are two possible inferences: (1) First Corinthians had already been written in the spring of 54. (2) Paul wrote 1 Corinthians in the spring of 55 and 2 Corinthians in the fall of 56 and did not arrive in Jerusalem until the spring of 57.

Second Corinthians is addressed not only to the Corinthian church but also to "all the saints throughout Achaia" (1:1). This expansion of the intended readership changes the character of the letter, for Paul addresses not only a local congregation but all Christians in Achaia (cf. 9:2; 11:10). This dual purpose is also important for evaluating the literary structure of 2 Corinthians. When compared with 1 Corinthians, a decisive change has occurred in the way the situation of the church is portrayed: false teachers have made their way into the church (cf. 11:4), who have quickly become influential and have slandered Paul. The apostle speaks of these opponents in the third person in order to distinguish them clearly from the congregation itself (cf. 10:1–2, 7, 10, 12; 11:4–5, 12–18, 20, 22–23).

10.2 The Unity of 2 Corinthians

The unity of 2 Corinthians is much disputed. The following phenomena within the text are presented as arguments for various partition hypotheses:

(1) The break between 2 Cor. 1–9 and 2 Cor. 10–13 is so spectacular that the two sections must have been written at different times, each representing a different attitude toward the church. This supposition is often combined with the assumption that 2 Cor. 10–13 is a fragment of a different letter.
(2) At 2:13 the discussion of an incident in Corinth is evidently interrupted by a long defense of Paul's apostleship (2:14–7:4), which is better explained if 2:13 was originally followed immediately by 7:5.
(3) The two exhortations, found in 2 Cor. 8 and 9, regarding the collection appear not to have originally belonged together.
(4) The passage 6:14–7:1 is quite different from the rest of the letter in both language and content, so that the Pauline origin of this text is doubtful.

The Hypotheses

Partition hypotheses require that different letters or letter fragments be reconstructed from the sections 2 Cor. 1:1–2:13; 2:14–6:13; 7:2–4; 7:5–16;

---

3. So, e.g., Windisch, *Korintherbrief,* 255–56 (eighteen months); Lüdemann, *Chronology,* 98.

2 Cor. 8; 2 Cor. 9; 2 Cor. 10–13. The most important variations of these attempts may be listed as follows:[4]

(1) Following J. S. Semler, A. Hausrath saw in chapters 10–13 part of the lost "tearful letter."[5] He thus transposed chapters 10–13 from the end of the extant letter to the beginning of the correspondence contained in 2 Corinthians. This hypothesis was widely accepted and in a modified form is still important today. Thus H.-J. Klauck and L. Aejmelaeus consider chapters 10–13 to be a part of the "tearful letter,"[6] advocating this sequence: "tearful letter" (chs. 10–13), "letter of reconciliation" (chs. 1–9). An additional modification of the Hausrath hypothesis is advocated by G. Dautzenberg, who regards 2 Corinthians as a collection of three letters or letter fragments. He places chapter 9 at the beginning of the correspondence, followed by chapters 10–13, then chapters 1–8.[7]

(2) The second important variation of the partition hypothesis also regards chapters 10–13 as part of a separate letter but does not consider it to have been part of the "tearful letter." Instead chapters 1–9 are seen as representing an intermediate stage in the apostle's relations with the Corinthian church. Then chapters 10–13 follow as the final letter, in which Paul attempted to get the Corinthians to accept him as an authentic apostle. H. Windisch, C. K. Barrett, and V. P. Furnish, among others, advocate, with somewhat differing arguments, this sequence: chapters 1–9, chapters 10–13.[8]

(3) Following J. Weiss,[9] R. Bultmann extracts 2:14–7:4 from the "letter of reconciliation" and attributes this text, along with chapter 9 and chap-

4. A survey of research is given in Windisch, *Korintherbrief,* 11–21; Ralph P. Martin, *2 Corinthians* (WBC 40; Waco: Word Books, 1986), xl–lii; Hans Dieter Betz, *2 Corinthians 8 and 9: A Commentary on Two Administrative Letters of the Apostle Paul* (Hermeneia; Philadelphia: Fortress, 1985), 3–36; R. Bieringer and Jan Lambrecht, eds., *Studies on 2 Corinthians* (BETL 112; Leuven: Leuven University Press, 1994), 67–105; Margaret E. Thrall, *A Critical and Exegetical Commentary on the Second Epistle to the Corinthians* (Edinburgh: T&T Clark, 1994), 1–76.

5. Adolf Hausrath, *Der Vier-Capitel-Brief des Paulus an die Korinther* (Heidelberg: Fr. Bassermann, 1870).

6. Hans-Josef Klauck, *2. Korintherbrief* (3rd ed.; NEchtB 8; Würzburg: Echter, 1994), 9; Lars Aejmelaeus, *Streit und Versöhnung: Das Problem der Zusammensetzung des 2. Korintherbriefes* (trans. Klaus-Jürgen Trabant; SESJ 46; Helsinki: Finnische Exegetische Gesellschaft, 1987); cf. also Francis Watson, "2Cor X–XIII and Paul's Painful Letter to the Corinthians," *JTS* 35 (1984): 324–46; Georg Strecker, "Die Legitimität des paulinischen Apostolates nach 2 Korintherbrief 10–13," *NTS* 38 (1992): 566.

7. Gerhard Dautzenberg, "Der zweite Korintherbrief als Briefsammlung," *ANRW* 25.5:3045–66.

8. Windisch, *Korintherbrief,* 5–21; C. K. Barrett, *A Commentary on the Second Epistle to the Corinthians* (HNTC; New York: Harper & Row, 1973), 21; Furnish, *II Corinthians,* 30–48.

9. Cf. Weiss, *Korintherbrief,* 265, 275.

ters 10–13, to the "tearful letter."[10] Bultmann thus advocates this order: "tearful letter" (2:14–7:4; ch. 9; chs. 10–13); "letter of reconciliation" (1:1–2:13; 7:5–16; ch. 8).

(4) In the apology 2:14–7:4, G. Bornkamm sees the section of 2 Corinthians that was written first, in which Paul attempted to influence the developments in Corinth. But the situation in Corinth degenerated to such an extent that he wrote the "tearful letter," which Bornkamm rediscovers in chapters 10–13. Following the success brought about by the "tearful letter" and the mission of Titus, Paul wrote the "letter of reconciliation," 1:1–2:13; 7:5–16. Bornkamm classifies 8:1–24 as an appendix to the "letter of reconciliation," and 9:1–15 as a circular letter to the churches in Achaia. The sequence of the correspondence collected in 2 Corinthians is thus represented as follows: (1) 2:14–7:4; (2) 10–13; (3) 1:1–2:13; 7:5–16; (4) 8:1–24; (5) 9:1–15.[11]

The Disputed Issues

The first issue that must be clarified in a responsible and appropriate evaluation of the various partition hypotheses regarding 2 Corinthians is whether chapters 10–13 could have been part of the "tearful letter." In 2:3ff. and 7:8, 12, Paul gives a precise description of what triggered the incident in Corinth, his abrupt return to Ephesus, and his writing the "tearful letter": A member of the Corinthian church deeply offended him, but the details of the event can no longer be reconstructed. Upon receiving the "tearful letter," the church punished the wrongdoer, and Paul then asks them to forgive the person (cf. 2:6–8). If chapters 10–13 are part of the "tearful letter," it is quite remarkable that Paul makes no reference to the incident that evoked this letter in the first place. The opponents against whom Paul struggles in chapters 10–13 have no connection at all to the individual member of the church involved in the incident of 2:3ff. While Paul forgives the ἀδικήσας (wrongdoer, 2 Cor. 7;12), so that the matter is over and done with so far as he is concerned (2:6–10), it is the dispute with his opponents that essentially determines not only the argumentation of chapters 10–13 but chapters 1–9 as well (compare 3:1–3 with 10:12, 18; cf. also 4:2–5; 5:12; 2:17). The "super-apostles" are "false apostles" and "deceitful workers" (11:13), and Paul does not extend the hand of reconciliation to them as he had to the person who offended him. While the ἀδικήσας

10. Rudolf Bultmann, "Exegetische Probleme des zweiten Korintherbriefes," in *Exegetica: Aufsätze zur Erforschung des Neuen Testaments* (ed. Erich Dinkler; Tübingen: Mohr Siebeck, 1967), 298–322; and *2 Corinthians,* 16–18.

11. Günther Bornkamm, "Die Vorgeschichte des sogenannten Zweiten Korintherbriefes," in *Geschichte und Glaube* (BEvT 53; Munich: Kaiser, 1968), 162–94; similarly, Betz, *2 Corinthians 8 and 9,* 251–56; Erich Grässer, *Der zweite Brief an die Korinther* (Gütersloh: Gütersloher Verlagshaus, 2002), 29–35.

doubtless belonged to the Corinthian church, Paul's opponents have intruded into the church from elsewhere (cf. 11:4: ὁ ἐρχόμενος, someone who comes [from elsewhere]"). The "tearful letter" was written in place of Paul's returning in person from Macedonia to Corinth (cf. 1:16; 1:23–2:4), whereas chapters 10–13 look forward to a third visit. Also, the criticism raised against Paul according to 10:1, 9–11; 13:2, that he appeared as a weakling when among them in person but came on strong in his letters, speaks against assigning chapters 10–13 to the "tearful letter." These accusations refer to the conflict with the individual church member and the "tearful letter" that followed, and so they presuppose the "tearful letter" and are not themselves a part of it. The plural αἱ ἐπιστολαί (letters, 10:10) includes 1 Corinthians and the tearful letter.[12] The second visit, mentioned in 13:2, also fits into this interpretation, for it is the visit between 1 and 2 Corinthians that triggered the "tearful letter." Paul spared the church by deciding not to visit them at that time, but he will spare them no longer, and is on the way to his third visit. And finally, if one considers chapters 10–13 to be part of the "tearful letter," then the reference to Titus in 12:17–18 presupposes that Titus had already been in Corinth before delivery of the "tearful letter." But this clearly contradicts 7:14, for, if Paul, in connection with the "tearful letter," there mentions that his boasting about the Corinthians to Titus has turned out to be correct, then Titus was not yet in Corinth before delivery of the "tearful letter." Next to Paul himself, it was especially Silvanus (cf. 1:19) and Timothy (cf. 1 Cor. 4:17; 16:10–11; 2 Cor. 1:1, 19) who had maintained contact with the church and had participated in the first phase of gathering the collection. Titus was not involved in organizing the collection until he came to Corinth bearing the "tearful letter" (cf. 2 Cor. 8:6). Advocates of the theory that chapters 10–13 are part of the "tearful letter" have often found it necessary to take refuge in the assumption that the passages in it that dealt with Paul's mistreatment by one of the church members have been lost.[13] There is not a reference to this incident in 10:1–11,[14] for Paul's line of argument here presupposes the "tearful letter." Moreover, the procedure of the purported redactor can hardly be explained, since, contrary to the postulated historical course of events, he placed chapters 10–13 at the conclusion of the Corinthian correspondence and thus leaves the impression that Paul's work in Corinth had been finally thwarted. In sum, chapters 10–13 cannot be seen as the "tearful letter" or a fragment thereof.[15]

12. Whoever considers 2 Cor. 10–13 to be part of the tearful letter must understand 2 Cor. 10:10 to refer to 1 Corinthians and the letter mentioned in 1 Cor. 5:9; cf. Klauck, *2. Korintherbrief*, 79. This prior letter, however, has nothing at all to do with the problems dealt with in 2 Corinthians.

13. For an argument along these lines, cf., e.g., Vielhauer, *Geschichte der urchristlichen Literatur*, 152.

14. So Watson, "Painful Letter," 343ff.; Klauck, *2. Korintherbrief*, 8.

15. Nor does the characterization of the tearful letter in 2 Cor. 2:4 fit 1 Corinthians, as supposed by Udo Borse, *"Tränenbrief" und 1. Korintherbrief* (SNTSU 9; Freistadt: Plöchl, 1984), 175–202.

The section 2:14–7:4 poses another central problem for the analysis of how 2 Corinthians attained its present literary form. Against the view that this section is an independent fragment of a separate letter, the first item to be noted is the series of motifs that relate it to 1:1–2:13: The theme of "sincerity" (εἰλικρινεία, 1:12) is taken up again in 2:17; 4:2; 6:3–10. The statements about suffering and comfort in 1:4ff. are extended and deepened in 4:8ff. Also, 5:12 takes up 1:14b, as in both places Paul deals thematically with the proper kind of καύχημα (boasting). The problematic of 5:1–10 (the death of the apostle before the parousia) is already clearly prepared for in 1:8–10. In both 1:1–2:13 and 2:14–7:4, Paul deals with a central theme: the apostle's ministry and his relation to the church. Precisely the discussions of the nature of Paul's apostolic ministry in chapters 3–5 are intended to neutralize the charges against the apostle and lead the church to a deepened understanding of the apostolic ministry.

Furthermore, 7:5 cannot be considered the direct continuation of 2:13.[16] There are linguistic connections between 7:4 and 7:5–7. (In 7:6, παρακαλῶν and παρεκάλεσεν connect with παρακλήσει in 7:4, as does παρακλήσει of 7:7; χαρῆναι in 7:7 takes up χαρᾷ of 7:4, and θλιβόμενοι in 7:5 likewise takes up θλίψει of 7:4.)[17] Second Corinthians 7:4 and 7:5–7 belong close together in terms of content, for the cause of the overwhelming joy mentioned in 7:4 is the arrival of Titus with good news from Corinth, reported in 7:5–7 (compare also 7:4 with 7:16). The travel report beginning with καὶ γάρ (for even) is not intended primarily to give information about the trip but to explain the reason for Paul's joy. The content of 7:4 is thus oriented to the context that immediately follows, so that the connection between 7:4 and 7:5ff. must be considered original. And finally, the apostle's comment in 6:11 ("We have spoken frankly to you Corinthians; our heart is wide open to you") shows that Paul is entirely aware of the way he has handled things in chapters 3–6. In order to neutralize the charges leveled against him and win the church back to him, Paul had found it necessary to give a comprehensive explanation of his own self-understanding as a minister of the new covenant and proclaimer of reconciliation with God.[18]

The Pauline authorship of 6:14–7:1 is disputed. This brief text contains numerous hapax legomena for the Pauline corpus and/or the New Testament as a whole (μετοχή [partnership], μερίς [share], καθαρίζω [cleanse], συμφώνησις [agreement], συγκατάθεσις [agreement], Βελιάρ [Beliar], παντοκράτωρ [Almighty], μολυσμός [defilement], ἑτεροζυγέω [mismatch]). There are additional ideas and expressions that stand out as unusual for Paul. Nowhere else does Paul use "Beliar" for Satan (cf. 1QM 13:11–12; *T. Sim.* 5.3; *T. Levi* 19.1; *T. Iss.*

---

16. Cf. also Wolff, *Der zweite Brief an die Korinther*, 155–56.

17. Cf. Lietzmann and Kümmel, *Korinther*, 131.

18. We may certainly consider the seventh letter of Plato to be a parallel, where the chronological recounting of events is also interrupted by longwinded digressions (compare *Ep.* 7.330b with 7.337e; in 7.344d Plato calls this manner of presentation a "digressive narration").

6.1), and "the Almighty" is found only here in Paul as a designation for God. The expression "defilement of body and spirit" (2 Cor. 7:1) is in tension with the antithetical relation of σάρξ and πνεῦμα elsewhere in Paul. Moreover, 7:2 connects seamlessly to 6:13. The distinctive elements of language and content, in particular their proximity to those of Qumran, *Jubilees,* and the *Testaments of the Twelve Patriarchs,* have repeatedly given scholars good reason to suppose that a Jewish Christian inserted 2 Cor. 6:14–7:1 in the letter in post-Pauline times.[19] Those who consider the text to be original usually explain the peculiarities as the apostle's use of traditional terms and motifs.[20]

Scholarship has often regarded chapters 8 and 9 as doublets, considering them to be separate writings, an appendix, or parts of a different letter.[21] The two main arguments for such partition hypotheses have been that there is a fresh beginning at 9:1 and that in 8:1ff. Paul holds up the Macedonians as an example for the Corinthians whereas in 9:2ff. Achaia is an example for the Macedonians.[22] These arguments are not persuasive. Although there is a fresh start in 9:1, it is not the beginning of an independent letter.[23] Paul wrote 2 Corinthians to the churches in Corinth and Achaia (2:1), so that it is not surprising that in chapter 9 he addresses Achaia directly in the important matter of the collection. Moreover, the γάρ (now, for) points back to the preceding; after the excursus in 8:16–24 about the messengers of the churches, Paul returns to the main subject with all Achaia in view. Paul wants to urge the Corinthian church as well as other churches in Achaia to become more active in gathering the collection. He thus gives the Corinthians an exuberant report of the activity in Macedonia (8:1–5) so that Titus can now facilitate the same kind of response in Corinth (8:6). Paul takes a different line of argument in addressing Achaia. He mentions his praise of them to the Macedonians (9:2), thereby encouraging Achaia to live up to this exemplary picture he has already given of them (cf. 9:4–5). There is no contradiction here; Paul is quite skillful in appealing to the

---

19. The secondary character of 2 Cor. 6:14–7:1 has been recently supported with extensive evidence: Joseph A. Fitzmyer, "Qumran and the Interpolated Paragraph in 2 Cor. 6:14–7:1," in *Essays on the Semitic Background of the New Testament* (Missoula, MT: Scholars Press, 1974); Joachim Gnilka, "2Kor 6,14–7,1 im Lichte der Qumranschriften und der Zwölf-Patriarchen-Testamente," in *Neutestamentliche Aufsätze: Festschrift für Prof. Josef Schmid zum 70. Geburtstag* (ed. Josef Blinzler et al.; Regensburg: Pustet, 1963), 86–99.

20. For this understanding, cf. Wolff, *Der zweite Brief an die Korinther,* 146–54 (Paul takes over a baptismal paraenesis); Jerome Murphy-O'Connor, "Philo and 2Cor 6:14–7:1," in *The Diakonia of the Spirit (2 Co 4:7–7:4)* (ed. Lorenzo De Lorenzi et al.; SMBenSP 10; Rome: St. Paul's Abbey, 1989), 133–46 (all expressions and motifs in this section have parallels in Hellenistic Judaism); Reck, *Kommunikation und Gemeindeaufbau,* 290–94. Among those who still argue that Paul composed the whole section entirely on his own are Gerhard Sass, "Noch einmal: 2Kor 6,14–7,1," *ZNW* 84 (1993): 36–64, and Franz Zeilinger, "Die Echtheit von 2 Cor. 6:14–7:1," *JBL* 112 (1993): 71–80.

21. On the individual hypotheses, cf. Lang, *An die Korinther,* 317.

22. See also the listing of arguments in Bultmann, *2 Corinthians,* 256.

23. One can understand 2 Cor. 9:1 as a paraleipsis (Blass and Debrunner, *Grammar,* § 495 [1]: "The orator pretends to pass over something which he in fact mentions").

honor and self-understanding of the Christians in Corinth and Achaia so that he can bring the gathering of the collection to a successful conclusion.

Still other observations speak in favor of the unity of chapters 8 and 9: (1) In 8:10 and 9:2, the same point in time is given for the beginning of the procedure for gathering the collection, the previous year. (2) Mentioning the brothers in 9:3 presupposes that the churches know them from the reference in 8:16ff. (3) The arrival of Titus to join Paul, referred to in 7:5ff., is the basis for the whole line of argument presupposed in chapters 8 and 9. (4) There is a clear internal connection between chapters 8 and 9, for Paul sends Titus and the coworkers (8:16ff.) so that the collection can already be completed by the time he arrives in Corinth with the Macedonians (9:3–4).

A Proposed Solution

Can the two major sections of 2 Corinthians be seen as a literary unit?[24] The reports about Titus and those who accompanied him, found in both chapters 1–9 and chapters 10–13, provide useful information for reconstructing the relationship between the two parts of the letter. Paul mentions in both 8:17–22 and 9:3–5 that he had sent Titus and "the brothers" to Corinth. The aorist verbs used, ἐξῆλθεν (he is going) and συνεπέμψαμεν (we are sending) are often understood as epistolary aorists (as in the NRSV translations here provided).[25] If the verbs are real aorists,[26] however, this presupposes that Paul first dictated chapters 1–9 after Titus and his companions had left for Corinth. Evidently the apostle wanted to forward the letter as quickly as possible to his coworkers who had been sent on ahead (cf. προέρχομαι [go ahead], 9:5). This is not done, however, and Paul retains chapters 1–9 in his own hands, as new reports from Corinth reach him through the Titus group. Second Corinthians 12:17–18

---

24. A survey of research is provided by R. Bieringer, "Der 2. Korintherbrief als ursprüngliche Einheit: Ein Forschungsüberblick," in *Studies on 2 Corinthians* (ed. R. Bieringer and Jan Lambrecht; BETL 112; Leuven: Leuven University Press, 1994), 107–30. Key positions of this view are represented by the following: (1) Kümmel and Feine, *Introduction*, 292, hold that "Paul dictated the letter with interruptions, so that the possibility of unevenness is antecedently present." (2) Wolff, *Der zweite Brief an die Korinther*, 193–94, assumes that 2 Cor. 8 and 9 were the planned conclusion of the letter but Paul composed 2 Cor. 10–13 after receiving new, unfriendly news from Corinth. R. Bieringer, "Plädoyer für die Einheitlichkeit des 2. Korintherbriefes," in *Studies on 2 Corinthians* (ed. Bieringer and Lambrecht), 131–79, refers 2 Cor. 2:14–7:4 to the same phase of the dispute as 2 Cor. 10–13 and sees the goal of the whole letter as Paul's attempt to come to a real reconciliation with the church. Paul Barnett, *The Second Epistle to the Corinthians* (NICNT; Grand Rapids: Eerdmans, 1997), 18ff., gives three arguments for the unity of 2 Corinthians: (1) the rhetorical structure of the letter is that of an "apologetic letter"; (2) the apostle's planned third visit in Corinth characterizes the argumentation of the whole letter; (3) there are numerous linguistic points of contact between 2 Cor. 1–9 and 10–13 that point to an original connection.

25. Windisch, *Korintherbrief*, 262; Furnish, *II Corinthians*, 421–22.

26. Blass and Debrunner, *Grammar*, § 334, rightly list none of these texts as examples of the epistolary aorist.

indicates that the Titus group is back with Paul, for this text looks back on the visit announced in 8:16ff.; 9:3–5. These verses cannot be referred to a different visit, for Titus had not been in Corinth before delivery of the "tearful letter" (cf. 7:14).[27] In 12:18 Paul names only the brothers who had been commissioned by the churches in Macedonia, not his coworker mentioned in 8:22. This is appropriate in the context of the accusations against him in Corinth that he was using the collection for his personal profit (cf. 8:20; 12:14, 16–17), for only Titus and those commissioned from Macedonia were officially responsible for organizing and carrying out the collection. In addition, in 12:17–18 there was no necessity to give once again the exact number of people in the Titus group.

Evidently Titus and "the brother" brought new information about the situation in Corinth that caused Paul to write chapters 10–13. Probably his opponents had in the meantime won over the majority of the church to their point of view, and Paul deals with them in chapters 10–13 in an extraordinarily sharp form, hoping thereby to win the church back to his own leadership. The invective elements in chapters 10–13 are not so unusual within the context of ancient literature; material of this kind is found especially in tragedies, comedies, and the speeches of famous orators such as Cicero.[28] Paul adds chapters 10–13 to 1–9 because the problems dealt with there (delay of his promised visit, the "tearful letter," the collection) must be convincingly explained, all the more so now that his opponents have become more influential in Corinth. Parallels for Paul's changing his tone within a single letter are found in 1 Cor. 8/9, Gal. 2/3; Rom. 11/12. The polemic in 2 Cor. 10–13 does not apply to the Corinthian church but to the opponents, who have interposed themselves in the relationship between apostle and church as a third party (cf. 10:1–2). In terms of *this* relationship (apostle-church), there is no fundamental difference between chapters 1–9 and chapters 10–13. In each section Paul attempts to persuade wavering church members and win them over to his side. A final piece of evidence for the unity of 2 Corinthians, presupposing that the church situation changed between Paul's writing chapters 1–9 and 10–13, is found in the letter's concluding words, 13:11–13. It maintains a surprisingly positive tone, uniting both parts of the letter (cf. 13:11a). Paul obviously won the church back to himself by writing 2 Corinthians, since in the spring of

27. Whoever considers 2 Cor. 10–13 part of the tearful letter must refer 2 Cor. 12:17–18 to an earlier visit of Titus in Corinth in connection with the collection; cf., e.g., Lang, *An die Korinther*, 354; Klauck, *2. Korintherbrief*, 98.

28. Cf. Severin Koster, *Die Invektive in der griechischen und römischen Literatur* (BKP 99; Meisenheim am Glan: Hain, 1980), 354: "Invective is a structured literary form, but at least in its main point, it is directed to πράξεις [practices]. Its goal is to belittle a particular person or persons against the background of the prevailing values, destroying them for good in the public consciousness. The person or persons may be explicitly named or only implied, though they could be named if necessary, and may be considered as individuals or as representing a group."

56 he was residing in Corinth, where he composed Romans, commenting in Rom. 15:26 that the collection in Macedonia and Achaia had been successfully completed.

No reconstruction of the events that preceded 2 Corinthians and occasioned its composition can be made without hypotheses. The explanatory model chosen here has two advantages: (1) The reference to Titus and his companions is the only sure indication found within the letter itself that can be cited as a basis for reconstructing the events underlying the letter. (2) The hypothesis of the unity of 2 Corinthians, presupposing a changed situation between chapters 1–9 and 10–13, has the great advantage that it does not require the postulation of additional letters or letter fragments that have no discernible beginnings or endings.

10.3 Paul's Life as Apostolic Existence

In 2 Cor. 6:11 the apostle lets us see that this is the most personal of all his letters: "We have spoken frankly to you Corinthians; our heart is wide open to you." Paul develops in 2 Corinthians the paradoxical form of his apostolic ministry. It takes place in the tensive force field between God/Christ, the church, his own self-understanding, and the world. Within this complex set of relationships, God's saving act in Jesus Christ lays the foundation for the life of both church and apostle. This is manifest in the basic doxological structure of 2 Corinthians.[29] Paul begins his confrontational argument to the Corinthians with praise to God, who is "God and Father of our Lord Jesus Christ, the Father of mercies and the God of all consolation" (1:3).[30] The grace of God is revealed in both the life of the church and the work of the apostle. The church responds to this grace by its prayers (1:11) and by its unreserved generosity (9:12–13), which increases thanksgiving to the glory of God (4:15). The response to God's gracious dealing with the apostle (2:14) and his coworkers (8:16) for the welfare of the church can only be grateful praise. Such praise is the expression of unshakable trust in the salvific, gracious action of God for the church and the apostle. It was God who united the Corinthians and the apostle with Jesus Christ in baptism and thus made possible the life of believers in the power of the Spirit (1:21–22). Church and apostle know that the promises of God find their fulfillment in Jesus Christ (1:19–20), in him God's power is revealed (4:6c), and he is the image of God (4:4).

29. Wolff, *Der zweite Brief an die Korinther*, 12.
30. On the interpretation of 2 Cor. 1:3–11, cf. Gerhard Hotze, *Paradoxien bei Paulus: Untersuchungen zu einer elementaren Denkform in seiner Theologie* (NTAbh NF 33; Münster: Aschendorff, 1997), 300–340; Johannes Krug, "Die Kraft des Schwachen: Ein Beitrag zur paulinischen Apostolatstheologie" (diss., Ruprecht-Karls-Universität, 2001), 179–97.

Power in Weakness

Paul knows in his innermost being that he has been called by Christ, who continues to direct his ministry, that he owes his apostolic existence to Christ, and that his apostolic ministry is stamped with Christ's own sovereignty and lowliness. Thus he says, "For we do not proclaim ourselves; we proclaim Jesus Christ as Lord and ourselves as your slaves for Jesus' sake" (2 Cor. 4:5). The lowliness of Christ imposes an obligation on both the apostle (10:1; 11:23, 33) and the church (8:9). The crucified and risen one paradoxically stamps apostolic existence with both his weakness and his power. This basic structure is concisely expressed in the *peristasis catalogues*; it is hardly an accident that of the four such catalogues, three are found in 2 Corinthians (1 Cor. 4:11–13; 2 Cor. 4:7–12; 6:4–10; 11:23–29).[31] The peristasis catalogues compactly express the motif that the whole life of the apostle is determined by the Christ event as God's saving act for humanity in both sovereignty and lowliness. In 2 Cor. 4:6 Paul understands the event of a person's coming to faith as an act of God's creative power (cf. Gen. 1:3). This saving, creative act grants a knowledge of the glory of God in the countenance of the crucified Christ. This illumination of the heart and the knowledge of the glory of God are not at the disposal of earthly power that wants to have things under its own control; instead, Christians have these treasures only in fragile earthly vessels. These vessels are the human beings themselves (cf. Gen. 2:7), to whom God has entrusted the priceless treasure of proclaiming the gospel. The gospel is contained in fragile, vulnerable vessels; it is dependent on ready access, for it lives by being shared. The power of the proclaimed gospel to bring the church into being does not depend on the competence of the apostle; it owes this power to God alone, who works in and through it. God's glory manifests itself in God's own dynamic power. In contrast, the external appearance of the apostle is that of a miserable human being who barely manages to get by—harassed, persecuted, thrown to the ground. But God's power is at work in him, so that again and again he is amazingly delivered from all his afflictions (cf. 2 Cor. 4:8–9).[32] The apostle always bears the death of Jesus in his own body "so that the life of Jesus may also be made visible in our bodies. For while we live, we are always being given up to death for Jesus' sake, so that the life of Jesus may be made visible in our mortal flesh. So death is at work in us, but life in you" (4:10b–12).

It belongs to the essence of apostolic existence that its participation in the event of Jesus' cross cannot be reduced to mere verbal preaching about it but

---

31. On the background of the peristasis catalogues in the history of religions, see above, section 3.3 ("The Religious and Cultural Background of Paul's Thought").

32. For analyses, see Erhardt Güttgemanns, *Der leidende Apostel und sein Herr: Studien zur paulinischen Christologie* (Göttingen: Vandenhoeck & Ruprecht, 1966), 94ff.; Ebner, *Leidenslisten und Apostelbrief,* 196ff.; Schiefer-Ferrari, *Peristasenkatalogen,* 201ff.; Hotze, *Paradoxien,* 252–87; Krug, "Kraft des Schwachen," 197–225.

is a reality that involves the apostle's whole existence. The life of the apostle is the *existential illustration of the kerygma*, so that the apostle can go no other way than his Lord. The apostle's sufferings in the service of preaching the gospel are participation in the cross of Jesus' own suffering, even to the point of leaving marks in his own body (cf. Gal. 6:17). Paul does not avoid these sufferings because they are the result of the way he understands his commission as preacher of the gospel and have only one goal: to enable the life of the church. In the experience of death, Paul encounters life; the apostle's existence is entirely incorporated into the soteriological dimension of the event of the cross. The constant dying contained in his ministry of preaching is not an end in itself; its only purpose is to reveal for both apostle and church the life of Jesus that makes itself present in the power of the Spirit as God's own power and glory.[33] Paul's apostolic existence in death is thus paradoxically not oriented to death but exclusively to life. Both apostle and church owe their existence to this post-Easter life of Jesus, which is itself life-giving power. This is why ministry in the service of the present Jesus Christ is the compass by which Paul's whole life is aligned.

The Apostle's Integrity

Because a clear connection exists between the credibility of the message and the conduct of the one who proclaims it, the splendor of the gospel can be clouded by the self-will of the preacher. Thus sincere service to the gospel shapes the whole existence of the apostle. Through numerous troubles and suffering, the apostle's patient endurance remains steadfast by "truthful speech, and the power of God; with the weapons of righteousness for the right hand and for the left; in honor and dishonor, in ill repute and good repute. We are treated as impostors, and yet are true; as unknown, and yet are well known; as dying, and see—we are alive; as punished, and yet not killed; as sorrowful, yet always rejoicing; as poor, yet making many rich; as having nothing, and yet possessing everything" (2 Cor. 6:7–10).[34] Paul knows himself to be supported and borne along by God in his whole existence, so that he can preach the gospel no matter what happens to him. For Paul, apostolic ministry is bound up with a particular understanding of reality. Human beings in their natural, unredeemed state perceive surface reality and make their decisions on that basis. In contrast, believers see God as the ultimate ground of reality and make their judgments about reality according to God's own judgment. Accordingly, one's external existence can be lowly and homely, even though it is the glory of God

---

33. Hotze, *Paradoxien*, 287: "The apostle functions as the divinely called medium of God's paradoxical revelation in Christ. The real goal of this revelation, however, is the church."

34. For interpretation, see Ebner, *Leidenslisten und Apostelbrief*, 243ff.; and Schiefer-Ferrari, *Peristasenkatalogen*, 218ff.

at work in and through it.[35] Externally, the life of the apostle is worn away and exhausted by the many sufferings he must endure in the course of his mission. At the same time, within this ἔξω ἄνθρωπος (outer nature, 4:16) the grace of God is at work through the Spirit. Believers know themselves to be determined by the Spirit of the present Lord, who strengthens and renews them in their ἔσω ἄνθρωπος (inner nature).[36] They are able to endure external suffering and hardships, because they participate in the life-giving power of the risen one and so overcome the troubles and the decline of the body. By ἔσω ἄνθρωπος Paul means the real "I," the true self of the person, which is open to the will of God and the work of the Spirit. Although Paul does not make a convincing external appearance, he nevertheless offers the church the true treasures of life: faith and hope in God. The apostle does not look at the visible and temporal but reaches for the invisible and eternal (cf. 4:17–18).

The peristasis catalogues articulate a concentrated form of Paul's own self-understanding. Paul knows himself to be supported and borne along in his whole existence by God and enabled by the post-Easter life-giving power of Jesus Christ to preach the gospel no matter what may happen to him.

The Earthly and Heavenly House

In the course of time, the almost superhuman labors of his missionary work and events such as the threat to his life in Asia (cf. 2 Cor. 1:8)[37] do not leave Paul untouched, and he longs to be eternally at home with God in heaven. Differently from 1 Thess. 4:13–18 and 1 Cor. 15:51–52, in 2 Cor. 5:1–10 the apostle for the first time reckons with the possibility of his own death before the parousia of the Lord. Utilizing traditional materials,[38] in 2 Cor.

---

35. Again we find a comparable position in the true (Stoic) philosopher, who holds his own in the most difficult situations on the strength of his knowledge; cf. Epictetus, *Diatr.* 2.1.34–39: "'Bring on death and you shall know; bring on hardships, bring on imprisonment, bring on disrepute, bring on condemnation.' This is the proper exhibition of a young man come from school. Leave other things to other people; neither let anyone ever hear a word from you about them, nor, if anyone praises you for them, do you tolerate it, but let yourself be accounted a nobody and a know-nothing. Show that you know this only—how you may never either fail to get what you desire or fall into what you avoid. Let others practice lawsuits, others problems, others syllogisms; do you practice how to die, how to be enchained, how to be racked, how to be exiled. Do all these things with confidence, but trust in Him who has called you to face them and deemed you worthy of this position, in which once having been placed you shall exhibit what can be achieved by a rational governing principle when arrayed against the forces that lie outside the province of the moral purpose" (*NW* 2/1:456–57).

36. See below, section 19.5 ("Centers of the Human Self").

37. Cf. Windisch, *Korintherbrief*, 157.

38. Evidence is provided especially by the hapax legomena in 2 Cor 5:1, ἀχειροποίητος (not made with hands), σκῆνος (tent); moreover, the words οἰκία (house), οἰκοδομή (building), and καταλύω (destroy) are used in the anthropological sense only here. Peter von der Osten-Sacken, *Römer 8 als Beispiel paulinischer Soteriologie* (Göttingen: Vandenhoeck & Ruprecht, 1975), attempts the reconstruction of a pre-Pauline tradition behind 2 Cor. 5:1–2, 6b, 8b (cf. pp. 121–22). The structure of the

5:1 Paul speaks of his present life as an earthly tent, and after it is destroyed there stands ready for him in heaven a building from God, a house not made with hands.[39] By καταλυθῆναι (be destroyed) the apostle means his own death before the parousia,[40] and because he now considers this a real possibility, he longs to be "further clothed" with the "heavenly dwelling" (5:2). Possibly Paul is here thinking of being clothed with the σῶμα πνευματικόν (spiritual body) immediately after death (cf. 1 Cor. 15:51ff.).[41] The real occasion for such thoughts comes into view in 2 Cor. 5:3–4: the apostle fears death as a possible hindrance interfering with the eschatological events. Thus he wishes to be "further clothed" and not to be found "naked" at that event.[42] Because death can occur as an act of "unclothing" (without a further act of clothing), the apostle hopes to be "further clothed," because only so does life swallow up what is mortal.[43] As a present deposit on the new life of the future, God has already given the Spirit to those who are baptized (cf. 2 Cor. 1:21–22). This gift of the Spirit is one that cannot be lost and that obviously endures beyond death (cf. 1 Cor. 3:15–16; 5:5), and the Spirit is the presupposition for being "further clothed" with the σῶμα πνευματικόν—the idea that possibly provides the background for Paul's thought here.[44] The Spirit assures human identity

---

argument of 2 Cor. 5:1ff., however, speaks against the use of a connected tradition here and points rather to Paul as the composer.

39. The idea of the body as a tent is of Greek-Hellenistic origin; cf. Plato, *Phaed.* 81C (which probably influenced Wis. 9:15); cf. also Isa. 38:12 LXX; *4 Ezra* 14:13–14; additional Hellenistic examples are found in Windisch, *Korintherbrief*, 158. Philipp Vielhauer, *Oikodome: Aufsätze zum Neuen Testament* (ed. Günter Klein; Munich: C. Kaiser, 1979), 32ff., 100ff., points to Mandean parallels. The most impressive parallel is found in a saying of the Socratic philosopher Bion of Borysthenes (first half of the third century BCE; transmitted in Teles, frg. 2), who compares death to moving out of a house: "'Just as we are ejected from our house,' says Bion, 'when the landlord, because he has not received his rent, takes away the door, takes away the pottery, stops up the well, in the same way,' he says, 'am I being ejected from this poor body when Nature, the landlady, takes away my eyes, my ears, my hands, my feet. I am not remaining, but as if leaving a banquet and not at all displeased, so also I leave life: when the hour comes, step on board the ship." This translation is from Edward O'Neill, *Teles (The Cynic Teacher)* (Texts and Translations: Graeco-Roman Religious Series 11/3; Missoula, Mont.: Scholars Press, 1977), 16–17.

40. Cf. Windisch, *Korintherbrief*, 158; Lietzmann and Kümmel, *Korinther* 118; Wiefel, "Eschatologischen Denken," 75. Differently, Lang, *An die Korinther* 286, who thinks Paul here emphasizes "only his confidence in being ready."

41. So, e.g., Windisch, *Korintherbrief*, 160. This is by no means clear, however, for Paul uses σῶμα in 2 Cor. 5:6–8 exclusively for the earthly body and does not take up the line of argument of 1 Cor. 15:51ff.; see below, section 22.2 ("The Course of the Final Events and Life after Death").

42. On the Greek-Hellenistic background of the image of nakedness as a result of the destruction of the earthly body, cf. the evidence in Windisch, *Korintherbrief*, 164–65; Wiefel, "Eschatologischen Denken," 75–76.

43. According to Windisch, *Korintherbrief*, 163, Paul here thinks that immediately in the act of dying he will be clothed with a heavenly garment "whose essence is 'life'" and will thereby evade the nothingness of death.

44. Wiefel, "Eschatologischen Denken," 76.

in being "unclothed" at death and, even if one is "found naked," provides the individual spirit the "further clothing" with the spiritual body.

Second Corinthians 5:6–10 continues the preceding eschatological discussion but shifts the focus mainly to paraenesis.[45] With new images (being in a strange land, being at home; emigration, immigration),[46] Paul describes once again earthly existence as being separated from Christ and then in 5:7 pointedly expresses the eschatological reservation: the fullness of salvation still belongs to the believer's future. Christian existence on earth takes place in the mode of faith, not sight (cf. 1 Cor. 13:12; Rom. 8:24). Whereas 2 Cor. 5:7 can characterize Christian life in general, in 5:8 Paul formulates his own wish to move out of his earthly body and to be at home with the Lord. Here death before the Lord's parousia appears not only as a possibility; it is even what the apostle longs for. Because the hoped-for being with Christ immediately after death is connected with judgment, Paul concludes the section with the admonition to live one's life in the light of this judgment to come (5:9).

The section 5:1–10 is characterized by a tendency toward dualism and individualization. This dualism is seen first in the imagery (earthly/heavenly dwelling; being at home/being away from home; being unclothed/being further clothed; mortality/life), which is based on an anthropology stamped with Hellenistic features. The image of the body as a tent and thus only the temporary dwelling of the self, the mystical understanding of "clothing," "nakedness" as the result of the separation of body and soul, the idea that one's real homeland is in the heavenly world and that living in the body is living in exile from one's true homeland—all point to Greek-Hellenistic influence (cf. esp. Epictetus, *Diatr.* 1.9.12–14).[47] Because the apostle would like to leave his earthly body, he here uses dualistic categories to evaluate bodily life in an unusually negative manner. The individualizing of eschatology manifests itself in the almost complete lack of apocalyptic ideas in 5:1–10,[48] in the use of imagery limited to the individual, and in the fact that here for the first time Paul reckons with his

45. Cf. the way the text is outlined in Bultmann, *2 Corinthians*, 129, 144; and C. H. Hunzinger, "Die Hoffnung angesichts des Todes im Wandel der paulinischen Aussagen," in *Leben angesichts des Todes: Beiträge zum theologischen Problem des Todes: Helmut Thielicke zum 60. Geburtstag* (ed. Bernhardt Lohse; Tübingen: Mohr Siebeck, 1968), 76ff.

46. Documentation for the Greek-Hellenistic ideas that stand in the background is found in Windisch, *Korintherbrief*, 166; and Wiefel, "Eschatologischen Denken," 76–77.

47. Epictetus's conversation partner addresses the philosopher: "Epictetus, we are not going to put up with it any longer, this being bound to this body, having to give it food and drink and let it rest, to wash it and take care of it in this or the other way. Does any of that really matter? Is not death our redemption? Are we not children of God, and don't we come from him? So let us return to where we came from. We want to untie the bonds that here bind and hinder us." Further examples in Windisch, *Korintherbrief*, 158–75; Lietzmann and Kümmel, *Korinther*, 117–23; Wiefel, "Eschatologischen Denken," 74–79.

48. At the most, we find echoes of expectation of the parousia in 2 Cor. 5:2b (ἐξ οὐρανοῦ [from heaven]). This speaks against Furnish, *II Corinthians*, 297, who wants to interpret 2 Cor. 5:1–10 not anthropologically but in an broader, eschatological sense (especially by appealing to Rom. 8).

death before the parousia of the Lord. This does not mean he has abandoned the expectation of the parousia (cf. 4:14; 5:10; 6:2; 13:4), but he places the accents differently: death before the parousia of the Lord now appears as the normal case that applies to Paul himself, and so 5:1–10 is evidence that *the acute expectation of the near end has been relaxed.* This reaching out to the future is for Paul, however, no flight from the reality of the present; it is, rather, the case that God's saving act in Jesus Christ determines both present and future. Paul experiences fellowship with the crucified and risen Jesus Christ already in the present, a fellowship that will find its fulfillment in future glory. This future glory is already evident in Paul's apostolic ministry.

10.4 The Glory of the New Covenant

In 2 Cor. 3 Paul engages his opponents in Corinth by presenting his God-given qualification to be a minister of the new covenant;[49] it is a matter of the integrity of his apostolic ministry (cf. 2:17; 4:1ff.).[50] The agitators who oppose him in Corinth bring letters of recommendation (cf. 3:1b),[51] evidently appeal to Moses to legitimize their claims, and disdain Paul's preaching ministry. In contrast, Paul does not find it necessary to impress people with letters of recommendation and pneumatic phenomena, for the Corinthian church is itself the visible proof of his apostleship. The existence of a new Christian congregation is a provocative sign in the midst of a world that is passing away. The Corinthians themselves are Paul's letter of recommendation, written with the Spirit of the living God.

Letter and Spirit

In 3:3 the contrasting pairs γράμμα/πνεῦμα (letter/spirit) and "tablets of stone" / "tablets of human hearts" appear as the working model that shapes the whole competitive argument as Paul attempts to outbid his opponents.[52] In the background of Paul's argument stands Ezek. 11:19, "I will give them

49. A concise survey of research is provided in Sini Hulmi, *Paulus und Mose: Argumentation und Polemik in 2 Kor 3* (SESJ 77; Göttingen: Vandenhoeck & Ruprecht, 1999), 4–16.

50. Cf. Jones, *"Freiheit,"* 61.

51. Epictetus, *Diatr.* 2.3.1 addresses the following anecdote about Diogenes to those who write letters of recommendation for other philosophers: "'That you are a man,' he says, 'he will know at a glance; but whether you are a good or a bad man he will discover if he has the skill to distinguish between good and bad, and if he is without that skill he will not discover the facts, even though I write him thousands of times.'"

52. The contrasting pair γράμμα/πνεῦμα was probably triggered by the opponents, who appeared on the scene with their letters of recommendation, i.e., with γράμματα (letters); cf. Horn, *Angeld des Geistes*, 317. Something of a parallel is found in Philo, *Abraham* 60: Abraham understood "by commands not only those conveyed in speech and writing, but also those made manifest by nature with

one heart, and put a new spirit within them; I will remove the heart of stone from their flesh and give them a heart of flesh" (cf. also Exod. 31:18; Deut. 9:10; Ezek. 36:26–27; 37:26–28; Jer. 31:33).[53] By receiving the Holy Spirit, the hearts of the Corinthians become the temple of the living God. The time of the stone tablets has passed; in the Christ event God writes on human hearts by the Holy Spirit. God utilizes the preachers of the gospel to do this, making them ministers of the new covenant, a covenant not of the letter but of the Spirit: "for the letter kills, but the Spirit gives life" (2 Cor. 3:6). Paul hardly has Jer. 31:31–34 in mind here, for the contrast between "letter" and "Spirit" is not found in that text.[54] The new covenant instituted by Jesus Christ is for Paul an eschatological reality; it is not determined by the letter but by the Spirit. The genitives γράμματος (of the letter) and πνεύματος (of the Spirit) have a qualifying character, describing the essential nature of each covenant. The singular τὸ γράμμα is "not simply identical with νόμος; it is the aspect of being-only-in-written-form that is significant" (cf. Rom. 2:27).[55] The written letter is not able to have a life-giving effect; it is the Spirit that enlivens and leads to life. Thus Paul breaks open the fundamental connection between the Spirit and what is written (Ezek. 36:26–27). There is a new access to God granted by the Spirit; it stands diametrically opposed to the old order represented by the stone tablets of Sinai.

The New Covenant

In 2 Cor. 3:7ff. Paul evaluates the fundamental letter/Spirit antithesis in contrasting pairs, using Exod. 34:29–35 LXX as his basic text.[56] Paul adjusts

---

clearer signs, and apprehended by the sense [the eye] which is the most truthful of all and superior to hearing, on which no certain reliance can be placed."

53. Cf. Erich Grässer, *Der Alte Bund im Neuen: Exegetische Studien zur Israelfrage im Neuen Testament* (Tübingen: Mohr Siebeck, 1985), 80–81; Räisänen, *Paul and the Law*, 244–45.

54. With Wolff, *Der zweite Brief an die Korinther*, 61; Grässer, *Der Alte Bund*, 81; contra Lang, *An die Korinther*, 270; Otfried Hofius, "Gesetz und Evangelium," in *Paulusstudien* (2 vols.; WUNT 51, 143; Tübingen: Mohr Siebeck, 1989–2002), 2:81; Vollenweider, *Freiheit als neue Schöpfung*, 265. Räisänen, *Paul and the Law*, rightly comments, "If Paul intended an allusion to Jer 31 in 2 Cor. 3.3 or 3.6, it is all the more conspicuous that he omits what Jer 31 says about the law."

55. Cf. Wolff, *Der zweite Brief an die Korinther* 62; cf. also Vogel, *Das Heil des Bundes*, 184–97 (the metaphors here adopted by Paul do not serve to critique the Torah); Jens Schröter, "Schriftauslegung und Hermeneutik in 2 Korinther 3," *NovT* 40 (1998): 236; Hulmi, *Paulus und Mose*, 107. Differently, Hofius, "Gesetz und Evangelium," 75–78, who pointedly interprets καινὴ διαθήκη (new covenant) as "what God has newly instituted," i.e., the gospel, and παλαιὰ διαθήκη (old covenant) as "that which God previously instituted," i.e., the Torah from Sinai, understanding the whole text in the antithetical categories "law"/"gospel." A similar interpretation is found in Scott J. Hafemann, *Paul, Moses, and the History of Israel: The Letter/Spirit Contrast and the Argument from Scripture in 2 Corinthians 3* (WUNT 81; Tübingen: Mohr Siebeck, 1995), 437, who simply equates γράμμα and νόμος.

56. For detailed analysis, see Hafemann, *Paul, Moses, and the History of Israel*, 255ff.; the argument that Paul adopted and edited a source from his opponents, as argued by Siegfried Schulz, "Die

the original statement of the Old Testament text to fit the goals of his own argument. The glory of Moses' face now appears as temporary (2 Cor. 3:7, 11), reflecting the temporal and material limitations of the old covenant itself. In contrast, the new covenant is radiant with brilliant light. If there was a glory that already belonged to the old covenant in the world of death, how much more does life and glory radiate from the new covenant! The new covenant, as the ministry of justification, surpasses and outshines the temporary first covenant in a fundamental way, so that it is not the idea of continuity but that of *radical antithesis* that primarily determines the Pauline argument. How is the expression διακονία δικαιοσύνης (ministry of justification) in 3:9 to be understood? The antithesis to κατάκρισις (condemnation) at first suggests an interpretation corresponding to Rom. 1:17: God's verdict of acquittal as the pronouncement of justification.[57] But Paul is not here speaking of the δικαιοσύνη θεοῦ (righteousness of/from God), and here there is a substantial difference from the usage in Rom. 1:17: the Romans text speaks of the righteousness of God in a universal dimension, but here it is entirely a matter of the preachers of the gospel, the apostolic ministry. Δικαιοσύνη (righteousness) here is a qualification of the apostolic ministry, just as θάνατος (death), ζωή (life), δόξα (glory), and πνεῦμα (Spirit) describe their respective ministries.[58] "Righteousness" or "justification" thus here describes the activity of the minister, the goal of ministry, and the Lord who commissions the ministry. There is no affinity to δικαιοσύνη γὰρ θεοῦ . . . ἐκ πίστεως εἰς πίστιν (righteousness of God . . . through faith for faith) of Rom. 1:17.

Contrary to the record of the Old Testament text, Paul states that Moses wore a veil to conceal the temporary, passing nature of the glory radiating from his face. The apostle obviously uses the veil motif to show the inferiority of the old covenant: to this very day there is a covering over the old covenant that can only be taken away in Jesus Christ. This covering is ultimately identical with the hardening of Israel (2 Cor. 3:14) revealed in its nonacceptance of the

---

Decke des Mose: Untersuchungen zu einer vorpaulinischen Überlieferung in II Cor 3,7–18," *ZNW* 49 (1958): 1–30; and Dieter Georgi, *The Opponents of Paul in Second Corinthians* (Philadelphia: Fortress, 1986), 246–313. I consider the contrasting thesis of Koch, *Die Schrift als Zeuge*, 332, more probable: "Second Corinthians 3:7–18 appears to be a literary 'interlude,' but it is clearly connected with the overarching theme of the letter (cf. the transition from v. 6 to v. 7); it gradually diverges from this main theme until 3:12–18 becomes an independent topic. This suggests that in 3:17–18 Paul has taken up his own reworked interpretation of Exod. 34:29–35, the substance of which is in fact independent of its present literary context."

57. The following scholars so argue, with some nuances in their individual arguments: Windisch, *Korintherbrief*, 116; Lietzmann and Kümmel, *Korinther*, 111; Wolff, *Der zweite Brief an die Korinther*, 68.

58. Cf. 1QS 4:9; 1QH 6:19. [Translator's note: Throughout this section the author distinguishes "justification" in the forensic sense, as God's pronouncement that guilty sinners are acquitted, as he understands Rom. 1:17 and 5:1, from "righteousness" as a quality of God and justified sinners. This distinction is not acknowledged in the NRSV translation, "justification," for δικαιοσύνη in this passage.]

gospel. It is only through faith in Jesus Christ that this barrier to understanding is overcome and the meaning and goal of the first covenant is revealed. In 3:16 Moses is pictured as the prototype for those in Israel who turn to Christ.[59] The antithesis old covenant / new covenant is for Paul finally reduced to the antithesis Moses/Christ. For Paul, Moses is the personification of the letter that kills when misunderstood as the way of salvation, whereas Christ is the personification of the new covenant in the power of the Spirit. The newness of the second covenant is manifest in the liberating presence of the Spirit, through whom the risen one himself is at work. The reality of the resurrection is revealed as the reality of the Spirit, for ὁ δὲ κύριος τὸ πνεῦμά ἐστιν (now the Lord is the Spirit, 3:17). This programmatic statement is illuminated by 3:16,[60] where the identification[61] of κύριος (Lord) with πνεῦμα is not to be understood as a static equation but as a way of describing the dynamic presence of the exalted Lord. This is made clear in 3:17b, where the Lord's action in the Spirit is understood as a liberating event. The exalted Lord is the Spirit as the life-giving, energizing power of God, inasmuch as he allows the church to participate in the life-giving power bestowed on him by God (cf. 1 Cor. 15:45). In 2 Cor. 3:17 Paul understands the freedom made possible by the Spirit not as freedom from the law/Torah; the apostle would have formulated such a fundamental principle more clearly and precisely, as shown by the later letters to the Galatians and Romans.[62] It is, rather, a matter of the freedom realized in the glory of the new covenant as the ministry of righteousness/justification. It is not only the apostle who participates in this freedom; the glory of Christ works in the transformative power of the Spirit within the whole church (3:18).

For Paul, the second covenant is *really new and not merely a renewed covenant,* for it is grounded in the presence and power of the Spirit. The risen one present in the Spirit is thus both the ground of salvation and the way one comes to a knowledge of salvation. The presence of the Spirit's work qualifies not only the letter as something standing under the power of death but at the same time grants the awareness of the new order of salvation in Jesus Christ. It is to this that the apostle's ministry is dedicated, and so the function of 2 Corinthians 3 is exclusively to demonstrate the God-given competency of the apostle as a minister of the new covenant. In this text Paul is not discussing the law/Torah. If he were, he could hardly have relinquished the νόμος terminology and the line of argument evident in Rom. 2:26–29 and 7:6.[63] Characteristically, Paul

59. The ἐν Χριστῷ of 2 Cor. 3:14 speaks in favor of understanding the κύριος of 3:16–17 as referring to Christ, not to God; for analysis, cf. Hulmi, *Paulus und Mose,* 96–98.

60. Cf. Ingo Hermann, *Kyrios und Pneuma: Studien zur Christologie der paulinischen Hauptbriefe* (SANT 2; Munich: Kösel, 1961), 49.

61. Correctly, so Hermann, ibid., 48ff.; for analysis, cf., most recently, Horn, *Angeld des Geistes,* 320–45.

62. Cf. Jones, *"Freiheit,"* 61–67.

63. Cf. Horn, *Angeld des Geistes,* 317.

does not here take up Jer. 38:33 LXX (Jer. 31:33) (δώσω νόμους μου εἰς τὴν διάνοιαν αὐτῶν καὶ ἐπὶ καρδίας αὐτῶν γράψω αὐτούς [I will put my laws into their mind, and write them on their hearts]) or the critique of the law in Ezek. 20:25–26.[64] The multilayered use of νόμος in Galatians (thirty-two times) and Romans (seventy-four times) and the related subtleties in the train of thought followed there show that when he is discussing the role of the law, Paul is capable of using the requisite terminological clarity and precision and that he could have done so in 2 Cor. 3. The absence of νόμος here is to be taken seriously and should not be ignored for the sake of constructing a system of Pauline theology.[65] The subject under discussion here is the Pauline understanding of apostolic ministry, not the law/Torah.

10.5 The Message of Reconciliation

In 2 Cor. 5:14–21 Paul develops the second major interpretation of his apostolic ministry, under the concept of reconciliation. Paul embeds it within a deep and thorough reflection on the basic event of salvation history and its continuing presence in the church. In the course of this explanation, it becomes clear that the love of Christ is the divine reality that determines both church and apostle. This love was revealed in the death of Jesus on the cross and is expressed in this passage with the idea of sacramental participation in his destiny:[66] "one has died for all; therefore all have died" (5:14b). Those who have been baptized (cf. Gal. 2:19–20; Rom. 6:3–4) participate fully in

64. Cf. also Schröter, "2 Korinther 3," 249: "The issue of the law can *not* be considered the comprehensive theme of this passage. Instead it is characteristic of this text that this theme, addressed by both Jeremiah and Ezekiel and in any case suggested by the phrase πλάκες λίθιναι ['stone tablets'], is *pointedly not* dealt with."

65. Contra Vollenweider, *Freiheit als neue Schöpfung*, 247–84, who deals with 2 Cor. 3 under the rubric "The Transcendent Splendor of the Law," making it into a text that already contains the whole Pauline doctrine of the law as found in Galatians and Romans, even though νόμος and ἁμαρτία are not found in this text. For a critique of Vollenweider, see Dautzenberg, "Streit um Freiheit," 270–71: "The dominant perspective of the apologetic-confessional line of thought in 2 Cor. 3:6–18 is Paul's divinely given competence as a minister of the new covenant. This is the only reason the relation of the two covenants is discussed. It is by no means a discussion of the law." See also Berger, *Theologiegeschichte*, 463; Schröter, "2 Korinther 3," 274–75. Of course, the statements in 2 Cor. 3 touch on the theme of the law if one systematizes them from our perspective today. Such treatment does not correspond to the data of the text itself, however, for not only is the word νόμος missing but the three central aspects of the discussion of law and justification in Galatians and Romans are absent as well: (1) the relation of ἁμαρτία and νόμος; (2) the antithesis πίστις / ἔργα νόμου (faith / works of the law); (3) the question of the significance of the Torah for Jewish Christians.

66. On the baptismal background of 2 Cor. 5:14–15, see Rudolf Schnackenburg, *Das Heilsgeschehen bei der Taufe nach dem Apostel Paulus: Eine Studie zur paulinischen Theologie* (MThSH 1; Munich: Zink, 1950), 110–11; Michael Wolter, *Rechtfertigung und zukünftiges Heil: Untersuchungen zu Röm 5,1–11* (BZNW; Berlin: de Gruyter, 1978), 74 n. 174.

the once-for-all saving event and are thereby placed in a new reality: they no longer live merely for themselves but for their Lord, who was killed and raised to new life.[67] The power of the resurrection of Jesus Christ is revealed wherever people are delivered from their own selfishness and in faith find their way to God and thereby to their true selves and their fellow human beings. One cannot be both self-centered and Christ-centered; the new reality of salvation represented by God's act in the Christ event takes concrete shape in the life of each person, not in some transcendent world beyond it. For Christians, there is no longer any knowledge or insight that does not have its basis and norm in the saving reality of the cross and resurrection of Jesus Christ. This is the only kind of knowledge that can claim to understand Jesus Christ, knowledge that is no longer κατὰ σάρκα (2 Cor. 5:16;[68] lit. according to the flesh; NRSV, "from a human point of view").[69] If anyone is in Christ,[70] that person is a "new existence" (καινὴ κτίσις;[71] NRSV, "there is a new creation"), for "everything old has passed away; see, everything has become new!" (5:17). Baptism and the conferral of the Spirit as incorporation into Christ's realm of life take on the dimensions of a new creation.[72] The creative activity of God for human

---

67. As in Rom. 6:3–4, here there is a break in the line of thought. The logic of 2 Cor. 5:14b suggests that believers are already risen with Christ. Paul avoids this inference and describes the present and future of those who have been baptized in ethical terms. On the numerous connections between 2 Cor. 5:14–17 and Gal. 2:19–21, see Udo Borse, *Der Standort des Galaterbriefes* (BBB 41; Cologne: P. Hanstein, 1972), 71–75.

68. Grammatically, κατὰ σάρκα must be understood adverbially as modifying οἴδαμεν (we regard) or ἐγνώκαμεν (we once knew); cf., e.g., Cilliers Breytenbach, *Versöhnung: Eine Studie zur paulinischen Soteriologie* (WMANT 60; Neukirchen-Vluyn: Neukirchener Verlag, 1989), 116.

69. Three relevant interpretive models exist for 2 Cor. 5:16 (for a survey of recent research, see Wolff, *Der zweite Brief an die Korinther*, 123–27): (1) "The Χριστὸς κατὰ σάρκα [Christ according to the flesh] is Christ as he can be encountered in the world, before his death and resurrection. He should no longer be viewed as such" (Bultmann, *2 Corinthians*, 155). (2) "There was a period in the life of Paul in which he evaluated Christ from a point of view that one can rightly call fleshly and sinful. . . . This 'fleshly' way of knowing Christ was overcome at his conversion. A spiritual image of Christ steps into its place" (Klauck, *2. Korintherbrief*, 54). (3) Paul's opponents charge him with having no knowledge of the earthly Jesus and dispute his claim to be an apostle on this basis. Paul calls this way of knowing Jesus Christ "fleshly" because it relativizes the cross and resurrection (the interpretation of Wolff, *Der zweite Brief an die Korinther*, 127, tends in this direction). This last interpretation has the advantage that it does not have to postulate Paul's disinterest in the historical Jesus (as in Bultmann's interpretation) and does not have to take recourse to the Damascus experience—for Paul does not mention his activity as a persecutor in 2 Cor. 5:16. Moreover, the first-person-plural verbs make clear that he is not making statements about his individual experience but making general, fundamental affirmations.

70. Ἐν Χριστῷ is to be understood in a local sense here and means being included in the sphere of the Christ reality that is constituted by the gift of the Spirit; cf. Umbach, *In Christus getauft*, 230–32.

71. On the analysis of καινὴ κτίσις in Paul (2 Cor. 5:17; Gal. 6:15), see Mell, *Neue Schöpfung*, 261–388; Hubbard, *New Creation*, 133–232.

72. Cf. Lietzmann and Kümmel, *Korinther*, 126; Hans Windisch, *Taufe und Sünde im ältesten Christentum bis auf Origenes: Ein Beitrag zur altchristlichen Dogmengeschichte* (Tübingen: Mohr Siebeck, 1908), 146ff.

beings is not limited to this one-time-only event of calling people into a new life, but by the gift of the Spirit, God continues to grant people participation in God's ongoing creative power. For Paul, the whole life of the Christian is embraced by God's continuing act of salvation in the present, as Christians find themselves in a new situation in a new time: in a situation of life that is real and in a time when the Spirit is real.

God makes this new reality possible by his reconciling act in Jesus Christ.[73] In 5:18 the apostle makes a precise distinction between the prior act of God and the human act that follows, while at the same time binding them most closely together. Second Corinthians 5:18a speaks of God's reconciling act, with God as the acting subject who accomplishes this reconciliation with human beings by the event of Jesus' cross. The exponent of the new reality made possible by God is the crucified and risen Jesus Christ, who was and is the locus of this reconciling act in the past, present, and future. The ministry of reconciliation is founded on this reconciling act (5:18b). The reconciling act of the cross makes possible the proclamation of the message of reconciliation, and reconciliation with God takes place together with this proclamation. The ministry of reconciliation takes place in the proclamation of the message of reconciliation; *the saving event is present in the word.*[74] Paul proclaims a coincidence of God's word on the cross and the apostolic word of reconciliation. The proclamation thus grows out of God's saving act of reconciliation, while being also itself a part of this act of God. *The* manifestation of the cross event in the present takes place in the word event of the proclamation. Paul sees his apostolic existence anchored in the saving event itself; God's act of reconciliation results in the apostle's ministry of reconciliation. Reconciliation with God takes place where the word of reconciliation is proclaimed in the ministry of reconciliation and is grasped, acknowledged, and accepted in faith by individuals as the new determination of their relation to God and the world.

In 5:19 Paul develops the cosmological dimension of the cross event. As a universal event, God's reconciling act can be limited neither to the individual nor the church, for it overcomes the alienation between God and the world grounded in universal human sinfulness.[75] God does not charge human transgressions to people's account but turns toward humanity from pure grace by establishing the word of reconciliation. It is not God who is reconciled or persuaded to change his mind by the act of Christ; God alone is the acting subject in the reconciling act, while human beings experience that "in Christ" they have been placed in a new relationship.[76] Second Corinthians 5:20 focuses on Paul's missionary existence as apostolic ambassador of reconciliation. As

---

73. For a basic analysis of 2 Cor. 5:18–20, cf. Breytenbach, *Versöhnung*, 107ff.

74. Cf. Bultmann, *Theology of the New Testament*, 1:301–2.

75. For the background of the Pauline doctrine of reconciliation in the history of religions, see below, section 16.6 ("The Death of Jesus Christ as Atoning Event").

76. Cf. Bultmann, *2 Corinthians*, 159.

ambassador of Jesus Christ, Paul proclaims God's reconciling act ἐν Χριστῷ (in Christ), so that his ministry becomes an integral element of God's work of reconciliation. The apostle acts with the authority of his Lord and reports for duty to carry out his mission. Because God is the one who creates and carries out this act of reconciliation, it is God who speaks through the mouth of his witnesses and calls people to accept the message of reconciliation by which they are reconciled to God.

Second Corinthians 5:21 once again emphatically stresses the heart and core of God's saving act of reconciliation. Because Jesus knew no sin, he could become sin for us, making the new being possible by taking our sins on himself. For understanding the expression that here appears for the first time, δικαιοσύνη θεοῦ (righteousness of God), it is important to note the textual setting of this phrase within ἵνα ἡμεῖς γενώμεθα . . . ἐν αὐτῷ (so that we might become the righteousness of God in him). God's righteousness is directed to making the believer righteous in Jesus Christ. This new being in Jesus Christ does not here consist of a judgment by God or of God's pronouncement of righteousness but names a new reality. God's righteousness proves itself to be making the sinner righteous (cf. 1 Cor. 1:30; 6:11). Realized on the cross, the act of making the individual Christian righteous occurs in baptism. This interpretation is supported by the phrase ἐν αὐτῷ (in him), which, analogously to the ἐν αὐτῷ of 1 Cor. 1:30, expresses incorporation into the realm of Christ as sacramental participation in his destiny.[77] In Christ, the believer participates in the substitutionary death of Jesus and receives a new life characterized by righteousness; it is mediated sacramentally and is an objective effect of baptism. The use of δικαιοσύνη θεοῦ here has no connotation critical of the law, as in Romans;[78] on the contrary, the expression in 2 Cor. 5:21 describes the new being of the one who has been baptized and thus the new reality of the church.

10.6 The Fool's Speech

The successful agitation in Corinth by Jewish-Hellenistic itinerant preachers compels Paul to provide in 2 Cor. 10–13, explicitly and emphatically, his own

---

77. The comment of Windisch, *Korintherbrief,* 199, is on target: "Then the righteousness of God has also entered into our being and has become a real quality of our 'new nature.' The concluding formula ἐν αὐτῷ also points to this. If we have become the righteousness of God 'in Christ' (Phil. 3:9), then this reality cannot be restricted to God's judgment and God's 'declaring' us to be righteous, for a new reality must actually have been created within us."

78. Karl Kertelge, *Rechtfertigung bei Paulus: Studien zur Struktur und zum Bedeutungsgehalt des paulinischen Rechtfertigungsbegriffs* (Münster: Aschendorff, 1967), 106 n. 223; Hans Hübner, *Law in Paul's Thought: A Contribution to the Development of Pauline Theology* (ed. John Kenneth Riches; trans. James C. G. Greig; SNTW; Edinburgh: T&T Clark, 1984), 125–26.

self-understanding as apostle of Jesus Christ.[79] Here Paul once more shows his ability to work out the systematic issues inherent in a multilayered process and to develop principles for the proper understanding of the gospel. The opponents accuse Paul of being strong in his letters but weak when he appears personally (10:1–10). Whereas the opponents boast, commend themselves, and compare themselves with each other, Paul places no emphasis on his personal traits (cf. 10:12–18). His opponents also interpret it as weakness that Paul obviously does not have at his command the means of putting himself forward means that are equally central in ancient and modern society. And finally, the opponents reproach Paul for not allowing himself to be supported by the church—from their perspective, an indication of his lack of love for the congregation.[80] The Corinthians were impressed by these objections and by the manner in which the opponents appeared before the congregation. They were fascinated by preachers who knew how to get along on the basis of their personality. Rhetorical training, the claim to special knowledge, and an imposing external appearance were probably characteristic features of these outsider missionaries (cf. 10:5). In addition, they boasted of their special abilities, for they experienced ecstatic visions and could do signs and wonders (cf. 11:6; 12:1, 12). Thus, from the point of view of the Corinthians, the opponents belonged to that category of itinerant preachers characteristic of the religious and intellectual scene in the urban centers of that time. They attempted to impress people by their unconventional appearance, by an independent, self-sufficient lifestyle, and by rhetorical pathos. The marketplaces and plazas of large cities were full of such people, who played up to the crowds and made their money from them.[81] Not the best specimens of humanity, they had their own reputation in mind. In the eyes of the Corinthians, these missionaries from foreign parts fit the familiar image of the religious or philosophical speakers who responded to the common human desire to be both impressed and flattered. After all, these missionaries could do amazing miracles that demonstrated their authority, and could also prove it with letters written in their behalf.

79. On the structure of 2 Cor. 10–13 and the organization of Paul's argument, see Ulrich Heckel, *Kraft in Schwachheit: Untersuchungen zu 2. Kor 10–13* (WUNT 2/56; Tübingen: Mohr Siebeck, 1993), 6–142.

80. If a philosopher did not accept money, that could be considered a sign of the worthlessness of his teaching; cf. Xenophon, *Mem.* 1.6.12, where Antiphon says to Socrates, "It is clear after all that you would not ask less for your instruction than it is worth, if you believed that it were really worth anything."

81. Cf. Lucian, *Icaromennipus* 5, who wants to be initiated by philosophers into the heavenly mysteries: "I thus looked around for the most distinguished among them, that is, those who stood out with the darkest face, the palest complexion, and the most tangled beard—for I thought it had to be so that men whose appearance and speech stood out so much from the others, must know more than others about heavenly things. So I turned myself over to them and their teaching, paid a substantial sum in advance, and obligated myself to pay the same amount later, after I had attained the peak of wisdom."

Paul was different. His weak external appearance and his lack of gifts in public speaking evidently caused many of the Corinthians to believe that the apostle's message was likewise to be disdained. The power of the gospel they wanted did not correspond to the weakness of the apostle.

The Opponents

How may the opponents in 2 Corinthians be classified from the point of view of the study of the history of religions? W. Lütgert saw them as libertine pneumatics and Gnostics.[82] This position was adopted by R. Bultmann and W. Schmithals.[83] E. Käsemann rightly objected against equating the opponents reflected in the two Corinthians letters, arguing that 2 Corinthians presupposes a new, more developed situation. For him, the opponents in 2 Corinthians are missionaries advocating a position close to that of the original Jerusalem church, who attempted to establish the authority of the original apostles over against that of Paul (cf. ὑπερλίαν ἀπόστολοι [super-apostles], 2 Cor. 11:5; 12:11). For Käsemann, the issue was focused on the dispute between two different understandings of apostleship in early Christianity, a dispute in which the Pauline apostolic office was opposed by the Jerusalem authorities' claims to church leadership. There is, however, no text in 2 Corinthians that clearly represents the agitators as real or presumed emissaries of the Jerusalem church. The expression πρὸς ὑμᾶς ἢ ἐξ ὑμῶν (to you or from you) in 3:1b already speaks against this, for if the opponents had arrived with letters of recommendation from Jerusalem, they would hardly have made claims based on letters *from* the Corinthians. D. Georgi judges the opponents in 2 Corinthians to be early Christian missionaries belonging to the types of itinerant prophet, healer, and wonder-worker widespread in antiquity. They honored the earthly Jesus as a triumphalistic pneumatic who was already filled with divine power, and made no distinction between the earthly Jesus and the exalted Lord. In a manner similar to pagan miracle workers who represented themselves as emissaries of their gods and praised their own powers, these early Christian missionaries displayed their powers by revelations and miracles. Georgi clearly underrates

---

82. Cf. Wilhelm Lütgert, *Freiheitspredigt und Schwarmgeister in Korinth: Ein Beitrag zur Charakteristik der Christuspartei* (BFCT 12/3; Gütersloh: C. Bertelsmann, 1908), 79. A survey of research on the identity of Paul's opponents in 2 Corinthians is given by Jerry L. Sumney, *Identifying Paul's Opponents: The Question of Method in 2 Corinthians* (JSNTSup 40; Sheffield: JSOT Press, 1990), 13–73; R. Bieringer, "Die Gegner des Paulus im 2 Korintherbrief," in *Studies on 2 Corinthians* (ed. R. Bieringer and Jan Lambrecht; BETL 112; Leuven: Leuven University Press, 1994), 181–221; and Hulmi, *Paulus und Mose*, 18–23.

83. Cf. Bultmann, *2 Corinthians*, 215. Cf. Walter Schmithals, *Gnosticism in Corinth: An Investigation of the Letters to the Corinthians* (trans. John E. Steely; Nashville: Abingdon, 1971), 113–16; and, more recently, the collection of essays in Walter Schmithals, ed., *Neues Testament und Gnosis* (EdF 208; Darmstadt: Wissenschaftliche Buchgesellschaft, 1984), 28–33.

the pointers to a militant Jewish Christian position, in contrast to other reconstructions where the line of argument is primarily based on them. Thus G. Lüdemann takes up the position of F. C. Baur that the opponents were Jewish Christians from Jerusalem who had participated in the apostolic council but had not acknowledged the agreement made there and had attacked Paul in the Gentile churches he had founded.[84] Such a characterization of the opponents is inadequate, for, although it does appreciate their Jewish origin (cf. 11:22), the decisive criterion for their credibility was their possession of the Spirit manifest in signs and wonders (cf. 12:12). They probably advocated a different Christology from Paul's. But Paul never indicates that his opponents demanded circumcision. Since the apostle deals with the activities and objections of his opponents, he would certainly have dealt with circumcision if his opponents had made this an issue. Therefore the opponents in 2 Corinthians cannot be called Judaists in the same sense as those in Galatians.[85] In 2 Corinthians, it is not circumcision, and thus not the law, that is the disputed issue. Nor do the opponents make any particular appeal to the historical Jesus, for otherwise in 2 Cor. 10:7 Paul would not have responded to their motto, "I belong to Christ," by saying οὕτως καὶ ἡμεῖς (so also do we). Paul's opponents in 2 Corinthians were early Christian itinerant missionaries of Jewish-Hellenistic origin who charged Paul with lacking spiritual power and who wanted to legitimate themselves as authentic apostles and bearers of the Spirit.[86] We can no longer perceive to what extent, if at all, they were connected with Jerusalem.[87]

Appearance and Reality

Paul does not combat his opponents on the surface level but analyzes the theological depths of the disputed issues of what is only apparently a personal conflict. The real difference between Paul and his opponents is not to be sought in the realm of their external appearances and operations but is a matter of their respective understandings of the gospel and its proclamation. The opponents obviously advocated a Christology of glory, in which they boasted of the splendor and glory of the resurrected Christ and made their own participation in this glory a matter of public observation. In 2 Cor. 11:5 and 12:11 Paul ironically calls them "super-apostles," since, with their privileges and advantages, they appear

84. Lüdemann, *Opposition to Paul*, 80–103. With slight modifications, Klauck, *2. Korintherbrief*, 11, advocates this position.

85. Cf. Windisch, *Korintherbrief*, 26; Furnish, *II Corinthians*, 53; Lang, *An die Korinther*, 357–59.

86. Cf. Sumney, *Identifying Paul's Opponents*, 190; differently, Horn, *Angeld des Geistes*, according to whom pneumatic phenomena were not an essential element in the way the opponents conducted themselves in Corinth.

87. Hulmi, *Paulus und Mose*, 62, has recently revived the argument for a connection with Jerusalem.

to stand above the other apostles. In contrast, Paul wants to be a weak apostle if thereby the power and might of the gospel itself can be revealed. The power of the risen one makes itself known in weakness (12:9a). With much imagination, the apostle rings the chimes on this fundamental idea throughout chapters 10–13, with impressive rhetorical power. The opponents and the Corinthian church should not deceive themselves, for, although Paul lives ἐν σαρκί (lit. in the flesh; NRSV, "as human beings"), he does not live and work κατὰ σάρκα (lit. according to the flesh; NRSV, "according to human standards," 10:3). He too has spiritual power at his disposal, for, in his struggle for the church, his weapons are mightily effective through the power of God. Paul contends for the sake of his church, not for his own sake but because the opponents falsify the gospel and thus deprive the church of σωτηρία (salvation/well-being). In this struggle Paul knows that he must not glorify himself and his own abilities; rather, the existence of the church in Corinth is itself the glory God apportions him (10:12–18). It is not the opponents who are "incomparable" but only the grace of God that has made Paul and his coworkers competent to the task of preaching the gospel and building up the churches. Competence is not a matter of self-commendation, for only those commended by the Lord are competent (10:18).

Paul thus uses a bit of cunning in order to open the eyes of the church. As a preacher of the gospel, Paul cannot boast of his own competence, but he can boast as fool and clown. The church in Corinth willingly puts up with the foolishness of the opponents, and so they should allow him to be foolish at least this one time (11:1ff.). The fool's speech (11:21b–12:10) is the center of chapters 10–13, framed by 11:16–21a and 12:11–13.[88] Paul assumes the role of a fool because this is the only way he can speak the truth to the church. By donning the fool's mask, he can indulge in self-glorification and self-praise. The community suffers fools gladly, for it allows itself to be taken in and exploited by the super-apostles. Paul is in no way behind them, for he too is a Hebrew and descendent of Abraham (11:22). If they represent themselves as ministers of Christ, Paul is a much better one. This polemical superclaim is followed not by a list of the apostle's personal abilities but by the longest peristasis catalogue in the New Testament (11:21b–29). Paul does not glory in his strengths but in his weakness. His life itself thus appears as an example of the theology of the cross. God's power is at work where human ability breaks down and human observation sees only weakness. Despite the manifold troubles that afflict his missionary work, the apostle is still alive, and this not because he is strong but only because the grace of God keeps him alive. Paul does not boast in his manifold missionary success but in his suffering and weakness so that the

---

88. On the various efforts at outlining this section, cf. Heckel, *Kraft in Schwachheit*, 22–23. He understands 2 Cor. 11:1–12:13 as the fool's speech "in the broader sense," with 11:21b–12:10 as the fool's speech "in the narrower sense." For an analysis, see Hotze, *Paradoxien*, 159–227.

power of God can be all the more revealed in him (11:30–33). At the center of the fool's speech stands his account of being taken to paradise (12:1–10).[89] Paul narrates this extraordinary event in the distancing third person singular in order to emphasize its character as an objective event. In paradise his ears heard inexpressible sounds that human beings cannot repeat. Regarding such revelations and evidences of God's grace, Paul remains faithful to his fundamental theological position. Whereas his opponents seek to impress the church with their special revelations and thus boast of their own abilities, Paul cannot do this because God afflicted him with a sickness or disease that prevents it (12:7–9).[90] Three times he prayed to God for recovery, but the answer to his prayer that came to him through Jesus has a programmatic character and determines the apostle's understanding of reality: "My grace is sufficient for you, for [my] power is made perfect in weakness" (12:9a). Paul is to be the weak apostle so that his work manifests the grace and power of God.

At the conclusion of the fool's speech, Paul takes off the mask and speaks directly to the Corinthians once again (12:11–13). As minister of the gospel of Jesus Christ, the apostle is not one bit inferior to the super-apostles. Signs, wonders, and mighty works happened among the Corinthians (12:12), which Paul alludes to with the catchphrase σημεῖα καὶ τέρατα (signs and wonders).[91] Paul too had worked miracles in Corinth, "in the first place healing sick people as well as converting people under special circumstances, impressive confrontations with unbelievers, glossolalia and other pneumatic phenomena, and punitive miracles among both church members and outsiders."[92] For the Spirit-inspired Paul, miracles were nothing exceptional; here also the super-apostles had no superior legitimation.[93] If the Corinthians insist on proof that Christ is at work

89. For a comprehensive exegesis, cf. Heckel, *Kraft in Schwachheit*, 56–120. As a parallel from the history of religions, see Plato, *Resp.* 10.614b–615c (*NW* 2/1:504–5).

90. The spectrum of explanations of Paul's sickness extends from a speech impediment through hearing difficulties, leprosy, rheumatism, hysteria, and epilepsy to headaches and migraines (cf. the survey in Windisch, *Korintherbrief*, 386–88). Of all these suggestions, the most likely is headaches or migraines; cf. Ulrich Heckel, "Der Dorn im Fleisch: Die Krankheit des Paulus in 2Kor 12,7 und Gal. 4,13f.," *ZNW* 84 (1993): 65–92.

91. On the opponents' understanding of apostleship and their image of Jesus as reflected in 2 Corinthians, cf. Bernd Kollmann, "Paulus als Wundertäter," in *Paulinische Christologie: Exegetische Beiträge: Hans Hübner zum 70. Geburtstag* (ed. Udo Schnelle et al.; Göttingen: Vandenhoeck & Ruprecht, 2000), 84–87.

92. Windisch, *Korintherbrief*, 397.

93. This fact is played down by Ernst Käsemann, "Die Legitimität des Apostels: Eine Untersuchung zu II Korinther 10–13," in *Das Paulusbild in der neueren deutschen Forschung* (ed. Karl Heinrich Rengstorf; 2nd ed.; Darmstadt: Wissenschaftliche Buchgesellschaft, 1969), 511, who argues that extraordinary phenomena are of interest to Paul "only as an aspect of his apostolic ministry whereas his opponents have them bursting into history unconditionally as revelations of the new age and regard them as 'miracles.'" Similarly Heckel, *Kraft in Schwachheit*, 298, according to whom Paul devalues "wonder-working activity as only an accompanying phenomenon of apostolic ministry." In contrast, cf. H. K. Nielsen, "Paulus' Verwendung des Begriffes δύναμις," in *Die paulinische Literatur*

in him, then Paul can provide it: "For he was crucified in weakness, but lives by the power of God. For we are weak in him, but in dealing with you we will live with him by the power of God" (13:4).[94] The δύναμις θεοῦ (power of God) is by no means always hidden, working only paradoxically in the weakness of the apostle. It manifests itself in the apostle's own signs and wonders and will be directly operative when Paul comes to Corinth for the third time to take action against the abuses in the church. Here Paul is not orienting himself to the model of power hidden in weakness; rather, through this weakness the power of God works visibly. If mighty works were for Paul manifestations of the presence of God in a world that is passing away (cf. 1 Thess. 1:5; 1 Cor. 2:4; 5:4; Gal. 3:5; Rom. 15:18–19), so Paul was himself also a miracle worker.

In 2 Corinthians Paul develops *the fundamental ideas of his theology in paradoxical form*:[95] the participation of the apostle and the church takes place in the same way as the transformation of the Son. God's glory is paradoxically revealed in the weakness and suffering of death. Just as the life-giving power of God is revealed in the cross, God's power is also at work in the weakness of the apostle. The ministry of the gospel corresponds to the suffering of Jesus; the suffering of the apostle is the intersection of divine revelation and earthly existence. Whereas the super-apostles orient themselves to God's glory and their own competence, Paul outlines a paradoxical model of identity: experiences of suffering do not contradict the new being in Christ; on the contrary, as the existential counterpart to the suffering of Christ, one's own suffering is a constitutive element of Christian existence. Both apostle and church are participants in the suffering endured by their Lord. The tensions between the world as presently perceived and the reality of God do not threaten the persuasive power of the gospel but are an essential element of it: the reality of the resurrection that cannot be seen by ordinary sight corresponds to God's hidden activity in the world.

---

und Theologie = The Pauline Literature and Theology: Anlässlich der 50. jährigen Gründungs-Feier der Universität von Aarhus (ed. Sigfred Pedersen; Århus: Aros, 1980), 153: "Paul clearly says, in a way that cannot be misunderstood, that he has done σημεῖα ['signs'], τέρατα ['wonders'], and δυνάμεις ['mighty works']; this may not be disguised."

94. The extraordinary aspects of this text are emphasized by Nielsen, "Δύναμις," 154–55; and Siber, *Mit Christus Leben*, 168–78.

95. For the fundamental importance of paradox as a reasonable thought form, cf. Hotze, *Paradoxien*, 341–60.

11

Paul and the Galatians

Discovery in Conflict

Sometimes a critical situation can be devastating, but it can also release unforeseen strength and lead to new insights. Paul never backed away from a confrontation when the truth of the gospel was at stake.

11.1 Prehistory

The Letter to the Galatians may have been written to churches in either of two places: the area inhabited by, and named after, ethnic Galatians (the North Galatian theory, or region hypothesis) or the southern part of the Roman province of Galatia (the South Galatian theory, or province hypothesis). The ethnic Galatians were the descendants of the Celtic tribes who began to move into Asia Minor in 279 CE, settling in the area of present-day Ankara. In 25 CE, this Galatian area became a constituent part of the province of Galatia, which also incorporated parts of the areas to the south, including Pisidia, Lycaonia, Isauria, Paphlagonia, Galatia Pontica, and (from time to time) Pamphylia.

The Province Hypothesis

According to the province hypothesis, the letter was addressed to Christians in the areas of Lycaonia, Pisidia and Isauria, where, according to Acts 13:13–14:27, Paul had founded churches and where he probably paid a second visit (cf. Acts 16:2–5). The following arguments can be advanced for this view:[1] (1) Galatian churches were among those who participated in the collection for Jerusalem (cf. 1 Cor. 16:1), and Acts 20:4 mentions only Christians from South Galatia, for example, Gaius of Derbe, as members of the delegation that delivered the collection. (2) That Paul's opponents in Galatia were able to disrupt the life of the churches there points to Jewish Christians in the congregations. The population of South Galatia included Jews, but it is not clear that this was the case in North Galatia.[2] (3) Paul often uses the provincial names (Asia, Achaia, Macedonia); he does not orient his mission to ethnic-geographical areas but to the large cities of the provinces.[3] (4) The sequence in the account of the trip in Acts 18:23 ("went from place to place through the region of Galatia and Phrygia") can be seen as evidence for the province hypothesis.[4]

The Region Hypothesis

Substantial arguments can also be presented for the region hypothesis:[5] (1) The province hypothesis presupposes the founding of the Galatian churches on the first missionary journey. Paul says nothing about this in Gal. 1:21, however, although this would have been strong support for his argument that his mission was independent of Jerusalem. Moreover, in Gal. 3:1ff. and 4:12ff. Paul speaks explicitly about his founding visit, so the addressees know that Gal. 1:21 and 3:1ff.; 4:12ff. refer to different events and that Paul did not establish churches in their area until the later period.[6] (2) Acts calls the southern areas of

---

1. A thorough and extensive argument for the province hypothesis is given in Carl Clemen, *Paulus: Sein Leben und Wirken* (2 vols.; Giessen: J. Ricker, 1904), 1:24–38. This is the dominant theory in Anglo-Saxon scholarship and is advocated in the German-speaking world by, e.g., Stuhlmacher, *Biblische Theologie*, 1:226; Riesner, *Paul's Early Period*, 281–91; Breytenbach, *Paulus und Barnabas*, 99ff.; Thomas Witulski, *Die Adressaten des Galaterbriefes: Untersuchungen zur Gemeinde von Antiochia ad Pisidiam* (FRLANT 193; Göttingen: Vandenhoeck & Ruprecht, 2000), 224.

2. This is an argument from silence, which cannot support the weight of a hypothesis with such far-reaching implications.

3. Cf. Ollrog, *Mitarbeiter*, 55–56.

4. Cf. Colin J. Hemer and Conrad H. Gempf, *The Book of Acts in the Setting of Hellenistic History* (Tübingen: Mohr Siebeck, 1989).

5. Cf. the extensive evidence and argument in Vielhauer, *Geschichte der urchristlichen Literatur*, 104–8.

6. This argument is not weakened by pointing to the expression τὰ κλίματα (τῆς Συρίας καὶ τῆς Κιλικίας) (the regions [of Syria and Cilicia]), for otherwise Paul's argument in Gal. 1 is very precise. It would have been an exquisite demonstration of his independence from Jerusalem if Paul could have pointed out that he had already founded the Galatian churches prior to the apostolic council.

the province of Galatia not Galatia but Pisidia (Acts 13:14; 14:24) and Lycaonia (Acts 14:6, 11); in contrast, in Acts 16:6 and 18:23 Γαλατικὴ χώρα (lit. the Galatian country; NRSV, "the region of Galatia") stands alongside Phrygia for the region (not the province) of Galatia in which, from the Lukan perspective, Paul carried on his missionary work.[7] Elsewhere in the New Testament the term "Galatia" always refers to Galatia in the regional sense (cf. 1 Pet. 1:1; 2 Tim. 4:10). (3) With the exception of the Letter to Philemon, Paul always addresses his letters to churches in particular locations. The lack of a particular place-name and the use of an ethnic designation in addressing the readers (Gal. 1:2; 3:1) speak in favor of the regional hypothesis.[8] (4) The ethnic groups incorporated into the province of Galatia maintained their distinctive cultural and linguistic traditions, so that, for example, the people of Lycaonia still spoke their own language (cf. Acts 14:11). It would have been a cultural faux pas and very poor rhetorical strategy if Paul had addressed people of Lycaonia or Pisidia as "foolish Galatians" (Gal. 3:1).[9] This reproach could have been on target only if Paul had been speaking to people who felt themselves to be Galatians in the full, traditional sense.[10] (5) In Paul's time, the term ἡ Γαλατία (Galatia) was used primarily not for the province but for the region of historical and ethnic Galatia.[11] (6) It is by no means the case that Paul always used the official names of Roman provinces; he also frequently used the older regional

7. Cf. Mussner, *Galaterbrief*, 3–5; Karl Strobel, *Die Galater: Geschichte und Eigenart der keltischen Staatenbildung auf dem Boden des hellenistischen Kleinasien* (Berlin: Akademie, 1996–), 1:118: "In Acts, the areas in the southern part of the province of Galatia are distinguished from ἡ Γαλατία χώρα ['the region of Galatia'] and are consistently called Pisidia and Lycaonia." Cf., in addition, Dietrich-Alex Koch, "Barnabas, Paulus, und die Adressaten des Galaterbriefes," in *Das Urchristentum in seiner literarischen Geschichte: Festschrift für Jürgen Becker zum 65. Geburtstag* (ed. Ulrich Mell and Ulrich B. Müller; BZNW 100; New York: de Gruyter, 1999), 89: "For Luke, the churches founded in Acts 13–14 are located not in Galatia but in Pisidia and Lycaonia (cf. Acts 13:14; 14:6). . . . Thus, for Luke, 'Galatia' is located farther in the interior of Asia Minor than Pisidia and Lycaonia. This means that although Barnabas and (!) Paul establish churches in Antioch of Pisidia, Iconium, Lystra, and Derbe, for Luke these are clearly not in 'Galatia,' just as they are not in Phrygia."

8. Cf. Strobel, *Galater*, 117–18, who, as a historian of antiquity, strongly advocates the regional hypothesis and, in disputing Anglo-Saxon scholarship, emphasizes, "If one considers Hellenistic usage, which had not changed in the time of Paul, who himself had a Hellenistic education, then one can only interpret his usage in the Letter to the Galatians in the sense of this general ethnic understanding of the word. For his contemporaries, this connotation of 'Galatia' was firmly established in history and literature, and its meaning was unmistakable. Thus the debate about the addressees of the Letter to the Galatians must be decided in favor of the historical ethnic group, especially so since the Galatians, along with the city of Ankyra, constituted a specific political organization within the larger province, the Galatian Koinon [Galatian Commonwealth]."

9. Cf. ibid., 118: "In this connection, we must underscore the fact that the traditional ethnic regions and historical areas continued to exist within the Roman provincial structure." This argument must also keep in mind the mixed population not only in the south but also in the north; cf. Breytenbach, *Paulus und Barnabas*, 154ff.

10. Cf. François Vouga, *An die Galater* (HNT 10; Tübingen: Mohr Siebeck, 1998), 11.

11. Documentation in Rohde, *Galater*, 11.

designations (cf. Gal. 1:21; 1:17; 4:25; 1 Thess. 2:14; Rom. 15:24). (7) The churches in South Galatia had been founded by Barnabas (!) and Paul (cf. Acts 13:1–2; 14:12–14). Galatians, however, is addressed to churches founded by Paul himself (Gal. 1:1, 8–9; 4:12–14).[12]

All in all, the arguments for the region hypothesis are more persuasive, and when taken with the well-considered plan of the letter as a whole, several arguments speak against the province hypothesis, especially the failure to mention the addressees in Gal. 1:21, the Lukan statements about Paul's work in "the region of Galatia" (Acts 18:23), the address in Gal. 3:1, and the presupposition that the churches were founded by Paul alone.[13]

The Founding of the Churches

When were the Galatian churches founded? According to Acts 16:6 and 18:23, at the beginning of both the second and third missionary journeys, Paul traveled through the "region of Galatia." Acts 16:6 is often regarded as referring to the initial visit to Galatia when the churches were founded, followed by a second visit for strengthening the churches (Acts 18:23). As evidence for this assumption, the phrase in Gal. 4:13 τὸ πρότερον is taken in the sense of "the first time," thus implying a second visit had taken place later. The Galatian churches would then have been founded on the second missionary journey.[14] But both texts are (at least for the most part) the products of Lukan redaction,[15] so that we can say nothing for certain about Pauline missionary activity in "the region of Galatia" except for the mere fact that he was there. If we restrict our conclusions to what can be inferred from the data of the letter itself, other interpretative possibilities emerge. Galatians 1:6 presupposes that the initial

12. On this point, see Koch, "Barnabas," 94–97.

13. The positions of individual exegetes on the regional or province hypotheses are catalogued in Rohde, *Galater*, 6–7. For the regional hypothesis, cf., most recently the extensive discussion of Betz, *Galatians*, 1–8; cf. also U. Wickert, "Kleinasien," *TRE* 19:251, "The North Galatia hypothesis is certainly to be preferred"; Strobel, *Galater*, 117ff.; Karl Löning, "Der Galaterbrief und die Anfänge des Christentums in Galatien," in *Forschungen in Galatien* (ed. Elmar Schwertheim; AMS 12; Bonn: Habelt, 1994), 132–33; Roloff, *Einführung*, 123; Becker et al., *Briefe*, 14–16; J. Louis Martyn, *Galatians: A New Translation with Introduction and Commentary* (AB 33A; New York: Doubleday, 1997), 16–17; Vouga, *Galater*, 11–12; Koch, "Barnabas," 106; Dieter Lührmann, "Galaterbrief," *RGG* 3:451.

14. So Schlier, *Galater*, 17–18; Albrecht Oepke, *Der Brief des Paulus an die Galater* (3rd ed.; THKNT 9; Berlin: Evangelische Verlagsanstalt, 1973), 25, 142; Mussner, *Galaterbrief,* 3–9, 306–7.

15. Acts 18:23c ("strengthening all the disciples") is often cited as evidence for a previous mission in Galatia; cf. Hans Hübner, "Galaterbrief," *TRE* 12:6. But precisely this expression is clearly redactional (cf. Luke 22:32; Acts 14:22; 15:32, 41; 16:5). Additional redactional elements in 18:23 are ποιεῖν χρόνον τινα (spend time; cf. Acts 15:33) and καθεξῆς (in order, sequentially; elsewhere in the New Testament only in Luke 1:3; 8:1; Acts 3:24; 11:4). Acts 16:6 must be understood as entirely a Lukan compositional note portraying the apostle's determined path toward Europe; cf. the analysis of Weiser, *Apostelgeschichte*, 2:404, 500. The differing order of stations in Acts 16:6 and 18:23 remains worthy of note; on the problems of Acts 18:18–23, see above, section 2.2 ("Relative Chronology").

visit on which the churches were founded had occurred in the not-too-distant past; at first the Galatians were "running well" (5:7), but now Paul is amazed that they "so quickly" are deserting his gospel (1:6). Paul does not mention a second visit, nor is one presupposed. The reference in 4:13, τὸ πρότερον, need not be understood as "the first time," as though it implied that a second visit had already taken place, but can be translated simply as "first" in the sense of "then, at that time" (so NRSV).[16] Moreover, 4:13–15, 18–19 likewise refers only to the initial founding visit, so that from the letter itself a second visit can only be a hypothetical inference.[17] As a result, only Acts 18:23 can be taken as reflecting the founding of the Galatian churches.[18] That the Galatian churches were founded at the beginning of the third missionary journey in the spring of 52 CE fits the internal data of Galatians and the statements from Acts and agrees with the dating of Galatians here presupposed—shortly before the composition of Romans.

The Galatians were primarily Gentile Christians (cf. Gal. 4:8; 5:2–3; 6:12–13) and probably belonged to the Hellenized population of the cities. The reception of the letter presupposes a certain level of education, and the initial effect of the Pauline message of freedom points to circles that were interested in cultural and religious emancipation. As locations of the Galatian churches, we may think of Pessinus, Germa, Ankyra, and Tavium.

Writing the Letter

Two serious possibilities offer themselves in determining the circumstances of the letter: (1) Galatians was written during Paul's stay in Ephesus, either before or after the writing of 1 Corinthians from the same city.[19] (2) Paul wrote Galatians during his trip through Macedonia (cf. Acts 20:2), which would mean it was written after 1 Corinthians (and 2 Corinthians as well), very near the time when Romans was written.[20] The sole criteria for determining the

---

16. Cf. Borse, *Galater,* 150.

17. Among those who vote against a second visit of Paul to the Galatian churches are Borse, ibid., 8ff.; and Betz, *Galatians,* 11.

18. Cf. Koch, "Barnabas," 100–105.

19. Oepke, *Galater,* 211–12 (Galatians after 1 Corinthians); Schlier, *Galater,* 18; Vielhauer, *Geschichte der urchristlichen Literatur,* 110–11; Lührmann, *Galatians,* 3 (Galatians after 1 Corinthians); Hübner, "Galaterbrief," *TRE* 12:11.

20. So, e.g., Joseph Barber Lightfoot, *Saint Paul's Epistle to the Galatians: A Revised Text* (10th ed.; London: Macmillan, 1890), 55; Otto Pfleiderer et al., *Primitive Christianity: Its Writings and Teachings in Their Historical Connections* (4 vols.; New York: G. P. Putnam, 1906), 1:138; Borse, *Galater,* 9–17; Mussner, *Galaterbrief,* 9ff.; Ulrich Wilckens, *Der Brief an die Römer* (3 vols.; EKKNT 6; Neukirchener-Vluyn: Neukirchener Verlag, 1978–1982), 1:47–48; Lüdemann, *Chronology,* 263; Becker et al., *Briefe,* 14–16; Dieter Zeller, *Der Brief an die Römer* (RNT; Regensburg: Pustet, 1985), 13; Jones, *"Freiheit,"* 25–26; Vollenweider, *Freiheit als neue Schöpfung,* 20 n. 40; Räisänen, *Paul and the Law,* 8; Rohde, *Galater,* 10–11; Georg Strecker and Johann Maier, *Neues Testament–antikes Judentum*

circumstances of the letter's composition are its striking proximity to Romans and the references to the collection in Gal. 2:10 and 1 Cor. 16:1.

Close contacts between Galatians and Romans become immediately visible when the two letters are compared in terms of structure:[21]

Gal. 1:15–16	Rom. 1:1–5	Set apart as an apostle
Gal. 2:15–21	Rom. 3:19–28	Righteousness through faith
Gal. 3:6–25, 29	Rom. 4:1–25	Abraham
Gal. 3:26–28	Rom. 6:3–5	Baptism
Gal. 4:1–7	Rom. 8:12–17	Slavery and freedom
Gal. 4:21–31	Rom. 9:6–13	Law and promise
Gal. 5:13–15	Rom. 13:8–10	Set free to love
Gal. 5:17	Rom. 7:15–23	Conflict between willing and doing
Gal. 5:16–26	Rom. 8:12ff.	Life in the Spirit

The main lines of the train of thought found in Romans is already anticipated in Galatians. The polemic of Galatians, conditioned by the particular situation, deals with the same basic issues as does Romans, but in Romans the argument is more reflective and the points are supported with more stringent evidence. Also, in Romans Paul is challenged with new questions that have emerged, as shown in Rom. 1:18–3:21 and Rom. 9–11. Above all, the doctrine of justification, integral to both letters, indicates a close relationship between Galatians and Romans. Only here do we find the alternative "by faith, not by works of the law," and only here do we find a reflective and thought-through understanding of the law. The differences in the way the law is understood in Galatians and Romans derive from the fact that Galatians is more conditioned by its particular situation. It is precisely the development of these particular ideas, which first emerge in Galatians, that are further developed in Romans.

According to 1 Cor. 16:1, in Galatia, too, Paul is organizing a collection for the saints in Jerusalem, probably not long before the composition of 1 Corinthians. Here there is no trace of a crisis between the apostle and the Galatian churches, a clear indication that Galatians was written at least after

---

(Stuttgart: Kohlhammer, 1989), 78; Eduard Schweizer, *A Theological Introduction to the New Testament* (trans. O. C. Dean Jr.; Nashville: Abingdon, 1991), 73; Thomas Söding, "Zur Chronologie der paulinischen Briefe," *BN* 56 (1991): 58; Horn, *Angeld des Geistes*, 346; Hans-Joachim Eckstein, *Verheissung und Gesetz: Eine exegetische Untersuchung zu Galater 2,15–4,7* (WUNT 86; Tübingen: Mohr Siebeck, 1996), 252. Even when Galatians is seen in immediate proximity to Romans, its relation to 2 Corinthians and Philippians can still be understood in different ways. Following U. Borse, some scholars locate Galatians between 2 Cor. 1–9 and 2 Cor. 10–13, e.g., Mussner, *Galaterbrief*, 10–11, and Rohde, *Galater*, 11. Becker, *Paul*, 314, argues for the sequence Galatians, Philippians B (Phil. 3:2–21; 4:8–9), Romans, describing Philippians B as a later "little Galatians"; Berger, *Theologiegeschichte*, 441, advocates the order Galatians, Philippians, Romans.

21. Cf. Borse, *Standort des Galaterbriefes*, 120–35; Wilckens, *Römer*, 1:48; Broer, *Einleitung*, 2:442–43.

1 Corinthians. Galatians 2:10 mentions the collection without any suggestion of polemic, within the context of the agreements made at the apostolic council. Since the collection was not a matter of dispute between the apostle and his opponents, or between apostle and the churches, and is otherwise not mentioned in Galatians, we may assume that the collection in Galatia was already complete at the time the letter was written. When Paul in Gal. 2:10b explicitly emphasizes that he was in full agreement with the provisions for the collection that had been worked out in Jerusalem, he thus presupposes the arrangements for the collection mentioned in 2 Corinthians (cf. Rom. 15:26).[22] Moreover, the whole procedure for gathering the collection speaks for dating Galatians immediately before Romans. In 1 Cor. 16:3–4 Paul is not yet certain whether he will have to travel to Jerusalem as a member of the delegation delivering the collection. In 2 Cor. 8:19 he does belong to the (future) group delivering the collection, and in Rom. 15:25–27 he regards delivering the collection as his current and top priority, about which he has deep anxieties (cf. Rom. 15:30–31). Between the time when Paul wrote 1 Corinthians and his composition of Romans, the relation between the apostle and the church in Jerusalem must have dramatically worsened, presumably as a result of Paul's heated reaction to the Galatian crisis, expressed in his letter to the Galatian churches.

Both the close proximity to Romans and the reports in Galatians about the collection speak for the view that Galatians was written *after* the two Corinthians letters and immediately *before* Romans, which would place it in the late autumn of 55 CE in Macedonia. This late date for the composition of Galatians has been attained solely from data in Paul's letters, but it is confirmed by considerations regarding the particular situation of the recipients.

11.2 The Galatian Crisis

The Letter to the Galatians emerges from a profound crisis between the Galatian churches and the apostle Paul. In addition, the letter marks a major change in Paul's thought. The structure of the letter itself already signals that the critical relationship between apostle and church is coming to a head. Thus the beginning of the letter lacks the conventional thanksgiving, since, in view of the situation in Galatia, Paul sees nothing for which to give thanks. By using

---

22. Cf. Rohde, *Galater*, 94. Paul's use of the first aorist ἐσπούδασα (I was eager) indicates "that he had already been engaged in activity that shows how concerned he was to fulfill the assignment" (Günther Harder, "σπουδάζω, κτλ.," *TWNT* 7:564). [Translator's note: The translation of *TWNT* in *TDNT* does not preserve the nuanced point here made.] In any case, Gal. 2:10b eliminates the possibility of dating Galatians early, making it the oldest Pauline letter, as advocated by Theodor Zahn, *Der Brief des Paulus an die Galater* (3rd ed.; Leipzig: Deichert, 1922), 20–21; *Introduction to the New Testament* (trans. John Moore Trout et al.; 3 vols.; Edinburgh: T&T Clark, 1909), 1:164–202.

his apostolic title in the opening line, Paul emphatically brings his authority into play. Only here within the Pauline letter corpus is sharp polemic found at the very beginning of a letter (Gal. 1:6–9), and it characterizes extensive sections of this letter. The conclusion of the letter is devoid of any sort of greeting from the apostle, closing instead with yet another argument with his opponents (6:12–14). The Letter to the Galatians has a clear apologetic character, aimed at changing the church's mind on the disputed issues. To achieve this goal, Paul makes much use of rhetorical elements and techniques.[23] In fact, Galatians offers the best possibility for analyzing a Pauline letter from the point of view of rhetorical criticism because Paul's dispute with his opponents and his relationship to the church explains the form of the letter. The letter takes the place of the absent Paul and substitutes for the apology, the speech for the defense, he would give if present. But regarding Galatians as an apologetic letter is not the exclusive key to understanding everything in it. An apologetic tendency doubtless predominates in the first two chapters, but 5:13–6:18 is deliberative rhetoric rather than forensic, and 3:1–5:12 cannot be placed neatly in any rhetorical classification.[24] The place of paraenesis within an apologetic letter also remains unclear. When making a speech for the defense before the court, who inserts paraenetic comments within the argument? The relation between ancient epistolography and rhetoric represents a further problem, for there are only a few points of contact that can be considered.[25] The apostle's

23. Betz, *Galatians*, 14–25, regards Galatians as an apologetic speech in letter form and thus divides the letter into the sections typical of such a speech: 1:1–5, *praescriptum* (epistolary prescript); 1:6–11, *exordium* (introduction); 1:12–2:14, *narratio* (narrative); 2:15–21, *propositio* (statement of what is to be proven); 3:1–4:31, *probatio* (proof); 5:1–6:10, *exhortatio* (exhortation); 6:11–18, *conclusio* (conclusion). Others whose rhetorical analyses place the accents differently, assigning Galatians to the *genus deliberativum* (deliberative rhetoric), include George A. Kennedy, *New Testament Interpretation through Rhetorical Criticism* (Chapel Hill: University of North Carolina Press, 1984), 144–52; François Vouga, "Zur rhetorischen Gattung des Galaterbriefes," *ZNW* 79 (1988): 291–92; J. Smit, "The Letter of Paul to the Galatians: A Deliberative Speech," *NTS* 35 (1989): 1–26; Ralph Brucker, "'Versuche ich denn jetzt, Menschen zu überreden . . . ?'—Rhetorik und Exegese am Beispiel des Galaterbriefes," in *Exegese und Methodendiskussion* (ed. Stefan Alkier and Ralph Brucker; TANZ 23; Tübingen: Francke, 1998), 211–36.

24. Cf. Johannes Schoon-Janssen, *Umstrittene "Apologien" in den Paulusbriefen: Studien zur rhetorischen Situation des 1. Thessalonicherbriefes, des Galaterbriefes, und des Philipperbriefes* (GTA 45; Göttingen: Vandenhoeck & Ruprecht, 1991), 66–113.

25. From the perspective of scholars of ancient philology, see C. J. Classen, "Paulus und die antike Rhetorik," *ZNW* 82 (1991): 1–33. Classen points out the difference between rhetoric and epistolography as understood in antiquity, doubts that the "genre of the apologetic letter" ever existed, and, regarding the "strict commitment to theory" presumed for ancient authors, comments that "it was precisely the 'art of dissimulation' that belonged to the theoretical challenges of every practitioner of the art of rhetoric, that is, the challenge of not allowing allegiance to rules to be noticed. Thus a clear application of rhetorical rules must have the effect of showing a lack of ability or experience, at least in the areas of *dispositio* and *elocutio*" (p. 31). Dieter Sänger, "'Vergeblich bemüht' (Gal. 4,11)? Zur paulinischen Argumentationsstrategie im Galaterbrief," *ZNW* 48 (2002): 377–99, is insistent that ancient rhetoricians regarded *oratio* and *epistula* as two distinct forms of communication: "The

candid admission in 2 Cor. 11:6 that he is "untrained in speech" (ἰδιώτης τῷ λόγῳ) but not in knowledge should be a warning against trying to see Paul's line of argument only in terms of formal rhetoric. Moreover, Paul addressed his letters to circumstances that were much more complex than the speech situations assumed in textbooks of rhetoric.[26] Paul incorporated rhetoric as one element of his cultural environment, but it did not become the determining factor in his line of reasoning.

The Occasion for the Crisis

Both the careful literary construction of Galatians and the unparalleled sharpness of the letter's polemic show that the dispute concerned a central theological issue. Jewish Christian missionaries (of the more stringent type) provoked the crisis between apostle and church.[27] They intruded into the churches and disturbed the good relationship between them and the apostle (cf. Gal. 5:7; 4:13–15). In order to avoid threatening persecutions by Jews (cf. 6:12), the opponents insisted on the practice of circumcision (cf. 5:3; 6:12–13; cf. also 2:2; 6:15)[28] and adherence

---

performance aspects reserved for oral delivery, *actio* and *pronuntiatio,* that is, gestures, imitation, volume and rhythm of one's speech, modulation of the voice, dramatic pause, and the like, cannot be reproduced in it [the letter]. It is precisely these elements, however, that are an essential factor in delivering a speech and that determine its success or failure on those addressed" (p. 389).

26. Aune's comment is on target: "Paul in particular was both a creative and eclectic letter writer. The epistolary situations he faced were often more complex than the ordinary rhetorical situations faced by most rhetoricians" (David E. Aune, *The New Testament in Its Literary Environment* [LEC; Philadelphia: Westminster, 1987], 203).

27. This understanding is represented by, e.g., Oepke, *Galater,* 27ff.; Kümmel and Feine, *Introduction,* 298–304; Mussner, *Galaterbrief,* 25; Otto Merk, "Der Beginn der Paränese im Galaterbrief," in *Wissenschaftsgeschichte und Exegese: Gesammelte Aufsätze zum 65. Geburtstag Otto Merks* (ed. Roland Gebauer et al.; Berlin: de Gruyter, 1998), 250; Lührmann, *Galatians,* 123–28; Hübner, "Galaterbrief," *TRE* 12:7–8; Betz, *Galatians,* 7; Lüdemann, *Opposition to Paul,* 99; Horn, *Angeld des Geistes,* 346–50; Broer, *Einleitung,* 2:440; Koch, "Barnabas," 87. Differently, Breytenbach, *Paulus und Barnabas,* 143, who argues that it was not itinerant Jewish Christian missionaries who had intruded into the churches: "It was rather an attempt by the synagogue associations to get the Galatians to practice circumcision and observance of the Torah, to make them into Jews and incorporate them into the existing Jewish community. It is a dispute with a group of Jewish Christians who had not yet separated from the synagogue and who had not agreed with the arrangements made at the apostolic council (Gal. 2:7–9), according to which the law-free Gentile mission had its theological legitimacy alongside the mission proclaiming the gospel to Jews." There is nothing in Galatians, however, about an integration into the synagogue. Moreover, Acts 15:1; Gal. 2:4, 11–14; 2 Cor. 3:1; 11:23ff.; 12:13; Phil. 3:1ff. presuppose the activities of strict Jewish Christian itinerant missionaries who directed their work against Paul. For a critique of Breytenbach's view, see also Koch, "Barnabas," 85–88.

28. Peder Borgen, "Observations on the Theme 'Paul and Philo': Paul's Preaching of Circumcision in Galatia (Gal. 5:11) and Debates on Circumcision in Philo," in *Die paulinische Literatur und Theologie = The Pauline Literature and Theology: Anlässlich der 50. jährigen Gründungs-Feier der Universität von Aarhus* (ed. Sigfred Pedersen; Århus: Aros, 1980), 85–102, refers to Philo's distinction between "ethical" and physical circumcision (*Migration* 86–93; *QE* 2.2) and infers, regarding Galatia, that the

to the cultic calendar (cf. 4:3, 9, 10).[29] The Qumran texts in particular document the great importance attributed to calendar issues in ancient Judaism, and the firm connection between Torah and the ordering of time (cf., e.g., 1QS 1:13–15; 9:26–10:8; 1QM 2:4; 10:15; CD 3:12–16; 16:2–4; 1QH 1:24; 12:4–9; *Jub.* 6:32, 36, 37; *1 En.* 72:1; 75:3–4; 79:2; 82:4, 7–10). The veneration of elemental spirits and the observation of special days, months, seasons, and years in Gal. 4:3, 9–10 thus speaks for regarding the opponents as Jewish Christians.[30] At the same time, the complex combination of service to the *stoicheia* (elemental spirits), ritual attention to the calendar, and Torah observance allows us to be more precise, since especially the significance of the elemental spirits points to Hellenistic influence; this means the opponents are Hellenistic Jewish Christians.[31] Large segments of the Galatian churches accepted the demands of the Jewish Christian missionaries (cf. 1:6–9; 4:9, 17, 21; 5:4; 6:12–13), which evokes sharp criticism from the apostle. Their conversion to the Christian faith obviously resulted in being uprooted from their previous surroundings, and they were not clear how their new identity in the elect people of God was to be defined.[32] They were susceptible to the arguments of Paul's opponents, four of which were evidently persuasive: (1) The person of Abraham shows that circumcision mediates membership in the divine covenant (cf. Gen. 17). (2) Faith in the God of Israel includes belonging to empirical, existing Israel. (3) Both Jesus and Paul had in fact accepted the command of circumcision. (4) Belonging to Judaism—that is, as Jewish Christians—grants those who are circumcised social identity and stability. This was an important point, since the fledgling congregations were exposed to great social and political pressure from

---

opponents persuaded some within the churches that Paul's preaching was to be considered "ethical" circumcision, which must now be followed by physical circumcision.

29. On the possible background of στοιχεῖα τοῦ κόσμου (elemental spirits of the universe), cf. Eduard Schweizer, "Die 'Elemente der Welt': Gal. 4,3.9; Kol 2,8.20," in *Beiträge zur Theologie des Neuen Testaments: Neutestamentliche Aufsätze (1955–1970)* (Zurich: Zwingli, 1970), 147–63; cf also D. Rusam, "Neue Belege zu den στοιχεῖα τοῦ κόσμου," *ZNW* 83 (1992): 119–25.

30. Cf. the extensive evidence in Dieter Lührmann, "Tage, Monate, Jahreszeiten, Jahre (Gal. 4,10)," in *Werden und Wirken des Alten Testaments: Festschrift für Claus Westermann* (ed. Rainer Albertz et al.; Göttingen: Vandenhoeck & Ruprecht, 1980), 428–45; Kuhn, "Bedeutung der Qumrantexte," 195–202.

31. Cf., e.g., Thomas Söding, "Die Gegner des Apostels Paulus in Galatien," *MTZ* 42 (1991): 315–16; like many other exegetes, he takes the opponents to be "Hellenistic Jewish Christians who advocated a syncretistic Christian nomism" (p. 316). Differently, Nikolaus Walter, "Paulus und die Gegner des Christusevangeliums in Galatien," in *L'apôtre Paul : personnalité, style, et conception du ministère* (ed. Albert Vanhoye; BETL 73; Leuven: Leuven University Press, 1986), 351–56, who argues that Paul was in conflict with a Jewish countermission. But Gal. 6:12 speaks against this: Paul's opponents insist on circumcision "that they may not be persecuted for the cross of Christ"; they were thus Jewish Christians.

32. Cf. the comprehensive discussion on this point by John M. G. Barclay, *Obeying the Truth: A Study of Paul's Ethics in Galatians* (ed. John Kenneth Riches; SNTW; Edinburgh: T&T Clark, 1988), 36–74.

several sides.[33] Despite the attractiveness of these arguments, Paul hoped to win the churches back by his reasoned arguments (cf. 3:4; 4:11–12, 19–20). The preservation and transmission of the Letter to the Galatians demonstrates that this was no unfounded hope.

What connection did the opponents have with the Jerusalem authorities, especially to James? We cannot establish a link to the "certain people from James" mentioned in 2:12, since they did not insist on circumcision.[34] Recently the hypothesis has once again emerged that Paul's opponents were identical with the "false brothers" at the apostolic council who unsuccessfully insisted on the circumcision of Titus.[35] In this view, they had not participated in the agreement worked out at the apostolic council, and they now obtruded themselves into the Pauline churches in Galatia, insisting on observance of the Torah and the cultic calendar. Here, too, the scanty sources do not permit a sure judgment. Certainly, 2:3–4 shows that within Jewish Christianity there were influential groups that programmatically advocated the circumcision of Gentile Christians. Their presence at the apostolic council signals that their claims extended beyond Palestine/Syria. Even if there is no direct literary evidence, one must proceed on the basis that there was some kind of connection between the Jerusalem authorities and Paul's opponents in Galatia. It is hardly conceivable that their actions in Galatia could have taken place without the awareness and approval of the Jerusalem church. As a result of the success of the Gentile mission that did not require circumcision, which in Jewish eyes meant in fact a Torah-free mission, the Jerusalem church came under increasing pressure of both a theological and a political nature. Theologically, its members had to explain how it could be that, on the one hand, they considered the new believers in Christ to be a part of Judaism while, on the other hand, an expanding wing of the new movement abandoned circumcision as a requirement for Gentile converts, thinking of itself as exclusively the true people of God. Politically, the actions of Agrippa I and the edict of Claudius show that it would be important to Judaism to let the new movement separate from the synagogue and appear to the world at large as an independent group.[36] Probably the Jerusalem church attempted to resist this dangerous development by strengthening or reactivating Jewish self-awareness. This included modifications of its previous stance toward the decisions made at the apostolic council. This would mean minimally that it gave its approval to the work of Jewish Christian missionaries (from

33. Barclay, ibid., 58, emphasizes that the precarious social situation could well have been an important reason that Gentile Christians were willing to accept circumcision.

34. Differently, e.g., Francis Watson, *Paul, Judaism, and the Gentiles: A Sociological Approach* (SNTSMS 56; Cambridge: Cambridge University Press, 1986), 59ff.

35. Cf. Lüdemann, *Opposition to Paul*, 99–103. This thesis had been previously advocated by, e.g., Oepke, *Galater*, 212–13.

36. On Agrippa and Claudius, see above, section 7.5 ("The Development of Early Christianity as an Independent Movement").

Palestine) within the Pauline mission territory, who regarded Paul's Gentile mission without the requirement of circumcision to be a blatant violation of the will of God revealed in the Torah. Their actions must be seen within the framework of a movement following the Pauline mission, a movement in which strict Jewish Christians in a variety of ways attempted to make faith in Jesus Christ *and* Torah observance, baptism *and* circumcision obligatory not only for Jewish Christians but for Gentile Christians as well.[37] Granted, there is no Jewish command for the circumcision of Gentiles, but by their entrance into the Christian community, those who were once Gentiles now belonged to the people of God, which, from the point of view of Paul's opponents, raised the issue of circumcision, among other matters. The Jerusalem church was mistaken in supposing that this development would bring about a reduction of pressure from the Jewish side and that its own theological position would prevail throughout the new Christian movement. The Galatian crisis thus testifies to a fundamental discussion in the history of the early Christian mission concerning the theological and political direction the new movement was to take.

Paul's Reaction

Paul was thus presented with a completely new situation. It appears that Paul's Jewish Christian opponents do not acknowledge the agreements made at the apostolic council, so that, in their understanding, Gentile Christians too must be subject to the prescriptions of the Torah. These Jewish Christian missionaries therefore jeopardized all of Paul's previous missionary work. The worldwide mission inaugurated by Paul in the prospect of Christ's return would be impossible if conditioned by the requirement of circumcision for Gentile Christians. Missionary strategy, however, was not the primary reason for Paul's advocacy of the Gentile mission free from the constraint of circumcision; it was, rather, the expression of his basic theological position: God saves Gentiles through faith in Jesus Christ. The dispute between Paul and his Jewish Christian opponents was ultimately concerned with the appropriate understanding of, and response to, God's saving act in Jesus Christ.[38] Does this really apply to all human beings, or is it bound to particular conditions? The significance of this problem corresponds to the apostle's careful, powerful, polemical argument of Galatians. Paul stakes out his position in the opening sentence: his apostleship is "neither by human commission nor from human authorities, but through Jesus Christ and God the Father" (Gal. 1:1). The opponents in Galatia obviously contest Paul's claim that his gospel comes directly from God. They

---

37. Cf. Wrede, *Paul*, 70.

38. An exclusively sociological interpretation of this conflict does not go far enough; contra Watson, *Paul, Judaism, and the Gentiles*, 69, who states, "Paul opposes circumcision because it is the rite of entry into the Jewish people, and for that reason alone."

probably put his preaching into the category of the apostle's personal opinion, contrasting it with the practice of the original Jerusalem church. Against this view Paul places a reality that connects him directly with the heavenly realm, from which he receives his legitimation.[39] Both Paul's apostleship and his gospel are based on a revelation from heaven, so that even angels would come under an ἀνάθεμα (curse) if they preach a different gospel (1:8). Paul's claim is unparalleled: in this letter he acts as divinely commissioned apostle, and the Galatians will act in accordance with their true being as church by accepting and orienting themselves only to the Pauline gospel.

Paul first counters the successful effects of his opponents' work with a narrative-autobiographical argument (1:10–24). By reading his story, the Galatians can judge the origin and quality of his gospel for themselves. He did not receive his gospel from human beings but only through the miraculous revelation and call from God.[40] He thus did not depend on an early meeting with the Jerusalem authorities in order to be instructed by them. God himself called Paul to be apostle to the Gentiles; both the divine origin of the Pauline gospel and the apostle's independence disprove the charge that he was acting on his own authority. The Jewish Christians in Judea already confirmed this, for they praised God for the divine intervention that had transformed the persecutor into a proclaimer of the gospel (1:22–24).

Paul then adds a historical-apologetic argument (2:1–14), likewise intended to demonstrate the independence of the Pauline gospel.[41] Paul's Gentile mission without the requirement of circumcision was explicitly acknowledged by the Jerusalem "pillars" at the apostolic council, where only the "false brethren" unsuccessfully attempted to suppress the freedom of the gospel (2:4). At the Antioch incident, Paul opposed the perversion of the truth of the gospel represented by Peter's hypocritical conduct, and he once again documented by his own conduct the independence and truth of his proclamation. This brings us to the theological heart of the Galatian letter; Paul wrestles with the question of what significance the law/Torah can have for Christians now that circumstances have changed, and with how the status of justification and sonship to God are attained.

11.3 The Doctrine of the Law and of Justification in Galatians

The first clear literary documentation for the fundamental Pauline doctrine of justification is found in Gal. 2:16. In 2:15 Paul recapitulates the traditional Jewish and/or Jewish Christian standpoint in order to lead from the negative

---

39. For analysis, see Alkier, *Wunder und Wirklichkeit*, 125–31.

40. On Gal. 1:15, see above, section 4.1 ("The Reports about the Damascus Event").

41. See above, chapter 6 ("The Apostolic Council and the Incident at Antioch: The Problems Remain Unresolved").

evaluation of Gentiles to the primary affirmation in 2:16—the ἡμεῖς (we) of 2:15 is taken up by the καὶ ἡμεῖς (and we) of 2:16b.

The Basic Idea

The hamartiological distinction between Jews and Gentiles is regarded as abolished,[42] since, in the light of justification in Christ, the nonsinful status of those who were previously Jews in contrast to those who were previously Gentiles no longer exists. What does exist is this: "yet we know that a person is justified not by the works of the law but through faith in Jesus Christ. And we have come to believe in Christ Jesus, so that we might be justified by faith in Christ, and not by doing the works of the law, because no one will be justified by the works of the law" (2:16). Here Paul possibly adopts elements from Ps. 142:2 LXX (Ps. 143:2), which states, οὐ δικαιωθήσεται ἐνώπιόν σου πᾶς ζῶν (no one living is righteous before you).[43] Granted, in Galatians the words ἐνώπιόν σου (before you) are missing, and Paul writes οὐ πᾶσα σάρξ (lit. not all flesh; NRSV, "no one") for the psalm's οὐ πᾶς ζῶν (no one living). The most significant difference between Paul's statement and the psalm text, however, consists in his addition of ἐξ ἔργων νόμου (by the works of the law). In Gal. 2:16 Paul takes a decisive step beyond the agreement made at the apostolic council and the disputed issue at the Antioch incident. Whereas there he still acknowledged the coexistence of faith in Christ and loyalty to the Torah for Jewish Christians, he now maintains that no one can be justified before God by works of the law/Torah.[44] This abolishes the privileged status of the Jews

---

42. Cf. Wechsler, *Geschichtsbild und Apostelstreit*, 383. In Gal. 2:15 ἁμαρτωλοί is not a noun of action: "The Gentile is [a sinner] both by his nature as a non-Jew and by the fact that his life is not oriented to the Torah as its norm" (Karl Heinrich Rengstorf, "ἁμαρτωλός," *TWNT* 1:329). [Translator's note: The translation of *TWNT* in *TDNT* does not convey the author's nuance reflected here in the text.]

43. Cf. Hübner, *Biblische Theologie*, 2:64–68. Contra the far-reading conclusions drawn by Hübner, it must still be emphasized with Mussner, *Galaterbrief*, 174–75, that in Gal. 2:16c we do *not* have a real quotation but only a "contextual reference."

44. The Pauline understanding of the law raises not only problems with regard to its content but linguistic issues as well. Paul's writings manifest an oscillating use of terminology; he never defines the content, scope, or precise meaning of (ὁ) νόμος. Paul can relate νόμος to Moses (cf. 1 Cor. 9:8–9; Gal. 3:17; Rom. 5:13–14), sharply distinguish it from the prophets (Rom. 3:21), and then in other passages designate texts from the prophets (1 Cor. 14:21), Psalms (Rom. 3:10–14), or Genesis (Gen. 4:17–18) all as words of the law (cf. Walter Gutbrod, "νόμος," *TDNT* 4:1069–71; Räisänen, *Paul and the Law*, 16–18; Hans Hübner, "νόμος," *EDNT* 2:475–77). Paul unquestionably stands in the tradition of the Septuagint, which translates תורה with νόμος about two hundred times (cf. Räisänen, *Paul and the Law*, 16, "The different occurrences can be compared to concentric circles: the radii can be different, but the Sinaitic centre remains the same"), and so in his writings νόμος is usually to be translated as "law" and refers to the Sinai tradition. Cf. Hübner, "νόμος," 2:477; Thomas R. Schreiner, *The Law and Its Fulfillment: A Pauline Theology of Law* (Grand Rapids: Baker, 1993), 33–34; Dunn, *Theology of Paul*, 131–33. The German word *Gesetz* [like the English word

as God's elect people, and now nothing in addition to faith in Jesus Christ makes it possible to be justified before God. Jewish Christians and Gentile Christians thus find themselves in the same hamartiological and soteriological situation.[45]

The virulent distinction between Jewish Christians and Gentile Christians made in Gal. 2:1–15 on the basis of salvation history is simultaneously restricted in 2:16 by both individualizing (ἄνθρωπος [a person]) and universalizing (οὐ πᾶσα σάρξ) qualifications,[46] and Paul moves the argument to a new level. Soteriology, nomology, and hamartiology are brought together in one coordinated system, the basis of which is Christology and which is stated in terms of anthropology. The question whether circumcision is an indispensable element in Christian self-definition is broadened out by Paul's restatement of the issue: which powers endanger Christian identity and existence, and which powers provide their basis? Paul states the question of Christian existence in terms of its source (ἐκ ["from," "out of," "by"] is found twenty times in 2:16–3:24). This question of origin is what determines the structure and orientation of human life. A life that can stand justified before God cannot result from works of the law. "By faith in Christ" (ἐκ πίστεως Χριστοῦ) and "by the works of the law" (ἐξ ἔργων νόμου) are diametrically opposed.

"law"] and associated expressions such as "freedom from the law" or "apart from the law," however, only partly overlap the Pauline standpoint. No one in the ancient world could think of the ordered world and its philosophy or religion apart from "law" or "laws" (see below, section 19.3 ["The Law"]). Nor was Paul by any means "apart from law" or "free from law," for he knew himself to be subject to the "law of Christ" (Gal. 6:2), the "law of faith" (Rom. 3:27) or the "law of the Spirit" (Rom. 8:2). It is rather the case that Paul's critique was directed exclusively against the Torah and its use by other missionaries; he did this in a variety of ways on the basis of his Christ hermeneutic. Such a critique is not the same as "being critical of law" in a general sense. In order to take account of this state of affairs, I speak of Torah when (ὁ) νόμος appears to mean the revelation on Sinai and its associated complex of traditions. When Paul makes statements about (ὁ) νόμος that include the Torah but at the same time go beyond its *foundational* character, "law/Torah" will be used. When by the word (ὁ) νόμος Paul means a law/rule/principle/norm *with no reference to the Torah*, this will be made explicit. I will continue to use expressions that include the word "law" (such as "understanding of the law") where the meaning is clear from the context. Although such distinctions still do not entirely obviate overlappings and ambiguities, they appear to me necessary from the subject matter.

45. This new level of argument speaks against the assumption that Gal. 2:16 derives from Antiochene theology and was handed on to Paul (as understood by Becker et al., *Briefe*, 96; Michael Theobald, "Der Kanon von der Rechtfertigung," in *Worum geht es in der Rechtfertigungslehre? Das biblische Fundament der "Gemeinsamen Erklärung" von katholischer Kirche und Lutherischem Weltbund* (ed. Thomas Söding and Frank-Lothar Hossfeld; QD 180; Freiburg: Herder, 1999), 131–38. Christoph Burchard, "Nicht aus Werken des Gesetzes gerecht, sondern aus Glaube an Jesus Christus—seit wann?" in Christoph Burchard, *Studien zur Theologie, Sprache, und Umwelt des Neuen Testaments* (Dieter Sänger; WUNT 107; Tübingen: Mohr Siebeck, 1998), 233–34, thinks Paul adopted the basic statement found in Gal. 2:16 from the Jerusalem "Hellenists."

46. Cf. Jens Schröter, "Die Universalisierung des Gesetzes im Galaterbrief," in *Das Verständnis des Gesetzes bei Juden, Christen, und im Islam* (ed. Udo Kern and Karl-Erich Grözinger; RTS 5; Münster: LIT, 2000), 37.

A Key Concept

The expression ἔργα νόμου (works of the law) plays a key role in Pauline argumentation (cf. Gal. 2:16; 3:2, 5, 10; Rom. 3:20, 28; in addition, cf. Phil. 3:9).[47] What does Paul mean by ἔργα νόμου, and what theological conception does he associate with it? Six interpretations may be distinguished in the current discussion: (1) R. Bultmann sees in the "works of the law" a misguided zeal for the law and understands Paul to have rejected such works "because *man's effort to achieve his salvation by keeping the Law only leads him into sin, indeed this effort itself in the end is already sin.*"[48] Thus, for Bultmann, Paul considers not merely the result of failing to keep the law to be sin but the intention to be righteous before God by keeping the law to be already sinful. (2) In contrast, U. Wilckens emphasizes that "it is by no means the case that he [Paul] condemns as such the human striving to fulfill the law and show that one is righteous before God; even less, then, would he dispute the righteousness of one who had really attained it on the basis of works. But Paul judges all human beings to be sinners, because all have in fact sinned."[49] (3) Differently than Wilckens, E. P. Sanders formulates his position in contrast to Bultmann: "It is not Paul's analysis of the nature of sin which determines his view, but his analysis of the way to salvation; not his anthropology, but his Christology and soteriology. Paul's own reason for maintaining that 'man shall not, must not, be "rightwised" by works of the Law' is not that man must not think of procuring his own salvation, but that if the law could save, Christ died for nothing (Gal. 2:21). . . . The conviction that only belonging to Christ brings salvation precedes the analysis of one's position before God and the change of one's self-understanding."[50] For J. D. G. Dunn, ἔργα νόμου are not the prescriptions of the Torah, the keeping of which earns one credit in God's eyes, but Jewish "identity markers" such as circumcision, the food laws, and the Sabbath, which distinguish Jews from Gentiles.[51] Paul evaluates these identity markers negatively only when they are

---

47. In addition to the works of J. D. G. Dunn and M. Bachmann mentioned in the bibliography, cf. esp. Ernst Lohmeyer, "Gesetzeswerk," in *Probleme paulinischer Theologie* (Stuttgart: Kohlhammer, 1955), 31–74; Josef Blank, "Warum sagt Paulus: 'Aus Werken des Gesetzes wird niemand gerecht'?" in *Evangelisch-katholischer Kommentar zum Neuen Testament: Vorarbeiten* (ed. Josef Blank et al.; 4 vols.; Neukirchen-Vluyn: Neukirchener Verlag, 1969–1972), 1:79–95; Wilckens, "Werken des Gesetzes," 77–109; Hans Hübner, "Was heißt bei Paulus 'Werke des Gesetzes'?" in *Biblische Theologie als Hermeneutik: Gesammelte Aufsätze: Hans Hübner zum 65. Geburtstag* (ed. Antje Labahn and Michael Labahn; Göttingen: Vandenhoeck & Ruprecht, 1995), 166–74; Thomas R. Schreiner, "'Works of Law' in Paul," *NovT* 33 (1991): 217–44; R. K. Rapa, *The Meaning of "Works of the Law" in Galatians and Romans* (SBL 31; New York: P. Lang, 2001).

48. Bultmann, *Theology of the New Testament,* 1:264.

49. Wilckens, "Werken des Gesetzes," 107.

50. E. P. Sanders, *Paul and Palestinian Judaism: A Comparison of Patterns of Religion* (Philadelphia: Fortress, 1977), 481–82.

51. In addition to the works listed in the Bibliography (esp. James D. G. Dunn, "The New Perspective on Paul," in *Jesus, Paul, and the Law: Studies in Mark and Galatians* (Louisville: Westminster

claimed as the basis for Jewish prerogatives and restrict the grace of God. "In sum, then, the 'works' which Paul consistently warns against were, in his view, Israel's misunderstanding of what her covenant law required."[52] Paul does not oppose the law as such, does not disparage works of the law, but votes against the law as a marker of national identification, directing his critique against an understanding of the Torah oriented to special privileges for those who observe it. Paul's doctrine of justification thus is not primarily concerned with the relation of the individual to God but is a matter of assuring the rights of Gentile Christians. (5) F. Watson proposes to confine the understanding of ἔργα νόμου to the purely sociological plane: "Faith in Christ is incompatible with works of the law because the church is separate from the synagogue."[53] (6) By appealing explicitly to 4QMMT, M. Bachmann supposes that ἔργα νόμου "refers to the prescriptions and regulations of the law, not to conduct that accords with these regulations."[54] Works of the law may not be simply identified with sin, for "works of the law are involved directly with the νόμος, which according to Rom. 7:12 is holy, and thus they have to do with God himself."[55]

The critique of Bultmann's view prevalent throughout the recent discussion is correct in that for Paul the possibility of attaining life by keeping the Torah is not merely a rhetorical concession. The Scripture explicitly affirms this way (cf. Lev. 18:5 in Gal. 3:12b; also Rom. 2:13; 10:5). Paul relegates neither the Torah itself nor fulfilling the commands of the Torah to the realm of sin, but the fact is that from the perspective of the curse of the law against those who fail to keep it, the ἔργα νόμου always bring one into the realm of sin because no one really lives by what is written in the Torah (Gal. 3:10b). The uniformly negative use of this phrase by Paul makes clear that the ἔργα νόμου are the results of the regulations of the Torah, regulations intended actually to be done, but the doing of them is always already conditioned by sin.[56] The realm of

---

John Knox, 1990), cf., most recently, James D. G. Dunn, "Yet once more—'the Works of Law': A Response," *JSNT* 46 (1992): 99–117; *A Commentary on the Epistle to the Galatians* (BNTC; London: A. & C. Black, 1993), 131–50.

52. Dunn, *Theology of Paul*, 366. On p. 358 he argues unequivocally, "To sum up thus far, the phrase 'the works of the law,' does, of course, refer to all or whatever the law requires, covenantal nomism as a whole. But in a context where the relationship of Israel with other nations is at issue, certain laws would naturally come more into focus than others. We have instanced circumcision and food laws in particular." But precisely this distinction is not found in Paul.

53. Watson, *Paul, Judaism, and the Gentiles*, 47.

54. Michael Bachmann, "Rechtfertigung und Gesetzeswerke bei Paulus," *TZ* 49 (1993): 30.

55. Ibid., 32.

56. The exact expression ἔργα νόμου is not found in Greek literature prior to and contemporaneous with Paul. There could be a linguistic parallel, also partially corresponding to the content of the phrase, in 4QMMT[a] C 27 (4Q398 frg. 14, col. 2), where it is stated in a letter about questions of the law, "We too have written you some prescriptions of the Torah, which we deem to be good for you and your people" (Kuhn, "Bedeutung der Qumrantexte," 209). Johann Maier and Kurt Schubert, eds., *Die Qumran-Essener: Texte der Schriftrollen und Lebensbild der Gemeinde* (Munich: Reinhardt, 1973), 375, translate, "We too have written you several Torah practices that we find good for you and your

human deeds is constitutive for Paul's argument (cf. the use of ποιέω [do], in 3:10–12), for it is only this realm that make's possible sin's assault. The "works of law" cannot lead to righteousness because the power of sin thwarts the Torah's promise of life. In contrast to the πνεῦμα, the Torah does not have the power to withstand the hostile intrusion of sin (cf. 5:18). Regarding its promise of life, the Torah falls short of its own promises; the power of sin reveals the weakness of the Torah.[57] Paul virtually makes the *insufficiency of the Torah* his point of departure. This is why the ἔργα cannot be separated from the Torah itself, as though Paul only intended to criticize a certain style of Torah observance,[58] a style "that does not mean living in accord with the Torah but simply makes the halakot its point of orientation."[59] Paul is not concerned with individual commands (of the Torah) but with the whole orientation of human life, as indicated by the prepositions ἐκ (out of, by, from) and διά (through, by means of),[60] the immediate context of 2:16, and the thrust of the letter's argument as a whole.[61] The identity concept Paul here criticizes understands one's relation to God to be, "out of" one's own act, bound up with certain privileges, whereas he casts his own vote for a concept in which one's relation to God is mediated "through" faith in Jesus Christ and/or granted by God. For Paul, there can no longer be a coexistence of faith in Christ with fulfilling the requirements of the

---

people"; E. Qimron and John Strugnell, *Qumran Cave 4. V* (DJD 10; Oxford: Oxford University Press, 1994), 62, 64, translate, "some of the precepts of the Torah." According to H.-W. Kuhn, "Qumran und Paulus: Unter traditionsgeschichtlichem Aspekt ausgewählte Parallelen," in *Das Urchristentum in seiner literarischen Geschichte: Festschrift für Jürgen Becker zum 65. Geburtstag* (ed. Ulrich Mell and Ulrich B. Müller; BZNW 100; Berlin: de Gruyter, 1999), 232, the expression מעשי התורה means "'some works of the law,' in the sense of 'some works that are to be done according to the law.'" These "prescriptions of the Torah" are not simply identical with the Pauline concept oriented to the results of one's actions, for in Paul the sense is determined by the preposition ἐκ, so that 4QMMT[a] C 27 is not really a parallel; cf. Vouga, *Galater*, 58. Nor can 4Q174Flor. be considered a parallel, for there the text is to be read "works of praise," not "works of law" (cf. Kuhn, "Bedeutung der Qumrantexte," 207). Especially instructive are 4QFlor 1 + 3 2.2; 1QS 5:21; 6:18; CD 20:6; cf. also *2 Bar.* 48:38; 57:2.

57. Differently, e.g., Helmut Merklein, "'Nicht aus Werken des Gesetzes . . .': Eine Auslegung von Gal. 2,15–21," in *Studien zu Jesus und Paulus* (2 vols.; WUNT 43, 105; Tübingen: Mohr Siebeck, 1987), 2:308, who argues it is the fault of human beings that no one is justified by "works of the law."

58. So Burchard, "Nicht aus Werken des Gesetzes," 236.

59. So Michael Bachmann, "4QMMT und Galaterbrief, מעשי התורה und ΕΡΓΑ ΝΟΜΟΥ," *ZNW* 89 (1998): 110. He thus infers, "If Paul's polemic against 'works of law' was concerned with an orientation to (specific) halakot, then it is easier to understand—as compared with the usual interpretation—that both the Torah as a whole and its unmitigated claim are evaluated in a thoroughly positive sense (one need only note Rom. 3:31 and Gal. 5:14)." Against this is to be emphasized that for Paul it is not a matter of just any halakah but of circumcision, so that he could hardly go on to evaluate "the demand of the Torah as a whole" in a positive sense. Moreover, Galatians as a whole excludes such an interpretation; one need only note Gal. 5:18.

60. Cf. Vouga, *Galater*, 58.

61. This is all the more true if Paul takes up ἔργα νόμου as a key concept of his opponents and gives it a completely new interpretation; cf. Heinrich Hoffmann, *Das Gesetz in der frühjüdischen Apokalyptik* (SUNT 23; Göttingen: Vandenhoeck & Ruprecht, 1999), 344–45.

law because the law/Torah no longer has any constitutive significance for one's relation to God. Δικαιοσύνη can therefore not be attained through the law/Torah; otherwise Christ would have died for nothing (2:21). Paul thus annuls the special status of the Jews as righteous, having a righteousness mediated by the Torah.[62] Gentiles are not per se sinners, and Jews do not have the status as righteous by virtue of their birth. On the contrary, in the new paradigm Paul places Jews and Gentiles in the same category, namely, that of sinners, a state they can quit only through faith in Jesus Christ.

Two Anthropological Approaches

In addition to the above considerations, we may now note that for Paul different approaches to understanding the nature of human existence are associated respectively with faith in Jesus Christ and life oriented to the law/Torah. The way of salvation aligned with the law/Torah assigns human beings an active role in their relation to God: their lives are always on the way to meeting the God who is their judge, and human deeds appear as an essentially positive element in their relation to God. Doubtless there existed in ancient Judaism the fundamental conviction that human beings as sinners are dependent on the mercy, goodness, and love of God (cf., e.g., 1QS 10:9–12; *4 Ezra* 8:32, 36). The concept of the covenant as a central way of expressing Israel's relation to God presupposes their prior election by God.[63] Nonetheless, the issue of salvation remained bound to human activity, to the extent that God was expected to be the righteous judge who would be merciful to the righteous and punish lawbreakers.[64] God's righteousness is revealed in his righteous judgments (cf., e.g., *Pss. Sol.* 14; *4 Ezra* 7:70–74, 105). Again, this just judgment manifests itself as mercy to those who are righteous and as condemnation of the godless, with Torah observance the material criterion for God's future act of judgment. Thus human deeds do not define one's relation to God in an exclusive sense, but they do have a fundamental importance both positively and negatively. Thus, in texts such as Rom. 2; Matt. 6:1–6, 16–18, the contradiction presupposed between orthodoxy and orthopraxy is tendentiously set forth.

---

62. Cf. Mikael Winninge, *Sinners and the Righteous: A Comparative Study of the Psalms of Solomon and Paul's Letters* (ConBNT 26; Stockholm: Almqvist & Wiksell International, 1995), 185ff.

63. Sanders, *Paul and Palestinian Judaism*, 33–428, interprets (one-sidedly) almost the whole of ancient Judaism's literature in terms of the covenant concept.

64. Cf. Friedrich Avemarie, *Tora und Leben: Untersuchungen zur Heilsbedeutung der Tora in der frühen rabbinischen Literatur* (TSAJ 55; Tübingen: Mohr Siebeck, 1996), 578: "The principle of retribution remains intact. Nowhere is it doubted that keeping the commandments is rewarded and breaking them is punished; still, it is repeatedly emphasized that true obedience is not a matter of looking for rewards but is practiced because it is God's will or for the sake of the command itself—and this even where acting for the sake of reward is explicitly approved."

In the light of God's revelation in Christ, Paul evaluates the human situation in a fundamentally different way than his Jewish (and Gentile) contemporaries. Human beings apart from faith always find themselves in the situation of enslavement; they are ὑπὸ νόμον (under the law/Torah, Gal. 3:23), ὑπὸ παιδαγωγόν (under the disciplinarian; NRSV, "subject to a disciplinarian," 3:25),[65] ὑπὸ ἐπιτρόπους . . . καὶ οἰκονόμους (under guardians and trustees, 4:2), and ὑπὸ τὰ στοιχεῖα τοῦ κόσμου (under the elemental spirits of the world, 4:3). This basic anthropological insight from the perspective of faith excludes any fundamental significance of human acts in establishing one's relation to God. On their own, human beings are not at all in the situation to establish a positive relation with God. The power of sin also dominates the law/Torah, qualifying and perverting it. If Paul proceeds, on the basis of this interpretation, from the human experience of being frustrated and defeated by the law/Torah, then we see the real basis for his statement in 3:22: συνέκλεισεν ἡ γραφὴ τὰ πάντα ὑπὸ ἁμαρτίαν (the scripture has imprisoned all things under the power of sin). The power of sin is such that it ultimately causes the law/Torah to lose its quality as the place where life[66] and righteousness are found.[67] The lostness of humanity that results from this is only revealed in the light of the Christ event. *The Pauline doctrine of the law and sin is not based on anthropology but on Christology and soteriology.*[68] If righteousness came through the law/Torah, then Christ would have died for nothing (2:21; cf. 3:21b). But since God has acted in Jesus Christ to establish salvation for those who believe, righteousness cannot come from the law/Torah.

In 2:17–18 Paul addresses a possible objection. If even Jews and Jewish Christians are found to be sinners, does not faith in Christ actually foster the power of sin? Does Christ himself become a servant of sin by exposing its real power and thus at the same time the insufficiency of the law/Torah? Paul emphatically rejects this implication; this would be the case only if the law/Torah still possessed soteriological quality. Only then would the one who believes in Christ but does not follow the law/Torah turn out to be a transgressor. But Paul has torn down the fence of the law/Torah and will not—like Peter in Antioch—rebuild it.

Participation in the Power of the Spirit

In Gal. 2:19 the apostle moves the argument and language to a new level: the actual effect of the law/Torah—its failure to provide salvation—serves to

---

65. Cf. Diogenes, *Epistle 29*, 1–2 (in Malherbe, *Cynic Epistles*).
66. On the idea of the Torah as source of life, cf., e.g., Ezek. 20:11, 13, 21; Deut. 4:1; 8:1, 3; 30:15–20; Ps. 119:116; Neh. 9:29; Sir. 17:11; Wis. 6:18; Bar. 3:9; 4:1; *4 Ezra* 7:21; 14:30; CD 3:15–16.
67. Hübner, *Law in Paul's Thought*, 27–29.
68. Cf. Sanders, *Paul and Palestinian Judaism*, 481–82.

take away its power, for the law/Torah played a role in the death of Jesus in that it brings out the meaning of his death (3:13; 4:5). The law/Torah thereby brought about its own end, and so it can no longer exercise power over Christ and those who have died with him in baptism. The saving knowledge mediated by this event is found in the affirmation Χριστῷ συνεσταύρωμαι (I have been crucified with Christ), which results in living for God. By being admitted through baptism into the sphere where the life of the resurrected one prevails (cf. Rom. 6:6, 8),[69] Paul prepares for the ideas that follow. The language is now no longer the legal language of the courtroom but the experiential language of participation. The communion between Christ and those who have been baptized is so close that they not only participate in his death; the risen Christ himself lives in them, directs and fulfills their lives (Gal. 2:20). The human ego is freed from being curved in on itself (Luther) and is incorporated in the encompassing reality of Jesus Christ. This is made possible by the cross of Christ, which is also the paradigm of the process of transformation in which those who are baptized participate: the cross as the place of God-forsakenness thus becomes the source of life.[70] These mystical formulations do not have as their goal the abolition of the believer's subjectivity, nor is the believer's subjectivity replaced by the Spirit; rather, the Spirit leads the believing subject to his or her true self. This is indicated by the expression ζῇ δὲ ἐν ἐμοὶ Χριστός (Christ lives in me), which names Christ as the source of new life but at the same time, through the words ἐν ἐμοί (in me), holds on to personal identity and individuality. As people who have been baptized, the Galatians have died to the law/Torah; as people who have been justified, they now live for God, and indeed Christ lives within them, so that any return to the law is an impossible choice. The place of life and righteousness is no longer the law/Torah but Jesus Christ. The Galatians cannot belong to Christ and at the same time trust in the flesh by having themselves circumcised (cf. 5:13).[71] Precisely by holding before the Galatians' eyes what had happened to them in baptism, in which alone their justification can consist, Paul makes clear to them how inconsistently they are acting. Galatians 2:21 clearly shows once again the standpoint from which he poses the issues and structures his own theology. The death and resurrection of Jesus Christ alone constitute the saving event; *Paul's Christ hermeneutic necessarily presupposes that the law/Torah as a soteriological principle has been annulled,* for otherwise Christ would have died for nothing. The fundamental change of status has already transpired in baptism; it is here that the Galatians are delivered

---

69. Among those who argue for a baptismal reference in Gal. 2:19–20 are Mussner, *Galaterbrief,* 180; Schnelle, *Gerechtigkeit und Christusgegenwart,* 54–56; Hans Halter, *Taufe und Ethos: Paulinische Kriterien für das Proprium christliches Moral* (Freiburg: Herder, 1977), 102ff.; Thomas Söding, "Kreuzestheologie und Rechtfertigungslehre," *Cath (M)* 46 (1992): 170; Strecker, *Die liminale Theologie des Paulus,* 254.

70. Samuel Vollenweider, "Großer Tod und Großes Leben," *EvT* 51 (1991): 373.

71. Schweitzer, *Mysticism,* 194, 198, 303.

from the power of sin and incorporated into the realm of Christ by the gift of the Spirit (cf. 3:26–28). They do not need circumcision as a supplement in order to be full members of the eschatological people of God.

Galatians 3:1–5 makes this connection explicit: the Galatians received the Spirit through preaching responded to in faith, not from works of the law. Paul appeals to this experience in order to hold before the eyes of the Galatians the foolishness (ἀνόητοι, 3:1, 3) of their conduct. Through the Spirit they are "sons of God" and thus legitimate heirs (4:6–7; 3:26); through the Spirit they eagerly await the hope of righteousness (5:5), and because they live in the Spirit, the Spirit guides their way of life (5:25) and they produce the fruit of the Spirit (5:22), so that it is ultimately true that εἰ δὲ πνεύματι ἄγεσθε, οὐκ ἐστὲ ὑπὸ νόμον (if you are led by the Spirit, you are not subject to the law, 5:18). The Galatians are πνευματικοί (those who have received the Spirit, 6:1) and as such no longer slaves to the flesh (6:8); they are a καινὴ κτίσις (new creation) in which neither circumcision nor uncircumcision is important (6:15). Christ is formed in them (4:19), they have put on Christ (3:27), and in Christ all ethnic, religious, and social distinctions are abolished (3:28). All this means a call to freedom, freedom that is expressed in love (5:13), freedom from every bondage (5:1). Adopting the practice of circumcision and the observance of a cultic calendar would, as *pars pro toto legis* (a part of the law stands for the whole), would rescind all this. They would move from freedom back into bondage; from living in the Spirit, they would once again live according to the flesh. Thus circumcision and observance of the cultic calendar are foolish in a double sense: (1) These practices by no means correspond to what the Galatians already in fact are, πνευματικοί, people who have received the Spirit. (2) Such practices nullify the life the Galatians are already living, characterized by freedom and the gift of the Spirit. The Galatians need no change of status because they are already in the status of those who have been justified. All Paul's expressions in Galatians about the law/Torah and righteousness by faith are to be seen against the background of the Galatians' Christian existence, already grounded in baptism and determined by the Spirit of freedom (on the connection between baptism and Spirit, one need only compare 2:19–20 with 3:2–5, and 3:26–28 with 4:6–7). It is a matter of living in accord with this new reality or failing to do so, and the statements about the law/Torah and righteousness are embedded in a line of argument that is above all conditioned by its particular situation. This argument is directed to showing the Galatians the foolishness of their conduct in view of the reality in which they already stand.

Abraham as Identification Figure

Whereas the Galatian Christians' experience of the Spirit forms the real horizon for the apostle's line of thought, he utilizes a multilayered approach in carrying out the details of his argument. Paul first attempts to use the figure of Abraham to show that his virtually antinomistic doctrine of justification is biblical. Abraham, to whom Paul's opponents could appeal as demonstrating the unity of circumcision and faith,[72] played a decisive role in their argument.[73] Their argument was a synthesis of elements from Scripture, against which Paul poses a series of antitheses. It is God's promise to Abraham for all peoples that brings salvation (3:6ff.), not the law of Moses only for the circumcised. Paul makes a specific application of Gen. 15:6 LXX (cf. Rom. 4:3) in that he interprets Abraham's trust in God's promises without regard to the testing of Abraham's own faith. Placing this particular accent on the Abraham story is foreign to the way it was understood in Jewish tradition, where God's election and Abraham's faithful obedience form a unit (cf., e.g., *4 Ezra* 3:13ff.; *2 Bar.* 57). Abraham was repeatedly tested by God, and because he followed the will of God, he is named faithful and righteous (cf. Sir. 44:20; 1 Macc. 2:52). In contrast, Paul restricts the gift of righteousness to Abraham's faith and thus breaks apart the Jewish unity of promise and obedience, law/Torah and works, reward and punishment. This is illustrated by the conclusion of the letter from the Teacher of Righteousness to the ruling high priest Jonathan.[74] The letter contains numerous halakot with which Jonathan is to comply regarding the Jerusalem temple. If he follows the instructions of the Teacher, then "it will be reckoned for you righteousness when you perform what is right and good before him, for your own good and for that of Israel" (4Q398 frg. 14, col. 2; Vermès, 182). In contrast, for Paul in Galatians, by his faith and the promises given to him, Abraham serves as a proleptic illustration of the Christ event and an argument for it. It is only in Christ that the promises made to Abraham are fulfilled (Gal. 3:16), and it is through faith in Jesus Christ that the church has received the saving gift of the Spirit (3:14), so that Christians are now the true heirs of the promise (3:7, 29). Paul thus postulates a universal history of salvation that began with Abraham and into which the particular history of Israel is incorporated. The temporal distance of 430 years between the promise to Abraham and the giving of the law shows the objective priority of the promise (3:17), which is fulfilled in the one true offspring (seed) of Abraham: Jesus Christ (3:16).[75]

The apostle's break with basic Jewish and/or Jewish Christian convictions is seen very clearly in the way Gal. 3:11b handles Hab. 2:4b.[76] Paul takes as his starting point that no one can be justified before God by the law/Torah (Gal. 3:11a), since this would require that one would have to do everything

---

72. It can hardly be a coincidence that Paul speaks of Abraham only in the dispute with his Judaist opponents (cf. 2 Cor. 11:22; Galatians, Romans).

73. Cf. Berger, *Theologiegeschichte*, 457.

74. On the historical background, see Stegemann, *Library of Qumran*, 104–7.

75. Paul here argues on the basis of the Hellenistic distinction between written and unwritten law; cf. Jones, *"Freiheit,"* 92ff.

76. For analysis, see Kuhn, "Bedeutung der Qumrantexte," 177–78.

prescribed in the book of the Torah (3:10). Since no one, however, is able to keep the Torah completely, he or she falls under its curse (cf. Deut. 27:26 LXX, "Cursed is every one who does not continue in all the words of this law to do them").[77] But the saving status of being counted righteous before God is made available only through faith, for ὁ δίκαιος ἐκ πίστεως ζήσεται (The righteous will live from faith, Hab. 2:4b LXX). The interpretation of this prophetic text in Qumran allows us to determine the precise scope of the Pauline line of argument. A contemporary Jewish interpretation of Hab. 2.4b is found in 1QpHab 7:17–8:3: "'But the righteous shall live by his faith.' Interpreted, this concerns all those who observe the Law in the house of Judah, whom God will deliver from the House of Judgment because of their suffering and because of their faith in the Teacher of Righteousness" (Vermès, 344). In contrast to the pious of Qumran, for whom faith and the observance of the Torah are an organic unity, Paul sharply distinguishes between them. Whereas only the doers of the law attain to salvation according to the understanding at Qumran and within Judaism in general, salvation for Paul is something that transcends Torah observance and is entirely a matter of faith. "There can be no doubt that the Pharisee Paul, with his interpretation of this prophetic text so important for his theology, has taken a step beyond Judaism and that he has done so by recourse to the Bible they held in common.[78]

The Function of the Torah

In Gal. 3:19 the apostle first deals with the question that has been pressing for a response and can no longer be avoided: what, then, is the function of the Torah? Paul the Pharisee lived by the fundamental Jewish conviction that the Torah had been given by God (cf., e.g., Sir. 45:5). He does not here advocate this clear position, however, but in an argument that is tortuous and complex both linguistically and intellectually, he claims that the Torah had only been given as a supplement "because of transgressions."[79] Here the Torah is not credited with having any positive revelatory function; it belongs

---

77. On the Pauline modifications to the text he cites, cf. Koch, *Schrift als Zeuge*, 163–65. On Gal. 3:13, cf. esp. 4QpNah 1:6–8; 11QT[a] 64:6ff.; on the interpretation of these texts, cf. Kuhn, "Bedeutung der Qumrantexte," 178–82.

78. H.-W. Kuhn, "Die drei wichtigsten Qumranparallelen zum Galaterbrief," in *Konsequente Traditionsgeschichte: Festschrift für Klaus Baltzer zum 65. Geburtstag* (ed. Rüdiger Bartelmus et al.; OBO 126; Göttingen: Vandenhoeck & Ruprecht, 1993), 249; cf. also Gert Jeremias, *Der Lehrer der Gerechtigkeit* (SUNT 2; Göttingen: Vandenhoeck & Ruprecht, 1963), 142–46, who points out that that in 1QpHab 8:2–3 the Teacher of Righteousness is an authority comparable to Jesus, for only here do we find אמנה with the preposition ב (πίστις ἐν) with reference to a person.

79. An analogous argument is found in Seneca, *Ep.* 90.5–14: after the end of the Golden Age, laws had to be introduced as a check on the degenerating culture.

to the sphere of transgressions, revealing them and even provoking them.[80] It was only ordained by angels[81] (Gal. 3:19b)[82] and delivered to human beings by the mediator Moses[83] (3:20). Paul evidently wants to keep God out of the event of giving the law,[84] for this is the only way the distinction in 3:20 can be understood, according to which Moses represents more than one party (the angels), not God. The angels are understood as demonic powers (cf. 1:8) who institute the Torah, in order to demonstrate its inferiority and to explain how its originally good intention was perverted.[85]

80. Χάριν (in order to; NRSV, "because of," Gal. 3:19) is probably to be translated as indicating purpose. Cf. Hübner, *Law in Paul's Thought*, 27, 36; Sanders, *Paul*, 92.

81. Διά with the genitive can designate the one who causes something or through whom something comes into being (cf. Gal. 1:1); evidence and examples are given in Albrecht Oepke, "διά," *TDNT* 2:65–67. Of course, neither the angels nor the Torah are explicitly called inferior, but this is exactly what results from Paul's line of argument; contra Eckhard J. Schnabel, *Law and Wisdom from Ben Sira to Paul: A Tradition Historical Enquiry into the Relation of Law, Wisdom, and Ethics* (WUNT 2/16; Tübingen: Mohr Siebeck, 1985), 272. A comparison with Philo reveals the offensive character of Paul's argument. Angels appear in Philo, *Giants* 6ff., as beings who were originally νοῦς (mind) but who lost their purity by their fall into zones near the earth or to the earth itself; in contrast to these, the divine Spirit continued to rest on the one who was the wise man par excellence, namely, Moses (*Giants* 55). Philo subordinates the revelatory function of the angels to that of Moses and believes that there are good and bad angels (*Giants* 16–17). Paul, however, subordinates Moses to the angels. Helmut Burkhardt, *Die Inspiration heiliger Schriften bei Philo von Alexandrien* (Giessen: Brunnen, 1988), has demonstrated the outstanding position of Moses within Philo's understanding of revelation and Scripture. He shows that in Philo's understanding the personality of the human author Moses was by no means switched off "but—in contrast—his work expresses his person in manifold ways" (p. 211). In Philo, Moses appears as a forerunner of what was later called personal inspiration.

82. Cf. Deut. 33:2 LXX; Josephus, *Ant.* 15.136; *Jub.* 1:29; *T. Dan* 6:2; and elsewhere. Rabbinic evidence is given by Strack and Billerbeck, *Kommentar*, 3:554ff. Martyn, *Galatians*, 354–56, points out that διατάσσω is never connected with νόμος in the Septuagint. Paul thus also shows semantically that he places the origin of the law in a special category while in fact taking the tradition that the Torah was given by angels, originally meant in a positive sense, and presenting it *negatively*.

83. Cf. esp. Lev. 26:46 LXX; and Albrecht Oepke, "μεσίτης," *TDNT* 4:603–24.

84. In Gal. 3:19 Paul de facto disputes the direct divine origin of the Torah, for only under this presupposition does the distinction in 3:20 make sense; cf. Schweitzer, *Mysticism*, 70, 209; Oepke, *Galater*, 116; Hans Lietzmann, *An die Galater* (4th ed.; HNT 10; Tübingen: Mohr Siebeck, 1971), 21–22; Luz, *Geschichtsverständnis*, 190; Hübner, *Law in Paul's Thought*, 26–28, 36; John William Drane, *Paul, Libertine or Legalist? A Study in the Theology of the Major Pauline Epistles* (London: SPCK, 1975), 34; Schulz, *Neutestamentliche Ethik*, 344; Rohde, *Galater*, 155–56; Räisänen, *Paul and the Law*, 130–31; E. P. Sanders, *Paul, the Law, and the Jewish People* (Philadelphia: Fortress, 1983), 68; Becker et al., *Briefe*, 54; Kari Kuula, *The Law, the Covenant, and God's Plan* (Göttingen: Vandenhoeck & Ruprecht, 1999), 104–7; Vouga, *Galater*, 83; Martyn, *Galatians*, 357. Among advocates of the opposing position are Schnabel, *Law and Wisdom*, 271ff.; Stuhlmacher, *Biblische Theologie*, 1:265; Eckstein, *Verheissung und Gesetz*, 200–202; and Dunn, *Theology of Paul*, 139–40, who consistently appeal to the positive tradition about angels in ancient Judaism so that they can see the text here as affirming the unqualified divine origin of the Torah. Galatians 3:21; Rom. 7:22; 8:7; 9:4 do show that Paul cannot continue to make this argument consistently and that he does not want to do so. These texts, however, cannot be permitted to determine the interpretation of Gal. 3:19–20.

85. Cf. the threefold distinction in Hübner, *Law in Paul's Thought*, 30–31 (God's intention, the immanent intention of the law, the intention of the lawgiver).

Also the means by which it was made known shows the secondary status of the Torah over against the promise. God gave the promise directly to Abraham (3:18), but the Torah was only mediated through angels.[86] Paul makes clear semantic distinctions:[87] Whereas God deals directly with Abraham, "speaks" with him (3:16; cf. previously 3:3, 6, 8), the Torah is "added" and "ordained" through angels (3:19). The promises were confirmed directly by God (3:17a, ὑπὸ τοῦ θεοῦ), but the Torah "came" only 430 years later (3:17b, γεγονώς). The point of the argument is clear: the promises to Abraham and his authentic descendants derive directly from God, in contrast to which the law/Torah was merely a later supplement.

Finally, a comparison with 1:8, 11ff. confirms the polemical thrust of this whole line of argument: the gospel was directly revealed to Paul without any mediators, and neither apostle nor angel may change it. In contrast, the Torah appears in 3:19–20 as clearly having only secondary significance, instituted by angels and by the hand of the human mediator, Moses. In addition to its function of provoking transgressions, the law/Torah has a second main function: it enslaves human beings. Before the revelation of Christ, the only kind of life available to human beings was one in slavery to the law and the powers. Christ alone liberated human beings from this slavery; the status of servitude (ὑπὸ ἁμαρτίαν, ὑπὸ νόμον, ὑπὸ παιδαγωγόν [under sin, under the law, under a disciplinarian]) was transformed by Christ into the status of participation (ἐν Χριστῷ). Baptized believers know that they have been delivered not only from the power of sin but from all religious, ethnic, and economic distinctions; the church is one in Christ Jesus.

Baptism as Change of Status

Paul develops these fundamental ideas in the baptismal tradition of 3:26–28.[88] It defines the new status before God of those who have been baptized; the unmediated new relationship to God effected by the Spirit and made one's own in baptism establishes the new status of believers: "for in Christ Jesus you are all children of God [υἱοὶ θεοῦ, lit. 'sons of God'] through faith"

86. By making this distinction, Paul turns away from a fundamental conviction of ancient Judaism; one need only note *Avot* 1:1–2: "Moses received Torah at Sinai and handed it on to Joshua, Joshua to elders, and elders to prophets. And prophets handed it on to the men of the great assembly. They said three things: 'Be prudent in judgment. Raise up many disciples. Make a fence for the Torah.' Simeon the Righteous was one of the last survivors of the great assembly. He would say: 'On three things does the world stand: On the Torah, and on the Temple service, and on deeds of loving kindness.'" This translation is that of Jacob Neusner, *The Midrash: A New Translation* (New Haven, Conn.: Yale University Press, 1988).

87. Cf. Martyn, *Galatians*, 364–65.

88. For analysis of the text, cf. Schnelle, *Gerechtigkeit und Christusgegenwart*, 57–62; Strecker, *Die liminale Theologie des Paulus*, 351–59.

(3:26).[89] The new being in Christ (εἶναι ἐν Χριστῷ) is constituted in baptism. Ἐν Χριστῷ Ἰησοῦ (in Christ Jesus) describes the sphere in which sonship is realized, it is a meaningful description of the relationship granted in baptism between Christ and those baptized. The imagery of 3:27 is also primarily spatial; the one who is baptized puts on Christ like a garment: "As many of you as were baptized into Christ have clothed yourselves with Christ." The clothing metaphor[90] illustrates the baptismal experience as initiation. The baptized are entirely encompassed by the reality of Christ; this is precisely what is meant by being "in Christ." Galatians 3:28 describes baptism in regard to salvation history and its social-political effects: "There is no longer Jew or Greek, there is no longer slave or free, there is no longer male and female; for all of you are one in Christ Jesus."[91] The change of status granted in baptism includes a real transformation of social relationships. The first pair of contrasts is directed against the distinctions that divide all humanity into two classes: for Jews, the Jew/Gentile distinction; and for Greeks, the Greek/barbarian[92] distinction. Although the Old Testament laws concerning slavery can be considered relatively humane[93] and, according to the Sophists, the distinction between δοῦλος and ἐλεύθερος is set by human culture instead of being a difference made by nature,[94] this contrasting pair functioned among both Jews and Greeks. The third pair of contrasts, ἄρσεν καὶ θῆλυ (male and female; cf. Gen. 1:27 LXX), likewise had fundamental significance for both Jews and Greeks because, in Jewish understanding, women were not fully capable of participation in the cult and Greek thought tended to follow the line emphasizing the superiority of men to women.[95] These new views in Galatians probably originated in those large Hellenistic cities where the Pauline mission was carried on; in any case, that is where there would be

89. The expression διὰ πίστεως is an interpretive Pauline addition; cf. Schnelle, *Gerechtigkeit und Christusgegenwart*, 58.

90. Cf. Nils A. Dahl and David Hellholm, "Garment-Metaphors: The Old and the New Human Being," in *Antiquity and Humanity: Essays on Ancient Religion and Philosophy Presented to Hans Dieter Betz on His 70th Birthday* (ed. Adela Yarbro Collins and Margaret Mary Mitchell; Tübingen: Mohr Siebeck, 2001), 139–58.

91. On the interpretation, cf. Gerhard Dautzenberg, "'Da ist nicht männlich noch weiblich': Zur Interpretation von Gal. 3,28," in Gerhard Dautzenberg, *Studien zur paulinischen Theologie und zur frühchristlichen Rezeption des Alten Testaments* (ed. Dieter Sänger; Giessen: Verlag der theologischen Fakultät, 1999), 69–99.

92. Cf. the documentation in *NW* 2/1:3–6.

93. One need only note Exod. 21:2–6, 26–27; Deut. 15:12–18; 23:16–17; Lev. 25:8ff., 39–40; Job 31:13, 15; on the whole subject, cf. Henneke Gülzow, *Christentum und Sklaverei in den ersten drei Jahrhunderten* (Hamburg: LIT, 1999), 9–21.

94. On the Greek and Hellenistic understanding of slavery, cf. the documentation in *NW* 2/1:1065–72; and Schumacher, *Sklaverei*.

95. On the status of women in the ancient world, cf. Stegemann and Stegemann, *The Jesus Movement*, 361–407.

the least resistance to setting aside older traditions.[96] The explosive force for religion, politics, and society found in these ideas is illustrated by a text that represents a deep feeling for these basic values of antiquity: "Hermippus in his *Lives* mentions something said by some of Socrates' followers. For they related that he said he was thankful to Fate for three things: 'First, that I was born human and not an animal; then that I was born male and not female; and third that I was born Greek and not barbarian'" (Diogenes Laertius 1.33). This commitment to the status quo by those who were privileged by it encountered early Christianity as a movement oriented to changing things. The new reality is expressed by "You are now one in Christ Jesus" (ὑμεῖς εἷς ἐστε ἐν Χριστῷ Ἰησοῦ). Since all (Gal. 3:26, πάντες) are "sons of God" by baptism, since all have put on Christ and are those for whom the previous alternatives are no longer valid, it is true for all (3:28, πάντες) that they are "one" in Christ Jesus; this means that as a result of the baptismal event, there is now only "one" humanity, namely, the one for whom these alternatives no longer count.

This conquest, occurring in baptism, of the ancient world's fundamental alternatives shows that for Paul εἶναι ἐν Χριστῷ always includes two dimensions: (1) A real, ontological communion is effected by the Spirit between Christ and those who have been baptized. (2) The new qualifications granted the baptized include their thinking, feeling, and acting; that is, communion with Christ always has an empirical-pragmatic dimension: one's way of life has been changed, and one's acts and activities must take new forms.[97] The ritually constituted communion with Christ not only opens a new understanding of reality but indeed creates a new reality that equally includes the cognitive, emotional, and pragmatic dimensions of human existence.

Conclusions

If the Galatians want to be subject to the law (4:21), they are lagging behind the state of salvation that they have already attained. Once more Paul wants to explain to the Galatians the foolishness of their conduct by scriptural proof, again in connection with the figure of Abraham (4:21–31).[98] The Abraham

---

96. There are comparable Cynic traditions; cf. Francis Gerald Downing, "A Cynic Preparation for Paul's Gospel for Jew and Greek, Slave and Free, Male and Female," *NTS* 42 (1996): 454–62. The Cynics saw themselves as cosmopolitan types (cf. Diogenes Laertius 6.63) who had a new understanding of slavery and freedom and who accepted the equality of women (cf. Crates, *Epistle 28* [in Malherbe, *Cynic Epistles*, 79], "Women are not by nature worse than men"; Musonius, *Diss.* 3; Diogenes Laertius 6.12).

97. Strecker, *Die liminale Theologie des Paulus*, 193–211, speaks of a vertical and a horizontal communion with Christ.

98. Gerhard Sellin, "Hagar und Sara: Religionsgeschichtliche Hintergründe der Schriftallegorese Gal. 4,21–31," in *Das Urchristentum in seiner literarischen Geschichte: Festschrift für Jürgen Becker*

theme is developed further by considering the second generation, that of the two sons. For him, the Torah itself testifies to Christian freedom from the Torah. There are two kinds of descent from Abraham: according to the flesh and according to the promise (4:23). Whereas the son born according to the flesh corresponds to the Sinai covenant, which leads to slavery and is manifest in the earthly Jerusalem, the son of the free woman is represented by the heavenly Jerusalem, the mother of Christians. The truth that applies to them is this: "Now you, my brothers and sisters, are children of the promise, like Isaac" (4:28), for the Galatian Christians are τέκνα . . . τῆς ἐλευθέρας (children . . . of the free woman). Thus everything depends on maintaining the freedom grounded in the Christ event, realized in the gift of the Spirit, and confirmed by the Scripture and on not perverting it into its opposite through Torah observance.

Accepting the practice of circumcision as *pars pro toto legis* would mean that Christ's death on the cross, under the curse of the law, was for nothing, since whoever adopts the practice of circumcision is obligated to obey "the entire law" (ὅλον τὸν νόμον, 5:3). Paul here proceeds on the basis that the law/Torah has been the ruin of every person who has attempted to keep it, because no one has ever been able to keep the whole law. A quantitative factor here shapes this understanding of the Torah (cf. 3:10); the Torah as a whole is present in every individual command, so that the failure to observe one command puts the soteriological aspect of the law/Torah out of commission.[99] Galatians 5:14 and 6:2 appear to be in tension with this negative interpretation of the law/Torah. By appealing to Lev. 19:18, Paul states in Gal. 5:14, "For the whole law [ὁ γὰρ πᾶς νόμος] is summed up in a single commandment, 'You shall love your neighbor as yourself.'" Paul concentrates the whole law/Torah into the love command, which is a radical reduction of its content and precisely thereby amounts to the same thing as an intentional abrogation of the Torah.[100] Here the term νόμος is used to designate what in any case characterizes the πνευματικοί in their new status as people who are justified before God, namely, love. What the law calls for has long since been attained by those who love. In 6:2 Paul plays with the term νόμος: "Bear one another's burdens, and in this way you will fulfill the law of Christ." Whereas elsewhere in Galatians νόμος consistently refers to the Torah with its negative connotations (5:14 is an exception), in 6:2 Paul intentionally uses it in the sense of "order," "norm."[101] This interpretation is

---

zum 65. Geburtstag (ed. Ulrich Mell and Ulrich B. Müller; BZNW 100; Berlin: de Gruyter, 1999), 59–84. Sellin emphasizes (p. 75), "Thus, as we read Gal. 4:21–31 today, this text appears as one of the sharpest anti-Jewish invectives in the New Testament."

99. Cf. 4 Macc. 5:20: "to transgress the law in matters either small or great is of equal seriousness."

100. Hübner, *Law in Paul's Thought*, 36–42.

101. Contra Ferdinand Hahn, "Das Gesetzesverständnis im Römer- und Galaterbrief," *ZNW* 67 (1976): 57 n. 89, who excludes the meaning "rule," "principle," or "norm," since in his understanding the law has received its intended purpose through Christ. Against this, Jost Eckert, *Die urchristliche Verkündigung im Streit zwischen Paulus und seinen Gegnern nach dem Galaterbrief* (Regensburg: Pustet,

supported above all by Hellenistic parallels that place 6:2 in the context of the ancient friendship ethic.[102] Νόμος is here entirely qualified and determined by "Christ" (genitive of source). The immediate context is also illuminating,[103] indicating that Paul understands νόμος Χριστοῦ in an ethical sense: those who allow themselves to be completely led by the Spirit and orient their lives to the standard of love fulfill the will of Christ. Paul thus signals to the Galatians that he, too, despite his sharp critique of the Torah, is not without law, for he knows himself to be subject to the norm of Christ.

The concept of love enables Paul to bring together Hellenistic Jewish and Greek-Hellenistic thinking about law and to press them into service for his argument. He gives a new definition of the Torah in terms of the love command, since, in contrast to Jewish tradition, the other commands and prohibitions completely lose their significance.[104] For Jewish thought, it was inconceivable that fulfilling the whole Torah by observing a single command would mean the annulment of all the other commands. By understanding the Torah in terms of ἀγάπη, its character and original meaning are changed, since now the Torah as a whole is exclusively determined by love and summarized in the concept of love, so that it now accords with the Hellenistic law of nature or reason.[105]

This multilayered[106] character of Paul's critique of the law/Torah in Galatians is held together only by pneumatology as its common denominator.[107] The gift of the Spirit means that, for Christians, the law is no longer essential and that it is impossible for Christians to place themselves under the law/Torah (cf. 5:18).[108] Since Christians have received the Spirit as the decisive mark of salvation not from works of the law/Torah but by believing the Christian message (3:2, 5),

---

1971), 160, rightly emphasizes, "When Paul now speaks of the 'law of Christ,' the paradoxical formulation is evident, and it is just as clear that he must be speaking of an entirely different law from the law of Moses."

102. Cf. Xenophon, *Mem.* 2.7.1: Socrates says to his ill-tempered friend Aristarchus, "You should share some of your burden with your friends. Perhaps we could make it easier for you." Menander, *Sent.* 534: "See, all burdens are [to be borne] in common with friends." Cf. further Epictetus, *Diatr.* 4.153–154, 159.

103. M. Winger, "The Law of Christ," *NTS* 46 (2000): 537–46.

104. Mussner, *Galaterbrief,* 373.

105. Cf. the exegesis of Rom. 13:8–10 below, in sections 12:10 ("The Shape of the New Life") and 19.3 ("The Law").

106. Schweitzer, *Mysticism,* 187, has a clear apprehension of the complexity of Paul's doctrine of the law: "He asserts roundly that the Law is no longer in force. But at the same time he admits its authority by his view that those who acknowledge the Law are subject to the Law, and so perish by the Law. And there is yet another unintelligible distinction. That believers from Judaism should continue to live according to the Law seems to him quite proper and in no way detrimental to their redemption. But if the believers from among the Gentiles do the same thing, this is for him a denial of the cross of Christ."

107. Cf. Kuula, *Law and Covenant,* 36–45, who rightly emphasizes "that the idea of participation in Christ or the Spirit as 'God's empowering presence' is a much more important category in Galatians than the language of justification" (p. 45).

108. On the relation of Spirit and law, cf. esp. Horn, *Angeld des Geistes,* 352–74.

circumcision and calendar observance are foolishness because they pervert back into its opposite the freedom granted by the Spirit. The contrast that determines Paul's argument in Galatians is νόμος/πνεῦμα. Circumcision and law/Torah *do not belong to Christianity's soteriological self-definition* because God has revealed himself directly in Jesus Christ and because those who believe and are baptized participate in this saving event through the gift of the Spirit.

11.4 The Ethic of Galatians: Freedom Active in Love

The major section of Galatians devoted to ethics begins with a resounding declaration as its basis: "For freedom Christ has set us free. Stand firm, therefore, and do not submit again to a yoke of slavery" (Gal. 5:1).[109] The new existence of believers—appropriated in baptism, lived in the power of the Spirit—excludes subjection to any other powers. Christians already serve the one Lord Jesus Christ, who has granted them freedom. Christian existence is in its very essence life in freedom, and so it is now up to the Galatians whether they will choose to distort this gift of freedom into its opposite by Torah observance and thereby lose it[110] or whether they will express it positively by Christian love. The only way of life that corresponds to the gift of freedom is the life that knows it is guided by the Spirit. In this context, an orientation to the Torah would mean nothing other than a perversion of the freedom of the Spirit into the slavery of the flesh.

Love as the central determining factor in the freedom attained through Christ obligates the Galatians to a course of life no longer oriented to the flesh but to the Spirit.[111] The σάρξ/πνεῦμα contrast appears in Paul not as a metaphysical dualism but as a historical dualism. Since there is no human existence outside the flesh and God's dealing with human beings takes place in the sphere of the flesh, the flesh appears as the place where human beings

---

109. For analysis, see Jones, *"Freiheit,"* 96–102; different emphases are found in Karl Kertelge, "Gesetz und Freiheit im Galaterbrief," in *Grundthemen paulinischer Theologie* (Freiburg: Herder, 1991), 184–96.

Precisely where the paraenetical section of Galatians begins is a disputed point. Some regard the beginning as Gal. 5:13 (e.g., Merk, "Beginn der Paränese," 238–59; Becker et al., *Briefe*, 83). Others opt for 5:1 (e.g., Betz, *Galatians*, 253–55). In addition to the characteristic οὖν (cf. Rom. 12:1), analogous opening styles of the three sections 5:1–12, 5:13–24, and 5:25–6:10 speak in favor of 5:1 as the beginning of the paraenetic section.

110. Cf. Karl Kertelge, "Freiheitsbotschaft und Liebesgebot im Galaterbrief," in *Grundthemen paulinischer Theologie* (Freiburg: Herder, 1991), 197–208.

111. On the ethic of Galatians, in addition to the standard commentaries, see esp. Merk, *Handeln*, 66–80; Barclay, *Obeying the Truth*, 106ff.; Wolfgang Harnisch, "Einübung des neuen Seins: Paulinische Paränese am Beispiel des Galaterbriefes," in *Die Zumutung der Liebe: Gesammelte Aufsätze* (ed. Ulrich Schoenborn; FRLANT 187; Göttingen: Vandenhoeck & Ruprecht, 1999), 149–68; Hans Weder, "Die Normativität der Freiheit," in *Paulus, Apostel Jesu Christi: Festschrift für Günter Klein zum 70. Geburtstag* (ed. Michael Trowitzsch; Tübingen: Mohr Siebeck, 1998), 130ff.

either persevere in their own selfishness or allow themselves to be drawn into God's service by the power of the Spirit. Human beings never live out of their own being but always find themselves already in a force field that qualifies their individual lives.[112] There is only one life, and it is lived "according to the flesh" (κατὰ σάρκα) or "according to the Spirit" (κατὰ πνεῦμα). In 5:25 Paul classically formulates the ethical dimension of the new reality in which those who have been baptized now live: Εἰ ζῶμεν πνεύματι, πνεύματι καὶ στοιχῶμεν (If we live by the Spirit, let us also be guided by the Spirit).[113] The Spirit is thus ground and norm of Christian being and action; it is the Spirit that creates and maintains the new being of the Christian. The Spirit has an effective monopoly on the Christian's inner being, including the will. Christians have entered the realm of life determined by the Spirit; now they must let themselves be guided by the Spirit. At the same time, it becomes clear: there is no new life without new actions. The Spirit given to the believers wants to be appropriated through deeds of love. Precisely because the Spirit has incorporated believers into the sphere of God's work and made them members of the church, they do not live their lives in a space free from all controls but stand under the demand of obedience made possible by the Spirit. Paul can thus consistently designate the marks of this new life as fruits of the Spirit (5:22): love, joy, peace, patience, kindness, generosity, faithfulness.[114] Living by the Spirit (πνεύματι περιπατεῖτε) separates itself from the desires of the flesh (5:16) and realizes its goal in love, which also fulfills the law/Torah (cf. 5:14). For those who live in the force field where the Spirit holds sway, God is no longer seen as an intruder from outside with commands that must be obeyed.[115] The newness of life takes place in the newness of the Spirit.

As those who are led by God, the Galatians have already decided on a particular way of life. Paul now emphatically insists that they not abandon this way of freedom and turn back to the old way of slavery. For the apostle, the way of freedom is open only by being bound to God, a freedom in which one finds one's true self, where others become our fellow human beings, and where one learns to respect the creation as God's gift. Freedom is an attribute that applies directly and absolutely to God alone, but God confers it on those who bind themselves to him and orient their lives to his will. Only God delivers human beings, through the power of the Spirit, from the power of sin and thereby enables them to do good.

---

112. Cf. Bultmann, *Theology of the New Testament*, 1:227–46.

113. For the interpretation of Gal. 5:25, see below, section 20.1 ("Life within the Sphere of Christ: Correspondence as Basic Ethical Category").

114. Harnisch, "Einübung des neuen Seins," 163, appropriately points out the plural "works of the flesh" in Gal. 5:19 and the singular "fruit of the Spirit" in 5:22: "And because the effects of the Spirit can all be summed up in ἀγάπη as their focal point, Paul can speak of the one 'fruit' of the Spirit in the singular."

115. Hans Lietzmann, *An die Römer* (5th ed.; HNT 8; Tübingen: Mohr Siebeck, 1971), 71.

11.5 Inclusive and Exclusive Doctrine of Justification in Paul

Paul's statements regarding the law/Torah go beyond what he has previously said in several different ways:

(1) He *universalizes* the statements about righteousness in the baptismal tradition, which had been oriented primarily to the individual (cf. Gal. 2:16, πᾶσα σάρξ; in addition, 3:22; 5:3, 14). The righteousness revealed in Jesus Christ and appropriated in faith is equally valid for Jews and Gentiles; every human being is directed to it as the means of escaping the coming wrath. Paul thus explicitly denies a special status to the Jews and Jewish Christians, mediated to them by the Torah. Jesus Christ alone is the source and locus of righteousness that comes from beyond ourselves. The distinction between Jews and Gentiles, grounded in ethnicity and salvation history, is no longer in force.

(2) Along with this universalizing goes a *radicalizing*: the righteousness conferred by God applies not only to those who are justified according to their own self-understanding but to all human beings. All stand under the power of sin (3:22) and are in need of the righteousness in Jesus Christ that comes from God.

(3) In the Letter to the Galatians, for the first time Paul's language takes on a *firm conceptual pattern* regarding the relation between righteousness/justification and law/Torah, so that we can now speak of a doctrine of justification whose central core can be seen in the antithesis ἐξ ἔργα νόμου / ἐκ πίστεως Ἰησοῦ (by works of the law / by faith in Jesus Christ). What prevents those who observe the law/Torah from receiving the promise found within it is not human striving per se, nor is it a defect in the law/Torah, but it is the power of sin. Only faith in Jesus Christ reveals this reality of the human situation.

(4) In Galatians Paul *evaluates the Torah in a fundamentally negative way*. Not only Gentile Christians but also Jewish Christians, as believers in Jesus Christ, are in every respect withdrawn from the Torah's power over them. Life is given to them outside the realm of the Torah.

The apostle's autobiographical statements about his call and commissioning at Damascus, as well as the textual data in 1 Thessalonians and the Corinthian letters, show that Paul has not previously thought of the law/Torah in the way that he now does in Galatians. Here he has an exclusively negative evaluation of the Torah but still does not consider himself and his churches to be "without law," for he knows that he is bound by the "law of Christ" and that love fulfills the law/Torah (Gal. 5:14).

The way the Pauline mission developed supports this judgment. The decisions at the apostolic council, the Antioch incident, and the testimony of his letters permit only one conclusion, that the individual groups had mostly preserved their religious customs. In 1 Cor. 7:18 Paul formulated this position programmatically regarding Jewish and Gentile Christians: "Was anyone at the time of his call already circumcised? Let him not seek to remove the marks of circumcision. Was anyone at the time of his call uncircumcised? Let him not seek circumcision." In Paul's predominantly Gentile Christian churches, except for maintaining the ethical core of the law, freedom from the Torah was the "basis, more or less taken for granted as obvious."[116] At the same time, in the Pauline churches also, the Jewish Christians and God-fearers at least partially continued their observance of the Torah, as evidenced by the conflicts about eating meat sacrificed to idols (1 Cor. 8, 10) in Corinth and the disputes between "weak" and "strong" in Rome (Rom. 14:1–15:3). The way the apostle deals with these problems is very informative. He no longer attaches any fundamental importance to the ritual laws (cf. 1 Cor. 6:12; 7:19; 9:20–22; 10:23; Rom. 14:14, 20) but regards consideration for the endangered group and mutual acceptance to be the right Christian conduct (cf. 1 Cor. 8:9, 12, 13; 10:23–24; Rom. 14:13, 15, 29–30; 15:7). The apostle carries on his mission without a theory about the Torah. In view of the imminent return of the Lord and the judgment that would then take place, Paul's only goal is to save Jews and Gentiles (1 Cor. 9:22b, "I have become all things to all people, that I might by all means save some"). He advises the Corinthians, "Give no offense to Jews or to Greeks or to the church of God, just as I try to please everyone in everything I do, not seeking my own advantage, but that of many, so that they may be saved" (1 Cor. 10:32–33). He can call the Galatians to "become as I am, for I also have become as you are" (Gal. 4:12).[117] The sarcastic comment in Gal. 5:12 (I wish those who unsettle you would castrate themselves!) shows how far Paul had distanced himself from core values of Judaism. Circumcision, the sign of God's election (cf. Gen. 17:10), is compared to castration.[118] The textual data shows that in practice Paul was neither nomist nor antinomist, that he handled the law/Torah as an adiaphoron.[119]

Gaining Insight in the Midst of Crisis

When strict Jewish Christian missionaries arrived in Galatia, the practical way in which Jewish Christians and Gentile Christians had lived and worked together for some time both in the Pauline churches and in early Christianity as a whole and which had never been entirely without its problems, now escalated into a real antagonism. The new missionaries' insistence that Gentile Christians, too, must be circumcised made it necessary for Paul to move the problematic of the law/Torah from the periphery of his theology to its center. New external challenges initiated an internal process of penetrating reflection that led to a more precise reformulation of his understanding of the law and its place in Christian life and thought.[120]

116. Ulrich Wilckens, "Zur Entwicklung des paulinischen Gesetzesverständnisses," *NTS* 28 (1982): 158; cf. also Räisänen, *Paul and the Law*, 73–83.

117. As a parallel in the Hellenistic friendship ethic, cf. Cicero, *Amic.* 20; Lucian, *Toxaris* 5; numerous other texts are cited in *NW* 1/2:715–25.

118. Betz, *Galatians*, 270.

119. Cf. Räisänen, *Paul and the Law*, 77.

120. A mediating position is maintained by Theissen, *Religion of the Earliest Churches*, 219, who, on the one hand, notes that the law must have become a problem to Paul immediately after

The doctrine of justification as found in Galatians is thus *a new response to a new situation*.[121] This understanding derives not only in contrast to the agreements at the apostolic council and the paucity of statements about law and justification in the Corinthian letters but also from Galatians itself. The demand that Gentile Christians be circumcised posed in a fundamental way the unavoidable question of the continuing relevance of the law/Torah not only for Gentile Christians but also for Jewish Christians. The solution of this problem led Paul to increased theological insight. The apostle did not stop with assuring Gentile Christians of their place in the ἐκκλησία θεοῦ; his fundamental critique of the Torah also made it problematical for Jewish Christians. Paul's antithesis of νόμος/πνεῦμα pulled the rug out from under the practical assumption that had previously prevailed in broad circles of early Christianity, namely that there were no insuperable problems involved in the coexistence of Torah observance and Christian faith in the Christian community. The way Paul argues in Galatians shows how deeply he struggles with what, in this form, is for him a new and insistent problem. Thus the very different kinds of reasons presented for the abrogation of the Torah do not generate the impression that they are the result of twenty years of reflection on the significance of the Torah. Likewise the considerable tensions within the variety of evidences and arguments Paul presents are a clear indication that his line of argument is conditioned by the new situation.[122] Paul obviously wants to use everything in his power to neutralize the false teaching of his opponents and salvage his own

---

his conversion but, on the other hand, states, "Only now did Paul activate his own conversion and introduce it as an argument into the public discussion—as a warning against accepting circumcision. He did this in two letters written against Judaistic countermissionaries, Galatians and Philippians. A (current) crisis in the communities and a (long past) personal crisis now came together" (p. 220). Did a fundamental insight remain buried for twenty years, only to emerge with explosive force in the confrontation with the Judaists? It seems to be more plausible that Galatians represents a really new insight and argumentation within Paul's thought.

121. From the older scholarship, cf. Wrede, *Paul*, 122ff.; Weiss, *Earliest Christianity*, 301–3; Schweitzer, *Mysticism*, 219–26; Schoeps, *Paul*, 183–84. From the current discussion, cf., e.g., Wilckens, "Entwicklung," 157–58; Wilckens, "Werken des Gesetzes," 84–85: "Evidently it was first in connection with the debate with the Judaistic opponents in his Galatian churches that Paul realized it was necessary to develop an explicit doctrine of justification." Cf. further Strecker, "Befreiung und Rechtfertigung," 237; Lüdemann, *Paulus und das Judentum*, 21. Räisänen, *Paul and the Law*, 9–10, formulates the matter as follows: "Whatever major development there was in Paul's theology of the law, must, in my view, have taken place by the time of the writing of Galatians." Cf. further Berger, *Theologiegeschichte*, 459: "Paul's real doctrine of justification was developed—conditioned by the situation—in connection with the problem of how far the validity of the Jewish way could be extended (Galatians, Romans). On the basis of Gen. 15:6, Paul thereby brings together elements of his own theology that had not previously been so connected and that thereby received a new meaning." So also Gnilka, *Apostel und Zeuge*, 237–44, assumes that the Galatian crisis—on the basis of traditions—led to the formulation of the specific doctrine of justification.

122. The tensions within the Pauline understanding of the law have been revealed, above all, by the work of H. Räisänen; cf. especially Heikki Räisänen, "Paul's Theological Difficulties with the Law," in Heikki Räisänen, *The Torah and Christ: Essays in German and English on the Problem of the Law in Early Christianity* (ed. Anne-Marit Enroth; SESJ 45; Helsinki: Finnish Exegetical Society, 1986), passim.

missionary work; this is why his debate with them has unparalleled sharpness and such an emotional tone. If Paul had been advocating the doctrine of justification, as found in Galatians, from the very beginning of his missionary work, then the Christians in Galatia would have been familiar with at least its basic outline since the time when Paul founded the churches there. Then it would be all the more remarkable that the Galatian Christians listened to the opposing teaching so readily, and Paul would be responding to them with an argument that they had already heard but of which he had not convinced them. Another explanatory model seems to me to be more probable: in his founding visit, Paul instructed the new converts in the importance of the Old Testament for Christian faith, but hardly with the sharp distinctions and predominantly negative statements found in Galatians. This initiated an intensive study of the Old Testament in the Galatian churches, a study that evidently prepared the ground for the message of the opponents. They were not simply propagators of false teaching; they proclaimed a gospel (cf. Gal. 1:6–9). Their message had greater drawing power than the original Pauline preaching that founded the churches. Evidently the strict Jewish Christians were able to persuade the Galatians that being "children of Abraham" and thus belonging to the people of God included the practice of circumcision, the observance of the ritual calendar, and the complete acceptance of the Old Testament. Paul in turn reacts to this attempt at changing the status of Gentile Christians by relativizing the previous status of Jewish Christians.

Inclusive and Exclusive Doctrine of Justification

Despite the fact that the doctrine of justification in Paul's letter to the Galatians is conditioned by the particular situation it addresses, it had presuppositions already present in Pauline theology. The theme of righteousness/justification within Paul's theology is primarily associated with baptismal traditions (cf. 1 Cor. 1:30; 6:11; 2 Cor. 1:21–22; Rom. 3:25; 4:25; 6:3–4), which develop a doctrine of justification that is in itself a consistent, well-rounded whole: in baptism the individual Christian is delivered from the dominance of sin through the power of the Spirit and thereby made righteous, so that within the horizon of the parousia of Jesus Christ he or she can live a life corresponding to the will of God. This doctrine of justification can be described as *inclusive* because it is oriented toward the effective making-righteous of the individual believer in baptism through the power of the Spirit, without any criteria of exclusion. Universal concepts were also already associated with pre-Pauline baptismal traditions. So also in Galatians, justification is grounded first of all in the death and resurrection of Jesus Christ (cf. Gal. 2:19–21).[123] The

---

123. Cf. Daniel G. Powers, *Salvation through Participation: An Examination of the Notion of the Believers' Corporate Unity with Christ in Early Christian Soteriology* (CBET 29; Leuven: Peeters, 2001), 121–22.

transformation of the Son and the participation of the baptized believer in the power of the Spirit, in Galatians as in all the other Pauline letters, form the foundation and deep structure of Paul's argumentation. It is on this basis that Paul attempts to conduct the debate forced upon him about the value of circumcision and Torah observance as conditions for entrance into the people of God. The results of his reflections can be described, in a twofold aspect, as an *exclusive doctrine of justification*: (1) Paul excludes the possibility that the νόμος can play a synergistic role in the event of justification. (2) He likewise now excludes the possibility that Jews and Jewish Christians have a privileged hamartiological status based on salvation history. The Judaists' insistence that also Gentile Christians must be circumcised compelled Paul to break with the compromise solution made at the apostolic council and, as a countermove, to call into question the importance of the Torah even for Jewish Christians.

The traditions and concepts associated with baptism not only formed the theological link between the inclusive and exclusive doctrines of justification. In addition, *Paul intentionally introduced the function of rituals in identity formation in order to stabilize the Galatians' endangered sense of identity.*[124] In this way he protects the exclusive doctrine of justification based on a radicalized anthropology and a universalized understanding of God from becoming a worldless abstraction, in that he presents baptism as the place where God's universal saving act in Jesus Christ can be experienced in the particularity of one's own existence and where one's new identity can be formed. The act of God postulated in Paul's doctrine of the justification of the sinner through faith alone had to be placed in some particular relation to the reality of human existence. This is what the baptismal traditions do, in that they designate baptism as the place where God lets himself be encountered and experienced. Moreover, the baptismal traditions guard the exclusive doctrine of justification from the danger of ethical indifference because they designate baptism as the place and the means of the tangible presence of God's act of forgiving sins and conferral of righteousness in the power of the Spirit, a reality to which one's life must now correspond. God's righteousness can thus be a power that determines human life only if it is an act of God tangible to human experience. By making himself available to human beings in the event of baptism, God claims them as his own and places them in the new being ἐν Χριστῷ. Thus the baptismal traditions serve Paul as the verification of fundamental affirmations within the community's experiential horizon. The universal saving act of God affirmed in the Christ event is thus guarded from the danger of being a reality that is only postulated but not tangibly experienced.[125]

---

124. Cf. Strecker, *Die liminale Theologie des Paulus*, 208–11.

125. On the changing and stabilizing function of rituals, cf. Clifford Geertz, "Thick Description: Toward an Interpretative Theory of Culture," in *The Interpretation of Cultures: Selected Essays* (New York: Basic Books, 1973), 3–30.

12

Paul and the Church in Rome

High-Level Encounter

As Paul's work in the eastern part of the empire came to an end, the church in Rome assumed an increasing priority in his thought. He hoped to receive material and spiritual support from it and sensed that Rome would play a portentous role in his own life.

12.1 The History and Structure of the Roman Church

The beginnings of Christianity in Rome cannot be understood apart from the history of the Roman Jewish community, mentioned for the first time in 139 CE. The Jews had experienced a varied and eventful history in Rome, full of ups and downs. The community grew very rapidly; Josephus mentions that eight thousand Roman Jews met the Jewish delegation sent to Rome after the death of Herod (*Ant.* 17.300). Augustus treated the Jews well, respected their customs, and sanctioned the legal status of their communities as *collegia licita*.[1]

1. Cf. Philo, *Embassy* 156–57: "He [Augustus] knew therefore that they have houses of prayer and meet together in them, particularly on the sacred sabbaths when they receive as a body training in their

Dio Cassius 60.6.6. reports that in 41 CE, because of their large numbers, Claudius had not expelled the Jews from Rome but that he had withdrawn their right of assembly. The Jews in Rome had organized themselves into independent congregations with their own assembly rooms and their own administration.[2] They were hard hit by the expulsions that occurred in 19 CE under Tiberius[3] and under Claudius in 49 CE.[4] The edict of Claudius presupposes disputes in Rome between Jews and Christians about "Chrestus" and documents the success of Christian missionaries in the synagogues.[5]

As had previously been the case with Judaism, Christianity came to Rome via the trade routes. It is hardly accidental that pre-Pauline churches are found in Puteoli (Acts 28:13) and in Rome itself (Rom. 1:7; Acts 28:15). Not only were large Jewish communities found in both locations; in addition, the main trade route between the eastern part of the empire and the city of Rome ran through Puteoli. Unknown early Christian missionaries who were engaged in business or commerce probably brought the gospel to Rome. The edict of Claudius not only affected the Roman Jews but was also important in several respects for the Christian community there: (1) The edict effected the final separation of Christians from the synagogue. (2) The expulsion of Jews and Jewish Christians from Rome had a decisive effect on the composition of the Christian congregations there. Before the edict, the majority had been Jewish Christians, but after 49 CE they were the minority. In the persecution of Christians under Nero in 64 CE, the authorities made a distinction between Jews and Christians.[6] (3) The edict had probably prevented Paul from coming to Rome earlier (cf. Rom. 1:13; 15:22). (4) The edict made it clear to the young Christian community that they would have to find their own way in the field of conflicting forces between the synagogue and the Roman authorities.

At the time when Paul wrote to the Roman church, Gentile Christians already formed the majority (cf. Rom. 1:5, 13–15; 10:1–3; 11:13, 17–32; 15:15, 16,

---

ancestral philosophy. . . . Yet nevertheless he neither ejected them from Rome nor deprived them of their Roman citizenship because they were careful to preserve their Jewish citizenship also, nor took any violent measures against the houses of prayer, nor prevented them from meeting to receive instructions in the laws, or opposed their offerings of the first fruits." Cf. also Juvenal, *Satirae* 3.10–18.

2. Cf. Wolfgang Wiefel, "The Jewish Community in Ancient Rome and the Origins of Roman Christianity," in *The Romans Debate* (ed. Karl P. Donfried; rev. and exp. ed.; Peabody, MA: Hendrickson, 1991), 89–92; Peter Lampe, *From Paul to Valentinus: Christians at Rome in the First Two Centuries* (ed. Marshall D. Johnson; trans. Michael Steinhauser; Minneapolis: Fortress, 2003), 90–94; Lichtenberger, "Josephus und Paulus," 247–48.

3. Cf. Tacitus, *Ann.* 2.85 (four thousand devotees of Egyptian and Jewish cults were deported to Sardinia to combat the banditry there); cf. also Suetonius, *Tib.* 36; Josephus, *Ant.* 18.83.

4. On the edict of Claudius, see above, section 2.1 ("Absolute Chronology").

5. On the relation between Christianity and Judaism in Rome, cf. Karl P. Donfried and Peter Richardson, eds., *Judaism and Christianity in First-Century Rome* (Grand Rapids: Eerdmans, 1998).

6. Cf. Tacitus, *Ann.* 15.44.

18). At the same time, one must reckon with a considerable and influential minority of Jewish Christians within the Roman church, as indicated particularly by Rom. 9–11 and 16:7, 11 (Andronicus, Junia[s], and Herodion as συγγενεῖς, Paul's fellow Jews). Jewish Christians were also a factor in the conflict between "strong" and "weak" (cf. Rom. 14:1–15:13), and many Gentile Christians had doubtless belonged to the group of God-fearers.

Romans 16:3–16 is particularly informative regarding the social levels represented in the Roman church, since the chapter refers to twenty-eight different persons, twenty-six of them by name.[7] Thus Prisca and Aquila (16:3–4) were independent business people who may have had employees or slaves working for them.[8] Romans 16:10b, 11b names as fellow Christians members of the households of Aristobulus and Narcissus, which may refer to slaves or freedmen who worked in the household of a non-Christian master. Analysis of the names in 16:3–16 that also occur in Roman inscriptions reveals that of thirteen comparable names, four refer to a freeborn origin, and nine to a slave origin, for the name holder.[9] Women looked after many tasks in the life of the church, for it is said only of them that they "worked very hard" (κοπιάω, 16:6, 12; cf. also 13b). Of the twenty-six persons named in 6:3–16, twelve came to Rome from the east and are personally known by Paul, indicating there was a significant influx of Christians from the east into the Roman church.

Romans 16:3–6 also provides information about the organizational structure of the Roman Christians. Not only does Paul mention the house church of Prisca and Aquila (16:5); at least 16:14–15 documents the existence of several independent house churches in Rome.[10] After his arrival in Rome, Paul's apartment, too, became a meeting place for Christians (cf. Acts 28:30–31). Thus the Roman church at this time did not consist of a single congregation that met in one large assembly room. Paul therefore does not direct his letter to a single ἐκκλησία in Rome but to "all God's beloved in Rome, who are called to be saints" (Rom. 1:7a).

At the time of the composition of Romans, the Christian community in Rome must have already become very large, since Paul expected from them both monetary support and coworkers to help in his mission. The persecution of Christians under Nero in 64 CE also presupposes a growing Christian movement known throughout the city.

7. On the hypothesis that Rom. 16 was originally addressed to the church in Ephesus (no longer advocated in the current discussion), see Schnelle, *New Testament Writings*, 116–20.

8. Cf. Lampe, *Christians at Rome*, 187–95.

9. Cf. ibid., 164–83.

10. Cf. Klauck, *Hausgemeinde und Hauskirche*, 26ff.; Lampe, *Christians at Rome*, 359–64; Peter Lampe, "Urchristliche Missionswege nach Rom: Haushalte paganer Herrschaft als jüdisch-christliche Keimzellen," *ZNW* 92 (2001): 123–27 (he calculates that in the 50s there must have been at least seven Christian islands in the sea that was metropolitan Rome).

12.2 The Letter to the Romans as a Contextualized Document

Romans was written at the decisive turning point in Paul's missionary career. The apostle regards his work in the eastern part of the empire as finished and now wants to continue his proclamation of the gospel in the west, especially in Spain (cf. Rom. 15:23–24). But first he must immediately make another trip to Jerusalem to deliver the offering from the churches in Macedonia and Achaia (cf. 15:28–29).

Romans was probably written in Corinth, where Paul dictated the letter in the spring of 56 CE while staying in the house of Gaius (cf. Acts 20:2–3; Rom. 16:1, 22–23; 1 Cor. 1:14).[11] Presumably the letter was delivered by Phoebe, deacon in the nearby congregation of Cenchrea (cf. Rom. 16:1–2).

The Situation of Paul

The occasion and goal of the Letter to the Romans are closely related to Paul's own situation. In order to carry out his planned mission to Spain, the apostle needs the support of the Roman church both financially and in terms of personnel. Thus he introduces himself to the Roman Christians, most of whom he does not know personally, by means of an extensive presentation of his own theology. Along with this motive, which he straightforwardly declares in the letter itself (Rom. 15:24), there are two other problem areas that gave Paul reason to compose the Letter to the Romans. Paul is clearly not sure that the Jerusalem church will accept the offering he is bringing, for only on this presupposition can we understand his request for the prayers of the Roman church and the doubts that continue to plague him (cf. 15:30, 31). The apostle understands the collection as material support for needy Christians in Jerusalem and at the same time as an acknowledgment of the preeminence of the original Jerusalem church in the history of salvation (cf. 15:27). Above all, the offering is intended to strengthen the bonds between Jewish Christians and Gentile Christians and thus reinforce the agreements made at the apostolic council (cf. Gal. 2:9). The intensifying agitation by his Judaist opponents, including within churches Paul himself had established, shows that after the apostolic council the position of these groups had gained in importance—especially in Jerusalem—so that Paul sees himself compelled to renew his opposition to these streams. Thus Romans, too, must be read as evidence of this debate, for Paul's line of argument is still visibly shaped by the disputes with the Galatians in the immediate past, and the church in Rome will also have already heard reports about Paul and his gospel from the mouths of his opponents (cf. Rom.

---

11. On this relatively broad scholarly consensus, one need only note, e.g., Zeller, *Römer*, 15; and Peter Stuhlmacher, *Paul's Letter to the Romans: A Commentary* (trans. Scott J. Hafemann; Louisville: Westminster John Knox, 1994), 5.

3:8, 31a; 6:1, 15; 7:7 [16:17–18?]). When Paul takes up the conflict between "strong" and "weak" (14:1–15:13), there is most likely some sort of connection to the works of the rigorous Jewish Christians.

The Situation of the Church

The church in Rome was also probably subject to increasing pressure from both the Jewish and the Roman sides. In the period between the edict of Claudius (49 CE) and the persecution of Christians under Nero (64 CE), the Roman house churches experienced considerable growth and became identifiable to outsiders as a distinct group. This development did not happen without an increase in external pressures, as indicated by Rom. 12:9–21.[12] Both the exhortation "Bless those who persecute you; bless and do not curse them" in 12:14 and the command to forego revenge in 12:19–21 cannot be seen as simply part of the conventional paraenesis-oriented tradition. What we have here is rather the reflection of conflicts with Roman Judaism, which, after the negative experiences of the edict of Claudius, sought to keep believers in Christ distant from the ambit of the synagogue and to indicate to the Roman authorities that the Christians were an independent and hostile group. The house churches at the time when Romans was written had not yet been declared to be heretics or criminals. The admonitions in 13:1–7, however, show that the relation to the state was a debated point in the churches. The juxtaposing in Rom. 13 of basic affirmation of the state (13:1–2) and instructions related to current issues (13:6–7) suggests that a variety of opinions existed on these issues in the house churches. Possibly Suetonius, Nero 16.2, is a reflection of increased pressure on Christians by the Roman state. In a listing of the measures Nero had taken to deal with various issues in the early part of his reign (e.g., prohibition of the sale of certain foods; prohibition of chariot drivers from harassing the population with their abusive behavior), we suddenly find this: "Punishment was inflicted on the Christians, a sect devoted to a new and mischievous superstition." This note is usually related to the fire in Rome, for the Christians were blamed, as in Tacitus, Ann. 15.44.[13] This is not at all necessary, however, for Suetonius, Nero 38.1–3, reports the burning of Rome without mentioning the Christians. Perhaps the Christians had already come into the sights of the Roman authorities, and Romans reflects the beginnings of this development.

Problems of Pauline Thought

Finally, yet another element was a factor in shaping the apostle's argumentation: problems in the logic and/or presentation of his thought, which evidently

---

12. Cf. the exposition by Alvarez Cineira, Claudius, 390–95.
13. See below, section 13.4 ("Paul the Martyr").

led to misunderstandings and allegations. Thus the apostle's wresting in Rom. 9–11 with the issue of Israel follows logically from his doctrine of justification. When Paul proclaims faith in the one God who justifies the ungodly (4:5), the question is forced on him with unrelenting sharpness: What about those to whom God has made promises? Does Paul's doctrine mean that God is unfaithful? Another question: In Paul's doctrine of justification, what is the relation of divine grace to human responsibility? If all are guilty as they stand before God's judgment (2:1) and if no one can appeal for justification to his or her own deeds, what is the meaning and function of ethical conduct? One's deeds have no positive significance in regard to salvation, but at the same time one can forfeit salvation by his or her deeds!

Major Positions in the History of Scholarly Research

The modern discussion of Paul's reason(s) for writing Romans began with the work of F. C. Baur.[14] Baur surmised that there was an anti-Pauline party in Rome that rejected Paul's universalistic message and wanted to exclude Gentiles from the grace of the gospel. Paul wrote Romans to oppose the false particularism of this Jewish Christian group.[15] The classic position of Baur generated a discussion that has been maintained until today with no end of hypotheses, only a few of which can be named here:[16] (1) From the fact that ἐκκλησία terminology is missing from Rom. 1–15, G. Klein infers that for Paul the Roman congregations still needed an apostolic foundation and that Romans is to be understood as Paul's proleptic act of the apostolic εὐαγγελίζεσθαι (evangelizing) that is yet to be accomplished.[17] Against this view is the objection that Paul acknowledges

---

14. Ferdinand Christian Baur, "Über Zweck und Veranlassung des Römerbriefes und die damit zusammenhängenden Verhältnisse der römischen Gemeinde," in Ferdinand Christian Baur, *Ausgewählte Werke in Einzelausgaben* (ed. Klaus Scholder; 5 vols.; Stuttgart: Frommann, 1963–1975), 1:147–266.

15. A. J. M. Wedderburn, *The Reasons for Romans* (Edinburgh: T&T Clark, 1988), has now once again picked up the thread of Baur's argument. He specifically emphasizes that there were several "reasons for Romans" but still considers the Jewish Christians in Rome to be the apostle's real conversation partners. They had charged Paul with preaching a gospel that violated God's righteousness. Cf. further Brändle and Stegemann, "Entstehung," 1–11.

16. Surveys of research are found in Otto Kuss, *Paulus: Die Rolle des Apostels in der theologischen Entwicklung der Urkirche* (2nd ed.; Auslegung und Verkündigung 3; Regensburg: Pustet, 1976), 178–204; Walter Schmithals, *Der Römerbrief als historisches Problem* (SNT 9; Gütersloh: Gütersloher Verlagshaus, 1975), 24–52; Markku Kettunen, *Der Abfassungszweck des Römerbriefes* (AASFDHL 18; Helsinki: Suomalainen Tiedeakatemia, 1979), 7–26; Michael Theobald, *Der Römerbrief* (Darmstadt: Wissenschaftliche Buchgesellschaft, 2000), 27–42; Angelika Reichert, *Der Römerbrief als Gratwanderung: Eine Untersuchung zur Abfassungsproblematik* (FRLANT 194; Göttingen: Vandenhoeck & Ruprecht, 2001), 13–75. A selection of important essays have been published in Karl P. Donfried, ed., *The Romans Debate* (rev. and exp. ed.; Peabody, MA: Hendrickson, 1991).

17. Cf. Günter Klein, "Paul's Purpose in Writing the Epistle to the Romans," in *The Romans Debate* (ed. Donfried), 29–43.

Roman Christianity with no reservations and that the letter has no indication of such a deficiency in the Roman congregations. (2) G. Bornkamm, J. Jervell, and U. Wilckens see the whole letter to be overshadowed by the concern, expressed in 15:30–31,[18] that the opposition by Judaist Christians in Jerusalem could influence the Jerusalem church to decline the offering Paul is bringing. Paul would, then, have conceived the Letter to the Romans as a kind of speech for the defense he intended to give in Jerusalem. Jerusalem would, then, be the secret addressee of the letter. This is in fact an important factor in the composition of the letter, but this view overrates its significance. (3) M. Kettunen and P. Stuhlmacher understand Romans as the apostle's comprehensive apologetic against his Judaistic rivals. The Judaists follow him everywhere, and he must assume that they have already been agitating against him in Rome. Romans would, then, be the apostle's attempt to neutralize the objections brought against him by his opponents in Rome and thereby to win the Roman church over to support his planned mission to Spain. (4) K. Haacker interprets Romans in the context of the increasing tensions between Rome and Jerusalem that would lead to the war of 66–73/74 CE. The Pauline thesis of the equality of Jews and Gentiles is to be understood "as intended to be a message of reconciliation in a time of growing polarization between Jerusalem and Rome."[19] (5) E. Lohse understands Romans as a "summary of the gospel" and thus, to a certain degree, a timeless exposition of the Christian faith determined only by this subject matter.[20] Here Paul presents a critical accounting of the way he has been preaching the gospel, without really going into particular current problems. (6) A. Reichert applies an intensified text-linguistic method as a means of clarifying the intention of Romans and arrives at this result: "By writing this letter, Paul wanted to form the disparate groups of addressees into a united Pauline church, forestall any hindrance in carrying out his further missionary work, and qualify them to develop his gospel further on their own."[21] Paul is interested in a potential mission of the Roman church in the western part of the empire and is equipping the church for it.

The Letter to the Romans is not a timeless elaboration of Pauline theology but a writing thoroughly conditioned by the situation in which it was written. Five factors shape its composition and its goal: (1) the help Paul needs from the Roman church for his planned mission to Spain; (2) the apostle's desire for their prayers (and support) in the debate he anticipates in Jerusalem when he presents the offering; (3) the agitation of Judaist opponents to Paul's work, whose influence he must presuppose both in Jerusalem and Rome; (4) the increasing

---

18. Cf. Günther Bornkamm, "The Letter to the Romans as Paul's Last Will and Testament," in *The Romans Debate* (ed. Donfried), 16–28.

19. Klaus Haacker, "Der Römerbrief als Friedensmemorandum," *NTS* 36 (1990): 34.

20. Eduard Lohse, *Summa evangelii: Zu Veranlassung und Thematik des Römerbriefes* (NAWGPH 3; Göttingen: 1993), 113ff.

21. Reichert, *Römerbrief*, 321.

distress of the church brought on by the Jewish community in Rome, and the conflict with the state already beginning to develop; and (5) problems inherent in understanding Paul's theology: only by neutralizing Jewish objections and by a persuasive presentation elaborating his own position could Paul count on the Jerusalem church accepting the offering and the Roman church adopting "his" gospel as their own.

12.3 The Gospel of Jesus Christ

In the letter to the Romans, Paul gives a comprehensive exposition of the εὐαγγέλιον, the *central concept of his theology of revelation and mission*. God called Paul to be an apostle and separated him for the mission of preaching the gospel (Rom. 1:1). Like the prophets Jeremiah (Jer. 1:5), Deutero-Isaiah (Isa. 49:1), and Moses (*As. Mos.* 1:14), Paul knows that he has been chosen by God. From the very beginning, this election was for the purpose of Paul's preaching the gospel among the Gentiles,[22] a fulfillment of the will of God already expressed in the prophets (Rom. 1:2–5).

The Gospel: Origin and Content

The gospel is about the Son of God, Jesus Christ, and his twofold origin: God declared Jesus of Nazareth, descended from David, to be Lord and Christ through his resurrection from the dead. The Jesus-Christ-history is a striking parallel to Paul's own life. "Just as by the revelation at Damascus Paul became what he was destined to be, so by the resurrection the human being Jesus became what God had declared him to be. Each had been previously appointed to his respective office by God (Paul, ἀφορίζειν ['set apart for']; Jesus, ὁρίζειν ['declare to be']). Neither exercised his office from birth but was installed in his respective office by a particular, miraculous act of God (Paul, καλεῖν ['call']; Jesus, ἐξ ἀναστάσεως νεκρῶν ['by resurrection from the dead'])."[23] By this paralleling of himself and Jesus and with the attributes mentioned in Rom. 1:1, Paul is not only emphasizing the continuity in God's saving acts. He is suggesting to the Romans that they see in the letter more than Paul's own introduction of himself; they should read it as the development and realization of the gospel instituted by God in Jesus Christ. The gospel did not come to Paul through human mediation but was revealed to him directly by God through the Christ event. Therefore the gospel is not at his own disposal; rather, Paul may and must serve it, and what he is to do with his life is already determined

---

22. Otfried Hofius, "Paulus—Missionar und Theologe," in *Paulusstudien* (2 vols.; WUNT 51, 143; Tübingen: Mohr Siebeck, 1989–2002), 2:1–16.

23. Alkier, *Wunder und Wirklichkeit*, 263.

for him by the gospel. Paul formulates this priestly dimension of his ministry in 15:15–16, where he returns to the theme of the prescript: "Nevertheless on some points I have written to you rather boldly by way of reminder, because of the grace given me by God to be a minister of Christ Jesus to the Gentiles in the priestly service of the gospel of God, so that the offering of the Gentiles may be acceptable, sanctified by the Holy Spirit." In contrast to the Levitical priests in the Jerusalem temple, Paul brings no material sacrifice to the altar; the Gentile believers are the acceptable offering he presents to God. Paul understands God's establishment of the gospel and God's calling of Paul to be apostle to the Gentiles to be acts of God's grace in salvation history that precede and initiate the faith of Jews and Gentiles. The apostle develops this fundamental insight in the thesis of the Letter to the Romans: "For I am not ashamed of the gospel; it is the power of God for salvation to everyone who has faith, to the Jew first and also to the Greek. For in it the righteousness of God is revealed through faith for faith; as it is written, 'The one who is righteous will live by faith'" (1:16–17).

The Gospel as Saving Power

Paul defines the gospel as δύναμις θεοῦ[24] and thereby designates its theo-centric nature as *the decisive structural feature of his Christology*. In the powerful event of Jesus Christ, God definitively reveals who he is. In the linguistic usage of both the Greek world and the Old Testament, power is a characteristic of deity. Psalm 67:12 LXX (Ps. 68:11)[25] is very close to the Pauline argumentation: "With much power the Lord will give his word to those who announce the good news" (κύριος δώσει ῥῆμα τοῖς εὐαγγελιζομένοις δυνάμει πολλῇ). In Rom. 1:17 the apostle cites Hab. 2:4, and so he could also have had Hab. 3:19 LXX in mind: κύριος ὁ θεὸς δύναμίς μου (God the Lord is my power). Finally, the common use of δύναμις and σωτηρία points to Ps. 139:8 LXX (Ps. 140:7): κύριε κύριε δύναμις τῆς σωτηρίας μου (O Lord God, the strength of my salvation). The plethora of allusions and citations shows clearly that behind Rom. 1:16–17 stands the Scripture, read from Paul's christological point of view. Paul finds it declared already here that God's message comes in power. The apostle brings this idea to a sharp point: the gospel is not mere information about God's saving plan but is itself a part of that plan because it is the powerful earthly representation of the God who saves. God's saving act takes place in the gospel, whose goal is the σωτηρία (salvation, deliverance) of Jews and Gentiles. Paul thereby designates the decisive motif of his evangelistic ministry and his concept of worldwide mission. In view of the fact that all humanity has fallen under the power of ἁμαρτία and the wrath of God already

24. Walter Grundmann, "δύναμαι, δύναμις," *TDNT* 2:284–317.
25. Hübner, *Biblische Theologie*, 1:174.

being revealed, the gospel must be proclaimed to all nations throughout the world so that they can be saved. This is why Paul orchestrates his missionary program, which extends from Jerusalem to Illyricum (15:19b),[26] then via Rome to Spain (15:28). He does this with the consciousness that it is the risen Christ who acts in Paul's word and deed (15:18), for the preaching of the gospel takes place "by the power of signs and wonders, by the power of the Spirit of God" (15:19a, ἐν δυνάμει σημείων καὶ τεράτων, ἐν δυνάμει πνεύματος). The power of God, which has already raised Jesus Christ from the dead, now continues to work visibly through signs and wonders in the apostle's worldwide preaching of the gospel.[27]

Human beings respond in faith to God's loving action on behalf of the world through the gospel (1:16–17). The apostle understands faith as a saving and thus life-giving power and gift of God that attains its goal when human beings accept the gospel according to God's will. The gospel changes the soteriological status of those who hear it, for faith comes by hearing the good news and knows itself to have been created by the gospel. With the phrase Ἰουδαίῳ τε πρῶτον καὶ Ἕλληνι (to the Jew first and also to the Greek) in 1:16, Paul views humanity in its polarity as a matter of salvation history, whereby Ἰουδαίῳ τε πρῶτον (to the Jew first) already signals the problematic of Rom. 9–11. The promise of God distinguishes Israel from all other peoples, it stands in a special relation to God, so that God's eschatological act of salvation in Jesus Christ raises the question of the destiny of Israel in a way that cannot be avoided. Only the saving gospel grants the believer the righteousness of God, which excludes any righteousness based on doing the works of the law.[28] In 1:16–17 Paul brings the concept of righteousness/justification directly into the image of God and makes it the basis of his argumentation. The present-tense ἀποκαλύπτεται indicates that this righteousness is not a reality that will appear only in the future but is already revealed in the here and now: in the Pauline preaching of the gospel of the crucifixion and resurrection of Jesus Christ. To show that these claims are scriptural, Paul again cites Hab. 2:4 (cf. Gal. 3:11). In contrast to Jewish tradition, the apostle does not refer the prophet's word to the intentional keeping of the laws, from

---

26. This statement does not describe the geographical outline of the Pauline mission, for according to Gal. 1:17ff. Paul did not begin his missionary activity in Jerusalem and proceed from there (cf. Wilckens, *Römer*, 3:119; differently, Riesner, *Paul's Early Period*, 241–55). Jerusalem appears here as the factual beginning point of the gospel of Jesus Christ. Nothing is known about Paul's activity in Illyricum (corresponding to parts of present day Slovenia, Croatia, Serbia, and Albania). One can suppose that Paul also had contacts with Illyricum during his stay in Macedonia.

27. Cf. Nielsen, "Δύναμις," 151–52.

28. On the expression ἐκ πίστεως εἰς πίστιν (NRSV, "through faith for faith," Rom. 1:17), cf. Wilckens, *Römer* 1:88: "The righteousness of God is established through faith (not through works); thus its purpose is directed toward faith, that is, that all people come to believe. The phrase εἰς πίστιν thus designates the universally intended effect of the preaching of God's righteousness that is received ἐκ πίστεως."

which righteousness would then follow.[29] For him, human righteousness is, rather, the result of the righteousness of God encountered in the gospel and accepted in faith. As in Gal. 3:11, here also Paul makes a sharp distinction between observance of the Torah and faith, thereby annulling a fundamental conviction of ancient Judaism.

The thesis expressed in Rom. 1:16–17 makes clear that the whole letter is to be read as a comprehensive unfolding of the Pauline gospel. With this thesis Paul prepares the reader to understand what follows, where the gospel of Jesus Christ will be developed as the righteousness by faith that leads to life. The Letter to the Romans should be read as an unfolding development of the various aspects of an irreversible line: gospel–faith and justification/righteousness–life.

12.4 Knowledge of God among Jews and Gentiles

In Rom. 1:18–3:20 Paul turns to the question of the addressees of his worldwide preaching of the gospel.[30] There is a striking parallel between the revelation of the righteousness of God (1:17) and the wrath of God (1:18), but this in itself does not indicate that they have the same scope. Paul does not understand the revelation of God's wrath as an aspect of the gospel, for wrath does not come from the gospel but "from heaven." The apostle can describe the gospel without speaking of God's wrath. Certainly, the humanity to whom this gospel is directed is in a state of cognitive and ethical perversion. But for all that, the immoral conduct of human beings is merely a symptom of their truly disastrous state: humans fail to acknowledge God and in this very way bring about the ruination of their own existence.[31] They suppress the truth (1:18) and thereby reveal the boundlessness of their own evil, for whoever disdains the truth knows what it is, but is not willing to acknowledge it. Humanity sets itself against what is clearly revealed: the revelation of God through and in the creation. God does not keep himself hidden either from his creatures or in creation, and so human beings are in a position to perceive this revelation. The knowledge of God thus appears not merely as a possibility but as the reality in which the whole world already finds itself. Paul is not concerned to prove the existence of God; for him, this is the self-evident presupposition that demonstrates the godlessness of humanity Those who believe in the gods while they, however, deny honor to the one God reveal their own godlessness.

29. Cf. ibid., 1:84–85.
30. For exegesis of this section, see, in addition to the standard commentaries, esp. M. Pohlenz, "Paulus und die Stoa," *ZNW* 42 (1949): 69–104; Günther Bornkamm, "Die Offenbarung des Zornes Gottes," in *Das Ende des Gesetzes: Paulusstudien* (BEvT 16; Munich: Kaiser, 1961), 9–33; Bussmann, *Paulinischen Missionspredigt,* 108–22.
31. Hübner, *Biblische Theologie,* 2:63.

In 1:18–32 Paul shows this by taking up the critique of Gentile life already elaborated by Hellenistic Diaspora Judaism.[32]

The Blindedness of Gentiles

In their foolishness and blindness, the Gentiles fail to recognize who is the only true God. In their false worship, they turn to transitory idols and exchange the glory of the one true God "for images resembling a mortal human being or birds or four-footed animals or reptiles" (Rom. 1:23). This astonishing conduct of humanity calls for an explanation, which Paul attempts to provide on several levels. He begins with the assertion that sin leads to more sin. Individual transgressions release the power of sin and lead to enslavement under sin. The apostle goes a step further: according to 1:24–27, God himself gives humanity over to blindness. God not only permits humanity to go astray but actively effects it himself (cf. Jer. 2:5; Ps. 93:11).[33] Wrath is thus inherently present in the revelation of God, and not only when it is seen simply as the negative foil for God's righteousness. God reacts to humanity's inconsistent conduct; God does not want human beings to come to him with such inconsistent conduct, for God is the Creator.[34]

Paul's demonstration that, in view of the present revelation of the righteousness of God in Jesus Christ, the Gentiles are without excuse is based on his fundamental anthropological and cosmological convictions.[35] For Paul, *persons first become what they essentially are as human beings when they stand in their proper relation to God as creatures to Creator.* People miss their life's goal and lose the standard by which they conduct their lives when they do not let God be for them the only true God. A false understanding of God results in a false understanding of what it means to be human. With this is associated a specific understanding of the nature of reality. Because for Paul Creator and creation belong most closely together, the creation in its present being can be recognized only in view of its having-been-created. For Paul, there is no knowledge of "nature" apart from God the Creator. Such a view would mean the destruction of nature because nature would be separated from its origin. When they deny their origin, which can be so clearly perceived, human beings and nature are equally alienated from God. For Paul, the godless world is a

---

32. Especially Wis. 13:1–9 appears to have affected Paul (texts in *NW* 2/1:13–22).

33. Cf. Ernst Käsemann, *Commentary on Romans* (trans. Geoffrey W. Bromiley; Grand Rapids: Eerdmans, 1980), 42–43.

34. It is striking that Paul argues on the basis of a theology of creation even in those places where he could cite passages from the Torah; cf., on the rejection of male homosexuality in Rom. 1:27, the prohibitions in Lev. 18:22; 20:13.

35. Cf. Udo Schnelle, *The Human Condition: Anthropology in the Teachings of Jesus, Paul, and John* (trans. O. C. Dean Jr.; Minneapolis: Fortress, 1996), 37–113.

profoundly chaotic, dreadful world because humanity and nature have turned
away from the power of God, who alone grants life.

The Blindedness of Jews

The gospel addresses not only the Gentiles in their blindness to the knowledge of God but also the Jews imprisoned in their sin (cf. Rom. 2:1–3:8). Paul
attempts to prove to them that possession of the Torah by no means saves
them from the wrath of God. In doing so, he employs the typical pattern of
thought he had previously used in his dialogue with the Gentiles. If the Gentiles disqualify themselves by their polytheism, the Jews do the same by their
fundamental contradiction between orthodoxy and orthopraxy (cf. 2:3). The
contrast between their advantages, which Paul does not deny, and their failure
leads to the judgment of God for Jews just as in the case of the Gentiles (cf.
2:5–10). Because God will repay according to each one's deeds (2:6),[36] Israel's
priority, based on the gift of the Torah, turns out ultimately to be a disadvan-
tage because Israel does not keep its commands. By taking up the concept of
judgment according to one's works, Paul adopts an idea widespread in ancient
Judaism (cf. Prov. 24:12; *Pss. Sol.* 9:5),[37] but he applies it in a specific way.
For example, whereas in *Pss. Sol.* 2:16–18 judgment according to one's works
is understood as God's righteous dealing with the Gentiles,[38] Paul now turns
this idea against the Jews themselves. Precisely because God is no respecter of
persons and judges people according to their works, only those will be justified who do the law/Torah (cf. Rom. 2:13b). In 2:13b Paul acknowledges the
possibility of one who does what the law requires, but how is this possibility
related to the concept that dominates the letter as a whole, that justification
comes by faith alone without works of the law/Torah? The problem becomes
sharper in 2:14, for Gentiles too can be doers of the law, since the law is written
on their hearts, and can thus attain salvation apart from the redemptive act of
Christ (cf. also 2:26). This tension clarifies the position from which Paul makes
his argument. He is not finally concerned with the theoretical possibility of
fulfilling the requirement of the law, even if he acknowledges this is possible
for both Jews and Gentiles, but only with the actual reality that the efforts of
all human beings are doomed by the law/Torah. This doom is the result of sin,
as shown by 3:9: προητιασάμεθα γὰρ Ἰουδαίους τε καὶ Ἕλληνας πάντας ὑφ'
ἁμαρτίαν εἶναι (we have already charged that all, both Jews and Greeks, are

36. Cf. Ps. 61:13 LXX (Ps. 62:12).
37. Cf. Wilckens, *Römer*, 1:127–31.
38. *Pss. Sol.* 2:16–18: "For you have rewarded sinners according to their actions, and according
to their extremely wicked sins. You have exposed their sins, that your judgment might be evident; you
have obliterated their memory from the earth. God is a righteous judge and will not be impressed by
appearances" (trans. R. B. Wright, *OTP* 2:653). On the idea of judgment according to works in the
realm of classical Greek, cf. Plato, *Phaed.* 113d–114c.

under the power of sin; cf. also 3:20). From this point of view, it becomes clear that judgment according to works and justification by faith alone without works belong together. Since, because of the power of sin, human beings can exhibit in the judgment no works that will justify them,[39] salvation comes exclusively through faith in Jesus Christ, the resurrected Son of God. God alone effects the justification of human beings by his grace because human beings are and remain sinners and are therefore always in need of God's justifying pronouncement of acquittal.[40] Standing before God in the judgment, no human being can achieve this pronouncement of acquittal by his or her own accomplishments but can only receive it as something freely granted in the gospel and given by faith in the saving act of God in Jesus Christ. This faith manifests its effective presence in love, and so the Christian's responsibility to give account for his or her life to the future Judge is not rendered superfluous.[41] The external possession of the law/Torah is not decisive in this happening if the hearer of the law is not at the same time a doer of the law. This fundamental principle applies to Jews and Gentiles alike.

In order to point out to the Jews their true situation, in 2:14–15 Paul takes up the Greco-Roman idea of the νόμος ἄγραφος (unwritten law).[42] This concept was also widespread in Hellenistic Judaism, where it affirmed that there are orders in nature, established by God and accessible to reason, that are identical with the commands of the Torah. With the help of reason, people can comply with God's will by observing the νόμος φύσεως (natural law), even though they do not possess the Torah. The law here appears as a constituent element of an orderly world, so that it gives Jews no advantage over Gentiles. Neither the Jews, who possess the law/Torah as an external object, nor the Gentiles, who have the law written on their hearts, are actually doers of the law/Torah,

---

39. Differently, Bultmann, *Theology of the New Testament*, 1:263: "But Paul goes much further still; he says not only that man *can* not achieve salvation by works of the Law, but also that he is not even *intended* to do so." This understanding does not capture the apostle's intention, for it is not the doing of works but being under the power of sin that prevents one from being justified.

40. Cf. Hans Conzelmann, *An Outline of the Theology of the New Testament* (trans. John Bowden; New York: Harper & Row, 1969), 248, where judgment according to works means in Paul that "here grace is no longer a compensation for what righteousness man still lacks, but the complete provision of righteousness by God."

41. Cf. Wilckens, *Römer*, 1:145: "The Pauline gospel is at its core by no means hostile to works."

42. Compare the texts in *NW* 2/1:71–85 with the whole complex of ideas; with ἑαυτοῖς εἰσιν νόμος compare Aristotle, *Eth. nic.* 4.1128a: "The refined and well-bred man, therefore, will be as we have described, being as it were a law to himself." Cf. also Aristotle, *Pol.* 1284a, according to which the law is not concerned with exceptional people, "for they are a law to themselves" (αὐτοὶ γάρ εἰσι νόμος). How strongly the idea of the νόμος ἄγραφος had impressed itself into people's consciousness is indicated by a pseudepigraphical letter of the Pythagorean Melissa to Kleareta: "For a husband's wishes ought to be an unwritten law [νόμος ἄγραφος] to an orderly wife, and she should live by them" (*Epistulae pythagoreorum* 3.2; trans. A. J. Malherbe, *Moral Exhortation: A Greco-Roman Sourcebook* [LEC; Philadelphia: Westminster, 1986], 83).

and therefore they fall under God's righteous judgment. So, too, circumcision does not justify a special place for the Jews, for, according to 2:25, ἡ περιτομή σου ἀκροβυστία γέγονεν (your circumcision has become uncircumcision). In 2:28–29 Paul even goes so far as to redefine the term Ἰουδαῖος: "For a person is not a Jew who is one outwardly, nor is true circumcision something external and physical. Rather, a person is a Jew who is one inwardly, and real circumcision is a matter of the heart—it is spiritual and not literal." Thus physical circumcision does not make one a Jew; only circumcision of the heart, a spiritual reality, indicates who is a Jew and who is not.[43] "The true Jew is thus—the Christian convert."[44] What, then, is the basis for Israel's special relation to God? It is the promises of God that form the foundation for Israel's special status (3:1). *Israel is and remains the chosen people of God but no longer has any soteriological priority in comparison with the Gentiles.* Instead, for both Jews and Gentiles, subjection to the power of sin reveals the difference between what one should be and what one is (cf. 3:9). For Paul, this fundamental anthropological state of affairs appears to be already clearly expressed in the Scripture (cf. 3:10–18).[45] When Paul concludes his wide-ranging argumentation with a combination of texts from the Old Testament, he incorporates God's previous authoritative pronouncements in order to legitimate and clarify his own main points. The reality of every human being is characterized by its hostility to God.

In 2:1–3:8 Paul places the Jewish self-understanding radically in question. Although he acknowledges the special position of Israel to which the Scripture testifies, he in fact limits it to the past. In order to make this argument work, the apostle constructs *a redefinition of the law and circumcision.*[46] Both gifts that originally distinguished Israel from all other peoples are universalized and spiritualized: the knowledge of the νόμος ἄγραφος and the practice of circumcision of the heart place Israel and the Gentiles in the same status. Now both the promises and the law/Torah are under the power of sin and become the Jews' accusers, and they paradoxically attain their goal not among the Jews but among the Christians as those spiritually "circumcised." Paul thus claims that God's original and eschatological will is fulfilled among the Christians alone. It is difficult to imagine a sharper criticism and challenge to Jewish self-understanding than 2:1–3:8. Paul never questions the validity of God's promises, but he does challenge the special status of Israel inferred from these promises. In practice this amounts to a reversal of the promises, since they now are fulfilled among Christians and become an accusation against Israel. For Jews and Jewish Christians, such an interpretation of the history of salvation as the history of disaster for Israel was unacceptable,

---

43. A thoroughly comparable position is found in Philo, where the rite is spiritualized in response to cultural pressure to conform; cf. *QE* 2.2: "The sojourner is one who circumcises not his uncircumcision but his desires and sensual pleasures and the other passions of the soul."

44. Wilckens, *Römer*, 1:157.

45. For analysis, cf. Hübner, *Biblische Theologie*, 2:272–74.

46. See below, section 19.3 ("The Law").

and so, despite Rom. 9–11, *Romans must be read as a document contributing to the separation of the early Christians from the synagogue.*

12.5 The Righteousness of God

The theological depth of the concept of sin expressed in Rom. 1:18–3:20 poses the unavoidable question of how Jews and Gentiles as sinners can escape the impending wrath of God or whether they are already delivered from it. Paul turns to this question in 3:21–31, taking up the expression previously used only in 2 Cor. 5:21, δικαιοσύνη θεοῦ and making it into *the key theological concept of the whole letter.*

Major Positions in the Scholarly Discussion

The meaning of δικαιοσύνη θεοῦ is a disputed point in recent research.[47] Whereas R. Bultmann and H. Conzelmann understand δικαιοσύνη θεοῦ in the anthropological context as gift, that is, as righteousness/justification imputed through faith (cf. Phil. 3:9),[48] E. Käsemann and P. Stuhlmacher interpret δικαιοσύνη θεοῦ as a *terminus technicus* already present in Jewish apocalyptic that Paul takes into his own theology.[49] As a key term in the Pauline doctrine of justification, it is crucial for how this doctrine is to be understood, and is thus decisive for Pauline theology as a whole.[50] They rightly object, against

---

47. For the history of research, cf., most recently, Seifrid, *Justification by Faith*, 1–75; R. Bieringer, "Sünde und Gerechtigkeit in 2 Korinther 5,21," in *Studies on 2 Corinthians* (ed. R. Bieringer and Jan Lambrecht; BETL 112; Leuven: Leuven University Press, 1994), 494–501, 511–14, for good bibliography; Theobald, *Römerbrief*, 206–12.

48. Cf. Bultmann, *Theology of the New Testament*, 1:285: "The reason why 'righteousness' is called 'God's righteousness' is just this: Its one and only foundation is God's grace—it is God-given, God-adjudicated righteousness (Rom. 1:17; 3:21–22, 26; 10:3)." Cf. further p. 271: "But it is possible to speak so of 'righteousness' not only because of the tight connection that exists between 'righteousness' (as condition) and 'life' (as result), but especially because *not merely salvation (the result) is the gift of God but even the condition for it is already the gift of God Himself.*" Conzelmann, *Theology of the New Testament*, 220: "Philippians 3.9 offers the key for the definition of the concept." This is elaborated in Hans Conzelmann, *Grundriss der Theologie des Neuen Testaments* (4th ed.; Tübingen: Mohr Siebeck, 1987), 244: "Here [in Phil. 3:9] this theme is fully developed. 'My righteousness' and 'the righteousness of God διὰ πίστεως Χριστοῦ ['through faith in Christ''] here stand diametrically opposite each other. The former represents human attainment through the Torah (ἐκ νόμου; cf. 3:6 and Rom. 10:5), in contrast, the latter comes from God (ἐκ θεοῦ; here the genitive is clearly explained as *genitivus auctoris,* i.e., genitive of source)."

49. Ernst Käsemann, "'The Righteousness of God' in Paul," in *New Testament Questions of Today* (London: SCM Press, 1969), 172; Peter Stuhlmacher, *Gerechtigkeit Gottes bei Paulus* (Göttingen: Vandenhoeck & Ruprecht, 1965), 73; more hesitantly, Stuhlmacher, *Romans*, 29–32.

50. Cf. Käsemann, "Righteousness of God," 176: "But I find myself totally unable to assent to the view that Paul's theology and his philosophy of history are oriented towards the individual."

Bultmann and Conzelmann, that an interpretation of δικαιοσύνη θεοῦ oriented primarily to the individual neglects the universal aspects of a theology of creation and history. But there are also significant objections to be raised against the approach of Käsemann and Stuhlmacher. The question of God's righteousness was indeed already raised for Paul from the Old Testament[51] and the literature of ancient Judaism,[52] but δικαιοσύνη θεοῦ was not a *terminus technicus* of traditional Jewish apocalyptic. The phrase "righteousness of God" is found in Jewish texts (cf. Deut. 33:21; *T. Dan* 6:10; 1QS 10:25; 11:12; 1QM 4:6), but not as a fixed formula.[53] The statements in the Qumran literature about the righteousness of God do present a parallel to Paul's but cannot be considered a presupposition of the apostle's own doctrine of justification.[54] There was intensive reflection on the subject of righteousness at Qumran, on the basis of a radicalized image of humanity and God, but this did not result in using "righteousness of God" as the predominant *terminus technicus* for God's act in establishing righteousness.[55] What is striking is, rather, that at Qumran divine and human righteousness was described in several different ways.

"Righteousness of God" as a Multidimensional Concept

The data in the Pauline texts shows that δικαιοσύνη θεοῦ is a multidimensional concept. In 2 Cor. 5:21 the gift character of δικαιοσύνη θεοῦ predomi-

51. Cf., most recently, Frank-Lothar Hossfeld, "Gedanken zum alttestamentlichen Vorfeld paulinischer Rechtfertigungslehre," in *Worum geht es in der Rechtfertigungslehre? Das biblische Fundament der "Gemeinsamen Erklärung" von katholischer Kirche und Lutherischem Weltbund* (ed. Thomas Söding and Frank-Lothar Hossfeld; QD 180; Freiburg: Herder, 1999), 13–26.

52. Cf. Seifrid, *Justification by Faith*, 78–133, who limits his analyses to the *Rule of the Community* (1QS) and the *Psalms of Solomon* on grounds of chronology and content. Both groups of texts show clearly "that an emphasis on 'mercy' did not necessarily exclude the idea that obedience was a prerequisite to salvation in early Judaism" (p. 133).

53. For evidence, see Schnelle, *Gerechtigkeit und Christusgegenwart*, 93–96, 217–19; Becker, *Paul*, 367; Seifrid, *Justification by Faith*, 99–107.

54. On the problematic of possible relations between Paul and Qumran thought, in addition to the works of H.-W. Kuhn listed in the bibliography, see the circumspect reflections of Herbert Braun, *Qumran und das Neue Testament* (2 vols.; Tübingen: Mohr Siebeck, 1966), 2:166ff. See further Joseph A. Fitzmyer, "Paul and the Dead Sea Scrolls," in *The Dead Sea Scrolls after Fifty Years: A Comprehensive Assessment* (ed. Peter W. Flint and James C. VanderKam; 3 vols.; Leiden: Brill, 1998), 2:599–621.

55. Cf. Hartwig Thyen, *Studien zur Sündenvergebung im Neuen Testament und seinen alttestamentlichen und jüdischen Voraussetzungen* (FRLANT; Göttingen: Vandenhoeck & Ruprecht, 1970), 57ff.; Eduard Lohse, "Die Gerechtigkeit Gottes in der paulinischen Theologie," in *Die Einheit des Neuen Testaments: Exegetische Studien zur Theologie des Neuen Testaments* (2nd ed.; Göttingen: Vandenhoeck & Ruprecht, 1973), 216. Moreover, it is questionable whether one can designate the Qumran texts in so wholesale a manner, as in Stuhlmacher's statement, as "the central core of the apocalyptic theology of late Judaism" (*Gerechtigkeit Gottes*, 148). On the relation of Paul to Qumran, see Hartmut Stegemann, "Die Bedeutung der Qumranfunde für die Erforschung der Apokalyptik," in *Apocalypticism in the Mediterranean World and the Near East: Proceedings of the International Colloquium on Apocalypticism, Uppsala, August 12–17, 1979* (ed. David Hellholm; Tübingen: Mohr Siebeck, 1983), 495–530.

nates; the "of" represents a *genitivus auctoris* (genitive of source).[56] Believers participate in the substitutionary death of Jesus Christ and are transferred by baptism and the gift of the Spirit into a new realm of existence. The character of δικαιοσύνη θεοῦ as power is clear in Rom. 1:17,[57] indicated linguistically by ἀποκαλύπτεται (is revealed).[58] Now Jesus discloses God's eschatological saving will, which makes itself known powerfully in the gospel of the righteousness of God in Jesus Christ for those who believe. In Rom. 3:5 human righteousness and the righteousness of God (subjective genitive) stand opposed to each other in a legal dispute. Here it is not a matter of the righteousness of God being revealed in the gospel,[59] but a quality of God's nature, who establishes his righteousness/justice in the judgment and proves the unrighteousness of humanity. In 3:21–22 δικαιοσύνη θεοῦ appears twice, but each instance has a different connotation. Δικαιοσύνη θεοῦ in 3:21 is to be read as a revelatory concept, meaning that in the Christ event God has made himself known as the one who makes (others) righteous and establishes justice. Here the term "righteousness of God" does not communicate something about God, but in it God's revelation takes place as an event. It is to this epoch-making event that the law and the prophets bear witness, so that the law itself confirms its own end as the source of righteousness. In 3:22 Paul is thinking of δικαιοσύνη θεοῦ in its anthropological aspect. Faith in Jesus Christ is the form in which the righteousness of God (i.e., the righteousness that comes from God) is appropriated. By faith, Jesus is the righteousness of God for all who believe. Whereas the righteousness of God appears in 3:21 as the universal power of God, in 3:22 the character of God's righteousness as gift is the predominant meaning.[60]

Romans 3:25 is of particular significance for understanding δικαιοσύνη θεοῦ and the Pauline doctrine of justification as a whole.[61] In 3:25–26a Paul quite intentionally integrates a baptismal tradition[62] into the decisive line of argument of the Letter to the Romans in order to relate the universal saving act of God

56. Cf., e.g., Windisch, *Korintherbrief,* 198; Bultmann, *Theology of the New Testament,* 1:277; C. E. B. Cranfield, *The Epistle to the Romans* (2 vols.; ICC; Edinburgh: T&T Clark, 1979), 1:97–98; Theobald, *Römerbrief,* 207.

57. Stuhlmacher, *Gerechtigkeit Gottes,* 78–84.

58. Zeller, *Römer,* 43, is on target with his comment: "The righteousness of God is made eschatologically available already in the present (present tense!)."

59. Cf. ibid., 78–79.

60. The classification of the nuances of content in terms of grammatical categories is not entirely satisfactory; Rom. 3:21 should be understood as *genitivus objectivus* and Rom. 3:22 as *genitivus auctoris.* Differently, e.g., Theobald, *Römerbrief,* 207–8, who wants to read all instances in Rom. 3:21–26 as *genitivus subjectivus.*

61. On the exegesis of Rom. 3:25, see below, section 16.6 ("The Death of Jesus Christ as Atoning Event").

62. For evidence and argument, cf. Schnelle, *Gerechtigkeit und Christusgegenwart,* 67–72, 197–201.

expressed in 3:21–22 to the personal experience of the individual Christian. The baptismal reference is indicated by the Pauline framework (3:24, δικαιόω, ἀπολύτρωσις, ἐν Χριστῷ Ἰησοῦ; 3:26, ἐν τῷ νῦν καιρῷ) and by the concept of the once-for-all forgiveness of sins found in the traditional material. Paul takes up terminology with ritual overtones as a way of relating the ritual experiences of the Roman church to his exclusive doctrine of justification. The subjective genitive in δικαιοσύνη θεοῦ does not merely designate a quality of God but means the righteousness appropriate to the God who reveals himself universally in the event of the cross, the righteousness realized in the remission of prior sins that takes place in baptism. Universal significance and individual appropriation of the saving event are seen as conditioning each other: God's saving act in Jesus Christ can be believed as universally true only when it is experienced in the particularity of one's own existence. The tradition highlights this conjunction in that, transcending any particular critique of the law, it holds together these two dimensions—God's universal act on the cross, and God's presence experienced in baptism—as the forgiveness of sins that makes righteous.

The universal dimension of δικαιοσύνη θεοῦ is also seen in 10:3. Here Israel is reproached for seeking its own righteousness, not the righteousness that comes from God. The chosen people closes itself off from the will of God revealed in Jesus Christ and does not submit to the δικαιοσύνη θεοῦ (subjective genitive).[63] Instead Israel undertakes the hopeless task of wanting to establish its own righteousness by works of the law. God's action here concerns peoples, so that an interpretation of δικαιοσύνη θεοῦ focusing exclusively on the individual and neglecting its cosmological dimension would not square with the textual data.[64] At the same time, Phil. 3:9 lets us see clearly that a choice between the individual and cosmic dimensions of δικαιοσύνη θεοῦ would be just as wrong. There Paul refers the justifying act of God entirely to the individual existence of the believer (Phil. 3:9a, καὶ εὑρεθῶ ἐν αὐτῷ [and be found in him], i.e., Christ). The righteousness of God (genitive of source: righteousness from God) does not result from the law/Torah but is given to human beings through faith in Jesus Christ.

Depending on the context, δικαιοσύνη θεοῦ is thus to be interpreted as a *universal-forensic concept* (Rom. 1:17; 3:5, 21, 25; 10:3) and as a *concept expressing transfer and participation* (2 Cor. 5:21; Rom. 3:22; Phil. 3:9). The "righteousness of God" concisely designates both the revelatory act and the act of the believer's incorporation and participation in God's justifying/rightwising act in Jesus Christ. The limited use and application of the expression,[65] the

---

63. Cf. Wilckens, *Römer*, 2:220.

64. Cf. Stuhlmacher, *Gerechtigkeit Goites*, 93.

65. The seven explicit instances of δικαιοσύνη θεοῦ (2 Cor. 5:21; Rom. 1:17; 3:5; 3:21, 22; 10:3; Phil. 3:9) may be contrasted with the vocabulary dealing with the realm of salvation: πνεῦμα, 120 times; ἐν Χριστῷ, 61 times; ἐν κυρίῳ, 37 times; πίστις, 91 times; πιστεύω, 42 times; δικαιοσύνη, 25 times; ζωή, 27 times; ἐλπίς, 25 times.

restrictive function apparent in the predominantly negative formulations,[66] its concentration in the letter to the Romans, and the variety of meanings, depending on the particular context in which the term is found, show clearly that δικαιοσύνη θεοῦ is *not* the *key concept* of Pauline theology *as a whole*.[67] Paul can fully set forth his theology without having to fall back on the expression δικαιοσύνη θεοῦ. In the Letter to the Romans, "righteousness of God" does function as a major theological concept because, in the wake of the Galatian crisis and in view of the delivery of the collection in Jerusalem, Paul must give his Christology a theocentric profile and provide a solution to the problematic of the law: the Christ event manifests the righteousness that comes from God and is appropriated by faith, the righteousness that alone allows human beings to stand justified before God and that thus removes any soteriological significance from the law/Torah (cf. Rom. 6:14b). Since designating the righteousness of God as δικαιοσύνη θεοῦ χωρὶς νόμου (the righteousness of God *apart from law*, 3:21) has abrogated the law/Torah as a way to salvation, in Romans Paul can arrive at a partially new evaluation of the law/Torah. This new evaluation can be interpreted, on the one hand, as purely antinomianism endangering the Christian community and, on the other hand, as preserving the central theological values resulting from his dispute with the Galatian Judaists.

The Law of Faith

In Rom. 3:27, in contrasting the hopeless situation of humanity enslaved to sin (3:20) with the saving potential of the righteousness of God that has appeared in Jesus Christ (3:26–21), there suddenly appears an expression significant for Paul's understanding of the law, νόμος πίστεως (the law of faith). Does νόμος here mean the Old Testament Torah, or is the word here used in the sense of "rule/order/norm"?[68] A decision can be made only on philological grounds, and on the basis of the data found in 3:27 itself, not by bringing in one's prior understanding of Paul's theology of the law. Philologically, the question διὰ ποίου νόμου; (through what sort of law?) presupposes a generic understanding of νόμος; that is, Paul here assumes there are a number of different kinds of laws.[69] This linguistic observation already indicates that νόμος here cannot refer

---

66. Cf. Sanders, *Paul and Palestinian Judaism*, 441, 491–92.

67. Cf. also Hübner, *Biblische Theologie*, 1:177: "This term, of course, does not occur elsewhere in the Pauline corpus with the meaning it has in Paul's usage in Romans. The 'righteousness of God' is thus for Paul a concept that developed out of the late phase of his theology."

68. Linguistic parallels to the use of νόμος in the sense of "order/norm" are given by Heikki Räisänen, "Sprachliches zum Spiel des Paulus mit Nomos," in *Glaube und Gerechtigkeit: In memoriam Rafael Gyllenberg (18 6 1893–29 7 1982)* (ed. Rafael Gyllenberg et al.; SFEJ 38; Helsinki: Suomen Eksegeettisen Seuran, 1983), 134–49.

69. Cf. Klaus Haacker, *Der Brief des Paulus an die Römer* (THKNT 6; Leipzig: Evangelische Verlagsanstalt, 1999), 93.

to the Torah given at Sinai. Regarding its content, νόμος appears in 3:27 as the means (διὰ) through which boasting is excluded. Moreover, the verb ἐκκλείω in the aorist passive (it has been excluded; NRSV, "it is excluded") refers to a single event in the past. The acting subject in this event is God, for it is not the right conduct of the believer with respect to the law/Torah or the revitalization of the law/Torah through faith that is up for discussion but νόμος as a means of a single event that excludes καύχησις (boasting). Then νόμος πίστεως can only mean God's saving act in Jesus Christ, for the Old Testament Torah is not the means chosen by God to exclude human boasting once and for all. Νόμος must thus here be translated as "rule/order/norm."[70] Faith appears as the new norm to which Christians are committed and that excludes any boasting of one's own achievements before God.

In 3:28 the expression νόμος πίστεως is taken up and continued with the words δικαιοῦσθαι πίστει ἄνθρωπον (a person is justified by faith) and interpreted under the aspect of works (χωρὶς ἔργων νόμου [apart from works prescribed by law]). The righteousness that comes through works of the Torah does not justify the person; faith in the justifying act of God in Jesus Christ opens to the person the status of δικαιοῦσθαι (being justified). The event of justification is thereby withdrawn from the sphere of human action; it occurs in the Christ event and can only be accepted by faith. Paul emphasizes the universal significance of this event by using the word ἄνθρωπος (person, human being), and righteousness/justification does not have the character of deed but that of a gift. Why? The immediate context provides no answer to this question, but Paul continues his argument under the premise of 3:20: because the law/Torah has been taken over by the power of sin, no one can be justified by the law/Torah. Paul emphasizes the universal dimension of this event in 3:30 with the affirmation of the one God (εἷς ὁ θεός [God is one]) who justifies both Gentiles and Jews by faith. Paul does not thereby deny the election of Israel but abolishes the particularism of salvation, for now the Gentiles, too, participate by faith in God's gift of election. Finally, if God is one, then all who believe in God, both Jews and Gentiles, are one. Does this removal of the barriers that had signified the exclusive election of Israel mean a removal of the law/Torah itself? In 3:31 Paul emphatically denies this inference, which seems to lie so close at hand, and affirms the opposite: μὴ γένοιτο· ἀλλὰ νόμον ἱστάνομεν (By no means! On the contrary, we uphold the law). This tension-filled line of argument becomes clear only when one observes Paul's overriding goal: he must integrate the Torah into his argument as the gift of God without thereby detracting from the exclusive soteriological function of Christology. He attains this through two arguments: (1) The Scripture itself says in Gen.

---

70. Cf. Räisänen, "Spiel des Paulus," 149–54; cf., further in this sense, Käsemann, *Romans*, 103; Zeller, *Römer*, 92–93; R. Weber, "Die Geschichte des Gesetzes und des Ich in Römer 7,7–8,4," *NZST* 29 (1987): 166; Haacker, *Der Brief an die Römer*, 93.

15:6 (cf. Rom. 4:3) that righteousness comes by faith. We may learn from the figure of Abraham that faith does not destroy the Torah.[71] (2) For Paul, the love command is the content, center, and fulfillment of the law/Torah (cf. Rom. 13:8–20). By pointing to ἀγάπη (love), the law/Torah changes its character and its original significance, for now it is determined by love and summed up in the one love commandment.[72] Through this *transformation of the Torah into the love commandment*, Paul reclaims fulfillment of the Torah for Christians without attributing to it any sort of soteriological quality. Moreover, the Torah as concentrated into the concept of love can now be combined with the Hellenistic conception of law and thus be integrated into the world of Gentile Christianity.[73]

12.6 Paul and the Old Testament

For Paul, the Old Testament (the Septuagint) is Holy Scripture that narrates the story of Israel as the saving activity of God. The new evaluation of God's dealing with Israel, necessitated by Paul's Christ hermeneutic, allowed him to interpret the Old Testament within a new framework of understanding that the Christ event had altered. *He reads the Old Testament christologically, approaching it with the question of how it bears witness to the Christ event.* Since he claims the Scripture as a witness for the gospel (Rom. 1:16; 3:21),[74] he must concentrate on the texts, images, and characters in the Old Testament that can be understood as announcements or prefigurations of the Christ event. This approach brings Hab. 2:4b and the figure of Abraham into prominence. For Paul, they represent a theological program, and by means of them, he illustrates the historical and theological anchoring of his doctrine of justification in the Old Testament.

Two Key Texts

Paul's interpretation of Gen. 15:6 and Hab. 2:4b means that all the other texts in the Old Testament are virtually invalidated.[75] He understands Hab. 2:4b LXX in Gal. 3:11 and Rom. 1:17 in such wise that πίστις (faith, faithfulness) refers not to the faithfulness of God to the righteous who live by the Torah but to faith in Jesus Christ as the justifying event. Paul presents the figure of Abraham to prove that Paul's exclusive doctrine of justification is according to

71. Cf. Hübner, *Biblische Theologie*, 2:287.
72. Hübner, *Law in Paul's Thought*, 83–85.
73. For an extensive supporting argument, see below, section 19.3 ("The Law").
74. Cf., on this topic, Koch, *Schrift als Zeuge*, 341–42.
75. Cf. Schweitzer, *Mysticism*, 208.

the Scripture[76] and to show that Abraham is already represented paradigmatically in the Bible as an authoritative model of justification by faith. The whole of ancient Judaism identified with Abraham as representing God's election,[77] for not only Israel (cf. *4 Ezra* 3:13ff.) but also the proselytes have him as their father.[78] Before Israel received the written Torah, Abraham was already following it (cf. Gen. 26; *2 Bar.* 57:2; *T. Benj.* 10:4). After all, Abraham had been repeatedly tested by God and each time found to be faithful and righteous (cf. Neh. 9:8; Sir. 44:20; *Jub.* 17:15–18; 18:16; 19:9). Because Abraham did the will of God, he received the attribute "righteous" (cf. *Jub.* 21:2–3). Especially his response to the command to sacrifice Isaac (Gen. 22) was regarded as an act of faithfulness and righteousness. Paul extracts from the Abraham traditions only what fits the goals of his argument, namely, the pronouncement of righteousness in Gen. 15:6, the promises in Gen. 15:5 and 17:5, and the sequence of the pronouncement of righteousness (Gen. 15:6) and circumcision (Gen. 17). Differently than in Judaism, Abraham was not credited with righteousness on the basis of the unity of Torah and works, faith and obedience, obedience and reward, earnings and blessing.[79] In contrast, because Abraham trusted the promise of God, this was reckoned to him as righteousness (Rom. 4:3b). In contrast to Jewish tradition (cf. *Jub.* 30:17–23; 1 Macc. 2:52; Ps. 69:28–29), Paul dissolves the connection between being reckoned (λογίζεσθαι) as righteous and human achievement. For him, everything depends on the sovereign act of God. There are no claims on God but only an appropriation of God's promise by faith. This was the way Abraham himself acted, against all human experience trusting the promise of God that his descendants would be as numerous as the stars. The innermost essence of faith is an unconditioned trust in the God who justifies the ungodly (Rom. 4:5). The act of faith is found precisely in acknowledging the righteous judgment of God on ungodly human beings. The grammatical form of ἐνεδυναμώθη τῇ πίστει (lit. he was made strong in faith; NRSV, "he grew strong in his faith," 4:20) is a divine passive, signaling that it was God who gave Abraham the power to trust in God's promise against all external appearance. So, too, on the issue of circumcision, Abraham functions for Paul as a witness to God's justifying action through faith alone (cf. Rom. 4:9–12). For Paul, the chronological gap between Gen. 15:6 and Gen. 17 has theological significance. Whereas, from the Jewish perspective, circumcision was considered a comprehensive proof of Abraham's faithfulness in response to God's command, Paul separates circumcision from the event of Abraham's being justified by faith. Justification by faith preceded circumcision, so that circumci-

---

76. Ernst Käsemann, "The Faith of Abraham in Romans 4," in *Perspectives on Paul* (Philadelphia: Fortress, 1971), 79: "Romans 4 holds a key place in the epistle. Here the scriptural evidence is marshalled for the theme of the righteousness of faith which has been expounded in 3:21–31."

77. Klaus Berger, "Abraham," *TRE* 1:372–82.

78. Cf. the evidence in Strack and Billerbeck, *Kommentar*, 3:195; Philo, *Virtues* 219.

79. Cf., e.g., *Pss. Sol.* 9:2–7; 13:5–12; 14.

sion can be understood as only a later acknowledgment and confirmation of the justification by faith Abraham had already received. Paul radicalized this view in Rom. 4:11b, where Abraham is first of all the father of the uncircumcised, so that he only becomes father of the circumcised somewhat belatedly in Rom. 4:12. Even here this happens not because they are circumcised but when they live by faith. Paul thus here presents a sharp contradiction to the thinking that was current in ancient Judaism about salvation history.[80]

"Promise" as a Key Category

Paul's abolition of Israel's understanding of election necessarily raises the question of the function of the Torah. To respond to this pressing question, Paul again takes up the concept of ἐπαγγελία (promise) he had already used in Gal. 3:[81] the promise becomes a prototype of the gospel. Abraham did not receive the promise through the Torah but only as believer and hearer.[82] For Paul, Torah obedience and attaining the promise are mutually exclusive actions (Rom. 4:14). Because no human being is in the situation of being able to fulfill the Torah, it turns against those who practice it: "For the law brings wrath; but where there is no law, neither is there violation" (4:15). Inheriting the promise is bound to faith, for in his word God himself has opened up the gospel to all peoples (4:13, 16). Righteousness therefore comes by faith, and Abraham becomes the archetype of all believers, both for Jewish Christians and for Gentile Christians (4:16–17).[83] The contemporizing tendency of Paul's handling of the Old Testament becomes clear in 4:23–25.[84] Genesis 15:6 is aimed at contemporary believers; it was for their sake that the text was written (Rom. 4:24, ἀλλὰ καὶ δι᾿ ἡμᾶς [but for ours also]). What happened to Abraham as an outstanding individual figure of prehistory is now put into effect in the eschatological time.[85]

---

80. Differently, Maria Neubrand, *Abraham, Vater von Juden und Nichtjuden: Eine exegetische Studie zu Röm 4* (FB 85; Würzburg: Echter, 1997), 293, who consistently affirms a special and unchanging election of Israel: "For Paul explains to his readers with the help of a rereading of the Abraham narratives that their election through Jesus Christ means neither that the special election of Israel is depreciated or replaced nor that non-Jewish disciples of Jesus are integrated into the special covenant of God with Israel."

81. Cf. Hübner, *Law in Paul's Thought*, 15–20, 51–57; Gerhard Sass, *Leben aus den Verheissungen: Traditionsgeschichtliche und biblisch-theologische Untersuchungen zur Rede von Gottes Verheissungen im Frühjudentum und beim Apostel Paulus* (FRLANT 164; Göttingen: Vandenhoeck & Ruprecht, 1995), 370ff.

82. Differently in the rabbinic tradition; cf. Strack and Billerbeck, *Kommentar*, 3:204–6.

83. It is disputed whether the expression τῷ ἐκ τοῦ νόμου (Rom. 4:16, to the adherents of the law) refers to the Jews as such; for discussion at this point, see Wilckens, *Römer*, 1:272.

84. For interpretation, cf. Luz, *Geschichtsverständnis*, 113–16.

85. For a critique of the promise/fulfillment schema, cf. Sass, *Leben aus den Verheissungen*, 22–24, 508–10.

Not only Jews but Gentiles, too, now come to faith in the God who raised Jesus Christ from the dead.

The Old Testament opens up to Paul in the light of the revelation in Christ, with the concept of promise as the determining hermeneutical category. He demonstrates this fundamental reality with the figure of Abraham. God is now fulfilling the promises made to Abraham, since the promise of many descendants is being fulfilled in the vast number of Gentiles who are coming to faith. Abraham functions not only as precedent for justification by faith but as father of the Pauline Gentile mission.[86] But Paul does not explicitly take up the promise/fulfillment schema; the figure of Abraham is, rather, an anticipatory representation of what is now achieving its goal in the Christ event. This does not mean that Paul is here the advocate of one continuous line of salvation history, for the sole point of comparison is the stance of faith shared by Abraham and Christians of the present. The continuum between then and now does not run through history but is grounded exclusively in the act of God, who then as now justifies the ungodly by faith. The only historical continuum is established by the promises of God; that is, only the divine "I" constitutes the continuity between the Old Testament and the New Testament.[87] For Paul, there is no history of salvation but only saving events that occur in history and give it direction and meaning. Precisely the figure of Abraham shows that God acts contingently and that it is not possible for any group to claim God's action exclusively for itself. Everything rests in God's own hands, whose promises may be trusted now, as they were then, despite all appearances to the contrary.

12.7 The Presence of Salvation: Baptism and Righteousness

The new reality of salvation in Jesus Christ proclaimed by Paul leads unavoidably to this question: where is this salvation concretely available, and how can it be experienced in a world that stands under the continuing power of sin and death? The fundamental change in the world situation and the new individual existence of the believer likewise call for a universal and biographical verification. Why does the world stand under the power of sin, how does the change of lordships from death to life take place, how do believers come to participate in this event, what is the power that determines the new life? Paul poses these questions in Rom. 5–8 in a very complex train of thought.[88] At the beginning stands the postulate of the new being: justification by faith

---

86. Cf. Alkier, *Wunder und Wirklichkeit*, 273.

87. Cf. Hübner, *Biblische Theologie*, 2:344; Koch, *Schrift als Zeuge*, 348.

88. On the outline of Rom. 5–8, in addition to the standard commentaries, see the survey of scholarly options and arguments on this point in Ulrich Luz, "Zum Aufbau von Röm. 1–8," *TZ* 25 (1969): 161–81; Theobald, *Römerbrief*, 47ff. The issue revolves around whether the break comes at 5:1, 5:12, or 6:1. Along with many others, I argue for 5:1 as the beginning of a new section. Here the

is a definitive reality that determines the actuality of the Christian's life (5:1). Jesus Christ makes possible access to God and thus to grace and salvation. Assurance of the new being eludes any attempt at demonstration by this-worldly criteria and knows itself to be borne by hope alone (cf. 5:2–4). Hope attains its power from God's love granted to the believer as a gift (5:5), which provides the courage to believe despite all appearances to the contrary. From this comes Paul's perspective: "For if while we were enemies, we were reconciled to God through the death of his Son, much more surely, having been reconciled, will we be saved by his life" (5:10).[89]

The Adam/Christ Typology

In view of this surpassing hope, the pressing question becomes even more urgent than before: how is the reality of death in the world to be understood? Paul turns to this fundamental problem, addressing it with the Adam/Christ typology of Rom. 5:12–21.[90] It answers the question of how death came into the world and how it was overcome and surpassed by Christ's redemptive act. Here Adam and Christ are antitheses sharply juxtaposed to each other, for they are contrasted in time, space, and being.[91] Through Adam sin entered the world, and thereby came death (5:12ab). All humanity and the cosmos itself are negatively determined by this event (5:12c), so that inevitably the reality of the power of sin in the world led to the concrete participation in sin in the case of every human life prior to the coming of Christ (5:12d).[92] The character of sin as a concrete

---

preceding argument is concisely summarized (Δικαιωθέντες οὖν [as those who are now justified]) and lifted to a new level in 5:2 by the motif of "access."

89. On the concept of reconciliation, see below, section 16.7 ("Jesus Christ as Reconciler").

90. The Adam/Christ typology gives the impression of being a coherent unit independent of this context; on the possible roots of Rom. 5:12–21 in pre-Pauline tradition, cf. Egon Brandenburger, *Adam und Christus: Exegetisch-religions-geschichtliche Untersuchung zu Röm. 5, 12–21 (1.Kor 15)* (WMANT 7; Neukirchen: Kreis Moers, 1962), 15–157; Wilckens, *Römer*, 1:305–37; Schade, *Apokalyptische Christologie*, 69–90, 239–44. It could be that standing in the background of the Adam/Christ contrast in 1 Cor. 15:22, 45 and Rom. 5:14 is the Alexandrian Jewish interpretation of Gen. 1:26–27 and 2:7, as found in Philo, *Alleg. Interp.* 1.31: "There are two types of men; the one a heavenly man, the other an earthly. The heavenly man, being made after the image of God, is altogether without part or lot in corruptible and terrestrial substance; but the earthly one was compacted out of the matter scattered here and there, which Moses calls 'clay'" (cf. *NW* 2/1:406; Boring et al., eds., *Hellenistic Commentary*, § 715); cf. also Philo, *Alleg. Interp.* 1.32, 42, 53, 88–89; *Creation* 134–135; 146. Of course, Paul places the accents differently, since for him the temporal sequence of the two ἄνθρωποι (men, human beings) is central (cf. 1 Cor. 15:46; Rom. 5:14b, 17). In Corinth there had evidently already been a discussion about Adam and Christ before Paul's writing 1 Corinthians (cf. 1 Cor. 14:46), and so Rom. 5:12–21 is to be read as the Pauline variation of a theme in the contextual requirements of the Letter to the Romans (cf. Umbach, *In Christus getauft*, 196–200).

91. Cf. Umbach, *In Christus getauft*, 197.

92. Bultmann, *Theology of the New Testament*, 1:251: "He holds to the idea that sin came into the world by sinning."

act is the result of its character as unavoidable destiny.[93] Adam and Christ are antithetical figures in both their essential reality and their actual acts. Whereas Adam is the representative of sin, death, and the fallen state of humanity in subjection to these powers, the possibility of eschatological life is revealed in and through Christ (cf. 5:17, 18, 21). The term τύπος (type, antitype, counterpart) in 5:14 signals the understanding Paul intends: "Adam is for Paul a τύπος, an advance presentation, through which God intimates the future Adam, namely, Christ in his universal work of salvation."[94] The argumentation is determined by antithesis and discontinuity, such that death and life, Adam and Christ are mutually exclusive realms of being that have only their opposites in common.[95] The law/Torah stand on the side of Adam by provoking and increasing sin (cf. 5:13, 20).[96] It does not initially entangle humanity in the web of sin and death, but it does activate it and make human beings aware of this entanglement. The sovereignty of Christ breaks the sovereignty of sin and death (cf. 5:17–21), so that now life reigns in Jesus Christ. It is this affirmation of the presence of new life that is the real goal of what 5:12–21 wants to say. This then raises the question of how Christians enter into this new life beyond the ruling power of θάνατος καὶ ἁμαρτία (death and sin). The universal-mythical representation needs to be concretely individualized. The relation of 5:12–21 and Rom. 6 is to be stated as follows: 5:12–21 is the factual and argumentative presupposition for Rom. 6, and Rom. 6, in turn, is the necessary explication of 5:12–21.[97]

Baptism as Transfer Event

Both the dethroning of sin and concrete incorporation into the realm where the soteriological, ecclesiological, ethical, social, and biographical dimensions

---

93. The fundamental problem of Rom. 5:12 is whether it presupposes that sin-as-inevitable-destiny and personal responsibility exist side by side. This is the understanding of Ernst Käsemann, e.g., who argues that "the real problem of interpretation lies in v. 12d, where the motif of destiny which dominates v. 12a–c is abruptly set aside by that of the personal guilt of all mankind" (Käsemann, *Romans*, 147). Then the inference as found in *2 Bar.* 54.15 would be inescapable: "For, although Adam sinned first and has brought death upon all who were not in his own time, yet each of them who has been born from him has prepared for himself the coming torment. And further, each of them has chosen for himself the coming glory" (trans. A. F. J. Klijn, *OTP* 2:640). Cf. also *4 Ezra* 7:118–119. To be sure, Paul's thinking in terms of spheres of power points in a different direction, for Adam's fall already decides definitively that all human beings will in fact be sinners. Cf. Otfried Hofius, "Die Adam-Christus-Antithese und das Gesetz," in *Paulusstudien* (2 vols.; WUNT 51, 143; Tübingen: Mohr Siebeck, 1989–2002), 2:81–82.

94. Leonhard Goppelt, "τύπος," *TDNT* 8:252.

95. Cf. Umbach, *In Christus getauft*, 203.

96. Cf. Hofius, "Adam-Christus-Antithese," 2:89–102.

97. Cf. Rudolf Schnackenburg, "Die Adam-Christus-Typologie (Röm 5,12–21) als Voraussetzung für das Taufverständnis in Röm 6,1–14," in *Battesimo e giustizia in Rom. 6 e 8* (ed. Michel Bouttier and Lorenzo De Lorenzi; SMBenSB 2; Rome: Abbazia S. Paolo fuori le Mura, 1974), 37–55; Umbach, *In Christus getauft*, 204.

of this event are effective happen as discrete, once-for-all historical events. Cross, resurrection, and baptism are related to each other not only as cause and effect but the original event is constantly present in its effects. The point of departure for the Pauline line of argument in Rom. 6 is the relation of sin and grace.[98] They stand antithetically over against each other, for the Christian lives in the realm of χάρις (grace) and is thus dead to sin. Paul justifies this claim by appealing to baptism, which functions as baptism into the death of Jesus and means that the Christian has also died to sin. Paul attempts to illustrate this decisive event in the Christian life with the help of traditional material (6:3b–5).[99] The expression ὅσοι ἐβαπτίσθημεν εἰς Χριστὸν Ἰησοῦν (all of us who have been baptized into Christ Jesus) designates the incorporation of the baptized into the saving work of Jesus Christ and into the realm where this salvation is operative. That the εἰς (into) should be understood in terms of an objectively real space is indicated by the parallel formulations εἰς τὸν θάνατον (into [his] death) in 6:3b and 4a and the expression in 6:2, πῶς ἔτι ζήσομεν ἐν αὐτῇ; (how can we . . . go on living in it [sin]?), which presuppose a force field or sphere of influence.[100] The images of incorporation and participation take up and expand the idea of a transfer from one legal sphere to another.[101] The death of Jesus Christ is made present in baptism, so that the individual Christian can understand what takes place in the baptismal event as a sacramental reexperiencing of the death of Jesus present in this event. Only the death of Jesus Christ ultimately overcame sin; it is now present and effective in baptism through the power of the Spirit, effecting the death of the Christian to sin as something that happens in reality (not merely "in symbol"). The death of Jesus Christ on Golgotha is not identical with the sacramental reexperiencing of this death resulting in the Christian's own death, but baptism is indeed the place where the salvific meaning of the death of Jesus becomes reality for the Christian. Here the body of sin is destroyed and the new life is constituted, a life that is lived κατὰ πνεῦμα (according to the Spirit).

98. On the interpretation of Rom. 6, cf. Schnelle, *Gerechtigkeit und Christusgegenwart*, 74–88, 203–15 (where the positions advocated in the literature are debated); Hans Dieter Betz, "Transferring a Ritual: Paul's Interpretation of Baptism in Romans 6," in *Paul in His Hellenistic Context* (ed. Troels Engberg-Pedersen; Minneapolis: Fortress, 1995), 84–118; David Hellholm, "Enthymemic Argumentation in Paul: The Case of Romans 6," in *Paul in His Hellenistic Context* (ed. Troels Engberg-Pedersen), 119–79; Strecker, *Die liminale Theologie des Paulus*, 177–89; Umbach, *In Christus getauft*, 230–57.

99. Cf., e.g., Lietzmann, *Römer*, 67; Käsemann, *Romans*, 166–67; Umbach, *In Christus getauft*, 239–40. Differently, Hans-Joachim Eckstein, "Auferstehung und gegenwärtiges Leben," *TBei* 28 (1997): 15, who regards Rom. 6:3–4 as an independent formulation by Paul himself.

100. Cf., in this sense, Erich Dinkler, "Römer 6, 1–14 und das Verhältnis von Taufe und Rechtfertigung bei Paulus," in *Battesimo e giustizia in Rom. 6 e 8* (ed. Michel Bouttier and Lorenzo De Lorenzi; SMBenSB 2; Rome: Abbazia S. Paolo fuori le Mura, 1974), 87; Käsemann, *Romans*, 166; Umbach, *In Christus getauft*, 240.

101. Eckstein, "Auferstehung und gegenwärtiges Leben," 13, wants to restrict the statement in the text to the idea of transfer.

Romans 6:4 enhances the image of participation already developed in 6:3b, because both the prefix σύν (with) and the explanatory ὥσπερ . . . οὕτως clause (just as . . . so) points to a substantial parallel between Christ and the one who is baptized. The expression συνετάφημεν . . . αὐτῷ (we have been buried with him) emphasizes the fully salvific character of baptism, for baptism is effective participation in the whole saving event, which includes the resurrection of Jesus Christ. This is clearly indicated by the purpose clause in 6:4b–c, introduced by ἵνα and structured by ὥσπερ . . . οὕτως. The idea that what happens to believers corresponds to Christ's resurrection in terms of both its actuality and its place on the time scale would have required that the initial part of the formulation be carried through consistently: ὥσπερ . . . οὕτως καὶ ἡμεῖς ἐκ νεκρῶν ἐγερθῶμεν (just as . . . so we also have been raised from the dead).[102] Paul does not draw this conclusion but determines the present and future being of the Christian with the expression οὕτως καὶ ἡμεῖς ἐν καινότητι ζωῆς περιπατήσωμεν (so we too might walk in newness of life)—characterizing the new life of the Christian in terms of ethics and oriented to the future.[103] The result of dying to sin is not a change in the substance of which human life is composed. People are not taken out of their previous network of connections; they continue to live under the conditions of a world that is passing away. The new reality of freedom from sin stands under an eschatological reservation; it is not demonstrable by this-worldly criteria and must be maintained within the conditions of history. Those who believe and have been baptized are not yet risen, but they still participate in a real way in the powers of Jesus' resurrection, which permeate and transform the whole cosmos (cf. 8:18ff.). By no means, however, does this qualification relativize the real transformations in the life of the baptized.[104]

The ideas developed in 6:3–4 point to the mystery cults as their milieu in cultural history.[105] The following text was stamped on two small gold leaves

102. Cf. Bultmann, *Theology of the New Testament*, 1:140–41; cf. also 1:178.

103. Here is the decisive difference from Col. 2:12; 3:1–4; Eph. 2:6, which speak of a resurrection (in faith) that already takes place in baptism. On the analysis of the texts, cf. Erich Grässer, "Kolosser 3,1–4 als Beispiel einer Interpretation secundum homines recipientes," in *Text und Situation: Gesammelte Aufsätze zum Neuen Testament* (Gütersloh: Gütersloher Verlagshaus G. Mohn, 1973), 129ff.

104. Cf. Umbach, *In Christus getauft*, 247. Strecker, *Die liminale Theologie des Paulus*, 177–89, accents the matter differently, insisting, on the one hand, that the baptized person is separated from sin and saying, on the other hand, on the basis of his presupposed understanding of death in terms of process, that the baptized are dead to sin in a way that is "symbolically effective" (p. 188).

105. Cf. Bultmann, *Theology of the New Testament*, 1:140–42; Niklaus Gäumann, *Taufe und Ethik: Studien zu Römer 6* (BEvT 47; Munich: Kaiser, 1967), 46; Schnelle, *Gerechtigkeit und Christusgegenwart*, 74ff.; Dieter Zeller, "Die Mysterienreligionen und die paulinische Soteriologie," in *Suchbewegungen: Synkretismus: Kulturelle Identität und kirchliches Bekenntnis* (ed. Hermann Pius Siller; Darmstadt: Wissenschaftliche Buchgesellschaft, 1991), 42–61; Umbach, *In Christus getauft*, 244–47; rather more skeptical regarding this derivation is the recent work of A. J. M. Wedderburn, *Baptism and Resurrection: Studies in Pauline Theology against Its Graeco-Roman Background* (WUNT 44; Tübingen: Mohr Siebeck, 1987), 90–163. Dunn, *Theology of Paul*, 446, 451–52, posits a connection between

found in a woman's grave from the late fourth century BCE: "Now you have died, and now you are born, thrice blessed, on this day. Say to Persephone that Bacchus himself redeems you. You are speeding to the milk like a bull. You are hurrying quickly to the milk. You rush to the milk like a ram. You have wine, you blessed one, without measure. And solemnities await you beneath the earth, with the other blessed ones."[106] Apuleius reports, in the context of an Isis initiation, "I drew near to the confines of death, treading the very threshold of Proserpine. I was borne through all the elements and returned to earth again. At the dead of night I saw the sun shining brightly. I approached the gods above and the gods below, and worshipped them face to face."[107] Firmicus Maternus transmits the saying of a priest of the mysteries: "'Rejoice, O mystai! Lo, our god appears as saved! And we shall find salvation, springing from our woes.'"[108] The connection between these texts and Rom. 6:3–4 lies in the concept of an identification of the initiate with the destiny of the deity. Although the New Testament ideas are not derived from these texts in terms of genealogy or analogy,[109] they do illustrate the intellectual milieu within which the imagery and concepts developed in 6:3–4 could be thought out and received.[110]

The idea that a uniform pattern embraces baptized believers and the destiny of Jesus Christ is continued in 6:5 by σύμφυτος (grown together with / united with) and ὡμοίωμα (likeness).[111] Baptism is the place of effective and full participation in the Christ event. In 6:6 Paul underscores the starting point for this line of thought, separation from sin, by speaking now of the παλαιὸς ἄνθρωπος (old human being; NRSV, "our old self"), whose body of sin is destroyed in baptism. Said positively, a life in righteousness follows being freed from sin. Paul gives a variation on this thought in 6:7 by again interpreting death in baptism as liberation from the power of sin. Romans 6:8–11 then summarizes the new situation of the baptized: because Jesus Christ has died and been raised from the dead and believers have been made by their baptism to share completely in this saving event, they are also freed from the sphere of influence ruled by death and sin. As those who have died to sin, they now live for God. This new life of the Christian has been made possible through the

---

Jesus and Paul: "As Christ had spoken of his death as baptism, so Paul could speak of the beginning of salvation as a baptism into Christ's death" (p. 452).

106. Text and interpretation in *NW* 2/1:122–23.

107. Apuleius, *Metam.* 11.23.8 (*NW* 2/1:125–26; Boring et al., eds., *Hellenistic Commentary*, § 387). For analysis of the whole textual complex, cf. D. Berner, "Initiationsriten in Mysterienreligionen, im Gnostizismus, und im antiken Judentum" (diss., Georg August Universität, 1972), 75ff.

108. Firmicus Maternus, *De errore profanarum religionum* 22.1, 3 (*NW* 2/1:124; Boring et al., eds., *Hellenistic Commentary*, § 571).

109. See additional texts in *NW* 2/1:123–27.

110. Within early Christianity, the pattern "as with Christ . . . so with his own" is found for the first time in 1 Thess. 4:14ff.; it could have been further developed independently in Corinth; cf. Schnelle, *Gerechtigkeit und Christusgegenwart*, 78–81.

111. For an extensive analysis, cf. ibid., 81–83.

cross and resurrection of Jesus Christ, appropriated in baptism and lived out in the power of the Spirit.

The Counterpart to the "New Being"

In 6:11 Paul urges the church, with the first imperative in the letter, to live a life that corresponds to its new being: "So you also must consider yourselves dead to sin and alive to God in Christ Jesus." Because what happens in baptism makes a difference in the way one lives, in 6:12–23 Paul's numerous imperatives emphasize the ethical aspect of the new being. Christians must not obey fleshly desires, for they are called to present their bodies as weapons of righteousness at God's disposal, not as weapons of unrighteousness in the service of sin (6:12–13). Have not those who have been baptized died to sin, as 6:2 explicitly claims? Yes, Christians have died to sin—but sin is not dead. Sin continues as a destructive power in the world, tempting the body and the spirit. It is our "old self" and the "body of sin" that have died (6:6), not sin as such.[112] Sin no longer rules over those who have believed and been baptized; for them, sin's power is a thing of the past. At the same time, sin continues to exist in the world and exercises its dominion over all those who do not live in the realm of Christ's rule. With the expression ὡσεὶ ἐκ νεκρῶν ζῶντας (as those who have been brought from death to life) in 6:13, Paul takes up the basic concern of 6:3–4: in baptism the Christian has in reality died to sin, and a righteous life must follow from the conferral of righteousness that happens in baptism.[113] Paul himself evidently cannot derive this proof of freedom from sin—a proof that is decisive for his exclusive doctrine of justification—from the abstract formulation δικαιοσύνη θεοῦ (righteousness of God / justification from God), which does not appear in Rom. 6, and so we may not drag it in here. Paul quite intentionally points to the rite of baptism in order to designate the actual presence of the new reality and the place where it becomes effective. The explicit emphasis on righteousness in 6:12ff. must be understood as a challenge to those who have been baptized to allow the act of God in the ritual to correspond to their own acts in everyday life. This is the presupposition of the heavy emphasis on obedience (6:13, 16, 18, 20), and on sanctification as what follows from δικαιοσύνη (6:19, 22). As δικαιοσύνη already in 6:13 means right human conduct, so the expression ὑπακοὴ εἰς δικαιοσύνην in 6:16 points in the same direction: obedience leads to righteousness. That is, δικαιοσύνη means the right conduct of those who

---

112. Cf. Umbach, *In Christus getauft*, 250–51.

113. This means at the same time that the whole of Rom. 6 is to be understood from the perspective of the baptismal event, which by no means separates 6:1–14 and 6:15–23; contra A. B. du Toit, "Dikaiosyne in Röm 6," *ZTK* 76 (1979): 263.

are baptized, the life lived corresponding to and maintaining the gift they have received in baptism.[114]

Chapter 6 has a key function within the structure of Romans: here Paul makes clear where the transfer into the new being takes place. The characteristic feature of Paul's theology that thinks of salvation in terms of participation is indicated semantically in Rom. 6 by the frequency of the preposition σύν and words compounded with σύν (6:4, 5, 6, 8). The change to the new life in the power of the Spirit has already begun, not only as a change in the way the world is perceived but in an objectively real sense. Through baptism believers are placed in a new realm, and entrance into eternal life has already taken place (6:23). Freedom from sin and the powerfully effective beginning of the new being include freedom from the law/Torah: "For sin will have no dominion over you, since you are not under law but under grace" (6:14).

12.8 Sin, Law, and Freedom in the Spirit

With the determination of the believer's status declared in Rom. 6:14 there is associated an almost unsolvable problem of Pauline thought: How is the election of Israel and the gift of the law/Torah related to the new, final, unsurpassed revelation of God in Jesus Christ? What function can the law/Torah still have? Whereas in Galatians this question received an almost completely negative answer, in Romans Paul's argument is more nuanced. Here, too, however, the point of departure is the basic conviction that life comes not through the law/Torah but through faith in Jesus Christ (cf. 3:21). Why is the law/Torah unable to comply with its original assignment? Paul attempts to resolve this decisive problem in Romans 7–8 by determining the relation of sin, law/Torah, and the Spirit.[115] One might expect at the outset that this attempt will involve secondary rationalizations, lack of conceptual and terminological sharpness, and risky constructions.

By Way of Introduction: One Example

In Rom. 7:1–4 Paul chooses as his starting point an example from Jewish marriage law in order to illustrate the working of the law/Torah and define its limit.[116] Because death always results in release from the requirements of the law

114. Cf. Hübner, *Law in Paul's Thought*, 130–32.

115. It is no accident that of fifty-nine instances of ἁμαρτία in Paul, forty-eight are found in Romans. Where Paul describes the role of the law in God's plan, there he must also develop a comprehensive hamartiology. In Paul's previous writings, only 1 Cor. 15:56 and Gal. 3:22 point in this direction.

116. Cf. Wilckens, *Römer*, 2:62–67; Umbach, *In Christus getauft*, 268–71; Otfried Hofius, "Der Mensch im Schatten Adams," in *Paulusstudien* (2 vols.; WUNT 51, 143; Tübingen: Mohr Siebeck, 1989–2002), 2:107–10.

(cf. 7:2–3), so also the death of Christ and the Christian's dying with him in baptism free from the law/Torah. Baptism is not only a dying to sin but also a dying to the law/Torah, which has now lost its claim on those who are baptized. Romans 7:4 antithetically summarizes the new reality, which is marked by the sharp contrast between the law/Torah and God. In 7:5 Paul represents this now past situation from the perspective of faith, then in 7:6 describes the believer's new form of existence grounded in the Christ event. In 7:5 he characterizes the being of the person prior to faith as a being in the flesh. The flesh appears as the point of attack for the "sinful passions" (τὰ παθήματα τῶν ἁμαρτιῶν) that are aroused by the law/Torah. Sin does not simply approach one as an external power but takes up residence in him or her (7:17, 20, ἡ οἰκοῦσα ἐν ἐμοὶ ἁμαρτία [sin that dwells within me]) in order to completely dominate the person. As a result of sin thus taking over, death appears. In 7:6 Paul marks the eschatological turning point with the phrase νυνὶ δέ (but now; cf. 3:21). Through the gift of the Spirit, the Christian is taken out of the realm of the law/Torah and is thereby freed from sin and death. Christians now know that they are led by the living Spirit, not by the perishable letter.[117] Paul will develop in Rom. 7:7–25a and Rom. 8:1ff. the "once"/"now" schema at the basis of 7:5–7.

Paradise Lost

Paul must first, however, in Rom. 7:7 vigorously ward off the identification of νόμος as itself ἁμαρτία, an inference one might make from his previous statements.[118] He himself had repeatedly associated law/Torah and sin very closely (cf. 3:20; 4:15; 5:13b; 7:5), so that it would not be a big step simply to equate νόμος and ἁμαρτία, which would be fatal for his exclusive doctrine of justification—especially for his Jewish Christian opponents. For Paul, however, the law/Torah is not to be identified with sin, but it does have an important function in the process of the revelation of sin and one's coming to know and experience sin. In order to clarify the actual connection of law and sin in human experience, Paul takes up the story of paradise[119] and introduces the category of ἐπιθυμία ([evil] desire) as an anthropological category.[120] Sin is able to gain a foothold in human life because it can make desire serve its own will.

---

117. Umbach, *In Christus getauft*, 270, appropriately summarizes Paul's intention in Rom. 7:1–6: "Thus here *hamartia, nomos*, and *thanatos* are terms that describe the Christian's past; in contrast, *Christos, theos, pneuma* indicate the present reality. The two lists stand antithetically opposite each other."

118. On Rom. 7:7, see esp. Hübner, *Law in Paul's Thought*, 71–76.

119. See the documentation in Luz, *Geschichtsverständnis*, 166–67.

120. On the Hellenistic Jewish background of the term ἐπιθυμία in this passage, see Weber, "Geschichte des Gesetzes," 154–55. On the negative function of "desire" in the Stoic doctrine of the passions, cf. Diogenes Laertius 7.113: "Desire is an unreasonable striving. Under this heading are to be subsumed longing, hate, jealousy, anger, love, wrath, and violent temper."

The law/Torah comes to the aid of sin in this regard, in that that it creates the necessary presuppositions whereby human desire can be aroused by sin and used for its own purposes. According to 7:7, the relation of sin, law/Torah, and desire is to be described in the following manner: The knowledge of sin comes through the law/Torah because the law/Torah becomes concrete in a particular command and sin becomes concrete in a particular desire. The law/Torah is itself not sin, but one would have never known sin as a particular desire if the command had not been there. In this event sin plays a most active role, for it uses the law/Torah, or the command, in order to pervert what God wills into its opposite (7:8). Precisely through the command, sin calls forth what the command forbids: the desire. Here it already becomes clear that the law/Torah and sin are opposed to each other and that the law/Torah has precedence both temporally and substantively. At the same time, the concept of "desire" turns out to be the conceptual key that makes it possible for Paul to speak positively of the law/Torah despite its proximity to sin (cf. 7:12).

In 7:7ff. Paul leans heavily on the story of the Garden of Eden as a way of characterizing the situation of people before they come to Christian faith. The "I" of 7:7ff. includes Adam and the whole human race, including the Jews.[121] The essential reality of sin cannot be described in a way that limits it in either time or space; it is a reality that infects and determines all human beings of all times and places prior to and apart from faith. Sin and law appear as trans-individual powers that are at work in individual events and circumstances. Paul intentionally chooses mythological language as a means of representing a general anthropological state of affairs. Sin already existed before the law/Torah and apart from the law/Torah, but it is through the law/Torah that sin first became a condemning power. Sin did not originate through the law/Torah and is thus not identical with it, but the power of sin first became manifest when the law aroused evil desire, desire that sin was able to coopt into its own service in order to rule in human life. Thus the encounter with the law dominated by sin takes place when one deals with the individual commandment.

Paul expresses the universality of this event by the way he uses the terms ἐντολή (command) and νόμος in 7:8–11.[122] While ἐντολή refers to God's command to Adam in Eden and νόμος means the Torah given at Sinai, Paul does not dwell on the point, for in Rom. 7 he is describing a fundamental conflict that applies to every kind of law. For him, there has never been an epoch in which sin did not use the commandment, or the law/Torah, as a means of provoking evil desire. The human "I" in every period of history always finds itself to be an "I" already dominated by sin. The active role of sin in this process is explicitly emphasized in 7:11, where the history of the human "I" is not a history of

---

121. Weber, "Geschichte des Gesetzes," 157; Hofius, "Der Mensch im Schatten Adams," 110–21.
122. On the details, cf. Hübner, *Law in Paul's Thought*, 72–76; Weber, "Geschichte des Gesetzes," 155–57.

salvation but by the power of sin has become the exact opposite. Through this line of argument, Paul is able to avoid a direct identification of the νόμος or ἐντολή with sin (7:12, "So the law is holy, and the commandment is holy and just and good"), for sin is the real cause that what is good (the law) has the final result of bringing about death (7:13). Sin can even pervert what is good into its opposite, which clearly shows how powerful it is. Thus, according to Paul, the law/Torah does not have the power to overcome sin. It can reveal the situation of humanity without being able to change it.

The Imprisoned Self

This fundamental insight is the basis for the apostle's anthropological argumentation of Rom. 7:14–25a,[123] which elaborates the way in which the power of sin inescapably ensnares the human "I," to show that the law/Torah is not itself responsible for its ungodly effects in the world. In 7:14 Paul names the general circumstance that prevails in the present world: human beings, as creatures of flesh, are enslaved to sin. The term σάρκινος (fleshly, belonging to the material world) refers to life as separated from God and in rebellion against God in contrast to the law/Torah, which belongs to the spiritual realm. The pair of contrasting modifiers πνευματικός/σάρκινος indicates that anthropology is the real level on which Paul develops his argument.[124] For Paul, this antithesis defines the two categories of human existence; here he is clearly already anticipating 8:1ff. The universality of the foundational statement in 7:14 underscores the ἐγώ (ego, I). It uses the first person singular as a literary device, parallel to the usage in the psalms of lament (cf. Ps. 22:7–8) and in the Qumran literature (cf. 1QH 1:21; 3:24–25; 1QS 11:9ff.).[125] This literary style of the first person singular as well as the general character of 7:14 and the reference to 8:1ff. suggest that the "I" should be seen as an exemplary, general "I," which portrays from the perspective of faith the situation of humanity before and apart from faith.[126] In 7:15 Paul explains that human beings simply find themselves to

123. Alongside the standard commentaries, cf. the analysis of Hofius, "Der Mensch im Schatten Adams," 135–52; Volker Stolle, *Luther und Paulus: Die exegetischen und hermeneutischen Grundlagen der lutherischen Rechtfertigungslehre im Paulinismus Luthers* (Arbeiten zur Bibel und ihrer Geschichte 10; Leipzig: Evangelische Verlagsanstalt, 2002), 210–32.

124. Recently the view of R. Bultmann has been taken up and developed, esp. by Karl Kertelge, "Exegetische Überlegungen zum Verständnis der paulinischen Anthropologie nach Römer 7," *ZNW* 62 (1971): 105–14, arguing that the real subject matter of Rom. 7 is to be located on the anthropological level. In contrast, Wilckens, *Römer*, 2:75, states that in Rom. 7:7–25 the theme continues to be the law. This is an inappropriate alternative, for in Paul the hermeneutic of human existence and the hermeneutic of history belong together; cf. Weber, "Geschichte des Gesetzes," 149, 163.

125. On this point, cf. Kümmel, *Römer 7*, 127–31; Theissen, *Psychological Aspects*, 190–201.

126. Kümmel, *Römer 7*, 74ff., thoroughly discusses this insight. Paul Althaus, *Paulus und Luther über den Menschen: Ein Vergleich* (3rd ed.; SLA 14; Gütersloh: Bertelsmann, 1958), 39, is also on target: "Romans 7 is thus the picture of human beings under the law, before and apart from Christ,

be already sold under the power of sin: the "I" finds itself in a fundamental conflict with itself, not doing what it wants to do but what it hates. Here Paul lays hold of the general human experience of the difference between one's good intentions and actual deeds, which the Greco-Roman tradition associates with the name Medea[127] and which is also found independently in Jewish tradition (cf. 1QS 4:20–21; 11:5).[128] From this contradiction Paul infers in 7:16 that the law/Torah in itself is good, for it is sin that brings about the contradiction between willing and doing. Paul underscores the character of sin as a power in 7:17 with the metaphor of the indwelling of sin in human beings. Here, too, the reference to Rom. 8 is unmistakable, for in 8:9–10 Paul says that the Spirit of God, the Spirit of Christ, or Christ dwells in the believers (all three expressions are equated). Sin and Christ appear as two competing powers, and the human being seems to function only passively as the place where powers dwell that may bring either life or death.[129] If sin prevails in human life, one comes to ruin, whereas Christ / the Spirit grants the person life (cf. 8:11).

In 7:18–20 Paul emphasizes the absolute hopelessness of the situation of humanity apart from faith, once again developing the contradiction between willing and doing. Although human beings can in fact will the good, they are not able to accomplish it because of the sin that dwells within them. In 7:21 the "I" itself draws up a summary account and confirms that an inherent law is in effect: the good will manifests itself concretely in an evil act. Here ὁ νόμος does not mean the Old Testament Torah but describes an inherent law[130] that will be explained in 7:22–23. Two sets of opposite laws clearly stand over against each other: νόμος τοῦ θεοῦ (the law of God) and νόμος ἁμαρτίας (the

---

but this picture is seen only after one comes to faith in Christ. Only the one who stands in Rom. 8 can write and fully affirm Rom. 7." Among those who see in Rom. 7 an echo of personal individual experiences are Hildebrecht Hommel, "Das 7. Kapitel des Römerbriefes," in *Sebasmata: Studien zur antiken Religionsgeschichte und zum frühen Christentum* (2 vols.; WUNT 31–32; Tübingen: Mohr Siebeck, 1983), 2:167; and Theissen, *Psychological Aspects*, 201. Differently, Sanders, *Paul*, 98: "Romans 7, in other words, does not actually describe anyone, except possibly the neurotic. Why, then, is it there? The cry of anguish is probably a cry of theological difficulty."

127. Cf. Euripides, *Medea* 1076–1080; Ovid, *Metamorphoses* 7.10–21 (cf. *NW* 2/1:142–48); additional examples in Hommel, "Das 7. Kapitel des Römerbriefes," 157–64; and Theissen, *Psychological Aspects*, 212–18.

128. For answers to the problem of evil in antiquity, see below, section 19.2 ("Sin and Death").

129. Cf. Günter Röhser, *Metaphorik und Personifikation der Sünde: Antike Sündenvorstellungen und paulinische Hamartia* (Tübingen: Mohr Siebeck, 1987), 119ff. Romans 7 does not portray a conflict within human beings but a transpersonal event; contra Althaus, *Paulus und Luther*, 41–49, who wants to understand Rom. 7 as a conflict within the individual human being; similarly Timo Laato, *Paulus und das Judentum: Anthropologische Erwägungen* (Åbo, Finland: Åbo Akademis Förlag, 1991), 163: "Romans 7 includes nothing that does not fit the Christian, or—formulated more sharply—everything included in Rom. 7 fits only the Christian." An English translation by T. McElwain has been published as *Paul and Judaism: An Anthropological Approach* (Atlanta: Scholars Press, 1995).

130. Cf. Zeller, *Römer*, 142; Weber, "Geschichte des Gesetzes," 159; Hofius, "Der Mensch im Schatten Adams," 142.

law of sin); νόμος τοῦ νοός μου (the law of my mind) and ἕτερος νόμος ἐν τοῖς μέλεσίν μου (another law in my members); and ἔσω ἄνθρωπος (my inmost self) and ἔξω ἄνθρωπος (my external self).[131] The law of God and the law of sin each have found vulnerable points in human life where they may launch their respective attacks, and a battle ensues (7:23, ἀντιστρατεύομαι [struggle, fight]; αἰχμαλωτίζω [take captive]) for control of the person. In this discussion the term νόμος by no means has a consistent referent (e.g., the Sinai Torah), but its meaning in each case is determined by its modifiers. The phrase νόμος τοῦ θεοῦ in 7:22 includes the Sinai Torah but probably extends beyond that to mean the law manifest in creation, given by God to the Gentiles (cf. 1:19ff.; 2:14–15).[132] Such an interpretation is found already in 7:7–13, where Paul also speaks of the same basic circumstances that apply to Jews and Gentiles. The content of the phrase νόμος τοῦ θεοῦ is the original will of God, with which human beings agree in their innermost being. The ἔξω ἄνθρωπος (external person) strives to fulfill this will of God. In 7:23 νόμος τοῦ νοός stands, on the one hand, in continuity with νόμος τοῦ θεοῦ in 7:22 and at the same time in sharp antithesis to ἕτερον νόμον ἐν τοῖς μέλεσίν μου and the νόμος ἁμαρτίας. Here Paul is playing with variations of the meaning of the term, for he is not referring to the Old Testament Torah but is designating structural qualities. This is obviously the case with νόμος ἁμαρτίας, where νόμος cannot refer to God's law given on Sinai. As a power opposing the original will of God, the term must here be understood in the sense of an inherent principle: sin is contrasted with the law of the Spirit (8:2) and enslaves those who are outside the realm of faith.[133]

Human beings are not able by their own power simply to choose the good and reject the evil because the sin dwelling and battling within completely dominates them. So also νόμος τοῦ νοός μου and νόμος ἐν τοῖς μέλεσίν μου designate the conflict that characterizes human existence between reason itself and the powers that subjugate it. Thus 7:23 portrays a fundamental anthropological state of affairs: human beings are torn in two and of themselves are not in the situation to restore their own integrity.[134] This is the reason the natural human being is in a hopeless situation, resulting in the apostle's cry in 7:24: "Wretched man that I am! Who will rescue me from this body of death?" The inner logic of Rom. 7 permits only one answer: "No one." For Paul, this is not the last word, as 7:25a indicates.[135] The deliverance of humanity from this

---

131. Cf. Weber, "Geschichte des Gesetzes," 160–61.

132. Cf. Walter Schmithals, *Die theologische Anthropologie des Paulus: Auslegung von Röm 7, 17–8, 39* (Stuttgart: Kohlhammer, 1980), 66.

133. Contra Wilckens, *Römer*, 2:90, who thinks that in Rom. 7:22–23 "νόμος refers throughout to different aspects of the contents of the Torah."

134. Cf. Weber, "Geschichte des Gesetzes," 159.

135. Romans 7:25b is a gloss, for it speaks again of the unredeemed person while 7:25a already leads to the redeemed situation of the person in Rom. 8. Moreover, this summary does not fit the

hopeless situation has appeared in Jesus Christ; therefore Paul thanks God for the deliverance from the realm of sin's rulership, a deliverance accomplished in Jesus Christ and made available through the Spirit. Romans 8 appears as the appropriate continuation of the Pauline argument in 7:7ff., indeed as its presupposition, for the perspectives elaborated by Paul in Rom. 8 have already been the basis for all that he says in Rom. 7.

The Liberated Person

In Rom. 8:2–3 Paul describes the present reality of the believer living in the realm where the power of the Spirit prevails. It is no accident that the problems of the Pauline understanding of the law culminate here, for in Paul's thought the relation between nomology and pneumatology is filled with tensions. Just as in 3:20; 4:15; 6:14; 7:7–11 Paul comes close to equating the law/Torah with sin and then in the countermove of 7:12 emphatically endorses the holiness of the law/Torah, so he now speaks of a νόμος τοῦ πνεύματος (law of the Spirit) that effectively determines and empowers the life of the believer. What does Paul mean by this expression? Linguistically, one could easily think in terms of a particular use of the genitive case, such that νόμος τοῦ πνεύματος τῆς ζωῆς (law of the Spirit of life) and νόμος τῆς ἁμαρτίας καὶ θανάτου (law of sin and of death) are construed as "genitives of direction and purpose," and the meaning would be "of the Spirit, which leads to life" and "of sin, which leads to death."[136] It is clear regarding their content that the genitives qualify how the νόμος is to be understood in each case. By no means can νόμος be understood as a consistent quantity with the same meaning in each case, for the verb ἠλευθέρωσεν clearly expresses that the one νόμος liberates one from the other. Clearly πνεῦμα and ἁμαρτία here stand over against each other, and the νόμοι (laws) with which they are associated also are related antithetically. Thus νόμος must here be translated with the "rule/norm" or "principle" that belongs to the Spirit or to sin, which means that in 8:2 νόμος does not refer to the Sinai Torah.[137] The first reference to the Sinai Torah is found in 8:3a, where Paul emphasizes the inability of the Torah to liberate from the power of

---

argument Paul has just made. The approval of, and consent to, the law/Torah in 7:16, 22 is not identical with the δουλεύω νόμῳ θεοῦ (I am a slave to the law of God) in 7:25b. Becoming a "slave of the law/Torah" is precisely what does *not* happen in Rom. 7:14ff. because this is what sin keeps from happening; contra Stuhlmacher, *Romans*, 113–14.

136. Blass and Debrunner, *Grammar*, § 166.

137. Understood in this sense by, e.g., Käsemann, *Romans*, 215–16; Heikki Räisänen, "Das 'Gesetz des Glaubens' (Röm 3,27) und das 'Gesetz des Geistes' (Röm 8,2)," *NTS* 26 (1980): 113ff.; Ulrich Luz and Rudolf Smend, *Gesetz* (Stuttgart: Kohlhammer, 1981), 104; Weber, "Geschichte des Gesetzes," 116; Umbach, *In Christus getauft*, 282–83. Contra Wilckens, *Römer*, 2:122–23; Hübner, *Law in Paul's Thought*, 145–46; Bernhardt Lohse, "Ὁ νόμος τοῦ πνεύματος τῆς ζωῆς: Exegetische Anmerkungen zu Röm. 8,2," in *Die Vielfalt des Neuen Testaments* (Göttingen: Vandenhoeck & Ruprecht, 1982), 285–86, who understand νόμος here too as referring to the Torah.

the σάρξ. Here it becomes completely clear that νόμος in 8:2 cannot mean the Old Testament Torah, for then 8:3a would take back what has just been said in 8:2: liberation from the power of sin and death. Because Christ himself entered into the realm of ἁμαρτία, by his resurrection he overcame the power of sin and death. This liberation takes place in the life of the Christian through the power of the Spirit[138] and is present in the Spirit, as indicated in 8:4. With the sending of the Son, the legal claim of the law/Torah was fulfilled. But what is meant by the phrase δικαίωμα τοῦ νόμου (NRSV, "just requirement of the law")? The answer is given in 13:8, which explicitly emphasizes that the law/Torah is fulfilled in keeping the love commandment.[139] According to the programmatic statements in 7:1–6, "fulfillment" here can mean neither the fulfillment of the legitimate claims of the Old Testament Torah nor its restitution.[140] It is, rather, the case that here νόμος is to be understood in the same sense as in Gal. 6:2—through the act of God's love in Jesus Christ, the power of sin was broken, and the law/Torah was fulfilled and at the same time transformed. The new being does not lead to lack of all restraints or to "lawlessness," for Paul knows himself to be constrained by love in living by the Spirit's norm.

Flesh and Spirit

In Rom. 7:7–8:4 Paul elaborates his understanding of the basic structures of human existence as they are revealed retrospectively from the point of view of faith. Prior to and apart from faith, human beings always find themselves under the power of sin. In relation to the commandment or the will to do the good, sin always has both a temporal head start and a functional advantage: it was in the world before the commandment and with the help of the law/Torah deceives human beings by perverting into its opposite their striving after the good. As creatures who belong to this world of flesh, human beings are helpless against the power of sin. Sin sets in motion a legal situation from which no one can extract himself or herself. Only the resurrection of Jesus Christ from the dead, which overcomes the power of death and sin, frees human beings from their hopeless situation. This can be perceived and experienced only by those who through the power of the Spirit in faith allow this saving act to be valid for them. Believers know that they are thereby delivered from the realm of the flesh and subject to the norm of the Spirit. Paul sets this forth in exem-

---

138. Contra Stuhlmacher, *Romans*, 124: "The law no longer stands over against them as something foreign and threatening, but moves them from within so that they stand in the knowledge of God's will and fulfill the legal demand of the law on the basis of the power of Christ (Rom. 8:4)."

139. Henning Paulsen, *Überlieferung und Auslegung in Römer 8* (WMANT 43; Neukirchen-Vluyn: Neukirchener Verlag, 1974), 65.

140. Cf. Käsemann, *Romans*, 217.

plary fashion in 8:5–8.[141] Here σάρξ and πνεῦμα stand over against each other as two mutually exclusive powers that surround human life and in each case take it into their service, whether a service that leads to life or a service that leads to death (8:5, "For those who live according to the flesh set their minds on the things of the flesh, but those who live according to the Spirit set their minds on the things of the Spirit"). Neither any sort of mediation between the two realms nor a natural transition from one to the other is possible, for two force fields, understood in ontological terms, stand sharply opposed to each other. The antithesis between σάρξ and πνεῦμα results from their respective goals: death, on the one hand, and life, on the other (8:13). Because the Spirit of God or Christ is actively at work in believers (8:9), they still live ἐν σαρκί but no longer κατὰ σάρκα. Their previous hostility to God is abrogated, and they live lives in accord with the new being through the work of the Spirit (cf. Gal. 5:22). In contrast, human beings in their natural state apart from faith are delivered over to the works of sin in the flesh: sexual immorality, idolatry, quarrels, factions, and such (Gal. 5:19b–21).

Paul had received the σάρξ/πνεῦμα way of thinking from Hellenistic Judaism, such as that found in the pre-Pauline tradition of Rom. 1:3b–4a but also Gal. 5:16ff.; 1 Pet. 3:18, and 1 Tim. 3:16.[142] From the history-of-religions perspective, the Jewish wisdom literature is probably the starting point for this antithetical pair (cf. Wis. 7:1–6, 7b–14; 9:5, 15, 17).[143] A carefully considered σάρξ/πνεῦμα dualism is found in Philo.[144] The flesh appears as the container for the real person (*Virtues* 78), is a burden to it (*Giants* 31), is the coffin of the soul (*Migration* 16). In contrast, God belongs to the incorporeal, fleshless world, so that turning to God means turning away from the flesh, with the result that one enters into the spiritual world. There are thus two classes of human beings and two ways of life: one leading to salvation and one leading to destruction (cf. *Unchangeable* 140–183). While the perfect proceed on the way opened by wisdom, the "comrades of the flesh" avoid this way (*Unchangeable* 143). Because they are imprisoned in the flesh, they cannot attain divine knowledge; "because they are flesh, the divine Spirit cannot dwell in them" (*Giants* 29).

In Paul the σάρξ/πνεῦμα antithesis represents a historical dualism, not a metaphysical one. Since there is no human existence outside the flesh and God's dealing with human beings takes place in the flesh, the flesh appears as the

---

141. On the interpretation of Rom. 8:5–8, in addition to the standard commentaries, cf. esp. Paulsen, *Überlieferung*, 33ff.; Schmithals, *Anthropologie*, 104ff.; Gordon D. Fee, *God's Empowering Presence: The Holy Spirit in the Letters of Paul* (Peabody, MA: Hendrickson, 1994), 515–56; Umbach, *In Christus getauft*, 293–98.

142. Paulsen, *Überlieferung*, 46.

143. See the foundational work of Brandenburger, *Fleisch und Geist*, passim. Differently, J. Frey, "Die paulinische Antithese von 'Fleisch' und 'Geist' und die palästinisch-jüdische Weisheitstradition," *ZNW* 90 (1999): 45–77, who traces the flesh/spirit contrast back to pre-Essenic wisdom traditions that have indirectly influenced Paul.

144. Cf. Brandenburger, *Fleisch und Geist*, 114ff.

place where human beings either harden themselves in self-centeredness or let themselves be placed in God's service through the power of the Spirit. God's new reality thus opens itself to human beings as the reality of the Spirit. The turn from the yoke of the σάρξ, which brings death, to the life-giving ministry of the Spirit takes place in baptism. This is a fundamental change, for entrance into Christ's life-giving realm has the dimension of a new creation (cf. 2 Cor. 5:17). God's creative act for human beings is not limited to the one-time act of being called into life, but by the gift of the Spirit God grants human beings participation in God's own creative power. Baptized believers live according to the norm of the Spirit, which gives them assurance of present salvation and the first installment of the full redemption still to come. The Spirit is both power (ἐν πνεύματι [in/by the Spirit]) and norm (κατὰ πνεῦμα [according to the Spirit]) of the new life and makes it possible for Christians to continue to be what they have already become.

Christians find themselves in a new situation and in a new time: the time of the Spirit. The changed reality in which Christians live, as the reality of the Spirit, thus determines past and present just as it determines the future. Romans 8:11, "If the Spirit of him who raised Jesus from the dead dwells in you, he who raised Christ from the dead will give life to your mortal bodies also through his Spirit that dwells in you." Here the resurrection of the believer appears as an act of creation in which God, so to speak, continues and completes a creative act already begun, in continuity with the divine reality already present in the Christian life: the Spirit conferred in baptism and dwelling in the Christian appears as the continuum of divine life-giving power. Through the power of the Spirit, God grants believers participation in the creative act of God already achieved in the Christ event.

12.9 Paul and Israel

The question of the validity of the promises to Israel in view of the revelation of the righteousness of God apart from the law/Torah is already raised in Rom. 1:16 and 2:9–10 ('Ιουδαίῳ τε πρῶτον [to the Jew first]), is also the theme of 3:1–8,[145] and is then taken up in Rom. 9–11 and dealt with at some length. Whereas the apostle seems to have previously devalued the prerogatives of Israel, 3:1–8 for the first time raises the question of Israel's advantages. Paul explicitly and emphatically affirms the exceptional status of Israel (πολὺ κατὰ πάντα τρόπον [much, in every way]), naming as the first of Israel's privileged gifts the promises and instructions of the Scripture (τὰ

145. On the exemplary references to Israel in Rom. 1–8, cf. Dieter Sänger, *Die Verkündigung des Gekreuzigten und Israel: Studien zum Verhältnis von Kirche und Israel bei Paulus und im frühen Christentum* (WUNT 75; Tübingen: Mohr Siebeck, 1994), 95–151; Kraus, *Das Volk Gottes*, 272–90; Reichert, *Römerbrief*, 149–66.

λόγια τοῦ θεοῦ [the oracles of God]). Paul himself then immediately raises an objection resulting from the previous chapter: the faithfulness of God is not nullified by the unfaithfulness of some of his people. The truthfulness of God abides despite human unrighteousness. The apostle presents variations on this basic affirmation in the form of a dialogical style of argument, attempting to show the absurdity of inferences his opponents might make.[146] His line of argument, however, is not tight and does not proceed step by step (the πρῶτον μέν [in the first place] of 3:2 is not continued), for 3:9 then sharply negates the positive answer to the question of the advantages of the Jews in 3:2a. This indicates that 3:1–8 is something of an excursus;[147] here Paul deals with the theme in a very streamlined manner that does not fit very well into his present train of thought (the contrast between sin and God's righteousness). On the other hand, 1:16, 2:9–10, and 3:1–8 make clear that the problematic of Rom. 9–11 was in view from the very beginning of the conception of the letter.[148] Paul sees the appropriate place for dealing with this theme as following the section that looks forward to God's final redemption of creation and humanity (8:18–39), for the destiny of Israel is a constituent element in the eschatological act of God.

God's Freedom and Faithfulness

The overarching theme of Rom. 9–11 is the question of the righteousness of God that has appeared in Jesus Christ, and thus the faithfulness of God in view of the promises made to Israel (9:14ff.; 10:3ff.).[149] If the election of Israel, the promises to the fathers, and the provisions of the covenant are no longer valid, then God's righteousness is at stake (9:6). Then the word of God would in fact have failed (9:6). Paul, of course, claims the opposite. The election of Israel continues, the promises are still valid, but in view of God's revelation in Jesus Christ, Israel faces a crisis. As the theological point of departure for the discussions in Rom. 9–11, this revelation is the crisis for every single privilege when these are falsely understood. Thus Paul is concerned to show that, in view of the faithfulness of God and the unfaithfulness of Israel, God stands in unbroken continuity with his promises, proves his faithfulness despite the unfaithfulness of Israel, is a righteous

---

146. For analysis, see Wilckens, *Römer*, 1:161ff.

147. Luz, "Röm. 1–8," 169.

148. Cf. ibid.; Werner Georg Kümmel, "Die Probleme von Römer 9–11 in der gegenwärtigen Forschungslage," in *Heilsgeschehen und Geschichte* (ed. Erich Grässer, Otto Merk, and Adolf Fritz; 2 vols.; MTS 16; Marburg: Elwert, 1965–1978), 2:246ff.; Theobald, *Römerbrief*, 261ff.

149. Luz, *Geschichtsverständnis*, 36; Heikki Räisänen, "Römer 9–11: Analyse eines geistigen Ringens," *ANRW* 25.4:2893; Theobald, *Römerbrief*, 260–61.

The name "Israel" is found in Romans only in chs. 9–11 (eleven times); cf., in addition, the concept of the people of God in Rom. 9:25–26; 10:21; 11:1–2.

and just God. Paul presents this in a train of thought that is dialectically determined, constantly takes up new points of view, and varies the ways it deals with the subject.

The hardening of the majority of Israel in unbelief in the face of the ultimate revelation of God in Jesus Christ causes Paul deep pain (9:1–2). With profound rhetorical impact, the assurance of salvation and the hymnic praise in 8:28–39 is set over against the apostle's willingness to sacrifice himself for the salvation of Israel. He is willing to be excluded from salvation himself if by doing so he could achieve the salvation of his own kindred people (9:3). Israel is the people chosen by God, to whom belongs the "adoption" (ἡ υἱοθεσία), the "glory" (ἡ δόξα), the "covenants" (αἱ διαθῆκαι), "the giving of the law" (ἡ νομοθεσία), "the worship" (ἡ λατρεία), and "the promises" (αἱ ἐπαγγελίαι). If large segments of Israel reject the revelation in Christ, one could then conclude that the promises of God have failed. But with a series of arguments in 9:6ff., Paul refutes this possible conclusion. He proceeds on the basis of his axiomatic conviction that it is not possible for God's word to fail (9:6a). Instead the fact of the matter is that empirical Israel is not identical with those who have received the promises of God (Rom. 9:6b, οὐ γὰρ πάντες οἱ ἐξ Ἰσραὴλ οὗτοι Ἰσραήλ [For not all Israelites truly belong to Israel]),[150] and so Israel is not defined ethnically.[151] For Paul, the true Israel is identical with those who accept God's promises and acknowledge that God's saving purpose is fulfilled in Jesus Christ. The Old Testament promises do not apply to the part of Israel that rejects the revelation in Christ, because it is not Israel in the theological sense. By redefining the people of God as the people of the promise in this sense,[152] Paul gains the room he needs for his argument to show that in view of God's contingent acts in history, God is indeed faithful.

In 9:7–9 Paul gives additional support to his thesis stated in 9:6b. In the sense of salvation history, the true descendants of Abraham are only those descended from Isaac. Genetic descent alone by no means guarantees a special status within the history of salvation, for only the τὰ τέκνα τῆς ἐπαγγελίας (the children of the promise) are counted as descendants. Because for Paul the promises of the old covenant have been realized in Jesus Christ, they are inherited only by those who grasp them through faith. Since the relation of Isaac to Ishmael

---

150. Cf. Hans Hübner, *Gottes Ich und Israel: Zum Schriftgebrauch des Paulus in Römer 9–11* (Göttingen: Vandenhoeck & Ruprecht, 1984), 17.

151. The idea that empirical Israel is not identical with elected Israel is found in developed form in the Qumran literature. Thus, e.g., CD 4:2c–5a states (commenting on Ezek. 44:15), "'The priests': they are the repentant of Israel, who go out of the land of Judah and the Levites are those accompanying them; 'and the sons of Zadok': they are the chosen of Israel, the ones called by name, who are to appear in the last days. This is the full list of their names by their generations, and the time they appeared."

152. Cf. Jürgen Roloff, *Die Kirche im Neuen Testament* (GNT 10; Göttingen: Vandenhoeck & Ruprecht, 1993), 127; Kraus, *Das Volk Gottes*, 298ff.; Sass, *Leben aus den Verheissungen*, 434–61.

already shows that it is the sovereignty of God over Israel that is the focal point, in 9:10–13 Paul provides a further illustration of the freedom exercised by the Creator God. Although Jacob and Esau have the same mother and father, God chose one and rejected the other. Even before Jacob and Esau were born, before they could have done anything either good or evil, God's choice was already firmly made. Paul gives the basis for God's behavior in 9:11b–12 ("so that God's purpose of election might continue, not by works but by his call"). The call is entirely a matter of God's decision, not on the basis of works. All statements in Paul about divine predestination must thus be regarded as the result of his doctrine of justification.

Both the exclusive doctrine of justification and the statements about predestination are directed toward a single affirmation: everything depends on God's gracious act.[153] This act of God occurs in divine freedom; no one can influence God or require that God act in a certain way on the basis of one's origin or achievements. The freedom and sovereignty of God prevail over against every human being, including the chosen people, Israel. The Scripture already takes note of the election of Jacob and the rejection of Esau (cf. Gen. 25:23; Mal. 1:2 LXX in Rom. 9:12–13).[154] In Rom. 9:14 Paul takes up the obvious human objection, that God is unjust. He parries this objection in 9:15 by quoting Exod. 33:19 LXX: "I will have mercy on whom I have mercy, and I will have compassion on whom I have compassion." We find here a central feature of Paul's argumentation. For Paul, the Scripture announces and confirms the divine predestination. In the Scripture God himself has made known his will, which human beings can hear and learn but not call in question.[155] In Rom. 9:16 Paul emphasizes once again God's independence, in what is virtually a dogmatic formula: "So it depends not on human will or exertion, but on God who shows mercy." In 9:17 Paul provides the scriptural grounding (Exod. 9:16) for the preceding thetical statement, then in Rom. 9:18 again summarizes: "So then he has mercy on whomever he chooses, and he hardens the heart of whomever he chooses." Again, God's being as God is the only basis for the way God acts.

In 9:19–21 Paul deals with an additional possible objection, since from his previous argument one could draw the conclusion that the arbitrary rule of God to which no one may object means that human beings are not responsible for their own actions or for their own destiny.[156] Why does God blame sinners and condemn them if everything depends on God's arbitrary will anyway and

---

153. Appropriately, Otto Michel, *Der Brief an die Römer* (11th ed.; EKKNT 4; Göttingen: Vandenhoeck & Ruprecht, 1957), 307: "According to Paul, God's justification is found in God's act and in his self-portrayal."

154. On the use of scriptural quotations in Rom. 9(–11), cf. esp. Hübner, *Gottes Ich*, 149ff.; Koch, *Schrift als Zeuge*, on each text.

155. Maier, *Mensch und freier Wille*, 337–38.

156. See below, section 15.3 ("God as the One Who Elects, Calls, and Rejects")

human beings cannot do anything to change their own destiny? Paul responds to this objection in 9:19–21 by holding the objectors' creatureliness before their own eyes and thus ruling the question itself out of order. Such questioners, consciously or unconsciously, place themselves on the same level as God, but they are God's creatures and thus have no "right" to bring charges against God. Paul here anchors anthropology in creation theology: the qualitative distinction between Creator and creature cannot be abrogated and is the positive basis for the sovereign act of the Creator, who can choose and reject according to God's own will.[157] Every presumption of the creature to be master of his or her own fate is always already an offense against the appropriate role and purpose of a human being and an illegitimate rejection of the will of the Creator, who reveals himself in a double manner as wrath and mercy (9:22–23). Over against those Jews who insist on their privileges, Paul makes clear that God is free to act as God pleases, completely free to call or reject both Jews and Gentiles, just as the Scripture has prophesied (cf. 9:25–29).[158] Within the argumentation of Romans, Paul advocates a double predestination,[159] for salvation and destruction are not matters for the creature to decide but for the Creator—who has already decided.

Israel's Conduct

A new perspective in Paul's argument emerges in Rom. 9:30–10:21, where he turns his eye to the conduct of Israel. He first contrasts the righteousness of the Gentiles through faith with the righteousness of the Jews through the law/Torah (9:30–33). Paul explains the failure of the Jews to attain righteousness in the terse statement that Israel wanted to attain righteousness by works, not through faith. Christ thus became a stumbling stone to Israel because it went the way of the law/Torah, not the way of faith. In contrast to 9:1–29, there is no more talk of the act of God that is not at human disposal; Paul instead speaks of the boundless possibilities of faith to obtain salvation or of unbelief to miss it. Nonetheless, the apostle once again solemnly avows his wish for Israel's salvation (10:1), and confirms Israel's zeal for God but also its lack of insight (10:2). This is revealed in its attempt to establish its own righteousness instead of submitting itself to the righteousness of God (10:3). For believers, in contrast, Christ is their righteousness, so that Christ is at the same time the end of the law/Torah, that is, to the extent that the law facilitates the vain attempt to establish one's own righteousness before

---

157. Cf. Maier, *Mensch und freier Wille*, 337–38.

158. On the history-of-religions parallels, see above, section 3.3 ("The Religious and Cultural Background of Paul's Thought").

159. Emphatically, Maier, *Mensch und freier Wille*, 356–57.

God.[160] In 10:4[161] there can be no talk of Jesus Christ as the "end and goal"[162] or "goal"[163] of the law/Torah, or of a "fulfillment of the Torah" by Christ.[164] Against this view is the juxtaposition of ἰδία δικαιοσύνη (their own righteousness) and δικαιοσύνη θεοῦ in 10:3,[165] the grammatical structure of 10:4 (εἰς δικαιοσύνην [lit. for righteousness], which is to be connected to the following participle [so that a somewhat literal translation would read, "for righteousness to every believing person"], at the same time referring to the whole preceding verse),[166] and the function of 10:4 as the basis for what is said in 10:5–8.[167] Especially the contrasting of the righteousness that comes through the law/Torah (10:5)[168] with righteousness that comes from faith (10:6)[169] underscores the fundamentally antithetical structure of the argumentation of the whole section. Righteousness through the law/Torah is indebted to the principle of one's own doing, and the promise appears to be the result of one's own deed; but for the personified righteousness that comes from faith (10:6a), its word comes near to human beings in the proclamation of the gospel and calls for nothing but saving faith.[170] Again, it is not "lawlessness" that is here meant; rather, Paul is reducing the productive capacity of the law/Torah and making it more precise: Jesus Christ alone is the place of life and righteousness, which are made available through faith.

160. Among those who understand the text in this sense are Lietzmann, *Römer*, 96; Bultmann, *Theology of the New Testament*, 1:263–64; Käsemann, *Romans*, 282–83, Michel, *Römer*, 326; Gerhard Delling, "τέλος, κτλ.," *TDNT* 8:56; Zeller, *Römer*, 185; Hans Hübner, "τέλος," *EDNT* 3:348; Räisänen, *Paul and the Law*, 56; Schulz, *Neutestamentliche Ethik*, 347; Hans-Martin Lübking, *Paulus und Israel im Römerbrief: Eine Untersuchung zu Römer 9–11* (Frankfurt: Lang, 1986), 83–84; Reichert, *Römerbrief*, 167–68. This interpretation is also confirmed by the linguistic usage in Romans (6:21–22), where τέλος always means "end."

161. On the history of the interpretation of Rom. 10:4, see Luz, *Geschichtsverständnis*, 139ff.; Robert Badenas, *Christ the End of the Law: Romans 10.4 in Pauline Perspective* (JSNTSup 10; Sheffield: JSOT, 1985), 7ff.

162. Cf. Wilckens, *Römer*, 2:223, where he describes Christ as the "end and goal of the Torah in faith"; cf., in addition, Theobald, *Römerbrief*, 218.

163. So, e.g., Cranfield, *Romans*, 2:519; Dunn, *Theology of Paul*, 369. Haacker, *Der Brief an die Römer*, 201, translates, "Christ is what the law is in fact about."

164. So esp. Osten-Sacken, *Römer 8*, 250ff.

165. The repeated γάρ (for) in Rom. 10:3–4 indicates a tight connection in the argument; cf. Schreiner, *The Law and Its Fulfillment*, 134–36.

166. Cf. Käsemann, *Romans*, 282–83.

167. One cannot learn Paul's understanding of the expression τέλος τοῦ νόμου (end of the law) from the lexicon alone, for neither the history of the word's usage (cf. the account in Badenas, *Christ the End of the Law*, 38–80) nor Pauline usage elsewhere (cf. Delling, "τέλος," *TDNT* 8:54–56) permits us to establish a consistent basic meaning. The majority of the instances of τέλος are to be understood in the sense of "end" (1 Cor. 1:8; 10:11; 15:24; 2 Cor. 3:13; 11:15; Rom. 6:21, 22; Phil. 3:19).

168. On the textual problems of Rom. 10:5, cf. Hübner, *Gottes Ich*, 78–80.

169. On the mixed citation in 10:6–8, cf. ibid., 86, 154–55.

170. Cf. Zeller, *Römer*, 186.

In 10:5–13 Paul again goes to the Scripture for proof that righteousness does not come through doing the law/Torah. Paul presents his proof that salvation comes only through the word of faith by having the personified figure of justification by faith introduce itself. Paul intentionally takes a text that originally referred to the Torah and plays it off against the law/Torah, since, for him, salvation comes only through faith in Jesus Christ, which has attained tangible form in the Christian confession. Because messengers of the gospel were presently under way, preaching the message of justification by faith in every land (10:14–17), Israel has no excuse. Then, why is not Israel converted? Once again the answer comes from Scripture, for the Torah and the prophets had already predicted that the ignorant Gentiles, a nonpeople, would someday overtake and surpass Israel (10:18–21). God has gone to a lot of trouble for his people, whose lack of knowledge consists in a willful ignorance of God's will. Israel has refused to cooperate and is thus itself responsible for its present disastrous situation. This logic of personal responsibility clearly stands in tension with the apostle's argumentation in 9:1–29.[171] Whereas there the unquestionable act of God is in complete control, here human beings are charged with being able to make a positive decision but not doing so. The tension between sovereign divine predestination and personal human responsibility is not merely the expression of a logical weakness in the Pauline argumentation; it is grounded in Paul's objective situation. He must explain something that is *not* really explainable. Why has the chosen people rejected the ultimate saving act of God in Jesus Christ? The mystery of unbelief that is the subject of debate eludes every human effort at a consistent explanation, for its resolution is found exclusively in God. Paul introduces every imaginable argument in his effort to make the paradoxical present situation understandable.

Moreover, talk of predestination also always has a social function, in that it explains to a group why it has not been successful in converting others. Both are necessary in a missionary situation: coming to terms with the actual situation by appeal to divine hardening, and the human possibility of making right or wrong decisions in order to be able to change the situation through preaching. Therefore Paul can regard neither God's negative predestination nor Israel's own negative decision as the last word on the matter, as Rom. 11 shows.

Israel's Salvation

In Rom. 11:1–2 Paul solemnly avows that under no circumstances will God "reject his people whom he foreknew." The apostle judges his own life to be evidence for this claim (11:1b). The Scripture also points to this conclusion, for, just as in Elijah's time, so also now there is "a remnant chosen by grace" (λεῖμμα κατ᾽ ἐκλογὴν χάριτος γέγονεν, 11:5). Paul here returns to the argu-

---

171. Räisänen, "Römer 9–11," *ANRW* 25.4:2910.

mentation of 9:6ff., that the majority of Israel has been hardened according to God's own will. By his own grace God chooses the Jewish Christians[172] as a remnant while the rest of Israel is hardened. Thus Israel is divided into two categories (9:7), "the elect" (ἡ ἐκλογή) and "the rest" (οἱ λοιποί). God himself brings about this division, for, according to 9:8, God has given those who are hardened "a sluggish spirit" that has prevented their hearing and understanding the gospel. The remnant concept provides Paul evidence for his thesis that Israel is and remains the elect people, that it can never be entirely rejected. On the other hand, the vast majority of Israel does remain at present in its state of having been hardened according to God's own will. According to this line of argument, it is still a long way to the salvation of Israel as a whole.

Romans 11:11–32 occupies a special position within this argumentation, where Paul thematizes the salvation of Israel in an augument divided into four subsections (11:11–16, 17–24, 25–27, 28–32).[173] In 11:11 he emphasizes that the hardening of Israel has a positive purpose in God's plan. Israel's stumbling provides the opportunity for salvation to come to the Gentiles as well. Israel's ἥττημα (defeat, loss, damage) becomes riches for the Gentiles because in this way the Gentiles come to participate in God's salvation alongside Israel. In contrast to the preceding argumentation, Israel's situation appears in a positive light, since it is playing its assigned role in its salvation, albeit with delays and detours. In 11:13–14 Paul defines his apostolic office in a new way and adapts it to the understanding of history expressed in Rom. 11. It is precisely as "apostle to the Gentiles" (11:13, εἰμι ἐγὼ ἐθνῶν ἀπόστολος) that he now preaches, explaining that the goal of his mission to the Gentiles is in the service of the salvation of Israel in that he provokes Israel to "jealousy" of Gentile Christians in order to save some of the people of Israel. This interpretation of his apostolic ministry hardly fits Paul's original understanding of his apostleship, for, according to Gal. 1:15–16, Paul received his call in order to win the Gentiles. According to Gal. 2:9, he was explicitly not a missionary to Israel. Here we have a "belated rationalization,"[174] which Paul sees himself compelled to adopt in view of the actual course of early mission history. In addition, in this way he can neutralize the charge that his stance toward the law has prevented Israel from accepting the Christian faith (cf. Acts 21:21, 28). It is probably the case that in the final phase of his missionary career, Paul developed from his reading of Deut. 32:21 the expectation that Israel would still be saved after all by becoming jealous of the Gentiles (cf. Rom. 10:19; 11:11, 14). The great hopes he associated with this view are indicated in Rom. 11:15: "For if their rejection is the reconciliation of the world, what will their acceptance be but life from the dead!" The history of Israel's election goes on despite their present

172. Wilckens, *Römer*, 2:238.
173. Reichert, *Römerbrief*, 200ff.
174. Räisänen, "Römer 9–11," *ANRW* 25.4:2913.

rejection; if Israel's rejection results in the reconciliation of the world to God, then Israel's acceptance introduces the eschatological events.

With the picture of the holiness of the roots and the resulting holiness of the branches (11:16), Paul makes the transition to the analogy of the olive tree (11:17–24). Here Israel appears in its original role as people of God whereas Gentile Christians merely join with the status of proselytes.[175] As the noble olive tree, Israel is the root of all salvation, including that of the Gentiles (11:18b). Although a few branches have been broken off this tree and branches from wild olive trees have been grafted in, Israel remains the real people of God. When Gentile Christians are accepted into the tree, they have no grounds for boasting. With this warning Paul is possibly reacting to a disdainful attitude of Gentile Christians in Rome to Jews and Jewish Christians there. The present status of Gentiles is not definitive, for they are likewise assigned their place by the gracious act of God. If God has the power to break branches off and graft them in again, they, too, can be broken off if they abandon the way of faith and love (11:20–22). Once again human wrongdoing serves to explain the current situation, so that giving up one's unbelief can introduce a new dimension in God's saving acts. Paul explicitly emphasizes this possibility in 11:23–24: if the branches that originally belonged to the olive tree do not persist in their unbelief, they will be regrafted into their "own" olive tree. The hardening of a part of Israel has a temporal limit, lasting only until the fullness of the Gentiles are converted, and so[176] πᾶς Ἰσραὴλ σωθήσεται (all Israel will be saved, 11:26a).[177] This pointedly maximal statement of Pauline eschatology and soteriology generates numerous problems.[178] First, there is not very much dispute about the time to which the stated event refers, since 11:26b points to the coming of Christ at the parousia (cf. 1 Thess. 1:10).[179] In the interpretation of πᾶς Ἰσραήλ (all Israel), the decisive clues are given by the immediate context and the corresponding expression πλήρωμα τῶν ἐθνῶν (full number of the Gentiles, 11:25). Romans 11:20 names unbelief as the reason for the present exclusion of Israel from salvation; according to 11:23, this must be overcome as the condition for the entrance of Israel into salvation. Thus especially 11:23 makes unlikely an interpretation

---

175. Käsemann, *Romans*, 308–9; Zeller, *Römer*, 197; Räisänen, "Römer 9–11," *ANRW* 25.4:2914.

176. On the understanding of καὶ οὕτως (and so), see the discussion in Hübner, *Gottes Ich*, 110; Otfried Hofius, "Das Evangelium und Israel," in *Paulusstudien* (2 vols.; WUNT 51, 143; Tübingen: Mohr Siebeck, 1989–2002), 1:192–93.

177. On the structure of Rom. 11:25–27, cf. Ferdinand Hahn, "Zum Verständnis von Röm 11,26a," in *Paul and Paulinism: Essays in Honour of C. K. Barrett* (ed. Morna Dorothy Hooker and S. G. Wilson; London: SPCK, 1982), 227; Luz, *Geschichtsverständnis*, 288–89; Theobald, *Römerbrief*, 178ff.

178. A history of research is found in Winfrid Keller, *Gottes Treue, Israels Heil—Röm 11, 25–27: Die These vom "Sonderweg" in der Diskussion* (SBB; Stuttgart: Katholisches Bibelwerk, 1998).

179. Cf. Wilckens, *Römer*, 2:256; Theobald, *Römerbrief*, 280. Differently, e.g., Zeller, *Römer*, 199; Reichert, *Römerbrief*, 208ff., who refer Rom. 11:26b to the "first coming" of Christ.

of 11:26a as something that happens apart from Christian faith.[180] In 11:25b πλήρωμα does not refer to the full number of Gentile Christians, for only then do the Pauline concept of faith and the apostle's preaching of judgment maintain their validity. So also πᾶς Ἰσραήλ does not simply imply ethnic Israel but only that part of Israel that comes to Christian faith in the eschatological acceptance of God's salvation. In addition to 11:23, this interpretation is also suggested by the distinction between the Israel of the promise and the Israel according to the flesh of 9:6, as well as the apostle's remark in 11:14b that he hopes to save some of his own people (καὶ σώσω τινὰς ἐξ αὐτῶν).[181]

Finally, the use of σῴζω/σωτηρία (save/salvation) makes clear that, for the apostle, there is no salvation apart from faith.[182] In 1:16 salvation applies only to those who believe, to the Jews first and also to the Greeks. The determination of σωτηρία by δικαιοσύνη θεοῦ and πίστις in the foundational theological statement of 1:16–17 is definitive for further understanding. In 5:9–10 righteousness by faith is parallel to the blood of Christ, which makes possible salvation from the coming wrath. The form σωθήσεται in the Isaiah quote in 9:27 is revealing, since it is explicitly applied only to the remnant of Israel and thus prejudices the understanding of σωθήσεται in 11:26a. Moreover, 10:9–13 emphasizes specifically that salvation is guaranteed through faith in Jesus Christ, and there alone. According to 10:12, there is no distinction between Jews and Gentiles; Christ is the Lord of both. Why should Jews be provoked to jealousy by Gentile Christians if, in any case, Israel already has what the Gentile Christians are just now receiving? Why is Paul so deeply troubled (9:2–3; 10:1) if Israel could bypass Christ and still attain salvation?

According to 11:25–27, Paul expects an act of God in the final events of history that will lead Israel to conversion and thus to salvation.[183] He sees in this the maintenance of God's identity and faithfulness, who does not reject Israel forever but who subjected Jews and Gentiles alike to disobedience in order to be merciful to both in Jesus Christ (11:32). God is righteous; it is up to human

---

180. On the meaning of 11:23, see also Hahn, "Röm 11,26a," 228–29. This verse speaks decisively against the thesis of F. Mussner, "'Ganz Israel wird gerettet werden' (Röm 11,26)," *Kairos* 18 (1976): 241ff., that in Rom. 11:26a Paul is pointing out a "special way" of salvation for Israel; similarly, Theobald, *Römerbrief*, 278, who also argues for a salvation of all Israel apart from the preaching of the gospel and thus necessarily relativizes the significance of 11:23a: "Accordingly, the only thing certain from 11:23a is that the future salvation of all Israel includes *turning away from unbelief* but not necessarily that Israel must *be converted to the gospel.*" An additional suggestion for resolving the problem is offered by Hofius, "Evangelium und Israel," 197, according to whom "all Israel" attains salvation neither through the preaching of the gospel nor by a "special way." "It is rather the case that Israel will hear the gospel directly from the mouth of the returning Christ—the saving word of his acceptance that generates the faith that lays hold of God's salvation." Hofius, too, must play down the importance of Rom. 11:20, 23 (cf. Hofius, "Evangelium und Israel," 188) in order to make his thesis plausible.

181. Cf. Hahn, "Röm 11,26a," 229.

182. Hübner, *Gottes Ich*, 117.

183. Cf. Käsemann, *Romans*, 305:"Its [Israel's] full conversion is undoubtedly expected . . . but is bound up with the fact that salvation has come first to the Gentiles."

beings to decide whether they will open themselves to God's righteousness or harden themselves in unbelief.

Paul as Prophet

The multilayered character of Paul's argumentation in Rom. 9–11 results from the complexity of the issue. Paul is the first within early Christianity to pose the basic question, a question that is finally unsolvable: how is God's fundamental and continuing promise of salvation to Israel related to God's ultimate promise of salvation in Jesus Christ? Paul had to balance and hold together two competing orders of salvation, two different soteriologies, each with an absolute claim to authority. This is an impossible venture: Paul had to be creative, to rationalize, to speculate, in order to prevent his argument from being completely derailed. The Pauline line of argument in Rom. 9–11 reflects this theological but also intellectual dilemma and attempts to overcome it with three different types of solutions: God has hardened the major part of Israel but also has elected a part (9:6–29; 11:3–10); Israel has rejected God's revelation in Jesus Christ (9:30–10:21); and God will save his elect people in his own eschatological act (11:1–2, 11–36). The third answer represents the attempt to overcome the partial solutions represented in the concepts of hardening and remnant. Paul speaks in 11:25b–26a obviously as a prophet, who shares knowledge that is not derived by inferential arguments from the kerygma.[184] Prophecy provides Paul with a way of gaining theological knowledge in order to fill an empty space left by theological reflection (1 Thess. 4:13–18). Continuity between the individual models is found only in the freedom, faithfulness, and selfhood of God, who in each case remains the director of the whole scenario. Paul is profoundly convinced that the decision made in God's unfathomable wisdom applies both to God's elect people Israel and to the new people of God composed of both Jews and Gentiles. He accepts the tensions that are necessarily present in the argument of Romans because the dominant conception, in Rom. 1–8 and 12, of the participation of believers in the Christ event cannot be logically combined with the prophetic expectations of Rom. 11.

12.10 The Shape of the New Life

In Rom. 12:1ff. Paul again takes up the idea already formulated in 6:11ff., that obedience to God is realized in bodily service,[185] and now develops his

---

184. Cf. Merklein, "Theologe als Prophet," 400–401; Theobald, *Römerbrief*, 279, sees in Rom. 11:28–31 the working out of the prophetic revelation in 11:25–26, which flows into 11:32.
185. Reichert, *Römerbrief*, 233–34.

understanding of the Christian life in its relation to God, its reality in the community of faith, and its relation to the world.

Reasonable Ethic according to the Will of God

The four-chapter section Rom. 12–15 begins with a caption, 12:1–2,[186] which makes clear the dialectical character of Christian existence: on the one hand, Paul challenges the Roman Christians to a worship corresponding to the essence of λόγος (word, reason) and thus to conducting their lives in a way that is reasonable and devoted to the world;[187] on the other hand, at the same time he makes it just as clear that this does not mean an accommodation to the essential values and perspectives of this world but a life that corresponds to the will of God, which can also be discerned in the world. This way of thinking is based on the ancient concept of offering a sacrifice to the gods as grateful response for some manifestation of divine deliverance. Paul summarizes the whole life of the Christian as such a thank offering, defined as λογικὴ λατρεία (reasonable service). As in the ancient world in general, so also in Paul: religion and intellect are not contrasted but penetrate each other, each able to interpret the other. Therefore it is by no means the case that the revelation of God's will in Jesus Christ can be perceived only within the limited area of the church, for its content is also fulfilled in the world ethos in a way that can be perceived by all, as τὸ ἀγαθὸν καὶ εὐάρεστον καὶ τέλειον (what is good and acceptable and perfect, 12:2).[188] Paul thus takes up the Hellenistic tradition of piety governed by reason and acting according to reason. Precisely in its orientation to the Spirit/spirit, the Christian ethic for Paul is also a reasonable ethic, for the Spirit takes away the defect in reasoning caused by the power of sin and thus restores it to its true self. Because the will of God is identical with the ethical good, the apostle is able to integrate the general human knowledge of good and evil into the Christian ethic and at the same time opens it up to the world ethos without thereby grounding it in reason or in a particular ethical tradi-

---

186. Haacker, *Der Brief an die Römer*, 254, speaks of a "preamble."

187. On λογικὴ λατρεία (reasonable service or spiritual worship, Rom. 12:1), cf. Lietzmann, *Römer*, 108–9. Texts relevant to this complex are found in *NW* 1/2:220–34; 2/1:177–80. For analyses of Rom. 12:1–2, in addition to the standard commentaries, see esp. Ernst Käsemann, "Worship in Everyday Life: A Note on Romans 12," in *New Testament Questions of Today* (London: SCM Press, 1969), 188–95; Wolfgang Schrage, *Die konkreten Einzelgebote in der paulinischen Paränese: Ein Beitrag zur neutestamentlichen Ethik* (Gütersloh: Gütersloher Verlagshaus, 1961), 49ff.; Betz, "Grundlagen der paulinischen Ethik," 193–203; Reichert, *Römerbrief*, 228–48.

188. Cf. Cicero, *Nat. d.* 2.71, "The best, purest, and holiest worship of the gods consists of our prayer to them with pure, uncorrupted, and unadulterated words and thoughts" (*NW* 1/2:224); Seneca, *Ep.* 95.50, "Do you want to make the gods well-disposed to you? Then do good. The one who strives to imitate them gives them adequate worship" (*NW* 2/2:1181); cf., in addition, Seneca, *Ben.* 1.6.3 (*NW* 1/2:225). According to Plato, *Resp.* 5.520c, philosophers should rule the state "because they have seen the Beautiful, the Good and Just, in the Truth." Cf. also Plato, *Leg.* 4.716c–d.

tion. Instead Christians are challenged to discern which ways of living one's life derive from the will of God.[189]

In 12:3–15:13 Paul illustrates how such ethical reflections might look. Paul first focuses his attention on internal problems of the community (12:3–8) and follows with more general instructions in 12:9ff., continued in 13:8–14, then in Rom. 14–15 turns back to primarily inner-church issues. The love commandment, central in both 12:9ff. and 13:8ff., thus shows that Paul's instructions are by no means limited only to the realm of church life; the Christian lives of church people can serve as models for the transformation of the world.

In 12:3 Paul first instructs the charismatics not to transgress the established limits, which also apply to them, but to conduct themselves in a level-headed and circumspect manner.[190] The philosophical cardinal virtues of φρόνησις (insight) and σωφροσύνη (level-headedness, composure), under the heading of the "renewing of your minds" (through the Spirit), are at the same time the cardinal ecclesial virtues.[191] With μέτρον πίστεως (measure of faith) Paul guides the train of thought in the direction of faith that comes to expression as defined in a particular instance and defined in a particular manner, a faith that must be aware of its boundaries; he does not want faith to slide off into effusive rapturous experiences. The differences of gifts and responsibilities must not be allowed to become divisive; instead the members of the community are as a whole ἓν σῶμα ἐν Χριστῷ (one body in Christ), although as individuals they conduct themselves in relation to each other as members. In Paul, as in the use of the imagery in the ancient world generally, the concept of an organism is directed toward order. Differently than in 1 Cor. 12:28, however, the point here is not priority in rank but the diversification of the charismatic gifts. Within the listing in Rom. 12:6–8, central offices and functions may be discerned: to the sphere of worship belong prophecy, service (at the table), teaching, and exhortation, while administration of charity, leadership, and care for the sick are in the area of church organization. For Paul, to have a spiritual gift means that one must decide how to use it in the service of others.

Paul rings the chimes on this basic idea in Rom. 12:9–21. At the beginning stands the programmatic word about Christian love as the functional center of all spiritual gifts (cf. 1 Cor. 13). The following chain of instructions provides a rich description of life within the Christian community that knows itself to be determined exclusively by love. Some admonitions are directed to insiders: to love one another (Rom. 12:10), contributing to the needs of one's broth-

---

189. Reichert, *Römerbrief*, 247, emphasizes the introductory function of Rom. 12:1–2: "The text functions to characterize the addressees as a community/congregation and to orient them to the effect of their lives beyond the community."

190. For the interpretation of Rom. 12:3–8, in addition to the standard commentaries, cf. Andreas Lindemann, "Die Kirche als Leib," in *Paulus, Apostel und Lehrer der Kirche: Studien zu Paulus und zum frühen Paulusverständnis* (Tübingen: Mohr Siebeck, 1999), 151–57; Reichert, *Römerbrief*, 248–58.

191. Cf. Aristotle, *Eth. nic.* 2.1105b (*NW* 2/1:183–84).

ers and sisters in the faith, to show hospitality (12:13), and to manifest unity (12:15–16). Here Paul challenges the Roman Christians to "be ardent in the Spirit" (12:11b). The way of life that prevails within the Christian community is also to be directed outward in its relation to the world.[192] The renunciation of vengeance (12:17, 19), the ability to live in peace with all other human beings (12:18), and finally the call to love even one's enemies (12:20) encourage the community of faith to allow the power of the Spirit to work without restraint in all areas of its life. Just as with the other admonitions, the fundamental principle "Do not be overcome by evil, but overcome evil with good" (12:21) appeals to the experience of love and is not merely one of a list of commands. The exhortation not to repay evil with evil presupposes that the Roman church is faced with considerable pressure from outside.[193] The edict of Claudius in 49 CE most likely caused the Jewish community in Rome to distance itself from the emerging Christianity and at the same time to oppose it as a potential source of danger. But one can also easily imagine that pressures were arising from the Roman state, for this presupposition provides an explanation for the surprising instructions in 13:1–7.

In the Shadow of the Roman Imperial Power

In Rom. 13:1–7 Paul deals with the relation of the Christian to the state. The section is intentionally permeated with secular terms and concepts, which make a direct christological interpretation impossible.[194] The Roman church should fit itself into the created structures of the world. Romans 13:1b emphasizes the divine origin of all authority, and 13:2 draws the consequence that whoever resists the authority resists the order God has established. Romans 13:3–4 explain the function of the divinely established authority. Because the authorities have the responsibility to punish evil, no one who does good need fear them. By punishing evil, the authorities are God's servants and are executing God's wrath. Therefore, so 13:5 declares, one must be subject to these authorities "not only because of wrath but also because of conscience." The general admonition calling for obedience is concretized with the example of 13:6: the Romans pay taxes and thereby acknowledge the authorities established by God. The imperial officials in charge of taxes and customs carry out their work as nothing less than λειτουργοὶ θεοῦ (God's servants). In 13:7 Paul concludes his instruction with a generalization: "Pay to all what is due them—taxes to whom taxes are due, revenue to whom revenue is due, respect to whom respect is due, honor

---

192. Differently, Reichert, *Römerbrief*, 258ff., who refers Rom. 12:9–13 exclusively to insiders and 12:14–21 exclusively to relations with outsiders.

193. Cf. Reichert, *Römerbrief*, 271.

194. The basic evidence is given by A. Strobel, "Zum Verständnis von Röm 13," *ZNW* 47 (1956): 67–93; cf. also Haacker, *Der Brief an die Römer*, 216–70; texts in *NW* 2/1:199–206.

to whom honor is due." The interpretation of this disputed passage must attend carefully to its location within the structure of Romans: it is paraenesis, not dogmatics.[195] Since the state accepts the tasks of administering and putting into effect the power assigned it by God, then Christians are responsible to support it in these tasks. Moreover, 13:1–7 manifests a political connotation currently relevant to Paul's readers, for his instruction to acknowledge the political authorities is probably to be understood against the background of the increasing tensions between the Roman authorities and the independent movement that was developing into a recognizably Christian community.[196] The Romans are beginning to perceive the Christians as a group that worships an executed criminal as a god and that proclaims the imminent end of the world. The Neronian persecution that occurred only eight years after Romans was written shows that there must have been increasing tensions between the Christians, on the one side, and the authorities and the population of Rome, on the other.[197]

With the keyword ἀγάπη (love), Paul takes up the thread of the instructions in 12:9–21, at the same time drawing a significant relationship between ἀγάπη and νόμος (law/Torah), for, according to the general understanding of antiquity, love comprises everything with which the law/Torah is concerned.[198] Love appears in 13:8a as the obligatory fundamental norm of all Christian conduct, and 13:8b then supplies the basis for this demand: ὁ γὰρ ἀγαπῶν τὸν ἕτερον νόμον πεπλήρωκεν (for the one who loves another has fulfilled the law).[199] With this

---

195. Cf. Käsemann, *Romans*, 353; extensive reflections on the textual pragmatism are found in Helmut Merklein, "Sinn und Zweck von Röm 13,1–7: Zur semantischen und pragmatischen Struktur eines umstrittenen Textes," in *Studien zu Jesus und Paulus* (2 vols.; WUNT 43, 105; Tübingen: Mohr Siebeck, 1987), 2:405–37.

196. With reference to Tacitus, *Ann.* 13.50–51 (lingering protests against the tax burden in 58 CE), Johannes Friedrich et al., "Zur historischen Situation und Intention von Röm 13,1–7," *ZTK* 73 (1976): 131–66, see the current background of Rom. 13:1–7 in the tax burden on the citizens at the time when Romans was composed. Michel, *Römer*, 403 n. 34, had already advocated this thesis; cf. also Merklein, "Röm 13,1–7," 431–34; and Theobald, *Römerbrief*, 309. The matter is accented differently by Haacker, *Der Brief an die Römer*, 269: "In Rom. 13:3–6 Paul evidently alludes to this interpretation of the Roman 'world order' (sc., tribute as gratitude of the subjected peoples for the achievements of the Romans, especially law and order) and presupposes that the readers of Romans share this conclusion, whether he here follows his own socialization as a Roman citizen or whether it is a matter of deferring to the milieu in which he would like to work next as a missionary." Elliott's thesis, that Paul's advice is purely a tactical measure in view of the prevailing power structure, is not persuasive (N. Elliott, "Romans 13:1–7 in the Context of Imperial Propaganda," in *Paul and Empire: Religion and Power in Roman Imperial Society* [ed. Richard A. Horsley; Harrisburg, PA: Trinity Press International, 1997], 184–204).

197. See above, section 7.5 ("The Development of Early Christianity as an Independent Movement").

198. Cf. Haacker, *Der Brief an die Römer*, 273.

199. Very probably τὸ ἕτερον (another) is the object of ἀγαπῶν (the one loving; cf. τὸν πλησίον [neighbor] in Rom. 13:9) and cannot be an attribute of νόμος, for Paul never uses ἀγαπάω without an object; cf. the discussion in Michel, *Römer*, 409 n. 5; and Wilckens, *Römer*, 3:68.

concentration of the law into the concept of love, Paul stands in the tradition of Jewish and Jewish Christian exposition of the Scripture (cf. Matt. 5:43; 7:12; 19:19; 22:39; Mark 12:28–34; Luke 10:27).[200] Romans 13:9 functions as an explanation; Paul cites first, in abbreviated form, four prohibitions (cf. Exod. 5:17–20, 21; Exod. 20:13–15, 17) as preliminary to introducing Lev. 19:18b as the positive testimony of Scripture. According to Paul, the individual commands should be understood in the light of the love command. Then Rom. 13:10b draws the programmatic concluding inference: πλήρωμα οὖν νόμου ἡ ἀγάπη (therefore, love is the fulfilling of the law). In 13:8–10 Paul chooses three fundamental points where his train of thought regarding the law comes to crucial junctures:

(1) He precisely *specifies and reduces the Torah by orienting it completely to the love command*[201] and claims that in this way it is fulfilled by Christians in its entire extent. There is thus no distinction between commands that are still valid and commands that have been annulled, although in fact the ritual laws are no longer observed (cf. 14:14, 20). Paul is concerned with the claim of the whole Torah. Through this line of argument Paul avoids the objection that his theology negates the Torah as divine revelation. From the Jewish perspective, however, this objection continues to be valid, for, in contrast to Jewish tradition, the rest of the commands and prohibitions of the Torah completely lose their importance for Paul.[202] This also applies to the Decalogue, for in 13:9 Paul does not cite *the* Decalogue but only illustratively *from* the Decalogue. Through this line of argument, the apostle leaves his Jewish thinking behind, for the claim to fulfill the whole Torah by keeping one command while failing to observe all the other commands is not imaginable and not verifiable in the Jewish thought world.

(2) Paul attempts to resolve the problematic of the law through *a new definition of the law/Torah.* He thinks he can appeal to a scriptural text for support (Lev. 19:18) and is persuaded that he can thereby do justice to both the continuity and the discontinuity of God's actions.

---

200. Documentation from Hellenistic Judaism and early rabbinic tradition is given by Klaus Berger, *Die Gesetzesauslegung Jesu: Ihr historischer Hintergrund im Judentum und im Alten Testament* (WMANT 40; Neukirchen-Vluyn: Neukirchener Verlag, 1972), 99–136; Andreas Nissen, *Gott und der Nächste im antiken Judentum: Untersuchungen zum Doppelgebot der Liebe* (WUNT 15; Tübingen: Mohr Siebeck, 1974), 224–46, 389–416; Strack and Billerbeck, *Kommentar,* 1:357–59; 3:306; O. Wischmeyer, "Das Gebot der Nächstenliebe bei Paulus," *BZ* 30 (1986): 162ff.

201. Cf. Räisänen, *Paul and the Law,* 27; Wischmeyer, "Nächstenliebe bei Paulus," 180–87. Differently, Karin Finsterbusch, *Die Thora als Lebensweisung für Heidenchristen: Studien zur Bedeutung der Thora für die paulinische Ethik* (SUNT 20; Göttingen: Vandenhoeck & Ruprecht, 1996),100–107, who thinks that through love Christians make effective the function of the law in regulating social order. The fulfilling of other Torah commands is not annulled by the love command; similarly, M. Stowasser, "Christus, das Ende welchen Gesetzes?" *PzB* 5 (1996): 6–9.

202. Cf. Mussner, *Galaterbrief,* 373.

(3) Through the transformation of the law/Torah into the love command, Paul succeeds in taking up *the nucleus of both Jewish and Greco-Roman thinking about the law* and thus in providing a means by which all groups in the community could find his understanding of the law acceptable.[203]

Just as the concept of love already forms the functional center of Rom. 12:9–13:14, so it also determines the apostle's argumentation in the conflict between the "strong" and the "weak" in 14:1–15:13.[204] It is no accident that the term ἀδελφός (brother/sister) is found especially often in this section (14:10, 13, 15, 21), for it is the love of brothers and sisters who accept one another within the one family of God, in which the love for neighbor Paul is calling for assumes concrete shape. Paul shares the position of the "strong" (14:14, 20; 15:1) but for love's sake requires that the strong be considerate of the "weak." Both groups live from the fact that Christ has welcomed them; therefore they should welcome each other. The inclusio of 14:3 and 15:7, which determines this whole section, highlights mutual acceptance as a fundamental ecclesiological principle. But the principle of mutual acceptance is not to be identified with the modern concept of tolerance,[205] for what is at stake here has to do with the differing evaluation of cultural presuppositions, not christological or sociological issues, about which Paul does not leave open a range of options. Each person has the right to remain committed to his or her own lifestyle (cf. 14:1–2), but because the brother or sister who thinks and acts differently on such matters has been welcomed by God, "Welcome one another, therefore, just as Christ has welcomed you, for the glory of God" (15:7). When love expresses itself in the concrete form of welcoming those who think differently, judging each other is excluded (cf. 14:4, 10, 13). Judgment is the prerogative of God alone (14:10–11), but every individual must give account to God (14:12). The unity of the church of Jewish Christians and Gentile Christians may not be obscured or even placed at risk by third-rate issues, for only then does the church maintain its drawing power for outsiders (15:8ff.).

203. For extensive supporting argument, see below, section 19.3 ("The Law").
204. For interpretation, see, most recently, Reichert, *Römerbrief,* 271–311.
205. Cf. Theobald, *Römerbrief,* 293.

13

Paul in Rome

The Old Man and His Work

In the world capital, a man who changed the world: in Paul's missionary program, Rome was supposed to be only a brief stop on the way to Spain, but it became his final stop. Rome did not, however, become the end of his missionary work, for not only did Paul continue to be active within the city of Rome, and in a way that made his influence felt from Rome, but also his martyrdom there sealed his work and assured its continuing effect.

13.1 Prehistory: Paul en Route to Rome

Although Luke provides an extensive account of Paul's stay in Jerusalem, his imprisonment, and the following trip to Rome (cf. Acts 21:15–28:31), many events during this period remain in the dark.[1] From a literary point of view, there is a noticeable lack of balance between the extensive account of the trip,

---

1. Friedrich Wilhelm Horn, "Die letzte Jerusalemreise des Paulus," in *Das Ende des Paulus: Historische, theologische, und literaturgeschichtliche Aspekte* (ed. Friedrich Wilhelm Horn; BZNW 106; New York: de Gruyter, 2001), 15–35, provides a critical introduction to the problems.

imprisonments, and trials (Acts 21–26), the detailed portrayal of the adventurous voyage to Rome (27:1–28:15), and the exceedingly brief report of Paul's stay in Rome itself (28:16–31).[2] Theologically important is the open ending of Acts. Even though Paul is the hero of the whole narrative, manifestly so from Acts 15 on, the reader does not learn from Acts how his story came to an end. Luke knows the real purpose of Paul's final trip to Jerusalem (cf. 24:17) and already in 20:24–25 has his death in view, but he does not explicitly refer to either. An explanation for this remarkable set of circumstances must take into account, besides the minimal (though valuable) information found in Paul's own letters, especially the amount and quality of information available to Luke but also his theological strategy.

What Happened to the Collection?

The first point to note is that for Paul the delivery of the collection must have become a matter of great urgency. According to 1 Cor. 16:3–4, the offering is to be delivered by a delegation (16:3, without Paul; 16:4, Paul will go if it seems advisable); according to 2 Cor. 8:19–20, Paul intends to deliver the offering accompanied by Titus. Now the apostle himself seems compelled to work into his missionary plans a detour via Jerusalem before he can continue his mission westward. Why does he intentionally enter a situation he knows is personally dangerous for him? Acts 20:1–21:14 gives no information regarding Paul's intention in making this last trip to Jerusalem; Luke does not mention the collection and lets Paul stop for a while in Miletus despite the necessary haste. At the same time, there are allusive hints of Paul's coming suffering and death (cf. Acts 20:23, 25; 21:11, 13), and a comparison of Luke 9:51 with Acts 19:21 shows that Luke considers Paul's trip to Jerusalem to be on the way to martyrdom.[3] Paul's discussion in Rom. 15:30–31 clearly reveals how strained the situation had become: "I appeal to you, brothers and sisters, by our Lord Jesus Christ and by the love of the Spirit, to join me in earnest prayer to God on my behalf, that I may be rescued from the unbelievers in Judea, and that my ministry to Jerusalem may be acceptable to the saints." Paul uses the verb ῥύομαι (deliver) explicitly in the context of deliverance when his life is in danger (2 Cor. 1:10) or needs eschatological salvation (1 Thess. 1:10; Rom. 7:24; 11:26). Paul fears violent actions from the Jews in Judea, whose hostility to the apostle also has a deep influence on the attitude and conduct of the Jerusalem church toward him. The tensions obviously escalated once Paul was in Jerusa-

---

2. Heike Omerzu, "Das Schweigen des Lukas: Überlegungen zum offenen Ende der Apostelgeschichte," in *Das Ende des Paulus* (ed. Horn), 128–44, surveys the history of scholarly attempts to explain this lack of proportion.

3. Cf. Horn, "Jerusalemreise," 24 note 33; and Omerzu, "Schweigen des Lukas," 128–44.

lem,[4] and with this trip Paul undertook his final and possibly even despairing attempt to refute the charges against himself in order to calm down the agitations of his Jewish Christian and Jewish opponents (in Jerusalem, Rome, and other places), to reestablish relations with the original church in Jerusalem by delivering the offering to them, and finally to assure their remaining within Judaism by providing a demonstration of his orthodoxy.[5]

In Acts 21:15ff. Luke reports Paul's arrival in Jerusalem, where he meets with James, the leader of the Jerusalem church (21:18). The Jerusalem church's faithfulness to the Torah is emphasized in 21:20, which notes the response to Paul's report of his successful mission among the Gentiles: "When they heard it, they praised God. Then they said to him, 'You see, brother, how many thousands of believers there are among the Jews, and they are all zealous for the law.'" Luke then repeats the charges against Paul that are circulating in Jerusalem: "They have been told about you that you teach all the Jews living among the Gentiles to forsake Moses, and that you tell them not to circumcise their children or observe the customs" (21:21). These charges against Paul probably have a historical nucleus that represents the real situation,[6] reflecting not only the hostility of Jews but also the strong reservations of Jewish Christians in Jerusalem regarding Paul. Moreover, they correspond to the reality of the situation of the churches in the Pauline mission. Some ethnic Jews who had been converted in the Pauline mission churches certainly did distance themselves from observing the Torah, including the command to circumcise their children.[7]

Another aspect of the account makes clear how tense and fragile the relation between Paul and the Jerusalem church had become despite the agreements made at the apostolic council. Luke is conspicuously silent on whether the real goal of the Jerusalem trip was attained: the delivery of the collection to the original Jerusalem church. Although, according to Acts 24:17, Luke was aware of the real purpose of the final trip to Jerusalem, he never mentions the collection, which could have been placed dramatically between 21:19 and 21:20. Three explanatory models have attempted to illuminate this remarkable state of affairs: (1) The collection was delivered, but only "unofficially" and with great difficulties.[8] (2) The collection was partially or gradually delivered or used in the context of paying the expenses of those who had taken Nazarite

---

4. Cf. Betz, *2 Corinthians 8 and 9*, 141–42.

5. Cf. Horn, "Jerusalemreise," 34.

6. Cf. Lüdemann, *Traditions in Acts*, 234.

7. Hengel, "Herrenbruder," 575.

8. So, e.g., Haenchen, *Acts*, 655–59 [translator's note: the author's reference to Ernst Haenchen, *Die Apostelgeschichte* (7th ed.; Göttingen: Vandenhoeck & Ruprecht, 1977), 586–88, is more specific on this point than the English translation referenced here, which is of the 1965 edition]; Dieter Georgi, *Remembering the Poor: The History of Paul's Collection for Jerusalem* (Nashville: Abingdon, 1992), 126 ("But as things turned out, the collection . . . was received as if 'on the side,' accompanied by whispers"); Wehnert, *Hintergrund des sogenannten Aposteldekrets*, 271 ("Apparently the delivery of the money was done unofficially and without Paul's participation"). Cf. also the reflections of Claus-

vows (cf. 21:23–24:26).[9] (3) Luke does not report the delivery and acceptance of the collection because it never took place.[10] There is much evidence that the Jerusalem church refused to accept the collection but that Luke is silent about this failure because it does not fit his ecclesiology, a united church of Jews and Gentiles. The understanding of the law found in Galatians and Romans would have been out of the question for strict Jewish Christians and would have been nothing short of a breach of church fellowship, since now the Torah even for Jewish Christians would have at most only a preliminary function (cf., e.g., Gal. 6:15). Not only for Jews but for strict Jewish Christians, there was no longer any difference between Paul and an out-and-out apostate who had betrayed the true spiritual home of both Jews and Jewish Christians, the synagogue. It was also probably consideration for the synagogue that provided another reason the Jerusalem church was unwilling to accept "unclean" money.[11] Moreover, the strict Jewish Christians whom Paul had just repudiated in Galatia probably had strong support in Jerusalem, and so, for them, refusing to accept Paul's offering would be a victory against Paul's concept of the one church of Jews and Gentiles. Finally, it is remarkable that Luke reports no efforts of the Jerusalem church to free Paul from prison or to stand by him during his trials. The relation between Paul and the Jerusalem church, which was never entirely free from tensions (cf. Gal. 1:18–19; 2:6), at the end of Paul's successful mission to the Gentiles developed into open hostility. The theological differences were too deep, the characters themselves too different. The founding epoch of early Christianity comes to its end not with unity but division.

Arrest and Trial

According to Acts 21:27–30, Paul was arrested because he was thought to have taken Trophimus, a Gentile Christian from Ephesus, with him into the temple.

Jürgen Thornton, *Der Zeuge des Zeugen: Lukas als Historiker der Paulusreisen* (WUNT 56; Tübingen: Mohr Siebeck, 1991), 347–51.

9. Cf. Friedrich Wilhelm Horn, "Paulus, das Nasiräat, und die Nasiräer," *NovT* 39 (1997): 117–37; Dietrich-Alex Koch, "Kollektenbericht, Wir-bericht, und Itinerar," *NTS* 45 (1999): 380. On the Nazarite as one dedicated to God (basic texts are Judg. 13; Num. 6), see Ludger Schwienhorst-Schönberger, "Nasiräer," *NBL* 2:901–2.

10. Cf. Lüdemann, *Traditions in Acts*, 234–35; Joachim Gnilka, "Die Kollekte der paulinischen Gemeinden für Jerusalem als Ausdruck ekklesialer Gemeinschaft," in *Ekklesiologie des Neuen Testaments: Für Karl Kertelge* (ed. Rainer Kampling and Thomas Söding; Freiburg: Herder, 1996), 301–15; Jacob Jervell, *Die Apostelgeschichte* (17. Auflage, 1. Auflage dieser Auslegung; KEK 3; Göttingen: Vandenhoeck & Ruprecht, 1998), 529–30; Roloff, *Apostelgeschichte*, 313; Rudolf Pesch, *Die Apostelgeschichte* (2 vols.; EKKNT; Neukirchen-Vluyn: Neukirchener Verlag, 1986), 222.

11. Cf. Josephus, *J.W.* 2.408–409, where the demand that the temple priests no longer accept money or sacrificial offerings from non-Jews is named as one of the events that triggered the war against the Romans; Haacker, *Der Brief an die Römer*, 314–15, argues that rebellion against Rome was the real motivation for refusing such gifts.

This would have been a violation of the temple law, which prohibited any non-Jew from entering the sacred area of the temple.[12] Luke explicitly points out that this was a false charge (Acts 21:29), and so Paul is arrested on false charges just as had previously been the case with Stephen. The exact circumstances of Paul's arrest and delivery into the hands of the Roman authorities can no longer be clearly illuminated.[13] Also, the following report of Paul's trial contains numerous historical inconsistencies.[14] Luke has at his disposal extensive traditions in which Paul's trials, with their speeches accusing him and his speeches of defense, are formulated as literary models of the forensic rhetoric of antiquity.[15] In this literary style, prominent political personalities seek out famous prisoners and engage them in discussion (cf. 24:24–27; 25:23–26:32), which gives Paul the opportunity to present his teaching. But why is a Roman citizen who has already been pronounced innocent kept under arrest for so long without any recognizable progress in the trial? Acts 24:26 mentions that Felix had hoped to receive a bribe from Paul, but this speculation can hardly be historical. As the time of Paul's imprisonment drags on, Festus replaces Felix in 58 CE. The new procurator takes up the case (cf. 25:1–12) and pronounces Paul not guilty. Festus's suggestion to initiate a new case against Paul in Jerusalem is legally questionable. If Festus is willing to deliver Paul over to the Jewish authorities, then it is no longer necessary to have any legal proceedings in his own jurisdiction. Or if Festus sees the issue as a matter of Roman law, then we must ask why a final decision could not have been given in Caesarea. Also, the appeal to Caesar (cf. 25:9–12) is difficult to explain in terms of legal history,[16] for Paul is neither

12. Cf. Philo, *Embassy* 212 ("Death without appeal is the sentence against those of other races who penetrate into its inner confines"; Josephus, *J.W.* 5.192–194. Cf. also the temple inscription discovered in 1871 (text in C. K. Barrett, *The New Testament Background: Selected Documents* [2nd ed.; London: SPCK, 1987], 53; Boring et al., eds., *Hellenistic Commentary*, § 527). For interpretation, cf. Klaus E. Müller, "Möglichkeit und Vollzug jüdischer Kapitalgerichtsbarkeit," in *Der Prozess gegen Jesus: Historische Rückfrage und theologische Deutung* (ed. Karl Kertelge and Josef Blank; QD 112; Freiburg: Herder, 1988), 68ff.

13. On the possible legal backgrounds, cf. Brian Rapske, *The Book of Acts and Paul in Roman Custody* (vol. 3 of *The Book of Acts in Its First Century Setting*; ed. Bruce W. Winter; Grand Rapids: Eerdmans, 1994), 135–49 (the events in Jerusalem); Omerzu, *Der Prozess des Paulus*, 309–84.

14. On the events in Caesarea, cf. Rapske, *Roman Custody*, 151–72; Omerzu, *Der Prozess des Paulus*, 396–501.

15. Whether behind Acts 21:17–26:32 there was already a connected account of Paul's arrest and imprisonment or only individual units of tradition is a disputed point. The former option is argued by, among others, Volker Stolle, *Der Zeuge als Angeklagter: Untersuchungen zum Paulusbild des Lukas* (BWA[N]T 102; Stuttgart: Kohlhammer, 1973), 260–67; Roloff, *Apostelgeschichte*, 316; Pesch, *Apostelgeschichte*, 2:224; Lüdemann, *Traditions in Acts*, 22; Omerzu, *Der Prozess des Paulus*, 507–8. Among those who argue for individual traditions are Haenchen, *Acts*, 632–732; Schneider, *Apostelgeschichte*, 2:311–79; Weiser, *Apostelgeschichte*, 2:390, 601.

16. Cf. Rapske, *Roman Custody*, 186–88, who votes for a *provocatio*, according to which Roman citizens and some others who were spending some time in the provinces could appeal for a trial in Rome when there was no authorized court in the province where they were staying. According to Omerzu, *Der Prozess des Paulus*, 485–97, Paul's *appellatio* was based "on a legal ruling that

acquitted nor convicted.[17] Then why does he appeal to Caesar? It is possible
that the Roman procurator did in fact condemn Paul as an agitator but that
Luke has suppressed this report in view of the way he wants the Roman public
to view the Christian movement. In such a case, the appeal to Caesar would
be consistent, for now the higher court must take action. Such an explanation
would fit the tendency of Luke's narrative as a whole, which wants to present
the Jews as exclusively responsible for the death of Jesus and the imprisonment
of Paul. In any case, Luke's goal is clear: Paul now takes the path from Jerusalem
to Rome, from the Jews to the Gentiles, from Israel to the new Israel, which
consists of both Jews and Gentiles.[18]

The trip from Caesarea to Italy is portrayed as filled with adventure, according to the literary taste of the time. At first the Roman officer and his prisoners sail along the coast of Asia Minor, then in Myra they board a ship from
Alexandria bound for Italy. Between Crete and Italy the ship is overtaken by
a hurricane, and Paul and the others are shipwrecked on the island of Malta.
Paul's journey passes through Syracuse and Rhegium en route to Puteoli, at that
time the largest harbor in the western half of the Roman Empire. Once again
center stage of this drama is occupied by the apostle Paul, presented by Luke as
a respected and righteous man who speaks up for his fellow travelers (cf. Acts
27:10, 21–26, 31, 33–36).[19] He not only is a person with social competence
but also has prophetic abilities, for he predicts the catastrophe (cf. 27:10, 22)
and their deliverance (27:26). Also the snakebite incident on Malta (28:3–6)
and his contacts with the elite leadership of the island (28:7–10) present Paul
as one who is righteous in God's sight. Luke has two goals in this portrait of
Paul, which his hearers and readers would recognize: (1) It is God's will that
with Paul the gospel comes to Rome (cf. the divine δεῖ ["it is necessary"] in
27:24). (2) Although, according to the general understanding in antiquity, as
a prisoner Paul had lost every shred of social reputation he might have had,[20]
he is shown to be one who is righteous in God's sight and in the eyes of his
fellow human beings, and enters Rome as one who can preach the gospel in
all freedom.

---

first originated in the principate and had no connection with the later forms of appeal found in
the republic (viz., the *provocatio ad populum* or the *appellatio ad tribunos*). The *appellatio* of the
imperial period, which we have here, is primarily based on the delegated authority of the emperor
to pronounce sentence in the provinces and on the usual procedure there for cases deemed *extra
ordinem*" (p. 504).

17. Differently, Omerzu, *Der Prozess des Paulus*, 491, who supposes that Paul's appeal was against
the death sentence that Festus had pronounced.

18. Cf. Weiser, *Apostelgeschichte*, 2:642: "The appeal to Caesar—and thus, in Luke's understanding, the opening of the way to Rome—is the high point toward which everything before had been
directed."

19. Cf. Labahn, "Paulus—ein homo honestus et iustus," 79–106.

20. Cf. Rapske, *Roman Custody*, 146.

Paul in Rome

The account of Paul's stay in Rome (28:17–31) likewise raises numerous legal, historical, and theological questions. Regarding the legal situation, the first point one notices is the relatively free circumstances of Paul's imprisonment. He does not live in a prison or barracks but in a rented apartment (cf. 28:16, 23, 30)[21] under the guard of a soldier (28:16). Although 28:20 presupposes that Paul was bound to his guard by chains, this does not hinder his having an extensive preaching ministry in Rome. One can only imagine such treatment if Paul was a Roman citizen and thus entitled to a privileged form of incarceration.[22] Moreover, it is remarkable that nothing is said of a trial in Rome. The real reason for his journey to Rome slips completely into the background. The chronological information about the two years (28:30) has no relevance for the legal aspects of his trial,[23] so that also from a legal point of view Paul's fate remains undecided. Historically, it is clear from Rom. 16 that Paul knew many members of the Roman church. Nonetheless, there is never any real meeting with the Roman Christian community (cf. Acts 28:16). Instead Paul first makes contact—as always in the Acts account—with the local synagogue (Acts 18:17ff.). It is the rejection of his message that first causes Paul to turn to the Gentiles. Thus the impression is given that Paul was the first founder of the church in Rome, although in Acts 28:15 the non-Pauline origin of the Roman church is presupposed. What caused Luke to tell the story in this way? We must assume that for this segment of Paul's ministry, Luke probably had only a few historically reliable traditions.[24] In addition, the tendency is apparent in the whole two-volume work to excuse the Romans from any guilt in the death of Jesus or in hindering the Christian mission. It is therefore likely that Luke remained silent about the guilty verdict Paul received in Rome though he knew the circumstances of the apostle's death (19:21; 20:23–25; 21:11). We can be confident of the historical veracity of only the following: Paul arrived in Rome as part of a transport of prisoners, and there he was able to continue some missionary work despite his confinement. The literary and theological strategy of Luke is clearly recognizable in 28:17–31. As in the previous narratives, Paul is presented, despite his imprisonment, as one with legal and social privileges, one with whom leading members of the Jewish community meet (cf. 28:17, 23) and who, as a worthy messenger of God, openly proclaims the gospel in the capital city of the world.[25]

21. Omerzu, "Schweigen des Lukas," 146.

22. On Paul's Roman imprisonment from the point of view of legal history, see Rapske, *Roman Custody*, 173–91; Omerzu, "Schweigen des Lukas," 144–51; Labahn, "Paulus—ein *homo honestus et iustus*," 98–104.

23. Cf. the argumentation in Omerzu, "Schweigen des Lukas," 147–49.

24. So Omerzu, ibid., 151–56, who sees the traditional kernel as 28:16, 23, 30–31.

25. Luke signals this linguistically with the adverb ἀκωλύτως (without hindrance, Acts 28:31; hapax NT).

13.2 Philippians

13.2.1 A Letter from Rome to Philippi

Is Paul still writing letters to his churches from the Roman imprisonment? The Letter to the Philippians was written while Paul was in prison (Phil. 1:7, 13, 17) but in a situation that did not prevent him from having a vigorous missionary activity (1:12–13). He had received a gift from Philippi brought by Epaphroditus (4:18; cf. also 2:25; 4:14), and he now sends Epaphroditus back with the letter expressing his gratitude (2:25, 28). During his stay in the city where Paul was imprisoned, Epaphroditus himself had become severely ill, which caused the church in Philippi great concern (2:26–30). Paul would like to visit the church himself (1:26; 2:24), but the outcome of his trial is still open. A trial has already taken place (1:7); Paul counts on a quick decision (2:23) and considers either acquittal or the death sentence to be possible (1:19–24), but he hopes for a positive verdict (1:25). In any case, he wants to send Timothy to Philippi (2:19–23) to learn how things are going in the church.

Philip II of Macedon had founded the city about 356 BCE.[26] An intensive Roman settlement in the city began in 42 BCE, which the events of 31 BCE (Octavian's defeat of Antony) strengthened. From 27 BCE onward, Philippi developed as a military colony, the Colonia Augusta Julia Philippensis, in which primarily veterans of the army were settled. The most influential segment of the population was the Romans, but Greeks and Thracians also contributed to the linguistic, cultural, and religious life of the city.[27] Philippi's economic importance (agriculture, crafts, commerce) resulted from its location on the Via Egnatia, the main artery connecting the eastern and western regions of the Roman Empire. Philippi is a good example of the religious syncretism of the first century CE (cf. Acts 16:16–22), for, alongside the Caesar cult and the Greek, Roman, and Egyptian gods, the indigenous fertility cults of the original Thracian inhabitants enjoyed great popularity.

The first Pauline church in Europe began in Philippi (cf. Acts 16:11ff.; Phil. 4:15), founded by the apostle in 49/50. The majority of the congregation was Gentile Christian (cf. Acts 16:33b and the names Epaphroditus [Phil. 2:25ff.; 4:18], Euodia, Syntyche, and Clement [Phil. 4:2–3]), but it also probably included God-fearers (cf. Acts 16:14) and Jewish Christians (cf. Acts 16:13).[28]

---

26. On the city and its history, cf. Elliger, *Paulus in Griechenland*, 23–77.

27. Lukas Bormann, *Philippi: Stadt und Christengemeinde zur Zeit des Paulus* (Leiden: Brill, 1995), 11–84, strongly emphasizes the Roman element; also Pilhofer, *Philippi*, 1:85–92, highlights the Roman character of Philippi but also emphasizes that the influence of Greeks and Thracians is not to be ignored.

28. We now have good evidence of a synagogue from the third century CE; cf. Chaido Koukouli-Chrysantaki, "Colonia Iulia Augusta Philippensis," in *Philippi at the Time of Paul and after His Death* (ed. Charalambos Bakirtzis and Helmut Koester; Harrisburg, PA: Trinity Press International, 1998), 5–35.

What location for the prison fits the apostle's situation described above? Of the locations proposed by scholars (Rome, Caesarea, Ephesus),[29] the greatest probability belongs to Rome. The portrayal of the Roman imprisonment in Acts 28:30–31 fits very easily into the mild sort of confinement presupposed in Philippians (cf. Phil. 1:13–14; 2:25; 4:10ff.).[30] Moreover, the references to the Praetorian guard (1:13 NRSV, "imperial guard")[31] and the slaves of the emperor (4:22 NRSV, "those of the emperor's household") are best understood in terms of a Roman imprisonment. There is additional evidence for Rome as the place where Philippians was written and thus for a late dating of the letter: (1) The lack of any reference to the collection indicates that at the time of the letter the collection was already complete.[32] (2) Philippians presupposes a lengthy confinement. If the letter had been written in Ephesus, the silence of Acts about a long imprisonment would be without explanation,[33] whereas the two year imprisonment in Rome (Acts 28:30) fits very well with the situation presupposed in the letter. Paul's allusion in 2 Cor. 1:8 to a life-threatening situation in the province of Asia provides no support for the hypothesis of an

29. For arguments for and against, cf. Kümmel and Feine, *Introduction*, 325–32; Gnilka, *Philipperbrief*, 18–25; Schade, *Apokalyptische Christologie*, 182ff.; Raymond E. Brown, *An Introduction to the New Testament* (ABRL; New York: Doubleday, 1997), 493–96. The Ephesus hypothesis founded by Deissmann, *Paul*, 17 n. 1, is advocated today by numerous exegetes (e.g., Bornkamm, *Paul*, 241; Gnilka, *Philipperbrief*, 199; Gerhard Barth, *Der Brief an die Philipper* [Zurich: Theologischer Verlag, 1979], 8–9; Wolfgang Schenk, *Die Philipperbriefe des Paulus: Kommentar* [Stuttgart: Kohlhammer, 1984], 338). Especially Ernst Lohmeyer, *Die Briefe an die Philipper, an die Kolosser, und an Philemon* (14th ed.; KEK 9/1; Göttingen: Vandenhoeck & Ruprecht, 1974), 3–4, has argued for Caesarea as the place of imprisonment (cf. also Marion L. Soards, *The Apostle Paul: An Introduction to His Writings and Teaching* [New York: Paulist, 1987], 114). The Roman hypothesis was revived in the last century by Josef Schmid, *Zeit und Ort der paulinischen Gefangenschaftsbriefe: Mit einem Anhang über die Datierung der Pastoralbriefe* (Freiburg: Herder, 1931), passim; and C. H. Dodd, "The Mind of Paul, II," in *New Testament Studies* (New York: Scribner, 1954; Manchester: Manchester University Press, 1966), 83–128 (Scribner), 85–108 (Manchester). In recent research this view is again winning more and more advocates—e.g., Merk, *Handeln*, 174; Hunzinger, "Hoffnung angesichts des Todes," 85 n. 30; Wiefel, "Eschatologischen Denken," 79; Strecker, "Befreiung und Rechtfertigung," 230; Lüdemann, *Chronology*, 104, 186 n. 135; Schade, *Apokalyptische Christologie*, 190; Roloff, *Einführung*, 139–40; Peter T. O'Brien, *The Epistle to the Philippians: A Commentary on the Greek Text* (NIGTC; Grand Rapids: Eerdmans, 1991), 19–26; Peter Wick, *Der Philipperbrief: Der formale Aufbau des Briefs als Schlüssel zum Verständnis seines Inhalts* (BWA[N]T 135; Stuttgart: Kohlhammer, 1994), 182–85; Gordon D. Fee, *Paul's Letter to the Philippians* (NICNT; Grand Rapids: Eerdmans, 1995), 34–37; Matthias Günther, *Die Frühgeschichte des Christentums in Ephesus* (ARGU 1; New York: P. Lang, 1995), 40, 43–47.

30. Cf., however, Acts 24:23 for Caesarea.

31. Thus, with emphasis, Fee, *Philippians*, 35, on πραιτώριον: "The word more naturally refers the Praetorian Guard, the emperor's own elite troops stationed in Rome. Those who favor an Ephesian imprisonment can only hypothesize the presence of the guard in Ephesus, since (a) there is no evidence to support it and (b) there was no praetorium in Ephesus."

32. Schade, *Apokalyptische Christologie*, 190.

33. On the difficulties of the Ephesian hypothesis, see esp. Schmid, *Gefangenschaftsbriefe*, 10ff., 72ff.

Ephesian imprisonment, since Paul indicates only that his life had been endangered, without giving any particular circumstances.[34] So also the fighting with "wild animals" in 1 Cor. 15:32 is no evidence for a lengthy imprisonment in Ephesus.[35] (3) The rather reserved portrayal of the relations with the church at the place of imprisonment (Phil. 1:12–18, esp. vv. 15, 17; cf. *1 Clem.* 5:5) indicates that the church there had not been founded by the apostle himself. (4) The term ἐπίσκοπος (overseer, supervisor), found only in Phil. 1:1 in the undisputed letters of Paul (cf. Acts 20:28; 1 Tim. 3:2; Titus 1:7), presupposes a development within the church in the direction of the Pastoral Letters.[36] (5) An analysis of Paul's vocabulary in Philippians[37] reveals distinctive elements in the greeting, in the use of the title "Christ," in the manner in which "we" and "I" are used, and the presence of rare words (cf. esp. Βενιαμίν [Benjamin], only Rom. 11:1; Phil. 3:5; Ἑβραῖος [Hebrew], only 2 Cor. 11:22; Phil. 3:5; ἐργάτης [worker], only 2 Cor. 11:13; Phil. 3:2; φυλή [tribe], only Rom. 11:1; Phil. 3:5). All these speak for the date of the composition of Philippians *after* that of Romans.

One objection to Rome as the place of composition is that the statements about the law and Israel in Philippians must have been written before Romans rather than later.[38] But Paul by no means takes back the actual result of the argument in Romans, which affirms that righteousness/justification is located in Jesus Christ alone (compare Rom. 10:3–4 with Phil. 3:9). The sharp statements about the break with his Jewish past are doubtless conditioned by the continuing agitation of Jewish Christian missionary opponents, and they are not a correction of Paul's hope for Israel in Rom. 11:25–26. Instead the location of Philippians within the chronology of Paul's letters points to the end of his career and thus to Rome: Whereas according to Rom. 15:24 Paul plans a mission to Spain, in Phil. 1:21 he is an old man in prison who longs for death.

---

34. Contra Furnish, *II Corinthians*, 123; Helmut Koester, *History and Literature of Early Christianity* (vol. 2 of *Introduction to the New Testament*; Philadelphia: Fortress, 1982), 130.

35. Contra Hans Conzelmann and Andreas Lindemann, *Interpreting the New Testament: An Introduction to the Principles and Methods of New Testament Exegesis* (trans. Siegfried S. Schatzmann; Peabody, MA: Hendrickson, 1988), 177. Ulrich B. Müller, "Der Brief aus Ephesus: Zeitliche Plazierung und theologische Einordnung des Philipperbriefes im Rahmen der Paulusbriefe," in *Das Urchristentum in seiner literarischen Geschichte: Festschrift für Jürgen Becker zum 65. Geburtstag* (ed. Ulrich Mell and Ulrich B. Müller; BZNW 100; Berlin: de Gruyter, 1999), 161, attempts to explain, on the basis of Luke's political expediency, the silence of Acts about the assumed lengthy imprisonment of Paul in Ephesus: "One must take into account the fact that the historical situation when Acts was written made it seem inadvisable for a conflict between pagan religion (polytheism) and Christianity that had almost led to a legal sentence against Paul as a Christian leader to be reported in such a manner that the 'no little disturbance concerning the Way' (Acts 19:23) could appear to Greco-Roman society in an all too suspicious light."

36. Cf. Jürgen Roloff, "Amt IV," *TRE* 2:522.

37. Cf. Schade, *Apokalyptische Christologie*, 184–90.

38. So, e.g., Müller, "Der Brief aus Ephesus," 170: "The third chapter of Philippians can be made plausible only if, like Galatians, it is located *before* the fundamental clarifications in Romans."

A further argument raised against Rome as the place where Philippians was written is the great distance between Rome and Philippi, which would not have allowed the lively traffic presupposed between Paul's prison and the church he addresses. Moreover, a Roman location would mean that Paul had changed his travel plans announced in Rom. 15:24–28, since he intends to visit Philippi after his release. Neither objection is well grounded. Paul could change his travel plans, as shown in the Corinthian correspondence (compare 1 Cor. 16:5–8 with 2 Cor. 1:15–16). At the time he wrote Romans, Paul could not have foreseen the years of imprisonment in Caesarea and Rome, but new contacts with the churches he had already established could lead Paul to change (not abandon) his previous plans. The planned journey to Spain would not necessarily be given up by making a trip to Philippi occasioned by present circumstances—only postponed. Moreover, the statement affirming that he wants to visit a particular church is part of the formal structure of Pauline letters (cf. 1 Thess. 2:17ff.; 1 Cor. 16:5–6; 2 Cor. 13:1; Gal. 4:20; Rom. 15:23–24; Philem. 22). The transportation links between Philippi and Rome were very good (on the Via Egnatia to Dyrrhachium, by ship to Brundisium, then continuing along the Via Appia).[39] A sea voyage from Philippi to Rome took about two weeks,[40] and a predominantly overland trip of about 672 miles[41] would take about four weeks, calculated at about 23 miles per day.[42] The travel time could be even less if one takes into consideration the good condition of the Roman roads, the possibility of favorable winds and good ship connections, and the possible use of a wagon. If we presuppose in Philippians four trips between Rome and Philippi (the Philippians hear of Paul's imprisonment; they send Epaphroditus; the Philippians hear of Epaphroditus's sickness; Paul sends Epaphroditus back to Philippi), this constitutes no difficulty for a location such as Rome, where Paul was in custody for a relatively long time. Philippians was probably written in Rome about 60 CE.[43]

13.2.2 Philippians as a Document of Later Pauline Theology

The Letter to the Philippians is a document of late Pauline theology in a twofold sense: (1) It was composed at the final stage of the apostle's missionary activity. (2) Its content also represents an advanced stage of Pauline thought,

39. Cf. Schmid, *Gefangenschaftsbriefe*, 77–83. On the excellent road conditions, see G. Radke, "Viae publicae romanae," PWSup 13:1477.

40. Cf. Friedlaender and Wissowa, *Sittengeschichte Roms*, 337ff.

41. Cf. Alfred Wikenhauser and Josef Schmid, *Einleitung in das Neue Testament* (6th ed.; Freiburg: Herder, 1973), 506.

42. Friedlaender and Wissowa, *Sittengeschichte Roms*, 333, estimates 37.5 km (ca. 23 miles) per day; other calculations are found in Reck, *Kommunikation und Gemeindeaufbau*, 85–87. Cf. Jewett, *Chronology*, 56–62.

43. When Ephesus is regarded as the place where Philippians was written, its writing is usually located at the end of this period; thus Müller, *Philipper*, 22, e.g., argues for the year 55 CE.

which is in no small way conditioned by the personal situation of the apostle. Especially the eschatological affirmations of the letter and the readiness of the apostle to die a martyr's death show that Paul understands himself to be at the end of not only his ministry but also his life (cf. Phil. 1:21; 2:17).

In this difficult situation, the Letter to the Philippians lets us see that Paul regards his situation as a vehicle for the proclamation of the gospel and for a challenge to his churches. In Philippians he develops the paradox of Christian existence by referring to his own person, proceeding from gratitude to God, who in his faithfulness both maintains and furthers the Philippians in their faith and also uses the present situation of the apostle for God's own good purposes. Paul felt closer to the Philippians than to any other church. Several particular features reflect the extremely good relationship between apostle and church: (1) Philippians has the longest *prooemium* (thanksgiving section) of all the Pauline letters (1:3–11); the content throughout bears the stamp of Paul's closeness to them in constant prayer and unreserved thanksgiving and praise.[44] The motif of thanksgiving, bound up with the call to rejoice, permeates the whole letter (cf. 1:3, 18; 2:29; 3:1a; 4:1, 4–6, 19–20) and provides its fundamentally positive tone. (2) Paul specifically emphasizes the close friendship of church and apostle. They have shared the ministry of the gospel with each other from the very beginning (1:5). From this there grew a mutual participation in giving and receiving that has endured until the present (4:15). (3) The apostle has granted to them alone the privilege of supporting his work with material gifts (cf. 4:18). Differently from his relationship with the Corinthian church (cf. 1 Cor. 9), he has no fear of a theological takeover by the Philippians. Also the threatening situation in prison is unable to detract from the apostle's joy and confidence, for it paradoxically calls forth further fearless proclamation of the gospel (Phil. 1:12, 14). Their common service in the gospel also binds together apostle and church in this difficult situation, which Paul presses into service in his own missionary cause. The news about his trial publicizes the gospel, so that in the place where he is imprisoned even rival missionary factions find the courage to proclaim Christ (cf. 1:15–18ab). Although Paul must reckon with the possibility that his death is near, he faces the future with joy, for he lives in the glad confidence that whether he lives or dies, Christ is glorified (cf. 1:18c ff.). Nonetheless, he is troubled by a deep inner conflict, for, although what he would really like to do is die and be with the Lord, his responsibility for the church keeps him in this world. In 1:20 the apostle at first expresses his hope that Christ will be glorified in his body, whether through life or death. Philippians 1:21 takes up this confidence in salvation with a sweeping identification of ζωή with Christ.[45] Now bodily death is by no means the end

44. This is signaled linguistically by the numerous forms of πᾶς (all, every, vv. 4, 7, 8, 9).

45. Formally, τὸ ζῆν (to live, life) is the subject, and Χριστός is the predicate nominative; cf. Blass and Debrunner, *Grammar*, § 399 (1). But cf. the appropriate comment of Paul Hoffmann, *Die Toten in Christus: Eine religionsgeschichtliche und exegetische Untersuchung zur paulinischen Eschatologie*

of life; rather, as the removal of the separation between apostle and Christ, it is preferred to continuing life in this body.[46] Thus the dilemma formulated in 1:22: on the one hand, the wish to die and be with Christ and, on the other hand, the possibility of continuing to do fruitful missionary work. The apostle's longing comes clearly to expression in 1:23 in ἐπιθυμίαν ἔχων (have a longing for) and the exclamatory interruption πολλῷ γὰρ μᾶλλον κρεῖσσον (for that would be far better): he would like to die and thus finally attain being with Christ. A conventional euphemism for death is ἀναλύω[47] (depart), which here receives its content from the phrase σὺν Χριστῷ εἶναι (to be with Christ).[48] Paul here expects being with Christ immediately after death, giving no further description of the future life with Christ that forms the content of his hope, since σὺν Χριστῷ εἶναι was clearly a common paraphrase in Pauline Christianity for the believer's new salvific status.[49] It is necessary, however, for the sake of the church that Paul remain in this life, and so he puts aside his own wish and will continue to help the church in Philippi (1:24–26).

Philippians 3:20–21 also reveals the apostle's orientation to the future heavenly existence. There Paul disputes with opponents (3:17–19) and contrasts them with the church's orientation to the heavenly reality. The term πολίτευμα (citizenship) designates the legal status of a citizen; just as the Roman citizens of Philippi are enrolled as members of the *tribus Voltinia* in Rome, so the Christians in Philippi are registered in a heavenly "citizenship list."[50] To this designation of the true location of Christians Paul adds a portrayal of the parousia, which begins with the coming of the Savior Jesus Christ and comes to its climax with the transformation of our present bodies of humiliation into glorious bodies like that of Christ, who will subject all things to himself.[51]

The apostle's (martyr) consciousness is seen also in 2:17. Paul sees himself as a libation "poured out" as an offering in both Jewish and pagan cultic worship.[52] If his life is now to come to an end, the apostle rejoices nonetheless for

---

(NTAbh NF 2; Münster: Aschendorff, 1966), 294: "In terms of content, Χριστός is the subject of the sentence: Christ is my life."

46. On the Greek background of Phil. 1:21b cf., e.g., Plato, *Apologia* 40c, d, where Socrates speaks about what happens after death: "Let us reflect in another way, and we shall see that there is great reason to hope that death is a good; for one of two things—either death is a state of nothingness and utter unconsciousness, or, as men say, there is a change and migration of the soul from this world to the other. Now if you suppose that there is no consciousness, but a sleep like the sleep of him who is undisturbed even by dreams, death will be an unspeakable gain."

47. Cf. BDAG 67.

48. Καί is here to be taken in the explicative sense; cf. Hoffmann, *Die Toten in Christus*, 289; BDAG, 495.

49. On the problem of an intermediate state, which cannot be found in Paul, cf. Hoffmann, *Die Toten in Christus*, 341ff.

50. Cf. Pilhofer, *Philippi*, 1:122–23; Bormann, *Philippi*, 218–19.

51. On the eschatological conception of Philippians (compared with the other Pauline letters), see below, section 22.2 ("The Course of the Final Events and Life after Death").

52. Cf. the documentation in *NW* 2/1:689–92.

the Philippians, who have brought their own spiritual offerings by the way they have lived their lives. When measured by the standards of human thinking, this results in the paradox that the apostle's suffering reveals the faithfulness, grace, and glory of God. The members of the Christian community respond to the goodness of God when they live their lives in a way that corresponds to Jesus Christ (1:27–30).

The Hymn as Paradigmatic History

This aspect is deepened in Phil. 2:1–5, 6–11, where Paul elucidates Christian life as oriented to the way of the Lord Jesus Christ, who originates, maintains, and consummates salvation. As the prototype [*Urbild*], Jesus Christ makes possible the new existence of Christians; as the exemplary model [*Vorbild*], he sets forth his own conduct as the example to be followed. Just as Christ did not look after his own welfare and gave himself up to death on the cross, so also Christians should not live in selfishness and quarreling but in humility and unity. The Son's transformation makes possible the believer's participation.

Since the analyses of E. Lohmeyer, it can be taken as probable that a pre-Pauline text has been incorporated in 2:6–11.[53] Evidence for a traditional unit is provided by the occurrence of vocabulary not found elsewhere in the New Testament (ὑπερυψόω [to exalt highly], καταχθόνιος [under the earth]) or found only here in Paul (μορφή [form], ἁρπαγμός [something to be exploited]), by the heaping up of participles and relative clauses, by the strophic construction of the text, by the interruption of the letter's train of thought, and by the contextual transitions in 2:1–5, 12–13. Most scholars regard 2:8c (θανάτου δὲ σταυροῦ [death on a cross]) as Pauline redaction, for in the hymn itself it is only the fact of Jesus' death, not its manner, that is important. The structure of the pre-Pauline unit is disputed. Lohmeyer arranges the traditional unit into six strophes of three lines each, which are divided into two equal stanzas by the new beginning made by διό (therefore) in 2:9. In contrast, J. Jeremias proceeds on the formal principle of *parallelismus membrorum* and advocates a structure of three sections of four lines each (2:6–7a; 2:7b–8; 2:9–11).[54] All

---

53. Cf. Ernst Lohmeyer, *Kyrios Jesus: Eine Untersuchung zur Phil. 2, 5–11* (2nd ed.; SHAW 4; Heidelberg: C. Winter, 1961).

For the history of research, see Ralph P. Martin, *An Early Christian Confession: Philippians 2:5–11 in Recent Interpretations* (London: Tyndale, 1960), 97ff. The more recent discussion has been critically summarized by Jürgen Habermann, *Präexistenzaussagen im Neuen Testament* (EHS, Reihe 23, Theologie 362; Frankfurt: Lang, 1990), 91–157. Ralph Brucker, *"Christushymnen" oder "epideiktische Passagen"?* (FRLANT 176; Göttingen: Vandenhoeck & Ruprecht, 1997), 304, 319, argues that Paul himself composed the "hymn."

54. Cf. Joachim Jeremias, "Zur Gedankenführung in den paulinischen Briefen (4. Der Christushymnus Phil. 2,6–11)," in *Abba: Studien zur neutestamentlichen Theologie und Zeitgeschichte* (Göttingen: Vandenhoeck & Ruprecht, 1966), 274–76; "Zu Philipper 2,7: ἑαυτὸν ἐκένωσεν," ibid., 56–62.

other reconstructions are simply variations of these two pioneering suggestions. The metric-strophic structure of 2:6–11 will continue to be disputed, but what remains clear is the bipartite structure of the text with 2:9 as the hinge: 2:6–8, 9–11. From the point of view of form criticism, the text is mostly called a "hymn," but other classifications have also emerged: "encomium,"[55] "epainos,"[56] or "didactic poem."[57] From the history-of-religions point of view, the hymn presents no unity, the second section (2:9–11) pointing to the thought world of Judaism by its Old Testament allusions and formal liturgical elements, and the first section (2:6–7) manifesting strong terminological and conceptual parallels to Hellenistic religio-philosophical writings.[58] The Sitz im Leben of the hymn is the church's liturgy (cf. Col. 3:16).

Already before Paul christological reflection had seen Christ's change of status as involving not only postexistence but preexistence, not only post-Easter but prebirth. The hymn explicitly emphasizes the juxtaposition of μορφὴ θεοῦ (form of God, Phil. 2:6) and μορφὴ δούλου (form of a slave, 2:7).[59] Jesus Christ leaves his divine status and places himself in the crassest, most opposite situation imaginable. The hymn portrays and reflects further on the stages of this fundamental event. Jesus Christ divests himself of his divine power and assumes the helpless status of a slave; not lordship but weakness and humiliation are now his lot.[60] Becoming human means renunciation of the power that is rightly his; it means humility and obedience even to death. The Pauline addition in 2:8c (death on the cross)[61] brings this line of thought to its climax: Jesus Christ not only renounces his equality with God and his life but dies in the most extreme shame conceivable.[62] Philippians 2:9 marks the turning point in this event, linguistically indicated by the new subject, ὁ θεός (God). Jesus Christ's exaltation to a new status occurs in the conferral of the new name (2:9b–10), followed by his installation and acknowledgment as Cosmocrator (2:10–11b).

---

55. Klaus Berger, *Formgeschichte des Neuen Testaments* (Heidelberg: Quelle & Meyer, 1984), 345.

56. Brucker, *Christushymnus*, 319–20, 330–31.

57. Nikolaus Walter et al., *Die Briefe an die Philipper, Thessalonicher, und an Philemon* (NTD 8/2; Göttingen: Vandenhoeck & Ruprecht, 1998), 56–62.

58. Cf. S. Vollenweider, "Die Metamorphose des Gottessohnes," in *Das Urchristentum in seiner literarischen Geschichte: Festschrift für Jürgen Becker zum 65. Geburtstag* (ed. Ulrich Mell and Ulrich B. Müller; BZNW 100; Berlin: de Gruyter, 1999), 107–31.

59. Cf. Strecker, *Die liminale Theologie des Paulus*, 163.

60. On the multilayered problems of this text from the history-of-religions perspective, see now S. Vollenweider, "Der 'Raub' der Gottgleichheit: Ein religions-geschichtlicher Vorschlag zu Phil. 2,6(–11)," *NTS* 45 (1999): 413–33. Vollenweider argues for a political reading of the text, primarily on the basis of the Hellenistic parallels to ἁρπαγμός and ἰσοθεία: "The Christ who humbles himself is presented in Phil. 2:6–11 as the exact opposite of the type of ruler who exalts himself."

61. For evidence for this view, which still seems to me to be the most likely, see Müller, *Philipper*, 105.

62. Cf. Otfried Hofius, *Der Christushymnus Philipper 2, 6–11: Untersuchungen zu Gestalt und Aussage eines urchristlichen Psalms* (WUNT 17; Tübingen: Mohr Siebeck, 1976), 63.

Acclamation as Lord and worship by the whole universe correspond to the will of God and redound to God's glory (2:11c). The new status of Jesus Christ is more than a mere restoration of his preexistent equality with God.[63] Only his willingness to enter into the humiliation that leads to the cross makes possible his exaltation to be ruler of the world, which means that even the preexistent one has undergone a transformation in order to attain his true identity.

Paul takes up the Christology of the traditional unit and embeds it in a paraenetic argumentation, as shown by 2:1–5. The hymn is connected to the preceding verses both compositionally and terminologically. Thus the humility of Christ expressed by ταπεινόω (to humble) in 2:8 illustrates the humility (ταπεινοφροσύνη) to which the church is called in 2:3. The obedience of the humiliated Christ appears as the foil to the self-interest and quarreling that the church must overcome (2:3). Finally, the summarizing formulation of the preexistent one's abasement (ἑαυτὸν ἐκένωσεν [he emptied himself], 2:7) points to the fundamental affirmation of 2:4, according to which a Christian should not seek his or her own interests but the interests of others. The hymn also has a connection to 2:12, which follows; there Paul takes up the idea of Christ's obedience as the basis for the ethical stance the church is called to adopt. The church is challenged to take what the Lord has done in the incarnation, crucifixion, and enthronement as a pattern to be imitated in its own ethics. Christ thus appears in Phil. 2 as both prototype and example. The church can and should follow Christ in the awareness that, just as is the case with the apostle himself, it does not yet stand in the state of fulfilled salvation but is on the way to the day of Christ's return, the judgment, and the resurrection (3:12ff.). God is the one who makes this possible, for it is God who is at work among the believers, enabling both their will and their deeds (2:13).

Against the background of a church influenced by its setting in a Roman colony, 2:6–11 also has a political dimension. One who was crucified by the Romans receives, by God's direct intervention, an unsurpassable status, so that worship and confession belongs to him alone. Whereas kings and rulers have gained power by violence and predatory aggressiveness, Jesus Christ humbled himself and thereby became the true sovereign. He thus embodies the exact opposite of the ruler who exalts himself.[64] Also, the Lord/Kyrios title in 2:11 and the Savior title in 3:20 each have anti-imperial connotations. A Greek inscription from the time of Nero has the formula "Nero, Lord of the Whole World,"[65] and the Roman emperors were praised as "saviors," especially in the

---

63. Cf. Günther Bornkamm, "Zum Verständnis des Christus-Hymnus Phil. 2,6–11," in *Studien zu Antike und Urchristentum* (3rd ed.; BEvT 28; Munich: Kaiser, 1970), 171–72.

64. Cf. Vollenweider, "Gottgleichheit," 431. In this context there are often references to Plutarch, *Alex. fort.*, 1.8.330d, where Plutarch defends Alexander the Great as the model world robber: "For he did not overrun Asia like a robber nor was he minded to tear and rend it, as if it were booty and plunder bestowed by unexpected good fortune."

65. Cf. *NW* 1/2:249.

eastern part of the empire.[66] Over against this politico-religious claim, the hymn sets a new reality that surpasses every earthly power. The Philippian Christians receive their citizenship not from the Roman authorities but from heaven (3:20–21), so that Paul is consistent when he describes their life with the verb πολιτεύομαι (conduct one's life as a citizen) only in 1:27. Paul, a prisoner in Rome, presents his church with an alternative model: weakness and rulership are in truth assigned completely differently from the way it appears at first glance.

Another Debate

A unique insight into the way Paul understood himself is found in Phil. 3:2–11, where Paul vehemently attacks the hostile missionaries who have intruded into the church. The apostle calls them "dogs," indicating the opponents' malicious and destructive intentions.[67] The expression βλέπετε τοὺς κακοὺς ἐργάτας (beware of the bad/evil workers) is illuminated by 2 Cor. 11:13, where ἐργάται δόλιοι (deceitful workers) is used as a polemical term for "apostles." In early Christianity, ἐργάτης (worker) was evidently a term used by missionaries to describe themselves (cf. Matt. 9:37–38; 10:10), which Paul qualifies negatively with the adjective κακός (bad, evil). The position advocated by the opponents is clearly recognizable in the word κατατομή (lit. "mutilation"), a sarcastic allusion to circumcision. When in Phil. 3:3a Paul reclaims the term "circumcision" for the church in a positive sense, he thus designates the central issue of the controversy: Jewish Christian missionaries had made inroads into the church in Philippi, insisting that Gentile converts be circumcised.[68] In intentionally polemical statements, in 3:4ff. Paul points to the advantages of his Jewish background, his belonging to the Pharisees, and his blameless fulfilling of the law. The justification terminology in 3:9, reminiscent of Galatians, suggests that the opponents were militant Jewish Christians. Paul includes in this attack a fundamental interpretation of his life and history, which the readers are to apply to themselves. What had transpired in the life of Paul is characteristic of

---

66. Cf. the documentation at John 4:42 in *NW* 1/2:239–56; cf. also Michael Labahn, "'Heiland der Welt': Der gesandte Gottessohn und der römische Kaiser—ein Thema johanneischer Christologie," in *Zwischen den Reichen: Neues Testament und römische Herrschaft: Vorträge auf der ersten Konferenz der European Association for Biblical Studies* (ed. Michael Labahn and Jürgen Zangenberg; TANZ 36; Tübingen: Francke, 2002), 149ff.

67. Cf. Hellenistic parallels for a derogatory use of "dog" in *NW* 2/1:693–97; for usage among Jews, cf. Strack and Billerbeck, *Kommentar*, 3:621: "The ignorant, the godless, and non-Israelites were called 'dogs.'"

68. Cf., most recently, Müller, *Philipper*, 186–91. A survey of research is provided in Günter Klein, "Anti-paulinismus in Philippi," in *Jesu Rede von Gott und ihre Nachgeschichte im frühen Christentum: Beiträge zur Verkündigung Jesu und zum Kerygma der Kirche: Festschrift für Willi Marxsen zum 70. Geburtstag* (ed. Andreas Lindemann et al.; Gütersloh: Gütersloher Verlagshaus, 1989), 297–300; Schnelle, *New Testament Writings*, 139–43.

the life of every Christian: the newness of a life determined by Christ casts the old life, despite its advantages, in a wholly negative light. Paul demonstrates to the Philippians that their departure from the conventional social and religious conditions of their setting, and the radical change in his own life, have one and the same goal: both leave behind their social, political, legal, and religious privileges in order to be registered as citizens of heaven (3:20–21).[69] The new life seems to be threatened by the experience of suffering and by the competing Judaistic missionaries. In 3:4b–11 Paul counters this threat with a line of argument oriented to the categories of belonging and participation. Belonging to the chosen people Israel grants one participation in its privileges: circumcision, law, righteousness. Paul by no means caricatures Jewish life but names precisely his self-confidence and self-understanding as a zealous Pharisee.[70] The radical turn in his life appears all the more dramatic against this positive background. With ζημία (loss) and σκύβαλα (dung, filth) the apostle gives a drastic description of his new perspective on reality; all previous privileges appear in a different light. Belonging to Christ and participation in his life-giving power radically surpass everything that was previously considered good, and so Paul interprets himself and the world anew. He has recognized who this Jesus Christ is and what he is able to give as Lord and Savior: righteousness and life.

Paul characteristically describes his new life by weaving together participatory and juridical categories. He speaks of being found in Christ and of participating in the power of his resurrection. He thereby grounds righteousness through faith, a righteousness that has its source not in the law/Torah but in God. Regarding the demand for circumcision made by the opponents, the antithesis ἐκ νόμου / ἐκ θεοῦ (from the law / from God) in 3:9 also underscores the new location of salvation: it is found in God and cannot be attained by human beings but only accepted as a gift. This is the emphasis of the expression καὶ εὑρεθῶ ἐν αὐτῷ (and be found in him), which, like ἐν Χριστῷ, means being incorporated into a saving relationship with Christ and participating in the new being that results from this relationship. From the time they were baptized and received the Spirit, a qualitative change has taken place in the life of Paul and every Christian: they now participate fully in the life-giving power of Jesus Christ, which grants righteousness and new life that extends beyond physical death. As in Rom. 6:3–5, Paul binds present participation in the sufferings of Christ with the confidence that Christians also participate in the power of his resurrection. For the apostle, it is precisely sufferings that designate one as belonging to Christ, for in them the power of God is already revealed, the power that also will bring the resurrection of the dead. At the end of his life, Paul attains a view of the past, present, and future in which everything is

---

69. M. Tellbe, "The Sociological Factors behind Philippians 3.1–11 and the Conflict at Philippi," *JSNT* 55 (1994): 97–121, rightly emphasizes the political, legal, and sociological dimensions of Paul's argument in Phil. 3:1–11.

70. Cf. Müller, *Philipper*, 148–49.

oriented to Christ. Paul evaluates his own glorious past in the light of Christ; in the certainty of the Lord's presence, the apostle endures the suffering that threatens him; in the hope of the parousia of Christ, he goes undaunted into the future. Such extraordinary composure, generated by his faith, could have caused misunderstandings. Thus Paul emphasizes in Phil. 3:12, "Not that I have already obtained this or have already reached the goal; but I press on to make it my own, because Christ Jesus has made me his own." In the present power of the Spirit (cf. 1 Cor. 2:6; 3:1), Paul numbers himself among the τέλειοι (perfect, mature, 3:15), but perfection/maturity does not imply, for him, a habitual life, as though salvation were already complete.

Like no other of Paul's letters, Philippians gives an insight into the apostle's personality. We see his fundamental convictions and his confidence but also his anxieties and fears. Paul lives in the confidence that he fully participates in the destiny of Christ, both in suffering and in glory. Thus external circumstances cannot finally affect him, for "I can do all things through him who strengthens me" (Phil. 4:13). The fact that he writes from a prison cell by no means hinders Paul from repeatedly calling the Philippians to prayer, thanksgiving, and joy. He is certain that everything that serves the preaching of the gospel is happening according to God's will. Paul speaks with joy even about the possibility of his being offered as a sacrifice, his own martyr's death (cf. 2:17–18). Nonetheless, a slight uncertainty creeps into his consciousness when he says "if somehow" (3:11, εἴ πως) he might attain to the resurrection of the dead, that is, die before the appointed time. This is an understandable reaction, for looking into the future when one stands in the presence of death calls forth not only confidence but anxiety. But for the sake of the Philippians, Paul chooses life; he knows that they and many other people need the preaching of the gospel to continue.

13.3 The Letter to Philemon

The Letter to Philemon is to be placed in immediate proximity to Philippians, for Paul is in prison (Philem. 1, 9, 13) and, as with the composition of Philippians, Timothy and other coworkers are with him (vv. 23–24). The mild situation of his custody is also comparable, for Paul can still gather his coworkers about him and continue his missionary activity (vv. 10, 23–24). These circumstances, like the unparalleled self-description πρεσβύτης (old man)[71] in verse 9, point to Rome as the place where the letter to Philemon was composed.[72] Although the

---

71. Πρεσβύτης is the designation not of an office but of age (cf. Luke 1:18; Titus 2:2); according to Philo, *Creation* 105, this term refers to ages forty-nine to fifty-six, after which one is a γέρων. Cf. *NW* 2/2:1064.

72. Among those who argue for Rome are Joseph Barber Lightfoot, *Saint Paul's Epistles to the Colossians and to Philemon: A Revised Text with Introductions, Notes, and Dissertations* (9th ed.; London: Macmillan, 1890), 310–11; Weiss, *Earliest Christianity*, 1:385; Schweitzer, *Mysticism*, 47; Adolf Jülicher,

chronological relationship to Philippians cannot be determined with certainty, the irony in verse 19 suggests that Paul is in a better mood and situation than at the time when Philippians was written, and so the letter to Philemon was probably written after Philippians (ca. 61). The occasion of the letter is the sending of the slave Onesimus back to his master, Philemon, a Christian from Colossae (cf. Col. 4:9, Onesimus; Col. 4:17/Philem. 2, Archippus).

The letter is directed primarily to Philemon, addressed by Paul as ἀδελφός (brother) and συνεργός (coworker) (Philem. 1). The letter is also addressed to Apphia, Archippus, and the church in Philemon's house. Speaking of the church as "in *your* house" (the "your" is singular in the Greek) indicates that Philemon, Apphia, and Archippus were not relatives but that Apphia and Archippus are singled out as leaders in the church addressed. It remains an open question whether Archippus served in the church as a deacon, as suggested by Col. 4:17. Philemon was a Christian (Philem. 5, 7) who worked actively in the church and owned at least one slave, and his house served as the assembly room for the church, so that he can be regarded as belonging to the handworker or tradesman middle class. In verse 19b, Paul mentions that Philemon still owes him something. That the two men were personally acquainted is thus quite possible but by no means necessary, since verse 19b can also be an element of Paul's subtle argument, which moves constantly back and forth between asking for a favor and giving an indirect command.[73] On the other hand, it could be the case that Paul converted Philemon and is alluding to this in verse 19b. In determining the location of the addressees, the agreements between Philem. 23–24 and Col. 4:10ff. are very important. Except for Jesus Justus, all those named in the conclusion of the Letter to Philemon also appear in Col. 4:10ff., in a different order and with additional information. Thus most interpreters consider Colossae Philemon's place of residence.[74]

Einleitung in das Neue Testament (7th ed.; Tübingen: Mohr Siebeck, 1931), 124–25; Gülzow, *Christentum und Sklaverei*, 29–30; Fischer and Schenke, *Einleitung*, 1:156. The following argue, somewhat tendentiously, for Caesarea: Martin Dibelius and Heinrich Greeven, *An die Kolosser, Epheser; An Philemon* (3rd ed.; HNT 12; Tübingen: Mohr Siebeck, 1953), 107; Thornton, *Der Zeuge des Zeugen*, 212. The majority of exegetes regard Ephesus as the place where Philemon was written—e.g., Peter Stuhlmacher, *Der Brief an Philemon* (Neukirchen-Vluyn: Benziger, 1975), 21; Eduard Lohse, *Colossians and Philemon: A Commentary on the Epistles to the Colossians and to Philemon* (trans. William R. Poehlmann and Robert J. Karris; Hermeneia; Philadelphia: Fortress, 1971), 188; Gnilka, *Philemonbrief*, 4–5; Hermann Binder, *Der Brief des Paulus an Philemon* (THKNT 11/2; Berlin: Evangelische Verlagsanstalt, 1990), 21–29; Michael Wolter, *Der Brief an die Kolosser; Der Brief an Philemon* (ÖTK 12; Gütersloh: Gütersloher Verlagshaus Gerd Mohn, 1993), 238; Lampe, in Walter et al, *Briefe*, 205; Joseph A. Fitzmyer, *The Letter to Philemon: A New Translation with Introduction and Commentary* (AB 32C; New York: Doubleday, 2000), 11. In this case, Philemon would have been written between 53 and 55 CE.

73. Cf. Alfred Suhl, *Der Brief an Philemon* (ZBKNT 13; Zurich: Theologischer Verlag, 1981), 20.

74. Cf., e.g., Kümmel and Feine, *Introduction*, 348; Vielhauer, *Geschichte der urchristlichen Literatur*, 173–74; Lohse, *Colossians and Philemon*, 186; Stuhlmacher, *Philemon*, 20; Gnilka, *Philemonbrief*, 6 (a church in the Lycus valley); Fitzmyer, *Philemon*, 12.

The letter to Philemon is *not* a private letter, for it is addressed simultaneously to Philemon and the church that meets in his house. As in his other letters, here also Paul brings his apostolic authority into play. In terms of form criticism, Philemon must be considered a letter of request (παρακαλέω, Philem. 9, 10a; an explicit request in v. 17), into which elements of a letter of recommendation have been inserted (cf. vv. 10b–13).

The structure of the letter is heavily influenced by rhetorical elements.[75] As in ancient rhetoric, so also in Paul, the introduction of the thanksgiving section has the function of putting the hearers or readers in a good mood. This becomes clear in verse 7, which functions as *captatio benevolentiae* in making the transition to the apostle's real argumentation. Rhetorical conventions also structure the body of the letter. Thus verses 9–10; 11–13; 11–14 illustrate the rhetorical arguments of pathos, logos (reasonable grounds), and ethos (considerations of usefulness, an appeal to honor). In particular, the identification of the apostle with Onesimus in verse 12 (and 17) is aimed at winning the addressee over by appealing to the emotions. In ancient rhetoric, the epilogue had the function of summarizing and underscoring what had been previously said, with intensified pathos. Just as verse 17 pulls the preceding argument together, so verses 19–20 clearly increase the element of pathos.

At first glance, the Letter to Philemon gives the impression of being a theologically insignificant letter. This would be an inadequate evaluation, for it is precisely the Letter to Philemon that permits an insight into the distinctive features of the way Paul argues his case. In the thanksgiving (vv. 4–7), Paul clearly attempts to win Philemon over to his side. He approaches him in terms of his life as a Christian, suggesting that he do for Christ the good that he is able to do (vv. 6–7). Whereas to this point he has only appealed to Philemon's own responsibility, in verses 8–9 he subtly brings his apostolic authority into play. He explicitly emphasizes that he does not want to make any use of his authority, and does not use his apostolic title (vv. 8b–9), but precisely in doing so, he uses his position all the more effectively. The real concern of the letter does not become clear until verse 10; Paul presents his petition on behalf of the slave Onesimus, whose master in the legal sense Philemon was and continues to be. Why is Onesimus staying with Paul? It may be that Onesimus ran away from his master after stealing something from him (cf. v. 18), then met Paul and was converted to the Christian faith by him (cf. v. 10). Then Onesimus would have possessed the status of a runaway slave (*fugitivus*) and had to count on receiving the necessary punishment, which Paul attempts to hinder. On this assumption, there is no satisfactory explanation as to why Onesimus appears at Paul's prison cell, of all places (coincidence? did he already know the apostle?), instead of attempting to maintain the freedom he had gained by

---

75. Cf. F. F. Church, "Rhetorical Structure and Design in Paul's Letter to Philemon," *HTR* 71 (1978): 17–33; Gnilka, *Philemonbrief,* 7–12.

submerging himself in a large city or a foreign country. Some have thus supposed that Onesimus was not a runaway slave[76] but that he had sought out Paul as his advocate in a domestic conflict. Then Onesimus would have taken the usual route in such circumstances, as illustrated in numerous ancient texts.[77] Onesimus's goal would then be to return to Philemon's household, which he attempts to facilitate by means of Paul's mediation. This is a plausible explanation for Onesimus's stay with Paul, but verse 13 still poses a problem, since it presupposes that the slave had already been serving Paul for some time. Why did Onesimus remain with Paul for this extended period if Paul was only to serve as his advocate (by means of a letter)? We can not be sure why Onesimus came to Paul or whether he met him accidentally. It is only clear that some event in the household of Philemon caused the slave Onesimus to leave,[78] that he met Paul in prison, that he assisted him there, and that now it had to be decided whether he would continue with Paul or return to the household of Philemon. Philemon is to acknowledge and accept the new status of the slave Onesimus as a beloved brother, "both in the flesh and in the Lord" (καὶ ἐν σαρκὶ καὶ ἐν κυρίῳ, v. 16). The apostle thus encourages Philemon to break through the ancient social structure of the household and confer on Onesimus a new social status as beloved brother while his legal status remains the same.[79] By explicitly identifying himself with Onesimus (vv. 12, 16, 17–20), he makes the new situation clear to Philemon, who is to recognize that he now has the same kind of relationship to the slave Onesimus as he has to the apostle Paul. Thus, when Paul now sends Onesimus back (vv. 12, 14) in accordance with the legal situation of the time (but contrary to Deut. 23:16), he is sending a part of himself to Philemon. The real goal of Paul's argument becomes clear in Philem. 13: he would like to have Onesimus remain with him in order to serve him and the preaching of the gospel. But Paul does not want to have this service of Onesimus without Philemon's voluntary agreement (v. 14), which, however, he already presupposes (v. 21). Paul hopes to visit Philemon soon himself (v. 22), but this does not make the present and future service of Onesimus superfluous. According to the evidence provided by the Letter to Philemon, Christian freedom does not abolish the prevailing social structures but finds its concrete realization within the life of the Christian community.

---

76. Cf. Lampe, in Walter et al., *Briefe*, 206.

77. Cf., e.g., Pliny the Younger, *Ep.* 9.21 (*NW* 2/2:1058–60).

78. According to Michael Wolter, *Der Brief an die Kolosser: Der Brief an Philemon* (ÖTK 12; Gütersloh: Mohn, 1993), 231, we can assume "that Onesimus had committed some offense in his master's household, but considered himself innocent and asked Paul's help in coming to terms with his master."

79. Cf. ibid., 233–34: "Philemon is to see his brother precisely in the slave Onesimus (pp. 15f.), and indeed without the radicality of this imposition being in any way moderated by a formal change in Onesimus's legal status by emancipation."

The name Onesimus is also mentioned in Col. 4:9, where Paul says that he is sending the faithful and beloved brother Onesimus to Colossae. If this is referring to the same person as the Letter to Philemon, it can be inferred that Philemon not only forgave his slave Onesimus but also placed him at Paul's disposal for service in the Pauline mission. This is the view of P. Stuhlmacher, who also supposes that the bishop Onesimus mentioned three times by Ignatius (Ign. *Eph.* 1.3; 2.1; 6.2) is the same person as the slave Onesimus of the Letter to Philemon.[80] The mere fact that the same name occurs in both places is, of course, not an adequate argument for such far-reaching conclusions.[81] Paul was probably not asking for the emancipation of Onesimus, for he defines freedom as inner freedom (cf. 1 Cor. 7:21–24), a freedom that is enabled by, and finds its goal in, Jesus Christ alone. Social structures are irrelevant for this concept of freedom, since they can neither bestow freedom nor abolish servitude. Maintaining the validity of the prevailing law does not, however, exclude a fundamental transformation in the situation of the slave, as shown by the argument of the Letter to Philemon. Paul wants to lead Philemon to see Onesimus as a beloved brother and to put Onesimus at the apostle's disposal in place of Philemon himself.

13.4 Paul the Martyr

When Paul arrived in Rome in 59 CE as a prisoner but was still allowed to continue his missionary activity, Jews and Christians in the world capital had already attained a clear differentiation in their respective understandings of their own identities: (1) The diminishing of the Jewish Christian segment within the Roman congregations had resulted in the increased influence of Gentile Christians, which finally forced a separation from the Jewish congregations. (2) The dominance of Gentile Christians in the Roman church probably also led to a situation in which the Roman authorities perceived the Christians to be an independent movement separate from Judaism. (3) We have no direct information about the relation of Jews and Christians in the 60s, but Augustine preserves a revealing comment by Seneca indicating that the Christians were already the hated enemies of the Jews: "Christianos tamen iam tunc Iudaeis inimicissimos" (Christians, however, who were already most inimical to the Jews, *Civ.* 6.11). The Jewish congregations in Rome probably actively encouraged the process of differentiation from the Christians in order to hinder any further missionary success of the Christians among the Jews. This strategy was obviously successful, for Jews remained unaffected when the persecution began against the Christians. (4) The reference in Tacitus, *Ann.* 15.44.4, to the

---

80. Cf. Stuhlmacher, *Philemon*, 18, 57.
81. Cf., in this sense, Lohse, *Colossians and Philemon*, 186–87; Gnilka, *Philemonbrief*, 6.

"enormous mass" of Christians who were arrested during the Neronian persecution presupposes that the Roman church had grown very rapidly.[82] If Nero, without further evidence and with the applause of the population, could hold the Christians responsible for the burning of Rome,[83] then this movement was already known throughout the city and was regarded by most of the population as worthy of punishment.

The Report of Tacitus

Tacitus's account of the burning of Rome confirms this, for he explicitly emphasizes, on the one hand, that the Christians were not involved in the fire but he states, on the other hand,[84]

> But all human efforts, all the lavish gifts of the emperor, and the propitiations of the gods, did not banish the sinister belief that the conflagration was the result of an order. Consequently, to get rid of this report, Nero fastened and inflicted the most exquisite tortures on a class hated for their abominations [*flagitia*], called Christians by the populace.[85] Christus, from whom the name had its origin, suffered the extreme penalty under the reign of Tiberius at the hands of one of our procurators, Pontius Pilatus, and a most mischievous superstition [*superstitio*], thus checked for the moment, again broke out not only in Judea, the first source of the evil [*mali*], but even in Rome, where all things hideous and shameful from every part of the world find their center and become popular. Accordingly, an arrest was first made of all who pleaded guilty, then, upon their information, an immense multitude was convicted, not so much of the crime of firing the city, as of hatred against mankind [*odio humani generis*]. Mockery of every sort was added to their deaths. Covered with the skins of beasts, they were torn by dogs and perished, or were nailed to crosses, or were doomed to the flames and burnt, to serve as a nightly illumination, when daylight had expired. Nero offered his gardens for the spectacle, and was exhibiting a show in the circus, while he mingled with the people in the dress of a charioteer or stood aloft on a car. Hence, even for criminals who deserved extreme and exemplary punishment, there arose a feeling of compassion; for it was not, as

---

82. This description is confirmed by *1 Clem.* 6.1, which reports the martyrdoms of Peter and Paul and in this context speaks of many other martyrs.

83. On Nero's intensification of the Caesar cult, cf. Clauss, *Kaiser und Gott*, 98–111.

84. Cf. Hildebrecht Hommel, "Tacitus und die Christen," in *Sebasmata: Studien zur antiken Religionsgeschichte und zum frühen Christentum* (2 vols.; WUNT 31–32; Tübingen: Mohr Siebeck, 1983), 174–99; D. Flach, "Plinius und Tacitus über die Christen," in *Imperium romanum—Studien zur Geschichte und Rezeption: Festschrift für Karl Christ zum 75. Geburtstag* (ed. Peter Kneissl and Volker Losemann; Stuttgart: F. Steiner, 1998), 218–32.

85. The best manuscripts read *Chrestianos* here, which must have sounded to Greek ears like "good/honest men"; cf. Hommel, "Tacitus," 178–80.

it seemed, for the public good, but to glut one man's cruelty, that they were being destroyed. (*Ann.* 15.44.2–5)[86]

Tacitus's accusations probably reflect the anti-Christian polemic at the beginning of the second century CE but at the same time may well reflect the hostile feelings of many Romans against the Christians in 64. The accusations are to be understood under the heading *flagitia* (abominations),[87] charges that had been made against Christians from earlier times: incest, murder of children, secret cults.[88] Offering divine honors to a criminal executed by crucifixion, together with the Eucharist and its strange words and practices as (mis-)understood by outsiders, could have generated such charges. The accusation of superstition (*superstitio*)[89] emerges repeatedly in anti-Christian polemic, since, to the Romans, it was absurd, and peculiar to the point of being antisocial, for the Christians to worship a crucified political agitator as the Son of God. The charge of *odium humani generis*, hatred of the human race, was also politically explosive.[90] Christians attracted this charge by their exclusive community organization, their social support of church members who had fallen into trouble, and their refusal to participate in the usual social, religious, and political life. Tacitus raises similar charges against the Jews (*Hist.* 5.3–5),[91] who were still basically accepted by the Romans as a national group. In contrast to the Christians, Judaism was an ancient ancestral religion.

The Report of Suetonius

Suetonius places the accents differently in his report of the persecution of Christians under Nero:

During his reign many abuses were severely punished and put down, and no fewer new laws were made: a limit was set to expenditures; the public banquets were confined to a distribution of food; the sale of any kind of cooked viands in the taverns was forbidden with the exception of pulse and vegetables, whereas before every sort of dainty was exposed for sale. Punishment was inflicted on the Christians, a class of men given to a new and mischievous superstition. He put an end to the diversions of the chariot drivers, who from immunity of long standing claimed the right of ranging at large and amusing themselves by cheat-

---

86. Tacitus, *The Annals and the Histories* (trans. A. J. Church and W. J. Brodribb; Great Books of the Western World 15; Chicago: Encyclopaedia Britannica, 1952), 168.

87. On *flagitia*, cf. Hommel, "Tacitus," 181–82.

88. Cf. R. Freudenberger, "Der Vorwurf ritueller Verbrechen gegen die Christen im 2. und 3. Jahrhundert," *TZ* 23 (1967): 97–107.

89. Cf. Dieter Lührmann, "Superstitio—die Beurteilung des frühen Christentums durch die Römer," *TZ* 42 (1986): 191–213.

90. Cf. Hommel, "Tacitus," 182–91 (p. 189: "an attitude absolutely opposed to the empire").

91. Cf. Lichtenberger, "Josephus und Paulus," 258.

ing and robbing the people. The pantomimic actors and their partisans were banished from the city. (*Nero* 16.2)

Suetonius obviously regards the persecution of Christians as the result of a new prohibition imposed by Nero and does not associate it with the burning of Rome, which he recounts in *Nero* 38.1–3. Whether Nero promulgated a special *mandatum* (mandate), unrelated to the fire, categorizing the Christians as a politically dangerous group is a disputed point.[92] This procedure would not have been unusual for Nero, who took action against both individuals and groups who did not participate properly in the public ceremonies of the state religion and in the worship of his own person. Thus in 66 CE Nero condemned the Stoic Thrasea Paetus to death because, as a philosopher committed to the republic, he publicly demonstrated his resistance to the Caesar cult, which brought upon him this charge: "He disdains our religious practices, and abolishes our laws" (Tacitus, *Ann.* 16.22).

From Nero's time on, the public confession *Christianus sum* (I am a Christian) was considered a capital offense. The basis for this charge is probably to be found in the fact "that Christianity, through the person of its 'founder,' an executed political agitator, and Christians as members of his group and bearers of his name had generally been criminalized from the very beginning."[93] Christians were punished in gruesome ways, and the manner of their execution (being eaten by wild dogs, crucifixion, death by fire) indicates that most of them were not Roman citizens. But when the pogrom atmosphere prevailed, no doubt Christians with the rights of citizenship were also killed.

Early Christian Traditions

The oldest traditions about Paul's fate presuppose that he died a martyr's death in Rome. Thus *1 Clem.* 5:5–7 states,

> Through jealousy and strife Paul showed the way to the prize of endurance; seven times he was in bonds, he was exiled, he was stoned, he was a herald both in the East and in the West, he gained the noble fame of his faith, he taught righteousness to all the world, and when he had reached the limits of the West he gave his testimony before the rulers, and thus passed from the world and was taken up into the Holy Place,—the greatest example of endurance.[94]

92. Vittinghoff, "'Christianus sum,'" 336, casts his vote against this view.
93. Ibid.
94. For an analysis of this text, see, most recently, H. Löhr, "Zur Paulusnotiz in 1 Clem 5, 5–7," in *Das Ende des Paulus: Historische, theologische, und literaturgeschichtliche Aspekte* (ed. Friedrich Wilhelm Horn; BZNW 106; New York: de Gruyter, 2001), 197–213.

The context of this passage already points clearly to martyrdom: "Through jealousy and envy the greatest and most righteous pillars [στῦλοι, cf. Gal. 2:9] of the Church were persecuted and contended unto death. Let us set before our eyes the good apostles" (*1 Clem.* 5:2–3). After presenting Peter and Paul as outstanding examples of such righteous ones, *1 Clem.* 6:1 continues, "To these men with their holy lives was gathered a great multitude of the chosen, who were the victims of jealousy and offered among us the fairest example of their endurance under many indignities and tortures." Also *1 Clem.* 5:5–7 contains several motifs pointing to Paul's martyrdom in Rome:[95] (1) The portrayal of Paul's death in terms of "prize" and "endurance" reflects the vocabulary of 4 Macc. 17:11–16 for the courage, faithfulness, and endurance necessary to gain the heavenly reward of the martyrs (cf. Phil. 3:14). (2) So also the expression "he gave his testimony before the rulers" refers to a martyr's death (cf. 1 Tim. 6:13; *Mart. Pol.* 1:1; 19:1–2; 22:1). (3) For *1 Clement,* the "limits of the west," that is, Rome,[96] and the place of martyrdom are identical. (4) Paul left this life and attained to the "Holy Place" of martyrs with God. As Peter before (*1 Clem.* 5:4), Paul is presented as an example to be imitated by all Christians.

First Clement does not connect the deaths of Peter and Paul with the burning of Rome. We should also note the repeated reference to ζῆλος (zeal, jealousy) and ἔρις (envy, strife) in *1 Clem.* 5–6, for it should not be referred exclusively to the current conflicted situation in Corinth. The text obviously presupposes that there were also disputes within the Roman church or between the Roman church and Judaism that played a decisive role in the deaths of both apostles. The way in which Acts 28 presents Paul's residence in Rome could support this interpretation. Paul appears as an isolated individual without any support from the Roman church and with only minimal success in his missionary work among the Jews. This situation fits the personal tradition handed on in 2 Tim. 4:10–17:

for Demas, in love with this present world, has deserted me and gone to Thessalonica; Crescens has gone to Galatia, Titus to Dalmatia. Only Luke is with me. Get Mark and bring him with you, for he is useful in my ministry. I have sent Tychicus to Ephesus. When you come, bring the cloak that I left with Carpus at Troas, also the books, and above all the parchments. Alexander the coppersmith did me great harm; the Lord will pay him back for his deeds. You also must beware of him, for he strongly opposed our message. At my first defense no one came to my support, but all deserted me. May it not be counted against

95. Cf. Andreas Lindemann, *Paulus im ältesten Christentum: Das Bild des Apostels und die Rezeption der paulinischen Theologie in der frühchristlichen Literatur bis Marcion* (BHT 58; Tübingen: Mohr Siebeck, 1979), 74–80.

96. If Paul had in fact made his proposed mission trip to Spain, *1 Clement* would have mentioned this; cf. Lindemann, *Paulus im ältesten Christentum,* 78. Differently, Löhr, "Paulusnotiz," 207–9, who understands the expression "limits of the West" to refer to Spain. Then *1 Clement* would be evidence for a still later Spanish mission by Paul.

them! But the Lord stood by me and gave me strength, so that through me the message might be fully proclaimed and all the Gentiles might hear it. So I was rescued from the lion's mouth.

Second Timothy presents itself as the testament of Paul written in Rome (cf. 1:17; also 1:8; 2:9) and develops a theology of martyrdom, in 4:7–9 characteristically adopting the athletic metaphor: Paul has fought the good fight and finished his course; there is now reserved for him the crown of righteousness from God. Then follows the personal tradition in 4:10–17, which fits Acts 28 in a decisive point: Paul is abandoned by his coworkers, and only Luke is with him. Even if the strands of tradition represented by Acts and 2 Timothy differ in the details of their argument, they agree in the fact that Paul had no support from his coworkers and also probably none from the Roman church. The emphasis on jealousy and envy in *1 Clem.* 5–6 confirms this picture; the previous disputes about Paul between Gentile Christians and Jewish Christians also continued in Rome. Paul probably died abandoned and alone as a martyr[97] in the setting of a persecution of Christians between 62 and 64 in the time of Nero.[98]

97. No competing tradition developed in the ancient church; this permits the inference that Paul died as a martyr in Rome. Cf., e.g., *Ep. Paul Sen.* 49; Eusebius presents a variation of this tradition, *Hist. eccl.* 22.2: "Tradition has it that after defending himself the Apostle was again sent on the ministry of preaching, and coming a second time to the same city suffered martyrdom under Nero." The ancient Christian texts are cited and analyzed by Zahn, *Introduction*, 2:54–84; cf. also W. Bauer, "The Picture of the Apostle in Early Christian Tradition," in *New Testament Apocrypha* (ed. Edgar Hennecke and Wilhelm Schneemelcher; 2 vols.; Philadelphia: Westminster, 1963–1964), 2:35–73. On the local historical traditions of the Roman church, cf. Hans Georg Thümmel, *Die Memorien für Petrus und Paulus in Rom: Die archäologischen Denkmäler und die literarische Tradition* (Arbeiten zur Kirchengeschichte 76; New York: de Gruyter, 1999).

98. For a different emphasis, see Omerzu, *Der Prozess des Paulus*, 508, who argues that Paul came to Rome in 60 CE "and spent two years in relatively mild custody before the emperor Nero confirmed the death sentence pronounced by Festus and Paul was executed."

Part Two

The Basic Structures
of Pauline Thought

The historiographical insight already developed,[1] namely, that no event is meaningful in and of itself but its *meaning potential must first be inferred and established*, provides the point of departure for the following considerations. This potential must be transferred from the realm of chaotic contingency into "an orderly, meaningful, intelligible contingency."[2] The fundamental construct that facilitates this is narration, for narrative sets up the meaning structure that makes it possible for human beings to come to terms with historical contingency.[3] Narrative brings things into a factual, temporal, and spatial relationship; "it arranges things ex post facto in a plausible structure that shows they necessarily or probably happened that way."[4] Narrative establishes insight by creating new connections and allowing the meaning of the event to emerge. Paul achieves this in the macrogenre of the letter with his Jesus-Christ-history,[5] for his encounter with the risen Christ near Damascus made it impossible to avoid restructuring the meaning of things. Paul transferred the chaotic contingency of cross and resurrection into a meaningful narrative-, argument-, and meaning-structure. It is now our task to delineate the load-bearing foundations of this intellectual structure, and the materials, the connections, the realms of meaning, and the principles by which it was erected. As we do this, the historical and theological results of part 1 are presupposed throughout.

1. See above, section 1.2 ("Reflections on Historiography")
2. Paul Ricoeur, *Zufall und Vernunft in der Geschichte* (Tübingen: Konkursbuchverlag, 1985), 14.
3. Cf. Straub, "Temporale Orientierung," 26–27.
4. Ibid., 30.
5. See above, section 5.1 ("Rehearsal and Coaching: Paul and Early Christian Tradition").

14

The Presence of Salvation

The Center of Pauline Theology

The eschatological presence of God's salvation in Jesus Christ is the basis and center of Pauline thought. Paul was overwhelmed by the experience and insight that in the crucified and risen Jesus Christ, who was soon to return from heaven, God had put into effect his ultimate purpose for the salvation of the whole world. God himself brought about the turn of the ages; God brought a new reality into being, in which the world and the situation of human beings in the world appear in a different light. A completely unexpected, singular event fundamentally changed Paul's thinking and his life. Paul was set before the task of interpreting afresh, from the perspective of the Christ event, the history of the world and God's saving activity within it—God's acts in the past, present, and future and his own role in God's plan. Pauline theology is thus equally an appropriation of the new and an interpretation of the past. Paul drafted an eschatological scenario: its foundation is God's saving will, its decisive act is the resurrection and parousia of Jesus Christ, its determining power is the Holy Spirit, its present goal is the participation of believers in the new being, and its final goal is transformation into spiritual existence with God. Since the resurrection of Jesus Christ, the Spirit of God is again at work in the world, and baptized Christians are delivered from sin and live in a qualitatively new relationship with God and the Lord Jesus Christ.[1] The election of Christians and their call to be participants in the gospel, manifest in their baptism and reception of the Spirit, are effective until the end, so that the present experience of salvation and future hope modulate into each other as one reality.[2] Paul's typical eschatological reservation (cf. 1 Cor. 13:12; 2 Cor. 4:7; 5:7; Rom. 8:24) by no means limits the reality of the believer's new life[3] but portrays the temporal structure of Christian existence and its fulfillment in the future event of the resurrection. Already in the present, baptized believers have truly left the realm of death and have truly arrived in the realm of life. It is not merely a new understanding of reality; rather, in the full sense of the word, the new reality itself has already begun. Believers thus already participate in a universal process of transformation, which began with the resurrection of Jesus Christ from the dead, continues in the present power and saving work of the Spirit, and will end with the transformation of the whole creation into the glory of God. Pauline theology as a whole is stamped with the idea of the presence of salvation.[4]

This basic model, consistent within itself, forms the basis of Paul's argumentation in all his letters. At the same time, it leaves unresolved questions, questions that increasingly became a burden to Paul: How does one become and remain a member of God's elect people? With this central question several individual problems are associated: How is God's first revelation related to the second? Must Gentile Christians be circumcised before they can be received into the people of God?[5] What significance does observation of the Torah have for Jewish Christians? for Gentile Christians? What is the relation of Christian believers to empirical Israel? The great success of his Gentile mission, which did not require circumcision, presented enormous problems for Paul, for he had to think disparate issues through and bring into some kind of consistency what could not really be harmonized: God's first covenant continues to be valid, but only the new covenant saves. God's people Israel must be converted to Christ

---

1. Cf. Kim, "Heilsgegenwart," 180: "For Paul, after the end of prophecy in Israel, the working of the Spirit of God in the world began anew with the death and resurrection of Jesus Christ. God affirmed the one who had been unjustly crucified by raising him from the dead; God set his Spirit to work again in the world in order to bring it to judgment and fulfillment. Since the death and resurrection of Christ, people are called to unite with the community in which the Spirit is at work."

2. Cf. Powers, *Salvation through Participation*, 234: "Paul even describes the believers' eschatological resurrection as a participation in Jesus' resurrection."

3. Differently, Strecker, *Die liminale Theologie des Paulus*, 211, according to whom the baptized are "liminal persons . . . among whom the new being is just beginning to dawn but who are in fact delivered from their old life under sin." On this problematic area, see below, section 17.1 ("The New Being as Participation in Christ").

4. Cf. Kim, "Heilsgegenwart," 177–86. From the theological and history-of-religions point of view, the author sees the distinctive element in Pauline thought to be Paul's belief that the Spirit has already been poured out on believers in baptism.

5. See above, chapter 6 ("The Apostolic Council and the Incident at Antioch: The Problems Remain Unresolved").

so that with the Gentile believers they could become the one true people of God. In order to affirm the unity of what was in fact separated, Paul was compelled to work out retrospective rationalizations, especially on the question of the law and the problematical issue of how Israel continues as the people of God. His understanding of God did not permit him to declare the abrogation of the first covenant. He could not accept, and did not want to accept, that God made or had to make a second attempt in order to bring deliverance and salvation for the world.[6] Therefore Paul *had to* accept lines of argument that were in part contradictory, vague, and artificial.[7] All this did not derive from his arbitrariness or lack of theological competence but was already objectively present in the issues that had to be dealt with, questions that at the heart of the matter are still with us. They cannot be answered, because God alone knows the answers. The significance of the Torah for Christians and their relation to Israel are, for Paul, historical and theological issues arising from his situation and to which he had to assume a stance. Although these issues became increasingly important as his missionary career approached its end, they nonetheless remained secondary phenomena in Paul's actual ministry. Even Galatians and Romans, shaped as they are by the themes of law and justification, still clearly show that it is not juridical categories but the concepts of transformation and participation that always provide the foundation of Pauline thought.

---

6. Cf. Sanders, *Paul*, 127–28, reflecting M. Eugene Boring, "The Language of Universal Salvation in Paul," *JBL* 105 (1986): 269–92. Both rightly emphasize that Paul's thought was guided by unshakable axioms that could not be brought into logical consistency.

7. This aspect is not noticed by Räisänen, *Paul and the Law*, 266–67, when he states, "It is a fundamental mistake of much Pauline exegesis in this century to have portrayed Paul as 'the prince of thinkers' and the Christian 'theologian par excellence.'" Paul was more than an original thinker, for despite the problems mentioned above, his work possesses a systematic quality that Räisänen's statement does not take into account.

15

Theology

The God Who Acts

The reality of God is the axiom of all Pauline theology, the all-determining point beyond which one cannot think or inquire, the point of departure for its all-encompassing worldview. The linguistic data already signal the significance of this theme, for in the undisputed Pauline letters ὁ θεός appears 430 times.[1] Paul never reflects or asks about the existence of God; the knowledge of God belongs to his natural experience of life and shapes his understanding of reality. God, however, never comes within Paul's purview in God's essential essence[2] but always as the one who acts. Paul's *theo*logy per se is in direct continuity with the fundamental Jewish affirmation: God is one, the Creator, the Lord who will bring his creative purpose to completion. At the same time, Christol-

---

1. 1 Thessalonians, 36 times; 1 Corinthians, 106 times; 2 Corinthians, 79 times; Galatians, 31 times; Romans, 153 times; Philippians, 23 times; Philemon, 2 times.
2. This question dominates the dialogue in Cicero's primary writing on the philosophy of religion, *De natura deorum*; cf., e.g., *Nat. d.* 1.2: "For many different claims are made about the form of the gods, their location and place of residence, and the manner of the divine life, and a bitter clash of opinions prevails among the philosophers."

ogy effects a basic change in Paul's *theo*logy, for Paul proclaims a christological monotheism.

15.1 The One God Who Creates and Concludes

The unity and uniqueness of God belong to the fundamental convictions of Jewish faith; there is only one God, beside whom there is no other (Deut. 6:4b LXX, "Hear, O Israel: The Lord is our God, the Lord alone!"; cf., e.g., Isa. 44:6; Jer. 10:10; 2 Kings 5:15; 19:19).[3] In *Let. Aris.* 132, a didactic section about the nature of God begins with the statement "that God is one, that his power is shown in everything, every place being filled with his sovereignty." In sharp contrast to the polytheism of antiquity, Philo emphasizes, "Let us, then, engrave deep in our hearts this as the first and most sacred of commandments, to acknowledge and honor one God who is above all, and let the idea that gods are many never even reach the ears of the man whose rule of life is to seek for truth in purity and guilelessness."[4] For Paul, the unity of God is the intellectual and practical foundation of all his thinking.[5] Granted, numerous so-called gods exist in heaven and on earth (cf. 1 Cor. 8:5; 10:20); at the same time, it is true that "for us there is one God, the Father, from whom are all things and for whom we exist" (1 Cor. 8:6a). The Christians in Thessalonica converted from idols to serve the one true God (1 Thess. 1:9–10), and Paul writes programmatically to the Roman church, "since God is one; and he will justify the circumcised on the ground of faith and the uncircumcised through that same faith" (Rom. 3:30). The fundamental criterion for distinguishing God, the law, Moses, and the angels in Gal. 3:19–20 is the creedal statement "God is one" (ὁ δὲ θεὸς εἷς ἐστιν). Outsiders, too, regard monotheism as the distinctive aspect of Judaism; thus Tacitus emphasizes, "The Jews have purely mental conceptions of Deity, as one in essence" (*Hist.* 5.5.4). The knowledge of God's unity also has practical results for Paul, for "we know that 'no idol in the world really exists,' and that 'there is no God but one'" (1 Cor. 8:4). The Galatians fall away from their knowledge of the one true God when they worship "the weak and beggarly elemental spirits" (Gal. 4:9). Jewish monotheism

---

3. On the development of monotheism in the history of Israelite religion, cf. Matthias Albani, *Der eine Gott und die himmlischen Heerscharen: Zur Begründung des Monotheismus bei Deuterojesaja im Horizont der Astralisierung des Gottesverständnisses im Alten Orient* (ABG 1; Leipzig: Evangelische Verlagsanstalt, 2000); and Wolfgang Schrage, *Unterwegs zur Einzigkeit und Einheit Gottes: Zum "Monotheismus" des Paulus und seiner alttestamentlich-frühjüdischen Tradition* (BTS 48; Neukirchen-Vluyn: Neukirchener Verlag, 2002), 1–35 (primary documentation of Old Testament and Jewish monotheism), 35–82 (important texts for pagan monotheism).

4. Philo, *Decalogue* 65; cf. also Josephus, *Ant.* 3.91. Pagan philosophers ridiculed the many gods of antiquity; cf. Cicero, *Nat. d.* 1.81–84.

5. Cf. Schrage, *Unterwegs zur Einzigkeit*, 43–90.

is the basis of the Pauline worldview: there is only one true God, whose being and actions are real.

God's deity is manifest first of all in his acts as Creator. For Paul, the whole world is God's creation (1 Cor. 8:6; 10:26),[6] and the Creator God of Genesis is none other than the one who acts in Jesus Christ and in Christian believers (2 Cor. 4:6). God "calls into existence things that do not exist," "gives life to the dead" (Rom. 4:17),[7] and is the "Father" of the world (1 Cor. 8:6; Phil. 2:11). Only about this God can it be said, "For from him and through him and to him are all things" (Rom. 11:36a). Prior to the world and history stands God, "who is over all" (Rom. 9:5) and of whom it is said that at the end he will be "all in all" (1 Cor. 15:28). All things are God's creation, and they remain so even when human beings, by worshiping idols, flee the destiny for which they were created.[8] God allows himself to be perceived in his created works (Rom. 1:20, 25), but even though human beings knew about God, "they did not honor him as God or give thanks to him, but they became futile in their thinking, and their senseless minds were darkened" (Rom. 1:21). Again and again human beings are drawn away to worship the powers who by their very nature are not gods (Gal. 4:8). Despite this compulsion to create gods for themselves or to set themselves in God's place, human beings (and the world) remain God's creation. It is true that since the fall of Adam, sin sets its traps (Rom. 5:12ff.) and Satan appears on the human scene in many deceptive forms (cf. 1 Thess. 2:8; 1 Cor. 5:5; 2 Cor. 2:11; 11:14), but God nevertheless does not abandon his creation to this evil power.[9] God the Creator still orders human life by providing political (Rom. 13:1–7) and social (1 Cor. 7) structures. Believers are called to discern and follow the will of God (1 Thess. 4:3; Rom. 12:1). As Lord of history, God guides its events and determines the time of salvation (Gal. 4:4), and as Judge, God has the last word on human destiny (Rom. 2:5ff.; 3:5, 19).

Believers need have no fear of the last judgment, for the apostle is sure "that neither death, nor life, nor angels, nor rulers, nor things present, nor things to come, nor powers, nor height, nor depth, nor anything else in all creation, will be able to separate us from the love of God in Christ Jesus our Lord" (Rom. 8:38–39). Not only do creation and humanity have the same origin; their future destiny is also bound together. For Paul, protology and eschatology, universal

6. On creation and cosmos in Paul, cf. G. Baumbach, "Die Schöpfung in der Theologie des Paulus," *Kairos* 21 (1979): 196–205; Heinrich Schlier, *Grundzüge einer paulinischen Theologie* (Freiburg: Herder, 1978), 55–63; Baumgarten, *Paulus und die Apokalyptik*, 159–79; Erich Grässer, "'Ein einziger ist Gott,'" in *Der Alte Bund im Neuen: Exegetische Studien zur Israelfrage im Neuen Testament* (Tübingen: Mohr Siebeck, 1985), 249ff.; O. Wischmeyer, "ΦΥΣΙΣ und ΚΤΙΣΙΣ bei Paulus," *ZTK* 93 (1996): 352–75; Dunn, *Theology of Paul*, 38–43.

7. On the concept of *creatio ex nihilo* in Rom. 4:17, cf. Käsemann, *Romans*, 121–22.

8. Cf. Becker, *Paul*, 379–82.

9. Wolfgang Schrage, "Die Stellung zur Welt bei Paulus, Epictet, und in der Apokalyptik," *ZTK* 61 (1964): 128, appropriately comments, "God does not abandon the world . . . to itself because it belongs to him and, as its Creator, he is still entitled to it."

history and individual history correspond to each other because God is the source and goal of all that is (cf. Rom. 8:18ff.).[10] Everything comes from God, everything is sustained in existence by God, and everything is on its way to God. The Creator God shows his life-giving power in the resurrection of Jesus Christ, in which he will also grant believers participation: "If the Spirit of him who raised Jesus from the dead dwells in you, he who raised Christ from the dead will give life to your mortal bodies also through his Spirit that dwells in you" (Rom. 8:11).[11]

15.2 God as the Father of Jesus Christ

In Paul's thought, theology is not replaced by Christology; rather, the question of Jesus' identity and status is answered in terms of God's act.[12] God's act in and through Jesus Christ is the foundation of Christology. God sent Jesus Christ (Gal. 4:4–5; Rom. 8:3–4), God delivered him over to death, and God raised him from the dead (Rom. 4:25; 8:32). Through Christ, God reconciled the world (2 Cor. 5:18–19) and justifies those who believe (Rom. 5:1–11).[13] The church is challenged to orient its life to God in Christ Jesus (Rom. 6:11). Jesus Christ demonstrated his own obedience to God (Phil. 2:8; Rom. 5:19). *The* distinguishing characteristic of the God proclaimed by Paul is that God raised Jesus Christ from the dead (cf. 1 Thess. 1:10; 4:14; 1 Cor. 15:12–19). God is the source of all χάρις (Rom. 1:7; 3:24; 1 Cor. 15:10) and the goal of redemptive history (1 Cor. 15:20–28). Behind the Christ event stands the saving will of God, and God alone, with effective power. At the same time, however, the act of God is the expression of the unique dignity and office of Jesus Christ. Paul does not reflect on the relation of God to Jesus Christ in the conceptual-ontological categories of later doctrinal developments, but two lines of thought are nonetheless obvious. On the one hand, there is a clear tendency toward subordination in Pauline Christology. Thus in 1 Cor. 11:3 Paul presupposes a graduated scale:[14] "Christ is the head of every man, and the husband is the head of his wife, and God is the head of Christ." A subordination on the part of Christ is also indicated in 1 Cor. 3:23 (you belong to Christ, and

---

10. On the interpretation of Rom. 8:18ff., cf. Vollenweider, *Freiheit als neue Schöpfung*, 375–96.

11. Statements about creation have a significant weight in Romans; in particular, the correspondence between Rom. 1 and Rom. 8 illustrates the theocentric approach to both protology and eschatology. Cf. Theobald, *Römerbrief*, 138–42.

12. Cf. Schrage, *Unterwegs zur Einzigkeit*, 200: "Jesus Christ can only be understood as from God and to God."

13. On διὰ Χριστοῦ (through Christ) in Paul, cf. Wilhelm Thüsing, *Gott und Christus in der paulinischen Soteriologie* (3rd ed.; Münster: Aschendorff, 1986), 164–237 (p. 237, "The phrase 'through Christ' is in itself already theocentric, as an expression of mediation in those passages that speak of the relation of the elect [or the world] to God").

14. For analysis, cf. ibid., 20–29.

Christ belongs to God)[15] and 15:28 (the Son himself will also be subjected to the one who put all things in subjection under him, so that God may be all in all). Especially 1 Cor. 15:23–28 speaks of a temporal limitation to the rule of Christ and thus clearly signals the subordination of the Son to the Father.[16] In Phil. 2:8–9 the obedience of the Son to the Father is the presupposition for his exaltation as Lord.

At the same time, the Pauline formulations can be seen as the beginnings of thinking of God and Christ as equals. In Phil. 2:6 the preexistent one is termed ἴσος θεῷ (equal with God), and in Rom. 9:5 Paul apparently identifies the Christ descended from Israel (Χριστὸς κατὰ σάρκα) with God (from them, according to the flesh, comes the Messiah, who is over all, God blessed forever).[17] The crucified one receives the predicate "Lord of glory" (1 Cor. 2:8; cf. Ps. 23:7–10 LXX [Ps. 24:7–10]; *1 En.* 22:14; 25:3, 7). Paul directs his prayers both to God (cf., e.g., 1 Thess. 1:2–3; Rom. 8:15–16; 15:30ff.) and to Jesus Christ (2 Cor. 12:8).[18] Christians are those who call on the name of the Lord (cf. 1 Cor. 1:2), and baptism in the name of Jesus Christ grants forgiveness of sins (cf. 1 Cor. 6:11; Rom. 6:3ff.). A coordination of God and Christ appears in 1 Cor. 8:6 and 1 Thess. 3:13 as well as in the *salutatio* already mentioned, "Grace to you and peace from God our Father and the Lord Jesus Christ" (1 Cor. 1:3; 2 Cor. 1:2; Gal. 1:3; Rom. 1:7b; Phil. 1:2; Philem. 3). The church looks to the Lord Jesus in the same way that it looks to God as the one who can provide it with the eschatological gifts of the Spirit.

The Son as Mediator

Paul can obviously portray without any sense of inconsistency the relation of Jesus Christ to God in terms of subordination, coordination, or belonging to the same category. These lines converge and meet in the role of mediator; Jesus Christ is the mediator of creation and salvation. The pre-Pauline tradition of 1 Cor. 8:6 develops this line of thought by boldly interrelating God's history with the history of Jesus Christ: "yet for us there is one God, the Father, from whom are all things and for whom we exist, and one Lord, Jesus Christ, through whom are all things and through whom we exist."[19] This text reflects

---

15. Cf. ibid., 10–20.

16. Cf. Schrage, *Korinther*, 4:152–89.

17. In any case, here it is a matter of an interpretation that is grammatically the most likely and yet the most difficult in terms of content; for arguments pro and con, cf. Wilckens, *Römer*, 2:189.

18. Cf. Roland Gebauer, *Das Gebet bei Paulus: Forschungsgeschichtliche und exegetische Studien* (Giessen: Brunnen, 1989), 20–29.

19. For evidence of its pre-Pauline character and for determining the numerous history-of-religions connections, cf. Schrage, *Korinther*, 2:216–25. For interpretation, in addition to the standard commentaries, see Thüsing, *Paulinischen Soteriologie*, 225–32; Christoph Demke, "'Ein Gott und viele Herren': Die Verkündigung des einen Gottes in den Briefen des Paulus," *EvT* 36 (1976): 473–84; Grässer, "Ein

the relation of theology proper and Christology within a monotheistic framework; the εἷς (one) predication applies not only to the Father but at the same time to the Lord Jesus Christ. This does not mean splitting the one God into two gods; it is, rather, the case that the one Lord is included in the category of the one God.[20] Regarding origin and essential being, Christ belongs entirely on the side of God. At the same time, the one Lord remains subordinate to the one God not only in terms of the order of the text,[21] for the Creator God is the Father of the Lord Jesus Christ.[22] A more precise determination of the sense expressed by the prepositions in 1 Cor. 8:6b and 6d develops the idea of subordinated parallelism. At first, creation and salvation are referred to God and the Lord by identical terminology (τὰ πάντα / ἡμεῖς [all things / we]), but then the use of the prepositions ἐκ and διά result in a fundamental distinction. The universe owes its existence to the one God alone; only God is the origin of all that is. The Lord/Kyrios is the preexistent mediator of creation; the one God creates "all things" through the one Lord.[23] The creation owes its character and essence to the mediation of Jesus Christ, "for 'the earth and its fullness are the Lord's'" (1 Cor. 10:26).[24] The whole creation is ineradicably bound to Jesus by the will of God: "Therefore God also highly exalted him and gave him the name that is above every name, so that at the name of Jesus every knee should bend, in heaven and on earth and under the earth, and every tongue should confess that Jesus Christ is Lord, to the glory of God the Father" (Phil. 2:9–11). It corresponds to the saving will of God for his creation that

---

einziger ist Gott,'" 249–54; Traugott Holtz, "Theo-logie und Christologie bei Paulus," in Traugott Holtz, *Geschichte und Theologie des Urchristentums: Gesammelte Aufsätze* (ed. Eckart Reinmuth and Christian Wolff; WUNT 57; Tübingen: Mohr Siebeck, 1991), 189–204; Otfried Hofius, "Christus als Schöpfungsmittler und Erlösungsmittler: Das Bekenntnis 1Kor 8,6 im Kontext der paulinischen Theologie," in *Paulinische Christologie: Exegetische Beiträge: Hans Hübner zum 70. Geburtstag* (ed. Udo Schnelle et al.; Göttingen: Vandenhoeck & Ruprecht, 2000), 47–58.

20. Cf. Holtz, "Theo-logie und Christologie," 191–92.

21. Wilhelm Thüsing, *Die Neutestamentlichen Theologien und Jesus Christus* (3 vols.; Düsseldorf: Patmos, 1981–1999), 3:371, appropriately comments, "Despite the incomprehensibly close unity with himself into which God brought the crucified Jesus by the resurrection, the specific relationships are preserved; more than that, it is those relationships that fundamentally structure and thereby reconstitute the unity in the first place. Only a mediator who lives in unity with God can be 'mediator of the divine immediacy.'"

22. Contra Hofius, "Christus als Schöpfungsmittler und Erlösungsmittler," 52: "The abundance of θεοί ['gods'] and κύριοι ['lords'] worshiped in the pagan world, referred to by the εἴπερ clause of 1 Cor. 8:5, is contrasted with the *one* God in the distinctiveness of the *one* Father and the *one* Son. This means that the 'Father' of Jesus Christ and the 'Son' of this Father are confessed in the creedal statement of 1 Cor. 8:6 as the *one God,* beside whom there is no other." Hofius introduces the categories of Father/Son, not contained in the text itself, in order to minimize the clear differential between the one God and the one Lord.

23. Hofius, ibid., 52, sees this merely as expressing "the irreversibility of the roles of Father and Son," which does not affect the "ontological status" of the Son. Once again the text is interpreted in terms of the ancient Christian creed, not in Paul's own terms.

24. The context indicates that κύριος refers to Christ; cf. Wolff, *Korinther*, 238.

powers, authorities, and human beings acknowledge Jesus Christ as mediator of both creation and salvation. Jesus stands at the beginning of creation and, as the resurrected one, is the prototype of the new creation. As the "image of God" (2 Cor. 4:4, εἰκὼν τοῦ θεου), Jesus Christ participates in the very being of God; the Son is the revelation of the true being of the Father. Christ takes up the believers into a historical process, at the end of which stands their own transformation; they are to "be conformed to the image of his Son, in order that he might be the firstborn within a large family" (Rom. 8:29). It is only in reference to Christ as the prototype that humanity lives up to its definition as "image of God." The meaning of being human is not exhausted in merely being a creature—the Creator confers on the creature the honor of participating in the special status of the Lord Jesus Christ. The statements about the role of Jesus Christ as mediator of creation are indebted to the experience of him as mediator of salvation; that is, protology points to soteriology from the very beginning. Redemption is no chance event but was built into creation from the foundation of the universe.[25]

Paul's understanding of the relation of Jesus Christ to God can best be expressed by saying that they belong to the same category.[26] Jesus Christ is at the same time subordinate to the Father and fully incorporated into his essence and status.[27] This dynamic may be shifted neither in the direction of preserving a presumed "pure" monotheism nor toward using the New Testament to establish the ontological doctrinal categories of the later church. Rather, this dynamic is the appropriate way to understand the factual subject matter that the post-Easter process of meaning formation could only express as a paradox that permits no monolinear solutions: the one God has fully revealed himself once and for all in the one human being Jesus of Nazareth.

Continuity and Discontinuity with Judaism

How are the continuity and discontinuity of Pauline *theo*logy and Christology with Judaism to be determined? In the first place, we can speak of continuity regarding several points: (1) Paul chooses as the beginning point of his theology not the life and ministry of Jesus of Nazareth but God's act through him in the cross and resurrection, and so this initial principle already points to the primacy of *theo*logy. (2) Paul affirms continuity in God's own acts. The

25. Cf. Hofius, "Christus als Schöpfungsmittler und Erlösungsmittler," 56.

26. Cf. Thüsing, *Paulinischen Soteriologie*, 258: "The Pauline Christocentrism is inherently oriented to God because Paul's Christology is already theocentric; and from this perspective, the orientation of his Christocentrism to God is just as thoroughly consistent as is Christ's κυριότης ['lordship'] and his work in the Spirit."

27. S. Vollenweider, "Zwischen Monotheismus und Engelchristologie," *ZTK* 99 (2002): 32–33, names five realms in which the attributes of God are transferred to Jesus Christ: name/title, creation, cosmic lordship, salvation, and worship.

concept of preexistence (cf. 1 Cor. 8:6; 10:4; Gal. 4:4; Rom. 8:3; Phil. 2:6), like the reflections on the history of God's promise in Gal. 3:15–18 and Rom. 4 and 9–11, shows that from the beginning Paul thinks of the history of God's mighty acts as the history of Jesus Christ.[28] Paul interprets the history of Israel consistently from the perspective of faith in Jesus Christ and as finding its goal in him—and theologically he must do so.[29] Only so can he show the selfhood of God present in his acts; only in this way can he avoid splitting the unified concept of God and history. Paul thinks through theologically and christologically the unity of creation, history, Scripture, and redemption; because God acts definitively in Jesus Christ, this activity embraces both eschatology and protology. Paul would not and could not question the identity of the God of Israel with the Father of Jesus Christ. It was impossible for him to separate the saving act of God in Jesus Christ from the history of Israel. There is only one divine history, which is determined from the beginning by the role of Jesus Christ as mediator of both creation and salvation. (3) In terms of the history of tradition, Paul takes up ideas from ancient Judaism into his understanding of the relation of God and Jesus Christ.[30] According to the Jewish conception, there is only one God, but God is not alone. God is constantly surrounded by numerous heavenly mediating figures, such as Wisdom, the Logos, the biblical patriarchs, and angels. They participate in God's heavenly world, are subordinate to God, and in no way threaten faith in the one God. Against this background, Jesus Christ had been incorporated into the worship of the "one God" already prior to Paul. In contrast to this history-of-religions continuity, there are material differences: Unlike Christ, the personified heavenly mediating figures were not persons on a par with God, with their independent fields of operation, and they did not receive cultic worship. Moreover, according to Jewish understanding, it was impossible to offer divine worship to one who had died on a cross.

Although the concept of God vouches for the continuity to Judaism, Christology warps and breaks open every category of unity and provides the basis for the theological and thus also the historical discontinuity between developing

---

28. On the Pauline idea of preexistence, cf. Habermann, *Präexistenzaussagen*, 91–223; Hermann von Lips, *Weisheitliche Traditionen im Neuen Testament* (WMANT 64; Neukirchen-Vluyn: Neukirchener Verlag, 1990), 290–317; Martin Hengel, "Präexistenz bei Paulus?" in *Jesus Christus als die Mitte der Schrift: Studien zur Hermeneutik des Evangeliums* (ed. Christof Landmesser et al.; BZNW; Berlin: de Gruyter, 1997), 479–517; Thomas Söding, "Gottes Sohn von Anfang an: Zur Präexistenzchristologie bei Paulus und den Deuteropaulinen," in *Gottes ewiger Sohn: Die Präexistenz Christi* (ed. Rudolf Laufen; Paderborn: Schöningh, 1997), 57–93.

29. Contra the undifferentiated statement of Paul-Gerhard Klumbies, *Die Rede von Gott bei Paulus in ihrem zeitgeschichtlichen Kontext* (Göttingen: Vandenhoeck & Ruprecht, 1992), 213: "For Paul, God is not to be defined in a way that transcends his acts in the history of Israel."

30. See below, section 16.9 ("God, Jesus of Nazareth, and Early Christology").

early Christianity and Judaism.[31] Paul's christological monotheism changes
and goes beyond fundamental Jewish concepts. Since, from the very beginning, the history of the crucified Jesus Christ was understood as the authentic
history of God,[32] a new image and understanding of God were formed: God
is God in the way he has revealed himself in Jesus Christ. The crucified God
of Paul and the God of the Old Testament, however, are not compatible with
each other. The Old Testament is silent about Jesus Christ even if by daring
exegesis Paul attempts to break this silence and have the Old Testament speak
as a Christian book. If God has made the ultimate revelation of himself in the
contingent event of the cross and resurrection, then the idea of a continuity in
the history of salvation and election, oriented to belonging to the elect people
of God, to the land, to the Torah or the covenant, can no longer bear the load
imposed upon it. Paul does not want to draw this conclusion and cannot do so,
but he attempts to avoid it through a redefinition of the people of God.[33] For
Jews and strict Jewish Christians, such attempts were not acceptable because
this would mean nothing less than a complete reinterpretation of their own
salvation history.[34] Regarding salvation, Jewish particularism and early Christian universalism could not both be true at the same time—the two symbolic
universes were incompatible. Thus, already for Paul, despite all protests to the
contrary, Christology is the explosive charge that demolished the initial unity
between Christian believers and Judaism.

15.3 God as the One Who Elects, Calls, and Rejects

God encounters human beings as the one who calls and elects but also
as the one who rejects.[35] Paul interprets his own history in these categories

31. One can hardly claim, however, as does Klumbies, *Die Rede von Gott*, 252, that Paul "inci-
dentally develops a fundamentally new formulation of theo-logical thought."

32. Cf. the appropriate comment of Hofius, "Christus als Schöpfungsmittler und Erlösungsmittler,"
58: "For it is *one thing* to speak of God's 'Wisdom' or 'Logos' as the highest powers of God, whether
as hypostatizations or personifications, and to ascribe a cosmological or soteriological function to
them but *an entirely different thing* to make these statements about a historical human being, and one
who had been crucified at that."

33. See below, section 21.1 ("Primary Vocabulary and Foundational Metaphors of Pauline
Ecclesiology").

34. In my opinion, we must distinguish between the intention and the actual effects of Paul's
christological redefinition of *theo*logy; the comment of Klumbies, *Die Rede von Gott*, 251, is a valid
statement regarding the way Paul's statements were perceived and the effects they produced: "Despite
his intention, however, he [Paul] fundamentally separated from the Jewish idea of God by his turning
away from an interpretation of God oriented to the law and turning to a soteriological-christological
explication of God."

35. For an analysis of Paul's statements about predestination, see Luz, *Geschichtsverständnis*,
227–64; Maier, *Mensch und freier Wille*, 351–400; Bernhard Mayer, *Unter Gottes Heilsratschluss:
Prädestinationsaussagen bei Paulus* (FB 15; Würzburg: Echter, 1974); Günter Röhser, *Prädestination und*

when he says that it pleased God "who had set me apart before I was born and called me through his grace . . . to reveal his Son to me" (Gal. 1:15–16). The apostle knows that he, like his churches, has been included in the divine history of election, a history that began with Abraham, reached its goal in the Christ event, and will find its fulfillment in the transformation of believers into the heavenly reality at the parousia. Paul already has this awareness when he develops his theology of election in his first letter (1 Thess. 1:4). The Thessalonian Christians should understand their call as God's gracious choice in the eschatological era; God appears as the "one who calls you" (2:12; 5:24). The church has turned from idols to the one true God (1:9), and it can now live toward its future heavenly existence in excited anticipation of the parousia (4:13–18). The Thessalonians can be confident: "For God has destined us not for wrath but for obtaining salvation through our Lord Jesus Christ" (5:9). God is not bound by human standards but chooses those who by human standards are foolish, weak, lowly, and despised (1 Cor. 1:27–28). According to God's will, salvation comes through the foolishness of the message of the cross, not through human wisdom (1 Cor. 1:18ff.). God is sovereign and almighty, and reality cannot be understood apart from its relation to God, for "the earth and its fulness are the Lord's" (1 Cor. 10:26). Humanity is divided into those who are to be saved and those who are to be lost (2 Cor. 2:15).

It is no accident that Paul's thinking on election and rejection find their culmination in Rom. 9–11. They are located here as the consistent development of the Pauline idea of freedom, the problem of Israel's role, and the doctrine of justification as these are elaborated in the Letter to the Romans. The apostle's reflections on God's eschatological determination of believers and the cosmos in Rom. 8:18ff. are going in the direction of the complex of problems involving predestination. We know that "those whom he predestined he also called; and those whom he called he also justified; and those whom he justified he also glorified" (Rom. 8:30). In Rom. 9–11 Paul clearly advocates a double predestination.[36] God calls whom he wills, and rejects whom he wills (cf. Rom. 9:16, 18; 2 Cor. 2:15). God's chosen people Israel suffers defeat and is again reestablished; the Gentiles come to share in salvation, but God can also remove this new branch from the olive tree (Rom. 11:17–24). "The predestinarian statements express the fact that the decision of faith does not, like other decisions, go back to this-worldly motives of any sort whatever—that, on the contrary, such motives lose all power of motivation in the presence of the encountered proclamation." "At the same time, this means that faith cannot appeal to itself

---

Verstockung: Untersuchungen zur frühjüdischen, paulinischen, und johanneischen Theologie (Tübingen: Francke, 1994), 113–76.

36. So Maier, *Mensch und freier Wille*, 356–57; differently, Röhser, *Prädestination*, 171 and elsewhere, who argues that for Paul God's will does not exclude human decision.

to establish its own decision."[37] The Pauline statements about predestination are by no means exhausted, however, by this interpretation centered on the believing life of individuals. They are primarily theological affirmations that communicate a reality revealed by God in the Scripture. God the Creator, in freedom beyond which there is no appeal, can choose and reject. Free will is thus for Paul an exclusive predicate of God. The infinite distinction between Creator and creature is the basis for the specific perspective from which Paul thinks of human beings. God meets human beings as the one who calls; "to be human is to be called and addressed by God."[38] Christian existence is grounded in the call of God. It is thus something not at the individual human being's own disposal but rather can only be appropriated by hearing. Ὁ καλέσας ἡμᾶς (the one who called us) becomes in Paul a central predicate of God (cf. 1 Thess. 2:12; 5:24; Gal. 1:6; 5:8). God encounters the individual human being as the calling "I," whose will is made known in the Scripture.[39] Regarding salvation, individual human beings can understand themselves only as ones who receive, only as ones who are given a gift. As creatures, they are fundamentally incapable of projecting what salvation and meaning would be and then executing this plan themselves. This would be to take God's own place, a dangerous and hopeless delusion. If human beings want to understand and assess their own situation appropriately and realistically, they must acknowledge and take seriously their creatureliness, which means knowing their limits. In hearing and doing the will of their Creator, creatures attain the goal determined for them. For Paul, God is always the God who acts.[40] Salvation and damnation are not matters that the creature can decide; the Creator has already decided.

What function do the statements about predestination have in the structure of Paul's thought as a whole? They were part of the given worldview within which the apostle lived, but were activated by him with differing degrees of intensity. On the one hand, Paul always thinks within a broad framework that presupposes salvation, rejection, and judgment; on the other hand, it is only in Rom. 9–11 that he plumbs the argumentative depths of this thematic complex.[41] The special communication situation of Romans requires that he provide an extensive discussion of predestination. Paul's aim is to preserve the freedom of God; this is why he specifically emphasizes a fundamental theological insight: God's act is independent of human deeds or presuppositions, God's will always precedes our own decision. God's electing grace is the same as God's justifying grace. The exclusive doctrine of justification and the statements about predes-

---

37. Bultmann, *Theology of the New Testament*, 1:330. The second statement, though in the German text, was not translated in the standard English translation.

38. Hübner, *Gottes Ich*, 31–32.

39. Ibid., 31–35.

40. Grässer, "'Ein einziger ist Gott,'" 233ff.

41. On the concept of judgment in Paul's thought, see below, section 20.2 ("The New Being in Practice").

tination are thus both in the service of preserving God's freedom and the gift nature of salvation, which is not at human disposal.[42] This goal of Paul's argument, together with the observation that the statements about predestination in Rom. 9–11 emerge as a function of the exclusive doctrine of justification and the Israel thematic, should be a warning against forcing them into a firmly structured, static doctrine of predestination. At the same time, against tendencies toward relativizing and leveling out Paul's theology, it is nonetheless true that Paul advocates a double predestination that understands free will regarding salvation as a predicate of God, not something belonging to human beings, that is organically integrated into Paul's theology as a whole, and that necessarily arises from it. Salvation and damnation are equally grounded in the decision of God, beyond which there is no appeal (differently James 1:13–15). They do not, however, stand alongside each other having the same rank, for God's universal saving will has been revealed in the gospel of Jesus Christ[43] whereas God's "No" is a mystery withdrawn from human knowledge.

15.4 The Gospel as God's Eschatological Good News of Salvation

The term εὐαγγέλιον (gospel, good news) in Paul represents a central concept in his theology of revelation.[44] Its significance is already indicated by vocabulary statistics: of the seventy-six occurrences of εὐαγγέλιον in the New Testament, forty-eight are found in Paul (the verb εὐαγγελίζομαι ["proclaim the gospel," "announce good news"] is found fifty-four times in the New Testament, nineteen of them in Paul).

The Origin of the Gospel

Regarding its origin and authority, the gospel is the εὐαγγέλιον (τοῦ) θεοῦ (gospel of God; cf. 1 Thess. 2:2, 8–9; 2 Cor. 11:7; Rom. 1:1; 15:16). Εὐαγγέλιον thus means much more than "good news"; it is an effective means by which

---

42. Cf. Luz, *Geschichtsverständnis*, 249: "Paul's statements about predestination are intended to be statements about God alone, not statements about human decisions and history."

43. God's "Yes" is specifically emphasized by Theobald, *Römerbrief*, 276: "The dialectic of election and rejection, call and hardening in Rom. 9–11 are eschatologically overruled by the confession of 11:32 to the God who 'has imprisoned *all* in disobedience so that he may be merciful to *all*.' This perspective, which constitutes the goal of the three chapters, cannot be disregarded in any discussion of the problematic of Paul's understanding of predestination."

44. Cf. Georg Strecker, "Das Evangelium Jesu Christi," in *Eschaton und Historie: Aufsätze* (Göttingen: Vandenhoeck & Ruprecht, 1979), 183–228; Stuhlmacher, *Biblische Theologie*, 1:311–48; Helmut Merklein, "Zum Verständnis des paulinischen Begriffs 'Evangelium,'" in *Studien zu Jesus und Paulus* (2 vols.; WUNT 43, 105; Tübingen: Mohr Siebeck, 1987), 1:279–95; Dunn, *Theology of Paul*, 163–81; Gnilka, *Apostel und Zeuge*, 229–37; Koch, *Schrift als Zeuge*, 322–53.

salvation is communicated, a faith-generating event and a faith-effecting power,[45] proceeding forth from God in the power of the Spirit, its goal being the salvation of human beings (cf. 1 Thess. 1:5; 1 Cor. 4:20; Rom. 1:16–17). The gospel was not transmitted to Paul by human agents but was revealed to him directly by God through the appearance of Jesus Christ (cf. Gal. 1:11ff.; 2 Cor. 4:1–6; Rom. 1:1–5). Paul is permitted to serve the gospel and must do so, for the decision is not at his own disposal (cf. Rom. 15:16). Granted, the gospel is mediated through the human word of the apostle, but it cannot be reduced to that; it is the word of God that encounters his hearers in his own preaching (cf. 1 Thess. 2:13; 2 Cor. 4:4–6; 5:20). Paul stands under the compulsion of the gospel itself, for "an obligation is laid on me, and woe to me if I do not proclaim the gospel" (1 Cor. 9:16). For Paul, God's initiating the proclamation of the gospel is itself part of God's saving work, which precedes the faith and salvation experience of the church of Jesus Christ.[46] As an eschatological event,[47] the gospel must be proclaimed to the whole world (cf. 2 Cor. 10:16; Rom. 10:15–16, which take up Isa. 52:7 LXX), for its goal is the salvation of humanity and thus has a soteriological quality in itself (cf. 2 Cor. 4:3–4). The church in Corinth was begotten by the gospel (1 Cor. 4:15); the service of the gospel unites Paul and his churches (2 Cor. 8:18; Philem. 13); Paul struggles for the gospel (cf. Gal. 1:6ff.; Phil. 1:7; 2:22; 4:3) and endures everything rather than place an obstacle in the way of the gospel of Christ (1 Cor. 9:12). His sole concern is to be a participant in the saving power of the gospel: "I do it all for the sake of the gospel, so that I may share in its blessings" (1 Cor. 9:23).

The Content of the Gospel

Regarding its content, the gospel is the εὐαγγέλιον τοῦ Χριστοῦ (cf. 1 Thess. 3:2; 1 Cor. 9:12; 2 Cor. 2:12; 9:13; 10:14; Gal. 1:7; Rom. 15:19; Phil. 1:27). This gospel has a very definite shape and a clearly determined content; Paul therefore fights mightily against anyone who preaches a different gospel. According to Paul, the content of the gospel (cf. 1 Thess. 1:9–10; 1 Cor. 15:3–5; 2 Cor. 4:4; Rom. 1:3b–4a) can be described as follows: From the very beginning, God intended to save the world through Christ (cf. 1 Cor. 2:7; Rom. 16:25); God announced this saving will through the prophets (cf. Rom. 1:2; 16:26) and had it witnessed through the Scripture (cf. 1 Cor. 15:3–4; Gal. 3:8).[48] When the time was fulfilled, God sent his Son, who achieved the salvation of the world and humanity by his death on the cross and his resurrection (cf. Gal. 4:4–5; Rom. 1:3–4; 15:8; 2 Cor. 1:20). Until the sending of the Son,

45. See above, section 12.3 ("The Gospel of Jesus Christ").
46. Stuhlmacher, *Biblische Theologie*, 1:315.
47. Merklein, "Verständnis des paulinischen 'Evangelium,'" 287ff.
48. Cf. Dunn, *Theology of Paul*, 169–73.

both Jews and Gentiles lived unaware of the true will of God, which is now proclaimed in the gospel by Paul, called by God to be apostle to the Gentiles. Thus, for Paul the ultimate saving will of God in Jesus Christ is summarized in the gospel, the message of the crucified Son of God (cf. 1 Cor. 1:17).[49] In the suffering and resurrection of his Son, God has made known his saving will, and he has entrusted the proclamation of this saving event to his apostles. The gospel definitively controls the preaching of the apostle and reveals itself as the eschatological saving power of God. Directly addressed to humanity (2 Cor. 5:20, "be reconciled to God!"), the gospel is the active and effective communication of salvation from God; it is equally valid for Jews and Gentiles when they acknowledge Jesus Christ as Savior. The gospel is "the power of God for salvation to everyone who has faith" (Rom. 1:16). For Paul, the proclamation of the gospel is inseparably related to the judgment: "according to my gospel, God, through Jesus Christ, will judge the secret thoughts of all" (Rom. 2:16). Salvation and judgment cannot be separated in Paul's thought. Because the gospel is the message of salvation, to reject it cannot be without consequences, just as the acceptance of it has consequences. Therefore in the gospel Jesus Christ appears not only as Savior but also as judge. At the same time, it is also clear that for Paul the gospel is above all a δύναμις θεοῦ that saves those who accept in faith the saving message of the crucified and risen Jesus Christ.

"Gospel" as a Politico-Religious Term

The Pauline churches appropriated the term εὐαγγέλιον in a cultural and political setting in which the word already had particular associations. The verb εὐαγγελίζομαι derives from a predominantly Old Testament and Jewish background.[50] It appears in the Septuagint as well as the writings of ancient Judaism, where it must be translated "to announce eschatological salvation." Εὐαγγελίζομαι in the religious sense is also documented in Hellenistic literature (cf. Philostratus, *Vit. Apoll.* 1.28; Philo, *Embassy* 18, 231). The substantive forms of this word are used in the Septuagint without any recognizable theological content, in contrast to the central role the word plays in the ruler cult.[51] Thus, in the Priene inscription (9 BCE), the birthday of Augustus is celebrated, among other ways, in the following words: "Since the birthday of the god Augustus was the beginning for the world of the good tidings [εὐαγγελίων] that

49. Cf. Merklein, "Verständnis des paulinischen 'Evangelium,'" 291–93.
50. The prehistory of the terms εὐαγγέλιον and εὐαγγελίζομαι in the Old Testament and Judaism is comprehensively presented by Stuhlmacher, *Das paulinische Evangelium*, 109ff.
51. The singular εὐαγγέλιον is not found in the Septuagint, and the plural εὐαγγέλια only in 2 Sam. 4:10; cf. also ἡ εὐαγγελία in 2 Sam 18:20, 22, 25, 27; 2 Kings 7:9. Gerhard Friedrich, "εὐαγγέλιον," *TDNT* 2:725, appropriately comments, "The NT use of εὐαγγέλιον does not derive from the LXX."

came by reason of him."[52] Josephus relates how the εὐαγγέλια of Vespasian's promotion to the emperor's office was celebrated with sacrifices: "Quicker than thought, rumor spread the news of the new emperor in the east. Every city kept festival for the good news and offered sacrifices on his behalf."[53] In first-century linguistic usage, the terms εὐαγγέλιον/εὐαγγελίζομαι were closely related to emperor worship,[54] so that when Christians used this terminology, it had politico-religious overtones and a virtually anti-imperial connotation.[55] The early churches were quite aware of these ideas when they adopted the gospel terminology from their cultural environs, but at the same time, by using the singular εὐαγγέλιον, they fundamentally distinguished their usage from the plural εὐαγγέλια used in their environment. Paul's usage, too, can be seen in the framework of this early Christian strategy, in which the culture's vocabulary was adopted only to be turned against it: the true and exclusive good news is the message of the cross and resurrection. It is not the advent of the emperor that saves but the Son of God who comes from heaven (cf. 1 Thess. 1:9–10). Paul consciously makes use of a *political*-religious semantics in order to describe this reality.

The variety inherent in Paul's proclamation of the gospel and the very limited function of the term in Galatians, Romans, and Philippians as critical of the law show that the Pauline gospel can by no means be understood as fundamentally a "gospel of freedom from the law" from the very beginning.[56] The issue of the law is a secondary theme within the gospel concept. The gospel that proceeds from God, at its core, is filled with christological-soteriological and eschatological content:[57] the event of Jesus' death and resurrection are, as such, the saving event (cf. 1 Cor. 15:3b–5) that determines the present and future of all humanity. The gospel appears on the stage of history as the power of God calling to salvation, a power that wants to liberate and save a world enslaved under the power of sin. God speaks in the gospel and defines himself through the gospel as the one who loves and saves. The gospel is the presence of the powerful God, the God who wants to lead human beings to faith.

52. Cf. *NW* 2/1:9; and Boring et al., eds., *Hellenistic Commentary*, §§ 225–26.

53. Josephus, *J.W.* 4.618; cf. also 4.656 (*NW* 2/1:9–10).

54. Cf. Strecker, "Evangelium Jesu Christi," 188–92.

55. This aspect is specifically emphasized by N. T. Wright, "Paul's Gospel and Caesar's Empire," in *Paul and Politics: Ekklesia, Israel, Imperium, Interpretation: Essays in Honor of Krister Stendahl* (ed. Richard A. Horsley; Harrisburg, PA: Trinity Press International, 2000), 160–83.

56. Contra Hahn, "Entwicklung," 344, who claims, "What the gospel is in terms of its content and its effect is elaborated with the help of the justification thematic." Similarly Lohse, *Summa evangelii*, 109: "For what Paul has to say about justification . . . is understood by the apostle—as he has summarized it in the Letter to the Romans—as the only adequate interpretation of the gospel proclaimed by Christianity as a whole." Here the position of the Letter to the Romans is elevated to the role of Paul's basic point of view, and freedom from the law becomes almost the very center of the gospel.

57. Cf. Strecker, "Evangelium Jesu Christi," 225; Merklein, "Verständnis des paulinischen 'Evangelium,'" 286.

15.5 The Newness and Attractiveness of the Pauline Talk of God

What made Paul's talk of God so attractive? Why, in a truly multireligious society, did both Jews and Gentiles turn to the early Christian proclamation of God? An essential reason was its monotheism, which was already the basis for antiquity's fascination with Judaism. The multiplicity of gods and the ways they were portrayed in the Greco-Roman world obviously suffered a loss of plausibility, reflected in Cicero's comment "The gods have as many names as mankind has languages."[58] Because the throng of gods could hardly be numbered, the question naturally arose as to which gods should be worshiped and in what ways.[59] The philosopher thus asks, "Then, if the traditional gods whom we worship are really divine, what reason can you give why we should not include Isis and Osiris in the same category? And if we do so, why should we repudiate the gods of the barbarians? We shall therefore have to admit to the list of the gods oxen and horses, ibises, hawks, asps, crocodiles, fishes, dogs, wolves, cats, and many beasts besides."[60] The absurdity to which this line of argument leads is obvious: the conventional religions and cults neutralize each other and can no longer satisfy the needs of those who are upwardly mobile economically and intellectually.[61] The middle-Platonist Plutarch attempted to avoid this danger by pointing out that the deity is named differently among different peoples yet is in fact the same for all human beings:

> So for that one rationality [λόγος] which keeps all things in order and the one Providence which watches over them and the ancillary powers that are set over all, there have arisen among different peoples, in accordance with their customs, different honors and appellations. Thus men make use of consecrated symbols, some employing symbols that are obscure, but others those that are clearer, in guiding the intelligence toward things divine. . . . Wherefore in the study of these matters it is especially necessary that we adopt, as our guide in these mysteries, the reasoning [λόγος] that comes from philosophy, and consider reverently each one of the things that are said and done, so that . . . we may not thus err by

---

58. Cicero, *Nat. d.* 1.84. On the nature of Greek religion, cf. the classic work of Ulrich von Wilamowitz-Moellendorff, *Der glaube der Hellenen* (2 vols.; Berlin: Weidmannsche Buchhandlung, 1931); Werner Wilhelm Jaeger, *Die Theologie der frühen griechischen Denker* (Darmstadt: Wissenschaftliche Buchgesellschaft, 1964); L. B. Zaidmann and P. Schmitt-Pantel, *Die Religion der Griechen* (Munich: Beck, 1994); Jan N. Bremmer, *Götter, Mythen, und Heiligtümer im antiken Griechenland* (trans. Kai Brodersen; Darmstadt: Wissenschaftliche Buchgesellschaft, 1996). On Roman religion, cf. Kurt Latte, *Römische Religionsgeschichte* (HAW 5/4; Munich: Beck, 1960); Hubert Cancik and Jörg Rüpke, *Römische Reichsreligion und Provinzialreligion* (Tübingen: Mohr Siebeck, 1997); Rüpke, *Religion der Römer*.

59. Cicero, *Nat. d.* 3.40–60.

60. Cicero, *Nat. d.* 3.47.

61. Cf. Stark, *The Rise of Christianity*, 37–45.

accepting in a different spirit the things that the laws have dictated admirably concerning the sacrifices and festivals.[62]

In contrast to this, Paul encourages his hearers to accept a new view of the world, a new God. This God is one but not alone; this God has a name and a face: Jesus Christ. The God proclaimed by Paul is a personal God, who acts in history and cares about human beings. He is neither withdrawn from the world nor immanent in it but in Jesus Christ has turned to the world (cf. Gal. 4:4–5; Rom. 8:3). It is not a universal myth but a concrete act that determines the early Christian picture of God. Here lies the definitive difference between the Christian message and the two leading philosophical schools at the time of Paul, the Stoa and Epicureanism (cf. Acts 17:18). Stoicism advocated a monistic pantheism, according to which the deity is present and active in all forms of existence. It is immanent within the world and omnipresent and precisely for this reason is not tangibly comprehensible. Chrysippus teaches, "The divine power is located in the reason, in the soul and spirit of all nature, and that the world itself and the world-soul that permeates it all is God."[63] Nothing exists beyond the material elements of all being; there is neither a transcendent Creator God nor a metaphysical grounding of the world.

An opposing concept of deity is found in Epicurus. For him, the gods live a carefree life beyond this world of time without being concerned with human beings. "For a god does nothing, is not involved in any business, not burdened with any work, but enjoys his own wisdom and virtue and abandons himself to living in eternal bliss."[64] As immortals, the gods can neither suffer nor turn themselves toward the world in love.[65] They have withdrawn from the seamy side of life and have nothing in common with human beings.

Obviously, at the beginning of the Christian era, the traditional ancient teaching about the gods had lost its persuasive power, so that even their existence was questioned.[66] The philosophical critique of polytheism prepared the way for Christian monotheism. The God proclaimed by Paul combined two attractive basic principles: this God is both the Lord of history and Lord of one's personal life. In the early Christian churches, both realms coalesced not only in their thinking but also in their religious practice. Christians lived in the awareness of belonging to the group of human beings whom God had

---

62. Plutarch, *Is. Os.* 67–68; cf. further tradition ascribed to Antisthenes by Philodemus of Gadara, *De pietate* 7a.3–8: "In his *Physikos* one reads that there are many gods according to tradition but only one God according to nature [τὸ κατὰ νόμον εἶναι πολλοὺς θεούς, κατὰ δὲ φύσιν ἕνα]" (trans. M.E.B.).

63. Cicero, *Nat. d.* 1.39.

64. Cicero, *Nat. d.* 1.51.

65. Cf. Cicero, *Nat. d.* 1.95, 121; Diogenes Laertius 10.76–77.

66. Cf. Cicero, *Nat. d.* 1.94: "If none of them [the philosophers] has seen the truth about the nature of the gods, it is to be feared that this nature does not in fact exist."

chosen to reveal to the world both his saving will and his judgment. They were convinced that God through Jesus Christ had conferred meaning and purpose on history as a whole and on each individual life. This meaning embraced both daily life and a living hope for what lies beyond this life. The early Christian proclamation was directed both to the everyday life of the believer and to the ultimate issues of life, such as the meaning of death. Here developing Christianity was considerably different from the prevalent ideas of its environment. The God of Christians was a God of life who demanded commitment but who also granted freedom, a God who was already experienced in the present but who also guaranteed the ultimate future. Early Christianity offered a comprehensive and reasonable framework for living one's life, one that took up the hopes of antiquity for eternal life beyond this world while giving at the same time a convincing perspective on life within this world.

16

Christology

The Lord Who Is Present

Unlike the Gospels, Paul does not set forth his Christology as a narrative Jesusology. Instead he chooses a variety of christological leitmotifs, takes up metaphors used in Christian preaching from a number of semantic fields and their related imagery, in order to elaborate the meaning of the Christ event in all its dimensions and interpret why the historical "once for all" became the eschatological "always." Paul's polyphonic christological language has a clear point of departure: the conviction that Jesus Christ and his cruel fate represent and portray the love of God as God's saving will for humanity. He liberates from the slavery to sin and death and already in the present grants authentic life. For Paul, Christology is the manifold conceptual-theological interpretation of the significance of an event at the same time unique and universal: the death and resurrection of Jesus Christ.

16.1 Transformation and Participation as the Basic Modes of Pauline Christology

One fundamental idea characterizes Paul's Christology: God has transferred the Jesus who was crucified and dead into a new mode of being. A change of status occurs here: Jesus of Nazareth did not remain in the status of those who are dead and distant from God's presence, but God conferred on him the status of equality with God. This overwhelming experience and insight were granted to Paul at Damascus, and his letters reflect the variety of ways Paul had pondered the significance of this transfer of Jesus from the realm of death to life with God. As was already the case with the earliest Christian tradition, so also for Paul, the conviction that God had raised Jesus from the dead was fundamental (e.g., 1 Thess. 1:10; 2 Cor. 4:14; Rom. 8:11). God and Jesus Christ were thought of together; the Son participates fully in the deity of the Father. Thus, already before Paul, christological reflection had extended the change in Jesus' status from the resurrection to include preexistence. It was only Jesus' own willingness to descend to the way of the cross that granted him his exalted status as Lord of the universe; that is, even the preexistent one underwent a transformation in order to become what he was to be (cf. Phil. 2:6–11).

The goal of the transformation of Jesus Christ is the participation of believers in this fundamental event: "For you know the generous act of our Lord Jesus Christ, that though he was rich, yet for your sakes he became poor, so that by his poverty you might become rich" (2 Cor. 8:9); "For our sake he made him to be sin who knew no sin, so that in him we might become the righteousness of God" (2 Cor. 5:21).[1] Easter is an act of God involving not only Jesus but disciples and apostles, for God has made them know that the one who was crucified now lives. The resurrection of Jesus Christ from the dead is thus for Paul a once-for-all act, but its effects continue and have effected a fundamental change in the world. The God of the resurrection is the one who "gives life to the dead and calls into existence the things that do not exist" (Rom. 4:17b). God so identifies himself with the crucified Jesus of Nazareth that the life-giving power revealed in the resurrection continues to be effective: "For to this end Christ died and lived again, so that he might be Lord of both the dead and the living" (Rom. 14:9). The power of the resurrection of Jesus Christ is at work in the present and generates its own assurance: "But if we have died with Christ, we believe that we will also live with him" (Rom. 6:8; cf. 2 Cor. 1:9; 5:15). Christ was "handed over to death for our trespasses and was raised for our justification" (Rom. 4:25). When Paul himself was near death, his participation in the power of the resurrection was the ground of his hope of attaining the resurrection from the dead (Phil. 3:10–11). With the resurrection of Jesus Christ from the dead, a universal dynamic was set in motion that affects not only the destiny of the individual believer but the whole cosmos (cf. Phil. 3:20–21). As the way of salvation, the way of Christ is aimed at the believers' participation; as the prototype, the way of Jesus Christ from death to

---

1. Cf. Schweitzer, *Mysticism*, 115: "The original and central idea of the Pauline Mysticism is therefore that the Elect will share with one another and with Christ a corporeity which is in a special way susceptible to the action of the powers of death and resurrection, and in consequence capable of acquiring the resurrection state of existence before the general resurrection of the dead takes place."

life opens up the way for humans to follow the same way and makes it possible for them to do so.[2] According to Paul's conviction, this way introduces a new epoch, at the end of which stands the universal transformation when God will be "all in all" (1 Cor. 15:28).

16.2 Jesus Christ as Crucified and Risen

Paul is the last direct witness of the transformation of Jesus of Nazareth from death to life. At Damascus he was granted an Easter appearance: "Last of all, as to one untimely born, he appeared also to me" (1 Cor. 15:8). God's grace was revealed to him, the small one (Latin *paulus* [small]), the least among the apostles (1 Cor. 15:9, ἐλάχιστος, superlative of μικρός [small]). The appearance of the risen one made Paul certain that Jesus had not remained in death as a crucified transgressor of the law but that he has taken his rightful place at God's side (cf., e.g., 1 Thess. 4:14; 2 Cor. 4:14; Rom. 6:9; Phil. 2:6–11). The resurrection of Jesus Christ from the dead is therefore the factual presupposition for the theological relevance of the cross, which means that *the person of the crucified one is first revealed in the light of the resurrection.*[3] We must therefore first deal with the Pauline understanding of the resurrection before the cross can come into view as historical locus and thematic theological symbol of God's act.

16.2.1 Jesus Christ as the Risen One

The resurrection of Jesus Christ from the dead is at once the central content of Paul's meaning formation and its most disputed element, never accepted as entirely credible.[4] Luke had already presented the Epicureans and Stoics as

2. Cf. the parallels both in motifs and in vocabulary between Phil. 2:6–11 and 3:6–10, 20–21; they point to the direct connection between the destiny of the Kyrios and that of believers; cf. Strecker, *Die liminale Theologie des Paulus,* 176.

3. Regarding terminology, because in the New Testament God is consistently the subject of the act and Jesus of Nazareth is the object, we will sometimes speak of the *raising* of Jesus Christ in order to emphasize this passive element. On the other hand, the term "resurrection" (*rising*) has pervasively established itself in the general discussion as a term describing the whole event. It is also used here without suggesting that Jesus played an active role in his own resurrection.

On the relationship between Jesus as crucified and Jesus as resurrected, cf. the different approaches in Wolfgang Schrage, "Der gekreuzigte und auferweckte Herr: Zur theologia crucis und theologia resurrectionis bei Paulus," *ZTK* 94 (1997): 25–38; K. Haldimann, "Kreuz–Wort vom Kreuz–Kreuzestheologie," in *Kreuzestheologie im Neuen Testament* (ed. Andreas Dettwiler and Jean Zumstein; WUNT 151; Tübingen: Mohr Siebeck, 2002), 1–25. Whereas Schrage prefers a dialectical coordination, for Haldimann the saving event is the cross and the cross alone.

4. As a selection from the extensive literature, cf. Hans Campenhausen, *Der Ablauf der Osterereignisse und das leere Grab* (4th ed.; SHAW; Heidelberg: C. Winter, 1977); Hans Grass, *Ostergeschehen und Osterberichte* (2nd ed.; Göttingen: Vandenhoeck & Ruprecht, 1961), 94ff.; Willi Marxsen, *The Resurrection of Jesus of Nazareth* (Philadelphia: Fortress, 1970); Becker, *Auferstehung der Toten,* 14–116; Karl Martin Fischer, *Das Ostergeschehen* (2nd ed.; Göttingen: Vandenhoeck & Ruprecht, 1980); Paul Hoffmann,

ridiculing Paul's preaching of the resurrection (cf. Acts 17:32). When it comes to integrating the idea of resurrection from the dead into human thought, the deficiency in the world of human experience requires that we proceed in an exploratory manner in three progressive stages: we will ask what reality content Paul ascribes to the resurrection of Jesus Christ from the dead, present relevant explanatory models, and finally discuss our own model for understanding the resurrection.

The Reality Content of the Resurrection Event

Paul leaves no doubt about the significance of the resurrection as the foundation of Christian faith: "if Christ has not been raised, then our proclamation has been in vain and your faith has been in vain" (1 Cor. 15:14); "If Christ has not been raised, your faith is futile and you are still in your sins. . . . If for this life only we have hoped in Christ, we are of all people most to be pitied" (15:17, 19). For Paul, there is an irreversible series of resurrection, appearance, kerygma, and faith. In 1 Cor. 15 Paul gives a literary elaboration of this chronological series of events. Although he is himself an authentic witness of the resurrection, here too he anchors his Christology in church tradition (cf. 15:1–3a), in order to make clear that the resurrection of Jesus Christ from the dead is the foundation of faith for all Christians. The gospel has a definite form, and only in this form does it manifest itself for the Corinthians as a gospel that saves, and so believers must hold fast to the confession "that Christ died for our sins in accordance with the scriptures, and that he was buried, and that he was raised on the third day in accordance with the scriptures, and that he appeared to Cephas, then to the twelve" (15:3b–5).[5] Neither Paul nor the Corinthians can simply have their own version of the gospel; both are directed to the one gospel already given. The content of the gospel is the tradition of the death and resurrection of Christ. Jesus Christ died for our sins according to the will of God; the statement about his burial functions to confirm the reality of his death. The event of Jesus' death as a whole, including his burial, has its counterpart in the event of Jesus' resurrection as a whole, including the appearances. This resurrection overcomes death, understood both as God's last enemy and as the end of every individual life. Both the idea of Jesus' burial and the idea of the visible appearances of the resurrected one point to the fact that both Paul and

---

"Die historisch-kritische Osterdiskussion von H. S. Reimarus bis zu Beginn des 20. Jahrhunderts," in *Zur neutestamentlichen Überlieferung von der Auferstehung Jesu* (ed. Paul Hoffmann; Darmstadt: Wissenschaftliche Buchgesellschaft, 1988), 15–67; Ingolf U. Dalferth, *Der auferweckte Gekreuzigte: Zur Grammatik der Christologie* (Tübingen: Mohr Siebeck, 1994); Lüdemann, *Resurrection of Jesus*, 33–120; Ingolf U. Dalferth, "Volles Grab, leerer Glaube?" *ZTK* 95 (1998): 379–409; Gerd Theissen and Annette Merz, *The Historical Jesus: A Comprehensive Guide* (trans. John Bowden; Minneapolis: Fortress, 1998), 474–511 (a survey of research on Easter and its interpretations).

5. For analysis of the text, see above, section 9.6 ("The Resurrection of the Dead").

the tradition understand the death and resurrection of Jesus as bodily events in space and time.[6] Likewise Paul's extension of the list of witnesses (15:6–9) functions to demonstrate the bodily, and thus verifiable, resurrection of Jesus Christ from the dead,[7] since many of the five hundred brothers and sisters are still alive and can be interrogated. Bultmann rightly understands the intention of this text when he emphasizes, "I can understand this text only as an attempt to make the resurrection of Christ credible as an objective historical fact."[8] But he then continues, "And I see that Paul is betrayed by his apologetic into contradicting himself. For what Paul says in 15:20–22 of the death and resurrection of Christ cannot be said of an objective historical fact."[9] What Paul understood as historical event Bultmann wants to relegate to the realm of myth in order to maintain the credibility of the gospel in the modern world. Paul, the only witness to the resurrection from whom we have written reports, however, obviously understood the resurrection of Jesus Christ from the dead as an event within history, an event that had completely changed his own life. By citing the tradition in 15:3b–5 and by filling out the list of witnesses, Paul is also defending his own authority as an apostle.[10] He brings the accepted tradition up to the time when the risen Christ appeared personally to him, and thus makes clear to the Corinthians that he saw the risen one in the same way as the other witnesses, including Cephas. Paul thereby touches on three problem areas: (1) the bodily resurrection of Jesus, (2) his own testimony to this event, and (3) an understanding, derived from this, of the bodily resurrection from the dead. For Paul, this understanding of the resurrection is not a question of interpretation but a constituent element of the gospel itself. Only if Jesus Christ was raised bodily, and therefore in reality, from the dead can Christians place their hope in God's eschatological act of salvation.

This is by no means contradicted by the fact that both Paul and his tradition also argue in a restrictive manner:[11] the resurrection event itself is never described; the materiality of the event remains unmentioned. Paul understands Easter strictly as a revelatory act (Gal. 1:15–16), in which God revealed Jesus to him (1 Cor. 9:1; 15:8). This revelation occurred as at once an event within the world of human experience and as an event that transcends space and time, an event that fundamentally changed those who accepted it. The act of God at

---

6. Here Paul stands in the tradition of Jewish anthropology and eschatology; cf. Wolff, *Korinther,* 375.

7. Cf. ibid., 369.

8. Rudolf Bultmann, "Karl Barth, 'The Resurrection of the Dead,'" in *Faith and Understanding* (ed. Robert W. Funk; trans. Louise Pettibone Smith; London: SCM, 1969), 83.

9. Ibid., 83–84.

10. This aspect is specifically emphasized by Osten-Sacken, "Apologie," 131–49.

11. For discussion of the material, cf. Gerhard Delling, "Die Bedeutung der Auferstehung Jesu für den Glauben an Jesus Christus: Ein exegetischer Beitrag," in *Die Bedeutung der Auferstehungsbotschaft für den Glauben an Jesus Christus* (ed. F. Viering; Berlin: Evangelische Verlagsanstalt, 1967), 63–88; Hoffmann, "Auferstehung I/3," *TRE* 4:452–58; Fischer, *Ostergeschehen,* 73–76.

Easter includes the disciples and apostles, for God had made known to them that the crucified one is now alive. The power of life that became manifest in the resurrection of Jesus Christ continues to work, transforming those who believe (cf. Rom. 6:8; 2 Cor. 1:9; 5:15). Paul understands the bodily resurrection of Jesus Christ from the dead as the act of God for the crucified one, which introduces the eschatological age and thus becomes the foundation for a new view of the world and history. Moreover, the resurrection of Jesus Christ visibly changed his own life, so that for Paul its reality content not only consists in a new evaluation about the act of God for Jesus of Nazareth but also expresses a new and experiential reality.[12]

Explanatory Models

The experiences of Paul near Damascus are not our own; his worldview does not belong to everyone.[13] How can one speak of the resurrection of Jesus Christ from the dead within the terms of the modern world? How is it possible to affirm the truth of the good news of the resurrection of Jesus Christ from the dead in a time when truth claims are exclusively bound to the rationalism of the methods of (natural) science?[14] What plausibility do the arguments of the disputers and the advocates of the reality of the resurrection possess? Three interpretative models are significant in the current discussion.

Projections of the disciples as the cause of the resurrection faith (subjective-visions hypothesis)

David Friedrich Strauss (1808–1874) presented arguments against the Easter faith that have set the agenda for the discussion up to the present day.[15] He

---

12. In the 1960s discussion that lingers today, this aspect is intentionally minimized or underestimated; cf., e.g., Marxsen, *Resurrection*, 111, who denies that 1 Cor. 15 intends to prove anything, and states, "Consequently one cannot appeal to Paul in any attempt to hold fast to the historical nature of Jesus' resurrection." [Translator's note: The German text has a parenthetical comment after "historical nature" left untranslated in the English edition: "(as it is sometimes expressed)."]

13. Cf. G. E. Lessing, "On the Proof of the Spirit and Power," in *Lessing's Theological Writings* (ed. and trans. Henry Chadwick; Library of Modern Religious Thought 2; London: Adam & Charles Black, 1956), 51: "Fulfilled prophecies, which I myself experience, are one thing; fulfilled prophecies, of which I know only from history that others say they have experienced them, are another."

14. Historical thought is also directly concerned with this methodological process; cf. Rüsen, "Historische Methode," 345: "By adopting a methodological procedure, historical thinking achieves, in the form of its own logic of memory, the process of rationalizing that historically constitutes the modern world."

15. Cf. Lüdemann, *Resurrection of Jesus*, 198 and elsewhere. Lüdemann follows Strauss in all essential points. He classifies the tradition of the empty tomb as an unhistorical apologetic legend and sees the basis of the Easter faith in the individual appearances to Peter and Paul, which he interprets psychologically. Peter's vision is explained as the completion of a grief process that had been blocked by the sudden death of Jesus; the vision then allowed him to overcome his guilt feelings due to his

strictly distinguished between the appearance tradition and the tradition of the empty tomb. In his opinion, the historical origin of the Easter faith lies in the visions of the disciples in Galilee, far removed from Jesus' burial place, which first became the empty tomb in a secondary legend. The appearance stories point to visions of the disciples that were evoked by their pious charismatic experiences and their stressful situation. Strauss is thus an advocate of the subjective-vision hypothesis, according to which the disciples' visionary experiences can be rationally explained on the basis of their specific historical situation.

> Consternation at the execution of their master had scared them far from the dangerous metropolis, to their native Galilee; here they may have held secret meetings in honor of his memory, they may have found strength for their faith in him, have searched Scripture through and through, and strained every nerve to reach unto light and certainty; these were spiritual conflicts which, in Oriental and especially female natures of an unbalanced religious and fanatical development, easily turned into ecstasies and visions. . . . Thus the disciples, by elaborating the conception of the resurrection of their slain master, had rescued his work; and, moreover, it was their honest conviction that they had actually beheld and conversed with the risen Lord. It was no case of pious deception, but all the more of self-deception; embellishment and legend, of course, although possibly still in good faith, soon became intermingled with it.[16]

The significance of this line of argument is found not only in the reversal of cause and effect of the resurrection faith but above all in its dissolution of the coincidence of reality and truth. To a considerable degree, Strauss makes Jesus' historicity evaporate into the realm of myth, with the result that a cavernous gap appears between the reality of the historical event and the truth claim of the resurrection faith. Strauss hoped to resolve the tension he had thereby created by transferring the core of the Christian faith from the realm of history to the realm of ideas.[17] This is a deceptive hope, for the apparently positive results

---

betrayal of his master. In the case of Paul the persecutor, a previously repressed, unconscious fascination with the figure of Jesus breaks through. All the other purported visions are dependent on these two, and those, such as the vision to the five hundred, can be explained only by mass suggestion. For a critique of the historiographical and theological deficiencies in Lüdemann's constructions, cf. Dalferth, "Grab," 381ff.

On David Friedrich Strauss and his theological development, cf. the portrayals in Albert Schweitzer, *The Quest of the Historical Jesus: A Critical Study of Its Progress from Reimarus to Wrede* (trans. W. Montgomery et al.; "First Complete" ed.; Minneapolis: Fortress, 2000), 65–73; Reinhard Slenczka, *Geschichtlichkeit und Personsein Jesu Christi: Studien zur christologischen Problematik der historischen Jesusfrage* (FSÖTh 18; Göttingen: Vandenhoeck & Ruprecht, 1967), 46–61; Dietz Lange, *Historischer Jesus oder mythischer Christus: Untersuchungen zu dem Gegensatz zwischen Friedrich Schleiermacher und David Friedrich Strauss* (Gütersloh: Gütersloher Verlagshaus, 1975).

16. David Friedrich Strauss, *The Old Faith and the New* (trans. Mathilde Blind; New York: H. Holt, 1873), 81–82.

17. Cf. David Friedrich Strauss, *The Life of Jesus Critically Examined* (ed. Leander Keck; London: SCM Press, 1973), 780: "This is the key to the whole of Christology, that, as subject of the predicate

stood before a fundamental deficit: If the disciples are the cause and subject of the resurrection faith, then this event can be integrated into our understanding of reality. But it thereby loses its claim to be the truth, for in the long run truth cannot be maintained when unrelated to historical reality.[18]

Various levels of objections are to be raised against this derivation of resurrection faith from internal psychological processes:

(1) The *historical* argument: G. Lüdemann follows Strauss in regarding the traditions of the empty tomb as late apologetic legends. Lüdemann supposes that even the earliest Christian community did not know the location of Jesus' grave.[19] This is a thoroughly questionable historical argument, for Jesus' crucifixion clearly attracted much attention in Jerusalem. Thus neither Jesus' opponents nor his disciples and sympathizers would have been unaware of the place where Joseph of Arimathea buried Jesus (Mark 15:42–47).[20] When, shortly after this event, Jesus' disciples emerged in Jerusalem with the message that Jesus had been raised from the dead, then the issue of Jesus' tomb must have occupied a place of central importance from the very beginning. The disciples' preaching could easily have been refuted by pointing to a tomb that still contained Jesus' body.

(2) The *history-of-religions* argument: There are no parallels from the history of contemporary religion to the concept of a person who had died appearing to his or her associates.[21] If the appearances are understood exclusively on the basis of internal psychological phenomena, then there would have been other models for conceiving the event in order to express Jesus' special position. From the history-of-religions perspective, the eschatological affirmations of the early Christians are a unique combination.

(3) The *methodological* argument: Strauss and Lüdemann in no way present an "objective" and historically cogent representation of the resurrection event but necessarily *their* own history with Jesus of Nazareth. Their argument is determined by their epistemologically unfounded assumption that *their* analysis of the *literary* process by which the event was communicated is completely authoritative in deciding its reality. Such an analysis, however, can produce no assured results, for it does not apply to the event itself but always only to

---

which the church assigns to Christ, we place, instead of an individual, an idea, but an idea which has an existence in reality, not in the mind only, like that of Kant."

18. It is thus consistent with this point of view that G. Lüdemann has taken leave not only from official church teaching but from Jesus himself; cf. Gerd Lüdemann, with Frank Schleritt and Martinal Janssen, *Jesus after Two Thousand Years: What He Really Said and Did* (Amherst, NY: Prometheus Books, 2001), 693: "So with this book I am putting him on file." [Translator's note: It is perhaps better translated in American English "I am closing the file on him" or "I am filing him away."]

19. Cf. Lüdemann, *Resurrection of Jesus*, 117: "The tomb was evidently unknown."

20. In my opinion, the redactional note about the flight of the disciples in Mark 14:50 (cf. the πάντες [all] motif in Mark 14:27, 31, 50) should by no means be understood to say that all Jesus' sympathizers left Jerusalem.

21. Cf. Karrer, *Jesus Christus*, 35–36.

its literary interpretations as found in particular texts, and the way these are interpreted is in turn dependent on the exegete's understanding of reality and history, which inevitably determines the actual results. The decision about the reality and truth content of the resurrection event thus always occurs within the premises of the worldview and the life history of the interpreters; these premises set forth the normative worldview and guiding interests of the interpretation and spring from within the interpreters themselves. In the subjective-vision hypothesis, the argument is based especially on psychological assumptions,[22] and historical postulates derived from them, without their advocates having thought through the hermeneutical deficits involved in this approach.[23]

Resurrection dissolved into the kerygma

Following the (negative) results of the nineteenth century's quest for the historical Jesus, Bultmann intentionally abandoned the attempt to illuminate the Easter faith by historical methods: "The church had to surmount the scandal of the cross and did it in the Easter faith. How this act of decision took place in detail, how the Easter faith arose in individual disciples, has been obscured in the tradition by legend and is not of basic importance."[24] Bultmann understands Easter as an eschatological event, that is, an event that puts an end to all previous history, an event whose source is God, who brings in a new world and a new time. As an eschatological event, Easter is misunderstood when one attempts to understand it by this-worldly criteria, for the resurrection is not a miracle that can be certified by evidence. This basic hermeneutical decision

22. This is clearly the case with Lüdemann, who simply identifies his historical judgments with the event itself and in an unreflective, popularizing form exalts the supposed insights of psychoanalysis into apparently assured results. The suppositions of a hobby psychologist are passed off as historical facts. Examples: He speaks of Paul's "Messianic complex . . . that may have been formally brought to a boil" (Lüdemann, *Resurrection of Jesus*, 83), without indicating which psychological theory is the basis of this diagnosis of someone who died almost two thousand years ago. The internal conflicts that generated Peter's vision are tendentiously analyzed (ibid., pp. 97–100) with the help of one book (Yorick Spiegel, *The Grief Process: Analysis and Counseling* [trans. Elsbeth Duke; Nashville: Abingdon, 1977]). Of course, there were psychological dimensions associated with the appearances to both Peter and Paul, but those did not necessarily become the trigger for the appearances themselves. Moreover, the ideological character of psychoanalysis seems to have escaped Lüdemann's notice; one need only note Pohlen and Bautz-Holzherr, *Psychoanalyse*, 14: "Freudian thinking, which originated from a writer's creative spirit, exalted its personally necessary principle of perception and cognition into a claim of universal validity."

23. For critique of Strauss and the subjective-vision hypothesis, cf. Grass, *Ostergeschehen*, 233ff.; Wolfhart Pannenberg, *Jesus, God, and Man* (trans. Lewis L. Wilkins and Duane A. Priebe; 2nd ed.; Philadelphia: Westminster, 1977), 93–98; for critique of Lüdemann, cf. Reinhard Slenczka, "'Nonsense' (Lk 24,11)," *KD* 40 (1994): 170–81; Ulrich Wilckens, "Die Auferstehung Jesu: Historisches Zeugnis–Theologie–Glaubenserfahrung," *Pastoraltheologie* 85 (1996): 102–20; Wolfhart Pannenberg, "Die Auferstehung Jesu—Historie und Theologie," *ZTK* 91 (1994): 318–28. On the deficits of historicism in general, see above, section 1.2 ("Reflections on Historiography").

24. Bultmann, *Theology of the New Testament*, 1:45.

Bultmann finds in the New Testament itself, for there the crucified one is not proclaimed in such a way "that the meaning of the cross is . . . disclosed from the life of Jesus as a figure of past history, a life that needs to be reproduced by historical research. On the contrary, Jesus is not proclaimed merely as the crucified; he is also risen from the dead. The cross and the resurrection form an inseparable unity."[25] But how exactly are cross and resurrection related to each other? The resurrection is nothing else than "an attempt to convey the meaning of the cross."[26] This eschatological event, once set in motion by God, continues to happen as the word is proclaimed and faith is generated. Thus it is correct to say that Jesus "has risen into the kerygma,"[27] inasmuch as the proclamation of the word is the continuation of God's eschatological act effective for believers. There is a way to apprehend an eschatological event only when one is inducted into the new world, that is, eschatological existence, and confesses in faith "that the cross really has the cosmic and eschatological significance ascribed to it."[28]

This procedural concept, specifically obligated to the thinking of the modern age, raises two necessary questions:

(1) In this coordination of cross and resurrection, what reality content is attributed to the resurrection? If the resurrection is "an attempt to convey the meaning of the cross," then it is not a matter of making a judgment about its objective reality but a reflective judgment of a subject, a judgment that marks the subject's own hermeneutical standpoint.[29] A reflective judgment that does not refer to anything that really happened finally evaporates, even if it is often discussed and reformulated.[30] Just how Bultmann thinks of Jesus having risen into the kerygma remains unclear. The reality of the resurrection and one's confession of it are intentionally no longer distinguished and are thus effectively identified as the same thing. We have here an elegant but

25. Rudolf Bultmann, "New Testament and Mythology," in *Kerygma and Myth* (ed. Hans Werner Bartsch; New York: Harper & Brothers, 1961), 38.

26. Ibid.

27. Rudolf Bultmann, "The Primitive Christian Kerygma and the Historical Jesus," in *The Historical Jesus and the Kerygmatic Christ: Essays on the New Quest of the Historical Jesus* (ed. and trans. Carl E. Braaten and Roy A. Harrisville; Nashville: Abingdon, 1964), 42.

28. Bultmann, "New Testament and Mythology," 39.

29. Cf. the astute reflections of H.-G. Geyer, "Die Auferstehung Jesu Christi. Ein Überblick über die Diskussion in der evangelischen Theologie," in *Die Bedeutung der Auferstehungsbotschaft für den Glauben an Jesus Christus* (ed. F. Viering; Berlin: Evangelische Verlagsanstalt, 1967), 93–94.

30. Reformulations and radicalizations of Bultmann's position are found in, e.g., Willi Marxsen, "Die Auferstehung Jesu als historisches und als theologisches Problem," in *Die Bedeutung der Auferstehungsbotschaft* (ed. Viering), 27: "Originally triggered by the visions, the 'Jesus thing' [Jesus' *Sache*, 'cause'] continues." Herbert Braun, *Jesus—der Mann aus Nazareth und seine Zeit* (2nd ed.; Gütersloh: Gütersloher Verlagshaus, 1989), 244: "That what he was about [his *Sache*] endures (expressed in the jargon of early Christianity, that he was resurrected)—this is what, when push comes to shove, we can get from no one else, including no apostle, simply on trust and faith.

vague formulation that consciously veils the reality affirmed.[31] Precisely at the spot where the fundamental relation between history and truth needs to be clarified, "the meaning of each delimiting statement remains stuck in unresolved ambiguity."[32]

(2) It is not possible to renounce the analysis of the historical dimensions of the resurrection event because both the oldest tradition and Paul himself understand the resurrection event as an event bound to space and time. Moreover, if the powers of the resurrection continue at work in Christian faith, they must have a historical beginning point. Whoever does not pose the question of the historical dimensions of the resurrection of Jesus Christ lags behind what had already happened in the New Testament.[33]

Resurrection as real event

W. Pannenberg understands the Easter appearances as the objective expression of the manifestations of the risen one.[34] He opposes the reductionistic worldview of modern times, which dogmatically excludes God from the world of reality. "Historicity does not necessarily mean that what is said to have taken place historically must be like other known events. The claim to historicity that is inseparable from the assertion of the facticity of an event simply involves the fact that it happened at a specific time. The question whether it is like other events may play a role in critical evaluation of the truth of the claim but is not itself a condition of the actual truth claim the assertion makes."[35] If the possibility of God's acting in time and history is held open, then there are also weighty historical arguments for the credibility of the Easter narratives. For Pannenberg, the tomb tradition, regarded historically, is just as original as the appearance tradition but is independent of it regarding the facts reported. It was first in the light of the appearances that the empty tomb became a witness of the resurrection; apart from the appearances, it remains ambiguous. There are thus two mutually confirming witnesses for the Easter event, which vouch for the objectivity of the event. "And in fact, not the report of the discovery of the empty tomb, taken by itself, but rather the convergence of the independent appearance tradition originating in Galilee with the Jerusalem tomb tradition has considerable

31. For critique, cf. Karl Barth, *The Doctrine of Creation* (vol. 3, part 2 of *Church Dogmatics*; ed. Geoffrey W. Bromiley and T. F. Torrance; trans. Geoffrey W. Bromiley et al.; Edinburgh: T&T Clark, 1960), 443–47.

32. Geyer, "Auferstehung Jesu Christi," 96.

33. Bertold Klappert, ed., *Diskussion um Kreuz und Auferstehung: Zur gegenwärtigen Auseinandersetzung in Theologie und Gemeinde* (9th ed.; Wuppertal: Aussaat, 1985), has documented the lively controversy since 1945 about the cross and resurrection.

34. Cf. Pannenberg, *Jesus, God, and Man*, 93–98.

35. Wolfhart Pannenberg, *Systematic Theology* (trans. Geoffrey W. Bromiley; 3 vols.; Grand Rapids: Eerdmans, 1991), 2:360–61.

weight in forming a historical judgment. In making historical judgments—to speak in general—the convergence of different findings has great importance."[36] Pannenberg does not avoid historical inquiry and argument and thus necessarily moves into the realm of judgment calls influenced by life history and worldview. The conclusiveness of *two* witnesses that he presupposes[37] may not, however, be able to bear the burden of proof, for Pannenberg himself thereby remains within the thought patterns of modern historical positivism.[38]

Resurrection as Transcendent Event

The historicization of thought in modern times and its associated subsuming of the concept of truth under the rational methods of the prevailing science have effected a fundamental change in the way biblical texts and their claims are perceived. "Historicization has removed the Bible into the far distant temporal context of its origin, so that between the past of its origin and its present meaning there opens a temporal gap that—and this is the decisive point—cannot be closed with the same methodological means."[39] The spotlights of the history of research have revealed decisive strategies for avoiding this dilemma or for constructing a bridge across the chasm that separates past record and present meaning. Some resulting methodological insights are these: (1) The problems cannot be resolved by declaring that the inquiry about the resurrection from the dead is historically impossible or theologically illegitimate. In each case, one simply avoids the question of whether the accounts of the resurrection event refer to something real; faith and reality are torn apart. The resurrection remains among the rubble of past history,[40] and faith becomes merely an ideological assertion if it severs the connection to the original event. (2) Hermeneutical and historiographical reflections must precede the necessary historical inquiry, for they determine the respective constructions of reality and the concept of truth associated with each. With these methodological presuppositions, the following discussion attempts to understand the resurrection as a transcendent event.

36. Wolfhart Pannenberg, "Die Auferstehung Jesu," 327–28.

37. Not only the coordination of appearances and empty tomb but also the proleptic element in the pre-Easter Jesus' claim to authority and God's raising him from the dead are mutually confirmatory; cf. Pannenberg, *Jesus, God, and Man*, 53–73.

38. For critique of Pannenberg, see esp. Eckart Reinmuth, "Historik und Exegese—zum Streit um die Auferstehung Jesu nach der Moderne," in *Exegese und Methodendiskussion* (ed. Stefan Alkier and Ralph Brucker; TANZ 23; Tübingen: Francke, 1998), 1–8.

39. Rüsen, "Historische Methode," 358.

40. So, e.g., Dalferth, "Grab," 385: "It is the cross, not the resurrection, that anchors the faith in history. One can ask historical questions about the cross but not about the resurrection."

Hermeneutical and historiographical considerations

When dealing with the topic of the resurrection, one must think in a special way about the question of the range and capability of historical knowledge, for it is beyond our experience of reality.[41] Historical knowledge always takes place in view of a temporal gap from the event itself. This temporal gap cannot be bridged— not by the availability of good sources, not by an intuitive grasp of historical events. On the contrary, historical understanding always takes place only as an act of getting as close as possible to the past events without ever actually being in their presence. It is impossible to visualize a past event in such a way that it, so to speak, repeats itself under the control of the historian. Hypotheses about the origin of traditions and texts cannot decide about what really happened.

In addition to the temporal gap, there is the fact that historical events must always be interpreted, which constitutes the relativity of all historical knowledge. History is first constructed in the interpretation of the knowing subject; history is always a constructed model of what really happened, a mock-up of the event itself. In this process the worldview of the historian necessarily serves as the lens through which the data are viewed; that is, the understanding of reality accepted by the historian, his or her religious or areligious disposition, necessarily determines what can and what cannot be counted as historical.[42] The prevailing worldviews are themselves subject to a constant process of change. No worldview can claim for itself a special place in history,[43] for it undergoes unavoidable changes, can never be an absolute, but itself always belongs to the relativities of history. Pointing out the differences between the contemporary worldview and that of the New Testament is not therefore an adequate argument to demonstrate its deficient character because every generation must articulate its understanding within its own worldview. And there is no reason to think that following generations can derive some sort of absolute cognitive advantage from their later, differing worldview.

41. Here we are presupposing and picking up on the statements above in sections 1.2 ("Reflections on Historiography") and 1.3 ("Methodological 'Handle': Meaning Formation in Continuity and Change").

42. Appropriately, Pannenberg, *Systematic Theology*, 2:362: "Our judgment regarding the historicity of the resurrection of Jesus depends not only on examining the individual data (and the related reconstruction of the event) but also on our understanding of reality, of what we regard as possible or impossible prior to any evaluation of the details."

43. Among the exegetes, the frequently dominant passion for the historical, in the sense of confirming the facts behind the texts, begins with the claim that reality and history have always been understood as they understand it, and can only be understood in this way. The concept of the "facts," however, is of modern origin and can be documented only since the middle of the eighteenth century, and it is no accident that it plays a decisive role in the work of G. E. Lessing; cf. R. Staats, "Der theologiegeschichtliche Hintergrund des Begriffes 'Tatsache,'" *ZTK* 70 (1973): 316–45. Earlier generations understood history in other ways, and generations to come will probably do the same.

History is never simply there for all to see but is always constructed only through the retrospective view of the knowing subject. In modern times, this process of construction is oriented to particular methods as markers of scientific rationality, so that the prevailing truism is, "No meaning without method."[44] Method breaks the spell of the meaning potential of historical memory and levels everything out to a uniform mass. In the case of the resurrection, this freeing of history from its magic spell goes under the name of "analogy." Historical events can be properly evaluated only when they have analogies, when they can be understood within the nexus of cause and effect.[45] This is not the case with the resurrection of Jesus Christ from the dead, for—regarded historically—it deals with a singular phenomenon. This immediately raises the question whether such a unique event is historically credible. The answer to this question depends on the theory of history[46] accepted by each exegete. Followers of nomological conceptions will declare everything unhistorical that lies outside the realm of law as defined by themselves. In contrast, if one sees the constitutive element of history in temporal experiences, this changes the horizon of one's perceptions. "For the sake of its orientation function, historical thinking takes recourse to temporal experiences that are disregarded within the schema of nomological explanation: experiences of changes that do not fit the internal regularity where change is always caused by the things themselves. It is a matter of temporal experiences that, in contrast to things perceptible from the nomological approach, have the status of contingency."[47] For our question, this means that the appearances of the risen Jesus and the resurrection events that lie behind them may not be proved by historical method, but neither can they be excluded if one includes the experiential category of contingency in one's construction of history. In addition, there is the fundamental epistemological insight that, in general, events of the past are not directly available to us, so that history, as a secondary interpretation of what happened, cannot claim the same reality content as the events from which it derives.[48] We can only say for historically certain that after the crucifixion and death of the Jewish itinerant preacher Jesus of Nazareth, some of his followers claimed that he had appeared to them as alive from the dead. Claims about the reality content of the resurrection event that go beyond this, in the case of both those who believe them and those who reject them, move *equally* on the level of life history experiences, epistemological positions, and historical considerations.

44. Rüsen, "Historische Methode," 345.
45. Extremely influential, even to the present day, on this point is the work of Ernst Troeltsch, "Historical and Dogmatic Method in Theology," in *Religion in History* (trans. James Luther Adams and Walter E. Bense; Minneapolis: Fortress, 1991), 11–32, who explains his views of historical criticism and analogy and their correlation to the basic concepts of the historical and thus to what is real.
46. Cf. Rüsen, *Rekonstruktion der Vergangenheit*, 22–86.
47. Ibid., 41.
48. Cf. Rüsen, *Historische Vernunft*, 58ff.

Resurrection as transcendent event

If one's theory of history allows the possibility of the resurrection of Jesus Christ from the dead, and admits that the following appearances of the risen one must be granted the same possible reality content as other events of the past, then the question arises as to the event's actual relation to reality. Although it cannot be placed within the categories of human reality, it can be classified with reference to them. It cannot be placed within human categories because for Paul, as for the New Testament as a whole, the resurrection is always understood strictly as the exclusive act of God (cf. 1 Thess. 4:14; 1 Cor. 6:14a, 15; Gal. 1:1; Rom. 4:24–25; 6:9; 8:11; 10:9).[49] The acting subject in the resurrection is God; that is, all talk of the resurrection of Jesus Christ is first of all a statement about God himself.[50] As the creative act of God on the crucified and dead Jesus of Nazareth, the reality of the resurrection must therefore be distinguished from human experiences, appropriations, and expressions of this reality.[51] If one combined and identified these two (divine act and its human experience and expression), then the question of the reality of this event could no longer be answered, and the possibility of divine act would be dependent on human confession.

Certainly, regarding the resurrection as God's act on Jesus of Nazareth does not do away with the question of the relation of this event to reality. Claiming that God himself speaks in the resurrection event and that God's act as such is not described but can only be confessed[52] must again be considered only an elegant avoiding of the problems. How is something supposed to be the foundation of my faith and thus of my understanding of reality if it cannot

49. On the so-called formula tradition, cf. Werner R. Kramer, *Christ, Lord, Son of God* (trans. Brian Hardy; SBT 50; London: SCM Press, 1966), 19–64; and Klaus Wengst, *Christologische Formeln und Lieder des Urchristentums* (Gütersloh: Gütersloher Verlagshaus, 1972), 92ff.

50. Cf. Christoph Schwöbel, "Auferstehung," *RGG* 1:926: "The act of God is the common reference point in speaking of the resurrection of the dead Jesus, in the faith of the earliest church that Jesus thereby comes to participate in the life of God and that he was certified as living by God himself, and in the commission to spread this message further."

51. Here lies the theological deficit inherent in speaking of the resurrection of Jesus as an interpretation, e.g., by Marxsen, *Resurrection*, 138–48. If the resurrection of Jesus is an interpretation [*Interpretament*], what is it that is being interpreted [*Interpretandum*]? Following Bultmann, Marxsen equates faith in the resurrection with the resurrection itself; he can even formulate it: "We must see exactly where the miracle lies. For the miracle is not the resurrection of Jesus, as one all too easily says; the miracle is the finding of faith" (p. 139).

52. So Dalferth, *Der auferweckte Gekreuzigte*, 56: "The theme of the confession of Jesus' resurrection, and thus what is expressed in the terminology of resurrection, is not an empirical content or a historical event, however this is defined, which then is interpreted or explained in a particular way, but something that can only be confessed by those who know that they have been incorporated in this act of God. It is not historical events and phenomena and, still less, subjective impressions, understandings, and interpretations of the first Christians that are here set forth and interpreted as God's resurrection act. Rather, exactly the opposite is the case: what is confessed in this way is an act of God, which as such is inexpressible and thus becomes the factual and linguistic basis of the resurrection confession."

be brought into some relation to my reality? In my opinion, this necessary coordination is achieved with the concept of transcendence. The resurrection is first of all and essentially an event that goes beyond (*transcendere*) normal experience, an event that originates in God. It does not emerge, however, as the transcendence of the absolutely Holy One or as the distancing monotheism of God the wholly Other but rather as the act of the God who transcends his own eternity and, without giving up his freedom, enters into the realm of the creaturely world, of which God is the Creator and which belongs to him.[53] Within the created world, human beings are the creatures whose being is permeated by experiences of transcendence. Human beings live in a world that is ultimately out of their reach, a world that was there before them and will be there after they are gone.[54] They can experience the world but not simply fuse themselves with it. The differences between experiences of one's own "I" and experiences that transcend one's self result not only in experiences of difference but in experiences of transcendence. Every experience at its core points to something absent and foreign to oneself, which evokes an experience of transcendence along with the experience of "ordinary" things. Thus, for example, love and pain (through the separation or death of a loved one) are experiences that are beyond us and nevertheless permeate and determine our lives; they transcend our previous experience of reality and evoke both the capacity and the necessity of meaning formation. Thus a somewhat oversimplified typology of experiences of transcendence can be formulated:

> In the first place, when what is not directly experienced in present experience is just as experientially real as what is presently experienced, we can speak of "small" transcendent elements within daily life. In the second place, when the present is basically only indirectly, never directly, experienced but is nonetheless experienced as a constituent element of the same everyday reality, we can speak of "medium" transcendent elements. In the third place, when something is experienced only as pointing to a different reality outside everydayness, a reality that cannot be experienced as such, we speak of "large" transcendent elements.[55]

53. Cf. Paul Tillich, *Reason and Revelation; Being and God* (vol. 1 of *Systematic Theology*; Chicago: University of Chicago Press, 1951): "God is immanent in the world as its permanent creative ground and is transcendent to the world through freedom. Both infinite freedom and finite human freedom make the world transcendent to God and God transcendent to the world."

54. Here I am following the reflections of Alfred Schutz and Thomas Luckmann, *Strukturen der Lebenswelt* (Frankfurt: Suhrkamp, 1984), 2:139ff.; and Luckmann, *Die unsichtbare Religion*, 167: "Already in our everyday mode of existence, the world is experienced by us all as a reality to which we belong but with which we are not identical. We can, it is true, get acquainted with it, but we cannot become one with it. The distinction between I-referential experiences and I-transcending experiences occurs to everyone without thinking much about it; it is the basis of our knowledge of transcendence." [The English version of vol. 2 of *Strukturen der Lebenswelt* was published before the German: *The Structures of the Life-World* (vol. 2; trans. R. M. Zaner and David J. Parent; Evanston: Northwestern University Press, 1983).]

55. Luckmann, *Die unsichtbare Religion*, 167–68.

To these large transcendent elements, alongside sleep and crises, belongs above all death,[56] whose reality cannot be doubted but nevertheless cannot be experienced. As the boundary situation of life, death is the location where resurrection, the transcendent event that proceeds from God, encounters the first witnesses' experiences of transcendence. God's creative act on the crucified and dead Jesus of Nazareth evokes in the first witnesses and also in Paul experiences of transcendence of its own kind.[57] The decisive experience and insight is that *in the resurrection of Jesus Christ from the dead, God has made death the place of his love for human beings.*

These special experiences of transcendence cannot be subsumed [*einordnen*] under the categories of our reality, but they can be coordinated [*zuordnen*] with them, for our reality is permeated throughout with different sorts of experience of transcendence. If one does not restrict the concept of experience to the natural sciences,[58] the experiences of the early witnesses of the resurrection are by no means so categorically different from "normal" experience as is commonly supposed. In particular, the early Christians processed their special experiences of transcendence in the way that experiences of transcendence fundamentally must be constructively processed: through meaning formation.[59]

A Plausible Historical Course of Events

If one's worldview allows the possibility of regarding the resurrection as an act of God, then the main features of a historically plausible course of events comes into view. A comparison of the Easter narratives in the Gospels with 1 Cor. 15:3b–5 reveals that the basic structure of the Easter narrative is composed of

56. Cf. Schutz and Luckmann, *Structures of the Life-World*, 2:127. See above, p. 100 n. 63.

57. Samuel Vollenweider, "Ostern—der denkwürdige Ausgang einer Krisenerfahrung," *TZ* 49 (1993): 34–53, interprets the experiences of the first witnesses as crisis experiences: "The disciples' crisis experience consequently does not regressively calm down but abruptly modulates into an extremely extraordinary experience, an expansion of consciousness in which they perceive a dimension of reality otherwise hidden" (p. 42).

58. Cf. Kurt Hübner, *Die Wahrheit des Mythos* (Munich: Beck, 1985), 340: "Whoever affirms that science has proved the uniformity and absolute validity of natural law is an advocate not of science but of a dogmatic metaphysic of science. Thereby every belief of 'modern consciousness' that, on the basis of better scientific insight, miracles are no longer credible is exposed as itself a mere faith, to which man may oppose the faith of this or that religion. The truth, however, is that scientific theory as such speaks neither for nor against miracle, unless one points out the trivial fact that a miracle cannot be the object of *scientific* experience because this, of course, is based on the regulative principle of *seeking* such a law wherever something happens that is not explainable in terms of natural law. But as has already been extensively shown in earlier sections of this book, scientific experience cannot claim for itself that its explanation is the only one possible."

59. Luckmann, *Die unsichtbare Religion*, 171, comments on the character of religious constructions: "These constructions build on communicative reconstructions of subjective experiences of transcendence."

three elements: a tomb narrative (in Paul at 1 Cor. 15:4, "and he was buried"); an appearance report (in Paul at 1 Cor. 15:5a, "and that he appeared to Cephas"); and an appearance to a group of disciples (in Paul at 1 Cor. 15:5b–7).

Like the Gospels (cf. Mark 16:1–8 par.; John 20:1–10, 11–15), Paul too presupposes the empty tomb.[60] He does not specifically mention it, but the logic of Jesus' burial and resurrection in 1 Cor. 15:4 (and also being "buried with him" in Rom. 6:4) points to the empty tomb, for Jewish anthropology would presuppose a bodily resurrection.[61] In addition, there is the argument already mentioned: the message of the resurrection could not have been so successfully preached in Jerusalem if Jesus' corpse had remained in a mass grave or in an unopened tomb.[62] Neither Jesus' opponents nor his disciples would have been unaware of the location of Jesus' burial.[63] Precisely when one thinks historically, the success of the Easter message in Jerusalem is inconceivable without an empty tomb. The discovery in Jerusalem of the remains of a victim of crucifixion from the time of Jesus shows[64] that the corpse of an executed criminal could be handed over to his relatives or friends for burial. The empty tomb by itself remains ambiguous, however, and only the appearances of the risen one reveal its significance.[65]

The point of departure for the appearance traditions[66] is the primary epiphany of Jesus to Peter (cf. 1 Cor. 15:5a; Luke 24:34), since it is the basis for the

---

60. Differently, Bultmann, *Theology of the New Testament*, 1:45: "The accounts of the empty grave, of which Paul still knows nothing, are legends."

61. Cf., most recently, the argumentation of Martin Hengel, "Das Begräbnis Jesu bei Paulus," in *Auferstehung = Resurrection: The Fourth Durham-Tübingen Research Symposium: Resurrection, Transfiguration, and Exaltation in Old Testament, Ancient Judaism, and Early Christianity* (ed. Friedrich Avemarie and Hermann Lichtenberger; WUNT 135; Tübingen: Mohr Siebeck, 2001), 139ff.

62. Cf. Paul Althaus, *Die Wahrheit des christlichen Osterglaubens* (BFCT; Gütersloh: Bertelsmann, 1940), 25: "In Jerusalem, at the site of the execution and burial of Jesus, and not long after his death, it was proclaimed that he had been raised from the dead. This fact requires that within the earliest church there was reliable evidence that the tomb had been found to be empty."

63. Differently, Gerd Lüdemann, *What Really Happened to Jesus: A Historical Approach to the Resurrection* (Louisville: Westminster John Knox, 1996), 23, who asserts, without mentioning any evidence, "As neither the disciples nor Jesus' next of kin bothered about Jesus' body, it is hardly conceivable that they were informed about its resting place." Joseph of Arimathea was one of Jesus' sympathizers, from a respectable Jerusalem family (cf. Mark 15:43; John 19:38), and he "bothered about Jesus' body." Ingo Broer, *Die Urgemeinde und das Grab Jesu: Eine Analyse der Grablegungsgeschichte im Neuen Testament* (SANT 31; Munich: Kösel, 1972), 294, after a penetrating analysis of all relevant texts, comes to the conclusion "that the earliest church knew the tomb of Jesus, although we do not know, for example, when and how the church learned that Joseph of Arimathea had buried Jesus."

64. Cf. H.-W. Kuhn, "Der Gekreuzigte von Givcat ha-Mivtar: Bilanz einer Entdeckung," in *Theologia crucis, signum crucis: Festschrift für Erich Dinkler zum 70. Geburtstag* (ed. Carl Andresen and Günter Klein; Tübingen: Mohr Siebeck, 1979), 303–34.

65. Cf. Dalferth, "Grab," 394–95. It is also to be maintained against Dalferth, however, that also from the theological point of view it is not irrelevant whether the tomb was empty.

66. For analysis of the texts, cf. Ulrich Wilckens, *Resurrection: Biblical Testimony to the Resurrection: An Historical Examination and Explanation* (trans. A. M. Stewart; Atlanta: John Knox, 1978), 6–73.

distinctive position of Peter in early Christianity.[67] In the Gospel of John, the appearance tradition begins with the appearance to Mary Magdalene (John 20:11–18), and it is only after this that Jesus appears to his male disciples (John 20:19–23). Mark announces that Jesus will meet his disciples in Galilee (Mark 16:7), without recounting this event in the narrative itself. In Matthew Jesus appears first to Mary Magdalene and the other Mary (cf. Matt. 28:9–10), and in Luke to the disciples on the road to Emmaus (Luke 24:13ff.). Still, the accounts suggest that Jesus probably appeared first to Peter and Mary Magdalene or several women. The appearance accounts obviously pursue no particular apologetic slant,[68] for, although women were not fully qualified to be witnesses according to Jewish law, they play an important role in almost all the reports of appearances found in the Gospels. After appearing to individuals, Jesus appeared before different groups of disciples, to the Twelve or to the group of more than five hundred (1 Cor. 15:7).[69] These group appearances were followed by other individual appearances, such as those to James and finally to Paul (cf. 1 Cor. 15:7–8).[70]

On the basis of these reflections, the discernible historical data may be quickly summarized. After Jesus' arrest, the disciples fled, probably back to Galilee. Only a few women dared to witness the crucifixion (from a distance) and later to seek out the grave. Jesus was buried by Joseph of Arimathea. Jesus' first appearances took place in Galilee (cf. Mark 16:7; 1 Cor. 15:6[?]), and there may also have been appearances in Jerusalem (cf. Luke 24:34; John 20). Peter probably regathered the members of the Twelve and other disciples, both men and women, to whom Jesus then appeared. Further individual appearances followed, such as those to James and to Paul. The appearance tradition was connected very early to the tradition of the empty tomb; in the light of the Easter appearances, this grave, located near the place of execution, became itself a witness of the resurrection.

What was the nature of the appearances? From the history-of-religions and history-of-traditions points of view, they are understood as visions in the context of apocalyptic ideas, according to which in the end times God will grant insight into his acts to a few chosen individuals.[71] Because of the paucity of available materials, the reality content of the appearances cannot be understood in psy-

---

67. Cf. Campenhausen, *Osterereignisse*, 15.

68. Ibid., 41.

69. Lüdemann, *Resurrection of Jesus*, 100–108, identifies the appearance to more than five hundred with the Pentecost event of Acts 2. There are no serious grounds for this construction, since 1 Cor. 15:6ff. and Acts 2:1–13 have nothing to do with each other from the point of view of the history of traditions.

70. Even Lüdemann, *Resurrection of Jesus*, 140, states, without reinterpreting with any pseudopsychological model, "Because of 1 Cor. 15:7 it is certain *that* James 'saw' his brother."

71. Cf. Ulrich Wilckens, "Der Ursprung der Überlieferung der Erscheinungen des Auferstandenen," in *Zur neutestamentlichen Überlieferung von der Auferstehung Jesu* (ed. Paul Hoffmann; Darmstadt: Wissenschaftliche Buchgesellschaft, 1988), 139–93.

chological terms, nor is an interpretation of the appearances as faith experiences adequate,[72] for this would minimize the special status of the appearances as forming the basis of faith. Like the resurrection itself, the appearances are to be understood as a transcendent event deriving from God that generated the disciples' transcendent experiences. Such experiences of transcendence can be processed and reconstructed in a twofold manner: "narratives, in which the experiences of transcendence are communicatively structured and prepared for retelling, and rituals, in which such experiences are commemorated and with which the transcendent reality is ritually invoked."[73] Both the formula traditions and the narrative traditions do this; in each case they are necessarily consolidated in a variety of forms conditioned by their own times and made available for the intersubjective discourse of the churches. Baptism, the Lord's Supper, and worship were ritual locations in which the experiences were renewed and confirmed.

Easter thus became the foundational story of the new movement.[74] The texts disclose to us what the events set in motion and the significance ascribed to them. Historically and theologically, it is most important to note that as an authentic witness of the appearances, Paul's transcendental experience is portrayed in a very restrained manner and points to the decisive theological realization: the crucified one is risen. The appearances of the risen one, as a particular kind of transcendent experience, become the basis for the sure conviction that God through his creative Spirit (cf. Rom. 1:3b–4a) has acted in Jesus Christ and has made him to be the decisive eschatological figure.

16.2.2 The Cross in Pauline Theology

For Paul, the risen one is the crucified one (2 Cor. 13:4, "For he was crucified in weakness, but lives by the power of God"). The salvific significance of the resurrection casts the death of Jesus in a new light. For Paul, there is an interaction between death and resurrection. The resurrection is the objective grounding for the saving significance of Jesus' death, while at the same time the resurrection kerygma in Paul's hermeneutic presents the ultimate meaning of the cross. Even after the resurrection, Jesus remains the crucified one (the perfect passive participle ἐσταυρωμένος, 1 Cor. 1:23; 2:2; Gal. 3:1).[75] "The risen one still bears the

---

72. In this sense, cf., e.g., Ingo Broer, "'Der Herr ist wahrhaft auferstanden' (Lk 24,34)—Auferstehung Jesu und historisch-kritische Methode: Erwägungen zur Entstehung des Osterglaubens," in *Auferstehung Jesu, Auferstehung der Christen: Deutungen des Osterglaubens* (ed. Lorenz Oberlinner; QD 105; Freiburg: Herder, 1986), 39–62.

73. Luckmann, "Religion–Gesellschaft–Transcendenz," 120–21.

74. Cf. R. von Bendemann, "Die Auferstehung von den Toten als 'Basic Story,'" *GL* 15 (2000): 148–62.

75. Cf. Blass and Debrunner, *Grammar*, § 340: the perfect tense "denotes the continuance of the completed action."

nail prints of the cross."[76] In Paul, a biographical experience attains theological quality. He persecutes Jesus' followers because of their claim that the Messiah is one who has been crucified.[77] In the context of Deut. 21:22–23, this message must be resisted as blasphemy. Paul was convinced that the curse pronounced by the Torah applied to one who had been crucified (Gal. 3:13). The revelation at Damascus reversed the coordinates of this theological system. Paul recognized that the accursed one on the cross is the Son of God; that is, in the light of the resurrection, the cross was transformed from the place of the curse to the place of salvation. Thus Paul can call out to the Corinthians, "we proclaim Christ crucified, a stumbling block to Jews and foolishness to Gentiles" (1 Cor. 1:23). In Paul's letters the cross appears as the historical location of the death of Jesus, as an argumentative-theological theme, and as a theological symbol.[78]

The Cross as Historical Place

Theology always permeates Paul's talk of the cross. This does not mean, however, that Paul detaches it from history but that his beginning point is the cross as the place of the death of Jesus of Nazareth. By using the expression σκάνδαλον τοῦ σταυροῦ (scandal / stumbling block of the cross, 1 Cor. 1:23; Gal. 5:11), Paul refers to the concrete, degrading manner of the crucifixion, which identifies someone as a criminal, not as Son of God. To revere a victim of crucifixion as Son of God appeared to the Jews as theologically scandalous,[79] and to the Greco-Roman world as lunacy.[80] The central place of the crucified one in the Pauline symbolic universe meant that every current cultural plausibility was stood on its head, for now the cross is the *signum* of divine wisdom.[81]

Crucifixion was regarded as a degrading punishment.[82] The offender was often forced to carry the crossbeam to the site of crucifixion,[83] was nailed to it

---

76. Friedrich, *Verkündigung des Todes Jesu*, 137.

77. See above, section 3.4 ("The Persecutor of the Earliest Churches").

78. Hans Wolfgang Kuhn, "Jesus als Gekreuzigter in der frühchristlichen Verkündigung bis zur Mitte des 2. Jahrhunderts," *ZNW* 72 (1975): 1-46, here 29ff., chooses another way of systematizing the data: (1) the cross of Christ and wisdom; (2) the cross of Christ and the law; (3) the crucified one and the believers' new existence.

79. On the translation of σκάνδαλον with "offense" [*Anstoß*], cf. ibid., 36–37.

80. Cf. Cicero, *Rab. perd.* 5.16 (*NW* 2/1:239); Pliny the Younger, *Ep.* 10.96.8: "muddled wild superstition."

81. There are, however, possible cultural points of contact; thus in Plato the just man appears as dishonored: "They will tell you that the just man who is thought unjust will be scourged, racked, bound—will have his eyes burnt out; and at last, after suffering every kind of evil, he will be impaled: Then he will understand that he ought to seem only, and not to be, just" (*Resp.* 2.361c [trans. Jowett, p. 312]).

82. Cf. Deut. 21:22–23; 11Q19 64:9–13; Josephus, *J. W.* 7.203; further documentation in Kuhn, "Jesus als Gekreuzigter," 7ff.

83. Documentation in H.-W. Kuhn, "σταυρός," *EDNT* 3:267–70. Jesus was probably crucified on a T-shaped cross, as evidenced in Palestine through the discovery at Giv'at ha-Mivtar.

(cf. John 20:25, 27),[84] and usually died only after a long and painful struggle.[85] The executioners had developed various means of prolonging or shortening the life of the victim.[86] Death could come within three hours or be delayed for three days. As a rule, death resulted from a combination of the following factors: traumatic shock; orthostatic collapse (blood settling into the lower part of the body because of the victim's vertical position); insufficient oxygen (suffocation); and blockage of the pericardium (collection of fluids around the heart).[87] In Palestine only the Roman officials could be responsible for a crucifixion, which was their preferred punishment for slaves and rebels.[88] In Palestine during the period between 63 BCE and 66 CE, the Romans carried out all the crucifixions of rebels and their sympathizers.[89]

Paul holds fast to the cross as the historical location of the love of God. He resists a complete kerygmatizing of the unique historical event. God's time-transcending act identifies itself as salvific because it has a real place and a real time, a name and a history.[90] Pauline theology's concentration on the exalted and present Kyrios Jesus Christ is based on his identity with the crucified and dead Jesus of Nazareth. Faith cannot flee into the mythical realm because it is rooted in this world by the cross, as the Pauline addition in Phil. 2:8c (θάνατος δὲ σταυροῦ) makes clear. The concrete, once-for-all uniqueness of the saving event and its unmistakable character (cf. Rom. 6:10) are indispensable for the identity of Christian faith. Thus Paul asks the Corinthians, "Was Paul crucified for you?" (1 Cor. 1:13a). If Pilate had known who Jesus of Nazareth truly is, he would not have crucified the "Lord of glory" (1 Cor. 2:8).[91] The offense of the cross has continuing effects; Paul is persecuted because he proclaims the cross (Gal. 5:11), while his opponents avoid persecution and thus abolish the scandal of the cross (Gal. 6:12; Phil. 3:18). Through the unique event of the past, the cross becomes the eschatological event, that is, the event that transcends time. The presence of the cross in preaching presupposes that only

84. Cf. further Josephus, *J.W.* 2.308; 5.451; Luke 24:39; Col. 2:14. The victim of crucifixion found at Giv'at ha-Mivtar was nailed through the feet; cf. H.-W. Kuhn, "Kreuz II," *TRE* 19:715; "Der Gekreuzigte von Giv'at ha-Mivtar," 320ff.

85. See Chr. M. Pilz, "Tod am Kreuz: Geschichte und Pathophysiologie der Kreuzigung" (diss.; Tübingen, 1986), 64ff.

86. Cf. ibid., 140ff.

87. Cf. ibid., 147. Pilz thereby rejects the previous (mostly monocausal) explanations: heat stroke, blood poisoning, starvation, thirst, loss of blood, and loss of the strength necessary to maintain breathing.

88. The basic works here are Martin Hengel, *Crucifixion* (trans. John Bowden; Philadelphia: Fortress, 1977); and H.-W. Kuhn, "Die Kreuzesstrafe während der frühen Kaiserzeit," *ANRW* 25.1:648–793.

89. Documentation in Kuhn, "Kreuz II," *TRE* 19:714–15.

90. Cf. Weder, *Das Kreuz Jesu bei Paulus*, 228ff.

91. For interpretation, cf. Wolff, *Korinther*, 55–57.

the crucified one is the risen one, and so the significance of the cross is always bound to its historical location.

The Cross as Argumentative and Theological Theme

The cross appears in several Pauline contexts as an argumentative and theological theme:

(1) In Corinth it has to do with rightly determining the identity of God's wisdom.[92] Paul attempts to make clear to this church striving for present fulfillment that wisdom is revealed at the place where human beings suppose only foolishness is to be found (1 Cor. 1:18ff.). God's way of working can be read off the cross, as the God who has chosen the weak and despised (1 Cor. 1:26–29) and who has led the apostle to a way of life and thought determined by the Lord (1 Cor. 2:2). If some in the church suppose that they are already in the state of fulfillment that is to occur only at the end of history (1 Cor. 4:8), then they have exchanged God's wisdom for their own or for the wisdom of the world. In contrast to Paul, they do not distinguish consistently between God's Spirit and the human spirit, between divine and human knowledge. Only the Spirit of God leads into the "deep things of God" (1 Cor. 2:10); the Spirit does not reveal special teachings about God's essence but the event of the cross as the deepest basis of divine wisdom.[93] The resurrection can only be declared as the resurrection of the one who was crucified; there are no wisdom and glory that can bypass the crucified one (1 Cor. 2:6ff.).

(2) The cross in Galatians also appears in a polemical context. Against the demand for circumcision advocated by his Jewish Christian opponents, Paul emphasizes that it is precisely the crucified one who has liberated baptized believers from the law (Gal. 3:13; 5:11). In his death on the cross, as our substitute (3:13, ὑπὲρ ἡμῶν [for us]), Christ took upon himself the curse pronounced in the law, the curse that applies to everyone who wants to gain life from the law. If the law characterizes the crucified one as accursed, the law cannot at the same time be the obligatory basis of the Christian life. Those who preach circumcision want to resolve this contradiction so that they will not be persecuted (by Jews) "for the cross of Christ" (6:12). The cross of Christ and the law are mutually exclusive alternatives, for the saving gift of the Spirit comes through faith in the crucified one (3:1–5).

(3) In paraenetic contexts, reference to the cross serves as the basis for the believer's new being. The radical change in the believer's life is causally related to the cross, for transfer into the new realm of being takes place as the believer participates in Christ's crucifixion at baptism. The old self, crucified with Christ,

---

92. See above, section 9.2 ("The Wisdom of the World and the Foolishness of the Cross").
93. Cf. Merklein, *Korinther*, 1:236.

is dead and delivered from sin (Gal. 2:19; Rom. 6:6). The new existence of baptized believers bears the sign of the cross.

The Cross as Symbol

In every place where the cross is introduced into Paul's argumentative contexts, it is also a symbol. Because it first of all continues to be a historical location, the cross is able to be both fact and symbol at the same time.[94] It has a referential character, pointing to an actual event of the past, but through the power of the Spirit, this past event is also made real in the present. As the place of the once-for-all transfer of Jesus Christ into the new realm of being, the present existence of the believer is also stamped with the reality of the cross. In each case it designates the crossing over from death to life and attains its present dimension in a twofold ritual context:

(1) In baptism, the believer is incorporated into the event of Christ's crucifixion and resurrection in that here the power of sin and death is overcome and the status of the new being is conferred. The perfect passive verb συνεσταύρωμαι (I have been crucified with) in Gal. 2:19, like σύμφυτοι γεγόναμεν (united with him in a death like his) in Rom. 6:5, underscores the reality and power of the baptismal event in which the believer is crucified with Christ, a power at work in the present and determining it anew.

(2) In Galatians Paul develops a critique of the Judaists' demand for circumcision, a critique based on his theological understanding of the cross. Circumcision was made a competitor with baptism as the initiation ritual into the people of God and thereby became a competitor with the cross. Circumcision maintained the ethnic differences between Jews and other peoples whereas the cross symbolized the transvaluation of all previous values and baptism specifically abolished all previous privileges (Gal. 3:26–28). The cross symbolizes God's surprising act that puts all human standards out of commission. The wisdom of the cross is incompatible with the wisdom of the world. The cross radically calls into question every human self-assertion and individualistic striving after salvation because it leads to weakness rather than power, to mourning rather than celebration, to shame rather than to glory, to the lostness of death rather than the glory of salvation already fulfilled in the present. This foolishness of the cross cannot be identified with any ideology or philosophy and refuses to be made the instrument of any program because it is grounded solely in the love of God.

This language of the cross is a distinctive element of Pauline theology. The apostle does not develop it from church tradition but from his own biography: at Damascus God revealed to him the truth about the crucified one, who did not remain in the realm of death. The word of the cross designates the

---

94. Cf. Strecker, *Die liminale Theologie des Paulus*, 262–63.

foundational transformation process in the Christ event and in the lives of baptized believers, and so it leads directly to the center of Pauline thinking.[95] The theology of the cross appears as a fundamental interpretation of God, the world, and life; it is the midpoint of the Pauline symbolic universe. It instructs one to interpret reality by beginning with the God who reveals himself in the crucifixion of Jesus and to orient one's thinking and acting by this revealed reality. Human values, norms, and categories receive a new interpretation in the light of the cross of Christ, for God's values are the revaluing of all human values. The gospel of the crucified Jesus Christ grants salvation through faith because this is where God reveals himself, the God who wants to be the savior of human beings precisely in their lostness and nothingness. In the cross, God reveals his love, which is able to suffer and therefore able to renew.

16.3 Jesus Christ as Savior and Liberator

As the crucified and risen one, Jesus Christ is for Paul the central figure of the end time. He completely determines the apostle's understanding of reality "For his sake I have suffered the loss of all things, and I regard them as rubbish, in order that I may gain Christ" (Phil. 3:8). Paul sees the world, life and death, present and future, all from the perspective of the Christ event, and it is already true that "all things are yours, whether Paul or Apollos or Cephas or the world or life or death or the present or the future—all belong to you, and you belong to Christ, and Christ belongs to God" (1 Cor. 3:21–23). Paul's symbolic universe is definitively shaped by the conception that in the end time Jesus Christ acts first of all as Savior and liberator; Savior from the coming wrath of God and liberator from the power of death.[96]

The Savior

Only the Son of God, Jesus Christ, saves believers from the wrath of God in the coming judgment (cf. 1 Thess. 1:10). It is not God's will that believers be subject to wrath; they will receive salvation through the Lord Jesus Christ (1 Thess. 5:9; Rom. 5:9).[97] The gospel is the power of God for the salvation of believers (Rom. 1:16). Paul prays for the people of Israel, that they too will be saved (Rom. 10:1). He himself lives in the awareness that salvation is

95. Contra Kuhn, "Jesus als Gekreuzigter," 40, who locates the Pauline statements about the cross exclusively in a polemical context; 1 Cor. 1:23; 2:2; Gal. 3:1 show clearly that the language of the cross was a constituent element of Paul's proclamation from the very beginning.

96. Cf. the foundational work of Wrede, *Paul*, 85–121; Schweitzer, *Mysticism*, 65–74; Sanders, *Paul and Palestinian Judaism*, 421–27; Georg Strecker, *Theology of the New Testament* (trans. M. Eugene Boring; New York: de Gruyter, 2000), 116–38.

97. Thüsing, *Paulinischen Soteriologie*, 203–6.

now nearer than the time when he and the Roman Christians became believers (Rom. 13:11). Because God has raised Jesus Christ from the dead, those who have been called to faith confidently hope for salvation at the imminent parousia (cf. 1 Thess. 4:14; 5:10). Thus Christians will be found blameless and holy when the "day of the Lord" arrives without warning (1 Thess. 3:13; 5:23; 1 Cor. 1:7–8; Phil. 1:6). Paul looks forward with great solemnity to the day of judgment, when the perfection of the church will be manifest. At the beginning of his letters, he often names the salvation of the churches in the context of the thanksgiving. The initial section of the communication is especially important, for it sets up the new common understanding of reality and essentially determines the mutual understanding between apostle and church for which he strives.[98] In his letter to the Thessalonians, Paul reminds them of their election as the presupposition of their salvation (1 Thess. 1:4). He assures the Corinthians that Jesus Christ will "strengthen you to the end, so that you may be blameless on the day of our Lord Jesus Christ. God is faithful; by him you were called into the fellowship of his Son, Jesus Christ our Lord" (1 Cor. 1:8–9). On the "day of the Lord" the Corinthian Christians will be Paul's boast (2 Cor. 1:14), and it is this confidence alone that comforts him in his present troubles (2 Cor. 1:5). Paul thanks God, "who in Christ always leads us in triumphal procession, and through us spreads in every place the fragrance that comes from knowing him" (2 Cor. 2:14). Although the thanksgiving is missing from the Letter to the Galatians, Paul nonetheless extends the greeting formula in his characteristic manner: "Grace to you and peace from God our Father and the Lord Jesus Christ, who gave himself for our sins to set us free from the present evil age, according to the will of our God and Father" (Gal. 1:3–4). Only through faith in the Son of God, Jesus Christ, do human beings have access to God and thus to salvation. Apart from this faith, rulership is exercised by "the god of this world" (2 Cor. 4:4) and by unbelief, which leads to ruin. In Phil. 1:5–6 the apostle explicitly portrays the temporal framework of God's act in the past and present up to the future judgment: "because of your sharing in the gospel from the first day until now. I am confident of this, that the one who began a good work among you will bring it to completion by the day of Jesus Christ." With the expression "from the beginning to the completion" Paul evidently adopts a conventional terminological pair (cf. 2 Cor. 8:6, 10–11; Gal. 3:3); on the "day of Jesus Christ," God will complete the act begun in the call to faith (Phil. 1:9–11; cf. 1:6). The apostle and his churches are convinced that their election, visibly manifest in baptism, and their call as participants in the gospel maintain their validity into the eschaton.

98. Cf. Bickmann, *Kommunikation gegen den Tod*, 47ff.; Alkier, *Wunder und Wirklichkeit*, 91ff.

The Liberator

The Christ event strips the power from death, personified as God's eschatological antagonist (cf. 1 Cor. 15:55), and Jesus Christ is manifest as the liberator from the power of death and the powers associated with it, σάρξ and ἁμαρτία.[99] As the last enemy, at the end of time death will be subjugated to Christ (1 Cor. 15:26), then the creation itself will be set free from its "bondage to decay" (Rom. 8:21). Paul develops these ideas extensively in his Adam/Christ typology (Rom. 5:12–21),[100] which is stamped with the conception of two figures that determine humanity as a whole: Adam and Christ. As death entered the world through the transgression of the first central figure, so the power of death is reversed and destroyed by God's gracious act in Christ. Of course, death continues to exist as a biological reality, but it has lost its eschatological dimension as a power that separates from God. Although, as individual figures, Adam and Christ each determine the destiny of humanity as a whole, at the same time Jesus surpasses Adam, for the disaster Adam brought about is more than abolished through God's eschatological gift of grace. So also the idea of ransom/redemption (ἀπολύτρωσις, Rom. 3:24; ἐξαγοράζω, Gal. 3:13; ἀγοράζω, 1 Cor. 6:20; 7:23) concisely expresses the liberating act of Jesus Christ: Jesus Christ took upon himself what held human beings in bondage; he paid "for us" the price of our liberation[101] from the powers of sin and death.

With liberation from death Paul associates deliverance from σάρξ and ἁμαρτία, powers that belong to the realm of death. The negative qualification of the flesh derives from the σάρξ/πνεῦμα antithesis[102] already present in Hellenistic Judaism and with no dependence on Paul's exclusive doctrine of justification.[103] Human beings whose lives are oriented to themselves and trust in their own resources Paul relegates to the realm of the flesh.[104] "Sarkish" (fleshly, belonging to the world of the flesh) people are characterized by self-centeredness and self-satisfaction; they rely on their own capabilities and make their own knowledge the standard of what is reasonable and what is real. Thus they do not perceive that it is precisely they who are helplessly delivered over to the all-dominating power of sin and death (cf. Rom. 7:5). A life κατὰ σάρκα means being imprisoned by what is earthly and transient, living a life without God.[105]

---

99. On the Pauline understanding of flesh, sin, law, and death, see below, chapter 19 ("Anthropology: The Struggle for the Self").

100. For analysis, see above, section 12.7 ("The Presence of Salvation: Baptism and Righteousness").

101. On the possible backgrounds in the history of religions (redemption of slaves), cf. Friedrich, *Verkündigung des Todes Jesu*, 82–86; Gerhard Barth, *Der Tod Jesu Christi im Verständnis des Neuen Testaments* (Neukirchen-Vluyn: Neukirchener, 1992), 71–75.

102. Cf. Schweitzer, *Mysticism*, 286–87; Strecker, "Befreiung und Rechtfertigung," 243–46.

103. Cf. Paulsen, *Überlieferung*, 46.

104. Cf. Bultmann, *Theology of the New Testament*, 1:232–39.

105. Cf. Alexander Sand, "σάρξ," *EDNT* 3:231.

The real subject of this life is sin and its unavoidable consequence, everlasting death (cf. Rom. 7:5). No human being can escape this fateful intertwining of sin and death on his or her own resources and abilities. God alone can liberate from the powers of sin and death and place believers in a new reality determined by the Spirit.[106] This liberation was brought about by the sending of the Son in that Jesus took upon himself the fleshly mode of existence in which the lordship of sin over humanity exercised its power (cf. Rom. 8:3, ἐν ὁμοιώματι σαρκὸς ἁμαρτίας [in the likeness of sinful flesh]). Jesus stripped sin of its power in the very place where its power was effective: in the flesh. As the sinless one (2 Cor. 5:21), he entered into the realm of sin and overcame it. The consequence of the freedom obtained by Christ is σωτηρία (salvation, deliverance). In worship, the congregation invokes Jesus Christ as "Savior," who as Cosmocrator will transform the earthly and transient body (Phil. 3:20–21). Salvation will occur at the imminent parousia of the Lord (Rom. 13:11); it is the consequence of repentance (2 Cor. 7:10) and the content of the Christian hope (1 Thess. 5:8–9). Salvation is already present in the proclamation of the apostle (2 Cor. 6:2) and takes place in the call of believers (cf. 1 Thess. 2:16; 1 Cor. 1:18; 15:2; 2 Cor. 2:15). The church can live in the confidence that their faith and their confession will save them (Rom. 10:9–10). The present experience of salvation and the confidence of future salvation collapse into each other: "For in hope were we saved" (Rom. 8:24, τῇ γὰρ ἐλπίδι ἐσώθημεν).

In the end time, Jesus Christ exercises his universal lordship in his function as Savior and liberator. His sovereignty relativizes all other claims, for it is not the emperor or the cult deities who save.[107] Paul lives in the certainty that God has acted in Christ for the salvation of humanity. Through their liberation from the powers of sin, the flesh and death, believers participate in the turn of the ages brought about by God in the death and resurrection of Jesus Christ. Christians may go to meet the coming judgment in confidence because they live in the assurance that the Savior Jesus Christ will not surrender them to eternal damnation.

16.4 Jesus as Messiah, Lord, and Son

Paul expresses Jesus' status as the risen one and his function as eschatological judge and liberator by the use of specific christological titles. The use of such titles belongs to the central means by which the Christ event was interpreted;

106. On this complex, see below, section 18.1 ("The Spirit as the Connectional Principle in Pauline Thought").

107. So, e.g., the hero in Apuleius, *Metam.* 10.25.1, to Isis: "O holy and blessed dame, the perpetual comfort of human kind, who by Thy bounty and grace nourishest all the world, and bearest a great affection to the adversities of the miserable as a loving mother."

they declare who and what Jesus is for the community of Christian faith.[108] The christological titles contain the basic ideas of Pauline Christology in concentrated form. Whereas central complexes of Pauline thought, such as the themes of reconciliation and justification, are limited to individual letters or segments of their text, the christological titles are documented throughout the Pauline letters in remarkable density. Thus, of the 531 occurrences of Χριστός (Christ) or Ἰησοῦς Χριστός (Jesus Christ) in the New Testament, 270 are found in the undisputed letters of Paul (1 Thessalonians, 10; 1 Corinthians, 64; 2 Corinthians, 47; Galatians, 38; Romans, 66; Philippians, 37; Philemon, 8).[109] Κύριος is found 719 times in the New Testament as a whole, 189 of them in Paul; that is, more than a fourth of all the instances are in Paul's letters (1 Thessalonians, 24; 1 Corinthians, 66; 2 Corinthians, 29; Galatians, 6; Romans, 44; Philippians, 15; Philemon, 5).[110] The title υἱὸς τοῦ θεοῦ (Son of God) appears relatively seldom in Paul (15 times), but in very significant contexts, so that this term, too, is important for Pauline Christology.

"Christ"

The central christological title in the undisputed letters of Paul is (Ἰησοῦς) Χριστός.[111] The title Χριστός derives from the royal messianic tradition of ancient Judaism, as is clear from such texts as *Pss. Sol.* 17–18; 1QS 9:9–11; CD 20:1;[112] *1 En.* 48:10; 52:4; *4 Ezra* 12:32; *2 Bar.* 39:7; 40:1; 72:2. The title Χριστός is an integral element in the oldest creedal traditions (cf. 1 Cor. 15:3b–5; 2 Cor. 5:19), combined with statements about the death and resurrection of Jesus, which express the Christ event as a whole (1 Cor. 15:3b–5 is a foundational text). Likewise statements about Jesus' crucifixion (1 Cor. 1:21; 2:2; Gal. 3:1, 13), death (Rom. 5:6, 8; 14:15; 15:3; 1 Cor. 8:11; Gal. 2:19,

108. A survey is found in Christfried Böttrich, "'Gott und Retter': Gottesprädikationen in christologischen Titeln," *NZST* 42 (2000): 217–36.

109. Statistics are based on Kurt Aland, ed., *Vollständige Konkordanz zum griechischen Neuen Testament* (3 vols.; Berlin: de Gruyter, 1983), 2:300–301.

110. Cf. ibid., 166–67.

111. On Χριστός, see esp. Kramer, *Christ, Lord, Son of God,* 19–64, 133–50; Ferdinand Hahn, *The Titles of Jesus in Christology: Their History in Early Christianity* (trans. Harold Knight and George Ogg; New York: World, 1969), 136–239; Géza Vermès, *Jesus the Jew: A Historian's Reading of the Gospels* (Philadelphia: Fortress, 1973), 129–59; Martin Hengel, "Erwägungen zum Sprachgebrauch von Χριστός bei Paulus und in der 'vorpaulinischen' Überlieferung," in *Paul and Paulinism: Essays in Honour of C. K. Barrett* (ed. Morna Dorothy Hooker and S. G. Wilson; London: SPCK, 1982), 135–59; Ferdinand Hahn, "Χριστός," *EDNT* 3:478–86; Martin Karrer, *Der Gesalbte: Die Grundlagen des Christustitels* (FRLANT 151; Göttingen: Vandenhoeck & Ruprecht, 1991); Dieter Zeller, "Messias/Christus," *NBL* 3:782–86; Marinus de Jonge, "Christ," *DDD* 192–200.

112. On messianic/anointed concepts at Qumran, cf. Johannes Zimmermann, *Messianische Texte aus Qumran: Königliche, priesterliche, und prophetische Messiasvorstellungen in den Schriftfunden von Qumran* (WUNT 2/104; Tübingen: Mohr Siebeck, 1998), 23ff.

21), resurrection (Rom. 6:9; 8:11; 10:7; 1 Cor. 15:12–17, 20, 23), preexistence (1 Cor. 10:4; 11:3ab), and earthly life (Rom. 9:5; 2 Cor. 5:16) are combined with the Christ title. From such foundational statements, which refer to the Christ event as a whole, Χριστός affirmations then branch off into different areas. Thus Paul speaks of πιστεύειν εἰς Χριστόν (to believe in Christ, Gal. 2:16; cf. Gal. 3:22; Phil. 1:29) and of the εὐαγγέλιον τοῦ Χριστοῦ (the gospel of Christ; cf. 1 Thess. 3:2; 1 Cor. 9:12; 2 Cor. 2:12; 9:13; 10:14; Gal. 1:7; Rom. 15:19; Phil. 1:27) and understands himself as apostle of Christ (cf. ἀπόστολος Χριστοῦ, 1 Thess. 2:7; 2 Cor. 11:13). For Paul, Χριστὸς Ἰησοῦς is a titular name, both title and name. The apostle knows that Χριστός was originally an appellative and that Ἰησοῦς is the real *nomen proprium*, for he never speaks of a κύριος Χριστός. When combined with᾽ Ἰησοῦς, Χριστός is thus to be understood as a cognomen (surname) that also always has the overtones of its original titular significance. At the same time, the title is fused so closely with the person of Jesus and his specific destiny that it soon became simply a name for Jesus and the basis of the epithet later applied to Christians (Acts 11:26).

It is no accident that the title Χριστός is used without further ado in letters to predominantly Gentile churches, for the addressees could appropriate Χριστός from its usage in their cultural background in the context of ancient anointing rituals. The anointing rituals widespread in the whole Mediterranean area point to a linguistic usage common to antiquity in general, according to which, "when someone or something is anointed, that person or thing becomes holy, near to God, given over to God."[113] Thus both Jewish Christians and Gentile Christians could understand the word Χριστός as affirming Jesus' unique holiness and nearness to God, so that precisely in its capacity as a titular name, Χριστός (or Ἰησοῦς Χριστός) became for Paul the ideal missionary term.

"Lord"

Paul brings a different perspective to the κύριος title.[114] By speaking of Jesus as "Lord," believers place themselves under the authority of the exalted Lord, who is present in the life of the church. It is most likely that Ps. 109 LXX (Ps. 110) played a key role in the adoption of the Kyrios title into the developing Christology:[115] "The Lord says to my lord, 'Sit at my right hand until I make your enemies your footstool.'" Here the early Christians found the definitive scriptural evidence for Jesus' heavenly status and function: he had been exalted

---

113. Karrer, *Gesalbte*, 211.

114. Cf. Kramer, *Christ, Lord, Son of God*, 65–107, 151–82; Hahn, *Titles of Jesus*, 68–135, 349–51; Joseph A. Fitzmyer, "Κύριος," *EDNT* 2:239–331; Vermès, *Jesus the Jew*, 103–28; David B. Capes, *Old Testament Yahweh Texts in Paul's Christology* (WUNT 2/47; Tübingen: Mohr Siebeck, 1992).

115. Cf. Martin Hengel, "Psalm 110 und die Erhöhung des Auferstandenen zur Rechten Gottes," in *Anfänge der Christologie: Festschrift für Ferdinand Hahn zum 65. Geburtstag* (ed. Cilliers Breytenbach et al.; Göttingen: Vandenhoeck & Ruprecht, 1991), 43–74.

to God's right hand, participates in the power and glory of God, and from there exercises his lordship. In this context, where God was commonly addressed as "Lord," the early Christians very early applied the title to Jesus (cf. the adoption of Joel 3:5 LXX [Joel 2:32] in Rom. 10:12–13; see also 1 Cor. 1:31; 2:16; 10:26; 2 Cor. 10:17) and thereby expressed his unique authority, marking it off from other claims.[116] The increasing religious reverence for the Roman emperor was combined with the Kyrios title (especially in the eastern part of the empire; cf. Acts 25:26; Suetonius, *Domitianus* 13.2), and κύριος (or the feminine κυρία) acclamations are also found in the mystery cults.[117] The Jewish background of the Kyrios title[118] was often combined with critical thinking in the Hellenistic reception: in the early Christian mission, the κύριος Ἰησοῦς Χριστός crossed the path of many gods, male and female, of whom the title "lord" was used; precisely for this reason, it was necessary to make clear that, for Christians, this title did not present Jesus as one of many such lords. There is only one God and only one Lord, Jesus Christ, as 1 Cor. 8:6 emphatically declares. In this pre-Pauline tradition, the εἷς κύριος Ἰησοῦς Χριστός (the one/only Lord Jesus Christ) appears as the one through whom everything was created and to whom everything is subject.[119]

The presence of the exalted Lord in the life of the church, an aspect associated with the Kyrios title, is seen most clearly in two anchor points of the tradition—the church's acclamation of Jesus as Lord and the eucharistic tradition. By its acclamation of Jesus as Lord, the church acknowledges the status of Jesus as Lord and confesses its own faith and obedience to him (cf. 1 Cor. 12:3; Phil. 2:6–11). The God of the Christians works through his Spirit, so that they cry out in the worship services κύριος Ἰησοῦς (Jesus is Lord) and not ἀνάθεμα Ἰησοῦς (Jesus be cursed). The title κύριος appears with particular frequency in the eucharistic tradition (cf. 1 Cor. 11:20–23, 26ff., 32; 16:22). The church assembles in the powerful presence of the Lord, whose salvific but also punitive powers are effective in the celebration of the Lord's Supper (cf. 1 Cor. 11:30). Alongside the liturgical dimension of the Kyrios title, Paul also includes an ethical component. The Kyrios is the ultimate authority, the reference point for deciding all the issues of daily life (Rom. 14:8, "If we live, we live to the Lord, and if we die, we die to the Lord; so then, whether we live or whether we die, we are the Lord's"). The Lord's power embraces every aspect

---

116. Cf. Marinus de Jonge, *Christology in Context: The Earliest Christian Response to Jesus* (Philadelphia: Westminster, 1988), 184–85.

117. Cf. Plutarch, *Is. Os.* 367, where Isis is named ἡ κυρία τῆς γῆς (ruler of the earth). [Translator's note: "Ruler" is here the feminine form of "lord."]

118. Cf. Joseph A. Fitzmyer, "The Semitic Background of the New Testament *kyrios*-Title," in *A Wandering Aramean: Collected Aramaic Essays* (SBLMS 25; Missoula, MT: Scholars Press, 1979), 115–42.

119. Dieter Zeller, "Der eine Gott und der eine Herr Jesus Christus," in *Der lebendige Gott: Studien zur Theologie des Neuen Testaments: Festschrift für Wilhelm Thüsing zum 75. Geburtstag* (ed. Thomas Söding; NTAbh NF 31; Münster: Aschendorff, 1996), 34–49.

of life; there is no dimension of life not under his authority. In particular, the lord/slave metaphor expresses the dependence of believers on their Lord (cf. Gal. 1:10; Rom. 1:1; Phil. 1:1). Paul can summarize the content of his whole proclamation in these words: "For we do not proclaim ourselves; we proclaim Jesus Christ as Lord and ourselves as your slaves for Jesus' sake" (2 Cor. 4:5).

The title has additional connotations in addition to the aspect of the Lord's present authority. Paul not only uses Kyrios for the earthly Jesus (e.g., 1 Thess. 1:6; 2:15; 1 Cor. 9:5; Gal. 1:19) and for the resurrected Lord (e.g., 1 Cor. 9:1) but also for the coming Lord, to whose "day" he joyfully looks forward. The Lord will come to judge the world and to call those who believe in him to participate in his lordship (cf. 1 Thess. 2:19; 3:13; 1 Cor. 1:7–8; 5:5; Phil. 3:20; 4:5). For the church, the exalted one who presently rules in power is the one who is to come, the one invoked in worship, "Our Lord, come!" (1 Cor. 16:22; cf. Rev. 22:20; *Did.* 10:6).[120]

"Son of God"

The title υἱὸς τοῦ θεοῦ is found only fifteen times in Paul.[121] The apostle took it over from the tradition (cf. 1 Thess. 1:9–10; Rom. 1:3b–4a); the formative history-of-religions context of the Son Christology was most likely provided mainly by Old Testament ideas (cf. Ps. 2:7, "I will tell of the decree of the Lord: He said to me, 'You are my son; today I have begotten you'"; cf. also 2 Sam. 7:11–12, 14).[122] The central importance of the Son title is seen in 2 Cor. 1:19, where the Son appears as the content of the apostle's message: "the Son of God, Jesus Christ, whom we proclaimed to you." The soteriological dimension of the Son title is underscored in Gal. 1:16; the content of Paul's call vision at Damascus is the revelation of God's Son. The Son of God gave himself for

120. Cf. de Jonge, *Christology*, 48.

121. The relevant material is discussed in Martin Hengel, *The Son of God: The Origin of Christology and the History of Jewish-Hellenistic Religion* (trans. John Bowden; Philadelphia: Fortress, 1976), 7–16, 57–84; Larry W. Hurtado, "Son of God," *DPL* 900–906; Hurtado, *Lord Jesus Christ*, 108–17; Labahn and Labahn, "Sohn Gottes bei Paulus," 97–120. On Qumran (in addition to 4QFlor 1:11–13 and 1QSa 2:11, see esp. *Apocryphon of Daniel* (4Q246), cf. Joseph A. Fitzmyer, "The 'Son of God' Document from Qumran," *Bib* 74 (1993): 153–74; Zimmermann, *Messianische Texte aus Qumran*, 128–70.

122. Here, too, it is important to note the context in which the material was received, for with reference to "Son of God," the predominantly Gentile churches would tend to think of the worship of the emperor as Son of God (for Augustus, cf. Deissmann, *Light from the Ancient East*, 346–48), heroes such as Hercules (cf. Epictetus, *Diatr.* 3.26.31, "God granted Hercules . . . His Son, nothing superfluous"), rulers such as Alexander the Great (Plutarch, *Alex.* 27–28), or miracle workers such as Apollonius of Tyana (Philostratus, *Vit. Apoll.* 1.6, "The inhabitants of the country declared that Apollonius was a son of Zeus"). Additional texts in Petr Pokorný, *Der Gottessohn: Literarische Übersicht und Fragestellung* (ThSt 109; Zurich: Theologischer Verlag, 1971), 11–17. These Hellenistic associations of the term are to be kept in mind even if they did not offer the model for the New Testament's Son of God Christology.

believers (cf. Gal. 2:20; Rom. 8:32). In Gal. 4:4 and Rom. 8:3 the sending of the Son is combined with the concept of preexistence (Gal. 4:4, "But when the fullness of time had come, God sent his Son, born of a woman, born under the law"). The continuing significance of the saving event is designated in Gal. 4:6; the presence of the Spirit enables believers to understand themselves as "sons": "And because you are children [υἱοί, 'sons'], God has sent the Spirit of his Son into our hearts, crying, 'Abba! Father!'" God has acted through the Son for the salvation and sonship of all humanity. The small number of occurrences of the Son of God title says little about its actual significance for Pauline theology.[123] The careful location of υἱός within the structure of Paul's arguments shows instead that he attributed great theological importance to this title. The Son title expresses both the close relationship of Jesus Christ with the Father and his function as the one who mediates God's salvation to human beings.

The Text-Pragmatic Function of the Christological Titles

Within the communicative dynamics of a letter, the christological titles designate the reality instituted by God and present in the work of the Spirit, the reality by which both apostle and churches know they are borne and determined. This is the reason they appear in particular density in the letter prescripts; the titles belong to the metacommunicative signals by which communication is established and universes of meaning are defined. The presupposition for a successful epistolary communication is a common understanding of reality between author and addressees. This reality, with its past, present, and future dimensions, is designated by the christological titles, which are reaffirmed and made present as the shared knowledge derived from the common faith.[124]

Obviously, the christological titles are a fundamental element of Pauline Christology and theology. Their intentional and repeated use shows that they are by no means only an element of conventional, tradition-bound communication and thus more like artificial communication but are bearers of basic theological convictions. As anchor points of fundamental theological affirmations, they formulate and actualize the new reality in which church and apostle live. In every Pauline letter except 1 Thessalonians, the *salutatio* reads, "Grace to you and peace, from God, our Father, and the Lord Jesus Christ" (1 Cor. 1:3; 2 Cor. 1:2; Gal. 1:3; Rom. 1:7b; Phil. 1:2; Philem. 3, χάρις ὑμῖν καὶ εἰρήνη ἀπὸ θεοῦ πατρὸς ἡμῶν καὶ κυρίου Ἰησοῦ Χριστοῦ). Thereby the religious dimension for each letter is already explicitly invoked in the prescript; the communication initi-

---

123. Contra Kramer, *Christ, Lord, Son of God*, 189, who claims that the title "Son of God" for Paul was "of relatively minor importance."

124. Udo Schnelle, "Heilsgegenwart: Christologische Hoheitstitel bei Paulus," in *Paulinische Christologie: Exegetische Beiträge: Hans Hübner zum 70. Geburtstag* (ed. Udo Schnelle et al.; Göttingen: Vandenhoeck & Ruprecht, 2000), 178–93.

ated with the prescript occurs within the framework of the reality determined by God and Jesus Christ. God and the present Lord are projected into the text as those who make communication possible; they are constantly implied as the communication partners in the conversation between apostle and church. Thus the christological titles designate the real center of Pauline theology: in Jesus Christ, the Son of God and Lord of the church, salvation is present.

16.5 The Substitutionary Death of Jesus Christ "for Us"

Paul makes use of differing interpretative models in order to portray the salvific meaning of the death of Jesus. The dominant basic model is the concept of substitution,[125] which is concisely expressed in the concept of Jesus' proexistence.[126] Semantically, however, the term "substitution"[127] itself is not unequivocal but points to a whole range of meanings that includes christological, soteriological, and ethical motifs. The concept combines phenomena that may be distinguished but cannot always be separated. In particular, the relation atonement/substitution is a problem in Pauline thought,[128] for Paul's terminology does not correspond precisely to the German word *Sühne* or the English word "atonement."[129] At the same time, "substitution" is associated with such motifs as forgiveness of sins, sacrifice, and suffering for others, which could be among the images of atonement included in the interpretative horizon of the word. So also linguistically, speaking of the death of Jesus "for" (ἀποθνήσκειν ὑπέρ) can be accentuated differently, for the preposition ὑπέρ with the genitive[130] can have the derived meaning "for the benefit of," "in the interest of," "for the sake of," or "in place of, instead of."[131] In order to avoid prejudicing the content, the relevant texts must be analyzed individually, beginning with

125. Cf. Cilliers Breytenbach, "Versöhnung, Stellvertretung, und Sühne," *NTS* 39 (1993): 77–78; Schröter, *Der versöhnte Versöhner*, 316; cf. Thüsing, *Neutestamentlichen Theologien*, 1:93 n. 73.

126. H. Schürmann coined the term *Pro-Existenz*; cf., e.g., Heinz Schürmann, *Gottes Reich—Jesu Geschick: Jesu ureigener Tod im Licht seiner Basileia-Verkündigung* (Freiburg: Herder, 1983), 205ff.

127. On the history of this term, evidently first used by G. F. Seiler in 1778/1779, cf. Bernd Janowski, *Stellvertretung: Alttestamentliche Studien zu einem theologischen Grundbegriff* (SBS 165; Stuttgart: Katholisches Bibelwerk, 1997), 97–129.

128. For the history of research, cf. F. Bieringer, "Traditionsgeschichtlicher Ursprung und theologische Bedeutung der ὑπέρ-Aussagen im Neuen Testament," in *The Four Gospels 1992: Festschrift Frans Neirynck* (ed. Frans van Segbroeck et al.; 3 vols.; Leuven: Leuven University Press, 1992), 1:219–48.

129. Cf. Breytenbach, "Versöhnung, Stellvertretung, und Sühne," 60ff.

130. Paul's statements on substitution are constructed primarily using ὑπέρ with the genitive (cf. 1 Thess. 5:10; 1 Cor. 1:13; 15:3; 2 Cor. 5:14, 15, 21; Gal. 1:4; 2:20; 3:13; Rom. 5:6, 8; 8:32; 14:15); with διά in 1 Cor. 8:11; Rom. 4:25.

131. The original meaning of ὑπέρ was "over" in the local sense; cf. Franz Ludwig Carl Friedrich Passow et al., *Handwörterbuch der griechischen Sprache* (2 vols. in 4; 5th ed.; Leipzig: Vogel, 1841–1857), 2/2:2066–67.

the pre-Pauline tradition. We will therefore presuppose the following under-standing of "substitution: "to do something for others, and thus also doing it in their stead, in order to produce a salvific effect."[132]

In the pre-Pauline tradition of 1 Cor. 15:3b, the substitutionary formula-tion refers to the removal of the sins of the confessing community (Χριστὸς ἀπέθανεν ὑπὲρ τῶν ἁμαρτιῶν ἡμῶν [Christ died for our sins]).[133] Because Christ is named as the specific subject of the event and there is no mention of sacrificial categories, we should not here speak of atonement.[134] Jesus' giving of himself ([διδόναι] ὑπὲρ τῶν ἁμαρτιῶν) in Gal. 1:4 is for the liberation of human beings from the power of the present evil age.[135] The apocalyptic motif again speaks for an interpretation that avoids bringing in the concept of atonement (as found in the Priestly document): Jesus Christ's giving of himself results in liberation from "our" imprisonment within the old aeon, an imprisonment evidenced by our sins.[136] The "handing over" formula in Rom. 4:25 is probably influenced by Isa. 53:12 LXX,[137] without bringing in the atonement theology of the Priestly document:[138] Jesus Christ's substitutionary self-giving removes the negative effects of "our" transgressions, just as his resurrection makes pos-sible "our" justification.

132. On the issue of definition, see also Janowski, *Stellvertretung*, 133, who, in debating with Kant's dictum that individual guilt is not transferable, formulates as follows: "Substitution accord-ingly does not mean to exonerate from his or her responsibility a person who has become guilty—a view that cannot be advocated because thereby the person's own dignity would be destroyed—but to seek out the guilty and failing in the place where they themselves are most deeply involved." Cf. further C. Breytenbach, "Gnädigstimmen und opferkultische Sühne im Urchristentum und seiner Umwelt," in *Opfer: Theologische und kulturelle Kontexte* (ed. Bernd Janowski and Michael Welker; 1st ed.; Frankfurt: Suhrkamp, 2000), 238–39: "Authentic substitution first emerges when one person by his or her voluntary death can save another person—for example, father, dear friend, or commu-nity—from death or destruction." G. Röhser, "Stellvertretung," *TRE* 32:141, suggests the following definition: "Substitution means an appropriate religious 'mediator' doing something for someone or taking someone's fate upon himself or herself, which the one represented could not do, or not do in the same way as the representative, and which directly, that is, without the person's own activities, . . . serves to establish or reestablish an intact relation to God for the one represented or to bring that person into any relation with God at all (by intercession)."

133. For analysis, cf., most recently, Thomas Knöppler, *Sühne im Neuen Testament: Studien zum urchristlichen Verständnis der Heilsbedeutung des Todes Jesu* (Neukirchen-Vluyn: Neukirchener Verlag, 2001), 127–29, who sees Isa. 53:4–5, 12 LXX and 1 Kingdoms 16:18–19 LXX (1 Kgs. 16:18–19) in the background.

134. Differently, Martin Gaukesbrink, *Die Sühnetradition bei Paulus: Rezeption und theologischer Stellenwert* (FB 32; Würzburg: Echter, 1999), 141, according to whom 1 Cor. 15:3b speaks "of Christ's death as a substitutionary atonement."

135. For analysis, cf. Knöppler, *Sühne im Neuen Testament*, 129–31.

136. More nuanced is Breytenbach, "Versöhnung, Stellvertretung, und Sühne," 68, according to whom 1 Cor. 15:3b and Gal. 1:4 "do not express the idea of substitution but that Jesus Christ gave himself, or that Christ died, in order to take away 'our sins.'"

137. So, e.g., Knöppler, *Sühne im Neuen Testament*, 132; differently, Koch, *Schrift als Zeuge*, 237–38.

138. Cf. Breytenbach, "Versöhnung, Stellvertretung, und Sühne," 70.

Coming from the pre-Pauline to the Pauline level, 1 Thess. 5:10 already shows the apostle's fundamental concept: Jesus' death "for" makes possible the new creation and salvation of human beings. Jesus Christ died "for us [ὑπὲρ ἡμῶν], so that whether we are awake or asleep we may live with him." The substitutionary concept can also have ecclesiological dimensions (1 Cor. 1:13, "Was Paul crucified for you?") and ethical aspects (Jesus died for the weak brother or sister; 1 Cor. 8:11, δι' ὃν Χριστὸς ἀπέθανεν [for whose sake Christ died]) without making use of the sin/atonement language and imagery. The substitutionary concept in the strict sense (instead of, in the place of) is found in 2 Cor. 5:14b–15, "we are convinced that one has died for all; therefore all have died. And he died for all, so that those who live might live no longer for themselves, but for him who died and was raised for them." Christ "loved me and gave himself for me [ὑπὲρ ἐμοῦ]" (Gal. 2:20), and so the present reality is this: "He who did not withhold his own Son, but gave him up for all of us, will he not with him also give us everything else?" (Rom. 8:32). In Gal. 3:13 Paul combines the imagery of substitution with that of redeeming someone from slavery: "Christ redeemed us from the curse of the law by becoming a curse for us [ὑπὲρ ἡμῶν]." Those who once were slaves have now become sons and daughters (Gal. 3:26–28; 4:4–6). Christ died in the place of the sinner in that "For our sake [ὑπὲρ ἡμῶν]he [God] made him to be sin who knew no sin, so that in him we might become the righteousness of God" (2 Cor. 5:21).[139] Jesus' death is not some sort of heroic achievement (cf. Rom. 5:7, "Indeed, rarely will anyone die for a righteous person—though perhaps for a good person someone might actually dare to die") but a dying for the godless (Rom. 5:6), "for us," for sinners (Rom. 5:8).[140] God sent his Son—"to deal with sin, he condemned sin [περὶ ἁμαρτίας κατέκρινεν]" (Rom. 8:3)—who entered into the realm where sin held the power in order to overcome it. From the point of view of the history of traditions, the mission Christology (Christ as the sent one) stands in the background (cf. Gal. 4:4–5; 1 John 4:9; John 3:16–17), so that the connotation is probably a general image of atonement, not the specific sacrificial cult of the Old Testament.[141] So also the idea that Christ's death is for our benefit (in the interest of, for the advantage of), in that it sets aside our sins, allows room for introducing the idea of atonement as a heuristic category. "Often it is the case that the two aspects can be separated only with difficulty. The substitutionary death is a dying for the benefit of

139. The ἁμαρτία of 2 Cor. 5:21 is by no means to be understood as a sin offering; cf. Karrer, *Jesus Christus*, 122: "While a sin offering atones for sins that have already happened, here the sinless one takes the place of sin as such and removes this power from its place."

140. In Rom. 5:7 there is clearly present the Hellenistic idea of one person dying to protect another person, the fatherland, or a virtue; cf. the texts in *NW* 1/2:592–97, 715–25; 2/1:117–19.

141. With Breytenbach, "Versöhnung, Stellvertretung, und Sühne," 71–72; contra Peter Stuhl-macher, *Biblische Theologie des Neuen Testaments* (2 vols.; Göttingen: Vandenhoeck & Ruprecht, 1992–1999), 1:291.

those who are spared, and the Christ who dies for the benefit of human beings takes upon himself what should apply to them, so that his atoning death is also a substitutionary death."[142]

We should strictly distinguish from the preceding imagery the tradition-historical background of the "for us" statements, which have nothing to do with the cultic offering of a sacrifice.[143] The idea of cultic atonement by no means forms the tradition-historical background of the Pauline ὑπέρ statements,[144] since it is precisely the characteristic expression of the Septuagint's Leviticus, ἐξιλάσκεσθαι περί (to make atonement for / on behalf of), that Paul does not employ as his term for atonement for sin (cf. Lev. 5:6–10 LXX).[145] Instead it is much more likely that the Greek idea of the substitutionary death of the righteous, whose death effects the expiation / taking away of sin, is the starting point for the formation of this tradition.[146] It is especially this idea that had already deeply influenced Jewish martyr theology, as we find, for example, in 2 Macc. 7:37–38; 4 Macc. 6:27–29; 17:21–22. In pre-Pauline Hellenistic Jewish Christianity,[147] the eucharistic tradition (1 Cor. 11:24b, τοῦτό μού ἐστιν τὸ σῶμα τὸ ὑπὲρ ὑμῶν, lit. "this is my body for you") had also influenced, with a limited adoption of the language of Isa. 53:11–12 LXX,[148] the development of the idea of the death of the righteous as a substitute for all, which breaks the irresolvable connection between sin and death and thereby makes possible a new and authentic life. This idea is particularly concentrated in the formulae of death (cf. 1 Thess. 5:10; 1 Cor. 1:13; 8:11; 15:3b; 2 Cor. 5:14–15; Gal. 2:21; Rom. 5:6–8, 14–15) and self-giving (cf. Gal. 1:4; 2:20; Rom. 4:25; 8:32);[149] Paul adopts it and emphasizes the universal dimensions of the event: the crucified one suffers the violence of death for humanity in order to deliver humanity from the ruinous powers of sin and death.

142. Friedrich, *Verkündigung des Todes Jesu*, 74.

143. Cf. ibid., 75; Barth, *Der Tod Jesu*, 59; cf. also Breytenbach, "Versöhnung, Stellvertretung, und Sühne," 66, who appropriately notes regarding Rom. 3:25, "Before composing this one passage, Paul manages without the language of 'atonement' and 'atone' when he is explaining to his churches the gospel he proclaims."

144. Contra Wilckens, *Römer*, 1:240, according to whom "throughout the New Testament the cultic idea of atonement is the horizon within which the saving significance of Jesus' death is thought through."

145. Cf. Breytenbach, "Versöhnung, Stellvertretung, und Sühne," 69.

146. Evidence is in *NW* 1/2:592–97, 715–25. On the substance of the matter, cf. Martin Hengel, *The Atonement: The Origins of the Doctrine in the New Testament* (Philadelphia: Fortress, 1981), 8–18; Barth, *Der Tod Jesu*, 59–64; H. S. Versnel, "Quid Athenis et Hierosolymis? Bemerkungen über die Herkunft von Aspekten des 'Effective Death,'" in *Die Entstehung der jüdischen Martyrologie* (ed. J. W. van Henten et al.; StPB 38; Leiden: Brill, 1989), 162–96.

147. Cf. Breytenbach, *Versöhnung*, 205–15.

148. Cf. Barth, *Der Tod Jesu*, 56–59.

149. For analysis, cf. Wengst, *Christologische Formeln*, 55–86.

16.6 The Death of Jesus Christ as Atoning Event

The structure of Pauline theology does not include as a part of its load-bearing framework the concept of atonement as understood in its context of temple and sacrifice.[150] Paul takes it up only once, though it is in a central theological passage; in Rom. 3:25–26 he speaks of Jesus Christ, "whom God put forward as a sacrifice of atonement [ἱλαστήριον, 'place or means of atonement'] by his blood, effective through faith. He did this to show his righteousness, because in his divine forbearance he had passed over the sins previously committed; it was to prove at the present time that he himself is righteous and that he justifies the one who has faith in Jesus." Which conceptual horizon provides the background for this pre-Pauline Jewish Christian tradition?[151] At the center of the task of answering this question stands the term ἱλαστήριον,[152] whose traditional origin and theological significance are both disputed. Two explanatory models have become important in recent exegesis:[153]

(1) In terms of tradition history, ἱλαστήριον is derived from the cultic ritual on the great Day of Atonement (cf. Lev. 16; further Ezek. 43). Christ would then be associated with the *kapporet* (mercy seat) of the Day of Atonement, which, as the golden plate on the ark of the covenant, is the place of atonement and (in a nonobjectifying sense) the location of Yahweh's presence. Christ becomes the theological location of eschatological atonement. A polemical accent would then be included, for the place of atonement is transferred from the temple to the cross, and the hiddenness of the *kapporet* and the yearly sacrifice on the Day of Atonement are invalidated. God has set forth Christ openly "as the place where his saving righteousness is made present."[154] There are weighty objections to this model: (a) A personal dimension is integral to the death of Jesus, which involves one who gave his life for other human beings in a way that effects atonement or forgiveness of sins; this is an aspect not straightforwardly derived from Lev. 16. (b) In addition, a typological interpretation of Lev. 16 leads to paradoxical imagery, so that if Christ is identified with the mercy seat, Christ as mercy seat

---

150. Differently, e.g., Gaukesbrink, *Sühnetradition*, 283: "Paul formulates and develops his Christology, which biographically goes back to the Damascus event, theologically in terms of the atonement tradition." Pauline semantics offers no support for this thesis, for the apostle does not use ἱλάσκομαι at all and does not relate the ἱλαστήριον of Rom. 3:25 with the idea of substitution.

151. For evidence of the pre-Pauline character of Rom. 3:25–26, cf. Schnelle, *Gerechtigkeit und Christusgegenwart*, 68–69.

152. On the morphology of ἱλαστήριον, cf. C. Breytenbach, "Sühne," *TBLNT* 2:1685–91, here 1686.

153. For the history of research, cf. Wolfgang Kraus, *Der Tod Jesu als Heiligtumsweihe: Eine Untersuchung zum Umfeld der Sühnevorstellung in Römer 3, 25–26a* (Neukirchen-Vluyn: Neukirchener Verlag, 1991), 1–9.

154. Wilckens, *Römer*, 1:193; cf. also Stuhlmacher, *Biblische Theologie*, 1:193–94; Kraus, *Tod Jesu*, 150–57; Gaukesbrink, *Sühnetradition*, 229–45; Knöppler, *Sühne im Neuen Testament*, 113–17; Breytenbach, "Sühne," *TBLNT* 2:1691.

would be sprinkled and cleansed with his own blood.[155] (c) Finally, the cultural horizon of the Roman church, composed predominantly of Gentile Christians, would certainly have suggested the idea of a heroic death for the people more readily than subtle allusions to the rites of Yom Kippur.[156]

(2) Romans 3:25 is to be understood against the background of 4 Macc. 17:21–22, where atoning power is attributed to the sacrificial death of martyrs.[157] Like the martyrs, Jesus gave his life as a sacrifice for others, and this substitutionary death has atoning potency. This model fits both the personal dimension of the event and the context of the Roman church for appropriating this image. In addition, Paul's own proximity to the martyr tradition supports this view (cf. Acts 22:3; Gal. 1:14; Phil. 3:6), and his lifelong self-understanding corresponds more to the martyr tradition than to cultic categories. But this explanation, too, has its problems: (a) Fourth Maccabees belongs in the first century CE and may not have been written until after 70 CE.[158] (b) The adjective ἱλαστήριος in 4 Macc. 17:22 LXX does not contribute much to the exact understanding of ἱλαστήριον in Rom. 3:25 because ἱλαστήριον is by no means a word whose meaning is determined by its cultic associations, but is semantically a complex term whose meaning is provided only by its context from case to case.[159]

155. Cf., most recently, Haacker, *Der Brief an die Römer*, 91.

156. Cf., e.g., Seneca, *Ep.* 76.27: "If the situation calls for you to die for your country, and the price of saving them is that you give your own life . . ."; cf. also *Ep.* 67.9; Cicero, *Fin.* 22.61; *Tusc.* 1.89; Josephus, *J.W.* 5.419.

157. In addition to 4 Macc. 17:21–22, see esp. 2 Macc. 7:30–38; 4 Macc. 6:27–29. For evidence and argument, cf. Eduard Lohse, *Märtyrer und Gottesknecht: Untersuchungen zur urchristlichen Verkündigung vom Sühntod Jesu Christi* (FRLANT 46; Göttingen: Vandenhoeck & Ruprecht, 1955), 151–52; J. W. van Henten, "The Tradition-Historical Background of Romans 3,25: A Search for Pagan and Jewish Parallels," in *From Jesus to John: Essays on Jesus and New Testament Christology in Honour of Marinus de Jonge* (ed. Martinus C. de Boer; JSNTSup; Sheffield: JSOT Press, 1993), 101–28 (analysis of all relevant texts with this result: "The traditional background of the formula probably consists of ideas concerning martyrdom" [p. 126]); Haacker, *Der Brief an die Römer*, 90–91.

158. Cf. Wolfgang Kraus, "Der Jom Kippur, der Tod Jesu, und die 'Biblische Theologie,'" *JBTh* 6 (1991): 158, who follows H.-J. Klauck in dating 4 Maccabees at the end of the first century CE and thus excludes 4 Macc. 17:21–22 as a possible background for Rom. 3:25. Two counterarguments should be noted, however: (1) The dating of 4 Maccabees at the end of the first century CE is by no means certain; cf., most recently, R. Weber, "Makkabäer-bücher," *NBL* 2:696, who speaks only hesitantly of the documents having been written in the first century CE, while K.-D. Schunck, "Makkabäer/Makkabäerbücher," *TRE* 21:742, completely abandons the attempt to date it more precisely because of inadequate textual data. (2) The study of the history of traditions indicates that the transfer of sacrificial imagery to the concept of the martyr's death is older than 4 Maccabees, as shown by 2 Macc. 7:37–38.

159. Cf. Adolf Deissmann, "Ἱλαστήριος und ἱλαστήριον: Eine lexikalische Studie," *ZNW* 4 (1903): 193–212, specifically emphasizes the complexity of the meanings of ἱλαστήριον and infers from this regarding Rom. 3:25, "The only statement that one may apply to this text from the perspective of linguistics is this: ἱλαστήριον means something that reconciles or makes atonement. Everything else must be decided on the basis of the context itself."

The breadth of the meaning of the word ἱλαστήριον and the problems of deriving its meaning from a unilinear understanding of its tradition history show that it is appropriate to understand ἱλαστήριον in Rom. 3:25 in the broad sense of "means of atonement."[160] It is God who created the possibility of atonement by setting forth Jesus Christ as the means of atonement. Both the tradition and Paul himself emphasize the theocentricity of the event, that the point from which salvation proceeds is the act of God. This reveals continuity with the Old Testament's basic perspectives regarding atonement. It by no means suggests a sadistic image of a deity who demands a sacrifice as satisfaction for the sins of humanity. On the contrary, atonement is the initiative of God himself: "For the life of the flesh is in the blood; and I have given it to you for making atonement for your lives on the altar; for, as life, it is the blood that makes atonement" (Lev. 17:11). God alone is the acting subject in the event of atonement, who provides the sacrifice through which humanity is ritually set free from sin and who breaks the ruinous connection between the sinful act and its consequences.[161] At the same time, the early Christian tradition already breaks through the Old Testament framework, within which sin was understood in multiple ways: whereas in the Old Testament cultus the atoning effect of the sacrifice was restricted to Israel, the Christ event brings universal forgiveness of sins; the sacrificial ritual of the Old Testament required yearly repetition, but Jesus' death on the cross is the eschatological, once-for-all event. What happened on the cross within salvation history is made real for the individual in baptism: forgiveness of previous sins. This is where the tradition attains its soteriological high point, for here it is a matter not only of proclaiming the Christ event but of its soteriological dimension made real in the believer's own experience: the forgiveness of sins that occurs in baptism.[162] The significance of the saving event and its individual appropriation are not seen here as alternatives but in their interrelatedness. The universality of God's saving act in Christ can be believed only when it is experienced in the particularity of one's own existence. The tradition indicates this connection by thinking of God's universal saving act on the cross and God's justifying act together. Paul takes up these fundamental ideas from the tradition and extends them through anthropological universality and ecclesiological specificity. Faith, as a human stance and outlook made possible by God, grants participation in the saving event. This faith, like its content, is universal, not bound to any sort

160. Cf. Lietzmann, *Römer*, 49–50; Schnelle, *Gerechtigkeit und Christusgegenwart*, 70–71; Barth, *Der Tod Jesu*, 38–41.

161. Cf. the foundational work of Bernd Janowski, *Sühne als Heilsgeschehen: Studien zur Sühnetheologie der Priesterschrift und zur Wurzel כפר im Alten Orient und im Alten Testament* (WMANT 55; Neukirchen-Vluyn: Neukirchener, 1982), who shows that atonement is not to be understood in terms of punishment but as the salvation event initiated by God. See also Reinhold Niebuhr, *The Nature and Destiny of Man* (2 vols.; Gifford Lectures; New York: Scribner, 1964), 1:142–43.

162. Schnelle, *Gerechtigkeit und Christusgegenwart*, 71.

of ideological preconditions, and as God's gift, it is still a human decision. In faith the person experiences a new purpose and orientation; in the forgiveness of sins received in baptism, the person is justified. The resulting righteousness, the being-right with God, was already understood in the pre-Pauline tradition not as a *habitus*, a static mode of life, but rather as an assignment to be fulfilled, corresponding to the act of God that had already occurred for the person. The reference to baptism, which Paul strengthens contextually,[163] emphasizes the ecclesiological locus of the righteousness of God. The church [*Gemeinde*] of the baptized is the community [*Gemeinschaft*] of those justified through faith.

Is the atonement model capable of adequately expressing the theological intentions of the tradition and the apostle? In particular, is the image of sacrifice an appropriate way of grasping the saving effect of the death of Jesus? These questions have arisen not only within the modern horizon but above all from the fundamental differences between Old Testament atonement theology and Rom. 3:25–26a.[164] For the atonement ritual, the laying on of hands by the one making the offering and the blood ritual enacted by the priest are constitutive (Lev. 16:21–22). Moreover, a ritual transfer of identity to the animal follows, and it is only through this that the killing of the animal becomes a sacrifice. There is nothing in the crucifixion of Jesus that really corresponds to these fundamental elements of the sacrificial ritual. The cross has God as its exclusive acting subject throughout; God acts on his own initiative at the cross and incorporates humanity into this event without any activity or previous achievement from the human side.[165] Paul never understands the death of Jesus as an appeasement of the wrath of God. It is not necessary for human beings to make contact with the holy; in Jesus Christ, God comes to human beings. *Sacrifice stands for something different; it points to something different from itself that mediates between two parties, whereas at the cross only God himself is involved. In Jesus' death at the cross God is totally present, and therein he is present with human beings.* The Philippians hymn (Phil. 6:2–11) shows that—in the categories of sacrificial offering—we must speak of God's offering himself. But Paul does not speak of the cross in these terms because the cross has abolished the soteriological relevance of every sacrificial cult. The concept of sacrificial offering is thus structurally inappropriate for the Pauline thought world, and it can hardly be an accident that it is only in the tradition found in Rom. 3:25–26 that Paul takes up a text that thinks in the categories of atonement and sacrifice. Here the reason for this reception is not the apostle's interest in this form of thought but a matter of textual pragmatics, for it functions to support the case the apostle is making to the Roman church for his

    163. Cf. Rom. 3:24: δικαιόω, χάρις, ἀπολύτρωσις, ἐν Χριστῷ Ἰησοῦ.
    164. Cf. Ingolf U. Dalferth, "Die soteriologische Relevanz der Kategorie des Opfers," *JBTh* 6 (1991): 173–94.
    165. For critique of the idea of atonement sacrifice, see also Ernst Käsemann, "Die Gegenwart des Gekreuzigten," in *Kirchliche Konflikte* (Göttingen: Vandenhoeck & Ruprecht, 1982), 78–80.

exclusive doctrine of justification. The Jewish Christian baptismal tradition in Rom. 3:25–26a indicates where χωρὶς νόμου δικαιοσύνη θεοῦ (apart from law, the righteousness of God, 3:21) is manifest for individuals, where they can effectively experience it. The universal saving act of God declared in Rom. 3:21–22 needs to become concrete within the horizon of the experience of the individual Christian so that it will not remain a mere abstract thesis but will become lived/experienced reality.

16.7 Jesus Christ as Reconciler

Another model by which the salvation mediated by Christ and its results may be visualized is the image of reconciliation. The noun καταλλαγή (reconciliation, 2 Cor. 5:18, 19; Rom. 5:11; 11:15) and the verb καταλλάσσω (reconcile, 1 Cor. 7:11; 2 Cor. 5:18; Rom. 5:10) are found in the New Testament only in Paul's letters. The derivation of the term "reconciliation" from within the history of the tradition and its exact semantic determination are both disputed points.

According to C. Breytenbach, Paul adopted essential elements of his statements about reconciliation from the language and thought world of Hellenistic diplomacy.[166] In classical Hellenistic texts, both διαλλάσσω and καταλλάσσω signify a reconciling action in political, social, and family contexts, without any religious or cultic component. "The Pauline καταλλάσσω concept and the Old Testament כפר tradition do not have any tradition-historical connection that could form the basis for biblical theological conclusions."[167] In contrast, O. Hofius emphasizes the—in his opinion—firm connections asserted in the Old Testament between "reconciliation" and cultic "atonement," especially as found in Deutero-Isaiah (cf. Isa. 52:6–10; 52:13–53:12).[168] In this view, Paul follows a linguistic usage already present in ancient Judaism. "The Pauline concept of reconciliation is . . . decisively stamped by the message of Deutero-Isaiah."[169]

The textual data speak in favor of a differentiation between καταλλάσσω and ἱλάσκομαι (atone) regarding both their respective histories and their semantic domains, since the two terms derive from different worlds of thought.[170] Whereas καταλλάσσω describes the event of reconciliation on the human plane,

166. Cf. the texts in *NW* 2/1:450–55.

167. Breytenbach, *Versöhnung*, 221; cf. C. Breytenbach, "Versöhnung," *TBLNT* 2:1777–80, here 1777: "it is a matter of reconciliation terminology, not of religious terminology."

168. But notice that καταλλαγή and καταλλάσσω are missing there.

169. Otfried Hofius, "Erwägungen zur Gestalt und Herkunft des paulinischen Versöhnungsgedankens," in *Paulusstudien* (2 vols.; WUNT 51, 143; Tübingen: Mohr Siebeck, 1989–2002), 1:14.

170. Cf. Friedrich, *Verkündigung des Todes Jesu*, 98–99; Breytenbach, "Versöhnung, Stellvertretung, und Sühne," 60ff.; Schröter, *Der versöhnte Versöhner*, 272 n. 2; Grässer, *Der zweite Brief an die Korinther*, 235–36; also Stuhlmacher, *Biblische Theologie*, 1:320, acknowledges a semantic distinction.

ἰλάσκομαι indicates an event in the sacred realm. To be sure, there is a fundamental difference in content between the postulated background in Hellenistic tradition and the Pauline concept of reconciliation: it is God himself who grants reconciliation as the creative acting subject. This is, in every way, more than a mere offer of reconciliation or an appeal for reconciliation.[171]

The point of departure for the affirmations in 2 Cor. 5:18–21 is the new reality of baptized believers as καινὴ κτίσις ἐν Χριστῷ (new creation/existence in Christ, 5:17a). Paul points to God, whose reconciling act has made possible a change in God's relationship to humanity. Paul develops the structure of this new relationship with the concept of reconciliation, which is thought of in strictly theocentric terms (5:18a, τὰ δὲ πάντα ἐκ τοῦ θεοῦ [all this is from God]) and is established christologically (διὰ Χριστοῦ [through Christ]). The overcoming of sin as the power that separates God and humanity requires God's initiative, for only God can put an end to sin (5:19). Within this reconciling event, the Pauline apostolate is given a special role. In 5:20, Paul designates it with the verb πρεσβεύω, which belongs to Hellenistic ambassadorial terminology.[172] Just as the ambassador plays a decisive role in the signing of a treaty of reconciliation, the message and office of the apostle are part of God's own reconciling work.[173] As a called apostle, Paul can proclaim to the world that God has acted in Jesus Christ to reconcile the world to himself (5:19).[174] God himself has thus created the presupposition for Paul's office, not only to announce to the world that reconciliation is possible but to make his appeal in Christ's stead: "be reconciled to God" (5:20b). In 5:21 Paul brings in the soteriological relevance of the Christ event as the basis that makes this surprising entreaty possible. God brings sin and righteousness into a new relationship in that Christ has taken our place: he becomes sin and in him we become God's righteousness. The parallelism of these two clauses speaks in favor of understanding ἁμαρτία as "sin," not in the sense of "sin offering."[175] Because Christ

171. Hofius, "Herkunft des paulinischen Versöhnungsgedankens," 14 n. 14, makes this argument.

172. Cf. Breytenbach, Versöhnung, 65–66. It is a hapax legomenon in the undisputed letters of Paul; otherwise only Eph. 6:20.

173. Particularly informative is Dio Chrysostom, Ad Nicomedienses (Or. 38) 17–18: "Indeed they are said to be, as it were, heralds sent by the gods, and for that reason among ourselves also, while peace is proclaimed by heralds, wars for the most part take place unheralded. Furthermore, men go unarmed into an armed camp as envoys to sue for peace and it is not permitted to wrong any of them, the belief being that all messengers in behalf of friendship are servants of the gods" (NW 2/1:455).

174. The thesis of Schröter, Der versöhnte Versöhner, 305, is overstated when he claims that Paul was concerned "to present his apostolate as a constituent element in the saving event itself and almost to make it equal to the Christ event." Against this is, above all, the general Christian διακονία (ministry) in 2 Cor. 5:18b; with Otfried Hofius, "'Gott hat unter uns aufgerichtet das Wort von der Versöhnung' (2 Kor 5,19)," in Paulusstudien (2 vols.; WUNT 51, 143; Tübingen: Mohr Siebeck, 1989–2002), 1:17 n. 8.

175. Cf. Breytenbach, Versöhnung, 136–41; Schröter, Der versöhnte Versöhner, 314ff.; differently, Stuhlmacher, Biblische Theologie, 1:195; and Wolfgang Kraus, "Der Tod Jesu als Sühnetod bei Paulus," ZNT 3 (1999): 26, who see the background here as atonement theology.

is in no way affected by the realm where sin is dominant, he can represent us in becoming sin, in order thereby to effect our incorporation into the realm where he is Lord.[176] It is not the idea of sin that dominates 5:21 but that of the righteousness of God—manifesting itself in the death of Jesus, sacramentally experienced in baptism. All the stress is placed on the ontological statement of 5:21b, whereby ἐν αὐτῷ (in him in the spatial sense) is decisive for interpreting the verse: in Christ the believer participates in the substitutionary death of Jesus, is separated from sin and separated to the righteousness of God; that is, in Christ the believer receives a new existence whose essential distinguishing characteristic is the righteousness of God.

Whereas Paul does not in 2 Cor. 5 directly connect reconciliation and sin, Rom. 5:1–11 extends the line of argument, already made in Rom. 3:21ff., about God's justifying act through the atoning death of Jesus and places justification, atonement, and reconciliation in relation to each other.[177] Justification by faith is seen in 5:1 as a definitive reality that determines the present life of Christians. It grants the peace of God that becomes reality in the gift of the Spirit (cf. 14:17). As those who have been baptized, believers stand in the grace of God and now have access to God (5:2). This presence of salvation gives the church the power not only to bear the troubles of the present but to attain a living hope stamped by faith and patient endurance. The existence of those who are justified and reconciled is thus simultaneously an existence in θλῖψις (troubles, sufferings) and an existence in hope that is shaped by its view of the eschatological act of God. Believers are not saved from the contradictions of life, the temptations and challenges to one's own existence and to one's faith, the threats of hopelessness and doubt, but the essence of faith reveals itself in the fact that believers can bear up under these threats and come through them. The power to do this comes from the Holy Spirit, received by believers at baptism, the Spirit that thenceforth effectively and powerfully determines the life of Christians (5:5). God's love is revealed in the death of Jesus "for us," which makes possible the justification of the sinner and reconciliation with God (5:6–8). In 5:9 Paul explicitly refers back to 3:25 by using the expression ἐν τῷ αἵματι αὐτοῦ (through his blood). The atoning death of the Son effects both justification and reconciliation (5:9–10). Both justification and reconciliation are thus ways of designating the new relation of human beings to God made possible by destroying the power of sin in the atoning death of Jesus Christ. Through it the godless become those who are justified, and God's enemies become those who are reconciled.

Both 2 Cor. 5 and Rom. 5 show that Christ's death "for us" makes possible the new relationship to God that Paul designates as reconciliation.

---

176. Cf. Umbach, *In Christus getauft*, 222–28.
177. On the connections between Rom. 3:21ff. and 5:1–11, cf. Wolter, *Rechtfertigung*, 11–34.

(1) Reconciliation for Paul is *the act of God alone*.[178] It is not human beings who propitiate God, encourage God to adopt a new attitude to us, or reconcile God to us through any of our own acts;[179] instead the new relationship to God and the resulting new being of those who are baptized, justified, and reconciled are due only to the once-for-all and continually present act of God in Jesus Christ.[180] (2) God's reconciliation with the world is *an act of universal peace* (2 Cor. 5:19; Rom. 11:15). It is limited neither to Israel nor to believers but is intended to apply to all human beings and the whole creation.[181] (3) Reconciliation occurs concretely in the *acceptance* of the message of reconciliation, the gospel. (4) This acceptance *effects a transformation* in the whole person. Those who were previously alienated from God now have access to God and are granted the privilege of life in the power of the Spirit.[182]

16.8 Jesus Christ as God's Righteousness/Justice

In all high cultures and in every effective religion, "Righteousness/Justice" is one of the names of deity. God is no more conceivable apart from righteousness/justice than is any form of culture, philosophy, law, or religion. These fundamental connections determine not only central sections of the Old Testament but also classical Greece and Hellenism.[183]

16.8.1 Cultural and Historical Milieu

Paul's statements about righteousness and justification stand in a complex cultural context.

178. The comment of Breytenbach, "Versöhnung," *TBLNT* 2:1779, is on target: "The acting subject of reconciliation is God (2 Cor. 5:18–19). This is the theologically new element in relation to the minimal 'religious' use in the few passages in Hellenistic Jewish texts, which know the deity only as the object of the reconciling act of human beings."

179. Cf., in this sense, 2 Macc. 1:5; 7:33; 8:29; Josephus, *Ant.* 6.151; 7.153; *J.W.* 5.415.

180. In contrast, the reconciliation of the cosmos must be achieved through the high priest year after year because sin again and again obscures the relation to God (cf. Philo, *Moses* 2.133ff.).

181. Ernst Käsemann, "Erwägungen zum Stichwort Versöhnungslehre im Neuen Testament," in *Zeit und Geschichte: Dankesgabe an Rudolf Bultmann zum 80. Geburtstag* (ed. Erich Dinkler and Hartwig Thyen; Tübingen: Mohr Siebeck, 1964), 47–59, emphasizes this aspect.

182. Cf. Friedrich, *Verkündigung des Todes Jesu*, 116–17.

183. [On righteousness/justification, see translator's note above, p. 72 n. 82.] On the area of Egypt, not dealt with here, cf. Jan Assmann, *Ma'at: Gerechtigkeit und Unsterblichkeit im alten Ägypten* (Munich: Beck, 1990); Klaus Koch, "Sädäq und Ma'at: Konnektive Gerechtigkeit in Israel und Ägypten?" in *Gerechtigkeit: Richten und Retten in der abendländischen Tradition und ihren altorientalischen Ursprüngen* (ed. Jan Assmann et al.; Munich: Fink, 1998), 37–64. Diogenes Laertius 1.11 reports of the Egyptians, "They also laid down laws on the subject of justice, which they ascribe to Hermas."

Old Testament

In the Old Testament, central theological themes cluster around the term צְדָקָה/δικαιοσύνη.[184] The connection between righteousness and right [justice and just] is obvious, for one cannot think of God's righteousness apart from God's acting on behalf of what is right.[185] "The Lord works vindication and justice for all who are oppressed" (Ps. 103:6; cf. 11:7). In the assembly of divine beings, Yahweh holds court, judging the other gods, and demands: "Give justice to the weak and the orphan; maintain the right of the lowly and the destitute" (Ps. 82:3). Among the basic instructions of the Torah is found this: "You shall not render an unjust judgment; you shall not be partial to the poor or defer to the great: with justice you shall judge your neighbor" (Lev. 19:15). The obligation to create justice for his people and to protect them from oppression rests especially on the king (cf. Jer. 22:3; Ps. 72:4; Prov. 31:8–9). Justice serves to preserve the integrity of community life and determines the relation of people to each other and to the society as a whole. Thus God intervenes against everything that obstructs this relationship, acting on behalf of those who suffer injustice, those who are economically oppressed and who suffer social discrimination (cf. Amos 5:7, 10–15; Isa. 1:23; 10:1–2; Jer. 22:13–17; Deut. 10:17–19). It is only consistent with this fundamental perspective that among the top priorities of the Messiah is that of establishing justice (Isa. 11:3b–4a), and the eschatological Prince of Peace will preside over a kingdom of justice and righteousness (Isa. 32:1, 15–17). The practice of righteousness and justice develops powers full of blessings: "Whoever is steadfast in righteousness will live, but whoever pursues evil will die" (Prov. 11:19).

The effective realm of God's justice extends over the righteous life: "Those who have clean hands and pure hearts, who do not lift up their souls to what is false, and do not swear deceitfully . . . will receive blessing from the LORD and vindication from the God of their salvation" (Ps. 24:4–5). The idea of righteousness as the beneficial gift of God is directly connected with universal images, and so justice and righteousness become elements of the divine epiphany. "The Lord is king! Let the earth rejoice; let the many coastlands be glad! Clouds and thick darkness are all around him; righteousness and justice are the foundation of his throne. . . . The heavens proclaim his righteousness; and all the peoples behold his glory" (Ps. 97:1–2, 6). Also God's creative power

---

184. A survey of this theme is given in J. Scharbert, "Gerechtigkeit," *TRE* 12:404–11; Spieckermann, "Rechtfertigung," *TRE* 28:282–86; Hossfeld, "Gedanken zum alttestamentlichen Vorfeld," 13–26; Mark A. Seifrid, "Righteousness Language in the Hebrew Scriptures and Early Judaism," in *Justification and Variegated Nomism* (ed. D. A. Carson et al.; 2 vols.; WUNT 2/140, 181; Grand Rapids: Baker Academic, 2001–2004), 1:415–42. For additional texts and secondary literature, see above, section 3.3 ("The Religious and Cultural Background of Paul's Thought").

185. Cf. Herbert Niehr, *Rechtsprechung in Israel: Untersuchungen zur Geschichte der Gerichtsorganisation im Alten Testament* (SBS 130; Stuttgart: Katholisches Bibelwerk, 1987).

and his continuing intervention for the good of creation are expressions of his righteousness (cf. Ps. 33:4–6; 85:10–14), so that the cosmic order is described as righteousness, which "unites cosmic, political, religious, social, and ethical aspects."[186] Salvation and righteousness/justice become synonymous with the universal acts of God, which include the nations. This idea is found in numerous psalms (cf. Ps. 98:2, "The Lord has made known his victory; he has revealed his vindication [צדקה (righteousness, justice)] in the sight of the nations." This is especially the case in Isa. 40–66. Deutero-Isaiah impressively proclaims to Israel the nearness of the righteousness/justice/vindication of God, who is now fulfilling his promises (Isa. 45:8, "let the earth open, that salvation may spring up, and let it cause righteousness to sprout up also; I the Lord have created it." Cf. also Isa. 46:12–13; 51:5–8). Monotheism and universalism combine to form a view of history in which God's righteousness appears as kingship, gift, claim, power, and salvation. "There is no other god besides me, a righteous God and a Savior; there is no one besides me" (Isa. 45:21–22). The prophet explicitly demands that his message be accepted: "Listen to me, you stubborn of heart, . . . I bring near my deliverance [צדקה], it is not far off, and my salvation will not tarry" (Isa. 46:12–13). In the tradition of the suffering servant, the concept of suffering on behalf of others is combined with statements about righteousness. Despite his shameful end, the prophet is an innocent righteous person who even makes righteous the many who are guilty: "The righteous one, my servant, shall make many righteous, and he shall bear their iniquities" (Isa. 53:11b).[187]

In a later and different historical situation, Trito-Isaiah intensifies Deutero-Isaiah's declarations of salvation and explicitly connects them with the demand for active human righteousness: (cf. Isa. 56:1, "Thus says the Lord: Maintain justice, and do what is right [צדקה], for soon my salvation will come, and my deliverance [צדקה] will be revealed").[188] He confronts Israel with the social situation after the exile (cf. Isa. 58:6–9) and sharply attacks injustice until the time that righteousness again streams forth from Jerusalem: "The nations shall see your vindication [צדקה], and all the kings your glory" (Isa. 62:2).

In addition to these universal tendencies in the Psalms, Paul is also strongly influenced by the themes of sin and righteousness, which the Psalms reflect in a variety of ways. The sinner praises God for the election of Israel, and places

---

186. Hans Heinrich Schmid, *Gerechtigkeit als Weltordnung: Hintergrund und Geschichte der alttestamentlichen Gerechtigkeitsbegriffes* (BHT 40; Tübingen: Mohr [Siebeck], 1968), 166. Among those critical of this conception is Frank Crüsemann, "Jahwes Gerechtigkeit im Alten Testament," *EvT* 36 (1976): 430–31.

187. For the background of Isa. 53 in the tradition and for the history of the interpretation of this text, cf. Bernd Janowski and Peter Stuhlmacher, *Der leidende Gottesknecht: Jesaja 53 und seine Wirkungsgeschichte, mit einer Bibliographie zu Jes 53* (FAT 14; Tübingen: Mohr Siebeck, 1996).

188. Cf. Crüsemann, "Jahwes Gerechtigkeit," 446–49, who sees Trito-Isaiah as having made a decisive innovation in the Old Testament understanding of the concept of righteousness in his tensive correlation of divine and human righteousness.

his hope on the goodness and righteousness of Yahweh (Ps. 65, 85); so also the righteous praise the goodness and righteousness of the Lord, whose actions are characterized by justice: "He loves righteousness and justice; the earth is full of the steadfast love of the LORD" (Ps. 33:5; cf. 51:14; 71:15). In Psalm 130 the sinner prays for mercy; may grace take precedence over justice because only so will the one burdened with guilt be able to live. In Ps. 51 the worshipper turns to God in prayer, asking unconditionally for God's grace and goodness: "Have mercy on me, O God, according to your steadfast love; according to your abundant mercy blot out my transgressions" (Ps. 51:1). It is not by chance that Paul cites Ps. 51:4 and 143:2, in which the insight of one's own lostness is combined with a prayer for justification by God in the judgment.[189] Finally, Gen. 15:6 and Hab. 2:4 are of exceptional importance as key texts for the Pauline doctrine of justification, for here "faith" and "righteousness / being righteous" are found together. Abraham is held up as an example for the Israelites of all time because of his attitude, for against all external appearances he held fast to the faithfulness of God.[190] In the way in which Paul appropriates this text, the coordinates are shifted;[191] under the influence of Gen. 15:6 LXX, Abraham appears as the acting subject who believes, and Yahweh appears as the acting subject who credits something to his account. God responds to Abraham's persistent attitude with a declaration of Abraham's righteousness. So also in Hab. 2:4, faithfulness is an outstanding indication of righteousness. It takes the form of adherence to Yahweh's instruction; that is, righteousness and law are a unity according to the Old Testament understanding. The law is the saving gift of Yahweh, the expression of Israel's unmerited election (Deut. 6:24–25; 7:6ff.), and Israel continues in righteousness by obedient fulfillment of the law.

Ancient Judaism

Ancient Judaism was decisively stamped by the profound transformations following the Babylonian exile. The consciousness of being the elect people of God, the hope in God's continuing faithfulness, the Torah as the saving gift of God, and the associated attempt of the Jewish people to redefine themselves by

189. In the Septuagint, particularly in the translation of the Psalms (cf. Ps. 34:23; 50:6; 72:13; 142:2), the forensic element and thus the concept of justification are strengthened; cf. Spieckermann, "Rechtfertigung," *TRE* 28:284.

190. On the interpretation of Gen. 15:6, cf. (with different emphases) M. Oeming, "Der Glaube Abrahams: Zur Rezeptions-Geschichte von Gen 15,6 in der Zeit des zweiten Tempels," *ZAW* 110 (1988): 16–33; R. Mosis, "'Glauben' und 'Gerechtigkeit': Zu Gen 15,6," in *Die Väter Israels—Beiträge zur Theologie der Patriarchenüberlieferungen im Alten Testament: Festschrift for Josef Scharbert* (ed. Manfred Görg and Augustin Rudolf Müller; Stuttgart: Katholisches Bibelwerk, 1989), 225–57.

191. Spieckermann, "Rechtfertigung," *TRE* 28:283, according to whom "one can hardly speak of justification in this passage, for neither is Abraham made righteous by God nor does Abraham, through his faith reckoned as righteousness, do anything for anyone else."

ritual demarcation from all other peoples became central elements of the Jewish religion.[192] God's binding himself to his people is expressed by the gift of the Torah,[193] which was understood as a gracious gift of God and as the document validating God's covenant (cf., e.g., Sir. 24; *Jub.* 1:16–18). The Torah is far more than rules for life or social order; by observing it, one enters into God's kingdom to acknowledge the rule of God and to enlist in its service. Loyalty to the Torah, as observing and respecting the will of God, is thus the response expected from Israel to God's election. The Torah does not mediate the relation to God; it is, rather, the divinely given guide within the divine order of creation. Within this comprehensive conception of things, righteousness is not the result of human achievement but God's promise to humanity (cf. *Jub.* 22:15, "And may he renew his covenant with you, so that you might be a people for him, belonging to his inheritance forever. And he will be God for you and for your seed in truth and righteousness throughout all the days of the earth" [trans. O. S. Wintermute, *OTP* 2:98]; cf. *1 En.* 39:4–7; 48:1; 58:4). Precisely because God "loves righteousness/justice" (*Let. Aris.* 209) and is a just judge, the religious person can expect righteousness only from God (cf. *2 En.* 42:7, "Happy is he who carries out righteous judgment, not for the sake of payment, but for justice, not expecting anything whatever as a result"). The standard for divine and human righteousness is the law. Moses gave the law "for unblemished investigation and amendment of life for the sake of righteousness" (*Let. Aris.* 144); "all the regulations have been made with righteousness in mind" (*Let. Aris.* 168; cf. 147). Faithfulness to the Torah preserves righteousness and life.[194]

Particularly at Qumran a deepened understanding of sin (cf. 1QH 4:30; 1QS 11:9–10) was combined with an elitist consciousness of election and a radicalized Torah obedience (cf. CD 20:19–21).[195] The community's repentance for ritual and ethical offenses responds to the gracious working of the righteousness of God in the end time through the revelation of his will among those predestined. Nevertheless, those who are faithful to their religious du-

---

192. On the historical process involved, cf. Maier, *Zwischen den Testamenten*, 191–247; on the basic theological presuppositions, cf. Nissen, *Gott und der Nächste*, 99–329; on the understanding of the law and righteousness, cf. Meinrad Limbeck, *Die Ordnung des Heils: Untersuchungen zum Gesetzesverständnis des Frühjudentums* (Düsseldorf: Patmos, 1971), passim; and Holger Sonntag, *ΝΟΜΟΣ ΣΩΤΗΡ: Zur politischen Theologie des Gesetzes bei Paulus und im antiken Kontext* (TANZ 34; Tübingen: Francke, 2000), 109–65.

193. On the theological and social history of the Torah, cf. Frank Crüsemann, *Die Tora: Theologie und Sozialgeschichte des alttestamentlichen Gesetzes* (Munich: Kaiser, 1992); and Nissen, *Gott und der Nächste*, 330ff.

194. Cf. J. Marböck, "Gerechtigkeit und Leben nach dem Sirachbuch," in *Gerechtigkeit und Leben im hellenistischen Zeitalter: Symposium anlässlich des 75. Geburtstags von Otto Kaiser* (ed. Jörg Jeremias; Berlin: de Gruyter, 2001), 21–51.

195. Cf. Otto Betz, "Rechtfertigung in Qumran," in *Rechtfertigung: Festschrift für Ernst Käsemann zum 70. Geburtstag* (ed. Johannes Friedrich et al.; Göttingen: Vandenhoeck & Ruprecht, 1976), 17–36; and Seifrid, *Justification by Faith*, 81–108.

ties still need God's mercy; the righteousness of God is God's faithfulness to his covenant and his people, from which human righteousness springs up in response: "I said in my transgression, I am abandoned by Your covenant. But, when I remembered the power of Your hand together with the abundance of Your mercies, I stood upright and firm and my spirit grew strong to stand against affliction. For [I] rested in Your mercies and the abundance of Your compassion. For You atone for iniquity and purif[y] man from guilt by Your righteousness" (1QH 12:35–37, trans. Wise et al.); "And what shall a man say concerning his sin? And how shall he plead concerning his iniquities? And how shall he reply to righteous judgment? For thine, O God of knowledge, are all righteous deeds" (1QH 1:26–27, trans. Vermès, 192; cf. further 1QH 3:21; 1QS 10:25; 11:11ff.). The confession of guilt points to dependence on God's righteousness and mercy, which God will reveal in the judgment (cf. 1QS 10:1ff.). God's righteousness leads to obedience to the law, but without thereby making it a matter of earning merit before God. Rather, God alone grants the devout assurance of salvation that comes from their belonging to the chosen people.[196]

The *Psalms of Solomon*, a collection of writings originating in Pharisaic circles in Palestine about the middle of the first century BCE, are particularly relevant for evaluating the theological content of the Pauline doctrine of justification.[197] They represent a kind of thinking that revolves around God's election, mercy, and righteousness. The linguistic data already points to their exceptional interest in the theme of righteousness: δίκαιος (righteous) appears thirty-four times and δικαιοσύνη (righteousness) twenty-five times. How do human beings attain righteousness? The *Psalms of Solomon* set forth a complex answer to this fundamental religious question.[198] The basic idea turns out to be the insight that those who trust in God receive righteousness through God's mercy: "Praise God, you who fear the Lord with understanding, for the Lord's mercy is upon those who fear him with judgment. To separate between the righteous and the sinner, to repay sinners forever according to their actions, and to have mercy on the righteous" (*Pss. Sol.* 2:33–34, trans. R. B. Wright, *OTP* 2:654). God is righteous, and God has mercy on those who subject themselves to his righteous judgment (8:7). The plumb line for God's mercy is the law, which provides the

---

196. For a structural comparison between Qumran and Paul, cf. Becker, *Das Heil Gottes*, 238–79.

197. Cf. Joachim Schüpphaus, *Die Psalmen Salomos: Ein Zeugnis Jerusalemer Theologie und Frömmigkeit in der Mitte des vorchristlichen Jahrhunderts* (Leiden: Brill, 1977), 137; S. Holm-Nielsen, ed. and trans., *Die Psalmen Salomos* (JSHRZ 4/2; Gütersloh: Güterloher Verlagshaus, 1977), 59; Winninge, *Sinners and the Righteous*, 12–16; Seifrid, *Justification by Faith*, 109–32; D. Falk, "Psalms and Prayers," in *Justification and Variegated Nomism* (ed. D. A. Carson et al.; 2 vols.; WUNT 2/140, 181; Grand Rapids: Baker Academic, 2001–2004), 1:7–56. J. L. Trafton, "The Psalms of Solomon in Recent Research," *JSP* 12 (1994): 3–19, gives a survey of research.

198. Cf. Udo Schnelle, "Gerechtigkeit in den Psalmen Salomos und bei Paulus," in *Jüdische Schriften in ihrem antik-jüdischen und urchristlichen Kontext* (ed. Hermann Lichtenberger and Gebern S. Oegema; SJSHRZ 1; Gütersloh: Gütersloher Verlagshaus, 2002), 365–75.

criteria for God's righteous judgment and in which his righteousness is revealed. "The Lord is faithful to those who truly love him, to those who endure his discipline, to those who live in the righteousness of his commandments, in the Law, which he has commanded for our life. The Lord's devout shall live by it forever; the Lord's paradise, the trees of life, are his devout ones" (14:1–3). Thus the righteous are those who are willing to live according to the law and to trust in God's mercy. What really makes righteousness possible, however, is that the devout belong to the elect people of God. The mercy of God to the devout and the gift of life that comes through the law are the expression and result of Israel's election (cf. 9:6, 10; 10:4). The basis for the theological thinking of the *Psalms of Solomon* is a contrasting pair: Israel as the righteous and Gentiles or unfaithful Jews as sinners (cf. 13.7–12).[199] The righteousness of the devout is a status concept that fundamentally separates them from the Gentiles. Admittedly, the devout also sin, but God's faithfulness and mercy is by no means abolished by unintentional sins. Instead God cleanses them from their sins and thus brings the repentant sinner to a righteous life oriented to the law (cf. 3:6–8; 9:6, 12; 10:3). Sin does not lead to the destruction of the righteous, for they continue to be sons and daughters of the elect people of God. Whereas sin has the character of an unchangeable status for the Gentiles and apostate Jews, for the devout it is only one aspect of the way God deals with them.[200] Consistent with this, the devout who commit sins are never referred to as "sinners" or "lawless," for through God's provision of atonement and reconciliation the possibility is provided for the righteous to maintain their status even though they sin.

Classical Greece and the Hellenistic World

Classical Greece and the Hellenistic Greek World are also profoundly stamped by reflection on the meaning of righteousness and justice.[201] In the early period of thought on the law, the right, and justice[202] under Draco and Solon (seventh to sixth centuries BCE),[203] the written law was established as the decisive norm

---

199. On the determination of "sinners" and "righteous" in the *Psalms of Solomon*, cf. Winninge, *Sinners and the Righteous*, 125–36.

200. Cf. ibid., 333: "One of the most important results of the present study is that the PssSol convey an inherent distinction between the act 'to sin' (aspect of dynamics) and the status 'sinner' (status aspect). . . . The important thing is that these 'sinfully righteous' Jews are basically righteous, granted that they do not leave the covenantal sphere in outright apostasy. The Gentiles, on the other hand, are sinners by definition."

201. A survey is provided in Albrecht Dihle, "Gerechtigkeit," *RAC* 10:233–360; cf. further Sonntag, *ΝΟΜΟΣ ΣΩΤΗΡ*, 7–108.

202. Cf. Karl-Wilhelm Welwei, *Die griechische Polis: Verfassung und Gesellschaft in archaischer und klassischer Zeit* (2nd, rev. and enl. ed.; Stuttgart: Steiner, 1998).

203. On Solon, cf. Diogenes Laertius 1.45–67; cf. further Pavel Oliva, *Solon, Legende und Wirklichkeit* (Konstanz: Universitätsverlag, 1988).

that surpassed and was meant to determine all other regulations of the polis. In each new case, just/righteous actions for the good of the community are now oriented to adjusting conflicting interests by means of the relevant laws, thus going beyond the principle of retribution and the laws and customs carried over from past times.[204] At the same time, this development makes possible the first beginnings in the direction of equality and democracy. The ideas of righteousness and justice play an important role in the constitutional theories of the fifth century BCE, for the question of monocracy, democracy, or oligarchy was directly related to the distribution and validity of rights (cf. Herodotus, *Hist.* 3.80ff.; Thucydides 4.78). Fundamental insights on the nature of righteousness/justice are found in Plato and Aristotle.[205] Whereas Socrates holds fast to the νόμοι of the polis, although he became their victim (cf. Plato, *Crito* 50a–54d), Plato, affected by the destiny of his teacher, anchored the norms of justice in the unchangeable order of being itself. Thereby the central issue is the relation of law and justice/righteousness, for justice is the norm of the law. In the myth of the origin of culture, justice and law are the presupposition for the participation of all human beings in justice and righteousness.[206] The lawgiver instructed by Zeus will be a person who "will always and above all things in making laws have regard to the greatest virtue; which, according to Theognis, is loyalty in the hour of danger, and may be truly called perfect justice" (Plato, *Leg.* 1.630c; cf. *Phaedr.* 277de; *Epistulae* 7.351c; Aristotle, *Pol.* 1281a). Justice stands in first place among the cardinal virtues,[207] for it has a key role as both a social and a universal category and is thus supremely important for ordering both the individual soul and the state. Aristotle does not distinguish between law and ethics; righteousness/justice as the general ordering principle comprehends both (*Eth. nic.* 5.1130a, "Justice in this sense, then, is not part of virtue but virtue entire").[208] In terms of content, the laws define what is right, for, "since the lawless man was seen to be unjust and the law-abiding man just, evidently all lawful acts are in a sense just acts" (*Eth. nic.* 5.1129b).[209] Because what is

---

204. Cf. Okko Behrends and Wolfgang Sellert, eds., *Nomos und Gesetz: Ursprünge und Wirkungen des griechischen Gesetzesdenkens* (AAWGPH 3/209; Göttingen: Vandenhoeck & Ruprecht, 1995).

205. Cf. Ada Babette Neschke-Hentschke, *Politik und Philosophie bei Plato und Aristoteles: Die Stellung der "Nomoi" im Platonischen Gesamtwerk und die politische Theorie des Aristoteles* (FWBKR 13; Frankfurt: Klostermann, 1971).

206. Cf. Plato, *Prot.* 322c–d, which portrays how Zeus commissioned Hermes to bring justice and law to humanity.

207. Cf. Plato, *Resp.* 4.433.d.e.

208. The distinction between natural law and positive law in Aristotle, *Eth. nic.* 5.1134–1135a, had a great impact on later history: "Of political justice part is natural and part legal: natural, that which everywhere has the same force and does not exist by people's thinking this or that; legal, that which is originally indifferent, but when it has been laid down is not indifferent."

209. Cf. also Plato, *Symposium* 196b–c; *Resp.* 1.338d–339a; *Gorg.* 489a–b; *Politicus* 294d–295a; *Leg.* 10.889e–890a. Cf. further Ps.-Plato, *Definitiones* 414E ("Right: That ordering according to the law that brings about justice"); *Min.* 317d ("Socrates: And therefore our statement was entirely cor-

lawful is identified with what is just, it follows that violation of the law is an offense against justice (cf. *Eth. nic.* 5.1130b). Particularly for Aristotle, it was true that, for human beings, righteousness and justice means living according to a particular norm, that is, conduct regulated by law. The law grants the polis and its members righteousness/justice and life.[210] Justice thus grows from the laws and is their effect, for just actions are oriented to the law and create justice.[211] In Hellenistic philosophy, in a culture that was taking on worldwide dimensions and thus focusing less on the polis and more on the individual, one of the effects was a shift in the understanding of justice itself. In this process, justice/righteousness and piety became in part synonyms without abolishing the connection with the law.[212]

The fundamental continuity between right, justice/righteousness, law, and a successful life also determined ethical thinking at the beginning of the first century CE. For Cicero, this was an unchangeable relationship: "Therefore Law is the distinction between things just and unjust" (*Leg.* 2.13). Righteousness/justice, indeed, is far more than behavior motivated by fear of punishment or expectation of reward. It is *the* virtue and comes from insight into the nature of things. "Thus all things honorable are to be sought for their own sake" (*Leg.* 1.48).

A pessimistic view of culture emerges when this order appears to be dissolving: "And in all probability the disappearance of piety toward the gods will entail the disappearance of loyalty and social union among men as well, and of justice itself, the queen of all the virtues" (Cicero, *Nat. d.* 1.4). At the same time, trust in justice as the power that orders life continues unbroken:

> It follows then, O Apollonius, that rightly judged, it is not the man who abstains from injustice that is just, but the man who himself does what is just, and also influences others not to be unjust; and from such justice as his there will spring up a crop of other virtues, especially those of the law-court and of the legislative chamber. For such a man as he will make a much fairer judge than people who take their oaths upon the dissected parts of victims, and his legislation will be similar to that of Solon and of Lycurgus; for assuredly these great legislators were inspired by justice to undertake their work.

---

rect, that the law is the discovery of what really is"); *Min.* 314D ("Socrates: And something supremely excellent is law and justice? Friend: So it is").

210. Cf. Aristotle, *Pol.* 1271a; 1325a: "The good lawgiver should inquire how states and races of men and communities may participate in a good life, and in the happiness which is attainable by them."

211. Cf. Aristotle, *Eth. nic.* 5.1130b: "For practically the majority of the acts commanded by the law are those which are prescribed from the point of view of virtue taken as a whole; for the law bids us practice every virtue and forbids us to practice any vice."

212. Cf. Dihle, "Gerechtigkeit," *RAC* 10:263–69.

Justice was also a central element of the *pax romana*; Augustus in particular connected his rule with this attribute. In 13 CE the temple of Iustitia Augusta was dedicated, and his imperial autobiography states,

> In my sixth and seventh consulates (28–27 B.C.E.), after putting out the civil war, having obtained all things by universal consent, I handed over the state from my power to the dominion of the senate and the Roman people. And for this merit of mine, by a senate decree, I was called Augustus and the doors of my temple were publicly clothed with laurel and a civic crown was fixed over my door and a gold shield placed in the Julian senate-house, and the inscription of that shield testified to the virtue, mercy, justice, and piety, for which the senate and Roman people gave it to me. After that time, I exceeded all in influence, but I had no greater power than the others who were colleagues with me in each magistracy. (*Res gestae divi Augusti* 34)[213]

It is informative to compare Paul with the reflections of Dio Chrysostom (Dio of Prusa), an intellectual and rhetorician who is representative of the intellectual elite of the period only a little later than Paul. For Dio, the ideal king receives his rulership from Zeus and, "keeping his eyes upon Zeus, orders and governs his people with justice and equity in accordance with the laws and ordinances of Zeus" (*1 Regn.* 45; cf. *De lege* 1). The law grants not only to both the society and the individual the justice and protection to which they are entitled; it is also true that "such is the righteousness and benevolence which pervades the law, that for the unfortunate it has proved even more helpful than blood relatives" (*De lege* 6). The divine unity of law and justice includes person and institution; as the ordering principle, justice always has an importance that is both an individual-moral and a universal principle.[214] These connections make it possible for Hellenistic Jewish thinkers such as Philo of Alexandria and Josephus to form a synthesis that combines Greek thinking about law and justice/righteousness with Jewish traditions. Philo combines the Greek doctrine of virtue with the Decalogue: "For each of the ten pronouncements separately and all in common incite and exhort us to wisdom and justice and godliness and the rest of the company of virtues" (*Spec. Laws* 4.134). Philo can reduce the innumerable individual Jewish laws to two basic principles: "one of duty to God as shown by piety and holiness, one of duty to men as shown by humanity and justice" (*Spec. Laws* 2.63; cf. 2.13–14). The Torah is subject to a strong ethical impulse that corresponds to the Greek and Hellenistic concentration on the concept of justice/righteousness but without giving up its universal aspect.[215]

---

213. Cf. Ovid, *Ex Ponto* 3.6: "And no god is milder than our Prince, for Justice tempers his strength. Her Caesar but recently installed in a marble temple; long ago he enshrined her in his heart."

214. Cf. Iamblichus, *Prot.* 6.1: "For all these compelling reasons, law and justice rule over humanity, and that will never change, for it is anchored in nature itself."

215. Cf. Reinhard Weber, *Das "Gesetz" bei Philon von Alexandrien und Flavius Josephus: Studien zum Verständnis und zur Funktion der Thora bei den beiden Hauptzeugen des hellenistischen Judentums*

16.8.2 The Genesis of the Pauline Doctrine of Justification

All relevant religious, philosophical, and political symbols and symbolic stories of antiquity are stamped with the comprehensive connection of law-justice-life. Paul did not want to break out of this foundational model of plausibility—and could not have done so if had wanted to—for the theme of righteousness/justification was a given in his cultural situation. At the same time, he had to make new classifications and combinations, for his Christ hermeneutic demanded that the three key concepts, law-righteousness-life, be brought together in a new system of coordinates.

How did Paul develop the theme righteousness/justification? Do the letters allow us to recognize a general and consistent doctrine of justification, or must we introduce terminological and conceptual differentiations into their content in order to do them justice?[216]

The linguistic data provides a first pointer in responding to this question:

	NT	Paul	1 Thess.	1 Cor.	2 Cor.	Gal.	Rom.	Phil.	Philem.
δικαιοσύνη	91	49	—	1	6[217]	4	34	4	—
δικαιόω	39	25	—	2	—	8	15	—	—
δικαίωμα	10	5	—	—	—	—	5	—	—
δικαίωσις	2	2	—	—	—	—	2	—	—
δίκαιος	79	10	—	—	—	1	7	2	—
δικαίως	5	2	1	1	—	—	—	—	—
νόμος	195	118	—	9	—	32	74	3	—

(ARGU 11; Frankfurt: Lang, 2001), 338: "Religion is a manner of orientation to *nomos*. Religion is accordingly always practical, but it is the practice of *pietas*, whereby piety is not something purely spiritual, nor merely cultic, but a way of life, a pattern of everyday existence, above all an ethical way of coming to terms with the world, in which something cosmic is manifest."

216. The conceptuality and terminology varies; thus, e.g., Hans Hübner, "Die paulinische Rechtferti-gungstheologie als ökumenisch-hermeneutisches Problem," in *Worum geht es in der Rechtfertigungslehre? Das biblische Fundament der "Gemeinsamen Erklärung" von katholischer Kirche und Lutherischem Weltbund* (ed. Thomas Söding and Frank-Lothar Hossfeld; QD 180; Freiburg: Herder, 1999), 86, distinguishes strictly between justification *theology* and the *doctrine* of justification "because, in the strict sense of the word, there is no doctrine of justification in Paul." Hahn, "Entwicklung," 344, 353, and passim, differentiates between the justification thematic already present in the tradition that came to Paul and the doctrine of justification; cf. further p. 346, statements about justification; 353, the understanding of justification; 359, the mes-sage of justification. Cf. further the terminological reflections in Dieter Lührmann, "Gerechtigkeit," *TRE* 12:414–15; Kertelge, *Rechtfertigung bei Paulus*, 286–87. I distinguish (1) between the righteousness and justification *thematic* already present in the culture and the tradition; (2) in terms of Paul's own linguistic usage, between *righteousness* (δικαιοσύνη, δίκαιος) and *justification* (δικαίωσις, δικαιόω); (3) between justi-fication *theology* in isolated statements and a *doctrine* of justification, when there is a self-contained thought complex. Because all aspects belong together and the terms "justification" and "doctrine of justification" are artificially coined theological terms, a precise distinction is often not possible.

217. Δικαιοσύνη in 2 Cor. 6:14 is not counted, since in my opinion it is part of a post-Pauline text fragment; see above, section 10.2 ("The Unity of 2 Corinthians").

It is evident that Paul speaks extensively about righteousness/justification only where he is at the same time engaged in intensive reflection on the significance of the law. How can the concentration of this thematic in the letters to the Galatians and Romans be explained? A first answer would seem to be that in each case the historical situation calls for increased engagement with this complex of problems.[218] Can we infer from this that Paul merely took up a program he had already thought out and made it available to each church situation? The analysis of the textual data above speaks against this, for it reveals two important points: (1) Paul does not generally connect the theme righteousness/justification with the question of the law as he does in Galatians and Romans. It may therefore not be reduced to the structure of the argument he follows in each of these two letters. (2) The statements about justification and the law in Galatians and Romans are not consistent with themselves or with each other; such contradictions[219] are a clear pointer that *this* variation of the theme is new and has been conditioned by its own situation.

A Diachronic Model

Righteousness/justification in Paul is obviously a complex phenomenon that calls for an explanatory model on the diachronic plane.[220]

Within Pauline theology, righteousness is primarily bound to the baptismal traditions (1 Cor. 1:30; 6:11; 2 Cor. 1:21–22; Rom. 3:25–26a; 6:3–4; 4:25).[221] The ritual anchoring of the righteousness thematic is no accident,[222] for baptism is the place where the fundamental change of status for the

218. See above, sections 11.3 ("The Doctrine of the Law and of Justification in Galatians") and 12.5 ("The Righteousness of God")

219. See above, section 11:3 (The Doctrine of the Law and of Justification in Galatians") and 12.8 ("Sin, Law, and Freedom in the Spirit").

220. Cf. Schnelle, *Gerechtigkeit und Christusgegenwart*, passim; Thomas Söding, "Kriterium der Wahrheit? Zum theologischen Stellenwert der paulinischen Rechtfertigungslehre," in *Worum geht es in der Rechtfertigungslehre? Das biblische Fundament der "Gemeinsamen Erklärung" von katholischer Kirche und Lutherischem Weltbund* (ed. Thomas Söding and Frank-Lothar Hossfeld; QD 180; Freiburg: Herder, 1999), 211–13.

221. Cf. Gerhard Delling, *Die Taufe im Neuen Testament* (Berlin: Evangelische Verlagsanstalt, 1963), 132; Kertelge, *Rechtfertigung bei Paulus*, 228–49; Eduard Lohse, "Taufe und Rechtfertigung bei Paulus," in *Die Einheit des Neuen Testaments* (Göttingen: Vandenhoeck & Ruprecht, 1973), 228–44; Ferdinand Hahn, "Taufe und Rechtfertigung," in *Rechtfertigung: Festschrift für Ernst Käsemann zum 70. Geburtstag* (ed. Johannes Friedrich et al.; Göttingen: Vandenhoeck & Ruprecht, 1976), 104–17; Ulrich Luz, "Gerechtigkeit," *EKL* 2:91: "The presupposition for the Pauline doctrine of justification was that the early Christian congregations understood baptism as an anticipation of God's final judgment and thus as a real making-righteous (1 Cor. 6:11). . . . The Pauline doctrine of justification is thus no innovation but is rooted in the church's interpretation of baptism."

222. Cf. Strecker, *Die liminale Theologie des Paulus*, 210.

Christian occurs, the place where one is transferred from the realm of sin
into the realm of righteousness. The baptismal tradition not only deals with
the theme of righteousness but develops a self-consistent sacramental-onto-
logical doctrine of justification: in baptism, as the place of participation in
the Christ event, the Spirit effectively separates believers from the power of
sin and grants them the status of righteousness so that, looking forward to
the parousia of Jesus Christ, they can live a life corresponding to the will
of God. This doctrine of justification can be described as inclusive because,
without any criteria of exclusion, it aims at making the individual righteous
and incorporating him or her into the church. Faith, the gift of the Spirit,
and baptism constitute one holistic event: in baptism the believer enters the
realm of the spiritual Christ, personal communion with Christ is established,
and redemption has really begun, which then continues in righteousness in
a life determined by the Spirit.[223] This form of the doctrine of justification
in the context of baptism is organically connected with the constitutive
foundational views of Pauline Christology: transformation and participation.
Through his resurrection from the dead, Jesus Christ has entered the realm
of God's life and power, and in baptism he grants to believers, through the
gift of the Spirit, participation in the new being already in the here and now.
Baptized believers live as those who have been delivered from the power of
sin in Christ's realm of salvation,[224] where the Spirit holds sway, and their
new being ἐν Χριστῷ is comprehensively determined by the life-giving powers of the risen one. As a ritual of status transformation, baptism brings into
being not only a new perception of reality; those who are baptized are truly
changed, as is reality itself.[225]

Within this conception, the law/Torah has neither a negative nor a positive
function; it is not a constituent element of the basic structure of the inclusive
doctrine of justification. In contrast, it is nomology (a doctrine of the law) that
determines the argumentation of the letters to the Galatians, the Romans, and

223. Cf. Schnelle, *Gerechtigkeit und Christusgegenwart*, 100–103; Umbach, *In Christus getauft*, 230–32.

224. Hübner, "Rechtfertigungstheologie," 93, goes further: "As soon as one thematizes the being of the justified in his or her historicality and existence in space and time, including his or her self-understanding, that is, as soon as one interprets in *this* existential sense, in Paul's theological under-standing, the distinction collapses between the pronouncement of the individual's justification and making the individual to be righteous."

225. Cf., from the theological perspective, Söding, "Kriterium der Wahrheit," 205; from the cultural anthropological perspective, cf. Geertz, "Thick Description," 122: "Having ritually 'lept' . . . into the framework of meaning which religious conceptions define, and the ritual ended, returned again to the common-sense world, a man is—unless, as sometimes happens, the experience fails to register—changed. And as he is changed, so also is the common-sense world, for it is now seen as but the partial form of a wider reality which corrects and completes it."

the Philippians.[226] This shift results from the current situation in each of the churches, not from a deficiency in the inner logic of the inclusive doctrine of justification. The demand of the Galatian Judaists that Gentile Christians also be circumcised not only represented a breaking of the agreements made at the apostolic council, and placed in question the success of the Pauline mission, but was directed against *the* fundamental principle of all Pauline theology: the locus of life and righteousness is Jesus Christ alone. If the law/Torah could give life (so, e.g., Sir. 17:11 LXX, προσέθηκεν αὐτοῖς ἐπιστήμην καὶ νόμον ζωῆς ἐκληροδότησεν αὐτοῖς [He bestowed knowledge upon them, and allotted to them the law of life]); cf. also Sir. 45:5), then Christ would have died in vain. For Paul, there can be only one form of the end time that is relevant for salvation: Jesus Christ. When the law is no longer regarded as an adiaphoron, as had been the case previously (as, e.g., in 1 Cor. 9:20–22), but receives a status that matters for salvation, then the issue of whether the law is in fact able to provide salvation must be moved to the center of the argument. Paul decides this in the negative, for "the scripture has imprisoned all things under the power of sin, so that what was promised through faith in Jesus Christ might be given to those who believe" (Gal. 3:22; cf. Rom. 3:9, 20). It corresponds to the will of God that the power of sin is stronger than the ability of the law/Torah to deliver from it. The law/Torah may no longer be thought of as the foundation of the special position of Israel in the history of election, and so the hamartiological differentiation between Jews and Gentiles is also invalidated "because no one will be justified by the works of the law" (Gal. 2:16; cf. Rom. 3:21, 28).

Universalizing

In Galatians, Romans, and Philippians, Paul extends the basic views of the inclusive doctrine of justification connected with baptism to an exclusive doctrine of justification characterized by universalism and antinomism (a polemic against the law).[227] On the sociological plane, it was directed at establishing the equality of Gentile Christians; in response to the Judaistic challenge, it guaranteed Gentile Christians, as baptized believers, unqualified membership in the elect people of God.[228] Theologically, the exclusive doctrine

226. Differently, Hahn, "Taufe und Rechtfertigung," 121, who sees the main difference between Paul and his tradition to be their respective understandings not of the law but of faith.

227. Cf. Söding, "Kriterium der Wahrheit," 203: "It is doubtful that the apostle advocated the theology of justification from the very beginning in the form found in Galatians and Romans." Cf. further Luz, "Gerechtigkeit," *EKL* 2:91. A mediating position is adopted by Kertelge, *Rechtfertigung bei Paulus*, 297: "We can already see from the sequence of the Pauline letters from 1 Thessalonians to Romans that the statements about justification become increasingly stronger in their linguistic explicitness and their conceptual clarity."

228. Cf. Dieter Zeller, *Charis bei Philon und Paulus* (SBS 142; Stuttgart: Katholisches Bibelwerk, 1990), 154–55.

of justification not only negated every sociological function of the law/Torah and summarized its ethical relevance in the love command;[229] it also removed every particularistic or national element from the consciousness of election and formulated a universal image of God: entirely apart from considerations of race, sex, and nationality, God gives to every human being through faith in Jesus Christ his sin-conquering righteousness. Thus the stance expressed in Gal. 2:19; 3:26–28; Rom. 3:25; 4:25; 6:3–4 shows that Paul intentionally plays off the inclusive and exclusive doctrines of justification against each other. He thus guards his exclusive doctrine of justification, based on a radicalized anthropology and a universalized understanding of God, from becoming an otherworldly abstraction by declaring baptism to be the place where God's universal saving act in Jesus Christ can be experienced in the particularity of one's own existence. Making-righteous and declaring-righteous thus collapse into two aspects of one event.[230]

An indirect confirmation of the interpretation presented above is provided in the history of effects of the exclusive doctrine of justification of Galatians and Romans, as these were interpreted in the later church. The receding of this doctrine in the deutero-Pauline letters need not be seen as caused primarily by the giving up of apocalyptic ideas and the increasing importance of problems of ethics and church structure;[231] it is also due to the polemical sharpening of Pauline theology related to the particular situation. Because the exclusive doctrine of justification of Galatians and Romans is not the center of Pauline theology as a whole, the authors of the deutero-Paulines did not adopt it in this form. On the other hand, the deutero-Paulines manifest a remarkable continuity with Paul, for they generally deal with the theme of justification in connection with baptismal texts (cf. Col. 2:12–13; Eph. 2:5, 8–10; Titus 3:3–7; 2 Tim. 1:9–11).[232]

16.8.3 The Theological Content of the Doctrine of Justification

If one keeps the Pauline statements on righteousness and justification *as a whole* in mind, then one sees a way of thinking that, with all its historical and theological distinctions, still has a systematic quality. The point of departure for such a line of thought is the insight, revolutionary in the ancient world, that righteousness is not essentially a matter of doing but a matter of *being*.

In the realm of Greek culture, actions defined righteousness/justice; Aristotle formulated the issue in exemplary fashion: "It is well said, then, that it is by doing just acts that the just man is produced, and by doing temperate acts the

---

229. See below, section 19.3 ("The Law").

230. Cf. Kertelge, *Rechtfertigung bei Paulus*, 295.

231. Luz, "Rechtfertigung bei den Paulusschülern," 380–81, presents this as the primary reason.

232. Cf. ibid., 369ff.

temperate man; without doing these no one would have even a prospect of becoming good."[233] Righteousness/justice appears as the highest human virtue, which is attained by one's actions. In ancient Judaism there was undoubtedly the basic conviction that sinful human beings are dependent on the mercy and goodness of God. The covenant idea, as the central form of expression of Israel's relation to God, is based on God's prior election of Israel. Nevertheless, the question of salvation continued to be connected to human actions inasmuch as God was expected as the righteous judge, the one who is merciful to the righteous and punishes the lawless and lawbreakers. Even in the theological conceptions of the *Psalms of Solomon*[234] and the Qumran writings,[235] God's mercy, as the ultimate ground of one's relation to God, does not exclude a positive function for works, for they *also* are the basis of righteousness/justification. In these writings, righteousness is thus *equally* a matter of doing and a matter of being. A further fundamental difference from Paul is that belonging to the realm of righteousness is determined differently. In the *Psalms of Solomon*, righteousness is a status concept, and righteousness is the result of belonging to the elect people of God.[236] Likewise at Qumran, participation in the righteousness of God finally is based on belonging to the elect people of God and the community that represents it.[237]

Paul knows the fundamental difference between Israel as the righteous and the Gentiles as sinners (cf. Rom. 9:30) but does not make it the foundation of his system of thought. Instead he completely redefines the relation between righteous and sinners: *no one* belongs to the group of the righteous, and *everyone,* Gentiles and Jews, belong to the group of sinners (cf. Rom. 1:16–3:20). But by faith in Jesus Christ, both Jews and Gentiles can attain righteousness. The Pauline status-schema is marked by a universal beginning point: all human beings are hopelessly subject to the power of sin (cf. Gal. 3:22; Rom. 3:9–10); that is, all human beings have the status of sinners even if they belong to a privileged group and practice justice. Righteousness can come only through the transfer from the realm where sin rules into the realm of Christ. In Jewish thought, deep insight into the power of sin, the

---

233. Aristotle, *Eth. nic.* 2.1105b.

234. Jens Schröter, "Gerechtigkeit und Barmherzigkeit: Das Gottesbild der Psalmen Salomos in seinem Verhältnis zu Qumran und Paulus," *NTS* 44 (1998): 576, underestimates this foundational function of works when he states, "The difference between Paul and the *Psalms of Solomon* can thus hardly be understood on the basis of their different evaluations of the relation between God's mercy and human works. For the *Psalms of Solomon*, too, the 'works' of the δίκαιοι are not the basis for one's relation to God, although, of course, there is still a connection between them."

235. The comment of Betz, "Rechtfertigung in Qumran," 36, is on target: "There is no justification of the sinner *contra legem* at Qumran, but there is also no justification through one's own works of the law."

236. See above, section 16.8.1 ("Cultural and Historical Milieu").

237. Cf. 1QS 4:22, which says of the devout members of the Qumran community, "For God has chosen them for an everlasting covenant"; cf. further 1QS 11:7; 1QSb 1:1–2.

consciousness of dependence on God's mercy, belonging to the elect people of God, and observance of the Torah all together necessarily form a unity in which each of these elements supplements the other. Righteousness is radically understood as coming from God, but at the same time, religious privileges in contrast to other peoples remain in place. In contrast, Paul negates every special religious status, for his Christ hermeneutic allows no distinctions at all regarding either sin or righteousness. The universality of the liberating act of God corresponds to the previous universality of bondage to sin. There can no longer be any ethnic or national prerogatives; righteousness is no longer grounded in belonging to a particular people and the privileges connected therewith but only in the act of faith. For Paul, righteousness is the result of the new life constituted by Christ in baptism. God grants participation in his life-giving power in that he annihilates sin by the gift of the Spirit and establishes the existence of baptized believers anew.

The basic thesis of Paul's doctrine of justification thus rests on *a theocentric and christological concentration, a deepening of hamartiology, and a universalizing of anthropology*: God himself has constituted Jesus Christ as *the* place of his righteousness for all human beings; only by faith in Jesus Christ do Jews and Gentiles attain an equal freedom from the powers of sin and death.[238] The revelation of Jesus Christ has fundamentally changed the situation of all human beings before God, since from God's side it has revealed God's universal saving will and from the human side it has revealed both the need for, and the possibility of, salvation for all human beings. For Paul the Christian, the situation of human beings before God is placed in a completely new light: the question of salvation has been answered once and for all through the death and resurrection of Jesus Christ. Human beings are justified by faith in Jesus Christ and have peace with God (Rom. 5:1). Thereby all past, present, and future efforts of human beings to obtain salvation from other sources or to realize it on their own have lost all significance. The Christ event likewise brings into being both the fundamental turning point in time and the new existence of human beings. Since Paul interprets the righteousness of God as a gift[239] but not as a rule or demand, he separates the question of salvation from human activity. Truth does not come to human beings from their own actions but is the gift of God.[240]

---

238. Cf. Thomas Söding, "Der Skopus der paulinischen Rechtfertigungslehre," *ZTK* 97 (2000): 404–33, who distinguishes within the doctrine of justification a christological point ("communion with the crucified Christ"), a theological point ("the magnitude of God's grace"), a missiological-ecclesiological point ("the salvation of Jews and Gentiles"), and an anthropological motif ("comfort for sinners—encouragement toward freedom").

239. Lietzmann, *Römer*, 95.

240. Appropriately, Hans Weder, "Gesetz und Sünde: Gedanken zu einem qualitativen Sprung im Denken des Paulus," in *Einblicke ins Evangelium—exegetische Beiträge zur neutestamentlichen Hermeneutik: Gesammelte Aufsätze aus den Jahren 1980–1991* (Göttingen: Vandenhoeck & Ruprecht, 1992), 344: "The question is whether my truth is something that is to be listened to, perceived, heard, and believed or something that I construct for myself."

Human beings no longer live out of their own resources; they owe their new life to the death of Jesus Christ, an event of great importance for both the relation of God to the world and for human self-understanding. God alone is the one who changes the human situation through his saving act in Jesus Christ, so that human beings now find access to God through faith.

Historically, the exclusive doctrine of justification found in Galatians represents a new response to a new situation. To this extent the statement of W. Wrede about the Pauline doctrine of justification holds true: "It is the polemical doctrine of Paul, is only made intelligible by the struggle of his life, his controversy with Judaism and Jewish Christianity, and is only intended for this. So far, indeed, it is of high historical importance, and characteristic of the man."[241] So also the famous dictum of Albert Schweitzer sees the matter rightly: "The doctrine of righteousness by faith is therefore a subsidiary crater, which was formed within the rim of the main crater—the mystical doctrine of redemption through the being-in-Christ."[242] Both Wrede and Schweitzer, however, unjustly relate these appropriate observations on the origin of the exclusive Pauline doctrine of justification to evaluations of its importance. Although it did indeed originate in the disputes with Judaism and Jewish Christianity, its theological capacity cannot be restricted to this dispute.

Within the Pauline symbolic universe, the doctrine of justification formulates fundamental insights that maintain their validity to this very day.[243] Its point of departure is the insight into the gift character of all being. Through faith in Jesus Christ, God grants participation in the new being. Human beings thus stand before God as undeserving recipients of a gift, as persons who are no longer compelled to find their own way in this world back to God and salvation. Rather, as those justified by faith and having their origin in God, they can do God's will in the world. With Paul, justification always designates the "prior" reality of God's own act. God has already acted in Jesus Christ, before human beings have done anything. Paul strictly separates and distinguishes this prior act of God from human deeds, which always follow.[244] It is only this previous act of God that creates salvation and meaning for human beings. Humans are thus relieved of the impossible task of

---

241. Wrede, *Paul*, 123.

242. Schweitzer, *Mysticism*, 225. Cf. also p. 383: "Justification by faith (which itself is only a fragment of the doctrine of redemption, owing its prominence to the controversy about the Law, not Paul's real doctrine of redemption)."

243. See below, chapter 23 ("Epilogue: Pauline Thought as Enduring Meaning Formation").

244. Thus theology or Christology is to be considered the constant, and anthropology is the variable; contra Herbert Braun, "The Meaning of New Testament Christology," *JTC* 5 (1967): 115, who affirms that "for Paul anthropology is the constant. . . . Christology, on the other hand, is the variable." Bultmann, "Primitive Christian Kerygma," 36, agrees with this thesis: "The constant is the self-understanding of the believer; the Christology is the variable." For justifiable criticism of this conception, cf. Ulrich Wilckens, "Christologie und Anthropologie im Zusammenhang der paulinischen Rechtfertigungslehre," *ZNW* 67 (1976): 67ff.

having to create meaning and salvation for themselves. Human life receives a new reference point, and humans are freed for the tasks that they can in fact accomplish. Also, before God, the human being is not the sum of his or her acts; people are distinguishable from their works. It is not the deed that defines what it means to be a human being but only one's relation to God. Righteousness/justification, like life itself, can be received only and exclusively by faith in Jesus Christ.

The doctrine of justification is related to fundamental ecclesiological, ethical, and anthropological insights, but above all and originally, it is a soteriological model with a core consisting of the theoretical understanding of one's own selfhood: the subject knows itself to be grounded directly on God's prior act; it is constituted by its reference to God and understands itself as embraced and maintained by God.

16.9 God, Jesus of Nazareth, and Early Christology

How could Paul and the churches hold fast to Jewish monotheism and at the same time regard the resurrected Jesus of Nazareth as the central figure of the end time? Pauline theology is in continuity with the basic affirmation of Jewish faith: God is one, the Lord, the Creator who made the world and continually maintains it in being. Traditions within ancient Judaism made it possible for Paul to hold together monotheism and Christology.[245] As noted above, there is only one God, according to Jewish thought, but God is not alone. Numerous heavenly mediating figures,[246] such as Wisdom (cf. Prov. 2:1-6; 8:22-31; Wis. 6:12-11:1),[247] the Logos,[248] or the name of God, are

245. Cf. Hengel, *Son of God*, 66-83; Larry W. Hurtado, *One God, One Lord: Early Christian Devotion and Ancient Jewish Monotheism* (Philadelphia: Fortress, 1988), 17-92; cf. further Carey C. Newman et al., *The Jewish Roots of Christological Monotheism: Papers from the St. Andrews Conference on the Historical Origins of the Worship of Jesus* (JSJSup 63; Leiden: Brill, 1999).

246. Cf. the survey in Schrage, *Unterwegs zur Einzigkeit*, 91-132.

247. Cf. here esp. Wis. 9:9-11: "With you is wisdom, she who knows your works and was present when you made the world; she understands what is pleasing in your sight and what is right according to your commandments. Send her forth from the holy heavens, and from the throne of your glory send her, that she may labor at my side, and that I may learn what is pleasing to you. For she knows and understands all things, and she will guide me wisely in my actions and guard me with her glory."

248. Cf., e.g., Philo, *Confusion* 146-147: "But if there be any as yet unfit to be called a Son of God, let him press to take his place under God's First-born, the Word, who holds the eldership among the angels, their ruler as it were. And many names are his, for he is called 'the Beginning,' and the Name of God, and his Word, and the Man after His image, and 'he that sees,' that is Israel." Philo is the Jewish author who has reflected most intensively on the divine powers, while at the same time explicitly emphasizing the oneness of God: "Now we must first lay down that no existing thing is of equal honor to God and that there is only one sovereign and ruler and king, who alone may direct and dispose of all things. For the lines, 'It is not well that many lords should rule; Be there but one,

at home in immediate proximity to God. Biblical patriarchs, such as Enoch (cf. Gen. 5:18–24)[249] or Moses, and the archangel Michael[250] surround God and now work at God's command. They testify to God's interest in the world and God's relation to it and show that God's power is everywhere present and that everything is under God's control. As participants in the heavenly world, they are subordinate to God and in no way endanger faith in the one God. As created and subordinate powers, they do not compete with God; as divine attributes, they describe, in the language of human hierarchy, God's activities for the world and in the world. At the same time, however, weighty differences are clear:[251] (1) The personified divine attributes were not persons on a par with God, with their independent spheres of activity. (2) They were not the objects of cultic worship. (3) Within the multiplicity of Jewish ideas, it was inconceivable that of all people, someone who had died a shameful death would be reverenced as divine.

Genuine Greek-Hellenistic ideas must also have influenced the origins of early Christology and facilitated its reception.[252] The idea that gods can become human and that human beings can become divine is a Hellenistic idea, not a Jewish one.[253] The mark of Greek religion is precisely an anthro-

---

one king' [Iliad, 2:204–205] could be said with more justice of the world and of God than of cities and men. For being one it must needs have one maker and father and master. . . . God is one, but He has around Him numerous Potencies, which all assist and protect created being, and among them are included the powers of chastisement. . . . Now the King may fitly hold converse with his powers and employ them to serve in matters which should not be consummated by God alone. It is true indeed that the Father of All has no need of aught, so that He should require the cooperation of others, if He wills some creative work, yet seeing what was fitting to Himself and the world which was coming into being, He allowed his subject powers to have the fashioning of some things, though He did not give them sovereign and independent knowledge for completion of the task, lest aught of what was coming into being should be miscreated" (*Confusion* 170, 171, 175).

249. Cf., e.g., *1 En.* 61.

250. Cf., e.g., Dan. 10:13–21; *1 En.* 20:5; 71:3; 90:21. On the possible importance of angel imagery for the formation of early Christology, cf. C. Rowland, *The Open Heaven* (New York: Crossroad, 1982); J. E. Fossum, *The Name of God and the Angel of the Lord* (WUNT 36; Tübingen: Mohr Siebeck, 1985); Loren T. Stuckenbruck, *Angel Veneration and Christology: A Study in Early Judaism and in the Christology of the Apocalypse of John* (WUNT 2/70; Tübingen: J. C. B. Mohr Siebeck, 1995). Vollenweider, "Monotheismus und Engelchristologie," 23ff., clearly sees the limits of an angelological interpretation: isolated individual texts form the basis for comprehensive reconstructions; risky lines of development with the tradition are postulated; Sophia imagery and Logos imagery fade out; and the New Testament adopts angel imagery in only partial and minimal ways. Nonetheless, he would like to understand angelophanies as *praeparatio christologica*.

251. Cf. Hurtado, *Monotheism*, 93–124; cf. further Schrage, *Unterwegs zur Einzigkeit*, 132–45.

252. The classical approach of tradition history must be extended to include the aspects of reception history; cf. Dieter Zeller, "New Testament Christology in Its Hellenistic Reception," *NTS* 46 (2001): 332–33.

253. Dieter Zeller, "Die Menschwerdung des Sohnes Gottes im Neuen Testament und die antike Religionsgeschichte," in *Menschwerdung Gottes, Vergöttlichung von Menschen* (ed. Dieter Zeller; NTOA 7; Göttingen: Vandenhoeck & Ruprecht, 1988), 141–76, rightly emphasizes this. Hengel, *Son of God*, 40, in his debate with the history of religions school and Bultmann, poses false alternatives when he

pomorphic polytheism.[254] Divine beings in human form already stand at the center of classical Greek thought; Homer reports, "And we know that the gods go about disguised in all sorts of ways as people from foreign countries, and travel about the world to see who do amiss and who righteously."[255] The origins of culture are traced back to the interventions of the gods, so that, for example, Zeus sends Hermes to teach humanity justice and shame;[256] Hermes, Hercules, and Apollo, as messengers of the gods, assume human form or are active among human beings as gods.[257] Gods in human form can be thought of as originating from this world or as coming from the eternal world. Plutarch can report on the origin of Apollo: "For my native tradition removes this god from among those deities who were changed from mortals into immortals, like Heracles and Dionysus, whose virtues enabled them to cast off mortality and suffering; but he [Apollo] is one of those deities who are unbegotten and eternal."[258] Hercules, as a son of the god Zeus, in obedience to Zeus destroys injustice and lawlessness on the earth.[259] Mythical figures of the primeval period such as Pythagoras[260] and famous miracle workers such as Apollonius of Tyana[261] appear as gods in human form, who use their divine powers in the service of humanity. Empedocles travels around as an immortal god, healing people and doing them good.[262] The hero cult continued in the ruler cult, which finally passed into the Roman cult of the emperor;[263] in the

---

states, concerning the Greek ideas of the gods, "All this gets us no nearer to the mystery of the origin of Christology." It is a matter of the cultural context in which the early christological affirmations originated and could be adopted; the Greek-Hellenistic *also* belongs here.

254. Walter Burkert, "Griechische Religion," *TRE* 14:238ff. The foundational legends of Greek religion are handed on in Herodotus, *Hist.* 2.53.2: "For Homer and Hesiod were the first to compose Theogonies, and give the gods their epithets, to allot them their several offices and occupations, and describe their forms" (Rawlinson).

255. Homer, *Od.* 17.485–486 (*NW* 2/2:1232); cf. also Plato, *Sophista* 216a–b (*NW* 2/2:1232); Diodorus Siculus 1.12.9–10 (*NW* 2/2:1232–33); Homer, *Od.* 7.199–210 (*NW* 1/2:55).

256. Cf. Plato, *Prot.* 322c–d (*NW* 1/2:56).

257. One only need note Acts 14:11–12, after Paul's miracle in Lystra: "When the crowds saw what Paul had done, they shouted in the Lycaonian language, 'The gods have come down to us in human form!' Barnabas they called Zeus, and Paul they called Hermes, because he was the chief speaker."

258. Plutarch, *Pel.* 16 (*NW* 1/2:57–58).

259. Cf. Epictetus, *Diatr.* 2.16.44, and Diodorus Siculus 4.15.1.

260. Cf. Iamblichus, *Vit. pyth.* 31, according to whom the Pythagoreans introduced the following distinction: "Of rational, living beings one kind is divine, another human, and another such as Pythagoras" (Dillon and Hershbell, 55). Pythagoras is described with the adjective θεῖος (cf. John 1:1–2), for he hands on to humanity the saving philosophy he has received from the gods (cf. Iamblichus, *Vit. pyth.* 1–2). On the historical Pythagoras, cf. Christoph Riedweg, *Pythagoras: Leben, Lehre, Nachwirkung: Eine Einführung* (Munich: Beck, 2002).

261. Cf. the texts in *NW* 1/2:59 and in Boring et al., eds., *Hellenistic Commentary,* §§ 7, 31, 55, 61, 88, 119, 132, 198, 228, 229, 230, 290.

262. Cf. Diogenes Laertius 8.62: "I go about among you as an immortal god, no more a mortal."

263. Cf. H. Funke, "Götterbild," *RAC* 11:659–828.

great cultural accomplishments and victories of history, deities are revealed in human form.[264] For Jews, however, the idea was intolerable that human beings such as the Roman Caesar would presume to consider themselves divine and would actually be worshiped.[265]

Plutarch's reflections are informative as he ponders the nature of the numerous real or ostensible gods:

> Better, therefore, is the judgment of those who hold that the stories about Typhon, Osiris, and Isis, are records of experiences of neither gods nor men, but of demigods [δαιμόνων μεγάλων], whom Plato and Pythagoras and Xenocrates and Chrysippus, following the lead of early writers on sacred subjects, allege to have been stronger than men and, in their might, greatly surpassing our nature, yet not possessing the divine quality unmixed and uncontaminated, but with a share also in the nature of the soul and in the perceptive faculties of the body, and with a susceptibility to pleasure and pain and to whatsoever other experience is incident to these mutations, . . . Plato calls this class of beings an interpretative and ministering class, midway between gods and men [ὅτε Πλάτων ἑρμηνευτικὸν τοιοῦτον ὀνομάζει γένος διακονικὸν ἐν μέσῳ θεῶν καὶ ἀνθρώπων], in that they convey thither the prayers and petitions of men, and thence they bring hither the oracles and the gifts of good things. (*Is. Os.* 360–361)

In the context of a growing (pagan) monotheism, Plutarch postulates a group of intermediate beings that maintain contact with the true deities and fill an indispensable function for human beings.[266] The concept of intermediate beings that were both divine and human was also acceptable to non-Jews on the basis of their own cultural background.

Within this complex of traditions already available in the culture, early Christians even prior to Paul could speak of the preexistence, incarnation, exaltation, and unique status of Jesus Christ the Son of God (cf. Phil. 2:6–11). Jesus was not honored as a "second" god but was included in the worship of the "one God" (Rom. 3:30, εἷς θεός). God is God in such a way that he reveals his essential being and character as the Χριστός, κύριος, and υἱός. In Jesus, God is encountered; God defines himself christologically. Paul advocates an exclusive monotheism in binitarian form. He does not reflect on the relation of God to Jesus in ontological categories but rather makes the experience of God's act in and through Jesus the beginning point for his thinking.[267]

---

264. Cf. Burkert, "Griechische Religion," *TRE* 14:247–48.

265. Cf. Philo, *Embassy* 118 (*NW* 1/2:54–55).

266. Cf. further Plutarch, *Is. Os.* 361: "She herself [Isis] and Osiris, translated for their virtues from good demigods into gods, as were Heracles and Dionysus later, not incongruously enjoy double honors, both those of gods and demigods, and their powers extend everywhere, but are greatest in the regions above the earth and beneath the earth."

267. On the relation of theology and Christology in Paul, see above, section 15.2 ("God as the Father of Jesus Christ").

The formation of early Christology did not occur in discernible spatial or temporal stages; on the contrary, within a very compressed period of time, the different christological views emerged alongside each other and partially interrelated with each other. There was no development from a "low" Jewish Christian Christology to a Hellenistic syncretistic "high" Christology.[268] It is rather the case that from the very beginning, central concepts were available within Hellenistic Judaism that were important for early Christianity's new deployment of intermediate beings and titles. Moreover, the central christological titles and the concept of a mediator between God and humanity were open to an independent Hellenistic reception. All essential christological statements about Jesus associated with titles of majesty had already been formed some time before Paul and were adopted by him from Christian tradition: the resurrected Jesus is the Son of God (1 Thess. 1:10; Gal. 1:16; Rom. 1:4); the name of God had been conferred on him (Phil. 2:9–10). He is identified with God or is the image of God (Phil. 2:6; 2 Cor. 4:4) and bearer of God's glory (2 Cor. 4:6; Phil. 3:21). As preexistent, he had participated in the divine act of creation (Phil. 2:6; 1 Cor. 8:6); expressions and citations that properly refer to God are applied to him (cf. 1 Cor. 1:31; 2:16; Rom. 10:13). His place is in heaven (1 Thess. 1:10; 4:16; Phil. 3:20) at the right hand of God (Rom. 8:24), and from there he exercises universal dominion (1 Cor. 15:27; Phil. 3:21), which includes the heavenly powers (Phil. 2:10). Sent from God, he is presently at work in the church (Gal. 4:4–5; Rom. 8:3); he is God's authorized representative at the last judgment, which will take place at his parousia (1 Thess. 1:10; 1 Cor. 16:22; 2 Cor. 5:10).

These views can neither be systematized nor traced back to a uniform, cohesive milieu. On the contrary, we should realize that early Christian communities in different places were originators and transmitters of these ideas, for the Jesus event was understood and appropriated in earliest Christianity in a variety of ways. The inclusion of Jesus in the worship of God originated from the overwhelming religious experiences of the earliest Christians, especially the resurrection appearances and the present working of the Spirit. The worship practice of the earliest churches must also be counted among the essential factors within this process. First Corinthians 16:22 (*Marana tha* [Our Lord, come!]) shows that the unique status and significance of the exalted Christ characterized congregational worship from the very beginning (cf. also 1 Cor. 12:3; 2 Cor. 12:8).[269] Liturgical practice included instruction to "glorify the God and Father of our Lord Jesus Christ" (Rom. 15:6). Baptism, Eucharist, and acclamation stand in an exclusive relation to

268. Kramer, *Christ, Lord, Son of God,* and Hahn, *Titles of Jesus,* are somewhat slanted in favor of this distinction; cf. the careful self-correction in Hahn, *Titles of Jesus,* 347–51.

269. On the significance of worship practice for the formation of early Christology, cf. Schrage, *Unterwegs zur Einzigkeit,* 158–67; Hurtado, *Lord Jesus Christ,* 111–18, 194–206, and passim.

the name of Jesus; this multiplicity of perspectives points to the new and revolutionary religious experience on which they are based. Alongside theological reflection, the liturgical invocation and ritual worship of Jesus were further points of contact for the construction, development, and expansion of christological ideas.

17

Soteriology

The Transfer Has Begun

The subject of Pauline theology is God's saving act in Christ, and so it bears a soteriological stamp throughout.[1] The two preceding chapters provide the foundation for the following change of perspective: the view shifts to the early Christians' new understanding of both self and time, their new self-understanding and their new understanding of history and their place within it.

Foundational for Pauline theology is the concept that by receiving the Spirit at baptism, believers in the here and now already fully participate in the salvation achieved through Jesus' death and resurrection. They are delivered from sin and live in the realm of grace. Not only a new understanding of being but the new being itself has already begun, in the sense that now all things have become new. Pauline Christianity was by no means only a religion of the transcendent future; it was deeply stamped by ritual experiences of the presence of salvation.[2] The fulfillment of salvation that was still to come in no way detracted from the conviction that the transfer into the new reality had already effectively occurred in power, for the heart and soul of the Pauline gospel are

1. Cf. also Dunn, *Theology of Paul*, 461–98.
2. Cf. Strecker, *Die liminale Theologie des Paulus*, 245ff.

not what is still to come but what had already happened. For Paul, the presence of salvation was real: "See, now is the acceptable time; see, now is the day of salvation!" (2 Cor. 6:2b). Christ's triumphal victory procession has already begun (cf. 2 Cor. 2:14); Paul again uses different metaphors to describe and interpret this reality: the present is the time of grace and salvation; participation in Christ changes being and time.

17.1 New Being as Participation in Christ

Just as Jesus Christ, by his resurrection and parousia, marks the beginning and end points of the saving event, he comprehensively determines the life of believers who live between the times. Paul communicates the idea of participation in salvation above all with the imagery of being σὺν Χριστῷ and ἐν Χριστῷ.

Participation in Baptism

The phrase σὺν Χριστῷ[3] and other such expressions using the preposition σύν describe primarily entrance into the realm of salvation and the transition into ultimate communion with Christ. In Rom. 6 the basic participatory character of Pauline theology is expressed semantically by the unusual frequency of σύν (6:8) or its compounds (6:4, 5, 6, 8).[4] Referring back to baptism does not serve as an illustration[5] but is the explication of a fundamental theological, biographical, and social set of circumstances: (1) In baptism believers fully participate in the soteriological power of the cross; they are incorporated into the somatic destiny of their Lord. (2) In baptism the factual-historical separation from the power of sin takes place. (3) The conferral of the Spirit and righteousness/justification takes place in baptism. (4) The new being in the power of the Spirit is a continuing result of baptism. (5) In baptism a new individual and social identity is conferred. The individual is taken out of the realm of secularity and receives a new understanding of self and world. (6) Incorporation into the new form of faith and society constituted by the body of Christ changes the thinking, acting, and feeling of those who are baptized.

Since rituals represent the consolidation of religious worldviews, baptism receives a fundamental importance for Pauline thought. *In the ritual, the theo-*

---

3. The expression σὺν Χριστῷ is found in Paul at 1 Thess. 4:14, 17; 5:10; 2 Cor. 4:14; 13:4; Rom. 6:8; Phil. 1:23. Combinations with σύν are found in Gal. 2:19; Rom. 6:4, 5, 6, 8; 8:17, 29; Phil. 3:10, 21.

4. For an analysis of Rom. 6, see above, section 12.7 ("The Presence of Salvation: Baptism and Righteousness").

5. Contra Haacker, *Der Brief an die Römer*, 126, who does not acknowledge baptism as a separate theme even in Rom. 6.

logical and social construction of the new person "in Christ" takes place.[6] Baptism is not salvation[7] but is related to the reality of salvation, for God has chosen baptism as the place where God's saving act in history becomes reality in the history of individual human beings. In baptism the death of Jesus and the powers of his resurrection are both equally present, so that the baptismal event must be understood as a sacramental reliving of the death of Jesus, which in baptism becomes present reality, and as incorporation into the reality of his resurrection.

The powers of the resurrection are also at work in the Lord's Supper, so that Paul can warn the Corinthian Christians, "For all who eat and drink without discerning the body, eat and drink judgment against themselves. For this reason many of you are weak and ill, and some have died" (1 Cor. 11:29–30). Thus the powers present in the sacrament can bring God's judgment on those who participate in it in an unworthy manner.[8]

The reality of the resurrection is not limited to the sacraments but permeates the believers' whole existence, determining their new being in the present and future. Jesus Christ died for those who have been called, so that they may "live with him" (cf. 1 Thess. 4:17, σὺν κυρίῳ ἐσόμεθα [we will be with the Lord]; 5:10, σὺν αὐτῷ ζήσωμεν [that . . . we may live with him]). God will act for the members of the eschatological community just as he acted for Jesus Christ (2 Cor. 4:14). Paul regards Christians as already having the status of sonship (cf. Gal. 3:26; 4:6–7; Rom. 8:16); they have put on Christ (Gal. 3:27; Rom. 13:14), so that Christ is formed in them (Gal. 4:19). As "heirs" of the promise (cf. κληρονομία, Gal. 3:18; κληρονόμος, Gal. 3:29; 4:1, 7; Rom. 4:13–14; cf. further 1 Cor. 6:9–10; 15:50), they already participate in God's saving work; they have been granted the status of God's children and the freedom that goes with it (Gal. 5:21). Regarding both suffering and glory, believers are "joint heirs with Christ" (Rom. 8:17, συγκληρονόμοι Χριστοῦ); they are destined to be conformed to the image of the Son of God (Rom. 8:29). The reality of the resurrection penetrates the existence of Christians, even into their bodily sufferings (cf. 2 Cor. 4:10–11; 6:9–10). Near the end of his life, Paul longs for unbroken, constant communion with Christ (Phil. 1:23, σὺν Χριστῷ εἶναι). He wants to participate in the power of both Christ's resurrection and his sufferings "by becoming like him in his death, if somehow I may attain the resurrection from the dead" (Phil. 3:10–11). Jesus Christ will transform "the body of our humiliation" to conform to "the body of his glory," for he

---

6. Cf. Theissen, "Taufe," 107ff.

7. In recent theological history, especially the alternatives posed by Markus and Karl Barth have led to immoderate theories; for a history of research, cf. Schnelle, *Gerechtigkeit und Christusgegenwart*, 11–32.

8. The realism of Paul's argumentation, foreign to our thinking, makes it difficult for modern interpreters to perceive the connection between the manner in which the meal was celebrated and God's acting in judgment; cf. Schrage, *Korinther*, 3:53–54.

has the power (ἐνέργεια) "that also enables him to make all things subject to himself" (Phil. 3:21).[9] Christians already, in the here and now, have been placed in a tension-filled force field that powerfully effects their lives both now and beyond death.

"In Christ"

The sphere within which the new life is lived between the beginning of salvation and its consummation Paul describes with the phrase εἶναι ἐν Χριστῷ. This expression is much more than a "formula"; it must be regarded as *the* continuum of his theology.[10] The external data are already significant: forms of ἐν Χριστῷ (Ἰησοῦ) (in Christ [Jesus]) occur sixty-four times in Paul's letters, and the derived expression ἐν κυρίῳ (in the Lord) thirty-seven times.[11] Paul is not the creator of the expression ἐν Χριστῷ, as shown by the pre-Pauline baptismal traditions in 1 Cor. 1:30, 2 Cor. 5:17, and Gal. 3:26–28.[12] Nonetheless, he can still be regarded as the real champion of this image, which not only was made by him into a concise definition of what it means to be Christian but must also be understood as his "core ecclesiological definition."[13] The primary meaning of ἐν Χριστῷ is to be understood in a local sense, indicating a sphere of being:[14] by baptism the believer is incorporated into the sphere of the pneumatic Christ, and the new life is constituted by the conferral of the Spirit as the down payment on salvation, which begins in the present and is fulfilled in the eschatological future redemption. Human beings are torn out

---

9. For analysis, cf. Siber, *Mit Christus Leben*, 110–34.

10. On ἐν Χριστῷ, cf. Adolf Deissmann, *Die neutestamentliche Formel "in Christo Jesu"* (Marburg: N. G. Elwert, 1892); Friedrich Büchsel, "'In Christus' bei Paulus," *ZNW* (1949): 141–58; Fritz Neugebauer, *In Christus = Ἐν Χριστῷ: Eine Untersuchung zum paulinischen Glaubensverständnis* (Göttingen: Vandenhoeck & Ruprecht, 1961); Wilhelm Thüsing, *Per Christum in Deum: Studien zum Verhältnis von Christozentrik und Theozentrik in den paulinischen Hauptbriefen* (2nd ed.; NTAbh NF 1; Münster: Aschendorff, 1969), 61–114; Schnelle, *Gerechtigkeit und Christusgegenwart*, 106–23, 225–35; A. J. M. Wedderburn, "Some Observations on Paul's Use of the Phrases 'in Christ' and 'with Christ,'" *JSNT* 25 (1985): 83–97; Wolfgang Schrage, "'In Christus' und die neutestamentliche Ethik," in *In Christus: Beiträge zum ökumenischen Gespräch* (ed. Josef Georg Ziegler; 1st ed.; MSSA 14; St. Ottilien: EOS, 1987), 27–41; Mark A. Seifrid, "In Christ," *DPL* 433–36; Roloff, *Kirche im Neuen Testament*, 86–99; L. Klehn, "Die Verwendung von ἐν Χριστῷ bei Paulus," *BZ* 74 (1994): 66–79; Georg Strecker, *Theologie des Neuen Testaments* (Berlin: de Gruyter, 1996), 117–23; Gnilka, *Apostel und Zeuge*, 255–60 ; Umbach, *In Christus getauft*, 215ff.; Strecker, *Die liminale Theologie des Paulus*, 189–211.

11. Cf. Klehn, "Die Verwendung von ἐν Χριστῷ," 68.

12. Cf. additional traditional images in 2 Cor. 5:21b; Gal. 2:17; 5:6; Rom. 3:24; 6:11, 23; 8:1; 12:5. From the history-of-religions point of view, Jewish wisdom traditions provide the background for the ἐν Χριστῷ imagery (cf., e.g., Sir. 6:28–31; 14:24–27; Wis. 5:15; 8:17–18; Philo, *Alleg. Interp.* 3.46, 152); evidence and arguments in Schnelle, *Gerechtigkeit und Christusgegenwart*, 108–9.

13. Hübner, "Rechtfertigungstheologie," 91.

14. Cf. Schnelle, *Gerechtigkeit und Christusgegenwart*, 109–17; Seifrid, "In Christ," 433–34; Umbach, *In Christus getauft*, 220–21; Strecker, *Die liminale Theologie des Paulus*, 191–92.

of their lives oriented to themselves and find their true selves in their relation to Christ. This local/sphere-of-being sense of ἐν Χριστῷ dominates in 1 Thess. 4:16; 1 Cor. 1:30; 15:18, 22; 2 Cor. 5:17; Gal. 2:17; 3:26–28; 5:6; Rom. 3:24; 6:11, 23; 8:1; 12:5. The variety and complexity of the ἐν Χριστῷ statements and the fact that such statements with different levels of meaning are found alongside one another can all be derived from this basic local/sphere-of-being sense.[15] With the expression ἐν Χριστῷ, Paul unites the vertical and horizontal realms:[16] from communion with Christ (cf. Gal. 3:27) grows a new *communitas* of baptized believers that now transcends fundamental gender, ethnic, and social alternatives (Gal. 3:28; 1 Cor. 12:13). Thus ἐν Χριστῷ appears as the sphere in which changes affecting reality take place and are lived out.[17] The baptized are determined by Christ in every aspect of life, and in their community the new being assumes visible form. *The world not only is declared to be different but has really been changed because the powers of the resurrection already are at work in the present through the gift of the Spirit.*

17.2 The New Time between the Times

The transformation of the Son and the participation of believers in this saving event change the way they perceive and understand time. Time is likewise subject to a transformative process, for "the ends of the ages have come" (1 Cor. 10:11c). The Pauline νυνὶ δέ (but now) impressively marks out the eschatological hinge of the ages:[18] "But in fact Christ has been raised from the dead, the first fruits of those who have died" (1 Cor. 15:20; cf. 2 Cor. 6:2; 13:13; Rom. 3:21; 6:22; 7:6). Baptized believers are now (νῦν) justified through the blood of Christ (Rom. 5:9) and have now (νῦν) received reconciliation (Rom. 5:11). Paul is certain that "salvation is nearer to us now than when we became believers" (Rom. 13:11). The present and future are the time of grace (χάρις) and salvation (σωτηρία).

"Grace"

Paul consistently uses χάρις (63 time in Paul, of 155 New Testament instances) in the singular; this linguistic usage already signals the fundamental idea of his doctrine of grace: χάρις proceeds from God, is concentrated in the

---

15. Cf. Albrecht Oepke, "ἐν," *TDNT* 2:542, "This underlying spatial concept gives us the clue to the true significance of the formula ἐν Χριστῷ ᾽ Ιησοῦ and its parallels"; Schnelle, *Gerechtigkeit und Christusgegenwart*, 117–22; Klehn, "ἐν Χριστῷ bei Paulus," 77.

16. Strecker, *Die liminale Theologie des Paulus*, 193ff., speaks of a vertical and horizontal community of Christ.

17. On the spatial aspect of Pauline theology, cf. Hübner, "Rechtfertigungstheologie," 90ff.

18. Cf. Luz, *Geschichtsverständnis*, 168–69.

Christ event, and is effective for baptized believers. Because Jesus Christ personifies the grace of God, Paul can use "grace" and "Christ" as parallels (Rom. 5:15). Believers already stand in a state of grace (cf. 1 Cor. 1:4; Rom. 5:21), for through the Christ event they have been lifted out of their entanglement in the past history of condemnation (Rom. 5:15–16); grace triumphs over the powers of sin and death.[19] The present truth is that "just as sin exercised dominion in death, so grace might also exercise dominion through justification leading to eternal life through Jesus Christ our Lord" (Rom. 5:21). All this happens "for your sake, so that grace, as it extends to more and more people, may increase thanksgiving, to the glory of God" (2 Cor. 4:15). The Spirit is given to those who believe and are baptized (1 Cor. 2:12, aorist passive participle χαρισθέντα), so that now through God's grace they recognize the new time in which they live. They participate in God's saving work through the faith they have received as a gift (cf. Rom. 4:16; Phil. 1:29). God's reconciliation with human beings through Jesus Christ is concretely realized in the gifts of righteousness and grace (cf. 2 Cor. 5:18–6:2; Rom. 5:1–11). Paul understands the collection for Jerusalem to be a work of grace because it confers a concrete form on God's saving work (cf. 1 Cor. 16:3; 2 Cor. 8:1, 4, 6–7, 19; 9:8, 14–15). The prototype for this χάρις is the grace of Christ, for through his poverty he confers riches on the community of faith (cf. 2 Cor. 8:9). Even the apostle's time in prison can be described as χάρις because it furthers the preaching of the gospel (cf. Phil. 1:7). The grace of God thus becomes the real bearer of the apostle's work (cf. 2 Cor. 1:12) and of the churches, for also the "spiritual gifts" (χαρίσματα, lit. "the effects of grace") owe their existence to the one grace (Rom. 12:6). When, at the beginning and conclusion of his letters, Paul emphasizes the grace in which his churches stand (cf. 1 Thess. 1:1; 5:28; 1 Cor. 1:3; 16:23; 2 Cor. 1:2; 13:13; Gal. 1:3; 6:18; Rom. 1:5; 16:20; Phil. 1:2; 4:23; Philem. 3), he is not only following a liturgical convention but naming an existing reality: both apostle (cf. 1 Cor. 3:10; Gal. 1:15; 2:9; Rom. 1:5; 12:3; 15:15) and church owe their existence and continuance to the grace of God alone. Paul contrasts his earlier life with his call to be an apostle: "But by the grace of God I am what I am, and his grace toward me has not been in vain. On the contrary, I worked harder than any of them—though it was not I, but the grace of God that is with me" (1 Cor. 15:10). It is grace that carries him through difficult situations, for grace shows its strength precisely in enduring severe tests and challenges (cf. 2 Cor. 12:9). It is not the goodwill of Caesar[20] that graces and changes the life

---

19. On the Pauline understanding of χάρις, cf. Bultmann, *Theology of the New Testament*, 1:279–85, 288–92; Hans Conzelmann, "χαίρω, χάρις, κτλ.," *TDNT* 9:393–96; Zeller, *Charis*, 138–96; Dunn, *Theology of Paul*, 319–23.

20. Cf. the catalogue of material in Gillis Petersson Wetter, *Charis: Ein Beitrag zur Geschichte des ältesten Christentums* (UNT 5; Leipzig: Brandstetter, 1913), 6–19; Conzelmann, "χαίρω, χάρις, κτλ.," *TDNT* 9:373–76; Zeller, *Charis*, 14–32. The enumeration of the emperor's achievements for the Roman people in Augustus, *Res gestae divi Augusti*, are worth reading in this regard.

of human beings but the gracious turning of God toward humanity in Jesus Christ. Grace is not a feeling, emotion, or quality of God but his unexpected, free, and powerful act. Grace is the expression of God's love, for "God proves his love for us in that while we still were sinners Christ died for us" (Rom. 5:8).[21] Therefore Paul constantly hopes that Israel, too, will share in the grace of God (Rom. 11:1ff.).

In his letters to the Galatians and the Romans, Paul relates χάρις statements to his exclusive doctrine of justification determined by nomology. He expresses surprise at how quickly the Galatians had turned aside from grace (Gal. 1:6) and says, "You who want to be justified by the law have cut yourselves off from Christ; you have fallen away from grace" (Gal. 5:4). Paul formulates the matter positively in Rom. 3:24: "they are now justified by his grace as a gift, through the redemption that is in Christ Jesus." Overflowing grace appears as a power by which the actual, unavoidable condemnation of humanity is averted (Rom. 5:16). Christians have been delivered from sin and death and find themselves in the objective status of saving grace. Because it is the Christ event and not the law/Torah that saves them, the apostle can designate the new status of Christians in Rom. 6:14 to mean that "sin will have no dominion over you, since you are not under law but under grace." Romans 6 makes it clear that the antinomian distortion of the Pauline concept of grace can also be based on the fundamental conception of the believer's participation in the grace of God through baptism (cf. Rom. 6:1, "Should we continue in sin in order that grace may abound?"). But Paul emphatically rejects this logic of his opponents and points to the basic salvific datum of Christian existence, namely, baptism. The fundamental conception of Pauline soteriology is not bound to a negative understanding of the law or a particular conception of justification but derives positively from the logic of transformation and participation.[22] *Through the Son's change of status, baptized believers are placed in a new status, namely, grace.*

"Deliverance"

Alongside χάρις, Paul takes up a second idea central to the religiosity of antiquity, namely, σωτηρία, as a means of interpreting the new time in which

---

21. For the internal connection between the concepts of love and grace, cf. Bultmann, *Theology of the New Testament*, 1:291–92.

22. Differently, e.g., Bultmann, ibid., 1:284, who practically identifies χάρις and δικαιοσύνη (θεοῦ) (the righteousness [of/from God]): "'Righteousness,' then, has its origin in God's grace." Similarly, Conzelmann, *Theology of the New Testament*, 213–20, and Dunn, *Theology of Paul*, 319–23, argue that the exclusive doctrine of justification as found in Romans is *the* complete statement of Paul's doctrine of grace. Bultmann's statements are doubtless correct regarding Romans, but the Pauline understanding of grace is not to be reduced to the conceptions of justification and law found in Romans. The grace of God in Jesus Christ is not identical with one of its interpretations. A more differentiated argumentation is found in Zeller, *Charis*, 154ff.

Christians know themselves to live. In New Testament times, the semantic field σωτήρ/σωτηρία/σῴζω (savior/salvation/save) has both political and religious connotations:[23] the Roman Caesar is the savior of the world who guarantees not only the political unity of the empire but grants its citizens prosperity, well-being, and meaning and purpose for their lives. Paul goes beyond these promises, for the gospel he proclaims encompasses all realms of time and being and saves from the just wrath of God (cf. Rom. 1:16ff.). Those who trust in this message are delivered from the unpredictable powers of the future. It is against this complex background that the early Christian message of the salvation of believers in Jesus Christ must be read. God has destined them not for wrath but for salvation (1 Thess. 5:9; Rom. 5:9); the foolishness of the preaching of the cross saves; on the cross God has shown the wisdom of the world to be foolishness (1 Cor. 1:18, 21). Paul proclaims the gospel in a variety of ways in order to save at least some (cf. 1 Cor. 9:22; 10:33); he prays for Israel, that it will be saved (cf. Rom. 10:1; 11:14), and finally attains the prophetic insight that at the Lord's return "all Israel" will be saved (Rom. 11:26).[24] The saving gospel has a particular form (cf. 1 Cor. 15:2); it is the power of God (Rom. 1:16), and every one who confesses it with the mouth (i.e., publicly) will be saved (Rom. 10:9, 13). How much Paul thought of σωτηρία as a real, tangible event is shown by 1 Cor. 3:15; 5:5, where the self of the baptized will be saved in the fire of judgment even if their works or bodies are lost; the sanctification of the unbelieving partner makes possible his or her salvation (7:16). Because the powers of the resurrection are already at work in the present and continue into the future, salvation is much more than a new kind of consciousness of those who consider themselves saved; σωτηρία is a concretely real and, at the same time, universal event that transforms being and time.

The new definition of the believers' understanding of time thus comprises three dimensions: (1) God's act in Jesus Christ as the climax of salvation history has introduced the transformation of the ages (cf., e.g., 2 Cor. 5:16; 6:2; Rom. 5:8–11). (2) Believers participate in this event through individual appropriation of salvation in baptism (cf. Rom. 6:19–22). (3) They thus find themselves in a new situation and a new time: the time of grace, the time of salvation, the time of the Spirit.

---

23. Cf. Franz Jung, ΣΩΤΗΡ: *Studien zur Rezeption eines hellenistischen Ehrentitels im Neuen Testament* (NTAbh NF 39; Münster: Aschendorff, 2002), 45–176; and Martin Karrer, "Jesus der Retter (σωτήρ)," *ZNW* 93 (2002): 153–76.

24. According to Rom. 9:27, only a remnant of Israel will be saved.

18

Pneumatology

The Spirit Moves and Works

Pauline theology is profoundly stamped with the insight that *since Jesus Christ has been raised from the dead, the Spirit of God is again at work.*[1] As the power of God's self-revelation in Jesus Christ, the Spirit is the determining element in the process of universal transformation that has already begun. Within the symbolic universes of antiquity, Paul gave a new definition of the divine presence by defining the Spirit as the unqualified creative presence of the one who is to come (cf. 2 Cor. 1:22; 5:5; Rom. 8:23). The presence of salvation is manifest through participation in the work of the Spirit. At the same time, confession of the risen Jesus Christ as κύριος functions as the criterion for authentic possession of the Spirit (cf. 1 Cor. 12:3).

18.1 The Spirit as the Connectional Principle of Pauline Thought

The surpassing importance of pneumatology in Paul's thought results from its internal connectional[2] role interrelating theology proper (the doctrine of

---

1. Cf. Kim, "Heilsgegenwart," 180: "After the cessation of prophecy in Israel, for Paul the Spirit of God begins to work anew in the world with the death and resurrection of Jesus Christ."
2. Translator's note: In this section I have used "connection" and related forms to to represent *Vernetzung, vernetzen,* etc. The German words suggest networks of connections.

God), Christology, soteriology, anthropology, ethics, and eschatology.[3] The integrative power of pneumatology is what first makes it possible for Paul to impart a systematic quality to his interpretation of the Jesus-Christ-history.

Theology

The reality of God in the world is the reality of the Spirit. By the πνεῦμα (spirit, breath), which is always primarily the Spirit that proceeds from God (cf. 1 Thess. 4:8; 1 Cor. 1:12–14; 2 Cor. 1:22; 5:5; Gal. 4:6; Rom. 5:5), the life-giving power of the Creator is manifest.[4] The Spirit of God not only effected the resurrection of Jesus (cf. Rom. 1:3b–4a) but is at the same time the new mode of being and working of the risen one himself, his dynamic and effective presence (cf. 2 Cor. 3:17; 1 Cor. 15:45). Through the working of the Spirit of God, believers are freed from the powers of sin and death (Rom. 8:9–11). The Spirit that Christians have received has its origin in God (cf. 1 Cor. 2:12; 6:19, "Or do you not know that your body is a temple of the Holy Spirit within you, which you have from God"). The new universal working of the Spirit of God is for Paul the foundation of his whole theology, for the act of God's Spirit in Jesus Christ and in the believers is *the* sign of the present time of salvation. Nonetheless, the Spirit, as the powerful gift of God, in all its manifestations is no independent force but remains united with its origin.[5] In all Paul's statements about the Spirit, the Spirit of God is the irreversible beginning point, so that theology proper, that is, his doctrine of God (and Christology), is always the basis for his pneumatology (and soteriology).

Christology

Jesus Christ was raised from the dead through the Spirit of God (cf. Rom. 1:3b–4a; Rom. 6:4; 2 Cor. 13:4), and the work of God's Spirit is the basis for the unique eschatological status of Jesus Christ. The being and ministry of the risen Lord as Pneuma (2 Cor. 3:18) are nourished by the Spirit's unique relation to God. The Spirit is also a decisively formative christological power, for Christ and the Spirit are in a sense equivalents (2 Cor. 3:17, ὁ δὲ κύριος τὸ πνεῦμά ἐστιν [now the Lord is the Spirit]).[6] The attribute of the Spirit applies even to the preexistent Christ (1 Cor. 10:4). As life-creating and life-sustaining power, the Lord is the Spirit; that is, pneumatology is not a separate topic but

---

3. On the integrating and organizing function of pneumatology, cf. also Schlier, *Grundzüge*, 179–94; Horn, *Angeld des Geistes*, 385–431; Dunn, *Theology of Paul*, 413–41.

4. Cf. Friedrich Wilhelm Horn, "Kyrios und Pneuma bei Paulus," in *Paulinische Christologie: Exegetische Beiträge: Hans Hübner zum 70. Geburtstag* (ed. Udo Schnelle et al.; Göttingen: Vandenhoeck & Ruprecht, 2000), 59.

5. Cf. the foundational work of Thüsing, *Per Christum in Deum*, 152–63.

6. Differently, Horn, "Kyrios und Pneuma," 66–67, who equates the reference to the Kyrios with a reference to the Spirit and infers, "The idea that in this passage Paul intends to say something about a possible identity of the Kyrios (Christ) and the Spirit is thus a bit bizarre" (p. 67).

describes the way in which the risen Lord is present and at work in the church (cf. Gal. 4:6, "And because you are children, God has sent the Spirit of his Son into our hearts, crying, 'Abba! Father!'"). The relation between the Spirit and Christ is so close that for Paul it is impossible to have one without the other (cf. Rom. 8:9b, "Anyone who does not have the Spirit of Christ does not belong to him"). Since the resurrection, Jesus Christ, as Pneuma and in the Pneuma, stands united with his own. The exalted Christ works as πνεῦμα ζῳοποιοῦν (life-giving Spirit)[7] and at the resurrection grants a σῶμα πνευματικόν (spiritual body) to his own (1 Cor. 15:44).[8] The Spirit of the Lord moves and forms the life of believers (cf. Phil. 1:19). They become part of his body; communion with the exalted Lord is a communion in the Spirit (1 Cor. 6:17, "anyone united to the Lord becomes one spirit with him").

Soteriology

By receiving the Spirit of God (cf. 1 Thess. 4:8; 1 Cor. 2:12; 2 Cor. 1:22; 11:4; Gal. 3:2, 14; Rom. 5:5; 8:15), baptized believers are already in the living present placed within the realm of communion with Christ and thus within the realm of salvation. Because Christ and his own belong on the side of the Spirit, they are not subject to the domination of the world of flesh, sin, and death. They can move forward toward the future judgment in the confidence that the gift of the Spirit is the first installment on what is yet to come (cf. 2 Cor. 1:22; 5:5), and future and present modulate into one reality in the saving work of the Spirit.

Anthropology

Baptized believers, through the gift of the Spirit of God/Christ, experience a new orientation and determination, for the Spirit is the creator and preserver of the new being. As the beginning of communion with Christ, reception of the Spirit in baptism marks (cf. 1 Cor. 6:11; 10:4; 12:13; 2 Cor. 1:21–22; Gal. 4:6; Rom. 8:14) the beginning of the believer's participation in the saving event. Baptism places the Christian in the realm of the spiritual Christ, and at the same time the exalted Lord (cf. Gal. 2:20; 4:19; 2 Cor. 11:10; 13:5; Rom. 8:10) and the Spirit (cf. 1 Cor. 3:16; 6:19; Rom. 8:9, 11) are at work in the believer. The statements in which Christ and Spirit are paralleled or identified designate for

---

7. The term πνεῦμα ζῳοποιοῦν is found only here in the New Testament; cf. Horn, *Angeld des Geistes*, 197–98; Dunn, *Theology of Paul*, 261. First Corinthians 15:46 shows that Paul is arguing against Spirit enthusiasm and intentionally relates the concept of the Spirit to that of the exalted Lord.

8. Johannes Sijko Vos, *Traditionsgeschichtliche Untersuchungen zur paulinischen Pneumatologie* (Assen: Van Gorcum, 1973), 81, appropriately formulates the matter: "As the eschatological Adam, Christ is Pneuma in his substance just as he is in his function. As Pneuma, Christ creates his own in his own image, and this means that he transforms them into his own spiritual mode of being."

Paul a fundamental reality:[9] just as the believer is incorporated in the Spirit of Christ, so Christ dwells in the believer as Spirit. Life in the Spirit appears as the consequence and effect of the baptismal event, which, as a saving event, is in turn an event in the power of the Spirit. Paul thereby points out a fundamental anthropological transformation, for the life of the Christian has taken a decisive turn: as those determined by the Spirit, Christians live in the sphere of the Spirit and orient their lives to the working of the Spirit. This life-changing experience brought about by the Spirit, and thus by God himself, reveals the true situation of Christians: they do not live out of their own resources but always experience themselves as living in a realm in which they have already been acted upon (cf. Rom. 8:5–11).[10] Life can be lived according to the flesh (κατὰ σάρκα) or according to the Spirit (κατὰ πνεῦμα). The Spirit also has a noetic function,[11] for only the Spirit of God grants insight into God's plan of salvation: "Now we have received not the spirit of the world, but the Spirit that is from God, so that we may understand the gifts bestowed on us by God" (1 Cor. 2:12). Participation in the Spirit of God does not abolish the individual human spirit (cf. 1 Cor. 5:4; 14:14; 16:18; 2 Cor. 2:13; 7:1; Gal. 6:18; Rom. 1:9, "my spirit"; Phil. 4:23; Philem. 25, "your spirit); rather, the human spirit is taken up within a dynamic event, borne along, embraced, transformed, and given a new orientation.[12] The knowledge given by God in the Spirit discloses an understanding of God's acts, an understanding that includes human knowledge and leads to a new way of living, but without minimizing or abolishing human responsibility.[13] The new self is formed in the interface between the divine and the bodily, which are to be thought of in creative and relational terms.

Ethics

The new being takes place in harmony with the Spirit, which appears as ground and norm of the new way of life (cf. Gal. 5:25; 1 Cor. 5:7; Rom.

---

9. Cf. Schnelle, *Gerechtigkeit und Christusgegenwart*, 120–22; and S. Vollenweider, "Der Geist Gottes als Selbst der Glaubenden," *ZTK* 93 (1996): 169–72.

10. Cf. Bultmann, *Theology of the New Testament*, 1:227–28.

11. As a pagan parallel, cf. Cicero, *Tusc.* 5.70, where, after listing the joys of the wise, it is said, "To the soul occupied day and night in these meditations there comes the knowledge enjoined by the god at Delphi [γνῶθι σεαυτόν, "know thyself"], that the mind should know its own self and feel its union with the divine mind, the source of the fullness of joy unquenchable."

12. Paul's statements on the relation of the Spirit of God to the human spirit are intentionally open and nonspecific because this mystery eludes static conceptuality. Reflections on this theme are found in Vollenweider, "Geist Gottes," 175ff.; cf. p. 189: "The Spirit moves the ego to stop thinking of itself in terms of its fleshly origin, to let itself go, to die, so that it can understand itself anew as pervaded by the divine Spirit (cf. Gal. 2:19–20; 6:14b). This elementary process alone brings one to the presence of the Pneuma/Spirit in one's self."

13. In this respect, the statement of Wolfgang Schrage, *The Ethics of the New Testament* (trans. David E. Green; Philadelphia: Fortress, 1988), 178, appears to be problematic: "The Spirit is rather the very essence of the new life, in all its apparently insignificant and mundane details."

6:2, 12; Phil. 2:12–13). The Spirit creates and maintains the new being of Christians, powerfully becoming the determining force in their character and intentions. Christians have entered life determined by the Spirit, and so they are henceforth to be led by the Spirit. The Spirit is the power and principle of the new life, and so Paul asks the Galatians in bewilderment, "The only thing I want to learn from you is this: Did you receive the Spirit by doing the works of the law or by believing what you heard?" (Gal. 3:2). At the same time, it becomes clear: there is no change without a new way of living. The Spirit conferred as a gift must be accepted. Precisely because the Spirit incorporates baptized believers into the sphere of God and the realm of the church, they are not in the vacuum of a world free of any ruling powers but instead stand under the call to new obedience made possible by the Spirit.[14] For those who live within the force field of the Spirit, God is no longer the one who makes demands as an outsider;[15] the law/Torah and the Spirit are opposing powers, for "if you are led by the Spirit, you are not subject to the law" (Gal. 5:18; cf. Rom. 6:14). The "newness of life" (Rom. 6:4) takes place in the "new life of the Spirit" (Rom. 7:6).

Eschatology

As the present gift of the one who is to come, the Spirit is the guarantor of God's eschatological faithfulness (cf. 2 Cor. 1:22; Rom. 8:23). The Spirit of God/Christ determines not only the present but the future, for in the final event of history, he grants the transition into the postmoral pneumatic mode of existence of the believers (cf. 1 Cor. 15:44–45) and bestows eternal life (Gal. 6:8, "but if you sow to the Spirit, you will reap eternal life from the Spirit"). Within this event, the Spirit even stands beside the creature and intercedes for the saints before God (cf. Rom. 8:26–27).[16] The Spirit conferred in baptism and living in the Christian appears as *the* continuing reality of the divine life-giving power. Through the Spirit, God will grant believers participation in what God has already done for Christ (cf. Rom. 8:11). The creative relation of the Spirit to the soma ensures the existence of the new being even beyond death.

18.2 The Gifts and Present Acts of the Spirit

The Spirit confers gifts and effectively operates in the life of the churches.[17] All baptized believers are given the basic gifts of the Spirit:

---

14. Käsemann consistently emphasizes this aspect (cf., e.g., *Romans*, 28: "For the apostle knows of no gift which does not also challenge us to responsibility, thereby showing itself as a power over us and creating a place of service for us").

15. Cf. Lietzmann, *Römer*, 71.

16. For exposition, cf. Horn, *Angeld des Geistes*, 294–97.

17. See above, section 9.5 ("The Power of the Spirit and Building Up the Church").

Freedom

It belongs to the essential distinctive marks of the Spirit that it bestows and creates freedom (2 Cor. 3:17b, "where the Spirit of the Lord is, there is freedom"). The life principle of the Spirit itself frees baptized believers from the enslaving powers of the law, sin, and death (Rom. 8:2). As those who have been "born according to the Spirit," baptized believers no longer belong to the realm of slavery but of freedom (cf. Gal. 4:21–31).

Adoption, inheritance

The new relation to God and Jesus Christ through the gift of the Spirit establishes believers in the status of adopted children (Rom. 8:15, "For you did not receive a spirit of slavery to fall back into fear, but you have received a spirit of adoption. When we cry, 'Abba! Father!'"). As children of God, believers are joint heirs with Christ both in suffering and in glory (cf. Rom. 8:17; Gal. 4:6–7).

Love

The power of love now shapes the lives of Christians "because God's love has been poured into our hearts through the Holy Spirit that has been given to us" (Rom. 5:5b). Love is first on the list of the fruits of the Spirit (cf. 1 Cor. 13; Gal. 5:22); love has its origin in God, attains concrete form in Christ, and gives hope to human beings (cf. Rom. 5:5a). Love is the ground of hope because the destiny of Jesus Christ is the embodiment of love. Participation in this destiny gives Christians the assurance that the effective power of life that comes from God continues beyond death, for their hope is in the "God who raises the dead" (2 Cor. 1:9). Apart from love, all human manifestations of life are nothing, for they lag behind the new reality God has brought into being.[18]

As the first and greatest gift, love is the criterion for identifying the current work of the Spirit.[19] Because Jesus Christ is the embodiment of the love of God, Paul binds the question of the validity of various spiritual works to an appropriate understanding of Christ (cf. 1 Cor. 12:1–3).[20] When in worship the community confesses its faith in the crucified and risen one with the acclamation Κύριος Ἰησοῦς (Jesus is Lord), it orients its own life to the way of love lived out by Jesus of Nazareth. Paul calls on the Corinthians, in particular, to

18. Appropriately, Hans Weder, "Die Energie des Evangeliums," in *Theologie als gegenwärtige Schriftauslesung* (ZTKB 9; Tübingen: Mohr Siebeck, 1995), 95, who argues that love has a reality "that is not created by those who love but who are themselves supported and carried along by love."

19. Cf. Günther Bornkamm, "Der köstlichere Weg," in *Das Ende des Gesetzes: Paulusstudien* (BEvT 16; Munich: Kaiser, 1961), 110: "Ἀγάπη is related to the variety of χαρίσματα as Christ is related to the many members of his body."

20. On 1 Cor. 12:1–3, cf. Matthias Pfeiffer, *Einweisung in das neue Sein: Neutestamentliche Erwägungen zur Grundlegung der Ethik* (Gütersloh: Gütersloher Verlagshaus, 2001), 211–15.

remember this fundamental fact when he points out to the congregation that the Spirit at work within it originates in and from God. God is the final cause of all activities and the giver of all spiritual gifts in their various workings (cf. 1 Cor. 12:6b, "it is the same God who activates all of them in everyone"; cf. also 1 Cor. 1:4; 7:7; 12:28–30), so that an anthropological monopolization of the Spirit does not increase the power of its works but rather silences them. The insight into the unity and indivisibility of the Spirit[21] produces the kind of life that knows it is in harmony with the creative work of the Spirit. Paul emphasizes the gift character and the Spirit, and the fact that its works are not at human disposal, by using the terms πνευματικά (lit., spiritual phenomena) and χαρίσματα (gifts) as synonyms in 1 Cor. 12:1 and 12:4;[22] the Spirit is the power of grace, and χαρίσματα grow out of χάρις (cf. Rom. 12:6). Paul underscores the indissoluble connection between the work of the Spirit and love by defining the church as σῶμα Χριστοῦ. The body, as the life space created by Christ, obligates the individual members to a kind of being and acting that is responsible only to love.[23] Therefore the variety of the Spirit's activities must correspond to the unity of the one church, for both have the same origin: God's love through the Son in the power of the Spirit. The Spirit produces what is useful to the church and leads to its edification, so that not the individualistic self-realization of the individual member but only the edification of the congregation as a whole corresponds to the work of the Spirit (cf. 1 Cor. 14:3, 5, 26). The Spirit integrates individuals into the orderly structures of the church, structures characterized by the power of love (cf. 1 Cor. 13) and the transvaluation of the structures of the old world (cf. 1 Cor. 12:13; Gal. 3:26–28).

18.3 Father, Son, and Holy Spirit

How does Paul think about the relation between God, Jesus Christ, and the Spirit? He is doubtless no advocate of a trinitarian *doctrine*[24] later fixed in ontological categories and expressed in the concept of persons, but there are nonetheless expressions and images that show the beginnings of reflections on how the three are related. The point of departure is the basic *theocentric* characteristic of all Pauline theology; everything comes from God and goes to God.[25] Also, Paul clearly distinguishes Christ and the Spirit and places them in a gradu-

---

21. Cf. Roloff, *Kirche im Neuen Testament*, 137.

22. In 1 Cor. 12:4 Paul abandons the obvious term πνευματικά and thus calls a halt to any attempt to base individual privileges on manifestations of the Spirit; cf. Hans Weder, *Neutestamentliche Hermeneutik* (Zurich: Theologischer Verlag, 1986), 34–35.

23. Cf. Pfeiffer, *Einweisung*, 221ff.

24. Cf. Fee, *God's Empowering Presence*, 829–42; Horn, *Angeld des Geistes*, 415–17 is more reserved in his analysis of the triadic expression in 2 Cor. 13:13 (cf. Gal. 6:18; Phil. 2:1; Philem. 25).

25. See above, section 15.2 ("God as the Father of Jesus Christ").

ated series. Of these three, it is said only of Christ that he is the Son of God (cf. Gal. 4:4; Rom. 1:3) who died for our sins in order to gain salvation for us (cf. 1 Cor. 15:3ff.; 2 Cor. 5:15; Rom. 5:8).[26] On the foundation of this primary ordering of theology proper and Christology, we can describe the internal unitive role of pneumatology: the Spirit certifies and represents the salvation willed by God and effected in the Christ event; it names, makes present, and powerfully determines the new being. The Spirit comes from God and is closely related to Jesus Christ in its works. As the power of God, it leads people to faith in Jesus Christ (cf. 1 Cor. 2:4–5), enables confession to the Kyrios (cf. 1 Cor. 12:3), and sanctifies the believers (cf. 1 Cor. 6:11; Rom. 15:16). The Spirit certifies the new status of adopted children (lit. "sons") of God (Gal. 4:4ff.), pours the love of God into the hearts of believers, and effects finally the transformation into the eschatological glory (cf. 1 Cor. 15:44–45; Rom. 8:18ff.). The Spirit of God, so creatively active in the resurrection that it also became the Spirit of Christ, encompasses and characterizes the new being of baptized believers.

This fundamental relatedness to God and Jesus Christ does not, however, exclude the Spirit from having a certain independent status for Paul. The relation of the Spirit to God and Jesus Christ cannot be satisfactorily described in the categories of subordination, coordination, or identity. As the one who proceeds from Christ, the Spirit also has its own personal reality, as 1 Cor. 12:11 shows: "All these are activated by one and the same Spirit, who allots to each one individually just as the Spirit chooses." The Spirit does not appear in Paul as an independent person but is still thought of in personal terms. The Spirit leads to the Father, for he/she/it[27] teaches believers to say "Abba" (cf. Rom. 8:15, 27),[28] makes intercession for the saints before God, and even searches out the depths of God (cf. 1 Cor. 2:10). Although the Spirit works only as a power from God and acts only on behalf of God and the Kyrios, it still has a personal aspect.

The internal interconnectedness of theology proper, Christology, and pneumatology constitutes the force field of Pauline thought and can be described as follows: *the Spirit is classified with God and Christ in that through God's Spirit, Christ becomes a life-giving Pneuma.* The Pneuma comes from God and binds baptized believers to God through Christ. Thus the concept of the salvific divine life-giving power links the three fundamental realms of Pauline thought.

26. Appropriately, Schlier, *Galater*, 249: "The Spirit is, of course, not a power given with existence itself but the power of Christ himself that overcomes existence along with Christ. The Spirit is Christ in the power of his emerging presence with us."

27. Translator's note: In German, as in Greek, the pronoun referring to the Spirit is determined by the grammatical gender of the word for "Spirit" (neuter in Greek; masculine in German). English is not so structured, and so the choice of pronoun seems to communicate whether the Spirit is thought of in personal terms (he, she) or not (it) and thus cannot communicate the way the term is used in either Greek or German. English translations of the Bible and of theological works in German (and other languages) must make choices not necessary or meaningful in Greek or German.

28. Cf. Horn, *Angeld des Geistes*, 418–22.

19

Anthropology

The Struggle for the Self

In the formation of philosophical and religious symbolic universes of antiquity, one issue was omnipresent: what does it mean to be a human being?[1] Paul understood the meaning of human existence from the perspective of his Christ hermeneutic, which resulted in new insights and solutions. Because only Christ has overcome the hostile powers of sin and death, the idea prevailed within the Pauline symbolic universe that human life by nature exists within a comprehensive set of connections. People cannot live out of themselves, on their own resources, for they always find themselves in a previously existing force field where various powers already hold sway. As a creature, the human being is not autonomous but is exposed to the powers that prevail in creation: God, and evil in the form of sin.[2]

1. Cf. Plato, *Alcibiades major* 1.129e: Τί ποτ' οὖν ὁ ἄνθρωπος; (So what is a human being?).
2. Cf. Ernst Käsemann, "Aspekte der Kirche," in *Kirchliche Konflikte* (Göttingen: Vandenhoeck & Ruprecht, 1982), 10: "What binds together Christology, anthropology, and sacramental doctrine . . . is the understanding of bodily existence as gift and participation, seen in cosmic perspective: belonging to a world, either of blessing or curse, God's world or the demonic world."

19.1 Human Being and Corporeality: σῶμα and σάρξ

For Paul, corporeality constitutes the essence of human existence in its creatureliness.[3] Because of the reality of sin, corporeality for Paul also always means endangered corporeality, and so he distinguishes between σῶμα and σάρξ.

"Body"

The key term σῶμα (body, corporeality) appears in Paul with three contextual meanings:[4]

(1) Paul uses σῶμα as a *neutral* designation of the human physical constitution.[5] Abraham had a body that was already practically dead (Rom. 4:19). When Paul issues his condemnation of the immoral person in Corinth, he is absent in body (1 Cor. 5:3, ἀπὼν τῷ σώματι; cf. also 2 Cor. 10:10) but present in spirit. Paul bears the marks of Jesus on his body (Gal. 6:17), such as from wounds that he had received in beatings during his mission work (cf. 2 Cor. 11:24–25). In a marriage each partner has a claim on the body of the other (1 Cor. 7:4, "For the wife does not have authority over her own body, but the husband does; likewise the husband does not have authority over his own body, but the wife does"). As the place of human desires and weaknesses, the body must be tamed (1 Cor. 9:27). Even giving one's body to be burned in martyrdom is of no use if one does not have love (1 Cor. 13:3). In 1 Cor. 15:38, 40 Paul elevates σῶμα existence to being essential to all existence as such, for God gives to every creature a body that fits its particular nature.

(2) Paul also uses σῶμα in a *negative* sense. In Rom. 6:6 the apostle speaks of the destruction of the body of sin in baptism. Here σῶμα τῆς ἁμαρτίας (body of sin) means nothing different from σῶμα τοῦ θανάτου (body of death) in Rom. 7:24: the human being totally exposed to the powers of sin and death. Even after they have been freed from these powers through the Christ event, Paul can challenge his readers not to let sin reign in their σῶμα θνητόν (mortal body; cf. Rom. 6:12). In Rom. 8:10 (σῶμα νεκρόν [the body (is) dead]) and 8:11 (σῶμα θνητόν), σῶμα is used in very much the same sense as σάρξ, describing

---

3. For the history of research, cf. Karl-Adolf Bauer, *Leiblichkeit, das Ende aller Werke Gottes* (Gütersloh: Gütersloher Verlagshaus, 1971), 13–64; Robert K. Jewett, *Paul's Anthropological Terms: A Study of Their Use in Conflict Settings* (AGJU 10; Leiden: Brill, 1971), 201–50; Udo Schnelle, "Neutestamentliche Anthropologie," *ANRW* 26.3:2658–2714.

4. The important foundational work is still Bultmann, *Theology of the New Testament*, 1:192–203; cf. further Schweizer and Baumgärtel, "σῶμα," *TDNT* 7:1024–94; Alexander Sand, *Der Begriff Fleisch in den paulinischen Hauptbriefen* (BU 2; Regensburg: Pustet, 1967); Robert Horton Gundry, *Soma in Biblical Theology: With Emphasis on Pauline Anthropology* (SNTSMS 29; Cambridge: Cambridge University Press, 1976); Schnelle, *Human Condition*, 55–59; Dunn, *Theology of Paul*, 55–61.

5. Extensive analyses of all relevant instances of σῶμα are found in Bauer, *Leiblichkeit*, 67–181; cf. further Gundry, *Soma*, 29–50.

the human body as it confronts the power of sin. Can Paul simply equate σάρξ and σῶμα? This seems to be indicated by their parallel use in 2 Cor. 4:11 and Rom. 8:13, where, analogously to σῶμα θνητόν, Paul speaks of "our mortal flesh" (θνητὴ σάρξ ἡμῶν; cf. 2 Cor. 5:4). So also ἐπιθυμίαι ([evil] desires) can have their source in the σῶμα (Rom. 6:12) as well as the σάρξ (Gal. 5:16–17, 24). Nonetheless, to simply equate the two misses Paul's own understanding, for in Rom. 8:9 the apostle explicitly emphasizes the change of existence that transpires in baptism from the realm of σάρξ into the realm of the πνεῦμα (Spirit). Thus Rom. 8:10–11, 13 can no longer speak of being determined by σάρξ but only of being confronted by σάρξ. Σῶμα as such has not become a slave to the alien powers of σάρξ and ἁμαρτία[6] and thus deprived of its own will, yet it finds itself in the constant danger of being taken over by them again. Those who have been baptized have really died to sin (cf. Rom. 6:1ff.), but sin is not dead. It lives on in the world and continues to tempt and test the body. This is why Paul can speak of the σῶμα θνητόν or the σῶμα τῆς ἁμαρτίας without abolishing the fundamental distinction between σάρξ and σῶμα. Σῶμα is the person himself or herself whereas σάρξ is an alien power claiming power over human beings.

(3) Paul uses the term σῶμα in a *positive* sense as his comprehensive expression for the human self.[7] The body is essentially much more than food and drink (1 Cor. 6:13a); it is not defined by biological functions but, rather, belongs to the Lord (1 Cor. 6:13b, "The body is meant not for fornication but for the Lord, and the Lord for the body"). As the locus of sexuality (cf. 1 Cor. 6:18; 7:4; Rom. 1:24), the body may not be defiled through sexual immorality; on earth Christians must instead place their bodies at the disposal of their Lord as "a living sacrifice, holy and acceptable to God, which is your spiritual worship" (θυσίαν ζῶσαν ἁγίαν εὐάρεστον τῷ θεῷ, τὴν λογικὴν λατρείαν ὑμῶν, Rom. 12:1b). It is precisely in bodily existence that faith acquires visible form. As the dwelling place of the Holy Spirit, the body is no longer available for one's own arbitrary disposition (1 Cor. 6:19). The autonomous "I" is no longer in control of the body of the believer because God himself has established the body as the place where he will be glorified: δοξάσατε δὴ τὸν θεὸν ἐν τῷ σώματι ὑμῶν (glorify God in your body, 1 Cor. 6:20; cf. Phil. 1:20). It is precisely in bodily existence that indicative and imperative, God's affirmation of us and God's claim upon us, are fused into a unity,[8] because that is the place where

6. Contra Bultmann, *Theology of the New Testament*, 1:197, who comments regarding Rom. 8:13 that here the σῶμα has fallen under the sway of an alien power and that the πράξεις τοῦ σώματος (passions of the body) are nothing else than ζῆν κατὰ σάρκα (to live according to the flesh). For critique, see Käsemann, *Romans*, 221–26; Bauer, *Leiblichkeit*, 168–69.

7. Bultmann, *Theology of the New Testament*, 1:194, formulates it concisely: "Man does not *have* a *soma*; he *is* a *soma*." For debate with Bultmann, cf. Gundry, *Soma*, 29–50.

8. Cf. Eduard Schweizer, "σῶμα," *EDNT* 3:323.

the new being is called to faithful obedience.[9] To withhold the body from the Lord's service is to withhold oneself completely.

For Paul, there is no human identity apart from bodily existence, and so he also thinks of the resurrection reality and thus postmortal existence in bodily terms.[10] Just as believers on earth are connected bodily to Christ, so the resurrected one effects the transition and transformation of human beings from pre-mortal to postmortal existence.[11] God's life-giving power, present in the Spirit, overcomes even death and creates a spiritual body (σῶμα πνευματικόν) into which the pre-mortal human self and thus one's personal identity are taken up into a qualitatively new mode of existence (cf. 1 Cor. 15:42ff.).[12] When Paul speaks of the redemption of our present body (Rom. 8:23), he is not expressing any hostility toward present bodily existence but longs for unbroken, enduring communion with the resurrected Christ. The present "body of our humiliation" (Phil. 3:21, τὸ σῶμα τῆς ταπεινώσεως ἡμῶν) will be conformed "to the body of his glory" (τῷ σώματι τῆς δόξης αὐτοῦ). What happened to Christ as "the first fruits of those who have died" (1 Cor. 15:20) will also happen to believers.

The σῶμα is the interface between the givenness of human existence in the world and the act of God for human beings. Precisely because a human being both is a body and has a body,[13] God's saving act in Jesus Christ embraces and determines the body and thereby the person's concrete existence and history. As the comprehensive definition of the human self, the σῶμα marks the place where the powers of the transitory world and God's saving intention for human beings encounter each other. Through the Spirit, believers are snatched away from their previous unredeemed history and placed in God's new reality grounded in the resurrection of Jesus Christ from the dead, a history that begins concretely, for the individual, in baptism and that will be fulfilled in the eschatological gift of the σῶμα πνευματικόν. For Paul, therefore, σῶμα means

---

9. Käsemann consistently emphasizes this aspect in his debate with Bultmann; cf. Käsemann, "Aspekte," 11: "He [Bultmann] is still indentured to the tradition of philosophical idealism when he explains the term 'body' as the relation of the person to oneself and thus gives the possibility of the self's distancing itself from itself. . . . In contrast to this view, for me everything has depended on seeing existence in the body as being related to others; it can never be isolated and regarded as an independent, responsible individual, so that also the possibility of self-transcendence is not applicable." Following Käsemann, K.-A. Bauer emphasizes that the body is the anthropological intersection of history and nature. Nature indicates solidarity with the whole creation; history is intended here to describe "the love of God that reveals itself in word and spirit to human beings, including their bodily existence" (Bauer, *Leiblichkeit*, 185 n. 14).

10. Cf. Gundry, *Soma*, 159–83.

11. See below, section 22.2 ("The Course of the Final Events and Life after Death").

12. See above, section 9.6 ("The Resurrection of the Dead").

13. Cf. Bauer, *Leiblichkeit*, 185: "The human being both is a body and has a body. The human being is thus called σῶμα inasmuch as, within the temporal sphere of Jesus Christ, one is able to differentiate oneself from oneself and thus to become the object of one's own experience."

both bodily existence, as one's self-understanding in the present world, and being incorporated into God's creative saving act.[14]

"Flesh"

Just as with σῶμα, Paul can use σάρξ (flesh, materiality) first in a *neutral* sense, to designate the physical aspect of the human condition.[15] Sicknesses are described as ἀσθένειαν τῆς σαρκός (lit. "weakness of the flesh"; NRSV, "physical infirmity," Gal. 4:13) or "thorn in the flesh" (2 Cor. 12:7, σκόλοψ τῇ σαρκί). Circumcision takes place "in the flesh," there is a "distress in this life" (so NRSV; θλῖψιν δὲ τῇ σαρκί [lit. distress in the flesh], 1 Cor. 7:28), and there are different kinds of flesh (1 Cor. 15:39, humans, fish, cattle, birds). In 1 Cor. 9:11 the "material benefits" to which the apostle can legitimately lay claim are called σαρκικός (cf. also Rom. 15:27). In the genealogical sense, σάρξ stands for membership in the people of Israel (Gal. 4:23, 29; Rom. 4:1; 9:3; 11:14).

The term σάρξ receives an explicitly *negative* connotation in the places where Paul assigns to the realm of the flesh those who live out of their own resources and trust in themselves.[16] He calls the Corinthians "fleshly" (σάρκινος), immature children in Christ (1 Cor. 3:1). They orient their lives to the superficial and external world, let themselves be blinded by what is merely visible to the physical eye, are incapable of penetrating through it to the hidden reality of God, which controls everything. Their discernment and evaluation of things takes place on the earthly level (2 Cor. 1:12). Paul designates the transient reality excluded from the kingdom of God as "flesh and blood" (σάρξ καὶ αἷμα, 1 Cor. 15:50; Gal. 1:16; cf. also 1 Cor. 5:5; 2 Cor. 4:11; Rom. 6:19).[17] The apostle speaks several times in negative form of a "life in the flesh" (cf. 2 Cor. 10:3; Gal. 2:20; Phil. 1:22, 24; Philem. 16). Fleshly people are characterized by self-centeredness and self-satisfaction, relying on their own abilities, making their own knowledge the standard of what is reasonable and real. They do not perceive that, precisely by doing so, they are helplessly delivered over to the power of sin. A life κατὰ σάρκα means life without access to God, a life imprisoned in what is earthly and transient. Paul speaks for the person living without faith when he says, ἐγὼ δὲ σάρκινός εἰμι πεπραμένος ὑπὸ τὴν ἁμαρτίαν (but I am of the flesh, sold into slavery under sin, Rom. 7:14b). Here σάρξ no longer merely describes physical existence but becomes the summary expres-

---

14. Paul makes a very close connection between one's relation to the world and one's self-understanding; eschatology and anthropology condition and supplement each other. Käsemann states the matter pointedly: "There is no such thing as man without his particular and respective world" (Ernst Käsemann, "On Paul's Anthropology," in *Perspectives on Paul* (Philadelphia: Fortress, 1971), 27.

15. A survey is provided in Sand, "σάρξ," *EDNT* 3:230–33.

16. The foundational treatment of this theme continues to be Bultmann, *Theology of the New Testament*, 1:232–39.

17. Cf. Wolff, *Korinther*, 205.

sion for a life separated from, and opposed to, God.[18] The real acting subject of life is sin, which results in death (Rom. 7:5, "While we were living in the flesh [ἐν τῇ σαρκί], our sinful passions, aroused by the law, were at work in our members to bear fruit for death").

On their own, human beings are unable to escape this fateful interplay of flesh, sin, and death. God alone can set them free from themselves and the powers of sin and death and set them in the new reality determined by the Spirit.[19] This liberation took place fundamentally in the sending of the Son "in the likeness of sinful flesh" (Rom. 8:3, ἐν ὁμοιώματι σαρκὸς ἁμαρτίας καὶ περὶ ἁμαρτίας). Jesus assumed the very mode of existence in which sin exercises its power over human beings. The death and resurrection of Jesus Christ disarmed sin of its power in the very place where it is effective: in the flesh. Although believers continue to live ἐν σαρκί, they no longer live κατὰ σάρκα (cf. 2 Cor. 10:3, "we live as human beings [ἐν σαρκί], but we do not wage war according to human standards [κατὰ σάρκα]"). Believers know that they have been snatched away from the realm of the flesh and subjected to the work of the Spirit (cf. Rom. 8:5–8). In Paul the σάρξ/πνεῦμα contrast is not a metaphysical but a historical dualism. Because there is no human existence outside the flesh and the act of God occurs for human beings in the realm of the flesh, the flesh appears as the location where human beings either stubbornly persist in their self-centeredness or through the Spirit let themselves be placed in the service of God. For Paul, it is precisely *not* the case that in their earthly existence believers are removed from the flesh; rather, the Spirit overcomes the natural self-assertion inherent in the flesh and blocks the access to sin.

19.2 Sin and Death

The distinctive features of the Pauline understanding of sin are manifest in the apostle's linguistic usage.[20] Paul characteristically uses the term ἁμαρτία in the singular (cf., e.g., 1 Cor. 15:56; 2 Cor. 5:21; Gal. 3:22; Rom. 5:21; 6:12; 7:11). Plural forms are found in pre-Pauline traditional formulations outside the Letter to the Romans (cf. 1 Thess. 2:16; 1 Cor. 15:3, 17; Gal. 1:4). In Romans, a document in which Paul reflects intensively on the nature of sin, the singular ἁμαρτία clearly dominates, with only three instances of the plural (the citations from the Septuagint in Rom. 4:7 and 11:27; and Rom. 7:5, qualified by τὰ παθήματα). The distribution of the word is striking: of the 173 occurrences of ἁμαρτία in the New Testament, 59 are in the undisputed Pauline letters; of these, 48 are found in Romans (1 Thessalonians, 1; 1 Corinthians, 4; 2 Corinthians, 3; Galatians, 3; the word is missing from Philippians and Philemon). In 1 Thessalonians Israel is considered

---

18. Cf. Sand, "σάρξ," *EDNT* 3:233.
19. See above, section 12.8 ("Sin, Law, and Freedom in the Spirit").
20. Cf. Röhser, *Metaphorik*, 7ff.

to be rejected because of its transgressions/misdeeds (1 Thess. 2:16),[21] but the basic idea of the Pauline doctrine of sin first clearly emerges in 1 Corinthians: Christ "died for our sins" (1 Cor. 15:3b; cf. 15:17); that is, he overcame the power of sin through the cross and resurrection. In passing and without systematic reflection, 1 Cor. 15:56 states that sin is the sting of death and gains its power through the law.[22] According to 2 Cor. 5:21, God made the nonsinner Jesus Christ to be sin for us "so that in him we might become the righteousness of God." The anarthrous ἁμαρτία in 2 Cor. 11:7 is to be understood in the sense of "mistake, error" (NRSV, "Did I commit a sin . . . ?" = "Did I do something wrong . . . ?").[23] The logic that becomes characteristic of Romans already appears in Galatians: according to the will of the Scripture (and thus of God), the Jews, too, stand under the power of sin, to which everything is subject, in order that the promises might be given to those who believe (Gal. 3:22). If the Galatians want to have themselves circumcised, they fall short of the liberating power of the death of Jesus "for our sins" (Gal. 1:4). Christ cannot be a servant of the power of sin (Gal. 2:17),[24] for through him it becomes clear that the law/Torah cannot set people free from sin. In Romans the connection between the extensive treatment of the righteousness/law theme and the doctrine of sin is obvious. When Paul gives a comprehensive statement of his nomology and declares the hamartiological equality of Jews and Gentiles (Rom. 1:18–3:20), he must also reflect on the nature and function of sin.

Sin as Antecedent Power

Two aspects are characteristic of the Pauline understanding of sin: concentration on the absolute use of the term ἁμαρτία and the refusal to make distinctions or differentiations within the concept of sin. Sin is an antecedent power with fateful character in every human life. In the linguistic usage of the apostle, the fundamental insight becomes clear that human beings in their natural state stand under the power of sin, from which there is no escape, and that this power determines their actions. Thus the plural "sins" (ἁμαρτίαι) in 1 Cor. 15:17/Rom. 7:5, the declarations of inexcusability in Rom. 1:20; 2:1, and the descriptions of the human condition in Rom. 3:23 ("all have sinned and fall short of the glory of God") and Rom. 14:23b ("whatever does not proceed from faith is sin") all refer to sinful acts / transgressions without thereby neutralizing the importance of ἡ ἁμαρτία as the antecedent force field in which every human being lives.[25] The power of sin precedes and is the

---

21. For analysis, cf. Umbach, *In Christus getauft*, 68–70.

22. See above, section 9.7 ("The Cross, Justification, and the Law").

23. Cf. Windisch, *Korintherbrief*, 334.

24. Cf. Umbach, *In Christus getauft*, 88–90.

25. Cf. Weder, "Gesetz und Sünde," 331: "The qualitative leap we see here in Paul's thinking thus consists in the fact that he goes beyond a quantitative statement of human sin of some (perhaps many) by the qualitative declaration that all human beings are, as such, sinners."

basis of individual sinful acts (cf. 5:12: "Therefore, just as sin came into the world through one man, and death came through sin, and so death spread to all because all have sinned").[26] The character of sin as a particular act has no substantial or temporal independence over against its fateful character.[27] Sin is much more than some sort of defect in the way one lives one's life. It has the character of an inescapable power (cf. 7:14–25a) to which every person apart from faith is enslaved.[28] Sin is even able to commandeer the law/Torah and to pervert its intended function as implementing the life-giving will of God into its opposite.[29] Paul thus ends up saying something he does not really intend: God's first covenant was not able to restrain the spreading power of sin and death. Living in the realm where sin rules, human beings are delivered into the hands of death and nothingness (cf., e.g., 5:12; 6:16, 21, 23; 8:2).

What caused Paul to develop such a hypostatization of sin? The point of departure for his reflections can hardly be found in his anthropology,[30] for his view of the human condition pictured above is not available for objective observation but can only be seen by faith. On the contrary, here too the logic is shaped by the fundamental idea of the Pauline Christ hermeneutic: only faith in Jesus Christ saves, and so alongside him no other authority can have a salvific function.[31] Not anthropology but Christology and soteriology provide the foundation for the Pauline doctrine of sin. In Galatians and especially in

26. Differently, Bultmann, *Theology of the New Testament*, 1:251: "He holds the idea that sin came into the world by sinning."

27. Cf. Umbach, *In Christus getauft*, 201, on Rom. 5:12: "By the sinning, or disobedience, of the one (Adam) ἡ ἁμαρτία came into the world, that is, to all human beings (12d) and since then has determined the general human condition in both action (ἥμαρτον ["they sinned"]) and its result (θάνατος)." Differently, e.g., Theobald, *Römerbrief*, 151ff., who emphasizes the dialectic in Paul's understanding of sin: "For him, sin is both: a power that determines history (5:12a) and a deed for which human beings are responsible (5:12d). . . . The presence of the power of sin in the world resulting from Adam's sin (5:12a) is not a mythical reality that hovers over history but sin's expression of its power and sin's on-stage appearance in the sinful acts of all human beings" (pp. 153–54).

28. See above, section 12.8 ("Sin, Law, and Freedom in the Spirit").

29. The law/Torah is only *one* aspect of the Pauline understanding of sin; in Bultmann, *Theology of the New Testament*, 1:242, however, it takes center stage: "The attitude of sinful self-reliance finds its extreme expression in man's 'boasting' (καυχᾶσθαι). It is characteristic both of the Jew, who boasts of God and the Torah (Rom. 2:17, 23), and of the Greek, who boasts of his wisdom (1 Cor. 1:19–31). It is also a natural tendency of man in general to compare himself with others in order to have his 'boast' thereby (Gal. 6:4). How characteristic boasting is for the Jew, Rom. 3:27 shows."

30. Bultmann, ibid., 1:191, seems close to sharing this misunderstanding when he emphasizes, "Therefore, Paul's theology can best be treated as his doctrine of man: first, of man prior to the revelation of faith, and second, of man under faith."

31. Appropriately, Helmut Merklein, "Paulus und die Sünde," in *Studien zu Jesus und Paulus* (2 vols.; WUNT 43, 105; Tübingen: Mohr Siebeck, 1987), 2:335ff., who points out the paradigm shift in Pauline thinking and notes, "This paradigm shift in Paul's thought confers on the thesis of universal human sinfulness a foundational character that it had never had within similar paradigms. Inquiry about the genesis of Pauline theology must therefore keep this paradigm shift in mind. It can even be considered its true basis."

Romans, Paul had to explain why the law/Torah is not able to deliver the life it promises. Paul attempted to support his thesis with the argument, unacceptable for Jews (and conservative Jewish Christians), that the law/Torah was secondary to sin both chronologically and substantially. The Pauline doctrine of sin is thus in practice the attempt at a later and supplementary rationalization for the already firmly fixed conclusion of an argument. Also, the relation between the character of sin as a power/fate and a particular deed, a problem that cannot finally be resolved, results from Paul's cognitive starting point: the magnitude of the saving act by which all human beings can be saved must correspond to the magnitude of the fate in which all human beings are enmeshed.

The Origin of Evil

The Pauline doctrine of sin cannot simply be reduced to nomology[32] or apologetics, however, for it also makes an original contribution to a debate that was carried on both in Judaism and in the Gentile Hellenistic world: the question of the origin of evil and the cause of defective human conduct.

According to Paul, sin is the real cause for the fact that the good intentions of human beings are perverted into their opposite, which can finally result only in death (Rom. 7:13). From this basic insight comes the apostle's anthropological argumentation in 7:14–25a, in which he elaborates on the ego's inescapable entanglement in the web of sin. In 7:14 Paul names a general circumstance that still applies in the present: as a physical being, every human is subject to the power of sin. Apart from faith, an awareness of this situation is just as impossible as is escape from it, for sin perverts the goodwill of human beings into its negative. Epictetus (*Diatr.* 2.26.1) also reflects on this typical difference between what one really wants to do and what one actually does:[33] "Every error [πᾶν ἁμάρτημα] involves a contradiction. For since he who is in error [ὁ ἁμαρτάνων] does not wish to err, but to be right, it is clear that he is not doing what he wishes [ὃ μὲν θέλει οὐ ποιεῖ]." A little later Epictetus says (*Diatr.* 2.26.4–5), "He, then, who can show to each man the contradiction that causes him to err, and can clearly bring home to him how he is not doing what he wishes, and is doing what he does not wish [πῶς ὃ θέλει οὐ ποιεῖ καὶ ὃ μὴ θέλει ποιεῖ], is strong in argument, and at the same time effective both in encouragement and in refutation. For as soon as anyone shows a man this, he will of his own accord abandon what he is doing. But so long as you do not point this out, be not surprised if he persists in his error; for he does it because he has an impression that he is right." For both Paul and Epictetus, there is a

---

32. Weder, "Gesetz und Sünde," 331, points this out: "The fact that sin is understood independently of the law corresponds to the other fact that righteousness is understood independently of the law."

33. On Rom. 7:15, 19 and the parallels in Epictetus, cf. esp. Theissen, *Psychological Aspects*, 216–26.

contradiction within the human person between the intention of the act and the practical carrying out of the intention. But there is a fundamental difference between Paul and Epictetus when they explain the reason for this contradiction. For Epictetus, wrong conduct can be overcome by right knowledge. Here we have an optimistic picture of human nature, a picture in which reason, as the standard of action, makes it possible to overcome such wrong conduct.[34] Paul does not share this confidence, since for him the acting subject is really sin, not the knowledgeable human being. Human beings by nature are not at all able to see what their situation actually is, for Jesus Christ alone is able to free human beings from this situation through the gift of the Spirit.

In a way different from Epictetus's, Cicero, in the context of his critique of the Stoic theology, reflects on the question of whether the evil in the world is the work of the gods. "For if the gods gave man reason, they gave him malice" (*Nat. d.* 3.75). Human beings use the divine gift of reason not for the good but in order to betray each other. It would thus have been better if the gods had withheld reason from humans (cf. *Nat. d.* 3.78). But now, when good people have troubles and things go well for bad people, stupidity prevails, and we find that "we, for whose welfare you say that the gods have cared most fully, are really in the depth of misfortune" (*Nat. d.* 3.79). The gods must therefore be subject to this charge: "They should have made everyone good, if they were really concerned for humanity" (*Nat. d.* 3.79). Seneca, a contemporary of Paul, has a predominantly pessimistic evaluation of the human situation. Both humanity as a whole (*Ep.* 97.1, "No epoch is free from guilt") and individual human beings (*Ira* 2.28.1, "Not one of us is without guilt") fail to attain true insight and moral goodness. Experience teaches that even the most circumspect transgress (cf. *Ira* 3.25.2), so that this insight is unavoidable: "We have all sinned [*peccavimus omnes*]—some in serious, some in trivial things; some by deliberate intention, some by chance impulse, or because we were led away by the wickedness of others; some of us have not stood strongly enough by good resolutions, and have lost our innocence against our will and though still clinging to it" (*Clem.*

---

34. Similarly, Dio Chrysostom, *Alex.* 14, 15, who answers the question of the origin of good and evil as follows: "All things which happen to men for their good are without exception of divine origin; not only is this true if a voyager has the luck to find a pilot with experience, or a nation or a city to secure good leaders, but also if a physician arrives in time to save his patient, we must believe that he is a helper come from god, and if one hears words of wisdom, we must believe that they too were sent by god. For in general, there is no good fortune, no benefit, that does not reach us in accordance with the will and the power of the gods; on the contrary, the gods themselves control all blessings everywhere and apportion lavishly to all who are ready to receive; but evils come from quite a different source, as it were from some other fount close beside us. Take for example the water of Alexandria—that which keeps us alive and nourishes us and is truly the author of our being: it descends from some region up above, from some divine fount; whereas the filthy, evil-smelling canals are our own creation, and it is our fault that such things exist. As physician and healer, it becomes the philosopher's task to bring people to right insight and appropriate action by instruction in reason."

1.6.3). The law as the norm of conduct and common life offers no protection: "Who is the man who can claim he has never violated any law? . . . How much is required by the sense of duty, love for humanity, generosity, righteousness [*iustitia*], loyalty [*fides*], all of which stand outside the written laws" (*Ira* 2.28.2). No one can pronounce his or her own acquittal; everyone is guilty when they examine their own conscience (cf. *Ira* 1.14.3). The unerring judgment of Seneca the philosopher and the experiences of Seneca the psychologist force the conclusion on him that human beings never live up to their potential.[35]

In a completely different cultural context, namely, in *4 Ezra* (after 70 CE), we also find a pessimistic argument about the state of the world and the human situation.[36] Although God has given the law/Torah, sin and ignorance still prevail. "For this reason, therefore, those who live on earth shall be tormented, because though they had understanding, they committed iniquity; and though they received the commandments, they did not keep them; and though they obtained the law, they dealt unfaithfully with what they received" (*4 Ezra* 7:72). There are only a few righteous (*4 Ezra* 7:17–18, 51) because the rule of sin is so pervasive, and so the question forces itself on the author, "For who among the living is there that has not sinned, or who is there among mortals that has not transgressed your covenant?" (*4 Ezra* 7:46). The author obviously has no confidence that the law can change this situation:[37] "For all who have been born are entangled in iniquities, and are full of sins and burdened with transgressions" (*4 Ezra* 7:68). Here an anthropological pessimism prevails (*4 Ezra* 4:38; 8:17, 35), which, although it does not infer from the given evil situation of the world and history that God is absent, evil, or incapable of changing things, nonetheless appears to take a somewhat skeptical stance toward the divine promises and saving acts.

Finally, in this regard the Qumran texts also manifest great similarities to Paul.[38] Here, too, the human creature is flesh and thus separated from God and delivered inescapably into the power of sin; the "flesh" belongs to the dominion of sin (cf. 1QS 4:20–21).[39] Not only blatant sinners but even the devout author

35. On the ideas of evil in Greco-Roman thought, cf. Fritz-Peter Hager, *Gott und das Böse im antiken Platonismus* (Würzburg: Königshausen & Neumann, 1987); and Gabriele Thome, *Vorstellungen vom Bösen in der lateinischen Literatur: Begriffe, Motive, Gestalten* (Stuttgart: Steiner, 1993).

36. For the theological potential in this text, cf. Wolfgang Harnisch, *Verhängnis und Verheissung der Geschichte: Untersuchungen zum Zeit- und Geschichtsverständnis im 4. Buch Esra und in der syr. Baruchapokalypse* (FRLANT 97; Göttingen; Vandenhoeck & Ruprecht, 1969); and Egon Brandenburger, *Die Verborgenheit Gottes im Weltgeschehen: Das literarische und theologische Problem des 4. Esrabuches* (ATANT 68; Zurich: Theologischer Verlag, 1981); *Das Böse: Eine biblisch-theologische Studie* (ThSt 132; Zurich: Theologischer Verlag, 1986).

37. Cf. Weder, "Gesetz und Sünde," 328: "Precisely because Ezra is beginning to raise doubts about the adequacy of the law for its task, the fatefulness of sin becomes the focus of his attention."

38. Cf. here H.-W. Kuhn, "Πειρασμός/ἁμαρτία/σάρξ im Neuen Testament und die damit zusammenhängenden Vorstellungen," *ZTK* 49 (1952): 209ff.; Kim, "Heilsgegenwart," 35–40.

39. On the understanding of sin in the Qumran texts, cf. Lichtenberger, *Studien zum Menschenbild*, 79–98, 209–12.

of the Qumran community belong "to wicked mankind, to the company of unjust flesh" (1QS 11:9]), and has in his flesh the perverse spirit (1QS 4:20–21), for the flesh is sin: (1QH 4:29–30, trans. Vermès], "But what is flesh [to be worthy] of this? What is a creature of clay for such great marvels to be done, whereas he is in iniquity from the womb and in guilty unfaithfulness until his old age?"). The "work of iniquity and deeds of deceit" prevail in the human race (1QH 1:27; cf. 1QS 4:10; 1QM 13:5, "their service of uncleanness"). Human beings are not able on their own to choose the good and reject the evil, but sin that dwells and struggles within them dominates them fully (cf. 1QS 4:20–21). Righteousness is thus not a human possibility that one can simply decide to choose and do. Rather, everything depends on God, who "shapes the [human] spirit" (1QH 15:22) and through the Holy Spirit (1QS 4:21) wipes out the spirit of wickedness that resides in human flesh.

Unreserved observance of the Torah (cf., e.g., 1QS 2:2–4; 5:8–11), along with complete dependence on the grace of God, makes it possible for the devout to follow God's will and to practice righteousness (1QS 11:12). The Essenes did not expect the ultimate destruction of the power of sin (including that within the Qumran community) to occur until the last judgment, still to come (cf. 11QMelch 2:6b–8a; CD 14:17–19).

The position of Paul within the religious and philosophical debates about the origin of evil and its conquest demonstrates originality not in its analysis but in its resolution. Like many of his contemporaries, the apostle sketched a gloomy picture of the human condition.[40] He derived this evaluation, however, not by observing the given situation or by insight into the inner nature of human beings but from God's liberating act in Jesus Christ. The magnitude of the saving act corresponds to the hopeless situation of those who were to be saved. The Pauline solution is distinguished by two components: (1) It takes up the contemporary religious-philosophical discourse and shows itself to be an attractive and competent conversation partner. (2) It opens up to human beings an insightful and practicable possibility of being freed from their situation. Paul differs from all other systems by the thesis that, for Christians, sin has already been overcome in baptism,[41] so that those who are baptized are essentially already liberated from the enslaving power of sin. Human beings are delivered from the deficiency and self-centeredness of their own thinking only when they anchor their existence in God; this means that *the new life cannot be a mere extension of the old, for a change of lordship brings about a changed life.* This possibility is opened up by the Christ event, which becomes concretely present in baptism, frees one from the power of sin, and places one in the freedom given by the Spirit.

40. Hommel, "Das 7. Kapitel des Römerbriefes," 166, rightly supposes that in Paul's portrayal of the inner conflicts to which humans are subject, he is taking up a topos familiar in antiquity.

41. Cf. Kim, "Heilsgegenwart," 108–11.

19.3 The Law

Paul grew up in a cultural context already familiar with numerous models of the positive function of the law or laws, not only in his Jewish mother religion but also in the originally Greco-Roman realm.[42] There was already a given connection between law, righteousness/justice, and life.

The Law in Greco-Roman Thought

Within the political communities of antiquity, the law[43] is the norm that fosters respect for the gods[44] and justice between human beings, thus making life possible.[45] According to Xenophon, *Mem.* 4.6.6, Socrates says, "We are rightly advised when we confirm that those are just who know the legal rules of relating to other human beings." According to Aristotle, justice receives its internal purpose and determination from the laws, so that he can state, "Whoever disdains the laws is unjust, and as we have seen those who respect them are just. This means therefore: everything lawful is in the broadest sense of the word just" (*Eth. nic.* 5.1138a).[46] Human justice results from living in accordance with a norm; a righteous life is a life that corresponds to the law. The laws, as the norms of justice, enable people in the polis to live together in a reasonable manner, and whoever violates the laws acts against the polis.[47] As the "gift of the gods" (Demosthenes, *Or.* 25.16, δῶρον θεῶν)

42. The importance of this area of research for Paul's understanding of the law has only been perceived gradually; in addition to the bibliography in Sonntag, *ΝΟΜΟΣ ΣΩΤΗΡ*, cf. esp. Haacker, "'Antinomismus' des Paulus," 387–404; and Francis Gerald Downing, *Cynics, Paul, and the Pauline Churches: Cynics and Christian Origins II* (London: Routledge, 1998), 55–84.

43. I use the terminology as follows (see above, section 11.3 ["The Doctrine of the Law and of Justification in Galatians"]): "Torah" is used here when (ὁ) νόμος appears to mean the revelation on Sinai and its associated complex of traditions. When Paul makes statements about (ὁ) νόμος that include the Torah but at the same time go beyond its *foundational* character, "law/Torah" is used here. When by the word (ὁ) νόμος Paul means a law/rule/principle/norm *with no reference to the Torah*, this will be made explicit. I will continue to use expressions that include the word "law" (such as "understanding of the law") where the meaning is clear from the context. When discussing Greco-Roman authors, I use "law" or "laws," and the meaning will be clear from the context.

44. Cf. Plato, *Leg.* 10.885b: "No one who in obedience to the laws believed that there were Gods, ever intentionally did any unholy act, or uttered any unlawful word." Cf. further *Leg.* 12.996b–e.

45. See, e.g., Euripides, *Hecuba* 799–801, "How mighty are the gods and their ruler, the law; for according to the law we believe in the gods and demarcate right and wrong, and so live!" Cf. further the textual examples and analyses in Sonntag, *ΝΟΜΟΣ ΣΩΤΗΡ*, 18–46.

46. Cf. also Aristotle, *Eth. nic.* 5.1134a: "For justice exists only between men whose mutual relations are governed by law; and law exists for men between whom there is justice." Cf. further *Eth. nic.* 10.1180: "But the law *has* compulsive power, while it is at the same time a rule proceeding from a sort of practical wisdom and reason."

47. Cf. Aristotle, *Eth. nic.* 5.1138a; further, Diogenes Laertius 6.72, "It is impossible for society to exist without law"; Sextus Empiricus, *Math.* 2.31, "For the community structure is held together

and a power that establishes and promotes culture,[48] the laws preserve the life of the individual and the polis as a whole from destruction;[49] the laws have a life-giving and salvific function (cf. Demosthenes, *Or.* 24.156, οἵ τε γὰρ σῴζοντες τὴν πόλιν εἰσὶ νόμοι [The salvation of state is its laws]).[50] The laws also regulate the relation of human beings to the gods. Piety results from relating to the gods according to the laws (cf. Socrates, "Thus whoever knows the legally prescribed conduct in relation to the gods can well honor the gods this way" (Xenophon, *Mem.* 4.6.4; cf. Plato, *Leg.* 10.885b).[51] In the ancient Greco-Roman world, there was *no* realm that was not determined by the wholesome authority and function of the laws. It is only the laws that grant to the individual and to the polis justice, unity, prosperity, happiness, and continued existence.

In the first century there was also a widespread awareness that in addition to the countless individual laws, there is *one* law: "For Justice is one; it binds all human society, and is based on one Law, which is right reason applied to command and prohibition" (Cicero, *Leg.* 1.42).[52] The law includes much more than rules, for it is the presupposition established by the gods for a successful life (Cicero, *Leg.* 1.58, "But it is certainly true that, since Law ought to be a reformer of vice and an incentive to virtue, the guiding principles of life may be derived from it. It is therefore true that wisdom is the mother of all good things; and from the Greek expression meaning 'the love of wisdom' philosophy has taken its name. And philosophy is the richest, the most bounteous and the most exalted gift of the immortal gods to humanity"). The true law already existed before the fixing of particular laws in writing, for it proceeds from reason, which originated at the same time as the divine spirit. "Wherefore the true and primal Law, applied to command and prohibition, is the right reason of supreme Jupiter" (Cicero, *Leg.* 2.10).

The one, true, and valid law is the "law of nature" (ὁ μὲν τῆς φύσεως νόμος), for it alone grants freedom (Dio Chrysostom, *Lib.* 4–5). The awareness of a distinction between the original law and the written law (cf. Cicero, *Leg.* 1.42;

---

by law, and if the soul collapses when the body is destroyed, so the states also collapse when the laws are set aside."

48. Cf. Isocrates, *Nicocles* (*Or. 3*) 6–7: "We have come together, founded cities, made laws, invented arts."

49. Cf. Aelius Aristides, *Orationes* 45.226: "The law, king of all immortals as well as mortals, conducts violence with a strong hand into the way of justice" (quote from Pindar, frg. 187).

50. Cf., in addition, the text analyses in Sonntag, ΝΟΜΟΣ ΣΩΤΗΡ, 47–105.

51. Cf. also Pseudo-Pythagoras, *Carmen aureum* 1: "First honor the immortal gods, as the law requires."

52. For the earlier period, cf., e.g., Isocrates, *Panathenaicus* (*Or. 12*) 144, who says regarding the ancestral laws, "For because they followed this principle they saw their code of laws completely written down in a few days—laws not like those which are established today, nor full of so much confusion and of so many contradictions that no one can distinguish between the useful and the useless." For criticism of unjust laws, cf. also Demosthenes, *Orations* 24.119–120, 137, 139, 156.

2.10; Dio Chrysostom, *Consuet.* 1–2) was just as widespread as the insight that numerous written laws do not correspond to the intention of *the* law (cf. Cicero, *Leg.* 2.11; Dio Chrysostom, *Consuet.* 2–4; *Lib.* 5; Pseudo-Diogenes, *Epistulae* 28.1).[53] Likewise the idea is frequently found that laws do not bring justice but injustice, not freedom but restriction.[54] Despite such a spectrum of experiences,[55] the unwavering conviction persisted that life for the individual and the community can only be attained when insight into the order willed by the gods is attained.[56] Thus Dio Chrysostom can launch into a song in praise of the law: "The law is a guide to life . . . , a good rule for how to live" (*De lege* 1; cf. *Lib.* 5). The gods themselves serve the law, for it guarantees order in the cosmos.[57] It goes without saying that law and justice/righteousness belong together, for both are the guarantors of life.[58] In Greek-Hellenistic thinking, the true law is seen as a power and ordering principle in being itself that facilitates and sustains life.[59]

The Law in Ancient Judaism

There is, of course, no question about the outstanding position held by the Torah[60] within ancient Judaism.[61] Still, within ancient Judaism there was

53. Skepticism goes yet a step further; Diogenes Laertius 9.61 reports a saying of Pyrrho: "He denied that anything was honorable or dishonorable, just or unjust. And so, universally, he held that there is nothing really existent, but custom and convention govern human action; for no single thing is any more than that."

54. Cf. Dio Chrysostom, *Lib.* 5; cf. also the distinction ascribed to Antisthenes: "The wise man will be guided in his public acts not by the established laws but by the law of virtue" (Diogenes Laertius 6.11).

55. Cf. also the view that it was necessary to introduce laws because of misconduct (e.g., of the kings) and thus law does not correspond to the ideal human situation (Lucretius, *Rer. nat.* 5.958–961, 1141–1147; Seneca, *Ep.* 90.6; Tacitus, *Ann.* 3.25–26; Sextus Empiricus, *Math.* 9.14–16).

56. Cf. Epictetus, *Diatr.* 1.26.1: "But much more important is the following law of life—that we must do what nature demands [τῆς φύσει πράττειν]."

57. Cf. Dio Chrysostom, *De lege* 2.

58. Cf. Dio Chrysostom, *De lege* 6: "But such is the righteousness and benevolence which pervades the law, that for the unfortunate it has proved even more helpful than blood relatives, and for the victims of injustice it has proved more potent than their own might"; cf. further *De lege* 8.

59. Cf. Dio Chrysostom, *1 Regn.* 42, according to which the universe is ordered, "guided by a good destiny and a like divine power, by foreknowledge and a governing purpose most righteous and perfect, and renders us like itself, since, in consequence of the mutual kinship of ourselves and it, we are marshalled in order under one ordinance and law and partake of the same polity. He who honors and upholds this polity and does not oppose it in any way is law-abiding, devout and orderly."

60. For a history of the formation of the Torah and its later role in the history of Israel and Judaism, cf. Crüsemann, *Tora*.

61. Cf. esp. Nissen, *Gott und der Nächste*; and Reinhard Weber, *Das Gesetz im hellenistischen Judentum: Studien zum Verständnis und zur Funktion der Thora von Demetrios bis Pseudo-Phokylides* (ARGU 10; Frankfurt: Lang, 2000).

a spectrum of theologies of the law[62] (e.g., cultural [Diaspora Judaism influenced by its Hellenistic environment]; apocalyptic; political-theological [the differing views of Pharisees, Sadducees, Essenes, and Zealots]), and isolated individual voices that may have challenged the law's ability to deliver what it promised.[63]

Philo's understanding of the law is important; in it he fuses into a unity the Sinai Torah, the creation Torah, and the law of nature.[64] In Philo's view, both φύσις (nature), as the world principle, and the Torah both go back to the Creator God of the Old Testament, so that both must be considered together. Because the creation of the world and the giving of the law both occurred together "in the beginning," the law of nature is just as divine as the Torah: "His [Moses'] exordium, as I have said, is one that excites our admiration in the highest degree. It consists of an account of the creation of the world, implying that the world is in harmony with the Law, and the Law with the world, and that the man who observes the law is constituted thereby a loyal citizen of the world, regulating his doings by the purpose and will of Nature, in accordance with which the entire world itself also is administered" (*Creation* 3). The written Sinai Torah is essentially much older, for both Moses, as the "living law,"[65] and the concept of the νόμος ἄγραφος (*Migration* 3–6)[66] allow Philo to emphasize, through

---

62. A survey is given in Hermann Lichtenberger, "Das Tora-Verständnis im Judentum zur Zeit des Paulus," in *Paul and the Mosaic law* (ed. James D. G. Dunn; Grand Rapids: Eerdmans, 2001), 7–23.

63. For Diaspora Judaism's understanding of the law, Weber, *Das Gesetz im hellenistischen Judentum*, 37–322, provides comprehensive analyses (without Philo and Josephus). For apocalypticism's understanding, the analyses by Hoffmann, *Gesetz*, 71ff., are foundational. On the understanding among the Zealots, cf. Hengel, *Zealots*, 149–228.

The point of departure for Gerd Theissen's thesis, explaining Paul's doctrine of justification from the religious and social problems of Judaism in the first century CE, is the possible problematizing of the law in such texts as Philo, *Migration* 89–90; *4 Ezra* 7:72; 8:20–36, 47–49; Josephus, *Ant.* 4.141–155; Strabo, *Geogr.* 16.2.35–38. To be sure, there are only a few texts one can call on to support this thesis, and their interpretation is in each case disputed (cf. Theissen, *Religion of the Earliest Churches*, 211–30). On *4 Ezra*, to which appeal is frequently made, cf., e.g., Hoffmann, *Gesetz*, 217–57, who vehemently rejects the idea that the content of the law is problematic for this author; what we have instead is a specific renewal of the Deuteronomic understanding of history and the law. "Despite the seer's statements critical of the law in the dialogue section of the document, the author of *4 Ezra* is no 'pre-Christian Paul.' When one attempts to chart the complex train of thought of this document, the conclusion is unavoidable that the author's own intention is to facilitate radical obedience to the law under changed conditions" (pp. 341–42).

64. Cf. Weber, *Das "Gesetz" bei Philon*, 42–164.

65. Cf. Philo, *Moses* 1.162: "Perhaps, too, since he was destined to be a legislator, the providence of God which afterwards appointed him without his knowledge to that work, caused him long before that day to be the reasonable and living impersonation of law."

66. The virtuous lives of the patriarchs appear as prototypes of the Torah: "For in these men we have laws endowed with life and reason, and Moses extolled them for two reasons. First he wished to show that the enacted ordinances are not inconsistent with nature; and secondly that those who wish to live in accordance with the laws as they stand have no difficult task, seeing that the first generations before any of the particular statutes was set in writing followed the unwritten law with perfect ease,

the idea of a protological creation-Torah, the continuity of God's activity both temporally and in terms of its content. Philo makes no distinction between ritual and ethical commands, but the "ten words" (δέκα λόγοι, the Decalogue) constitute the foundation and summary of the individual ritual commands (cf. Philo, *Spec. Laws* 1.1). Philo consistently interprets the individual commands as formulations of the Decalogue, which in turn are interwoven with natural law. By means of the idea of (natural) morality, Philo is able to understand both the natural law and the individual commands of the Torah in ethical terms and thus accomplishes a major effort at synthesizing Jewish and Greek-Hellenistic thought.[67]

In their cultural context it was absolutely inconceivable that Paul and his churches, according to their self-understanding, would live "lawlessly," that is, without life-giving and salvific norms. As with righteousness/justice, so also the theme of the law was already a given in his cultural milieu. At the same time, the course of Paul's life from zealous Pharisee to battle-scarred apostle to the Gentiles is broken by numerous fault-lines, which have also influenced his statements about the law/Torah. It is thus necessary to distinguish between a diachronic and a synchronic approach to this thematic complex. We shall first step along the path of the apostle's life in connection with his statements about the law/Torah, which will enable us then to approach the issue on the synchronic plane and ask whether and how one may speak of a comprehensive, integrated, and/or changing Pauline understanding of the law.

19.3.1 Diachronic Analysis

From the diachronic point of view, we must first note the statements in which Paul speaks of his past life as a Pharisee.[68] The autobiographical statements in Gal. 1:13–14 and Phil. 3:5–9 permit three conclusions: (1) Paul was a zealot for the Torah who perceived himself as blameless regarding Torah observance and surpassed all his contemporaries in his dedication to the traditions of the fathers. This self-characterization is congruent with what we otherwise know about the understanding of the law by the Pharisees, who followed the traditions of the fathers in a special way, distinguishing themselves by the exact manner in which they interpreted and obeyed the law.[69] (2) If, as a ζηλωτής (zealot),

---

so that one might properly say that the enacted laws are nothing else than memorials of the life of the ancients, preserving to a later generation their actual words and deeds" (Philo, *Abraham* 5).

67. Cf. Weber, *Das "Gesetz" bei Philon*, 337: "The Torah is thus here understood as a moral law to which human beings must conform their conduct, in what they must do and what they must endure, because its observance leads to a life in social harmony, in psychological balance, in religious devotion, and thus in a wholesome communion with God and humanity and in peace with oneself."

68. Diachronic analyses of Paul's understanding of the law are found only sporadically; Wilckens, "Entwicklung," 154, points the way forward when he speaks explicitly against the exaltation of Romans as the only standard of Pauline thought and insists on a chronological way of considering the issue.

69. See above, section 3.2 ("Paul: Pharisee in the Diaspora").

Paul tended toward the radical wing of Pharisaism, then he was thoroughly at home in the world of the Torah and its interpretation. It is very probable that he knew the whole spectrum of Jewish exegesis of the law,[70] and so the thesis that Paul misunderstood or misrepresented the Jewish understanding of the law[71] must be considered very improbable. (3) His rootedness in Pharisaic tradition would lead us to expect that the problem of the law continued to be an important and sensitive theme for the apostle to the Gentiles.

The Early Period

It is thus all the more noticeable that there is no direct criticism of the law in Paul's own accounts of his call at Damascus[72] to be apostle to the Gentiles.[73] What we have instead is that God revealed to Paul the persecutor that the crucified Jesus of Nazareth is now exalted as Son of God at the Father's side where he belongs, where he continues to reign, and from where he exercises his saving power. If the core of the Damascus event is to be interpreted in christological-soteriological terms, this naturally raises the question of what consequences such a revolutionary event must have for the former Pharisee's understanding of the law. For the earliest period of the apostle's work, speculations are all that are possible;[74] Paul joined the Antiochene Gentile mission, which was already expanding (cf. Acts 11:25–26), and so the beginning point is his adoption of the theory and practice of evangelism already in practice there.[75] To begin with, the position of the Antiochene believers in Christ who had come from Hellenistic Judaism (cf. Acts 11:20–21) was critical of the temple, not critical of the law.[76] They made the overwhelming discovery that God also gives the Holy Spirit to the Gentiles (cf. Acts 10:44–48; 11:15), so that a reevaluation of the place in salvation history for believers in Christ from paganism was unavoidable. They then abandoned the requirement of circumcision,[77] a decision that carried with it an indifference to the Torah regarding the question of salvation. The fact that believers in Christ who had come from Judaism and paganism made the same confession, κύριος Ἰησοῦς (Jesus is Lord; cf. Acts 11:20), overruled previous criteria of precedence and subordination. What role did the Torah play in this

---

70. Cf. Hoffmann, *Gesetz,* 337.

71. So Schoeps, *Paul,* 213.

72. On the analysis of the texts, see above, section 4 ("The Call to Be Apostle to the Gentiles: The New Horizon").

73. Cf. Sonntag, *ΝΟΜΟΣ ΣΩΤΗΡ,* 187.

74. Cf. also the outline in Wilckens, "Entwicklung," 154–57.

75. Following W. Wrede, Heikki Räisänen, "Freiheit vom Gesetz im Urchristentum," *ST* 46 (1980): 58, formulates the matter thus: "In the beginning was the praxis."

76. This is specifically emphasized by Rau, *Von Jesus zu Paulus,* 79.

77. Differently, Rau, ibid., 81–83, who believes that circumcision was not abandoned until later, and in passing, not as a central issue.

context of the Gentile mission, which no longer required circumcision? Here
we must distinguish between the ethical core of the Torah and ritual commands. The abandonment of circumcision was connected with giving up the
ritual laws (cf. Acts 10:14–15, 28; 11:3), but on the other hand, the ethical
core of the Torah (the Decalogue) was unproblematically adopted by Gentile
Christians (including the God-fearers; cf. Rom. 7:7; 13:9). Moreover, when
Gentile Christians oriented their lives by the "law of Christ" (Gal. 6:2), the
"law of faith" (Rom. 3:27), or the "law of the Spirit" (Rom. 8:2), they were
not, according to their own self-understanding, without rules or norms and
thus also not without law.

The Apostolic Council

The apostolic council with its apostolic decree (Acts 15:29) tends to confirm
this picture.[78] Those at the apostolic council who insisted on circumcision for
Gentile Christians were unsuccessful, and the apostolic decree represents the
attempt of some Jewish Christian circles to at least maintain a minimum of the
ritual law as still in force for Gentile Christians, which in turn means they had
not previously been observed by Gentile Christians. Traditions such as 1 Cor.
7:19; Gal. 3:26–28; 5:6; 6:15 emphasize the new status of all baptized believers
before God, quite apart from circumcision or uncircumcision. Paul himself
likewise makes it clear that life together in the churches is not to be regulated
by specific prescriptions of the law (cf. 1 Cor. 10:33; Gal. 2:18; 4:12; Rom.
14:14, 20).[79] His stance toward the Torah in the early and middle periods of
his missionary work thus seems to be that Gentile Christians are included in
the people of God through faith and baptism, not by circumcision and the
ritual observance of the Torah that would follow. Faith and the Spirit, which
include an orientation to the basic ethical tradition of the Old Testament,
come forward as new norms regulating the relation of God to human beings.
Baptism, not circumcision, functions as the decisive initiation rite. According
to their own understanding, Paul and his churches were never "lawless," even
though this is the way they were seen from the perspective of militant Jewish
Christians and Jews.

Paul's understanding was that the apostolic council confirmed this arrangement, but at the same time Paul accepted the older, strict Jewish Christian
way practiced by the Jerusalem church and its sympathizers. The distinction
between the Pauline "gospel for the uncircumcised" and the Petrine "gospel for

---

78. See above, chapter 6 ("The Apostolic Council and the Incident at Antioch: The Problems
Remain Unresolved").

79. Cf. Räisänen, "Freiheit vom Gesetz," 58.

the circumcised" (Gal. 2:7)[80] is not a new arrangement that first came into force in 48 CE but the continuation of different concepts of mission that had already been practiced for some time. This means for Paul's understanding of the law that as the real newcomer, he acknowledged the full scope of the coexistence of different initiation rites and thus of different conceptions of the law that had been in place for some time and were already a part of Christian history when he came on the scene. Acts 11:3 and the conflict at Antioch indicate that the difference in these two conceptions concerned primarily the evaluation of the food laws and their consequences (e.g., regarding the eucharistic celebrations). Moreover, the Jerusalem church increasingly found itself in a completely different cultural and political situation than did Paul. Its goal was to find a way to remain within Judaism; it thus wanted and needed to attach a different importance to the Torah than was the case for Paul.

The compromise at the apostolic council, then, turned out to be only a pseudo-solution, for it was either interpreted differently by opposite sides of the issue or only provisionally accepted. Moreover, the agreement did not resolve the problems of mixed congregations (cf. the Antioch conflict), and for the Jerusalem church, it increasingly aggravated the political pressure against its continuing acceptance of the Gentile mission that did not require circumcision and for renouncing its connection to the—in Jewish eyes—apostate Paul. With at least the endorsement of the Jerusalem church, a countermission began with the goal of accepting Gentile Christians into proselyte status on the condition that they be circumcised, thus leaving the whole new movement of believers in Christ in Judaism or, as the case may be, integrating them into it.

The Galatian Crisis

The unresolved or repressed problems surfaced with full force in the Galatian crisis, and Paul saw that he was challenged to think through and resolve the problematic of the law under changed presuppositions. Thus a differentiation is unavoidable: Until the Galatian crisis, Paul acknowledged two streams of early Christianity, with the Jerusalem church (and its sympathizers) on the one side and the younger, predominantly Gentile Christian churches on the other side, each with its own way of relating to others and with its own evaluation of the Torah. Paul and his churches were free from the requirement of circumcision; the ethical core of the Torah in the form of the Decalogue was acknowledged without question, and the new norms of faith and the Spirit provided orientation for Christians' lives together, so that in practice the multitude of individual

---

80. This fundamental distinction, so important for Paul's understanding of the law, is mostly minimized in Pauline research; thus, e.g., Theissen, *Religion of the Earliest Churches*, 369 n. 8.

commandments of the Torah played only a subordinate role or none at all.[81] The data of the letters themselves confirms this assessment, for in 1 Thessalonians and the Corinthian letters, the law/Torah is either not mentioned at all (1 Thessalonians, 2 Corinthians) or only referred to in passing. Except for the allusion in 1 Cor. 15:56, Paul makes no reference to the function of the law/Torah; that is, Paul felt no need for a doctrine of the law because the law/Torah was not an urgent topic. Ethical instruction was not based primarily on the Torah,[82] and the new concept of righteousness was connected not with the Torah but with baptism. The Galatian crisis changed the situation abruptly and dramatically because now the problem of the law was massively forced upon them from outside. In the predominantly Gentile churches also, the Torah shifted from the periphery to the center, and Paul saw himself compelled to do what the Jerusalem Christians had already done: to abandon the concept that there were different ways to deal with the issue of the law and to provide a fundamental clarification of the significance of the Torah for Jews and Gentiles.

The downright breathtaking, highly emotional, and tense argumentation of Galatians, like the corrections to it provided in Romans, shows that in the Letter to the Galatians Paul for the first time advocates this form of a doctrine of justification and the law.[83] Paul universalizes and demotes the Torah in that he evaluates it as secondary both chronologically (Gal. 3:17) and materially (3:19–20). Its role in history was only to be a custodian and disciplinarian (cf. 3:24). This time of bondage has now come to an end in Christ, who liberated human beings into the freedom of faith (Gal. 5:1). Believers from both Judaism and paganism are legitimate heirs of the promises to Abraham on another basis than circumcision and the Torah (3:29). In Galatians Paul abolishes the privileged hamartiological status of Jews and Jewish Christians (2:16) and places them in the same category as humanity as a whole—in a history determined by sin (cf. 3:22).

Compared with Galatians, Paul's letter to the Romans manifests substantial changes on three levels:[84] (1) Paul introduces δικαιοσύνη θεοῦ (righteousness/

---

81. Theissen, ibid., 219ff., advocates another variation, that although the law had been a problem for Paul since his conversion, the Galatian crisis was also fundamentally important: "Only now did Paul activate his own conversion and introduce it as an argument into the public discussion—as a warning against accepting circumcision. He did this in two letters written against Judaistic counter-missionaries, Galatians and Philippians. A (current) crisis in the communities and a (long past) personal crisis now come together. The one interpreted the other."

82. See below, section 20.2 ("The New Being in Practice").

83. On the line of argument of Galatians, see above, section 11.5 ("Inclusive and Exclusive Doctrine of Justification in Paul").

84. It is by no means merely a matter of "deeper discussions" found in Romans, as supposed by Becker, *Paul*, 395. Nor is the objection persuasive that the brief temporal interval between Galatians and Romans speaks against changes in the meantime (so Dunn, *Theology of Paul*, 131), for both the textual data of each letter and the apostle's changed historical situation point to the fact that Paul had developed his position further.

justification of/from God) as a major theological term in order to underpin the theological substructure of the argument in Galatians (cf. Rom. 3:21, δικαιοσύνη θεοῦ χωρὶς νόμου [the righteousness of God *apart from law*]; cf. also Rom. 6:14b; 10:1–4). (2) This makes it possible for him to have a partially new evaluation of the law/Torah (cf. Rom. 3:31; 7:7, 12; 13:8–10); the law/Torah is no longer criticized as such but has itself now become primarily the victim of the power of sin. (3) Paul fundamentally rethinks the relation of God's righteousness to the election of Israel. These changes derive from the apostle's particular historical situation in relation to the Jerusalem and Roman churches (delivery of the collection; mission to Spain) but also from the polemically one-sided argument of the Letter to the Galatians. The Letter to the Philippians takes up the results of the doctrine of justification as set forth in Romans (cf. Phil. 3:5, 6, 9), and its understanding of the law also stands in continuity with that preceding letter.

This diachronic sketch shows how closely each stage of Paul's understanding of the law is connected with the course of his life and ministry. We cannot, therefore, speak of *the* understanding of the law held by the apostle, for Paul necessarily and appropriately worked out the application of the theme of the law in different ways corresponding to his historical situation.[85] The letters to the Galatians and to Rome document a late phase of this process, which represents a final stage of development both chronologically and materially. They provide the point of departure for the synchronic analysis of Paul's understanding of the law.

19.3.2 Synchronic Analysis

Is it possible to summarize the apostle's statements about the law/Torah in a consistent doctrine of the law? The answer to this question has considerable consequences for the systematic capability of Pauline thought.[86]

Statements about the Law/Torah

We begin with the observation that Paul speaks in very different ways about the law/Torah:

(1) Paul makes *positive* statements about the character of the law (Rom. 7:12, "So the law is holy, and the commandment is holy and just and good"; cf. also Rom. 7:16b, 22) and the possibility of obeying it (Gal. 3:12, "Whoever

---

85. Hahn, "Entwicklung," 365, has a different emphasis: "The fact that statements about justification and the law are partially lacking by no means permits the conclusion that this theme was only gradually taken into Pauline theology, whether as a result of disputes or because of reflection on the subject itself."

86. A survey of the current discussion is provided in Schreiner, *The Law and Its Fulfillment*, 13–31.

does the works of the law will live by them"; Rom. 2:13, "the doers of the law
. . . will be justified"; cf. also Gal. 5:3, 23; Rom. 2:14–15). Galatians 5:14 and
Rom. 13:8–10 explicitly emphasize the positive connection between the love
commandment and fulfilling the law.

(2) He also makes *negative* statements about the law/Torah, regarding its
character and its function. The law/Torah is deficient in both its substance (cf.
Gal. 3:19, 23, 24; 4:5; 5:4; Rom. 6:14b, "you are not under law but under
grace") and its chronological status (cf. Gal. 3:17, 430 years after the promise;
Gal. 3:24, a "custodian/disciplinarian" until Christ came; Rom. 5:20a, "But
law came in [later]"; Rom. 7:1–3), in contrast to the promise fulfilled in Jesus
Christ. The law/Torah is contrasted with the Spirit (Gal. 3:1–4; 5:18), faith
(Gal. 3:12, 23), the promise (Gal. 3:16–18; Rom. 4:13), and righteousness
(Gal. 2:16; 3:11, 21; 5:4; Rom. 3:28; 4:16). It has the function of revealing sin
(Rom. 3:20–21a, "For 'no human being will be justified in his sight' by deeds
prescribed by the law, for through the law comes the knowledge of sin. But
now, apart from law, the righteousness of God has been disclosed"; Rom. 4:15b,
"where there is no law, neither is there violation"; cf. 1 Cor. 15:56; Rom. 5:13,
20; 7:13).[87] Thus it is true that Christ, as the only locus of righteousness and
life, is the "end" of the law/Torah (Rom. 10:4). Additional functional descriptions of the law/Torah are these: "For the law brings wrath" (Rom. 4:15a); the
law/Torah evokes sinful passions (7:5); the law/Torah imprisons (7:6a, "But
now we are discharged from the law, dead to that which held us captive"). The
law/Torah is the standard in the coming judgment (2:12–13; 3:19); Israel was
given the Torah (9:4), but through its present conduct subjects itself to the
law's condemning judgment (2:17–29) and did not attain the righteousness
based on the law (9:31).

The law/Torah is incapable of breaking through the power of sin. What
was once given to provide life (cf. Deut. 30:15–16) now shows itself to be the
accomplice of death. According to Gal. 3:22, this corresponds to the Scripture
and the will of God; in contrast, Rom. 7:14ff.; 8:3, 7 only affirms the weakness
of the law/Torah over against the power of sin.

Is the law/Torah itself sin? In Rom. 7:7 Paul himself raises this objection,
which had been suggested by his own argument, so that he may emphatically
reject it. All the same, Rom. 4:15; 5:13; 7:5, 8, 9 does evoke this inference, for
here Paul attributes an active role to the law, which activates sin and thus sets
the fateful process in motion that ends in eschatological death.

(3) Paul makes *paradoxical* statements about the law, in which a law/rule/
norm is described that does not refer to the Torah (Gal. 6:2, "the law of Christ";
Rom. 3:27, "the law of faith"; Rom. 8:2, "the law of the Spirit of life in Christ
Jesus has set you free from the law of sin and of death").

87. Cf. Ps. 19:13; 32; 51; 119.

(4) We also see texts in which the term νόμος does not explicitly appear but that touch on the problem of the law thematically (1 Cor. 7:19, "Circumcision is nothing, and uncircumcision is nothing; but obeying the commandments of God is everything"; cf. also 1 Cor. 10:23–33; 2 Cor. 3).

(5) Paul uses νόμος in the *neutral* sense as a description of Jewish life (cf. Gal. 4:4; Phil. 3:5) or to introduce a quotation (cf. 1 Cor. 9:8–9; 14:21).

Can these different series of statements be brought together conceptually without harmonization, or must we simply say that Paul has differing doctrines of the law?[88] Are Paul's positions on the law/Torah perhaps even in such conflict with each other that a comprehensive view is impossible, so that one can only relegate them to the status of later rationalizations?[89] The attempt to resolve this problematic complex should proceed in two steps: First, one must have in view the conceptual problems Paul faced. One must then ask how the individual lines of Paul's understanding of the law are related to each other and whether they can be brought together into a consistent overall understanding.

Conceptual Problems

The objective beginning point for Paul's understanding of the law is the knowledge that God's ultimate will for humanity is its salvation in Jesus Christ. But then how is God's initial revelation in the Torah related to the Christ event? Paul could not affirm a direct or even a gradual contrast between the two revelations unless he also wanted to accept irreconcilable contradictions in his image of God. Was the first revelation inadequate to grant life to humanity?[90] Why did God first concern himself with the people of Israel, and only later with the whole world? What value is there in the Torah if Gentiles can completely fulfill the will of God even without circumcision? These and other questions forced themselves on Paul, for he wanted to hold fast to both convictions: the validity of the first revelation and the exclusive salvific character of the second revelation. Paul stood before two opposing fundamental principles, neither of which he could give up: (1) a valid divine institution had already been established, and (2) only faith in Jesus Christ can save. Paul thus stood before an unsolvable problem; he both wanted and needed to prove a continuity that did not exist: the continuity of the saving act of God in the first covenant with

---

88. Cf. Sanders, *Paul*, 84: "He did not have, however, one single theology of the law. It was not the starting point of his thought, and it is impossible to give one central statement about the law which explains all his other statements." Cf. further pp. 92–95.

89. Cf. Räisänen, *Paul and the Law*, 199–202, 256–63; Sanders, *Paul, the Law, and the Jewish People*, 68: "This is the best explained by hypothesizing that he thought backwards, from solution to plight, and that his thinking in this, as in many respects, was governed by the overriding conviction that salvation is through Christ"; cf. further pp. 35–36, 144–48.

90. On the power of the Torah to save and give life, cf., e.g., Sir. 17:11; 45:5; Bar. 3:9; 4:1; *Pss. Sol.* 14:2; *4 Ezra* 7:21ff.; 9:7ff.; 14:22, 30; *2 Bar.* 38:2; 85:3ff.

that of the second covenant. For "if God's own people must be converted in order to remain the people of God, then the previously established covenant cannot be satisfactory as such."[91] The conceptual problems were intensified by open questions in the praxis of the attempts of Jewish Christians and Gentile Christians to establish a common life. This situation, which the Torah did not foresee and for which it provided no regulations, thus meant that conflicts were preprogrammed. Moreover, the law problematic played a central role in the separation of early Christian congregations from Judaism. Thus the law problematic also brought pressure on Paul and his churches from outside, for both militant Jews and Jewish Christians stood in opposition to Paul.

The specific historical situation of the apostle Paul consisted of the fact that he was the first within early Christianity to see himself confronted with the full scope of this problem and therefore had to find a solution for it.[92] In the process, he had to maintain the freedom of the Gentile Christians from the require-ment of circumcision, the ritual and soteriological inadequacy of the Torah for both Jewish and Gentile Christians, at the same time postulating that the law/Torah is also fulfilled by Christians. Only so was it possible to affirm the continuing validity of the first covenant and the exclusive salvific character of the new covenant. Moreover, it was necessary for him to refute the charge of "lawlessness" that had certainly been raised by the line of argument pursued in Galatians. This unique beginning point, bound up with almost unsolvable problems inherent in the subject matter itself, should keep us from accusing Paul too quickly of distorting the Jewish understanding of the Torah or of inconsistencies or contradictions within his own understanding of the law.

Solution by Redefinition

The different lines followed by Paul's statements on the law/Torah cannot simply be harmonized or explained exclusively by attributing them to the dif-ferent church situations to which they were addressed. Paul struggled with the issue that had been forced upon him and arrived at a solution that, though incomplete, was moving in the direction of integration and consolidation. This solution consisted in redefining the essential nature of the law. A first step in this direction is represented by Gal. 5:14: "For the whole law is summed up in a single commandment, 'You shall love your neighbor as yourself.'" This idea first attains a systematic quality in the Letter to the Romans, in which Paul has gained some distance from the polemical agitation of Galatians and can also describe the positive importance of the law/Torah for Christian believers.

---

91. Cf. Heikki Räisänen, "Der Bruch des Paulus mit Israels Bund," in *The Law in the Bible and in Its Environment* (ed. Timo Veijola; Göttingen: Vandenhoeck & Ruprecht, 1990), 167.

92. Cf. Räisänen, ibid., 170, who concedes that he did not sufficiently take this aspect into consideration in his previous publications.

Romans 13:8–10 is a key text in this regard; the thesis that love is the fulfilling of the law/Torah (Rom. 13:10, πλήρωμα οὖν νόμου ἡ ἀγάπη) secures the
Pauline argument in a fourfold perspective: (1) It permits the claim of bringing the law to full validity in its innermost essence and fulfilling it, without
attributing any sort of soteriological function to it. (2) At the same time, this
idea facilitates the necessary reduction of the law/Torah into this one principle
in view of the Gentile mission that did not require circumcision. (3) Both by
concentrating the law/Torah into one command or a few basic ethical principles[93] and by defining the essence of the law as love, Paul stands within the
tradition of Hellenistic Judaism. There the tendency prevailed to identify the
commands of the Torah with a doctrine of virtue oriented to human reason,[94]
an approach that allowed Hellenistic Judaism both to preserve the Torah and
to open it up to a more universal application. Εὐσέβεια (piety, religious devotion), as the highest form of virtue, included the virtue of love, and so love of
God and love of neighbor were directly related.[95] Their cultural background
thus made it easier for Jewish Christians and proselytes to appropriate the
Pauline solution to the problem posed by the law.[96] (4) But also in the Greco-
Roman cultural context, the conviction was prevalent that kindness and love
represent the true form of righteousness/justice and the fulfilling of the laws:[97]
"And also when nature prescribes that one should care for his fellow men"
(Cicero, *Off.* 3.5.27).[98] The law that is identical with reason and in harmony
with nature can be no different in Rome from that in Athens, for "one eternal

93. Cf. *Let. Aris.* 131, 168; *T. Dan* 5.1–3; *T. Iss.* 5.2; Philo, *Spec. Laws* 1.260; 2.61–63; *Decalogue* 154ff.; Josephus, *Ag. Ap.* 2.154; *Ant.* 18.117. Differently than in Paul, however, the exaltation
of particular commands did not repeal the authority of the other commandments; on this point, cf.
Weber, *Das Gesetz im hellenistischen Judentum*, 236–39.

94. Cf. Weber, *Das Gesetz im hellenistischen Judentum*, 320: "Thus the Nomos is basically a form
of the doctrine of virtue, for the purpose of virtue is the formation of character."

95. Cf., e.g., Philo, *Spec. Laws* 2.63: "But among the vast number of particular truths there studied, there stand out practically high above the others two main heads: one of duty to God as shown
by piety and holiness, one of duty to men as shown by humanity and justice, each of them splitting
up into multiform branches, all highly laudable." Cf. also Philo, *Decalogue* 108–110, where, in the
context of his exposition of the command to honor one's parents, he mentions people who direct
their love either entirely to God or entirely to human beings: "These may be justly called lovers of
men, the former sort lovers of God. Both come but halfway in virtue; they only have it whole who
win honor in both departments."

96. Although in Jewish ethical instruction the love commandment was not of outstanding importance, it did have a significant position; cf. Karl-Wilhelm Niebuhr, *Gesetz und Paränese: Katechismusartige Weisungsreihen in der frühjüdischen Literatur* (WUNT 2/28; Tübingen: Mohr Siebeck, 1987),
122ff. and passim.

97. On the connection of ethical conduct toward God and that toward other human beings,
cf. Albrecht Dihle, *Der Kanon der zwei Tugenden* (Arbeitsgemeinschaft für Forschung des Landes
Nordrhein-Westfalen, Geisteswissenschaften 144; Cologne: Westdeutscher Verlag, 1968).

98. Cf. Cicero, *Off.* 3.5.21, 23 (it is not permitted to harm another person: "For it is to this
that the laws have regard; this is their intent, that the bonds of union between citizens should not be
impaired; and any attempt to destroy these bonds is repressed by the penalty of death, exile, imprison-

and unchangeable law will be valid for all peoples and all times" (Cicero, *Resp.*
3.22). Those who attend to the law of reason can do no harm to their fellow
human beings; they are in harmony with God, nature, and themselves. This
law of nature is not simply identical with laws promulgated by human beings,
which can lead to bondage rather than freedom (cf. Dio Chrysostom, *Lib.* 5,
ὁ μὲν οὖν τῆς φύσεως νόμος ἀφεῖται [The law of nature is eclipsed for you]).[99]
The differentiation between enslaving legal rules and the true meaning of law
is also an insight of enlightened ancient philosophy.

At the stage when he was composing Romans, Paul developed an understanding of the law that took account of the demands of the current historical situation and at the same time could be appropriated by both Jewish and
Gentile Christians. For Paul, the law/Torah continued to be the word and will
of God but not a basis or condition for salvation. Negatively, he repealed the
soteriological dimension of the law by his claim that the law itself was under
the domination of sin (cf. Gal. 3:22; Rom. 7:8); positively, he formulated the
abiding significance of the law in the love commandment (cf. Gal. 5:14; Rom.
13:8–10). Concentrating on the concept of love made it possible for Paul to
continue to advocate in Romans the theological position he had developed in
Galatians, but without being branded as "lawless." Moreover, by speaking in
Rom. 3:27 of the "law of faith" and in Rom. 8:2 of the liberating "law of the
Spirit of life in Christ Jesus" (cf. also Gal. 6:2, "law of Christ), he provides norms
that in this intentionally open-ended form could be appropriated within both
Jewish and Greco-Roman cultural contexts. Since Christians were already living
by these norms, Paul could also claim that they have by no means overthrown
the law/Torah but uphold it (Rom. 3:31). Paul sets out a new definition in
that he formulates his interpretation of the Torah (partially from his own strict
Jewish perspective) as "the law," thus at the same time integrating the Torah into
an overriding concept of law that was equally accessible to Jewish and Gentile
Christians on the basis of their respective cultural backgrounds. By means of
the concept of love, the apostle synthesizes Jewish and Greco-Roman understandings of law and thus attains a consistent, well-rounded integration of the
law thematic within his project of meaning formation.[100] By this rewriting of
the basic terminology, Paul manages to combine what cannot be combined, in

---

ment, or fine"). Cf. further Aristotle, *Eth. nic.* 5.1137b: "The same thing, then, is just and equitable,
and while both are good the equitable is superior."

99. Cf. further Cicero, *Leg.* 1.42: "But the most foolish notion of all is the belief that everything
is just which is found in the customs or laws of nations. Would that be true, even if these laws had
been enacted by tyrants? . . . For Justice is one; it binds all human society, and is based on one Law,
which is right reason applied to command and prohibition. Whoever knows not this law, whether it
has been recorded in writing anywhere or not, is without Justice."

100. Cf. above, the subsection "History as Meaning Formation" within section 1.2 ("Methodological 'Handle': Meaning Formation in Continuity and Change").

order to provide the necessary means for communicating his message within his cultural situation.

It is helpful to note that Paul also follows this path when dealing with other central theological questions. In Rom. 2:28–29 he redefines what it means to be a Jew and what circumcision is: "For a person is not a Jew who is one outwardly, nor is true circumcision something external and physical. Rather, a person is a Jew who is one inwardly, and real circumcision is a matter of the heart—it is spiritual and not literal." In Rom. 4:12 he takes up this new definition of circumcision when he states that Abraham became "the ancestor of the circumcised who are not only circumcised but who also follow the example of the faith that our ancestor Abraham had before he was circumcised." And finally, in Rom. 9:6–7 Paul issues a new definition of Israel: "It is not as though the word of God had failed. For not all Israelites truly belong to Israel, and not all of Abraham's children are his true descendants." Redefinition, which means rewriting the basic vocabulary with new content, is always necessary when symbolic universes are incompatible as previously formulated but must be brought together on a higher plane.

19.4 Faith as the New Qualification of the Self

By faith the person enters the realm of God's love for the world; faith is a new qualification of the self. The foundation and possibility of faith are given in God's saving initiative in Jesus Christ.

Faith as Gift

Faith does not rest on human decision but is a gift of God's grace.[101] This was already true for Abraham: "For this reason it depends on faith, in order that the promise may rest on grace [Διὰ τοῦτο ἐκ πίστεως, ἵνα κατὰ χάριν] and be guaranteed to all his descendants, not only to the adherents of the law but also to those who share the faith of Abraham (for he is the father of all of us . . .)" (Rom. 4:16). The basic structure of the Pauline concept of faith is clearly revealed in Phil. 1:29: "For he has graciously granted you the privilege [ὅτι ὑμῖν ἐχαρίσθη] not only of believing in Christ [οὐ μόνον τὸ εἰς αὐτὸν πιστεύειν], but of suffering for him as well." Faith is numbered among the fruits of the Spirit (cf. 1 Cor. 12:9; Gal. 5:22), for "no one can say 'Jesus is Lord' except by

---

101. Cf. the foundational reflections of Gerhard Friedrich, "Glaube und Verkündigung bei Paulus," in *Glaube im Neuen Testament: Studien zu Ehren von Hermann Binder anlässlich seines 70. Geburtstags* (ed. Ferdinand Hahn and Hans Klein; BTS 7; Neukirchen-Vluyn: Neukirchener Verlag, 1982), 100ff.

the Holy Spirit" (1 Cor. 12:3b).[102] Faith, like love, cannot be commanded, but only received, experienced, and lived out. Faith opens up a new relationship to God, a relationship human beings can only gratefully receive. The gift character of πίστις/πιστεύω (faith/believe) also determines the close relationship between faith and preaching in Paul's thought. Faith is ignited by the gospel, the power of God (Rom. 1:16). It pleased God, "through the foolishness of our proclamation, to save those who believe" (1 Cor. 1:21). Early on, the word was spread about the apostle: "The one who formerly was persecuting us is now proclaiming the faith he once tried to destroy" (Gal. 1:23). According to Rom. 10:8, Paul preaches the "word of faith" (τὸ ῥῆμα τῆς πίστεως). Faith grows out of preaching, which in turn goes back to the word from/about Christ (Rom. 10:17, "So faith comes from what is heard, and what is heard comes through the word of Christ"). Thus Christ himself in active in the word of preaching; "the hearing of faith" takes place in the preaching of the gospel (Gal. 3:2, 5, ἡ ἀκοὴ πίστεως; NRSV, "believing what you heard"). In 1 Cor. 15:11b Paul concludes his basic instruction with the words "so we proclaim and so you have come to believe." It is not the rhetorical arts of the preacher or the enthusiastic human "yes" in response that leads to faith but the Spirit and power of God (cf. 1 Cor. 2:4–5). The Spirit mediates the gift of faith and at the same time gives its content a characteristic stamp, thus giving unity to the church. Spirit and faith are related in Paul's thought as cause and effect inasmuch as the Spirit opens the door to faith and the believer then leads his or her life in the power of the Spirit. Thus Paul testifies, "For through the Spirit, by faith, we eagerly wait for the hope of righteousness" (Gal. 5:5). Finally, Gal. 3:23, 25 indicates that for Paul "faith" has dimensions that go far beyond the individualistic coming-to-believe: "coming" to faith possesses a quality related to salvation history, for faith replaces the Torah as a soteriological entity and opens up for humanity a new access to God.

The basic structure of the Pauline concept of faith as a saving and thus life-giving power and gift of God shows that it is inappropriate to understand faith as a "condition,"[103] "free deed of obedience . . . this sort of decision,"[104] "reception and preservation of the message of salvation,"[105] "communication process,"[106] or "desired human response to the Christian missionary message"[107] or even "to speak of faith as though it had the character of a meritorious achievement."[108] Such language does in part name important aspects of the Pauline

---

102. Contra Bultmann, *Theology of the New Testament*, 1:330, who states "that Paul does not describe faith as inspired, attributable to the Spirit."

103. Adolf Jülicher, *Der Brief an die Römer* (3rd ed.; SNT 2; Göttingen: Vandenhoeck & Ruprecht, 1917), 232.

104. Bultmann, *Theology of the New Testament*, 1:316.

105. Käsemann, *Romans*, 107.

106. Axel von Dobbeler, *Glaube als Teilhabe: Historische und semantische Grundlagen der paulinischen Theologie und Ekklesiologie des Glaubens* (WUNT 22; Tübingen: Mohr Siebeck, 1987), 20.

107. Becker, *Paul*, 412.

108. Schoeps, *Paul*, 205.

concept of faith, but at the same time it reverses cause and effect, for it is God's act that first makes faith possible.[109] It is God who "is at work in you, enabling you both to will and to work for his good pleasure" (Phil. 2:13). Thus faith originates from God's saving initiative; it is God who calls human beings into the service of preaching the gospel (cf. Rom. 10:13–14, "For, 'Everyone who calls on the name of the Lord shall be saved.' But how are they to call on one in whom they have not believed? And how are they to believe in one of whom they have never heard? And how are they to hear without someone to proclaim him?"). Whoever comes to faith has always already begun to believe and traces this faith back to God. God alone is the giver, and human beings are receivers, so that Paul can consistently contrast life that comes from faith and life that comes from the law/Torah (cf. Gal. 2:16; 3:12; Rom. 3:21–22, 28; 9:32). Justification διὰ πίστεως Ἰησοῦ Χριστοῦ (through faith in Jesus Christ) takes place as a gift through the grace of God (Rom. 3:24, δωρεὰν τῇ αὐτοῦ χάριτι). As the gift of God's grace, faith is that which is absolutely new, which opens up to human beings the possibility of letting God's act be effectively valid and thus of entering into the realm of this act.

A vigorous debate rages around the meaning of the expression πίστις Ἰησοῦ Χριστοῦ (see Gal. 2:16, 20; 3:22; Rom. 3:22, 26; Phil. 3:9).[110] Should we understand it as *genitivus subjectivus* ("the faith of Jesus Christ," in the sense of his obedience to God)[111] or as *genitivus objectivus* ("faith in Jesus, Christ")? The most likely meaning is *genitivus objectivus*:[112] (1) in the *genitivus subjectivus* we should expect the definite article; (2) the context of the respective passages points clearly to faith in Jesus Christ; and (3) in no Pauline text does Jesus Christ ever receive the predicate πιστός (faithful).[113]

Structural Elements of Faith

Faith attains its form in the act of confession, as programatically formulated by Paul in Rom. 10:9–10: "if you confess with your lips that Jesus is Lord and believe in your heart that God raised him from the dead, you will be saved.

109. Friedrich, "Glaube und Verkündigung," 109: "Faith is a decision made by God."

110. On the extensive debate, including comprehensive bibliographies, cf., on the one side, Richard B. Hays, "PISTIS and Pauline Christology," in *Looking Back, Pressing On* (ed. E. Elizabeth Johnson and David M. Hay; vol. 4 of *Pauline Theology*; SBLSymS 4; Atlanta: Scholars Press, 1997), 35–60 (votes for the subjective genitive); and, on the other side, Dunn, *Theology of Paul*, 61–81 (votes for the objective genitive).

111. Cf. Hays, "PISTIS and Pauline Christology," 37: "His death, in obedience to the will of God, is simultaneously a loving act of faithfulness (πίστις) to God and the decisive manifestation of God's faithfulness to his covenant promise to Abraham. Paul's use of πίστις Ἰησοῦ Χριστοῦ and other similar phrases should be understood as summary allusions to this story, referring to Jesus' fidelity in carrying out this mission."

112. Cf. the argumentation in Dunn, *Theology of Paul*, 379–85.

113. Haacker, *Der Brief an die Römer*, 87.

For one believes with the heart and so is justified, and one confesses with the mouth and so is saved." *Faith is thus only faith when it is confessed.* There is no neutral stance toward the content of the faith—it can only be confessed or denied. Precisely in the act of confession, the believer turns away from himself or herself and turns toward God's saving act, so that the believer begins to participate in the ultimate salvation of the future. Faith does not remain by itself but communicates itself, stepping over boundaries. Thus the believer cannot keep silent; rather, "'I believed, and so I spoke' [Ps. 115:1 LXX (Ps. 116:10)]—we also believe, and so we speak [καὶ ἡμεῖς πιστεύομεν, διὸ καὶ λαλοῦμεν]" (2 Cor. 4:13b).

For Paul, the content of faith is not to be separated from the act of faith, which brings one into relationship with God and others. If the content of faith is the resurrection of Jesus Christ from the dead (cf. 1 Thess. 4:13; 1 Cor. 15:14), then the acceptance of this saving message does not occur in a detached manner separate from one's own existence; rather, "faith in Jesus Christ" means to acknowledge him as Lord and to enter into a personal relationship with him. Closely connected with the content of faith is the knowledge included in faith, as Paul frequently reminds his churches (cf. 1 Thess. 4:13; 1 Cor. 3:16; 6:1–11, 15–16, 19; 10:1; 12:1; 2 Cor. 5:1; Gal. 2:16; Rom. 1:13; 11:25; and passim).

As a gift of God, faith always at the same time includes the individual factor of each particular person's religious life and activates human responsibility.[114] Paul frequently speaks of "your faith" (1 Thess. 1:8; 3:2, 5–7, 10; 1 Cor. 2:5; 2 Cor. 1:24; 10:15; Rom. 1:8, 12; Phil. 2:17; and passim), by which he emphasizes especially the missionary dimension of the faith of the churches of Thessalonica and Rome. For the apostle, there was a "growing in faith" (2 Cor. 10:15); new insights and knowledge increase, purify, and change faith. Faith is subject to changes but does not abandon its fundamental convictions. In Rom. 12:3 Paul admonishes the charismatics not to go beyond the boundaries to which they too are subject but to think with sober judgment according to the measure of faith (μέτρον πίστεως) that God has assigned.[115] Thus Paul introduces the idea of a faith that realizes itself in a particular place in a particular way, a faith that must remember its limitations, for he does not want faith to slide off into an enthusiastic, exaggerated evaluation of itself. Believers must discern and assess which gifts they have been given, and each must find his or her appropriate place in the life of the church.

Faith is grounded in the love of God made known in Jesus Christ (cf. Rom. 5:8), so that love appears as the active and visible side of faith. Because love is the essential characteristic of faith, all that does not come from faith is sin

---

114. Concisely stated by Adolf von Schlatter, *Der Glaube im Neuen Testament* (5th ed.; Stuttgart: Calwer, 1963), 371: "The will grounded in faith is love."

115. On this concept, see Käsemann, *Romans*, 334.

(Rom. 14:23). Paul insists on concord between thinking and acting, conviction and deed.[116] At the same time, he is aware that believers sometimes fail (Gal. 6:1), speaks of those who are "weak in faith" (Rom. 14:1), promises the Philippians progress in faith (Phil. 1:25), and challenges his readers to stand fast in the faith (1 Cor. 16:13; 2 Cor. 1:24; Rom. 11:20). Faith does not confer on people any visibly new quality but sets them into a historical movement and situation where they can demonstrate it, resulting in obedience (Rom. 1:5, "we have received grace and apostleship to bring about the obedience of faith among all the Gentiles for the sake of his name"). In turn, the obedience of faith manifests itself in the acceptance and preservation of the gospel.

"Faith/Believing" in Cultural Contexts

When Paul and early Christianity used the terms πίστις/πιστεύω to describe one's relation to God, they adopted and adapted a vocabulary and conceptuality that already had a wide range of connections. Thus the Septuagint regularly translates the Hebrew/Aramaic root אמן with the Greek πιστ- word group, in which the predominant meanings are "believe in" and "place confidence in."[117] Philo takes up this linguistic usage of the Hellenistic Jewish wisdom tradition (Jesus ben Sirach, Wisdom of Solomon, 4 Maccabees)[118] and develops it further, so that faith now appears as the highest virtue.[119] "How should one come to believe in God [πῶς ἄν τις πιστεύομαι θεῷ]? By learning that all other things change but He is unchangeable" (*Alleg. Interp.* 2.89). Trust in God is set over against trust in the world of external appearances, and Abraham is seen as the prototype of this kind of trust. In his interpretation of Gen. 15:6, Philo emphasizes, "Faith in God [πρὸς θεὸν πίστις], then, is the one sure and infallible good, consolation of life, fulfilment of bright hopes, dearth of ills, harvest of goods, inacquaintance with misery, acquaintance with piety, heritage of happiness, all-around betterment of the soul which is firmly stayed on Him Who is the cause of all things and can do all things yet only wills the best" (*Abraham* 268).[120] In the Greek world, the words "faith" and "believe" are first of all associated with more than fifty oracle shrines.[121] The reality of oracles had been a widespread cultural phenomenon from

116. Appropriately, Stuhlmacher, *Romans*, 77: "In accordance with all of this, faith, for the apostle, is an all-encompassing act of life which is upheld by the Holy Spirit."

117. Cf. G. Bertram, "πιστεύω κτλ.," *TDNT* 6:197ff.; Dieter Lührmann, "Pistis im Judentum," *ZNW* 64 (1973): 20–25.

118. Cf., e.g., Sir. 2:6, 8, 10; 4:16; 11:21; Wis. 16:26; 4 Macc. 7:19, 21; 15:24; 16:22.

119. Cf. Lührmann, "Pistis im Judentum," 29–34; Egon Brandenburger, "Pistis und Soteria," in *Studien zur Geschichte und Theologie des Urchristentums* (ed. Egon Brandenburger; SBAB 15; Stuttgart: Katholisches Bibelwerk, 1993), 251–88.

120. *NW* 2/1:108; see further Philo, *Heir* 90–101; *Moses* 1.83.90; *Alleg. Interp.* 2.89.

121. Cf. Veit Rosenberger, *Griechische Orakel: Eine Kulturgeschichte* (Darmstadt: Wissenschaftliche Buchgesellschaft, 2001).

around the seventh or sixth centuries BCE and continued to have an influence on all realms of public and private life into late antiquity. In this context, "faith" meant "to believe in revelations from the gods"[122] that served to interpret the future destiny of a person, especially in crisis and times of upheaval.[123] The trial of Socrates is an especially good example of the extent to which faith in oracles was also connected to political options; Xenophon portrays Socrates as a model Greek who acknowledged the gods and was himself an unparalleled advocate of the art of fortune-telling: "But in such circumstances, what else could one do than call on the gods? Thus he trusted in the gods [πιστεύων δὲ θεοῖς]. So how could he have believed that the gods did not exist [as his opponents charged]?" (*Mem.* 1.5). Oracles are the expression of a personal relation to deities, for they presuppose faith that the gods are involved in the fate of human beings and are concerned about their affairs; happiness and unhappiness, good luck and bad are perceived as the effect of the power of the gods. That πίστις/πιστεύω had strong religious connotations[124] in the non-Jewish Hellenistic world is seen in Lucian and especially in Plutarch, who about 95 CE took over the office of one of the two high priests in the oracle shrine of Apollo in Delphi. For Plutarch, faith is self-evident, for the gods are the guarantors of social and individual stability; he refers to "the reverence and faith implanted in nearly all mankind at birth" (*Mor.* 359–360). The content of faith is the foreknowledge of the gods and their help for human beings, especially in times of distress or in the border situations of life, such as sickness and death. In the whole of human life, the gods are those who "witness and direct, who lead and help us" (*Mor.* 757D). Thus atheism is criticized just as sharply by Plutarch as is superstition; both result from an inadequate knowledge of the deities (cf. *Alex.* 75; *Mor.* 164E). It is a matter of finding true piety between these two extremes, the "true religion that lies in between" (*Mor.* 171F; these are the closing words of *De superstitione*).

New Accents

Both the early Christian missionary proclamation and Paul go beyond the boundaries of the linguistic usage of Hellenistic Judaism and pagan Hellenism

---

122. Iamblichus, *Vit. pyth.* 138, reports of the Pythagoreans, "Hence they take serious interest in divination, for this alone is the means of interpreting the god's purpose. And this diligent study of theirs would seem equally worthwhile to one who believes there are gods, but to those who believe that either of these (i.e., divination or the god's existence) is silliness, both are silliness" (trans. Dillon and Hershbell).

123. The central texts are presented and interpreted in Gerhard Barth, "Pistis in hellenistischer Religiosität," in *Neutestamentliche Versuche und Beobachtungen* (Waltrop: Spenner, 1996), 173–76; and W. Schunack, "Glaube in griechischer Religiosität," in *Antikes Judentum und frühes Christentum: Festschrift für Hartmut Stegemann zum 65. Geburtstag* (ed. Bernd Kollmann et al.; BZNW 97; Berlin: de Gruyter, 1999), 299–317.

124. Here, too, cf. Barth, "Pistis," 175–85; Schunack, "Glaube in griechischer Religiosität," 317–22.

in that they make πίστις/πιστεύω the central and exclusive description of one's relation to God.[125] A second distinctive characteristic is the orientation of faith to Jesus Christ. For Paul, faith is always faith in the God who has raised Jesus Christ from the dead (cf. Rom. 4:17, 24; 8:11). Jesus Christ is at one and the same time the one who generates faith and the content of this faith.[126] The center of faith is thus not the believer but the one believed in. Because faith grows out of the preaching of the gospel, it is ultimately the act of God, grounded only in the Christ event. Therefore faith cannot be the means by which human beings create the presupposition for God's saving act. Rather, God places human beings in faith and sets them on a new way, the ground and goal of which is Jesus Christ. Although for human beings faith is not something they can generate by themselves, it is something that can be lived, experienced, and carried out in one's own deeds. *Faith thus appears as a creative act of God in human beings*, which in turn makes possible human action—indeed demands such action. Doubtless, faith also includes biographical and psychological elements and the factor of human decision, but it is preceded by God's fundamental decision. God's facilitating act of grace precedes and leads to the acceptance of the gospel, an acceptance that in turn is to be seen as a gift of God. Whoever comes to faith can only be grateful to the gospel that comes from God, the gospel that seeks acceptance and powerfully overcomes the resistance it finds in human beings.

Believers thus understand their own decision as an act of God's grace.[127] Faith does not close off human decisions but incorporates them and gives them a new orientation. In faith human beings understand themselves and the world anew. A new relation to the world is opened up[128] because now God's reality in Jesus Christ is the standard of knowledge and action. This is confirmed by the phenomenon of doubt, which originates in the opposition between the hidden reality of faith (2 Cor. 5:7, "for we walk by faith, not by sight") and the criteria of the world as generally perceived. Faith can orient itself only to the promises of the gospel message, and it receives from there the power to accept the hiddenness of its truth. Faith always takes place in the tension-filled interweaving of the experience of God and the world, whereby God's saving act in Jesus Christ is seen as the basis of all reality and is resolutely set in relation to the empirical world.

125. Cf. Gerhard Barth, "πίστις," *EDNT* 3:95.

126. Cf. Friedrich, "Glaube und Verkündigung," 102–6.

127. It is thus not possible to equate the believer's new self-understanding with God; contra Herbert Braun, "The Problem of a New Testament Theology," in *The Bultmann School of Biblical Interpretation: New Directions?* (ed. Robert W. Funk; trans. Irvin W. Batdorf et al.; JTC 1; New York: Harper & Row, 1965): 179–83, whose reduction of theology to anthropology consistently leads to the statement "Man as man, man in relation with his fellow man, implies God" (p. 183).

128. The alternative posed by Dobbeler, *Glaube als Teilhabe*, 276, is thus not applicable: "Πίστις is therefore not about a new self-understanding but a new group understanding or social understanding of those . . . made equal before God."

19.5 Centers of the Human Self

Paul designates and characterizes the innermost self of human beings in different ways. In the process, he can make connections with both Old Testament and Greco-Roman ideas.

"Conscience"

At the center of human self-awareness is the conscience. The term συνείδησις (conscience) appears thirty times in the New Testament, fourteen of them in Paul. The most intensive concentration (eight times) is found in the dispute about food sacrificed to idols in 1 Cor. 8 and 10. There are three more occurrences of συνείδησις in 2 Corinthians and in Romans; one instance of the verb σύνοιδα is found in 1 Cor. 4:4.[129]

The Old Testament and ancient Judaism know no linguistic equivalent for the Greek term συνείδησις.[130] Analogous functions can be expressed, however, with the word לֵב (heart). Thus the pounding of the heart can be regarded as the expression of a bad conscience (1 Sam. 24:5; 2 Sam. 24:10), one's heart can be pure or stained (*T. Jos.* 4:6a; *T. Benj.* 8:2), and the heart can accuse (Job 27:6). Paul probably adopted the term συνείδησις from popular Hellenistic philosophy. Here συνείδησις mostly means the awareness that one's own actions are morally condemned or approved.[131] Because the gods have given wisdom to human beings, they are capable of self-awareness. "For he who knows himself will realize, in the first place, that he has a divine element within him, and will think of his own inner nature as a kind of consecrated image of God; and so he will always act and think in a way worthy of so great a gift of the gods" (Cicero, *Leg.* 1.59). Since God has equipped human beings with their own inherent capabilities, they are able to distinguish between good and evil, for God has "placed a monitor at the side of each one of us, namely the guardian angel [δαίμων] of each person, a monitor who never slumbers, and who cannot be gotten around" (Epictetus, *Diatr.* 1.14.12; cf. *Diatr.* 2.8.11–12; Seneca, *Ep.* 41.1–2; 73.76). So also the phenomenon of a bad conscience (cf., e.g., Seneca, *Ep.* 43.4–5; 81.20;

---

129. The concentration of Pauline instances of συνείδησις in the two Corinthian letters leads Klauck to surmise that the conscience problematic was "handed off" to Paul by the Corinthians (see Klauck, "Der Gott in dir,'" 30).

130. Cf. Eckstein, *Syneidesis*, 105ff.

131. On the concept of conscience in Roman and Greek authors, cf. H. Böhlig, "Das Gewissen bei Seneca und Paulus," *TSK* 87 (1914): 1–24; P. W. Schönlein, "Zur Entstehung eines Gewissensbegriffes bei Griechen und Römern," *RMP* 112 (1969): 289–305; Henry Chadwick, "Gewissen," *RAC* 10:1025–1107; Klauck, "'Der Gott in dir,'" passim; Hans-Josef Klauck, "Ein Richter im eigenen Innern: Das Gewissen bei Philo von Alexandrien," in *Alte Welt und neuer Glaube: Beiträge zur Religionsgeschichte, Forschungsgeschichte, und Theologie des Neuen Testaments* (NTOA 29; Göttingen: Vandenhoeck & Ruprecht, 1994), 33–58; H. Cancik-Lindemaier, "Gewissen," *HRWG* 3:17–31.

105.8) points to an authority resident in each person, intertwined with virtue and reason, that insists on conduct that accords with the law of nature: "We should, therefore, have a guardian, as it were, to pluck us continually by the ear and dispel rumors and protest against popular enthusiasms" (Seneca, *Ep.* 94.55). At the turn of the first century CE, a deepening of moral self-awareness can be clearly perceived; the moral autonomy that began to solidify in human consciousness is understood as the divine representative in the human self and thus as a being and acting in harmony with reason and nature.

The central complex of texts that communicates the Pauline meaning of συνείδησις is the dispute about eating meat sacrificed to idols in 1 Cor. 8 and 10.[132] In these passages Paul means by συνείδησις neither "bad conscience"[133] nor "consciousness of God";[134] rather, συνείδησις appears as the authority of making one's own judgments. The subject about which conscience makes judgments is human conduct, which is tested regarding its agreement with traditional norms.[135] When the "strong" make use of the freedom available to them by continuing to eat meat that has been sacrificed to idols, they mislead the "weak" into doing the same. This brings the weak into an internal conflict of conscience, who now themselves eat meat consecrated by pagan sacrificial rituals even though this does not correspond to their own will and self-understanding. When the strong thus sin against their brothers and sisters, they sin against Christ (1 Cor. 8:13), who also died for the weak members of the community (8:12). The freedom of the individual is clearly limited by the conscience of the other person, who must not be placed in such a stressful circumstance. Paul can assure the strong that they need not search their own consciences every time they go to the meat market, for "the earth and its fullness are the Lord's" (10:26). Likewise, when invited to a dinner party among non-Christian Gentiles, the Christian need raise no questions of conscience but can eat whatever is served in good conscience. At the same time, however, if a weak Christian points out that the meat has been sacrificed to idols and if by eating it the strong would burden the conscience of the weak, then strong Christians are called upon to forego their own freedom. Συνείδησις thus does not here describe a feeling, a state of consciousness, or a capacity for making religious or moral judgments but an authoritative court that judges the person's conduct by given norms.[136]

In 2 Cor. 1:12, Paul must respond to objections from the Corinthian church about his own person. Some charge that he is unreliable, that he changes his travel plans, and that he is not to be trusted. Paul brings forward his conscience

132. See above, section 9.4 ("Freedom and Obligation in Christ").

133. Bultmann, *Theology of the New Testament*, 1:217.

134. Walter Gutbrod, *Die paulinische Anthropologie* (BWA[N]T 67; Stuttgart: Kohlhammer, 1934), 63.

135. Cf. Eckstein, *Syneidesis*, 242–43.

136. On the consistency of Paul's line of argument, cf. ibid., 271.

as an independent witness for the truth of his statements, so that here the overtones of the original meaning (co-knowledge) can still be heard.[137] The apostle speaks the truth not only subjectively but also objectively, for his conscience evaluates positively his way of life and his missionary work in the Corinthian church. In 2 Cor. 4:2 συνείδησις is used in a similar way: "We have renounced the shameful things that one hides; we refuse to practice cunning or to falsify God's word; but by the open statement of the truth we commend ourselves to the conscience of everyone in the sight of God." Paul sets himself before the Corinthians' decision in all candor and appeals to their conscience as a human court of appeal (cf. 2 Cor. 5:11).

In Rom. 2:14–16 συνείδησις appears as a universal human phenomenon: "When Gentiles, who do not possess the law, do instinctively what the law requires, these, though not having the law, are a law to themselves. They show that what the law requires is written on their hearts, to which their own conscience also bears witness; and their conflicting thoughts will accuse or perhaps excuse them." Here conscience, as an awareness of norms, includes the capacity to make moral judgments about one's own conduct, one's knowledge about one's self and one's conduct.[138] As a phenomenon inherent in human beings, conscience confirms for Paul the existence of the law among the Gentiles. In Rom. 9:1–2 the apostle expresses the truthfulness of his feelings as a solemn vow: "I am speaking the truth in Christ—I am not lying; my conscience confirms it by the Holy Spirit—I have great sorrow and unceasing anguish in my heart" (cf. also 2 Cor. 1:23; 2:17; 11:38; 12:19). Here conscience steps forth as an independent, personified witness for the truth and examines the agreement between convictions and conduct. According to Rom. 13:5,[139] insight into the meaning of political power and order should lead Christians to subject themselves to institutionalized authority: "Therefore one must be subject, not only because of wrath but also because of conscience." Inasmuch as it resists evil and promotes good, political authority originates in the will of God. As in Rom. 2:15, Paul is here thinking about the conscience resident in every human being, not about a specifically Christian conscience. Responsibility to the order established by God and reasonable insight into the necessity of the function of the state in maintaining law and order are already enough to cause the conscience to affirm the existence of this office.

Paul understands συνείδησις as a neutral authority for evaluating actions already done (both one's own acts and those of others), on the basis of values and norms that have been internalized. For Paul, conscience does not itself contain the basic knowledge of good and evil but rather a coknowledge, a

---

137. Cf. Lang, *An die Korinther*, 255.
138. Cf. Zeller, *Römer*, 70.
139. Cf. Eckstein, *Syneidesis*, 276–300.

knowledge-with, of norms that serve as the basis for making judgments that can be either positive or negative.[140] As a relational concept, the conscience does not itself set norms but makes judgments as to whether given norms are in fact observed. Neither can conscience be seen as distinctive of Christians, pagans, or Jews; it is a general human phenomenon. Its function is the same for all human beings, but the norms that are presupposed in making judgments can be very different. Love, and reason renewed by the Spirit—these are the relevant and decisive norms for Christians, on the basis of which they make judgments about their own conduct and that of others.

"Icon"

Paul expresses the special dignity of human beings with the εἰκών (image, reflection, prototype) motif. The εἰκών concept receives fundamental theological significance by being used in speaking of Christ as the image of God. In 2 Cor. 4:4 the apostle explains how it came about that the gospel is veiled to unbelievers;[141] the god of this age has blinded their minds "to keep them from seeing the light of the gospel of the glory of Christ, who is the image of God [ὅς ἐστιν εἰκὼν τοῦ θεοῦ]." Here εἰκών appears as a category of participation: the Son participate in the δόξα of the Father; in him the true nature of God becomes visible because he is the image of the God who is compassionately concerned for humanity.

Parallels to the εἰκών concept are found particularly in the wisdom literature.[142] Thus wisdom is the "pure emanation of the glory of the Almighty" (Wis. 7:25). She/it is "a spotless mirror of the working of God, and an image of his goodness" (Wis. 7:26 LXX, καὶ εἰκὼν τῆς ἀγαθότητος αὐτοῦ). For Philo, the Logos as God's Son is also God's image; cf. *Flight* 101, αὐτὸς [λόγος θεῖος] εἰκὼν ὑπάρχων θεοῦ (He is himself the image of God); cf. also *Alleg. Interp.* 1.31–32; *Creation* 25; *Confusion* 62–63, 97. In pagan debates about the philosophy of religion, the concept of a relationship of human beings with God also played an important role. Thus, according to Cicero, the gods implanted the soul in human beings: "Moreover, virtue exists in man and God alike, but in no other creature besides; virtue, however, is nothing else than Nature perfected and developed to its highest point; therefore there is a likeness between man and God [*est igitur homini cum deo similitudo*]."[143]

All the statements about the relation of believers to the image of Christ are based on the concept of Christ as the image of God. In 1 Cor. 15:49 Paul

---

140. Cf. ibid., 311ff.

141. Cf. Jacob Jervell, *Imago Dei: Gen 1, 26 f. im Spätjudentum, in der Gnosis, und in den paulinischen Briefen* (FRLANT 76; Göttingen: Vandenhoeck & Ruprecht, 1960), 214–18.

142. Cf. the extensive discussions of history-of-religion connections in Friedrich Wilhelm Eltester, *Eikon im Neuen Testament* (BZNW 23; Berlin: Töpelmann, 1958), 15–170.

143. Cicero, *Leg.* 1.25.

emphasizes, in contrast to the Corinthians' understanding of salvation, an understanding oriented to the present, that they will not bear the image of the heavenly man Jesus Christ until the eschatological event, for the earthly man Adam still determines the present.[144] At the resurrection believers will be stamped with the image of the risen one and thereby participate in his immortal nature. According to Rom. 8:29, the goal of God's election is that believers "be conformed to the image of his Son, in order that he might be the firstborn within a large family." Although this event first takes place at the future resurrection of believers, it has a present dimension as well, for in baptism believers already participate in the reality of Christ as the image of God (Rom. 6:3–5). The subject matter of 2 Cor. 3:18 is very close to Rom. 8:29.[145] Through the work of the Spirit, believers see the glory of the risen one "as in a mirror" and are thereby being changed into the image of their Lord. The divine glory rests on the risen one in all its fullness, so that he is at once both the prototype and the goal of the Christian's transformation. Paul does not explain this as a material transformation[146] but as a historical-eschatological event, for the power of God is already at work in the life of the believer, the power that will be fully revealed and effective at the eschaton.

If the declaration of Gen. 1:26–27 that human beings are created in God's image already stands in the background in Rom. 8:29 and 2 Cor. 3:18, in 1 Cor. 11:7–8 Paul refers explicitly to this idea: "For a man ought not to have his head veiled, since he is the image and reflection of God; but woman is the reflection of man. Indeed, man was not made from woman, but woman from man." Paul directs this statement against the custom, evidently widespread in Corinth, of women participating in worship without the customary head covering. He is probably dealing with a new practice, unknown in other congregations (cf. 1 Cor. 11:16), which may have originated in efforts toward women's emancipation by segments of the Corinthian church, efforts they saw as directly inspired by the Spirit.[147] Paul argues against this abolition of previous conventions on the basis of creation theology, basing the distinction between men and women and its practical consequences on the fact that the man was created in the image of God. The man participates in the glory of God, is the "reflection" of God. In contrast, the woman is the "reflection" of

144. Cf. Wolff, *Korinther*, 203. Paul transposes the image of God given to human beings at creation into the eschatological dimension of the new creation of humanity already present in the Spirit and completed at the parousia; cf. Jost Eckert, "Christus als 'Bild Gottes' und die Gottebenbildlichkeit des Menschen in der paulinischen Theologie," in *Vom Urchristentum zu Jesus: Für Joachim Gnilka* (ed. Hubert Frankemölle and Karl Kertelge; Freiburg: Herder, 1989), 350ff.

145. On the problems of 2 Cor. 3:18, cf. Klauck, *2. Korintherbrief*, 41–42.

146. Windisch, *Korintherbrief*, 129, supposes Paul is here influenced by ideas from the mystery cults.

147. Cf. Wolff, *Korinther*, 70–71.

the man because she was created from man (cf. Gen. 2:22). Paul's interpretation of Gen. 1:27 follows the Jewish exegesis of his time, in which the tension between the statements about one person in Gen. 1:27a–b ("So God created man in his own image, in the image of God he created him") and the statement of 1:27c ("male and female he created them") is resolved in favor of the first half of the verse.[148] That exegesis observed that creation in the image of God is spoken of only in 1:27a–b (regarding the man), not in 1:27c (regarding the male and the female). This interpretation does not do justice to the intended meaning of the original, for אדם in 1:27a must be understood as a collective term for humanity. Thus 1:27a–b and 1:27c mutually interpret each other and must be seen as a functional unity.[149] The statement that man/Adam/humanity is made in the image of God is not gender-specific but a statement that transcends gender.

The εἰκών concept is for Paul a category of participation: the participation of the Son in the glory of the Father is completed in the believers' participation in the glory of Christ. Christ, as εἰκὼν τοῦ θεοῦ (2 Cor. 4:4), incorporates believers in a historical process at the end point of which stands their own transformation. In their relationship to Christ, human beings each attain their own destiny as the εἰκὼν τοῦ θεοῦ they were created to be. The meaning of being human is not exhausted in mere creatureliness; only in becoming like God do human beings realize their intended purpose of being made in God's image, the course that was set for them by their creation and made possible through faith in Jesus Christ as the image of God.

"Heart"

In Pauline thought, the καρδία (heart) is another center of the human self.[150] The love of God is poured out into human hearts through the Holy Spirit (Rom. 5:5). God sent the Spirit of his Son "into our hearts" (Gal. 4:6), and in baptism gave us the Spirit "in our hearts" as the ἀρραβών (first installment, 2 Cor. 1:22). Baptism leads to an obedience from the heart (Rom. 6:17), and human beings stand in a new relationship of dependence that brings salva-

148. Examples are given in Jervell, *Imago Dei*, 107–12. [Translator's note: The NIV, which preserves the gender-specific language of the original, is cited here. The NRSV's interest in gender-inclusive language here obscures Schnelle's point, which is clear in the Hebrew text and the German translation he cites.]

149. On the interpretation of Gen. 1:27, cf. esp. Gerhard von Rad, *Genesis: A Commentary* (OTL; Philadelphia: Westminster, 1972), 57–61.

150. Paul's use of καρδία stands in the tradition of Old Testament anthropology. The Septuagint translates the Hebrew לב (ca. 850 times in the Old Testament) mostly with καρδία. In the Old Testament, the heart designates the dynamic midpoint of the person, the innermost center, the locus of one's willing, thinking, and striving; cf. Hans Walter Wolff, *Anthropology of the Old Testament* (Philadelphia: Fortress, 1974), 40–58.

tion: they now serve God, which means righteousness and justice. There is a circumcision of the heart, a circumcision that is spiritual and not literal (Rom. 2:29), an inner change within the person from which a new relationship with God grows. The church in Corinth is a letter of Christ, written not with ink but with the Spirit of the living God, not on tablets of stone but on tablets of human hearts (2 Cor. 3:3). Faith is located in the heart, and into the heart God has sent "the light of the knowledge of the glory of God in the face of Jesus Christ" (2 Cor. 4:6). Hearts are strengthened by God (1 Thess. 3:13), and the peace of God, "which surpasses all understanding, will guard your hearts and your minds in Christ Jesus" (Phil. 4:7).[151] The heart can open itself to the saving message of Jesus Christ or close itself off from it (2 Cor. 3:14–16). Repentance and confession begin in the heart: "if you confess with your lips that Jesus is Lord and believe in your heart. . . . For one believes with the heart and so is justified, and one confesses with the mouth and so is saved" (Rom. 10:9–10). Here mouth and heart are related to each other on the one side as are the acts of confession and faith on the other; that is, the saving act of God in Christ grasps the whole person.

Precisely as the innermost organ, the heart determines the whole person. In both the positive and the negative sense, the heart is the center of one's being; there crucial decisions are made (1 Cor. 4:5). The heart knows the will of God (Rom. 2:15); it stands fast in resisting the passions (1 Cor. 7:37) and is eager to help the needy (2 Cor. 9:7). All the same, the heart can also be darkened and without understanding (Rom. 1:21; 2:5) and can be hardened (2 Cor. 3:14–15). God searches and tests the heart (1 Thess. 2:4; Rom. 8:27), and reveals its intentions (2 Cor. 4:5). The heart is the seat of feelings and perceptions, the place of anxiety (2 Cor. 2:4), of love (2 Cor. 7:3), of candor, and of earnest longings (Rom. 9:2; 10:1). The especially close relation of the apostle to the Philippians is manifest in the fact that he has them in his heart (Phil. 1:7). In contrast to his opponents, Paul makes no use of letters of recommendation. The Corinthian church itself is his letter of recommendation, "written on our hearts, to be known and read by all" (2 Cor. 3:2). Paul's opponents in 2 Corinthians boast in matters of external appearance, not of the heart (2 Cor. 7:2). He opens his heart to the church (2 Cor. 6:11) and assures them, "you are in our hearts, to die together and to live together" (2 Cor. 7:3). When Paul uses the word καρδία, he designates the deepest inner core of the person, the seat of the understanding, feelings, and will, the place where the ultimate decisions of life are made and where God's act through the Spirit begins.

151. In both Phil. 1:7–8 (φρονέω ["think"], σπλάγχνα ["one's insides"]) and Phil. 4:7 (νόημα ["thought"], νοῦς ["mind," "reason"]), Paul can connect καρδία with Greek ideas.

"Psyche"

Relatively seldom (eleven times) do we find the term ψυχή (life, person, soul) in Paul. In the Septuagint it appears mainly as the translation of נֶפֶשׁ (soul, life, person). Paul, too, can use ψυχή to mean a living being as a whole (Rom. 2:9) or the life of all human beings (Rom. 13:1). Ψυχή appears frequently in contexts that speak of giving one's life; for example, Paul is ready to give his life for the church (2 Cor. 12:15). Epaphroditus risked his life for the work of Christ and almost died (Phil. 2:30). Prisca and Aquila risked their necks for Paul's life (Rom. 16:4). In 2 Cor. 1:23 Paul offers the Corinthians his life as a guarantee that his invocation of God as witness for his plans is true. In the quote from 1 Kings 19:10, 14 in Rom. 11:3, Elijah's enemies are seeking his life. Paul grants the Thessalonians a share of his life when he lets them participate in his gifts and his ministry (1 Thess. 2:8). In 1 Cor. 15:45a the first man Adam, in contrast to Christ, is described as a living *psyche* (ψυχὴ ζῶσα) and thus as a mortal being. The natural, physical human being (ψυχικὸς ἄνθρωπος) is incapable of perceiving the works of God through the Spirit (1 Cor. 2:14). Parallel to ἐν ἑνὶ πνεύματι (in one Spirit) stands μιᾷ ψυχῇ (one psyche; NRSV: "one mind") in Phil. 1:27, in the sense of "as one person, unanimously."

A particular problem of Pauline anthropology is presented by 1 Thess. 5:23: "May the God of peace himself sanctify you entirely; and may your spirit and soul and body be kept sound and blameless at the coming of our Lord Jesus Christ." This expression, which seems to echo a tripartite understanding of human being (τὸ πνεῦμα καὶ ἡ ψυχὴ καὶ τὸ σῶμα) is not based on the Hellenistic anthropology that divides human being into body, soul, and spirit. Paul is merely emphasizing that God's saving work affects the whole person. This interpretation is suggested both by the use of the adjectives ὁλοτελής (entirely) and ὁλόκληρος (completely) as well as by the observation that in 1 Thessalonians πνεῦμα is for Paul not a constituent part of human nature but expresses and signals the new, creative act of God in and for human beings. By ψυχή and σῶμα, Paul means only the individual human being as a whole, what constitutes each individual as a whole person. That which is really new and determinative here is the Spirit of God.[152] In his use of ψυχή, Paul stands in the tradition of the Old Testament, where נֶפֶשׁ designates the person as a whole.[153] A human being is not the sum of individual parts; rather, the whole can be concentrated in each "part."

---

152. Holtz, *Thessalonicher*, 265.
153. Wolff, *Anthropology*, 10–25.

"Nous"

The Hebrew language has no equivalent for νοῦς (thinking, reason, mind, understanding), a central term in Hellenistic anthropology.[154] Paul uses νοῦς in 1 Cor. 14:14–15, in his discussion of glossolalia as the authority of critical reason in contrast to the uncontrolled and unintelligible speaking in tongues. Prayer and praise take place both in the divine Spirit and in the human mind (14:15). In 14:19 νοῦς means a clearly understood communication by which the church is instructed: "In church I would rather speak five words with my mind, in order to instruct others also, than ten thousand words in a tongue." In Phil. 4:7 νοῦς designates the rational mind, the human capacity for understanding, which is surpassed by the peace of God. In 1 Cor. 1:10 Paul appeals for the unity of the Corinthian church, that they have one mind and one purpose. Paul speaks in 1 Cor. 2:16 of the νοῦς Χριστοῦ (mind of Christ) and in Rom. 11:34 of the νοῦς κυρίου (mind of the Lord), in each case referring to the Holy Spirit, which transcends human judgment.[155] In the context of the dispute between the "strong" and "weak" in Rome, Paul challenges each group "to be fully convinced in their own minds" (Rom. 14:5). According to Rom. 7:23, the law in one's members fights against the law of the mind. Regarding content, the νόμος τοῦ νοός (law of my mind) corresponds to the νόμος τοῦ θεοῦ (law of God) in Rom. 7:22 and means the person who is oriented to God. In the mind, this person wants to serve God, but the sin dwelling within shatters these good intentions. In Rom. 12:2 Paul warns the church not to accommodate itself to this sinful and transient world but to let God work a transformation in its whole existence, which takes place as a renewing of the νοῦς.[156] By νοῦς Paul here means reasonable knowing and thinking that maintain a new orientation through the work of the Spirit. Christians receive a new power and capacity for making judgments that enable them to discern the will of God. Human beings can perceive God's invisible nature because God himself has graciously turned to them and has given them this revelation (Rom. 1:19). The mind cannot renew itself out of its own resources but is dependent on the initiative of God, who places the mind in his service, for which it was originally intended.[157]

---

154. Classically, Plato, *Phaedr.* 247c–e, presents the mind as the highest and best part of the soul, making the moral life possible by its ability to discern what virtue is; cf. further Aristotle, *Eth. nic.* 10.1177a (the mind as the epitome of the divine, the most valuable part of the inner life); Diogenes Laertius 7.54 (according to Zeno, reason is the primary criterion of truth); Epictetus, *Diatr.* 2.8.1–2 (the essence of divine being is νοῦς); further documentation in *NW* 1/2:230ff.

155. Cf. Lang, *An die Korinther*, 47.

156. The exegesis of Käsemann remains foundational; cf. Käsemann, *Romans*, 325–32.

157. Cf. Günther Bornkamm, "Faith and Reason in Paul's Epistles," *NTS* 4 (1958): 93–100.

"Inner" and "External" Person

With the distinction between the ἔσω ἄνθρωπος and the ἔξω ἄνθρωπος,[158] Paul makes use of an image from Hellenistic philosophy.[159] It enables him to take up a philosophical ideal of his time and at the same time recoin it in terms of his theology of the cross.

It is not possible to delineate a clear tradition-historical derivation of the ἔσω/ἔξω ἄνθρωπος imagery.[160] The beginning point is probably Plato, *Resp.* 9.588A–589B, where he states in 589A: "To him the supporter of justice makes answer that he should ever so speak and act as to give the man within him [τοῦ ἀνθρώπου ὁ εντὸς ἄνθρωπος] the most complete mastery over the entire human creature" (trans. Jowett). In Hellenistic philosophy around the beginning of the first century CE, the idea was prevalent that the authentic, thinking person, who can distinguish the essential from the unessential, lives a disciplined life free from the passions and makes himself or herself inwardly independent from external circumstances. In contrast, the "external" person is imprisoned by the senses of the external world, with the result that he or she is dominated by passions and anxiety. Thus the Hellenistic Jewish philosopher of religion Philo of Alexandria, can say, "This 'man,' dwelling in the soul of each of us . . . convicts us from within (Philo, *Worse* 23; cf. also *Prelim. Studies* 97; *Planting* 42). In Seneca there are repeated references to the internal divine power, which preserves and builds up the fragile body: "If you see a man who is unterrified in the midst of dangers, untouched by desires, happy in adversity, peaceful amid the storm, who looks down upon men from a higher plane, and views the gods on a footing of equality, will not a feeling of reverence for him steal over you? Will you not say: 'This quality is too lofty to be regarded as resembling this petty body in which it dwells? A Divine power has descended upon that man.'"[161]

In contrast to Hellenistic anthropology, Paul does not understand the distinction between the ἔσω ἄνθρωπος and the ἔξω ἄνθρωπος as an anthropological dualism. Instead the apostle regards the life of the believer from different perspectives.[162] In the context of a peristasis catalogue (2 Cor. 4:8–9), Paul

158. For the history of research, cf. Jewett, *Paul's Anthropological Terms*, 391–95; Theo K. Heckel, *Der innere Mensch: Die paulinische Verarbeitung eines platonischen Motivs* (WUNT 2/53; Tübingen: Mohr Siebeck, 1993), 4–9; Hans Dieter Betz, "The Concept of the 'Inner Human Being' (ὁ ἔσω ἄνθρωπος) in the Anthropology of Paul," *NTS* 46 (2000): 317–24.

159. The distinction of Christoph Markschies, "Innerer Mensch," *RAC* 18:279–80, between the image of the inner person and the term ἔσω ἄνθρωπος is followed here. The image is found before Paul, but the term itself is not.

160. A comprehensive discussion of further examples is found in Heckel, *Der innere Mensch*, 266ff.

161. Seneca, *Ep.* 41.4–5 (*NW* 2/1:439f.); cf. further *Ep.* 71.27; 102.27; and Epictetus, *Diatr.* 2.7.3.

162. Cf. Gutbrod, *Die paulinische anthropologie*, 85–92.

says in 2 Cor. 4:16,[163] "So we do not lose heart. Even though our outer nature [ἔξω ἄνθρωπος] is wasting away, our inner nature [ἔσω ἄνθρωπος] is being renewed day by day." Externally the apostle is being worn away by the many sufferings entailed in his mission work. But at the same time the δόξα θεοῦ (glory of God, 4:15) works in the ἔσω ἄνθρωπος, so that believers in their inner selves know that their lives are determined by the Lord who is present with them, who strengthens and renews them. They can thus bear external suffering and hardship because they participate in the life-giving power of the risen one and so overcome the troubles and decline of the body.[164] In Rom. 7:22 the ἔσω ἄνθρωπος agrees joyfully with the will of God and thus lives in peace with himself or herself. The power of sin, however, perverts the actual existence of believers, who in their striving after the good are subject to the "law of sin" in their members. With the term ἔσω ἄνθρωπος Paul designates the "I" within the human self that is open for the will of God and the work of the Spirit.[165]

19.6 The New Freedom

The formation of a sense of individual freedom belongs among the outstanding cultural achievements of Hellenism.[166] It became the hallmark of the philosopher to live a life of freedom from external constraints (cf. Epictetus, *Diatr.* 2.1.23); it was thus said of Diogenes that "the manner of life he lived was the same as that of Hercules when he preferred liberty to everything" (Diogenes Laertius 6.71). In the context of Stoic-Cynic and middle Platonic concepts of freedom, Paul's mission could only flourish if it could give a plausible basis for how human freedom can be obtained and lived out.

163. Betz, "Inner Human Being," 329ff., argues that Paul made the concept of the "inner person" more conceptually and terminologically precise in his dispute with the dualistic Corinthian anthropology.

164. On the difference between Rom. 7:22 and 2 Cor. 4:16, cf. Markschies, "Innerer Mensch," *RAC* 18:280–82.

165. Bultmann, *Theology of the New Testament*, 1:203, does not do justice to the meaning of ἔσω ἄνθρωπος in Paul when he understands the expression as the "formal designation for . . . his real self . . . the subject of his own willing and doing."

166. See the descriptions and interpretations in Dieter Nestle, *Eleutheria: Studien zum Wesen der Freiheit bei den Griechen und im Neuen Testament* (HUT 6; Tübingen: Mohr Siebeck, 1967); "Freiheit," *RAC* 8:269–306; M. Pohlenz, *Griechische Freiheit: Wesen und Werden eines Lebens-ideals* (Heidelberg: Quelle & Meyer, 1955); Maximilian Forschner, *Die stoische Ethik: Über den Zusammenhang von Natur-, Sprach,- und Moralphilosophie im altstoischen System* (Stuttgart: Klett-Cotta, 1981), 104–13; Vollenweider, *Freiheit als neue Schöpfung*, 23–104; Hans Dieter Betz, *Paul's Concept of Freedom in the Context of Hellenistic Discussions about the Possibilities of Human Freedom: Protocol of the Twenty-Sixth Colloquy, 9 January 1977* (Berkeley: The Center for Hermenuetical Studies in Hellenistic and Modern Culture, 1977).

The Ultimate Starting Point

Paul has no unified, consistent doctrine of freedom but can deal with the theme of freedom in different social and theological contexts, making use of a variety of traditions.[167] At the same time, a single idea lies at the basis of all his statements: freedom is the result of a liberating event. Christian freedom results from the act of God in Jesus Christ that frees from the powers of sin and death, an act concretely appropriated in baptism. Freedom is not a matter of human potential; human beings can neither attain it for themselves nor provide it to others, for the universal power of sin excludes freedom as a goal of human striving. It is true that human beings can have a feeling of individual freedom and deny the existence of powers hostile to human life, but this changes nothing regarding their actual servitude to the lordship of sin and death over their lives. Only the saving act of God in Jesus Christ can be grasped as an event of comprehensive liberation because only here are the powers that oppress human life overcome. In baptism, as a once-in-a-lifetime historical act, human beings become participants in the liberating act of God in Jesus Christ, and they themselves are now liberated from sin's domination. The new identity of believers does not stop at the freedom of the individual, for its goal is the overcoming of the ethnic, gender, and social distinctions that dominate life. From this ultimate starting point, Paul deals with the theme of freedom in its different dimensions:[168]

Freedom as love in the service of Christ

Especially in his debate with the Corinthians, Paul makes clear that freedom is not the realization of individual potential but can be expressed only in love for others. This ethical dimension of the Pauline concept of freedom shapes his argument with the Corinthians in the conflict about eating meat sacrificed to idols (cf. esp. 1 Cor. 8:1–13; 10:33).[169] Paul takes up the motto of the "strong," πάντα μοι ἔξεστιν (All things are lawful for me), only in order to immediately relativize it and make it more precise (6:12, "'All things are lawful for me,' but I will not be dominated by anything"; 10:23, "'All things are lawful,' but not all things build up").[170] The goal of Christian freedom is not indifference, for it is essentially a term of participation and relationship: baptized believers par-

---

167. In contrast to the older studies, Jones, *"Freiheit,"* 138–41, emphasizes this aspect.

168. Cf. the methodological reflections of Jones, ibid., 19–24, who chooses a chronological approach; he is followed by Dautzenberg, "Freiheit im hellenistischen Kontext," 58–59.

169. For elaboration, see above, section 9.4 ("Freedom and Obligation in Christ"); cf. further Dautzenberg, "Freiheit im hellenistischen Kontext," 66–69.

170. Cf. the Diogenes tradition in Diogenes Laertius 6.72: "He maintained that all things are the property of the wise, and employed such arguments as those cited above. All things belong to the gods; the gods are friends of the wise; and friends share all property in common; all things, therefore, are the property of the wise." For additional parallels, cf. Downing, *Pauline Churches*, 98–104, 114–27.

ticipate in the freedom attained through Christ, a freedom that only becomes authentic in relation to other Christians and the Christian community. The model for this concept of freedom is given by Jesus Christ as the crucified one, the one who died for his brothers and sisters (cf. 8:11; Rom. 14:15, "If your brother or sister is being injured by what you eat, you are no longer walking in love. Do not let what you eat cause the ruin of one for whom Christ died"). Christian freedom is for Paul the freedom given by Jesus Christ as a gift, so that a misuse of this freedom, as a sin against one's fellow Christians, is at the same time a sin against Christ.

In 1 Cor. 9, Paul presents himself as a model for the kind of freedom that is willing to give up its own rights for the sake of others. The apostle does not claim his legitimate right to support by the churches, so that thereby he might further the preaching of the gospel (cf. 9:12, 15–16). Whereas in antiquity freedom and servitude were mutually exclusive alternatives, for Paul they mutually condition and complement each other, which is to say that the way Paul handles his social freedom is christologically grounded.[171] The apostle's freedom is realized precisely in the service of the gospel, which means active love for others (cf. 9:19; Gal. 5:13). Here, too, freedom is attained first of all through participation in Christ; paradoxically, it can realize itself in servitude because it receives its essence and content from Christ, who himself entered into a life of servitude (Phil. 2:6–7). Servitude as such does not constitute freedom, but freedom in Christ takes place in the mode of service to the gospel.

The free and the slave

The social reality of the churches required that Paul think through the relation of social/political freedom and theological freedom.[172] In so doing, he could make contact with a broad stream of ancient thought in which true freedom was understood as internal freedom. "It is not possible that that which is by nature free should be disturbed or thwarted by anything outside itself" (Epictetus, *Diatr.* 1.19.7). Therefore, the threats of tyrants to imprison one in chains brings no fear: "'If it seems more profitable to you to do so, chain it [my leg].' 'Do you not care?' 'No, I do not care.' 'I will show you that I am master.' 'How can *you* be my master? Zeus has set me free'" (*Diatr.* 1.19.8–9). For Paul, slaves should remain in their social status (1 Cor. 7:21b), for in Christ and in the church the fundamental alternatives presented by society have long

---

171. In my opinion, the alternative given by Dautzenberg, "Freiheit im hellenistischen Kontext," 65, is not appropriate: "The distinctive thing about the statements in 1 Cor. 9 dealing with freedom is not an understanding of freedom as Christian freedom but the exemplary manner in which Paul handles his social freedom."

172. It is no accident that most of the instances of the word "freedom" are placed in opposition to δοῦλος (slave), δουλεύω (serve as a slave), δουλόω (enslave); cf. 1 Cor. 7; 9; 12; Gal. 4, 5; Rom. 6).

since been abolished (cf. 1 Cor. 12:13; 2 Cor. 5:17; Gal. 3:26–28; 5:6; 6:15).[173] The letter to Philemon shows, however, that Paul's recommendations are not ideologically bound, for there he by no means excludes the option of freedom for a Christian slave. But when Christian slaves do gain their freedom, they still know that they have long since been set free in Christ.

Freedom from the world within a world that is passing away

Because, through the Christ event, the present is already proleptically quali-fied by the future (1 Cor. 7:29–31), Paul challenges Christians to bring their self-understanding and ethical conduct into line with the eschatological turn of the ages. The ordering structures of this world, which is passing away, must still be acknowledged in their historical reality, but at the same time Paul calls for an inner freedom and independence.[174] Baptized believers should thus remain in their present social status, but without attaching any great importance to it. The institution of marriage, like the status of slaves, belongs to the structures of the old age. Whoever still allows himself or herself to be too involved in them has not understood the signs of the times (cf. 7:1, 8); on the other hand, those already married should remain so (cf. 7:2–7). The Pauline ὡς μή (as if not) aims at participation in this world, but with a certain distancing of oneself from it; participation in the life of the world without falling victim to it—a kind of freedom from the world while living in the world. Because what is to come already shapes the present, the present loses its determinative character.

Freedom as the liberation of creation

The universal-apocalyptic dimensions of the Pauline concept of freedom are manifest in Rom. 8:18ff.,[175] where the liberation of believers and the liberation of creation converge and are embedded in a comprehensive perspective on the future. Through Adam's transgression, the creation was involuntarily subjected to futility, but still with hope (Rom. 8:20; cf. *4 Ezra* 7:11–12). Creation itself participates in the hope of believers: "the creation itself will be set free from its bondage to decay and will obtain the freedom of the glory of the children of God" (Rom. 8:21). The present δουλεία (bondage) and the future ἐλευθερία (freedom) stand in opposition to each other as "decay" and "glory." God's es-chatological creative act will include not only believers but the whole creation (8:22, πᾶσα κτίσις). Like creation itself, believers groan under the futility and decay of this-worldly, earthly reality. They long for the redemption of their

---

173. For elaboration and interpretation, see above, section 9.4 ("Freedom and Obligation in Christ"); cf. further Dautzenberg, "Freiheit im hellenistischen Kontext," 60–62.

174. Cf. Epictetus, *Ench.* 15, where he says in the analogy of the banquet, "But if you do not take these things even when they are set before you, but despise them, then you will not only share the banquet of the gods, but share also their rule. For it was by so doing that Diogenes and Heracleitus, and men like them, were deservedly divine and deservedly so called."

175. Cf. Jones, *"Freiheit,"* 129–35; Vollenweider, *Freiheit als neue Schöpfung*, 375–96.

body (8:23) and look forward to the transition into God's very presence. The assurance of this future event is given by the Spirit, which, as the initial gift, is not only the pledge and guarantee that the Christian hope is authentic but also comes to the help of believers who struggle to hold on to their hope in difficult situations (8:26–27). The Spirit intercedes for the saints before God in a language commensurate with the situation. The confidence of faith makes it possible for Paul in 8:28–30 to give a comprehensive portrayal of the "glorious liberty of the children of God": "We know that all things work together for good for those who love God, who are called according to his purpose. For those whom he foreknew he also predestined to be conformed to the image of his Son, in order that he might be the firstborn within a large family. And those whom he predestined he also called; and those whom he called he also justified; and those whom he justified he also glorified." God himself will call for the freedom of the children of God, which will attain its goal in the believers' participation in the glory of God that has appeared in God's own Son. Although for Paul the relation of present and past is determined by discontinuity, present and future stand in the continuity of the Spirit. To believers and to the whole creation, God himself opens a perspective that leads to God as the source and fulfiller of all that is.

Freedom from the disastrous results of the law/Torah

In no text in the Corinthian letters is freedom understood as "freedom from the law."[176] Neither is this idea found in Galatians and Romans, for Paul knows no "freedom from the law" in a general sense,[177] but he does have a conviction about liberation, through the Spirit, from the disastrous consequences brought about by sin's use of the law.[178] In sharply polemical terms, Paul deals with this fundamental connection for the first time in his letter to the Galatians[179] with its exclusive doctrine of justification:[180] human beings are not able to keep all the commands of the Torah, and this failure brings them under its curse (Gal. 3:10–12). Christ has redeemed us from the curse of the Torah by taking its curse upon himself (3:13). This annuls the Torah itself, so that it no longer has power over us, for we have died with Christ. Those who have been crucified with him in baptism have died to the

176. With Jones, *"Freiheit,"* 67–69 and others; against Vollenweider, *Freiheit als neue Schöpfung*, 21, and others, who consistently understand freedom in Paul to include freedom from the law. For critique of a one-sided fixation of Paul's concept of freedom on the problematic of the law, cf. also Dautzenberg, "Streit um Freiheit," 265–76; "Freiheit im hellenistischen Kontext," 75.

177. See above, section 19.3 ("The Law").

178. Bultmann, *Theology of the New Testament,* 1:240–45, is also incorrect when he speaks of "Freedom from the Law" without making differentiations.

179. On the understanding of the law and freedom in Galatians, cf. Kertelge, "Gesetz und Freiheit," 184–96.

180. See above, section 11.5 ("Inclusive and Exclusive Doctrine of Justification in Paul").

law/Torah and now live for God alone (2:19–20). The Galatians received the Spirit not from the law/Torah but from the preaching that calls for faith (3:1–5). As those who have received the Spirit (πνευματικοί, 6:1) and as new creatures in Christ (6:15), the Galatians are no longer under the law/Torah (5:18). If they want to be under the Torah (4:21), then they lag behind the status of salvation and freedom they have already reached. What matters now is this: "Now you, my friends [so NRSV; ἀδελφοί (brothers and sisters)], are children of the promise, like Isaac" (4:28). At the same time, the Galatians are thereby τέκνα τῆς ἐλευθέρας (children of the free woman, 4:31),[181] so that everything depends on preserving the freedom grounded in the Christ event, appropriated in the gift of the Spirit, and confirmed by the Scripture and on not perverting it into its opposite through observance of the Torah. The essence of the Christian life is freedom: Τῇ ἐλευθερίᾳ ἡμᾶς Χριστὸς ἠλευθέρωσεν (For freedom Christ has set us free, 5:1; cf. 5:13). Despite his sharp critique of the Torah, in Galatians, too, Paul does not understand himself to be "without law," for he is bound to the "law of Christ" (6:2) and thus to the norms of the Spirit and of love.

In Romans, a derivative of the word "freedom" appears for the first time in 6:18, 22, whereby this passage, as also the passive form of ἐλευθερόω (set free) receive a programmatic character. Freedom from sin, as liberation by God through Jesus Christ, also includes for Paul a liberation from the negative effects of the law/Torah. Paul develops this theme extensively in Rom. 7,[182] where freedom appears as the impossible possibility for human beings in the situation between sin and Torah. Human beings are torn between the powers of sin, the commandeered Torah, and death; their will to do good is frustrated and perverted into its opposite. They are embedded in an enslaving pattern from which they cannot extricate themselves. Only the saving act of God in Jesus Christ can free them from their hopeless situation (cf. Rom. 8:2). The Spirit breaks through the legal pattern that leads to disaster and places persons in a new pattern: the pattern of life that has appeared in Jesus Christ. At the center of his letter to the Romans, Paul uses the term ἐλευθερόω to designate precisely the breakthrough from the level of the law/Torah, dominated by sin, to the level of the Spirit, a breakthrough that was accomplished on Golgotha and was appropriated to the individual believer in baptism and freedom from sin and freedom from the inadequacies of the law/Torah. Now this holds true: οὐκ ἐσμὲν ὑπὸ νόμον ἀλλὰ ὑπὸ χάριν (we are not under law but under grace, Rom. 6:14b).

---

181. Cf. Gerhard Dautzenberg, "Die Freiheit bei Paulus und in der Stoa," *TQ* 176 (1996): 65–76.

182. On the interpretation of Rom. 7, see above, section 12.8 ("Sin, Law, and Freedom in the Spirit").

Ancient Theories of Freedom

Paul removes freedom from the sphere of human activity; for him it has the character of a gift, not an act. From this point of departure, the apostle advocates an independent position in the ancient debate about freedom. At the very same time early Christianity was developing, two theories about the nature of freedom were having powerful effects:[183] Epictetus composed an entire book entitled Περὶ ἐλευθερίας (*About Freedom*, in *Diatr.* 4.1), and three of Dio Chrysostom's speeches were on slavery and freedom (*De servitute et libertate 1, 2* [*Or.* 14, 15]; *De libertate* [*Or.* 80]). Both Epictetus and Dio began with a popular understanding of freedom: freedom as freedom to act without any constraints.[184] They chose this point of departure for their reflections in order to destroy an externally oriented concept of freedom.

Epictetus put forward arguments based on experience and insight: a rich senator is still the slave of the emperor (*Diatr.* 4.1.13), and any free man who falls in love with a beautiful young slave becomes her slave: "Did you never cozen your pet slave? Did you never kiss her feet? Yet, if someone should compel you to kiss the feet of Caesar, you would regard this as insolence and most extravagant tyranny" (*Diatr.* 4.1.17). Who can be free when even the kings and their friends are not free? Because freedom is not adequately understood in terms of external freedom, what matters is to distinguish between the things we can control and the things over which we have no power (*Diatr.* 4.1.81). The given circumstances of life are not really at our disposition, but we can have control over our attitude to them.

> Purify your judgments, for fear lest something of what is not your own may be fastened to them, or grown together with them, and may give you pain when it is torn loose. And every day while you are training yourself, as you do in the gymnasium, do not say that you are "pursuing philosophy" (indeed an arrogant phrase!) but that you are a slave presenting your emancipator in court; for this is the true freedom. This is the way in which Diogenes was set free by Antisthenes, and afterwards said that he could never be enslaved again by any man. How, in consequence, did he behave when he was captured? How he treated the pirates! He called none of them master, did he? And I am not referring to the name! It is not the word that I fear, but the emotion, which produces the word. (*Diatr.* 4.1.112–115)

True freedom is thus inner freedom from things; it manifests itself in my attitude to the given realities of life. The only free people are those who are not slaves to their passions and have not been imprisoned by their desires for external,

---

183. Cf. Dautzenberg, "Freiheit bei Paulus und in der Stoa," 65–76.

184. Cf. Epictetus, *Diatr.* 4.1.1 (*NW* 2/1:281); Dio Chrysostom, *1 Serv. lib.* 3 (if one were to ask the crowd "what the nature of freedom is, they would say, perhaps, that it consists of being subject to no one and acting simply in accord with one's own judgment").

material things. Socrates and Diogenes were really free[185] because they lived in harmony with the will of God and nature; they recognized which goods God had entrusted to them, and the things over which they had no control.[186]

Dio Chrysostom argued similarly when he refused to define freedom and slavery as objective states concerning one's birth or external, clearly perceivable circumstances.[187] "And so when a man is well-born in respect to virtue, it is right to call him 'noble,' even if no one knows his parents or his ancestors either. . . . We should make no distinction between the two classes. Nor is it reasonable to say that some are of ignoble birth and mean, and that others are slaves" (*2 Serv. lib.* 31). Whoever turns away from the true law, the law of nature, perhaps still observes tables of written law but no longer lives in freedom (*Lib.* 5). Such people are, rather, the slaves of laws and conventions, so that they inevitably go to ruin, burdened down with all the things on which they depend.

Epictetus and Dio Chrysostom represent a broad stream of tradition in the history of ancient philosophy that flows through the Stoics and Epicureans all the way to the Skeptics:[188] true freedom is the inner independence of the wise, those who have made peace with their own feelings (ἀταραξία), who have placed themselves under the will of God (and thus the law of nature) by a knowledge of their own emotions and by refusing to be dominated by them. Paul takes up this concept of inner freedom but makes decisive modifications in its meaning structure. He describes *freedom as a supporting reality external to a person: God.* Paradoxically, the only true freedom comes by being tied down to God, that is, being committed to God as Lord of one's life, for freedom in the full sense of the word belongs to God alone—the concept of God and the concept of freedom determine each other. Freedom is not located in human beings themselves but has an external basis. Freedom does not come as the result of one's own resolute decision but is a gift that can only be received from God and is realized in love. The norm for freedom is love.[189] Those set free by God and placed in the expanse of freedom live their lives by the standard of love that has appeared in Jesus Christ. Love recognizes other human beings as God's children and orients itself to what they and the world need. The acknowledgment of this freedom bestowed from outside oneself thus becomes an integrating factor in one's own freedom. Freedom is more than being able to do what I choose; it is revealed in acts of loving concern for others. Thus the truth of the matter is this: *only those are truly human who become fellow human beings with others.*

---

185. Cf. Cicero, *Parad.* 5: "Only the wise man is free, and every fool is a slave" (ὅτι μόνος ὁ σοφὸς ἐλεύθερος καὶ πᾶς ἄφρων δοῦλος).

186. Cf., e.g., Epictetus, *Diatr.* 1.152–154 (*NW* 2/1:567).

187. Cf. Dio Chrysostom *2 Serv. lib.* 2.

188. For the Stoics, cf. Diogenes Laertius 7.88, 117, 119, 121, and passim. For the Epicureans, cf. Diogenes Laertius 10.82, 117–121, and passim. For the Skeptics, cf. Diogenes Laertius 9.68, 107, and passim.

189. Weder, "Die Normativität der Freiheit," 136ff., emphasizes this aspect.

20

Ethics

The New Being as Meaning Formation

The processes of meaning formation are always connected with the ways one attains orientation in the world; they mediate values and norms and make possible the availability of standpoints and their revision.[1] For baptized believers, life has been transformed; this is why the new being opens up new possibilities for action and thus new challenges to act. God accepts human beings through faith in Jesus Christ; this acceptance is unconditional but not inconsequential. Paul does not outline his ethic from the perspective of a subject who acts autonomously but, in accord with his theology as a whole, begins with the image of participation in the new being. This image takes concrete form in new actions, the bases and accomplishment of which Paul constantly calls to mind to the churches.

20.1 Life within the Sphere of Christ: Correspondence as Basic Ethical Category

Interpreters often express the basic idea of Paul's ethic on the model of indicative and imperative.[2] In this view, it is considered characteristic for Paul

---

1. Cf. Straub, "Geschichten erzählen," 130ff.
2. Friedrich Wilhelm Horn, "Ethik des Neuen Testaments," *TRu* 60 (1995): 32–86, gives a survey of research.

to reduce his ethical statements to those dealing with God's act for humanity (indicative) and those explicating the human actions called for in response (imperative). The imperative speaks of the implementation of the new being, which is both based on the divine act and results from it. "The indicative is the foundation for the imperative."[3] The strengths of this explanatory model are located on two different levels: God's act for human beings and the acts of human beings themselves are distinguished but also interrelated; and the character of the new being as having inherent obligations is expressed in a way that cannot be missed. Nonetheless, the indicative-imperative schema is not really the right way to grasp the dynamic structures of the Pauline ethic as a whole.[4] (1) The indicative-imperative schema has a static nature; it makes an artificial division in what Paul presents as a more sweeping continuity embracing being and life.[5] (2) What is the bridge between indicative and imperative?[6] The usual reference to the Spirit in this context is no solution to the problem, for the Spirit cannot at the same time be both gift and obligation [*Gabe und Aufgabe*]. (3) How does the gift of salvation become an obliga-

---

3. Bultmann, *Theology of the New Testament*, 1:332. In recent exegesis, the indicative-imperative model is adopted by, among others, Schrage, *Ethics*, 167–71; Rudolf Schnackenburg, *The Moral Teaching of the New Testament* (trans. J. Holland-Smith and W. J. O'Hara; New York: Seabury, 1973), 188–94; Merk, *Handeln*, 91 and passim; Stuhlmacher, *Biblische Theologie*, 1:374–75; Strecker, *Theology of the New Testament*, 194–96; Dunn, *Theology of Paul*, 625–31; Friedrich Wilhelm Horn, "Ethik," *RGG* 2:1608–9.

4. The problems of the indicative-imperative schema have often been noticed, most sharply by Hans Windisch, "Das Problem des paulinischen Imperativs," *ZNW* 23 (1924): 271: "Here the problematic of the Pauline imperative comes clearly in focus. It is attached to the indicative but still has the same content: you have been transformed, therefore be transformed; you have been freed from sin, so therefore free yourselves from sin; your sinful body is dead, therefore do not serve sin any longer." From the more recent discussion, cf. Hans Weder, "Gesetz und Gnade," in *Ja und Nein—christliche Theologie im Angesicht Israels: Festschrift zum 70. Geburtstag von Wolfgang Schrage* (ed. Klaus Wengst et al.; Neukirchen-Vluyn: Neukirchener Verlag, 1998), 171–73, who holds on to the indicative-imperative schema despite all his criticism of it; K. Backhaus, "Evangelium als Lebensraum: Christologie und Ethik bei Paulus," in *Paulinische Christologie: Exegetische Beiträge: Hans Hübner zum 70. Geburtstag* (ed. Udo Schnelle et al.; Göttingen: Vandenhoeck & Ruprecht, 2000), 9–14, who is consistent with his critique by abandoning the schema.

5. Here lies the primary weakness in Rudolf Bultmann's argument in his influential essay "Das Problem der Ethik bei Paulus," in *Exegetica: Aufsätze zur Erforschung des Neuen Testaments* (ed. Erich Dinkler; Tübingen: Mohr Siebeck, 1967), 36–54. He speaks throughout of an "antinomy" or "paradox" regarding indicative and imperative in Paul's theology, and his own solution is stamped with this idea: "Just as the moral demand expressed in the imperative is God's command to him [sc. the one who has been justified], so the obedient attitude that corresponds to this command is likewise the gift of God, brought about by the πνεῦμα, without the demand losing its imperatival character" (pp. 53–54). The attitude of obedience is at the same time God's gift and human responsibility; it remains unclear how these work together.

6. Cf. Schweitzer, *Mysticism*, 295: "In the doctrine of justification by faith, redemption and ethics are like two roads, one of which leads up to one side of a ravine, and the other leads onwards from the opposite side—but there is no bridge by which to pass from one side to the other."

tion?[7] Must the newness of the new being first be realized? (4) Are baptized believers set in the freedom of the new life only "on probation"? (5) In what does the respective soteriological quality of the indicative and the imperative consist? If the indicative has the salvific content, this raises the question of the soteriological status of the imperative. It cannot bring about salvation [*erwirken*], yet it can cause it to be forfeited [*verwirken*], so that a (negative) soteriological quality must be attributed to it. (6) The issue of what one *can* do and what one *should* do in Paul's ethical argument is marginalized. (7) Is the paradigm "obedience out of gratitude" a convincing and workable model of Paul's line of argument? In the long run, can obedience replace insight?

This severe challenge suggests that it would be reasonable to keep some distance from the indicative-imperative schema as *the* structural model of Paul's ethics. Instead the valid elements of this schema should be integrated into the basic paradigm "transformation and participation": the participation in Christ effected in baptism has direct consequences for the contents of Christian ethics, since incorporation into the death and resurrection of Jesus Christ is not limited to the act of baptism but, through the gift of the Spirit, determines the present and future life of those who are baptized (cf. Gal. 3:2, 3; 5:18; Rom. 6:4). Those whose lives are now located within the sphere of Christ are new creations (cf. 2 Cor. 5:7); where Paul speaks of the newness of life, he bases this on a christological foundation, not an ethical one (cf. 2 Cor. 4:16; 5:17; Gal. 6:15; Rom. 6:4; 7:6). Those who have been baptized have put on Christ (Gal. 3:27) and are entirely determined by him, for Christ lives in them and wants to be formed in them (cf. Gal. 4:19). Jesus Christ is both prototype and model [*Urbild und Vorbild*], as the ethical interpretation of the Christ hymn in Phil. 2:6–11 makes clear. For Paul, Christ himself appears as the content and continuum of ethics.[8] The theme of ethics is the aspect of the new being, the new life in the sphere of Christ, expressed in what one does and the way one lives. What has happened to baptized believers has placed its stamp on their whole life. Just as Christ died to sin once and for all, so those who have been baptized are no longer under the power of sin (Rom. 6:9–11). Just as Jesus obediently walked the way of the cross and overcame sin and death (Rom. 5:19; Phil. 2:8), so Paul challenges the Roman Christians to be obedient servants of righteousness (Rom. 6:16; cf. 1 Cor. 9:19). Christ gave himself up for our sins; he was not concerned for his own advantage (Gal. 1:4; Rom. 3:25; 8:32), and so believers too are to live not in a way oriented to their own selfish interests but for the salvation of the many who are being lost (1 Cor. 10:24, 33). Because

---

7. Cf. Weder, "Gesetz und Gnade," 172. [Translator's note: English cannot reproduce the important wordplay between *Gabe* (gift) and *Aufgabe* (assignment, obligation, duty); so also with the pairs *erwirken* and *verwirken*, *Urbild* and *Vorbild* in the next sentences.]

8. Cf. Heinz Schürmann, "'Das Gesetz des Christus' Gal. 6,2: Jesu Verhalten und Wort als letztgültige sittliche Norm nach Paulus," in Heinz Schürmann, *Studien zur neutestamentlichen Ethik* (ed. Thomas Söding; SBAB 7; Stuttgart: Katholisches Bibelwerk, 1990), 53–77.

Christ died out of love for humanity and this love now controls and sustains the church (2 Cor. 5:14; Rom. 8:35, 37), it determines the Christian life as a whole (1 Cor. 8:1; 13; Gal. 5:6, 22; Rom. 12:9–10; 13:9–10; 14:15). Just as Christ became the servant of humanity by going to the cross (Rom. 15:8; Phil. 2:6ff.), so Christians are to serve one another (Gal. 2:6). What began in baptism continues in the lives of those baptized: they have been placed on the way of Jesus, they imitate Christ, so that the apostle can even say, "Be imitators of me, as I am of Christ" (1 Cor. 11:1, μιμηταί μου γίνεσθε καθὼς κἀγὼ Χριστοῦ; cf. 1 Thess. 1:6; 1 Cor. 4:16).[9] The Christian life is founded on Jesus' way to the cross, which is at the same time the essential criterion of this life.[10] The ethical *proprium christianum* is thus Christ himself,[11] and for Paul ethics thus means the active dimension of participation in Christ.[12] This means that *the* theme of the Pauline ethic is correspondence to the new being.

This is made clear by the texts in which the apostle speaks explicitly of the relation between Christology (or soteriology) and ethics. In 1 Cor. 5:7a Paul at first formulates in the imperative ("Clean out the old yeast so that you may be a new batch") and only then adds the first basis for this action: "as [καθώς] you really are unleavened." The content of the admonition to the Corinthians is identical with the affirmation of what they already are; that is, it is a matter

---

9. On the Pauline concept of mimesis, see esp. Hans Dieter Betz, *Nachfolge und Nachahmung Jesu Christi im Neuen Testament* (BHT 37; Tübingen,: Mohr Siebeck, 1967), 137–89; Karl Martin Fischer, *Tendenz und Absicht des Epheserbriefes* (FRLANT 111; Göttingen: Vandenhoeck & Ruprecht, 1973), 125ff. On the determinative concept, taken from the history of religions, that stands in the background here, cf. Klaus Döring, *Exemplum Socratis: Studien zur Sokratesnachwirkung in der kynisch-stoischen Popularphilosophie der frühen Kaiserzeit und im frühen Christentum* (HE 42; Wiesbaden: F. Steiner, 1979), E42.

10. Contra Schrage, *Einzelgebote*, 241, who argues, "Thus Paul did not introduce the historical life and work of Jesus as the concrete norm of the Christian life."

11. On the problem of the *proprium* (that which is characteristically Christian) of the Pauline and New Testament ethic, cf. Georg Strecker, "Strukturen einer neutestamentlichen Ethik," *ZTK* 75 (1978): 136ff.; Halter, *Taufe und Ethos*, 8, 13–32, 455–92.

12. Cf. also Christof Landmesser, "Der paulinische Imperativ als christologisches Performativ," in *Jesus Christus als die Mitte der Schrift: Studien zur Hermeneutik des Evangeliums* (ed. Christof Landmesser et al.; BZNW; Berlin: de Gruyter, 1997), 543–77, who holds fast to the indicative-imperative schema but resolutely wants to understand the two as a unity. Faith and the life determined by faith are equally gifts of God, so that for the imperative one can say, "The imperative that sounds forth in the proclamation of the gospel, καταλλάγητε τῷ θεῷ, shows itself to be a prime example of performative language, a kind of language by which hearers are effectively made to be what they are addressed as" (p. 575). Michael Wolter, "Die ethische Identität christlicher Gemeinden in neutestamentlicher Zeit," in *Woran orientiert sich Ethik?* (vol. 13 of *Marburger Jahrbuch Theologie*; MTS 67; Marburg: Elwert, 2001), 68, takes the relation of ethos and identity as the point of departure for his new determination of indicative and imperative: "The imperative formulates a normative ethos that is not a sort of challenge to 'preserve' the indicative. Rather, it has the function of facilitating for believers an objectification of their newly attained identity. In other words, the indissoluble dependence of the imperative on the indicative is indebted to the interest inherent in every determination and every claim of identity, that this identity be made *visible* (and indeed externally as well as from within) if it is not to remain a mere postulate."

of two aspects of a single reality, which Paul then names in the second basis for this action: "For [καὶ γάρ] our paschal lamb, Christ, has been sacrificed" (1 Cor. 5:7b). The new being gained through Christ does not permit the purity and holiness of the church to be violated; baptized believers are to live out what they are already. This is made possible by the Spirit, whose effective power determines the whole life of baptized believers. The passage often cited as the *locus classicus* for the indicative-imperative schema, Gal. 5:25, also points in this direction: "If we live in the Spirit, let us also be in harmony with the Spirit"[13] (εἰ ζῶμεν πνεύματι, πνεύματι καὶ στοιχῶμεν). By no means is the verb στοιχέω to be taken merely as a synonym for περιπατέω (walk) but means "agree with," "be in harmony with."[14] The accent is thus not placed on the demand; rather, it is a matter of a relationship, which is expressed with the dative πνεύματι (in/by the Spirit). When Paul urges the Galatians not to fall back into their life "according to the flesh" (cf. Gal. 3:3) but to live in the freedom they have been given (Gal. 5:1), then the Spirit has the power to make this possible. It is the Spirit of God,[15] who is able "both to will and to work for his good pleasure" (Phil. 2:13; cf. 1:6). What they have already attained should now be lived out (Phil. 3:16). It is thus not a matter of realizing a gift but of abiding and living in the realm of grace. "To be a Christian is mimesis of Christ,"[16] and the form of the new life that corresponds to Christ is love. "For the love of Christ urges us on, because we are convinced that one has died for all; therefore all have died. And he died for all, so that those who live might live no longer for themselves, but for him who died and was raised for them" (2 Cor. 5:14–15; cf. 4:10–11; Rom. 15:7). Conformity to Christ that belongs to the new being and living consists of love (cf. Gal. 5:13); in the Pauline ethic, love is the critical principle of interpretation by which everything is to be oriented and the goal of every action.[17] Whoever does not act out of love is out of step with the new being. Paul repeatedly points to this fundamental fact in his instruction and admonition. If baptized believers do not attend to the aspect of their new, graced existence that results in particular actions, they are not living in accord with the new being (cf. 1 Cor. 3:17; 6:9–10; 8:9–13; 10:1ff.; 2 Cor. 6:1; 11:13–15; Gal. 5:2–4, 21; Rom. 6:12ff.; 11:20–22; 14:13ff.). Love is not a constraint on human freedom but its consistent outcome; Christian freedom means, therefore, to be productive for others and not just for oneself. The other is always the one for whom Christ died (cf. 1 Cor. 8:11–12; Rom. 14:15). Love is not oriented to the consumer principle or to dominating others, for it understands the world and humanity to be God's good creation, which does not need to be changed so as to become even more perfect.

13. The translation reflects Gerhard Delling, "στοιχέω κτλ.," *TDNT* 7:667–69.

14. Cf. the evidence cited ibid., 666–69; Delling is followed by, e.g., Mussner, *Galaterbrief*, 391; Weder, "Gesetz und Gnade," 179–80.

15. The ἐν ὑμῖν (in/among you) of Phil. 2:13 points to the working of the Spirit.

16. Backhaus, "Evangelium als Lebensraum," 24.

17. Cf. Weder, "Normativität," 136ff.; Pfeiffer, *Einweisung*, 240–49.

Paul designates this new existence with the verb φρονέω, which occurs twenty-six times in the New Testament, twenty-two of them in Paul.[18] This word describes the direction and goal of one's thinking, the "striving and meaning" of life: "Do the kind of thinking among yourselves that those do who are in Christ Jesus" (Phil. 2:5 [following Schnelle's German; cf. NRSV, "Let the same mind be in you that was in Christ Jesus"]). The inner orientation and will of Christians are prefigured by what has already occurred in Christ, and the new being and life are stamped in conformity to Christ. This inner orientation is directed toward the unity of the church and its ethical growth toward perfection. "May the God of steadfastness and encouragement grant you to live in harmony with one another, in accordance with Christ Jesus" (Rom. 15:5; cf. also 2 Cor. 13:11; Rom. 12:16; Phil. 2:2, 5; 4:2). Because the church participates in the spiritual mode of being of the risen one, it strives toward ethical perfection (cf. Phil. 3:13–15), but without overestimating itself (cf. Phil. 3:12).

Paul counters the fallacy of overestimating one's present Christian attainment and status by pointing to the particular temporal structure of the Christian life as eschatological existence: the advent of Jesus Christ means that the end time has broken in (cf. 1 Cor. 7:29, 31; 10:11; 2 Cor. 5:17; 6:2; Gal. 4:4); he is "the first fruits of those who have died" (1 Cor. 15:20) and has already entered into his lordship over death and sin (cf. Rom. 5:12ff.). All the same, the conditions of existence in this life and the structures of this world have not changed, and the lordship of Christ takes place within this earthly reality, which is already passing away. The forgiveness of sins, the establishment of righteousness, and the conferral of the Spirit and εἶναι ἐν Χριστῷ that take place in baptism mean that the consummation of history in the perfection of God's kingdom has really begun, but Christians are still exposed to the trials and temptations of the world and do not yet live in this state of final perfection. Baptized believers have been placed in the time between the cross and the parousia and are to live in harmony with the new reality, though in a world that is apparently unchanged.

The beginning point and foundation of Paul's ethic are the *unity of life and action of the new being as participation in the Christ event.* Jesus Christ provides both the foundation and the character for the Christian life, and Christians are those who live in the sphere of Christ by the power of the Spirit and whose actions correspond to this new being.

20.2 The New Being in Practice

What instructions does Paul give for the Christian life, and on what does he base them? The answers to these questions vary from letter to letter. In 1 Thessalonians the near parousia of the Lord and the related understanding of

18. Cf. Backhaus, "Evangelium als Lebensraum," 28–30.

judgment function as the motivation for a blameless life in holiness (cf. 1 Thess. 3:13; 4:3, 4, 7; 5:23).[19] Paul explicitly acknowledges the ethical status of the church but at the same time encourages it to make further progress (cf. 4:1–2). In 4:3–8, the contents of Paul's admonitions to live a moral and honorable life remain within the framework of the ethic of Hellenistic Judaism, and the exhortation to avoid greed and immorality are firmly established elements of his own instructions (cf. 1 Cor. 5:9–11; 6:9–10; 2 Cor. 12:20–21; Gal. 5:19–21; Rom. 1:29–31; 2:21–22; 13:13).[20] In accordance with the conventional ethics prevalent in the whole letter, the church is instructed to live quietly and unobtrusively (1 Thess. 4:11) so that outsiders are not offended (4:12). The ethical competence of non-Christian Gentiles that Paul here presupposes shows that he is not striving for some sort of ethical superiority in the church. He does not base his instructions on the Old Testament and makes his point of departure the ethos already valued by both Christians and the surrounding pagan world.

The two Corinthian letters present a differentiated picture.[21] After his call for the unity of the congregation, in 1 Cor. 4:16 Paul pleads with the church to "be imitators of me." The reason Timothy is coming to Corinth is "to remind you of my ways in Christ Jesus, as I teach them everywhere in every church" (4:17).[22] The Corinthians are exhorted, like all the other churches, to adopt the life and teaching of Paul as the pattern of their own lives. That Paul again takes up the word ὁδός (way) in 12:31 shows that he intends the way or ways of love.[23] He lives by what he teaches, the love of Christ that has been received, and the churches should adopt him as their model. The instructions Paul adds in the section 1 Cor. 5–7 dealing with various conflicts reveal the very different sorts of argument Paul might use to support his ethics. Although in 5:13b Paul can support his case for excluding the immoral person from the church by citing Deut. 17:7b LXX,[24] what really bothers him is that such things do not occur even among non-Christian Gentiles (cf. 1 Cor. 5:1b). Paul's prohibition, in 1 Cor. 6:1–11, of settling legal disputes among Christians by going to pagan courts has no parallel in Jewish tradition.[25] Paul supports the warning against

19. Cf. Schnelle, "Ethik des 1 Thessalonikerbriefes," 295–305. The motif of sanctification and the related concept of judgment are also found in 1 Cor. 1:8; 7:34; 2 Cor. 7:1; Phil. 1:9–11; 2:15–18.

20. For a comprehensive analysis, cf. Eckart Reinmuth, *Geist und Gesetz: Studien zu Voraussetzungen und Inhalt der paulinischen Paränese* (TA 44; Berlin: Evangelische Verlagsanstalt, 1985), 12–47.

21. For analysis, cf. Lindemann, "Toragebote," 95–110.

22. Although God's commands can be designated ὁδοί (cf. Ps. 24:4; 26:11; 118:3, 26; Isa. 55:3), the expression αἱ ὁδοί μου (my ways) is unique: Paul calls for orientation not to the commandments but to his person.

23. Otherwise ὁδός is found only in Old Testament quotations (Rom. 3:16, 17) or else in a prayer (1 Thess. 3:11) and a hymnic segment (Rom. 11:33).

24. We should still note that Paul does not introduce appropriate texts from the Torah dealing with the same subject, such as Deut. 23:1; 27:20 and Lev. 18:8.

25. As a parallel, cf. Plato, *Gorg.* 509c (*NW* 2/1:278).

immorality in 1 Cor. 6:12–20 not with relevant biblical texts dealing with the same subject matter, such as Prov. 5:3; 6:20–27; Sir. 9:6; 19:2, but instead cites Gen. 2:24, a text that originally had nothing to do with the theme of immorality. So also in 1 Cor. 7, Old Testament texts play no role as bases for his ethical instructions and recommendations. There is, in fact, no suggestion in the Old Testament in favor of the apostle's tendentious line of argument critical of marriage as such, but it does have some parallels with Cynic instruction: marriage and children hinder the Cynic from his real mission of being the gods' scout and herald among human beings (cf. Epictetus, *Diatr.* 3.67–82). The prohibition of divorce given by the Lord (1 Cor. 7:10–11) contradicts explicit regulations of the Torah (one need only see Deut. 24:1). In 1 Cor. 7:17–24 Paul develops the ethical maxim of remaining in the status in which one was called (7:17, "let each of you lead the life that the Lord has assigned, to which God called you. This is my rule in all the churches"), which is likewise to be understood against a Cynic-Stoic background.[26] One's actions must always be oriented to existing circumstances, for a false understanding of things produces suffering. "Therefore, one must not attempt to change the surrounding conditions themselves, but to adapt oneself to circumstances, just as sailors do. They don't try to change the wind and the sea, but they prepare themselves in advance to deal with them as they may come. . . . This is the way you are to relate to circumstances. You are a grown man; leave play to children. You are weak; withdraw your hands from work that requires strength" (Teles, frg. 2). Likewise 1 Cor. 7:19 reflects Hellenistic influence, for "obeying the commandments of God" (τήρησις ἐντολῶν θεοῦ) cannot refer to the Torah, for the Torah commands circumcision instead of considering it a matter of indifference as in 1 Cor. 7:19a. Paul again proceeds on the basis of a general understanding of what is considered ethical; there is direct access to the commands of God, into which human beings as such can have insight. Epictetus argues similarly: "What directions shall I give you? Has not Zeus given you directions?" (*Diatr.* 1.25). It is hardly an accident that in the context of the conflict over eating meat sacrificed to idols, Paul does *not* cite the Old Testament (cf., e.g., Deut. 14:3, "You shall not eat any abhorrent thing"; cf. also Exod. 20:5; 34:13ff.; 32:17) but points to a general ethical maxim.[27] He can even give instructions that directly oppose commands of the Torah.[28] Scriptural quotations (cf. 1 Cor.

---

26. Extensive evidence is given in Deming, *Marriage and Celibacy*, 159–65.

27. Compare 1 Cor. 10:24 ("Do not seek your own advantage, but that of the other") with Menander, *Sent.* 775 ("This means life: not to live only for yourself"), and Seneca, *Ep.* 48.2 ("And no one can live happily who has regard to himself alone and transforms everything into a question of his own utility. You must live for your neighbor, if you would live for yourself").

28. Compare 1 Cor. 10:27 ("If an unbeliever invites you to a meal and you are disposed to go, eat whatever is set before you without raising any question on the ground of conscience") with Exod. 34:15 ("You shall not make a covenant with the inhabitants of the land, for when they prostitute themselves to their gods and sacrifice to their gods, someone among them will invite you, and you will eat of the sacrifice").

10:7, 26) and allusions (cf. 11:3, 8, 9) do have some weight in the argumentation of 10:1–11:1. Even here, however, Paul does not derive his instructions directly from Scripture. Likewise the Isaiah text (Isa. 28:11–12) introduced as a citation of the Torah in 1 Cor. 14:21 has no normative function. "Paul's concrete instructions in 1 Corinthians show that he does not orient himself to the contents of the Torah when he deploys ethical norms or makes decisions on disputed points."[29] Second Corinthians confirms this judgment, for the only two relevant citations of Scripture in 2 Cor. 8:15 and 9:9 merely provide the basis for the promise that those who contribute to the collection will receive surpassing grace from God.

In Gal. 5:14 Paul cites Lev. 19:18b, where it is clearly a matter of the love that has appeared in Jesus Christ (cf. Gal. 5:6). The norm of the new being is exclusively the Spirit, who explicitly appears in 5:18 as *the* contrast to the Torah. The Christian virtues of love, joy, peace, patience, kindness, generosity, faithfulness, gentleness, and self-control (5:22–23a) are traced back exclusively to the Spirit. As an addendum, Paul notes, "There is no law against such things" (5:23b). Paul's line of argument is remarkable in two respects: he describes the content of Christian conduct with the general ethical concepts of Hellenism,[30] and their validity is derived from the fact that they are the fruits of the Spirit, not because they are commands of the Torah. It is only as a supplementary comment that Paul indicates that the qualities and ways of life characteristic of the new being are not in conflict with the Torah. In particular, the catalogues of virtues and vices (cf. 1 Cor. 5:10–11; 6:9–10; 2 Cor. 12:20–21; Gal. 5:19–23; Rom. 1:29–31) develop an ethical model that is interested in fitting in with the conventions of the time. They originated in Hellenistic philosophy, found acceptance in Hellenistic Jewish literature, and were very popular, especially in New Testament times.[31]

In Rom. 2:14–15 Paul proceeds on the basis of a common moral standard among Jews, pagans, and Christians (cf. also 13:13). He adopts the Hellenistic idea that ethical instruction comes through nature, the reason/logos, apart from external, that is, written laws.[32] So also in 12:1–2, Paul does not derive the will of God from the Torah.[33] These first two verses constitute a kind of title for this

---

29. Lindemann, "Toragebote," 110.

30. For analysis, cf. Betz, *Galatians*, 480–91.

31. Cf. the materials treated in Siegfried Wibbing, *Die Tugend- und Lasterkataloge im Neuen Testament und ihre Traditionsgeschichte unter besonderer Berücksichtigung der Qumran-Texte* (BZNW 25; Berlin: Töpelmann, 1959); and Ehrhard Kamlah, *Die Form der katalogischen Paränese im Neuen Testament* (WUNT 7; Tübingen: Mohr Siebeck, 1964). Sample texts are given in *NW* 2/1:54–66, 575–76.

32. Cf. the examples in *NW* 2/1:71–85.

33. In Rom. 12:3, too, Paul argues with the conceptuality of Hellenistic popular philosophy; cf. Dieter Zeller, "Konkrete Ethik im hellenistischen Kontext," in *Der neue Mensch in Christus: Hellenistische Anthropologie und Ethik im Neuen Testament* (ed. Johannes Beutler; QD 190; Freiburg: Herder, 2001), 89.

major division of the letter devoted to ethics and serve to guide the reader; they define the framework of reference within which the following statements are to be understood. The Roman Christians should themselves determine what the will of God is, on the basis of their own investigation and reflection (12:2, δοκιμάζειν ὑμᾶς τί τὸ θέλημα τοῦ θεοῦ [discern what is the will of God]), and they thereby undertake a task also given to philosophers when they inquire what is good, evil, or indifferent. "Therefore, the first and greatest task of the philosopher is to test the impressions [δοκιμάζειν τὰς φαντασίας] and discriminate [διακρίνειν] between them, and to apply none that has not been tested" (Epictetus, *Diatr.* 1.20.6–7). Paul labels the will of God with the standard categories of popular philosophy: the good, the acceptable, the perfect.[34] Plato had already long since declared that in human life, God is only pleased with what is reasonable, "for it is like God, while thoughtless and impulsive acts are unlike him, conflict with the divine nature, and are unjust" (*Leg.* 4.716c, trans. Jowett). According to Aristotle, passion does not obey reason, but reason submits to passion, "so the state of the soul that inclines to virtue must be there first, in which one loves good and avoids evil" (*Eth. nic.* 10.1179b). Human beings are truly friends of God, according to Plutarch, "when their refined and chastened mind recognizes God as the ultimate source of all good, the Father of all beauty, the one who can neither do evil nor tolerate it. He is good, and knows nothing of malevolence, fear, wrath, or hate."[35]

The basic ethical attitude commended by Paul in Rom. 12:1 likewise has noteworthy parallels in the popular philosophy of the time. In the tradition of philosophical critique of the cult,[36] Christians are challenged to present their bodies as acceptable sacrifices to God, for this is their "reasonable worship" (λογικὴ λατρεία; NRSV, "spiritual worship"). The new understanding of God has a corresponding reasonable worship, oriented to the reason that is itself the gift of God. Philo states that "what is precious in the sight of God is not the number of victims immolated but the true purity of a rational spirit in him who makes the sacrifice (*Spec. Laws* 1.277). Of the just ruler Dio Chrysostom declares that "he believes that the gods also do not delight in the offerings or sacrifices of the unjust, but accept the gifts made by the good alone. Accordingly, he will be zealous to worship them with these also without stint. Of a truth he will never cease honoring them with noble deeds and just acts" (*3 Regn.* 52; 53; cf. also 13.35; 31.15; 43.11). Paul and the early Christians see themselves as sent into the world by God and serve him in a new mode of worship. In a comparable manner, the philosopher knows himself to be bound only to

34. Cf. Delling, "τέλος," *TDNT* 8:69–77.
35. Plutarch, *Mor.* 1102.
36. Further examples are in Hans Wenschkewitz, *Die Spiritualisierung der Kultusbegriffe* ([Aggelos]; Archiv für neutestamentliche Zeitgeschichte und Kulturkunde, Beiheft 4; Leipzig: E. Pfeiffer, 1932), 74–151.

the one "who sent him, and whom he serves, that is, Zeus" (Epictetus, *Diatr.* 3.22.56, ὁ καταπεπομφὼς αὐτὸν καὶ ᾧ λατρεύει, ὁ Ζεύς).

Paul most clearly takes up the terminology of popular philosophy in Phil. 4:8:[37] "Finally, beloved, whatever is true, whatever is honorable, whatever is just, whatever is pure, whatever is pleasing, whatever is commendable, if there is any excellence and if there is anything worthy of praise, think about these things." In Paul's list, εὔφημος (commendable) and ἔπαινος ([worthy of] praise) are notable as political-social terms; they are aimed at social acceptance, which Paul expects from the church in Philippi. When he uses ἀρετή (virtue), he is adopting the key concept in Greek educational theory[38] and integrating the life of the Philippians thoroughly into the contemporary ethos. It is, after all, the task of the philosopher who is active in the political and social scene to make clear "what justice is, what a sense of duty is, what the capacity to suffer is, what bravery, disdain for death, knowledge of God is, and what a precious good a good conscience is."[39] Because a moral life is synonymous with philosophy and because philosophy teaches how to live, it can be thoroughly compared with the paraclesis of the apostle.[40] As a lifestyle and technique for happiness, as the "science of life,"[41] it becomes the task of philosophy to enliven the capacity for virtue already present in humanity or to cultivate insight in human beings so that they may orient their lives to these virtues. "Human beings are the only earthly beings who bear the image of God and have virtues similar to him. For among the gods too, we can imagine nothing better than insight, justice, courage, and wise, sober thought [φρονήσεως καὶ δικαιοσύνης, ἔτι δὲ ἀνδρείας καὶ σωφροσύνης]."[42] Musonius develops the idea of a similarity in nature between God and human beings into an ethic of emancipation. He proceeds on the basis that human beings are by nature free and without defects (ἀναμαρτήτως) and

37. Cf. Zeller, "Konkrete Ethik," 84.

38. One need only note Cicero, *Tusc.* 5.67: "For that 'best' of which you are in search must necessarily have its place in what is the best part of man. But what is there in man better than a mind that is sagacious and good? . . . The good of the mind is virtue: therefore happy life is necessarily bound up with virtue."

39. Seneca, *Tranq.* 3.4.

40. Cf. Seneca, *Ep.* 20.2: "Philosophy teaches to act, not to speak"; cf. further Musonius, *Diss.* 3, where it is not only men who should seek "how to live a moral life, which means the same thing as philosophy."

The term "paraclesis" better expresses the basic Pauline approach than "paraenesis": (1) Paraclesis is used by Paul himself (παρακαλέω, thirty-nine times; παράκλησις, eighteen times), but not paraenesis. (2) As the result of accepting the gospel, paraclesis unites encouragement and demand; cf. Anton Grabner-Haider, *Paraklese und Eschatologie bei Paulus: Mensch und Welt im Anspruch der Zukunft Gottes* (NTAbh NF 4; Münster: Aschendorff, 1968), 4–5, 153–54.

41. Cicero, *Fin.* 3.4: "Philosophy is the science of life." In *Fin.* 3 Cicero presents an impressive general view of Stoic ethics, whose basic idea is that "the highest good consists in living in accord with the natural givens, deciding for what is natural . . . i.e., living in harmony and agreement with nature" (*Fin.* 3.31).

42. Musonius, *Diss.* 17 (trans. M.E.B. after Schnelle).

so are capable of living in accord with virtue. The "seed of virtue" (σπέρμα ἀρετῆς) has been planted in every human being (*Diss.* 2). Therefore women too participate in virtue and are capable of studying philosophy (*Diss.* 3). Daughters and sons should be educated in the same way, for both men and women must be able to live according to justice (*Diss.* 4). All vices are found in both men and women, so that both are also in the position to overcome them. This happens through instruction, especially through habituation (*Diss.* 5), for learning the principles of virtue must always be followed by practice (*Diss.* 6).[43] Here the philosopher himself serves as example, for his students can see in his life the unity of doctrine and life (*Diss.* 11). For Musonius, philosophy is liberating instruction for life; it is the art of activating by art, insight, and practice the virtues that slumber in human beings.[44]

The material content of the paraclesis of the Pauline letters is not basically different from the ethical standards of the surrounding world. Paul uses the Old Testament as a normative ethical authority only in a very reserved manner;[45] the Torah is concentrated into the love command (cf. Rom. 13:8–10) and thus integrated into the contemporary ethos.[46] Even when Paul speaks of the "law of Christ" (Gal. 6:2), he remains within the context of the Hellenistic friendship ethic.[47] The function of the Pauline admonitions also is comparable with that of the philosophical instruction of his contemporaries; in each case the goal is to call to mind what people already know and to work through new problems. "I admit that precepts [*praecepta*] alone are not effective in overthrowing the mind's mistaken beliefs; but they do not on that account fail to be of service when they accompany other measures also. In the first place,

43. See also Seneca, *Ep.* 94.47: "A part of moral perfection consists in schooling, a part in practice; you must learn, and confirm what you have learned by practice."

44. Cf. also Iamblichus, *Prot.* 3.1–2: "When one has reached the goal toward which he strives and has mastered it, whether in eloquence, knowledge, or bodily strength, then he must put it into practice in the sense of the good and the laws. . . . Just as a person, who masters one of these abilities, will be entirely good when he applies it to good causes, and one who uses it for evil, will himself be completely evil."

45. Differently, Karl-Wilhelm Niebuhr, "Tora ohne Tempel: Paulus und der Jakobusbrief im Zusammenhang frühjüdischer Torarezeption für die Diaspora," in *Gemeinde ohne Tempel = Community without Temple: Zur Substituierung und Transformation des Jerusalemer Tempels und seines Kults im Alten Testament, antiken Judentum, und frühen Christentum* (ed. Beate Ego et al.; WUNT 118; Tübingen: Mohr Siebeck, 1999), 427–60, who sees the Pauline Torah reception as analogous to the Torah reception in the Jewish Diaspora: "When particular individual commands or whole parts of the Torah are not cited, this does not imply a rejection of the Torah in principle or even that its validity has been only partially accepted. Instead in each case one must ask to what extent such parts of the Torah were relevant for the situation of the addressees or were important for the specific intentions of the author."

46. Wolter, "Ethische Identität," 82–84, rightly points out that Paul does not derive the love command from the Torah: "It is, rather, the other way around, inasmuch as it is the love commandment of Lev. 19:18 that first makes possible an integration of the Torah into the Christian ethic, where the love command already prevails."

47. See above, section 11.3 ("The Doctrine of the Law and of Justification in Galatians").

they refresh the memory" (Seneca, *Ep.* 94.21).[48] When Paul begins to speak of the aspects of the new being that call for ethical action, he too activates the memory of his hearers and readers and strives for solutions to their problems. Paul does not emphasize that the material content of his ethical instruction is new, but that it has a new basis.[49] He evaluates the human capacity for action and its development in the light of the Christ event and proceeds from there to a new interpretation of life and history: only participation in the Christ event frees from the power of sin and enables, by the power of the Holy Spirit, a life lived in love that conforms to Christ's own life, a life that will endure beyond death and the judgment.

The indicative-imperative schema also shows itself to be inadequate to grasp the practice of the new being appropriately, for the imperative linguistic mode sets forth no really new content. Nor is this to be expected, for early Christianity participates in a highly reflective Jewish-Hellenistic and Greco-Roman ethical tradition; what is essentially human must not be newly created and thought through. Moreover, the formation of the Pauline churches from people who had been Jews, proselytes, God-fearers, and Gentiles would not lead us to expect anything else, for in the formation of a new identity, an interplay of Old Testament, Hellenistic-Jewish, and Greco-Roman norms is entirely natural. These norms, however, are bound together in the Pauline Christ hermeneutic, so that love alone receives the fundamental priority and all conventional distinctions in status lose their significance.[50] *The norm of Pauline meaning formation is love.* Pauline paraclesis aims at a life lived in accord with the Christ event and points to an inner concord between the gospel that is believed and the gospel as lived. It is not a matter of "deriving" an imperative from the indicative but of the innate unity of faith and life in the power of the Spirit. The Pauline ethic is not first of all an ethic of command but an ethic of insight.

---

48. Cf. also Seneca, *Ep.* 94.33–34: "For although we may infer by proofs just what Good and Evil are, nevertheless precepts have their proper role. Prudence and justice consist of certain duties; and duties are set in order by precepts. Moreover, judgment as to Good and Evil is itself strengthened by following up our duties, and precepts conduct us to this end."

49. Cf. Betz, "Grundlagen der paulinischen Ethik," 201, who emphasizes that Paul does not ground ethics directly in reason and unity with nature.

50. Wolter, "Ethische Identität," 86, sees the decisive new character of Pauline ethics to be reciprocity and the abolition of dependence on status.

21

Ecclesiology

The Church as a Demanding and Attracting Fellowship

The church is the place where baptized believers are joined together in their common relation to God and Jesus Christ. *For Paul, participation in the salvation they have in common can only exist in the fellowship of believers.* For him, being a Christian is identical with being in the church;[1] his mission is a church-founding mission, and his letters are church letters. Because the exalted Lord himself constitutes his church and is its foundation (1 Cor. 3:11), the Pauline ecclesiology, with its concepts, motifs, and imagery, is always the interpretation of a previously given reality.

21.1 Primary Vocabulary and Foundational Metaphors of Pauline Ecclesiology

The formation and consolidation of a new movement includes a necessary semantic strategy: the coining of new words and the reminting of old ones.

---

1. The general truth also applies to Paul: "Religion requires a religious community, and to live in a religious world requires affiliation with that community" (Berger and Luckmann, *Social Construction*, 158).

Primary Vocabulary

Of the 114 instances of ἐκκλησία (church, congregation) in the New Testament, 44 are found in the undisputed letters of Paul, and of these, 31 are found in the Corinthian letters. In adopting the term ἐκκλησία as the designation of the local assemblies of the new community, Paul takes up a word with political overtones. In the Greek-Hellenistic realm, ἐκκλησία refers to the assembly of free men with the right to vote, a usage also found in the New Testament (Acts 19:32, 39).[2] First Thessalonians 2:14, 1 Cor. 15:9, Gal. 1:13, and Phil. 3:6 (a persecutor of the church) show that the designation ἐκκλησία τοῦ θεοῦ (assembly of God) had already been used in Jerusalem for the new movement of believers in Christ. On the one hand, ἐκκλησία is taken from the Septuagint as the translation of קָהָל,[3] relating the Christian community to Israel as the people of God, and on the other hand the fact that συναγωγή was *not* taken over shows that the self-understanding of the earliest church distinguished itself from Judaism.

With the semantic neologism ἐκκλησία τοῦ θεοῦ, the new movement identified itself as an independent reality.[4] Paul intentionally orients his own understanding to the basic secular meaning of ἐκκλησία, for he considers the local assembly of believers to be of primary importance, as indicated by the local designations in 1 Thess. 1:1; 1 Cor. 1:2; 2 Cor. 1:1; Gal. 1:2.[5] At the same time, it is the one church of God that is represented in each local manifestation, so that the designation ἐκκλησία τοῦ θεοῦ can be applied to the local congregation (1 Thess. 1:1; 1 Cor. 1:2), to the group of congregations in the same area (2 Cor. 1:1; Gal. 1:2), and to Christianity as a whole (1 Thess. 2:14; 1 Cor. 10:32; 11:16, 22; 12:28; 15:9; Gal. 1:13; Phil. 3:6).[6] For Paul, the local

---

2. Cf. the inscription from the first century CE, where, in the context of honoring the Corinthian lady Junia Theodora, an assembly of citizens in Patara in Asia Minor is called an ἐκκλησία ("For this reason also most of our citizens came before the *assembly* and spoke on your behalf"); for translation and interpretation of the text, cf. Hans-Josef Klauck, "Junia Theodora und die Gemeinde in Korinth," in *Kirche und Volk Gottes: Festschrift für Jürgen Roloff zum 70. Geburtstag* (ed. Martin Karrer et al.; Neukirchen-Vluyn: Neukirchener Verlag, 2000), 42–57.

3. Cf. Deut. 23:2–4; Num. 16:3; 20:4; Mic. 2:5; 1 Chron. 28:8; קָהָל can also be translated as συναγωγή; cf., e.g., Isa. 56:8; Jer. 38:4; Ezek. 37:10. On the various derivation theories, cf. Roloff, "ἐκκλησία," *EDNT* 1:411–12; Kraus, *Das Volk Gottes*, 124–26.

4. The Greek construction ἐκκλησία τοῦ θεοῦ is found only in Paul (1 Thess. 2:14; 1 Cor. 1:2; 10:32; 11:16, 22; 15:9; 2 Cor. 1:1; Gal. 1:13) and in literature dependent on him (Acts 20:28; 2 Thess. 1:1, 4; 1 Tim. 3:5, 15); the only comparable expressions in the Septuagint are Judg. 20:2; Neh. 13:1; 1 Chron. 24:1; 28:8; Mic. 2:5; Deut. 23:1–2; cf. also Philo *Alleg. Interp.* 3.8.5. The expression קְהַל אֵל is found in 1Q33 4:10; 14:5; 1Q29a 2:4; 4Q271 frg. 5, 1:21.

5. Cf. Roloff, *Kirche im Neuen Testament*, 98–99.

6. Paul speaks of the ἐκκλησία (τοῦ) θεοῦ (cf. 1 Cor. 1:2; 10:32; 11:22; 15:9; 2 Cor. 1:1; Gal. 1:13), the ἐκκλησίαι (τοῦ) θεοῦ (cf. 1 Thess. 2:14; 1 Cor. 11:16), and the ἐκκλησία ἐν θεῷ (1 Thess. 1:1). In Gal. 1:22 and Rom. 16:16, he refers to the ἐκκλησίαι ἐν Χριστῷ or τοῦ Χριστοῦ.

congregation represents the whole church in a particular location;[7] he knows no hierarchical structure that connects local congregations and the whole church, but each part or manifestation of the church can in turn stand for the whole. The whole church is present in the local congregation, and the local congregation is a part of the whole church. Thus, terminologically, ἐκκλησία as the assembly of Christians in one location should be translated "congregation" [*Gemeinde*], and when it means the worldwide group of Christians as a whole, it should be translated "church" [*Kirche*].[8]

Paul also uses ecclesiological terminology adopted from the tradition history of Old Testament–Jewish imagery and from the pre-Pauline tradition, such as "the saints" (οἱ ἅγιοι)[9] and "the elect" (οἱ ἐκλεκτοί).[10] Very often the prescript of the letters includes a designation of the congregation as ἅγιοι (1 Cor. 1:2; 2 Cor. 1:1; Rom. 1:7; Phil. 1:1), which, like ἐκκλησία τοῦ θεοῦ, can be used alternatively for individual congregations (1 Cor. 16:1; 2 Cor. 8:4; Rom. 15:26) and for the whole church (1 Cor. 14:33, ταῖς ἐκκλησίαις τῶν ἁγίων [the churches of the saints]). For Paul, "saints" are the Christians ἐν Χριστῷ (1 Cor. 1:2; Phil. 1:1), that is, not on the basis of a special ethical quality but as those who have been incorporated by baptism into God's saving act in Jesus Christ. They belong to God, the Spirit of God dwells in them (1 Cor. 3:16; 6:19), and their body is holy because it is the temple of God (1 Cor. 3:17b). In direct connection with ἐκκλησία and in close proximity to ἅγιος stands the word group κλητός (called), κλῆσις (calling), ἐκλογή (election), and ἐκλεκτός (elect);[11] this word group is of great significance for Pauline ecclesiology. In 1 Thess. 1:4 Paul gives thanks for the election (ἐκλογή) of the Thessalonian Christians, who had previously been Gentiles and who had become an example to other churches. God's act of election is at the same time universal and historically real;[12] it includes Jews and Gentiles and has a discernible effect in shaping the life of the congregation. In 1 Cor. 1:26ff. Paul interprets the calling (κλῆσις) of the weak, foolish, and disdained of this world as the confirmation of the paradoxical act of God on the cross. The observable form of the church, however, provides no evidence of God's call, positive or negative, for election is entirely a matter of grace (Gal. 1:6; Rom. 1:6). Thus Paul can speak of a

7. Cf. Käsemann, *Romans*, 336.

8. Cf. Roloff, "ἐκκλησία," *EDNT* 1:413. [Translator's note: this distinction is much more important in Europe, where there is a long tradition of an established church, than in North America and other English-speaking areas, where "church" has always been used for the local congregation, for groups of congregations, for the denomination, and for the church as a whole. I have therefore not attempted to maintain this distinction consistently in the English translation.]

9. On the Old Testament and Jewish background of this term, cf. Deut. 33:3; Dan. 7:18, 21–22, 25, 27; *T. Levi* 18:11, 14; *2 En.* 100:5; *Pss. Sol.* 11:1; 1QM 10:10.

10. Cf. Isa. 65:9, 15, 22; Ps. 105:6, 43; 106:5; 1 Chr. 16:13; Sir. 46:1; 1QpHab 5:4; 9:12; 10:13; 1QH 14:15.

11. Cf. Conzelmann, *1 Corinthians*, 25–29.

12. Cf. Jost Eckert, "ἐκλεκτός," *EDNT* 1:417–19.

predestination of believers that, though not apparent in the present, will be eschatologically validated (Rom. 8:29–39; cf. 1 Cor. 2:7). One can see how closely calling and sanctification belong together for Paul by noting 1 Cor. 1:2 and Rom. 1:7, where he speaks of "called saints." Those whom God has called, separated (cf. Gal. 1:15; Rom. 1:1), and laid hold of are indeed holy. The eschatological overtones that can be overheard in all the ecclesiological designations of early Christianity are impressively clear in Rom. 8:33: the elect need not fear accusation or condemnation in the judgment, for God is the one who justifies them. The church understands itself as the eschatological people of God, as God's flock that God has elected and sanctified in the end time, the community that has been incorporated into Jesus' victory over sin and death and that will endure through the coming judgment.

Foundational Metaphors

Alongside the primary ecclesiological vocabulary, Paul's statements about the church are characterized by three foundational metaphors: "in Christ" (ἐν Χριστῷ), "body of Christ" (σῶμα Χριστοῦ), and "people of God" (λαός θεοῦ).[13] Their space and time aspects provide a comprehensive portrayal of the location and nature of Christian existence in the community of believers.

(1) As a special description of Christian existence, ἐν Χριστῷ designates the close and salvific fellowship of every individual Christian and of the church as a whole with Jesus Christ.[14] By baptism believers are incorporated into the sphere of the spiritual Christ and are ἐν Χριστῷ a new creation (2 Cor. 5:17). This incorporation into the sphere of Christ's lordship works itself out both in the life of the individual believer and in shaping the life of the community of faith as a whole, and it does this in a way that is realistic and not merely theoretical. Being included in the sphere of Christ not only means communion with Christ but also makes possible a new fellowship of believers with each other (cf. Gal. 3:26–28). The baptized have "in Christ" a participation in the κοινωνία (fellowship, communion) of the one Spirit (2 Cor. 13:13; Phil. 2:1), which

13. It is, of course, possible to arrange the data differently. Thus Herman N. Ridderbos, *Paul: An Outline of His Theology* (trans. John Richard de Witt; Grand Rapids: Eerdmans, 1975), 327, sees two main aspects of Pauline anthropology, the concept of the people of God and the image of the body of Christ; Heinrich Schlier, "Ekklesiologie des Neuen Testaments," in *Das Heilsgeschehen in der Gemeinde* (ed. Wolfgang Beinert et al.; 2 vols.; MySal 4; Einsiedeln: Benziger, 1972–1973), 1:152ff., adopts a threefold outline of Paul's ecclesiology (people of God and ἐκκλησία; body of Christ; and temple of God); Ollrog, *Mitarbeiter*, 132ff., finds four main lines of Pauline ecclesiological understanding (descendants of Abraham; the saints, the temple of God; God's field and planting; the body of Christ); Roloff, *Kirche im Neuen Testament*, 86ff., distinguishes two focal points of Pauline ecclesiology (body of Christ and people of God), which he develops in five subpoints: baptism and "being in Christ"; the ἐκκλησία as the local assembly "in Christ"; the "body of Christ"; the eschatological temple and its edification; the people of God and the church.

14. On ἐν Χριστῷ, see above, section 17.1 ("New Being as Participation in Christ").

now determines their life in the church. This life is stamped by the liberating power of the Spirit, which grasps individuals in the particularity of their bodily existence and characterizes the life of the church as a whole. Ecclesial existence "in Christ" is a life derived from baptism, a life that knows itself to be obligated and enabled to do God's will in the church and in the world.

(2) The christological foundation of Paul's ecclesiology is also seen in the σῶμα Χριστοῦ imagery, for the idea of incorporation into the body of Christ emphasizes the priority of Christology to ecclesiology.[15] The point of departure for the ecclesiological use of σῶμα in Paul is the way σῶμα Χριστοῦ is spoken of in Rom. 7:4 and in the eucharistic tradition (1 Cor. 10:16; 11:27). This is where one should look for the origin of the term "body of Christ" and where the transition to its use as an ecclesiological designation may be noted: whereas σῶμα Χριστοῦ in 1 Cor. 10:16; 11:27 and Rom. 7:4 means the body of Christ given on the cross for the church, in 1 Cor. 10:17 the ecclesiological inference is drawn from ἓν σῶμα οἱ πολλοί ἐσμεν (we who are many are one body). The fundamental identification of the church with the body of Christ is explicitly found only in 1 Cor. 12:27: Ὑμεῖς δέ ἐστε σῶμα Χριστοῦ (Now you are the body of Christ). Paul also makes use of this image in 1 Cor. 1:13; 6:15–16; 10:17; Rom. 12:5; and 1 Cor. 12:12–27.[16] In 1 Cor. 12:13 ("For in the one Spirit we were all baptized into one body"), Paul develops the idea of the σῶμα Χριστοῦ in a characteristic manner: (a) In regard to its members, the body of Christ is preexistent. It does not come into being by human decisions and mergers but is a pre-given reality that first makes these possible. (b) By baptism the individual Christian is integrated into the body of Christ that already existed. Baptism does not constitute the body of Christ but is the historical location of reception into this body and the concrete expression of the unity of the church grounded in Christ. The one who is baptized is placed within the body of Christ, whose reality and unity is established by Christ and testified to by the one baptized. The exalted Christ does not exist without his body, the church. So also, participation in the σῶμα Χριστοῦ manifests itself precisely in the corporeality of the believer: "Do you not know that your bodies are members of Christ?" (1 Cor. 6:15, οὐκ οἴδατε ὅτι τὰ σώματα ὑμῶν μέλη Χριστοῦ ἐστιν;). Because believers, including their bodies, belong totally to their Lord, they are at the same time members of the body of Christ. Just as for Paul there is neither a bodiless crucified one (Rom. 7:4) nor a bodiless risen one (Phil. 3:21), so also participation in the body of Christ is for him inconceivable apart from the glorification of God in the σῶμα of the believer.

Paul applies the universal concept of the body of Christ to the individual congregation in order to help clarify the challenging problem of the church,

15. On the interpretation of 1 Cor. 12, see above, section 9.5 ("The Power of the Spirit and Building Up the Church").

16. Cf. Schweizer and Baumgärtel, "σῶμα," *TDNT* 7:1063–66.

which is united by having received a common baptism but also has received a variety of spiritual gifts: just as the body is one even though it has many members, so in the church there are many callings and gifts but only one church (1 Cor. 1:10–17; 12:12ff.; Rom. 12:5). Likewise the relation of individual members to each other may illustrate the concept of the body: they are not all the same, but all are interconnected and need each other, and thus they are all of equal value. The presupposition for this paraenetic function of the body imagery is the indicative identification of the one body with Christ himself. The church does not form the body by its own actions, but its actions are to correspond to this body in which all are members.

(3) The programmatic proclamation of the gospel to Gentiles without the requirement of circumcision set Paul before the problem of how to understand the continuity and discontinuity of the church with Israel.[17] In this context, the linguistic usage of the apostle is notable, for Paul refers to the "people [of God]" (λαὸς [Θεοῦ]) only in five citations from the Old Testament, and it is not accidental that four of these are found in his letter to the Romans (1 Cor. 10:7 = Exod. 32:6; Rom. 9:25–26 = Hos. 2:25; Rom. 10:21 = Isa. 65:2; Rom. 11:1–2 = Ps. 93:14 LXX [Ps. 94:14]; Rom. 15:10 = Deut. 32:43).[18] Moreover, the apostle explicitly avoids speaking of one people of God composed of Jews and Gentiles, or of the "old" and "new" people of God. Nonetheless, showing the unity of God's acts in history and the continuity of the people of God in salvation history is a central theme of Pauline ecclesiology. The apostle wrestled with this theme his whole life, as shown by the different positions he assumes in his letters and by his organizing the collection for the Jerusalem church.

In 1 Thess. 2:16 Paul makes a definitive judgment: the wrath of God has already fallen on the Jews because they hinder the preaching of the message of salvation to the Gentiles. The idea of discontinuity prevails; Paul speaks of the election of the Thessalonians (cf. 1 Thess. 1:4; 2:12; 4:7; 5:24) but says nothing about Israel and does not cite the Old Testament.[19] In 1 Cor. 10:1–13, on the one hand, the rootedness of the church in Israel is expressed (1 Cor. 10:1, "our ancestors" [cf. 1 Cor. 5:7, "our paschal lamb, Christ, has been sacrificed"]; 1 Cor. 10:18, "Consider the people of Israel according to the flesh" [τὸν Ἰσραὴλ κατὰ σάρκα, empirical Israel]); on the other hand, Paul transcends this image and leaves it behind, for the events of the exodus can

17. In the Old Testament and the literature of ancient Judaism, numerous texts testify to reflection on the integration of the Gentiles into the people of God (for an analysis, cf. Kraus, *Das Volk Gottes*, 16–110). The Gentile mission with no requirement of circumcision, however, represented a completely new phenomenon that is illuminated by these texts but cannot be reduced to what is already found in them.

18. In 2 Cor. 6:16 we have a post-Pauline citation (see above, section 10.2 ["The Unity of Second Corinthians"]).

19. For an analysis of the text from the perspective of the people-of-God imagery, cf. Kraus, *Das Volk Gottes*, 120–55, who, however, minimizes the aspect of discontinuity.

only now be rightly understood—they were written down as warnings for the ἐκκλησία. Now the end of the ages has come (1 Cor. 10:11c), and it becomes obvious that the goal of God's action in history has been the ἐκκλησία all along. The statement in 1 Cor. 10:4 presupposing the preexistence of Christ again combines continuity and discontinuity: the ancestors of the wilderness generation are at the same time the ancestors of the Christians, but God was not pleased with them and punished them. Paul's understanding of Scripture consistently applies God's dealing with Israel to the current situation of the church because he proceeds on the assumption that these prior acts for Israel were always done with the future church in view and that they are now fulfilled in the life of the church.[20] In 2 Cor. 3:1–18 Paul sets forth these ideas explicitly: the covenant promises are disclosed only by a christological rereading because until the present day a barrier to understanding lies over the Scripture (2 Cor. 3:16–18).[21] Moses is the representative of a glory that has faded away whereas Christ represents the liberating new covenant in the power of the Spirit (cf. 2 Cor. 3:6; 1 Cor. 11:25).

The idea of the superiority of the new covenant is also dominant in the Letter to the Galatians, for although Paul does emphasize the continuing validity of God's covenant with Abraham (cf. Gal. 3:15–18), he regards it as only truly fulfilled in Christ. Therefore only those who believe the Christian message are the legitimate descendants of Abraham and heirs of God's promises (3:7, 29). In contrast, Jews oriented to the law/Torah are illegitimate children of Abraham, descendants of Ishmael, who was rejected by God, and their status is that of slaves (cf. 4:21–31). Here Paul advocates a consistent theory of disinheritance;[22] the true Israel, the "Israel of God" (6:16; cf. 4:26; Phil. 3:3), are those who believe, for only they have the legitimate status of descendants of Abraham.

In the Letter to the Romans, Paul abandons this rigorous standpoint and, by means of a complex argument, attains a new vision.[23] Christ was born of the seed of David according to the flesh (Rom. 1:3), so that God's saving act for believers is accomplished through Israel. The gospel is for the Jews first, then for the Gentiles (1:16; 2:9–10; 3:9, 29; 9:24); the covenant with Abraham retains its validity (Rom. 4); and the law/Torah is "holy and just and good" (7:12). But Jews can no longer appeal to the privileges of circumcision and the law/Torah (2:17ff.), for according to the will of God it is only one's stance toward the gospel that decides who belongs to the true Israel. Neither Jews nor Gentiles have an advantage, for both are equally under the power of sin (cf. 3:9, 20). With the intentional use of Old Testament and Jewish traditions, in Rom. 9–11 Israel is no longer confined to the empirical

---

20. Cf. Roloff, *Kirche im Neuen Testament*, 120–21.

21. For the interpretation of 2 Cor. 3:1–18, see above, section 10.4 ("The Glory of the New Covenant").

22. Cf. Roloff, *Kirche im Neuen Testament*, 125–26.

23. For the interpretation of Rom. 9–11, see above, section 12.9 ("Paul and Israel").

national group (cf. 9:6ff.), and the reception of the Gentiles appears as the
natural consequence of God's will after the Jews rejected the gospel (2:17ff.;
11:25, 31–32). Paul has hope for his people, however, that at the end of
time they will still be converted to Christ. At the parousia, God himself will
unveil the mystery of the anointed one; then the time of Israel's hardening
will come to an end, and all Israel will be saved (11:25–36). Paul sketches a
plausible vision: only God himself can reveal to his chosen people who this
Jesus Christ truly is.

These three foundational metaphors,[24] like the primary vocabulary, express
the basic approach of Paul's ecclesiology: participation in the Christ event takes
shape in the life of the church. Christology and ecclesiology do not merely
coincide or collapse into each other, but Christology determines ecclesiology
because "no one can lay any foundation other than the one that has been laid;
that foundation is Jesus Christ [ὅς ἐστιν Ἰησοῦς Χριστός]" (1 Cor. 3:11).[25]

21.2 Structures and Tasks in the Church

God, Jesus Christ, the apostle, and the churches are involved together in a
dynamic process of creation, working, leading, struggling, and suffering. The
churches have their origin in God, as indicated by the genitive ἐκκλησία τοῦ
θεοῦ (church of/from God; genitive of origin); their present life is grounded
in Jesus Christ, who bears the church as the σῶμα Χριστοῦ and determines it
by the gift of the Spirit. Within this dynamic event, Paul too receives a decisive
assignment, for as a called apostle of Jesus Christ, when he establishes churches,

24. Käsemann argues that the people-of-God image competes with the body-of-Christ image;
he starts from the priority of Christology over salvation history and sees in the body-of-Christ image
Paul's real ecclesiological concept (cf. Käsemann, *Romans*, 337; "Body of Christ," 102–21). Other
scholars see the concept of God as the predominate concept and the center of Paul's ecclesiology—e.g.,
Albrecht Oepke, *Das neue Gottesvolk* (Gütersloh: Gütersloher Verlagshaus, 1950), 198–230; Nils A.
Dahl, *Das Volk Gottes* (2nd ed.; Darmstadt: Wissenschaftliche Buchgesellschaft, 1963), 226; Neugebauer, *In Christus*, 93ff. The interrelationship between the two motifs is emphasized by Roloff, *Kirche
im Neuen Testament*, 130–31; Kraus, *Das Volk Gottes*, 350–61. Whereas the body metaphor has the
present growth of the church in view, the people-of-God image anchors it "in the depths of the divine history" (Kraus, *Das Volk Gottes*, 351). That Gal. 3:26–28 can be immediately followed by Gal.
3:29 shows that Paul is capable of thinking of the spatial and historical dimensions of ecclesiology
as belonging together.

25. Very strictly and pointedly, Käsemann, "Body of Christ," 113–14: "Pauline ecclesiology is
part of the apostle's theology of the cross, and to that degree can only be understood in the light of
his Christology."

On Paul's use of the temple metaphor, cf. Roloff, *Kirche im Neuen Testament*, 110–17; Christfried
Böttrich, "'Ihr seid der Tempel Gottes': Tempelmetaphorik und Gemeinde bei Paulus," in *Gemeinde
ohne Tempel = Community without Temple: Zur Substituierung und Transformation des Jerusalemer
Tempels und seines Kults im Alten Testament, antiken Judentum, und frühen Christentum* (ed. Beate Ego
et al.; WUNT 118; Tübingen: Mohr Siebeck, 1999), 411–25.

he is carrying out the will of God (1 Cor. 1:1; 2 Cor. 1:1; Gal. 1:1). Thus the churches realize that they are always dependent on God, Jesus Christ, and the apostle for their orientation.

Jesus Christ as Model

Paul constantly reminds the churches of God's loving act in Jesus Christ that provided salvation and delivered them from the coming wrath (1 Thess. 5:9), reconciled the world to himself (2 Cor. 5:18–21), and gives it peace, righteousness, and life (cf. Rom. 5). Jesus' own conduct became for Paul a structuring principle of his ecclesiology.[26] Through his proexistence Jesus overcame the kind of thinking that operates with the categories of domination and violence, and replaced them with the principle of a life of service for others (cf. Phil. 2:1–11). The church knows itself to be called to a kind of life determined by love for others, which finds its visible expression in the unity and fellowship of baptized believers. They are to be like-minded in both their thinking and their pursuits (2 Cor. 13:11; Rom. 12:16; Phil. 2:2), to admonish and encourage one another (1 Thess. 5:14; Gal. 6:1–2; Rom. 15:14), and always attempt to discern the will of God (Rom. 12:2; Phil. 1:9–10; 4:8). Christians should attempt to do good always and for everyone but especially for their brothers and sisters of the Christian community (Gal. 6:10; cf. 1 Thess. 3:12). The love of brothers and sisters within the family of God is the mark of Christian existence (1 Thess. 4:9; Rom. 12:10). The Christian brother or sister imposes a limit on one's own actions, for where their freedom begins, there one's own freedom ends (1 Cor. 8–10; Rom. 14); one must be concerned for them (1 Cor. 12:25; Rom. 12:13; 16:2) and share their joys and sorrows (1 Cor. 12:26; 13:7; 2 Cor. 7:3; Rom. 12:15; Phil. 2:18). In humility, one should "regard others as better than yourselves" (Phil. 2:3; cf. Rom. 12:10). None should look out for their own advantage and live only for themselves (1 Thess. 4:6; 1 Cor. 10:24, 33–11:1; 13:5; 2 Cor. 5:15; Rom. 15:2ff.; Phil. 2:4), but each should bear the burden of the other (Gal. 6:2). Christian love, as the determining power in the life of the church, is essentially unlimited (1 Cor. 13) and applies to everyone. It knows no egotistic selfishness, no quarreling, and no divisive party spirit, for love builds up the church (1 Cor. 8:1). This love changes even the social structures of the church because believers have all things in common (Gal. 6:6) and because they help those in need (cf. Gal. 4:10ff.) and practice hospitality (Rom. 12:13). The abundance of one supplies for the lack of another (2 Cor. 8:13–14).

---

26. Cf. Roloff, *Kirche im Neuen Testament*, 133.

Discipleship as Imitation

When Paul calls on his churches to imitate him as he himself imitates Christ (1 Thess. 1:6; 1 Cor. 4:16; 11:1), he sees himself holding a middle position in the chain, linking the model to be imitated (Christ) and the followers who imitate. In this sense Paul also commends himself as model in two respects:

(1) Paul's engagement for the gospel and the welfare of the churches surpasses that of all other apostles (cf. 1 Cor. 15:10, "I worked harder than any of them—though it was not I, but the grace of God that is with me"; cf. 2 Cor. 11:23; 6:4–5). He struggles tirelessly for the preservation and well-being of the churches (cf. 1 Thess. 2:2; 1 Cor. 9:25; Phil. 1:30)[27] and works day and night in order not to be a burden to them (cf. 1 Thess. 2:9; 1 Cor. 4:12). He runs the race and strives for the victor's crown (cf. 1 Thess. 2:19; 1 Cor. 9:24–26; Phil. 2:19; 3:14); his greatest worry is that he will have worked in vain and that on the day of the Lord he will have nothing to show for his labors (cf. 1 Thess. 3:5; Gal. 4:11; Phil. 2:16).

(2) Paul presents himself as a model to the churches also regarding his sufferings.[28] He always carries about in his body the death of Jesus (2 Cor. 4:10; cf. Gal. 4:17), sees himself constantly exposed to death διὰ Ἰησοῦ (for Jesus' sake) or for the sake of the gospel (2 Cor. 4:11; cf. 1 Cor. 4:10; 9:23; Philem. 13), and wants to become like Jesus in his death (cf. Phil. 3:10; 1:20). Paul understands his sufferings to be a constituent element in his apostolic mission and sees them in close relationship to Christ's own sufferings (cf. 1 Thess. 2:2; 2 Cor. 4:11; Phil. 1:7, 13; 2:17; Philem. 9, 13). All this happens "for your sake" (2 Cor. 4:15); Paul's sufferings are a sacrifice on behalf of the churches (cf. 2 Cor. 12:15). But the church, too, is exposed to experiences of suffering, for it is constantly threatened from outside and from within (cf. 1 Thess. 1:6; 2:14; 2 Cor. 1:7; Phil. 1:29–30). *Participation in the suffering of Jesus corresponds to Christian existence* (cf. Rom. 6:3–4), *just as does participation in the powers of his resurrection* (cf. Rom. 6:5), and so both shape the self-understanding of the church. Although apostle and church both participate in the sufferings of Christ, here also Paul embodies the model of Christian existence: he was called as apostle by the suffering Lord and demonstrates to his churches that not only

---

27. On the ἀγών (struggle) motif, cf. Victor C. Pfitzner, *Paul and the Agon Motif: Traditional Athletic Imagery in the Pauline Literature* (NovTSup 16; Leiden: Brill, 1967); and Rainer Metzner, "Paulus und der Wettkampf: Die Rolle des Sports in Leben und Verkündigung des Apostels (1Kor 9,24–7; Phil 3,12–16)," *NTS* 46 (2000): 565–83.

28. This point is elaborated, with differing accents, by Michael Wolter, "Der Apostel und seine Gemeinden als Teilhaber am Leidensgeschick Jesu Christi," *NTS* 36 (1990): 535–57; Hermann von Lips, "Die 'Leiden des Apostels' als Thema paulinischer Theologie," in *". . . Was ihr auf dem Weg verhandelt habt"—Beiträge zur Exegese und Theologie des Neuen Testaments: Festschrift für Ferdinand Hahn zum 75. Geburtstag* (ed. Peter Müller et al.; Neukirchen-Vluyn: Neukirchener Verlag, 2001), 117–28.

the resurrection but suffering determines the life of the individual Christian and the shape of the church's life.[29]

Charisma and Office

The dynamic nature of the basic structure of Paul's ecclesiology is also revealed in the relation between prescribed, orderly leadership tasks and charismatic gifts. Paul classifies the congregational meetings clearly within the realm of the Spirit. The vocabulary he chooses clearly reveals the apostle's own emphasis: the terms πνευματικός (spiritual person) and πνευματικά (spiritual things) and χάρισμα or χαρίσματα (gift[s] of grace) are found exclusively in the authentic letters of Paul and the literature dependent on them.[30] They appear to be words newly coined within early Christianity and are used exclusively to describe the spiritual gifts in their various dimensions. Whereas πνευματικός and πνευματικά portray the powerful, effective presence of the divine, χάρισμα and χαρίσματα point to the gift character and source of the extraordinary phenomena that break out in the church's life. Paul himself probably introduced the term χάρισμα into the debate[31] in order to make the true nature of the charismatic phenomena clear to the Corinthians who were especially endowed with such gifts. The Corinthians spoke of *pneumatika* (cf. 1 Cor. 12:1), emphasizing thereby their individual capabilities as the media of the divine power, whereas Paul points to the external origin of the work of the Spirit and derives from this the priority of the Spirit's work for the "edification" (οἰκοδομή) of the whole congregation (cf. 1 Cor. 14:12). Because the Spirit is one and indivisible, it is the nature of the Spirit's gifts to further the unity of the church. The multiplicity and variety of the charisms (cf. 1 Cor. 12:28) document, each in its own way, the richness of the Spirit's work, and charisms are misused when they lead to showmanship and disputes about rank. Moreover, the more extraordinary charisms such as glossolalia, prophecy, and the gift of healing only represent a fragment of the spectrum of the work of the Spirit in the life of the church. Love, as the purest and highest form of the presence of the divine, rejects domination and places itself in the service of others (cf. 1 Cor. 13), so that everything that serves the οἰκοδομή of the church demonstrates that it is an authentic gift of the Spirit.

29. Differently from the understanding of Güttgemanns, *Der leidende Apostel und sein Herr*, 323ff., this does not mean that Paul made a qualitative distinction between the sufferings of the church and his own sufferings; he is only emphasizing his special apostolic function and task.

30. Πνευματικός or πνευματικά is found twenty-six times in the New Testament: in the undisputed letters of Paul, nineteen times, of which fifteen are found in 1 Corinthians (seven times in Colossians, Ephesians, 1 Peter). Χάρισμα or χαρίσματα is found seventeen times in the New Testament: fourteen in the undisputed letters of Paul, of which seven are in 1 Corinthians and six in Romans (once in 2 Corinthians; and once each in 1 Timothy, 2 Timothy, and 1 Peter).

31. Cf. Brockhaus, *Charisma und Amt*, 189–90; Roloff, *Kirche im Neuen Testament*, 137.

If the Spirit effects, furthers, and orders the building up of the church, then for Paul there can be no conflict between individual-pneumatic capabilities and the tasks of administration and teaching, for all have their source in the same Spirit. The image of the organism (cf. 1 Cor. 12:12–31) makes clear that the individual gifts, capabilities, and tasks can carry out their ministry only in reference to the whole and for its good. The alternative frequently posed between charisma and office[32] does not exist for Paul because the work of the Spirit is indivisible. In 1 Cor. 12:28 the functions assigned to particular persons and the extraordinary capabilities given to others are equally considered the activity of God, who works to order the church as a whole: "And God has appointed in the church first apostles, second prophets, third teachers; then deeds of power, then gifts of healing, forms of assistance, forms of leadership, various kinds of tongues." The verb ἔθετο (install [someone], make [someone] to be something), the enumeration and juxtaposition of gifts that grow from a call spontaneously and extraordinarily and those that are mediated by being assigned a particular task in the church's life show that, for Paul, Spirit and law (in the sense of binding regulations and structures in the church) are not opposed to each other.[33] So also the list of charisms in Rom. 12:6–8 documents the basic tendency of Paul's approach: the charisms concretize God's gracious turning to the world, so that abilities to organize, administer, and encourage are naturally considered the workings of God's Spirit. In 1 Cor. 12:28 Paul formulates the first three charisms in terms of persons and thus signals that a definite group exercises particular responsibilities for a set time. In this sense, one can speak of offices playing a role in Paul's ecclesiology.[34]

Offices

The apostolic office focuses on exceptional aspects of certain early Christian missionaries: their calling, their competence to establish churches, and their leadership abilities. In the earliest period, this office was concentrated in Jerusalem (cf. 1 Cor. 15:3–11; Gal. 1:17, 19), but by no means can it be restricted to the Twelve or the Jerusalem church. The expression "then to all the

32. Cf. Rudolf Sohm, "Begriff und Organisation der Ekklesia," in *Das Kirchliche Amt im Neuen Testament* (ed. Karl Kertelge; WF 439; Darmstadt: Wissenschaftliche Buchgesellschaft, 1977), 53: "The ἐκκλησία is Christianity as a whole, the body of Christ, the Lord's bride—a spiritual reality withdrawn from earthly norms, including that of law."

33. The comment of Roioff, *Kirche im Neuen Testament*, 139, is on target: "The Spirit itself sets law by establishing particular functions as obligatory."

34. Cf. ibid., 139ff. Andrew D. Clarke, *Serve the Community of the Church: Christians as Leaders and Ministers* (Grand Rapids: Eerdmans, 2000), has a comprehensive treatment of the influence of Greco-Roman social structures (esp. the patron-client system) on the constitution and leadership structures of early Christianity, in order then to argue that in principle the *diakonia* established by Jesus as the norm represents the *proprium* (characteristic nature) of the structures of the new movement.

apostles" in the list of witnesses to the resurrection appearances (1 Cor. 15:7), the reference to Andronicus and Junia[s], who were already apostles before Paul (Rom. 16:7), the call of Paul to be "apostle to the Gentiles" (cf. Gal. 1:1; Rom. 15:15ff.), the concept and terminology of apostleship associated with Antioch (cf. Acts 13:1–3; 14:4, 14), the dispute in 2 Cor. 11:5, 13; 12:11 regarding how apostleship is to be defined, and the image of apostles in the sayings source Q (cf. Luke 10:4; Matt. 10:8)—all these show that the circle of apostles had expanded within the early Christian mission.[35] An appearance by, or legitimization from, the risen Christ by no means was sufficient authorization for apostleship; otherwise the "more than five hundred brothers and sisters" of 1 Cor. 15:6 would all have been apostles. Moreover, the only early Christian missionary that Paul really accepted is not called an apostle, namely, Apollos (cf. 1 Cor. 3:5ff.; 4:6; 16:12). In the long run, it is not calling and sending that legitimize the apostolic office but the capacity of the apostle to establish churches and to represent the gospel convincingly as the norm of God's grace among the churches, through which the apostle himself assumes a normative role (cf. 1 Thess. 1:6; 1 Cor. 4:16; 11:1; Phil. 3:17). The apostle embodies, in his person and his work, the servant form of the gospel (cf. 2 Cor. 4:7–18); he is himself the exemplar of the new being, and the churches are the seal of his apostleship and his glory in the last judgment (cf. 1 Thess. 2:19; 1 Cor. 2:9; 2 Cor. 3:2). Paul, too, manifests this apostolic competence to found, lead, and guide the churches, but in his case, after the initial preaching and basic instruction that had founded the churches, he continued to be present among them through his coworkers and his letters.

Prophetic speech belongs to the normal ingredients of early Christian church life. Already in 1 Thess. 5:20 Paul exhorts, "Do not despise prophetic speech" (NRSV, "Do not despise the words of prophets"). Early Christian prophets appear as distinctive groups in various strands of early Christian tradition: Acts 13:1; 15:32; 20:23; 21:4, 10 presupposes early Christian prophets in Greece and Asia Minor; Eph. 3:5; 4:11 and 1 Tim. 1:18; 4:14 look back on the beginnings of the church, when prophets were obviously at work; and Rev. 11:18; 16:6; 18:24; 22:9 regards the prophets as the central independent group within the worldwide church.[36] The prophetic office probably originated in the early Palestinian church (cf., e.g., Acts 11:28, Agabus); in Jerusalem the experience of the church convinced it that the time of the cessation of prophecy was over and that the Spirit of God was now at work again (cf. Acts 2:17–18). Likewise,

---

35. For the most part, scholars tend to see a historical line of development from the Jerusalem apostolate, based on resurrection appearances, to the charismatic itinerant apostolate as seen in the traditions of the sayings source Q and the Antiochene traditions (cf. Roloff, "Apostel I," *TRE* 3:433ff.).

36. See the comprehensive treatment of Boring, *Continuing Voice of Jesus*; see also Gerhard Dautzenberg, *Urchristliche Prophetie: Ihre Erforschung, ihre Voraussetzungen im Judentum, und ihre Struktur im ersten Korintherbrief* (BWA[N]T; Stuttgart: Kohlhammer, 1975); and Aune, *Prophecy in Early Christianity*.

in the original Greco-Roman cultural realm, prophecy belonged to the familiar forms of religious communication.[37]

What functions were exercised by the early Christian prophets? First of all, they interpreted God's past and future saving acts in Jesus Christ (cf. Acts 20:23; 21:4; Eph. 3:5), revealed the will of the risen Jesus for the church, and gave their testimony for Jesus (cf. Acts 19:10). Thus the early Christian prophets also participated in the process of handing on and interpreting the tradition, for they transmitted sayings of Jesus and gave them new interpretations in the awareness that the Spirit was present with them.[38] Their testimony for Jesus was evidently presented in different forms, so that ecstatic speech, visions, the contemporizing of sayings of Jesus as the word of the present Lord, and new instructions of the exalted Lord for the church were all expressions of their prophetic abilities.

Paul listed prophecy among the forms of intelligible speech and distinguished it from glossolalia (cf. 1 Cor. 14:5). When several prophets were present in the same worship service, their messages should be critically evaluated by the other members of the church (cf. 14:29). Here too the edification of the church served as the critical norm (14:26), for prophetic speech could not be permitted to disrupt the order and unity of the worship service (cf. 14:31).

Whereas the prophets are the vehicle of the exalted Lord, present in the Spirit, who speaks his revelatory word for the present, the task of the early Christian teachers was concerned with interpreting the (oral or written) kerygma and with the exposition of traditional texts (e.g., the Septuagint).[39] In 1 Cor. 12:28, Gal. 6:6, and Rom. 12:7b, Paul presupposes the existence of teachers in the congregation (cf. also Eph. 4:11; Acts 13:1; James 3:1; *Did.* 11–15). They had to be able to read and write and needed to be familiar with the Jesus traditions and the Septuagint as well as the conventional rules of interpretation in order to be able to interpret the new eschatological times for the church. The tasks of a teacher presuppose a high degree of personal presence and continuity, related to a particular time, subject matter, and place, and so here too we may speak of a particular "office" in the early church.

In Phil. 1:1 Paul mentions, without further explanation, ἐπίσκοποι (overseers, supervisors) and διάκονοι (helpers, servants). He obviously refers to several persons who carry out generally recognized tasks in the life of the community and whose special position is underscored by being mentioned in the letter's greeting. This linguistic usage suggests that the ἐπίσκοποι had a position of

37. Cf. Kai Brodersen, ed., *Prognosis: Studien zur Funktion von Zukunftsvorhersagen in Literatur und Geschichte seit der Antike* (AKG 2; Münster: LIT, 2001).

38. On early Christian prophets as creative transmitters of the Jesus tradition, cf. Boring, *Continuing Voice of Jesus*, 189–265.

39. Cf. Alfred Zimmermann, *Die urchristlichen Lehrer: Studien zum Tradentenkreis der Didaskaloi im frühen Urchristentum* (WUNT 2/12; Tübingen: Mohr Siebeck, 1984).

leadership within the congregation.[40] The term probably refers to leaders of house churches (cf. 1 Cor. 1:14; 16:15–16, 19; Rom. 16:5, 23; Acts 18:8) who made their homes available for the church meetings and who supported the congregations in various ways as their patrons.[41] Their normal authority predisposed them for this office as the church in Philippi grew and was divided into several house churches.[42] The διάκονοι functioned as helpers of the ἐπίσκοποι; especially in the celebration of the eucharistic meals, they may have assumed responsibility for the preparations, and their duties included the collection and administration of the offerings.[43]

21.3 The Church as the Realm of Freedom from Sin

If Jesus Christ is the foundation, builder, and preserver of the ἐκκλησία, the question is raised whether and in what sense sin continues to be present in the sphere of the church. Can sin still exercise its power within the church? What is the meaning of the ethical shortcomings that doubtless continue within the life of the church? Paul's linguistic usage gives some pointers for answering these questions.

As a rule, Paul does not use the singular ἁμαρτία to describe human misconduct. In 1 Thess. 4:3–8 he warns the Thessalonian Christians against πορνεία (fornication), ἐπιθυμία (lustful passion), and πλεονεξία (greed [4:6, πλεονεκτεῖν; NRSV, "exploit"]), but without speaking of sin. The life of holiness Paul calls for has as its opposite not "sin" but "impurity" (4:7, ἀκαθαρσία).[44] Paul deals with the flagrant case of immorality in 1 Cor. 5 under the aspect of the purity of the church. Because this holiness is endangered, the evildoer must be excluded for the sake of the community and for his own sake. The body (σάρξ) of the evildoer will be given over to Satan on the day of judgment, but his spirit will remain in the realm of σωτηρία (1 Cor. 5:5b). The purity of the church is the basis for the procedure of excommunication portrayed in 5:3–5. Likewise the legal disputes in court before pagan judges are not in accord with the purity of the church (6:11). Only at the end of his argument in 1 Cor. 5–6 (at 6:18), does Paul use ἁμαρτάνω (to sin) and ἁμάρτημα (offense; NRSV, "sin")—once each—but he still avoids using the word "sin" (ἁμαρτία) in this context. Be-

40. On the linguistic usage, cf. H. W. Beyer, "ἐπισκέπτομαι, ἐπίσκοπος, κτλ.," *TDNT* 2:603–14; on the Pauline and post-Pauline conceptions, cf. Roloff, *Timotheus*, 169–89. Worthy of note is the description of the Cynics as "scouts [κατάσκοπος] and heralds of the gods" in Epictetus, *Diatr.* 3.22.69.

41. Cf. the comprehensive analyses of Gehring, *House Church and Mission*, 185–228.

42. Cf. ibid., 352–59.

43. Cf. Roloff, *Kirche im Neuen Testament*, 143.

44. For analysis, cf. Umbach, *In Christus getauft*, 67–81. The plural ἁμαρτίαι in 1 Thess. 2:16 reflects the tradition used in this passage.

cause believers are united most closely with Christ precisely in their bodily existence, sexual misconduct endangers this union and is not compatible with the purity of the church. Thus Paul can recommend marriage as a means of avoiding sexual misconduct (ἁμαρτάνω, 7:28, 36). In 8:12 Paul makes a direct connection between the way one conducts oneself with fellow Christians and one's relation to Christ. Whoever sins against a brother or sister (ἁμαρτάνοντες εἰς τοὺς ἀδελφούς) sins against Christ (εἰς Χριστὸν ἁμαρτάνετε). Because the church is a sphere of sanctification and holiness, offenses have not only ethical dimensions but also soteriological aspects. This is an idea that Paul elaborates in 10:1–13, touches on in 15:34, and formulates in 15:17 as follows: "If Christ has not been raised, your faith is futile and you are still in your sins."[45] In 11:27ff. Paul sharply attacks the abuses at the eucharistic meal, but without speaking of "sin." Instead what is going on there is "unworthy" (11:27, ἀναξίως) and results in the church becoming "guilty" (11:27, ἔνοχος) and incurring punishment. In 2 Cor. 12:19–13:10 Paul specifically warns the Corinthian Christians that when he comes to them the third time, he will not spare those "who previously sinned and have not repented of the impurity, sexual immorality, and licentiousness that they have practiced" (2 Cor. 12:21). Paul uses the verb προαμαρτάνω (to sin previously) only in 12:21 and 13:2; in each case it is a perfect participle that describes the misconduct of church members that had not yet been set aside.[46] Paul does not dispossess these church members of their status as Christians; instead he insists that they and the church as a whole finally let their actions correspond to the new being in which they participate. "Examine yourselves to see whether you are living in the faith. Test yourselves. Do you not realize that Jesus Christ is in you?" (13:5). Likewise Paul does not relate the conflict with the ἀδικήσας (someone who has done wrong) in 2:5–11 to the concept and terminology of sin. The culprit had been excluded by the congregation (2:6) and may now be readmitted to their fellowship. Forgiveness is necessary, for Satan is just waiting for the discord to continue so that he can again infiltrate the church (cf. 2:11).[47]

The letter to the Galatians confirms that Paul does not use ἁμαρτία as a designation of human failures. The apostle here carries on an extremely sharp debate with his Judaistic opponents who have invaded the church, but without using the word "sin" to describe their actions. Likewise the false conduct of Peter is not described as ἁμαρτία (cf. Gal. 2:14), and in the context of the admonitions in the paraenetic section of the letter in 6:1, Paul merely uses the term παράπτωμα (transgression). The plural ἁμαρτίαι is the term for human deeds in the traditional formula in 1:4. But this is in contrast to the specific Pauline use of the singular. In Paul's usage, "sin" denotes a sphere of power, a

---

45. In 1 Cor. 15.17, the plural ἁμαρτίαι reflects the traditional usage in 1 Cor. 15:3; cf. Conzelmann, *1 Corinthians*, 266.

46. Cf. Umbach, *In Christus getauft*, 141.

47. For analysis, cf. ibid., 170–82.

force field, opposed to the sphere in which Christ exercises lordship. Christ is not a servant of sin (2:17), but sin has commandeered the law, so that it now enslaves human beings and deprives them of true freedom (3:22ff.).

The distinctive profile of the Pauline concept of sin also shapes the line of argument in the Letter to the Romans, for Paul's references to sin concern strictly the past.[48] He reminds the church members of their baptism, the place where they experienced a fundamental transformation of their lives; there believers died to sin, there they were placed in the sphere of Christ and righteousness (Rom. 6:3ff.). Paul uses antithetical terms to portray dramatically the new reality in which the baptized live: "So you also must consider yourselves dead to sin and alive to God in Christ Jesus" (6:11). For the church, sin is a reality that belongs to the past, and 6:14a states expressly, "For sin will have no dominion over you." This corresponds with the fact that Paul never associates the Lord's Supper with the forgiveness of sins. Because Christians have been freed from sin, they have now become servants of righteousness (6:18). The power of grace surpasses the effectiveness of sin (cf. 5:12–21), which has now been conquered and now perceived by the baptized as a destructive power of the past (cf. 7:7–8, 14). Faith in Jesus Christ and sin are mutually exclusive powers, for πᾶν δὲ ὃ οὐκ ἐκ πίστεως ἁμαρτία ἐστίν (whatever does not proceed from faith is sin, 14:23).

The Letter to the Philippians also confirms the Pauline conception of the church as a realm free from sin, for the singular of ἁμαρτία and related terms are not found in the letter although misbehavior and problems in the church are addressed. Paul is critical of the preaching of his rivals in the location where he is imprisoned (cf. Phil. 1:17) and sharply attacks the strict Jewish Christian missionaries (cf. 3:2ff.), but without speaking of sin. The admonitions in 2:1–5 and the smoothing over of a quarrel in 4:2–3 also stay within the bounds of traditional terminology (selfish ambition or conceit, 2:3). Because the new being in Christ in the power of the Spirit has begun not merely in name only but in reality,[49] the baptized are no longer in the realm of sin's power but in the force field of the resurrected Lord, in whose power Paul hopes to participate at the resurrection (cf. 3:10–11).

Baptized believers know themselves to have been essentially separated from the world, for they live in the realm of Christ's power and thus in the church as a realm free from sin. The sanctification of the church includes drawing a sharp boundary between itself and the world, and this also shapes the empirical form of the church, for Paul does not know the ecclesiological concept of the church as a *corpus mixtum*.[50] The church belongs on the side of light and has

---

48. For extensive analysis of Rom. 6–8, see above, sections 12.7 ("The Presence of Salvation: Baptism and Righteousness") and 12.8 ("Sin, Law, and Freedom in the Spirit"); cf. also section 19.2 ("Sin and Death"). The plural ἁμαρτίαι in Rom. 4:7 and 11:27 in each case belongs to a quotation.

49. Windisch, *Taufe und Sünde*, 104.

50. Cf. Ollrog, *Mitarbeiter*, 137.

cast off the works of darkness (1 Thess. 5:1ff.; Rom. 13:11–14). It does not conform to the world (Rom. 12:2), no longer practices the works of the flesh (Gal. 5:19ff.), and shines with a heavenly light in a dark world (Phil. 2:14–15). Because the Lord is near (Phil. 4:5) and τὸ σχῆμα (the "form," "schema") of this world is already passing away (1 Cor. 7:31), Christians are no longer oriented to what is transient.

If Paul understands the church as a holy realm free from sin, the question of the function of the Pauline paraenesis naturally arises. The Pauline admonitions and imperatives (e.g., 1 Cor. 6:18, φεύγετε τὴν πορνείαν [shun fornication]; 7:23; 8:12; and passim) testify that Christians can again fall under the power of sin. Paul knows the temptations to which Christians are exposed (cf. 1 Cor. 7:5; 10:9, 13; Gal. 6:1). Satan appears as an angel of light and attempts to deceive the church (cf. 2 Cor. 11:13–15). The church in Galatia falls from grace if it places itself back under the servitude of the law, which in turn is only an instrument of sin. In baptism, according to Rom. 6:6, the "old self" (παλαιὸς ἄνθρωπος) was crucified with Christ and "the body ruled by sin" (τὸ σῶμα τῆς ἁμαρτίας) was destroyed, but sin itself was not driven from the world.[51] The defeat of the old reality does not mean for baptized believers that they are taken out of the world as such, for they continue to live ἐν σαρκί and still must confront the temptations of sin. The power of the Spirit enables them to withstand these temptations, however, if they attune their thinking and acting to the new being. The imperative demands that life be brought into harmony with the new being, and only so does the power of sin remain a past reality and the church a realm free from sin.

---

51. Cf. Umbach, *In Christus getauft*, 250–51.

22

Eschatology

Expectation and Memory

The meaning formation included in the construction of every symbolic universe projects a temporal order that structures its understanding of the world.[1] In order to represent the meaning of things and how they are interrelated, it is necessary to arrange the individual temporal stages in some sort of order that makes sense of the present. The past must be brought into meaningful relation to the present before it can become history and remain such for our understanding.[2] This is clearly the case for Paul, for with the resurrection of Jesus Christ from the dead, a past event definitively determines the future and thus places its stamp on the present as well. Paul lived with an intense expectation: the impending advent of the crucified and risen Jesus Christ was a factor that shaped his symbolic universe until his life's end (cf. Phil. 4:5, "The Lord is near").[3] All creation is moving to that consummation, and Paul saw himself

---

1. Cf. Straub, "Temporale Orientierung," 33–34.

2. Cf. Jörn Rüsen, "Die Historisierung des Nationalsozialismus," in *Zerbrechende Zeit: Über den Sinn der Geschichte* (Cologne: Böhlau, 2001), 221: "Historiographically, it makes good sense to say that only a past that does not and cannot fade away is history and continues to be history."

3. On the structure of Pauline eschatology, cf. Becker, *Paul*, 440–49; Helmut Merklein, "Eschatologie im Neuen Testament," in *Studien zu Jesus und Paulus* (2 vols.; WUNT 43, 105; Tübingen: Mohr Siebeck, 1987), 2:87–95; Dunn, *Theology of Paul*, 461–98.

as riding the crest of this movement. Only those who expect something from the future keep the memory alert. And finally, the death of others presents to the living the question of their own destiny, and so eschatology must always also provide a persuasive answer to the questions of life and death.

22.1 The Future in the Present

The basis and point of departure for what is to come are for Paul something that has already happened: the death and resurrection of Jesus Christ provide the foundation for all eschatological affirmations; that is, *Christology is the foundation of eschatology and gives it its definitive shape.*[4]

Participation in the Life of the Risen One

In 1 Thess. 4:13–18 the threat to the symbolic universe on the occasion of church members' deaths is countered by the apostle with the fundamental confession of faith: "Since we believe that Jesus died and rose again" (4:14a; cf. 1:10). He derives a soteriological logic from this confession, which is determined by the concept of participation. Baptized believers participate in the destiny of the decisive figure of the end time, Jesus Christ. Just as God raised him from the dead, death is not the last word for church members who have died; like the living, they will be received into eternal communion with the risen Jesus (4:17, πάντοτε σὺν Κυρίῳ ἐσόμεθα, "we shall be with the Lord forever"). The assurance of this future determines the present. Paul explicitly emphasizes this eschatological qualification of the present in 5:1–11. Baptized believers are already "children of light and children of the day" (5:5) and thus eschatological persons; in 5:10 the cross is explicitly pointed out as the basis that makes this new being possible.[5] Likewise in 1 Cor. 15:20–22 Paul bases what he says on the fundamental Christian confession (cf. ἐγήγερται [he was raised], 1 Cor. 15:4a, 20a), and he infers from this the turn of the ages. Christ was raised as the "first fruits of those who have died"; that is, he not only is the first of all the resurrected in chronological terms but is himself the resurrection paradigm.[6] The temporal and material aspects are complementary; Jesus is the first one to whom God's eschatological act of salvation applies. First Corinthians 15:21 emphasizes the universal dimension of this event: "For since death came through a human being, the resurrection of the dead has also come through a human being." For Paul there are two bearers of human destiny, each of which is a prototype who determines the being of those who belong within

---

4. Cf. Baumgarten, *Paulus und die Apokalyptik*, 93.
5. Cf. Harnisch, *Eschatologische Existenz*, 151–52.
6. Cf. Lindemann, *Der erste Korintherbrief*, 343.

his category. Just as Adam was the ultimate cause of death, Jesus Christ, as the one who has overcome death, brings life (cf. 15:45–50; Rom. 5:12–21). Adam preceded Christ both chronologically and functionally, for by his transgression he brought about the hopeless situation that has now been taken away in Christ. Paul formulates the antithetical superiority of Christ's act in universal terms: "for as all die in Adam, so all will be made alive in Christ" (1 Cor. 15:22). The repeated πάντες (all) raises the question of not only whether all human beings must die because of Adam's transgression but whether all human beings will also be made alive in/through Christ.[7] Such a universal actuality of salvation would be singular for Paul; it is at odds with his general approach and is also probably excluded by the immediate context,[8] for in 15:23 it is explicitly those who "belong to Christ" (οἱ τοῦ Χριστοῦ) who will be saved at his parousia. By πάντες in 15:22, Paul emphasizes the universal significance of the Christ event; it potentially applies to all human beings, but they must appropriate it for themselves through faith. The consistent orientation of the eschatological event to Christ is obvious: it was for Christ as the "first fruits" that God acted to initiate the new being, it was through Christ that humanity's unavoidable subjection to death was abolished, and it is those belonging to Christ who participate in present and future salvation (cf. also 1:9; 4:14; Gal. 1:1; Rom. 4:17, 24; 10:9; 14:9).

The fundamentally participatory character of Pauline eschatology and the related qualification of the present as the time of salvation determined by the future are also evident in Rom. 6:4–5; 8:11. In Rom. 6:4–5 Paul infers from participation in Jesus' death in baptism a participation in the reality of his resurrection, which is already manifest in the present as transformation into a new existence. The apostle intentionally avoids speaking of a present resurrection of baptized believers, a view that was probably advocated in Corinth (cf. 1 Cor. 4:8; 10:1ff.; 15:12) and is found in various forms in later literature of the Pauline school (Col. 2:12; 3:1–4; Eph. 2:6; 2 Tim. 2:18) as well as elsewhere (cf. *1 Clem.* 23:1–27; *Barn.* 11:1; Pol. *Phil.* 7:1; *2 Clem.* 9:1; Justin, *Dial.* 80.4). The eschatological reservation thereby expressed (cf. 1 Cor. 13:12; 2 Cor. 4:7; 5:7; Rom. 8:24) imposes no limitation on the full participation of Christians in the new being[9] but expresses the temporal structure of Christian existence:[10] Christians live their lives between the world-changing acts of the

---

7. Emphasized by Lindemann, ibid.

8. Cf. Powers, *Salvation through Participation*, 153.

9. Differently, Strecker, *Die liminale Theologie des Paulus*, 452, who argues that "the aspect of threshold existence is fundamental" for all levels of Pauline theology. This underestimates the present reality of the new being for Paul.

10. It is thus inappropriate to speak of an "already and not yet of salvation," as done, e.g., by Günter Klein, "Eschatologie," *TRE* 10:283; Dunn, *Theology of Paul*, 466–72. It is also subject to misunderstanding to speak of an "eschatological reservation" (so, e.g., Andreas Lindemann, "Eschatologie," *RGG* 2:1556, for regarding the eschaton Paul has no "reservation" but, rather, a temporal qualification because the final consummation has not yet arrived. The way forward on this point is found in the

resurrection of Christ and his parousia, so that we may speak of the presence and assurance of salvation but not yet of the full reality of salvation. Although believers live in the end time, the end has not yet come.

The distinctive structure of Christian existence is based in God's eschatological act: God gives the Spirit to baptized believers; God is the one who through the Spirit raised Jesus from the dead and who will also give life to the mortal bodies of those who are bound to Christ by this same Spirit (cf. Rom. 8:11). The assurance of the presence of salvation and its future consummation is thus grounded in union with the Spirit of God, the God who has acted by the Spirit to attach us to himself, so to speak, when he grounds the new existence in baptism and renews it again after death.

Eschatological Existence

The relation of Christians to the world and their actions in the world are likewise defined by their specific location in time. They know that they have already been delivered from the enslaving powers of the world and that they can use the things of the world without lapsing back into their power (cf. 1 Cor. 7:29–31). The manner in which they live their lives is oriented to their new being ἐν Χριστῷ (cf. Gal. 3:26–28), and they know that all they do must be done in love (Gal. 5:22). Also, the exemplary destiny of the apostle illustrates how powerfully the events of the eschatological future already shine into the present as a source of strength, how the reality of the future already fully determines the present.[11] Present sufferings can be endured in the confidence that the God who raised Jesus from the dead will also raise up the believers. The great extent to which Paul's thought is shaped by his conviction that the ages already overlap and determine each other is seen in 2 Cor. 4:14: "we know that the one who raised the Lord Jesus will raise us also with Jesus [καὶ ἡμᾶς σὺν Ἰησοῦ ἐγερεῖ], and will bring us with you into his presence." Paul thinks of Jesus' resurrection, which has already happened, and the resurrection of baptized believers, which is yet to come, as a functional unity; the past is synchronous with the future, which in turn shapes the present.[12]

---

suggestion of Sören Agersnap, *Baptism and the New Life: A Study of Romans 6:1–14* (Århus: Aarhus University Press, 1999), 401, that "already"/"not yet" be replaced with "already"/"even more."

11. Cf. Bultmann, *Theology of the New Testament*, 1:129–30.

12. Because past and future both shape the present, Paul can take up the doctrine of the two ages only partially and in a broken form, as he does when speaking of the "wisdom of this age" (cf. 1 Cor. 1:20; 2:6; 3:18) or of the "ruler" of this world (cf. 1 Cor. 2:8; 2 Cor. 4:4; Gal. 1:4; Rom. 12:2). The dominant role of Christology for Paul makes it impossible for him to take over whole eschatological schemes from Judaism, and so he consistently avoids speaking of the "new" or the "coming" age; on Paul's appropriation of the doctrine of the two ages, cf. Baumgarten, *Paulus und die Apokalyptik*, 181–89.

The characteristic interlocking of present and future also appears in Phil. 3:10–11. It is not the case that present participation in the suffering of Jesus provides access to the future; rather, contrariwise, the reality of the future, which is grounded in God's past act, makes it possible to persevere through the sufferings of the present. Within the conditions of present life, the power of Jesus' resurrection already makes itself felt and mediates the assurance of participation in the process of transformation in the future. Christian expectation of the future is therefore a well-grounded hope (cf. 1 Thess. 1:3; 2 Cor. 3:12; Gal. 5:5; Rom. 5:2, 4; 8:24),[13] for it is not subject to the ambiguities of what is to come. Whereas in Greek thought the future and thus hope were perceived as both attractive and threatening, believers live in the unqualified confidence that the future has lost its threatening character.[14] Hope, like faith and love, belongs to the fundamentals of Christian existence (1 Cor. 13:12).

The new being of baptized believers can be described in both functional and temporal aspects as eschatological existence: they participate fully in the ultimate turn of the ages brought about by God's act in Jesus Christ, and know that they live their lives in a present already determined by the future. The resurrection and parousia of Jesus Christ, as functional and temporal turning points of God's saving acts, are the foundation of the Christian's eschatological existence, which is founded on, and bound to, Christology.

22.2 The Course of the Final Events and Life after Death

Paul's letters reveal clearly to what a great extent the differing church situations affected the shape of his eschatological thinking. That the new movement had only existed for a short time as well as the fact that both questions and answers had not yet become entirely clear indicate that this central area of early Christian meaning formation was still under construction. Although, for Paul himself, the resurrection of Jesus Christ from the dead and the parousia, expected in the near future, were the firm chronological and material cornerstones of his understanding of the final events, he obviously continued to think through how these events should be described, and ventured to make midcourse corrections in order to maintain a consistent view.[15]

---

13. Cf. Gottfried Nebe, *"Hoffnung" bei Paulus: Elpis und ihre Synonyme im Zusammenhang der Eschatologie* (SUNT 16; Göttingen: Vandenhoeck & Ruprecht, 1983).

14. Classically, Sophocles, *Antigone* 615–619: "Hope flits about on never-wearying wings [ἡ γὰρ δὴ πολύπλαγκτος ἐλπίς]; / Profit to some, to some light love she brings; / But no man knoweth how her gifts may turn, / Till 'neath his feet the treacherous ashes burn." Cf. further Plato, *Philebus* 33c–34c, 39a–41b. The masterly survey of Rudolf Bultmann, "ἐλπίς κτλ.," *TDNT* 2:517–23, is still very valuable.

15. Scholars have long noted development and changes in Paul's eschatology. See, e.g., Heinrich Julius Holtzmann, *Lehrbuch der neutestamentlichen Theologie* (2nd ed.; Sammlung theologischer Lehrbücher; Tübingen: Mohr Siebeck, 1911), 2:215ff.; Windisch, *Korintherbrief*, 172–75; Dodd, "Mind

Transformations

The first extant expression of this theme was already forced upon Paul by the unexpected fact that some members of the church in Thessalonica had died before the Lord's parousia (1 Thess. 4:13–18).[16] Paul responds with an explanation that for the first time combines the parousia with the resurrection of dead Christians. After an introduction to the problem (4:13) and a preliminary answer falling back on the kerygma of the death and resurrection of Jesus (4:14), in 4:15–17 Paul provides a second answer consisting of a summary of a traditional saying of the Lord (4:15) and its quotation (4:16–17). The instruction then concludes with the exhortation to encourage and comfort one another with the answer he has given to their question about the premature deaths (4:18). The goal of the whole event is "being with the Lord," which directly presupposes that all will be taken up to be with him, which in turn indirectly presupposes the resurrection of those who have died in Christ. It is first of all the problematic of the delay of the parousia and the historicity of Christian faith that compel Paul to introduce the concept of a resurrection of dead believers.[17] But in 4:13–18 he also holds on to his original eschatological conception that at the parousia all believers will be taken up to be with the Lord. Here the resurrection of believers who have died before the parousia functions only to make it possible for them to be taken up at the parousia. In 1 Thessalonians the death of Christians before the parousia is clearly the exception, and Paul thinks of himself and most of the church as among those who will be alive when the Lord returns (4:15, 17, "we who are alive, who are left until the coming of the Lord"), probably in the conviction that when he wrote 1 Thessalonians, the parousia was very near. There is no discussion of the question of how the resurrection of dead church members will take place or how to think of the residence of all believers with Jesus in the heavenly world.[18]

---

of Paul II," 109–13; Bammel, "Judenverfolgung," 310–15; Walter Grundmann, "Überlieferung und Eigenaussage im eschatologischen Denken des Paulus," *NTS* 8 (1961): 17ff.; Hunzinger, "Hoffnung angesichts des Todes," passim; Wiefel, "Eschatologischen Denken," passim; Becker, *Auferstehung der Toten*, 66ff.; Schade, *Apokalyptische Christologie*, 210–11; Siegfried Schulz, "Der frühe und der späte Paulus," *TZ* 41 (1985): 229–30; Roloff, *Einführung*, 143; Strecker, *Theology of the New Testament*, 209–16; cf. further the survey of the history of research in Friedrich Gustav Lang, *2. Korinther 5, 1–10 in der neueren Forschung* (BGBE 16; Tübingen: Mohr Siebeck, 1973), 64–92). Among those who are skeptical about theories of development in Paul's eschatology are Hoffmann, *Die Toten in Christus*, 323–29; Luz, *Geschichtsverständnis*, 356–57; Siber, *Mit Christus Leben*, 91ff.; Baumgarten, *Paulus und die Apokalyptik*, 236–38; Lindemann, "Eschatologie," *RGG* 2:1556.

16. On the interpretation of 1 Thess. 4:13–18, see above, section 8.2 ("The Theology of 1 Thessalonians").

17. Cf. Marxsen, *Thessalonicher*, 64–65.

18. Cf. Nikolaus Walter, "Leibliche Auferstehung? Zur Frage der Hellenisierung der Auferweckungshoffnung bei Paulus," in *Paulus, Apostel Jesu Christi: Festschrift für Günter Klein zum 70. Geburtstag* (ed. Günter Klein and Michael Trowitzsch; Tübingen: Mohr Siebeck, 1998), 110–11.

As time marches on, we see this theme in a different light as it appears in the Corinthian letters, with changes brought about by the passing of time, by the independent theological developments among the Corinthian Christians, and by Paul's reflections that take the changed situation into account.[19] Paul continues to hold fast to his unbroken acute expectation of the near parousia (cf. 1 Cor. 7:29; 10:11; 16:22), but instances of Christians who die before the Lord's return are no longer considered unusual (cf. 1 Cor. 7:39; 11:30; 15:6, 18, 29, 51). For the Corinthians, the σῶμα theme was apparently of decisive importance, for 56 of the 74 instances of σῶμα in Paul's letters are found in 1–2 Corinthians (142 times in the New Testament). Paul responded to this situation presented by the Corinthian theological interest, and he made the issue of corporeality a central aspect of his eschatology. He first anchors eschatology in Christology (1 Cor. 15:3–5), and after rejecting the thesis that there is no resurrection with arguments based on logic, he returns to the christological kerygma as his basis (cf. 15:20).[20] The destiny of Christ as the prototype requires the insight that baptized believers will also be raised (15:21–22). Everything, however, must take place within the prescribed order: because the final events have already begun with the resurrection of Christ and since that event Christ has been appointed by God as Lord, the resurrection of Christians will not take place until the parousia of Christ, which in turn will bring about the end, in which all hostile powers will be destroyed and God will be all in all.[21]

The question that now becomes important for the Corinthians, the "how" of the resurrection, Paul works through in 1 Cor. 15:35–56 in a broadly-conceived anthropological argumentation. The occasion was an antagonistic question: "But someone will ask, 'How are the dead raised? With what kind of body do they come?'" (15:35). Paul begins his line of thought with the idea, widespread in antiquity, that death is the necessary condition for new life. In 15:38 Paul applies the element of discontinuity, already inherent in this view, to God's free creative act, which gives to each creature its own σῶμα (body, corporeality) according to God's own will. Here the apostle's basic position becomes clear: for him there is no existence without corporeality, so that the question of the "how" of the resurrection can only be the question of the nature of the resurrection body. This leads Paul to differentiate between two different categories of bodies; by means of an antithetical analogy, he infers from the earthly body to the heavenly body (15:40), so that if there is a perishable body, there must also be an imperishable body (15:43–44). The spiritual body is of higher quality than the earthly body (15:46) because each type of body goes back to a

---

19. On the following, cf. Udo Schnelle, "Der erste Thessalonicherbrief und die Entstehung der paulinischen Anthropologie," *NTS* 32 (1986): 214–18; on the changed argumentation in 1 Corinthians, see also Walter, "Leibliche Auferstehung," 112–13.

20. On 1 Cor. 15, see above, section 9.6 ("The Resurrection of the Dead"). On the logical structure of 1 Cor. 15:12–19, cf. Schade, *Apokalyptische Christologie*, 193ff.

21. Cf. Schrage, *Korinther*, 4:152–89.

prototype: Adam and Christ (15:45, 47). Believers still bear the image of the earthly, but soon they will be in the likeness of the man of heaven (15:49). In 15:50–54, with the metaphor of transformation, Paul introduces a new category compared with 1 Thess. 4:13–18 and the preceding argumentation of 1 Cor. 15.[22] Both those who have already died and those who are still alive at the parousia will receive imperishable bodies. Although the σῶμα concept no longer appears and the categorical difference between two kinds of bodies no longer fits the metaphorical framework in 1 Cor. 15:52–54,[23] the argument as a whole indicates that the imperishable, immortal postmortal existence is probably identical with the σῶμα πνευματικόν of 15:44.

Whereas in 1 Thess. 4:13–18 and 1 Cor. 15:51ff. Paul made it clear that he expected to be among the living at the Lord's return (cf. ἡμεῖς [we], 1 Thess. 4:17; 1 Cor. 15:52), in 2 Cor. 5:1–10 for the first time he reckons with the possibility of his own death before the parousia.[24] This decisive adjustment in the apostle's situation is reflected in the decline of apocalyptic elements in the portrayal of the final events and the increased appropriation of Hellenistic conceptuality with its dualistic and individualistic tendencies. Now the σῶμα terminology is used exclusively for the earthly body (5:6, 8) and is seen in a negative light.[25] The idea of departure from the present body has its closest parallel in the Greek view that the true homeland of the soul is in the transcendent world[26] and that existence in the body is living in a foreign country.[27] Paul intentionally avoids using the term "soul" but at the same time no longer defines resurrection existence explicitly as "bodily" existence, thus coming closer to the Corinthians' own thinking. In terms of his worldview, Paul uses the metaphor of "seeing" (5:7) in order to maintain an intended vagueness. It is the divine Spirit alone that guarantees continuity (5:5), which, in the imagery of 5:2–4, makes possible being "further clothed" with the "heavenly dwelling." Second Corinthians 5:10 documents the connection between eschatology and the final judgment, a connection already present in pre-Pauline tradition[28] but also affirmed by Paul: "For all of us must appear before the judgment seat of Christ, so that each may receive recompense for what has been done in the body, whether good or evil."

22. Cf. Walter, "Leibliche Auferstehung," 114–15.

23. This is rightly emphasized by Walter, ibid., 115.

24. On the interpretation of 2 Cor. 5:1–10, see above, section 10.3 ("Paul's Life as Apostolic Existence").

25. Cf. Wiefel, "Eschatologischen Denken," 77; Walter, "Leibliche Auferstehung," 116: "'Body' is now no longer a concept that can describe both the earthly *and* the heavenly mode of being, and thus Paul also develops the auxiliary concept of 'transformation' (of one corporeality into another, new corporeality)."

26. Cf., e.g., Seneca, *Ep.* 102.24, on the future life: "Another realm awaits us, another situation. Still, we can tolerate heaven only from a distance. Therefore, every time of decision waits without fear: it is not the last hour for the soul, but for the body" (*NW* 2/1:944–45).

27. Cf., e.g., Plato, *Phaedr.* 67c–d.

28. Cf. Synofzik, *Vergeltungsaussagen*, 106.

The concept of the last judgment gives theological expression to the conviction that God is not finally indifferent to the way people live their lives nor to history as a whole. If there is to be no judgment, then a person's deeds remain forever in a twilight zone without evaluation. Murderers would finally triumph over their victims, and the oppressors would get away with their oppression. If there were no final judgment, then world history and the life of each human being would themselves constitute the judgment. But because no deed or failure to act is without consequences and because they must be evaluated for the sake of human life itself, the concept of the last judgment must itself be evaluated positively. It preserves the dignity of human life and shows that God has not abandoned God's creation. Still, in Jesus Christ human beings may hope that God's grace will have the last word.[29]

In the Letter to the Romans also, death before the parousia is no longer the exception but already the rule (cf. Rom. 14:8b, "so then, whether we live or whether we die, we are the Lord's").[30] The parousia of the Lord, it is true, is still thought of as imminent (cf. 13:11–12; 16:20), but the comparative in the expression "For salvation is nearer to us now than when we became believers" (13:11c) suggests an awareness of its delay. As an affirmation of eschatological hope, the phrase ζωὴ αἰώνιος (eternal life, the life of the age to come) gains increasing significance in Romans, which contains four of the five Pauline instances (cf. Gal. 6:8; Rom. 2:7; 5:21; 6:22, 23). This expression designates the future mode of being of those who are saved, which no longer is subject to any temporal limitation.[31] In Romans Paul gives no programmatic presentation on the course of the final events, but Rom. 8:11 and 8:23 clearly indicate that once again the concept of a transformation of the body stands in the foreground. The Spirit of God not only effected the resurrection of Jesus from the dead but will also "give life to your mortal bodies also through his Spirit that dwells in you" (8:11). Thus the revealed assurance that one is accepted by God includes the confidence of the transformation of the body by the power of the Spirit.[32]

In Philippians we see the consolidation of two tendencies already visible in Paul's previous writings: Paul now reflects openly on the possibility of his death before the parousia, and he concentrates his eschatological imagery on the destiny of the individual.[33] In Phil. 1:20 the apostle speaks of his earthly body, in which Christ will be glorified "whether by life or by death." In 1:21–24 Paul

---

29. Cf. ibid., 108–9: "No human being can achieve this acquittal in the last judgment by himself or herself; one can only receive it as pronounced in the gospel and by faith in the saving act of Christ."

30. On the eschatology of Romans, cf. G. Storck, "Eschatologie bei Paulus" (diss., Göttingen, Georg August Universität, 1979), 117–59.

31. Cf. Baumgarten, *Paulus und die Apokalyptik*, 129, who appropriately points out that as in the case of the doctrine of the two ages, so also Paul adopts the concept of 'eternal life,' only in a broken manner because for him life has already been revealed through the Christ event.

32. The comment of Walter, "Leibliche Auferstehung," 120, is on target: "Thus not redemption *from* the body or out of the body but the salvific *transformation* of the body."

33. Wiefel, "Eschatologischen Denken," 79–81.

wavers between the expectation of further life in this world and his own soon death, which is bound up with his confidence that immediately after death he will be with Christ (1:23, σὺν Χριστῷ εἶναι).[34] Philippians 1:23 has in view being in the presence of Christ immediately after death, without reference to the parousia and the resurrection. The singular formulation "if somehow I may attain the resurrection from the dead" (3:11, εἰς τὴν ἐξανάστασιν τὴν ἐκ νεκρῶν), with its double use of ἐκ (out of, from), likewise points to an early resurrection immediately after death.[35] In Philippians, as in all Paul's letters, the parousia is the horizon of all the apostle's eschatological statements (cf. 4:5b; 1:6, 10; 2:16; 3:20b), but as Paul nears the end of his life, he reconsiders his own destiny. Because he now thinks that he may die before the parousia, the parousia and the resurrection of the dead that is to happen then can no longer be the one and only point of orientation.[36] Paul here identifies his own destiny so closely with Christ that he unites himself completely with the passion and resurrection of his Lord. In 3:20–21, in contrast, the eschatological horizon is once more the parousia; Paul speaks of the transformation of our body of humiliation into conformity with Christ's glorious body through the power of God and thus interprets the believer's postmortal mode of existence in continuity with 1 Cor. 15 and Rom. 8.

By now it has probably become clear that in central areas of Paul's eschatology, we can speak of *transformations*, that is, of *progressive steps in the apostle's thought* that correspond to the changing historical situations with which he was dealing.[37] For all that, the acute expectation of the near end remained the horizon of his thought, as the present and future Christ event continued to be the foundation of Pauline eschatology, even when the status of the individual and the course of the final events themselves were adjusted as it became apparent that time was continuing. Paul's holding on to his expectation of the parousia is no counterargument, for experiencing a delay in the parousia is not the same as abandoning the idea of the parousia itself. Paul obviously continued to hold fast to his conviction of the soon coming of the Lord, while simultaneously making appropriate adjustments in his eschatological affirmations. Also, the objection that the changes were entirely conditioned by the various situations faced by

34. On the interpretation of Phil. 1:21–24, see above, section 13.2.2 ("Philippians as a Document of Later Pauline Theology").

35. Cf. Hunzinger, "Hoffnung angesichts des Todes," 87.

36. This divergence has often been explained by assuming that in Phil. 1:23 Paul is thinking of a martyr's death in particular whereas Phil. 3:10–11 and 3:21 represent, so to speak, the normal case. For an extensive argument in favor of this view, cf. Müller, *Philipper*, 64–71. Nothing in Phil. 1:23 suggests, however, that only a privileged group enters into the presence of Christ immediately after death, before the Lord's parousia. Cf. Gnilka, *Philipperbrief*, 75. A consistent understanding is attained when it is noted that in Phil. 1:23 and 3:10–11 Paul speaks in the first person singular but 3:20–21 uses the first person plural. Paul evidently considered his own destiny and that of others who die before the parousia as exceptions.

37. Schnelle, *Wandlungen*, 37–48.

the apostle[38] handles the issue too easily. The situations of the addressees are, of course, different, but Paul's thinking further and deeper is more than mere tinkering. As long as he firmly believed he would still be alive to experience the Lord's parousia, he portrayed the final events in terms of a broadly conceived apocalyptic scenario (cf. 1 Thess. 4:13–18; 1 Cor. 15:51ff.). But when he realized that he might die before the parousia, this led to eschatological statements oriented to his own individual destiny. This is an appropriate transformation in his thought, for as he began to experience the temporality and finitude of Christian existence, Paul was compelled to rethink the destiny of Christians who died before the parousia and finally to reckon with his own destiny. This working through of an individual eschatology oriented to the person of the apostle himself then receives an exemplary significance as a model for his general eschatological thought, as death before the parousia increasingly became the rule rather than the exception. The apostle could not ignore the fact that time was continuing, and was thus compelled to make appropriate changes in his eschatological views. At the same time, σὺν Χριστῷ εἶναι, "being with the Lord" / "being with Christ" (1 Thess. 4:17 / Phil. 1:23) continued to be the constant foundational element of Pauline eschatology.

Corporeality and Life after Death

Paul also attained new and transformed insights on the question of the "how" of postmortal existence, insights that to no small degree were influenced by the way bodily existence was evaluated in Greek thought. Such thought was largely under the influence of Platonic ideas (classically expressed in Plato, *Phaed.* 80a, "Now what is the soul like? —Obviously, Socrates, the soul corresponds to the divine and the body to the mortal [ἡ μὲν ψυχὴ τῷ θείῳ, τὸ δὲ σῶμα τῷ θνητῷ]").[39] Accordingly, the prevalent view was that immediately after death the immortal soul separated from the perishable body and so the body could have no significance for postmortal existence.[40] Thus Cicero, *Resp.* 3.28, states regarding the death of Hercules and Romulus and their going to the heavenly world, "Their bodies were not taken up to heaven, for Nature would not allow that which comes from the earth to be removed from the earth." Seneca emphasizes that the body is laid aside at death: "Why love such a thing as though it were your own possession? It was merely your covering. The day will come

38. So Lindemann, "Eschatologie," *RGG* 2:1556.
39. Cf. Cicero's ironical comments on Plato's influence in *Tusc.* 1.24, where a participant in the discussion emphasizes that he has carefully studied Plato's book on the soul: "I have done so, be sure, and done so many times; but somehow I am sorry to find that I agree while reading, yet when I have laid the book aside and begin to reflect in my own mind upon the immortality of souls, all my previous sense of agreement slips away."
40. On the large number of doctrines of the soul that existed at the turn of the first century CE, cf. esp. Cicero, *Tusc.* 1.17–25, 26–81.

which will tear you forth and lead you away from the company of the foul and noisome womb" (*Ep.* 102.27). It is clear for Epictetus, too, that the body hinders freedom (*Diatr.* 22.40ff.), so that the cry of the philosophy student is understandable: "Epictetus, we can no longer endure to be imprisoned with this paltry body, giving it food and drink, and resting and cleansing it, and, to crown all, being on its account brought into contact with these people and those. Are not these things indifferent—indeed, nothing—to us? And is not death no evil? Are we not in a manner akin to God, and have we not come from him?" (*Diatr.* 1.9.12–13). According to Plutarch, the only thing that survives is the image originally derived from the gods: "Yes, it comes from them, and to them it returns, not with its body, but only when it is most completely separated and set free from the body, and becomes altogether pure, fleshless, and undefiled" (*Rom.* 28; cf. also *Mor.* 382E). Likewise in Hellenistic Judaism, the view was widespread that at death the perishable body is left behind and only the soul survives (cf., e.g., Wis. 9:15; Philo, *Migration* 9.192).[41]

It was against the cultural background of this historical situation that Paul had to give an answer to the question of the nature of life after death, an answer that, on the one hand, avoided the idea of the immortality of the soul but, on the other hand, could not entirely do away with the negative evaluation of bodily existence.[42] Whereas in 1 Thess. 4:13–18 the question is not touched on at all and 1 Cor. 15 presents Paul's initial answer, especially 2 Corinthians shows how Paul partly came to terms with the (Hellenistic) argumentation of the churches.[43] At the same time, the Roman and Philippian letters show that the line taken in 1 Cor. 15 continued to be the dominate one: the body transformed by the divine Spirit preserves the identity of the self and as σῶμα πνευματικόν belongs to the divine world.

22.3 The Destiny of Israel

The relation to Israel is, for Paul, at one and the same time a biographical, a theological, and—at the end of his life—an eminent eschatological problem. The transition of salvation from the Jews to the Christians forcefully posed the question of God's relation to the people of Israel and the validity of his promises.

41. Further examples in Schweizer and Baumgärtel, "σῶμα," *TDNT* 7:1048–51

42. The statement of Helmut Merklein, "Eschatologie," *LTK* 3:870 is thus not correct: "As a consequence of his expectation of the near end, Paul had not reflected on the state of the individual's death with reference to the general resurrection (including 2 Cor. 5:1–10 and Phil. 1:21–24)."

43. Cf. Nikolaus Walter, "Hellenistische Eschatologie bei Paulus," *TQ* 176 (1996): 63: "All in all, we must conclude that the development of eschatological ideas in Paul took a clear step in the direction of hellenization. And so we should probably also say regarding 2 Cor. 5:1–10 that a development of Paul's ideas of eschatological matters can in no way be denied."

The earliest extant statement of the apostle regarding Israel, in 1 Thess. 2:14–16, already makes clear the interrelationship of biography and theology.[44] Paul charges the Jews with what he himself had previously done: putting obstacles in the way of the saving proclamation of the gospel. At the time of the composition of 1 Thessalonians, the greatest danger for the expansion of Christian churches was evidently the harassment and persecution by the Jews, so that the sharpness of Paul's polemic is to be explained in the light of this historical situation. For Paul, God had already pronounced judgment on the Jews; God's wrath had already descended on them.[45]

In 1 Corinthians Paul has no extensive discussion of the relation of the young Christian movement to Israel, only referring in 1 Cor. 10:1ff. to the wilderness generation as a negative example warning the Corinthian enthusiasts.[46] In contrast, 2 Cor. 3 offers an insight into Paul's self-understanding as an apostle and his christological interpretation of the Old Testament.[47] By means of the antithesis "letter"/"Spirit" (2 Cor. 3:6), Paul designates the fundamental difference between the old covenant and the new. The glory of the office of proclamation of the gospel far surpasses the glory on the face of Moses, which he had to conceal from the people by veiling his face (cf. Exod. 34:29–35). In 3:14 Paul explains the blindness of Israel as it encounters the glory of the revelation in Christ: ἀλλὰ ἐπωρώθη τὰ νοήματα αὐτῶν (But their minds were hardened). This puts the spotlight directly on the present guilt of Israel: not Moses but Israel itself is responsible for its unbelief.[48] Since it refuses to accept the revelation in Christ, the Old Testament also remains a closed book to it, for the veil that lies over the Old Testament to this very day can only be removed in Christ (3:14b–15). For Paul, the Old Testament promises point to Christ, and only from the perspective of faith in him is an authentic understanding of the Old Testament possible. God remains faithful, Israel is hardened, but the apostle reckons with the possibility of its turning to Christ, and so two important changes may be observed in the view expressed in 1 Thess. 2:14–16: God's final judgment on Israel has not been pronounced, for Israel can still convert; and the Old Testament is fulfilled in Christ because God stands by his promises.

For the stance of the apostle to Israel, the expression Ἰσραὴλ τοῦ θεοῦ (Israel of God) in Gal. 6:16 is revealing: "As for those who will follow this rule, peace be upon them, and mercy, and upon the Israel of God." The meaning is revealed

---

44. On the interpretation of 1 Thess. 2:14–16, see above, section 8.1 ("Prehistory and Initial Preaching").

45. Cf. Haufe, *Thessalonicher*, 48: "Because of their resistance to the divine plan of salvation, the Jews have already fallen under the wrath of God, even if this situation is not yet externally observable and is still hidden from them as well."

46. Cf. Schnelle, *Gerechtigkeit und Christusgegenwart*, 155–56.

47. On the analysis of 2 Cor. 3, see above, section 10.4 ("The Glory of the New Covenant").

48. Cf. Furnish, *II Corinthians*, 233.

by the immediate context. Paul once again speaks polemically against his opponents (6:12–14), and then in Gal. 6:15 adds his credo on which his polemic is based, that neither circumcision nor uncircumcision counts for anything, for all that matters is the new existence in Jesus Christ (cf. 3:26–28; 1 Cor. 7:19; 2 Cor. 5:17). Those who agree with this rule (κανών, lit. "canon") are those to whom the conditional blessing (καὶ ὅσοι) in Gal. 6:16 applies. When one notes the function of 6:15 as the interpretative key to 6:16, the correspondence of granting the blessing with the conditional curse in 1:8,[49] the textual agreements with Jewish prayers,[50] and the copulative meaning of καὶ (and) before ἐπὶ τὸν Ἰσραὴλ τοῦ θεοῦ (on the Israel of God),[51] then Ἰσραὴλ τοῦ θεοῦ can only mean the Galatian church in the inclusive sense: the whole church of Jews and Gentiles, to the extent that they understand themselves to be committed to the new existence described in 6:15.[52] The "Israel of God" is this inclusive church, not empirical Israel (cf. 1 Cor. 10:18, lit. "Israel according to the flesh"). This interpretation fits into the flow of thought in the Letter to the Galatians as a whole, for the debate with the Judaists also includes a sharp separation from unbelieving Judaism. In Gal. 4:25 the earthly Jerusalem represents the people of Israel, which not only belongs to the realm of slavery but is traced back by the apostle to Hagar and Ishmael, so that Abraham and Sarah have no connection to empirical Israel. A more radical demarcation can hardly be imagined. In 4:30–31 Paul concludes by formulating the result of his allegory of Sarah and Hagar by stating his view of God's saving acts: God has rejected the Jews, and only the Christians are heirs of the promise.

In Romans the theological and biographical problems involved in the Paul-Israel relation become more intense and then modulate into a new eschatological dimension. The question of the validity of the promises made to Israel, in view of the revelation of the righteousness of God apart from the law, is already broached in Rom. 12:16 and 2:9–10 (Ἰουδαῖος τε πρῶτον [to the Jew first]), is thematized in 3:1–8, and then is taken up in Rom. 9–11 as a specific issue requiring thorough discussion.[53] If the election of Israel, the promises to the patriarchs, and the covenants are no longer valid (9:4–5), what, then, is at stake is God's own righteousness. The word of God would then have failed (9:6). But Paul argues the converse: the election of Israel is still in effect, the promises are still valid, but God's revelation in Jesus Christ has brought Israel to a crisis point.

49. Cf. Betz, *Galatians*, 544–45.

50. Cf. the nineteenth benediction of the Shemoneh Esreh (Babylonian recension), "Let peace, happiness and blessing, grace, love and mercy come on your people Israel"; cf. Strack and Billerbeck, *Kommentar*, 4:214.

51. Cf. Schlier, *Galater*, 283.

52. Cf. Oepke, *Galater*, 204–5; Betz, *Galatians*, 547–48; Lüdemann, *Paulus und das Judentum*, 29; Hübner, *Gottes Ich*, 133 (who also provides a critique of Mussner, *Galaterbrief*, 416–17, who interprets "the Israel of God" from Rom. 9–11).

53. For analysis of Rom. 9–11, see above, section 12.9 ("Paul and Israel").

For Paul, this revelation means a crisis for any false understanding of privilege. In Rom. 9–11 Paul wants to demonstrate the faithfulness of God in contrast to the unfaithfulness of Israel that has so far prevailed. He sets forth his ideas in a train of thought that is filled with tensions, repeatedly adopting new viewpoints and ways of considering the issue. He begins by distinguishing empirical Israel (Israel according to the flesh) and the Israel defined by the promise, which alone is the true Israel (9:6–8). Then he affirms that only a remnant of Israel is elect while the rest remain hardened (11:5ff.). Finally, through the idea that the election of the Gentiles will ultimately bring salvation to Israel, he comes to his crowning thesis in 11:26a: πᾶς Ἰσραὴλ σωθήσεται (all Israel will be saved). It is precisely the plurality of solutions that shows how rigorously Paul has struggled with this theme and how deeply he was personally involved in it.[54] If God does not hold fast to the continuity of his promises, then how can the gospel be credibly proclaimed? For Paul, the destiny of Israel was the test case for God's righteousness in general, Thus in Rom. 9–11 the ultimate issue is the deity of God, God's righteousness and faithfulness in the face of human unfaithfulness, but it also concerns Paul's own credibility and the meaning of his own life and personal destiny. Paul is certain that God remains true to himself and that in the final days will by his miraculous power bring Israel to conversion and thus to salvation. Paul thus at the same time admits that this problem cannot be solved by human beings in the present but calls for an extraordinary act of God in the future. At Christ's parousia, Israel will be converted and with the believing Gentiles will enter into the fullness of salvation (cf. 11:23, 26–32).

The position of the apostle regarding Israel has undergone radical changes. First Thessalonians 2:14–16 is irreconcilable with Rom. 11:25–26, and so we must speak of a revision of Paul's stance on the issue.[55] Whereas in the former passage God has already rejected his people, in the latter he will save them. All attempts to harmonize the tension between these two statements are misplaced and only conceal the historical truth. Why did Paul revise his judgment about

---

54. Cf. Gerd Theissen, "Röm 9–11—eine Auseinandersetzung des Paulus mit Israel und sich selbst: Versuch einer psychologischen Auslegung," in *Fair Play: Diversity and Conflicts in Early Christianity: Essays in Honour of Heikki Räisänen* (ed. Ismo Dunderberg, Christopher Tuckett, and Kari Syreeni; NovTSup 103; Leiden: Brill, 2002), 326: "When Paul engages in such intellectual struggles concerning the salvation of all Israel, he is wrestling with the issue of his own salvation."

55. Among those who understand the matter in this sense are Räisänen, "Römer 9–11," *ANRW* 25.4:2925; Lüdemann, *Paulus und das Judentum*, 41–42; Roloff, *Einführung*, 138. Also Wilckens, *Römer*, 2:209, rightly emphasizes that "the result of the first move in Paul's thought in Rom. 9 (and then also the result of his second step in Rom. 10) is superseded and neutralized when he finally reaches the goal of his thought in chapter 11." Objections to this interpretation are raised by Holtz, *Thessalonicher*, 108–13 and Egon Brandenburger, "Paulinische Schriftauslegung in der Kontroverse um das Verheißungswort Gottes (Röm 9)," *ZTK* 82 (1985): 43–47. Whereas Brandenburger emphasizes the internal unity of Rom. 9–11, Holtz sees no fundamental contradiction between 1 Thess. 2:14–16 and Rom. 9–11, for 1 Thess. 2:16 "does not give eschatological sanction to the judgment on the Jews" (p. 110). The aorist tense ἔφθασεν (has come) in 1 Thess. 2:16 speaks against this, however, for it indicates a state of affairs that has already occurred and is already valid.

Israel? Again, the way in which each situation conditioned his thinking called
for new reflections on Israel, which then led to new judgments about the facts
of the matter. The polemic in 1 Thess. 2:14–16 is solely conditioned by the
Jewish opposition to the Gentile mission. But 2 Cor. 3 already shows that for
Paul a new situation again evokes different statements. The Letter to the Galatians, where the confrontation with the Judaists must necessarily influence the
theological evaluation of Israel, confirms this. Finally, the Letter to the Romans
itself speaks for the way the situation conditions Paul's stance on the issue, for
here Paul is dealing with a church, unknown to him personally, in which there
were obvious disputes between Jewish Christians and Gentile Christians (cf.
Rom. 14:1–15:13), a church in which he must assume that his Jewish Christian opponents had already exercised some influence. In addition, there is the
personal situation of the apostle: he sees his mission in the east as complete
(Rom. 15:23) and wants to deliver the collection to Jerusalem so that he can
then continue his work in the west (Rom. 15:24ff.). Both the collection, as a
visible bond of unity between Jewish Christians and Gentile Christians, and
the actual numerical predominance of Gentile Christians in the churches established in Paul's previous missionary work made it necessary for him to reflect
afresh on the destiny of Israel. Inseparably bound up with the existence of the
original church in Jerusalem as the holy remnant of Israel was the theological
question of the destiny of the part of Israel that had so far failed to accept the
revelation in Christ. When Paul, despite his statement in 1 Cor. 16:3, decided
to go to Jerusalem himself in order to make good on his promised service to the
church there—a decision that he knew involved some danger—this also posed
the theological problem of the faithfulness and righteousness of God to Israel,
which, for the most part, was hardened in unbelief. This was all the more so
since the Judaists in Galatia were certainly in contact with the Jerusalem church,
so that he could expect there theological debates about observing the law and
circumcision as well as about the theological meaning of Israel as such.

In addition, Paul had gained a different view of his Gentile mission. Whereas
in 1 Thess. 2:14–16 hindrance to this mission still served as the occasion for
vigorous polemic, Paul saw a different function for the Gentile mission as he
finished his work in the east: its purpose is to provoke the Jews so that they
too will come to faith and be saved (Rom. 11:13–15). The Pauline Gentile
mission had always had in view one church of Jews and Gentiles, and so the
foreseeable development of an almost purely Gentile church could not have
been an indifferent matter for the apostle.

22.4 Eschatology as Time Construal

Every symbolic universe requires a construal of time, for a horizon of meaning can only be outlined when the structure and quality of the time of the

meaningful events associated with it are made clear.[56] God's act in raising Jesus Christ from the dead is in several respects an event that calls for reflection on the nature and meaning of time:[57] (1) It transcends human experience in that it postulates an event that transcends time as an event in space and time. (2) It gives a new qualification to time, for from that point on, all time has the quality of the time of God. (3) It gives a new structure to time because with the resurrection there comes a radical, irreversible turn in the course of time. A past event determines the present and anticipates the future as the paradigm of what is to come.

Paul was faced with the task of developing a plausible construal of time that, on the one hand, incorporates the three basic elements named above and, on the other hand, is able to respond flexibly to the questions, raised by the church, that had been evoked by the problematic death of some members of the community. In this process he could incorporate some motifs from Jewish apocalyptic, but by no means could he take over self-contained systems for structuring meaning and time, for the uniquely new aspects of the event required an independent solution.[58] It called for an outline of an eschatological scenario whose functional and temporal anchor points were formed by the resurrection of Jesus Christ from the dead and his imminent return from God,

56. Cf. Aleida Assmann, *Zeit und Tradition: Kulturelle Strategien der Dauer* (Cologne: Böhlau, 1999), 4.

57. On the New Testament understanding of time, cf. Gerhard Delling, *Das Zeitverständnis des Neuen Testaments* (Gütersloh: Bertelsmann, 1940); *Zeit und Endzeit: Zwei Vorlesungen zur Theologie des Neuen Testaments* (Neukirchen-Vluyn: Neukirchener Verlag, 1970). Whereas Delling reclaims the qualitative understanding of time (καιρός, *kairos*) in contrast to the quantitative understanding of the Greek χρόνος (*chronos*), Kurt Erlemann, *Endzeiterwartungen im frühen Christentum* (Tübingen: Francke, 1996), 33–59, stresses that such general distinctions are not possible (see also James Barr, *The Semantics of Biblical Language* [London: Oxford University Press, 1961]; *Biblical Words for Time* [SBT 33; Naperville, IL: Alec R. Allenson, 1962]). Erlemann sees the primary differences between the ancient/New Testament and modern understanding of time in the following four points: the qualitative aspect is more prevalent than the chronological aspect; God is the Lord of time; things have a temporal "specific mass"; and the perception of time is a matter of the emotions.

58. Whereas Ernst Käsemann, "On the Subject of Primitive Christian Apocalyptic," in *New Testament Questions of Today* (London: SCM Press, 1969), 124–37, resolutely understands Paul as an apocalyptist, and apocalyptic as "the mother of all Christian theology," Rudolf Bultmann, "Ist die Apokalyptik die Mutter der christlichen Theologie?" in *Exegetica: Aufsätze zur Erforschung des Neuen Testaments* (ed. Erich Dinkler; Tübingen: Mohr Siebeck, 1967), 482, is willing to concede only that one could say "that eschatology, but not apocalyptic, is the mother of early Christian theology." On this debate and its theological relevance, cf. Baumgarten, *Paulus und die Apokalyptik*, who understands the disputed relation between tradition and interpretation as follows: "Interpretation through present eschatology, which thinks of eschatological existence as beginning with the Christ event, is inconceivable apart from the tradition that makes it possible to interpret the eschatological existence of the baptized as oriented to the future" (p. 239). On the temporal structure of Jewish apocalypticism and its reception in the New Testament, cf. also Erlemann, *Endzeiterwartungen*, 60–134. See also the essays in Carl E. Braaten and Roy A. Harrisville, *The Historical Jesus and the Kerygmatic Christ: Essays on the New Quest of the Historical Jesus* (Nashville: Abingdon, 1964).

whose confidence was nourished by the present experience of the Spirit, and whose perspective lies in the hope of an analogous act of God: Jesus of Nazareth serves as prototype for God's creative, life-giving power. Within this model, the Spirit, as the mode of the continuing presence of God and Jesus Christ in the church, guarantees the necessary functional and temporal continuity or duration between the two anchor points, so that baptized believers live in the consciousness of contemporaneity with these events, which factually are past and still to come.

The theme of death played an important role not only for Paul (the resurrection of Jesus Christ from the dead, the destiny of dead Christians) but also for competing systems of meaning and construals of time. Particularly in the Greco-Roman world, there existed a multiplicity of ideas about death and the possibility of life after death.[59] We find not only faith that the immortal soul continues to live[60] but also numerous skeptical variations on this theme. In philosophical systems, the discussion focused on the nature and continuation of the soul.[61] Over against the Platonic model,[61] there were numerous other proposals that denied the immortality of the soul or minimized its vital capacities after the death of the body. Thus Cicero mentions (*Tusc.* 1.77) that the Stoics do not believe in the immortality of the soul, in contrast to his own view: "The Stoics, on the other hand, grant us, as though to make us crows, a generous lease of life: they say that souls will survive a long time, but not forever." The Stoic understanding of the soul is also related to their periodic model of time: "Cleanthes indeed holds that all souls continue to exist until the general conflagration, while Chrysippus says that only the souls of the wise do so" (Diogenes Laertius 7.157).[62] Lucretius attempts to prove that the soul is mortal and experiences nothing after death. It cannot exist apart from the body and has no sense organs of its own: "Besides, if the nature of the mind is immortal and can feel when separated from our body, we must, I think, assume that it is endowed with the five senses; in no other way can we imagine the spirits below to be wandering in Acheron.

59. Cf. the classic presentation of Erwin Rohde, *Psyche: The Cult of Souls and Belief in Immortality among the Greeks* (trans. W. B. Hillis; Freeport, NY: Books for Libraries Press, 1972). Cf. also Nilsson, *Greek Religion*, 498–535; Walter Burkert, *Greek Religion* (Cambridge: Harvard University Press, 1985); and *Ancient Mystery Cults* (Cambridge: Harvard University Press, 1987).

60. The Greek soul-cults were transmitted primarily by the mystery cults (at first the Eleusinian, later the Orphic-Pythagorean and Dionysian); cf. Burkert, *Greek Religion*, 190–215, 276–304.

61. Cf. Rohde, *Psyche*, 263–95; Heinrich Barth, *Die seele in der philosophie Platons* (Tübingen: Mohr Siebeck, 1921).

62. Cf. Seneca, *Marc.* 26.7, where A. Cremutius Cordus concludes his speech with the Stoic conception that ultimately everything is destroyed in the final conflagration (ἐκπύρωσις), including the souls of the blessed dead: "We too, happy souls that we are, who gain eternity—if it pleases God, this [the final conflagration] to put in operation again, since everything falls into movement, will ourselves become a tiny part of the enormous dissolution at the end of the age in which all the elements will be changed."

Painters, therefore, and the earlier generations of writers, have introduced the spirits thus provided with senses. But apart from the body there can never be either eyes or nose or hand by itself for the spirit, nor tongue apart from the body, nor can the ears by themselves perceive by hearing or exist" (*Rer. nat.* 3.624–633).[63]

Epicurus developed an independent and still fascinating theory of death as the absence of time: "Death is nothing to us; for the body, when it has been resolved into its elements, has no feeling, and that which has no feeling is nothing to us" (*Ratae sententiae* 2 [in Diogenes Laertius 10.139]).[64] Cicero repeats a mixture of Platonic and Epicurean ideas: "In what sense then, or for what reason do you say that you consider death an evil, when it will either render us happy if our souls survive, or free from wretchedness if we are without sensation?" (*Tusc.* 1.25). Nor does Seneca express any fear of death: "And what is death? It is either the end, or a process of change [*Mors quid est? Aut finis aut transitus*]. I have no fear of ceasing to exist; it is the same as never having begun. Nor do I shrink from changing into another state, because I shall, under no conditions, be as cramped as I am now. Farewell" (*Ep.* 65.24).[65] According to Epictetus, death is neither an evil nor the state of nonbeing but only the transition from one state of being to another: "This is the meaning of death, a greater change of that which now is, not into what is not, but into what is not *now*.—Shall I then be no more?—No, you will not be, but something else will be, something different from that of which the universe now has need. And this is but reasonable, for you came into being, not when *you* wanted, but when the universe had need of you" (*Diatr.* 3.24.93–95.) Dio Chrysostom sees the matter as follows: "God, therefore, looking upon these things and observing all the banqueters, as if he were in his own house, how each person has comported himself at the banquet, ever calls the best to himself; and, if he happens to be especially pleased with any one, he bids him remain there and makes him his boon and companion" (*Charid.* 44).

Besides philosophical reflection, there was the kind of popular piety[66] whose widespread influence was especially lamented by Plutarch:

---

63. According to Diogenes Laertius 7.156, Zeno taught the following regarding the nature of the soul: "The soul is a nature capable of perception. And they regard it as the breath of life, congenital with us; from which they infer first that it is a body and secondly that it survives death. Yet it is perishable, though the soul of the universe, of which the individual souls of animals are parts, is indestructible."

64. The Epicurean doctrine that there is no life after death was also very popular among the elements of the Roman population with less philosophical education, as illustrated by this tomb inscription: "Dedicated to the divine spirits of the dead. To Aurelia Vercella, the sweetest wife who lived about 17 years. I was not, I was, I am not, I miss [it] not [Non fui, fui, non sum, non desidero]. Anthimus, her husband" (*ILS* 2:883, no. 8162).

65. Cf. Seneca, *Ep.* 54.3–5; 99.29–30; *Marc.* 19.4–5.

66. Cf. Rohde, *Psyche*, 336–96.

The great majority, however, have an expectation of eternity undisturbed by any myth-inspired fear of what may come after death; and the love of being, the oldest and greatest of all our passions, is more than a counterpoise for that childish terror. . . . Yet such doctrines as these, as I said, are not feared by very many, being the doctrine and fabulous argument of mothers and nurses; and even those who fear them hold that there is an answering remedy in certain mystic ceremonies and rituals of purification, and that when cleansed by these they will pass their time in the other world in play and choral dancing in regions where there is radiance and a sweet breeze.[67]

In view of the number of quite attractive answers to the problem of death, there arises the question of the Pauline model's ability to hold its own. In Judaism prior to the destruction of the temple, the concept of resurrection was the dominant but by no means the only model.[68] Among the Greeks, skepticism prevailed concerning any sort of continuing bodily existence after death, however it was conceived. Already in Aeschylus, *Eumenides* 545, one can read this about the finality of death: "For once the dust soaks up a man's blood, there is no resurrection for him [οὔ τις ἔστιν ἀνάστασις]." Especially among the Cynics is there great hesitation regarding theories of life after death.[69] A tradition about Diogenes reports, "It is also said that as Diogenes was dying, he commanded that his body be left out for wild animals to eat, or to stick it in a grave and throw a little dirt over it" (Diogenes Laertius 6.79; cf. 6:52; Lucian, *Demonax* 35.66). Here too Paul transcended intellectual and cultural boundaries by combining the Jewish concept of resurrection with the Greek view of the spirit as the present and enduring divine power of life[70] and thus facilitated the reception of his views in the Hellenistic world.

Rituals are also essential factors in the construal of a culture's time and identity.[71] Especially baptism, as the place where the Spirit is conferred and the new life begins, stamps Christian existence with an unmistakable character of the "I" that endures even beyond death through the life-giving power of God. In death, my relationship to myself and to other human beings comes to an end, but not God's relation to me. Thus narratives, too, confer lasting meaning on a unique event and so facilitate a particular construal of time. By presenting the Jesus-Christ-history as the model for God's love and creative power that

67. Plutarch, *Mor.* 1104–1105 (*NW* 2/1:405–6). Cf. the whole of Plutarch's *De superstitione*.

68. Cf. Günter Stemberger, "Auferstehung 3: Antikes Judentum," *RGG* 1:916–17.

69. Cf. Downing, *Pauline Churches*, 242–49.

70. On the Spirit as the divine power of life, cf. the texts at John 4:24, πνεῦμα ὁ θεός, in *NW* 1/2:226–34.

71. Cf. Assmann, *Zeit und Tradition*, 15. On the importance of social influences on the origin and development of ideas of death and what lies beyond, cf. Burkhard Gladigow, "Naturae Deus humanae mortalis: Zur sozialen Konstruktion des Todes in römischer Zeit," in *Leben und Tod in den Religionen: Symbol und Wirklichkeit* (ed. Gunther Stephenson; Darmstadt: Wissenschaftliche Buchgesellschaft, 1980), 119–33.

overcomes even death, Paul opens up to people from all ethnic and national groups and from all social levels the possibility of trusting the continuity of God's love, which transcends all traditional ideas of how it could be. Time is not abolished but entrusted to God's righteousness, goodness, and mercy. Neither Hellenism's cultural-imperial construal of time nor Jewish apocalypticism's destruction of time in the eschatological catastrophe were able to arouse a comparable assurance.

23

Epilogue

Pauline Thought as Enduring Meaning Formation

———————————————————

The preceding discussions indicate that the formation of symbolic universes can only begin, become successful, and endure if they manifest plausibility, the ability to make contact with and incorporate new concepts, and the capacity for renovation and renewal. This is doubtless the case with Paul, for the apostle belongs to the small group of human beings of the last two thousand years whose life and thought have made lasting changes in the world. Which elements in the Pauline dynamic of meaning formation have these particular abilities and are constitutive for the religion of the future? This question can be answered only in debate with the dominant intellectual streams of our epoch. Epochs creep in without fanfare, entering history at first unnoticed and letting their effects first be seen in retrospect. This is also true of postmodernism, but—in accord with its nature—much more quickly.[1] One feature is common to the Enlightenment of the early days of the modern world, the modernism of the nineteenth and twentieth centuries, and the postmodernism of the present: they define them-selves from an anthropocentric standpoint; for them all, human being itself is

———

1. On postmodernism, cf. P. V. Zima, *Moderne/Postmoderne: Gesellschaft, Philosophie, Literatur* (Tübingen: Francke, 1997).

the basis of its own subjectivity and freedom. The human spirit understands itself as its own project, to be managed under its own responsibility.

The study of Paul takes us back into another world. He anchors the ground of all being in God and shapes his understanding of humanity exclusively in terms of its relation to God. This is an intriguing contrast: here the deontologization, deconstruction, and deregulation of entangled postmodernism; there a person of antiquity who portrays reality on the basis of a theocentric symbolic universe and feels at home within it. Is it worthwhile in the twenty-first century to hear the voice of a man who lived in a mythological symbolic universe but who, at the same time, by his life and thought became an enabler of modern subjectivity and freedom? The question of the significance of the Pauline meaning formation for the religion of the future culminates precisely in this understanding of freedom and the images of God, the world, and humanity bound up with it. Freedom is the central promise of all meaning-formation. It grounds every particular way of experiencing life and each individual's pathway through life in the postmodern world. But what is the real basis of individual freedom, and how can it be distinguished from its counterfeits, which only make people dependent and lead them into bondage? How can the worth of creation and thus of humanity be protected from human aggression?

In the modern age, freedom has been understood as in principle a human product, as breaking out of dependence for which human beings themselves are responsible, as the overcoming of binding traditions and authorities, including the Bible.[2] This process is historically understandable, for the modern freedom movement has in fact taken place in the liberation from oppressive structures. But what does this mean for the concept of liberation itself if it is understood as a human product? Is the human subject independent? Of course not, for it is determined by its biological features and its life history. Freedom must necessarily be adapted to the given realities of each case. If freedom is located exclusively in the human subject, it then ultimately falls victim to dependence on this subject. The history of the last three hundred years teaches that when the human subject becomes the norm of freedom, it always tends to extend its own territory. It succumbs to the compulsion to live a life with no restrictions, no boundaries, a life that must assert itself against nature and against its own creatureliness. This means that human beings always attempt to extend their own maneuvering room and understand this as freedom but at the same time can no longer anticipate and assess the results of their action for the world and for the concept of freedom itself.[3] The restriction of the understanding of humanity and the concept of freedom to the autonomy of the subject leads to a constant effort to perfect and extend production. The idea of production

2. On this process, cf. Henning Reventlow, *Von der Aufklärung bis zum 20. Jahrhundert* (vol. 4 of *Epochen der Bibelauslegung*; 4 vols.; Munich: Beck, 1990).

3. Cf. Hans Jonas, *The Imperative of Responsibility: In Search of an Ethics for the Technological Age* (trans. Hans Jonas and David Herr; Chicago: University of Chicago Press, 1984).

and consumption dominates society, so that freedom is shown in the capacity for production and the necessity for consumption. Humanity understands the whole of creation as raw material for production and consumption and does not exclude other human beings from this perspective. The operations of science and research, with promises of the good life and ever new consumer demands, increasingly accelerate the reduction of human beings to their function as consumers and producers. In view of this ever more efficient human attack on human freedom, what can be the basis for inherent human dignity and worth?

A Philosophical Model

J. Habermas presents an important attempt to respond to this question.[4] The point of departure for his reflections is the question of how it is (still) possible to justify moral judgments in a postmodern world.[5] The perceiving and acting subject's will toward morality is no longer adequate by itself to put its ethical judgments into practice and to make them last. Also, the postmetaphysical hesitation regarding the nature of human being leads to an evaporation of moral standards. Modern philosophy, in contrast to its early history among the Greeks, no longer trusts itself to make any normative statements about how individuals or societies should conduct their lives. According to Habermas, the social changes that have come about as the result of biomedicine have brought about a fundamental cultural turning point. But the previous hesitation can no longer be maintained "as soon as questions of a 'species ethics' arise. As soon as the ethical self-understanding of language-using agents is at stake *in its entirety*, philosophy can no longer avoid taking a substantive position."[6] Not only the individual self-understanding as one who belongs to a particular culture but the identity of the individual as a member of the human species is endangered when the latest biotechnological interventions continue to move the boundary between what has inherent worth (and thus may not be used for other purposes) and what may be manipulated. The concept "species ethic" functions for Habermas as a description of anthropological principles and boundaries regarding the question of how far and how broadly humanity as a human community may push its own making of itself into a means (rather than an end) when the members of this community still want to understand themselves as autonomous and equal beings.

---

4. Jürgen Habermas, *The Future of Human Nature* (Cambridge: Polity, 2003); cf. also his *Religion and Rationality: Essays on Reason, God, and Modernity*, edited with an introduction by Eduardo Mendieta (Cambridge: Polity, 2002).

5. Cf. Habermas, *Future of Human Nature*, 4: "Deontological theories after Kant may be very good at explaining how to ground and apply moral norms; but they are still unable to answer the question of why we should be moral *at all.*"

6. Ibid., 11.

Finally, with the possibilities and limitations of individual autonomy—the authoring of one's own life story—the issue of freedom itself becomes a debatable issue. When the distinction between "the grown" and "the made"[7] is changed—a distinction that is crucial for the concept of freedom—then the issues of what it means to have "grown" and what it means to be an object that can be used for other purposes stand in a new relation to each other, for then it is not only the self-understanding of an individual that is at stake but also the species "human being."[8] The possibility of human self-optimization and the use of evolution as a tool of human self-realization dissolves the distinction between subject and object, between what grows according to its own nature and what is manufactured, resulting not only in a new self-description of the individual but in a redefinition of the whole species.[9] The subjection of human nature to technology gives rise to the misgivings that genetically manipulated human beings will be limited in their own freedom to act and develop as they will, in contrast to those whose natural birth plays a decisive role.

Habermas works through the fundamental problems of the modern concepts of the autonomous subject and freedom and brings them sharply into focus. The decisive question is: in the future, what kind of arguments can be given as the basis for understanding human life as something that cannot be made the object of some other purpose, for the right to compose one's own life story? According to Habermas, religious arguments with a universal claim are prohibited in a postmodern pluralistic society.[10] The concept of a "species ethic" provides a substitute basis for a plausible solution: humanity as a species can remain human only if it recognizes its specific essential nature in the face of the biomedical epoch and refuses to inscribe alien, nonhuman intentions into the genetic program of life histories. If the human race does not continue to follow the kind of thinking oriented to the concepts of freedom, self-determination, and the refusal to be disposed of for other purposes, then it will no longer be what it has been in the past.

Do these arguments deliver what they claim? Can the concept of a "species ethic," understood as a normative self-description of what it means to be human, provide the basis for establishing and maintaining human freedom?

7. Cf. ibid., 44–53.

8. Cf. ibid., 42: "What is so unsettling is the fact that the dividing line between the nature we *are* and the organic equipment we *give* ourselves is being blurred. My perspective in the examination of the current debate over the need to regulate genetic engineering is therefore guided by the question of the meaning, for our own life prospects and for our self-understanding as moral beings, of the proposition that the genetic foundations of our existence should not be disposed over."

9. Cf. ibid., 37–42.

10. Habermas thus holds himself to a fundamental directive of postmodern intellectualism, which Slavoj Zizek, *Die gnadenlose Liebe* (trans. Nikolaus G. Schneider; Frankfurt: Suhrkamp, 2001), 9, so describes: "Another of these unwritten rules has to do with religious convictions. One must act as though one had no faith. If one acknowledges one's own faith openly, it is perceived as something shameless, something that exhibitionists do."

The answer must be in the negative because the insights connected with the concept "species ethic" are by no means unchangeable. When the majority of the species prefers a different ethic from what Habermas would like, then the "species ethic" is likewise changed. The concept of the self-optimizing of humanity is based on the logic of self-determination as the sole and all-controlling factor, which no longer permits any sort of moral boundaries. The logic of (genetic-engineering) progress is not only consistent but unavoidable because it promises an even greater fulfillment of human potential. The "species ethic" as the metalevel need give no ultimate justification for itself and cannot ward off abuses because it is itself subject to changing cultural standards. If the idea that the characteristics of a particular human being may be engineered before birth gains social acceptance, then the postulated "species ethic" is unable to hinder the limitation of human freedom that is involved.

Habermas' inspiring proposal, carried out with religious overtones, is defeated by the fact that once again all the attributes of human being are anchored in the human subjects themselves. But the idea of the inviolable dignity and freedom of human beings cannot be derived from the subjects themselves; they can only be postulated. The fact is that the ultimate grounding of these attributes can be found only in God.

God as Meaningful Ultimate Explanation

The Pauline construction proves itself quite capable of holding its own even in this postmodern world. By anchoring human life in God, he preserves its inherent worth and does not allow any human life to be at the disposable of some "higher" purpose. To put the matter in only slightly exaggerated terms: it not only is theologically valid but also makes philosophical sense to fall back on God as the ultimate authority and the unquestionable guarantor of human freedom. The critique, made by one form of the Enlightenment, that explains religion as entirely a private affair but at the same time tolerates its evaporation as a resource for the life of humanity is inadequate to ward off the powers of postmodernism that destroy every tradition. So long as the idea of God as the guarantor of human reality is allowed to fade out, the idea that human beings cannot be made into objects cannot be established. Where God no longer appears as the one who gives freedom and meaning, human beings must find a new orientation. Humans then unintentionally (or, increasingly, intentionally) step into God's place and realize themselves in the process of active formation, domination, and consumption of the world. The problem with the modern concept of freedom is its anchoring in the individual subject, thought of as without relations to others. Since the Enlightenment, human beings have believed that they are the creators of good and thus the creators of freedom.

In contrast, Paul portrays freedom as the revelation of an alien, powerful, external reality: God. Freedom has an external foundation; it is not located in human beings themselves. Freedom is not one's own individual power to act but the gift granted by God. The "new humanity" must not be constructed and thus manipulated by human beings, for the new humanity has already become reality in Jesus Christ (cf. Gal. 3:26–28). All the attributes that human beings in the postmodern world ascribe to their own subjectivity are anchored by Paul in God: love, freedom, justice, and meaning. Paul thinks in paradoxes; for him, true subjectivity is a gift and not something attained and to which one may appeal. Only God, as the ground of human existence that rests on something outside itself, is able to establish and preserve the freedom and dignity of the human subject. Thus, for Paul, the "for us" of the salvation obtained in Jesus Christ becomes a basic form of his theological grammar. Paul presents human beings with the idea that if they would truly be themselves and truly be free, they must anchor themselves in God.

This understanding of the concept of freedom makes it possible to include ethical dimensions in one's view and to determine the relation of freedom and love. Only a concept of freedom that is not a priori corrupted by one's own interests will not find it necessary to create the conditions of its own realization itself—only such a freedom can uninhibitedly and productively take up the needs of the world about it, and do so in love. Love is the norm of freedom. The person liberated by God and set by God in the sphere of freedom acts by the standard of love. Love perceives other human beings as God's creatures and orients itself to the needs of other people and the world. Freedom does not consist in the power of choice but in a life governed by love. Love is not a limitation on human freedom but its consistent outcome. Within the Christian picture of what it means to be human, love thus becomes the critical principle of judgment to which every action is to be aligned and that is the norm and judge of every action. Christian freedom thus means to be productive for others and not merely for oneself. The outside world is not perceived as the limitation of my own freedom but as the field of operation in which love can be active. Love is not oriented to the consumer principle; it does not perceive the world and humanity as something that must be changed in order to become more perfect. Love, rather, understands that God has equipped this creation with everything that humanity and nature need in order to live. Love refrains from expanding the human ego in order to make it easier to enforce one's own power and create one's own reality. It respects what has "grown" as the gift of God, and is not interested in the "made."

The future of the human species will depend on whether it will again anchor its identity in its origin: in God. Paul was and is the standard-bearer of this conception, and his thought possesses the quality of a lasting symbolic universe because it points to freedom granted as a gift, to righteousness freely conferred, and to love as the ground of all being.

Selected Bibliography

I. Texts

Aland, Barbara, et al., eds. *Novum Testamentum Graece*. 27th ed. Stuttgart: Deutsche Bibelgesellschaft, 1994.

Apuleius. *Metamorphoses*. Translated by John Arthur Hanson. 2 vols. Loeb Classical Library. Cambridge: Harvard University Press, 1989.

Aristotle. *Generation of Animals*. Translated by A. L. Peck. Loeb Classical Library. Cambridge: Harvard University Press, 1943.

———. *History of Animals: Books VII–X*. Translated by D. M. Balme. Loeb Classical Library. Cambridge: Harvard University Press, 1991.

———. *Meteorologica*. Translated by H. D. P. Lee. Loeb Classical Library. Cambridge: Harvard University Press, 1952.

———. *Nicomachean Ethics*. Translated by H. Rackham. Loeb Classical Library. New York: Putnam, 1926.

———. *Nicomachean Ethics*. Translated by W. D. Ross. Great Books 9. Chicago: Encyclopaedia Britannica, 1952.

———. *On Sophistical Refutations; On Coming-to-Be and Passing Away*. Translated by E. S. Forster. Loeb Classical Library. Cambridge: Harvard University Press, 1955.

———. *Politics*. Translated by H. Rackham. Loeb Classical Library. Cambridge: Harvard University Press, 1944.

———. *Politics*. Translated by Benjamin Jowett. Great Books 9. Chicago: Encyclopaedia Britannica, 1952.

Barrett, C. K. *The New Testament Background: Selected Documents*. 2nd ed. London: SPCK, 1987.

Boring, M. Eugene, et al., eds. *Hellenistic Commentary to the New Testament*. Nashville: Abingdon, 1995.

Charlesworth, James H., ed. *The Old Testament Pseudepigrapha*. 2 vols. Garden City: Doubleday, 1983–1985.

Cicero. 28 vols. Loeb Classical Library. Cambridge: Harvard University Press, 1969.

Dio Chrysostom. Translated by J. W. Cohoon and H. L. Crosby. 5 vols. Loeb Classical Library. Cambridge: Harvard University Press, 1932–1951.

Diogenes Laertius. *Lives of Eminent Philosophers*. Translated by R. D. Hicks. 2 vols. Loeb Classical Library. Cambridge: Harvard University Press, 1931, 1972.

Ehrman, Bart D., trans. *The Apostolic Fathers*. 2 vols. Loeb Classical Library. Cambridge: Harvard University Press, 2003.

Epictetus. *The Discourses, as Reported by Arrian*. Translated by W. A. Oldfather. 2 vols. Loeb Classical Library. Cambridge: Harvard University Press, 1928.

Eusebius. *The Ecclesiastical History*. Translated by Kirsopp Lake. 2 vols. Loeb Classical Library. Cambridge: Harvard University Press, 1926.

Herodotus, *The History*, and Thucydides, *The History of the Peloponnesian War*. Translated by George Rawlinson and Richard Crawley. Great Books 5. Chicago: Encyclopaedia Britannica, 1952.

Holmes, Michael W. *Apostolic Fathers*. Grand Rapids: Baker, 1992.

Homer. *Iliad*. Translated by A. T. Murray. 2nd ed. 2 vols. Loeb Classical Library. Cambridge: Harvard University Press, 1999.

———. *Odyssey*. Translated by A. T. Murray. 2 vols. Loeb Classical Library. Cambridge: Harvard University Press, 1995.

Iamblichus. *On the Pythagorean Way of Life*. Translated by John Dillon and Jackson Hershbell. Edited by Hans Dieter Betz and Edward N. O'Neill. Texts and Translations: Graeco-Roman Religion 29/11. Atlanta: Scholars Press, 1991.

Lake, Kirsopp, trans. *The Apostolic Fathers*. Loeb Classical Library. Cambridge: Harvard University Press, 1970.

Lohse, Eduard. *Die Texte aus Qumran*. 4th ed. Darmstadt: Wissenschaftliche Buchgesellschaft, 1986.

Maier, Johann, and Kurt Schubert, eds. *Die Qumran-Essener: Texte der Schriftrollen und Lebensbild der Gemeinde*. Munich: Reinhardt, 1973.

Malherbe, Abraham J. *The Cynic Epistles: A Study Edition*. Society of Biblical Literature Sources for Biblical Study 12. Missoula, MT: Scholars Press, 1977.

Meyer, Marvin W., ed. *The Ancient Mysteries: A Sourcebook*. San Francisco: Harper, 1987.

O'Neill, Edward. *Teles (The Cynic Teacher)*. Texts and Translations: Graeco-Roman Religious Series 11/3. Missoula, Mont.: Scholars Press, 1977.

Philo. Translated by Francis Henry Colson et al. 12 vols. Loeb Classical Library. Cambridge: Harvard University Press and London: Heinemann, 1929–1962.

Plato. *The Dialogues*. Translated by Benjamin Jowett and J. Harward. Great Books 7. Chicago: Encyclopaedia Britannica, 1952.

Plato. *The Republic*. Translated by Paul Shorey. 2 vols. Loeb Classical Library. Cambridge: Harvard University Press, 1943.

Plutarch. *Lives*. Translated by Bernadotte Perrin. 11 vols. Loeb Classical Library. Cambridge: Harvard University Press, 1914–1926.

———. *Moralia*. Translated by F. C. Babbitt. 15 vols. Loeb Classical Library. Cambridge: Harvard University Press, 1914–1926.

Robinson, James M., ed. *Nag Hammadi Library in English*. 3rd ed. San Francisco: Harper & Row, 1988.

Schneemelcher, Wilhelm, ed. *New Testament Apocrypha*. Translated by R. McL. Wilson. 2nd ed. Louisville: Westminster John Knox, 1991.

Seneca. *Moral Essays*. Translated by John W. Basore. 3 vols. Loeb Classical Library. Cambridge: Harvard University, 1917.

———. *Naturales quaestiones*. Translated by Thomas H. Corcoran. 2 vols. Loeb Classical Library. Cambridge: Harvard University Press, 1971.

Seneca the Elder. *Declamations*. Translated by Michael Winterbottom. 2 vols. Loeb Classical Library. Cambridge: Harvard University Press, 1974.

Siegert, Folker, trans. *Drei hellenistisch-jüdische Predigten: Ps.-Philon, "Über Jona," "Über Simson," und "Über die Gottesbezeichnung 'wohltätig verzehrendes Feuer.'"* 2 vols. Wissenschaftliche Untersuchungen zum Neuen Testament 20, 61. Tübingen: Mohr Siebeck, 1980–1992.

Strack, Hermann, and Paul Billerbeck. *Kommentar zum Neuen Testament aus Talmud und Midrasch*. 6 vols. in 7. Munich: Beck, 1924.

Suetonius. Translated by John Carew Rolfe. 2nd ed. 2 vols. Loeb Classical Library. Cambridge: Harvard University Press, 1997.

Tacitus. Translated by M. Hutton et al. 5 vols. Loeb Classical Library. Cambridge: Harvard University Press, 1914–1937.

Vermès, Géza, ed. *The Dead Sea Scrolls in English*. 4th ed. London: Penguin Books, 1995.

Wettstein, Johann, *Neuer Wettstein: Texte zum Neuen Testament aus Griechentum und Hellenismus*. Edited by Georg Strecker et al. Berlin: de Gruyter, 1996–.

Wise, Michael O., et al., eds. *The Dead Sea Scrolls: A New English Translation*. New York: HarperCollins, 1996.

Xenophon. Translated by Carleton L. Brownson et al. 7 vols. Loeb Classical Library. Cambridge: harvard University Press, 1918–1968.

II. Lexica, Dictionaries, Concordances, Reference Works

Aland, Kurt, ed. *Vollständige Konkordanz zum griechischen Neuen Testament.* 3 vols. Berlin: de Gruyter, 1983.

Balz, Horst Robert, and Gerhard Schneider, eds. *Exegetical Dictionary of the New Testament.* Translated by James W. Thompson and John W. Medendorp. 3 vols. Grand Rapids: Eerdmans, 1990–1993.

Balz, Horst Robert, et al., eds. *Theologische Realenzyklopädie.* Berlin: de Gruyter, 1977–.

Bauer, W., F. W. Danker, W. F. Arndt, and F. W. Gingrich. *Greek-English Lexicon of the New Testament and Other Early Christian Literature.* 3d ed. Chicago, 1999.

Betz, Hans Dieter, et al., eds. *Religion in Geschichte und Gegenwart: Handwörterbuch für Theologie und Religionswissenschaft.* 4th ed. Tübingen: Mohr Siebeck, 1998–.

Blass, Friedrich, and A. Debrunner. *A Greek Grammar of the New Testament and Other Early Christian Literature.* Translated by Robert W. Funk. Chicago: University of Chicago Press, 1961.

Botterweck, G. Johannes, and Helmer Ringgren, eds. *Theological Dictionary of the Old Testament.* Translated by John T. Willis, G. W. Bromiley, and David E. Green. Grand Rapids: Eerdmans, 1974–.

Cancik, Hubert, Burkhard Gladigow, and Matthias Laubscher, eds. *Handbuch religionswissenschaftlicher Grundbegriffe.* 5 vols. Stuttgart: Kohlhammer, 1988–2001.

Coenen, L., and K. Haacker, eds. *Theologisches Begriffslexikon zum Neuen Testament.* Rev. ed. Wuppertal: Brockhaus, 1997–.

Fahlbusch, Erwin, et al., eds. *Evangelisches Kirchenlexikon.* 3d ed. Göttingen: Vandenhoeck & Ruprecht, 1985–1997.

Freedman, David Noel, ed. *The Anchor Bible Dictionary.* 6 vols. New York: Doubleday, 1992

Görg, Manfred, and Bernhard Lang, eds. *Neues Bibel-Lexikon.* Zurich: Benziger, 1988–.

Kittel, Gerhard, and Gerhard Friedrich, eds. *Theological Dictionary of the New Testament.* Translated by Geoffrey W. Bromiley. 10 vols. Grand Rapids: Eerdmans, 1964–1976.

Klauser, Theodor, et al., eds. *Reallexikon für Antike und Christentum: Sachwörterbuch zur Auseinandersetzung des Christentums mit der antiken Welt.* Stuttgart: Hiersemann, 1950–

Passow, Franz, et al. *Handwörterbuch der griechischen Sprache.* 2 vols. in 4. 5th ed. Leipzig: Vogel, 1841–1857.

Toorn, K. van der, B. Becking, and P. W. van der Horst, eds. *Dictionary of Deities and Demons in the Bible.* 2nd ed. Leiden: Brill, 1999.

III. Commentaries, Monographs, Essays, Articles

Agersnap, Sören. *Baptism and the New Life: A Study of Romans 6:1–14.* Århus: Aarhus University Press, 1999.

Aland, K., "Die Entstehung des Corpus Paulinum." Pages 302–50 in *Neutestamentliche Entwürfe.* Munich: Kaiser, 1979.

———. "Der Schluß und die ursprüngliche Gestalt des Römerbriefes." Pages 284–381 in *Neutestamentliche Entwürfe.* Munich: Kaiser, 1979.

Alkier, Stefan. *Wunder und Wirklichkeit in den Briefen des Apostels Paulus: Ein Beitrag zu einem Wunderverständnis jenseits von Entmythologisierung und Rehistorisierung.* Wissenschaftliche Untersuchungen zum Neuen Testament 134. Tübingen: Mohr Siebeck, 2001.

Althaus, Paul. *Die Wahrheit des christlichen Osterglaubens.* Beiträge zur Förderung christlicher Theologie. Gütersloh: Bertelsmann, 1940.

Alvarez Cineira, David. *Die Religionspolitik des Kaisers Claudius und die paulinische Mission.* Herders biblische Studien 19. Freiburg: Herder, 1999.

Asher, Jeffrey R. *Polarity and Change in 1 Corinthians 15: A Study of Metaphysics, Rhetoric, and Resurrection.* Hermeneutische Untersuchungen zur Theologie 42. Tübingen: Mohr Siebeck, 2000.

Assmann, Aleida. *Zeit und Tradition: Kulturelle Strategien der Dauer.* Cologne: Böhlau, 1999.

Assmann, Aleida, and Heidrun Friese, eds. *Identities: Time, Difference, and Boundaries.* Making Sense of History 2. New York: Berghahn Books, 2001.

Assmann, Jan. *Ma'at: Gerechtigkeit und Unsterblichkeit im alten Ägypten.* Munich: Beck, 1990.

———. *Das kulturelle Gedächtnis: Schrift, Erinnerung, und politische Identität in frühen Hochkulturen.* Munich: Beck, 1992.

Aune, David E. *Prophecy in Early Christianity and the Ancient Mediterranean World.* Grand Rapids: Eerdmans, 1983.

———. *The New Testament in Its Literary Environment.* Library of Early Christianity 8. Philadelphia: Westminster, 1987.

———. "Romans as a logos protreptikos." Pages 91–124 in *Paulus und das antike Judentum: Tübingen-Durham-Symposium im Gedenken an den 50. Todestag Adolf Schlatters (19 Mai 1938).* Edited by Martin Hengel and Ulrich Heckel. Wissenschaftliche Untersuchungen zum Neuen Testament 58. Tübingen: Mohr Siebeck, 1991.

Avemarie, Friedrich, and Hermann Lichtenberger, eds. *Auferstehung = Resurrection: The Fourth Durham-Tübingen Research Symposium: Resurrection, Transfiguration, and Exaltation in Old Testament, Ancient Judaism, and Early Christianity.* Wissenschaftliche Untersuchungen zum Neuen Testament 135. Tübingen: Mohr Siebeck, 2001.

Bachmann, Michael. *Sünder oder Übertreter: Studien zur Argumentation in Gal. 2,15ff.* WUNT 59, Tübingen 1992.

———. "Rechtfertigung und Gesetzeswerke bei Paulus." *Theologische Zeitschrift* 49 (1993): 1–33.

Backhaus, K. "Evangelium als Lebensraum: Christologie und Ethik bei Paulus." Pages 9–31 in *Paulinische Christologie: Exegetische Beiträge: Hans Hübner zum 70. Geburtstag.* Edited by Udo Schnelle et al. Göttingen: Vandenhoeck & Ruprecht, 2000.

———. "Mitteilhaber des Evangeliums." Pages 44–71 in *Christologie in der Paulus-Schule: Zur Rezeptionsgeschichte des paulinischen Evangeliums.* Edited by Klaus Scholtissek. Stuttgarter Bibelstudien 181. Stuttgart: Katholisches Bibelwerk, 2000.

Badenas, Robert. *Christ the End of the Law: Romans 10.4 in Pauline Perspective.* Journal for the Study of the New Testament: Supplement Series 10. Sheffield: JSOT, 1985.

Baird, William R. "'One against the Other': Intrachurch Conflict in 1 Corinthians." Pages 116–36 in *The Conversation Continues: Studies in Paul and John.* Edited by Robert T. Fortna and Beverly R. Gaventa. Nashville: Abingdon, 1990.

Balch, David L., and Carolyn Osiek. *Families in the New Testament World: Households and House Churches.* Louisville: Westminster John Knox, 1997.

Balz, Horst Robert. *Der Tod Jesu Christi im Verständnis des Neuen Testaments.* Neukirchen-Vluyn: Neukirchener, 1992.

———. "Pistis in hellenistischer Religiosität." Pages 169–94 in *Neutestamentliche Versuche und Beobachtungen.* Edited by Gerhard Barth. Waltrop: Spenner, 1996.

Bammel, E. "Judenverfolgung und Naherwartung." *Zeitschrift für Theologie und Kirche* 56 (1959): 294–315.

Barclay, John M. G. *Obeying the Truth: A Study of Paul's Ethics in Galatians.* Edited by John Kenneth Riches. Studies of the New Testament and Its World. Edinburgh: T&T Clark, 1988.

Barnett, Paul. *The Second Epistle to the Corinthians.* New International Commentary on the New Testament. Grand Rapids: Eerdmans, 1997.

Barr, James. *The Semantics of Biblical Language.* London: Oxford University Press, 1961.

———. *Biblical Words for Time.* Studies in Biblical Theology 33. Naperville, IL: Alec R. Allenson, 1962.

Barrett, C. K. *A Commentary on the Second Epistle to the Corinthians.* Harper's New Testament Commentaries. New York: Harper & Row, 1973.

———. *The New Testament Background: Selected Documents.* 2nd ed. London: SPCK, 1987.

Barth, Gerhard. *Der Brief an die Philipper.* Zurich: Theologischer Verlag, 1979.

———. *Die Taufe in frühchristlicher Zeit.* Biblisch-theologische Studien 4. Neukirchen-Vluyn: Neukirchener Verlag, 1981.

Barth, Karl. *The Doctrine of Creation.* Vol. 3, part 2 of *Church Dogmatics.* Edited by Geoffrey W. Bromiley and T. F. Torrance. Translated by Geoffrey W. Bromiley et al. Edinburgh: T&T Clark, 1960.

Barthes, Roland. *The Semiotic Challenge.* Translated by Richard Howard. New York: Hill & Wang, 1988.

Bauer, Karl-Adolf. *Leiblichkeit, das Ende aller Werke Gottes.* Gütersloh: Gütersloher Verlagshaus, 1971.

Bauer, W. *Die Briefe des Ignatius von Antiochia und der Polykarpbrief.* Edited by H. Paulsen. 2nd ed.

Handbuch zum Neuen Testament 18. Tübingen: Mohr, 1985.

Baumann, Rolf. *Mitte und Norm des Christlichen: Eine Auslegung von 1 Korinther 1, 1–3, 4.* Neutestamentliche Abhundlungen: Neue Folge 5. Münster: Aschendorff, 1968.

Baumgarten, Jörg. *Paulus und die Apokalyptik: Die Auslegung apokalyptischer Überlieferungen in den echten Paulusbriefen.* Wissenschaftliche Monographien zum Alten und Neuen Testament 44. Neukirchen-Vluyn: Neukirchener Verlag, 1975.

Baur, Ferdinand Christian. "Über Zweck und Veranlassung des Römerbriefes und die damit zusammenhängenden Verhältnisse der römischen Gemeinde." Pages 1:147–266 in *Ausgewählte Werke in Einzelausgaben.* 5 vols. Edited by Klaus Scholder. Stuttgart: Frommann, 1963–1975.

Baur, Ferdinand Christian, and Eduard Zeller. *Paul the Apostle of Jesus Christ: His Life and Works, His Epistles and Teachings: A Contribution to a Critical History of Primitive Christianity.* Translated by Allan Menzies. 2nd ed. Theological Translation Fund Library. 2 vols. London: Williams & Norgate, 1873.

Becker, Jürgen. *Das Heil Gottes: Heils- und Sündenbegriffe in den Qumrantexten und im Neuen Testament.* Studien zur Umwelt des Neuen Testaments 3. Göttingen: Vandenhoeck & Ruprecht, 1964.

———. *Auferstehung der Toten im Urchristentum.* Stuttgarter Bibelstudien 82. Stuttgart: KBW, 1976.

———. *Paul: Apostle to the Gentiles.* Translated by O. C. Dean. Louisville: Westminster John Knox, 1993.

Becker, Jürgen, et al. *Die Briefe an die Galater, Epheser, Philipper, Kolosser, Thessalonicher, und Philemon.* 14th ed. Das Neue Testament Deutsch 8. Göttingen: Vandenhoeck & Ruprecht, 1976.

Beker, Johan Christiaan. *Paul the Apostle: The Triumph of God in Life and Thought.* Philadelphia: Fortress, 1980.

———. "Paul's Theology: Consistent or Inconsistent?" *New Testament Studies* 34 (1988): 364–77.

Bendemann, Reinhard von. "Die Auferstehung von den Toten als 'Basic Story.'" *Glaube und Lernen* 15 (2000): 148–62.

———. "'Frühpaulinisch' und/oder 'spätpaulinisch'? Erwägungen zu der These einer Entwicklung der paulinischen Theologie am Beispiel des Gesetzesverständnisses." *Evangelische Theologie* 60 (2000): 210–29.

Berger, Klaus. *Die Gesetzesauslegung Jesu: Ihr historischer Hintergrund im Judentum und im Alten Testament.* Wissenschaftliche Monographien zum Alten und Neuen Testament 40. Neukirchen-Vluyn: Neukirchener Verlag, 1972.

———. *Formgeschichte des Neuen Testaments.* Heidelberg: Quelle & Meyer, 1984.

———. *Theologiegeschichte des Urchristentums: Theologie des Neuen Testaments.* Tübingen: Francke, 1994.

———. *Paulus.* Munich: Beck, 2002.

Berger, Peter L. *The Sacred Canopy: Elements of a Sociological Theory of Religion.* Garden City, NY: Doubleday, 1967.

Berger, Peter L., and Thomas Luckmann. *The Social Construction of Reality: A Treatise in the Sociology of Knowledge.* New York: Random House, 1966.

Betz, Hans Dieter. *Nachfolge und Nachahmung Jesu Christi im Neuen Testament.* Beiträge zur historischen Theologie 37. Tübingen: Mohr Siebeck, 1967.

———. *Der Apostel Paulus und die sokratische Tradition: Eine exegetische Untersuchung zu seiner Apologie 2 Korinther 10–13.* Beiträge zur historischen Theologie 45. Tübingen: Mohr Siebeck, 1972.

———. *Paul's Concept of Freedom in the Context of Hellenistic Discussions about the Possibilities of Human Freedom: Protocol of the Twenty-Sixth Colloquy, 9 January 1977.* Berkeley: The Center, 1977.

———. *Galatians: A Commentary on Paul's Letter to the Churches in Galatia.* Hermeneia: A Critical and Historical Commentary on the Bible. Philadelphia: Fortress, 1979.

———. *2 Corinthians 8 and 9: A Commentary on Two Administrative Letters of the Apostle Paul.* Hermeneia: A Critical and Historical Commentary on the Bible. Philadelphia: Fortress, 1985.

———. *The Greek Magical Papyri in Translation, Including the Demotic Spells.* Chicago: University of Chicago Press, 1986.

————. "Das Problem der Grundlagen der paulinischen Ethik." Pages 184–205 in *Paulinische Studien.* Tübingen: Mohr Siebeck, 1994.

————. "Transferring a Ritual: Paul's Interpretation of Baptism in Romans 6." Pages 84–118 in *Paul in His Hellenistic Context.* Edited by Troels Engberg-Pedersen. Minneapolis: Fortress, 1995.

Beutler, J., ed., *Der neue Mensch in Christus: Hellenistische Anthropologie und Ethik im Neuen Testament.* Quaestiones disputatae 190. Freiburg: Herder, 2001.

Bickmann, Jutta. *Kommunikation gegen den Tod: Studien zur paulinischen Briefpragmatik am Beispiel des ersten Thessalonicherbriefes.* Forschung zur Bibel 86. Würzburg: Echter, 1998.

Bieringer, R., and Jan Lambrecht, eds. *Studies on 2 Corinthians.* Bibliotheca ephemeridum theologicarum lovaniensium 112. Leuven: Leuven University Press, 1994.

Blank, Josef. *Paulus und Jesus: Eine theologische Grundlegung.* Studien zum Alten und Neuen Testament 18. Munich: Kösel, 1968.

Böhlig, H. *Die Geisteskultur von Tarsos im augusteischen Zeitalter mit Berücksichtigung der paulinischen Schriften.* Forschungen zur Religion und Literatur des Alten und Neuen Testaments 19. Göttingen: Vandenhoeck & Ruprecht, 1913.

————. "Das Gewissen bei Seneca und Paulus." *Theologische Studien und Kritiken* 87 (1914): 1–24.

Borgen, Peder. "Observations on the Theme 'Paul and Philo': Paul's Preaching of Circumcision in Galatia (Gal. 5:11) and Debates on Circumcision in Philo." Pages 85–102 in *Die paulinische Literatur und Theologie = The Pauline Literature and Theology: Anlässlich der 50. jährigen Gründungs-Feier der Universität von Aarhus.* Edited by Sigfred Pedersen. Århus: Aros, 1980.

Boring, M. Eugene. *Sayings of the Risen Jesus: Christian Prophecy in the Synoptic Tradition.* Society of New Testament Studies Monograph Series 46. Cambridge: Cambridge University Press, 1982.

————. "The Language of Universal Salvation in Paul." *Journal of Biblical Literature* 105 (1986): 269–92.

————. *The Continuing Voice of Jesus: Christian Prophecy and the Gospel Tradition.* Louisville: Westminster John Knox, 1991.

Boring, M. Eugene, et al., eds. *Hellenistic Commentary to the New Testament.* Nashville: Abingdon, 1995.

Bormann, Lukas. *Philippi: Stadt und Christengemeinde zur Zeit des Paulus.* Leiden: Brill, 1995.

Bormann, C. von, et al. "Denken." Pages 60–102 in vol. 2 of *Historisches Wörterbuch der Philosophie: Völlig neubearbeitete Auflage des "Wörterbuchs der philosophischen Begriffe" von Rudolf Eisler.* Edited by Karlfried Gründer et al. Darmstadt: Wissenschaftliche Buchgesellschaft, 1971–.

Bornkamm, Günther, "Faith and Reason In Paul's Epistles." *New Testament Studies* 4 (1958): 93–100.

————. "Der köstlichere Weg." Pages 93–112 in *Das Ende des Gesetzes: Paulusstudien.* Beiträge zur evangelischen Theologie 16. Munich: Kaiser, 1961.

————. "Die Offenbarung des Zornes Gottes." Pages 9–33 in *Das Ende des Gesetzes: Paulusstudien.* Beiträge zur evangelischen Theologie 16. Munich: Kaiser, 1961.

————. "Die Vorgeschichte des sogenannten Zweiten Korintherbriefes." Pages 162–94 in *Geschichte und Glaube.* Beiträge zur evangelischen Theologie 53. Munich: Kaiser, 1968.

————. "Zum Verständnis des Christus-Hymnus Phil. 2,6–11." Pages 177–87 in *Studien zu Antike und Urchristentum.* 3rd ed. Beiträge zur evangelischen Theologie 28. Munich: Kaiser, 1970.

————. *Paul, Paulus.* Translated by D. M. G. Stalker. New York: Harper & Row, 1971.

————. "The Letter to the Romans as Paul's Last Will and Testament." Pages 16–28 in *The Romans Debate.* Edited by Karl P. Donfried. Rev. and exp. ed. Peabody, MA: Hendrickson, 1991.

Börschel, Regina. *Die Konstruktion einer christlichen Identität: Paulus und die Gemeinde von Thessalonich in ihrer hellenistisch-römischen Umwelt.* Bonner biblische Beiträge 128. Berlin: Philo, 2001.

Borse, Udo. *Der Standort des Galaterbriefes.* Bonner biblische Beiträge 41. Cologne: P. Hanstein, 1972.

————. *Der Brief an die Galater.* Regensburg: Pustet, 1984.

————. *"Tränenbrief" und 1. Korintherbrief.* Edited by Albert Fuchs. Studien zum Neuen Testament und seiner Umwelt 9. Freistadt: Plöchl, 1984.

Botermann, Helga. *Das Judenedikt des Kaisers Claudius: Römischer Staat und Christiani im 1. Jahrhundert.* Hermes: Einzelschriften 71. Stuttgart: Steiner, 1996.

Böttrich, Christfried. "'Ihr seid der Tempel Gottes': Tempelmetaphorik und Gemeinde bei Paulus." Pages 411–25 in *Gemeinde ohne Tempel = Community without Temple: Zur Substituierung und Transformation des Jerusalemer Tempels und seines Kults im Alten Testament, antiken Judentum, und frühen Christentum.* Edited by Beate Ego et al. Wissenschaftliche Untersuchungen zum Neuen Testament 118. Tübingen: Mohr Siebeck, 1999.

———. "'Gott und Retter': Gottesprädikationen in christologischen Titeln." *Neue Zeitschrift für systematische Theologie* 42 (2000): 217–36.

Bousset, Wilhelm. *Kyrios Christos: A History of the Belief in Christ from the Beginnings of Christianity to Irenaeus.* Translated by John E. Steely. Nashville: Abingdon, 1970.

Brandenburger, Egon. *Adam und Christus: Exegetisch-religions-geschichtliche Untersuchung zu Röm. 5, 12–21 (1.Kor 15).* Wissenschaftliche Monographien zum Alten und Neuen Testament 7. Neukirchen: Kreis Moers, 1962.

———. *Fleisch und Geist: Paulus und die dualistische Weisheit.* Wissenschaftliche Monographien zum Alten und Neuen Testament 29. Neukirchen-Vluyn: Neukirchener Verlag des Erziehungsvereins, 1968.

———. *Die Verborgenheit Gottes im Weltgeschehen: Das literarische und theologische Problem des 4. Esrabuches.* Abhandlungen zur Theologie des Alten und Neuen Testaments 68. Zurich: Theologischer Verlag, 1981.

———. "Paulinische Schriftauslegung in der Kontroverse um das Verheißungswort Gottes (Röm 9)." *Zeitschrift für Theologie und Kirche* 82 (1985): 1–47.

———. *Das Böse: Eine biblisch-theologische Studie.* Theologische Studiën 132. Zurich: Theologischer Verlag, 1986.

———. "Pistis und Soteria." Pages 251–88 in *Studien zur Geschichte und Theologie des Urchristentums.* Stuttgarter biblische Aufsatzbände: Neues Testament 15. Stuttgart: Katholisches Bibelwerk, 1993.

Branham, Robert Bracht, and Marie-Odile Goulet-Cazâe, eds. *The Cynics: The Cynic Movement in Antiquity and Its Legacy.* Hellenistic Culture and Society 23. Berkeley: University of California Press, 1996.

Braun, Herbert. "The Problem of a New Testament Theology." Pages 169–83 in *Bultmann School of Biblical Interpretation: New Directions?* Edited by Robert W. Funk. Translated by Irvin W. Batdorf et al. Journal for Theology and the Church 1. New York: Harper & Row, 1965.

———. "The Meaning of New Testament Christology." *Journal for Theology and the Church* 5 (1967): 89–127.

———. *Gesammelte Studien zum Neuen Testament und seiner Umwelt.* 3rd ed. Tübingen: Mohr Siebeck, 1971.

Breytenbach, Cilliers. *Versöhnung: Eine Studie zur paulinischen Soteriologie.* Wissenschaftliche Monographien zum Alten und Neuen Testament 60. Neukirchen-Vluyn: Neukirchener Verlag, 1989.

———. "Paul's Proclamation and God's 'Thriambos': Notes on 2 Corinthians 2:14–16b." *Neotestamentica* 24 (1990): 257–71.

———. "Gnädigstimmen und opferkultische Sühne im Urchristentum und seiner Umwelt." Pages 217–43 in *Opfer: Theologische und kulturelle Kontexte.* Edited by Bernd Janowski and Michael Welker. 1st ed. Frankfurt: Suhrkamp, 2000.

———. "Versöhnung, Stellvertretung, und Sühne." *New Testament Studies* 39 (1993): 59–79.

———. *Paulus und Barnabas in der Provinz Galatien: Studien zu Apostelgeschichte 13f.; 16,6; 18,23 und den Adressaten des Galaterbriefes.* Arbeiten zur Geschichte des antiken Judentums und des Urchristentums 38. Leiden: Brill, 1996.

Brockhaus, Ulrich. *Charisma und Amt: Die paulinische Charismenlehre auf dem Hintergrund der frühchristlichen Gemeindefunktionen.* Wuppertal: Brockhaus, 1972.

Broer, J. "'Antisemitismus' und Judenpolemik im Neuen Testament: Ein Beitrag zum besseren Verständnis von 1.Thess. 2,14–16." Pages 734–72 in *Religion und Verantwortung als Elemente gesellschaftlicher Ordnung: Für Karl Klein zum 70. Geburtstage.* Edited by Bodo B. Gemper. 2nd ed. Siegen: Vorländer, 1983.

Brown, Raymond E. *An Introduction to the New Testament.* Anchor Bible Reference Library. New York: Doubleday, 1997.

Buck, C. H., and Greer Taylor. *Saint Paul: A Study of the Development of His Thought.* New York: Scribner, 1969.

Bultmann, Rudolf. *Glauben und Verstehen: Gesammelte Aufsätze.* 4 vols. Tübingen: Mohr Siebeck, 1933–.

———. *Theology of the New Testament.* Translated by Kendrick Grobel. 2 vols. New York: Scribner, 1951.

———. "The Primitive Christian Kerygma and the Historical Jesus." Pages 15–42 in *The Historical Jesus and the Kerygmatic Christ: Essays on the New Quest of the Historical Jesus.* Edited and translated by Carl E. Braaten and Roy A. Harrisville. Nashville: Abingdon, 1964.

———. *Exegetica: Aufsätze zur Erforschung des Neuen Testaments.* Edited by Erich Dinkler. Tübingen: Mohr Siebeck, 1967.

———. "Ist die Apokalyptik die Mutter der christlichen Theologie?" Pages 476–82 in *Exegetica: Aufsätze zur Erforschung des Neuen Testaments.*

———. "Das Problem der Ethik bei Paulus." Pages 36–54 in *Exegetica: Aufsätze zur Erforschung des Neuen Testaments.* Edited by Erich Dinkler. Tubingen: Mohr, 1967.

———. *Faith and Understanding.* Edited by Robert W. Funk. Translated by Louise Pettibone Smith. London: SCM Press, 1969.

———. "Paul." Pages 169–214 in *Themes of Biblical Theology.* Edited by Jaroslav Pelikan. Twentieth Century Theology in the Making 1. New York: Harper & Row, 1969. Reprinted from *Existence and Faith: Shorter Writings of Rudolf Bultmann* (translated by Schubert M. Ogden; New York: Meridian, 1960), 130–72. = "Paulus," RGG² 1019–45.

———. *The Second Letter to the Corinthians.* Edited by Erich Dinkler. Translated by Roy A. Harrisville. Minneapolis: Augsburg, 1985.

Burchard, Christoph. *Der dreizehnte Zeuge: Traditions- und kompositionsgeschichtliche Untersuchungen zu Lukas' Darstellung der Frühzeit des Paulus.* Forschungen zur Religion und Literatur des Alten und Neuen Testaments 103. Göttingen: Vandenhoeck & Ruprecht, 1970.

———. "Nicht aus Werken des Gesetzes gerecht, sondern aus Glaube an Jesus Christus—seit wann?" Pages 230–40 in Christoph Burchard, *Studien zur Theologie, Sprache, und Umwelt des Neuen Testaments.* Edited by Dieter Sänger. Wissenschaftliche Untersuchungen zum Neuen Testament 107. Tübingen: Mohr Siebeck, 1998.

Burfeind, C. "Paulus *muß* nach Rom." *New Testament Studies* 46 (2000): 75–91.

Burkert, Walter. *Ancient Mystery Cults.* Cambridge: Harvard University Press, 1987.

Bussmann, Claus. *Themen der paulinischen Missionspredigt auf dem Hintergrund der spätjüdisch-hellenistischen Missionsliteratur.* Europäische Hochschulschriften, Reihe 23, Theologie 3. Bern: Lang, 1971.

Cadbury, Henry J. *The Book of Acts in History.* New York: Harper, 1955.

Capes, David B. *Old Testament Yahweh Texts in Paul's Christology.* Wissenschaftliche Untersuchungen zum Neuen Testament 2/47. Tübingen: Mohr Siebeck, 1992.

Carson, D. A., et al., eds., *Justification and Variegated Nomism.* 2 vols. Wissenschaftliche Untersuchungen zum Neuen Testament 2/140, 181. Grand Rapids: Baker Academic, 2001–2004. Vol. 1.

Chow, J. K. "Patronage in Roman Corinth." Pages 104–25 in *Paul and Empire: Religion and Power in Roman Imperial Society.* Edited by Richard A. Horsley. Harrisburg, PA: Trinity Press International, 1997.

Christ, Karl. *Geschichte der römischen Kaiserzeit: Von Augustus bis zu Konstantin.* Munich: Beck, 1988.

Church, F. F. "Rhetorical Structure and Design in Paul's Letter to Philemon." *Harvard Theological Review* 71 (1978): 17–33.

Classen, C. J. "Paulus und die antike Rhetorik." *Zeitschrift für die neutestamentliche Wissenschaft und die Kunde der älteren Kirche* 82 (1991): 1–33.

———. "Philologische Bemerkungen zur Sprache des Apostels Paulus." *Wiener Studien* 107–8 (1994–1995): 321–35.

Clauss, Manfred. *Kaiser und Gott: Herrscherkult im römischen Reich.* Stuttgart: Teubner, 1999.

Clemen, Carl. *Paulus: Sein Leben und Wirken.* 2 vols. Giessen: J. Ricker, 1904.

Cohen, Shaye J. D. *From the Maccabees to the Mishnah.* Philadelphia: Westminster, 1987.

Collins, Adela Yarbro. *Crisis and Catharsis: The Power of the Apocalypse.* Philadelphia: Westminster, 1984.

Collins, Raymond F. *Studies on the First Letter to the Thessalonians*. Bibliotheca ephemeridum theologicarum lovaniensium 66. Leuven: Leuven University Press, 1984.

———, ed. *The Thessalonian Correspondence*, Bibliotheca ephemeridum theologicarum lovaniensium 87. Leuven: Leuven University Press, 1990.

Conzelmann, Hans. "On the Analysis of the Confessional Formula in 1 Corinthians 15:3–5." *Interpretation* 20 (1966): 15–25.

———. *An Outline of the Theology of the New Testament*. Translated by John Bowden. New York: Harper & Row, 1969.

———. *History of Primitive Christianity*. Translated by John E. Steely. Nashville: Abingdon, 1973.

———. "Paulus und die Weisheit." Pages 177–90 in *Theologie als Schriftauslegung: Aufsätze zum Neuen Testament*. Beiträge zur evangelischen Theologie 65. Munich: Kaiser, 1974.

———. *1 Corinthians: A Commentary on the First Epistle to the Corinthians*. Translated by James W. Leitch. Hermeneia: A Critical and Historical Commentary on the Bible. Philadelphia: Fortress, 1975.

———. "Die Schule des Paulus." Pages 85–96 in *Theologia crucis, signum crucis: Festschrift für Erich Dinkler zum 70. Geburtstag*. Edited by Carl Andresen and Günter Klein. Tübingen: Mohr Siebeck, 1979.

———. *Acts of the Apostles: A Commentary on the Acts of the Apostles*. Translated by James Limburg et al. Hermeneia: A Critical and Historical Commentary on the Bible. Philadelphia: Fortress, 1987.

———. *Gentiles, Jews, Christians: Polemics and Apologetics in the Greco-Roman Era*. Translated by M. Eugene Boring. Minneapolis: Fortress, 1992.

Cranfield, C. E. B. *The Epistle to the Romans*. 2 vols. International Critical Commentary. Edinburgh: T&T Clark, 1979.

Cumont, Franz. *The Oriental Religions in Roman Paganism*. Chicago: Open Court, 1911.

Dahl, Nils A. *Das Volk Gottes*. 2nd ed. Darmstadt: Wissenschaftliche Buchgesellschaft, 1963.

Dahl, Nils A., and David Hellholm. "Garment-Metaphors: The Old and the New Human Being." Pages 139–58 in *Antiquity and Humanity: Essays on Ancient Religion and Philosophy Presented to Hans Dieter Betz on His 70th Birthday*. Edited by Adela Yarbro Collins and Margaret Mary Mitchell. Tübingen: Mohr Siebeck, 2001.

Dauer, Anton. *Paulus und die christliche Gemeinde im syrischen Antiochia: Kritische Bestandsaufnahme der modernen Forschung mit einigen weiterführenden Überlegungen*. Weinheim: Beltz Athenäum, 1996.

Dautzenberg, Gerhard, *Urchristliche Prophetie: Ihre Erforschung, ihre Voraussetzungen im Judentum, und ihre Struktur im ersten Korintherbrief*. Beiträge zur Wissenschaft vom Alten (und Neuen) Testament. Stuttgart: Kohlhammer, 1975.

———. "Freiheit im hellenistischen Kontext." Pages 57–81 in *Der neue Mensch in Christus: Hellenistische Anthropologie und Ethik im Neuen Testament*. Edited by Johannes Beutler. Quaestiones disputatae 190. Freiburg: Herder, 2001.

———. *Studien zur paulinischen Theologie und zur frühchristlichen Rezeption des Alten Testaments*. Edited by Dieter Sänger. Giessen: Verlag der theologischen Fakultät, 1999.

Deissmann, Adolf. *Die neutestamentliche Formel "in Christo Jesu."* Marburg: N. G. Elwert, 1892.

———. *Light from the Ancient East: The New Testament Illustrated by Recently Discovered Texts of the Graeco-Roman World*. Translated by Lionel R. M. Strachan. New York: Doran, 1927.

———. *Paul: A Study in Social and Religious History*. Translated by William E. Wilson. New York: Harper, 1957.

Delling, Gerhard. *Das Zeitverständnis des Neuen Testaments*. Gütersloh: Bertelsmann, 1940.

———. *Die Bewältigung der Diasporasituation durch das hellenistische Judentum*. Göttingen: Vandenhoeck & Ruprecht, 1987.

Deming, Will. *Paul on Marriage and Celibacy: The Hellenistic Background of 1 Corinthians 7*. 2nd ed. Grand Rapids: Eerdmans, 2003.

Demke, Christoph. "'Ein Gott und viele Herren': Die Verkündigung des einen Gottes in den Briefen des Paulus." *Evangelische Theologie* 36 (1976): 473–84.

Dettwiler, Andreas, and Jean Zumstein, eds., *Kreuzestheologie im Neuen Testament*, Wissenschaftliche Untersuchungen zum Neuen Testament 151. Tübingen: Mohr Siebeck, 2002.

Dibelius, Martin. *An die Thessalonicher I, II*. 3rd ed. Tübingen: Mohr Siebeck, 1937.

———. *Paul.* Edited by W. G. Kümmel. Translated by Frank Clarke. Philadelphia: Westminster, 1953.

Dibelius, Martin, and Heinrich Greeven. *An die Kolosser, Epheser, an Philemon.* 3rd ed. Handbuch zum Neuen Testament 12. Tübingen: Mohr Siebeck, 1953.

Dietzfelbinger, Christian. *Die Berufung des Paulus als Ursprung seiner Theologie.* Wissenschaftliche Monographien zum Alten und Neuen Testament 58. Neukirchen-Vluyn: Neukirchener Verlag, 1985.

Dinkler, Erich. "Der Brief an die Galater." Pages 270–82 in *Signum crucis: Aufsätze zum Neuen Testament und zur christlichen Archäologie.* Tübingen: Mohr Siebeck, 1967.

———. "Zum Problem der Ethik bei Paulus." Pages 204–40 in *Signum crucis: Aufsätze zum Neuen Testament und zur christlichen Archäologie.* Tübingen: Mohr Siebeck, 1967.

———. "Römer 6, 1–14 und das Verhältnis von Taufe und Rechtfertigung bei Paulus." *Battesimo e giustizia in Rom 6 e 8.* Edited by Michel Bouttier and Lorenzo De Lorenzi. Serie monographica di Benedictina: Sezione biblico-ecumenica 2. Rome: Abbazia S. Paolo fuori le mura, 1974.

Dobbeler, Axel von. *Glaube als Teilhabe: Historische und semantische Grundlagen der paulinischen Theologie und Ekklesiologie des Glaubens.* Wissenschaftliche Untersuchungen zum Neuen Testament 22. Tübingen: Mohr Siebeck, 1987.

Dodd, C. H. "The Mind of Paul II." Pages 85–108 in *New Testament Studies.* New York: Scribner, 1954. Reprint, Manchester: Manchester University Press, 1966, "with minor corrections." Pages here refer to the 1966 edition.

———. *New Testament Studies.* New York: Scribner, 1954.

Donfried, Karl P. "Cults of Thessalonica and the Thessalonian Correspondence." *New Testament Studies* 31 (1985): 336–56.

———, ed. *The Romans Debate.* Rev. and exp. ed. Peabody, MA: Hendrickson, 1991.

Donfried, Karl P., and I. H. Marshall. *The Theology of the Shorter Pauline Letters.* Cambridge: Cambridge University Press, 1993.

Donfried, Karl P., and Peter Richardson, eds. *Judaism and Christianity in First-Century Rome.* Grand Rapids: Eerdmans, 1998.

Downing, Francis Gerald. "A Cynic Preparation for Paul's Gospel for Jew and Greek, Slave and Free, Male and Female." *New Testament Studies* 42 (1996): 454–62.

———. *Cynics, Paul, and the Pauline Churches: Cynics and Christian Origins II.* London: Routledge, 1998.

Drane, John William. *Paul, Libertine or Legalist? A Study in the Theology of the Major Pauline Epistles.* London: SPCK, 1975.

Droysen, Johann Gustav. *Historik: Rekonstruktion der ersten vollständigen Fassung der Vorlesungen.* Edited by Peter Leyh. Stuttgart–Bad Cannstatt: Frommann-Holzboog, 1857. Reprint, 1977.

———. *Outline of the Principles of History.* Translated by E. Benjamin Andrews. New York: Fertig, 1893. Reprint, 1967.

Dudley, Donald Reynolds. *A History of Cynicism: From Diogenes to the 6th Century A.D.* London: Methuen, 1937. Reprint, Hildesheim: G. Olms, 1967.

Dunn, James D. G. *Romans.* 2 vols. Word Bible Commentary 38A–B. Dallas: Word Books, 1988.

———. *Jesus, Paul, and the Law: Studies in Mark and Galatians.* Louisville: Westminster John Knox, 1990.

———. *A Commentary on the Epistle to the Galatians.* Black's New Testament Commentaries. London: A. & C. Black, 1993.

———. "Paul: Apostate or Apostle of Israel?" *Zeitschrift für die neutestamentliche Wissenschaft und die Kunde der älteren Kirche* 89 (1998): 256–71.

———. *The Theology of Paul the Apostle.* Grand Rapids: Eerdmans, 1998.

———, ed. *Paul and the Mosaic Law.* Wissenschaftliche Untersuchungen zum Neuen Testament 89. Tübingen: Mohr-Siebeck, 1996.

Dux, Günter. "Wie der Sinn in die Welt kam und was aus ihm wurde." Pages 195–217 in *Historische Sinnbildung: Problemstellungen, Zeitkonzepte, Wahrnehmungshorizonte, Darstellungsstrategien.* Edited by Klaus E. Müller and Jörn Rüsen. Reinbek bei Hamburg: Rowohlt, 1997.

———. *Historisch-genetische Theorie der Kultur: Instabile Welten: Zur prozessualen Logik im kulturellen Wandel.* Weilerswist: Velbrück Wissenschaft, 2000.

Ebner, Martin. *Leidenslisten und Apostelbrief: Untersuchungen zu Form, Motivik, und Funktion der Peristasenkataloge bei Paulus.* Forschung zur Bibel 66. Würzburg: Echter, 1991.

Eckert, Jost. *Die urchristliche Verkündigung im Streit zwischen Paulus und seinen Gegnern nach dem Galaterbrief.* Regensburg: Pustet, 1971.

———. "Christus als 'Bild Gottes' und die Gottebenbildlichkeit des Menschen in der paulinischen Theologie." Pages 337–357 in *Vom Urchristentum zu Jesus: Für Joachim Gnilka.* Edited by Hubert Frankemölle and Karl Kertelge. Freiburg: Herder, 1989.

Eckstein, Hans-Joachim. *Der Begriff Syneidesis bei Paulus: Eine neutestamentlich-exegetische Untersuchung zum "Gewissensbegriff."* Wissenschaftliche Untersuchungen zum Neuen Testament 2/10. Tübingen: Mohr Siebeck, 1983.

———. *Verheissung und Gesetz: Eine exegetische Untersuchung zu Galater 2,15–4,7.* Wissenschaftliche Untersuchungen zum Neuen Testament 86. Tübingen: Mohr Siebeck, 1996.

———. "Auferstehung und gegenwärtiges Leben." *Theologische Beiträge* 28 (1997): 8–23.

Eichholz, Georg. *Die Theologie des Paulus im Umriss.* 2nd ed. Neukirchen: Neukirchener Verlag, 1977.

Elliger, Winfried. *Ephesos: Geschichte einer antiken Weltstadt.* Stuttgart: Kohlhammer, 1985.

———. *Paulus in Griechenland: Philippi, Thessaloniki, Athen, Korinth.* Stuttgart: Katholisches Bibelwerk, 1987.

Elliott, N. "Romans 13:1–7 in the Context of Imperial Propaganda." Pages 184–204 in *Paul and Empire: Religion and Power in Roman Imperial Society.* Edited by Richard A. Horsley. Harrisburg, PA: Trinity Press International, 1997.

Ellis, E. Earle. *Paul's Use of the Old Testament.* Edinburgh: Oliver & Boyd, 1957.

Engberg-Pedersen, Troels, ed. *Paul in His Hellenistic Context.* Minneapolis: Fortress, 1995.

Erlemann, Kurt. *Endzeiterwartungen im frühen Christentum.* Tübingen: Francke, 1996.

Evans, Craig A., and James A. Sanders, eds. *Paul and the Scriptures of Israel.* Journal for the Study of the New Testament: Supplement Series 83. Sheffield: JSOT Press, 1993.

Falk, D. "Psalms and Prayers." Pages 7–56 in vol. 1 of *Justification and Variegated Nomism.* Edited by

D. A. Carson et al. 2 vols. Wissenschaftliche Untersuchungen zum Neuen Testament 2/140, 181. Grand Rapids: Baker Academic, 2001–2004.

Fee, Gordon D. *The First Epistle to the Corinthians.* New International Commentary on the New Testament. Grand Rapids: Eerdmans, 1987.

———. "Toward a Theology of 1 Corinthians." Pages 37–58 in *1 and 2 Corinthians.* Edited by David M. Hay. Vol. 2 of *Pauline Theology.* Society of Biblical Literature Symposium Series 22. Minneapolis: Fortress, 1991.

———. *God's Empowering Presence: The Holy Spirit in the Letters of Paul.* Peabody, MA: Hendrickson, 1994.

———. *Paul's Letter to the Philippians.* New International Commentary on the New Testament. Grand Rapids: Eerdmans, 1995.

Finegan, Jack. *Handbook of Biblical Chronology: Principles of Time Reckoning in the Ancient World and Problems of Chronology in the Bible.* Rev. ed. Peabody, MA: Hendrickson, 1998.

Finsterbusch, Karin. *Die Thora als Lebensweisung für Heidenchristen: Studien zur Bedeutung der Thora für die paulinische Ethik.* Studien zur Umwelt des Neuen Testaments 20. Göttingen: Vandenhoeck & Ruprecht, 1996.

Fischer, Karl Martin. *Tendenz und Absicht des Epheserbriefes.* Forschungen zur Religion und Literatur des Alten und Neuen Testaments 111. Göttingen: Vandenhoeck & Ruprecht, 1973.

———. *Das Ostergeschehen.* 2nd ed. Göttingen: Vandenhoeck & Ruprecht, 1980.

Fitzmyer, Joseph A. "Qumran and the Interpolated Paragraph in 2 Cor. 6:14–7:1." Pages 205–20 in *Essays on the Semitic Background of the New Testament.* Missoula, MT: Scholars Press, 1974.

———. "The Semitic Background of the New Testament *kyrios*-Title." Pages 115–42 in *A Wandering Aramean: Collected Aramaic Essays.* Society of Biblical Literature Monograph Series 25. Missoula, MT: Scholars Press, 1979.

———. "The 'Son of God' Document from Qumran." *Biblica* 74 (1993): 153–74.

———. "Paul and the Dead Sea Scrolls." Pages 599–621 in vol. 2 of *The Dead Sea Scrolls after Fifty Years: A Comprehensive Assessment.* Edited by Peter W. Flint and James C. VanderKam. 3 vols. Leiden: Brill, 1998.

————. *The Letter to Philemon: A New Translation with Introduction and Commentary.* Anchor Bible 32C. New York: Doubleday, 2000.

Fossum, J. E. *The Name of God and the Angel of the Lord.* Wissenschaftliche Untersuchungen zum Neuen Testament 36. Tübingen: Mohr Siebeck, 1985.

Forbes, Christopher. "Comparison, Self-Praise, and Irony: Paul's Boasting and the Conventions of Hellenistic Rhetoric." *New Testament Studies* 32 (1986): 1–30.

Friedlaender, Ludwig, and Georg Wissowa. *Sittengeschichte Roms.* Vienna: Phaidon, 1919.

Friedrich, Gerhard. *Auf das Wort kommt es an: Gesammelte Aufsätze zum 70. Geburtstag.* Edited by Johannes H. Friedrich. Göttingen: Vandenhoeck & Ruprecht, 1978.

————. "Glaube und Verkündigung bei Paulus." Pages 93–113 in *Glaube im Neuen Testament: Studien zu Ehren von Hermann Binder anlässlich seines 70. Geburtstags.* Edited by Ferdinand Hahn and Hans Klein. Biblisch-theologische Studien 7. Neukirchen-Vluyn: Neukirchener Verlag, 1982.

————. *Die Verkündigung des Todes Jesu im Neuen Testament.* Biblisch-theologische Studien 6. Neukirchen-Vluyn: Neukirchener Verlag, 1982.

Friedrich, Johannes, et al. "Zur historischen Situation und Intention von Röm 13,1–7." *Zeitschrift für Theologie und Kirche* 73 (1976): 131–66.

Furnish, Victor Paul. *II Corinthians.* Anchor Bible. Garden City, NY: Doubleday, 1984.

————. "Theology in 1 Corinthians." Pages 59–89 in *1 and 2 Corinthians.* Edited by David M. Hay. Vol. 2 of *Pauline Theology.* Society of Biblical Literature Symposium Series 22. Minneapolis: Fortress, 1991.

Gager, John G. *Kingdom and Community: The Social World of Early Christianity.* Englewood Cliffs, NJ: Prentice-Hall, 1975.

Garnsey, P., and R. Saller. "Patronal Power Relations." Pages 96–103 in *Paul and Empire: Religion and Power in Roman Imperial Society.* Edited by Richard A. Horsley. Harrisburg, PA: Trinity Press International, 1997.

Gäumann, Niklaus. *Taufe und Ethik: Studien zu Römer 6.* Beiträge zur evangelischen Theologie 47. Munich: Kaiser, 1967.

Gebauer, Roland. *Das Gebet bei Paulus: Forschungsgeschichtliche und exegetische Studien.* Giessen: Brunnen, 1989.

Geertz, Clifford. "Thick Description: Toward an Interpretive Theory of Culture." Pages 3–30 in *The Interpretation of Cultures: Selected Essays.* New York: Basic Books, 1973.

Gehring, Roger W. *House Church and Mission: The Importance of Household Structures in Early Christianity.* Peabody, Mass.: Hendrickson, 2004.

Gehrke, Hans-Joachim. *Geschichte des Hellenismus.* 2nd ed. Oldenbourg Grundriss der Geschichte 1A. Munich: Oldenbourg, 1995.

Georgi, Dieter. *The Opponents of Paul in Second Corinthians.* Philadelphia: Fortress, 1986.

————. *Remembering the Poor: The History of Paul's Collection for Jerusalem.* Nashville: Abingdon, 1992.

Giebel, M. *Reisen in der Antike.* Düsseldorf: Artemis & Winkler, 1999.

————, ed. *Das Orakel von Delphi: Geschichte und Texte.* Stuttgart: Reclam, 2001.

Gill, W. J. "Corinth: A Roman Colony in Achaea." *Biblische Zeitschrift* 37 (1993): 259–64.

Gnilka, Joachim. *Der Philipperbrief.* 3rd ed. Herders theologischer Kommentar zum Neuen Testament 10/3. Freiburg: Herder, 1980.

————. *Der Philemonbrief.* Herders theologischer Kommentar zum Neuen Testament 10/4. Freiburg: Herder, 1982.

————. "Die Kollekte der paulinischen Gemeinden für Jerusalem als Ausdruck ekklesialer Gemeinschaft." Pages 301–15 in *Ekklesiologie des Neuen Testaments: Für Karl Kertelge.* Edited by Rainer Kampling and Thomas Söding. Freiburg: Herder, 1996.

————. *Paulus von Tarsus, Apostel und Zeuge.* Herders theologischer Kommentar zum Neuen Testament 6. Freiburg: Herder, 1996.

Goertz, Hans-Jürgen. *Umgang mit Geschichte: Eine Einführung in die Geschichtstheorie.* Reinbek: Rowohlt, 1995.

————. *Unsichere Geschichte: Zur Theorie historischer Referentialität.* Stuttgart: Reclam, 2001.

Goldhahn-Müller, Ingrid. *Die Grenze der Gemeinde: Studien zum Problem der Zweiten Busse in Neuen Testament unter Berücksichtigung der Entwicklung im 2. Jh. bis Tertullian.* Göttinger theologische Arbeiten 39. Göttingen: Vandenhoeck & Ruprecht, 1989.

Goodman, Martin. *Mission and Conversion: Pros-elytizing in the Religious History of the Roman Empire.* Oxford: Clarendon, 1994.

Goppelt, Leonhard. *Typos: The Typological Interpreta-tion of the Old Testament in the New.* Translated by Donald H. Madvig. Grand Rapids: Eerdmans, 1982.

Grass, Hans. *Ostergeschehen und Osterberichte.* 2nd ed. Göttingen: Vandenhoeck & Ruprecht, 1961.

Grässer, Erich. *Der Alte Bund im Neuen: Exeget-ische Studien zur Israelfrage im Neuen Testament.* Tübingen: Mohr Siebeck, 1985.

———. *Der zweite Brief an die Korinther.* Gütersloh: Gütersloher Verlagshaus, 2002.

Grundmann, Walter. "Überlieferung und Eigen-aussage im eschatologischen Denken des Paulus." *New Testament Studies* 8 (1961): 12–26.

Gülzow, Henneke. *Christentum und Sklaverei in den ersten drei Jahrhunderten.* Ausgewählte Werke 2. Edited by Bärbel Dauber et al. Hamburg: LIT, 1999.

———. *Kirchengeschichte und Gegenwart: Studien, Aufsätze, Predigten, Meditationen.* Ausgewählte Werke 2. Edited by Bärbel Dauber. Hamburg: LIT, 1999.

Gundry, Robert Horton. *Soma in Biblical Theology: With Emphasis on Pauline Anthropology.* Society of New Testament Studies Monograph Series 29. Cambridge: Cambridge University Press, 1976.

Gutbrod, Walter. *Die paulinische Anthropologie.* Bei-träge zur Wissenschaft vom Alten (und Neuen) Testament 67. Stuttgart: Kohlhammer, 1934.

Güttgemanns, Erhardt. *Der leidende Apostel und sein Herr: Studien zur paulinischen Christologie.* Göt-tingen: Vandenhoeck & Ruprecht, 1966.

Haacker, Klaus. "Die Berufung des Verfolgers und die Rechtfertigung des Gottlosen." *Theologische Beiträge* 6 (1975): 1–19.

———. "Der Römerbrief als Friedensmemo-randum." *New Testament Studies* 36 (1990): 25–41.

———. "Zum Werdegang des Apostels Paulus." Pages 815–938 in *Aufstieg und Niedergang der römischen Welt.* Part 2. *Principat,* 26.2. Edited by Hildegard Temporini and Wolfgang Haase. Berlin: de Gruyter, 1995.

———. "Der 'Antinomismus' des Paulus im Kon-text antiker Gesetzestheorie." Pages 387–404 in *Geschichte–Tradition–Reflexion: Festschrift für Martin Hengel zum 70. Geburtstag.* Edited by Hubert Cancik et al. Tübingen: Mohr Siebeck, 1996.

———. *Der Brief des Paulus an die Römer.* Theolo-gischer Handkommentar zum Neuen Testament 6. Leipzig: Evangelische Verlagsanstalt, 1999.

Habermas, Jürgen. *The Future of Human Nature.* Cambridge: Polity, 2003.

Haenchen, Ernst. *The Acts of the Apostles: A Com-mentary.* Philadelphia: Westminster, 1971.

Hafemann, Scott J. *Paul, Moses, and the History of Israel: The Letter/Spirit Contrast and the Argument from Scripture in 2 Corinthians 3.* Wissenschaftli-che Untersuchungen zum Neuen Testament 81. Tübingen: Mohr Siebeck, 1995.

Hager, Fritz-Peter. *Gott und das Böse im antiken Platonismus.* Würzburg: Königshausen & Neu-mann, 1987.

Hahn, Ferdinand. *The Titles of Jesus in Christology: Their History in Early Christianity.* Translated by Harold Knight and George Ogg. New York: World, 1969.

———. "Das Gesetzesverständnis im Römer- und Galaterbrief." *Zeitschrift für die neutestamentliche Wissenschaft und die Kunde der älteren Kirche* 67 (1976): 29–63.

———. "Gibt es eine Entwicklung in den Aussagen über die Rechtfertigung bei Paulus?" *Evangelische Theologie* 53 (1976): 342–66.

———. "Taufe und Rechtfertigung." Pages 95–124 in *Rechtfertigung: Festschrift für Ernst Käsemann zum 70. Geburtstag.* Edited by Johannes Fried-rich et al. Göttingen: Vandenhoeck & Ruprecht, 1976.

———. "Zum Verständnis von Röm 11,26a." Pages 221–36 in *Paul and Paulinism: Essays in Honour of C. K. Barrett.* Edited by Morna Dorothy Hooker and S. G. Wilson. London: SPCK, 1982.

———. *Exegetische Beiträge zum ökumenischen Gespräch.* Göttingen: Vandenhoeck & Rupre-cht, 1986.

Halter, Hans. *Taufe und Ethos: Paulinische Kriterien für das Proprium christliches Moral.* Freiburg: Herder, 1977.

Hanson, Anthony Tyrrell. *Studies in Paul's Technique and Theology.* London: SPCK, 1974.

———. *The New Testament Interpretation of Scripture*. London: SPCK, 1980.

Harnack, Adolf von. *What Is Christianity?* Translated by Thomas Bailey Saunders. New York: Harper & Row, 1900. Reprint, 1957.

———. *The Mission and Expansion of Christianity in the First Three Centuries*. Translated by James Moffatt. 2nd ed. New York: Putnam, 1908.

———. *Das Alte Testament in den paulinischen Briefen und in den paulinischen Gemeinden*. Sitzungsberichte der Preussischen Akademie der Wissenschaften: Philosophisch-historische Klasse 12. Berlin: Reimer, 1928.

Harnisch, Wolfgang. *Eschatologische Existenz: Ein exegetischer Beitrag zum Sachanliegen von 1. Thessalonicher 4, 13–5, 11*. Forschungen zur Religion und Literatur des Alten und Neuen Testaments 110. Göttingen: Vandenhoeck & Ruprecht, 1973.

———. "Einübung des neuen Seins: Paulinische Paränese am Beispiel des Galaterbriefes." Pages 149–68 in *Die Zumutung der Liebe: Gesammelte Aufsätze*. Edited by Ulrich Schoenborn. Forschungen zur Religion und Literatur des Alten und Neuen Testaments 187. Göttingen: Vandenhoeck & Ruprecht, 1999.

Harrill, James Albert. *The Manumission of Slaves in Early Christianity*. 2nd ed. Hermeneutische Untersuchungen zur Theologie 32. Tübingen: Mohr Siebeck, 1998.

Haufe, Günter. *Der erste Brief des Paulus an die Thessalonicher*. Theologischer Handkommentar zum Neuen Testament 12/1. Leipzig: Evangelische Verlagsanstalt, 1999.

Hay, David M. "Philo's References to Other Allegorists." *Studia philonica* 6 (1979–1980): 41–75.

———, ed. *1 and 2 Corinthians*. Vol. 2 of *Pauline Theology*. Society of Biblical Literature Symposium Series 22. Minneapolis: Fortress, 1991.

Hays, Richard B. *Echoes of Scripture in the Letters of Paul*. New Haven: Yale University Press, 1989.

———. "PISTIS and Pauline Christology." Pages 35–60 in *Looking Back, Pressing On*. Edited by E. Elizabeth Johnson and David M. Hay. Vol. 4 of *Pauline Theology*. Society of Biblical Literature Symposium Series 4. Atlanta: Scholars Press, 1997.

Heininger, Bernhard. *Paulus als Visionär: Eine religionsgeschichtliche Studie*. Freiburg: Herder, 1996.

———. "Einmal Tarsus und zurück (Apg 9,30; 11,25–26): Paulus als Lehrer nach der Apostelgeschichte." *Münchener theologische Zeitschrift* 49 (1998): 125–43.

Heitmüller, Wilhelm. *Taufe und Abendmahl bei Paulus: Darstellung und religionsgeschichtliche Beleuchtung*. Göttingen: Vandenhoeck & Ruprecht, 1903.

Hellholm, David. "Enthymemic Argumentation in Paul: The Case of Romans 6." Pages 117–79 in *Paul in His Hellenistic Context*. Edited by Troels Engberg-Pedersen. Minneapolis: Fortress, 1995.

Hemer, Colin J., and Conrad H. Gempf. *The Book of Acts in the Setting of Hellenistic History*. Tübingen: Mohr Siebeck, 1989.

Hengel, Martin. *Die Zeloten: Untersuchungen zur jüdischen Freiheitsbewegung in der Zeit von Herodes I. bis 70 nach Christus*. Leiden: Brill, 1961.

———. "Die Ursprünge der christlichen Mission." *New Testament Studies* 18 (1971–1972): 15–38.

———. *Judaism and Hellenism: Studies in Their Encounter in Palestine during the Early Hellenistic Period*. Translated by John Bowden. 2 vols. London: SCM Press, 1974.

———. "Zwischen Jesus und Paulus: Die 'Hellenisten,' die 'Sieben,' und Stephanus." *Zeitschrift für Theologie und Kirche* 72 (1975): 151–206.

———. *The Son of God: The Origin of Christology and the History of Jewish-Hellenistic Religion*. Translated by John Bowden. Philadelphia: Fortress, 1976.

———. *Crucifixion*. Translated by John Bowden. Philadelphia: Fortress, 1977.

———. *The Atonement: The Origins of the Doctrine in the New Testament*. Philadelphia: Fortress, 1981.

———. "Erwägungen zum Sprachgebrauch von Χριστός bei Paulus und in der 'vorpaulinischen' Überlieferung." Pages 135–59 in *Paul and Paulinism: Essays in Honour of C. K. Barrett*. Edited by Morna Dorothy Hooker and S. G. Wilson. London: SPCK, 1982.

———. *The Zealots: Investigations into the Jewish Freedom Movement in the Period from Herod I until 70 A.D.* Translated by David Smith. Edinburgh: T&T Clark, 1989.

———. "Psalm 110 und die Erhöhung des Auferstandenen zur Rechten Gottes." Pages 43–74 in *Anfänge der Christologie: Festschrift für Ferdinand Hahn zum 65. Geburtstag.* Edited by Cilliers Breytenbach et al. Göttingen: Vandenhoeck & Ruprecht, 1991.

———. "Das früheste Christentum als eine jüdische messianische und universalistische Bewegung." *Theologische Beiträge* (1997): 197–210.

———. "Präexistenz bei Paulus?" Pages 479–517 in *Jesus Christus als die Mitte der Schrift: Studien zur Hermeneutik des Evangeliums.* Edited by Christof Landmesser et al. Beihefte zur Zeitschrift für die neutestamentliche Wissenschaft. Berlin: de Gruyter, 1997.

———. "Die Ursprünge der Gnosis und das Urchristentum." Pages 190–223 in *Evangelium, Schriftauslegung, Kirche: Festschrift für Peter Stuhlmacher zum 65. Geburtstag.* Edited by Otfried Hofius et al. Göttingen: Vandenhoeck & Ruprecht, 1997.

———. "Das Begräbnis Jesu bei Paulus." Pages 119–183 in *Auferstehung = Resurrection: The Fourth Durham-Tübingen Research Symposium: Resurrection, Transfiguration, and Exaltation in Old Testament, Ancient Judaism, and Early Christianity.* Edited by Friedrich Avemarie and Hermann Lichtenberger. Wissenschaftliche Untersuchungen zum Neuen Testament 135. Tübingen: Mohr Siebeck, 2001.

———. "Die Stellung des Paulus zum Gesetz in den unbekannten Jahren zwischen Damaskus und Antiochien." Pages 25–52 in *Paul and the Mosaic law.* Edited by James D. G. Dunn. Grand Rapids: Eerdmans, 2001.

———. "Jakobus, der Herrenbruder—der erste 'Papst'?" Pages 549–82 in *Paulus und Jakobus.* Wissenschaftliche Untersuchungen zum Neuen Testament 141; Kleine Schriften 3. Mohr Siebeck, 2002.

———. *The Septuagint as Christian Scripture: Its Prehistory and the Problem of Its Canon.* Translated by Mark E. Biddle. Old Testament Studies. Edinburgh: T&T Clark, 2002.

Hengel, Martin, and Roland Deines. *The Pre-Christian Paul.* Translated by John Bowden. Philadelphia: Trinity Press International, 1991.

Hengel, Martin, and Anna Maria Schwemer. *Paul between Damascus and Antioch: The Unknown Years.* Translated by John Bowden. Louisville: Westminster John Knox, 1997.

Hennecke, Edgar, and Wilhelm Schneemelcher, eds. *New Testament Apocrypha.* 2 vols. Philadelphia: Westminster, 1963–1964.

Henten, J. W. van. "The Tradition-Historical Background of Romans 3,25: A Search for Pagan and Jewish Parallels." Pages 101–28 in *From Jesus to John: Essays on Jesus and New Testament Christology in Honour of Marinus de Jonge.* Edited by Martinus C. de Boer. Journal for the Study of the New Testament: Supplement Series. Sheffield: JSOT Press, 1993.

Hermann, Ingo. *Kyrios und Pneuma: Studien zur Christologie der paulinischen Hauptbriefe.* Studien zum Alten und Neuen Testament 2. Munich: Kösel, 1961.

Hock, Ronald F. *The Social Context of Paul's Ministry: Tentmaking and Apostleship.* Philadelphia: Fortress, 1980.

Hoffmann, Heinrich. *Das Gesetz in der frühjüdischen Apokalyptik.* Studien zur Umwelt des Neuen Testaments 23. Göttingen: Vandenhoeck & Ruprecht, 1999.

Hoffmann, Paul. *Die Toten in Christus: Eine religionsgeschichtliche und exegetische Untersuchung zur paulinischen Eschatologie.* Neutestamentliche Abhandlungen: Neue Folge 2. Münster: Aschendorff, 1966.

———. "Die historisch-kritische Osterdiskussion von H.S. Reimarus bis zu Beginn des 20. Jahrhunderts." Pages 15–67 in *Zur neutestamentlichen Überlieferung von der Auferstehung Jesu.* Edited by Paul Hoffmann. Darmstadt: Wissenschaftliche Buchgesellschaft, 1988.

Hofius, Otfried. *Paulusstudien.* 2 vols. Wissenschaftliche Untersuchungen zum Neuen Testament 51, 143. Tübingen: Mohr Siebeck, 1989–2002.

———. "Christus als Schöpfungsmittler und Erlösungsmittler: Das Bekenntnis 1Kor 8,6 im Kontext der paulinischen Theologie." Pages 47–58 in *Paulinische Christologie: Exegetische Beiträge: Hans Hübner zum 70. Geburtstag.* Edited by Udo Schnelle et al. Göttingen: Vandenhoeck & Ruprecht, 2000.

Holtz, Traugott. *Der erste Brief an die Thessalonicher.* Neukirchen-Vluyn: Neukirchener Verlag, 1986.

————. *Geschichte und Theologie des Urchristentums: Gesammelte Aufsätze.* Edited by Eckart Reinmuth and Christian Wolff. Wissenschaftliche Untersuchungen zum Neuen Testament 57. Tübingen: Mohr Siebeck, 1991.

Holtzmann, Heinrich Julius. *Lehrbuch der neutestamentlichen Theologie.* 2nd ed. Sammlung theologischer Lehrbücher. Tübingen: Mohr Siebeck, 1911.

Hommel, Hildebrecht. "Das 7. Kapitel des Römerbriefes." Pages 141–73 in vol. 2 of *Sebasmata: Studien zur antiken Religionsgeschichte und zum frühen Christentum.* 2 vols. Wissenschaftliche Untersuchungen zum Neuen Testament 31–32. Tübingen: Mohr Siebeck, 1983.

Horn, Friedrich Wilhelm. "1 Korinther 15,56—ein exegetischer Stachel." *Zeitschrift für die neutestamentliche Wissenschaft und die Kunde der älteren Kirche* 82 (1991): 88–105.

————. *Das Angeld des Geistes: Studien zur paulinischen Pneumatologie.* Forschungen zur Religion und Literatur des Alten und Neuen Testaments 154. Göttingen: Vandenhoeck & Ruprecht, 1992.

————. "Ethik des Neuen Testaments." *Theologische Rundschau* 60 (1995): 32–86.

————. "Paulusforschung." Pages 30–59 in *Bilanz und Perspektiven gegenwärtiger Auslegung des Neuen Testaments: Symposion zum 65. Geburtstag von Georg Strecker.* Edited by Friedrich Wilhelm Horn. Beihefte zur Zeitschrift für die neutestamentliche Wissenschaft 75. New York: de Gruyter, 1995.

————. "Paulus, das Nasiräat, und die Nasiräer." *Novum Testamentum* 39 (1997): 117–37.

————. "Kyrios und Pneuma bei Paulus." Pages 59–75 in *Paulinische Christologie—exegetische Beiträge: Hans Hübner zum 70. Geburtstag.* Edited by Udo Schnelle et al. Göttingen: Vandenhoeck & Ruprecht, 2000.

————. "Die letzte Jerusalemreise des Paulus." Pages 15–35 in *Das Ende des Paulus: Historische, theologische, und literaturgeschichtliche Aspekte.* Edited by Friedrich Wilhelm Horn. Beihefte zur Zeitschrift für die neutestamentliche Wissenschaft 106. New York: de Gruyter, 2001.

Horrell, David G. "'No Longer Jew or Greek': Paul's Corporate Christology and the Construction of Christian Community." Pages 321–44 in *Christology, Controversy, and Community: New Testament Essays in Honour of David R Catchpole.* Edited by David G. Horrell and C. M. Tuckett. Leiden: Brill, 2000.

Horsley, Richard A. "Pneumatikos vs. Psychikos." *Harvard Theological Review* 69 (1976): 269–88.

————. "Wisdom of Word and Words of Wisdom in Corinth." *Catholic Biblical Quarterly* 39 (1977): 224–39.

————. "1 Corinthians: A Case Study of Paul's Assembly as an Alternative Society." Pages 242–52 in *Paul and Empire: Religion and Power in Roman Imperial Society.* Edited by Richard A. Horsley. Harrisburg, PA: Trinity Press International, 1997.

————. *1 Corinthians.* Abingdon New Testament Commentaries. Nashville: Abingdon, 1998.

————. "Rhetoric and Empire—and 1 Corinthians." Pages 72–102 in *Paul and Politics: Ekklesia, Israel, Imperium, Interpretation: Essays in Honor of Krister Stendahl.* Edited by Richard A. Horsley. Harrisburg, PA: Trinity Press International, 2000.

Hotze, Gerhard. *Paradoxien bei Paulus: Untersuchungen zu einer elementaren Denkform in seiner Theologie.* Neutestamentliche Abhandlungen: Neue Folge 33. Münster: Aschendorff, 1997.

Hubbard, Moyer V. *New Creation in Paul's Letters and Thought.* Cambridge: Cambridge University Press, 2002.

Hübner, Hans. "Paulusforschung seit 1945." Pages 2649–2840 in *Aufstieg und Niedergang der römischen Welt.* Part 2. *Principat*, 25.4. Edited by Hildegard Temporini and Wolfgang Haase. Berlin: de Gruyter, 1972.

————. "Gal. 3,10 und die Herkunft des Paulus." *Kerygma und Dogma* 19 (1973): 215–31.

————. *Gottes Ich und Israel: Zum Schriftgebrauch des Paulus in Römer 9–11.* Göttingen: Vandenhoeck & Ruprecht, 1984.

————. *Law in Paul's Thought: A Contribution to the Development of Pauline Theology.* Edited by John Kenneth Riches. Translated by James C. G. Greig. Studies of the New Testament and Its World. Edinburgh: T&T Clark, 1984.

————. *Biblische Theologie des Neuen Testaments.* 3 vols. Göttingen: Vandenhoeck & Ruprecht, 1990.

———. "Was heißt bei Paulus 'Werke des Gesetzes'?" Pages 166–74 in Hans Hübner, *Biblische Theologie als Hermeneutik: Gesammelte Aufsätze: Hans Hübner zum 65. Geburtstag.* Edited by Antje Labahn and Michael Labahn. Göttingen: Vandenhoeck & Ruprecht, 1995.

———. "Die paulinische Rechtfertigungstheologie als ökumenisch-hermeneutisches Problem." Pages 76–105 in *Worum geht es in der Rechtfertigungslehre? Das biblische Fundament der "Gemeinsamen Erklärung" von katholischer Kirche und Lutherischem Weltbund.* Edited by Thomas Söding and Frank-Lothar Hossfeld. Quaestiones disputatae 180. Freiburg: Herder, 1999.

Hübner, Kurt. *Die Wahrheit des Mythos.* Munich: Beck, 1985.

Hulmi, Sini. *Paulus und Mose: Argumentation und Polemik in 2 Kor 3.* Schriften der finnischen exegetischen Gesellschaft 77. Göttingen: Vandenhoeck & Ruprecht, 1999.

Hunzinger, C. H. "Die Hoffnung angesichts des Todes im Wandel der paulinischen Aussagen." Pages 69–88 in *Leben angesichts des Todes: Beiträge zum theologischen Problem des Todes: Helmut Thielicke zum 60. Geburtstag.* Edited by Bernhardt Lohse. Tübingen: Mohr Siebeck, 1968.

Hurtado, Larry W. *One God, One Lord: Early Christian Devotion and Ancient Jewish Monotheism.* Philadelphia: Fortress, 1988.

———. "Convert, Apostate, or Apostle to the Nations." *Studies in Religion* 22 (1993): 273–84.

———. "Son of God." Pages 900–906 in *Dictionary of Paul and His Letters.* Edited by Gerald F. Hawthorne et al. Downers Grove, IL: InterVarsity, 1993.

———. *Lord Jesus Christ: Devotion to Jesus in Earliest Christianity.* Grand Rapids: Eerdmans, 2003.

Hyldahl, Niels. *Die paulinische Chronologie.* Acta theologica danica 19. Leiden: Brill, 1986.

Instone-Brewer, David. *Techniques and Assumptions in Jewish Exegesis before 70 CE.* Texte und Studien zum antiken Judentum 30. Tübingen: Mohr Siebeck, 1992.

Iser, Wolfgang. *The Act of Reading: A Theory of Aesthetic Response.* Baltimore: Johns Hopkins University Press, 1978.

Jaeger, Friedrich, and Jörn Rüsen. *Geschichte des Historismus: Eine Einführung.* Munich: Beck, 1992.

Jaeger, Werner Wilhelm. *Die Theologie der frühen griechischen Denker.* Darmstadt: Wissenschaftliche Buchgesellschaft, 1964.

Jeremias, Gert. *Der Lehrer der Gerechtigkeit.* Studien zur Umwelt des Neuen Testaments 2. Göttingen: Vandenhoeck & Ruprecht, 1963.

Jeremias, Joachim. *The Eucharistic Words of Jesus.* Translated by Norman Perrin. New York: Scribner, 1966.

———. *Jerusalem in the Time of Jesus: An Investigation into Economic and Social Conditions during the New Testament Period.* Translated by F. H. Cave and C. H. Cave. Philadelphia: Fortress, 1975.

Jervell, J. "Der unbekannte Paulus." Pages 20–49 in *Die paulinische Literatur und Theologie = The Pauline Literature and Theology: Anlässlich der 50 jährigen Gründungs-Feier der Universität von Aarhus.* Edited by Sigfred Pedersen. Århus: Aros, 1980.

———. *Die Apostelgeschichte.* 17. Auflage, 1. Auflage dieser Auslegung. Kritisch-exegetischer Kommentar über das Neue Testament 3. Göttingen: Vandenhoeck & Ruprecht, 1998.

Jewett, Robert K. *Paul's Anthropological Terms: A Study of Their Use in Conflict Settings.* Arbeiten zur Geschichte des antiken Judentums und des Urchristentums 10. Leiden: Brill, 1971.

———. *A Chronology of Paul's life.* Philadelphia: Fortress, 1979.

———. *The Thessalonian Correspondence: Pauline Rhetoric and Millenarian Piety.* Philadelphia: Fortress, 1986.

Jobes, Karen H., and Moises Silva. *Invitation to the Septuagint.* Grand Rapids: Baker, 2000.

Jonas, Hans. *The Imperative of Responsibility: In Search of an Ethics for the Technological Age.* Translated by Hans Jonas and David Herr. Chicago: University of Chicago Press, 1984.

Jones, F. Stanley. *"Freiheit" in den Briefen des Apostels Paulus: Eine historische, exegetische, und religionsgeschichtliche Studie.* Göttinger theologische Arbeiten 34. Göttingen: Vandenhoeck & Ruprecht, 1987.

Jonge, Marinus de. *Christology in Context: The Earliest Christian Response to Jesus.* Philadelphia: Westminster, 1988.

Judge, E. A. "The Early Christians as a Scholastic Community." *Journal of Religious History* 1 (1960): 4–15, 125–37.

Jürgens, Burkhard. *Zweierlei Anfang: Kommunikative Konstruktionen heidenchristlicher Identität in Gal 2 und Apg 15.* Berlin: Philo, 1999.

Karrer, Martin. *Der Gesalbte: Die Grundlagen des Christustitels.* Forschungen zur Religion und Literatur des Alten und Neuen Testaments 151. Göttingen: Vandenhoeck & Ruprecht, 1991.

———. *Jesus Christus im Neuen Testament.* Grundrisse zum Neuen Testament 11. Göttingen: Vandenhoeck & Ruprecht, 1998.

Käsemann, Ernst. "Erwägungen zum Stichwort Versöhnungslehre im Neuen Testament." Pages 47–59 in *Zeit und Geschichte: Dankesgabe an Rudolf Bultmann zum 80. Geburtstag.* Edited by Erich Dinkler and Hartwig Thyen. Tübingen: Mohr Siebeck, 1964.

———. *Essays on New Testament Themes.* Studies in Biblical Theology 41. London: SCM Press, 1964.

———. *New Testament Questions of Today.* London: SCM Press, 1969.

———. *Perspectives on Paul.* Philadelphia: Fortress, 1971.

———. *Commentary on Romans.* Translated by Geoffrey W. Bromiley. Grand Rapids: Eerdmans, 1980.

Kennedy, George A. *New Testament Interpretation through Rhetorical Criticism.* Chapel Hill: University of North Carolina Press, 1984.

Kertelge, Karl. *Rechtfertigung bei Paulus: Studien zur Struktur und zum Bedeutungsgehalt des paulinischen Rechtfertigungsbegriffs.* Münster: Aschendorff, 1967.

———. *Grundthemen paulinischer Theologie.* Freiburg: Herder, 1991.

Kettunen, Markku. *Der Abfassungszweck des Römerbriefes.* Annales Academiae scientiarum fennicae: Dissertationes humanarum litterarum 18. Helsinki: Suomalainen Tiedeakatemia, 1979.

Kim, Seyoon. *The Origin of Paul's Gospel.* Tübingen: Mohr Siebeck, 1981.

———. "Heilsgegenwart bei Paulus: Eine religionsgeschichtlich-theologische Untersuchung zu Sündenvergebung und Geistgabe in den Qumrantexten sowie bei Johannes dem Täufer, Jesus,

und Paulus." Diss., Georg August Universität, Göttingen, 1996.

Klauck, Hans-Josef. *Hausgemeinde und Hauskirche im frühen Christentum.* Stuttgarter Bibelstudien 103. Stuttgart: Katholisches Bibelwerk, 1981.

———. *Herrenmahl und hellenistischer Kult: Eine religionsgeschichtliche Untersuchung zum ersten Korintherbrief.* Neutestamentliche Abhandlungen: Neue Folge 15. Münster: Aschendorff, 1982.

———. *1. Korintherbrief.* 3rd ed. Neue Echter Bibel 7. Würzburg: Echter, 1992.

———. *2. Korintherbrief.* 3rd ed. Neue Echter Bibel 8. Würzburg: Echter, 1994.

———. "'Der Gott in dir' (Ep 41,1): Autonomie des Gewissens bei Seneca und Paulus." Pages 11–31 in *Alte Welt und neuer Glaube: Beiträge zur Religionsgeschichte, Forschungsgeschichte, und Theologie des Neuen Testaments.* Novum Testamentum et orbis antiquus 29. Göttingen: Vandenhoeck & Ruprecht, 1994.

———. "Ein Richter im eigenen Innern: Das Gewissen bei Philo von Alexandrien." Pages 33–58 in *Alte Welt und neuer Glaube.*

———. "Junia Theodora und die Gemeinde in Korinth." Pages 42–57 in *Kirche und Volk Gottes: Festschrift für Jürgen Roloff zum 70. Geburtstag.* Edited by Martin Karrer et al. Neukirchen-Vluyn: Neukirchener Verlag, 2000.

———. *The Religious Context of Early Christianity: A Guide to Graeco-Roman Religions.* Translated by Brian McNeil. Minneapolis: Fortress, 2003.

Klausner, Joseph. *From Jesus to Paul.* Translated by William F. Stinespring. New York: Macmillan, 1943.

Klehn, L. "Die Verwendung von ἐν Χριστῷ bei Paulus." *Biblische Zeitschrift* 74 (1994): 66–79.

Klein, Günter. "Galater 2,6–9 und die Geschichte der Jerusalemer Urgemeinde." Pages 99–117 in *Rekonstruktion und Interpretation: Gesammelte Aufsätze zum Neuen Testament.* Beiträge zur evangelischen Theologie 50. Munich: Kaiser, 1969.

———. "Die Verleugnung des Petrus." Pages 49–89 in *Rekonstruktion und Interpretation: Gesammelte Aufsätze zum Neuen Testament.* Beiträge zur evangelischen Theologie 50. Munich: Kaiser, 1969.

———. "Anti-paulinismus in Philippi." Pages 297–313 in *Jesu Rede von Gott und ihre Nachgeschichte im frühen Christentum: Beiträge zur Verkündigung Jesu und zum Kerygma der Kirche: Festschrift für*

Willi Marxsen zum 70. Geburtstag. Edited by Andreas Lindemann et al. Gütersloh: Gütersloher Verlagshaus, 1989.

———. "Paul's Purpose in Writing the Epistle to the Romans." Pages 29–43 in *The Romans Debate.* Edited by Karl P. Donfried. Rev. and exp. ed. Peabody, MA: Hendrickson, 1991.

Klumbies, Paul-Gerhard. *Die Rede von Gott bei Paulus in ihrem zeitgeschichtlichen Kontext.* Göttingen: Vandenhoeck & Ruprecht, 1992.

Knöppler, Thomas. *Sühne im Neuen Testament: Studien zum urchristlichen Verständnis der Heilsbedeutung des Todes Jesu.* Neukirchen-Vluyn: Neukirchener Verlag, 2001.

Koch, Dietrich-Alex. *Die Schrift als Zeuge des Evangeliums: Untersuchungen zur Verwendung und zum Verständnis der Schrift bei Paulus.* Beiträge zur historischen Theologie 69. Tübingen: Mohr Siebeck, 1986.

———. "'. . . Bezeugt durch das Gesetz und die Propheten': Zur Funktion der Schrift bei Paulus." Pages 169–79 in *Sola scriptura: Das reformatorische Schriftprinzip in der säkularen Welt.* Edited by Hans Heinrich Schmid and Joachim Mehlhausen. Gütersloh: Mohn, 1991.

———. "'Seid unanstößig für Juden und für Griechen und für die Gemeinde Gottes' (1Kor 10,32)." Pages 35–54 in *Paulus, Apostel Jesu Christi: Festschrift für Günter Klein zum 70. Geburtstag.* Edited by Michael Trowitzsch. Tübingen: Mohr Siebeck, 1998.

———. "Barnabas, Paulus, und die Adressaten des Galaterbriefes." Pages 85–106 in *Das Urchristentum in seiner literarischen Geschichte: Festschrift für Jürgen Becker zum 65. Geburtstag.* Edited by Ulrich Mell and Ulrich B. Müller. Beihefte zur Zeitschrift für die neutestamentliche Wissenschaft 100. New York: de Gruyter, 1999.

———. "Kollektenbericht, Wir-bericht, und Itinerar." *New Testament Studies* 45 (1999): 367–90.

———. "Die Christen als neue Randgruppe in Makedonien und Achaia im 1. Jahrhundert n. Chr." Pages 155–88 in *Antike Randgesellschaften und Randgruppen im östlichen Mittelmeerraum: Ringvorlesung an der Westfälischen Wilhelms-Universität Münster.* Edited by Hans-Peter Müller and F. Siegert. Münsteraner judaistische Studien 5. Münster: Universitätsverlag, 2000.

Koester, Helmut. *Introduction to the New Testament.* 2nd ed. 2 vols. New York: de Gruyter, 1995.

Kollmann, Bernd. "Paulus als Wundertäter." Pages 76–96 in *Paulinische Christologie: Exegetische Beiträge: Hans Hübner zum 70. Geburtstag.* Edited by Udo Schnelle et al. Göttingen: Vandenhoeck & Ruprecht, 2000.

Kramer, Werner R. *Christ, Lord, Son of God.* Translated by Brian Hardy. Studies in Biblical Theology 50. London: SCM Press, 1966.

Kraus, Wolfgang. "Der Jom Kippur, der Tod Jesu, und die 'Biblische Theologie.'" *Jahrbuch für biblische Theologie* 6 (1991): 155–72.

———. *Der Tod Jesu als Heiligtumsweihe: Eine Untersuchung zum Umfeld der Sühnevorstellung in Römer 3, 25–26a.* Neukirchen-Vluyn: Neukirchener Verlag, 1991.

———. *Das Volk Gottes: Zur Grundlegung der Ekklesiologie bei Paulus.* Wissenschaftliche Untersuchungen zum Neuen Testament 85. Tübingen: Mohr Siebeck, 1996.

———. "Der Tod Jesu als Sühnetod bei Paulus." *Zeitschrift für Neues Testament* 3 (1999): 20–30.

———. *Zwischen Jerusalem und Antiochia: Die "Hellenisten," Paulus, und die Aufnahme der Heiden in das endzeitliche Gottesvolk.* Stuttgarter Bibelstudien 179. Stuttgart: Katholisches Bibelwerk, 1999.

Kuhn, H.-W. "Πειρασμός—ἁμαρτία—σάρξ im Neuen Testament und die damit zusammenhängenden Vorstellungen." *Zeitschrift für Theologie und Kirche* 49 (1952): 200–22.

———. "Der Gekreuzigte von Giv'at ha-Mivtar: Bilanz einer Entdeckung." Pages 303–34 in *Theologia crucis, signum crucis: Festschrift für Erich Dinkler zum 70. Geburtstag.* Edited by Carl Andresen and Günter Klein. Tübingen: Mohr Siebeck, 1979.

———. "Die Kreuzesstrafe während der frühen Kaiserzeit." Pages 648–793 in vol. 25/1 of *Aufstieg und Niedergang der römischen Welt: Geschichte und Kultur Roms im Spiegel der neueren Forschung.* Edited by Joseph Vogt et al. Berlin: De Gruyter, 1982.

———. "Die drei wichtigsten Qumranparallelen zum Galaterbrief." Pages 227–54 in *Konsequente Traditionsgeschichte: Festschrift für Klaus Baltzer zum 65. Geburtstag.* Edited by Rüdiger Bartelmus et al. Orbis biblicus et orientalis 126. Göttingen: Vandenhoeck & Ruprecht, 1993.

———. "Die Bedeutung der Qumrantexte für das Verständnis des Galaterbriefes." *New Qumran Texts and Studies: Proceedings of the First Meeting of the International Organization for Qumran Studies, Paris, 1992*. Edited by George J. Brooke and Florentino García Martínez. Studies on the Texts of the Desert of Judah 15. Leiden: Brill, 1994.

———. "Qumran und Paulus: Unter traditionsgeschichtlichem Aspekt ausgewählte Parallelen." Pages 227-46 in *Das Urchristentum in seiner literarischen Geschichte: Festschrift für Jürgen Becker zum 65. Geburtstag*. Edited by Ulrich Mell and Ulrich B. Müller. Beihefte zur Zeitschrift für die neutestamentliche Wissenschaft 100. Berlin: De Gruyter, 1999.

———. "Jesus als Gekreuzigter in der frühchristlichen Verkündigung bis zur Mitte des 2. Jahrhunderts." *Zeitschrift für die neutestamentliche Wissenschaft und die Kunde der älteren Kirche* 72 (1975): 1–46.

Kümmel, Werner Georg. "Jesus und Paulus." Pages 81–106 in vol. 1 of *Heilsgeschehen und Geschichte*. Edited by Erich Grässer, Otto Merk, and Adolf Fritz. Marburger theologische Studien 3. Marburg: Elwert, 1965.

———. "Die Probleme von Römer 9–11 in der gegenwärtigen Forschungslage." Pages 245–60 in vol. 2 of *Heilsgeschehen und Geschichte*. Edited by Erich Grässer, Otto Merk, and Adolf Fritz. Marburger theologische Studien 16. Marburg: Elwert, 1978.

———. "Das Problem der Entwicklung in der Theologie des Paulus." *New Testament Studies* 18 (1971–1972): 457–58.

———. *Römer 7 und das Bild des Menschen im Neuen Testament: Zwei Studien*. Theologische Bücherei: Neudrucke und Berichte aus dem 20. Jahrhundert 53. Munich: C. Kaiser, 1974.

Kümmel, Werner Georg, and Paul Feine. *Introduction to the New Testament*. Translated by Howard Clark Kee. 2nd ed. New Testament Library. London: SCM Press, 1975.

Kuss, Otto. *Paulus: Die Rolle des Apostels in der theologischen Entwicklung der Urkirche*. 2nd ed. Auslegung und Verkündigung 3. Regensburg: Pustet, 1976.

Kuula, Kari. *The Law, the Covenant, and God's Plan*. Göttingen: Vandenhoeck & Ruprecht, 1999.

Laato, Timo. *Paulus und das Judentum: Anthropologische Erwägungen*. Åbo, Finland: Åbo Akademis Förlag, 1991. ET: *Paul and Judaism: An Anthropological Approach*. Translated by T. McElwain. South Florida Studies in the History of Judaism 115. Atlanta: Scholars Press, 1995.

Labahn, Antje, and Michael Labahn. "Jesus als Sohn Gottes bei Paulus." Pages 97–120 in *Paulinische Christologie: Exegetische Beiträge: Hans Hübner zum 70. Geburtstag*. Edited by Udo Schnelle et al. Göttingen: Vandenhoeck & Ruprecht, 2000.

Labahn, Michael. "Paulus—ein homo honestus et iustus: Das lukanische Paulusportrait von Act 27–28 im Lichte ausgewählter antiker Parallelen." Pages 75–106 in *Das Ende des Paulus: Historische, theologische, und literaturgeschichtliche Aspekte*. Edited by Friedrich Wilhelm Horn. Beihefte zur Zeitschrift für die neutestamentliche Wissenschaft 106. New York: de Gruyter, 2001.

———. "'Heiland der Welt': Der gesandte Gottessohn und der römische Kaiser—ein Thema johanneischer Christologie." Pages 147–73 in *Zwischen den Reichen: Neues Testament und römische Herrschaft: Vorträge auf der ersten Konferenz der European Association for Biblical Studies*. Edited by Michael Labahn and Jürgen Zangenberg. Texte und Arbeiten zum neutestamentlichen Zeitalter 36. Tübingen: Francke, 2002.

Lampe, Peter. "Paulus-Zeltmacher." *Biblische Zeitschrift* 31 (1987): 256–61.

———. "Das korinthische Herrenmahl im Schnittpunkt hellenistisch-römischer Mahlpraxis und paulinischer theologia crucis." *Zeitschrift für die neutestamentliche Wissenschaft und die Kunde der älteren Kirche* 82 (1991): 183–213.

———. "Wissenssoziologische Annäherung an das Neue Testament." *New Testament Studies* 43 (1997): 347–66.

———. "Urchristliche Missionswege nach Rom: Haushalte paganer Herrschaft als jüdisch-christliche Keimzellen." *Zeitschrift für die neutestamentliche Wissenschaft und die Kunde der älteren Kirche* 92 (2001): 123–27.

———. *From Paul to Valentinus: Christians at Rome in the First Two Centuries*. Edited by Marshall D. Johnson. Translated by Michael Steinhauser. Minneapolis: Fortress, 2003.

Lang, Friedrich Gustav. *2. Korinther 5, 1–10 in der neueren Forschung*. Beiträge zur Geschichte der biblischen Exegese 16. Tübingen: Mohr Siebeck, 1973.

————. *Die Briefe an die Korinther*. 17th ed. Das Neue Testament Deutsch 7. Göttingen: Vandenhoeck & Ruprecht, 1994.

Lessing, G. E. "On the Proof of the Spirit and Power." Pages 51–56 in *Lessing's Theological Writings*. Edited and translated by Henry Chadwick. Library of Modern Religious Thought 2. London: Adam & Charles Black, 1956.

Lichtenberger, Hermann. *Studien zum Menschenbild in Texten der Qumrangemeinde*. Studien zur Umwelt des Neuen Testaments 15. Göttingen: Vandenhoeck & Ruprecht, 1980.

————. "Josephus und Paulus in Rom." Pages 245–61 in *Begegnungen zwischen Christentum und Judentum in Antike und Mittelalter: Festschrift für Heinz Schreckenberg*. Edited by Dietrich-Alex Koch et al. Schriften des Institutum judaicum delitzschianum 1. Göttingen: Vandenhoeck & Ruprecht, 1993.

————. "Das Tora-Verständnis im Judentum zur Zeit des Paulus." Pages 7–23 in *Paul and the Mosaic law*. Edited by James D. G. Dunn. Grand Rapids: Eerdmans, 2001.

Liefeld, Walter L. *The Wandering Preacher as a Social Figure in the Roman Empire*. Ann Arbor, MI: University Microfilms, 1967.

Lietzmann, Hans. *An die Galater*. 4th ed. Handbuch zum Neuen Testament 10. Tübingen: Mohr Siebeck, 1971.

————. *An die Römer*. 5th ed. Handbuch zum Neuen Testament 8. Tübingen: Mohr Siebeck, 1971.

Lietzmann, Hans, and Werner Georg Kümmel. *An die Korinther I, II*. 5th ed. Handbuch zum Neuen Testament 9. Tübingen: Mohr Siebeck, 1969.

Lightfoot, Joseph Barber. *Saint Paul's Epistle to the Galatians: A Revised Text*. 10th ed. London: Macmillan, 1890.

————. *Saint Paul's Epistles to the Colossians and to Philemon: A Revised Text with Introductions, Notes, and Dissertations*. 9th ed. London: Macmillan, 1890.

Limbeck, Meinrad. *Die Ordnung des Heils: Untersuchungen zum Gesetzesverständnis des Frühjudentums*. Düsseldorf: Patmos, 1971.

Lindemann, Andreas. *Paulus im ältesten Christentum: Das Bild des Apostels und die Rezeption der paulinischen Theologie in der frühchristlichen Literatur bis Marcion*. Beiträge zur historischen Theologie 58. Tübingen: Mohr Siebeck, 1979.

————. *Der erste Korintherbrief*. Handbuch zum Neuen Testament 9/1. Tübingen: Mohr Siebeck, 2000.

————. *Paulus, Apostel und Lehrer der Kirche: Studien zu Paulus und zum frühen Paulusverständnis*. Tübingen: Mohr Siebeck, 1999.

Lips, Hermann von. *Weisheitliche Traditionen im Neuen Testament*. Wissenschaftliche Monographien zum Alten und Neuen Testament 64. Neukirchen-Vluyn: Neukirchener Verlag, 1990.

Lohmeyer, Ernst. "Gesetzeswerk." Pages 31–74 in *Probleme paulinischer Theologie*. Stuttgart: Kohlhammer, 1955.

————. *Kyrios Jesus: Eine Untersuchung zur Phil. 2, 5–11*. 2nd ed. Sitzungen der heidelberger Akademie der Wissenschaften 4. Heidelberg: C. Winter, 1961.

————. *Die Briefe an die Philipper, an die Kolosser, und an Philemon*. 14th ed. Kritisch-exegetischer Kommentar über das Neue Testament 9/1. Göttingen: Vandenhoeck & Ruprecht, 1974.

Lohse, Eduard. *Märtyrer und Gottesknecht: Untersuchungen zur urchristlichen Verkündigung vom Sühntod Jesu Christi*. Forschungen zur Religion und Literatur des Alten und Neuen Testaments 46. Göttingen: Vandenhoeck & Ruprecht, 1955.

————. *Colossians and Philemon. A Commentary on the Epistles to the Colossians and to Philemon*. Edited by Helmut Koester. Translated by William R. Poehlmann and Robert J. Karris. Hermeneia: A Critical and Historical Commentary on the Bible. Philadelphia: Fortress, 1971.

————. "Die Gerechtigkeit Gottes in der paulinischen Theologie." Pages 209–27 in *Die Einheit des Neuen Testaments: Exegetische Studien zur Theologie des Neuen Testaments*. 2nd ed. Göttingen: Vandenhoeck & Ruprecht, 1973.

————. "Taufe und Rechtfertigung bei Paulus." Pages 228–44 in *Die Einheit des Neuen Testaments*. Göttingen: Vandenhoeck & Ruprecht, 1973.

————. *Summa evangelii: Zu Veranlassung und Thematik des Römerbriefes*. Nachrichten der Akademie der Wissenschaften in Göttingen 1:

Philologisch-historische Klasse 3. Göttingen: Vandenhoeck & Ruprecht, 1993.

———. *Paulus: Eine Biographie*. Munich: Beck, 1996.

Longenecker, Richard N. *Galatians*. Word Biblical Commentary 41. Dallas: Word Books, 1990.

Lübking, Hans-Martin. *Paulus und Israel im Römerbrief: Eine Untersuchung zu Römer 9–11*. Frankfurt: Lang, 1986.

Luck, Georg. "Die Bekehrung des Paulus und das paulinische Evangelium." *Zeitschrift für die neutestamentliche Wissenschaft und die Kunde der älteren Kirche* 76 (1985): 187–208.

Luckmann, Thomas. *Die unsichtbare Religion*. 2nd ed. Frankfurt: Suhrkamp, 1993.

———. "Religion–Gesellschaft–Transzendenz." Pages 112–27 in *Krise der Immanenz: Religion an den Grenzen der Moderne*. Edited by Hans-Joachim Höhn and Karl Gabriel. Philosophie der Gegenwart. Frankfurt: Fischer, 1996.

Lüdemann, Gerd. *Paulus und das Judentum*. Theologische Existenz Heute. Munich: Kaiser, 1983.

———. *Paul, Apostle to the Gentiles: Studies in Chronology*. Translated by F. Stanley Jones. Philadelphia: Fortress, 1984.

———. *Early Christianity according to the Traditions in Acts: A Commentary*. Translated by John Bowden. Minneapolis: Fortress, 1989.

———. *Opposition to Paul in Jewish Christianity*. Translated by M. Eugene Boring. Minneapolis: Fortress, 1989.

———. *The Resurrection of Jesus: History, Experience, Theology*. Minneapolis: Fortress, 1994.

———. *Paul, the Founder of Christianity*. Amherst, NY: Prometheus Books, 2002.

Lührmann, Dieter. "Pistis im Judentum." *Zeitschrift für die neutestamentliche Wissenschaft und die Kunde der älteren Kirche* 64 (1973): 19–38.

———. *Galatians*. Translated by O. C. Dean. Minneapolis: Fortress, 1992.

Luz, Ulrich. *Das Geschichtsverständnis des Paulus*. Beiträge zur evangelischen Theologie: Theologische Abhandlungen 49. Munich: Kaiser, 1968.

———. "Zum Aufbau von Röm. 1–8." *Theologische Zeitschrift* 25 (1969): 161–88.

———. "Rechtfertigung bei den Paulusschülern." Pages 365–83 in *Rechtfertigung: Festschrift für Ernst Käsemann zum 70. Geburtstag*. Edited by

Johannes Friedrich et al. Göttingen: Vandenhoeck & Ruprecht, 1976.

Luz, Ulrich, and Rudolf Smend. *Gesetz*. Stuttgart: Kohlhammer, 1981.

Mack, Burton L. *Logos und Sophia: Untersuchungen zur Weisheitstheologie im hellenistischen Judentum*. Studien zur Umwelt des Neuen Testaments 10. Göttingen: Vandenhoeck & Ruprecht, 1973.

Maier, Gerhard. *Mensch und freier Wille: Nach der jüdischen Religionsparteien zwischen Ben Sira und Paulus*. Wissenschaftliche Untersuchungen zum Neuen Testament 12. Tübingen: Mohr Siebeck, 1971.

Maier, Johann. *Zwischen den Testamenten: Geschichte und Religion in der Zeit des zweiten Tempels*. Neue Echter Bibel: Ergängzungsband zum Alten Testament 3. Würzburg: Echter, 1990.

Malherbe, Abraham J. *Paul and the Popular Philosophers*. Minneapolis: Fortress, 1989.

———. *The Letters to the Thessalonians: A New Translation with Introduction and Commentary*. Anchor Bible 32B. New York: Doubleday, 2000.

Marshall, Peter. *Enmity in Corinth: Social Conventions in Paul's Relations with the Corinthians*. Wissenschaftliche Untersuchungen zum Neuen Testament 2/23. Tübingen: Mohr Siebeck, 1987.

Martin, Luther H. *Hellenistic Religions: An Introduction*. New York: Oxford University Press, 1987.

Martin, Ralph P. *An Early Christian Confession: Philippians 2:5–11 in Recent Interpretations*. London: Tyndale, 1960.

———. *2 Corinthians*. Word Biblical Commentary 40. Waco: Word Books, 1986.

Martyn, J. Louis. *Galatians: A New Translation with Introduction and Commentary*. Anchor Bible 33A. New York: Doubleday, 1997.

Marxsen, Willi. *Introduction to the New Testament: An Approach to Its Problems*. Translated by G. Buswell. Philadelphia: Fortress, 1968.

———. *The Resurrection of Jesus of Nazareth*. Philadelphia: Fortress, 1970.

———. *Der erste Brief an die Thessalonicher*. Zurich: Theologischer Verlag, 1979.

Meeks, Wayne A. *The First Urban Christians: The Social World of the Apostle Paul*. New Haven: Yale University Press, 1983.

Meggitt, Justin J. *Paul, Poverty, and Survival.* Studies of the New Testament and Its World. Edinburgh: T&T Clark, 1998.

Meier, John P. *Companions and Competitors.* Vol. 3 of *A Marginal Jew: Rethinking the Historical Jesus.* Anchor Bible Reference Library 3. New York: Doubleday, 2001.

Mell, Ulrich. *Neue Schöpfung: Eine traditionsgeschichtliche und exegetische Studie zu einem soteriologischen Grundsatz paulinischer Theologie.* Berlin: de Gruyter, 1989.

Merk, Otto. *Handeln aus Glauben: Die Motivierungen der paulinischen Ethik.* Marburg: Elwert, 1968.

Merklein, Helmut. "Die Einheitlichkeit des ersten Korintherbriefes." Pages 345–75 in vol. 1 of *Studien zu Jesus und Paulus.* 2 vols. Wissenschaftliche Untersuchungen zum Neuen Testament 43, 105. Tübingen: Mohr Siebeck, 1987.

———. "Eschatologie im Neuen Testament." Pages 87–95 in vol. 2 of *Studien zu Jesus und Paulus.* 2 vols. Wissenschaftliche Untersuchungen zum Neuen Testament 43, 105. Tübingen: Mohr Siebeck, 1987.

———. "'Nicht aus Werken des Gesetzes . . .': Eine Auslegung von Gal. 2,15–21." Pages 303–15 in vol. 2 of *Studien zu Jesus und Paulus.*

———. "Paulus und die Sünde." Pages 316–56 in vol. 2 of *Studien zu Jesus und Paulus.*

———. "Sinn und Zweck von Röm 13,1–7: Zur semantischen und pragmatischen Struktur eines umstrittenen Textes." Pages 405–37 in vol. 2 of *Studien zu Jesus und Paulus.*

———. "Der Theologe als Prophet." Pages 377–404 in vol. 2 of *Studien zu Jesus und Paulus.*

———. "Zum Verständnis des paulinischen Begriffs 'Evangelium.'" Pages 279–95 in vol. 1 of *Studien zu Jesus und Paulus.*

———. *Der erste Brief an die Korinther.* Ökumenischer Taschenbuch-Kommentar zum Neuen Testament 7. Gütersloh: Gütersloher Verlagshaus, 1992–.

Meyer, Rudolf. *Zur Geschichte und Theologie des Judentums in hellenistisch-römischer Zeit: Ausgewählte Abhandlungen.* Edited by Waltraut Bernhardt. Neukirchen-Vluyn: Neukirchen, 1989.

Michel, Otto. *Paulus und seine Bibel.* Gütersloh: C. Bertelsmann, 1929. Reprint, Darmstadt: Wissenschaftliche Buchgesellschaft, 1972.

———. *Der Brief an die Römer.* 11th ed. Evangelisch-katholischer Kommentar zum Neuen Testament 4. Göttingen: Vandenhoeck & Ruprecht, 1957.

Müller, Klaus E. "Möglichkeit und Vollzug jüdischer Kapitalgerichtsbarkeit." *Der Prozess gegen Jesus: Historische Rückfrage und theologische Deutung.* Edited by Karl Kertelge and Josef Blank. Quaestiones disputatae 112. Freiburg: Herder, 1988.

Müller, Peter. *Anfänge der Paulusschule: Dargestellt am zweiten Thessalonicherbrief und am Kolosserbrief.* Abhandlungen zur Theologie des Alten und Neuen Testaments 74. Zurich: Theologischer Verlag, 1988.

Müller, Ulrich B. *Der Brief des Paulus an die Philipper.* Theologischer Handkommentar zum Neuen Testament 11/1. Leipzig: Evangelische Verlagsanstalt, 1993.

———. "Der Brief aus Ephesus: Zeitliche Plazierung und theologische Einordnung des Philipperbriefes im Rahmen der Paulusbriefe." Pages 155–71 in *Das Urchristentum in seiner literarischen Geschichte: Festschrift für Jürgen Becker zum 65. Geburtstag.* Edited by Ulrich Mell and Ulrich B. Müller. Beihefte zur Zeitschrift für die neutestamentliche Wissenschaft 100. Berlin: de Gruyter, 1999.

Murphy-O'Connor, Jerome. *St. Paul's Corinth: Texts and Archaeology.* Wilmington, DE: Michael Glazier, 1983.

———. "Philo and 2Cor 6:14–7:1." Pages 133–46 in *The Diakonia of the Spirit (2 Co 4:7–7:4).* Edited by Lorenzo De Lorenzi et al. Série monographique de Benedictina: Section paulinienne 10. Rome: St. Paul's Abbey, 1989.

———. "Paul in Arabia." *Catholic Biblical Quarterly* 55, no. 4 (1993): 732–37.

———. *Paul: A critical Life.* Oxford: Oxford University Press, 1997.

Mussies, Gerard. "Greek as the Vehicle of Early Christianity." *New Testament Studies* 29 (1983): 356–69.

Mussner, Franz. "'Ganz Israel wird gerettet werden' (Röm 11,26)." *Kairos* 18 (1976): 241–55.

———. *Der Galaterbrief.* Herders theologischer Kommentar zum Neuen Testament 9. Freiburg: Herder, 1974.

Neirynck, Frans. "Paul and the Sayings of Jesus." Pages 511–68 in Frans Neirynck, *Collected Es-*

says, 1982–1991. Vol. 2 of *Evangelica: Gospel Studies = Evangelica: Études d'évangile*. Edited by Frans van Segbroeck. Bibliotheca ephemeridum theologicarum lovaniensium 99. Leuven: Leuven University Press, 1991.

Neusner, Jacob. *The Rabbinic Traditions about the Pharisees before 70*. 3 vols. Leiden: Brill, 1971.

———. *From Politics to Piety: The Emergence of Pharisaic Judaism*. Englewood Cliffs, NJ: Prentice-Hall, 1973.

———. *Judaism in the Beginning of Christianity*. Philadelphia: Fortress, 1984.

Newman, Carey C., et al. *The Jewish Roots of Christological Monotheism: Papers from the St. Andrews Conference on the Historical Origins of the Worship of Jesus*. Journal for the Study of Judaism in the Persian, Hellenistic, and Roman Periods: Supplements 63. Leiden: Brill, 1999.

Niebuhr, Karl-Wilhelm. *Gesetz und Paränese: Katechismusartige Weisungsreihen in der frühjüdischen Literatur*. Wissenschaftliche Untersuchungen zum Alten und Neuen Testament 2/28. Tübingen: Mohr Siebeck, 1987.

———. *Heidenapostel aus Israel: Die jüdische Identität des Paulus nach ihrer Darstellung in seinen Briefen*. Wissenschaftliche Untersuchungen zum Neuen Testament 62. Tübingen: Mohr Siebeck, 1992.

———. "Die paulinische Rechtfertigungslehre in der gegenwärtigen exegetischen Diskussion." Pages 106–30 in *Worum geht es in der Rechtfertigungslehre? Das biblische Fundament der "Gemeinsamen Erklärung" von katholischer Kirche und Lutherischem Weltbund*. Edited by Frank-Lothar Hossfeld and Thomas Söding. Quaestiones disputatae 180. Freiburg: Herder, 1999.

Niebuhr, Reinhold. *The Nature and Destiny of Man*. 2 vols. Gifford Lectures. New York: Scribner, 1964.

Nilsson, Martin P. *A History of Greek Religion*. Translated by F. J. Fielden. Westport, CT: Greenwood, 1980.

Nissen, Andreas. *Gott und der Nächste im antiken Judentum: Untersuchungen zum Doppelgebot der Liebe*. Wissenschaftliche Untersuchungen zum Neuen Testament 15. Tübingen: Mohr Siebeck, 1974.

Noethlichs, Karl-Leo. *Das Judentum und der römische Staat: Minderheitenpolitik im antiken Rom*.

Darmstadt: Wissenschaftliche Buchgesellschaft, 1996.

———. "Der Jude Paulus—ein Tarser und Römer?" Pages 53–84 in *Rom und das himmlische Jerusalem: Die frühen Christen zwischen Anpassung und Ablehnung*. Edited by Raban von Haehling and Paul Mikat. Darmstadt: Wissenschaftliche Buchgesellschaft, 2000.

O'Brien, Peter T. *The Epistle to the Philippians: A Commentary on the Greek Text*. New International Greek Testament Commentary. Grand Rapids: Eerdmans, 1991.

Oepke, Albrecht. *Das neue Gottesvolk*. Gütersloh: Gütersloher Verlagshaus, 1950.

———. *Der Brief des Paulus an die Galater*. 3rd ed. Theologischer Handkommentar zum Neuen Testament 9. Berlin: Evangelische Verlagsanstalt, 1973.

Ogden, Schubert M., ed. *Existence and Faith: Shorter Writings of Rudolf Bultmann*. New York: Meridian Books, 1960.

Ollrog, Wolf-Henning. *Paulus und seine Mitarbeiter: Untersuchung zu Theorie und Praxis der paulinischen Mission*. Wissenschaftliche Monographien zum Alten und Neuen Testament 50. Neukirchen-Vluyn: Neukirchener Verlag, 1979.

Omerzu, Heike. *Der Prozess des Paulus: Eine exegetische und rechtshistorische Untersuchung der Apostelgeschichte*. Beihefte zur Zeitschrift für die neutestamentliche Wissenschaft 115. Berlin: de Gruyter, 2002.

Osten-Sacken, Peter von der. *Römer 8 als Beispiel paulinischer Soteriologie*. Göttingen: Vandenhoeck & Ruprecht, 1975.

———. "Die Apologie des paulinischen Apostolats in 1 Kor 15,1–11." Pages 131–49 in *Evangelium und Tora: Aufsätze zu Paulus*. Theologische Bücherei: Neudrucke und Berichte aus dem 20. Jahrhundert 77. Munich: Kaiser, 1987.

Otto, Rudolf. "Mystische und gläubige Frömmigkeit." Pages 140–77 in *Sünde und Urschuld, und andere Aufsätze zur Theologie*. Munich: Beck, 1932.

Pannenberg, Wolfhart. *Jesus, God, and Man*. Translated by Lewis L. Wilkins and Duane A. Priebe. 2nd ed. Philadelphia: Westminster, 1977.

———. *Systematic Theology.* Translated by Geoffrey W. Bromiley. 3 vols. Grand Rapids: Eerdmans, 1991.

Paulsen, Henning. *Überlieferung und Auslegung in Römer 8.* Wissenschaftliche Monographien zum Alten und Neuen Testament 43. Neukirchen-Vluyn: Neukirchener Verlag, 1974.

Pesch, Rudolf. *Die Apostelgeschichte.* 2 vols. Evangelisch-katholischer Kommentar zum Neuen Testament. Neukirchen-Vluyn: Neukirchener Verlag, 1986.

Pfeiffer, Matthias. *Einweisung in das neue Sein: Neutestamentliche Erwägungen zur Grundlegung der Ethik.* Gütersloh: Gütersloher Verlagshaus, 2001.

Pfleiderer, Otto, et al. *Primitive Christianity: Its Writings and Teachings in Their Historical Connections.* 4 vols. Theological Translation Library 22, 26–27, 31. New York: G. P. Putnam, 1906.

Pfitzner, Victor C. *Paul and the Agon Motif: Traditional Athletic Imagery in the Pauline Literature.* Novum Testamentum Supplements 16. Leiden: Brill, 1967.

Pilhofer, Peter. *Philippi.* 2 vols. Wissenschaftliche Untersuchungen zum Neuen Testament 87, 119. Tübingen: Mohr Siebeck, 1995.

Plevnik, J. "Pauline Presuppositions." Pages 50–61 in *The Thessalonian Correspondence.* Edited by Raymond F. Collins and Norbert Baumert. Bibliotheca ephemeridum theologicarum lovaniensium 87. Leuven: Leuven University Press, 1990.

Pohlen, Manfred, and Margarethe Bautz-Holzherr. *Psychoanalyse: Das Ende einer Deutungsmacht.* Reinbek: Rowohlt, 1995.

Porter, Stanley E. "Jesus and the Use of Greek in Galilee." Pages 123–54 in *Studying the Historical Jesus: Evaluations of the State of Current Research.* Edited by Bruce Chilton and Craig A. Evans. Leiden: Brill, 1994.

Powers, Daniel G. *Salvation through Participation: An Examination of the Notion of the Believers' Corporate Unity with Christ in Early Christian Soteriology.* Contributions to Biblical Exegesis and Theology 29. Leuven: Peeters, 2001.

Price, S. R. *Rituals and Power: The Roman Imperial Cult in Asia Minor.* Cambridge: Cambridge University Press, 1984.

Qimron, E., and John Strugnell. *Qumran Cave 4.V. Discoveries in the Judean Desert 10.* Oxford: Oxford University Press, 1994.

Rad, Gerhard von. *Genesis: A Commentary.* Old Testament Library. Philadelphia: Westminster, 1972.

Radl, Walter. *Ankunft des Herrn: Zur Bedeutung und Funktion der Parusieaussagen bei Paulus.* Beiträge zur biblischen Exegese und Theologie 15. Frankfurt: Lang, 1981.

Räisänen, Heikki. "Das 'Gesetz des Glaubens' (Röm 3,27) und das 'Gesetz des Geistes' (Röm 8,2)." *New Testament Studies* 26 (1980): 101–17.

———. "Sprachliches zum Spiel des Paulus mit Nomos." Pages 131–54 in *Glaube und Gerechtigkeit: In memoriam Rafael Gyllenberg (18 6 1893–29 7 1982).* Edited by Rafael Gyllenberg et al. Suomen Eksegeettisen Seuran julkaisuja 38. Helsinki: Suomen Eksegeettisen Seuran, 1983.

———. "The 'Hellenists'—a Bridge between Jesus and Paul?" Pages 242–306 in Heikki Räisänen, *The Torah and Christ: Essays in German and English on the Problem of the Law in Early Christianity.* Edited by Anne-Marit Enroth. Suomen Eksegeettisen Seuran julkaisuja 45. Helsinki: Finnish Exegetical Society, 1986.

———. "Paul's Call Experience and His Later View of the Law." Pages 55–92 in Heikki Räisänen, *The Torah and Christ.*

———. "Paul's Theological Difficulties with the Law." Pages 3–24 in Heikki Räisänen, *The Torah and Christ.*

———. *Paul and the Law.* 2nd ed. Wissenschaftliche Untersuchungen zum Neuen Testament 29. Tübingen: Mohr Siebeck, 1987.

———. "Paul's Conversion and the Development of His View of the Law." *New Testament Studies* 33 (1987): 404–19.

———. "Römer 9–11: Analyse eines geistigen Ringens." Pages 2891–2939 in *Aufstieg und Niedergang der römischen Welt.* Part 2. *Principat,* 25.4. Edited by Hildegard Temporini and Wolfgang Haase. Berlin: de Gruyter, 1987.

———. "Der Bruch des Paulus mit Israels Bund." Pages 156–72 in *The Law in the Bible and in Its Environment.* Edited by Timo Veijola. Göttingen: Vandenhoeck & Ruprecht, 1990.

———. "Freiheit vom Gesetz im Urchristentum." *Studia theologica* 46 (1980): 55–67.

———. *Neutestamentliche Theologie? Eine religionswissenschaftliche Alternative.* Stuttgarter Bibelstudien 186. Stuttgart: Katholisches Bibelwerk, 2000.

Ramsay, William M. *St. Paul, the Traveller and the Roman Citizen.* New York: G. P. Putnam, 1896. Reprint, Grand Rapids: Baker, 1962.

———. *The Cities of St. Paul: Their Influence on His Life and Thought.* London: Hodder & Stoughton, 1907; repr. Grand Rapids: Baker, 1979.

Rapa, R. K. *The Meaning of "Works of the Law" in Galatians and Romans.* Studies in Biblical Literature 31. New York: P. Lang, 2001.

Rapske, Brian. *The Book of Acts and Paul in Roman Custody.* Vol. 3 of *The Book of Acts in Its First Century Setting.* Edited by Bruce W. Winter. Grand Rapids: Eerdmans, 1994.

Rau, Eckhard. *Von Jesus zu Paulus: Entwicklung und Rezeption der antiochenischen Theologie im Urchristentum.* Stuttgart: Kohlhammer, 1994.

Reck, Reinhold. *Kommunikation und Gemeindeaufbau: Eine Studie zu Entstehung, Leben, und Wachstum paulinischer Gemeinden in den Kommunikationsstrukturen der Antike.* Stuttgarter biblische Beiträge 22. Stuttgart: Katholisches Bibelwerk, 1991.

Reichardt, Michael. *Psychologische Erklärung der paulinischen Damaskusvision? Ein Beitrag zum interdisziplinären Gespräch zwischen Exegese und Psychologie seit dem 18. Jahrhundert.* Stuttgart: Katholisches Bibelwerk, 1999.

Reichert, Angelika. *Der Römerbrief als Gratwanderung: Eine Untersuchung zur Abfassungsproblematik.* Forschungen zur Religion und Literatur des Alten und Neuen Testaments 194. Göttingen: Vandenhoeck & Ruprecht, 2001.

Reinbold, Wolfgang. *Propaganda und Mission im ältesten Christentum: Eine Untersuchung zu den Modalitäten der Ausbreitung der frühen Kirche.* Forschungen zur Religion und Literatur des Alten und Neuen Testaments 188. Göttingen: Vandenhoeck & Ruprecht, 2000.

Reinmuth, Eckart. *Geist und Gesetz: Studien zu Voraussetzungen und Inhalt der paulinischen Paränese.* Theologische Arbeiten 44. Berlin: Evangelische Verlagsanstalt, 1985.

———. "Narratio und Argumentatio—zur Auslegung der Jesus-Christus-Geschichte im Ersten Korintherbrief." *Zeitschrift für Theologie und Kirche* 92 (1995): 13–27.

Reiser, Marius. "Hat Paulus Heiden Bekehrt?" *Biblische Zeitschrift* 39 (1995): 76–91.

———. *Jesus and Judgment: The Eschatological Proclamation in Its Jewish Context.* Translated by Linda M. Maloney. Minneapolis: Fortress, 1997.

Richard, Earl. "Early Pauline Thought: An Analysis of 1 Thessalonians." Pages 39–51 in *Thessalonians, Philippians, Galatians, Philemon.* Edited by Jouette M. Bassler. Vol. 1 of *Pauline Theology.* Minneapolis: Fortress, 1991.

Ricoeur, Paul. *Time and Narrative.* Translated by Kathleen McLaughlin and David Pellauer. 3 vols. Chicago: University of Chicago Press, 1984.

Ridderbos, Herman N. *Paul: An Outline of His Theology.* Translated by John Richard de Witt. Grand Rapids: Eerdmans, 1975.

Riesner, Rainer. *Paul's Early Period: Chronology, Mission Strategy, Theology.* Translated by Douglas W. Stott. Grand Rapids: Eerdmans, 1998.

Rissi, Mathias. *Die Taufe für die Toten: Ein Beitrag zur paulinischen Tauflehre.* Abhandlungen zur Theologie des Alten und Neuen Testaments 42. Zurich: Zwingli, 1962.

Rohde, Erwin. *Psyche: The Cult of Souls and Belief in Immortality among the Greeks.* Translated by W. B. Hillis. Freeport, NY: Books for Libraries Press, 1972.

Rohde, Joachim. *Der Brief des Paulus an die Galater.* Theologischer Handkommentar zum Neuen Testament 9. Berlin: Evangelische Verlagsanstalt, 1989.

Röhser, Günter. *Metaphorik und Personifikation der Sünde: Antike Sündenvorstellungen und paulinische Hamartia.* Tübingen: Mohr Siebeck, 1987.

———. *Prädestination und Verstockung: Untersuchungen zur frühjüdischen, paulinischen, und johanneischen Theologie.* Tübingen: Francke, 1994.

Roloff, Jürgen. *Die Apostelgeschichte.* 17th ed. Das Neue Testament Deutsch 5. Göttingen: Vandenhoeck & Ruprecht, 1981.

———. *Der erste Brief an Timotheus.* Evangelisch-katholischer Kommentar zum Neuen Testament 15. Neukirchen-Vluyn: Neukirchener Verlag, 1988.

———. "Die Paulus-Darstellung des Lukas." Pages 255–278 in Jürgen Roloff, *Exegetische Verantwortung in der Kirche: Aufsätze*. Edited by Martin Karrer. Göttingen: Vandenhoeck & Ruprecht, 1990.

———. *Die Kirche im Neuen Testament*. Grundrisse zum Neuen Testament 10. Göttingen: Vandenhoeck & Ruprecht, 1993.

———. *Einführung in das Neue Testament*. Stuttgart: Reclam, 1995.

Rowland, C. *The Open Heaven*. New York: Crossroad, 1982.

Rüsen, Jörn. *Historische Vernunft*. Grundzüge einer Historik 1. Göttingen: Vandenhoeck & Ruprecht, 1983.

———. *Rekonstruktion der Vergangenheit: Die Prinzipien der historischen Forschung*. Grundzüge einer Historik 2. Göttingen: Vandenhoeck & Ruprecht, 1986.

———. *Lebendige Geschichte: Formen und Funktionen des historischen Wissens*. Grundzüge einer Historik 3. Göttingen: Vandenhoeck & Ruprecht, 1989.

———. *Konfigurationen des Historismus: Studien zur deutschen Wissenschaftskultur*. Frankfurt: Suhrkamp, 1993.

———, ed. *Western Historical Thinking: An Intercultural Debate*. New York: Berghahn Books, 2002.

Rüsen, Jörn, et al., eds. *Studies in Metahistory*. Pretoria: HSRC, 1993.

Safrai, Shemuel. "Education and the Study of the Torah." Pages 945–70 in *The Jewish People in the First Century*. (See following item.)

Safrai, Shemuel, and M. Stern, eds. *The Jewish People in the First Century: Historical Geography, Political History, Social, Cultural, and Religious Life and Institutions*. Compendia rerum iudaicarum ad Novum Testamentum 1. Assen: Van Gorcum, 1974.

Saldarini, Anthony J. *Pharisees, Scribes, and Sadducees in Palestinian Society: A Sociological Approach*. Biblical Resource Series. Grand Rapids: Eerdmans, 2001.

Saliba, John A. *Understanding New Religious Movements*. 2nd ed. Walnut Creek, CA: AltaMira, 2003.

Sanders, E. P. *Paul and Palestinian Judaism: A Comparison of Patterns of Religion*. Philadelphia: Fortress, 1977.

———. *Paul, the Law, and the Jewish People*. Philadelphia: Fortress, 1983.

———. *Paul*. Oxford: Oxford University Press, 1991.

Sandnes, Karl Olav. *Paul, One of the Prophets? A Contribution to the Apostle's Self-Understanding*. Wissenschaftliche Untersuchungen zum Neuen Testament 2/43. Tübingen: Mohr Siebeck, 1991.

Schade, Hans-Heinrich. *Apokalyptische Christologie bei Paulus: Studien zum Zusammenhang von Christologie und Eschatologie in den Paulusbriefen*. Göttinger theologische Arbeiten 18. Göttingen: Vandenhoeck & Ruprecht, 1981.

Schäfer, Peter. *The History of the Jews in Antiquity: The Jews of Palestine from Alexander the Great to the Arab Conquest*. Translated by David Chowcat. Luxembourg: Harwood Academic Publishers, 1995.

Schäfers, Bernhard. "Entwicklung der Gruppensoziologie und Eigenständigkeit der Gruppe als Sozialgebilde." Pages 19–36 in *Einführung in die Gruppensoziologie: Geschichte, Theorien, Analysen*. Edited by Bernhard Schäfers. 2nd ed. Heidelberg: Quelle & Meyer, 1994.

Schenk, Wolfgang. *Die Philipperbriefe des Paulus: Kommentar*. Stuttgart: Kohlhammer, 1984.

Schenke, Hans-Martin, and Karl Martin Fischer. *Einleitung in die Schriften des Neuen Testaments*. Gütersloh: Gütersloher Verlagshaus, 1978–.

Schenke, Ludger. *Die Urgemeinde: Geschichtliche und theologische Entwicklung*. Stuttgart: Kohlhammer, 1990.

Schiefer-Ferrari, Markus. *Die Sprache des Leids in den paulinischen Peristasenkatalogen*. Stuttgarter biblische Beiträge 23. Stuttgart: Katholisches Bibelwerk, 1991.

Schlatter, Adolf von. *Der Glaube im Neuen Testament*. 5th ed. Stuttgart: Calwer, 1963.

Schlier, Heinrich. *Der Brief an die Galater*. 10th ed. Göttingen: Vandenhoeck & Ruprecht, 1949.

———. *Grundzüge einer paulinischen Theologie*. Freiburg: Herder, 1978.

Schmeller, Thomas, and Christian Cebulj. *Schulen im Neuen Testament? Zur Stellung des Urchristentums in der Bildungswelt seiner Zeit*. Freiburg: Herder, 2001.

Schmid, Josef. *Zeit und Ort der paulinischen Gefangenschaftsbriefe: Mit einem Anhang über die Datierung der Pastoralbriefe.* Freiburg: Herder, 1931.

Schmidt, Siegfried J. *Der Diskurs des radikalen Konstruktivismus.* 8th ed. Frankfurt: Suhrkamp, 2000.

Schmithals, Walter. *Gnosticism in Corinth: An Investigation of the Letters to the Corinthians.* Translated by John E. Steely. Nashville: Abingdon, 1971.

———. *Der Römerbrief als historisches Problem.* Studien zum Neuen Testament 9. Gütersloh: Gütersloher Verlagshaus, 1975.

———. *Die theologische Anthropologie des Paulus: Auslegung von Röm 7, 17–8, 39.* Stuttgart: Kohlhammer, 1980.

———, ed. *Neues Testament und Gnosis.* Erträge der Forschung 208. Darmstadt: Wissenschaftliche Buchgesellschaft, 1984.

Schnabel, Eckhard J. *Law and Wisdom from Ben Sira to Paul: A Tradition Historical Enquiry into the Relation of Law, Wisdom, and Ethics.* Wissenschaftliche Untersuchungen zum Neuen Testament 2/16. Tübingen: Mohr Siebeck, 1985.

Schnackenburg, Rudolf. *Das Heilsgeschehen bei der Taufe nach dem Apostel Paulus: Eine Studie zur paulinischen Theologie.* Münchener theologische Studien, 1: Historische Abteilung 1. Munich: Zink, 1950.

———. *The Moral Teaching of the New Testament.* Translated by J. Holland-Smith and W. J. O'Hara. New York: Seabury, 1973.

Schneemelcher, Wilhelm. *Das Urchristentum.* Stuttgart: Kohlhammer, 1981.

Schneider, Gerhard. *Die Apostelgeschichte.* Herders theologischer Kommentar zum Neuen Testament 5. Freiburg: Herder, 1980–.

Schnelle, Udo. *Gerechtigkeit und Christusgegenwart: Vorpaulinische und paulinische Tauftheologie.* Göttinger theologische Arbeiten 24. Göttingen: Vandenhoeck & Ruprecht, 1983.

———. "Der erste Thessalonicherbrief und die Entstehung der paulinischen Anthropologie." *New Testament Studies* 32 (1986): 207–24.

———. *Wandlungen im paulinischen Denken.* Stuttgarter Bibelstudien 137. Stuttgart: Katholisches Bibelwerk, 1989.

———. "Die Ethik des 1 Thessalonikerbriefes." Pages 295–305 in *The Thessalonian Correspondence.* Edited by Raymond F. Collins and Norbert Baumert. Bibliotheca ephemeridum theologicarum lovaniensium 87. Leuven: Leuven University Press, 1990.

———. "Der historische Abstand und der Heilige Geist." Pages 87–103 in *Reformation und Neuzeit: 300 Jahre Theologie in Halle.* Edited by Udo Schnelle. Berlin: de Gruyter, 1994.

———. *The Human Condition: Anthropology in the Teachings of Jesus, Paul, and John.* Translated by O. C. Dean Jr. Minneapolis: Fortress, 1996.

———. "Neutestamentliche Anthropologie." Pages 2658–2714 in *Aufstieg und Niedergang der römischen Welt.* Part 2. *Principat,* 26.3. Edited by Hildegard Temporini and Wolfgang Haase. Berlin: de Gruyter, 1996.

———. *The History and Theology of the New Testament Writings.* Translated by M. Eugene Boring. Minneapolis: Fortress, 1998.

———. "Heilsgegenwart: Christologische Hoheitstitel bei Paulus." Pages 178–93 in *Paulinische Christologie: Exegetische Beiträge: Hans Hübner zum 70. Geburtstag.* Edited by Udo Schnelle et al. Göttingen: Vandenhoeck & Ruprecht, 2000.

———. "Gerechtigkeit in den Psalmen Salomos und bei Paulus." Pages 365–75 in *Jüdische Schriften in ihrem antik-jüdischen und urchristlichen Kontext.* Edited by Hermann Lichtenberger and Gerbern S. Oegema. Studien zu den jüdischen Schriften aus hellenistisch-römischer Zeit 1. Gütersloh: Gütersloher Verlagshaus, 2002.

Schoeps, Hans Joachim. *Paul: The Theology of the Apostle in the Light of Jewish Religious History.* Translated by Harold Knight. Philadelphia: Westminster, 1961.

Scholtissek, Klaus. "'Geboren aus einer Frau, geboren unter das Gesetz' (Gal. 4,4): Die christologisch-soteriologische Bedeutung des irdischen Jesus bei Paulus." Pages 194–219 in *Paulinische Christologie: Exegetische Beiträge: Hans Hübner zum 70. Geburtstag.* Edited by Udo Schnelle et al. Göttingen: Vandenhoeck & Ruprecht, 2000.

———. "Paulus als Lehrer." Pages 11–36 in *Christologie in der Paulus-Schule: Zur Rezeptionsgeschichte des paulinischen Evangeliums.* Edited by Klaus Scholtissek. Stuttgarter Bibelstudien 181. Stuttgart: Katholisches Bibelwerk, 2000.

Schrage, Wolfgang. *Die konkreten Einzelgebote in der paulinischen Paränese: Ein Beitrag zur neu-*

testamentlichen Ethik. Gütersloh: Gütersloher Verlagshaus, 1961.

———. "Die Stellung zur Welt bei Paulus, Epictet, und in der Apokalyptik." *Zeitschrift für Theologie und Kirche* 61 (1964): 125–54.

———. "'In Christus' und die neutestamentliche Ethik." Pages 27–41 in *In Christus: Beiträge zum ökumenischen Gespräch.* Edited by Josef Georg Ziegler. 1st ed. Moraltheologische Studien: Systematische Abteilung 14. St. Ottilien: EOS, 1987.

———. *The Ethics of the New Testament.* Translated by David E. Green. Philadelphia: Fortress, 1988.

———. *Der erste Brief an die Korinther.* 4 vols. Evangelisch-katholischer Kommentar zum Neuen Testament 7. Zurich: Benziger, 1991.

———. "Der gekreuzigte und auferweckte Herr: Zur theologia crucis und theologia resurrectionis bei Paulus." *Zeitschrift für Theologie und Kirche* 94 (1997): 25–38.

———. *Unterwegs zur Einzigkeit und Einheit Gottes: Zum "Monotheismus" des Paulus und seiner alttestamentlich-frühjüdischen Tradition.* Biblisch-theologische Studien 48. Neukirchen-Vluyn: Neukirchener Verlag, 2002.

Schreiner, Thomas R. "'Works of Law' in Paul." *Novum Testamentum* 33 (1991): 217–44.

———. *The Law and Its Fulfillment: A Pauline Theology of Law.* Grand Rapids: Baker, 1993.

Schröter, Jens. *Der versöhnte Versöhner: Paulus als unentbehrlicher Mittler im Heilsvorgang zwischen Gott und Gemeinde nach 2 Kor 2,14–7,4.* Texte und Arbeiten zum neutestamentlichen Zeitalter 10. Tübingen: Francke, 1993.

———. "Schriftauslegung und Hermeneutik in 2 Korinther 3." *Novum Testamentum* 40 (1998): 231–75.

———. "Die Universalisierung des Gesetzes im Galaterbrief." Pages 27–63 in *Das Verständnis des Gesetzes bei Juden, Christen, und im Islam.* Edited by Udo Kern and Karl-Erich Grözinger. Rostocker theologische Studien 5. Münster: LIT, 2000.

Schulz, Siegfried. "Der frühe und der späte Paulus." *Theologische Zeitschrift* 41 (1985): 228–36.

———. *Neutestamentliche Ethik.* Zurich: Theologischer Verlag, 1987.

Schumacher, Leonhard. *Sklaverei in der Antike: Alltag und Schicksal der Unfreien.* Beck's archäologische Bibliothek. Munich: Beck, 2001.

Schunack, W. "Glaube in griechischer Religiosität." Pages 296–326 in *Antikes Judentum und frühes Christentum: Festschrift für Hartmut Stegemann zum 65. Geburtstag.* Edited by Bernd Kollmann et al. Beihefte zur Zeitschrift für die neutestamentliche Wissenschaft 97. Berlin: de Gruyter, 1999.

Schürer, Emil. *The History of the Jewish People in the Age of Jesus Christ (175 B.C.–A.D. 135).* Edited by Géza Vermès and Fergus Millar. 2nd ed. 3 vols. Edinburgh: T&T Clark, 1973.

Schutz, Alfred. *The Phenomenology of the Social World.* Translated by George Walsh and Frederick Lehnert. London: Heinemann, 1972.

Schutz, Alfred, and Thomas Luckmann. *The Structures of the Life-World.* Translated by Richard M. Zaner and H. Tristram Engelhardt Jr. Northwestern University Studies in Phenomenology and Existential Philosophy. Evanston, IL: Northwestern University Press, 1973.

———. *Strukturen der Lebenswelt.* Neuwied: Luchterhand, 1975.

———. *Strukturen der Lebenswelt.* Vol. 2. Frankfurt: Suhrkamp, 1983.

———. *The Structures of the Life-World.* Vol. 2. Translated by Richard M. Zaner and David J. Parent. Northwestern University Studies in Phenomenology and Existential Philosophy. Evanston, IL: Northwestern University Press, 1989.

Schweitzer, Albert. *The Mysticism of Paul the Apostle.* Translated by William Montgomery. London: A. & C. Black, 1931.

———. *The Quest of the Historical Jesus: A Critical Study of Its Progress from Reimarus to Wrede.* Edited by John Bowden. Translated by William Montgomery et al. "First Complete" ed. Minneapolis: Fortress, 2000.

Schweizer, Eduard. "Die 'Elemente der Welt': Gal. 4,3.9; Kol 2,8.20." Pages 147–63 in *Beiträge zur Theologie des Neuen Testaments: Neutestamentliche Aufsätze (1955–1970).* Zurich: Zwingli, 1970.

Seifrid, Mark A. *Justification by Faith: The Origin and Development of a Central Pauline Theme.* Supplements to Novum Testamentum 68. Leiden: Brill, 1992.

———. "In Christ." Pages 27–41 in *Dictionary of Paul and His Letters*. Edited by Gerald F. Hawthorne et al. Downers Grove, IL: InterVarsity, 1993.

———. "Righteousness Language in the Hebrew Scriptures and Early Judaism." Pages 415–42 in vol. 1 of *Justification and Variegated Nomism*. Edited by D. A. Carson et al. 2 vols. Wissenschaftliche Untersuchungen zum Neuen Testament 2/140, 181. Grand Rapids: Baker Academic, 2001–2004.

Sellin, Gerhard. *Der Streit um die Auferstehung der Toten: Eine religionsgeschichtliche und exegetische Untersuchung von 1 Korinther 15*. Forschungen zur Religion und Literatur des Alten und Neuen Testaments 138. Göttingen: Vandenhoeck & Ruprecht, 1986.

Sherwin-White, A. N. *Roman Society and Roman Law in the New Testament*. Sarum Lectures, 1960–1961. Grand Rapids: Baker, 1978.

Siber, Peter. *Mit Christus Leben: Eine Studie zur paulinischen Auferstehungshoffnung*. Zurich: Theologischer Verlag, 1971.

Siegert, F. "Gottesfürchtige und Sympathisanten." *Journal of Jewish Studies* 4 (1973): 109–64.

Smallwood, M. *The Jews under Roman Rule from Pompey to Diocletian*. Studies in Judaism in Late Antiquity 20. Leiden: Brill, 1981.

Smit, J. "The Letter of Paul to the Galatians: A Deliberative Speech." *New Testament Studies* 35 (1989): 1–26.

Smith, Dennis E. "Egyptian Cults at Corinth." *Harvard Theological Review* 70 (1977): 201–31.

———. *From Symposium to Eucharist: The Banquet in the Early Christian World*. Minneapolis: Fortress, 2003.

Soards, Marion L. *The Apostle Paul: An Introduction to His Writings and Teaching*. New York: Paulist, 1987.

Soden, Hans von. "Sakrament und Ethik bei Paulus: Zur Frage der literarischen und theologischen Einheitlichkeit von 1.Kor. 8–10." Pages 338–79. *Das Paulusbild in der neueren deutschen Forschung*. Edited by Karl Heinrich Rengstorf and Ulrich Luck. Wege der Forschung 24. Darmstadt: Wissenschaftliche Buchgesellschaft, 1964.

Söding, Thomas. "Der erste Thessalonicherbrief und die frühe paulinische Evangeliumsverkündigung: Zur Frage einer Entwicklung der paulinischen

Theologie." *Biblische Zeitschrift* 35 (1991): 184–209.

———. "Die Gegner des Apostels Paulus in Galatien." *Münchner theologische Zeitschrift* 42 (1991): 305–21.

———."Zur Chronologie der paulinischen Briefe." *Biblische Notizen* 56 (1991): 31–59.

———. "'Die Kraft der Sünde ist das Gesetz' (1 Kor 15,56): Anmerkungen zum Hintergrund und zur Pointe einer gesetzeskritischen Sentenz des Apostels Paulus." *Zeitschrift für die neutestamentliche Wissenschaft und die Kunde der älteren Kirche* 83 (1992): 74–84.

———. "Kreuzestheologie und Rechtfertigungslehre." *Catholica* (Münster) 46 (1992): 31–60.

———. *Die Trias Glaube, Hoffnung, Liebe bei Paulus: Eine exegetische Studie*. Stuttgarter Bibelstudien 150. Stuttgart: Katholisches Bibelwerk, 1992.

———. "Das Geheimnis Gottes im Kreuz Jesu (1 Kor)." *Biblische Zeitschrift* 38 (1994): 174–94.

———. "Starke und Schwache." *Zeitschrift für die neutestamentliche Wissenschaft und die Kunde der älteren Kirche* 85 (1994): 69–92.

———. *Das Liebesgebot bei Paulus: Die Mahnung zur Agape im Rahmen der paulinischen Ethik*. Neutestamentliche Abhandlungen 26. Münster: Aschendorff, 1995.

———. "Apostel der Heiden (Röm 11,13): Zur paulinischen Missionspraxis." Pages 185–95 in *Das Wort vom Kreuz: Studien zur paulinischen Theologie*. Wissenschaftliche Untersuchungen zum Neuen Testament 93. Tübingen: Mohr Siebeck, 1997.

———. "Gottes Sohn von Anfang an: Zur Präexistenzchristologie bei Paulus und den Deuteropaulinen." Pages 57–93 in *Gottes ewiger Sohn: Die Präexistenz Christi*. Edited by Rudolf Laufen. Paderborn: Schöningh, 1997.

———. "Kriterium der Wahrheit? Zum theologischen Stellenwert der paulinischen Rechtfertigungslehre." Pages 193–246 in *Worum geht es in der Rechtfertigungslehre? Das biblische Fundament der "Gemeinsamen Erklärung" von katholischer Kirche und Lutherischem Weltbund*. Edited by Thomas Söding and Frank-Lothar Hossfeld. Quaestiones disputatae 180. Freiburg: Herder, 1999.

———. "Der Skopus der paulinischen Rechtfertigungslehre." *Zeitschrift für Theologie und Kirche* 97 (2000): 404–33.

Stanley, Christopher D. *Paul and the Language of Scripture: Citation Technique in the Pauline Epistles and Contemporary Literature*. Society of New Testament Studies Monograph Series 69. Cambridge: Cambridge University Press, 1992.

Stark, Rodney. *The Rise of Christianity: A Sociologist Reconsiders History*. Princeton: Princeton University Press, 1996.

Stegemann, Ekkehard, and Wolfgang Stegemann. *The Jesus Movement: A Social History of Its First Century*. Translated by O. C. Dean Jr. Minneapolis: Fortress, 1999.

Stegemann, Hartmut. "Die Bedeutung der Qumranfunde für die Erforschung der Apokalyptik." Pages 495–530 in *Apocalypticism in the Mediterranean World and the Near East: Proceedings of the International Colloquium on Apocalypticism, Uppsala, August 12–17, 1979*. Edited by David Hellholm. Tübingen: Mohr Siebeck, 1983.

———. *The Library of Qumran, on the Essenes, Qumran, John the Baptist, and Jesus*. Grand Rapids: Eerdmans, 1998.

Stegemann, Wolfgang. "War der Apostel Paulus ein römischer Bürger?" *Zeitschrift für die neutestamentliche Wissenschaft und die Kunde der älteren Kirche* 78 (1987): 220–29.

Stemberger, Günter. *Der Leib der Auferstehung: Studien zur Anthropologie und Eschatologie des palästinischen Judentums im neutestamentlichen Zeitalter (ca. 170 v. C[h]r.–100 n. Chr.)*. Analecta biblica 56. Rome: Biblical Institute Press, 1972.

———. *Jewish Contemporaries of Jesus: Pharisees, Sadducees, Essenes*. Translated by Allan W. Mahnke. Minneapolis: Fortress, 1995.

Stern, Menahem. *Greek and Latin Authors on Jews and Judaism*. 3 vols. Jerusalem: Israel Academy of Sciences and Humanities, 1974.

———. "The Jewish Diaspora." Pages 117–83. *The Jewish People in the First Century: Historical Geography, Political History, Social, Cultural, and Religious Life and Institutions*. Edited by Shemuel Safrai and M. Stern. Compendia rerum iudaicarum ad Novum Testamentum 1. Assen: Van Gorcum, 1974.

Stolle, Volker. *Der Zeuge als Angeklagter: Untersuchungen zum Paulusbild des Lukas*. Beiträge zur Wissenschaft vom Alten (und Neuen) Testament 102. Stuttgart: Kohlhammer, 1973.

Stowers, Stanley K. *The Diatribe and Paul's Letter to the Romans*. Society of Biblical Literature Dissertation Series 57. Chico, CA: Scholars Press, 1981.

———. "Social Status, Public Speaking, and Private Teaching: The Circumstances of Paul's Preaching Activity." *Novum Testamentum* 16 (1984): 59–82.

Strauss, David Friedrich. *The Old Faith and the New*. Translated by Mathilde Blind. New York: H. Holt, 1873.

———. *The Life of Jesus Critically Examined*. Edited by Leander Keck. Lives of Jesus Series. London: SCM Press, 1973.

Strecker, Christian. "Paul aus einer neuen 'Perspektiv.'" *Kirche und Israel* 11 (1996): 3–18.

———. *Die liminale Theologie des Paulus: Zugänge zur paulinischen Theologie aus kulturanthropologischer Perspektive*. Göttingen: Vandenhoeck & Ruprecht, 1999.

Strecker, Georg. "Strukturen einer neutestamentlichen Ethik." *Zeitschrift für Theologie und Kirche* 75 (1978): 117–46.

———. "Befreiung und Rechtfertigung: Zur Stellung der Rechtfertigungslehre in der Theologie des Paulus." Pages 229–59 in *Eschaton und Historie: Aufsätze*. Göttingen: Vandenhoeck & Ruprecht, 1979.

———. "Das Evangelium Jesu Christi." Pages 183–228 in *Eschaton und Historie*.

———. "Die sogenannte zweite Jerusalemreise des Paulus (Act. 11,27–30)." Pages 132–41 in *Eschaton und Historie*.

———. "Die Legitimität des paulinischen Apostolates nach 2 Korintherbrief 10–13." *New Testament Studies* 38 (1992): 566–86.

———. "Der vorchristliche Paulus." Pages 713–41 in *Texts and Contexts: Biblical Texts in Their Textual and Situational Contexts: Essays in Honor of Lars Hartman*. Edited by Tord Fornberg et al. Boston: Scandinavian University Press, 1995.

———. *Theologie des Neuen Testaments*. Berlin: de Gruyter, 1996.

———. *History of New Testament Literature*. Translated by Calvin Katter and Hans-Joachim Mollenhauer. Harrisburg, PA: Trinity Press International, 1997.

———. *Theology of the New Testament*. Translated by M. Eugene Boring. New York: de Gruyter, 2000.

Strecker, Georg, and Johann Maier. *Neues Testament–antikes Judentum*. Stuttgart: Kohlhammer, 1989.

Stuckenbruck, Loren T. *Angel Veneration and Christology: A Study in Early Judaism and in the Christology of the Apocalypse of John*. Wissenschaftliche Untersuchungen zum Neuen Testament 2/70. Tübingen: J. C. B. Mohr Siebeck, 1995.

Stuhlmacher, Peter. *Gerechtigkeit Gottes bei Paulus*. Göttingen: Vandenhoeck & Ruprecht, 1965.

———. *Das paulinische Evangelium*. Forschungen zur Religion und Literatur des Alten und Neuen Testaments 95. Göttingen: Vandenhoeck & Ruprecht, 1968.

———. *Der Brief an Philemon*. Neukirchen-Vluyn: Benziger, 1975.

———. "Das Gesetz als Thema biblischer Theologie." Pages 136–65 in *Versöhnung, Gesetz, und Gerechtigkeit: Aufsätze zur biblischen Theologie*. Göttingen: Vandenhoeck & Ruprecht, 1981.

———. "Jesustraditionen im Römerbrief?" *Theologische Beiträge* 14 (1983): 240–50.

———. *Biblische Theologie des Neuen Testaments*. 2 vols. Göttingen: Vandenhoeck & Ruprecht, 1992–1999.

———. *Paul's Letter to the Romans: A Commentary*. Translated by Scott J. Hafemann. Louisville: Westminster John Knox, 1994.

Suhl, Alfred. *Paulus und seine Briefe: Ein Beitrag zur paulinische Chronologie*. Studien zum Neuen Testament 11. Gütersloh: Gütersloher Verlagshaus, 1975.

———. *Der Brief an Philemon*. Zürcher Bibelkommentare: NT 13. Zurich: Theologischer Verlag, 1981.

Sumney, Jerry L. *Identifying Paul's Opponents: The Question of Method in 2 Corinthians*. Journal for the Study of the New Testament Supplement Series 40. Sheffield: JSOT Press, 1990.

Synofzik, Ernst. *Die Gerichts- und Vergeltungsaussagen bei Paulus: Eine traditionsgeschichtliche Untersuchung*. Göttinger theologische Arbeiten 8. Göttingen: Vandenhoeck & Ruprecht, 1977.

Tcherikover, Victor. *Hellenistic Civilization and the Jews*. Philadelphia: Jewish Publication Society of America. 1959. Peabody, MA: Hendrickson, 1999.

Tellbe, M. "The Sociological Factors behind Philippians 3.1–11 and the Conflict at Philippi." *Journal for the Study of the New Testament* 55 (1994): 97–121.

Theissen, Gerd. *Psychological Aspects of Pauline Theology*. Translated by John P. Galvin. Philadelphia: Fortress, 1987.

———. *The Gospels in Context: Social and Political History in the Synoptic Tradition*. Translated by Linda M. Maloney. Minneapolis: Fortress, 1991.

———. "Judentum und Christentum bei Paulus." Pages 331–56 in *Paulus und das antike Judentum: Tübingen-Durham-Symposium im Gedenken an den 50. Todestag Adolf Schlatters (19 Mai 1938)*. Edited by Martin Hengel and Ulrich Heckel. Wissenschaftliche Untersuchungen zum Neuen Testament 58. Tübingen: Mohr Siebeck, 1991.

———. "Social Stratification in the Corinthian Community." Pages 69–119 in *The Social Setting of Pauline Christianity*. Translated and edited by John H. Schütz. Philadelphia: Fortress, 1982.

———. "Die Starken und Schwachen in Korinth." Pages 272–89 in *Studien zur Soziologie des Urchristentums*. Wissenschaftliche Untersuchungen zum Neuen Testament 19. Tübingen: Mohr Siebeck, 1992. ET: "The Strong and the Weak in Corinth: A Sociological Analysis of a Theoretical Quarrel." Pages 121–43 in *The Social Setting of Pauline Christianity*. Edited and translated by John H. Schütz. Philadelphia: Fortress, 1982.

———. *The Religion of the Earliest Churches: Creating a Symbolic World*. Translated by John Bowden. Minneapolis: Fortress, 1999.

———. "Die urchristliche Taufe und die soziale Konstruktion des neuen Menschen." Pages 87–114 in *Transformations of the Inner Self in Ancient Religions*. Edited by Gedaliahu A. G. Stroumsa and Jan Assmann. Studies in the History of Religions 83. Leiden: Brill, 1999.

———. "Röm 9–11—eine Auseinandersetzung des Paulus mit Israel und sich selbst: Versuch einer psychologischen Auslegung." Pages 311–42. *Fair Play: Diversity and Conflicts in Early Christianity: Essays in Honour of Heikki Räisänen*. Edited by Ismo Dunderberg, Christopher Tuckett, and Kari

Syreeni. Supplements to Novum Testamentum 103. Leiden: Brill, 2002.

Theissen, Gerd, and Annette Merz. *The Historical Jesus: A Comprehensive Guide.* Translated by John Bowden. Minneapolis: Fortress, 1998.

Theobald, Michael. "Der Kanon von der Rechtfertigung." Pages 131–38 in *Worum geht es in der Rechtfertigungslehre? Das biblische Fundament der "Gemeinsamen Erklärung" von katholischer Kirche und Lutherischem Weltbund.* Edited by Thomas Söding and Frank-Lothar Hossfeld. Quaestiones disputatae 180. Freiburg: Herder, 1999.

———. *Der Römerbrief.* Darmstadt: Wissenschaftliche Buchgesellschaft, 2000.

Thielmann, F. "The Coherence of Paul's View of the Law: The Evidence of First Corinthians." *New Testament Studies* 38 (1992): 235–53.

Thompson, Leonard L. *The Book of Revelation: Apocalypse and Empire.* Oxford: Oxford University Press, 1990.

Thornton, Claus-Jürgen. *Der Zeuge des Zeugen: Lukas als Historiker der Paulusreisen.* Wissenschaftliche Untersuchungen zum Neuen Testament 56. Tübingen: Mohr Siebeck, 1991.

Thrall, Margaret E. *A Critical and Exegetical Commentary on the Second Epistle to the Corinthians.* Edinburgh: T&T Clark, 1994.

Thüsing, Wilhelm. *Per Christum in Deum: Studien zum Verhältnis von Christozentrik und Theozentrik in den paulinischen Hauptbriefen.* 2nd ed. Neutestamentliche Abhandlungen: Neue Folge 1. Münster: Aschendorff, 1969.

———. *Die neutestamentlichen Theologien und Jesus Christus.* 3 vols. Düsseldorf: Patmos, 1981–1999.

———. *Gott und Christus in der paulinischen Soteriologie.* 3rd ed. Münster: Aschendorff, 1986.

Tillich, Paul. *Reason and Revelation; Being and God.* Vol. 1 of *Systematic Theology.* Chicago: University of Chicago Press, 1951.

———. "The Meaning and Justification of Religious Symbols." Pages 165–72. *The Interpretation of Texts.* Edited by David E. Klemm et al. Hermeneutical Inquiry 1. Atlanta: Scholars Press, 1986.

Trafton, J. L. "The Psalms of Solomon in Recent Research." *Journal for the Study of the Pseudepigrapha* 12 (1994): 3–19.

Troeltsch, Ernst. "Historical and Dogmatic Method in Theology." Pages 11–32 in *Religion in History.* Translated by James Luther Adams and Walter E. Bense. Minneapolis: Fortress, 1991.

Umbach, Helmut. *In Christus getauft, von der Sünde befreit: Die Gemeinde als sündenfreier Raum bei Paulus.* Göttingen: Vandenhoeck & Ruprecht, 1999.

Unnik, W. C. van. "Tarsus or Jerusalem: The City of Paul's Youth." Pages 259–320 in vol. 1 of *Sparsa collecta.* 3 vols. Supplements to Novum Testamentum 29–31. Leiden: Brill, 1973–1983.

Vermès, Géza. *Jesus the Jew: A Historian's Reading of the Gospels.* Philadelphia: Fortress, 1973.

Vielhauer, Philipp. *Geschichte der urchristlichen Literatur: Einleitung in das Neue Testament, die Apokryphen, und die Apostolischen Väter.* Berlin: de Gruyter, 1975.

———. *Oikodome: Aufsätze zum Neuen Testament.* Edited by Günter Klein. Munich: C. Kaiser, 1979.

Vittinghoff, Friedrich. "'Christianus sum': Das 'Verbrechen' von Außenseitern der römischen Gesellschaft." *Historia* 33 (1984): 331–57.

Vogel, Manuel. *Das Heil des Bundes: Bundestheologie im Frühjudentum und im frühen Christentum.* Texte und Arbeiten zum neutestamentlichen Zeitalter 18. Tübingen: Francke, 1996.

Vollenweider, Samuel. *Freiheit als neue Schöpfung: Eine Untersuchung zur Eleutheria bei Paulus und in seiner Umwelt.* Forschungen zur Religion und Literatur des Alten und Neuen Testaments 147. Göttingen: Vandenhoeck & Ruprecht, 1989.

———. "Großer Tod und Großes Leben." *Evangelische Theologie* 51 (1991): 365–82.

———. "Der Geist Gottes als Selbst der Glaubenden." *Zeitschrift für Theologie und Kirche* 93 (1996): 163–92.

———. "Zwischen Monotheismus und Engelchristologie." *Zeitschrift für Theologie und Kirche* 99 (2002): 21–44.

Vos, Johannes Sijko. *Traditionsgeschichtliche Untersuchungen zur paulinischen Pneumatologie.* Assen: Van Gorcum, 1973.

Voss, Florian. *Das Wort vom Kreuz und die menschliche Vernunft: Eine Untersuchung zur Soteriologie des 1. Korintherbriefes.* Forschungen zur Religion und Literatur des Alten und Neuen Testaments 199. Göttingen: Vandenhoeck & Ruprecht, 2002.

Vouga, François. "Zur rhetorischen Gattung des Galaterbriefes." *Zeitschrift für die neutestamentliche Wissenschaft und die Kunde der älteren Kirche* 79 (1988): 291–92.

———. *An die Galater.* Handbuch zum Neuen Testament 10. Tübingen: Mohr Siebeck, 1998.

Walker, William O., Jr. "Galatians 2:7b–8 as a Non-Pauline Interpolation." *Catholic Biblical Quarterly* 65, no. 4 (2003): 568–87.

Walter, Nikolaus. "Paulus und die urchristliche Jesustradition." *New Testament Studies* 31 (1985): 498–522.

———. "Leibliche Auferstehung? Zur Frage der Hellenisierung der Auferweckungshoffnung bei Paulus." Pages 109–27 in *Paulus, Apostel Jesu Christi: Festschrift für Günter Klein zum 70. Geburtstag.* Edited by Günter Klein and Michael Trowitzsch. Tübingen: Mohr Siebeck, 1998.

———. "Alttestamentliche Bezüge in christologischen Ausführungen bei Paulus." Pages 246–71 in *Paulinische Christologie: Exegetische Beiträge: Hans Hübner zum 70. Geburtstag.* Edited by Udo Schnelle et al. Göttingen: Vandenhoeck & Ruprecht, 2000.

Walter, Nikolaus, et al. *Die Briefe an die Philipper, Thessalonicher, und an Philemon.* Das Neue Testament Deutsch 8/2. Göttingen: Vandenhoeck & Ruprecht, 1998.

Watson, Francis. *Paul, Judaism, and the Gentiles: A Sociological Approach.* Society of New Testament Studies Monograph Series 56. Cambridge: Cambridge University Press, 1986.

Watzlawick, Paul. *The Invented Reality: How Do We Know What We Believe We Know? Contributions to Constructivism.* New York: Norton, 1984.

Weber, Reinhard. "Die Geschichte des Gesetzes und des Ich in Römer 7,7–8,4." *Neue Zeitschrift für systematische Theologie* 29 (1987): 147–79.

———. *Das Gesetz im hellenistischen Judentum: Studien zum Verständnis und zur Funktion der Thora von Demetrios bis Pseudo-Phokylides.* Arbeiten zur Religion und Geschichte des Urchristentums 10. Frankfurt: Lang, 2000.

———. *Das "Gesetz" bei Philon von Alexandrien und Flavius Josephus: Studien zum Verständnis und zur Funktion der Thora bei den beiden Hauptzeugen des hellenistischen Judentums.* Arbeiten zur Religion und Geschichte des Urchristentums 11. Frankfurt: Lang, 2001.

Wechsler, Andreas. *Geschichtsbild und Apostelstreit: Eine forschungsgeschichtliche und exegetische Studie über den antiochenischen Zwischenfall (Gal. 2, 11–14).* Beihefte zur Zeitschrift für die neutestamentliche Wissenschaft 62. Berlin: de Gruyter, 1991.

Wedderburn, A. J. M. "Some Observations on Paul's Use of the Phrases 'in Christ' and 'with Christ.'" *Journal for the Study of the New Testament* 25 (1985): 83–97.

———. *Baptism and Resurrection: Studies in Pauline Theology against Its Graeco-Roman Background.* Wissenschaftliche Untersuchungen zum Neuen Testament 44. Tübingen: Mohr Siebeck, 1987.

———. *The Reasons for Romans.* Edited by John Kenneth Riches. Edinburgh: T&T Clark, 1988.

———. "Paul and the Story of Jesus." Pages 161–189 in *Paul and Jesus: Collected Essays.* Journal for the Study of the New Testament: Supplement Series 37. Sheffield: JSOT Press, 1989.

Weder, Hans. *Das Kreuz Jesu bei Paulus: Ein Versuch, über den Geschichtsbezug des christlichen Glaubens nachzudenken.* Göttingen: Vandenhoeck & Ruprecht, 1981.

———. "Gesetz und Sünde: Gedanken zu einem qualitativen Sprung im Denken des Paulus." Pages 171–82 in *Einblicke ins Evangelium: Exegetische Beiträge zur neutestamentlichen Hermeneutik: Gesammelte Aufsätze aus den Jahren 1980–1991.* Göttingen: Vandenhoeck & Ruprecht, 1992.

———. "Die Energie des Evangeliums: Hermeneutische Überlegungen zur Wirklichkeit des Wortes," in *Theologie als gegenwärtige Schriftauslegung.* Zeitschrift für Theologie und Kirche: Beiheft 9. Tübingen: Mohr Siebeck, 1995.

———. "Gesetz und Gnade." Pages 171–82 in *Ja und Nein: Christliche Theologie im Angesicht Israels: Festschrift zum 70. Geburtstag von Wolfgang Schrage.* Edited by Klaus Wengst et al. Neukirchen-Vluyn: Neukirchener Verlag, 1998.

———. "Die Normativität der Freiheit." Pages 129–45 in *Paulus, Apostel Jesu Christi: Festschrift für Günter Klein zum 70. Geburtstag.* Edited by Michael Trowitzsch. Tübingen: Mohr Siebeck, 1998.

Wehnert, Jürgen. *Die Reinheit des "christlichen Gottesvolkes" aus Juden und Heiden: Studien zum historischen und theologischen Hintergrund des sogenannten Aposteldekrets.* Forschungen zur

Religion und Literatur des Alten und Neuen Testaments 173. Göttingen: Vandenhoeck & Ruprecht, 1997.

Wehr, Lothar. *Petrus und Paulus, Kontrahenten und Partner: Die beiden Apostel im Spiegel des Neuen Testaments, der apostolischen Väter, und früher Zeugnisse ihrer Verehrung.* Neutestamentliche Abhandlungen 30. Münster: Aschendorff, 1996.

Weiser, Alfons. *Die Apostelgeschichte.* 2 vols. Ökumenischer Taschenbuch-Kommentar zum Neuen Testament 5. Würzburg: Echter, 1981–1985.

———. "Zur Gesetzes- und Tempelkritik der 'Hellenisten.'" Pages 146–68 in *Das Gesetz im Neuen Testament.* Edited by Johannes Beutler and Karl Kertelge. Quaestiones disputatae 108. Freiburg: Herder, 1986.

Weiss, Johannes. *Der erste Korintherbrief.* 9th ed. Kritisch-exegetischer Kommentar über das Neue Testament. Göttingen: Vandenhoeck & Ruprecht, 1910. Reprint, 1970.

———. *Earliest Christianity: A History of the Period A.D. 30–150.* Translated by Frederick C. Grant. 2 vols. New York: Harper, 1959.

Wengst, Klaus. *Pax romana: And the Peace of Jesus Christ.* Philadelphia: Fortress, 1987.

Wenham, David. *Paul: Follower of Jesus or Founder of Christianity?* Grand Rapids: Eerdmans, 1995.

Wernle, Paul. *Die Anfänge unserer Religion.* 2nd ed. Tübingen: Mohr Siebeck, 1904.

White, Joel R. "Baptized on account of the Dead." *Journal of Biblical Literature* 116 (1997): 487–99.

Wiefel, Wolfgang. "Die Hauptrichtung des Wandels im eschatologischen Denken des Paulus." *Theologische Zeitschrift* 30 (1974): 65–81.

———. "Paulus und das Judentum." *Zeichen der Zeit* 40 (1986): 142–47.

———. "The Jewish Community in Ancient Rome and the Origins of Roman Christianity." Pages 85–101 in *The Romans Debate.* Edited by Karl P. Donfried. Rev. and exp. ed. Peabody, MA: Hendrickson, 1991.

Wikenhauser, Alfred, and Josef Schmid. *Einleitung in das Neue Testament.* 6th ed. Freiburg: Herder, 1973.

Wilckens, Ulrich. *Weisheit und Torheit: Eine exegetisch-religionsgeschichtliche Untersuchung zu 1. Kor. 1 und 2.* Beiträge zur historischen Theologie 26. Tübingen: Mohr Siebeck, 1959.

———. "Was heißt bei Paulus: 'Aus Werken des Gesetzes wird kein Mensch gerecht'?" Pages 77–109 in *Rechtfertigung als Freiheit: Paulusstudien.* Neukirchen-Vluyn: Neukirchener Verlag, 1974.

———. "Christologie und Anthropologie im Zusammenhang der paulinischen Rechtfertigungslehre." *Zeitschrift für die neutestamentliche Wissenschaft und die Kunde der älteren Kirche* 67 (1976): 64–82.

———. *Der Brief an die Römer.* 3 vols. Evangelisch-katholischer Kommentar zum Neuen Testament 6. Neukirchen-Vluyn: Neukirchener Verlag, 1978–1982.

———. *Resurrection: Biblical Testimony to the Resurrection: An Historical Examination and Explanation.* Translated by A. M. Stewart. Atlanta: John Knox, 1978.

———. "Zur Entwicklung des paulinischen Gesetzesverständnisses." *New Testament Studies* 28 (1982): 154–90.

———. "Der Ursprung der Überlieferung der Erscheinungen des Auferstandenen." Pages 139–93 in *Zur neutestamentlichen Überlieferung von der Auferstehung Jesu.* Edited by Paul Hoffmann. Darmstadt: Wissenschaftliche Buchgesellschaft, 1988.

———. "Die Auferstehung Jesu: Historisches Zeugnis–Theologie–Glaubenserfahrung." *Pastoraltheologie* 85 (1996): 102–12.

Wilk, Florian. *Die Bedeutung des Jesajabuches für Paulus.* Forschungen zur Religion und Literatur des Alten und Neuen Testaments 179. Göttingen: Vandenhoeck & Ruprecht, 1998.

Wilken, Robert L. "Collegia, Philosophical Schools, and Theology." Pages 268–91 in *The Catacombs and the Colosseum.* Edited by Stephen Benko and John J. O'Rourke. Valley Forge, PA: Judson, 1971.

Windisch, Hans. *Taufe und Sünde im ältesten Christentum bis auf Origenes: Ein Beitrag zur altchristlichen Dogmengeschichte.* Tübingen: Mohr Siebeck, 1908.

———. "Das Problem des paulinischen Imperativs." *Zeitschrift für die neutestamentliche Wissenschaft und die Kunde der älteren Kirche* 23 (1924): 265–81.

———. *Der zweite Korintherbrief.* 9th ed. Göttingen: Vandenhoeck & Ruprecht, 1924.

Winger, M. "The Law of Christ." *New Testament Studies* 46 (2000): 537–46.

Winninge, Mikael. *Sinners and the Righteous: A Comparative Study of the Psalms of Solomon and Paul's Letters.* Coniectanea biblica: New Testament Series 26. Stockholm: Almqvist & Wiksell International, 1995.

Winter, Bruce W. *After Paul Left Corinth: The Influence of Secular Ethics and Social Change.* Grand Rapids: Eerdmans, 2001.

Wischmeyer, Oda. "Das Gebot der Nächstenliebe bei Paulus." *Biblische Zeitschrift* 30 (1986): 153–87.

———. "ΦΥΣΙΣ und ΚΤΙΣΙΣ bei Paulus." *Zeitschrift für Theologie und Kirche* 93 (1996): 352–75.

———. *Der höchste Weg: Das 13. Kapitel des 1. Korintherbriefes.* Studien zum Neuen Testament 13. Gütersloh: Gütersloher Verlagshaus, 1981.

Wiseman, J. "Corinth and Rome, I: 228 B.C.–A.D. 267." Pages 438–548 in *Aufstieg und Niedergang der römischen Welt.* Part 2. *Principat,* 25.4. Edited by Hildegard Temporini and Wolfgang Haase. Berlin: de Gruyter, 1972.

Wolff, Christian. "'Nicht über das hinaus, was geschrieben ist.'" Pages 187–94 in *". . . Das tiefe Wort erneun": Festgabe für Jürgen Henkys zum 60. Geburtstag.* Edited by Harald Schultze. Berlin: Wichern, 1989.

———. *Der zweite Brief des Paulus an die Korinther.* Theologischer Handkommentar zum Neuen Testament 8. Berlin: Evangelische Verlagsanstalt, 1989.

———. *Der erste Brief des Paulus an die Korinther.* Theologischer Handkommentar zum Neuen Testament 7. Leipzig: Evangelische Verlagsanstalt, 1996.

Wolff, Hans Walter. *Anthropology of the Old Testament.* Philadelphia: Fortress, 1974.

Wolter, Michael. *Rechtfertigung und zukünftiges Heil: Untersuchungen zu Röm 5,1–11.* Beihefte zur Zeitschrift für die neutestamentliche Wissenschaft. Berlin: de Gruyter, 1978.

———. "Der Apostel und seine Gemeinden als Teilhaber am Leidensgeschick Jesu Christi." *New Testament Studies* 36 (1990): 535–57.

———. *Der Brief an die Kolosser; Der Brief an Philemon.* Ökumenischer Taschenbuchkommentar zum Neuen Testament 12. Gütersloh: Gütersloher Verlagshaus Gerd Mohn, 1993.

———. "Die ethische Identität christlicher Gemeinden in neutestamentlicher Zeit." Pages 61–90. *Woran orientiert sich Ethik?* Vol. 13 of *Marburger Jahrbuch Theologie.* Marburger theologische Studien 67. Marburg: Elwert, 2001.

Wrede, William. *Paul.* Translated by Edward Lummis. Boston: American Unitarian Association, 1908.

Wright, N. T. "Paul's Gospel and Caesar's Empire." Pages 160–83 in *Paul and Politics: Ekklesia, Israel, Imperium, Interpretation: Essays in Honor of Krister Stendahl.* Edited by Richard A. Horsley. Harrisburg, PA: Trinity Press International, 2000.

———. *The Climax of the Covenant.* Minneapolis: Fortress, 1991.

Würthwein, Ernst. *The Text of the Old Testament: An Introduction to the Biblia Hebraica.* Translated by Erroll F. Rhodes. Grand Rapids: Eerdmans, 1979.

Zahn, Theodor. *Introduction to the New Testament.* Translated by John Moore Trout et al. 3 vols. Edinburgh: T&T Clark, 1909.

Zeller, Dieter. *Der Brief an die Römer.* Regensburger Neues Testament. Regensburg: Pustet, 1985.

———. "Die Menschwerdung des Sohnes Gottes im Neuen Testament und die antike Religionsgeschichte." Pages 141–76 in *Menschwerdung Gottes, Vergöttlichung von Menschen.* Edited by Dieter Zeller. Novum Testamentum et orbis antiquus 7. Göttingen: Vandenhoeck & Ruprecht, 1988.

———. *Charis bei Philon und Paulus.* Stuttgarter Bibelstudien 142. Stuttgart: Katholisches Bibelwerk, 1990.

———. "Die Mysterienreligionen und die paulinische Soteriologie." Pages 42–61 in *Suchbewegungen: Synkretismus: Kulturelle Identität und kirchliches Bekenntnis.* Edited by Hermann Pius Siller. Darmstadt: Wissenschaftliche Buchgesellschaft, 1991.

———. "Der eine Gott und der eine Herr Jesus Christus." Pages 34–49 in *Der lebendige Gott: Studien zur Theologie des Neuen Testaments: Festschrift für Wilhelm Thüsing zum 75. Geburtstag.* Edited by Thomas Söding. Neutestamentliche Abhandlungen: Neue Folge 31. Münster: Aschendorff, 1996.

————. "Konkrete Ethik im hellenistischen Kontext." Pages 82–98 in *Der neue Mensch in Christus: Hellenistische Anthropologie und Ethik im Neuen Testament.* Edited by Johannes Beutler. Quaestiones disputatae 190. Freiburg: Herder, 2001.

————. "New Testament Christology in Its Hellenistic Reception." *New Testament Studies* 46 (2001): 312–33.

Zeller, Eduard, and Wilhelm Nestle. *Outlines of the History of Greek Philosophy.* Translated by L. R. Palmer. 13th ed. International Library of Psychology, Philosophy, and Scientific Method. New York: Humanities Press, 1931. Reprint, 1963.

Ziesler, J. A. *The Meaning of Righteousness in Paul: A Linguistic and Theological Enquiry.* Society of New Testament Studies Monograph Series 20. Cambridge: Cambridge University Press, 1972.

Zimmermann, Alfred. *Die urchristlichen Lehrer: Studien zum Tradentenkreis der Didaskaloi im frühen Urchristentum.* Wissenschaftliche Untersuchungen zum Alten und Neuen Testament 2/12. Tübingen: Mohr Siebeck, 1984.

Zimmermann, Johannes. *Messianische Texte aus Qumran: Königliche, priesterliche, und prophetische Messiasvorstellungen in den Schriftfunden von Qumran.* Wissenschaftliche Untersuchungen zum Neuen Testament 2/104. Tübingen: Mohr Siebeck, 1998.

Index of Subjects

Abraham, 109, 270 (table), 401, 457, 514, 525; in Galatians, 274, 286–87, 290, 292–93, 300, 565, 590; in Romans, 323–26, 344, 521

Acts of Paul and Thecla, 58n4

Acts of the Apostles: as a document of the Pauline school, 44, 151; value for Pauline biography, 48; and Luke's ecclesiology, 52; on the Damascus road event, 94–96. *See also* contradictions between Paul and Acts

Adam: as type of Christ, in Romans, 327–28, 335, 436; as type of Christ, in 1 Corinthians, 584; mortal, in 1 Corinthians, 535; in the image of God, inclusive of male and female, 533; effects of the sin of, 74, 277, 394, 532, 541, 579

Agrippa I, 113n47, 119n75, 122, 165, 275

Agrippa II, 55n30

Albinos (procurator), 55n32

Alexander Janneus, 65

allegory, 109, 130, 590

Ananias, 112

Ananus. *See* Annas

Andronicus, 304, 571

Annas (Ananus), 55, 123

anthropology, 336, 346, 494–545, 562n13; of Paul's Corinthian opponents, 225, 250; and the Spirit, 488–89

Antioch (on the Orontes): Paul's return to, from Macedonia, 53; geography of, 113; founding of the church at, 113–15; significance in early Christian theology, 116–118. *See also* Paul, life of: Antioch incident

Antioch in Pisidia, 119

Antipatrus of Tarsus, 59

Antony, Mark, 59, 366

Apollonius of Tyana, 59, 441n122, 474

Apollos, 124, 131, 149, 151, 170n124, 195, 198, 203, 204n40, 571

apostleship, Paul's, 88–90; in Paul's self-understanding, 115, 158–59, 375–77; in 2 Corinthians, 245–51

apostolic council, 121–37, 275; date of, 50–51, 56 (table); Barnabas's role at, 115; consequences of, for Paul's mission, 138, 145; and the separation of Christianity from Judaism, 165; issue unresolved at, 189; aftermath at Galatia, 275–78, 301; and the offering for Jerusalem, 305, 361, 467; in the development of Paul's anthropology, 512–13

Aquila. *See* Prisca and Aquila

Arabia, 50–51, 84, 111, 114n51

Aretas IV, King, 51n13, 112

Aristarchus (Paul's coworker), 149

Artemis, 151, 193

Asclepius, 142, 193

Athens, 50, 146, 194

atonement, 443–54

Attis, 141

Augustine, 26

Augustus, 59, 78, 142, 405, 441n122, 463; and the Jews, 62n29, 161, 302. *See also Res gestae divi Augusti*

authentic letters, 41

baptism: in Jewish-Christian understanding, 127; pre-Pauline tradition regarding, 105, 148; and

643

Index of Greek Words and Phrases

651

Index of Modern Authors

Index of Ancient Sources

3. New Testament

2 Corinthians

Colossians

1 Thessalonians

4. Old Testament Pseudepigrapha

5. Dead Sea Scrolls

6. Mishnah, Talmud, and Related Literature

7. Apostolic Fathers

Erased - 8/15 MP.